Child Development

*Educating and Working with
Children and Adolescents*

Child Development

Educating and Working with Children and Adolescents

SECOND EDITION

Teresa M. McDevitt
University of Northern Colorado

Jeanne Ellis Ormrod
University of Northern Colorado (Emerita)
University of New Hampshire

PEARSON

Merrill
Prentice Hall

Upper Saddle River, New Jersey
Columbus, Ohio

Library of Congress Cataloging in Publication Data
McDevitt, Teresa M.
    Child development: educating and working with children and adolescents/Teresa M.
McDevitt, Jeanne Ellis Ormrod.—2nd ed.
        p. cm.
    Rev. ed. of: Child development and education. c2002.
    Includes bibliographical references and indexes.
    ISBN 0-13-110841-7 (pbk.)
    1. Child development. 2. Adolescent psychology. 3. Educational psychology. I. Ormrod,
Jeanne Ellis. II. McDevitt, Teresa M. Child development and education. III. Title.

LB1115.M263 2004
305.231—dc21

                                                                        2003050446

Vice President and Executive Publisher: Jeffery W. Johnston
Publisher: Kevin M. Davis
Development Editor: Julie Peters
Editorial Assistant: Autumn Crisp
Production Editor: Mary Harlan
Copy Editor: Barbara Lyons
Design Coordinator: Diane Lorenzo
Photo Coordinator: Valerie Schultz
Text Design: Bryan Huber and Carlisle Publishers Services
Cover Design: Bryan Huber
Cover Image: Getty One
Illustrations: Rolin Graphics and Carlisle Publishers Services
Production Manager: Laura Messerly
Director of Marketing: Ann Castel Davis
Marketing Manager: Amy June
Marketing Coordinator: Tyra Poole

This book was set in Berkeley by Carlisle Communications, Ltd. It was printed and bound by Courier Kendallville, Inc. The cover was printed by Phoenix Color Corp.

Photo Credits: Photo credits appear on p. P-1, facing the Name Index.

Pearson Education Ltd.   Pearson Education Australia Pty. Limited
Pearson Education Singapore Pte. Ltd.   Pearson Education North Asia Ltd.
Pearson Education Canada, Ltd.   Pearson Educación de Mexico, S.A. de C.V.
Pearson Education–Japan   Pearson Education Malaysia Pte. Ltd.

10 9 8 7 6 5 4 3 2 1
ISBN: 0-13-110841-7

DEDICATION

To our children and husbands,
Connor, Alexander, and Eugene Sheehan
and
Christina, Alex, Jeffrey, and Richard Ormrod

About the Authors

Teresa M. McDevitt is a psychologist with specializations in child development and educational psychology. She received a Ph.D. and M.A. in child development from Stanford University's Psychological Studies in Education program, an Ed.S. in educational evaluation from Stanford University, and a B.A. in psychology from the University of California, Santa Cruz. Since 1985 she has served the University of Northern Colorado in a variety of capacities—in teaching courses in child and adolescent psychology, human development, educational psychology, program evaluation, and research methods; in advisement of graduate students; in administration and university governance; and in research and grant writing. Her research interests include children's listening and communication skills, families, teacher education, and science education. She has published articles in such journals as *Child Development, Learning and Individual Differences, Child Study Journal, Merrill-Palmer Quarterly, Youth and Society,* and *Science Education,* among others. She has gained extensive practical experience with children, including raising two children with her husband and working in several capacities with children—as an early childhood teacher of toddlers and preschool children, an early childhood special education teacher, a scout leader, and a volunteer in school and community settings. When she has the chance, Teresa enjoys traveling internationally with her family, and spending time with her children and husband.

Jeanne Ellis Ormrod is an educational psychologist and the author of *Educational Psychology: Developing Learners* and *Human Learning* (now both in their 4th editions) and co-author of *Practical Research* (soon to be released in its 8th edition), all published by Merrill/Prentice Hall. She received her Ph.D. and M.S. in educational psychology at The Pennsylvania State University and an A.B. in psychology from Brown University; she also earned certification in school psychology through postdoctoral work at Temple University and the University of Colorado, Boulder. She was Professor of Educational Psychology at the University of Northern Colorado from 1976 until 1998, when she moved east to return to her native New England. She is now affiliated with the University of New Hampshire, where she teaches courses in educational psychology. She has worked as a middle school geography teacher and school psychologist, and has conducted research in cognition and memory, cognitive development, spelling, and giftedness. When Jeanne is not teaching, writing, reading professional books and journals, or monitoring the diverse activities of her three grown children, she enjoys boating, playing racquetball, and walking on the beach with her husband.

Preface

As psychologists and teacher educators, we have been teaching child and adolescent development for many years. A primary goal in our classes has been to help students translate developmental theories into practical implications for professionals who nurture the development of young people. In past years, the child development textbooks available to us and our students have often been quite thorough in their descriptions of theory and research, but they have offered few concrete suggestions for working with infants, children, and adolescents in applied settings.

With this book, we bridge the gap between theory and practice. We draw from innumerable theoretical concepts, from research studies conducted around the world, and from our own experiences as parents, teachers, psychologists, and researchers to identify strategies for promoting children's and adolescents' physical, cognitive, and social-emotional growth. Whereas the first edition of the book focused largely on strategies for educators, this second edition expands our audience to include practitioners in many professions, including infant care, health care, social work, counseling, family education, youth services, and community agencies. Furthermore, whereas the first edition focused on ages 2 through 18, we have expanded our coverage to include infancy as well.

Several features make this book different from other comprehensive textbooks about child and adolescent development. In particular, the book

- Continually relates abstract theories to professional strategies in applied settings
- Not only describes but also *demonstrates* developmental phenomena
- Uses several central themes to show patterns in diverse developmental domains

In the next three pages, we provide examples of how the book accomplishes these goals.

Dana, age 6

THE DIFFERENCE BETWEEN ABSTRACT UNDERSTANDING AND APPLICATION

This book focuses on concepts and principles that are important to developmental theorists *and* to professionals who are involved in protecting and nurturing the development of children and adolescents. More so than in any other development text, in McDevitt/Ormrod concepts are contexualized within schools, agencies, and other authentic settings where the day-to-day lives of children play out. And more so than in any other text, McDevitt/Ormrod spells out the practical implications of developmental theory and research and provides concrete applications for those who teach and work with children and adolescents. The result is a text that is uniquely useful to those who are interested in practical applications of developmental scholarship.

Professional Implications   Throughout every chapter, you will find extensive discussion of the relevance of material to teachers, child care providers, counselors, caseworkers, and others who work with children and adolescents. Most major topics contain sections that examine in depth the professional implications of the developmental research and theory being presented. As a result, the reader comes away not only understanding current views of concepts, such as how children learn to solve problems and express emotions, but also seeing the relevance and application of these ideas to working with children.

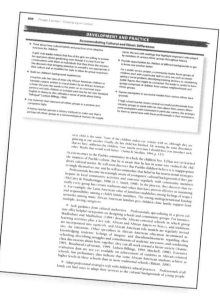

Development and Practice   In addition to discussing applications throughout the text itself, we provide "Development and Practice" features that offer concrete strategies for facilitating children's development. To help readers move from research to practice, each strategy is followed by an actual example of a professional using that strategy in an authentic setting.

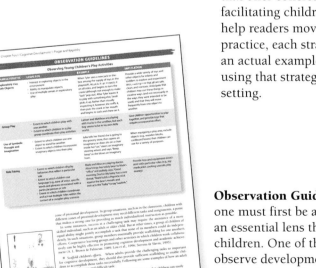

Observation Guidelines   To work productively with children and adolescents, one must first be able to see them accurately. Knowledge of development provides an essential lens through which professionals must look if they are to understand children. One of the foundational goals of this text is to help professionals observe developmental nuances in the infants, children, and adolescents with whom they work. To this end, throughout the book, we give readers "Observation Guidelines." These offer specific characteristics to look for, present illustrative examples, and provide specific recommendations for practitioners.

THE DIFFERENCE BETWEEN READING ABOUT DEVELOPMENT AND SEEING IT

Another central focus of this text is to illustrate concepts and research with frequent examples of real children and adolescents. Authentic case studies begin and end each chapter, and there are often separate, shorter vignettes within the bodies of chapters. In addition to these types of illustrations, the text, much more than any other similar text, also makes frequent use of real artifacts from children's journals, sketchbooks, and schoolwork. It is among real children and adolescents and in the midst of the work they produce that developmental content becomes meaningful to professional practitioners. More than any other text, McDevitt/Ormrod brings this context to life.

Case Studies Each chapter begins with a case that, by being referenced throughout the chapter, is used to illustrate and frame that chapter's content. A chapter ending case provides readers with an opportunity to apply chapter content. The questions that accompany each of these end-of-chapter cases help the reader in this application process.

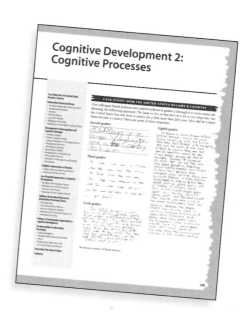

Artifacts from Children and Adolescents The frequent use of actual artifacts provides another forum for illustrating developmental abilities and issues. Throughout the text, actual examples of artwork, poetry, and school assignments are integrated into discussions of various concepts and applications. Not only do these artifacts offer readers authentic illustrations of chapter content, but they also help contextualize developmental research and theory.

Observation CD-ROMs Integrated into every chapter are video clips from a new collection of 3 CDs that accompany the book. Activities on the CDs allow students to explore 14 topics—such as Memory, Friendship, and Families—from the perspective of children from five age groups. The opportunity to see children and adolescents at different levels of development perform the same task or talk about a topic, such as what it means to be a friend, is unique and extremely powerful in demonstrating developmental differences.

THE DIFFERENCE A CONSISTENT THEMATIC APPROACH MAKES

The other core goal of *Child Development: Educating and Working with Children and Adolescents* is to help readers come to a broad conceptual understanding of the field of development, to make them aware of the foundational ideas and issues that frame the field, and to provide them with a broad sense of how and when children acquire various characteristics and abilities. Throughout all of its chapters, the book consistently examines theories and concepts from the perspective of three core developmental issues—biological and environmental influences on development, universality and diversity of developmental changes, and the qualitative and quantitative nature of developmental change. Though organized topically, the book also provides overviews of the distinctive features of each chronological period within the topical areas.

Basic Developmental Issues Every chapter examines ways in which development is the complex product of interacting forces—nature, nurture, and children's own efforts. We also spotlight circumstances that reveal fairly universal developmental trends and areas marked with substantial diversity. Finally, the text analyzes the underlying nature of developmental changes: Do they take the form of dramatic qualitative changes, or are they the outcome of many small, trend-like quantitative changes?

Developmental Trends The book is organized around substantive topics of development to allow for an in-depth examination of each area of development. In the context of this topical approach, however, we also identify the unique characteristics of children during particular periods of growth. In the narrative, we frequently provide detailed chronological examples of children's abilities to give professionals a flavor of what children can do at specific ages. In each chapter, a "Developmental Trends" table summarizes typical features of five developmental periods: infancy, early childhood, middle childhood, early adolescence, and late adolescence. These tables explain common types of individual and group differences and point out implications for practice.

Supplementary Materials

FOR INSTRUCTORS

Online Course Management Systems

Blackboard and CourseCompass are perfect course management solutions that combine quality Merrill/Prentice Hall content with state-of-the-art Blackboard technology. These products allow you to teach this material in an easy-to-use customizable format and add updates instantaneously.

The Videotape Package

Accompanying the textbook are seven videotapes:

Observing Children and Adolescents in Classroom Settings Videotape segments portray a wide variety of teachers and students in action, from kindergarten through senior year. By observing hours of interactions, viewers develop their ability to see where students are developmentally. The tape and its accompanying material also provide opportunities for students to analyze the developmental appropriateness of teaching methods and curriculum.

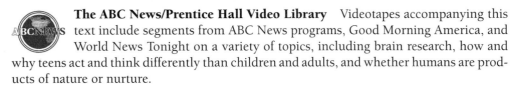 **The ABC News/Prentice Hall Video Library** Videotapes accompanying this text include segments from ABC News programs, Good Morning America, and World News Tonight on a variety of topics, including brain research, how and why teens act and think differently than children and adults, and whether humans are products of nature or nurture.

Insights Into Learning Three one-hour videotapes provide an in-depth examination of specific aspects of cognitive development:

■ *Using Balance Beams in Fourth Grade.* Students problem solve using weights on a balance scale and defend solutions in both small-group and whole-class sessions. Viewers can observe students acquiring understanding of balance beam principles at different rates.

■ *Finding Area in Elementary Math.* Fifth-graders engage in an authentic problem-solving activity in which they must calculate the area of an irregular shape using problem-solving steps. A teacher presents transfer tasks and probes students' reasoning.

■ *Designing Experiments in Seventh Grade.* Students conduct experiments in small groups and discuss how factors affect a pendulum's oscillation rate, then a teacher conducts a lesson on separating and controlling variables.

Double-Column Addition: A Teacher Uses Piaget's Theory Second graders construct creative strategies for adding and subtracting two-digit numbers and reveal a true understanding of place value. Rather than teaching specific strategies, the teacher helps the students develop their own strategies by presenting problems, asking for possible solutions, and encouraging discussion of various approaches. (20 min.)

A Private Universe This video illustrates the pervasiveness of misconceptions in high school students and in graduates and faculty at Harvard about the seasons of the year and the phases of the moon. One student's explanations are portrayed both before and after instruction. Questions probing her reasoning after instruction reveal she still holds onto some prior misconceptions. (18 min.)

NEW Test Bank

The completely rewritten test bank now contains more application items per chapter. In addition, items emphasize assessing key concepts. An average of 50 items per chapter are categorized and marked as lower-level or higher-level. Lower-level questions ask students to identify or explain the concepts and principles they have learned. Higher-level questions require students to apply their knowledge of developmental concepts and research to specific settings and situations and make developmentally appropriate decisions. The test bank is available printed and on disk, for PC and Macintosh, in *TestGen*, a test management system.

Instructor's Manual

This manual contains an outline of the primary chapter headings and sections, with a corresponding list of instructional materials to be used for each section; suggestions and resources for learning activities, supplemental lectures, case study analyses, group activities, handouts, and transparency masters. Over 35 titles of new Supplementary Readings have been integrated in the Chapter Outlines. (See the *Study Guide and Reader* for the actual readings.)

Transparencies

Over 120 acetate transparencies include key concept summarizations, diagrams, organizational tables, and other graphic aids to enhance learning. They are designed to help students understand, organize, and remember concepts, developmental theories, and developmental trends. The transparencies are also available as PowerPoint slides on CD-ROM.

Multimedia Guide

The *Multimedia Guide* will help you enrich your students' interpretation and understanding of what they see in the videos, on the Simulations CD, on the new interactive "Observing Children and Adolescents" CDs, and on the Companion Website. Observation Record tables, similar to the Observation Guidelines tables in the text, help students record their observations and apply their knowledge of development.

Instructor's CD-ROM

This user-friendly CD-ROM provides lecture-enhancing color PowerPoint transparencies; black-and-white Transparency Masters that can be used as handouts; handouts; and all other materials found in the *Multimedia Guide* and *Instructor's Manual.*

FOR STUDENTS

NEW Observing Children and Adolescents CD-ROMs: Guided Interactive Practice in Understanding Development

This unique new set of three CDs is packaged with every copy of the textbook and integrated into every chapter. In more than 50 activities, students view video clips of real children from infancy through adolescence, reflect on their observations, and record their interpretations. Students can explore 14 topics, including Memory, Intrinsic Motivation, Cognitive Development, Emotional Development, Families, Friendship, and Intelligence. Viewing these clips and responding to a series of questions across five age groups will familiarize students with the abilities and concerns of children at every developmental level—and reinforce key concepts.

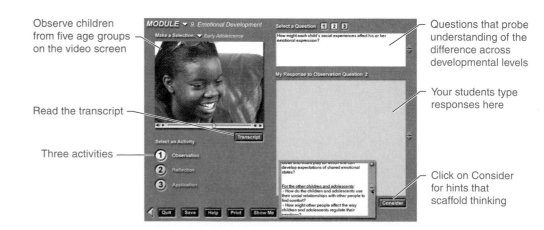

Observe children from five age groups on the video screen

Read the transcript

Three activities

Questions that probe understanding of the difference across developmental levels

Your students type responses here

Click on Consider for hints that scaffold thinking

Interactive Computer Simulations in Child Development

This problem-solving simulation CD-ROM allows students to participate in two "virtual" experiments—manipulating variables with a virtual pendulum to learn more about Piaget's theory of cognitive development and assessing moral reasoning using Kohlberg's theory of moral development—and then apply their knowledge.

NEW ASCD/Merrill Website

A joint Web site between Merrill and ASCD at www.educatorlearningcenter.com offers students and faculty many resources, including instructional strategies, video segments, case studies, and hundreds of articles from *Educational Leadership*. The site now includes a link to Research Navigator, allowing students to search hundreds of academic journals. A four-month subscription to this virtual "library" of resources is available to anyone who purchases a Merrill education textbook.

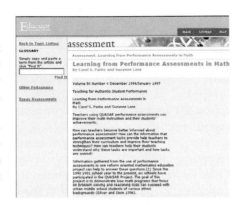

Companion Website

Our Web site at www.prenhall.com/mcdevitt enables instructors to manage their course online and helps students master course content with Practice Quizzes and Essay Questions, explore topics in WebLinks, and more.

NEW Study Guide and Reader

Features to help students focus their learning include (1) a chapter overview to give students an overall picture of chapter topics, (2) discussions of common student beliefs and misconceptions to alert students to widely held beliefs that may interfere with mastery of developmental concepts and theories, (3) focus questions for students to answer as they read the chapter and test themselves about their comprehension of chapter content, (4) application exercises to give students practice in recognizing concepts and principles being acted out in the classroom and other settings, (5) over 35 new supplementary readings and research study descriptions to extend the content found in the textbook, (6) chapter glossary, and (7) sample test questions.

ACKNOWLEDGMENTS

Although we are listed as the sole authors of this textbook, in fact many individuals have contributed in significant ways to its content and form. Our editor, Kevin Davis, saw the need for an applied child development book and continued to encourage us until we agreed to write one. Kevin has been the captain of our ship throughout both the first and second editions, charting our journey and alerting us when we drifted off course. We thank Kevin for his continuing encouragement, support, insights, task focus, high standards, and friendship.

We have been equally fortunate to work with Julie Peters, our development editor for both the first and second editions. Julie has seen us through the day-to-day challenges of writing the book—for instance, offering creative ideas for improving the manuscript, locating artifacts to illustrate key concepts, pushing us to condense when we were unnecessarily wordy, insisting that certain concepts be clarified and illustrated, being a willing ear whenever we needed to vent our frustrations and, in general, coordinating the entire writing effort until the book went into production. We thank Julie for her advice, support, and good humor, and also for her willingness to drop whatever else she was doing to come to our assistance at critical times.

Others at Merrill/Prentice Hall have also been key players in bringing the book to fruition. Barbara Lyons worked diligently to keep the manuscript focused, concise, and clear. Mary Harlan guided the manuscript through the production process; without a complaint, she let us continue to tweak the book in innumerable small ways even as production deadlines loomed dangerously close. Becky Savage secured permissions for the excerpts and figures we borrowed from other sources and was flexible and dependable when we added to our list at the eleventh hour. Valerie Schultz sifted through many images to identify those that could best capture key developmental principles in a visual form. Autumn Crisp handled logistical details quickly and smoothly. Marketing whizzes Ann Davis, Amy June, Joe Hale, Amy Judd, Suzanne Stanton, Barbara Koontz, and others helped us get out the word about the book.

We are also deeply indebted to the first two authors of the three compact disks that comprise *Observing Children and Adolescents: Guided Interactive Practice in Understanding Development.* Jayne Downey, now at Montana State University, labored diligently and effectively to translate a good concept into a better reality. Jayne shared our desire to represent children and adolescents in a natural and positive light so that adults could understand them more deeply and sympathetically; among the many tasks she undertook were recruiting children, securing the services of interviewers, drafting questions and setting up tasks for children, filming children in their homes, editing video clips, and interpreting children's thoughts and actions. Stuart Garry brought his technological know-how, in-depth knowledge of developmental theory, artistic talents, and keen attention to detail to bear in designing the CDs themselves. Others were vital contributors, as well. Jason Cole, now at San Francisco State University, expertly programmed the complex package. We extend our appreciation to Greg Pierson, Director of University Schools (formerly UNC Laboratory School), and to Keli Cotner, Director of the Campus Child Care Center at the University of Northern Colorado, for granting permission and assistance to Jayne Downey in filming classrooms and facilities. Dana Snyder and Kelle Nolke, teachers at the UNC Laboratory School, now University Schools, kindly assisted with videotaping in their classroom; Dana Snyder also permitted her own lessons to be taped. We also acknowledge the excellent job done by interviewers Stacey Blank, Tara Kaysen, Addie Lopez, Laura Sether, and Lisa Blank. Thanks also to Randy Lennon, Chair of the Department of Educational Psychology at the University of Northern Colorado, for making equipment available for editing. Finally, the children and families were especially generous in allowing Jayne and the interviewers to come into their homes and to film the children.

Several other colleagues around the country have contributed in significant ways to the book and its ancillary materials. Janet Gonzalez-Mena, Professor Emerita, Napa Valley College, and Julie Law, at the University of California, Davis, offered many concrete ideas for our expanded coverage of infancy in the second edition. Teresa DeBacker, at the University of Oklahoma, constructed our test bank, including many creative, scenario-based items that will challenge readers to apply concepts and theories to real-world situations. Cara Wicks-Ortega, at Central Michigan University, revised an instructor's manual, acetate transparencies, and PowerPoint® slides to guide veteran and novice instructors as they teach their classes. L. Brook Ervin, Stacy Droessler, and Melissa Storm, all at the University of Virginia, very ably and creatively developed the book's Companion Website assessment items to help students monitor and expand on their learning as they study various topics in child development. Sara Rimm-Kaufman at the University of Virginia reviewed their work, and we thank her for her generous efforts. We thank all of our ancillary authors for fitting these projects into their busy academic schedules.

Children, Adolescents, and Practitioners Equally important contributors to the book were the many young people and practitioners who provided the work samples, written reflections, other artifacts, and verbal responses that appear throughout the fourteen chapters and in the observation CD package. The work of the following young people contributed immeasurably to the depth and richness of our discussions:

Davis Alcorn	Geoff Alkire	Madison Blank	Eric Campos
Jacob Alcorn	Brenda Bagazuma	Brent Bonner	Leif Carlson
Curtis Alexander	Andrew Belcher	Diamond Bonner	Zoe Clifton
Kyle Alexander	Katie Belcher	Ricco Branch	Wendy Cochran
David Alkire	Kayla Blank	Marsalis Bush	Jenna Dargy

Noah Davis
Shea Davis
Brandon Doherty
Daniel Erdman
Rachel Foster
Eddie Garcia
Palet Garcia
Veronica Garcia
James Garrett, III
Mayra de la Garza
Amaryth Gass
Andrew Gass
Tony Gass
Dana Gogolin
Kenton Groissaint
Acadia Gurney
Amanda Hackett
Jared Hale
Cody Havens

Tyler Hensley
Elisabet Deyanira
  Hernandez
Lauryn Hickman
Sam Hickman
William Hill
Brandon Jackson
Rachel Johnson
Jordan Kemme
Marianne Kies
Sarah Luffel
Jessica Lumbrano
Krista Marrufo
Steven Merrick
Margaret Mohr
Tchuen-Yi Murry
Mike Newcomb
Malanie Nunez

Dustin O'Mara
Alex Ormrod
Jeff Ormrod
Tina Ormrod
Shir-Lisa Owens
Isiah Payan
Isabelle Peters
Michelle Pollman
Laura Prieto-Velasco
Ian Rhoades
Talia Rockland
Oscar Rodriguez
Elizabeth Romero
Amber Rossetti
Bianca Sanchez
Daniela Sanchez
Corwin Sether
Alex Sheehan

Connor Sheehan
Aftyn Siemer
Karma Marie Smith
Eric Spence
Connor Stephens
Megan Lee Stephens
Joe Sweeney
Grace Tober
Sarah Toon
David Torres
Joseph Torres
Samuel Torres
Madison Tupper
Danielle Welch
Brady Williamson
Joey Wolf
Lindsey Woollard
Anna Young

We also thank the children in the first- and second-grade classroom of Dana Snyder and Kelle Nolke at the Laboratory School, Greeley, CO (now University Schools).

To ensure that we included children's work from a wide variety of geographic locations and backgrounds, we contacted organizations north and south, east and west to obtain work samples that would reflect ethnic, cultural, and economic diversity. We want to thank these individuals for their assistance and coordination efforts: Don Burger at Pacific Resources for Education and Learning (PREL), Michelle Gabor of the Salesian Boys' and Girls' Club, Rita Hocog Inos of the Commonwealth of the Northern Mariana Islands Public School System, Bettie Lake of the Phoenix Elementary School District, Heidi Schork and members of the Boston Youth Clean-Up Corps (BYCC), Ann Shump of the Oyster River School District. Furthermore we thank the many teachers, counselors, principals, and other professionals—a child welfare case worker, a neurologist, a public health educator—who were so helpful in our efforts to identify artifacts, anecdotes, dialogues, and professional strategies to illustrate developmental concepts; key among them were Janet Alcorn, Rosenna Bakari, Trish Belcher, Paula Case, Michael Gee, Jennifer Glynn, Evie Greene, Diane Haddad, Betsy Higginbotham, Betsy Hopkins, Dinah Jackson, Jesse Jensen, Mike McDevitt, Erin Miguel, Michele Minichiello, Andrew Moore, Dan Moulis, Annemarie Palincsar, Kellee Patterson, Elizabeth Peña, Jrene Rahm, Nancy Rapport, Karen Scates, Cindy Schutter, Karen Setterlin, Jean Slater, Julie Spencer, Nan Stein, Sally Tossey, Pat Vreeland, and Cathy Zocchi.

Colleagues and Reviewers In addition, we received considerable encouragement, assistance, and support from our professional colleagues. Faculty and administrators at the University of Northern Colorado—especially Marlene Strathe, Steven Pulos, Randy Lennon, and Allen Huang—unselfishly provided information, advice, resources, and time. Developmentalists and educational psychologists at numerous institutions around the country have offered their careful and insightful reviews of one or more chapters. We are especially indebted to the following reviewers:

Karen Abrams, Keene State College
Jan Allen, University of Tennessee
Lynley Anderman, University of Kentucky
David E. Balk, Kansas State University
Tom Batsis, Loyola Marymount University
Heather Davis, University of Florida
Teresa DeBacker, University of Oklahoma
Eric Durbrow, The Pennsylvania State
  University
William Fabricius, Arizona State University

Daniel Fasko, Morehead State University
Sherryl Browne Graves, Hunter College
Michael Green, University of North
  Carolina–Charlotte
Glenda Griffin, Texas A & M University
Deborah Grubb, Morehead State University
Melissa Heston, University of Northern
  Iowa
James E. Johnson, The Pennsylvania State
  University

Michael Keefer, University of Missouri–St. Louis
Judith Kieff, University of New Orleans
Nancy Knapp, University of Georgia
Mary McLellan, Northern Arizona University
Sharon McNeely, Northeastern Illinois University
Kenneth Merrell, University of Iowa
Tamera Murdock, University of Missouri–Kansas City
Bridget Murray, Indiana State University
Kathy Nakagawa, Arizona State University
Virginia Navarro, University of Missouri–St. Louis
Larry Nucci, University of Illinois–Chicago

Jennifer Parkhurst, Duke University
Sherrill Richarz, Washington State University
Kent Rittschof, Georgia Southern University
Linda Rogers, Kent State University
Stephanie Rowley, University of Michigan
Richard Ryan, University of Rochester
Sue Spitzer, California State University, San Bernardino
Benjamin Stephens, Clemson University
Bruce Tuckman, The Ohio State University
Kathryn Wentzel, University of Maryland–College Park
Allan Wigfield, University of Maryland–College Park
Thomas D. Yawkey, The Pennsylvania State University.

Our Families Finally, our families have been supportive and patient over the extended period we have been preoccupied with reading, researching, writing, and editing. Our children gave of themselves in anecdotes, artwork, and diversions from our work. Our husbands picked up the slack around the house and gave us frequent emotional boosts and comic relief. Much love and many thanks to Eugene, Connor, and Alex (from Teresa) and to Richard, Tina, Alex, and Jeff (from Jeanne).

T.M.M.
J.E.O.

EDUCATOR LEARNING CENTER:
AN INVALUABLE ONLINE RESOURCE

Merrill Education and the Association for Supervision and Curriculum Development (ASCD) invite instructors to take advantage of a new online resource, one that provides access to the top research and proven strategies associated with ASCD and Merrill—the Educator Learning Center. At www.EducatorLearningCenter.com you will find resources that will enhance your students' understanding of course topics and of current educational issues, in addition to being invaluable for further research.

How the Educator Learning Center will help your students become better teachers

With the combined resources of Merrill Education and ASCD, you and your students will find a wealth of tools and materials to better prepare them for the classroom.

Research

- More than 600 articles from the ASCD journal *Educational Leadership* discuss everyday issues faced by practicing teachers.
- A direct link on the site to Research Navigator™ gives students access to many of the leading education journals, as well as extensive content detailing the research process.
- Excerpts from Merrill Education texts give your students insights on important topics of instructional methods, diverse populations, assessment, classroom management, technology, and refining classroom practice.

Classroom Practice

- Hundreds of lesson plans and teaching strategies are categorized by content area and age range.
- Case studies and classroom video footage provide virtual field experience for student reflection.
- Computer simulations and other electronic tools keep your students abreast of today's classrooms and current technologies.

Look into the value of Educator Learning Center yourself

Preview the value of this educational environment by visiting www.EducatorLearningCenter.com and clicking on "Demo." For a free 4-month subscription to the Educator Learning Center in conjunction with this text, simply contact your Merrill/Prentice Hall sales representative.

Brief Contents

Contents

CHAPTER 14

Growing Up in Context   595

NOTE: Every effort has been made to provide accurate and current Internet information in this book. However, the Internet and information posted on it are constantly changing, so it is inevitable that some of the Internet addresses listed in this textbook will change.

Special Features

Child Development
Educating and Working with Children and Adolescents

Zoe, age 5

Myra, age 13

Making a Difference in the Lives of Infants, Children, and Adolescents

CASE STUDY: TONYA

When Mary Renck Jalongo thinks back to her years as a novice teacher, one student often comes to mind:

Not only was she big for her age, she was older than anyone else in my first-grade class because she had been retained in kindergarten. Her name was Tonya and she put my patience, my professionalism, and my decision making on trial throughout my second year of teaching. Tonya would boss and bully the other children, pilfer items from their desks, or talk them into uneven "trades."

Matters worsened when I received a hostile note from a parent. It read, "This is the fourth time that Tommy's snack cake has been taken from his lunch. What are you going to do about it?"

What I did was to launch an investigation. First, I asked if anyone else was missing items from lunchboxes and discovered that many other children had been affected. Next, I tried to get someone to confess—not in the way that *my* teachers had done it, by sitting in the room until the guilty party or an informant cracked, but simply by asking the perpetrator to leave a note in my classroom mailbox. My classroom was antiquated, but it included an enclosed hallway, now equipped with coat racks and shelves that led to a restroom. Apparently, while I was preoccupied teaching my lessons, a child was stealing food. Three days later, several other children reported that they had seen Tonya "messing around people's lunchboxes." I asked her, but she denied it. At recess, I looked in her desk and found it littered with empty food wrappers. Then Tonya and I discussed it again in private and examined the evidence.

I consulted my principal about what to do. He suggested that I punish her severely; a month without recess seemed warranted, he said. I thought it might be better to call her mother, but they had no telephone and the principal assured me that, based on her failure to attend previous school functions, Tonya's mother would not come to school. Then I said I would write a note and set up a home visit. He strongly advised against that, telling me that Tonya's mother had a disease, that the house was a mess, and that she had a live-in boyfriend.

All these things were true, but I understand them differently now. Tonya's mother had lupus and was at a debilitating stage of the disease that prevented her from working, much less maintaining a spotless home. Tonya's family now consisted of mother, unofficial stepfather (also permanently disabled), and a three-year-old brother. They lived on a fixed income, and Tonya qualified for free lunches.

As a first-year teacher [at this school], I was reluctant to go against the principal's wishes, but I did draw the line at harsh punishment. When I asked Tonya *why* she took things from the other children's lunches, she simply said, "'Cause I was hungry." I asked her if she ate breakfast in the morning, and she said, "No. I have to take care of my little brother before I go to school." I asked her if having breakfast might solve the problem and she said, "Yes. My aunt would help." And so, my first big teaching problem was solved by an eight-year-old when instead of foraging for food each morning, Tonya and her brother walked down the block to her unmarried aunt's house before school and ate breakfast.

There was still the matter of repairing Tonya's damaged reputation with the other children, who had accumulated a variety of negative experiences with her and had labeled her as a thief. I stood with my arms around Tonya's shoulder in front of the class and announced that Tonya had agreed not to take things anymore, that she could be trusted, and that all was well.

Two weeks later, a child's candy bar was reported missing, and the class was quick to accuse Tonya. I took her aside and inquired about the missing candy bar. "No," she said firmly, "I didn't eat it." As I defended Tonya's innocence to her peers, I noticed how Tonya, the child who had learned to slouch to conceal her size, sat up tall and proud in her seat.

I must confess that I was wondering if Tonya might be lying when Kendra, the child who reported the stolen candy bar, said she was ill and wanted to go home. Then, with a candor only possible in a young child, Kendra said, "I have a stomachache, and you want to know why? Because I just remembered that *I* ate my candy bar on the bus this morning."

Tonya's confidence and competence flourished during the remainder of her first-grade year and throughout second grade. Then, in third grade, she had a teacher who was sarcastic and unfair. When I passed by the third-grade room, I often saw Tonya seated off by herself or washing the walls, desks, or floors as punishment for her misbehavior. She would stop at my first-grade classroom after school, and when I asked her about it, she said she just didn't like third grade and wished she could come back to first grade. Ms. M., Tonya's third-grade teacher, had the habit of choosing certain children—always the ones whose parents were influential and wealthy—for all of the classroom privileges. One day as I was passing by her classroom, the third-grade teacher said, "Alyssa, you have on such a pretty dress today, why don't you be our messenger? Be sure to show Mr. B [the principal] how nice you look!" I caught a glimpse of Tonya's face as she sat there in her secondhand clothes and felt bitter tears in my eyes. . . .

From *Teachers' Stories: From Personal Narrative to Professional Insight* (pp. 114–117), by M. R. Jalongo, J. P. Isenberg, & G. Gerbracht, 1995, San Francisco: Jossey-Bass. Copyright © 1995 by Jossey-Bass, Inc. This material is used by permission of John Wiley & Sons, Inc.

How easy it might have been for a teacher to write Tonya off as a bully and a thief and, as the principal suggested, to punish her severely for her transgressions. Fortunately, Ms. Jalongo instead looked beneath the surface to find a child who was hungry and eager to please. She was then able to identify a simple strategy—arranging for Tonya and her brother to eat breakfast with their aunt—that not only eliminated the lunch-pilfering episodes but also started Tonya on the road to establishing positive relationships with her classmates.

Infants, children, and adolescents need caring adults in their lives to support all aspects of their development. Professionals who work daily with youngsters play an important—in fact, a critical—role in the directions children's lives take. These adults can help young people to develop social skills, self-confidence, a love of learning, and health-promoting habits. In some cases, and perhaps in Tonya's, a single person may provide the caring, stable environment that truly makes a difference.

In this book, we explore the childhood years, extending from birth through late adolescence. Throughout our exploration, we connect what theorists and researchers have learned about child development to what adults can do to help infants, children, and adolescents become all that they are capable of becoming—not only academically, but also physically, socially, and emotionally. We frequently illustrate these connections between theory and practice with examples and case studies. We also draw on our own experiences as teachers, mothers, psychologists, and volunteers; thus, you will see references to the two of us, Teresa and Jeanne, throughout the book.

Our exploration in this chapter begins with an overview of the field of child development and an examination of basic issues that the field addresses. We also survey the various perspectives that psychologists and other theorists have used to describe and explain why youngsters behave and think as they do and how their behaviors and thought processes change over time. We then preview distinctive features of various age groups and consider recommendations for practice made by professionals who work with these age groups. Finally, we identify some general strategies through which professionals can make a difference in children's lives.

Child Development as a Field of Inquiry

What does it mean for children to "develop"? When we talk about **development**, we are referring to systematic, age-related changes in the physical and psychological functioning of human beings. Sometimes we are talking about changes that nearly everyone undergoes, such as acquiring increasingly complex language skills and developing consideration for other people's feelings. At other times, we are talking about changes that differ considerably among individuals. For example, over time, some children spontaneously develop effective study skills, but others gain little insight into learning strategies without explicit instruction. Similarly, some children learn to resolve conflicts with peers openly and tactfully, whereas others lash out or withdraw.

Development can also be characterized by the persistence of its changes. Learning to speak a language, to tie one's shoes, and to think abstractly are all changes that endure. Such developmental changes can be contrasted with short-lived physiological changes. For example, a cranky young boy may eat lunch, take an afternoon nap, and awaken pleasantly agreeable. This change in mood, albeit appreciated by his caregivers, is not an age-related change that persists. Predictably, this boy will become cranky again when he runs low on food and sleep.

That developmental abilities persist does not mean they become permanent states, however. Active and curious beings, children try out their new abilities, improve on them, and eventually replace or supplement them with new skills. For example, many infants learn to crawl before they learn to walk. As infants gain balance, muscular control, and confidence in walking, they walk more and crawl less. Eventually, crawling virtually disappears. As another example, a young girl may believe that she should follow rules because doing so shields her from her parents' punishment. Later, she realizes that following rules is valuable because it makes her inherently good. This new idea might last for some time, even years, but eventually be replaced with the insight that rules are essential to protect people's rights, even though they sometimes fail to safeguard everyone.

Finally, when we talk about development, we are typically referring to children's becoming increasingly proficient and responsible. Learning to speak, to tie shoes, and to think about abstract ideas are positive developments. Not every developmental change, however, is healthy or desirable. Through repeated rejection by family members, for instance, a child may learn to interact in a confrontational and accusatory manner, a style that will not help her to make or keep friends. Or, a young person may, through interactions with disillusioned peers, shift from idealism about his future to despair and depression. As you will learn throughout this book, practitioners can follow many strategies to support good developmental outcomes in children and to give second chances to children when they develop unhealthy patterns.

Three Developmental Domains

The study of human development is typically organized into three general areas, or domains: physical development, cognitive development, and social-emotional development. In upcoming chapters, we will examine developmental changes in these three domains. In our discussion of **physical development**, we will investigate patterns of physical growth and maturation, the genetic basis for some human characteristics and abilities, neurological (brain) development, the acquisition of motor skills (e.g., throwing a ball, using scissors), and healthy and unhealthy behaviors. As you may recall from the opening case study, Tonya was taller than her classmates. She may have been taller simply because she was a year older than her peers; she may also have been genetically inclined to be tall. Environmental factors also can influence physical development. For example, nutrition affects physical growth and energy level.

Cognitive development refers to the systematic changes that occur in children's reasoning, concepts, memory, and language. Tonya spent two years in kindergarten before moving on to first grade, perhaps because she initially lacked the cognitive skills that her kindergarten teacher thought would be essential for success in first grade. Also, Tonya responded to Ms. Jalongo's questions with short, simple responses. Was her language development delayed? Probably not; as you will discover, basic language skills develop normally at different rates and under a wide range of circumstances.

development
Systematic, age-related changes in physical and psychological functioning.

physical development
Physical and neurological growth and age-related changes in motor skills.

cognitive development
Systematic changes in reasoning, concepts, memory, and language.

We will use the term **social-emotional development** to refer to changes in children's feelings, ways of coping, social relationships, and moral functioning—for instance, changes in self-esteem, social skills, and beliefs about right and wrong. Notice how Tonya became increasingly self-confident during her year in first grade, to the point where she "sat up tall and proud in her seat" (Jalongo et al., 1995, p. 116). Furthermore, because Tonya's stealing episodes stopped once she was getting breakfast at her aunt's house, it appears that she had a basic respect for other children's possessions. Ms. Jalongo's efforts to repair Tonya's reputation may have helped her begin to forge friendships with classmates. Peer relationships are important to all children, and Tonya's situation reminds us of the pain that children experience when rejected by classmates and others.

Effect of Contexts on Development

Although it may appear that the three domains are three separate areas of development, they are in fact closely interrelated. For example, physical development (e.g., neurological growth) allows cognitive advancements to take place, and increases in the ability to look at situations from multiple perspectives (a cognitive ability) make possible more effective social relationships. And all areas of development are increasingly recognized as depending on children's experiences in schools, families, neighborhoods, clubs, community organizations, and society at large—the contexts in which they grow. The broad social environment, including culture, ethnicity, neighborhood, family, community, socioeconomic status, religious affiliation, and historical events, provides many **contexts** that influence and shape children's development.

Some sort of "family" or other cluster of close, caring relationships—one context—is a critical condition for optimal development. We know a few things about Tonya's family—that Tonya assumed responsibilities beyond her years in caring for her younger brother, that her mother was physically unable to give her much support, and that an aunt was, fortunately, able to provide the physical (and perhaps psychological) nurturance that she so desperately needed. Another context, the financial circumstances of Tonya's family, prevented her from buying pretty dresses like those admired by her third-grade teacher; it is troubling to think about what long-term repercussions this thoughtless teacher's actions may have had on Tonya's emotional and academic growth. The effects of context on children's development will be addressed throughout the book and particularly in Chapter 12, "Families," and Chapter 14, "Growing Up in Context."

As we describe the course of child development and the factors that promote or alter it, we will base our discussions on research primarily in psychology but also in sociology, anthropology, and applied fields, such as early intervention, education, juvenile justice, counseling, social work, and health promotion. In some cases, research findings are consistent with common sense. At other times, they may be surprising and perhaps even inconsistent with commonly held beliefs about child development. In all cases, however, developmental research gives professionals a solid foundation on which to build effective practical strategies. To help cultivate your appreciation for developmental research, we explore research principles early in the book (Chapter 2). In later chapters, we occasionally describe specific research studies to illustrate how researchers have reached their conclusions.

Figure 1–1 gives an overview of the book, identifying chapters in which we will examine developmental research methods, the three domains of development (physical, cognitive, and social-emotional), and the nature of the contexts in which children and adolescents grow.

social-emotional development
Systematic changes in emotional, social, and moral functioning.

context
The broad social environments, including culture, ethnicity, neighborhood, family, community, socioeconomic status, religious affiliation, and historical events, that influence children's development.

Basic Issues in the Study of Development

In their attempts to describe and explain the changes that take place during childhood, developmental theorists have grappled with, but not yet resolved, three key issues. First, they disagree about the relative influences of heredity and environment on various aspects of development. Second, they speculate about the extent to which certain developmental phenomena are true for everyone, or, conversely, unique to particular individuals. Third, when they describe how certain characteristics change, some theorists portray development as

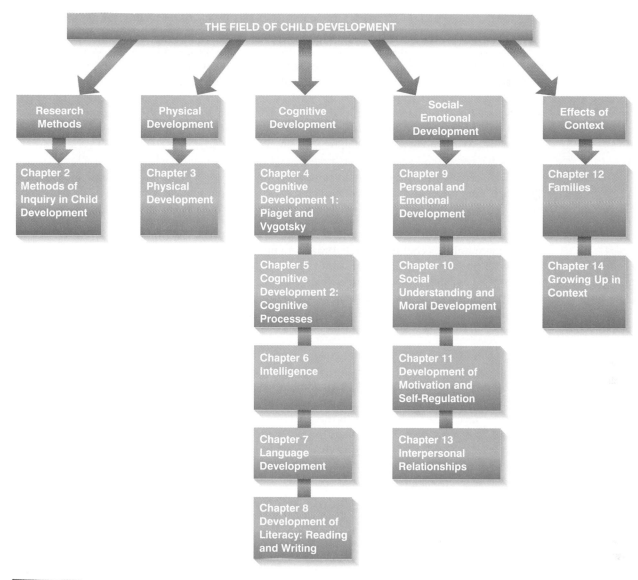

THE FIELD OF CHILD DEVELOPMENT

| Research Methods | Physical Development | Cognitive Development | Social-Emotional Development | Effects of Context |

Chapter 2
Methods of Inquiry in Child Development

Chapter 3
Physical Development

Chapter 4
Cognitive Development 1: Piaget and Vygotsky

Chapter 9
Personal and Emotional Development

Chapter 12
Families

Chapter 5
Cognitive Development 2: Cognitive Processes

Chapter 10
Social Understanding and Moral Development

Chapter 14
Growing Up in Context

Chapter 6
Intelligence

Chapter 11
Development of Motivation and Self-Regulation

Chapter 7
Language Development

Chapter 13
Interpersonal Relationships

Chapter 8
Development of Literacy: Reading and Writing

FIGURE 1–1 Overview of the book

occurring in major transformations, or *stages*, whereas others depict development as a series of more gradual, continuous *trends*. Let's now look more closely at these three issues, which are referred to by theorists as questions of (1) nature and nurture, (2) universality and diversity, and (3) qualitative and quantitative change.

Nature and Nurture

In the study of development, **nature** refers to inherited (genetic) influences on growth and functioning. Some inherited characteristics appear in virtually everyone. For instance, almost all children have natural talents for upright locomotion (walking, running, etc.), language, imitation, and the use of simple tools. Other inherited characteristics differ from one individual to another: these include stature, physical appearance, and athletic ability. Such psychological traits as temperament (e.g., the tendency to be shy instead of outgoing), aggression, and intelligence may also be partly influenced by genetics (Petrill & Wilkerson, 2000; Plomin, 1989; D. C. Rowe, Almeida, & Jacobson, 1999).

Inherited characteristics and tendencies are not always evident at birth. Many emerge gradually through the process of **maturation**, the genetically controlled changes that occur over the course of development. Although basic kinds of environmental support, such as food, are necessary for maturation to take place, people's genetic makeup provides powerful instructions for certain changes to occur under a range of circumstances.

nature
Effects of heredity and genetically controlled maturational processes on development.

maturation
Genetically controlled changes that occur over the course of development.

Expert coaching (nurture) can enhance children's natural abilities (nature).

Nature's partner is **nurture,** the influence of factors in children's environments. Nurture includes the effects of family, peers, schools, neighborhoods, culture, the media, the broader society, and the physical environment. Nurture affects children's development through multiple channels—physically through nutrition and activity; intellectually through informal experiences and formal instruction; socially through adult role models and peer relationships.

Historically, defining the relative influences of nature and nurture has created controversy among developmental theorists. You will find examples of this controversy in our discussions of intelligence (Chapter 6), language development (Chapter 7), temperament (Chapter 9), and aggression (Chapter 13). Increasingly, those who study development believe that nature and nurture intermesh in ways that we may never fully tease apart. There are, nonetheless, some important principles to keep in mind:

■ *The relative effects of heredity and environment vary for different domains of development.* Some domains seem to be governed primarily by genetically controlled systems in the brain. For example, depth perception and the ability to distinguish among various speech sounds develop without training and under a wide range of environmental conditions (Flavell, 1994; Gallistel, Brown, Carey, Gelman, & Keil, 1991). Development in other domains, such as traditional school subject areas (e.g., reading, geography) and advanced artistic and physical arenas (e.g., playing the piano, playing competitive soccer), depend on specific types of instruction and practice (Gardner, Torff, & Hatch, 1996; Olson, 1994; R. Watson, 1996).

■ *Inherited tendencies may make children more or less responsive to particular environmental influences.* Because of their genetic makeup, some children may be easily affected by certain conditions in the environment, whereas others are less affected (M. L. Rutter, 1997). For example, children who are, by nature, timid and inhibited may be quite shy if they have few social contacts. If their parents and teachers encourage them to make friends, however, they may become more socially outgoing (Arcus, 1991; J. Kagan, 1998). In contrast, children who have more extroverted temperaments may be sociable regardless of the environment in which they grow up: They will persistently search for peers with whom they can talk, laugh, and spend time.

■ *Environment may play a greater role when conditions are extreme rather than moderate.* When youngsters have experiences typical for their culture and age group, heredity often accounts for differences in their physical and psychological characteristics. But when they have experiences that are quite unusual—for instance, when they experience extreme deprivation—the role of environment may outweigh the possible influence of heredity (D. C. Rowe, Almeida, & Jacobson, 1999). You will discover in Chapter 6 that when children grow up with adequate nutrition, a loving and stable home environment, and appropriate educational experiences, heredity influences the rate at which they acquire certain intellectual abilities. But when they grow up with inadequate nutrition and harsh physical and psychological stimulation, heredity may have little effect on their intellectual development (Plomin & Petrill, 1997; D. C. Rowe, Jacobson, & Van den Oord, 1999).

■ *Some environmental experiences play a greater role at some ages than at others.* Sometimes the members of a species need a particular kind of stimulation at a particular age to develop normally. For example, classic studies with goslings and ducklings who were exposed to a mother figure (a mother goose, human being, or moving wooden duck decoy) during a particularly narrow age span, or *critical period,* found that these newborns instinctively followed the mother figure and formed an emotional attachment to it. This phenomenon, called *imprinting,* did not occur after the age span passed (Lorenz, 1981; Hess, 1958).

Evidence has since emerged that other species may also have critical periods for certain aspects of development, such as visual perception (Blakemore, 1976; Bruer, 1999; Hubel & Wiesel, 1965). In human beings, too, some kinds of environmental stimulation have a greater effect during particular age ranges. In most cases, however, these age ranges reflect the optimal time, rather than the only time, when such stimulation is effective. In other words, human beings may be most receptive to a certain type of stimulation at one point in their lives but be able to benefit from it to some degree later as well. Furthermore, enriching experiences or explicit training at a later time can often make up for experiences missed

nurture
Effects of environmental conditions on development.

at an earlier period (Bruer, 1999). Hence, some theorists prefer to use the term **sensitive period** (rather than critical period) when talking about the ideal time frames, determined by heredity, for certain environmental experiences.

■ *Children make choices that affect the environments they encounter.* In addition to the influences of nature and nurture, children's own characteristics and behaviors affect their development. They make active choices, seek out information and events that they can understand, modify concepts when confronted with inconsistent information, and, over time, develop ideas about people and the world that they continue to embellish on and refine (Flavell, 1994; Piaget, 1985). This is apparent in children's language development. Children ask for definitions ("What 'cooperate' mean, Mommy?"), seek out people they think can answer their questions ("Uncle Kevin, what is this word in your computer magazine?"), and test their own informal hypotheses about concepts and their boundaries ("Daddy called that a donkey, not a horse. I wonder what the difference is"). Children may even create environments that exacerbate their genetic tendencies. For example, a child with an irritable disposition may pick fights with peers and adults, thereby creating a more aggressive climate in which to grow.

As children get older, they are better able to seek out stimulation and create environments that suit their inherited tendencies. For example, imagine that Marissa has an inherited talent for verbal skills—learning vocabulary, comprehending stories, using sophisticated grammatical structures, and so on. As a baby, she must rely heavily on her parents to talk to her. As a toddler, she can move around independently and ask her parents for particular kinds of stimulation ("Read book, Mommy!"). In elementary school, she may seek out particular books to read and make friends with others who share her interest in books. As a teenager, she is even more capable of defining her own environment; for instance, she may baby-sit to earn money, take the bus to the bookstore, and choose books by a favorite author. Marissa's experience would suggest that genetic tendencies become more powerful as children grow older—an expectation that is in fact consistent with genetic research (Scarr & McCartney, 1983).

In many ways, nature and nurture are inextricably intertwined in their effects on human development. While theorists continue to debate the relative influences of nature and nurture, children usually manage to combine these forces skillfully and naturally (Keating, 1996b). For example, imagine an adolescent girl who is growing rapidly, thanks to genetic instructions activated by puberty (nature); she is also fueled by tasty meals prepared by her parents and extended family (nurture). She is less inclined to be athletic compared to many of her peers (nature) but still joins the girls' basketball team because she is encouraged to do so by her best friend (nurture).

Universality and Diversity

Developmental changes that occur in just about everyone are said to reflect a certain degree of **universality**. For instance, unless physical disabilities are present, all young children learn to sit, walk, and run, almost invariably in that order. Other developmental changes are highly individual, reflecting **diversity**. For instance, children differ in their strength, agility, and endurance as they engage in strenuous physical activities.

Theorists differ in the extent to which they believe that developmental sequences and accomplishments are universal among all human beings or unique to particular individuals. Some propose that heredity and maturation—products of nature—quite logically lead to universality in development (e.g., Gesell, 1928). They point out that, despite widely varying environments, virtually all human beings acquire basic motor skills, a capacity for counting at least small numbers of objects, proficiency in language, an ability to inhibit immediate impulses, and so on.

Heredity and maturation are not necessarily the only route to universality, however. The developmental psychologist Jean Piaget believed that children acquire similar ways of thinking about the world because, despite their unique interactions with objects and people, they are all apt to observe similar phenomena. For example, objects always fall down rather than up and people often get angry when their possessions are snatched away. (We will look at Piaget's theory in depth in Chapter 4.)

Although some developmental changes are universal, others (e.g., tastes in clothing and music) reflect diversity in children's talents, temperaments, interests, relationships, and experiences. Art by Ricco, age 13.

sensitive period
A period in development when certain environmental experiences have a more pronounced influence than is true at other times.

universality
Characteristics and developmental progressions shared by virtually all human beings.

diversity
Characteristics and developmental progressions that differ from one individual to another.

Yet other theorists have been impressed by diversity in cognitive and social functioning during childhood and adolescence (e.g., Baltes, Reese, & Lipsitt, 1980; R. M. Lerner, 1989). Some individual differences can be traced to the historical eras in which people grew up, such as those marked by war, economic depression, counterculture movement, societal apathy, a computer revolution, or terrorism. Differences also occur as a result of events unique to individuals and their families: Did their parents divorce? Did drug dealers invade their neighborhood? Did their parents win the lottery? Finally, cultural settings are significant sources of diversity, as we will see throughout the book and especially in Chapter 14. Children differ in competencies they acquire based on the particular cultural tools, symbols, communication systems, and values that pervade their lives (Rogoff, 1990; Wertsch & Tulviste, 1994).

Earlier, we mentioned that the relative influences of nature and nurture depend on domain. The same point can be made about universality and diversity. Development tends to be more universal in physical development. Diversity is more prevalent in other domains, such as cognitive, social, and moral development. Furthermore, there is always some diversity, even in physical development. Obviously, children vary in height, weight, and skin color, and some are born with physical disabilities or become injured. Throughout the book, we will find instances of developmental universality, but, perhaps more often, we will see divergences from typical pathways.

To be effective with children, professionals draw on universals of children's development; they are also sensitive to the many ways in which children are likely to be different from one another and from what is "average" for a particular age group. As we saw in the opening case study, Ms. Jalongo was well aware that Tonya was in some ways different from her classmates: she was taller, her bullying behavior was unusual for a first grader, and her ability to cajole her classmates into uneven "trades" indicated possible sophistication in persuasion. But Ms. Jalongo also suspected that Tonya, like nearly all children, had a basic desire to make friends, and so she paved the way for her to repair her reputation once the stealing stopped.

One theorist has offered a simple analogy that may help you understand the roles of universality and diversity in development:

> Development is like a game of Scrabble. The fundamental rules of the game and the strategies for maximizing progress are essentially the same for all players. However, because everyone starts with a different set of tiles and plays a different pattern of words, each player faces unique challenges and opportunities throughout the course of the game. That is why effective educational policies and practices must be based on notions of diversity and individuality, not on norms and group averages. Although education often occurs in group settings, development always proceeds one child at a time. (M. E. Ford, 1997, p. 124)

As professionals work with children, they should keep in mind not only typical age trends but also the diversity in children's abilities and developmental progress.

Qualitative and Quantitative Change

Sometimes development is characterized by a rather sudden, dramatic change in behavior or thinking; this is a **qualitative change**. For instance, when children learn to run, they propel their bodies forward in a way that is distinctly different from walking. When they begin to talk in two-word sentences rather than with single words, they are, for the first time, using rudimentary forms of grammar that govern the ways in which they combine words.

Not all development involves dramatic change. In fact, development more frequently occurs as a gradual progression, or *trend,* with many small additions to behaviors and thought processes. This progression is **quantitative change**. For example, children grow taller gradually over time, and with both age and experience they slowly learn more about such diverse realms as the animal kingdom and friendship.

Stage Theories Theorists associate qualitative change with a systematic revamping of previously acquired knowledge and skills. Often, they use the term **stage** to refer to a period of development characterized by a particular way of behaving or thinking. According to a **stage theory** of development, individuals progress through a series of stages that are qualitatively

qualitative change
Relatively dramatic developmental change that reflects considerable reorganization or modification of functioning.

quantitative change
Developmental change that involves a series of minor, trendlike modifications.

stage
A period of development characterized by a particular way of behaving or thinking.

stage theory
Theory that describes development as involving a series of qualitatively distinct changes, with these changes occurring in the same sequence for everyone.

different from one another. Most stage theories are *hierarchical*. In other words, each stage is seen as providing the essential foundation for the next one.[1] Stage theories often assume that children act and reason in one stage at a time; during periods of transition, children may move back and forth between two stage levels until they become proficient at the higher level.

Developmental theorists have been attracted to the concept of stages ever since the field of developmental psychology was founded (Parke, Ornstein, Rieser, & Zahn-Waxler, 1994). You will learn about several stage theories in this book, including Piaget's theory of cognitive development in Chapter 4, Erikson's theory of social-emotional development in Chapter 9, and Kohlberg's theory of moral development in Chapter 10.

Research does not entirely support the notion that children and adolescents proceed through one stage at a time or that they always move in the same direction. Children often display characteristics of two or more stages during a single period of time, depending on circumstances (e.g., Ceci & Roazzi, 1994; Kurtines & Gewirtz, 1991; Metz, 1995). For example, a 9-year-old girl may show an advanced ability to plan ahead while playing chess, her hobby, but she cannot easily plan ahead while writing a complex essay, an unfamiliar activity. Nor do stage progressions always appear to be universal across cultures or educational contexts (e.g., Glick, 1975; Triandis, 1995). For example, 13-year-olds in vastly different cultures learn to think differently because of the society in which they are raised; children in different cultures or academic environments do not progress through stages at the same age. Because of these and other exceptions to stages, few contemporary developmentalists support strict versions of stage theories (Parke et al., 1994).

At the same time, most theorists do not choose to abandon all notions of qualitative change (Flavell, 1994). It is obvious, for example, that the actions of adolescents at age 15 differ consistently from those of 2-year-old children. Fifteen-year-olds are not simply taller and more knowledgeable about the world; they go about their day-to-day living in a qualitatively different style. Maturation-based developments, such as neurological increases in memory capacity and efficiency, plus an ever-expanding accumulation of knowledge and experience, probably permit and promote both gradual and occasionally dramatic changes in thinking and behaving (Case et al., 1996; Flavell, 1994).

As you read this book, you will find that debate about the three basic developmental issues resurfaces periodically within individual chapters and in Basic Developmental Issues tables. (The first of these tables, "Illustrations in the Three Domains," provides examples of how the three basic developmental issues are reflected in the domains of physical, cognitive, and social-emotional development.) Continually revisiting the issues will remind us that development is the outcome of both natural forces (nature) and environmental influences (nurture), that it displays common pathways (universality) and exceptions (diversity), and that it reflects many minor changes (quantitative change) as well as occasional major reorganizations (qualitative change).

Theories of Child Development

In the 18th and 19th centuries, many scholars began to investigate the nature of change, looking at the histories of such varied phenomena as animal species, geological features, culture, and ideas (Dixon & Lerner, 1992). Charles Darwin's theory of natural selection and evolution provided an influential framework for looking at change in living beings, including humans (Charlesworth, 1992; Dixon & Lerner, 1992). Darwin and other early theorists articulated key ideas that have provided the foundation on which many current theories of human development rest. These ideas include the following:

- Knowledge about an individual's past can help us understand the individual's present functioning.

---

[1] Note that developmentalists use the term *stage* in a somewhat narrower way than we use it in everyday speech. Parents and other adults often make comments such as "He's at the terrible twos stage" or "She's at that stage when she really worries about what her friends think." Such comments reflect the idea that children are behaving typically for their age group, but they don't necessarily imply that a *qualitative* change has taken place.

BASIC DEVELOPMENTAL ISSUES

Illustrations in the Three Domains

ISSUE	PHYSICAL DEVELOPMENT	COGNITIVE DEVELOPMENT	SOCIAL-EMOTIONAL DEVELOPMENT
Nature and Nurture	Nature governs the maturational unfolding of specific parts of the brain in a particular order. Genetic factors also determine certain physical pre-dispositions, such as a tendency toward thinness or a susceptibility to diabetes. On the other hand, the importance of nutrition for health and training for athletic skills shows nurture at work (Chapter 3).	Some aspects of intelligence and language seem to be genetically based. However, many contemporary theorists emphasize the significance of environmental influences (nurture), such as informal learning experiences, adult modeling and mentoring, and formal schooling (Chapters 4, 5, 6, 7).	Individual differences in temperament appear to be partly controlled by heredity (nature). Environmental influences (nurture) are evident in the development of self-esteem and ethnic identity (Chapter 9).
Universality and Diversity	The emergence of key physical features (e.g., gender-specific features appearing during puberty) is universal. Diversity is evident in the ages at which children and adolescents undergo key physical developments, as well as in their general state of physical health (Chapter 3).	The components of the human information processing system (e.g., the mechanisms that allow learning and memory) are universal. However, diversity is evident in the fact that some children have more effective ways of learning and remembering academic information than others (Chapter 5).	The need for peer affiliation represents a universal aspect of development in children and adolescents. However, there are considerable individual differences in expression of prosocial behavior and aggression (Chapter 13).
Qualitative and Quantitative Change	Some aspects of physical development (e.g., transformations in puberty) reflect dramatic qualitative change. Most of the time, however, physical development occurs gradually as a result of many small changes (e.g., young children slowly grow taller, then experience a rapid growth spurt in adolescence) (Chapter 3), which are considered quantitative change.	Children's logical reasoning skills show some qualitative change; for instance, children acquire new and increasingly sophisticated ways of solving problems. Quantitative change occurs as children gradually gain knowledge in various academic disciplines (Chapters 4 and 5).	Some evidence suggests that, with appropriate social experience, children's understanding of morality undergoes qualitative change, often in conjunction with changes in logical reasoning ability. In a more quantitative manner, children gradually come to understand how other people's minds work and discover that others' knowledge, beliefs, and desires may be different than their own (Chapter 10).

- Both biological capacities and environmental experiences contribute to an individual's present characteristics.
- The nature of children's development is best investigated through systematic and scientific methods of inquiry.
- The changes that children exhibit as they grow older lead to improvements in their ability to function and adapt to environmental circumstances.

The last of these ideas, that change leads to progressive improvements, has been called into question in recent decades. As you may recall from our earlier discussion of developmental change, developmental transformations do not necessarily reflect increases in maturity or effective functioning. In other words, some developmental changes are probably not for the best. Nevertheless, the notion of progressive change has long been a guiding principle in the field of child development (Bronfenbrenner, Kessel, Kessen, & White, 1986).

In the first few decades of the twentieth century, explicit **theories**—organized systems of principles and explanations of child development—began to emerge. Over the years, these theories have governed the questions that developmental scientists ask, provided ground rules for research methods, and helped researchers make sense of their observations. In the next few pages, we survey the currently dominant theoretical perspectives of development. We urge that you, in turn, take advantage of these diverse perspectives in your attempts to understand infants, children, and adolescents, and to work more effectively with them.

theory
Organized system of principles and explanations regarding a particular phenomenon.

Theoretical Perspectives of Development

Nine theoretical approaches have dominated academic discussions about children and adolescents. We examine them briefly here and then revisit them in later chapters as they become relevant to our discussions of particular topics.

Maturational Perspectives   Developmental scholars working within **maturational perspectives** emphasize genetic and physiological contributions to developing structures of the body, neurological pathways in the brain, and motor abilities. Historically, the best known maturational theorist was Arnold Gesell, who focused on developmental changes that occur almost automatically, without learning or instruction (Gesell, 1928). According to this perspective, children walk when they are physiologically ready to do so, and puberty begins when a biological clock triggers the appropriate hormones. On the basis of our earlier discussion about the contributions of nature and nurture to development, you will be able to see that theorists who adopt a maturational perspective are emphasizing the nature side of the continuum. The influence of maturational perspectives is discussed in Chapter 3. Most contemporary theorists believe that genetically controlled maturational forces also require some degree of nurture. Although children's bodies and motor skills may develop largely as a result of preprogrammed instructions, children also need ongoing nutrition, exercise, and affection to make optimal physical development possible.

Psychodynamic Perspectives   Theorists taking a **psychodynamic perspective** believe that early experiences play a critical role in later characteristics and behavior. They typically focus on social and personality development and, often, on abnormal development.

Sigmund Freud, the earliest psychodynamic theorist, argued that there is more to childhood than innocent play. According to Freud, young children continually find themselves embroiled in internal conflicts between impulses toward sexuality and aggression, on the one hand, and socially sanctioned pressures to gain parental approval and be productive, on the other. Through ongoing negotiations with parents, children progress through a series of qualitatively distinct stages, eventually learning to channel their biological impulses in socially appropriate ways. You will find examples of psychodynamic perspectives in Erik Erikson's psychosocial theory in Chapter 9 and in Freud's ideas about moral development in Chapter 10.

Today, psychodynamic perspectives are seldom in the spotlight of developmental thinking. Nonetheless, some of Freud's core ideas remain influential: early social experiences can put children onto a healthy or unhealthy trajectory; forceful and repeated efforts may be needed to dislodge children from an abnormal path; and children do wrestle with particular issues during certain phases of their life.

Cognitive-Developmental Perspectives   Cognitive-developmental perspectives emphasize thinking processes and how they change, qualitatively, over time. According to cognitive-developmental perspectives, children typically play an active role in their own development: They seek out new and interesting experiences, try to make sense of what they see and hear, and work actively to reconcile any discrepancies between new information and what they have previously believed to be true. Through these impulses, children's thinking becomes more abstract and systematic.

The earliest and best known cognitive-developmental theorist was Jean Piaget. With a career that spanned decades and spawned thousands of research studies around the world, Piaget touched on many aspects of children's lives, including emotional development, peer relationships, and moral reasoning. However, his main focus and contributions were in cognitive development. He investigated the nature of children's logical thinking about such topics as numbers, physical causality, geographical formations, and time. We will describe Piaget's work in Chapter 4. A second cognitive-developmental perspective, Lawrence Kohlberg's theory of how moral reasoning develops, is presented in Chapter 10.

In the last few decades, cognitive-developmental perspectives have been vigorously critiqued. As we already suggested in the discussion of qualitative change, researchers have found that children's development does not necessarily coincide with the neat stage progressions that some theorists outline. Instead, children move from level to level and back again. Indeed, when tested, they are affected by minor changes in the questions they are asked and by simple substitutions to the materials they are analyzing. Such factors really shouldn't matter from a stage

Children develop, in part, by actively seeking out new and interesting experiences. Art by Margot, age 6.

maturational perspective
Theoretical perspective that emphasizes genetically guided unfolding of developmental structures, neurological organizations, and motor abilities.

psychodynamic perspective
Theoretical perspective that focuses on how early experiences affect social and personality development.

cognitive-developmental perspective
Theoretical perspective that focuses on qualitative changes in thinking processes over time.

orientation. Cognitive-developmental perspectives have also been criticized because of their assumption that all children are heading in the same direction toward abstract thinking. Despite these serious limitations, cognitive-developmental theories provide compelling descriptions of how thinking generally changes with age. They also convey children's active role in their own development as they search for meaning in experience.

Behavioral Learning Perspectives   A fourth position, the **behavioral learning perspective**, stands in sharp contrast to the earlier perspectives we have described by crediting developmental changes almost exclusively to environmental influences (nurture). Conducting research with humans and other species (e.g., dogs, rats, pigeons), behavioral learning theorists have shown that many behaviors can be modified through environmental stimuli. For example, theorists have demonstrated that children actively "work" for rewards such as food, praise, or physical contact, and tend to avoid behaviors that lead to punishment.

Behavioral learning theorists recently have begun to realize that children do not necessarily respond mindlessly to environmental events but, instead, actively think about and interpret those events. They have discovered that children can learn a great deal by observing others. Children can, furthermore, anticipate the consequences of their actions and choose their behaviors accordingly. We will present the ideas of one prominent behavioral learning theorist, B. F. Skinner, in our discussions of language development (Chapter 7) and motivation (Chapter 11). A second theorist, Albert Bandura, built his social cognitive theory on behaviorist foundations but has increasingly incorporated elements of cognition in recent years; we will consider Bandura's ideas in our discussions of self-regulation (Chapter 11) and families (Chapter 12).

Evolutionary Perspectives   Reflecting the influence of Charles Darwin, **evolutionary perspectives** focus on inherited behavior patterns that enhance a child's chances for survival and eventual reproduction. Characteristics and behaviors that increase likelihood of survival and reproduction are likely to be passed on genetically to future generations.

Two general types of evolutionary perspectives are ethology and sociobiology. *Ethological theorists* study behavior patterns they believe are inherited. From an ethological perspective it makes sense that parents and infants form emotional bonds to each other ("Isn't my baby adorable?!"), that people react alertly to threat signals ("Fire!"), that they engage in courtship rituals ("Dinner at my place?"), and that they safeguard their young ("A prison in my neighborhood? Never!"). *Sociobiologists* have similar concerns, but are more interested in behaviors that occur within a social group, such as childrearing, cooperation, and self-sacrifice, and that affect the long-term survival and proliferation of the group.

Evolutionary researchers cannot go back in time, and so must painstakingly re-create the pressures of long-gone environments. Often, they conduct research with other species and draw parallels to humans. Because much of their research and theorizing is after-the-fact, their evidence can seem speculative. Even so, evolutionary theorists make powerful arguments that childhood behaviors must be adaptations to the environments our ancestors inhabited eons ago. For example, our ancestors' children probably did not survive their early years unless they formed social-emotional bonds with caregivers who protected them. We will see in Chapter 9 that children form intense bonds with their caregivers and fear strangers at a time when they are especially vulnerable—able to crawl, explore, and unwittingly encounter danger. Also, children's need for physical activity, examined in Chapter 3, is almost certainly a product of selection. From an evolutionary perspective, children had to be physically fit to keep up with parents while they hunted, searched for food, and outran predators.

Information Processing Perspectives   Information processing perspectives focus on the nature of human cognitive processes—for instance, how people transform and remember the information they receive—and on how these processes change during childhood and adolescence. Early information processing theories, which emerged in the 1960s, modeled human thinking processes on the linear way in which computers operate. More recently, however, many theorists have acknowledged that computers and human beings probably "think" very differently (Derry, 1996; Mayer, 1996). Whether or not they use a computer metaphor, information processing theorists all attempt to describe children's and adolescents' thought processes with a fair amount of precision.

behavioral learning perspective
Theoretical perspective that focuses on environmental stimuli and learning processes that lead to developmental change.

evolutionary perspective
Theoretical perspective that focuses on inherited behavior patterns that enhance the survival and reproduction of the species.

information processing perspective
Theoretical perspective that focuses on the precise nature of human cognitive processes.

Information processing perspectives now dominate much of the research in cognitive development, and they will be the focus of much of our discussion of cognitive development in Chapter 5. You will also see the influence of information processing theory in our discussions of intelligence (Chapter 6), language development (Chapter 7), literacy (Chapter 8), and social cognition (Chapter 10). A drawback of some information processing approaches is that they neglect the social-emotional factors and contexts of children's lives, factors that many other modern developmental viewpoints consider to be significant.

Sociocultural Perspectives   Sociocultural perspectives illuminate the social and cultural systems in which children and adolescents develop. These perspectives show how parents and other adults encourage children to participate in meaningful activities. Depending on children's particular culture, these activities might include cooking, shopping, selling goods, caring for younger children, repairing a car engine, running a meeting, weaving a basket, or some other tasks. By participating in such activities and gradually taking on higher levels of responsibility, children learn to become responsible citizens.

Lev Vygotsky is the pioneering figure credited for advancing our knowledge of how children's minds are shaped by everyday experiences in social settings. In addition to emphasizing participation in everyday activities, Vygotsky suggested that the tools children learn to use affect their cognitive development. Depending on their culture, children may learn to use alphabets, number systems, computer technologies, pottery supplies, automotive equipment, or some other set of tools. Children learn to use such tools through close contact and activity with adults and others in their community. Side-by-side, children talk new ideas over with peers, brothers and sisters, younger and older children, and adults. Because Vygotsky emphasized the importance of society and culture for promoting children's cognitive growth, his theory is referred to as a *sociocultural perspective*. We describe Vygotsky's views on cognitive development in Chapter 4.

Children and adolescents learn a lot from participating in routine, purposeful activities with adults and others.

In the last two decades, there has been a virtual explosion of research conducted within sociocultural perspectives. This research is often well received by professionals who work with children because it is written about real children in real settings, in a manner that feels authentic. Furthermore, many professionals appreciate the beneficial effects these perspectives attribute to the environment (nurture is emphasized). Another strength of sociocultural perspectives is that they uncover substantial diversity in development—they show concretely how different cultural groups encourage children to use distinct modes of thinking. As with any theoretical approach, sociocultural perspectives have limitations. Its theorists, for example, have described children's thinking with less precision than have theorists working within information processing perspectives.

Developmental Systems Perspectives   Developmental systems perspectives show how multiple factors combine to steer children's development in dynamic and sometimes unpredictable ways. Systems perspectives emphasize the organizational structures of which children are made (e.g., their bodies), and the settings in which they reside and to which they contribute (e.g., their families). The child is a *changing system* because he or she constantly finds new ways to operate on the world. For example, a baby once had to be carried but now crawls and explores the house independently. Similarly, a high school student previously relied on parents to take her places but now begs for car keys. The child is also an *embedded system* because he or she relies on other people and the earth's natural resources to grow.

From systems perspectives, no single factor rules—whether genes, children's own efforts at understanding, social experiences, rewards from adults, circuits in the brain, cultural tools, practice, or conversation. All of these factors, and more, govern children's learning, thinking, feeling, growing, and relating to others. Systems perspectives are complex and can be difficult to grasp. However, they represent a promising way to think about development (Ford & Lerner, 1992; R. M. Lerner, 1998).

Dynamic systems theories clarify elements inside children and in their environment that influence how children carry out specific actions, such as reaching for objects, searching for hidden objects, learning new words, and expressing emotions. These theories specify that when children act, they integrate the many forces that impinge on them, including their own understandings, habitual ways of acting, body weight and motor strength, existing brain connections, and encouragement from adults.

sociocultural perspective
Theoretical perspective that focuses on children's learning of tools and communication systems through practice in meaningful tasks with other people.

developmental systems perspective
Theoretical perspective that focuses on the multiple factors, including systems inside and outside children, that combine to influence children's development.

Depending on their developmental levels, children's style of acting may be easily disrupted by factors both internal and external to them. For example, a toddler with an unsteady gait cannot maintain upright mobility all the time; when he is tired, distracted, or faced with obstacles on the floor, he is especially likely to fall. Other patterns of behavior may be far more consistent. This same toddler, when frightened, routinely calms down when comforted by the loving touch of a caregiver. This latter pattern of behavior is much more stable and resistant to change.

Dynamic systems theorists describe developmental change as being continual, somewhat unpredictable, and highly individual. Even universal motor milestones, such as infants' learning to reach for objects, show significant individual differences in the ways that children go about mastering them. In reflecting on these dynamic, ever-changing patterns in children, Thelen and Smith (1998) have likened development to a mountain stream, with smooth flowing water in some places, quiet whirlpools in others, and turbulent waves and water spray in yet other areas. Like mountain streams, children are systems that create order—mixed with a bit of chaos—out of their own resources, contact from other people, and opportunities presented in the outside world. In Chapter 3, we refer to dynamic systems theories when describing principles of physical development and changes in the brain.

A second important systems perspective we refer to is Bronfenbrenner's (1979) *ecological systems theory.* Bronfenbrenner (1979) described the natural environments of childhood, including children's immediate and extended families, neighborhoods, schools, parents' workplaces, mass media, community services, and political systems and practices. (Recall our description of *contexts* earlier in this chapter.) These social systems often interact with one another as they affect children. For example, out-of-home caregivers assist many parents with their children during the day. However, if child care is not responsive, safe, and stable, parents may become anxious about the welfare of their children and experience stress. Parents' stress may in turn lead them to be less patient and effective with their children. You will see the influence of ecological perspectives in our discussion of "Families" in Chapter 12 and "Growing Up in Context" in Chapter 14.

Life-Span Perspectives **Life-span perspectives** track developmental changes from conception to death. Some of these changes are predictable and age-related, others are more dependent on particular historical events (e.g., war, economic depression), and still others are the result of individual life events (e.g., divorce of parents, death of a close friend). Life-span theorists depict development as the result of dynamic interactions among maturational, contextual, historical, and cultural forces, a process that does not stop once people reach adulthood (Baltes, Lindenberger, & Staudinger, 1998). Life-span perspectives are similar, in their complexity, to developmental systems perspectives.

Life-span perspectives are a useful way to look at development, particularly as they remind us of the many forces that impinge on development and the diversity of developmental paths people take. For those of us concerned primarily with childhood and adolescence, life-span perspectives are also useful in pinpointing the interesting things that happen *after* adolescence. This is particularly important when youngsters are seriously troubled in their adolescent years. Because development continues throughout adulthood, troubled individuals may eventually find the resolve they need to rebuild their lives. We refer to one life-span theorist, Erik Erikson, in discussions of personal and emotional development in Chapter 9. (Earlier, we referred to Erikson as a psychodynamic theorist; he is also known for examining developmental change from infancy through old age.)

Life-span perspectives also draw attention to the growing and changing that take place in children's parents and guardians. Through tactful and culturally sensitive communication with professionals, parents can learn new ways to think about children. We examine partnerships with families in Chapter 12.

Taking an Eclectic Approach

The nine perspectives just described are summarized in Table 1–1. With so many theories, it would be tempting to ask, Which one is right? The answer is that, to some extent, they all are. Each theory provides unique insights into the nature of child development that no other approach can offer. At the same time, no single theory can adequately explain all aspects of

---

life-span perspective
Theoretical perspective that looks at developmental patterns from conception until death.

TABLE 1-1	Theoretical Perspectives on the Development of Infants, Children, and Adolescents	
THEORETICAL PERSPECTIVES	**EMPHASES OF PERSPECTIVES**	**ILLUSTRATIONS IN THE LIVES OF INFANTS, CHILDREN, AND ADOLESCENTS**
Maturational Perspectives	The development of many physical abilities depends on the genetically controlled unfolding of physiological and neurological structures.	• The pencil grip of kindergarten children depends on their level of neurological development. • During adolescence, physical changes associated with puberty are guided by maturational forces.
Psychodynamic Perspectives	Children and adolescents experience impulses related to sexuality and aggression, on the one hand, and desires for receiving social approval and making productive contributions to society, on the other. Through a series of qualitatively different stages, they learn to channel their impulses in socially acceptable ways.	• When young children cannot satisfy their immediate desires, they may lash out at others (e.g., by hitting another child). • Adolescents can release their frustrations through vigorous physical activity.
Cognitive-Developmental Perspectives	Children and adolescents actively contribute to their own intellectual development. As they discover difficulties or contradictions in their own thinking, they formulate new ways of understanding the world. With development, intellectual operations are increasingly abstract and systematic.	• Young children better understand the nature of numbers when they can see how counting and arithmetic operations play out with concrete manipulatives. • Through relationships with peers, children and adolescents learn to appreciate the rights of others and negotiate rules that ensure fairness for all.
Behavioral Learning Perspectives	Children and adolescents actively work for rewards such as food, praise, and physical contact. They learn a great deal from observing others, and as they learn which behaviors are likely to have successful outcomes, they eventually begin to regulate their own behavior.	• Many preschoolers and elementary school students eagerly seek the praise of their teachers, counselors, religious leaders, and recreation specialists. • Adolescents vigilantly observe and often imitate the ways of speaking, manner of dress, and activities of their friends.
Evolutionary Perspectives	Characteristics and behaviors that enhance an individual's chances for survival and reproduction may have a genetic basis.	• Parents react quickly when they believe that their infants are in danger. • Adolescents often engage in courtship rituals, trying to attract the attention of the opposite sex.
Information Processing Perspectives	The ways in which children perceive, interpret, and remember information change over time. With age, children become increasingly aware of and able to control their own cognitive processes.	• Young children often experience information overload when they first begin a new and complex task. • Adolescents often benefit from explicit instruction in how to study effectively.
Sociocultural Perspectives	The cultures in which children live have a significant influence on their learning and development. Children learn to use tools favored by their families and communities as they practice meaningful tasks with others.	• Children tend to acquire the skills and attitudes that their communities value (e.g., if their parents are active readers, children may read voluntarily). • Children often learn a great deal when working in a one-on-one mentoring relationship with an experienced adult.
Developmental Systems Perspectives	Multiple factors inside and outside the child combine to influence developmental patterns. In some domains, children may use different means to achieve the *same* milestone; in other domains, they take varied developmental paths and end up with *different* skills and dispositions.	• Infants may achieve a milestone, such as grasping an object, through a variety of means: mastering different muscle groups, using one or both arms, and perfecting a grasp quickly or over an extended time. • The ability of families to help children meet their needs is affected by the support families enjoy from friends, extended family, neighbors, child care providers, and community leaders.
Life-Span Perspectives	Developmental changes occur in individuals from conception to death. Some of these changes are predictable and age-related, others are dependent on particular historical events, and still others result from individual life events.	• Children growing up in the 21st century may have childhood experiences very different from those of adults who grew up in earlier times. • Parents' own life changes and events (e.g., marriage, relocation) affect their relationships with children.

development. In a sense, any theory is like a lens that brings certain phenomena into sharp focus but leaves other phenomena blurry or unrecognizable.

Throughout the book, we introduce a variety of theoretical explanations for the phenomena we are addressing. We urge you to take an eclectic attitude, looking for the best or most useful ideas that each theory has to offer. Each of the theories can help you understand some aspects of children's development, and each can give you some useful ideas about how to promote optimal development during the infancy, early childhood, and school years.

Developmental Periods

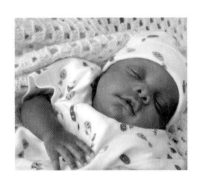

We can make our task of exploring child development more manageable by dividing the developmental journey into specific time periods. But how do we divide the "pie" of childhood into meaningful "slices"? Age cutoffs are somewhat arbitrary because universal stages with precise timetables cannot be found in any domain of development. Nonetheless, infants are very different from 8-year-olds, who in turn are very different from teenagers. Therefore, in our upcoming discussions, we will often compare different age groups. When we do so, we will consider five age periods: infancy (birth to 2 years), early childhood (2–6 years), middle childhood (6–10 years), early adolescence (10–14 years), and late adolescence (14–18 years). Here, we will look briefly at each period and at viewpoints of professionals who educate and care for young people in each age group.

Infancy (Birth–2 Years)

Infancy is a truly remarkable period, a time during which basic human traits—emotional bonds to other human beings, nonverbal communication and language expression, motor exploration of the physical environment, and systematic approaches to learning about people, places, and things—burst onto the scene.

Distinctive Developmental Features   Looking at a newborn, it is hard to grasp the enormous changes that will take place in the next two years. That small being, attached snugly to a caregiver, is completely dependent on others. But baby is also equipped with an arsenal of skills that gain comfort and stimulation from caregivers—a distinctive cry, physical reflexes, an attractive smile, and a brain alert to both novelty and sameness. As the caregiver responds warmly and consistently, attachment grows.

This security nourishes infants' desire to learn. Babies want to know everything: what keys taste like, what older family members do in the kitchen, what lurks on the other side of an electrical outlet, what happens when they drop their bowl of peas, and how other children respond when they pull their hair. Infants' growing facility with language builds on interests in concrete things—the sensation of warm water in the bathtub, the bounce of the ball, a parent's laughter.

Intellectual curiosity also fuels babies' drive to use physical skills—they reach, crawl, and climb to get objects they desire. The urge to explore coincides with a budding sense of mastery ("I can do it!") and a sense of independence ("*I* can do it!"). Physical development is accompanied by emotional reactions that guide behavior, such as a legitimate fear of heights and uneasiness in the presence of strangers.

Professional Viewpoints   Professionals who work with infants realize that each baby is unique, develops at his or her own rate, and is hungry for loving interaction. Infant caregivers emphasize *quality* of care, a position supported by research on the long-term effects of early care (NICHD Early Child Care Research Network, 2002). Caregivers who emphasize quality of care give individualized, responsive, and affectionate care to growing babies. (We examine quality of care in more detail in Chapter 14.) For example, in a recent article in a journal published by the National Center for Infants, Toddlers, and Families, Chazan-Cohen, Jerald, and Stark (2001) make these recommendations:

During the first two years, many dramatic developmental changes occur.

Attention must be given to the individual needs of the infant and the parents. Responsive caregiving of the infant that acknowledges and addresses the infant's needs and behavioral temperament will convey the respect and security essential for early emotional development.

Responsivity to parents' individual circumstances and life histories can enable parents to more comfortably engage in a beneficial relationship with their infant. (p. 9)

The authors are suggesting that professionals who work with infants also form supportive relationships with parents. Through these relationships, caregivers can learn about infants' home routines as well as educate parents about their children's rapidly changing abilities and needs.

In addition, infant caregivers design the physical environment so babies and toddlers can explore toys, objects, and surroundings freely. In the Environments/Infancy clip of the Observation CD that accompanies this textbook (see description to the right), you can observe one setting where crawling infants can speed up and down cushioned ramps and walking infants can strut around open spaces.[2] When infants stumble, furniture poses little threat since it has been crafted with smooth, rounded edges. Caregivers also design environments to foster infants' cognitive development and promote social interaction. In this video clip, notice a mirror that attracts attention; colorful toys with complex textures that beg to be touched; mobiles over cribs that encourage looking and studying; a tunnel that invites entering, exiting, and playing peek-a-boo games; and simple books for examination with caregivers while cuddling in a rocking chair.

These features of early care—affectionate, individualized, and responsive attention to infants; positive relationships with parents and other family members; and provision of a safe and interesting environment—help get infants off to a good start. They prepare infants for the expanded learning opportunities they will encounter in early childhood.

Early Childhood (2–6 Years)

Early childhood is a period of incredible creativity, fantasy, wonder, and play. Preschool-aged children see life as a forum for imagination and drama: They reinvent the world, try on new roles, and struggle to play their parts in harmony.

Distinctive Developmental Features Language and communication skills develop rapidly during early childhood. New vocabulary, appropriate use of language in social contexts, and facility with syntax (grammar) are noticeable advancements. Language builds on daily increases in knowledge about the world and, especially, the habits and patterns of daily life.

Physical changes are apparent as well. The cautious movements of infancy give way to fluid rolling, tumbling, running, and skipping. High levels of energy radiate from preschool-aged children's activities. Young children don't walk; they run, dance, and skip. They don't talk; they chatter, sing, and moan. They don't sit quietly on the sidelines; they handle, pour, and paste.

Socially and emotionally, preschoolers are often endearing, trusting, and affectionate. They become progressively more interested in others, eagerly spend time with playmates, and infuse social interactions with fantasy. However, their concern for others coexists with aggressive and self-centered impulses, which occasionally interfere with effective interactions.

Professional Viewpoints Practitioners working with young children wish to inspire and channel children's natural energy. They are respectful of young children's curiosity, spontaneity, and desires to try on new roles. As an example, the National Association for the Education of Young Children (NAEYC) offers these recommendations regarding appropriate practice for promoting cognitive development in 4- and 5-year-olds:

> Children develop understanding of concepts about themselves, others, and the world around them through observation, interacting with people and real objects, and seeking solutions to concrete problems. Learnings about math, science, social studies, health, and other

Observe the Environments/ Infancy clip to see a setting that is safe and interesting for infants. This clip is part of a three-CD set that accompanies this textbook. You can use this set, Observing Children and Adolescents: Guided Interactive Practice in Understanding Development (version 1.0), to enhance your understanding of developmental concepts and to refine your observation skills of children.

Preschool children learn from handling concrete objects, from pretending, and from talking with adults and other children.

---

[2] Appreciation is extended to Greg Pierson, University Schools, and Keli Cotner, Campus Child Care Center, both of Greeley, CO, for granting permission to film their facilities.

content areas are all integrated through meaningful activities such as those when children build with blocks; measure sand, water, or ingredients for cooking; observe changes in the environment; work with wood and tools; sort objects for a purpose; explore animals, plants, water, wheels and gears; sing and listen to music from various cultures; and draw, paint, and work with clay. Routines are followed that help children keep themselves healthy and safe. (Bredekamp, 1987, p. 56)

Environments for young children can be designed to encourage the active and purposeful learning advocated by the NAEYC. For example, in the Environments/Early Childhood clip of the Observation CD, you can see a classroom where children can draw and paint creatively. Play structures encourage children to climb, hide, stand tall, and spot one another. Tables and chairs make it possible for children to sit and talk together during mealtimes and group activities. A dramatic play area, furnished with kitchen appliances and dress-up clothes, encourages children to share fantasies with friends. Elsewhere in the room they can sit and look at books and take turns on a computer. Mats let children recharge their batteries with sleep and rest; a separate bathroom area is available for toilet needs and hand washing. Outdoors, children can scoot on vehicles, ride bicycles, and play in the sand.

Given ample chances to explore their environment and to converse with others, young children gain valuable knowledge about themselves and their world. They become ready to apply this knowledge to realistic tasks.

In the Environments/Early Childhood clip, observe a setting that encourages active, creative movement, pretend play, and hands-on learning in young children.

Middle Childhood (6–10 Years)

Whereas in early childhood interests are often transient and fleeting, middle childhood is a time of sustained attention to real-world tasks. Pretending is not abandoned, but it plays less of a role than it did earlier. Instead, children display motivation and persistence in mastering the customs, tools, and accumulated knowledge of their community and culture. For example, children of this age often learn to read and write, cook and clean house, apply rules in games and sports, care for younger brothers and sisters, and use computer technology.

Distinctive Developmental Features   Serious commitments to peers, especially to playmates of the same age and gender, emerge. Friendships are important, and children learn much from interactions with friends and resolutions of disputes.

Children also begin to compare their performance to that of others: Why do I have fewer friends than Janie and Maria? Am I good enough to be picked for the baseball team? Will I ever learn to read like the other kids? When they routinely end up on the losing side in such comparisons, they are more hesitant to try new academic tasks. Individual differences in academic performance become more noticeable with each passing year.

In the elementary school years, children internalize many prohibitions they've heard repeatedly ("Don't play near the river," "Keep an eye on your little brother," "Look both ways before crossing the street"). They gain a sense of what is expected of them, and most are inclined to live up to these expectations. Rules of games and required classroom behavior become important. Basic motor skills are notably stable during middle childhood, but many children gain increasing proficiency in athletic skills.

Professional Viewpoints   The National Council for Accreditation of Teacher Education (NCATE) published *Program Standards for Elementary Teacher Preparation* (2000). Although they focus on what teachers should do, the standards include recommendations about types of learning that are appropriate for elementary school students. As an example, they suggest that students in the upper elementary grades should be able to

Middle childhood is a time of sustained attention to realistic tasks.

examine a variety of sources (e.g., primary and secondary sources, maps, statistical data, and electronic technology-based information); acquire and manipulate data; analyze points of view; formulate well-supported oral and written arguments. (NCATE, 2000)

Such recommendations reveal professionals' confidence in the systematic thinking skills of young people in the middle-childhood range. As we will see in Chapters 4 and 5, children of this age do their best thinking when they already understand something about a topic and can rely on concrete objects to bolster their reasoning. Hence, adults can nurture children's skills by asking them to sort and analyze objects and events, to develop an interest and proficiency in reading, writing, mathematics, science, and other subjects, and to see the relevance of what they already know for the academic concepts they are learning.

In the Environments/Middle Childhood clip of the Observation CD, you can see a classroom that provides tangible support to children as they go about learning academic skills. For example, world maps are visible in several places, suggesting the importance of the world's geography. Frequently used words are posted on cabinets for children to refer to while writing. Small objects are stored in plastic canisters and drawers; children can manipulate, count, and classify objects according to shapes and other properties. Children's projects showcase their abilities to identify important events and to put them in a meaningful order. Books, a computer, chalkboards, and other resources are available to extend children's learning. Tables and chairs permit group work, and couches encourage relaxation while reading.

Having learned to think systematically, children are ready for the next big tasks, growing an adult body and speculating on what it means to hold a job, date, become intimate, and raise a family. This transition between childhood and adulthood takes time and effort; there are growing pains along the way.

Observe the Environments/ Middle Childhood clip for a setting that supports children's academic learning with concrete objects, displays of language rules, tables and chairs for group work, couches for relaxed reading, and other resources.

Early Adolescence (10–14 Years)

In early adolescence, youngsters slowly lose their childlike bodies and make strides toward reproductive maturation. Physical changes are accompanied by equally dramatic reorganizations in learning processes and relationships with parents and peers.

Distinctive Developmental Features   The physical changes of puberty are orderly and predictable, but boys and girls alike often experience them as puzzling, disconcerting events. Young adolescents sometimes look and feel awkward, and hormonal changes can lead to unpredictable mood swings. Adolescents show increasing reflectivity about their changing selves and a heightened sensitivity to what other people think about them. Whereas they compared themselves to peers in middle childhood, they now consider how their peers might view them. They wonder, What are they thinking of me? Why are they looking at me? How does my hair look? Am I one of the "cool" kids? Peers become a sounding board through which adolescents gain social support and seek assurance that their appearance and behaviors are acceptable.

Cognitive strides include expansion in abilities to think logically, abstractly, and exhaustively. Furthermore, the world view of young adolescents broadens well beyond family and peer group. A sense of power and idealism flickers, and adolescents feel entitled to challenge the existing order. They often become critical of social organizations, wondering why schools, neighborhoods, governments, and the earth's ecosystem cannot be improved overnight.

Early and late adolescence are times for many physical, cognitive, and social-emotional changes.

Diversity is present in every developmental phase, but individual differences are especially pronounced in early adolescence. Although the physical changes of puberty occur in a fairly predictable manner, the age at which they emerge can vary considerably from one individual to the next. Thus, not all "early adolescents" fall into the 10–14 age range. Some, girls especially, may begin puberty before 10. Others, boys in particular, may not begin puberty until the end of this age span.

Professional Viewpoints   The National Middle School Association (NMSA) offers guidelines for meeting the developmental needs of 10- to 15-year-olds (NMSA, 1995). These include a key recommendation that every student be supported by one adult (an *advisor*) who keeps an eye on his or her academic and personal development, perhaps within the context of a "home base" period or other group meeting time. The advisor-student relationship, when stable and positive, can help young adolescents weather the rapid developmental changes—not only physical but also cognitive and social—that they are likely to experience. In addition, NMSA suggests that large middle schools be subdivided into "houses" or other small units in which students share several classes with the same classmates and get to know

Observe the Environments/Early Adolescence video for a setting that encourages young adolescents to focus on academic learning, to work together in groups, to talk privately with advisors, and to follow a code of conduct emphasizing kindness and respect.

a few teachers well. NMSA also advocates teaching techniques that are varied, engaging, and responsive to students' cultural backgrounds, prior knowledge, and individual talents:

> Since young adolescents learn best through engagement and interaction, learning strategies feature activities that provide hands-on experiences and actively involve youngsters in learning. While direct instruction is still important, varied approaches are needed, including experiments, demonstrations, opinion polls, simulations, and independent study. (NMSA, 1995, p. 25)

An environment designed to meet the developmental needs of young adolescents is shown in the Environments/Early Adolescence clip of the Observation CD. Classrooms are equipped with a rich array of resources, including overhead projectors, a television and video cassette recorder, clocks, an easel, chalkboards, maps, binders, and a computer. Adolescents' artwork, papers, and a diorama are displayed for all to admire. A code of conduct reminds adolescents to treat themselves, others, and the environment with kindness and respect. A small room is set aside with two comfortable chairs and two school desks, allowing private conversations with familiar adults as recommended by the NMSA. Hallways are clean and uncluttered, school colors are obvious, and rows of lockers give adolescents places to store personal supplies and congregate between classes.

First steps toward maturity are often hesitant ones. With affection from parents and professionals, young adolescents gradually gain confidence that the adult world is within their reach. There is still more work to be done, however.

Late Adolescence (14–18 Years)

As teenagers continue to mature, they lose some of the gawky, uneven appearance of early adolescence and blossom into attractive young adults. And, resembling young adults, late adolescents often feel entitled to make decisions. Common refrains often include the word *my:* "It's *my* hair, *my* body, *my* clothes, *my* room, *my* education, *my life!*"

Distinctive Developmental Features   Late adolescence can be a confusing time to make decisions. Mixed messages abound. For instance, teenagers may be encouraged to abstain from sexual activity or practice "safe sex," yet they continually encounter inviting, provocative sexual images and activities in the media. Similarly, parents and teachers urge healthy eating habits, yet junk food is everywhere—in vending machines at school, at the refreshment stand at the movie theater, and often in kitchen cabinets at home.

Fortunately, many high school students make wise decisions. They try hard in school, explore career possibilities, gain job experience, and refrain from seriously risky behaviors. Others, however, are less judicious in their choices, experimenting with alcohol, drugs, sex, and violence and in general thinking more about here-and-now pleasures than potential long-term consequences.

Peer relationships remain a high priority in late adolescence and, as we will see in Chapter 13, they can be either a good or bad influence, depending on youngsters' choices of peer groups. At the same time, most adolescents continue to savor their ties with trusted adults and preserve fundamental values championed by their parents and teachers, such as the importance of a good education and the need to be honest and fair.

Individual differences in academic achievement are substantial during the high school years. Indeed, wide variations in students' abilities are among the biggest challenges faced by high schools today. Some low-achieving students drop out of high school altogether, perhaps to shield themselves from the stigma of academic failure. Many of the low achievers who stay hang out with students who share their own pessimistic views of education.

Professional Viewpoints   Adolescents, who are beginning to take on grown-up responsibilities, need intelligent, behind-the-scenes support from adults. The National Association of Secondary School Principals (NASSP), in partnership with the Carnegie Foundation for the Advancement of Teaching, has published a landmark book that offers guidance to teachers and other practitioners working with high school students. *Breaking Ranks: Changing an American Institution* (1996) offers more than 80 recommendations for improving schools for adolescents. It conveys a consistent message that schools must become more student-centered and personalized. Specific recommendations related to personalizing instruction include the following:

Each student will have a Personal Plan for Progress to ensure that the high school takes individual needs into consideration and to allow students, within reasonable parameters, to design their own methods for learning in an effort to meet high standards. (NASSP, 1996, p. 11)

Teachers will convey a sense of caring to their students so that their students feel that their teachers share a stake in their learning. (p. 21)

Every high school student will have a Personal Adult Advocate to help him or her personalize the educational experience. (p. 29)

High schools will create small units in which anonymity is banished. (p. 45)

School environments can help meet adolescents' needs for personalized attention by doing several things. As you can see in the Environments/Late Adolescence clip of the Observation CD, classrooms can sometimes be arranged so students face one another, making it hard for anyone to remain anonymous. Of course, physical arrangements must be adapted to instructional formats, and what matters more than layout is that professionals communicate affection and high expectations to *all* adolescents. In the science classrooms in this clip, numerous types of equipment, resources, and materials are present; these can be used flexibly to meet individual learning needs. Probably all students are expected to learn fundamental scientific facts (see the table of chemical elements) and to conduct classic experiments (see the goggles, beakers, and funnels). Statements of responsibility and citizenship are posted on a wall. A mural contains images appealing to a range of interests, including music, drama, and athletics. The message seems to be that *everyone* belongs here.

Observe the Environments/Late Adolescence clip for a setting that encourages older adolescents to become proficient in primary subjects, to achieve deeper understandings in areas of personal interest, and to follow a code of conduct emphasizing responsibility and citizenship.

Having been nurtured and guided by family, peers, and professionals during their childhood and adolescent years, young people are ready for new tasks, demands, and opportunities.

The five periods of development just identified appear regularly in Developmental Trends tables throughout the book. These tables summarize key developmental tasks, accomplishments, and milestones at different age levels, as well as manifestations of diversity at each level. In addition, they suggest implications for professionals who work with children in the five age periods. The first of these tables, "Accomplishments and Diversity at Different Age Levels," summarizes the accomplishments of infants, children, and adolescents in the domains of physical, cognitive, and social-emotional development; it also highlights areas of diversity in these domains and practical implications for those who work with children.

From Theory to Practice

As developmental scholars have studied the hows and whys of human development, their efforts have been motivated, in large part, by a keen interest in the welfare of children. Early developmentalists actively worked with educators and policy makers to improve schools for children and to establish national and regional centers that supported children and families (Beatty, 1996; S. H. White, 1992). They embraced a variety of children's causes, including support for child labor laws and improvements in elementary and secondary curricula (R. B. Cairns, 1983).

Contemporary scholars in child development build on this historical concern for children's welfare. Sadly, many children remain in harm's way. Hence, current developmentalists study and write about such topics as the effects of poverty and racism, inequities in school resources, substandard early care arrangements, drug and alcohol use by youngsters, abuse and sexual exploitation of children, community violence, and abandonment of children. To enhance their impact on child welfare, developmental scholars work with professionals who wish to make a difference in the lives of infants, children, and adolescents. This book is a case in point. Throughout the book, we highlight practical applications for those who advocate for children, particularly teachers and caregivers, educational specialists and administrators, family educators, mental health professionals, youth service providers, community leaders, health educators, and health-care providers.

The following sections describe these positions, the kinds of issues that particular groups of professionals might face, and examples of places in the book where we address such issues.

AGE	WHAT YOU MIGHT OBSERVE	DIVERSITY	IMPLICATIONS
Infancy (Birth–2) 	**Physical development** • Motor skills including rolling over, sitting, crawling, standing, walking • Growing ability to reach for, grab, manipulate, and release objects • Rudimentary self-feeding by the end of infancy **Cognitive development** • Ability to distinguish faces • Rapid growth in communication, including crying, using gestures and facial expressions, synchronizing attention with caregivers, babbling, forming one-word sentences, constructing multiple-word sentences • Ability to imitate simple gestures with a model present, moving to complex imitation of actions and patterns from memory • Remembering people and things out of sight • Forming mental representations of familiar spatial environments **Social-emotional development** • Ability to connect with people through nonverbal communication • Use of words to name people, things, needs, and desires • Playing side-by-side with peers but also interacting at times • Increasing awareness of ownership and boundaries of self ("Me!" "Mine!") • Developing sense of power and will ("No!")	• Considerable diversity exists in age when, and manner in which, babies reach early milestones. • Self-feeding and self-help skills emerge later when families encourage children to rely on others for meeting basic needs. Families who do this may value children's trust in them. • Children's temperament and physical abilities affect their exploration of the environment. • In unsafe environments, families may limit children's exploration. • Some young children learn two or three languages, especially when multilingualism is valued by their caregivers. • Ability to pretend is displayed early by some children and later by others. • Nonverbal communication varies with culture. For instance, a child may be discouraged from making eye contact with an elder, as a sign of respect. • Children who have few experiences with peers may appear tentative, detached, or aggressive. • Infants and toddlers who spend time in multi-age settings interact differently than do those accustomed to same-age groups. • Children may be encouraged to share possessions rather than respect rights of property.	• Provide a safe, appropriate, sensory-rich environment so infants can move, explore surroundings, and handle objects. • Avoid rushing infants toward milestones, such as walking. • Learn what each family wants for its children and try to provide culturally sensitive care. • Recognize that children's early images of themselves are influenced by unconscious messages from adults (e.g., "I enjoy holding you," "I'm sad and depressed"). • Speak to infants regularly to enrich their language development. • Find out which languages families speak at home. • Communicate regularly with families about infants' daily activities, including how much and what they eat and drink, how well they sleep, and what their moods are during the day.
Early Childhood (2–6)	**Physical development** • Increasing abilities in such motor skills as running and skipping, throwing a ball, building block towers, and using scissors • Increasing competence in basic self-care and personal hygiene **Cognitive development** • Dramatic play and fantasy with peers • Ability to draw simple figures • Some knowledge of colors, letters, and numbers • Recounting of familiar stories and events **Social-emotional development** • Developing understanding of gender • Emerging abilities to defer immediate gratification, share toys, and take turns • Some demonstration of sympathy for people in distress	• Children master physical milestones (e.g., skipping) at different ages. • Individual differences in fine motor and gross motor agility are substantial. • Some children enter kindergarten with few prior experiences with age-mates; others have been in group child care since infancy. • Family and cultural backgrounds influence the kinds of skills that children have mastered by the time they begin school. • Some children have difficulty following rules, standing quietly in line, and waiting for their turn.	• Provide sensory-rich materials that encourage exploration (e.g., water table, sand box, textured toys). • Read to children regularly to promote vocabulary and pre-literacy skills. • Give children frequent opportunities to play, interact with peers, and make choices. • Hold consistent expectations for behavior so that children learn to follow rules. • Communicate regularly with parents about children's academic and social progress.

AGE	WHAT YOU MIGHT OBSERVE	DIVERSITY	IMPLICATIONS
Middle Childhood (6–10) 	**Physical development** • Ability to ride a bicycle • Successful imitation of complex physical movements • Participation in organized sports **Cognitive development** • Development of basic skills in reading, writing, mathematics, and other academic subject areas • Ability to reason logically when aided by concrete objects **Social-emotional development** • Increasing awareness of how one's own abilities compare with those of peers • Desire for time with age-mates, especially friends of the same gender • Increasing responsibility in household chores • Adherence to rules in games • Understanding of basic moral rules	• Children begin to compare their academic and physical performance to that of others, and children who perceive they are doing poorly may lose motivation. • Individual differences are evident in children's performance in academic areas. • Many children are unable to sit quietly for long periods. • Children differ in temperament and sociability; some are outgoing, others are more reserved and shy. • A few children may show disturbing levels of aggression toward others.	• Tailor instructional methods (e.g., cooperative groups, individualized assignments, choices in activities) and materials to meet diversity in children's talents, background knowledge, and interests. • Address deficiencies in basic skills (e.g., in reading, writing, and math) before they develop into serious delays. • Provide moderately challenging tasks that encourage children to learn new skills, perform well, and seek additional challenges. • Provide the guidance necessary to help children interact more successfully with peers (e.g., by suggesting ways of resolving conflicts, and finding a "buddy" for a newcomer to the school or club).
Early Adolescence (10–14) 	**Physical development** • Onset of puberty • Significant growth spurt **Cognitive development** • Emerging capacity to think and reason about abstract ideas • Preliminary exposure to advanced academic content in specific subject areas **Social-emotional development** • Continued (and perhaps greater) interest in peer relationships • Emerging sexual interest in the opposite gender or same gender, depending on orientation • Occasional challenges to parents, teachers, and other authorities regarding rules and boundaries	• Young adolescents exhibit considerable variability in the age at which they begin puberty. • Academic problems often become more pronounced during adolescence; those who encounter frequent failure become less engaged in school activities. • Adolescents seek out peers whose values are compatible with their own and who will give them recognition and status. • Some young adolescents begin to engage in deviant and risky activities (e.g., unprotected sex, cigarette smoking, use of drugs and alcohol).	• Suggest and demonstrate effective study strategies as adolescents begin to tackle challenging subject matter. • Give struggling adolescents the extra support they need to be academically successful. • Provide a regular time and place where young adolescents can seek guidance and advice about academic or social matters (e.g., offer your classroom or office as a place where students can occasionally eat lunch). • Provide opportunities for adolescents to contribute to decision making in clubs and recreation centers. • Hold adolescents accountable for their actions, and impose appropriate consequences when they break rules.
Late Adolescence (14–18) 	**Physical development** • Achievement of sexual maturity and adult height • For some teens, development of a regular exercise program • Development of specific eating habits (e.g., becoming a vegetarian, consuming junk food) **Cognitive development** • In-depth study of certain academic subject areas • Consideration of career tracks and possibilities **Social-emotional development** • Dating • Increasing independence (e.g., driving a car, making choices for free time) • Frequent questioning of existing rules and societal norms	• Some adolescents make poor choices regarding the peers with whom they associate. • Older adolescents aspire to widely differing educational and career tracks (e.g., some aspire to college, others anticipate seeking employment immediately after high school, and still others make no plans for life after high school). • Some teens participate in extracurricular activities; those who do are more likely to stay in school until graduation. • Some teens become sexually active, and some become parents. • Teenagers' neighborhoods and communities offer differing opportunities and temptations.	• Communicate caring and respect for all adolescents. • Allow choices in academic subjects and assignments, but hold adolescents to high standards for performance. • Provide the guidance and assistance that low-achieving students may need to be more successful. • Help adolescents explore higher education opportunities and a variety of career paths. • Encourage involvement in extracurricular activities. • Arrange opportunities for adolescents to make a difference in their communities through volunteer work and service learning projects.

Teachers and Caregivers   Teachers and caregivers work with infants, children, and adolescents in school settings and early childhood programs, including family child care and center-based settings. They offer educational instruction and are responsible for the general welfare of infants, children, and adolescents for several hours daily. Teachers and caregivers educate and care for children by helping them meet their basic physical needs, stimulating their intellectual curiosity, and building their sense of self and ability to get along with other people. Teachers and caregivers include early childhood professionals, K–12 teachers, teacher aides, special education teachers, and early childhood special education teachers. Professionals in this category might encounter situations such as these:

My students aren't at all realistic about what it takes to learn something thoroughly. When I ask them to study for spelling tests or read their history chapters carefully, they glance briefly at the material. How can I encourage them to become active learners?

Practical Applications:

- Model and teach effective problem-solving and learning strategies.
- Provide opportunities for children to evaluate their own learning, and help them develop mechanisms for doing so effectively.
- Expect and encourage increasingly independent learning over time. (See pp. 213–215.)

I want to create an environment that is attractive and enriching for the infants in my care. I wonder what they really see and hear. Are fancy decorations really necessary? What kind of stimulation do they need?

Practical Applications:

- Give infants some choice and control in their sensory experiences.
- Be aware of the dangers of too much stimulation.
- Read cues.
- Recognize that temperamental and cultural differences determine the optimum amount of stimulation for each child. (See p. 191.)

Educational Specialists and Administrators   Educational specialists and administrators work in schools and other educational settings. Some provide hands-on specialized services to children and adolescents; others offer administrative and supervisory support to teachers and other professionals. Educational specialists and administrators include school psychologists, early-care licensing personnel, school counselors, career and guidance counselors, school librarians, educational technology specialists, school media specialists, early intervention consultants, child development disabilities specialists, principals, and child care center directors. Such specialists might encounter the following situation when working with children:

I can usually spot kids who are socially excluded at my school. Some have disabilities, and others are just immature, impulsive, or aggressive. Teachers work hard to integrate these children into the classroom, but they aren't sure about the next step—encouraging other kids to include them. I'm often called upon to offer advice. What can I tell them?

Practical Applications:

- Help rejected children learn basic social skills, such as how to join a conversation. Place them in cooperative groups with children who are likely to be sensitive and accepting. If children are aggressive, give appropriate consequences, and teach self-regulatory strategies to help them keep their impulses in check. Publicly compliment all youngsters (including those who are rejected) about the things they do well. (See p. 573.)

Family Educators   Family educators support and educate family members regarding the care of children and adolescents and the maintenance of healthy relationships within families. They include parent educators, family support specialists, and family advocates. A family educator might wonder:

I know it's all about partnerships with families. Several families I work with do not entirely trust me yet and put up emotional walls. How can I work more effectively with them?

Practical Applications:

- When two or more family members are primary caregivers, encourage them to stay in touch.
- Take parents' work schedules and other commitments into account.
- Establish rapport. Look for signs of discomfort, use friendly body language, display a sense of humor, and treat parents as authorities about their children.
- Be a listener as well as a talker.
- Step in their shoes.
- Remember that most parents view their children's behavior as a reflection of their own competence.
- Be alert for possible philosophical and cultural differences.
- Accommodate language and literacy differences.
- Curb your own biases.
- Inform parents of services available to them. (See pp. 535–536.)

Mental Health Professionals   Mental health professionals care for the mental health and other psychological needs of children, adolescents, and their families. They consult with families, teachers, and other experts to identify and address individual needs. Mental health professionals include counselors and clinical psychologists, clinical social workers, homeless shelter counselors, child advocates at family crisis centers, and counselors of crime victims. Mental health professionals often handle situations such as this one:

Many children referred to me have trouble with emotional outbursts—they explode when they're angry. Others seem to internalize their negative feelings—they blame themselves for their problems. It seems as if they've missed some critical lessons about dealing with anger, disappointment, and frustration. How can I help kids express their emotions in healthy ways?

Practical Applications:

- Help crying infants find comfort.
- Create an atmosphere of warmth, acceptance, and trust.
- Encourage young people to express their feelings.
- Discuss emotions experienced by characters you study in literature and history.
- Take cultural differences into account.
- Help children keep anxiety at a manageable level.
- Model appropriate ways of dealing with negative emotions. (See pp. 385–387.)

Youth Service Providers   Youth service providers arrange for legal and institutional intervention for children and adolescents. They include family social workers, caregivers in residential treatment facilities, substance abuse specialists, family crisis center child advocates, directors of child abuse and prevention centers, drug and alcohol intervention specialists, residential care managers, adoption and foster care agency personnel, law enforcement officers, probation authorities, prison guards, and other juvenile justice professionals, such as intake officers and attorneys representing minors. These professionals help children by addressing serious problems in their families and by guiding them through legal proceedings. They often encounter children who are troubled and need special guidance, as we see in the example below:

Some of the kids I work with seem "hardened" beyond their years. Is empathy a trait that you either have or lack? Can it be cultivated?

Practical Applications:

- Model sympathetic responses; explain what you are doing and why you are doing it.
- Recognize that young children's selfish and territorial behaviors are part of normal development.
- Alert children to needs of others, and encourage them to see such needs as a reason for providing assistance.
- Let adolescents know that giving, showing, and caring for others are high priorities.
- Encourage adolescents to do community service and to reflect on their commitment to helping others. (See p. 551.)

Community Leaders   Community leaders promote the development of youngsters in numerous ways. They include scout leaders, personnel from youth organizations, religious leaders, coaches, recreation directors, directors of museum programs for children, activity directors, community services specialists, and camp counselors. They offer a variety of services, including athletic events, cultural enrichment, religious education, and leisure pursuits. A community leader might face this kind of challenge:

Recently, a major employer in our community closed shop, laying off hundreds of workers. The kids dropping into my community center are really discouraged by this event. How do I keep them on a positive course?

Practical Applications:

- Identify and build on strengths of children and adolescents. Focusing on what's right with children can generate optimism, enthusiasm, and a definite commitment to learning on the part of adults and children alike.
- Create a sense of community.
- Establish clear and consistent expectations for children's behavior.
- Place a high priority on developing reading skills.
- Show relevance of academic skills to children's lives and needs.
- Communicate high expectations for children's success.
- Make sure children's basic needs are met. (See pp. 618–619.)

Health Educators and Health-care Providers   Health educators and health-care providers offer health education programs, diagnostic evaluations, medical treatments, and therapies. These services support the physical and psychological well-being of children and adolescents. Health educators and health-care providers include pediatric nurses, physicians, school nurses, audiologists, speech and language therapists, occupational therapists, physical therapists, family planning specialists, child life specialists, behavioral health advisors, youth exercise specialists, and directors of outpatient services for children. The following situation is a common one encountered by health educators and health-care providers:

Parents in my community are in total denial that adolescents are sexually active. I see increasing rates of gonorrhea, syphilis, and herpes. I can't substantiate it yet, but I'm also worried that kids are spreading HIV infections. We'll treat everyone we can, but prevention would be far more effective. What can I tell other professionals about encouraging young people to participate in constructive activities and avoid serious risks?

Practical Applications:

- Provide appropriate places for adolescents to "hang out" before and after school.
- Identify mechanisms (e.g., cooperative learning groups, public service projects) through which teenagers can fraternize productively as they work toward academic or prosocial goals.
- Be alert to the specific peer groups with which teenagers are associating. If they associate with troubled age-mates who discourage academic achievement or prosocial behavior, encourage them to join extracurricular activities and in other ways make them feel an integral part of the school and community. (See pp. 589–590.)

All professionals who work with children have opportunities to nourish the full spectrum of children's developmental needs—cognitive, physical, and social-emotional. Nurturing individual children is best accomplished with sensitivity to their unique needs, but also with knowledge of how children tend to progress developmentally. In the opening case study, Ms. Jalongo showed such knowledge. She integrated what she learned about Tonya with her extensive knowledge of children in general. The outcome was a more supportive social environment for Tonya.

Sensitivity to both individual needs and general developmental trends is addressed in the notion of **developmentally appropriate practice**: awareness of, and adaptations to, the age, characteristics, and developmental progress of students. It enables growing children to be active learners, recognizes that adult-level functioning is neither realistic nor valuable for

developmentally appropriate practice
Adapting instructional practices and materials to the age, characteristics, and developmental progress of children.

children to imitate, and encourages children to work together in an ethical and democratic fashion (Kohlberg & Mayer, 1972).

In this final section of the chapter, we identify several general strategies to encourage you to think like a developmentalist—in other words, to promote a *developmental mind-set*. We then offer strategies for maintaining this mind-set over the long run.

Acquiring a Developmental Mind-set in Professional Practice

In later chapters, we will pinpoint concrete strategies that relate to specific aspects of development. Here we offer general strategies to help you start thinking like a developmentalist:

■ *Remember that "weaknesses" of childhood and adolescence may, from a developmental standpoint, serve a purpose.* Human beings take longer to reach physical maturity than do members of any other species. For instance, although girls and boys become physiologically capable of conceiving offspring in their early teens, many continue to gain height after that time, and their brains continue to mature during the late teens and early twenties (Giedd, Blumenthal, Jeffries, Castellanos, et al., 1999, Giedd, Blumenthal, Jeffries, Rajapakse, et al., 1999; Sowell & Jernigan, 1998; Sowell, Thompson, Holmes, Jernigan, & Toga, 1999). Such a lengthy childhood allows children to learn what they need to know to become effective participants in adult society—from survival skills to the basic patterns, beliefs, and tools of their culture (Gould, 1977; Leakey, 1994).

From a developmental perspective, the "weaknesses" children and adolescents display and the "mistakes" they make often serve a purpose and promote development over the long run (Bjorklund & Green, 1992; Bruner, 1972). For example, a two-day-old baby's cries of hunger bring a parent running to feed and cuddle him, and in the process a strong parent-child emotional bond begins to form. And an eight-year-old's tendency to overestimate what he is capable of learning and accomplishing seems a bit naive, but his overly optimistic outlook encourages him to persist in new tasks despite setbacks he may face along the way.

■ *Remain confident that the environment makes a difference.* Throughout the book, we will identify multiple ways in which environmental factors influence the course of development. Even when early life circumstances have not been ideal (as was certainly the case for Tonya), thoughtful and systematic interventions can make a world of difference. A body of recent research suggests that children exhibit a certain amount of **resilience**, an ability to overcome effects of harmful early experiences. Some children "beat the odds," growing into healthy adults despite the high-risk environments they call home (E. Werner, 1989). Resilience seems to be fostered by a close relationship with a caring adult—perhaps a youth counselor, teacher, or caseworker—who serves as a role model, friend, and source of advice and support (McLoyd, 1998b; E. E. Werner, 1995). Professionals who work with children are most likely to foster resilience when they show affection and respect for youngsters, are available and willing to listen to their views and concerns, hold high expectations for performance, and provide the encouragement and support necessary for success in school and in society (Masten & Coatsworth, 1998; McMillan & Reed, 1994; E. E. Werner, 1995).

■ *Use the universals of development to make predictions about what children and adolescents probably can and cannot do at a particular age, but expect diversity at every turn.* Some developmental pathways are common to all, but exceptions are everywhere. If there are 25 children in a community recreation program, there will be 25 unique profiles of talents and needs. Children do not fit a single developmental mold, and adults need to plan activities that respect individual differences.

■ *Realize that children face different issues than you did as a child.* All too often, adults rely on their own childhood memories to predict the kinds of issues that children face. "What worked for us will work for others," they may assume. Yet the challenges children face today may not be the ones that either troubled or inspired children in previous generations. Consider the following trends:

• The majority of American parents with children are employed, as we will see in Chapter 12. More and more frequently, children receive out-of-family care in childcare settings or other people's homes. Many of these out-of-home settings are

Melanie (age 11) perceives Mrs. Lorenzo's classroom to be warm and supportive. Teachers and other professionals who are affectionate, respectful, and mindful of children's strengths can make a difference in children's lives.

resilience
Tendency of some children and adolescents to thrive and develop despite adverse environmental conditions.

high-quality environments, but others are understaffed, unsafe, and unresponsive to children's needs. Furthermore, many children have no supervision at all during the after-school hours.

- Children and professionals who work with them often come from different backgrounds. Students of color represent 30% of the population of students in American elementary and secondary schools (G. Gay, 1993). At the same time, teachers of color make up less than 15% of the teaching force. Only about 8% of all K–12 teachers are African Americans, 3% are Hispanic Americans, 1% are Asian Americans or individuals of Pacific Islander descent, and 1% are Native Americans (Status of the American School Teacher, 1992). In addition, the number of children living in large urban areas is increasing, whereas teachers tend to live in suburban communities. More than 72% of teachers are female (G. Gay, 1993). Coming from different backgrounds can mean that professionals sometimes misunderstand the children with whom they work. For example, some service providers hold unconscious biases toward poor children and families, biases they express as pity and a feeling of superiority (McLoyd, 1998a).

Professionals can effectively meet the needs of immigrant children when they learn about children's backgrounds, cultures, and families.
Art by Belinda, age 12.

- The number of children of immigrant families is increasing. Today's immigrant families come from a broad array of countries, especially countries in Central and South America and Southeast Asia (Board on Children and Families, 1995). By the year 2010, children of immigrants may make up 22% of the school-aged population, and most of those children will speak a language other than English (Fix & Passel, 1994). Despite the rich composition of cultures represented in American classrooms, individual teachers tend to be familiar with only one cultural perspective (C. C. Shaw, 1993).

- Almost 25% of children in the United States grow up in poverty (Hamburg, 1992). The percentage is even higher in some groups; for instance, 38% of Hispanic and 44% of African American children under the age of 18 live in poverty (Statistical Abstract of the United States, 1991). Although many children fare well despite very limited financial resources, in general, children who grow up in extreme poverty are at higher risk for death, malnutrition, disease, injury, disability, father absence, and exposure to violence.

- Requirements for federal assistance to poor families have changed in recent years. For example, more stringent work requirements and time limits have been imposed since establishment of the 1996 Temporary Assistance for Needy Families block grants. The effects on children are uncertain, but may include increases in child neglect, as poor parents who work outside the home are often unable to find adequate child care (Greenberg, Levin-Epstein, Hutson, Ooms, Schumacher, Turetsky, & Engstrom, 2002).

- Students with disabilities make up 11% of the students in the United States (M. M. Wagner, 1995b). Increasingly, such students are educated for part or all of the school day within the general education classroom—a practice called **inclusion**.[3]

As we describe developmental trends in this book, we will continually consider various sources of diversity. As you read the upcoming chapters, we ask you to pay particular attention to how developmental principles depend on culture and context (and in some cases disability). We also urge you to think about your professional responsibility to children who come from backgrounds different from your own. Marian Wright Edelman, the president of the Children's Defense Fund, offers a poignant moral imperative to us all:

inclusion
Practice of educating all students, including those with severe and multiple disabilities, in neighborhood schools and general education classrooms.

---

[3] In the United States, federal legislation known as the *Individuals with Disabilities Education Act* (IDEA), passed in 1975 and updated several times since, mandates that children with disabilities be educated in the *least restrictive environment*—in the most typical and standard educational environment that can reasonably meet their educational needs. As a result of such legislation, more than two-thirds of students with disabilities are now educated in general education classrooms for part or all of the school day (U.S. Department of Education, 1996).

We cannot continue as a nation to make a distinction between our children and other people's kids. Every youngster is entitled to an equal share of the American Dream. Every poor child, every black child, every white child—every child living everywhere—should have an equal shot. We need every one of them to be productive and educated and healthy. (Edelman, 1993, p. 235)

■ *Keep in mind that children and adolescents are, in many respects, very different from adults.* By knowing the characteristics and thinking abilities of children at a particular age, adults can better tailor instruction to address their developmental needs. The previous Developmental Trends table, like the others throughout this book, includes an "Implications" column that gives practitioners suggestions for working with young people at various age levels.Development and Practice features, which also appear throughout the book, provide additional ideas for working with children at one or more age levels. The first of these, "Engaging in Developmentally Appropriate Practice with Infants, Children, and Adolescents," appears on the following page.

■ *Look for and capitalize on children's strengths.* Children can sometimes make life difficult for adults, as Tonya initially did in our introductory case study. In such situations, educators and other specialists may be tempted to throw up their hands in despair. However, with extra effort, a change in tactics, and a solid faith in children's ability to overcome the odds, they can find areas of strength in all children and help them draw upon their own resources. As an illustration, consider how one teacher acquired a new appreciation for a student named Crystal when observing her in social play:

> Crystal really surprised me in the social learning center. Frankly, I always thought that Crystal was quiet and listless because you hardly hear anything from her and she seldom shows interest in anything in the class. Oh, no, you just can't believe, when doing dress-up Crystal was constantly moving, talking, and singing! When doing puppets she was constantly giving the directions! I would have never known where her strength lies if the social learning area were not available in the classroom. (J. Q. Chen, Krechevsky, & Viens, 1998, p. 58)

When adults tap into students' talents, they can use such strengths as a bridge to weaker areas. For instance, Crystal's teacher took advantage of Crystal's social skills to foster her improvement in mathematics. She asked Crystal to pose questions to classmates, tally their responses, and compare differences between groups (J. Q. Chen et al., 1998).

■ *Nudge children toward more advanced levels of thinking and behaving.* To some extent, adults must *meet children where the children are*—that is, at their current level of functioning. But to promote development, adults must also introduce tasks of increasing complexity and responsibility. A counselor, for instance, may work with a shy child to set specific goals that will promote her inclusion by peers. One such goal might be to stand close to a small group of children and make a point of saying something complimentary. Initially, children may need occasional reminders and words of praise for such behaviors, but eventually they should initiate these behaviors on their own, without any prodding or encouragement from adults.

By introducing tasks that involve increasing difficulty and responsibility, caregivers nudge children toward more advanced ways of thinking and behaving.

We intentionally say *nudge*, rather than *push*, children toward more advanced levels. Unreasonable expectations—expectations for behavior well beyond what children are currently capable of doing—will often lead to unnecessary failure, accompanied by stress and frustration, rather than the positive benefits that gentle prodding is likely to produce.

Maintaining the Mind-set over the Long Run

A developmental mind-set isn't something that, once acquired, necessarily lasts forever. Furthermore, researchers continue to advance the frontiers of knowledge about the nature and course of child development. Therefore, professionals who work with infants, children, and adolescents can—and must—work to keep a developmental mind-set alive. Here are some useful things you can do:

■ *Continue to take courses in child development and professional practice.* Additional coursework is one sure way of keeping up to date (1) on the latest theoretical perspectives and research results on child and adolescent development and (2) on their practical implications for work with young people. In general, such coursework has been shown to enhance professional effectiveness with children (Darling-Hammond, 1995).

Infancy

- Set up a safe and stimulating environment for exploration.

  A caregiver in an infant center designs her environment so infants can safely crawl, walk, and climb, inside and on the playground. A quiet corner is reserved for small infants not yet able to move around. A variety of materials and toys are carefully arranged to be in reach and to invite use. Duplicates of heavily used toys are left out.

- Arrange clean and quiet areas for meeting physical needs.

  A teacher in an early intervention program sets up his environment so that he can help toddlers meet their physical needs in a hygienic and quiet area. He talks to children during caregiving routines such as feeding, diapering, grooming, and toileting, explaining what they are doing and encouraging them when they take small steps toward self-care.

- Provide culturally sensitive care and support families' home languages.

  A family child-care provider who is bilingual in Spanish and English uses both languages with infants and toddlers in her care. She has cloth and cardboard books in both languages (some of the books are homemade), as well as audio tapes with songs and stories.

Early Childhood

- Provide reassurance to children who have difficulty separating from their families.

  A child-care provider establishes a routine for the morning. After children say goodbye to their parents, they stand at the window with him, watch their parents walk to their cars, and then find an activity to join.

- Create a classroom environment that permits children to explore their physical and cultural world.

  A preschool teacher has several "stations" available to children during free-choice time, including a water table and areas for playing with blocks, completing puzzles, doing arts and crafts, engaging in dramatic play, and listening to books on tape.

- Introduce children to the world of literature.

  A preschool teacher reads to the children at least once each day. She chooses books with entertaining stories and vivid illustrations that readily capture the children's attention, interest, and imagination.

- Encourage self-reliance and responsibility.

  A kindergarten teacher rotates daily jobs among the children. For instance, during snack time, one child hands out napkins, another pours milk into plastic cups, and a third sponges down the table after everyone has finished eating.

Middle Childhood

- Encourage family members to become active participants in their children's activities.

  A religious educator invites children's parents and other family members to contribute in some small way to "Sunday School." Different parents assist with musical performances, bake cookies, and give hands-on help during lessons.

- Ensure that all students acquire basic academic skills.

  A second-grade teacher individualizes reading instruction for her students based on their current knowledge and skills. She works on mastery of letter identification and letter-sound correspondence with some, reading of simple stories with others, and selection of appropriate books with a few students who are already reading indepen-

dently. She makes sure that all children have regular opportunities to listen to stories in small groups and on tape.

- Give children the guidance they need to establish and maintain positive relationships with their peers.

  When two children are quarreling, their camp counselor gives them several suggestions that can help them identify a reasonable compromise.

- Encourage children to be critical learners.

  When a fourth-grade teacher describes the Europeans' early explorations and settlements in the New World, he asks children to think about what various Native American groups might have been thinking and feeling at that time.

Early Adolescence

- Design a curriculum that is challenging and motivating and that incorporates knowledge and skills from several content areas.

  A middle school teacher designs a unit on "war and conflict," integrating writing skills and knowledge of social studies. He encourages students to bring in newspaper clippings about current events and to talk and write about local political events.

- Assign every student an advisor who looks after the student's welfare.

  During homeroom with her advisees, a seventh-grade teacher personally makes sure that each adolescent is keeping up with assignments. She also encourages her advisees to talk with her informally about their academic and social concerns.

- Show sensitivity to youngsters who are undergoing the physical changes of puberty.

  A sports coach makes sure that adolescents have privacy when they dress and shower after physical activities.

- Allow adolescents to make some decisions about policies and procedures that influence them.

  A counselor asks teenagers about the type of schedule they believe would be most helpful for them to follow together in their counseling sessions.

Late Adolescence

- Expect students to meet high standards for achievement, but give them the support and guidance they need to meet those standards.

  An English composition teacher describes and then posts the various steps involved in writing—planning, drafting, writing, editing, and revising—and asks his students to use these steps for their essays. He then monitors his students' work, and gives feedback and suggestions as necessary, making sure that they execute each step in a way that enhances the quality of their writing.

- Reach out to adolescents socially and emotionally.

  A leader in a youth development program talks about the social and political movements of her own adolescence and invites her students to talk about current social practices that they find troubling.

- Encourage adolescents to give back to their communities.

  A high school requires all students to participate in 50 hours of volunteer work or service learning in their town.

- Educate adolescents about the academic requirements of jobs and colleges.

  A drop-in community center posts vacant positions in the area, listing the work experience and educational requirements for each.

■ *Find information through professional organizations.* Many professional organizations hold regular meetings at which researchers and practitioners can exchange information and ideas. Such meetings enable professionals to learn about the latest research findings and theoretical advances in development, and to discover new methods for supporting youngsters. Professional organizations also publish journals with new research findings and standards for professional practice with young people. We recommend that you use these standards as useful guidelines, but remain alert to how they should be altered for specific populations of youngsters. Some guidelines reflect the values of particular cultures and may not always be as universally applicable as they first appear (Dahlberg, Moss, & Pence, 1999).

■ *Consult and collaborate regularly with professional colleagues.* Practitioners often gain a better understanding of the strengths and needs of individual children when they meet to exchange insights and ideas. Through the process, they may also gain a more optimistic view of their own ability to bring about positive changes in children's social development and academic achievement (e.g., Weinstein, Madison, & Kuklinski, 1995). In an approach that one school uses, 10 to 12 teachers, administrators, specialists, and parents meet every 2 or 3 weeks to discuss students' developmental needs (Squires, Howley, & Gahr, 1999). The following example illustrates the kinds of insights that emerge:

> [W]e began to notice recurring patterns of behavior. For example, when Jordan was upset, he would usually withdraw from the group and from me for awhile. Pat pointed out that these behavior patterns are clues . . . to what the child is working on in his or her development. From . . . observations I had made, I thought that Jordan was trying to understand how to deal with conflict. Other children were trying to learn about making "friends" with other students, or dealing with issues of responsibility in homework, classwork, and on the playground. All those details that we wrote in our journals started to make more sense as they were woven into recurring patterns.
>
> . . . I found it surprising that the children's developmental work generally had little to do with what we were studying in math, science, or social studies. . . .
>
> We discussed this in the group, as others felt the same way. . . . If Jordan has his own developmental agenda, then, of course, other students in the class did, too. And what I was doing in the classroom, all that content, didn't match well with what they were dealing with. I felt I was trying to show a movie at the beach at noon. It would be difficult for kids to see the movie (the content of the lessons) when the sun (their developmental agendas) was so strong and bright.
>
> . . . I found myself searching for and trying different ways to make my classroom and my teaching more attuned to students' needs. (Squires et al., 1999, p. 200)

Throughout this chapter, we have argued that developmental journeys are not universal. To a large degree, youngsters develop in their own individual fashions. Furthermore, the outcomes of development are not predetermined at the onset; instead, developmental paths depend significantly on the environments that caring adults create for and with children. Development happens one child at a time, and it doesn't happen without "nurture." As you will discover throughout this book, adults can do much to help children navigate their individual developmental journeys.

Find guidance through professional organizations such as Zero to Three, and the National Center for Infants, Toddlers, and Families, which publishes a journal by the same name. Subscribe to professional journals such as Child Development (published by the Society for Research in Child Development), Journal of Early Adolescence, and a host of others.

CASE STUDY: LATISHA

Latisha, who is 13 years old, lives in a housing project in an inner-city neighborhood in Chicago. An adult asks her to describe her life and family, her hopes and fears, and her plans for the future. She responds as follows:

> My mother works at the hospital, serving food. She's worked there for 11 years, but she's been moved to different departments. I don't know what my dad does because he don't live with me. My mother's boyfriend lives with us. He's like my step father.
>
> In my spare time I just like be at home, look at TV, or clean up, or do my homework, or play basketball, or talk on the phone. My three wishes would be to have a younger brother and sister, a car of my own, and not get killed before I'm 20 years old.
>
> I be afraid of guns and rats. My mother she has a gun, her boyfriend has one for protection. I have shot one before and it's like a scary feeling. My uncle taught me. He took us in the country and he had targets we had to like shoot at. He showed us how to load and cock it and pull the trigger. When I pulled the trigger at first I feel happy because I learned how to

shoot a gun, but afterward I didn't like it too much because I don't want to accidentally shoot nobody. I wouldn't want to shoot nobody. But it's good that I know how to shoot one just in case something happened and I have to use it.

Where I live it's a quiet neighborhood. If the gangs don't bother me or threaten me, or do anything to my family, I'm OK. If somebody say hi to me, I'll say hi to them as long as they don't threaten me. . . . I got two cousins who are in gangs. One is in jail because he killed somebody. My other cousin, he stayed cool. He ain't around. He don't be over there with the gang bangers. He mostly over on the west side with his grandfather, so I don't hardly see him. . . . I got friends in gangs. Some of them seven, eight years old that's too young to be in a gang. . . . They be gang banging because they have no one to turn to. . . . If a girl join a gang it's worser than if a boy join a gang because to be a girl you should have more sense. A boy they want to be hanging on to their friends. Their friends say gangs are cool, so they join.

The school I go to now is more funner than the school I just came from. We switch classes and we have 40 minutes for lunch. The Board of Education say that we can't wear gym shoes no more. They say it distracts other people from learning, it's because of the shoe strings and gang colors.

My teachers are good except two. My music and art teacher she's old and it seems like she shouldn't be there teaching. It seem like she should be retired and be at home, or traveling or something like that. And my history teacher, yuk! He's a stubborn old goat. He's stubborn with everybody.

When I finish school I want to be a doctor. At first I wanted to be a lawyer, but after I went to the hospital I said now I want to help people, and cure people, so I decided to be a doctor.

From "'I Wouldn't Want to Shoot Nobody': The Out-of-School Curriculum as Described by Urban Students," by J. Williams and K. Williamson, 1992, *Action in Teacher Education,* 14(2), pp. 11–12. Adapted with permission of Association of Teacher Educators.

- In what ways do we see the contexts of family, school, neighborhood, and culture affecting Latisha's development?
- Based on your own experiences growing up, what aspects of Latisha's development would you guess are probably universal? What aspects reflect diversity?
- What clues do we have that Latisha's teachers can almost certainly have a positive impact on her long-term development and success?

Now go to our Companion Website to assess your understanding of chapter content with a Practice Quiz, apply what you've learned in Essay Questions, and broaden your knowledge with links to related Developmental Psychology Web sites. Go to: www.prenhall.com/mcdevitt.

SUMMARY

Child Development as a Field of Inquiry

The term *development* refers to systematic, age-related changes in the physical and psychological functioning of human beings. Developmental theorists typically focus on the nature and progression of development in three domains—physical, cognitive, and social-emotional—and look at how a variety of environmental contexts (families, neighborhoods, culture, etc.) affect its course.

Basic Developmental Issues

Three basic issues characterize the study of developmental change during childhood and adolescence: (1) nature and nurture (the extent to which development involves a genetically controlled unfolding of characteristics or is guided by environmental factors); (2) universality and diversity (cases in which developmental progressions are common to all young people and others for which individuals differ because of inherited endowments and unique environmental conditions); and (3) qualitative and quantitative change (the extent to which development involves major reorganizations in functioning as opposed to a series of minor, trendlike modifications).

Theories of Child Development

Developmentalists have proposed a wide variety of explanations as to how and why children and adolescents change over time. These explanations can be categorized into nine general theoretical frameworks: maturational, psychodynamic, cognitive-developmental, behavioral learning, evolutionary, information processing, sociocultural, developmental systems, and life-span perspectives. These perspectives often focus on different domains of development and may place greater or lesser importance on nature versus nurture, universality versus diversity, and qualitative versus quantitative change.

Developmental Periods

Infancy (birth to 2 years) is a remarkable time of rapid growth and emergence of basic human traits, including emotional bonds to other people, language, and motor mobility. Early childhood (2–6 years) is a time of imaginative play, rapid language development, advances in gross motor and fine motor skills, and expansion of social skills. During middle childhood (6–10 years), children begin to tackle in earnest the tasks and activities that they will need to participate effectively in adult society; they also develop long-term relationships with age-mates and internalize many of society's rules and prohibitions. In early adolescence (10–14 years), youngsters are somewhat preoccupied with the physical changes of puberty and are often sensitive to how they might appear to others; at the same time, they are beginning to think in the abstract, logical, and systematic ways that allow a critical look at society and an exploration of complex academic topics. Late adolescence (14–18 years) is for most a period of intensive interaction with peers and greater independence from adults. Although many older adolescents make wise choices, others engage in risky and potentially dangerous behaviors.

Acquiring and Maintaining a Developmental Mind-set

Professional practice with infants, children, and adolescents is best guided by knowledge of universal developmental pathways and respect for individual differences. Age-related physical characteristics, thinking abilities, and social skills must be important considerations in how schools and other environments are structured for young people. Adults can use various strategies to acquire and maintain a developmental mind-set in their work. For instance, they can identify and capitalize on individual children's strengths. They can consider how children's "weaknesses" may ultimately foster development over the long run. Through ongoing education and participation in professional organizations, they can keep up to date on advancements in the field. And through regular collaboration with colleagues, they can maintain an optimistic outlook concerning their ability to have a positive impact on young people.

KEY CONCEPTS

development (p. 5)
physical development (p. 5)
cognitive development (p. 5)
social-emotional development (p. 6)
context (p. 6)
nature (p. 7)
maturation (p. 7)
nurture (p. 8)

sensitive period (p. 9)
universality (p. 9)
diversity (p. 9)
qualitative change (p. 10)
quantitative change (p. 10)
stage (p. 10)
stage theory (p. 10)
theory (p. 12)
maturational perspective (p. 13)

psychodynamic perspective (p. 13)
cognitive-developmental perspective (p. 13)
behavioral learning perspective (p. 14)
evolutionary perspective (p. 14)
information processing perspective (p. 14)

sociocultural perspective (p. 15)
developmental systems perspective (p. 15)
life-span perspective (p. 16)
developmentally appropriate practice (p. 28)
resilience (p. 29)
inclusion (p. 30)

Isabelle, age 4

Eddie, age 7

Elizabeth, age 14

Methods of Inquiry in Child Development

CASE STUDY: MICHAEL

Two teachers, Barb Cohen and Ted Delgado, sit down to compare notes after a long and busy day.

"Ted, I need your ideas about Michael," Barb says. Despite being the youngest child in the class, Michael is one of the tallest. He also has a relatively sophisticated vocabulary (chamber, cauldron, ghoul) for a 5-year-old. But Michael's young age does seem to be a factor in other arenas. He is impulsive, rarely pays attention during group activities, can't cut with scissors, has great difficulty writing letters and numbers, and refuses to paint at the easel. But what disturbs Barb most is that he seems to be an unhappy child.

Michael is usually Barb's responsibility, but Ted has plenty of opportunity to observe him as well. This is Barb's second year as a teacher, and so she often relies on the insights that her more experienced partner has gleaned from fifteen years in the classroom.

Barb digs out her teaching log and reads aloud her notes on Michael. "Jagged edges in his cutting." "Walks around just watching other children." "Doesn't make choices during free time." "Obnoxious today." "Delays in fine motor skills." "Jabbed Devon with a pencil." "Threw scissors on floor today and said, 'I hate scissors!'" "Possibly lacks self-esteem?" There are few work samples in Michael's portfolio folder, indicating that he hasn't turned in much in the way of artwork, stories, or other written products. Those that he has turned in appear to have been completed in a hurried, careless fashion.

"Not a picture of positive adjustment to kindergarten," Barb concludes.

"He does seem to be having a hard time, I agree," Ted responds. "What other ways might you look at Michael? What other observations could help you?"

"At his parent-teacher conference, his mother said that he doesn't like school," Barb recalls. "But his parents don't seem to be too concerned about his lack of progress. When I mentioned Michael's difficulty cutting in a straight line, his father laughed and said, 'I'm not much better. You should see how I cut grocery coupons out of the newspaper!'"

Silently, Barb wonders if Michael's parents are causing his problems. Certainly, they don't seem to support *her* objectives for their son. She cringes as she remembers how his mother mentioned that not only did Michael dislike school, he didn't seem to like his teachers either.

Barb refocuses on Ted's recommendation. "I like your question, Ted. What other observations could help me? Let me think about that."

The next day, during an art lesson, Barb asks the children to draw pictures of themselves. After school, she shows Ted the picture Michael drew. "Look, he's frowning in his self-portrait. He's angry. He's showing us that he doesn't feel good about himself. He has no self-esteem."

"Possibly," Ted responds thoughtfully. "But what other explanations are there for that expression? Think about it, Barb. Are there any optimistic ways to look at Michael?"

Angered, Barb wonders why Ted won't admit that Michael is having self-esteem problems that prevent him from learning at school. Furthermore, Barb's feelings are hurt by Ted's apparent implication that Barb has a negative perception of Michael. She is, after all, spending a lot of time observing him and trying to understand and help him. Is she missing something?

arb Cohen is concerned, perhaps justifiably, about Michael's immaturity. She perceives him to be inattentive, disagreeable, unhappy, and delayed in fine-motor skills. "Not a picture of positive adjustment to kindergarten," she concludes.

When professionals develop a serious concern about a struggling child, they often drop everything to learn more about the child's needs. Barb has been showing this disposition, collecting additional work samples from Michael, reflecting on parent-teacher conferences, and seeking insights from a colleague. Like Barb, we can all learn more about individual children through observations, interviews, assessments, and research on the job. In this chapter, we offer recommendations for gathering information about children during everyday professional practice. By following these recommendations, you can enhance your abilities to draw appropriate conclusions about young people's needs and to select professional strategies that help them meet these needs.

Professionals rely on two other influential sources of information as well: their own beliefs about child development, and the results of developmental research. We'll discuss both in this chapter. Barb's suspicion that poor self-esteem is at the root of Michael's problem is preventing her from evaluating his situation fully. Like Barb, when adults collect information from children, they make sense of what they see and hear on the basis of what they already believe. We take the position that professionals can become more effective with young people when they gain insight into their own views about child development. Fortunately for Barb—and most certainly for Michael—she has a colleague who is reminding her to think about his strengths as well as his limitations. Perhaps she can learn to look beyond her firmly held beliefs about self-esteem to see Michael and his family more sympathetically.

This chapter also gives us an opportunity to examine developmental research. Had Barb examined research with 5-year-olds, she would have been struck by the incredible diversity evident in children's fine-motor control, ability to restrain aggressive impulses, and family experiences. This perspective might well have enhanced her understanding of Michael's situation. New discoveries about children are constantly occurring, and researchers are making solid advances in describing how practitioners like Barb can better facilitate the physical, cognitive, and social-emotional development of children. Developmental scholars design their investigations to magnify the accuracy and impact of their research. Therefore, we will explore the primary features of strong research.

Beliefs About Child Development

All of us have beliefs about what children are like and how adults can best work with them. By the time prospective teachers and others preparing for careers with children begin college, they have well-established beliefs about teaching and caring for children, and they become increasingly comfortable with their views as they enter the workforce (Astington & Pelletier, 1996; D. Kagan, 1992; M. F. Pajares, 1992). Indeed, future professionals may believe that they already understand children and that anything they read is "just theory" that doesn't relate to the real world of professional practice.

Our beliefs about children are often so ingrained that we're not even aware of them; in a sense, they've gone "underground." They do, however, frequently surface in everyday behaviors (Olson & Bruner, 1996). For example, one prevalent belief about teaching is that it is primarily a process of communicating information (perhaps about history, geology, or mathematics) in a simplified manner to willing and attentive learners (Brookhart & Freeman, 1992; Strauss & Shilony, 1994). This belief often translates into relatively ineffective teaching strategies (Beatty, 1996; Clinchy, 1994). It implies that teaching is little more than "telling" and ignores children's existing understandings, reasoning abilities, interests, and needs. It may also lend itself to an overly simple focus on teaching and assessing basic skills.

Common Ideas about Infants, Children, and Adolescents

Many college students hold beliefs about youngsters that are favorable. For example, they often see children as curious, innocent, and endearing. Those wishing to work with adolescents are frequently drawn to their thoughtful and idealistic nature. Such beliefs can

have positive effects in later professional practice: Adults holding these beliefs may communicate positive regard to young people and endeavor to help
them extend the many good qualities they already possess.

On the other hand, adults' beliefs occasionally can be naïve and even
counterproductive. Consider, for example, these beliefs that are typical
of many prospective teachers:

- They are inclined to value the emotional needs of children but
  neglect the cognitive and academic variables that influence
  learning and behaving (C. S. Weinstein, 1988). (This is the
  counterproductive belief leading Barb Cohen to focus solely on
  Michael's self-esteem instead of considering also his cognitive and
  neurological abilities and limitations.)
- They hold unrealistic views about the classroom problems they will face and
  assume that they already have all the knowledge and skills they will need to teach
  effectively (Brookhart & Freeman, 1992; Pajares, 1992).
- They tend to support conventional teaching practices and see little need for change
  in education (Edmundson, 1990; Ginsburg & Newman, 1985; Lortie, 1975).
- They find it easy to believe that youngsters who are "different" in some way should
  adapt to the existing educational system, instead of seeing themselves as social
  activists who can change the system to reduce discrimination (Nel, 1993).

What are your assumptions about how children develop and learn? Your effectiveness with children depends, in part, on your willingness to explore—and sometimes revise—your beliefs.

Some typical beliefs about child development, like these, are at odds with research perspectives on children's needs. In Table 2–1, we list faulty conceptions that we have occasionally encountered in college students preparing for work with children. Sometimes
students have readily admitted that these beliefs might be flawed; at other times, their actions have revealed a clear commitment to them.

The importance of adults' beliefs about children raises a key question: How are they
formed? Often, adults' beliefs are a product of the culture in which they grew up (Kruger
& Tomasello, 1996). For instance, cultures vary widely in their views about physical development. Some believe that children's physical skills develop naturally and so need not
be taught, whereas others deliberately teach such basic skills as sitting and walking (Mead,
1930; Super, 1981).

Adults who work with children also pick up some ideas from co-workers. For example,
one myth that circulated in the Australian legal system is that some divorcing parents are
tempted to make false claims that their partner abused their child (T. A. Brown, Frederico,
Hewitt, & Sheehan, 2001). As a result, professionals occasionally discounted child abuse
allegations, believing that the parents simply were trying to "get back" at one another. Unfortunately, many of the claims were true but went uninvestigated and untreated. A second
illustration concerns girls and women victimized by sexual harassment and sexual violence. Counselors and legal officers occasionally believe that the victims may have been
partly responsible because they did not resist vigorously (Schulhofer, 1998). Therefore,
their claims may not be handled with the seriousness they deserve.

Clearly, some beliefs are harmful to children. Others are benign, or even helpful. And
some are simply a matter of cultural preference. How, then, are beliefs about children, development, learning, and teaching to be addressed?

Identifying and Confronting One's Beliefs

Because our beliefs about children often color what we see, it is essential that we examine
carefully our own assumptions. Consider the following observation by Frances Hawkins, a
former preschool teacher. She had been watching 5-year-old Jack from behind a one-way
mirror. Jack's teacher had just given Ms. Hawkins an earful about his chronic misbehaviors
in class, then left the room for a few minutes. At this point, Ms. Hawkins observed Jack's
careful and thoughtful examination of seeds in a cattail and his subsequent delight in blowing them off his hands and watching them fall to the floor. When Jack's teacher returned to
the classroom, and before Hawkins could recount Jack's exploration, the teacher exclaimed,
"Look at him wandering about . . . can't settle down to anything . . . does nothing . . .

TABLE 2-1 Beliefs About Infants, Children, and Adolescents Challenged by Research

BELIEF	RESEARCH FINDINGS THAT CHALLENGE THIS BELIEF	IMPLICATION
The wounds of childhood scar people for life.	Although adverse circumstances put children at risk, serious negative outcomes are most common when negative factors persist over a long period of time. Furthermore, some children are remarkably resilient to life's stresses (Cicchetti & Garmezey, 1993; Sameroff, Seifer, Baldwin, & Baldwin, 1993; D. S. Shaw, Vondra, Hommerding, Keenan, & Dunn, 1994).	Be sensitive to the difficult circumstances facing children, but do not assume that present hardships doom children to lasting misfortune or failure.
The best way for professionals to help children is to mimic their home environment. If there is a mismatch between the two environments, children suffer.	Sometimes it's good for there to be differences between home and other contexts in which children spend time (e.g., child care centers, family child care settings, schools, recreation centers, clubs, and community organizations). In one study, middle school students who had few opportunities for independence and decision making at home performed better in schools that fostered and encouraged initiative and decision making (J. L. Epstein, 1983).	Keep in mind the compensatory roles that schools and services can play in children's lives. For example, read to young children even when they are not read to at home.
Placing children in a literature-rich environment— one with many books and opportunities to listen to stories—virtually ensures they will learn to read by themselves.	Research studies attest to the importance of early reading experiences and availability of good children's literature. However, many children benefit from explicit instruction in letter-sound correspondences, decoding skills, and comprehension strategies; this is especially true for children who come to school with limited experience with books and other forms of written language (Gough & Wren, 1998; Hulme & Joshi, 1998; Stanovich, 2000). Furthermore, without intervention, early difficulties in reading often become more debilitating as children get older (Stanovich, 2000).	Immerse children in a literate environment, but also offer them explicit instruction in learning to decode and make sense of text. Be particularly attentive to the needs of children who struggle with reading.
The best environment for young children is an academically rigorous one. Given early training in basic skills, young children have a boost for life.	Some instruction in basic skills can be beneficial for young children, but too much academic pressure is detrimental. Young children thrive in learning environments that build on their natural curiosity; allow them to make choices; incorporate hands-on activities; and encourage play, small-group interaction, and personal expression (L. G. Katz, 1999a, 1999b; Shephard & Smith, 1988).	Temper your zeal in teaching basic skills to young children; give them opportunities to explore, experiment, and play.
Children and adolescents who fail to make eye contact with adults are devious and disrespectful.	Patterns of language and communication vary from one culture to another. In some cultures, it is disrespectful to look an adult in the eye or to initiate a conversation with an adult (Gilliland, 1988; Irujo, 1988; Lomawaima, 1995). Furthermore, some children with disabilities (e.g., autism) may routinely avoid eye contact.	Learn about the behavior patterns and communication styles of children whose cultural backgrounds are different from your own.
Adolescence is a time of storm and stress that must simply be endured by the adults in their lives.	Adolescence is a period of rapid physical, emotional, and social growth. Conflicts increase with parents as youths struggle to carve out individual identities. Yet only in about one in five families does the turmoil of adolescence lead to prolonged, extreme conflict (Montemayor, 1982). Serious conflict in adolescence is associated with juvenile delinquency, dropping out of school, and drug abuse (Brook, Brook, Gordon, Whiteman, & Cohen, 1990).	Never underestimate the emotional needs of troubled youth, but remember that juvenile delinquency and drug abuse are not inevitable outcomes of adolescence.
Schools spend too much time teaching students' "left brains." In doing so, they're asking students to use only half of their brain power.	The left and right hemispheres of the human brain have different specializations, as we see in Chapter 3. Nevertheless, the two hemispheres are in constant communication, and studies of efforts to strengthen a particular hemisphere indicate that such "training" is relatively ineffective (Ornstein, 1997; Pressley & McCormick, 1995).	Diversify instructional tasks, formats, and materials for all children, but remember that most activities involve both hemispheres.
Adults are smarter than adolescents, adolescents are smarter than children, and children are smarter than infants.	Thousands of research studies document that children become increasingly capable. However, the superior learning and memory capabilities that come with age are sometimes a function of individuals' *knowledge* rather than age per se. For instance, when children know more about a topic than adults do, their ability to learn and remember new information about it surpasses that of adults (Chi, 1978; Rabinowitz & Glaser, 1985). Furthermore, what appear to be limitations in thinking may actually be beneficial for development. The naïve optimism young children bring to learning tasks may help them to persist despite frequent failure. Likewise, the more limited memory capacity of young children may help them segment language into manageable pieces, making it easier to decipher (Bjorklund & Green, 1992).	Keep in mind that limitations in children's thinking may sometimes serve a purpose in their long-term development.

trouble to all" (Hawkins, 1997, p. 323). Ms. Hawkins believed that children were naturally curious about their world and would take action to satisfy their curiosity. In contrast, Jack's teacher apparently believed that some children, Jack among them, were restless and disruptive.

Developing self-confidence in one's beliefs about supporting children is an important part of becoming a professional. But as the attitude of Jack's teacher illustrates, it is equally important that practitioners identify beliefs that are just plain wrong, or that at least are not universally true. Following are five strategies that can help you better understand your own assumptions about how children develop and learn:

■ *Identify metaphors that best reflect your views about the nature of children.* Perhaps you think that children are like some of the following:

Empty buckets waiting to be filled
Dry sponges soaking up whatever moisture comes their way
Plants in a garden seeking shelter from the elements
Thoughtful philosophers questioning what they see and hear
Restless movie-goers wanting to be entertained
Stray cats following their own mysterious agendas
Prisoners conspiring against their wardens
Caged animals needing to be trained

We might guess that in the preceding scenario, Ms. Hawkins thought of children, including Jack, as "thoughtful philosophers." In contrast, Jack's teacher may instead have subscribed to a "stray cat" or "caged animal" point of view.

Certainly no single metaphor represents the "correct" way of thinking about children, but some metaphors are more productive than others for capturing specific aspects of children's development. For instance, you might read the summary in Chapter 4 of Piaget's theory of cognitive development and compare the child to a mason building his or her own house (Martínez, Sauleda, & Huber, 2001). The overview in Chapter 5 of the information processing system might inspire you to compare learning to a video camera recording the world (Martínez et al., 2001). As you read the upcoming chapters, we urge you to add to your store of metaphors relating to children. By expanding your ideas, you may be better prepared to select metaphors that meet the demands of particular children in specific situations.

■ *Identify metaphors that best capture your beliefs about effective interactions with children.* How would you best describe the role of a *teacher*? Consider the following possibilities:

Friend	Quality control inspector	Entertainer
Parent	Counselor	Scientist
Tour guide	Drill sergeant	Gardener
Cheerleader	Religious leader	Doctor

These various metaphors yield different implications about what a teacher should do. For example, the "counselor" metaphor suggests that a teacher should focus primarily on social and emotional development and pay little heed to cognitive development. The "quality control inspector" metaphor might lead to an emphasis simply on measuring, rather than improving, children's abilities. Perhaps Barb Cohen, in our introductory case, saw herself as a traditional "doctor," diagnosing disorders in Michael.

Metaphors can be applied to other professions, as well. For example, service providers might see themselves as missionaries (converting delinquents to a righteous path), prison wardens (depriving them of freedom), advertisers (persuading them of the value of other ways of living), bank tellers (dispensing goods in a relatively quick and impersonal manner), or healers (repairing damage through special powers).

Educators in early childhood centers and family providers also wrestle with metaphors that characterize their work. Models of "babysitter" and "surrogate mother" are rejected in favor of titles such as "teacher" that acknowledge the knowledge base of their profession. Similarly, health-care providers may reject the metaphor of "loyal soldiers in the battle against disease" and instead educate patients to protect their own health (Winslow, 1984).

When deciding which metaphors guide their work with children, professionals can evaluate those that might be too simple (Mackey, Fredericks, & Fredericks, 1993). For instance, social workers assigned to juveniles convicted of crimes may need to play "police officer," making sure these youngsters follow through with their treatments, but they are also "healers" because they help to rehabilitate them. Selecting only one of these roles could backfire for them and for the youngsters in their care.

Professionals can also avoid metaphors that are downright harmful to youngsters. For instance, social workers, principals, special educators, and classroom teachers sometimes treat defiant children as if they were isolating ("containing") dangerous environmental substances (Nybell, 2001). Practitioners using a containment metaphor are motivated to separate troubled children from others as engineers might do with contaminants. The containment metaphor is reflected in this description of a professional group's responses to 12-year-old Jimmy:

> The teacher, vice-principal, psychologist, three social workers, Jimmy's father and the wrap-around coordinator assembled as a "team" in the school cafeteria after the third suspension. At the core of the meeting was an incident in which Jimmy "flipped Allan out of his chair" and responded with anger to a prolonged series of staff efforts to contain him. According to the vice-principal, "Jimmy was disrupting an entire hallway. It was an ugly situation in which he was screaming obscene language . . . saying things that were permeating the entire building." The school personnel agreed to continue to try to work with Jimmy, but saw the situation as dangerous. The assistant director of special education stopped by the wrap-around office the day after the meeting. "I was over at Roosevelt Middle School today. That classroom does fine when Jimmy is gone, but he destabilizes things. Margaret [the teacher] is sitting on a powder keg over there." From the point of view of the school personnel, things did not improve as the day wore on. That afternoon, the school social worker left a voice mail message at the wrap-around office: "We need to do something about the situation over at Roosevelt Middle right away. *Jimmy's at meltdown.*" (Nybell, 2001, p. 223)[1]

According to Nybell (2001), the staff's view of Jimmy as unpredictable caused them to manage his crises rather than plan for his future. Had they been able to confront their beliefs, they might have seen a boy who was troubled but sought understanding from adults:

> "Do you know," the probation officer said, "that any assault, any assault whatsoever, means you go back to the youth home?"
> Jimmy looked down, defiantly.
> "Do you know that any threat, that threatening somebody, that's assault?" the probation officer persisted.
> "I know," said Jimmy, "that I am a twelve year old boy, but everyone will act like I'm something else." (p. 226)[2]

Jimmy had to be held accountable for his actions but he also needed strategies that would give him hope, affection, and practice in resolving conflicts without resorting to name calling or fighting. We hope that the professionals who worked with him eventually considered other metaphors, such as counselor, friend, and parent.

■ *Build on children's strengths.* When tempted to blame children for their problems, practitioners can step back and consider what they can do to get children onto a better path. For example, rather than wondering what is wrong with children who lag behind in kindergarten, teachers can make school a friendlier, more suitable environment for them (Stipek, 2002). For Michael, in Barb Cohen's classroom, this might mean less time in "Scissors 101" and more time in discussions centered on his interests. Rather than labeling children and adolescents as slow, delinquent, or unable to learn, educators and other professionals can change conventional practices that perpetuate failure for some (Deschenes, Tyack, & Cuban, 2001).

[1,2] Reprinted by permission of Sage Publications Ltd from "Meltdowns and Containments: Constructions of Children at Risk as Complex Systems," by L. Nybell, 2001, *Childhood, 8(2),* pp. 213–230. Copyright © Sage Publications Ltd, 2001.

A related tactic for practitioners is to learn how youngsters see their own lives. For instance, western counselors working with Arab clients can learn how clients think about gender roles, stress, and commitments to family and community (Al-Krenawi & Graham, 2000). Having gained such insights into clients' beliefs, counselors are in a better position to explain how therapy will help clients deal with stress and achieve personal goals. Being careful not to stereotype cultural groups, professionals can try to understand how young people and their families express basic moral commitments and communication patterns *differently*, not poorly.

■ *Talk with other professionals about their beliefs.* Preparing for a job with children, you can learn a great deal from experienced practitioners. Remember, however, that myths about children exist in the workplace, even among experienced practitioners. Fortunately, most practitioners remain open to new ideas—if the right people persuade them. Adults tend to rely on individuals whom they know for knowledge about child development (Granger, 2002). As a growing expert on child development, you can help instill faith in other adults that young people can achieve good outcomes—with guidance.

■ *Use the results of research to generate new ideas.* Over many decades, developmental research has corrected many misconceptions about children. For example, at the end of the 1800s and beginning of the 1900s, psychologists and people in general viewed infants as mindless, helpless creatures easily molded by adults (J. Kagan, 1984). The psychologist William James expressed this view when he asked his readers to "suppose a new-born mind, entirely blank and waiting for experience to begin" (James, 1890, p. 287). Psychologists now know that some aspects of perception are quite sharp almost from birth. Infants, for instance, can imitate facial expressions within the first few days of life (T. Field, Woodson, Greenberg, & Cohen, 1982) and they can detect changes in the appearance of simple shapes within the first few months (McCall & Kagan, 1967).

Research also gives reason for hope. Innumerable studies have demonstrated that under the right conditions most children and adolescents want to achieve in school, serve their families, and become loyal friends and productive citizens. By reading the research literature, professionals can discover how, and also how substantially, they can be positive agents in children's lives (G. Gay, 1993; R. S. Weinstein et al., 1995). For instance, the research literature reveals methods that help children understand the information they encounter in textbooks and classroom lessons (Palincsar & Brown, 1984; Paris & Jacobs, 1984; Pressley, Goodchild, Fleet, Zajchowski, & Evans, 1989). Moreover, advances in developmental research suggest how school and community environments can be improved by focusing on children's developmental needs (e.g., Wong Fillmore, 1993). Thus, instead of accepting the way things are, professionals can, through familiarity with research, learn new ways of working with children.

Developmental Research Methods

In the opening case study, Barb Cohen's deliberations about Michael illustrate three essential aspects of research in child development. First, Barb forms hypotheses that might explain Michael's difficulties adjusting to kindergarten. She suspects that Michael suffers from poor self-esteem and speculates that his parents are doing little to encourage his skill development. Second, she collects data by recording her observations of Michael's behavior in the classroom and keeping a portfolio of his work. Finally, she scrutinizes the data for patterns to support or disprove her hypotheses and she interprets these patterns: "Not a picture of positive adjustment to kindergarten" and "He has no self-esteem."

In many respects, Barb's efforts are similar to those of academic experts when they investigate children's development. They, too, pose questions about children's development, agonize over the kinds of information that best address their questions, collect information from and about children, interpret what the information might mean, and discuss conclusions with colleagues. There is an important difference, however, between how practitioners and scientists conduct research. Practitioners inquire about how particular children act and perceive events; their ultimate aim is to alter tactics so as to be more in sync with the needs of children with whom they work. In contrast, developmental scholars inquire about how children develop generally; their aims are to enhance the knowledge base about child development and to make broad recommendations for education and care that are applicable to many children in numerous settings.[3]

Key Features of Developmental Research

In preparing to conduct research, developmental scholars spend years studying cognitive, physical, and social-emotional development and the contexts in which young people develop. Budding developmental scholars also learn to think deeply and critically about basic developmental issues: how nature and nurture combine in children's growth, how youngsters are similar in some age-related progressions and highly individual in others (i.e., universality and diversity), and how age-related changes include both complete overhauls and many tiny increments (qualitative and quantitative development). In addition, developmental scholars become experts in one or more specific areas, such as children's memory, language, motor skills, sexual maturation, peer relationships, family relationships, experiences in cultural communities, or other areas of specialization.

Scientific Method   As they gain knowledge in their field, developmental scholars become intrigued with aspects of children's development that have not previously been examined. To investigate, they follow the *scientific method*. The scientific method prescribes these steps:

1. *Pose a question.* Researchers clearly state a question that captures their interest. When they can make predictions about the outcomes of their study, they also state their expectations in the form of hypotheses.
2. *Design an investigation.* Once the question is clear, researchers must figure out what kind of information will help answer the question and, if applicable, test any hypotheses.
3. *Collect data.* Researchers carry out their investigation, recruiting children and families, gathering data, and following carefully defined procedures.
4. *Analyze the data.* Having collected the data, researchers organize it, categorize children's responses, look for themes in the data, and when appropriate, perform statistical tests. After making sense of the data, they draw conclusions relevant to their original research question.
5. *Publish results.* Researchers make reasonable claims about the meaning and significance of their methods and results. They present the findings at conferences and in journals.

When they follow the scientific method, developmental scholars combine a passion for their subject with a critical frame of mind. As they plan and conduct their investigations, scholars constantly wonder how they might look differently at the data they collect from children and adolescents. When they can, they make adjustments that will increase the clarity of their results. When they cannot rule out problems, scholars describe limitations in final reports so readers can make their own judgments as to the value of the study.

Designing a Research Study   In the remainder of this section, we examine four decisions developmental scholars make when immersed in the second step of the scientific method

---

[3] This difference in motivations (solving practical problems with particular children, or contributing to the knowledge base generally) does not always hold true. Increasingly, practitioners publish the results of their research with children; when they do, they also add to academic literature about children and tactics for helping them learn. Furthermore, many practitioners share their results with colleagues and thereby create a forum for discussing best practice. Thus, practitioners often contribute to the knowledge base. Their primary responsibility, however, remains serving children, adolescents, and their families. Conversely, developmental scholars sometimes focus on one or a few children; when they do, they may derive implications for caring for and working with these particular children. In addition, many developmental scholars draw on their personal experiences with children when they conduct research. Thus, scholars often share with practitioners a commitment to improve the daily lives of children. Nonetheless, the primary job of developmental scholars is to obtain high-quality information about young people. The implications of their research must be carefully reviewed by professionals directly responsible for the well-being of young people before it can be utilized with them.

(designing the study): Who will participate in my study? How can I collect information from these participants? How can I protect the rights of participants? How can I ensure that my data collection will result in information that is technically sound?

Research participants. To add to the knowledge base about child development, researchers need the cooperation of infants, children, adolescents, and their parents and guardians. In deciding whom to recruit, researchers identify a particular population about which they want to draw conclusions, and then select a subgroup, or **sample**, of that population. For example, imagine a team of developmental scholars interested in how older adolescents think about their future jobs and careers. These scholars are interested in all younger adolescents in public middle and junior high schools in Denver, Colorado. With the help of district-level and school-building administrators, the researchers obtain a list of advisors; they randomly select 10% of these advisors. Next, researchers ask selected advisors to help them distribute letters, consent forms, surveys, and instructions to students and parents. If the return rate ends up being fairly high, the researchers can be reasonably confident that their *sample* of adolescents is representative of the larger *population* of young adolescents in public schools in Denver.

Ideally, individuals in the sample reflect the characteristics of people in the population in question, in roughly the same proportion. However, potential participants frequently decide not to join the study. Furthermore, it is easier to recruit some youngsters and families for research studies than others. For example, Teresa once conducted a series of studies to investigate the development of children's beliefs about listening. She asked questions such as "What do you think it means to be a good listener?" and "Whose fault is it when a listener does not understand the speaker?" She found that it was easy to recruit first graders; relatively easy to recruit third graders, although they were not quite as accessible; and harder still to recruit fifth graders, who had less free time. When researchers cannot be confident that their sample represents the population to which they want to generalize, they must identify characteristics of the sample, such as age, gender, income level, and ethnic background, that may influence the outcome of their study. That way, readers can judge for themselves to whom the research may apply.

Because some people are more accessible and willing than others, developmental researchers are inclined to recruit children and adolescents who come from backgrounds similar to their own. The unfortunate result is that we have less information about the development of youngsters who come from ethnic and racial minority groups, language environments other than English-only families, and low-income communities (e.g., Coll et al., 1996; C. B. Fisher, Jackson, & Villarruel, 1998). Fortunately, many developmental researchers are now working vigorously to study hard-to-find populations, such as migrant and homeless families. These outreach efforts will eventually strengthen the conclusions we can draw about child development.

Sometimes, researchers recruit a small number of people whom they study in depth. Their goal is not generalizing results to a larger population but rather portraying, with insight and candor, life as an individual child or small group of children experience it. Researchers who study one child or a limited number of children in depth must be particularly thoughtful about the kinds of children and families that will provide desired information. For example, researchers may look for children who have experienced particular events, such as witnessing community violence or having a sibling with a disability. These scholars also try to recruit individuals who will be willing to talk to them and are able to articulate their experiences. As you encounter studies focused on small numbers of children, you will want to reflect on whether the experiences of these children are relevant to the young people with whom you will work.

Systematic collection of data. Barb Cohen has collected data about Michael in a somewhat unsystematic fashion: She has made notes about whatever she has happened to see and collected whatever Michael has happened to turn in. Furthermore, she has accepted information uncritically, immediately interpreting Michael's frowning self-portrait as an indication of low self-esteem. In fact, Barb has noted that Michael shows "delays in fine motor skills," and that the work samples in his portfolio appear to have been completed hurriedly.

sample
The specific participants in a research study; their performance is often assumed to indicate how a larger population of individuals would perform.

Perhaps an undiagnosed disability, either in certain cognitive skills or in fine motor coordination, limits his ability to translate what he sees or imagines onto paper.

In developmental research, data collection is typically more planned and systematic than Barb's efforts. Researchers take precautions to minimize bias in their data collection. For example, they may administer tests under timed conditions and administer questionnaires with standard questions. They also think through the many ways in which their data might be interpreted, eliminating any explanations not warranted by the data. When developmental scholars report on how children act in natural settings, such as clubs, street-corners, and playgrounds, they may have little control over how children provide them with data, but they can do other things to ensure their study's integrity, such as:

- Spending extended time with children (e.g., making a point to observe children in an after-school program two days a week for three months)
- Collecting multiple sources of information (e.g., having conversations with children about their friendships and observing their interactions with friends)
- Asking children to confirm or disagree with a researcher's impressions (e.g., asking a child whether he intentionally avoids being home during scheduled visits with the family's social worker)
- Intentionally looking for evidence that would lead them to revise their interpretations (e.g., asking teachers whether preschool children typically play on the playground as cooperatively as a researcher has observed)

Later in this chapter we will present helpful tools frequently used by practitioners to collect data when working with children in various settings.

Ethical conduct. A paramount concern for developmental researchers is that they conduct their research in an ethical manner, in particular that they are honest and respectful of the rights of participants in their studies. Before conducting research, investigators submit plans to *review boards,* committees of scholars who scrutinize plans for potential dangers to participants and deny approval to any studies that may put participants at undue risk. Researchers must inform participants (and, in the case of minors, parents or guardians) of procedures that will be used, allow participants to withdraw from a study at any time, and keep individual responses anonymous and confidential. Ethics must have precedence over knowledge building whenever a research project potentially puts children in harm's way.[4] Furthermore, when describing research studies to others, researchers must represent their methods and results accurately.

Public scrutiny and critical analysis. Developmental researchers conduct their research in public. When they believe they have learned something about children, they present their methods, observations, and conclusions to other scholars in the field. Their colleagues eagerly consume the results, identify limitations, spot holes in the logic, recast the results in alternative theoretical perspectives, and think about implications for their own work. Experienced researchers have learned to anticipate criticisms and to eliminate as many problems as they can in their research designs.

We hope that you, too, will learn to analyze critically the developmental research studies that you read, rather than taking researchers' conclusions at face value. In order to do this, you must be familiar with data collection techniques and developmental research designs. We turn to these two topics next.

Data Collection Techniques

Researchers rely on four primary strategies for collecting information: self-reports (interviews and questionnaires), tests and other methods of assessment, physiological measures,

---

[4] You can read more about ethical decision making by researchers in "Ethical Standards for Research with Children," published by the Society for Research in Child Development (available online at http://www.srcd.org). Also review ethical principles for psychological research in "Ethical Principles of Psychologists and Codes of Conduct, 2002," published by the American Psychological Association (available online at http://www.apa.org).

and observations of behavior. As you read our discussion of these strategies, be alert to consider the advantages and disadvantages that each has as a window into the minds and habits of children and adolescents.

Self-Reports   To learn about children's beliefs, intentions, hopes, and frustrations, researchers frequently listen to children. In fact, some of the most informative research data come in the form of children's and adolescents' own statements about themselves—that is, in the form of **self-reports**.

Sometimes researchers pose questions in face-to-face **interviews**. For example, Jean Piaget once asked children of various ages to explain what they thought *thinking* was. Here is a conversation with 7-year-old "Monte":[5]

Adult: You know what it means to think?
Monte: Yes.
Adult: Then think of your house. What do you think with?
Monte: The mouth.
Adult: Can you think with the mouth shut?
Monte: No.
Adult: With the eyes shut?
Monte: Yes.
Adult: With the ears stopped up?
Monte: Yes.
Adult: Now shut your mouth and think of your house. Are you thinking?
Monte: Yes.
Adult: What did you think with?
Monte: The mouth. (dialogue from Piaget, 1929, p. 39)

Contrast Monte's views with those of 11-year-old "Victor":

Adult: Where is thought?
Victor: In the head.
Adult: If someone opened your head, would he see your thought?
Victor: No.
Adult: Could he touch it?
Victor: No.
Adult: Feel it as if it was air?
Victor: No . . .
Adult: What is a dream?
Victor: It's a thought.
Adult: What do you dream with?
Victor: With the head.
Adult: Are the eyes open or shut?
Victor: Shut.
Adult: Where is the dream whilst you are dreaming?
Victor: In the head.
Adult: Not in front of you?
Victor: It's as if . . . you could see it.
Adult: Is there anything in front of you when you dream?
Victor: No, nothing.
Adult: What is inside the head?
Victor: Thoughts.
Adult: Is it the eyes which see something inside the head?
Victor: No. (dialogue from Piaget, 1929, p. 54)

From these and other interviews, Piaget concluded that when children begin to conceptualize the nature of thinking (sometime around age 6), they view thoughts as concrete entities that occur in the mouth or ears. By age 11, their conceptualization has become more abstract; *thought* no longer has tangible, material qualities.

Seven-year-old Grace drew this picture of an apple tree. What kinds of interview questions might you ask her if you wanted to learn more about her understandings of how apples and trees grow?

self-report
Data collection technique whereby participants are asked to describe their own characteristics and performance.

interview
Data collection technique that obtains self-report data through face-to-face conversation.

---

[5] In reports of his interviews, Piaget often abbreviated or in other ways shortened the names of the children (A. Karmiloff-Smith, personal communication, October, 2000; S. Pulos, personal communication, September, 2000). Here and throughout the book we substitute for his abbreviations actual, but probably incorrect, names.

Interviews have the advantage of allowing a researcher to explore the reasoning of individual children in considerable depth. When interviewers succeed in making children feel safe and comfortable, they can learn a lot about how children think about things. In the Research/Early Adolescence module of the Observation CD, the interviewer gently but persistently asks 12-year-old Claudia a series of questions about why she grouped seashells in a particular way. The interviewer begins the discussion in this way:

Interviewer: All right. Why did you make the groups that you did?
Claudia: Mm, some, they were the ones that looked the most alike.
Interviewer: How did you decide which shells to put where?
Claudia: Um, I looked at them, like, and how they looked on every side. And I put them with the ones that looked closest like each other.
Interviewer: Okay. So what were you looking for when you were grouping them?
Claudia: Um, details.

Up until this point, Claudia describes her reasoning in a fairly general way. After a series of questions and requests for information from the interviewer, Claudia gives more detailed descriptions about the shells:

Interviewer: Why are those in a group?
Claudia: Um, they looked kind of the same. Feel like they both, they have the little thing there. And they fold over like that and have a tip.
Interviewer: Okay. What makes them different from the other ones?
Claudia: They're longer kind of. And they're smoother than the other ones.
Interviewer: Oh, okay. And then those ones at the far corner over there. . . . Now tell me about those ones.
Claudia: They were smaller than these, so I put them together. And they both pretty much, or all of 'em pretty much, had the same kind of thing.
Interviewer: Like what?
Claudia: Like, they all had the cone at the top. The kind of pocket area.

Listen to an interviewer use several different types of requests for information to elicit descriptions from Claudia in the Research/Early Adolescence clip.

Interviews can uncover children's thinking, but they have the disadvantage of being time-consuming. Another option researchers have is to use written **questionnaires** when they need to gather responses from a large number of participants. When young people complete questionnaires, they typically read specific questions or statements and choose from defined options that represent their feeling, attitude, action, or other response. As an illustration, let's examine an early study by Lynd and Lynd (1929), who administered a 12-item checklist to 730 students in grades 10 through 12. The Lynds asked adolescents to check the issues "about which you and your parents disagree." Students most often picked "the hours you get in at night" and "the number of times you go out on school nights during the week." Sound familiar? This study was replicated by Caplow, Bahr, Chadwick, Hill, and Williamson (1982), with most frequently checked items being "the hours you get in at night" and "home duties." Responses from these two questionnaires, administered more than five decades apart, indicate that parent-adolescent conflicts tend to center on everyday concerns, including completion of schoolwork, social life and friends, home chores, disobedience, disagreements with siblings, and personal hygiene (Montemayor, 1983). Some questionnaires include open-ended items, in which descriptive comments or opinions are encouraged; in contrast, items with defined options or yes or no answers do not provide this opportunity for people completing the questionnaire to express their thoughts fully.

Interviews and questionnaires have definite limitations. Without actually observing children and adolescents in their natural environments, researchers cannot check on the accuracy or meaning of their statements, and the information they get is limited by the particular questions that they ask. For example, Teresa once asked her son Connor, then 10, if he had made his bed that morning, and he answered that he had. Later that day, as Teresa brought Connor's laundry into his bedroom, she had to tiptoe carefully to avoid the many toys and clothes strewn on the floor. Yes, he had made his bed (albeit not to military standards), but he had done little else to get his room in order. Researchers, like parents and practitioners, get the most accurate and useful information when they ask the right questions (Teresa, of

questionnaire
Data collection technique that obtains self-report data through a paper-pencil inventory.

course, should have asked Connor if he had made his bed and picked up his room). Also, they must find a means of double-checking the veracity of what children are telling them.

Despite such difficulties, self-report techniques can give researchers vivid glimpses into the thoughts and actions of growing youths. Valuable insights can emerge when researchers ask children to express their views, verify children's understanding of the questions being asked, probe their understandings in a thorough yet sensitive fashion, and confirm the patterns they see with other types of data.

Tests and Other Assessment Devices   A test is an instrument designed to assess knowledge, abilities, or skills in a fairly consistent fashion from one individual to the next. Although tests inevitably involve observable behaviors (researchers cannot measure what they cannot see), they allow researchers and practitioners to draw inferences about learning, reasoning, and other nonobservable mental phenomena. Some tests involve paper and pencil, whereas others do not, but all typically yield a decision in the form of a number (e.g., a score on an IQ test) or category (e.g., "alert," "proficient," or "left-hand dominant").

Tests are prevalent in Western society, even at the moment of birth. For example, the *Apgar Scale* is commonly administered by medical personnel to infants one minute and five minutes after birth; scores from 0 to 2 are given on color, heart rate, reflexes, muscle tone, and respiration (yielding a maximum score of 10 points). Total scores predict some serious medical risks (B. M. Casey, McIntire, & Leveno, 2001). For example, Casey and colleagues examined birth records of live-born babies, excluding twins and other multiple births, in an inner-city hospital over a ten-year period. Out of 13,399 infants born 2 to 12 weeks early, 315 out of each 1000 infants with five-minute Apgar scores of 0 to 3 died within 28 days after birth, compared to 5 out of 1000 infants with five-minute Apgar scores of 7 to 10. For infants born "on time" (at least 37 weeks after conception), 244 infants out of 1000 with Apgar scores of 0 to 3 died, compared with 0.2 per 1000 for infants with scores from 7 to 10.

Tests also have long histories in schools; teachers and other school personnel often use them to determine what children do and do not know, and what they can and cannot do. Tests are often used in research as well. For example, in a study by F. A. Campbell and Ramey (1994), intelligence tests and other measures of cognitive development were administered at regular intervals to a sample of children from ages 3 months to 12 years. All of the children came from low-income families, and most of their mothers had not completed high school. As infants, half of the children were randomly selected to attend a child care center until they were 5 years old. There, they participated in activities designed to promote their cognitive, perceptual, linguistic, motor, and social development. The other half of the children were assigned to a control group in which they received nutritional formula and disposable diapers as long as such items were needed, but they did not attend child care. Test scores indicated that children who participated in the experimental child care program made greater cognitive gains than nonparticipants, beginning soon after the program began. They maintained this advantage at least through age 12, when data collection ended. A second intervention, beginning at age 5 and lasting for 3 years, was less effective. Thus, these tests were valuable in revealing that interventions may be most effective when they begin when children are young and when services provided are comprehensive and developmentally appropriate.

Some of the tests that researchers use are similar or identical to those used by practitioners. Others are designed specifically for research purposes. For instance, researchers have developed numerous instruments to assess aspects of children's motivation, self-esteem, personality, social skills, and moral development. Such instruments often have little or no usefulness to practitioners but help researchers test specific hypotheses about the nature or possible causes of children's development.

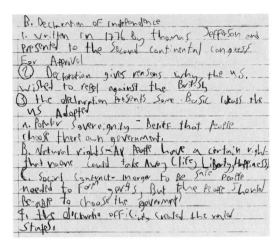

Fourteen-year-old Connor took these notes in his history class. How might you design a test that examines Connor's understanding of the abstract concepts he recorded (e.g., "popular sovereignty" and "social contract")?

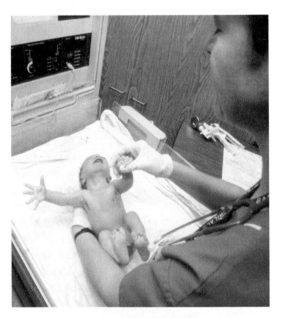

Infants are administered tests from the moment they are born. Minutes after birth, the numerical Apgar scale is often administered to provide an indication of a newborn's physical condition.

test
Instrument designed to assess knowledge, understandings, abilities, or skills in a consistent fashion across individuals.

Developmentalists also measure children's accomplishments and abilities in ways that we would not necessarily think of as "tests." They make use of a variety of **assessments**, tasks that children complete and which are then carefully reviewed by researchers for the understandings and skills children display. For instance, developmental scholars conducting separate investigations might record children's reaction times in decision-making tasks, precision in navigating through a maze, accuracy in detecting emotional expressions in others, and understanding of commonly used verbal expressions. You can see an example of an interviewer assessing 14-year-old Alicia's comprehension of proverbs in the Cognitive Development/Late Adolescence clip:

Observe an interviewer assess Alicia's comprehension of proverbs in the Cognitive Development/Late Adolescence clip.

Interviewer:	What does it mean when someone says, "Better to light a candle than to curse the darkness"?
Alicia:	Well, it means, probably, that you're actually getting somewhere than just complaining about it and not doing anything about it.
Interviewer:	What does it mean when someone says, "An ant may well destroy a dam"?
Alicia:	I think it probably means that even though they're really small, they can still change things.

Physiological Measures   To learn about children's physical development, researchers turn to **physiological measures**, measures of bodily functions or conditions such as heart rate, hormone levels, bone growth, brain activity, eye movements, body weight, and lung capacity. In recent decades, knowledge of infancy has advanced rapidly because of the ingenuity of physiological measures. In particular, researchers have learned a great deal about infants' attention, perception, and memory by exploiting their tendency to respond differently to familiar and unfamiliar stimuli. You can get a sense of what researchers might learn from watching infants' eye movements by observing 7-month-old Madison in the Emotional Development/Infancy clip. During a period when she is alone, she examines toys and books, intently studying their visual properties. Madison selects objects to manipulate and chooses new ones when she loses interest. When infants are shown the same thing repeatedly, they grow used to it and lose interest (M. Bornstein, 1989). This tendency, called **habituation**, can be assessed through changes in heart rate, sucking, and eye movements. Typically, young infants will show habituation through a decreased heart rate (detected with a small electronic stethoscope placed on their chest), a decreased rate of sucking (a nipple with a cord attached measures bursts and intensity of sucking), and eye movements that indicate they are looking elsewhere (their gaze is tracked electronically).

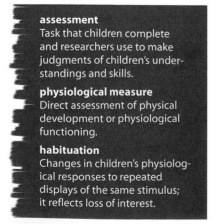

Observe 7-month-old Madison studying objects visually in the Emotional Development/Infancy clip. What might developmental scholars learn from Madison's eye movements?

Habituation studies have revealed amazing abilities in young learners. For example, these methods indicate that infants can tell differences between similar musical melodies and between pictures of dots that differ in number (Aldridge, Stillman, & Bower, 2001; H. Chang & Trehub, 1977; Hayne, Rovee-Collier, & Borza, 1991; McCall & Kagan, 1967; Xu & Spelke, 2000). Likewise, fetuses grow "bored" (they stop reacting) when they feel the same low-intensity vibration repeatedly on their mother's abdomen (van Heteren, Boekkooi, Jongsma, & Nijhuis, 2001). Without ingenious physiological measures, knowledge of infants' abilities would be far less advanced.

Recent advances in medical technologies have also greatly improved our understanding of brain development, a topic we examine in Chapter 3. We have learned of fascinating developmental patterns through animal research, analyses of brains of youngsters who died during childhood, and new technologies that can be safely and ethically implemented with living children. An example of the latter is magnetic resonance imaging (MRI), which measures blood flow and permits comparison of parts of the brain (Johnson, 1999). A recent investigation relied on MRI data to examine developmental changes in the brains of healthy individuals from age 7 to age 30 (Sowell, Delis, Stiles, & Jernigan, 2001). Among other results, MRI patterns revealed a trend for adults' brains to strengthen connections devoted to judgment and restraint and to let unused connections die out; as a result, adults can guide their behavior with thoughts of the future more easily than adults can with small children (Figure 2–1).

assessment
Task that children complete and researchers use to make judgments of children's understandings and skills.

physiological measure
Direct assessment of physical development or physiological functioning.

habituation
Changes in children's physiological responses to repeated displays of the same stimulus; it reflects loss of interest.

Observations   Researchers conduct **observations** when they carefully watch the behavior of youngsters. Observations can offer rich portraits of "slices" of children's lives, particularly when they take place over an extended time and are supplemented with interviews and analyses of the products that children create, such as drawings and essays.

Many researchers conduct observations of children and adolescents in their natural, everyday settings. When they do so, researchers generally keep an ongoing, detailed record of significant events that take place in a particular setting, such as a neighborhood playground, a youth center, classroom, or family home. The following observation records interactions between a father and his five-year-old daughter, Anna:

11:03 AM   Anna looks at her father, who is sitting on the couch reading the newspaper: "Wanna play Legos, Dad?" Dad says, "Sure" and puts down the paper and gets on the floor. Anna pushes a pile of Legos toward Dad and says, "Here. You can build the factory with the volcanoes."

The Bayley Scales of Infant Development are administered to infants between 1 and 42 months of age, particularly if there is a concern about a delay in the child's development or possible need for intervention (Bayley, 1993). The scales include observing such behaviors as turning to sound, looking for a hidden object, building a tower with cubes, playing pat-a-cake, sitting alone, and jumping in place.

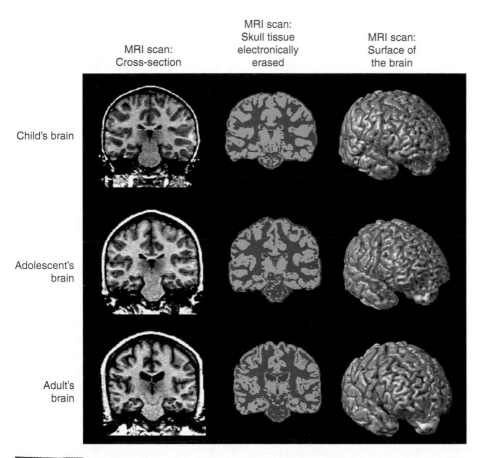

| | MRI scan: Cross-section | MRI scan: Skull tissue electronically erased | MRI scan: Surface of the brain |

Child's brain

Adolescent's brain

Adult's brain

FIGURE 2-1   Images of three brains from magnetic resonance imaging (MRI). A child's brain is shown in the first row, an adolescent's brain in the middle row, and an adult's brain in the bottom row. Researchers can see typical age-related patterns in these three types of scans. For example, comparisons of the three brains in the middle column reveal typical maturation of parts of the brain: the "gray matter" shown in green reveals decreases in neurons (which may be representative of increasing specialization in brain function in adults relative to children), the "white matter" shown in blue reveals increases in cells that insulate and protect neurons (which may be representative of faster, more efficient processing), and the red reveals increases in cerebrospinal fluid. (Cerebrospinal fluid fills in the gaps around the brain, protecting and nourishing it; fluid expands in volume when brain connections become more efficient and take up less space.)

From E. R. Sowell, P. M. Thompson, D. Rex, D. Kornsand, K. D. Tessner, T. L. Jernigan, and A. W. Toga, "Mapping Sulcal Pattern Asymmetry and Local Cortical Surface Gray Matter Distribution *in vivo*: Maturation in the Perisylvian Cortices," 2002, *Cerebral Cortex, 12*, pp. 17–26. Reprinted by permission of Oxford University Press.

observation
Data collection technique whereby a researcher carefully observes and documents the behaviors of participants in a research study.

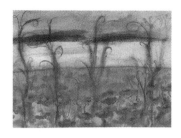

Ten-year-old Laura drew this field of poppies. How might you conduct observations to learn about her techniques in planning, drawing, and coloring her pictures? How would you record and interpret the observations you made?

Observe Claudia sorting seashells in the Research/Early Adolescence clip. How might the presence of an unfamiliar adult filming her affect Claudia's thinking, feeling, and acting?

11:06 AM   Dad looks puzzled and says, "What factory?" Anna laughs and says, "The one where they make molten steel, silly!" Dad says "Oh, I forgot" and picks up a gray Lego and fits a red one to it." (Pellegrini, 1996, p. 22)

Although they hope to describe events as faithfully as possible, observers must always make decisions about what to include and what to ignore. To illustrate, the observer who writes about Anna and her father may focus on Anna's ability to come to a joint understanding with her father. With this focus, the observer would prioritize conversations between Anna and Dad, recording their negotiations over what to play and what to pretend. Other events, such as Anna dropping toys or her father scratching his head, would receive less attention.

Observations are frequently used to document characteristics and behaviors that young people display in public settings (e.g., hairstyles, dress codes, "bullying" behaviors). They are also helpful for studying actions and interactional styles of which individuals may be unaware or unable to articulate (e.g., the frequency and types of questions that teachers direct toward boys and girls) and behaviors that violate social norms (e.g., temper tantrums, petty thefts). Occasionally, observations are used in settings that have been created by the researchers. For example, Feigenson, Carey, and Hauser (2002) observed choices made by infants when experimenters placed different numbers of graham crackers in opaque buckets. Ten- and twelve-month-old infants watched experimenters intently as they placed different numbers of crackers in the buckets. They were then permitted to crawl toward the buckets. Infants reliably crawled toward containers in which they had seen experimenters drop three crackers, passing over those with only two crackers. These results show that infants can distinguish "more" from "less," even though they may not be counting as adults would.

Observations have their weaknesses, however. For one thing, the presence of an observer might actually change the behaviors under investigation. For example, children will sometimes be deterred from showing typical patterns of behavior because they are distracted by the presence of an observer. They may misbehave or, alternatively, stay on task more than usual. Young people may also become self-conscious or even anxious. To return to the video clip of 12-year-old Claudia, Claudia is focused, cooperative, and efficient in her classification of seashells into piles. Nonetheless, the presence of the camera, lights, and an unfamiliar adult in her living room may affect her thinking and behaviors. To minimize children's reaction to the presence of observers, researchers often spend considerable time in the setting before they begin to observe formally. That way, children grow accustomed to them and their equipment, they begin to relax, and they are more inclined to carry on as they usually would.

Another weakness of observations is that biases and expectations of researchers can influence their notes and conclusions. For example, if an observer perceives children to be combative and hostile, she may categorize an interaction between two boys as hitting, whereas another observer who perceives children as playful may see the same scuffle as energetic play. Researchers handle this problem by spending as much time as possible in the setting, discussing their observations with one another, making independent observations and then checking on their agreement, and carefully defining the events and behaviors they observe. For example, after a lengthy time observing children's playground behavior, one researcher came up with specific behaviors that could help distinguish "aggression" (kicking, swearing, taking a toy from another child) from "rough-and-tumble play" (smiling while participating in harmless wrestling) (Pellegrini, 1996).

The four data-gathering strategies we have just described—self-reports, tests and other methods of assessment, physiological measures, and observations of behavior—must be implemented with care. Table 2–2 identifies possible distortions in each that can affect the accuracy of the conclusions.

Using Multiple Data Collection Techniques   In addition to trying to eliminate possible distortions, researchers often strengthen their conclusions by using a combination of several different measurement techniques. The information collected is often more persuasive as a result. In their research with children in Brazil, Campos and her colleagues (1994)

TABLE 2-2 **Distortions of Information Collected from Children and Adolescents**

SOURCE OF INFORMATION	POSSIBLE DISTORTION	EXAMPLE	IMPLICATION FOR PRACTITIONERS
Self-Reports (Interviews and Questionnaires)	Memory of research participants	In a study of children's informal experiences with science in their families, a 9-year-old forgets about his family's frequent trips to the local natural history museum.	When soliciting information from children (perhaps about their life experiences or their understandings of concepts), describe exactly what kind of information you are seeking.
	Interpretations by research participants	When asked if she has encountered any sexual harassment at her school, a teenager focuses only on unwanted physical contacts. She does not share the researcher's more general definition, which also includes verbal harassment.	When asking children and adolescents for their opinions and experiences, define your terms carefully.
	Defensiveness of research participants	In an anonymous survey, a young adolescent prefers not to admit that she has experimented with marijuana.	Respect children's right to privacy, but recognize that they may not always be honest with you about sensitive issues.
Tests and Other Assessment Devices	Response style of research participants	Children rush through a test, responding quickly and not very carefully, so that they can have a longer recess.	Encourage children to work carefully and thoroughly on tests, and give them reasons and incentives for performing at their best.
	Cultural bias in test content	Some children taking a mathematics test have difficulty with two questions—one asking them to calculate the perimeter of a football field and another asking them to calculate the area of a baseball diamond—because they have little familiarity with these sports.	Carefully screen test content and eliminate any items that may either penalize or offend children from particular backgrounds.
	Participants' familiarity with test format	Some children in a third-grade class have never taken tests involving a matching-item format and so skip all items using this format.	Give children ample practice with the test formats you will be using.
Physiological Measures	Attention to stimuli	In a study on infants' habituation, half of the babies tested are sleepy and do not attend to the array of objects shown to them.	When you want to draw conclusions about whether infants can make distinctions among stimuli, present them with tasks only when they are rested, fed, and alert.
	Motivation	In a study of lung capacity of adolescents, participants are not motivated to perform at their best.	Establish rapport with participants and encourage them to do their best on physical tasks.
	Instrumentation problems	A computer operator examining images from an MRI investigation fails to separate images of brain matter from that of surrounding tissues. The result is that the estimates of brain matter are confounded with the data on total brain volume.	Ensure that physiological data you examine is produced with the highest technical standards. Do not interpret information you are not adequately trained to analyze.
Observations	Bias of observers	In a study of gender differences in sharing behavior, an observer expects girls to share their possessions more often than boys and so is more apt to notice such actions in girls.	Think about your own biases about children and how they may color what you "see."
	Attention limitations of observers	In a study of nonverbal communication in older adolescents, a researcher misses a third of the smiles, gestures, winks, and other subtle communication behaviors that they display.	Keep in mind that you can take in only a limited amount of information at any given period of time.
	Effects of the observer's presence	During a researcher's observations of an after-school science club, young adolescents are unusually quiet, attentive, businesslike, and on task.	Be alert to ways that children might change their behavior when they know that you are watching.

Source: Distortions in self-reports, tests, and observations identified by Hartmann & George, 1999.

demonstrated nicely the value of multiple data sources. These researchers interviewed children and adolescents who worked, and in some cases also lived, on the streets of a large city. They supplemented open-ended interviews and group discussions with structured interviews and in-depth observations of youths in locations throughout the city. As an example, researchers learned through self-reports that young people who lived on the streets faced more serious problems than those who lived at home: 75% of the street-based youths but only 15% of the home-based youths reported engaging in illegal activities. The observations they conducted gave depth to these verbal reports. Here is an observation conducted by a member of the research team that aptly captures the desperation of drug dependency:

> I was in the square, the kids were sniffing thinner. L.A. was very agitated because the can had finished. L.R. said, "Look at that, just because the thinner's gone, he's in the mood, the first necklace that appears, he'll grab it." D.R. added, "It's true, when the thinner's gone they all get nervous until they get money for another can; when they buy it they . . . are calm again." (Campos et al., 1994, p. 325)

Collecting information in several formats is common practice among researchers working within sociocultural perspectives (see Chapter 1). Typically, sociocultural scholars document how children learn in a meaningful way while doing concrete tasks, with people they know, in familiar environments. One researcher, for example, studied the learning opportunities inner-city youth had in a gardening program sponsored by the 4-H program (Rahm, 2002). The researcher followed a team of six young adolescents, from 11 to 14 years in age, over an eight-week period during the summer. She videotaped their activities and conversations, wrote field notes, and supplemented these observations with interviews with the adolescents. In addition, she interviewed children on other teams and spoke with adults in the program. In the following excerpt, Will, a 14-year-old boy, shows a strong interest in the program, Marc is a master gardener, and Rahm is the researcher and interviewer:

> Will: What are flies really good for?
> Marc: Flies? Well, they pollinate some flowers for us. They teach us patience. . . . [giggle] What else can I think of?
> Will: They get on people's nerves!
> Rahm: They just test your nerves!
> Marc: Actually, they do play a good part in the ecology. They are food for other animals like birds and other insects. And they also help break down old plant material and things like that.
> Will: What do they eat?
> Marc: Flies themselves probably don't eat much of anything. But their larvae, the maggots, get into all kinds of decaying material, and it will decay faster. You can find maggots in the compost piles.
> Will: Are we gonna make a compost?
> Marc: Yes, everybody is gonna take part in it.
> Will: I did compost, but I didn't see any maggots.
> Marc: Actually, most of the time you won't see them much; they hide in places where nobody can see them, like on the edge of the pile and stuff. (Rahm, 2002, p. 172)[6]

Rahm's familiarity with the program, its activities, and the adolescents who took part in it is evident in her interpretation of the conversation:

> This exchange . . . shows how a casual question about flies by a participant became rephrased in a manner that made it more relevant to the City Farmers program. Marc, a master gardener, could have discussed in greater detail the role of flies in pollination, something typically talked about in science classrooms. . . . Instead, Marc focused on the flies' role in breaking down old material, which led Will to wonder about what flies eat. That caused Marc to link the ongoing

---

[6] From "Emergent Learning Opportunities in an Inner-City Youth Gardening Program," by J. Rahm, 2002, *Journal of Research in Science Teaching, 39*(2), 164–184 . Copyright © 2002 by John Wiley & Sons, Inc. Reprinted with permission of Wiley-Liss, Inc., a subsidiary of John Wiley & Sons, Inc.

TABLE 2-3 · Questions of Validity and Reliability in Data Collection

ISSUE	QUESTION ADDRESSED	EXAMPLE OF PROBLEM IN VALIDITY OR RELIABILITY
Validity		
Content Validity	Does the technique yield information that reflects the entire domain being assessed?	A researcher uses a questionnaire to identify study strategies high school students use to prepare for tests. The instrument includes questions about what students do when they study at school but omits questions about how they study at home, where distractions, resources, and supervision are different.
Construct Validity	Does the technique measure the underlying characteristic it is intended to measure?	A researcher uses children's activity level (e.g., the degree to which they move around the classroom during free play) as a measure of curiosity, neglecting the fact that activity level may also reflect other characteristics, such as hyperactivity or a desire to affiliate with energetic classmates.
Predictive Validity	Does the technique allow the researcher to make predictions?	A researcher finds that 4-year-olds' scores on a kindergarten "readiness" test have little relation to how well children perform in a kindergarten classroom.
Reliability		
Test-retest Reliability	Have the effects of temporary fluctuations in participants' performance been minimized?	A researcher who is asking children about their beliefs about the nature of thinking finds that their responses change considerably from one day to the next, depending on how the researcher phrases the questions.
Interrater Reliability	Do two researchers classify or rate aspects of participants' performance in the same way?	As two researchers classify the behaviors they see on the playground, one "sees" aggression (Sasha intentionally slammed into Maria) while the other "sees" clumsiness (Sasha slipped and tripped into Maria).
Internal Consistency Reliability	Do different items or questions yield consistent information?	In a questionnaire designed to assess overall self-esteem, many participants respond to some questions in ways that reflect high self-esteem but respond to others in ways that reflect low self-esteem.
Alternate Forms Reliability	Do two different forms of an instrument yield similar results?	A researcher is assessing adolescents' moral reasoning by presenting one of two moral dilemmas, situations with no obvious "right" answer. The adolescents show more advanced reasoning when given a dilemma about teens their own age than when given a dilemma involving adults.

dialogue to compost, something with which City Farmers were familiar. . . . Marc managed to treat Will's question as a teachable moment in light of gardening. (Rahm, 2002, p. 172)[7]

The insights that Rahm constructed were made possible by her access to several kinds of data—observations, conversations, and her own personal knowledge of science education and children's learning. Such an extensive array of data is not always available, but when it is, developmental scholars can be fairly confident in their conclusions about children.

Accuracy in Data Collection   As they collect their data, developmental researchers must continually ask themselves how they know they are getting accurate information. In other words, they are concerned with **validity**, the extent to which a data collection technique actually assesses what it is intended to assess. Validity takes several forms, each of which is more or less important in different situations. The top portion of Table 2–3 presents examples of situations in which the various forms of validity are suspect.

In addition to looking for evidence that their techniques measure certain things, researchers rule out the influence of other, irrelevant traits. For instance, do scores on a test of mathematical ability reflect children's knowledge of a particular culture (e.g., are there too many questions about American sports?)? Does a test of young children's reasoning capabilities assess desire to please the experimenter as much as finesse in reasoning skills?

---

[7] From "Emergent Learning Opportunities in an Inner-city Youth Gardening Program," by J. Rahm, 2002, *Journal of Research in Science Teaching, 39(2)*, 164–184 . Copyright © 2002 by John Wiley & Sons, Inc. Reprinted with permission of Wiley-Liss, Inc., a subsidiary of John Wiley & Sons, Inc.

validity
Extent to which a data collection technique actually assesses what it is intended to assess.

Only when researchers can say "no" to such questions do they have some assurance that their data collection methods are valid.

Sound developmental research also takes into account the perspectives and motives of participants. Skilled researchers recognize that young people bring their own expectations and agendas to their interactions with researchers. These may decrease the validity of information collected by researchers. Some participants (adolescents especially) may give responses to shock a researcher or in some other respect undermine the research effort. For example, Jeanne's daughter Tina once came home from high school reporting that, as a lark, she and her friends had written nonsensical (and definitely inaccurate) answers on a schoolwide questionnaire. Others may tell a researcher what they think the researcher wants to hear. Furthermore, children and adolescents may understand words and phrases differently than do the researchers. Probing in perceptive ways, searching for confirmation through a variety of sources, and reassuring children that they are not being evaluated are strategies researchers use to put children at ease and improve the validity of the data they collect.

Researchers must also ask whether their data collection methods are yielding consistent, dependable results—in other words, whether their methods have **reliability**. Like validity, reliability takes several forms. There are situations in which the different forms of reliability are questionable; examples of these are shown in the bottom portion of Table 2–3.

In general, reliability is lower when unwanted influences (usually temporary in nature) affect the results obtained. Children and adolescents, like adults, inevitably perform differently on some occasions than on others; they may be more or less rested, well fed, cheerful, attentive, cooperative, thoughtful, honest, and articulate. Their performance is also influenced by characteristics of the researcher (e.g., gender, educational background, ethnic origin, mode of dress) and conditions within the research setting (e.g., how quiet the room is, how instructions are worded, what kinds of incentives are given for participation).

Developmental Research Designs

While they are thinking about suitable ways to collect data, developmental scholars must simultaneously formulate a research design that addresses their foremost interests. Selecting a design requires researchers to set priorities. They must decide what their objective is, such as one of these: identifying effects of new treatments on children, determining elements of children's development that tend to occur together, charting traits that stay constant and others that tend to be replaced with time, or portraying children's experiences and relationships in everyday life.

Studies That Identify Causal Relationships In an **experimental study**, a researcher manipulates one aspect of the lives of children and measures its impact on a particular characteristic children display. Experiments typically involve an intervention, or *treatment*, of some sort. Participants are divided into two or more groups, with different groups receiving different treatments or perhaps with one group (a **control group**) receiving either no treatment or a presumably ineffective one. Following the treatment(s), the researcher looks at the groups for differences in the characteristic in question.

In a true experimental design, participants are assigned to groups on a *random* basis; they have essentially no choice in the treatment (or lack thereof) that they receive. Random assignment ensures that any differences among the groups (perhaps differences in motivations or personalities of group members) are due to chance alone. Furthermore, with the exception of administering a particular treatment, the experimenter tries to make all conditions of the research experience identical or very similar for all of the groups. The researcher thus tries to ensure that the only major difference among the groups is the experimental treatment. Any differences in children's subsequent behaviors will therefore almost certainly be the *result* of the treatment differences.

A classic study illustrates the use of an experimental design (Bandura, Ross, & Ross, 1963). Young children, from almost 3 years of age to just under 6 years, were brought to a playroom. Children were randomly assigned to one of four conditions. Children in the *Real-Life Aggression* condition watched an adult model act aggressively toward an inflated Bobo doll (a 5-foot plastic figure). The model punched the doll in the "nose," sat on it, hit it with

reliability
Extent to which a data collection technique yields consistent, dependable results—results that are only minimally affected by temporary and irrelevant influences.

experimental study
Research study in which a researcher manipulates one aspect of the environment (a treatment), controls other aspects of the environment, and assesses the treatment's effects on participants' behavior.

control group
A group of participants in a research study who do not receive the treatment under investigation; often used in an experimental study.

Photographs of children, ages three to six years, imitating aggressive acts made by an adult model, from a study by Bandura, Ross, and Ross (1963). Researchers found that children who viewed aggressive models behaved more aggressively than those who did not view aggressive acts. Experimental studies, such as this one, are useful to practitioners because they clearly identify causal effects.

From "Imitation of Film-mediated Aggressive Models," by A. Bandura, D. Ross, and S. A. Ross, 1963, *Journal of Abnormal and Social Psychology, 66,* pp. 3–11. Reprinted with permission.

a mallet, tossed it in the air, and kicked it. The model also made verbally aggressive comments such as, "Sock him in the nose." Children in the *Human Film-Aggression condition* watched a movie of a model who performed the same actions as in the previous condition. Children in the *Cartoon Film-Aggression condition* watched a televised "cartoon" character (a woman dressed as a black cat) doing the same things as models in the other two conditions; the film was accompanied by cartoon music. In the *Control condition,* children had no exposure to aggressive models. Thus, children in the three experimental conditions observed a model and then went to a different room for the test phase. For the control children, the test phase was their first participation in the study.

At the beginning of the test phase, children were given toys by the experimenter to play with; subsequently she told them that these were her very best toys and that she was going to reserve them for some other children (Bandura and colleagues wanted children to be mildly frustrated going into the final part of the study). After this attempt at frustration, the experimenter did paperwork and moved to a corner of the room to become "as inconspicuous as possible" (p. 5). Researchers then observed children's responses, watching for their aggressive acts.

The results of the study are more complicated than we can fully describe here, but the gist is that children in the experimental groups were more aggressive than were children in the control group. Children imitated specific aggressive acts more often in the live model condition than they did in the cartoon model condition (recall the rather specific and unusual acts of aggression the models used, such as sitting on the doll and punching it in the nose). Overall, though, children in the three experimental conditions were roughly equal in their total number of aggressive acts, which included aggressive acts they had seen as well as their own novel acts, such as spanking and pretending to shoot the doll, which the model had not done.

Experiments are unique among research designs because of the degree to which outside influences are controlled and therefore eliminated as possible explanations for the results obtained. For this reason, experiments are the method of choice when a researcher wants to explore possible cause-effect relationships. However, in many situations experiments are impossible, impractical, or unethical. When random assignment isn't a viable strategy, researchers may conduct a **quasi-experimental study,** which administers one or more experimental treatments but does not tightly control other possible influences on the results (D. T. Campbell & Stanley, 1963). For example, imagine that a team of researchers wants to examine the possible effects of an after-school recreation program in reducing aggressive behavior in high school students. The researchers might establish such a program at one high school and then enlist a second high school to serve as a control group. Before starting the after-school program, the researchers would collect data to ensure that students at

quasi-experimental study
Research study in which one or more experimental treatments are administered but in which random assignment to groups is not possible.

both high schools share certain characteristics potentially related to aggressive behavior (type of community and family income levels, for example). The researchers cannot, however, make sure that the two groups are similar in every respect. The possibility exists that some other, unmeasured variable, such as the presence of gangs in one school, may account for any eventual difference in students' aggressive behavior at the two schools.

Studies That Identify Associations   Some studies are aimed at uncovering patterns that exist in the world, that is, identifying associations or correlations. By **correlation**, we mean the extent to which two variables are related to each other, such that one variable changes when the other variable does, in a somewhat predictable fashion. The direction (positive or negative) and strength of a correlation are often summarized by a statistic known as a **correlation coefficient**, which we describe in Figure 2–2.

In a **correlational study**, investigators do not try to change anything, as they do in an experiment. Instead, they look for naturally occurring associations among existing characteristics, behaviors, or other variables. For example, in a study with 8- to 11-year-old children, Shavers (2000) found an association between children's exposure to community violence and their own expressions of aggression. Children who had seen a lot of violence in their neighborhoods tended to act aggressively themselves.

Correlational studies, like that conducted by Shavers, allow us to identify associations among variables. They do not enable us to draw conclusions about cause-effect relationships among variables. The data in Shavers's study provide no definitive clues as to what factors might lead children exposed to violence to become aggressive themselves. Although community violence might have triggered aggression in children, other conditions closer to home, in their own families, could have been the cause. Or perhaps a third factor affects the two variables. For example, high unemployment rates in the community might incite frustration and violence in adults. High unemployment could also increase stress in parents, who might act out physically to children; children in turn imitate parents' aggressive acts. In this explanation, high unemployment increases community violence in adults by triggering their frustration and it has its effects on children's aggression through the stress it creates in parents. In other words, community violence does not *directly* affect children. The complicated manner in which variables are associated in real life means we can never draw definitive conclusions about causation from correlational data alone.

A second type of design that identifies associations, the **causal-comparative study**,[8] permits researchers to examine how two or more groups of people who *already* differ with respect to certain characteristics or prior experiences also differ with regard to other factors. For example, Mansavage (1999) compared incarcerated and nonincarcerated male adolescents between the ages of 14 and 18. She found that the two groups did not differ on some variables, such as incidence of "bad behaviors" or experience with punishment. The two groups did differ on hostility and humor: The incarcerated adolescents showed greater hostility and less use of humor than did the adolescents who were not incarcerated. The incarcerated adolescents were also more pessimistic than were nonincarcerated adolescents.

Causal-comparative studies provide helpful glimpses into conditions of life for youngsters. For example, Mansavage's study raises an important question about how young people may develop the habit of dwelling on their own problems, on the one hand, or making light of their struggles and maintaining hope, on the other. However, causal-comparative studies do not allow us to draw firm conclusions about cause-effect relationships. Mansavage's study, for example, does not allow us to conclude that hostility, pessimism, and a poor sense of humor caused the incarcerated youngsters to take the paths that led to their wrongdoings. Many other explanations are possible: Adolescents who were incarcerated may have had families who offered little guidance about appropriate behavior, or perhaps their families were poor, genetically inclined to be combative, or inadequately educated.

correlation
Extent to which two variables are related to each other, such that when one variable increases, the other either increases or decreases in a somewhat predictable fashion.

correlation coefficient
A statistic that indicates the nature of the relationship between two variables.

correlational study
Research study that explores relationships among variables.

causal-comparative study
Research study in which relationships are identified between existing conditions in children's lives and one or more aspects of the children's behavior.

---

[8] Don't be misled by the name, *causal-comparative study.* Causal-comparative designs involve no direct manipulation of a variable: The presumed cause has already occurred by the time the researcher conducts the investigation.

Consider the following questions:

- Do children with high self-esteem perform better in school than children with low self-esteem?
- Do two different intelligence tests given at the same time yield similar scores?
- How is children's aggressiveness related to their popularity?
- Are highly aggressive children more or less likely than less-aggressive children to feel guilty about inflicting harm?

Each of these questions asks about a relationship between two variables—between self-esteem and school performance, between two sets of intelligence test scores, between aggressiveness and popularity, or between aggressiveness and the presence of a conscience. The nature of such relationships is sometimes expressed in terms of a particular number—a statistic known as a **correlation coefficient**.

A correlation coefficient is a number between -1 and $+1$; most correlation coefficients are decimals (either positive or negative) somewhere between these two extremes. A correlation coefficient simultaneously tells us about the direction and strength of the relationship between two variables.

Direction of the relationship. The sign of the coefficient ($+$ or $-$) tells us whether the relationship is positive or negative. In a *positive correlation,* as one variable increases, the other variable also increases. In a *negative correlation,* as one variable increases, the other variable decreases. Here are several examples:

Positive correlations.
- Children with higher self-esteem achieve at higher levels at school (e.g., Marsh, 1990a).
- Children tend to get similar scores on different intelligence tests, especially when the tests have similar content (e.g., McGrew, Flanagan, Zeith, & Vanderwood, 1997).

Negative correlations.
- Children who are more aggressive are less popular with their peers (e.g., J. D. Coie, Dodge, Terry, & Wright, 1991).
- Children who display low levels of aggression are more likely to have a guilty conscience about their aggressive acts than are children who display higher levels of aggression (e.g., Eron, 1987).

Strength of the relationship: The size of the coefficient tells us how strong the relationship is. A number close to either $+1$ or -1 (e.g., $+.89$ or $-.76$) indicates a *strong correlation*: The two variables are closely related, so knowing the level of one variable allows us to predict the level of the other variable with considerable accuracy. A number close to 0 (e.g., $+.15$ or $-.22$) indicates a *weak correlation*: Knowing the level of one variable allows us to predict the level of the other variable, but we cannot predict with much accuracy. Coefficients in the middle range (e.g., those in the .40s and .50s, whether positive or negative) indicate a *moderate correlation.*

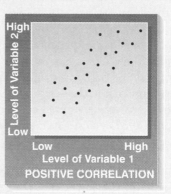

POSITIVE CORRELATION

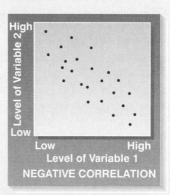

NEGATIVE CORRELATION

In the graphs above, each dot shows the degree to which a particular person shows Variables 1 and 2.

Studies That Show Developmental Stability and Change   Developmental studies examine how children grow, change, or stay the same as they become older and have more experiences. In a **cross-sectional study**, a researcher compares individuals at two or more age levels at the same point in time and assesses the same characteristic or behavior for each age group. For example, in a study with first- and third-grade boys, Coie, Dodge, Terry, and Wright (1991) found that first graders were more likely to be targets of aggression than were third graders.

Cross-sectional designs are frequently used to discover how children's and adolescents' thinking abilities, social skills, and other characteristics and behaviors change over time. Their major weakness is that, even though they reveal differences at different age levels, they do not necessarily indicate that age itself is the reason for the differences. Here's a hypothetical example. Imagine that a researcher goes to a high school and recruits two groups, freshmen and seniors. Students in the two age groups take a questionnaire measuring "school spirit." The researcher finds that seniors respond with more enthusiasm for their school than do freshmen. Does this mean that students become more invested in school during their high school years? Not necessarily. Students who stay in school through four years tend to be higher achievers than those who drop out. The entering freshman class is more diverse—it contains those who will stay and those who will eventually drop out. Those freshmen who will later drop out may already be disenchanted with school, thus showing little enthusiasm on the school spirit survey. Thus, what appear on the surface to be age comparisons are tainted by other differences in the populations.

Another option for studying developmental stability and change is the **longitudinal study**. In a longitudinal study, a researcher takes one group of children or adolescents and studies them over a lengthy period of time, often for several years and sometimes even for decades. The two most common uses of longitudinal designs are to examine the persistence of certain characteristics, abilities, and behaviors over time; and to identify factors in children's early lives that predict their later performance. An example of a longitudinal study is Eron's (1987) investigation into factors potentially related to aggressive behavior. These included family relationships, television viewing habits, attitudes about aggression, and police records. He collected data at three points in time, first when the participants in his study were in third grade, a second time 10 years later, and a third time 12 years after that. He found that aggressive behavior persisted from childhood to adulthood. Aggressive children were more likely to become aggressive adults, as manifested in aggressiveness toward spouses, punitive actions toward children, and arrests for criminal behavior. Furthermore, conditions present when the participants were children, including a punitive style by their parents, a tendency to watch violent television shows, and an apparent lack of a guilty conscience about aggressive acts, predicted their aggressiveness 10 and 22 years later.

Many longitudinal studies indicate that early development and events predict later tendencies and abilities. For example, children's experiences in high-quality, developmentally appropriate preschools are associated with social and academic competence several years later (Consortium for Longitudinal Studies, 1983; A. J. Reynolds, Mavrogenes, Bezruczko, & Hagemann, 1996; Schweinhart, Barnes, & Weikart, 1993). However, longitudinal research also suggests that benefits of attending preschool may diminish over time unless youngsters also enjoy positive school and family experiences in later years (Reynolds et al., 1996). Early progress does not necessarily guarantee life-long advantages, it seems.

Nor does early adversity seal a fate of hardship. For instance, troubled children who later experienced positive school experiences, received encouragement in a harmonious family setting, and avoided deviant peer groups functioned better as adults and were more likely to steer clear of antisocial individuals than were children who did not have these advantages (Rutter, Champion, Quinton, Maughan, & Pickles, 1995). Similarly, girls growing up in the 1950s and 1960s who encountered their parents' divorce and economic hardship later developed high self-esteem and good social skills when their mothers modeled good coping skills (Moen & Erickson, 1995). In general, longitudinal data indicate that young people continue to be affected by past experiences, but the later choices they make and new environments they encounter can either sustain or diminish the impact of the past.

cross-sectional study
Research study in which the performance of individuals at different ages is compared.

longitudinal study
Research study in which the performance of a single group of people is tracked over a period of time.

To strengthen certain kinds of inferences that can be made about change and stability in child development, some researchers have creatively modified developmental designs. To address questions about short-term learning, some researchers have tried *microgenetic methods,* which you might think of as brief longitudinal designs. Researchers implementing microgenetic methods may study children's actions and strategies—from beginning to end—over a few hours, days, or weeks (Siegler & Stern, 1998; Vygotsky, 1978). Other variations include the combining of cross-sectional and longitudinal designs. For instance, a *cohort-sequential design* replicates a longitudinal study with new *cohorts,* that is, with new populations of people born the same year. Cohort-sequential designs are advantageous when developmental scholars wish to know whether specific patterns of change and stability hold up with young people born at different times in history. To illustrate, Suhr (1999) conducted a cohort-sequential study to examine patterns of change in the mathematics, reading recognition, and reading comprehension scores of children. Scores were collected every two years for four groups of children, who varied by year of birth (the children were born in 1980, 1981, 1982, and 1983). Data were collected in 1988, 1990, 1992, and 1994. Suhr found that a single statistical model adequately portrayed the four cohorts and she was able to combine them into a single large group. In this large group, she found that growth in skills was rapid between ages 5 and 10, and slowed down after 10. Because the data included children from four birth years and Suhr examined growth in each cohort, she could be reasonably confident that the spurt of learning that occurred between 5 and 10 years is a reasonably accurate result and not an anomaly of one particular group.

Studies That Describe Children's Experiences in Natural Contexts   The research designs we've considered up until now typically involve considerable use of numbers such as test scores, tallies of questionnaire responses, or ratings of behavior. They therefore are sometimes referred to as **quantitative research**. In contrast, many studies rely heavily on non-numerical aspects of people's behavior—for example, verbal descriptions of what people do each day, how they interact with one another, what unspoken rules they follow—and may also make use of existing tools, documents, and other objects that shed light on participants' worlds. These studies are often described as **qualitative research**.

In the field of child development, qualitative studies are often conducted in everyday, non-laboratory settings. In a **naturalistic study**, a researcher examines development in natural contexts, as children and adolescents behave and interact in their families, peer groups, neighborhoods, schools, clubs, and elsewhere. Some of these studies, known as *ethnographies,* look at the everyday rules of behavior, beliefs, social structures, and other cultural patterns of an entire group of people—perhaps a community, a classroom, or an adolescent gang. Other naturalistic studies take the form of *case studies,* wherein the researcher looks at a single child or adolescent in considerable depth over a period of time. (The latter are not to be confused with the case studies in this book, which are more limited in scope.)

Naturalistic studies vary greatly in nature, as the methods they incorporate are limited only by the researcher's imagination. However, a description by Ember and Ember (1994) of the Kapauku, who lived in the central highlands of western New Guinea, can give you a feel for the naturalistic approach. War and homicides were frequent among the Kapauku, and the Embers attributed such aggressiveness to the childhood experiences of the Kapauku:

> At about 7 years of age, a Kapauku boy begins to be under the father's control, gradually sleeping and eating only with the men and away from his mother. His father gives him a garden plot to cultivate and later a pig to raise. The father tries to train his son to be a brave warrior. His training begins when the father engages his son in mock stick fights. Gradually the fights become more serious and possibly lethal when the father and son shoot real war arrows at each other. Groups of boys play at target shooting; they also play at hitting each other over the head with sticks. Boys from neighboring villages (in the same political unit) play at war by fighting with blunt arrows and sticks. (Ember & Ember, 1994, pp. 639–640)

This brief qualitative description of the Kapauku would have been possible only by extended observations in this society. Often, qualitative researchers spend a great deal of time observing and talking with the people they study. Researchers learn as much as they can

quantitative research
Research study in which the data collected are predominantly numerical in nature.

qualitative research
Research study in which the data collected are largely non-numerical in nature.

naturalistic study
Research study in which individuals are observed in their natural environment.

about the rules by which people live; qualitative scholars work hard to capture the details of people's relationships, conversations, and beliefs. Furthermore, they tend to view the context of people's lives as significant. When describing any particular aspect of people's lives, such as their religious practices, gender roles, or in this case, aggressive actions, qualitative researchers reflect on how it fits within the broader culture and community.

In the research designs we have examined in this section, we have included several studies focused on one topic, children's aggression. From an experimental study, we learned that children imitate role models who act aggressively; from a correlational investigation, we learned that exposure to community violence is associated with how aggressive children become; from longitudinal data we found long-term associations between extreme aggression in middle childhood and the same characteristic in adulthood; and from naturalistic research, we found that some societies purposefully prepare children for war and homicide. The developmental research designs we've just described have different strengths and weaknesses (Table 2–4). Together, these designs give us a more complete picture of how children experience life and change both in predictable and sometimes very individual ways.

TABLE 2-4 **Developmental Research Designs**

DESIGN	ADVANTAGES AND DISADVANTAGES	EXAMPLE
Studies That Identify Causal Relationships	• Well-designed experiments enable researchers to be relatively confident that a particular intervention is the cause of changes in thinking or behavior. • The tight controls required for firm conclusions about cause-effect relationships may lead to experimental conditions that do not resemble, and so may not generalize to, real-world settings. • Quasi-experiments provide an alternative when true experiments are not possible, practical, or ethical. • Because other possible explanations for observed changes cannot be ruled out, conclusions about cause-effect relationships in quasi-experiments are speculative at best.	A school district is unsure which of two textbook series is more effective for teaching scientific reasoning skills in its 10 elementary schools. It gives copies of one series to 5 schools and copies of the other series to the other 5 schools, with the schools using each series being chosen randomly. At the end of the school year, it administers a test of scientific reasoning skills to students at all 10 schools and compares the average scores of students using the two series.
Studies That Identify Associations	• Correlational studies are relatively inexpensive to conduct and can yield a large body of data regarding relationships among variables. • Cause-effect relationships cannot be determined from correlations alone. • Causal-comparative studies provide a second alternative when true experiments are not possible. • In causal-comparative studies, observed differences among groups cannot be traced to the particular factor being investigated.	A high school teacher gives students a questionnaire that assesses their attitudes toward mathematics and then looks at the relationship between their responses to the questionnaire and the number of elective math courses in which they enroll.
Studies That Show Developmental Stability and Change	• Cross-sectional designs offer an efficient snapshot of how characteristics or behaviors probably change with age. • In cross-sectional designs, age differences can be explained in a variety of ways, including physiological maturation, exposure to different schooling experiences, and important historical events. • Longitudinal studies demonstrate how individuals change as they grow older; they also allow prediction of later characteristics and behaviors from earlier characteristics and experiences. • Longitudinal studies are very expensive and time-consuming, and it is difficult to maintain a sizable sample of research participants over the duration of the study (people move, lose interest in the research, etc.).	A counselor assesses conflict-resolution skills during adolescence and determines whether they predict job stability and lasting marriages during adulthood.
Studies That Describe Children in Natural Contexts	• Naturalistic studies capture the complexities and subtle nuances of children's environments and experiences. • Naturalistic studies are difficult and time-consuming to conduct, as they generally take a long time and involve extended, in-depth data collection.	A preschool teacher is interested in the ramps that children make in the block area. She spends weeks observing children build ramps, run cars down them, talk about height and incline in simple terms, and extend structures into bridges.

Analyzing Research Studies

As you read this chapter, you may be studying research methods in child and adolescent development for the very first time. Nevertheless, if you ask yourself a few simple questions when you read the research literature, you can analyze research studies in much the same way experts do. Following are several questions to keep in mind:

■ *Do the data have high validity for the purpose of the research?* The data collected should provide reasonable indicators or measures of the characteristics or behaviors under investigation. No data collection method is perfect, of course. However, researchers should describe the procedures they took to make it likely that their measures gave them the kind of data they sought. For example, developmental scholars might report using a published test of writing ability with these features: It had been carefully constructed to provide clear instructions and standard procedures for administration, it was previously tested on a large population similar to the sample in their study, and children's essays were evaluated with a scoring rubric reflecting high-quality writing criteria. As another example, developmental scholars examining infants' responses to caregivers' emotional expressions might report how they examined infants only when infants were in a rested and alert state and how they further followed standard procedures for categorizing infants' responses to anger, sadness, and happiness in caregivers.

Many professional journals are available to help you learn more about infant, child, and adolescent development.

■ *Do the data have high reliability?* The data should have been influenced only minimally by temporary characteristics and other chance factors affecting participants' performance. Reliability is especially an issue with research involving young children, whose limited language skills, short attention spans, and relative inexperience with tests may lead to considerable variation in performance from one day to the next. Reliability is also a concern when judgments must be made. For example, observers asked to code for aggression and rough-and-tumble play in young children must be trained to spot behaviors and facial expressions that effectively distinguish these different interactions. Two observers' judgments would be considered to produce reliable information when they observed the same events and categorized them in a similar way.

■ *Does the research design warrant the conclusions drawn?* Experimental studies often enable researchers to draw conclusions about cause-effect relationships, but other designs rarely do. If you are reading about data from quasi-experimental, correlational, and causal-comparative studies, you should expect to see that the authors speculate about several reasons for any associations they obtain. If you are reading about qualitative research, you should expect the authors to explain the procedures that purportedly give their study integrity (e.g., conducting observations over a reasonably long period of time, checking patterns they initially notice by obtaining additional information, and interpreting events with references to context). Whenever you read a research report, ask yourself this question: *Have the researchers considered and justifiably eliminated other reasonable explanations for their results?*

■ *How substantial and compelling are the results?* Sometimes researchers find major differences between groups or observe dramatic effects from particular methods, which make their findings compelling. For example, in a classic study by Palincsar and Brown (1984), six seventh-grade students with poor reading comprehension skills participated in twenty 30-minute sessions involving *reciprocal teaching,* a procedure whereby students learn to ask themselves and one another thought-provoking questions about what they read. After this relatively short intervention, the students showed remarkable improvement in their reading comprehension skills, sometimes even surpassing the performance of their classmates (A. L. Brown & Palincsar, 1987; Palincsar & Brown, 1984). The effectiveness of reciprocal teaching has subsequently been documented in numerous other studies, and so we will revisit this technique in our discussion of literacy development in Chapter 8.

At other times, researchers report differences or effects that are probably too small to worry about. For instance, as you will discover in Chapter 6, many studies have found gender differences in verbal ability (a difference favoring females) and visual-spatial thinking (a difference favoring males). However, the differences are fairly small and are based only on group averages, so they tell us little if anything about how *individual children* are likely to perform on verbal and visual-spatial tasks. In fact, many boys have exceptional verbal ability (remember Michael in our earlier case study), and many girls are excellent visual-spatial thinkers.

Keep in mind, too, that our knowledge base about children is fallible and ever-changing. The new research findings that appear each year sometimes support what we have previously thought to be true and sometimes call into question our earlier conclusions. Therefore, ideally, we must look for consistent patterns across many studies and not rely too heavily on the results of any single study.

■ *How might the researchers' biases have influenced their data collection, analyses, and interpretations?* Much as researchers strive to be impartial in their work, their methods and interpretations are often influenced by their own expectations. For example, researchers are more likely to focus on research findings that support, rather than contradict, their beliefs and hypotheses. Unless researchers are exceptionally open-minded, they are likely to downplay results that contradict their original expectations when they write up their final reports. As a reader, you cannot always know the biases of the researcher, but you can be skeptical of conclusions that do not seem well supported by the data.

Furthermore, just as many developmental studies have used predominantly White, middle-class samples (see the earlier description of research participants), so, too, have the researchers been predominantly White, middle-class and, until recently, male. The unique perspectives of ethnic minority groups, members of alternative cultural groups, and women have been underrepresented in psychology and other disciplines (Bohan, 1995). Fortunately, cross-cultural perspectives on the development of children and adolescents are increasingly available. We will highlight many of them throughout the book as we summarize evidence on particular topics. Nonetheless, we invite you to remain vigilant to cultural gaps in the literature and the necessity of adapting instruction to the particular backgrounds of youngsters with whom you work.

■ *Do the conclusions seem reasonable in light of your own experiences with children?* Sometimes well-meaning researchers and theorists offer advice that flies in the face of what common sense tells us is reasonable and appropriate. For example, John Watson, a trailblazing and influential psychologist in the early twentieth century, warned mothers about the perils of excessive "mother love" and advised them not to "hug or kiss" their children or "let them sit in your lap" (J. Watson, 1928, pp. 81, 87). His ideas about parenting are questionable today, yet he touted his position with vigor to a generation of parents and nursery school teachers. Similarly, Arnold Gesell, a psychologist best known for his maturational view of physical development (e.g., 1923, 1929), operated a nursery school in which he modeled rigorous methods of "habit training" for parents and asked them to adjust their childrearing routines to comply with regimented procedures (Beatty, 1996). Years later, some of these mothers expressed regret about following the advice of such "experts."

Be aware that some professional practices are derived from research in one area but they are not informed by equally valid findings in other areas. For example, having children who are making slower-than-average progress repeat a grade level makes some educational sense if we look at the practice from the standpoint of cognitive development only. If Justin repeats first grade, the assumption goes, he'll get a chance to "catch up." In fact, recent research findings have unveiled many negative social and emotional consequences associated with not allowing children to move from one grade to the next with their peers (Shephard & Smith, 1987, 1989; R. Watson, 1996). From a social-emotional standpoint, the practice does not make sense.

As a newcomer to the technically rich world of developmental research, you may find it difficult to determine what constitutes a reasonable translation of research to practice with children. However, you can begin to try out your growing knowledge base of children's physical, cognitive, and social-emotional development by making a point of evaluating the meaning of research for all aspects of children's lives. By regularly thinking through how an intervention fits with children's physical, cognitive, and social-emotional development, you will develop good habits that can pay off not only in critiquing research applications but also in designing appropriate everyday environments for children.

■ *Are the results generalizable to infants, children, or adolescents with whom you will be working?* Fortunately, researchers typically describe the specific characteristics (e.g., age, gender, ethnicity, family income level) of the participants in their studies. If their samples are different in important ways from the children in your charge, be cautious in your use of their results. Following are some examples of questions you might ask yourself:

- A researcher finds a relationship between middle-class parents' disciplinary strategies and their children's social skills. Would a similar relationship also exist in families living in extreme economic poverty?
- A researcher finds a hospital's bereavement program helps children mourn the loss of parents who died after lengthy illnesses. Would the same program work for children whose parents died suddenly from accidents or suicide?
- A researcher finds a relationship between how openly fathers express emotions and their children's skill in resolving conflicts with their peers. Would this relationship apply to children who do not live full-time with their fathers?
- A researcher reports results obtained for Hispanic children who are fluent in both Spanish and English. Are the results likely to apply also to Hispanic children who speak only Spanish or only English?
- A researcher finds that a particular method of teaching science is highly effective with academically inclined, highly motivated children who attend a charter school. Would the same method be effective within a traditional public school with larger class sizes and more diverse populations of students?

Ultimately, professionals who work with infants, children, and adolescents must consider which research findings are applicable and potentially useful in their relationships, strategies, and interventions with them.

Gathering Information During Professional Practice

As you have seen, academic researchers work diligently to collect information about children and adolescents in ways that are sensitive, ethical, valid, and reliable. Practitioners who work with children do the same, although their strategies are somewhat different. In this final section, we consider techniques for gathering information that can be used by the many professionals who work with children. We conclude the chapter by offering ethical guidelines on data collection.

Collecting Information from Children and Adolescents

Adults who work with children and adolescents can use the same methods of data collection we examined for researchers, namely observations, surveys and interviews, tests and other assessment devices, and occasionally, physiological measures. Unlike researchers, however, busy practitioners do not have the luxury of controlled conditions for collecting information, and they almost always have numerous and competing demands on their time. Their primary motivations, of course, are teaching, caring for, and providing services to young people. Collection of data must take a lower priority. Given these work conditions and motivations of practitioners, we offer the following recommendations:

■ *Observe how children respond to the demands of particular settings.* Depending on their jobs, practitioners watch children in particular contexts, such as the classroom, in the cafeteria, on the playground, on field trips, during extracurricular activities, in court hearings, in private discussions, in recreation centers, in health clinics, in religious instruction,

Caregivers and other professionals can collect valuable information about children by observing their choices and reactions in everyday environments—what they look at, what they choose to play with, what they find distressing, and what makes them laugh.

Professionals who work with children can learn a lot from watching children's facial expressions, postures, and other nonverbal behaviors. These two girls appear to be enjoying their time together on the computer.

and with family members. As you observe children and adolescents in such settings, ask yourself what they are doing, why they might be behaving as they are, how they might be interpreting events, and how the setting may be affecting their behavior. Keep in mind that the settings in which you see children may not permit them to act their best—in other words, naturally, intelligently, and kindly.

■ *Observe nonverbal cues from youngsters.*   Careful observation of children's posture, actions, and emotional expressions can provide important information about their preferences and abilities. For example, an infant caregiver may learn that one 18-month-old toddler slows down, pulls at his ear, and seeks comfort when he's sleepy, whereas another child of the same age speeds up, squirms, and becomes irritable when ready for a nap. A 5-month-old baby may look away and close her eyes tightly when she is overstimulated; another child may cry in distress. During an interview with a teenage boy, a counselor senses that he is withdrawn and despondent; in response, she inquires sympathetically about his feelings toward family members, teachers, and friends at school.

■ *Use all your senses, not just your eyes.*   Through years of experience working with infants, children, or adolescents, practitioners often develop strong intuitions about how youngsters feel and think in particular situations. New professionals do not have the benefit of years of experience, but they can be as open as possible to the clues children give off, intentionally or not, as to their feelings and interests. For example, adults who care for infants can often guess fairly accurately which baby is crying from hunger, pain, fear, or exhaustion. But they need not rely on a mysterious sixth sense—they can keep records on notepaper of times for diaper changes, ounces of "formula" babies consume, and duration of naps. When infants become agitated, caregivers can refer to these records to help determine the nature of the unmet physical or emotional need.

■ *Realize you may be wrong.*   As you interact with children, search for evidence that both confirms your expectations and makes you change your ideas. Teresa recalls the case of an infant she cared for who was agitated one day. She figured the infant was cranky because she had caught a cold. Many of the other children in the room had colds, so that seemed plausible. Later, she realized she was wrong. Changing the baby girl's diaper, she discovered an abscess (an inflamed sore) on her bottom. Naturally, she regretted that she had not immediately investigated other causes for the girl's discomfort. These kinds of mistakes are common even though they can be highly distressing to caregivers. Knowing that you may sometimes be wrong about children's motivations, emotional states, physical well-being, and intellectual abilities, you can constantly look for clues from children that will help you to understand them more fully.

■ *Focus your observations on developmental states.*   When you sense an unmet need, analyze the situation using your knowledge of child development. For example, when an after-school care provider is uneasy about the social relationships among children in his care, he can respond by observing how in daily interchanges children are accepted or rejected by peers (we examine peer relationships in Chapter 13). A high school teacher who sees that her encouragement of critical thinking in social studies is proving unsuccessful may, by focused observations, determine that her efforts are undermined by students' desire to get the "right" answer on forthcoming tests (we examine motivation in Chapter 11). Similarly, a school counselor faced with a child who disregards the feelings of peers can remember to consider how children typically come to understand the perspectives and feelings of other people (we examine perspective taking in Chapter 10).

Knowledge of specific areas of development can help you to target your observations with children. Throughout the book you will find Observation Guidelines tables that can assist you in observing children and adolescents more effectively. The first of these, "Watching and Listening to Children," suggests some general behaviors to look for. You will also have many opportunities to look for specific developmental concepts in the three-volume Observation CD set that accompanies this textbook. We encourage you to take advantage of both of these resources to deepen your knowledge of developmental concepts as well as to practice your observation skills with infants, children, and adolescents.

OBSERVATION GUIDELINES
Watching and Listening to Children

CHARACTERISTIC	LOOK FOR	EXAMPLE	IMPLICATION

Preferred Activities	• Exploration of entire environment
	• Engagement with objects through age-appropriate means, for example:
	  • mouthing (infancy)
	  • manipulation and visual examination (early childhood)
	  • classification of objects into categories (middle childhood)
	  • explanations of groupings (early adolescence)
	  • conjecture about the physical origins of objects (late adolescence)
	• Interest in people, including initiating interactions as well as responding to those initiated by others
	• Quiet periods of self-absorption
		Nine-month-old Jamie is similar to other children in his infant-toddler room in that he busily explores the toys and room when he is rested and well fed. His teachers observe him on one day watching the shadows of the trees and rubbing his fingers over textures of tiles in the playroom. He also seeks interaction from familiar adults, and to some degree shows interest in the other children.	Provide a safe environment with interesting and attractive objects for active exploration. Make changes to the environment based on the preferred activities of children who inhabit it.

Activity Level	• Activity level appropriate to the assigned task (might indicate motivation to do well and an understanding of the assigned task) • High activity level but little sustained attention to the task (might indicate boredom, frustration, anxiety or, in some cases, a disability) • Listlessness (might indicate boredom, fatigue, or poor nutrition) • Requesting or volunteering for additional work (probably indicates high motivation)	In her recreation program, Molly sits on the sidelines, appearing bored and indifferent.	Determine the probable source of unexpected activity levels in children. Make sure assigned tasks are geared to each child's knowledge, abilities, and areas of interest. Follow up with children who appear listless to see if they are getting adequate meals and sleep.
Body Language	• Facial expressions (reflecting enjoyment, excitement, sadness, confusion, anger, or frustration) • Tenseness of limbs (might indicate intense concentration or excessive anxiety) • Slouching in seat (might indicate fatigue, boredom, or resistance to an activity) • Head on desk (might indicate intense concentration, boredom, depression, or fatigue)	Whenever his teacher engages the class in a discussion of controversial issues, Jamal participates eagerly. When she goes over the previous night's homework, however, he crosses his arms, slouches low in his seat, pulls his hat low over his eyes, and says nothing.	Use children's body language as a rough gauge of interest, and modify activities that do not appear to be engaging children's attention and interest. Speak individually and confidentially with children who often show signs of sadness or anger, and if necessary seek assistance from a mental-health professional.
On-task and Off-task Behaviors	• Ability to work well on independent assignments and in group activities (probably indicates high motivation to learn and achieve) • Frequent chattering or horseplay with peers (might indicate low motivation to learn, lack of confidence about an assigned task, or a strong need for social interaction with peers) • Focus on irrelevant, and perhaps meaningless, activities (might indicate boredom, lack of confidence about performing a task, or disability) • Daydreaming (might indicate unwillingness or inability to complete an assigned task; might also indicate creative thinking about a task)	During a cooperative group activity, three members of a group are actively planning the group's upcoming oral presentation. Nathan, the fourth group member, doesn't participate in the discussion; instead, he fiddles with a paperclip he has found on the floor.	Identify the specific reason(s) for children's off-task behaviors, and modify lessons and assignments to be appropriate for individual children's ability levels and needs. Incorporate opportunities for social interaction for youngsters who enjoy working with others toward common goals.
Questions and Comments	• Asking thoughtful and insightful questions about the topic at hand (indicates high task engagement and motivation) • Asking questions that have already been answered (might indicate inattentiveness or lack of understanding) • Complaining about the difficulty of an assignment (might indicate low motivation, lack of ability or confidence, or an overloaded schedule of academic and social obligations)	In a whining tone, Danusia asks, "Do we really have to include *three* arguments in our persuasive essays? I've been thinking really hard and can only come up with one!"	Read between the lines in the questions children ask and the comments they make. Consider what their questions and comments indicate about their existing knowledge, skills, motivation, and self-confidence.

(continued)

OBSERVATION GUIDELINES

Watching and Listening to Children *(continued)*

CHARACTERISTIC	LOOK FOR	EXAMPLE	IMPLICATION
Test Scores, Assessment Results, and Work Products	• Careful and thorough work (indicates high motivation) • Unusual and creative ideas, artwork, or constructions (indicates high motivation and a willingness to take risks) • Numerous sloppy errors (might indicate that a young person did an assignment hurriedly, has poor proofreading skills, or has a learning disability)	When Martin's social studies teacher gives several options for how students might illustrate the idea of *democracy*, Martin creates a large poster of colorful, cartoon-like characters engaging in such activities as voting, free speech, and making new laws.	When looking at and evaluating children's work, don't focus exclusively on "right" and "wrong" answers. When assessing several distinct abilities (e.g., accuracy, neatness, creativity), however, do not combine them into a single "grade" for an assignment; such a grade would be meaningless and impossible to interpret.

■ *Separate observations from inferences.* It is hard to do, but you can practice recording what you see, and writing separately what you think it means. Here are some observation notes from a student teacher, Ana, who practiced making this distinction ("Notetaking" refers to her observations, and "Notemaking" indicates her interpretations):

Notetaking	Notemaking
A child is working at the computer. There are fourteen students working at their desks. Six students are working with another teacher (aide) in the back of the room. It is an English reading/writing group she is working with—speaking only in English. I see a mother working with one child only and she is helping the student with something in English. There is a baby in a carriage nearby the mother. I hear classical music playing very lightly. I can only hear the music every once in a while when the classroom is really quiet. I stand up and move around the room to see what the children at their desks are working on. They are writing scary stories. The baby makes a funny noise with her lips and everyone in the class laughs and stares for a few seconds, even the teacher. . . .	The class seems to be really self-directed. . . . I am not used to seeing students split up into different groups for Spanish and English readers because in my class they are Spanish readers, but it is really good for me to see this because it happens in a lot of upper grade settings, and I will be working in an upper grade bilingual setting next placement. I really like the idea of putting on music during work times. I know that when I hear classical music it really helps me to relax and calm as well as focus. I think that it has the same effect on the students in this class. I'm noticing more and more that I really cherish the laughter in a classroom when it comes from a sincere topic or source. It is also nice to see the students *and* the *teacher* laughing. . . .

(C. Frank, 1999, pp. 11–12)[9]

It is impossible to separate objective observations completely from interpretations. Nonetheless, trying to make this distinction can lead professionals to appreciate how a particular scene can be interpreted in many different ways. Also, reflective observers can learn as much about themselves as they do about what they see, as Ana's "notemaking" comments reveal.

■ *Try out different kinds of observations.* The kinds of observations you conduct will depend on what you hope to gain from watching and listening to children. *Running records* are narrative summaries of a child's activities during a single period of time (Nicolson & Shipstead, 2002). Running records provide practitioners with opportunities to focus on a particular child and to draw conclusions about the child's emerging developmental abilities. In Figure 2–3, you can see an excerpt from a running record prepared by a language

---

[9] From *Ethnographic Eyes: A Teacher's Guide to Classroom Observation* (pp. 11–12) by Carolyn Frank, 1999, Portsmouth, NH: Heinemann. Copyright 1999 by Carolyn Frank. Reprinted with permission.

Center/Age level:	Center for Speech and Language/3- to 6-Year-Olds		
Date:	7/17	Time:	10:20–10:26 AM
Observer:	Naoki	Child/Age:	Taki/5;1
		Teacher:	Camille

	Comments
Taki is seated on the floor with Kyle (4;8) and Camille, the teacher, in a corner of the classroom; both children have their backs to the center of the room. Taki sits with her right leg tucked under her bottom and her left leg bent with her foot flat on the floor. The Listening Lotto card is in front of her on the floor, and she holds a bunch of red plastic markers in her right hand. Camille begins the tape.	10:20
The first sound is of a baby crying. Taki looks up at Camille, who says, "What's that?" Taki looks at Kyle, who has already placed his marker on the crying baby. Camille says, "That's a baby crying," and points to the picture on Taki's card. Taki places the marker with her left hand as the next sound, beating drums, begins.	No intro of game. Hearing aid working.
Taki looks at Kyle as the drumming continues. Camille points to the picture of the drums on Taki's card, and Taki places her marker.	Understands process.
The next sound is of a toilet flushing. Taki looks at Kyle and points to the drums. Kyle says, "Good, Taki. We heard drums banging." Taki smiles. Camille says, "Do you hear the toilet flushing?" as she points to the correct picture. Taki places her marker and repositions herself to sit cross-legged. She continues to hold the markers in her right hand and place them with her left. . . .	10:22 Kyle supportive of Taki.
Conclusions: Taki's receptive language was on display when she followed the teacher's directions in Listening Lotto (put markers on the appropriate spots), but she did not demonstrate success on her own. Her fine motor control was in evidence as she adeptly handled small markers.	

FIGURE 2–3 Running record for Taki during Listening Lotto. *Note:* Developmentalists often list a child's age in both years and additional months, separating the two numbers by a semicolon. For instance, Taki's age of 5 years and 1 month is indicated as "5;1."

From *Through the Looking Glass: Observations in the Early Childhood Classroom* (3rd ed.) (pp. 118–119), by S. Nicolson and S. G. Shipstead, 2002, Upper Saddle River, New Jersey: Merrill/Prentice Hall. Copyright 2002 by Pearson Education. Reprinted with permission.

specialist. After writing this running record, the language specialist concluded that Taki understood some aspects of spoken language when she followed directions. However, Taki needed help when completing the Listening Lotto game. These kinds of conclusions can offer professionals good ideas about the kinds of interventions they should try next with children. Possibly, the language specialist observing Taki realized she might conduct further assessments into Taki's hearing ability.

Anecdotal records are brief incidents observed and described by a practitioner (Nicolson & Shipstead, 2002). Anecdotal records are typically made when a practitioner notices an action or statement on the part of a child that is developmentally significant. For example, anecdotal records are sometimes made of children's fears, accomplishments, physical milestones, social interaction patterns, and ways of thinking. Anecdotal records tend to be far briefer than running records and they may be written up later in the day. In other words, the practitioner does not typically generate anecdotal records by sitting down and writing notes; instead, the practitioner may simply be struck by a child's statement or action and reflect on it afterwards. Anecdotal records are useful because they can help identify individual needs; practitioners can also accumulate notes about children and share them with family members during conferences, informal conversations, and meetings. In Figure 2–4, teachers have prepared anecdotal records from young children.

Observers sometimes use *checklists* and *rating scales* when they wish to evaluate the degree to which children's behaviors reflect specific criteria. Checklists allow observers to

FIGURE 2–4 Anecdotal records for young children

From *Through the Looking Glass: Observations in the Early Childhood Classroom* (3rd ed.) (p. 139), by S. Nicolson and S. G. Shipstead, 2002, Upper Saddle River, New Jersey: Merrill/Prentice Hall. Copyright 2002 by Pearson Education. Reprinted with permission.

10/5 Tatiana (2;0):	While sitting on the floor in the art area peeling the wrappers off crayons, she looked up as the caregiver grew near and said, "I making the crayons all naked."
1/15 Maggie (4; 8):	I listened as Maggie chattered on and on while the two of us cleaned up the block area. Finally I winked and said, "It all sounds like baloney to me." Maggie quickly asked, "What's baloney?" I replied, "It's a word that means you made all that up!" She thought for a few seconds and said, "No, it's salami!"
2/24 Matthew (7;4):	While discussing *In a Dark, Dark Room and Other Scary Stories* by Alvin Schwartz, Matthew thoughtfully shared, "Do you know what kind of scary things I like best? Things that are halfway between real and imaginary." I started to ask, "I wonder what . . . " Matthew quickly replied, "Examples would be aliens, shadows, and dreams coming true."

FIGURE 2–5 Checklist for evaluating an oral presentation

From *Writing Instructional Objectives for Teaching and Assessment,* (7th ed.) (pp. 82–83), by Norman E. Gronlund, 2004, Upper Saddle River, NJ: Merrill/Prentice Hall. Copyright 2004 by Pearson Education. Reprinted with permission.

Directions: On the space in front of each item, place a plus sign (+) if performance is satisfactory; place a minus sign (−) if the performance is unsatisfactory.

_____ 1. States the topic at the beginning of the report.
_____ 2. Speaks clearly and loudly enough to be heard.
_____ 3. Uses language appropriate for the report.
_____ 4. Uses correct grammar.
_____ 5. Speaks at a satisfactory rate.
_____ 6. Looks at the class members when speaking.
_____ 7. Uses natural movements and appears relaxed.
_____ 8. Presents the material in an organized manner.
_____ 9. Holds the interest of the class.

note whether a child's actions or work products reflect a series of specific standards. For example, a community center supervisor can determine whether an adolescent follows proper procedures for building and varnishing a wooden table. Figure 2–5 shows a checklist a debate club leader can use to evaluate a youngster's oral presentation. Rating scales are similar to checklists but these ask observers not simply whether a child shows a particular behavior but rather how often or consistently the child shows the behavior. In Figure 2–6, a teacher can indicate how often a child shows particular behaviors relating to being on-task during seatwork (Pellegrini, 1996).

One means of recording observations is not necessarily better than another. Instead, each observational system has a distinct purpose. As you gain experience in observing youngsters, you are likely to see how your own understanding of individual children grows when you use several observational methods and supplement these with conversations with children.

■ *Ask children and adolescents about their experiences.* Unless adults ask questions of children and adolescents, they cannot fully understand how young people experience life. Sometimes children share perspectives with adults, but at other times, they have vastly different worldviews. For example, Wilson and Corbett (2001) found that sixth-grade students in six schools in Philadelphia shared many values with adults. Adolescents stated that they wanted teachers to push them to complete assignments (even when they resisted), to maintain order (even when they misbehaved), and to ensure they understood material (even when they struggled). Despite their apparent desire to succeed, these youngsters were unaware of what it took to do well when subjects became difficult, and they were naïve

FIGURE 2–6 Rating scale of a child's concentration during seatwork

Adapted from *Observing Children in Their Natural Worlds: A Methodological Primer*, by A. D. Pellegrini, 1996, Mahwah, NJ: Erlbaum. Used with permission.

Directions: For each item, indicate how frequently the child shows this type of behavior during seatwork by circling the appropriate description.

1. Settles quietly during beginning of task.

   Never   Seldom   Sometimes   Frequently   Always

2. Shows strong interest in completing task.

   Never   Seldom   Sometimes   Frequently   Always

3. Concentrates on task despite difficulties and interruptions.

   Never   Seldom   Sometimes   Frequently   Always

4. Works through task from beginning until end.

   Never   Seldom   Sometimes   Frequently   Always

about getting into college, as revealed in this excerpt. ("S" refers to the Student and "I" to the Interviewer.)

S: I'm going to high school and college.
I: Think you will finish both?
S: Yep.
I: What will it take?
S: Good grades.
I: How are your grades now?
S: They're bad, but I'm trying to pull them up.
I: Is that hard to do?
S: I just haven't felt like doing it. (B. L. Wilson & Corbett, 2001, p. 23)

When practitioners learn how children and adolescents actually experience school, social services, entertainment, and health care, they can better help young people meet their needs. For example, from Wilson and Corbett's study, we realize that teachers need to have high expectations for students' performance and provide sufficient support to enable students to learn successfully (we'll address these issues in more detail in Chapters 4, 5, and 11). Children also have much to say to professionals in other fields, such as social work. They indicate, for example, that they dislike frequent changes in the social workers assigned to them and resent adults' failures to protect their confidentiality (Munro, 2001). Taking these children seriously by listening to them can help them to feel important and to take initiative in their own education and treatment (Cook-Sather, 2002).

■ *Develop your interviewing skills.* Too often, conversations between adults and children are short, ask-a-question-and-get-an-answer exchanges. Lengthier dialogues, perhaps with an individual child or a small group of children, can be far more informative. To find out what young people think, believe, know, and misunderstand, adults must not only encourage them to talk but also follow up with probing questions and frequent reassurances that their ideas and opinions are important and valued. For example, Pramling (1996) urges teachers

to become skilled at letting the children expose their ideas and also at getting the children to feel that they want to share their ideas with the teacher and the other children. Children must feel it is enjoyable to express themselves and to be thrilled by others' ideas. To achieve this means that both the teacher and the children must learn to communicate on equal terms and to share their experiences. (p. 570)

Getting children to talk takes experience, but there are a few things you can do (Graue & Walsh, 1998). For instance, try a combination of open-ended questions ("How was your day?") and close-ended questions ("Did you watch TV when you went home from school?"). Also, include some general requests for information that are not in question form ("Tell me more about that."). Try not to ask an unremitting series of questions; your probing may then seem like an inquisition. Sometimes it is appropriate to ask children how *other children* view life; this can be an effective way to help them feel safe in speaking their mind. For example, rather than asking children how they feel about standardized tests, ask them how other children feel ("Can you tell me how kids at your school felt when they took the CSAP—remember that Colorado achievement test?").

When talking with children, always consider factors that affect how they respond to your questions. Certainly the relationship between adult and child is significant, but so are other variables, including ethnicity, gender, and physical features such as height and attractiveness (Holmes, 1998). Children's age is also significant. Many younger children become confused with abstract terms, and some adolescents may hide their true feelings and actions.

■ *Keep in mind both the advantages and limitations of paper-pencil tests.* Paper-pencil tests are often a quick and efficient way of determining what children have and have not learned. Furthermore, a well-designed test—perhaps one that probes children's reasoning and problem-solving skills—can reveal a great deal about thinking processes. However, appraisals of children that rely exclusively on test scores often paint a lopsided picture of their abilities. For instance, those who have limited reading and writing skills (perhaps because they have a learning disability, or perhaps because they have only recently begun to learn English) are likely to perform poorly. Furthermore, paper-pencil tests, by their very nature, cannot provide certain kinds of information. For instance, they tell us little if anything about children's self-confidence, motor skills, ability to work with others, or expertise at using equipment.

■ *Assess and modify environments so they better support children's needs.* Assessment strategies can identify the strengths, priorities, and weaknesses of families, communities, classrooms, agencies, and other settings. For example, special educators, social workers, family educators, and other professionals can learn about the perspectives of families by talking informally with them over the telephone, interviewing them, and asking them to complete surveys and rating scales. Practitioners can then address questions families might have regarding services available to children with particular disabilities, agencies that maintain lists of well-trained caregivers, and strategies for communicating with strangers about their children's disabilities.

Assessments of environments can also be made to evaluate the degree to which they meet children's needs (Karp, 1996). For example, the Neonatal Intensive Care Unit (NICU) of hospitals tends to be a noisy, bright, busy, and even chaotic place, one designed to keep infants alive, but not for providing the reassuring stimulation craved by infants (High & Gorski, 1985; VandenBerg, 1982). Continuing advances in technology mean hospital environments for infants are constantly changing; these changes make it important to conduct ongoing assessments of hospital environments.

Finally, assessment strategies are vital to prevention programs and other community initiatives. For example, teams of community members planning a program to prevent substance abuse may need to identify conditions in the community that increase and decrease drug use by youngsters (U.S. Department of Health and Human Services, 2001). Specifically, among other factors, teams need to assess the availability of drugs in their community, laws and common practices that make drug use possible and even accepted, and local economic and social problems that make drugs an attractive escape. At the same time, the teams should evaluate community factors that protect youngsters, including cultural norms that set high expectations for youth, stable and nurturing social networks in the community, and positive recreation opportunities for youngsters (U.S. Department of Health and Human Services, 2001).

■ *Continually question the validity and reliability of the information you collect.* Validity and reliability are and must be ongoing concerns not only for researchers but also for practitioners. Practitioners must have some assurance that the data they gather about children and the conclusions they reach on the basis of those data are accurate and dependable.

Earlier we mentioned that virtually any method of obtaining data about children and adolescents has its weaknesses. Table 2–2 on page 53 provides several suggestions as to how professionals can minimize the influences of such distortions in data collection.

■ *Always, always use multiple sources of information.* Because no single source of data ever has "perfect" validity and reliability, professionals who work with children must use many sources of information—self-reports, tests, observations, homework, in-class creations, attendance patterns in drop-in community centers, and anything else that might be of value—to understand and draw conclusions about children's development. For example, they may look at facial expressions and body language for signs of comprehension, insight, engagement, or boredom (D. E. Hunt, 1981; Pinnegar, 1988). Juvenile caseworkers may look at other indicators, such as adolescents' compliance rates for treatment and reports of their job-seeking pursuits. In the classroom, teachers watch closely during laboratory activities, cooperative groups, and independent seatwork to see if students understand instructions and assignments. They examine children's work, listen to their discussions in class, and consider the questions they ask, all the while trying to determine not only *if* the students are learning but also *what* they are learning (Heuwinkel, 1998; S. M. Wilson, Shulman, & Richert, 1987).

As professionals gain experience with young people, they become better able to draw inferences about their perspectives on life. Adults must remember, however, that no single behavior or statement is likely to be a valid and reliable reflection of the understandings and values that young people have.

■ *Reflect on how your beliefs about children might influence your conclusions.* At the beginning of the chapter, we explored common beliefs about children and education. We also considered some of the metaphors that professionals might use to capture the nature of children and their own roles with them. These beliefs and metaphors are likely to influence how you interpret children's behavior. For example, if you are a teacher and think of your role as that of an "entertainer," you may be inclined to focus on children's enthusiasm. If you want to be "drill sergeant," you will be more apt to look at whether children comply with your instructions. Try to vary and change your focus over time—perhaps using particular metaphors as "lenses"—to learn from the various types of clues that children provide. Be particularly alert to clues from children whose backgrounds are different from your own, as you are less likely to be accurate in interpreting their behavior.

■ *Form multiple hypotheses.* In your efforts to observe infants, children, and adolescents, never be content with a single interpretation, no matter how obvious that interpretation might seem to you. Always consider multiple possible explanations for the behaviors you observe and resist the temptation to settle on one of them as "correct" until you've had a chance to eliminate other possibilities. In essence, try to behave as a researcher would: Hold your opinions in abeyance until the data are fairly compelling.

■ *Conduct research as a practitioner.* Professionals often encounter serious problems in their research that stop them in their tracks. For example, youngsters may be rebellious, aggressive, or withdrawn. In these situations, complex and repeated methods of data collection may be needed to obtain the depth of knowledge required to address the issues. Such research, referred to as **action research**, takes numerous forms, such as assessing the effectiveness of a new teaching technique, tracking the effectiveness of a counseling measure with a particular child, gathering information about adolescents' opinions on a school-wide issue, or conducting an in-depth case study of a particular child (Cochran-Smith & Lytle, 1993; G. E. Mills, 2003). Practitioner research often requires you to take the following steps (G. E. Mills, 2003):

1. *Identify an area of focus.* The practitioner-researcher begins with a problem and gathers some preliminary information that might shed light on the problem. Usually this involves perusing the literature for investigations of related problems and perhaps also surfing the Internet or conducting informal interviews of colleagues or students. He or she then identifies one or more questions and develops a research plan (data collection techniques, necessary resources, schedule, etc.) for answering those questions. At this point, the practitioner seeks permissions from supervisors and review boards (if applicable).

action research
Systematic study of an issue or problem in one's own situation, with the goal of bringing about improved practice and more productive outcomes.

2. *Collect data.* The practitioner-researcher collects data relevant to the research questions. Such data might be obtained from questionnaires, interviews, achievement tests, children's journals or portfolios, existing records (e.g., school attendance patterns, rates of referral for discipline problems, hours spent by volunteers in community projects), or observations. Many times, the practitioner-researcher uses two or more of these sources in order to answer research questions from various angles.

3. *Analyze and interpret the data.* The practitioner-researcher looks for patterns in the data. Sometimes the analysis involves computing particular statistics (e.g., percentages, means, correlation coefficients); at other times, it involves an in-depth, nonnumerical inspection of the data. In either case, the practitioner-researcher relates the patterns observed to the original research questions.

4. *Develop an action plan.* The final step distinguishes practitioner research from the more traditional research studies we considered earlier: The practitioner-researcher uses the information collected to select a new practical strategy—for instance, to change instructional techniques, counseling practices, home visiting schedules, or school policies.

A good example of research by a practitioner is a case study conducted by a teacher, M. Sims (1993). Initially concerned with why middle school students of average intelligence struggle to comprehend classroom material, Sims began to focus on one of her students, a quiet boy named Ricardo. She tapped a diverse array of data sources, including interviews with Ricardo, conversations with other teachers, dialogues with university faculty, her own journal reflections, and her notes of Ricardo's work. The more she learned, the better she understood who Ricardo was as an individual and how she could better foster his learning and development. She also became increasingly aware of how often she and her fellow teachers overlooked the needs of quiet students:

> We made assumptions that the quiet students weren't in as much need. My colleague phrased it well when she said, "In our minds we'd say to ourselves—'that child will be all right until we get back to him.'" But we both wanted desperately for these children to do more than just survive. (Sims, 1993, p. 288)

Action research and other kinds of practitioner research can be powerful tools, and we urge you to pursue opportunities to learn more about them. Research conducted by practitioners provides a forum for solving problems, broadening and deepening perspectives on adults' relationships with children, fostering a community spirit among practitioners, drawing attention to the legitimacy of the knowledge and practice of professional groups, and making schools and communities more just (Noffke, 1997). Conducting research is also a thoughtful way to improve one's abilities to meet the needs of youngsters. The Development and Practice feature "Getting a Flavor for Research as a Practitioner" offers some suggestions regarding initial steps practitioners can take to gather information as professionals.

Ethical Guidelines for Data Collection as a Practitioner

Regardless of how professionals collect data from children—whether through informal observation or the more formal conduct of practitioner research—they must behave in ways that protect children, their families, and professional colleagues. We recommend that you learn as much as possible in your professional program in college about your legal and ethical responsibilities as a practitioner. In addition, we offer the following guidelines:

■ *Collect multiple sources of information, and be tentative in your conclusions.* Never put too much weight on any single piece of information (remember Barb Cohen's conclusion, based heavily on a self-portrait, that Michael had low self-esteem). Instead, collect a variety of data sources—for example, writing samples, test scores, projects, and informal observations of behavior—and look for general trends. Even then, be cautious in the conclusions you draw and consider multiple hypotheses to explain the patterns you see. Finally, when shar-

DEVELOPMENT AND PRACTICE

Getting a Flavor for Research as a Practitioner

■ Keep a journal of your observations and reflections.

A high school English teacher keeps a daily log of students' comments and insights about the novels they are reading.

■ Talk with other practitioners about what you are observing and hypothesizing.

A social worker notices that girls in a local community organization are excited about their participation. She asks colleagues for their ideas about why the girls are so interested.

■ Encourage children and families to contribute to your inquiry.

A teacher in an infant room hears parents complain that their employers do not grant them time off to care for their children when they are sick. She asks three parents who have been most vocal to help her look into federal and corporate policies regarding family leave.

■ Collect information and write about children you seem unable to reach.

A middle school teacher keeps a journal of her observations of students who sit in the back of the room and appear to be mentally "tuned out." After a few weeks, she begins to form hypotheses about strategies that might capture the interest and attention of these students.

■ Conduct informal research on issues to which children or families can contribute.

A recreation director examines his community's employment rates and enlists the help of adolescents to survey local businesses about possible needs that youngsters could serve in after-school jobs.

ing your perceptions of children's talents and abilities with parents, acknowledge that these are your *interpretations,* based on the data you have available, rather than irrefutable facts.

■ *Administer and interpret tests or research instruments only if you have adequate training.* Many instruments, especially psychological assessments, physiological measures, and standardized achievement tests, must be administered and interpreted by individuals trained in their use. In untrained hands, they yield results that are highly suspect and, in some cases, potentially harmful.

■ *Be sensitive to children's perspectives.* Children are apt to notice any unusual attention you give them, either individually or collectively. For instance, when Michele Sims was collecting data about Ricardo, she made the following observation:

> I'm making a conscious effort to collect as much of Ricardo's work as possible. It's difficult. I think this shift in the kind of attention I'm paying to him has him somewhat rattled. I sense he has mixed feelings about this. He seems to enjoy the conversations we have, but when it comes to collecting his work, he may feel that he's being put under a microscope. Maybe he's become quite accustomed to a type of invisibility. (Sims, 1993, p. 285)

When data collection makes children feel so self-conscious that their performance is impaired, a practitioner must seriously consider whether or not the value of the information collected outweighs possible detrimental effects.

■ *Keep your supervisor informed of your research initiatives.* Supervisors are ultimately responsible for your actions with children. Furthermore, they are knowledgeable about policies in your school or agency that relate to research. In addition, supervisors can give you a fresh set of eyes when it comes to interpreting the data you eventually collect.

■ *Maintain confidentiality at all costs.* It may be appropriate for practitioners to share results of their research with colleagues. Some also make their findings known to an audience beyond the walls of their agency or school; for instance, they may make presentations at regional or national conferences, post their findings on a Website, or write journal articles describing what they have learned and how such knowledge has changed their interactions with children. However, you must never broadcast research findings in ways that violate children's anonymity. Practitioners must likewise protect their data sources from examination by onlookers. For example, it would be unwise to leave a notebook containing running records or completed checklists on a table where other children would have access to them. Protecting children's rights must be a high priority at all times.

Knowledge about effective tactics with children comes from a variety of sources—not only from research and theories about development and learning, but also from professionals' memories of their own childhood, insights and intuitions, conversations with other practitioners, policy statements of school systems and governmental agencies, personal moral codes, and direct observations of children. None of these sources is adequate in and of itself; each becomes more powerful and effective when complemented by other approaches. Effective practitioners draw from as many resources as possible when deciding how best to meet the needs of children and families.

If you were to extract but one theme from this chapter, we hope that it would be "critical analysis." When researchers and professionals working to gather information about children apply critical analysis, they thoughtfully scrutinize their assumptions, consider carefully how they can frame their questions, brainstorm possible methods for obtaining relevant information at every step of the way, and evaluate the many possible ways to accomplish their goals.

CASE STUDY: THE STUDY SKILLS CLASS

In spring semester, Deborah South is asked to teach study skills to a class of 20 low-achieving and seemingly unmotivated eighth graders. Later she describes a problem she encountered and her attempt to understand the problem through action research:

My task was to somehow take these students and miraculously make them motivated, achieving students. I was trained in a study skills program before the term started and thought that I was prepared. . . .

Within a week, I sensed we were in trouble. My 20 students often showed up with no supplies. Their behavior was atrocious. They called each other names, threw various items around the room, and walked around the classroom when they felt like it. . . .

Given this situation, I decided to do some reading about how other teachers motivate unmotivated students and to formulate some ideas about the variables that contribute to a student's success in school. Variables I investigated included adult approval, peer influence, and success in such subjects as math, science, language arts, and social studies, as well as self-esteem and students' views of their academic abilities.

I collected the majority of the data through surveys, interviews, and report card/attendance records in an effort to answer the following questions:

- How does attendance affect student performance?
- How are students influenced by their friends in completing schoolwork?
- How do adults (parents, teachers) affect the success of students?
- What levels of self-esteem do these students have?

As a result of the investigation, I learned many things. For example, for this group of students attendance does not appear to be a factor—with the exception of one student, their school attendance was regular. Not surprisingly, peer groups did affect student performance. Seventy-three percent of my students reported that their friends never encouraged doing homework or putting any effort into homework.

Another surprising result was the lack of impact of a teacher's approval on student achievement. Ninety-four percent of my students indicated that they never or seldom do their homework to receive teacher approval. Alternatively, 57 percent indicated that they often or always do their homework so that their families will be proud of them.

One of the most interesting findings of this study was the realization that most of my students misbehave out of frustration at their own lack of abilities. They are not being obnoxious to *gain* attention, but to *divert* attention away from the fact that they do not know how to complete the assigned work.

When I looked at report cards and compared grades over three quarters, I noticed a trend. Between the first and second quarter, student performance had increased. That is, most students were doing better than they had during the first quarter. Between the second and third quarters, however, grades dropped dramatically. I tried to determine why that drop would occur, and the only common experience shared by these 20 students was the fact that they had been moved into my class at the beginning of the 3rd quarter. . . .

When I presented my project to the action research class during our end-of-term "celebration," I was convinced that the "cause" of the students' unmotivated behavior was my teaching. . . . This conclusion, however, was not readily accepted by my critical friends and colleagues . . . who urged me to consider other interpretations of the data.

From "What Motivates Unmotivated Students?" by D. South. In *Action Research: A Guide for the Teacher Researcher* (2nd ed., pp. 1–2), by G. E. Mills, 2003, Upper Saddle River, NJ: Merrill/Prentice Hall. Reprinted with permission of the author.

 Now go to our Companion Website to assess your understanding of chapter content with a Practice Quiz, apply what you've learned in Essay Questions, and broaden your knowledge with links to related Developmental Psychology Web sites. Go to: www.prenhall.com/mcdevitt.

- What methods did Deborah use to collect her data? What were the potential strengths and limitations of each method?
- Deborah tentatively concluded that her own teaching led to the dramatic drop in grades from the second quarter to the third. Is her conclusion justified? Why or why not?

SUMMARY

Beliefs About Child Development

By the time people begin college, they already have well-established beliefs about children and learning. They become increasingly comfortable with their views as they proceed through college and into jobs. Unfortunately, not all of their beliefs are accurate portrayals of growing children and adolescents, and some may lead new practitioners to use relatively ineffective—perhaps even counterproductive—strategies. By carefully considering their own beliefs, practitioners can revise their thinking about how children and adolescents develop and how they most effectively learn.

Developmental Research Methods

Developmental researchers use various methods for collecting data, including self-reports (interviews and questionnaires), tests and other assessments, physiological measures, and observations. Regardless of the method, the data collected should be accurate measures of the characteristics or behaviors being studied (a matter of *validity*) and should be only minimally influenced by temporary, irrelevant factors (a matter of *reliability*). Researchers often collect two or more kinds of data relative to the same research question and look for converging patterns.

In their attempts to answer their research questions, developmental researchers use a variety of research designs,

including experimental, quasi-experimental, correlational, causal-comparative, cross-sectional, longitudinal, and naturalistic designs. These designs differ in the extent to which they allow researchers to draw conclusions about cause-effect relationships, find associations that already exist, trace age trends over time, determine the stability of particular characteristics, identify early predictors of later performance, and observe children and adolescents in their natural environments.

Developmental research helps professionals in many ways, for instance, by illuminating effective and ineffective practices, promoting new ways of thinking about child development, and engendering optimism about making a difference in the lives of youngsters. However, professionals must critically analyze the research they read to judge whether the conclusions are warranted from the data reported and whether the findings are applicable to their own situations.

Gathering Information During Professional Practice

Practitioners who work with infants, children, and adolescents often gather their own data about youngsters. Sometimes they do it very informally, such as when they watch children for possible clues about their learning and thinking. At other times, they may conduct more formal research to answer specific questions they may have about children or about strategies that most effectively support their development.

KEY CONCEPTS

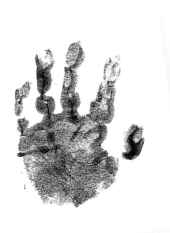

Lauryn, age 8 months

Isabelle, age 4

Alex, age 7

Connor, age 15

All handprints are shown at 50% actual size.

Physical Development

CASE STUDY: THE SOFTBALL LEAGUE

Two brothers, Tom (age 13) and Phillip (age 15) are talking with psychologist William Pollack about the impact of organized sports on their lives:

"There used to be nothing to do around here," Tom told me [Dr. Pollack], referring to the small, economically depressed town where he and his brother live.

"There was like just one bowling alley, and it was closed on weekends. We had nothing to do, especially during the summer," Phillip agreed.

"Not quite a year ago," Tom explained, "three of our best friends died of an OD."

Indeed, the autumn before, three teenage boys in the same sleepy town had all drunk themselves into oblivion and then overdosed on a lethal cocktail of various barbiturates. Sure, the town had always had its problems—high unemployment, poorly funded schools, and many broken families. But this was different. Three boys, the oldest only sixteen, were gone forever.

The mood in the town was sullen the summer following the deaths, and Tom and Phillip were resolved to change things. "We went to the mayor and to the priest at our church, and we asked if we could set up a regular sports program for kids around here," Phillip explained.

"A softball league," Tom added.

"What a great idea," I told the boys.

"Yeah. At first we were just ten guys," said Tom.

"But then, like, everybody wanted to sign up—girls too," explained Phillip. "Now there are too many kids who want to play. More than a hundred. But the state government offered to help with some money and coaches."

"So it is making a difference, to have this new league?" I asked the boys.

"Hell, yeah," Phillip replied. "Now, we've got a schedule. We've got something to do."

"I'm not sure I'd be here anymore if it wasn't for the league," added Tom. "For a long time I couldn't deal with things. Now I've got a place to go." (Pollack, 1998, p. 274)

From *Real Boys: Rescuing Our Sons from the Myths of Boyhood,* by William Pollack, © 1998 by William Pollack. Used by permission of Random House, Inc.

Art by Eric, age 12

erhaps the most obvious changes of human development are physical ones. As children get older, they grow taller, stronger, and more agile. They become increasingly able to perform such complex physical tasks as using scissors, riding a bicycle, and playing softball. But physical development occurs in tandem with social, emotional, and cognitive transformations. Certainly, Tom and Phillip enjoyed the physical activities involved in playing softball—throwing and catching a ball, swinging a bat, and running. As adolescents, they had muscles to move, a cardiovascular system to exercise, and energy to burn. But the benefits they gained from sports were not purely physical ones. The softball league became a way to forge friendships, develop teamwork and leadership skills, and gain ties to the community; the league also provided a schedule that helped the boys use time productively. Mind, body, and spirit are not always a single, integrated entity, but neither are they separate kingdoms.

In this chapter, we explore physical development: how genes and the environment influence children's growth, how the brain develops throughout childhood and what the implications are for practitioners, how the body changes during specific age periods, how children's health is affected by their activities and support from adults, and how professionals can help children with special physical needs.

Nature and Nurture in Physical Development

Genetic instructions determine children's physical characteristics and abilities, but environmental factors can influence how these instructions are carried out. Let's begin by looking at the effects of both heredity and environment on physical development and at important ways in which their influences are inextricably interwoven.

Genetic Foundations

People are all born with a set of hereditary instructions inherited from their parents. These instructions originate in their **genes.** A gene is a small unit of chemical directions that combines in an orderly way with other genes to make up a rodlike structure called a **chromosome.** Human beings have up to 100,000 genes (B. Lewin, Siliciano, & Klotz, 1997). They are dispersed among 46 chromosomes that reside in the center, or *nucleus,* of every cell in the body. The chromosomes are organized into 23 distinct pairs that are easily seen with a high-powered microscope (Figure 3–1). One chromosome of each pair is inherited from the mother, the other from the father.

Genes are made up of deoxyribonucleic acid, or **DNA.** A DNA molecule is structured like a twisted ladder—a *double helix*—with pairs of chemical substances comprising each rung of the ladder (see Figure 3–2). The configuration of chemical pairings that make up each rung of the ladder gives cells instructions to make specific proteins. These proteins, in turn, trigger critical chemical reactions throughout the body. These genetically controlled chemical reactions influence thousands of traits that vary among individuals, such as height, weight, activity level, intellectual capability, and style of emotional responding. Thus, genes make each child unique. But genes also give children a common human heritage, including a capacity for language, a need for social relationships, and a receptivity to learning the practices and beliefs of a culture (Bugental & Goodnow, 1998).

Routes to Genetic Individuality   As we have said, normal human cells contain 46 chromosomes. There is an important exception: Male and female reproductive cells, called **gametes,** have only 23 chromosomes each—half of each chromosome pair. Gametes, which take the form of *sperm* in men and *ova* in women, are formed by a process of cell division called **meiosis** (see Figure 3–3).

Meiosis begins when the 46 chromosomes within a male or female *germ cell* (a precursor to a gamete), pair up into 23 matched sets. The germ cell then duplicates each chromosome, and pairs of duplicated chromosomes line up side by side. Next, segments of

gene
Basic unit of genetic instruction in a living cell; segments of genes are contained on chromosomes.

chromosome
Rodlike structure that resides in the nucleus of every cell of the body and contains genes that guide growth and development; each chromosome is made up of DNA.

DNA
Short for deoxyribonucleic acid, a double-helix shaped "ladder" of four chemicals that specifies how to build specific proteins, which in turn direct growth and developmental change.

gamete
Reproductive cell that, in humans, contains 23 chromosomes rather than the 46 present in other cells in the body; a male gamete (sperm) and a female gamete (ovum) join at conception.

meiosis
The process of cell reproduction and division by which gametes are formed.

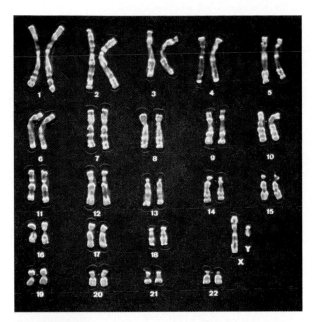

FIGURE 3-1 Photograph of human chromosomes that have been extracted from a human cell, colored, magnified, and arranged in order of size

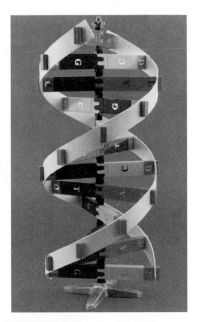

FIGURE 3-2 A DNA molecule is structured like a twisted ladder.

genetic material are exchanged between each pair. This *crossing-over* of genetic material shuffles genes between paired chromosomes and produces new hereditary combinations that do not exist in either parent's chromosomes. The effect is that a child's chromosomes are never exactly the same as those of parents or siblings.[1]

After crossing-over takes place, the pairs of duplicated chromosomes separate and the cell divides into two new germ cells with half from each pair. Chance determines which duplicated chromosome from each of the 23 pairs ends up in one of the two new cells. This step thus provides a second route to genetic individuality. During this first cell division, one of the two new female germ cells gets the bulk of the cell matter and is viable; the second, smaller cell disintegrates. Both new male germ cells are viable.

A second cell division takes place and the duplicated chromosomes are separated. Each new cell receives one of the duplicate chromosomes from each pair. The resulting male germ cells are ready to mature and become male gametes (sperm). The female germ cell undergoes this second division only after it is fertilized by a sperm. When the female cell divides, once again, only one of the two new cells, a female gamete (an ovum), is viable. The process of meiosis thus produces one ovum and four sperm.[2]

Conception Conception provides yet another route to genetic individuality because chance determines which gametes unite and combine their genes. When one sperm and one ovum unite at conception, the 23 chromosomes from each parent come together and form a **zygote** with 46 chromosomes. The 23rd chromosome pair determines the gender of the individual: Two *X chromosomes* (one each from the mother and father) produce a female, and a combination of an *X chromosome* and a *Y chromosome* (from the mother and father, respectively) produce a male. If you look at the photograph of human chromosomes

---

[1] Partway through meiosis, the process halts in female fetuses, germ cells rest, and meiosis resumes years later with the onset of puberty and ovulation. In males, the process continues without delay.
[2] We've simplified the complex process of meiosis by tracing gametes produced by one male and one female germ cell. In men, sperm are produced continuously throughout the reproductive years. During sexual intercourse, between 200 and 600 million sperm are deposited in the woman's vagina. In girls, up to 2 million germ cells are present at birth. Many subsequently decay, and between 40,000 and 400,000 remain at the beginning of adolescence. About 400 ova will be released during ovulation over the woman's lifetime (Moore & Persaud, 1998; Sadler, 2000).

zygote
Cell formed when a male sperm joins with a female ovum; with healthy genes and nurturing conditions in the uterus, it may develop into a fetus and be born as a live infant.

General Process of Meiosis

Each germ cell has 46 chromosomes. Chromosomes begin to move together and pair up into 23 matched sets in the germ cells.

Each chromosome replicates (duplicates) itself. Notice that the single strands in the previous step have doubled in this step.

"Crossing over" occurs: Pairs of duplicated chromosomes temporarily unite and exchange segments of chromosomes. This shuffling of genes between paired chromosomes—known as *crossing over*—ensures unique combinations of genes that differ from those of both the mother and the father.

The pairs of doubled chromosomes separate and the cell divides, forming two new cells, each containing 23 double-structured chromosomes. Chromosomes randomly join with others in one of the two new cells. This process is called the *first meiotic division*. It further ensures genetic individuality.

The second meiotic division takes place. The cell divides in two and the double-structured chromosomes are separated. Chromosomes are now single-structured: the new cell now has one chromosome from each pair, and a total of 23 chromosomes. Resulting cells are now gametes that mature and become ready to unite at conception.

During conception, the sperm enters the ovum.

The two sets of 23 chromosomes, one from the father and one from the mother, unite to form a zygote

Sperm in Men

Production of sperm begins for boys at puberty. During this initial phase, germ cells are formed. *Only one pair from the 23 pairs of chromosomes is shown here.*

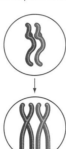

In the male, these first three steps have occurred sometime after puberty and continue to occur throughout the male's reproductive years.

Two cells are formed, each with 23 double chromosomes.

There are now four male gametes (sperm).

Ova in Women

Production of ova begins for girls during prenatal development. During this initial phase, germ cells are formed. *Only one pair from the 23 pairs of chromosomes is shown here.*

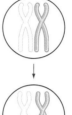

In the female, these first three steps have occurred during prenatal development. At the completion of crossing over, germ cells will rest until puberty.

Meiosis resumes during puberty. With each ovulation, the germ cell will complete the first meiotic division producing two cells, each with 23 double chromosomes. One cell receives the majority of cell material and becomes viable. The other cell may reproduce but neither it nor its progeny will be a viable gamete.

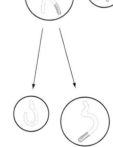

Only one potentially viable ovum, which has 23 chromosomes, remains. This step of the second meiotic division occurs only if the ovum is fertilized with a sperm.

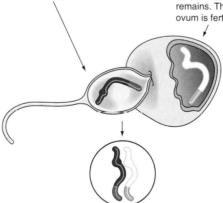

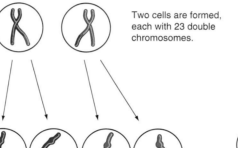

FIGURE 3–3 Meiosis: formation of gametes with unique genes. During meiosis, unique combinations of genes occur during two distinct phases—"crossing over" (when genes are exchanged between chromosomes) and cell division (when particular chromosomes randomly combine with others in new cells). Human genetic variability is also enhanced at conception, when chance affects which gametes unite and combine their genetic instructions.

Sources: Moore & Persaud (1998); Sadler (2000).

in Figure 3–1, you can see the XY pair near the bottom right corner, which makes this individual a male. When genes are reasonably healthy and conditions are sufficiently nurturing, the zygote begins to grow. The zygote divides into two cells; these two cells also divide, and the process is repeated many times over. Gradually, the growing cluster of cells develops into an *embryo* implanted into the uterine lining (3–4 weeks) and a *fetus* (9 weeks) that continues to undergo predictable changes until birth at about 38 weeks.

How Twins Are Created   Occasionally, a zygote splits into two separate cell clusters, resulting in two offspring instead of one. *Identical,* or **monozygotic twins**, come from the same fertilized egg and so have the same genetic instructions. At other times, two ova from the mother simultaneously unite with two sperm cells from the father, again resulting in two offspring. These **dizygotic twins**, also known as *fraternal* twins, are as similar to one another as ordinary siblings. They share some genetic traits but not others.

Because monozygotic and dizygotic twins differ in the degree to which they share a common genetic heritage, researchers have studied them extensively. Twin studies permit estimates of the relative effects of heredity and environment on human characteristics. In many cases, monozygotic twins are quite similar to one another in terms of how sociable they are and how they express emotion, whereas dizygotic twins are less similar (Plomin & DeFries, 1985). Even so, identical twins are not identical in all psychological characteristics—an indication that environment, experience, children's own choices, and even random factors also affect development.

Genes and Passing on of Traits   When the two sets of 23 chromosomes combine into matched pairs during conception, the corresponding genes inherited from each parent pair up. Each gene pair includes two forms of a gene—two **alleles**—related to a particular physical characteristic. Sometimes the two genes in an allele pair give the same instructions ("Have dark hair!" "Have dark hair!"). At other times, they give very different instructions ("Have dark hair!" "Have blond hair!"). When two genes give different instructions, one gene is often more influential than its counterpart. **Dominant genes** manifest their characteristic, in a sense overriding the instructions of a **recessive gene** with which they are paired. A recessive gene influences growth and development only when its partner is also recessive. For example, genes for dark hair are dominant and those for blond hair are recessive; thus, a child with a dark hair gene and a blond hair gene will have dark hair, as will a child with two dark hair genes. Only when two blond hair genes are paired together will a child have blond hair.

However, when two genes of an allele pair "disagree," one gene doesn't always dominate completely. Sometimes one gene has a stronger influence, but not total domination, a phenomenon known as **codominance.** *Sickle cell disease,* a blood disease, is an example. The disease develops in its full-blown form only when a person has two (recessive) alleles for it. However, when an individual has one recessive allele for sickle cell disease and one "healthy" allele, he or she may experience temporary, mild symptoms when short of oxygen (L. W. Sullivan, 1987).

The influence of genes is sometimes even more complex. Many physiological traits and most psychological ones are dependent on multiple genes rather than on a single pair of alleles. In **polygenic inheritance,** many separate genes each exert some influence on the expression of a trait. Height is an example: An individual's final height as an adult is not the result of a single allele pair, but instead the combined outcome of several genes that each individually have small effects (Tanner, 1990). (Of course, height and other complex traits are also affected by nutrition, experience, and other environmental influences.)

Problems in Genetic Instructions   Sometimes problems occur in the genetic instructions that children receive (see Table 3–1). There are two primary types of genetic disorders, chromosome abnormalities and single-gene defects. A child with a *chromosome abnormality* may have an extra chromosome, a missing chromosome, or a wrongly formed chromosome. Because each chromosome holds thousands of genes, a child with a chromosomal abnormality tends to have many affected genes and the result can be major physical problems and mental retardation (Burns, Brady, Dunn, & Starr, 2000). Chromosomal

These monozygotic twins share the same genetic instructions. Identical twins are usually quite similar in physical appearance and share many psychological characteristics, such as being particularly intelligent or gregarious. However, despite their many similarities, identical twins make their own choices, experience some different environments, form some separate friendships, and as a result, develop into distinctly unique individuals.

monozygotic twins
Twins that began as a single zygote and so share the same genetic makeup.

dizygotic twins
Twins that began as two separate zygotes and so are as genetically similar as two siblings conceived and born at different times.

alleles
Genes located at the same point on corresponding (paired) chromosomes and related to the same physical characteristic.

dominant gene
Gene that overrides any competing instructions in an allele pair.

recessive gene
Gene that influences growth and development only if the other gene in the allele pair is identical to it.

codominance
Situation in which the two genes of an allele pair, though not identical, both have some influence on the characteristic they affect.

polygenic inheritance
Situation in which many genes combine in their influence on a particular characteristic.

TABLE 3-1 **Common Chromosomal and Genetic Disorders**

METHOD OF TRANSMISSION	EXAMPLES	CHARACTERISTICS[1]	IMPLICATIONS AND TREATMENT	INCIDENCE
Chromosome abnormalities *Number of Chromosomes* Children are born with more than or fewer than the normal 46 chromosomes.	Down syndrome	Children with Down syndrome have one extra chromosome. Physical characteristics include a protruding tongue, thick lips, flat nose, short neck, wide gaps between toes, short fingers, specific health problems, and risks for heart problems and hearing loss. Mental retardation can range from mild to severe. Children often have good visual discrimination skills and may be better at understanding verbal language than producing it.	Provide explicit instruction in skills such as language when they are delayed. Address health issues such as heart problems and potential feeding difficulties.	1 per 700 to 1,000 births
	Klinefelter syndrome	Only boys have Klinefelter syndrome; they have one Y chromosome and two X chromosomes. Diagnosis may not occur until adolescence, when testes fail to enlarge. Boys tend to have long legs, to grow modest breast tissue, and to remain sterile. They tend to show lower than average verbal ability and some speech and language delays.	Offer an enriched verbal environment. Medical treatment may be given to support development of male sexual characteristics.	1 per 500 to 1,000 boys
	Turner syndrome	Only girls have Turner syndrome; they have one X chromosome and are missing the second sex chromosome. They have broad chests, webbed necks, short stature, and specific health problems. They do not show normal sexual development. These girls may show normal verbal ability but lower than average ability in processing visual and spatial information.	Provide instruction and support related to visual and spatial processing. Hormone therapy helps with bone growth and development of female characteristics.	1 per 2,500 to 5,000 girls
Structure of Chromosomes Children are born with deletions from or duplications to parts of an individual chromosome, or a part of one chromosome moves to another location.	Prader-Willi syndrome	Children have a deletion from a segment of genes on chromosome 15 inherited from the father. Children with this syndrome tend to become mentally retarded and obese; they also have small hands and feet and are short in stature. They often develop maladaptive behaviors such as throwing frequent temper tantrums and picking at their own skin. Beginning at 1–6 years of age, children may eat excessively, hoard food, and eat unappealing substances.	Create developmentally appropriate plans to help children regulate eating, decrease inappropriate behaviors, and increase acceptable emotional expression. Seek medical care as necessary.	1 per 10,000 to 25,000 births
	Angelman syndrome	Children have a deletion from a segment of genes on chromosome 15 inherited from the mother. Children who have this syndrome show mental retardation, a small head, seizures, jerky movements. They show unusual, recurrent bouts of laughter not associated with happiness.	Provide appropriate educational support suited to children's skills and developmental levels. Seek medical care as necessary.	1 per 10,000 to 30,000 births
Single-gene defects *Dominant Defects* Children have a dominant defect on one of the 22 paired chromosomes (all chromosomes except X and Y).	Neurofibro-matosis	Children develop benign and malignant tumors in the central nervous system. The condition appears to be caused by an error in a gene that would normally suppress tumor growth. Learning disabilities are somewhat common and mental retardation occurs occasionally. The majority of individuals experience only minor symptoms, such as having colored and elevated spots on their skin.	Address learning disabilities; offer adaptive services to children with mental retardation. Tumors may need to be removed or treated. Surgery or braces may be needed if the spine becomes twisted.	mild form occurs in 1 per 2,500 to 4,000 births; severe form occurs in 1 per 40,000 to 50,000 births

METHOD OF TRANSMISSION	EXAMPLES	CHARACTERISTICS[1]	IMPLICATIONS AND TREATMENT	INCIDENCE
Single-gene defects, continued	Huntington disease (HD)	Children have progressive disorder of the central nervous system. Signs typically appear by age 35 to 45, though age of first symptoms has varied between 2 and 85 years. It may be caused by a defect in the gene that produces a protein that destroys brain cells. Early signs include irritability, clumsiness, depression, and forgetfulness. Eventually, loss of control over movements of arms, legs, torso, or facial muscles occurs, speech becomes slurred, and severe mental disturbances arise.	Medicine may be given to alleviate movement problems and depression. Design the physical environment to remove sharp edges. When memory deteriorates, provide visual instructions about daily tasks.	3 to 7 per 100,000 births
Recessive Defects Children have a recessive defect on both chromosomes in one of the 22 matched pairs (all chromosomes except X and Y).	Phenylketon-uria (PKU)	Children with PKU are at risk for developing mental retardation, eczema, seizures, and motor and behavioral problems such as aggression, self-mutilation, and impulsiveness. When children have both recessive genes for PKU, their livers cannot produce an enzyme that breaks down phenylalanine (an amino acid); this substance accumulates and becomes toxic to the brain.	When phenylalanine is restricted from diet, children develop much more normally, and mental retardation is avoided. Subtle problems may still result (e.g., awkward pencil grip, learning disabilities, difficulty staying focused during complex tasks). Provide educational materials to enhance planning and memory skills and compensate for limitations.	1 per 15,000 births with rates highest in people of Celtic origin (e.g., from Ireland and Scotland)
	Sickle cell disease	Children have problems with blood circulation. The disease causes red blood cells to grow rigid; passage through small blood vessels causes pain. Children may experience many serious conditions, including stroke, infection, tissue damage, and fatigue. Symptoms become obvious during the first or second year of life.	Treatments include blood transfusions, medication for pain and infections, other medicines to reduce frequency of medical crises. Be alert to medical crises, such as strokes. Offer comfort to children who are tired or in pain.	1 per 500 to 600 children from African (Black) descent; rates are also elevated in people from Mediterranean descent
	Cystic fibrosis	Children with CF have glands that produce large amounts of abnormally thick, sticky mucus that create serious problems for breathing and digestion. The disease is usually noticed in infancy due to persistent coughing, wheezing, pneumonia, and big appetite with little weight gain.	The condition is often treated with physical therapy, medication, and bronchial drainage. Many individuals with the condition now live well into their 40s.	1 per 3,300 children from European American backgrounds and 1 per 9,500 children from Hispanic American backgrounds
	Tay-Sachs disease	Children have a fatal and degenerative condition of the central nervous system. Children lack an enzyme required to break down a fatty substance in cells in the brain. At about 6 months of age, children slow down in development, lose vision, display an abnormal startle response, and go into convulsions. Typically, other functions are gradually lost, children become mentally retarded, cannot move, and die by 3 or 4 years of age.	No known cure or treatment. Offer love and attention as you would to other children. Be alert to new accommodations that may be needed in the environment, such as stabilizing and securing the surroundings when children lose sight.	1 per 2,500 to 3,600 children among Ashkenazi Jews (of Eastern European ancestry)

(continued)

TABLE 3–1   **Common Chromosomal and Genetic Disorders**   *(continued)*

METHOD OF TRANSMISSION	EXAMPLES	CHARACTERISTICS[1]	IMPLICATIONS AND TREATMENT	INCIDENCE
Single-gene defects, continued	Thalassemia (Cooley's anemia)	Children have a disease of blood cells in which oxygen cannot be transmitted effectively. Children become pale, fatigued, and irritable. Symptoms may appear within the first few months of life. There may be feeding problems, diarrhea, and eventually enlargement of the spleen and heart.	Treatment may include blood transfusions and occasionally bone marrow transplant. Individuals with this condition often die by adolescence or early adulthood. Help children to cope with their health problems.	1 in 800 to 2,500 individuals of Greek or Italian descent in the U.S.; rates are lower in other groups
X-linked recessive defects[2] Boys who have an X-linked recessive gene defect show the disorder. In some X-linked disorders, girls develop symptoms if they have the problem gene on both of their X chromosomes.	Duchenne muscular dystrophy	Only boys experience this disease, a progressive muscular weakness caused by a gene's failure to produce an essential protein needed by muscle cells. Between 2 and 5 years, boys with this condition begin to stumble and walk on their toes or with another unusual gait. They may lose the ability to walk between 8 and 14 years and may later die from respiratory and cardiac problems.	Treatments include physical therapy, orthopedic devices, surgery, and medicines to reduce muscle stiffness. Watch for respiratory infections and heart problems.	1 per 3,000 to 4,000 boys

Sources: Blachford, 2002; Burns, Brady, Dunn, & Starr, 2000; Cody & Kamphaus, 1999; Dykens & Cassidy, 1999; Massimini, 2000; K. L. Moore & Persaud, 1998; Nilsson & Bradford, 1999; Powell & Schulte, 1999; J. T. Smith, 1999; Waisbren, 1999; Wynbrandt & Ludman, 2000.

[1]The table includes typical symptoms for children with particular chromosomal and genetic problems. Children's actual level of functioning depends on the medical treatments they receive, their experiences with families, teachers, other caregivers, and other children, and other genetic instructions they might possess. New medical treatments and educational interventions are constantly being tested, and many of these will increase the quality of life of these children.
[2]X-linked dominant defects also occur but are rare.

abnormalities can occur when chromosomes divide unevenly during meiosis. They can also occur when the zygote's cells divide unevenly, with the result that the growing zygote contains some cells with normal chromosomes and others with abnormal chromosomes. Chromosomal abnormalities may also occur when parents' exposure to viruses, radiation, and drugs prior to conception causes pieces of chromosomes in their germ cells to break off; the resulting damage can be passed along to their offspring.

Chromosome abnormalities occur in 1 per 150 births (Burns et al., 2000). To illustrate, children with *Down syndrome* have an extra 21st chromosome, or an extra piece of one. Children with Down syndrome typically show delays in mental growth and are susceptible to heart defects and other health problems. Apparently, the extra 21st chromosome causes biochemical changes that redirect brain development (N. R. Carlson, 1999). The severity of disabilities caused by Down syndrome and many other chromosomal abnormalities varies considerably from one child to the next.

A second type of genetic disorder occurs when a child inherits a *single-gene defect* from one or both parents. The resultant problems tend to be more specific and subtle than those caused by chromosomal abnormalities (Burns et al., 2000). Nonetheless, some single-gene defects are quite serious. The usual pattern of inheritance is that children who inherit a dominant gene defect show the problem; those who inherit a recessive gene defect show the problem if both genes in the allele pair are defective (transmission is slightly different in X-linked transmission). When we earlier talked about passing on of traits, we used the example of sickle cell disease as an illustration of a recessive trait. This disease and other single-gene defects, both dominant and recessive, are presented in Table 3–1.

There are some variations to these two primary causes of genetic problems. For instance, some conditions may be mild or severe depending on the particular sequence of chemical compounds on a gene. An example is *Fragile X syndrome*, a genetic defect on a part of the X chromosome. When a defect is small and limited, people who carry the problem gene may show no symptoms or only mild learning disabilities. But the defect can intensify as it is passed on from one generation to the next and lead to Fragile X syndrome (Hagerman &

Lampe, 1999). Children with Fragile X syndrome develop major learning disabilities, emotional problems, and mental retardation; physically, they develop prominent ears, long faces, double-jointed thumbs, flat feet, and other health conditions (Hagerman & Lampe, 1999). In addition, these children tend to be socially anxious, sensitive to touch and noise, and inclined to avoid eye contact and to repeat certain activities over and over again (e.g., spinning objects, waving their arms, saying the same phrase). Girls tend to have less mental retardation than boys because they have a second X chromosome that can compensate for the fragile X; however, girls may have learning disabilities and problems with attention and organization.

Many physical problems occur as well when several genes act together to make the fetus vulnerable to poor nutrition, trauma, and other adverse conditions in the uterus. Spina bifida (the spinal cord is malformed) and cleft palate (a split occurs in the oral cavity) are examples of such conditions, which tend to run in some families but do not follow simple patterns of genetic transmission. Instead, they occur because of interactions between nature and nurture.

Positive attitudes of teachers and other professionals, advocacy by parents, and federal legislation have improved educational services and opportunities for many children with genetic abnormalities and other physical disabilities.

All children require individualized care, but those with chromosomal abnormalities, single-gene defects, and other genetic conditions may need interventions tailored to their conditions. In several places in this book, you will find specific recommendations. Chapter 6 includes recommendations for fostering the development of children with mental retardation, which is sometimes caused by chromosomal or genetic defects. Chapter 7 suggests strategies for enhancing the skills of children with communication disorders, which sometimes have a genetic basis. Chapter 9 offers suggestions for working with children who have serious emotional problems, some of which arise in part because of genetic factors. In addition to creating tailored interventions, you can apply your knowledge of typical developmental progressions, since many children with genetic problems are more similar to those without such problems than they are different.

Maturation and Canalization   Some genes have an immediate influence on physical characteristics, beginning at birth, but many others don't manifest themselves until later in the course of development, when provoked to do so by hormones (Tanner, 1990). Genetically controlled changes that occur over the course of development are known as **maturation**. Height is again an example. Children's length at birth is determined largely by prenatal conditions in the mother's uterus and is only minimally influenced by heredity. By 18 months of age, however, we see a definite correlation between children's heights and the heights of their parents, presumably because genetic factors have begun to exert their influence (Tanner, 1990).

Some emerging characteristics are tightly controlled by genetic instructions, a phenomenon known as **canalization** (Waddington, 1957). For instance, basic motor skills are highly canalized: Crawling, sitting, and walking appear under a wide range of circumstances. They almost invariably appear without training or encouragement, and only extremely unusual environmental conditions can stifle them. For instance, a young child exposed to heavy doses of a toxic substance (e.g., lead paint) may fail to show typical motor and psychological milestones (G. Gottlieb, 1991, 1992).

Not all human traits are canalized, however. Most of the abilities that children acquire at school—reading, writing, mathematical problem solving, and so on—are highly susceptible to experiences children have both in and out of the classroom. Social skills tend also to rely on environmental support: For example, figuring out other people's intentions, learning to anticipate others' actions, and taking turns during conversation are competencies developed with social experience.

Environment and Its Interaction with Heredity

Many genes are active only under certain conditions. Most of the time, specific genes reside in inactive regions of the cell, and only a small subset of available genes guides the formation of proteins (Brown, 1999). You might think of genes as resembling data in a

maturation
Genetically controlled changes that occur over the course of development.
canalization
Tight genetic control of a particular aspect of development.

computer's memory, which are silent and inactive unless conditions are right (B. Brown, 1999). To use data in a computer, an operator must turn the computer on (in other words, adequate energy and nutrients must be available) and then intentionally and accurately seek out the information (hormones, messenger proteins secreted by the endocrine glands, must trigger the expression of individual genes).

Numerous environmental factors influence genetic expression. These include nutrition, illness, medication, stressful events, temperature, exposure to light, and intensity of stimulation (B. Brown, 1999; J. D. Wilson & Foster, 1985). For example, Guatemalan children raised in the United States tend to grow taller than their parents did in Guatemala, presumably because of more abundant and diverse nutritional resources in the United States (Bogin, 1988). The environment may also affect the hormones that provoke genes into action. For example, stressful events suppress the release of certain hormones and so can indirectly suppress growth in tissues of the body and nervous system (B. Brown, 1999). Long-term, excessive stress can also lead to the death of neurons in the hippocampus, a component of the brain essential for memory and other cognitive functions (Lombroso & Sapolsky, 1998). In such a circumstance, the environment affects a biological system, which in turn affects cognitive and social-emotional development.

Complex psychological traits, such as personality characteristics and intellectual talents, are the outcomes of both polygenic inheritance (nature) and environmental experience (nurture). For instance, there appear to be genetic origins to becoming particularly cheerful, outgoing, moody, anxious, or aggressive, and to becoming a risk taker (Henderson, 1982; Rothbart & Bates, 1998; Tellegren, Lykken, Bouchard, & Wilcox, 1988). Yet these traits are clearly influenced as well by the environment (Plomin, Owen, & McGuffin, 1994). We're not born wild or shy; instead, we're born with certain tendencies that our environments may or may not encourage. For example, children who, genetically, have high energy levels are sensation seekers, impulsive, and more likely to become highly aggressive (Goldsmith & Gottesman, 1996). The aggression of these children may be triggered by caregivers who allow them to hit others and do not encourage them to show empathy, or by caregivers who carry out punitive, destructive, and bitter exchanges with them (Goldsmith & Gottesman, 1996; G. R. Patterson, 1986, 1995).

Sandra Scarr has described three ways in which environments may interact with genetic predispositions (Scarr, 1992, 1993; Scarr & McCartney, 1983). A *passive gene-environment relation* occurs when parents' genetic tendencies correlate with the kind of setting in which they raise their children. Especially when their children are young, parents select environments based on their own preferences and genetic tendencies. For example, a father with a strong imagination and a love of drama may bring his son to theater performances. The father's drive toward dramatic expression has some genetic basis, and the child shares some of this genetically based talent. Thus, the boy's genes correlate with his environment, but the association is considered passive because the boy is not determining the environment—his father is. In an *evocative gene-environment relation*, children's own characteristics elicit specific kinds of reactions from the environment. For example, a calm and compliant child may have a soothing effect on caregivers, who respond with warmth. A child who is quick to argue may instead provoke hostile reactions from both adults and peers. Finally, an *active gene-environment relation* occurs when children have particular talents that influence environments made accessible to them. For instance, an athletic youngster may join a baseball team, organize neighborhood games, request sports equipment from parents, and otherwise create occasions for athletics.

Sensitive Periods: When Environment Has Its Greatest Effects

In Chapter 1, we introduced the concept of the *sensitive period*, an age range during which certain environmental experiences are especially important for normal development. The timing of sensitive periods is dictated by heredity, which determines *when* particular kinds of environmental stimulation can come into play.

Sensitive periods are more frequently observed in physical and perceptual development than in other developmental domains. For example, normal visual experiences in the first two years of life are critical for visual perception. And, children who are born with cataracts (cloudy lenses that allow sensitivity to light but impede perception of shapes) are more likely to have normal vision if their condition is treated *before* the age of 2 (Bruer, 1999).

Some aspects of temperament, such as shyness, have a genetic basis but are also influenced by the environment. Although this boy is shy around his peers and has trouble separating from his mother, his parents and teachers have worked out a way to ease the transition from home to school each morning.

Furthermore, some environmental influences may be highly detrimental at one phase of development yet have little or no effect at other phases. For example, fetuses exposed to rubella (German measles) in the first 12 weeks of pregnancy are frequently born with cataracts, hearing loss, heart defects, and other abnormalities; those exposed to this disease considerably later in pregnancy remain relatively unscathed.

As you can see, we are all products of nature and nurture. Genes do not determine appearance, behavior, or even cell functioning in any simple, predetermined fashion. Genes act in concert with one another; are affected by nutrition, stress, and other environmental agents; and are triggered by hormones and physiological events. Furthermore, they may be influential at different points in development, suddenly bringing out characteristics "from nowhere." In general, genes provide rough guidelines that may be either stretched or compressed, depending on the influence of other genes and opportunities present in the environment.

Implications of Genetic and Environmental Influences

Genetic influence may seem like a very theoretical topic compared to the world of real children in classrooms, community centers, and counseling offices. Nevertheless, anyone working closely with children and adolescents must understand the power and limits of genetic factors. At the same time, recognition that the environment also guides human development should give practitioners considerable optimism for all children. With these points in mind, we offer the following recommendations:

■ *Expect and make allowances for individual differences.* Practitioners who value a multitude of physical characteristics, personality types, and talents can put youngsters at ease. Children who are tall and short, chubby and thin, coordinated and clumsy, shy and outgoing, calm and irritable all have a rightful place in the hearts of adults who nurture them.

■ *Remember that environmental factors influence virtually every aspect of development.* Genes have a strong effect on physiological growth and a modest effect on complex psychological characteristics. Therefore, viewing development as the simple outgrowth of biology is simplistic and can have devastating effects on children (Eisenberg, 1998). Children often live up to—or, perhaps more accurately, *down* to—the low expectations that adults have for them. In Chapter 11, we will look more closely at the effects of such expectations on children's development.

Even if children have inherited potential for certain talents and temperaments, their path is unpredictable: Environmental factors— physical conditions, social interactions, educational experiences, and so on—affect the course of development. For instance, children who are genetically predisposed to be irritable, distractible, or aggressive can, with guidance, learn more adaptive and prosocial ways of responding (e.g., DeVault, Krug, & Fake, 1996; T. R. Robinson, Smith, Miller, & Brownell, 1999).

■ *Encourage children to make growth-promoting choices.* Especially as they grow older, youngsters actively seek experiences compatible with their natural tendencies. Adults can help them find activities and resources that allow them to use and nurture their talents and address their limitations. For instance, a socially outgoing child with an excessive amount of energy and little self-control may frequently interrupt adults and peers. He might be encouraged to join the school drama club, a community sports team, or other groups in which he can exercise his leadership skills while increasing his self-control.

Some young people have genetically based temperaments that make them somewhat prone to withdraw from social contact, to be impulsive, or to respond to conflict aggressively. Adults can help these young people learn new ways to form and maintain productive social relationships.

Principles of Physical Development

Thanks, in part, to genetic influences, physical development is somewhat predictable. Researchers have identified several general principles that characterize physical growth:

■ *Children's bodies are dynamic systems.* As we described in Chapter 1, dynamic systems theories characterize children's actions as the outcome of factors inside and outside themselves.

Observe 7-month-old Madison reach for objects in the Emotional Development/Infancy clip.

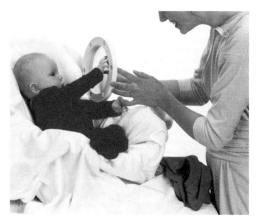

Reaching follows an uneven path of development, with sizable individual differences among infants, improvements and some regressions, and eventual stabilization of speed.

As one or more of these factors change, children respond by trying out new styles of acting. Gradually, children progress toward more mature levels, but there can be long periods of steady functioning, and even occasions when they return to more primitive styles of behaving.

Early motor skills show these kinds of dynamic changes. Infants move their limbs spontaneously from birth and even before (in later stages of pregnancy, many women feel the limbs of their developing babies thumping against their uterus). When they are about 3½ to 4 months old, infants begin to reach for objects (Thelen & Smith, 1998). Their initial efforts are shaky but gradually improve. After some small improvements, though, infants often show a period with *declines* in speed, directness, and smoothness in their reaching. Possibly, they must figure out how to integrate changes in muscle tone or a change in some other specific factor. By 12 months, however, most can reach easily and quickly. For example, in the Emotional Development/Infancy clip on the Observation CD, 7-month-old Madison adeptly reaches for objects. Notice that she not only reaches successfully for objects, but she can transfer objects between her two hands, and she can hold onto one object while reaching for another with her other hand.

Curiously, even nearly universal accomplishments, such as reaching for objects, show dramatic individual differences in the pathways children take to proficiency. For example, infants who make large and vigorous movements spontaneously in their first few months of life must learn to control such movements before they can successfully reach for objects (Thelen, Corbetta, & Spencer, 1996; Thelen, Corbetta, Kamm, Spencer, Schneider, & Zernicke, 1993). In contrast, infants who generate few and slow movements spontaneously in their first few months have a different set of problems to solve: They must learn to apply muscle tone to extend their arms forward and hold them stiffly.

■ *Different parts of the body mature at different rates.* Typical growth curves for height and weight reveal rapid increases in the first two years, slow but steady growth during early and middle childhood, an explosive spurt during adolescence, and a leveling off to mature, adult levels (Hamill, Drizd, Johnson, Reed, Roche, & Moore, 1979). Patterns of growth are similar for boys and girls, although girls tend to have their adolescent growth spurts about one and one-half years earlier, and boys, on average, end up a bit taller and heavier.

Such increases are, of course, a manifestation of the growth of individual bodily systems. However, specific parts of the body grow at different rates, and in the early years, some parts are closer than others to their ultimate adult size. Heads are proportionally closer to adult size than are trunks, which are more advanced than arms and legs. In the upper limbs, the hand is closer to adult size than the forearm; the forearm is closer than the upper arm. Likewise in the lower limbs, the foot is more advanced than the calf, which is more advanced than the thigh. Figure 3–4 illustrates how relative body proportions change throughout childhood and adolescence.

Internally, different systems grow at different rates as well (Tanner, 1990). For instance, the lymphoid system (e.g., tonsils, adenoids, intestines, lymph nodes) grows rapidly throughout childhood and then decreases somewhat in adolescence. This system helps children to resist infection, which is particularly important during the school years when children are exposed to many contagious illnesses for the first time. In contrast, the reproductive system shows fairly slow growth until adolescence, when there's a substantial burst of growth.

■ *Functioning becomes increasingly differentiated.* Every cell in the body (with the exception of gametes) contains all 46 chromosomes and so has the same genetic instructions. But as cells grow, they take on specific functions, some aiding with digestion, others transporting oxygen, still others transmitting information to various points in the body, and so on. Thus, individual cells "listen" to only a subset of the many instructions they have available. This change from general to more specific cell functioning is known as **differentiation.**

Differentiation characterizes other aspects of physical development as well. For instance, during prenatal development, the bud of an arm becomes longer, with hands emerging slowly, then fingers. Motor skills, too, become increasingly differentiated over time: They first appear as global, unsteady actions but gradually evolve into more specific, controlled

differentiation
An increase from general to more specific functioning over the course of development.

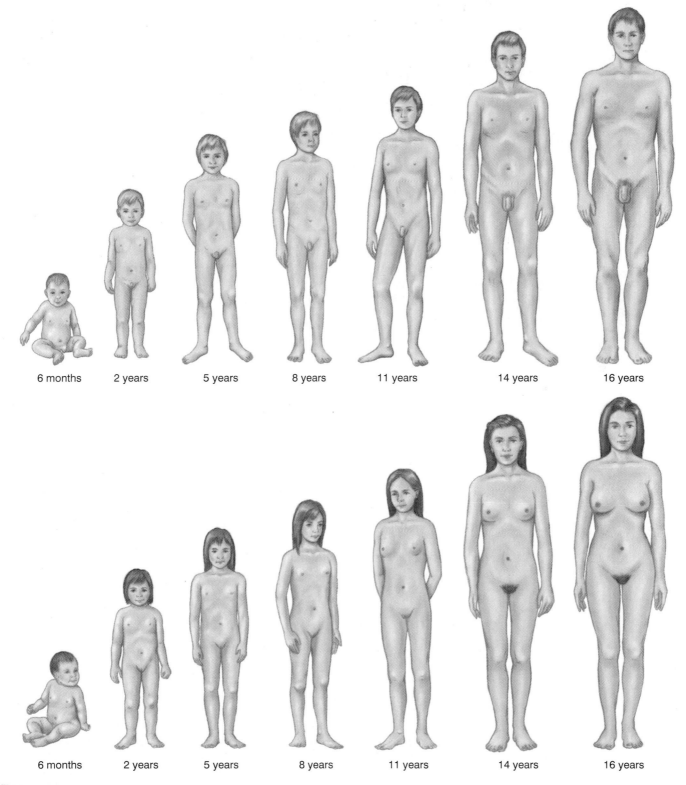

| 6 months | 2 years | 5 years | 8 years | 11 years | 14 years | 16 years |

| 6 months | 2 years | 5 years | 8 years | 11 years | 14 years | 16 years |

FIGURE 3-4 Physical development during childhood and adolescence. Children grow taller and heavier as they develop, and the characteristics and relative proportions of their bodies change as well.

Based on The Diagram Group (1983).

Development of a young boy at (left to right) ages 1, 5, 9, and 13. Notice the gradual, systematic changes. The boy grows taller, his face becomes more angular, his trunk elongates, and his hair color darkens.

Observe a developmental differentiation in hand grip by comparing three children holding writing utensils in the Observation CD: 16-month-old Corwin in the Literacy/Infancy clip, 4-year-old Zoe in the Neighborhood/Early Childhood clip, and 9-year-old Elena in the Neighborhood/Middle Childhood clip.

motions. For example, when trying to throw a ball, toddlers are apt to use their entire body in an intense but clumsy effort to move the ball forward. Preschoolers are more likely to move just a single arm and hand in an attempt to concentrate their efforts. As another example, you can see a clear developmental progression toward fine-motor control by comparing the writing-implement grips of three children in the Observation CD: 16-month-old Corwin in the Literacy/Infancy clip, 4-year-old Zoe in the Neighborhood/Early Childhood clip, and 9-year-Elena in the Neighborhood/Middle Childhood clip.

■ *Functioning becomes increasingly integrated.* As cells and body parts differentiate, they must work together. Their increasingly coordinated efforts are known as **integration** (Tanner, 1990). For instance, to throw a ball effectively, a child must carefully orchestrate movements of the entire body—the legs and torso along with the arm and hand propel the ball toward a particular target.

■ *Each child follows a unique growth curve.* Children appear to have target heights—perhaps not as specific as 4′ 9″ or 6′ 2″, but a definite, limited target, nonetheless. Growth curves are especially evident when things go temporarily awry in children's lives. Circumstances such as illness or poor nutrition may briefly halt height increases. But when health and adequate nutrition are restored, children grow rapidly. Before you know it, they're back on track—back to where we might have expected them to be, given their previous rate of growth. Exceptions to this self-correcting tendency occur when severe malnutrition is present very early in life or extends over a lengthy period of time. For instance, children who are seriously undernourished during the prenatal phase tend not to catch up completely, and they are at risk for later mental and behavioral deficiencies, motor difficulties, and psychiatric problems (e.g., schizophrenia; A. L. Brown et al., 1996; Chavez, Martinez, & Soberanes, 1995; M. Sigman, 1995).

■ *Physical development is characterized by both quantitative and qualitative changes.* Many physical changes are outcomes of a series of minor refinements. Motor skills, which may seem to the casual observer to appear overnight, are in most cases the result of numerous gradual advancements. For example, when Teresa's son Alex was 4, he wanted to snap his fingers like his older brother. Alex diligently practiced finger snapping several times a day for two months yet was unable to make the desired sound. With practice, however, his movements became more adept, and one day, much to his delight, snap, he got it right. In Alex's eyes, the accomplishment was a quantum leap forward, but in reality it was probably the result of repeated practice. Because he improved gradually in making the desired movements, this development might be considered as a quantitative change in motor proficiency.

However, qualitative changes are seen as well. To illustrate, Figure 3–5 shows how both walking and throwing change over time. Early on, toddlers have difficulty maintaining balance and upright posture, take short steps, make flat-footed contact with toes turned outward, and flex their knees as their feet contact the ground (Gallahue & Ozmun, 1998). A few years later, they increase their stride, make heel-toe contact, swing their arms a bit, lift themselves vertically as they proceed, and show increased pelvic tilt. The mature pattern of walking, achieved between ages 4 and 7, is characterized by a reflexive arm swing, a narrow base of support, a relaxed and long stride, minimal vertical lift, and a decisive heel-toe contact. Throwing a ball shows qualitative changes as well (Figure 3–5), as do such skills as jumping, galloping, and sliding (Gallahue & Ozmun, 1998).

integration
An increasing coordination of body parts over the course of development.

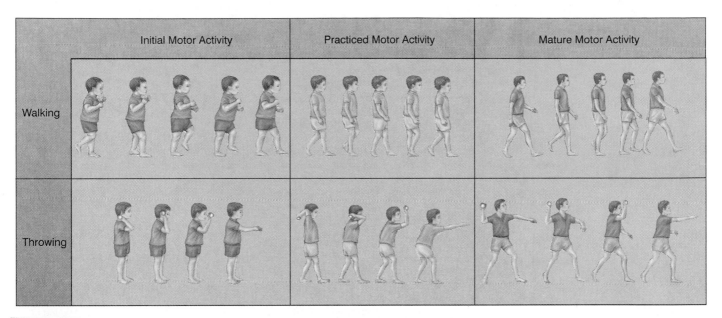

	Initial Motor Activity	Practiced Motor Activity	Mature Motor Activity
Walking			
Throwing			

FIGURE 3-5 Developmental sequences showing qualitative change in walking and overhand throwing. In walking, children tend to progress from (a) difficulty maintaining balance and using short steps with flat-footed contact, to (b) a smoother pattern, where arms are lower and there is heel-toe contact, to (c) a relaxed gait, with reflexive arm swing. In overhand throwing, the trend is from (a) stationary feet and action mainly from the elbow, to (b) ball held behind head, arm swung forward and high over shoulder, and a definite shift forward with body weight, to (c) movement of foot on same side as throwing arm; definite rotation through hips, legs, spine, and shoulders; and a step with foot opposite to the throwing arm as weight is shifted.

Based on Gallahue & Ozmun (1998)

In the Basic Developmental Issues table "Physical Development," we summarize the ways in which physical development is both qualitative and quantitative, as well as the ways in which nature, nurture, universality, and diversity come into play.

The Brain and Its Development

The brain is the switchboard, command center, and computer of human functioning. It is a *switchboard* in the sense that it transmits a huge amount of information to, and receives an equal amount of information from, all parts of the body. It is a *command center* in that it regulates and coordinates the activities of various bodily systems. It is a *computer* in that it stores, organizes, and tries to make sense of the masses of data that the body collects as it interacts with the physical and social environments. Not surprisingly, the brain is the most complex organ in the human body. As you will see in the following discussion, the brain is guided both by genetic instructions and by experience.

Altogether, the brain has approximately 180 billion cells (Teeter & Semrud-Clikeman, 1997). Many brain cells take the form of **neurons,** cells that transmit information to other cells. Neurons do their work through both architecture (Figure 3–6) and chemistry. With branchlike structures called **dendrites,** they reach out to receive information from other cells. With long, armlike structures called **axons,** they send information on to other neurons. The dendrites and axons of neurons come together at junctions known as **synapses.** Neurons activate one another to "fire," and in some cases prevent one another from firing, by sending chemical substances known as **neurotransmitters** across the synapses that join them.

Neurons in the brain are organized as communities that interact with other communities. In other words, groups of neurons grow together and communicate with other groups of neurons elsewhere in the brain and the body. Most neurons have hundreds or even thousands of synapses linking them with other neurons (R. R. Thompson, 1975), so obviously a great deal of cross-communication is possible.

Neurons are assisted by other kinds of brain cells, called **glial cells.** These cells give neurons structural support and protect the connections among neurons. They also produce chemicals that neurons need to function properly, and they help to repair injured neurons as well as dispose of seriously damaged ones (Carlson, 1999; Teeter & Semrud-Clikeman, 1997).

neuron
Cell that transmits information to other cells; also called nerve cell.

dendrite
Branchlike part of a neuron that receives information from other neurons.

axon
Armlike part of a neuron that sends information to other neurons.

synapse
Junction between two neurons.

neurotransmitter
Chemical substance through which one neuron sends a message to another neuron.

glial cell
Cell in the brain or other part of the nervous system that provides structural or functional support for one or more neurons.

BASIC DEVELOPMENTAL ISSUES

Physical Development

ISSUE	PHYSICAL GROWTH	MOTOR SKILLS	PHYSICAL HEALTH AND ACTIVITY
Nature and Nurture	Genetic instructions specify how cells divide and where they migrate during prenatal development; they also provide basic targets for mature height and weight. Yet normal progressions are contingent on healthful environmental conditions and experiences, such as adequate nutrition, movement, stimulation, affection, and protection from toxic substances.	Nature sets firm boundaries as to the motor skills a child can execute at any given period of time; for instance, a 6-month old cannot run and a 10-year-old cannot clear 15 feet in the standing high jump. However, organized sports programs and other opportunities for regular exercise allow children to expand, refine, and polish their developing motor skills.	Nature influences children's activity level (e.g., 3-year-olds tend to be more physically active than 17-year-olds) and susceptibility to infection and illness. Children learn habits of eating and exercise from their parents and others in their community.
Universality and Diversity	Children tend to show similar sequences in physical development (e.g., in the emergence of sexual characteristics associated with puberty) across a wide range of environments and cultures. However, the rate of development differs considerably from one child to the next, with differences being partly the result of genetic diversity and partly the result of diverse cultural practices with respect to food, exercise, and so on.	Motor skills often develop in the same, universal sequence. For example, children can, on average, pick up crumbs at age 1, scribble with a crayon at age 2, and build a tower 10 blocks high at age 4 (Sheridan, 1975). Diversity is present in the specific ages at which children master motor skills, due in part to genetic differences and in part to variations in environmental support (or lack of support).	All children and adolescents need good nutrition, plenty of rest, and a moderate amount of physical activity to be healthy. Huge variation is present in the activity levels and eating habits of youngsters. In addition, children differ in their susceptibility to illness.
Qualitative and Quantitative Change	Many physical advancements are the result of a series of quantitative physiological changes (e.g., gradual increases in physical strength and dexterity). Qualitative changes are revealed in the different rates of change that occur in different systems in the body and in the characteristics that emerge at puberty.	As a general rule, children must practice motor skills for a long time before they can execute them easily and gracefully, and a series of quantitative improvements allow more complex skills to emerge. Some motor skills, such as walking and throwing a ball, also change qualitatively with maturity and practice.	During the middle childhood years, children gradually gain control over what they eat and how they spend their leisure time (a quantitative change). Reorganization in thinking about safety and danger sometimes occurs in adolescence. Young people may shift from a preoccupation with safety to a thrill-seeking mindset (a qualitative change).

hindbrain
Part of the brain controlling the basic physiological processes that sustain survival.

midbrain
Part of the brain that coordinates communication between the hindbrain and forebrain.

forebrain
Part of the brain responsible for complex thinking, emotions, and motivation.

cortex
Part of the forebrain that houses conscious thinking processes (executive functions).

executive functions
Conscious thinking processes within the brain (e.g., reasoning, communicating, decision making).

Structures and Functions

The brain is organized into three main parts—the hindbrain, the midbrain, and the forebrain (Figure 3–7)—and each of these parts is organized further into specialized systems with identifiable functions.

- The **hindbrain** controls basic physiological processes that sustain survival, including breathing, blood pressure, sleep, arousal, balance, and movement (thank your hindbrain for your slow, methodical breathing as you sleep blissfully at night).
- The **midbrain** connects the hindbrain to the forebrain and acts as a kind of relay station between the two; for instance, it sends messages to the forebrain about priorities for attention ("Hello! Alarm clock ringing! Hello! Alarm clock ringing!").
- The **forebrain** produces complex thinking, emotional response, and the driving forces of motivation ("6:00 A.M.? Ugh! I can sleep another 10 minutes if I skip breakfast!").

Resting like a cap upon other parts of the brain is a portion of the forebrain known as the **cortex**. The cortex is where interpreting, reasoning, communicating, goal setting, planning, decision making, and other conscious thinking processes (collectively known as **executive functions**) take place. The cortex is also the seat of many personality traits and of habitual ways of responding to physical events and other human beings. For example, a

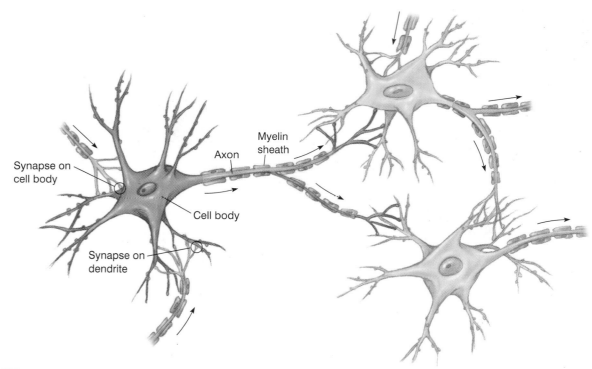

FIGURE 3-6 Neurons in the brain. The neuron on the left is receiving information from other cells. It then fires and incites other neurons to fire. Arrows show the direction of messages being sent.

Based on N. R. Carlson (1999).

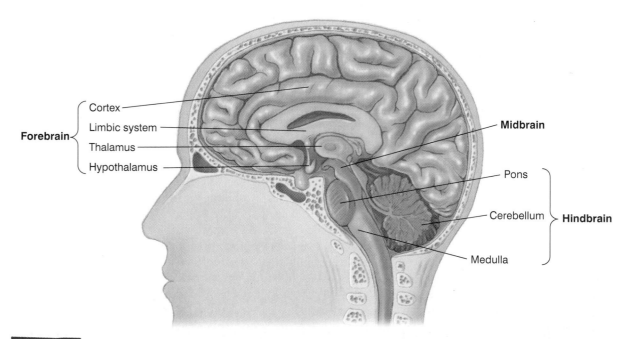

FIGURE 3-7 Structure of the human brain. The human brain is an enormously complex and intricate structure with three main parts: the hindbrain, the midbrain, and the forebrain.

Based on N. R. Carlson (1999).

10-year-old's cortex would include the ways she snuggles up to her father on the couch in the evening, her concerns for her mother's chronic health problems, her understanding of how to read, her knowledge of sailing, and of course, much more.

Physiologically, the cortex is extremely convoluted. Bundles of neurons repeatedly fold in on themselves. This physical complexity permits a huge capacity for storing information as well as for transmitting information throughout the brain. Consistent with the principle of differentiation, various parts of the cortex have specific functions, such as distinguishing among sounds, understanding spoken language, and planning speech.

Left and Right Hemispheres   The cortex is divided into two halves, or hemispheres. In most people, the **left hemisphere** dominates in *analysis,* breaking up information into its constituent parts and extracting order in a sequence of events (Carlson, 1999; Uba & Huang, 1999). Talking, understanding speech, reading, writing, mathematical problem solving, and computer programming are all beneficiaries of left-hemisphere processing. It is usually the **right hemisphere** that excels in *synthesis,* pulling together information into a coherent whole (especially nonlinguistic information such as body language, three-dimensional images, and other visual patterns). The right hemisphere therefore usually dominates in recognizing faces, detecting geometrical patterns, reading maps, and drawing. It is also key to appreciating musical melodies, understanding humor in physical events, noticing emotions in other people, and expressing one's own emotions.

The specializations of the two hemispheres are assured by the physical layout of neural circuits. The left hemisphere has neurological connections to fewer regions of the brain than does the right; this layout permits application of rules in specific, structured domains such as language and mathematics. It does its work close to home, so to speak. The right hemisphere is more amply connected with distant areas in the brain, permitting associations to all kinds of thinking and feeling (Goldberg & Costa, 1981; Semrud-Clikeman & Hynd, 1991; Teeter & Semrud-Clikeman, 1997).

Researchers have been studying the specialization of the two hemispheres for many years, and their findings have been widely disseminated among scientists and the general public. However, the body of evidence is often oversimplified or in other ways misrepresented by non-specialists. You may occasionally hear someone say, "I'm trying to reach children's right brains," or, "Billy's a left-brain kid." Such well-intentioned comments imply that various forms of thinking are confined to particular sides of the brain and that, for many individuals, one side is more proficient than the other. In reality, the two hemispheres are in constant communication, trading information back and forth, and so no single mental activity is exclusively the domain of one hemisphere or the other (Carlson, 1999). For example, the right hemisphere may process a complex emotion, such as the mixed feelings people often experience at high school graduation, while the left hemisphere searches for words to communicate the feelings.

Having discussed typical forms of hemispheric specialization, we have news for our left-handed readers. It is common for left-handed individuals to have reversed patterns, with the right hemisphere dominant in language and the left hemisphere more involved in visual synthesis (Carlson, 1999). Moreover, a few individuals distribute cognitive functions in different ways (Sheehan & Smith, 1986; Witelson, 1985). For instance, people who are ambidextrous (i.e., they use both hands equally well for fine motor tasks) are more likely to blend functions within hemispheres than are people who are definitely right-handed or left-handed (Sheehan & Smith, 1986). Thus, they may distribute language functions in both hemispheres rather than having one hemisphere predominate in language. Some evidence suggests that ambidextrous individuals are more creative than average (Gribov, 1992), although they may have greater difficulty with certain basic skills, such as discriminating left from right (Ladavas, 1988; Storfer, 1995). In addition, left-handed and ambidextrous individuals are somewhat more accident prone (Daniel & Yeo, 1994).

Malformations in Brain Development   Some individual differences in brain structure are far more extreme in their effects. In a few cases, people's brains have unusual circuits or missing or distorted structures, malformations that often interfere with effective learning and behavior. Some neurological disorders are not obvious at birth, or even in the first few years of life. For example, **schizophrenia**, a serious psychiatric disorder that affects one in a hundred people, often does not surface until adolescence or adulthood (Carlson, 1999). Individuals with schizophrenia display symptoms such as thought disorders (e.g., irrational ideas and disorganized thinking), hallucinations (e.g., "hearing" nonexistent voices), delusions (e.g., worrying that "everyone is out to get me"), and social withdrawal (e.g., avoiding eye contact or conversation with others). Such symptoms appear to be the

left hemisphere
Left side of the cortex; largely responsible for sequential reasoning and analysis, especially in right-handed people.

right hemisphere
Right side of the cortex; largely responsible for simultaneous processing and synthesis, especially in right-handed people.

schizophrenia
A psychiatric condition characterized by irrational ideas and disorganized thinking.

TABLE 3-2   Examples of Risk Factors for Healthy Neurological Development

PHASE OF DEVELOPMENT	RISK FACTOR	POSSIBLE OUTCOMES
Prenatal development	Alcohol	*Fetal alcohol syndrome:* Disruption of neuron development, growth delays, facial abnormalities, mental retardation, impulsivity, behavioral problems
	Marijuana	Premature birth, low birth weight, tremors, oversensitivity to certain kinds of stimuli
	Cocaine	Premature birth, low birth weight, small head size, lethargy, and irritability (cocaine alters the metabolism of some neurotransmitters and may influence the formation of brain structures that depend on these substances; it also reduces blood flow to the brain)
	Heroin	Premature birth, small head circumference, respiratory complications, irritability, death
	HIV infection and AIDS	Delays in motor skills, visual perception, language, and reasoning; long-term cognitive impairment; microencephaly (condition in which children have an exceptionally small head and fail to grow at normal rates)
	Maternal stress	Low birth weight, irritability, colic, restlessness
Birth	Serious birth complications (e.g., oxygen deprivation)	Cognitive, behavioral, and/or psychiatric disorders
Postnatal development	Nutritional deficiencies	Destruction of neurons and myelin sheaths, sometimes resulting in learning and memory problems
	Exposure to lead	Cognitive and behavioral problems, epilepsy, severe motor difficulties, blindness

Sources: Chasnoff, Burns, Burns, & Scholl, 1986; E. Hunt, Streissguth, Kerr, & Olson, 1995; Korkman, Autti-Raemoe, Koivulehto, & Granstroem, 1998; Kraemingk & Paquette, 1999; Mayes & Bornstein, 1997; Teeter & Semrud-Clikeman, 1997.

result, at least in part, of structural abnormalities or overactive synapses in certain parts of the brain (Carlson, 1999; Giedd, Jeffries, Blumenthal, Castellanos, Vaituzis, Fernandez, Hamburger, Liu, Nelson, Bedwell, Tran, Lenane, Nicolson, & Rapoport, 1999; L. K. Jacobsen, Giedd, Berquin, Krain, Hamburger, Kumra, & Rapoport, 1997; Jacobsen, Giedd, Castellanos, Vaituzis, Hamburger, Kumra, Lenane, & Rapoport, 1997).

What causes serious malformations in brain development? Earlier we learned that errors in chromosomes and single genes can cause mental retardation; these learning delays occur when genes trigger problems in brain chemistry and architecture. In the case of schizophrenia, genetic factors, viral infections during prenatal development, and childbirth complications may be causes (Carlson, 1999). Other neurological abnormalities may be due to drugs, alcohol, illness, or maternal stress during prenatal development; oxygen deprivation or other complications during childbirth; or inadequate nutrition or exposure to toxins (e.g., lead paint) after birth. Table 3–2 lists the possible effects of such factors.

Developmental Changes

To understand changes in the brain associated with particular periods of development, it is helpful to start with the basic principles that govern the brain as it is transformed from one ordered state to the next. In fact, brains mature according to principles much the same as those outlined earlier for general physical development:

■ *The brain operates as a dynamic system.* As a dynamic system, the brain is composed of structures that interact with each other and with the outside world (Thelen & Smith, 1998). Over time, the brain creates order as its parts find ways to relate to one another and with the environment. This order is temporary, however, and certain experiences and

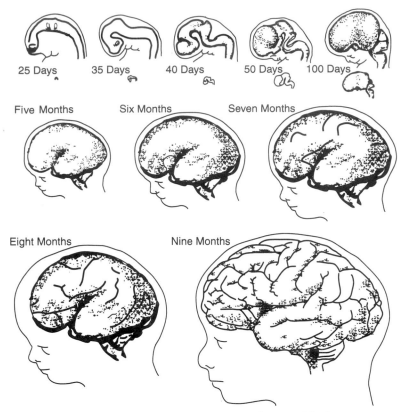

25 Days 35 Days 40 Days 50 Days 100 Days

Five Months   Six Months   Seven Months

Eight Months   Nine Months

FIGURE 3-8 Changes in the human brain during prenatal development. During the first few months, the basic structures appear. During the middle months of prenatal development, these structures become more distinct. During the final few months, prior to birth, the cortex folds in and out of itself, preparing the fetus for learning as a baby.

From "The Development of the Brain" by W. Maxwell Cowan, 1979, *Scientific American, 241*, p. 106. Illustration copyright 1979 by Tom Prentiss. Reproduced by permission.

structural changes make possible new ways of operating, thinking, and feeling.

■ *Different parts of the brain mature at different rates.* The timetable for development is *somewhat* area- and function-specific. Different parts of the brain are ready—eager, in fact—to learn at particular times. For example, infants' brains mature in sensory areas before motor areas. Similarly, inner portions of the brain mature before the outer cortex.

■ *The brain becomes increasingly differentiated.* What is first simple in the brain becomes complex. As shown in Figure 3–8, round bumps on a simple tube emerge early in prenatal development and then gradually are transformed into the brain's highly distinct and complex structures. (We'll say more about this transformation shortly.) Similarly, the two hemispheres of the brain, initially alike in appearance and composition, gradually become associated with distinct functions.

■ *The parts of the brain become integrated.* During brain growth, bundles of neurons gradually begin to work together. For instance, during adolescence maturation in circuits in the front part of the cortex (near the forehead) makes it increasingly possible for youngsters to channel strong emotional drives into appropriate directions, those that take into account the long-term consequences of actions. (Of course, good judgment is most likely to develop when it is not only possible, but also practiced!)

■ *Rates of growth vary greatly among populations of children.* The formation of pathways in children's brains is very dependent on their individual experiences, genetic factors, and nutrition. Each child's brain develops its own unique, habitual ways of processing information and responding to people and events.

■ *Brain development is characterized by both qualitative and quantitative changes.* The brain grows both by leaps and bounds and through slow, steady progress. Qualitative transformations are evident when the brain shifts from forming new connections among neurons during infancy to strengthening those that are truly active (and needed) during childhood and adolescence. Quantitatively, driven by new learning, the brain adds additional synapses throughout childhood, adolescence, and adulthood.

Changes During Developmental Periods Having outlined principles of developmental change in the brain, we can now examine the specific transformations that occur during particular growth periods.

Prenatal development. During prenatal development, the brain's most basic parts are formed. The brain begins as a tiny tube approximately 25 days after conception. This seemingly simple tube grows longer in places and folds inward to form pockets (Cowan, 1979; Rayport, 1992). Three bulges can be recognized early on; these bulges become the forebrain, midbrain, and hindbrain.

During prenatal development, neurons, the building blocks of the brain, are formed. Neuron cells reproduce in the inner portion of the tube; between the 5th and 20th weeks of prenatal development, they do so at the astonishing rate of 50,000 to 250,000 new cells per second (Cowan, 1979; M. Diamond & Hopson, 1998). More neurons than the brain will ever use are formed during the first 7 months of prenatal development (Johnson, 1998; Rakic, 1995).

Newly formed neurons move, *migrate,* to specific locations in the brain where they will do their work. Some push old cells outward, creating brain structures underneath the cor-

Newborn   1-Month-Old   3-Month-Old   6-Month-Old

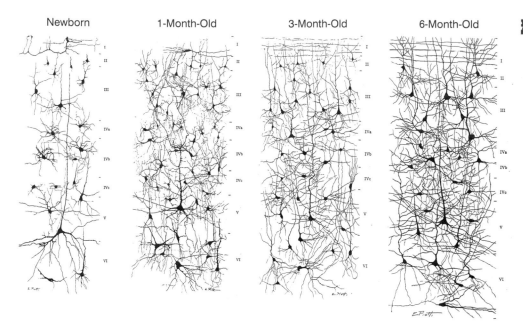

FIGURE 3–9 Drawings of the cellular structure of an infant's visual cortex. Comparison of these drawings at four different ages reveals the rapid and extensive growth of dendrites during infancy. Drawings based on Golgi stain preparations from Conel (1939–1967).

Reprinted by permission of the publisher from *The Postnatal Development of the Human Cerebral Cortex,* Vols. I–VIII, by Jesse LeRoy Conel, Cambridge, MA: Harvard University Press, Copyright © 1939, 1975 by the President and Fellows of Harvard College.

tex. Others actively seek out their destination, climbing up pole-like glial cells and ultimately giving rise to the cortex. Once in place, neurons send out axons in efforts to connect with one another. Groups of axons grow together as teams, reaching toward other groups of target neurons and spurred on by particular chemicals secreted by the target cells (different types of cells secrete different chemicals; Carlson, 1999).

As axons get close to their targets, they begin to form branches that become synapses with the target cells. The target cells do their part as well, forming small receptors that will receive stimulation from the other cells. Only about half of neurons make contact with other cells. Those that make contact survive; the others die. Nature's tendency to overproduce neurons and eliminate those that fail to connect ensures that its connections work well (M. Diamond & Hopson, 1998; Huttenlocher, 1990).

When genes are healthy and prenatal conditions have been good, the fetus's brain grows ready to survive and learn in the outside world. In the final two months of prenatal growth, the outer surface of the brain, the cortex, takes on its convoluted appearance, folding in and out (Cowan, 1979). The majority of neurons are in the right place (Johnson, 1999). It is time for birth.

Infancy. At birth, the infant's brain has two important tasks: (1) implementing survival mechanisms outside the womb and (2) learning about people, things, language, sensations, emotions, and events. Coming from healthy prenatal environments, most newborns are well prepared to breathe, suck, swallow, cry, and form simple associations. With survival taken care of, the brain concentrates on forming countless connections among neurons, prodigiously creating dendrites, synapses, and fiber bundles (Johnson, 1998). These will make learning possible. You can see, for example, the rapid development of dendrites in areas of the cortex that support vision in Figure 3–9. In general, inner areas of the brain become dense with dendrites before similar development occurs in outer layers, closer to the skull (Johnson, 1998).

Synapses also become plentiful during infancy. In the first three and one-half years of life, so many new synapses appear (a phenomenon known as **synaptogenesis**) that their number far exceeds adult levels (Bruer, 1999). During infancy, synaptic growth is especially rich in areas of the brain devoted to vision and hearing (Huttenlocher, 1990). Then, following this fantastic proliferation of synapses, frequently used connections strengthen, and connections not often used wither away in a process known as **synaptic pruning.** As with many phases of brain growth, particular regions of the brain take their turns growing and shedding synapses. For example, shortly after the first year, synapses decrease in number in the visual cortex, while the number of synapses in other areas of the cortex remains constant (Huttenlocher, 1990).

Another trend in brain development occurs in infancy and continues through adulthood (Bruer, 1999). Glial cells grow around axons, forming a fatty sheath, *myelin,* which insulates

synaptogenesis
A universal process in brain development whereby many new synapses appear, typically in the first 3½ years of life.

synaptic pruning
A universal process in brain development whereby many previously formed synapses wither away, especially if they have not been used frequently.

neurons and thereby enables them to transmit messages more quickly. This process of **myelination** is most pronounced in the early years, but it continues in certain areas of the brain well into adolescence and adulthood (Benes, 2001). It occurs in particular regions of the brain in a fairly predictable sequence (Yakovlev & Lecours, 1967). Myelination starts with neurons involved in basic survival skills during the prenatal period; then, beginning in infancy, it occurs with neurons that activate sensory areas, motor skills, and higher thinking processes (M. Diamond & Hopson, 1998).

Infancy is noteworthy because the brain connections that are formed will become the foundation of many later abilities. For example, in the first year of life infants activate neurological circuits that permit very basic skills in visually scanning objects, recognizing faces, distinguishing novel and familiar stimuli, and detecting sounds used by care-givers (Johnson, 1999). When these rudimentary abilities first appear, they seem rather automatic and reflex-like. A 2-month-old baby may visually track a ball thrown by his older brother, but he is unlikely to anticipate the path the ball will take or reflect on what he's seeing. With maturation and experience, infants can think about their perceptions and use them to guide their behavior. In the Emotional Development/Infancy clip of the Observation CD, you can observe 7-month-old Madison intently studying the properties of a blue toy. Although you cannot see the neurons firing in her brain, it is clear that learning is taking place.

The magnificent neurological advances of infancy are best promoted when caregivers are affectionate, consistent, responsive, and reassuring. We will explore infants' attachments to caregivers in Chapter 9, but emphasize here that these bonds help infants to develop not only emotionally but also physically and intellectually. To illustrate, responsive adults are inclined to give infants proper nutrition and to protect them from danger—essential conditions for healthy brain growth. In addition, responsive adults are able to soothe distressed infants, who can then relax and explore their surroundings. Similarly, responsive adults are likely to notice what infants care about—what they attend to and specifically what they see, hear, feel, smell, and taste. When adults routinely talk about the patterns that infants seem to be noticing (e.g., "Do you see the teddy bear's eyes?"), infants may spot new perceptual features, eventually learn adults' labels, and develop a keen desire to share new discoveries with them ("See this, Gamma!"). Finally, responsive adults are enthusiastic about sharing social and material worlds with infants, continuously placing them in situations where they are likely to learn.

Childhood. During childhood, the brain continues to distinguish neurological bundles that are used regularly from those that seldom fire. It nurtures active connections, those relating to core skills, understandings, and emotional responses, and allows under-utilized connections to shrivel. Synaptic pruning of under-utilized connections, which begins in certain regions during infancy, becomes a major force of change during childhood.

This sequence of rich proliferation of synaptic connections, followed by synaptic pruning, makes sense because of the complexity of human children's worlds. The early, over-connected state prepares children for a host of possible physical and cultural environments (M. Diamond & Hopson, 1998). Then, because children actually live in a single (admittedly very elaborate) environment, they keep and strengthen the synapses most likely to serve them well in that context (M. Diamond & Hopson, 1998).

This neurological pattern—in which connections are formed for repeated actions and thoughts—explains the rapid and sustained learning of children. Children quickly become knowledgeable about whatever strikes their fancy—comic books, dance movements, cake decorating, or hunting strategies. Likewise, they learn much about the habits and motives of people in their lives; this knowledge helps them to fit comfortably into family and peer networks. Children also become fluent in their native tongue, flexibly and expertly using increasingly sophisticated words and grammatical structures.

In middle childhood and adolescence, most neurological development occurs in the cortex, the seat of the executive functions through which people plan and control their own behavior (Casey, Giedd, & Thomas, 2000; Sowell, Delis, Stiles, & Jernigan, 2001). It appears that the building of neurological circuits that support executive functions peaks during middle childhood (6 to 8 years) and continues to be refined into adolescence (Passler, Isaac, & Hynd, 1985). In part because these circuits are still being constructed, children can lack the ability to

Observe 7-month-old Madison using her emerging perceptual skills to learn about the properties of a toy in the Emotional Development/Infancy clip.

myelination
The growth of a fatty sheath around neurons that allows them to transmit messages more quickly.

plan realistically for the future. Despite good intentions, they cannot easily sustain commitments to goals when other events and motives intervene. For example, they occasionally forget things when they leave home in the morning. In addition, their emotions are being processed at lower levels of the brain; the cortex of the forebrain is not yet fully developed.

Other kinds of changes in the brain occur steadily during childhood. The two hemispheres become increasingly distinct (Sowell, Thompson, Rex, Kornsand, Tessner, Jernigan, & Toga, 2002). Also, new synapses are formed in the cortex (National Research Council, 1999). Thus, while unused synapses are being pruned back, new ones continue to be formed as children learn new ideas. In addition, the process of myelination continues, protecting neurons and speeding up transmission of messages (Yakovlev & Lecours, 1967).

The net result of neurological changes in childhood is that young people become capable of completing more intellectual operations simultaneously. For example, they can keep more ideas in mind, an expanding capacity we examine in Chapter 5. To see this capacity being tapped, you can observe 6-year-old Brent listen to 12 words and try to recall them in the Memory/Early Childhood Clip of the Observation CD (he is able to recall 6 words). Quite possibly, a year or so earlier he would not have been able to recall so many words, and in a few more years, his recall will likely be even better.

Observe 6-year-old Brent trying to keep a few words in mind in the Memory/Early Childhood clip.

Professionals can support the brain development of children by giving them many varied opportunities to learn. Young children often learn best at play, but in the middle childhood years, professionals can explicitly teach many skills. For example, neurological changes during childhood prepare youngsters to read: they become increasingly able to move their eyes smoothly across a page, notice nuances in visual shapes, and integrate information about sounds, letters, and word meanings (Janowsky & Carper, 1996; Thatcher, 1994). By about age 5 or 6 and typically not much before, the brain has matured to such an extent that formal instruction in reading is likely to be beneficial. (See Chapter 8.)

The brain's tendency to nourish regularly used abilities also has implications. Teachers and other practitioners can effectively teach children by building on what they already understand. By helping children see new material in the context of familiar skills and concepts, adults facilitate learning. (We explore this application in greater detail in the presentation of cognitive development in Chapters 4 and 5.)

In addition, professionals can offer guidance in planning ahead and remembering obligations. Practitioners can post calendars, break up assignments into manageable pieces, and encourage children to use simple, concrete memory aids. To illustrate, when Teresa's son Alex was 7, his teachers sent home a bright orange packet called the "Friday Folder." At the end of each school week, they placed newsletters, assignments, and other papers in the folder. After a few weeks, Alex learned to empty his backpack on Friday afternoon and to show his parents the Friday Folder.

Adolescence. During adolescence, the brain ignites new passions, imagines the future, and tempers impulses with thoughts of long-term consequences. Continued development in the front part of the cortex makes this possible, causing a shift in how the brain analyzes emotional expressions. Adolescents become increasingly able to analyze emotions at higher levels of the brain, in the cortex, rather than responding to emotions more spontaneously, as in childhood (Killgore, Oki, & Yurgelun-Todd, 2001). Because these analytical abilities take some time to mature and also depend on experience, adolescents may be thoughtful one moment and rash the next. In the Emotional Development/Late Adolescence clip of the Observation CD, you can listen to 15-year-old Greg describe both impulsive reactions to anger and more controlled responses:

Listen to 15-year-old Greg describe both impulsive and controlled reactions to anger in the Emotional Development/Late Adolescence clip.

Interviewer:	What are some things kids do when they're angry?
Greg:	Hit lockers at school. They just get mad . . .
Interviewer:	Okay.
Greg:	And they don't want you to be around 'em. They just are not pleasant to be around.
Interviewer:	Okay. What are some things that kids can do to calm themselves down?
Greg:	I don't know. Usually give it a night, 'cause they, if they're mad they usually don't get unmad by the end of the day.

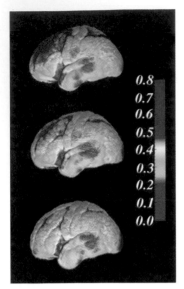

FIGURE 3–10 As humans develop, their brains become more efficient. The images show the average proportion of gray matter (neurons) in the left hemisphere of brains of children (top), adolescents (middle), and adults (bottom). Researchers conducted magnetic resonance imaging (MRI's) on individuals, then took averages for each age group and coded the proportion of gray matter in the cortex, which is reflected in the images. Warm colors (red and yellow) show high proportions of gray matter and cool colors (blue and green) show low proportions. Notice the decreased amount of red and yellow (neurons) in the adult brain as compared to the child's brain. This shows a developmental decline in the proportion of the cortex devoted solely to neurons. With development, unused neurons die out and active neurons become stronger and more efficient due to increases in myelination.

From E. R. Sowell, P. M. Thompson, D. Rex, D. Kornsand, K. D. Tessner, T. L. Jernigan, and A. W. Toga, "Mapping Sulcal Pattern Asymmetry and Local Cortical Surface Gray Matter Distribution *in vivo*: Maturation in the Perisylvian Cortices," 2002, *Cerebral Cortex, 12,* pp. 17–26. Reprinted by permission of Oxford University Press.

Myelination and the process of synaptic pruning continue into adulthood, as shown vividly in brain scans by Sowell and colleagues (see Figure 3–10). The result is that adolescents' and adults' brains are more efficient, compared to children's brains, both in terms of the connections (neurons, dendrites, and synapses) and the insulation of these connections (through myelination). If you look back at the photos of three brains in Chapter 2 (p. 51), you will literally see these fundamental differences: increases in the adult brain's "white matter" (the outcome of glial cells and myelination) and decreases in the adult brain's "gray matter" (neurons) because of synaptic pruning. The practical outcome of such progressive sculpting of the brain is that as young people grow older, they can hold more information in memory and apply their mental energy more effectively.

Yet other changes in the adolescent brain are the culmination of progressions that began in childhood. For example, pathways that support motor skills and speech continue to mature during late childhood and adolescence (Paus, Zijdenbos, Worsley, Collins, Blumenthal, Giedd, Rapoport, & Evans, 1999). Also, fibers connecting language centers within the cortex continue to grow during adolescence, but at a slower rate (P. M. Thompson, Giedd, Woods, MacDonald, Evans, & Toga, 2000). Myelination in the front region of the cortex, where planning, executive functions, and other complex cognitive processes occur, continues well into puberty (Giedd, Blumenthal, Jeffries, Castellanos et al., 1999; Kolb & Fantie, 1989). Taking into account the effects of one's actions before acting and planning ahead several steps are developments that seem to rely on these brain changes.

Although enhanced brain circuits are operational during adolescence, they do not necessarily function at maximum productivity. As you will discover in Chapter 5, adolescents can benefit from instruction showing them how to learn more effectively. Moreover, the brain will continue to change in systematic ways into adulthood. As we've already mentioned, the brain can add synapses at any time, and particular regions of the brain change predictably during adulthood (Sowell, Thompson, Holmes, Jernigan, & Toga, 1999).

Professionals who work with adolescents can take into account the neurological changes characteristic of this age level. For example, adults can communicate expectations for controlled behavior as well as coach adolescents in appropriate ways to vent their anger and frustrations. Thus, teachers who find Greg or his friends pounding on a locker can brainstorm alternative actions with them, such as letting out steam on the athletic field. Adults can also encourage young people to be optimistic about their future and to make plans for jobs, higher education, leisure activities, and personal lives—if they are planning for the future, adolescents have reason to avoid the temptations of the present. Finally, adolescents still need assistance with breaking up tasks into parts and setting interim goals for ambitious projects. Although adolescents are increasingly able to plan ahead, they still need practice in doing so.

We summarize key neurological changes during developmental periods in Table 3–3, where we also suggest the implications of these changes for practitioners working with young people in particular age groups. Some general applications of research on brain development are also discussed in the following section.

TABLE 3–3   Developmental Changes in the Brain

DEVELOPMENTAL PERIOD	DISTINCTIVE NEUROLOGICAL CHANGES	IMPLICATIONS FROM NEUROLOGICAL AND PSYCHOLOGICAL RESEARCH
Prenatal Development	*During prenatal development, the brain's most basic parts are constructed:* • The primary structures of the brain emerge within the first few months of prenatal growth. • Neurons, the building blocks of the brain, are formed. They migrate to the places where they will do their work. • With maturation of the cortex, the brain readies itself to learn in the outside world.	• Encourage pregnant adolescents to protect themselves from toxins, drugs, alcohol, injury, and excessive stress. • Encourage pregnant adolescents to seek prenatal care from a physician. • Encourage all adolescents—and especially pregnant adolescents—to obtain adequate nutrition.

TABLE 3-3   **Developmental Changes in the Brain** *(continued)*

DEVELOPMENTAL PERIOD	DISTINCTIVE NEUROLOGICAL CHANGES	IMPLICATIONS FROM NEUROLOGICAL AND PSYCHOLOGICAL RESEARCH
Infancy	*The developing brain ensures the infant's survival and makes it possible for him or her to absorb and respond to a world of people, things, language, sensations, feelings, and events:* • With a full array of neurons present at birth, the brain now concentrates on forming connections. • In the first year of life, dendrites expand their reach and complexity. Inner areas of the brain become dense with dendrites before this happens in outer layers, closer to the skull. • During the first year of life, synapses grow in density, especially in areas of the brain devoted to vision and hearing. • In certain areas, synaptic pruning begins. • The infant brain searches for certain kinds of stimuli, such as human faces. • Myelination occurs during infancy and continues through childhood, adolescence, and adulthood.	• Provide infants with the nutrition they need to build healthy bodies and brains. • Offer infants stimulating environments that include rich visual patterns and human voices—but don't overdo it. Infants are hungry to learn about the world, but they need to do it in their own way, on their own timetable. • Carefully observe infants' reactions to stimuli to determine their preferences. Be sensitive to their interests. • Talk to infants. They are able to learn a lot about language even when they are still unable to talk themselves. • Form stable and affectionate relationships with infants—their brains are as busy forming emotional circuits as they are learning to perceive objects, physical events, and properties of language.
Childhood	*During childhood, the brain strengthens neurological bundles that are used regularly and allows under-utilized ones to shrivel:* • Synaptic pruning occurs at different rates in different areas of the brain. Overall, though, brains actively prune synapses during childhood. • The front part of the cortex (closest to the forehead), used for learning new information, controlling behavior, and planning ahead, shows synaptic pruning throughout childhood and into adulthood. • Myelination continues to protect neurons and speed transmission of signals. • The brain continues to specialize, with the two halves (hemispheres) becoming more distinctly responsible for separate abilities rather than duplicating functions. • Although synapses are pruned during childhood, adolescence, and adulthood, the brain also forms new synapses throughout this extended period. These new synapses may reflect learning through experience.	• Encourage children to learn more than one language—most children can easily learn a second language (or more). • Take advantage of children's growing awareness of patterns in their environment. For example, ask children to think about the nature and origin of the seasons, tidal movements, holidays, and immigration patterns. • In informal contexts, expose children to advanced cultural and aesthetic systems, such as music, poetry, and geometric patterns; exposure to these systems may sensitize them to ways of thinking they can use in the future.
Adolescence	*During adolescence, the brain forms new emotional connections, makes thinking about the future easier, and makes rational judgment more likely:* • Synapses continue to decline in density through synaptic pruning. New synapses can be formed, though, when adolescents learn. • Myelination continues to protect neurons and speed transmission of signals, especially in the front region of the cortex (near the forehead), where planning and other complex cognitive processes occur. • The two sides (hemispheres) of the brain continue to become specialized for particular purposes. • Having begun in childhood, synaptic pruning in the front part of the cortex continues, making possible improvements in memory and attention. • The cortex matures between childhood and adolescence, helping adolescents to integrate information from different sensory systems and engage in planning, decision making, and higher-order thinking. • Fiber pathways that support motor and speech functions continue to mature during late childhood and adolescence. • Fibers connecting language centers of the cortex slow down in growth rate during adolescence. • The brain undergoes a shift in how it analyzes emotional expressions—adolescents become increasingly able to analyze emotions at higher levels of the brain rather than automatically responding from lower and more primitive centers of the brain.	• Recognize the positive features of adolescents' newfound passions, such as creative artwork, interests in politics, fascination with sports. • Help adolescents to think about the consequences of their actions for the future. • Encourage adolescents to use their developing ability to think abstractly. For example, adolescents can imagine irrational numbers in mathematics classes, hold variables constant in science, contemplate the complex motivations of characters in literature, and envision multiple causes of political conflict in history classes. • Provide opportunities for adolescents to participate in physical activity and, when they show an interest, to seek advanced training. • Encourage adolescents to attend to the emotional expressions, experiences, and plights of other people.

Sources. Carlson, 1999; Casey, Giedd, & Thomas, 2000; Cowan, 1979; Diamond & Hopson, 1998; Huttenlocher, 1979, 1990; Huttenlocher & de Courten, 1987; M. H. Johnson, 1998; Killgore, Oki, & Yurgelun-Todd, 2001; National Research Council, 1999; Paus et al., 1999; Rakic, 1995; Sowell, Delis, Stiles, & Jernigan, 2001; Sowell et al., 2002; Sowell, Thompson, Tessner, & Toga, 2001; Thompson et al., 2000; Yakovlev & Lecours, 1967.

Applications of Research on Brain Development

We sometimes hear colleagues talk about the implications of brain research for work with children in classrooms and other settings. In fact, research in brain development is still in its infancy (Bruer, 1997; Mayer, 1998; O'Boyle & Gill, 1998). Thus, it makes sense to derive practical applications from neurological evidence that is backed up with psychological research on children's learning. In the previous section, we cautiously made such recommendations for each of the developmental periods. Here are some additional recommendations pertaining to two or more age periods:

■ *Educate prospective parents about the harmful effects of alcohol and drugs on their developing fetuses.* Adolescent girls and women who are pregnant may not understand how brain development in their fetuses could be disrupted with harmful substances. Professionals who work with prospective parents have a responsibility to point out how even small amounts of alcohol, marijuana, and drugs can cause harm to fetuses.

■ *Be optimistic that high-quality experiences can have an impact throughout childhood and adolescence.* The brain is less strongly influenced by sensitive periods than many people have assumed. This misconception has arisen because some kinds of stimulation *are* required for some functions. For instance, cats, monkeys, and people who have reduced or abnormal visual stimulation when they are quite young have lifelong difficulties with visual perception, apparently as a result of irreversible neurological change (Bruer, 1999). On the other hand, everyday experience provides sufficient stimulation for normal development in these visual areas of the brain. Clearly, an intensive and "enriched" environment is not required (Bruer, 1999; Greenough, Black, & Wallace, 1987). Furthermore, there is no evidence that sensitive periods exist for areas of the brain that support learning and performance in reading, mathematics, music, or other culture-specific intellectual pursuits (Bruer, 1999; Greenough et al., 1987). Even in adulthood, the brain adapts to changing circumstances (Mühlnickel, Elbert, Taub, & Flor, 1998; C. A. Nelson, 1999; Ramachandran, Rogers-Ramachandran, & Stewart, 1992; Sowell et al., 1999). We know from countless studies, as well as from our own everyday observations, that human beings continue to learn new information and skills quite successfully throughout the lifespan.

Professionals who work with youngsters can therefore reasonably assume that the brain remains plastic and adaptable throughout childhood and adolescence, and that educational experiences and constructive social relationships at any age can have an important impact. Early years are learning years, but so are later ones.

Neurological development in childhood and adolescence supports more sophisticated executive functions, such as setting goals and planning future actions. Guidance from practitioners can help youngsters use these functions effectively.

■ *Give children many opportunities to learn spontaneously.* In their everyday experiences, children learn a great deal on an informal basis about the physical world, social relationships, language, and practices of their culture. They don't necessarily have to be taught everything they need to learn, although they do need to be exposed to it. In many cases, opportunities for play and informal experimentation are just as beneficial as, and sometimes even more beneficial than, planned and systematic instruction (R. D. Brown & Bjorklund, 1998; Bruer, 1999; Chafel, 1991).

In fact, because some neurological changes do not take place until middle childhood and later, youngsters may not even be able to benefit from certain kinds of educational experiences until middle childhood at the earliest. Sustaining attention on a single topic and inhibiting inappropriate actions are capacities that improve with experience but also depend on brain development. Accordingly, some expectations may be quite reasonable for older children yet unreasonable for younger ones. (In Chapters 4 and 5, we will look more closely at cognitive abilities and limitations of youngsters of various ages and at the practical implications.)

■ *Accommodate individual differences in neurological functioning.* Individualizing care is especially important for children who have a neurological exceptionality. For example, children who have difficulty distinguishing among the various sounds of speech may have brains with circuits that are not fully formed to permit this activity. Intensive training in speech processing seems to benefit these children, presumably because of its effects on brain pathways (C. A. Nelson, 1999). Special educators, school psychologists, and other specialists can often provide suggestions about effective strategies for working with children who have various neurological deficits.

■ *Provide extra guidance and support for children who have had early exposure to drugs and alcohol.* Children who were exposed to alcohol, cocaine, and other drugs during pre-natal development often have unique needs. These youngsters may need extra assistance in understanding abstract ideas, inhibiting inappropriate responses (such as impulsively hitting bothersome classmates), and applying rules to multiple settings (e.g., "keep your hands to yourself" applies to the lunchroom and playground as well as to the classroom) (Lutke, 1997). Furthermore, if children's mothers have abused alcohol or drugs during preg-nancy, there is a high probability that they are continuing to do so (O'Connor, Sigman, & Kasari, 1993). Substance-abusing parents tend to have dysfunctional relationships with their children, physically abuse and neglect them, and use harsh and ineffective disciplinary strate-gies (Mayes & Bornstein, 1997). Teachers, other school personnel, counselors, community volunteers, recreation leaders, after-school providers, or social workers may be among the few dependable sources of affection and structure that these children have.

Ultimately, adults must remember that, with proper guidance and instruction, many children of alcohol- and drug-abusing parents can lead productive and fulfilling lives. One 17-year-old girl with fetal alcohol syndrome expressed this idea eloquently:

> There are two things I want you to know: Do not call me a victim, and do not tell me what I cannot do. Help me to find a way to do it. (Lutke, 1997, p. 188)

■ *Encourage children and adolescents to think about the consequences of their actions.* To take full advantage of emerging abilities to temper impulses, young people need to practice these skills. Long-term planning and self-control do not ap-pear on the scene—or in the brain—fully formed. Therefore, you can encour-age young people to plan in a range of areas—keeping track of assignments at school, planning to meet graduation requirements, determining steps they need to land certain jobs, and deciding the optimal time to raise a family.

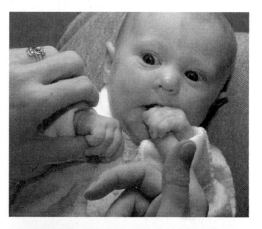

Physical Development Across Childhood

As you have seen, changes take place in size, bodily proportions, and neuro-logical structures throughout childhood and adolescence. With these changes come new opportunities to practice motor skills, take care of one's own health, engage in physical activity, and relate to peers in unprecedented ways. We list key characteristics of each age group in the Developmental Trends table "Phys-ical Development at Different Age Levels," and we describe developmental pe-riods in more detail in the next few pages.

Babies are born with an arsenal of reflexes that enhance their chances of survival. In the upper photo, a baby grasps an adult's fingers; in the lower photo, a newborn baby nurses.

Infancy (Birth–Age 2)

Infancy is an impressive period of rapid growth and development. However, even at birth, infants display remarkable **reflexes**—inherited, automatic re-sponses to certain kinds of stimulation—that enhance their chances of survival. Before the umbilical cord is cut, the first reflex, *breathing,* begins, providing oxy-gen and removing carbon dioxide (Gundy, 1981). Another permanent reflex is *eyeblinking,* rapid closing of eyes to bright lights and other unpleasant stimuli.

Some other reflexes are temporary. The *grasping* reflex is revealed when you place your finger in the baby's palm—his or her fingers close tightly around it. Infants show the *moro,* or *startle,* reflex in response to a loud, alarming noise or vibration. Their eyes open wide, arms and legs flare out with fingers and toes spread widely, and limbs move quickly inward, toward the torso, as if to catch mother and hold on for dear life. Perhaps in our human an-cestors' evolutionary history, infants needed to cling to mothers to survive (Peiper, 1963). In the *rooting* reflex, infants turn their head toward an object (perhaps bottle, breast, or hand) that stimulates their cheek. If you place a finger or nipple in their mouth, infants display an-other reflex, *sucking* (later replaced by voluntary sucking). Rooting and sucking prepare in-fants to obtain life-sustaining milk. In the *swimming* reflex, infants fan out their arms and legs when placed face down, as if paddling in water. The *babinski* reflex, whose survival purpose

reflex
An automatic response to a par-ticular kind of stimulation.

DEVELOPMENTAL TRENDS

Physical Development at Different Age Levels

AGE	WHAT YOU MIGHT OBSERVE	DIVERSITY	IMPLICATIONS
Infancy (Birth–2) 	• Rapid growth and change in proportions • Emergence of reflexes • General decline in crying • Increasing ability to move around, first by squirming, then rolling, crawling, creeping, or scooting; finally by walking • Increasing ability to coordinate small muscles of hands and eyes • Increasing self-help skills such as feeding, dressing, washing, toileting, and grooming	• Children vary in timing and quality of gross motor skills (e.g., rolling over, crawling, and sitting up) depending on genetic and cultural factors. • Children vary in timing of mobility as well as in methods they use to get around (some children never crawl or creep) • Fine motor skills and eye-hand coordination may come in earlier or later depending on genetic make-up and encouragement from caregivers. • Self-help skills come in earlier when encouraged, though virtually all children learn them eventually, and sooner is not necessarily better.	• Celebrate each child's unique growth patterns, while keeping an eye on unusual patterns and disabilities that require accommodation. • Provide a choice of appropriate indoor and outdoor experiences to help children practice their developing fine and gross motor skills. • Don't push infants to reach milestones. Allow children to experience each phase of physical development thoroughly. • Be aware of serious developmental delays that call for professional intervention.
Early Childhood (2–6) 	• Loss of rounded, babyish appearance, with arms and legs lengthening and taking on more mature proportions • Boundless physical energy for new gross motor skills, such as running, hopping, tumbling, climbing, and swinging • Acquisition of fine motor skills, such as functional pencil grip and use of scissors • Transition away from afternoon nap, which may initially be marked by periods of fussiness in the afternoon	• Children differ considerably in the ages at which they master various motor skills. • Boys are more physically active than girls, but girls are healthier overall; these differences will continue throughout childhood and adolescence. • Some home environments (e.g., small apartments and larger houses when parents restrict movement) limit the degree to which children can engage in vigorous physical activity; others may present hazardous environmental conditions (e.g., lead paint, toxic fumes). • Children with mental retardation have delayed motor skills.	• Provide frequent opportunities to play outside or (in inclement weather) in a gymnasium or other large indoor space. • Intersperse vigorous physical exercise with rest and quiet time. • Encourage fine motor skills through puzzles, blocks, doll houses, and arts and crafts. • Choose activities that accommodate diversity in gross and fine motor skills.
Middle Childhood (6–10)	• Steady gains in height and weight • Loss and replacement of primary teeth • Refinement and consolidation of gross motor skills, and integration of such skills into structured play activities • Participation in organized sports • Increasing fluency in fine motor skills, such as handwriting and drawing	• Variations in weight and height are prominent at any single grade level. • Children begin to show specific athletic talents and interests. • Gender differences appear in children's preferences for various sports and physical activities. • Some neighborhoods do not have playgrounds or other safe play areas that foster gross motor skills. • Some children have delays in fine motor skills (e.g., their handwriting may be unusually uneven and irregular) as a result of neurological conditions or lack of opportunity to practice fine motor tasks. • Some children spend much of their non-school time in sedentary activities, such as watching television or playing video games.	• Integrate physical movement into academic activities. • Provide daily opportunities for children to engage in self-organized play activities. • Teach children the basics of various sports and physical games, and encourage them to participate in organized sports programs. • Encourage practice of fine motor skills, but don't penalize children whose fine-motor precision is delayed.

DEVELOPMENTAL TRENDS

Physical Development at Different Age Levels *(continued)*

AGE	WHAT YOU MIGHT OBSERVE	DIVERSITY	IMPLICATIONS
Early Adolescence (10–14) 	• Periods of rapid growth • Beginnings of puberty • Self-consciousness about resulting physical changes • Some risk-taking behavior	• Onset of puberty may vary over a span of several years; puberty occurs earlier for girls than for boys. • Leisure activities may or may not include regular exercise. • Young teens differ considerably in strength and physical endurance, as well as in their specific talents for sports. Noticeable gender differences begin to appear, with boys being faster, stronger, and more confident about their physical abilities than girls. • Peer groups may or may not encourage risky behavior.	• Be a role model in terms of physical fitness and good eating habits. • Provide privacy for changing clothes and showering during physical education classes. • Explain what sexual harassment is, and do not tolerate it, whether it appears in the form of jokes, teasing, or physical contact. • Encourage after-school clubs and sponsored leisure activities that help teenagers spend their time constructively.
Late Adolescence (14–18) 	• In girls, completion of growth spurt and attainment of mature height. • In boys, ongoing increases in stature. • Ravenous appetites • Increasing sexual activity • Greater risk-taking behavior (e.g., drinking alcohol, taking illegal drugs, engaging in unprotected sexual contact, driving under the influence of drugs or alcohol), due in part to greater independence and acquisition of drivers' licenses	• Gender differences in physical abilities increase; boys are more active in organized sports programs. • Boys more actively seek sexual intimacy than girls do. • Some teens struggle with issues related to sexual orientation. • Some teens begin to rebound from earlier risky behaviors and make better decisions. • Eating disorders may appear, especially in girls. • Adolescents are less likely than younger children to get regular medical care.	• Make sure that adolescents know "the facts of life" about sexual intercourse and conception. • Encourage young people to form goals for the future (e.g., going to college, developing athletic skills) as a way of helping them curb risky behaviors. • Develop policies related to sexual harassment.

Sources: Black, Hutcheson, Dubowitz, & Berenson-Howard, 1994; Bredekamp & Copple, 1997; Dennis, 1960; Eaton & Enns, 1986; Edwards, Gandini, & Giovaninni, 1996; Eisenberg, Martin, & Fabes, 1996; Gallahue & Ozmun, 1998; Gerber, 1998; Hopkins & Westra, 1998; Jacklin, 1989; Linn & Hyde, 1989; Logsdon, Alleman, Straits, Belka, & Clark, 1997; National Research Council, 1993a; Pellgrini & Smith, 1998; M. P. Sadker & Sadker, 1994; Sheridan, 1975; Simons-Morton, Taylor, Snider, Huang, & Fulton, 1994; Tanner, 1990; J. R. Thomas & French, 1985; Wigfield, Eccles, & Pintrich, 1996.

is not yet clear, is activated when you run your fingers on the bottom of an infant's foot—the toes fan out and then curl. All of these reflexes are reflections of normal neurological development, and their absence is a matter of concern to physicians (Touwen, 1974).

As they grow older, infants add motor skills to their physiological repertoire. Motor skills at first appear slowly, then more rapidly. In the first 12 to 18 months, infants learn to hold up their head, roll over, reach for objects, sit, crawl, and walk. In the second year, they walk with increasing balance and coordination, manipulate small objects, and begin to run, jump, and climb. In the Cognitive Development/Infancy clip of the Observation CD, you can observe 16-month-old Corwin walking confidently and competently. Corwin holds his arms high to maintain balance, but he is also agile enough to walk quickly as well as stay upright while reaching down into a bag.

Observe 16-month-old Corwin showing good balance while walking in the Cognitive Development/ Infancy clip.

Motor skills emerge in a particular order, following **cephalocaudal** and **proximodistal** trends (Robbins, Brody, Hogan, Jackson, & Green, 1928). The cephalocaudal pattern refers to the vertical growth of skills, which proceeds from the head downward. This pattern is clear in infants, who learn first to control their heads, then shoulders and trunk, and later their legs. The proximodistal pattern refers to the inside-outside pattern in which growth progresses outward from the spine. Infants, for example, first learn to control their arms, then their hands, and finally, their fingers.

Crying allows infants to express discomfort and seek relief. The time infants spend crying tends to decrease by the fourth or fifth month (St. James-Roberts & Halil, 1991). Parents and

cephalocaudal trend
Vertical ordering of motor skills and physical development; order is head first to feet last.

proximodistal trend
Inside-outside ordering of motor skills and physical development; order is inside first and outside last.

Infant/Toddler Needs and Services Plan

Date: _____

Child's Name: _____ Birth Date/Age of Child _____ _____

Parent(s) Name: _____

Primary Caregiver: _____

Homebase: _____

Sleeping Routine

Pre-nap routines/rituals: _____
_____

How many naps per day (typical):   a.m. _____ to _____ p.m. _____ to _____

Length of nap: _____

What position does your child prefer: _____

Waking behavior/routine: _____

Special concerns: _____

Eating Routine

Solid Food: _____ Time of day you want given: _____

Special meals to be served in homebase: _____

Allergies: _____

Food dislikes or eating problems: _____

Food likes and eating preferences: _____

Special diet/requests: _____

Special concerns: _____

Bottle/Cup Routine

Circle: Bottle   Cup

Formula: Brand _____   Amount _____

                                              Time of day you want given _____

Juice: Type _____   Amount _____

                                              Time of day you want given _____

Milk: _____   Amount _____

                                              Time of day you want given _____

Breast Milk: _____   Amount _____

                                              Time of day you want given _____

Introducing Solid Foods

We recommend introducing infant cereal at 4–6 months, vegetables, fruits, and their juices at 5–7 months, protein such as cheese, yogurt, cooked beans, meat, fish, chicken, and egg yolk at 6–8 months, whole egg at 10–12 months, and milk at 12 months. We also can introduce the use of a cup and spoon at 8–10 months.

If you do not wish to follow our recommendations, please sign:

_____

Comforting/Distress

Does you child have a security object?   Name? _____

Does your child use a pacifier?   When? _____

Other information? _____

Diapering Routine

Please circle which type of diaper to use: Disposable   Cloth

If the child needs lotion or ointment, please specify which brand: _____

Does you child have any services that are different from those provided by the center's routine program? i.e., special exercises, special materials, accommodation of special services.

_____

_____

_____

Other Information

_____

_____

_____

The Needs and Services Plan will be updated every three months or sooner if requested by parent/guardian.

Parent Signature _____ Date _____

Staff Signature _____ Date _____

Date of change _____ Parent Initials _____ Staff Initials _____

Date of change _____ Parent Initials _____ Staff Initials _____

Date of change _____ Parent Initials _____ Staff Initials _____

FIGURE 3–11 Service plan for infants and toddlers

Adapted by permission. Roots and Wings. © 1991 Stacy York. Redleaf Press. St. Paul, Minnesota. www.redleafpress.org

other caregivers are physiologically primed to respond to cries, especially intense cries indicating extreme pain (R. M. Wood & Gustafson, 2001). Sensitive caregivers learn to identify urgency in infants' crying and to use information about infants' habits, daytime schedules, and time elapsed since last feeding to determine when—and how quickly—to respond. (You will read more about crying as an emotional response in Chapter 9.)

When infants are difficult to soothe, caregivers may become aggravated. Adults can become especially frustrated when infants show **colic**—persistent crying prevalent during the first three months of life (Hide & Guyer, 1982). In a study of 843 infants, 14.2% of the infants showed colic during the first 6 weeks of life; 8.9% showed colic during the next 7–12 weeks, 2.4% showed colic at 13–26 weeks; and prevalence declined thereafter (Hide & Guyer, 1982). The causes of colic are uncertain, but may include abdominal distress and disturbances in the brain's regulation of cycles of sleeping and waking (American Academy of Pediatrics Committee on Nutrition, 1998; Papousek & Papousek, 1996). Rates do not differ between breast- and bottle-fed babies, but rates are somewhat higher if cereals and other solid foods are introduced during the first three months (Hide & Guyer, 1982). There also seem to be occasions when intolerance of cow's milk perpetuates colic (Hide & Guyer, 1982).

colic
Persistent crying by infants; it is most prevalent in the first three months of life.

OBSERVATION GUIDELINES

Assessing Physical Development During Infancy

CHARACTERISTIC	LOOK FOR	EXAMPLE	IMPLICATION
Eating Habits	• Ability to express hungry feelings to adults • Developing ability to suck, chew, and swallow • Ability to enjoy and digest food without abdominal upset • Cultural and individual differences in how families feed infants	Wendy Sue is a listless eater who doesn't seem as interested in food as other infants in the child care program. The caregiver tells the director she is worried and the two decide to talk with the parents. It is possible that professional intervention might be needed.	To understand an infant's health, talk with parents and families. Find out what they believe about appropriate care of infants.
Mobility	• Use of hands and fingers to explore objects • Developing ability to coordinate looking and feeling • Growing ability to move toward objects • Temperamental factors that might affect exploration • Physical challenges that might affect exploration, including hearing and visual impairments • Temporary declines in exploration, such as when separating from parents	Daniel is a new child to the child care center. Due to neurological damage at birth, his left arm and leg are less strong than those on his right side. He scans the child care room visually, but does not move around. During a home visit, the teacher finds that he crawls with energy and enthusiasm, touching every object in his path. His movements are lopsided and he favors his right arm, but he is not stifled in his exploration. The teacher realizes that Daniel needs to feel secure in the program before he can explore freely.	Set up the environment so infants will find it safe, predictable, attractive, and interesting. Help individual children to find challenge and opportunities that meet their abilities.
Resting Patterns	• Methods babies use to put themselves to sleep • Families' expectations for sleeping arrangements • Difficulties in falling asleep • Evidence that families understand risk factors for Sudden Infant Death Syndrome (SIDS)	Angy cries a lot when falling asleep, in part because she is used to sleeping on her stomach, a practice not followed at her child care center because it is a risk factor for SIDS. Her teacher explains to Angy's parents why she needs to place Angy on her back; she gives Angy special attention, rubbing her head, as she adjusts to the new sleeping position.	Talk to parents about risk factors for SIDS. Explain why you place babies on their backs when they are falling asleep.
Health Issues	• Possible symptoms of temporary infections, such as unusual behavior, irritability, respiratory difficulty, changes in stool or urine, reduced appetite, fever or vomiting • Suspicious injuries and unusual behaviors that may indicate abuse • Possible symptoms of prenatal drug exposure, including difficulty sleeping, extreme sensitivity, and irritability • Physical disabilities requiring accommodation	The child care teacher enjoys having Michael, age 18 months, in her care. Michael has cerebral palsy, making it difficult for him to scoot around. His teacher encourages him to move toward objects, but also brings things to him to examine and play with. When he has a fever, she calls his mother or father, as she would with any child.	Remain alert to signs of illness and infection in children. Contact family members when infants have a fever or show other unusual physical symptoms.

Because infants cannot use words to communicate physical needs, practitioners must seek information from families about infants' sleeping, eating, drinking, diapering, and comforting preferences and habits (Greenman & Stonehouse, 1996). In Figure 3–11, you can see a service plan that can be completed by a family member and submitted to a caregiver.

Of course, the most detailed plan will not always be sufficient to meet infants' changing needs throughout the day. Thus, caregivers must also attend to the signals that infants give regarding their comfort and distress. We offer ideas of what to look for in the Observation Guidelines table "Assessing Physical Development During Infancy."

Early Childhood (Ages 2–6)

When you visit a local playground, you are likely to see preschool children engaged in non-stop physical activity. Physical movement is a hallmark of early childhood, and dramatic changes occur in both gross motor skills and fine motor skills. **Gross motor skills** (e.g., running, hopping, tumbling, climbing, and swinging) permit locomotion around the environment. **Fine motor skills** (e.g., drawing, writing, cutting with scissors, and manipulating small objects) involve more limited, controlled, and precise movements, primarily with the hands.

gross motor skills
Large movements of the body that permit locomotion around the environment.

fine motor skills
Small, precise movements of particular parts of the body, especially the hands

Observe two 4-year-old children, Acadia and Cody, playing actively and spontaneously at the park in the Physical Activity/Early Childhood clip.

FIGURE 3–12 Given access to paper and crayons or markers, most children begin scribbling when they are 18 to 24 months of age. This drawing by Tina, age 2½, shows early practice in making circular shapes.

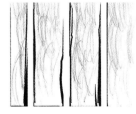

FIGURE 3–13 Isabelle, age 3½, showed great interest in practicing her drawing, writing, and cutting in preschool. In the left artwork, she traced shapes and wrote her name. She made a good attempt at the letters, but missed the sequence of the final four letters. Notice, though, that she was aware that her name has two *E*'s and two *L*'s, sensibly grouping letter pairs. In the artwork at right, she practiced cutting, attempting to follow the black lines. She corrected her work in the third rectangle from the left; she initially cut in too far and then started over on the black line, showing that she tried to meet a standard of straightness.

During the preschool years, children typically learn such culture-specific motor skills as riding a tricycle and throwing and catching a ball. Over time, these skills become smoother and better coordinated as a result of practice, longer arms and legs, and genetically guided increases in muscular control. Optimism and persistence in motor tasks play a role as well. For instance, when Teresa's son Alex was 4, he repeatedly asked his parents to throw him a baseball as he stood poised with his bat. Not at all deterred by an abysmal batting average (about .05), Alex would frequently exclaim, "I almost got it!" His efforts paid off, as he gradually did learn to track the ball visually and coordinate his swing with the ball's path.

A lot of chatter, fantasy, and sheer joy accompany gross motor activity in early childhood. You can observe such creative interactions between two 4-year-old children, Acadia and Cody, playing on climbing equipment in the Physical Activity/Early Childhood clip of the Observation CD. The two children practice a variety of gross-motor skills (running, climbing, throwing the ball), all in the name of play.

Often, young children infuse pretend roles into their physical play. For example, they may become superheroes and villains, cowboys and cowgirls, astronauts and aliens. During *chase play,* a young child may run after another child, pretending to be a lion or other predator (S. A. Owens, Steen, Hargrave, Flores, & Hall, 2000; Steen & Owens, 2000). Both the child doing the chasing and the one being chased work hard to keep the game going. The child wishing to be chased may yell "Chase me!," make a taunting face, and then sprint to avoid capture. The chaser joins in the game and often slows down rather than capture the other, thereby prolonging the fun. The eventual capture occurs in a friendly, if dramatic, manner, with the "victim" often squealing in excitement.

Young children also make strides in fine motor skills. For example, many begin to scribble with a pencil or crayon when they are 18 to 24 months in age (see Figure 3–12 for shapes by Tina, aged 2½ years). Many children can draw circles and squares when they are about 3. Some children spend considerable time drawing and cutting as early as 3½ or 4. Isabelle, aged 3½, regularly practiced her cutting and drawing; the fruits of her labor are shown in Figure 3–13. By age 4 or 5, children can draw rudimentary pictures, perhaps of a "person" consisting of a circle for a head, two smaller circles and a curvy line for eyes and a mouth, and four lines sprouting from the circle to represent arms and legs (J. J. Beaty, 1998; R. Kellogg, 1967; McLane & McNamee, 1990). In writing activities, children create wavy lines or connected loops ("pseudowriting" resembling adult cursive) at about 4, and given sufficient experience with written language, they can often write some letters of the alphabet by age 5 (Graham & Weintraub, 1996).

Children's fine motor skills improve gradually with experience, practice, and normal neurological development. Some progressions involve cognitive as well as physical development; for instance, children become more competent at drawing as they are increasingly able to identify basic shapes and contours in the people and objects they want to represent on paper (N. R. Smith, Cicchetti, Clark, Fucigna, Gordon-O'Connor, Halley, & Kennedy, 1998).

We often find large individual differences in young children's fine motor skills. Some children, such as those born with certain chromosomal conditions (e.g., Down syndrome) and those exposed to alcohol during prenatal development, tend to progress more slowly than age-mates (H. M. Barr, Streissguth, Darby, & Sampson, 1990; Bruni, 1998; Goyen, Lui, & Woods, 1998). Furthermore, some evidence indicates that some fine motor activities (e.g., cursive handwriting) may be easier for girls than boys (M. R. Cohen, 1997). Fortunately, explicit instruction and practice can help children improve fine motor skills, although some differences in dexterity inevitably persist (Bruni, 1998; Case-Smith, 1996).

Middle Childhood (Ages 6–10)

Over middle childhood, youngsters typically show slow but steady gains in height and weight. Body proportions change less than in infancy or early childhood. With these slow, continuous gains come a few losses. Consider the gap-toothed smiles so common in children's elementary school pictures. One by one, children lose their 20 primary ("baby") teeth, replacing them with permanent teeth that at first appear oversized in the small mouths of 6-, 7-, and 8-year-olds. Girls mature somewhat more quickly than do boys, erupting permanent teeth sooner and progressing toward skeletal maturity earlier.

In middle childhood, children build on their emerging physical capabilities. Many gross motor skills, once awkward, are now executed systematically. Whereas preschoolers may run for the sheer joy of it, elementary school children put running to use in organized games and sports. They intensify their speed and coordination in running, kicking, catching, and dribbling. Becoming proficient in athletic skills can be gratifying for children. As you will see in Figure 3–14, 6-year-old Alex chose five athletic movements when asked by his teacher to identify five things that he liked to do. You can also observe the pleasure that 9-year-old Kyle and 10-year-old Curtis experience as they practice basketball skills in the Physical Activity/Middle Childhood clip of the Observation CD.

Stopping frequently to negotiate over rules, children accompany physical exercise with important social lessons ("Whose turn is it?" and "The ball was outside the white line. I saw it!"). Although gender differences in gross motor skills are fairly small at this age, boys begin to outperform girls on some athletic tasks, such as speed in walking long distances (National Children and Youth Fitness Study II, 1987).

Within this age range, children also improve in fine motor skills. Their drawings, fueled by physiological maturation and cognitive advances, are more detailed and complex (Case, Okamoto, et al., 1996; N. R. Smith et al., 1998). Their handwriting becomes smaller, smoother, and more consistent (Graham & Weintraub, 1996). They also begin to tackle such fine-motor activities as sewing, model building, and arts and crafts projects.

As children progress through middle childhood, they become increasingly aware of and sensitive about their physical appearance. Consider this fourth grader's self-critical viewpoint:

> I am the ugliest girl I know. My hair is not straight enough, and it doesn't even have the dignity to be curly. My teeth are crooked from sucking my thumb and from a wet-bathing-suit-and-a-slide accident. My clothes are hand-me-downs, my skin is a greenish color that other people call "tan" to be polite, and I don't say the right words, or say them in the right way. I'm smart enough to notice that I'm not smart enough; not so short, but not tall enough; and definitely, definitely too skinny. (Marissa Arillo, in Oldfather & West, 1999, p. 60)

Physical appearance is a major force in social interactions throughout childhood and adolescence. People respond more favorably to children that they perceive to be physically attractive, and differential treatment leads to variations in how children feel about themselves. In a variety of cultures, physical attractiveness is correlated with, and probably a causal factor in, self-esteem (Chu, 2000; Harter, 1999).

In the Development and Practice feature "Accommodating the Physical Needs of Infants and Children," we give examples of strategies for meeting individual and group needs for physical care, creating a hazard-free environment, and integrating physical activity into the curriculum.

Early Adolescence (Ages 10–14)

The most obvious aspect of physical change in early adolescence is the onset of **puberty**. Ushered in by a cascade of hormones, puberty involves a series of biological changes that lead to reproductive maturity. It is marked not only by the maturation of sex-specific characteristics but also by a **growth spurt**, a rapid increase in height and weight. The hormonal increases of adolescence have other physiological repercussions as well, such as increased oil production in the face (often manifested as acne), increased activity in the sweat glands, mood swings, and emotional sensitivity (Buchanan, 1991).

Just as girls mature more quickly than boys in middle childhood, so, too, they reach puberty earlier. Puberty begins in girls sometime between ages 8 and 13 (on average, at age 10).

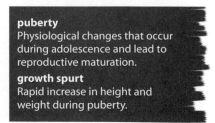

FIGURE 3–14 When asked to choose five things he liked to do, 6-year-old Alex chose five athletic activities: kicking, running, swimming, skating, and boating.

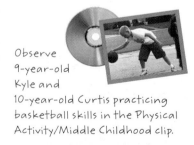

Observe 9-year-old Kyle and 10-year-old Curtis practicing basketball skills in the Physical Activity/Middle Childhood clip.

puberty
Physiological changes that occur during adolescence and lead to reproductive maturation.

growth spurt
Rapid increase in height and weight during puberty.

■ Meet the physical needs of individual infants rather than expecting all to conform to a universal and inflexible schedule.

A caregiver in an infant program keeps a schedule of times infants receive their bottles and nap. That way, she can plan her day to rotate among individual infants, giving each as much attention as is possible.

■ View meeting the physical needs of infants as part of the overall curriculum for their care and education.

An infant-toddler caregiver understands the importance of meeting physical needs in ways that establish and deepen relationships with each child. She uses one-to-one activities such as diaper changing and bottle feeding as occasions to interact.

■ Make sure that the classroom is free of sharp edges, peeling paint, and other environmental hazards to which young children may be particularly vulnerable.

After new carpet is installed in his classroom, a preschool teacher notices that several children complain of stomachaches and headaches. He suspects that the recently applied carpet adhesive may be to blame and, with the approval of the preschool's director, asks an outside consultant to evaluate the situation. Meanwhile, he conducts most of the day's activities outdoors or in other rooms.

■ Provide frequent opportunities for children to engage in physical activity.

A preschool teacher schedules "Music and Marching" for mid-morning, "Outdoor Time" before lunch, and a nature walk to collect leaves for an art project after naptime.

■ Plan activities that will help children develop their fine motor skills.

An after-school caregiver invites children to make mosaics that depict different kinds of vehicles. The children glue a variety of small objects (e.g., beads, sequins, beans, colored rice) onto line drawings of cars, trains, boats, airplanes, bicycles, and so on.

■ Design physical activities so that students with widely differing skill levels can successfully participate.

During a unit on tennis, a physical education teacher has children practice the forehand stroke using tennis rackets. First she asks them to practice bouncing and then hitting the ball against the wall of the gymnasium. If some students master these basic skills, she asks them to see how many times in succession they can hit the ball against the wall. When they reach 5 successive hits, she tells them to vary the height of the ball from waist high to shoulder high (Logsdon, Alleman, Straits, Belka, & Clark, 1997).

■ Integrate physical activity into academic lessons.

When teaching about molecules and temperature, a fifth-grade teacher asks children to stand in a cluster in an open area of the classroom. To show children how molecules behave when something is cold, she asks them to stay close together and move around just a little bit. To show them how molecules behave when something is hot, she asks them to spread farther apart and move more actively.

■ Give children time to rest.

After a kindergarten class has been playing outside, their teacher offers a snack of apple slices, crackers, and milk. Once they have cleaned up their milk cartons and napkins, the children gather around him on the floor while he reads them a story.

■ Respect children's growing ability to care for their own bodies.

In an after-school program, a teacher allows the children to go to the restroom whenever they need to. He teaches children to hang a clothespin with their name on an "out rope" when they leave the room and then remove the pin when they return.

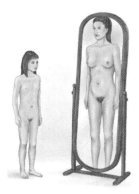

IN GIRLS
Initial elevation of breasts and beginning of growth spurt (typically between 8 and 13 years; on average, at 10 years)
Appearance of pubic hair (sometimes occurs before elevation of breasts)
Increase in size and structure of uterus, vagina, labia, and clitoris
Further development of breasts
Peak of growth spurt
Menarche, or onset of menstrual cycle (typically between 9 and 15 years)
Completion of height gain (about two years after menarche) and attainment of adult height
Completion of breast development and pubic hair growth

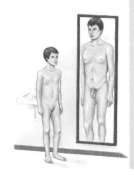

IN BOYS
Enlargement of the testes and changes in texture and color of scrotum (typically between 9 and 14 years; on average, at $11^1/2$ years)
Increase in penis size and appearance of pubic hair
Beginning of growth spurt (on average, at $12^1/2$ years)
Spermarche, or first ejaculation
Peak of growth spurt, accompanied by more rapid penis growth
Appearance of facial hair
Deepening voice, as size of larynx and length of vocal cords increase
Completion of penis growth
Completion of height gain and attainment of adult height
Completion of pubic hair growth

FIGURE 3–15 Maturational sequences of puberty

© Zits Partnership. Reprinted with special permission of King Features Syndicate.

During the adolescent growth spurt, appetites increase considerably.

It starts with a growth spurt, "budding" of the breasts, and the emergence of pubic hair. Whereas such changes are typically gradual, the onset of menstruation, **menarche**, is an abrupt event that can be either positive or frightening, depending on a girl's awareness and preparation. The first menstrual period tends to occur rather late in puberty, usually between 9 and 15 years of age. Nature apparently delays menstruation, and with it the possibility of conception, until girls are physically strong and close to their adult height and therefore are physiologically better able to have a successful pregnancy.

For boys, puberty gets its start between 9 and 14 years (on average, at 11½ years), when the testes enlarge and the scrotum changes in texture and color. A year or so later, the penis grows larger and pubic hair appears; the growth spurt begins soon after. At about 13 to 14 years, boys have their first ejaculation experience, **spermarche**, often while sleeping. Boys seem to receive less information from parents about this milestone than girls do about menstruation, and little is known about their feelings about it. Later developments include growth of facial hair, deepening of the voice, and eventually the attainment of adult height. (The course of puberty for both boys and girls is depicted in Figure 3–15.)

Notice that for girls the growth spurt is one of the first signs of puberty, but for boys it occurs relatively late in the sequence. The result of this discrepancy is that boys end up taller: They have a longer period of steady prepubescent growth. Also, they grow a bit more than girls do during their adolescent growth spurt. With the onset of puberty, boys also gain considerably more muscle mass than girls, courtesy of the male hormone *testosterone* (J. R. Thomas & French, 1985).

Accompanying the physical changes of puberty are changes in adolescents' cognitive capacities, social relationships, and feelings about themselves (Brooks-Gunn, 1989; Brooks-Gunn & Paikoff, 1992). Puberty also seems to loosen restraints on problem behaviors. For example, the onset of puberty in boys is associated with increased aggression (Olweus, Mattson, Schalling, & Low, 1988), alcohol and cigarette use (Reifman, Barnes, & Hoffman, 1999), and augmentation of such behaviors as lying, shoplifting, and burglary (Cota-Robles & Neiss, 1999).

To some extent, biology affects psychology in young adolescents. Continuing development of the cortex allows more complex thought as we have seen, and hormonal fluctuations affect emotions. Adolescents' rapidly changing physical characteristics can be a source of either excitement or dismay. For instance, Anne Frank looked positively on puberty, as this entry in her diary shows:

> I think what is happening to me is so wonderful, and not only what can be seen on my body, but all that is taking place inside. I never discuss myself or any of these things with anybody; that is why I have to talk to myself about them.
>
> Each time I have a period—and that has only been three times—I have the feeling that in spite of all the pain, unpleasantness, and nastiness, I have a sweet secret, and that is why,

menarche
First menstrual period in an adolescent female.

spermarche
First ejaculation in an adolescent male.

although it is nothing but a nuisance to me in a way, I always long for the time that I shall feel that secret within me again. (Frank, 1967, p. 146)

Others are not at all happy with their changing bodies. In *Reviving Ophelia,* therapist Mary Pipher (1994) describes ninth-grader Cayenne's perspective:

She hated her looks. She thought her hair was too bright, her hips and thighs too flabby. She tried to lose weight but couldn't. She dyed her hair, but it turned a weird purple color and dried out. She felt almost every girl was prettier. She said, "Let's face it. I'm a dog." (pp. 32)[3]

Curiously, psychology also affects biology, in that life experiences influence biological growth in adolescence. Family conflict seems to accelerate puberty in girls, although not in boys (Kenneth, Smith, & Palermiti, 1997). However, pubertal maturation seems to be delayed in girls who grow up in low-income families, perhaps because of less adequate nutrition (Tremblay, 1999). Also influencing physical well-being is a phenomenon known as the **personal fable:** Young teenagers tend to imagine themselves as unique, invincible members of the human race (Elkind, 1981a). Because they are like no one else (or so they think), they wrongly assume they are not vulnerable to dangers that harm others. The resulting sense of invulnerability may lead them to take foolish risks, such as experimenting with drugs and alcohol and having unprotected sexual intercourse (DeRidder, 1993; S. P. Thomas, Groër, & Droppleman, 1993). (In Chapter 9, we will revisit the personal fable when we talk about sense of self in adolescence.)

Diversity in the Onset of Puberty Compared to boys, girls get a one and one-half year head start on puberty. This gender difference is apparent in both the height advantage and the preoccupation with the opposite sex that many girls have in the middle school grades.

Do not be surprised at the wide range of development you observe in young adolescents. Typically, puberty begins sometime between 8 and 14 years, earlier on average for girls than for boys.

Considerable variation exists in the timing of puberty within groups of girls and boys, and this causes problems for some teenagers. Researchers have focused primarily on the potential vulnerabilities of *early-maturing girls* and *late-maturing boys,* whose bodies, the researchers hypothesize, are inconsistent with cultural ideals of attractiveness in the Western world. Early-maturing girls become heavier and more curvaceous earlier and are therefore less likely to resemble the slim, angular professional models idealized in the popular media. Late-maturing boys, on the other hand, are still "boys" when some of their peers are beginning to show signs of adultlike masculinity.

Some evidence indicates that early-maturing girls are, on average, less happy and feel less good about themselves than late-maturing girls (Susman, Nottelmann, Inoff-Germain, Dorn, & Chrousos, 1987). In addition, their more mature appearance may arouse older boys, ushering them into precocious sexual activity (Hayes & Hofferth, 1987; Stattin & Magnusson, 1990). Early-maturing girls are more likely to engage in other risky behaviors as well, including substance abuse and reckless driving (C. E. Irwin & Millstein, 1992).

As for late-maturing boys, research indicates that they get off to a slower start than other boys in important aspects of development. For instance, they tend to be less athletically inclined and less popular with peers, and they less frequently seek leadership positions at school (Gross & Duke, 1980; H. F. Jones, 1949; Simmons & Blyth, 1987). On the plus side, however, they are less likely to engage in risk-taking behaviors such as smoking, drinking, and delinquent activities (P. D. Duncan, Ritter, Dornbusch, Gross, & Carlsmith, 1985; Susman et al., 1985).

The timing of puberty does not necessarily establish lifelong patterns, however. For instance, the relative popularity of late-maturing girls and early-maturing boys brings only short-term advantages. Admired as teens, these girls and boys may become somewhat rigid,

personal fable
Tendency for adolescents to think of themselves as unique beings invulnerable to normal risks and dangers.

_____

[3] From *Reviving Ophelia* by Mary Pipher, Ph.D., copyright 1994 by Mary Pipher, Ph.D. Used by permission of Putnam Berkley, a division of Penguin Putnam Inc.

DEVELOPMENT AND PRACTICE

Accommodating the Physical Needs of Adolescents

■ Accommodate the self-conscious feelings that adolescents have about their changing bodies.

A middle school basketball coach gives adolescents plenty of time to change clothes before and after practice. He also makes sure that all showers have curtains so that each adolescent can shower in private.

■ Keep in mind that menstruation can begin at unexpected times.

An eighth-grade adolescent girl comes into class obviously upset, and her best friend approaches their teacher to explain that the two of them need to go to the nurse's office right away. The teacher realizes what has probably just happened and immediately gives them permission to go.

■ Make sure adolescents understand what sexual harassment is, and do not tolerate it when it occurs.

A high school includes a sexual harassment policy in its student handbook, and homeroom teachers explain the policy very early in the school year. When an adolescent unthinkingly violates the policy by teasing a classmate about her "big rack," his teacher takes him aside and privately explains that his comment not only constitutes sexual harassment (and so violates school policy) but also makes the girl feel unnecessarily embarrassed. The boy admits that he spoke without thinking and, after class, tells the girl he's sorry.

■ Be sensitive to adolescents' feelings about early or late maturation.

In its health curriculum, a middle school clearly describes the typical sequence of biological changes that accompanies puberty. It also stresses that the timing of these changes varies widely from one person to the next and that being "normal" takes many forms.

conforming, and discontented as adults (Livson & Peshkin, 1980; Macfarlane, 1971). In contrast, early-maturing girls and late-maturing boys may develop strategies for coping with the trials and tribulations of adolescence that help them to become independent, flexible, and contented adults.

Adolescents' adjustment to puberty is, to some degree, influenced by their culture, parents, and school setting (Blyth, Simmons, & Zakin, 1985; Hill, Holmbeck, Marlow, Green, & Lynch, 1985; A. C. Peterson & Taylor, 1980; Stattin & Magnusson, 1990). In some cultures, puberty is joyously welcomed by formal celebrations, such as the bar mitzvahs and bat mitzvahs for 13-year-olds of the Jewish faith and *quinceañeras* for 15-year-old girls in Mexican and Mexican American communities. School personnel can help to ease the transition by giving some advance warning about the physiological changes that young adolescents are likely to experience and reassuring students that considerable variations in timing are all well within the "normal" range.

In the Development and Practice feature "Accommodating the Physical Needs of Adolescents," we give examples of strategies that accommodate both the changes of puberty and the diversity that exists among young adolescents.

Late Adolescence (Ages 14–18)

At about age 15 for girls and age 17 for boys, the growth spurt ends, and in the later teenage years, most adolescents reach sexual maturity. (However, because of individual differences, especially among boys, some show few signs of puberty until the high school years.) With sexual maturation comes increasing interest in sexual activity, including hugging, kissing and, for many teens, more intimate contact as well (DeLamateur & MacCorquodale, 1979). Later in this chapter, we will consider health risks associated with sexual activity. (In Chapter 13, we will look at social and emotional aspects of adolescent sexuality.)

As you have learned, the processes of growth and maturation continue during late adolescence. The brain in particular continues to refine its pathways, permitting more thoughtful control of emotions and more deliberate reflection about possible consequences of various behaviors (Chugani, 1998; Giedd, Blumenthal, Jeffries, Rajapakse, et al., 1999). Perhaps as a result, the false sense of invulnerability associated with the personal fable tends to decline in later adolescence (Durkin, 1995; Lapsley, Jackson, Rice, & Shadid, 1988). Nevertheless, many older adolescents continue to engage in behaviors that could undermine their long-term physical health—for instance, smoking cigarettes, abusing alcohol and drugs, eating too many high-salt and high-fat foods or, worse still, eating little at all—without thinking about

FIGURE 3–16 As children grow older, they become more knowledgeable about what "good health" entails. Grace (age 11) drew this rendition of healthy and unhealthy people.

Modeled after Mayall, Bendelow, Barker, Storey, & Veltman (1996).

the potential repercussions (B. J. Guthrie, Caldwell, & Hunter, 1997). These kinds of problems give us reason, in the next section, to go into more detail on practices that contribute to good health and, conversely, the choices that undermine it.

Physical Well-Being

With age, children and adolescents become more aware of "good health" (Figure 3–16). But they also become increasingly independent decision makers and, even in late adolescence, don't always make decisions that are best for their health. In the following sections we consider issues related to health and well-being, including eating habits, physical activity, and rest and sleep, as well as health-compromising behaviors. We also identify strategies that adults can use to encourage young people to develop a more healthful lifestyle.

Eating Habits

As you have learned, children's nutrition affects their physical growth, brain development, and sexual maturation. Their diet also influences their energy level, ability to concentrate, and capacity for performing physical and mental tasks. Given the importance of nutrition, an essential question is, How do children learn to eat well?

Good eating habits start at birth. Breastfeeding is the preferred method of feeding infants unless mothers have a medical condition, such as being HIV positive, that would make it risky (American Academy of Pediatrics Committee on Nutrition, 1999). There are many advantages. Vitamins C, A, and iron are higher in breast milk than in milk from cows and goats. Breast milk provides antibodies against illnesses the mother has overcome. It is easier to digest than formula, and breast-fed babies have fewer allergies, colds, stomachaches, and other common ailments (Beaudry, Dufour, & Marcoux 1995; Dewey, Heinig, & Nommsen-Rivers 1995; Isolauri, Sutas, Salo, Isosonppi, & Kaila, 1998). Of course, not all mothers can easily breastfeed, others do not want to, and for some it is impossible. These families may select iron-fortified or soy protein-based formulas, or other milk substitutes from which infants can gain adequate nutrition (American Academy of Pediatrics Committee on Nutrition, 1998, 1999). Practitioners who work with families of infants will want to support families' preferences and explain to them their own practices, such as introducing soft cereals and fruits with adequate vitamins and iron around 4 to 6 months of age and avoiding hard foods that infants cannot easily swallow.

Unfortunately, practitioners often encounter children who are poorly fed, perhaps because their parents have few financial resources, are homeless, are physically or mentally ill, or simply do not have access to appropriate nutrition. Even in more fortunate financial circumstances, parents may rush to work in the morning and neglect to feed either themselves or their children. Anemia (iron deficiency) is the most common nutritional deficiency in children worldwide (Centers for Disease Control and Prevention, 1997). Anemia in children is associated with developmental delays and behavioral disturbances.

As students gain increasing independence from adults, they also gain more control over what they do and do not eat. Unfortunately, many adolescents choose relatively nonnutritious meals that are high in fat and sodium.

As children grow older and make their own decisions about what and when to eat, their nutrition may deteriorate. For instance, in a large-scale study of American children, 24% of children ages 2 to 5 had a good diet, as compared to only 6% of adolescents ages 13 to 18 (Interagency Forum on Child and Family Statistics, 1999). Generally speaking, adolescents (especially boys) eat far too much "bad" stuff, such as high-fat and high-sodium foods, and far too little "good" stuff, such as fruits, vegetables, and whole grains (T. N. Robinson &

Killen, 1995; Simons-Morton, Baranowski, Parcel, O'Hara, & Matteson, 1990; Subar et al., 1992).

Part of the problem is that children don't understand how eating habits relate to health. At age 5, children know that some foods (e.g., fruits, vegetables, milk) are good for them but have no idea why (Carey, 1985b). Figure 3–17 shows an assignment 7-year-old Alex completed in school; it reveals his emerging understanding of food groups. Even at ages 9 to 11, the vast majority of children have not learned that the body breaks food down into the essential nutrients it needs to grow and thrive (Carey, 1985b). We have seen that such ignorance can continue well into adolescence. Jeanne's son Jeff, at 17, maintained that he could get through an entire day on a few donuts and several cans of cola.

Well-balanced diets are essential not only for the short run but also for long-term well-being. Excessive intake of fat, cholesterol, and sodium increases the probability of obesity and high blood pressure later in life (Nicklas, Webber, Johnson, Srinivasan, & Berenson, 1995). A good diet may be particularly important for youth of color, who are statistically more prone to have an elevated risk for such serious medical conditions as cardiovascular disease, diabetes, and cancer (D. K. Wilson, Nicholson, & Krishnamoorthy, 1998).

Obesity   Children are considered **obese** if their body weight exceeds their "ideal" weight (a figure that takes into account their age, gender, height, and body build) by 20% or more (Rallison, 1986). The prevalence of childhood obesity has increased over the last few decades, as has the number of children who are extremely overweight (Gortmaker, Dietz, Sobol, & Wehler, 1987). In one recent study, 22% of children between the ages of 6 and 17, more than one-fifth of the sample, were identified as obese (Troiano, Flegal, Kuczmarski, Campbell, & Johnson, 1995). Amazingly, 8.6% of American children as young as 2 to 6 years old are overweight (Centers for Disease Control and Prevention, 1997).

Some obese children outgrow their baby fat, but others do not. Approximately 40% of obese 7-year-olds are obese as adults, but 70% of obese 10- to 13-year-olds become obese adults (L. H. Epstein, Wing, & Valoski, 1985). Childhood obesity is a concern because it may lead to serious health risks, especially in adulthood (Kedesdy & Budd, 1998). It has social consequences as well. Peers may torment obese youngsters, calling them names and excluding them from activities.

Obesity seems to have some genetic basis, but environmental factors, such as family eating patterns, also play a role (Kedesdy & Budd, 1998). Fortunately, interventions, including dietary counseling, calorie restriction combined with increases in physical activity, and behavioral techniques (e.g., setting specific goals, monitoring progress toward goals, and recognizing and rewarding progress) are often effective (Kedesky & Budd, 1998). Such interventions are more successful with obese children than with obese adults, possibly because children continue to grow in height whereas adults do not, and they have a briefer history of poor eating habits (cf. L. H. Epstein, 1990).

Eating Disorders   Whereas some young people eat too much, others eat too little. Some develop eating disorders that seriously threaten their health. People with **anorexia nervosa** eat little, if anything. In contrast, people with **bulimia** eat voraciously, especially fattening foods, and then purge their bodies by taking laxatives or forcing themselves to vomit. Individuals with eating disorders often have a distorted body image (feeling as if they are "fat" even when they appear grossly thin to others), and they may exercise compulsively to lose additional weight (Attie, Brooks-Gunn, & Petersen, 1990; Kedesdy & Budd, 1998). In addition to jeopardizing physical health, eating disorders may slow down the bodily changes associated with puberty (Rallison, 1986).

Eating disorders are most common in adolescence and early adulthood, but they are also sometimes seen at younger ages. Particularly when they appear before puberty, eating

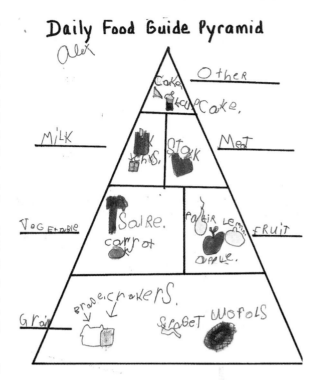

FIGURE 3–17   Children may learn about food groups before they understand why they should consume more of some foods and less of others. Alex (age 7) drew this picture of food groups for a lesson at school. He places bread, crackers, spaghetti, and waffles in *grains*, the bottom layer of the food group; celery and carrots in *vegetables*; pears, lemons, and apples in *fruits*; milk and cheese in the *milk* group; steak in *meat*; and in the top, restricted portion of the food pyramid, cake and cupcakes (his favorites!).

obesity
Condition in which a person weighs at least 20% more than what is optimal for good health.

anorexia nervosa
Eating disorder in which a person eats little or nothing for weeks or months and seriously jeopardizes health.

bulimia
Eating disorder in which a person, in an attempt to be thin, eats a large amount of food and then purposefully purges it from the body by vomiting or taking laxatives.

disorders are associated with feelings of loneliness and depression; hence, they are a manifestation of serious emotional as well as physical problems (Alessi, Krahn, Brehm, & Wittekindt, 1989; Attie et al., 1990). Girls are more likely to have eating disorders than boys, but 5% of anorexics are male (D. M. Stein & Reichert, 1990).

Many experts believe that society's obsession with thinness is partly to blame for anorexia nervosa and bulimia (Attie et al., 1990; C. B. Fisher & Brone, 1991; Streigel-Moore, Silberstein, & Rodin, 1986). It is fashionable for girls and women in particular to be slender; thin is "in." Psychological factors also come into play. Individuals may use their thinness to gain attention, stifle their growing sexuality, or maintain a sense of control in the face of overbearing parents. In some cases, inherited conditions predispose people to eating disorders (Attie & Brooks-Gunn, 1989; C. B. Fisher & Brone, 1991).

Occasionally, school personnel and other adults unwittingly contribute to eating disorders. For instance, Mary Pipher (1994) describes the roots of 16-year-old Heidi's bulimia. Heidi is a gymnast whose coach weighed her weekly and insisted that she remain thin. One day, Heidi, the coach, and the other gymnasts went to a restaurant where Heidi ate a double cheeseburger and onion rings. After eating, she regretted the meal, imagined the next day's weigh-in, went to the bathroom, and forced herself to vomit. Here's how she described the experience:

> "It was harder than you would think. My body resisted, but I was able to do it. It was so gross that I thought, 'I'll never do that again,' but a week later I did. At first it was weekly, then twice a week. Now it's almost every day. My dentist said that acid is eating away the enamel of my teeth."
>
> Heidi began to cry. "I feel like such a hypocrite. People look at me and see a small, healthy person. I see a person who gorges on food and is totally out of control. You wouldn't believe how much I eat. I shove food into my mouth so fast that I choke. Afterwards, my stomach feels like it will burst." (p. 167)[4]

Anorexia nervosa and bulimia frequently require intensive and long-term intervention by medical and psychological specialists (Linscheid & Fleming, 1995). These conditions are not easily corrected simply by encouraging individuals to change their eating habits. Thus, practitioners should be alert to common symptoms such as increasing thinness, complaints of being "too fat," and a lack of energy. When they suspect an eating disorder, they should consult with a counselor, a school psychologist, another mental health specialist, or a supervisor.

Promoting Better Eating Habits   We end this section with thoughts about what professionals can do to foster better nutrition and eating habits:

■ *Provide between-meal snacks when children are hungry.*   Children need periodic snacks as well as regular meals. Crackers, healthy cookies, and fruit slices can reinvigorate active children. Nutritious snacks are particularly important for children who are growing rapidly and those who receive inadequate meals at home. In providing snacks, practitioners must be aware of food allergies, family food preferences, and possible limitations in chewing and swallowing hard substances.

■ *Regularly review the basics of good nutrition, and ask children to set goals for improving their eating habits.*   Well planned school-based programs can be quite effective in changing children's eating habits and reducing their fat, sodium, and cholesterol intake (Bush et al., 1989; Perry et al., 1989; Resnicow, Cross, & Wynder, 1991). Such programs are more likely to be successful when they ask youngsters to set specific goals (e.g., reducing consumption of salty snacks), encourage them to chart their progress toward these goals, show them that they can stick with new eating patterns, and take cultural practices into account (Schinke, Moncher, and Singer, 1994; D. K. Wilson et al., 1998).

A logical first step is to introduce children to basic food groups and ask them to evaluate their own diets based on recommended servings for each group. Figure 3–18 shows a third grader's analysis of her eating habits on the preceding day.

I think I have ate to many sweets on Sunday. I had 1 to many things from the dairy groop. I had the right amount of meat, but not anof vegetables, I had only one vegetble. You wone't belve this, I had no fruits at all! I realy need to eat more fruits and vegetbles. If I ate two more things from bread groop I would have had anof.

FIGURE 3–18   Charlotte (age 8) reflects on her eating habits over the weekend.

─────────

[4] From *Reviving Ophelia* by Mary Pipher, Ph.D., copyright 1994 by Mary Pipher, Ph.D. Used by permission of Putnam Berkley, a division of Penguin Putnam Inc.

■ *Educate children about eating disorders.* Teachers and other professionals can take the glamour out of being excessively thin by educating youngsters about eating disorders. For instance, Teresa's son Connor first learned about anorexia nervosa when his third-grade teachers talked about eating disorders as part of a unit on the human body.

■ *Follow up when you suspect chronic nutritional problems.* Malnutrition can occur as a result of many factors. When low family income is at fault, practitioners can encourage families to apply for free or reduced-cost lunch programs at school. When parental neglect or mental illness is possibly involved, practitioners may need to report their suspicions to principals, counselors, social workers, school nurses, or supervisors to find the best approach for protecting vulnerable children.

■ *Convey respect for the feelings of children and adolescents.* Children and adolescents who struggle with obesity or eating disorders are certainly as sensitive as their peers—and often even more so—when others make unflattering comments about their appearance. Adults must insist that their classrooms, child care centers, after-school programs, and clubs are a "no-tease zone" regarding weight and other physical conditions.

In addition, children who are eligible for free lunches at school may be embarrassed about their limited financial circumstances. In response, educators can minimize the extent to which these children feel that they stand out. For instance, a considerate staff member at one school took subsidized lunches and placed them in students' own lunch-boxes, enabling children to save face when eating with classmates from higher-income families (Mayall et al., 1996).

Physical Activity

Infants and toddlers are highly motivated to master new physical skills and explore their environment with all their senses. As they wiggle, squirm, reach, and grasp, they exercise physical skills and also learn a lot about the world. For young children, physical activity is so enjoyable—and increasingly controllable—that they become even more active during early childhood. Activity level then decreases in middle childhood and adolescence, sometimes by as much as 50% (D. W. Campbell, Eaton, McKeen, & Mitsutake, 1999; Rowland, 1990).

A common feature of physical activity in early and middle childhood is **rough-and-tumble play,** or good-natured "fighting." Children wrestle each other to the ground, push and shove, and roll around together. Perhaps in our evolutionary past, rough-and-tumble play prepared children for the fights they were likely to encounter as adolescents and adults (A. P. Humphreys & Smith, 1987). In today's world, it seems to serve other purposes, such as providing breaks from demanding intellectual tasks and establishing who is dominant in a group of children (Bjorklund & Brown, 1998; Pellegrini & Smith, 1998). Whatever the functions of rough-and-tumble play, children often derive considerable pleasure from it, and when adults insist that they stop fighting, children are likely to maintain that they are just "playing" or "messing around."

In schools, child care centers, after-school programs, and recreation settings, such rough play is rarely considered acceptable, in large part because of the risk of injury. Yet children do need outlets for their seemingly boundless energy. Unfortunately, at most schools, opportunities for physical activity are quite limited. Even in physical education classes, children spend much of their time listening and watching demonstrations and waiting in line for their turn to try a new skill. Elementary students spend less than 10% of physical education class time in moderate or vigorous physical activity, and middle school students spend only 17% of class time in such activity (Simons-Morton, Taylor, Snider, & Huang, 1993; Simons-Morton et al., 1994).

As children reach adolescence, exercise can help them to maintain physical fitness and to cope more effectively with life's frustrations and stresses (J. D. Brown & Siegel, 1988). However, school tasks become increasingly sedentary in middle school and high school, and so adolescents are most likely to find opportunities for vigorous activity outside of school walls (Pate, Long, & Heath, 1994). Many do not get the exercise they need. For instance, only about one in five (19%) of American high school students is physically active

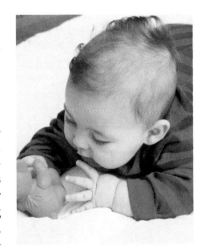

Infants are highly motivated to master new physical skills and to explore their environment.

rough-and-tumble play
Playful physical "fighting" typical in early and middle childhood.

for 20 minutes or more five days a week during physical education classes (U.S. Department of Health and Human Services, 1996).

Throughout childhood, and especially in adolescence, boys tend to be more active than girls. They are more active on the playground and have more difficulty sitting still in class (Eaton & Enns, 1986; Sallis, 1993). During early and middle childhood, gender differences in motor skills are typically quite small and are probably due more to environmental factors (such as opportunities to practice specific skills) than hereditary influences (Gallahue & Ozmun, 1998; J. R. Thomas & French, 1985). After puberty, however, boys have a significant advantage over girls in many physical activities, especially those requiring height and muscular strength (Eisenberg, Martin, & Fabes, 1996; Linn & Hyde, 1989; J. R. Thomas & French, 1985).

Organized Sports   In our opening case study, two enterprising teenagers were the driving force in establishing a softball league in a small, lower-income town. The league provided both a constructive use of time and an appropriate outlet for physical energy for the town's younger residents. As Tom and Phillip put it, "Now, we've got a schedule. We've got something to do . . . a place to go" (Pollack, 1998, p. 274). Organized sports have other benefits as well. They provide a means for maintaining and enhancing physical strength, endurance, and agility. They also promote social development by fostering communication, cooperation, and leadership skills.

Organized sports can have a downside when adults promote unhealthy competition, put excessive pressure on children to perform well, and encourage athletically talented children at the expense of their less gifted teammates. Well-meaning parents and coaches can bolster children's confidence and athletic skills, but they can also rob children of their intrinsic enjoyment of sports (R. E. Smith & Smoll, 1997).

Generally speaking, boys are more confident than girls about their ability to play sports, and boys are almost twice as likely as girls to belong to an organized sports team (Sadker & Sadker, 1994; Wigfield et al., 1996). For boys especially, participation in sports is a prestigious activity, and talented athletes are usually quite popular with classmates (Sadker & Sadker, 1994).

Regular recess and breaks for physical movement not only promote children's physical well-being but also lead to improved attention and concentration in more cognitively oriented activities. Art by Grace, age 11

Encouraging Physical Activity   Researchers still have much to learn about how adults can best promote healthful physical activity in children and adolescents (W. C. Taylor, Beech, & Cummings, 1998). Some information is available, though. Interventions with small groups tend to be more successful than programs delivered to larger audiences, and school-based interventions are more likely to be successful than those at other sites (W. C. Taylor et al., 1998). Here we offer strategies for promoting physical activity in youngsters:

■ *Be "pro-ACTIVE."*   Practitioners in many professions can incorporate physical movement into their activities. Regular breaks that include physical activity can actually increase children's attention to demanding cognitive tasks (Pellegrini & Bjorklund, 1997).

■ *Provide appropriate equipment and guidance so children can safely engage in physical activity.*   Open space, playground equipment, balls, and other athletic props encourage physical exercise. Equipment should be chosen carefully to allow children to experiment freely yet safely, ideally reducing times when adults have to say "no" (M. B. Bronson, 2000). Equipment should be adequate in scale so that all children can have access without crowding, yet sufficiently limited in number so that children must interact and cooperate as they use it (Frost, Shin, & Jacobs, 1998).

Expectations should not exceed the developmental abilities of children. For example, swimming "lessons" for infants are questionable because infants who paddle around independently can swallow too much water (American Academy of Pediatrics Committee on Sports Medicine and Fitness and Committee on Injury and Poison Prevention, 2000). This water intoxication can be fatal. Swimming lessons for babies can also create a false sense of security in families ("my baby is drown-proof"), whereas infants and children can easily get into trouble and must be supervised constantly. Figure 3–19 shows a swim record given by an instructor to parents of a 3½-year-old child; notice that the expectations are realistic for many children of preschool age.

By the middle elementary years, children can do much of the structuring of physical activities and games themselves. Coaches, teachers, recreation directors, and other practitioners should tolerate some bickering as children fuss over rules and in other ways learn to get along. Even so, they may occasionally need to intervene to minimize physical aggression and to help integrate children who do not readily join in.

■ *Make exercise an enjoyable activity.* By the time they reach high school, many young people have had some unpleasant experiences with physical exercise and, as a result, associate exercise with discomfort, failure, embarrassment, competitiveness, boredom, injury, or regimentation (Rowland, 1990). Furthermore, the majority of adolescents do not see physical exercise as a regular part of the daily lives of their parents or other family members (Feist & Brannon, 1989).

Youngsters are more likely to engage in a physical activity if they enjoy it and find it reasonably challenging while still being within their ability levels (W. C. Taylor et al., 1998). They may have intrinsic interest in developing particular skills (e.g., in karate), take pleasure in self-expression through a sport (e.g., through dance), or appreciate the camaraderie and peer support they gain from team sports and other group activities.

■ *Plan physical activities with diversity in mind.* Not everyone can be a quarterback, and not everyone likes football. In fact, it's probably a minority of youngsters who are drawn to competitive sports at all. But nearly all children can find enjoyment in physical activity in some form. Offering a range of activities, from dance to volleyball, and modifying them for children with special needs can maximize the number of youngsters who participate. For example, a child who is unusually short might look to activities such as soccer, cycling, or gymnastics that do not require exceptional height (Rudlin, 1993). Similarly, a girl in a wheelchair might go up to bat in a softball game and then have a classmate run the bases for her.

■ *Focus on self-improvement rather than on comparison with peers.* As you will discover in Chapter 11, focusing on one's own improvement is, for most children, far more motivating than focusing on how well one's performance stacks up against that of peers. Focusing too much on comparison with others may lead children and adolescents to believe that physical ability is largely a matter of "natural talent," when in fact most physical skills are primarily the result of considerable practice (Ames, 1984; Proctor & Dutta, 1995).

One obvious way to promote self-improvement is to teach skills in progression, from simple to complex (Gallahue & Ozmun, 1998). For example, a preschool teacher might ask children to hop on one foot as they pretend to be the "hippity hop bunny." Once they have mastered that skill, the teacher can demonstrate more complex skills, such as galloping and skipping. Carefully sequenced lessons give children feelings of success and mastery that enhance their enjoyment of physical activities. Even in competitive sports, the emphasis should be more on how well children have "played the game"—on whether they worked well together, treated members of the opposing team with respect, and were all-around good sports—than on whether they won or lost (Gallahue & Ozmun, 1998).

Another tactic is to ask children to chart their progress on particular athletic skills and exercises (Centers for Disease Control and Prevention, 2002). In Figure 3–20, 15-year-

PRESCHOOL

PROGRESS REPORT

✓ I LOVE TO COME TO CLASS AND MOM OR DAD DOES NOT HAVE TO STAY AROUND

✓ I LISTEN TO MY INSTRUCTOR

___ I CAN WAIT MY TURN

✓ I CAN PUT MY FACE IN THE WATER FOR 3 SECONDS

✓ I CAN KICK WITH THE KICKBOARD WITH A LITTLE HELP/ OR BY MYSELF

___ I CAN BLOW BUBBLES

✓ I CAN GO UNDERWATER ALL BY MYSELF

✓ I CAN FLOAT ON MY FRONT LIKE SUPERMAN WITH A LITTLE HELP / OR BY MYSELF

___ I CAN FLOAT ON MY BACK WITH A LITTLE HELP / OR BY MYSELF

✓ I CAN DO MY WINDMILL ARMS WITH A LITTLE HELP / OR BY MYSELF

FIGURE 3–19 Progress report for a 3½-year-old girl in a preschool swimming class. Standards appear developmentally appropriate for this age level. Depending on a child's cultural experiences and individual temperament, the first standard, not wanting parents poolside, might be a difficult one to meet.

Adults can help adolescents to see how enjoyable and worthwhile exercise can be.

Your Name: _Connor_   Your Age: _15_   Adult Supervising: _Mom_

Record of Physical Activity

Day 1-5: Exercise	Activity 1: _Sit ups_		Activity 2: _Push ups_		Activity 3: _up-downs_	
	How many did you do?	How did it feel?	How many did you do?	How did it feel?	How many did you do?	How did it feel?
1	37	Good	26	Hard to keep Back Straight	21	Hard to keep balance
2	22	Stomach sore from yesterday. Sore	30	Busy	25	Harder
3	26	Stomach is better OK	22	Sore	23	Sore
4	15	Hurt really Bad!	20	Sore	25	Hard
5	30	tried to beat #1 But to sore to	31	Beat it	25	use a lot of Energy
Day 6: Reflect	What parts of your body did you use? _Stomach Muscles!_		What parts of your body did you use? _Upper Body._		What parts of your body did you use? _A Full body Work out_	
	What did you do to prevent injury? _stopped when it hurt._		What did you do to prevent injury? _Tried to keep Balance_		What did you do to prevent injury? _Stopped when I needed to_	

FIGURE 3-20 Record of physical activity. Fifteen-year-old Connor kept a record of the number of sit-ups, push-ups, and up-downs he could complete on each of five successive days. Notice the drop in sit-ups on the second day, as compared to the first day. Connor complained that his stomach muscles hurt after the first day and only gradually recovered.

Form adapted from *Planning for Physical Activity,* a resource of BAM! Body and Mind, Summer 2002. Centers for Disease Control and Prevention. Available online at http://www.bam.gov/teachers.index.htm. Downloaded July 1, 2002.

old Connor kept a record of his performance on three activities, sit-ups, push-ups, and up-downs, for a five-day period. He enjoyed the challenge of trying to beat his own records.

■ *Make sure that children don't overdo it.* Becoming excessively involved in sports and exercise can present medical problems for children. The soft and spongy parts of bones in growing children are susceptible to injury from repeated use, and especially from excessive weight-bearing forces (Micheli & Melhonian, 1987). Weight-training machines are almost always designed for larger bodies, exacerbating chances for injury. Overuse injuries are also seen in distance running, distance swimming, and gymnastics (Gallahue & Ozmun, 1998). Furthermore, excessive concern about being successful in athletics can lead youngsters to make health-compromising choices (taking steroids, gaining or losing weight too quickly, etc.), as the case of Heidi, the 16-year-old gymnast described earlier, illustrates. Medical experts recommend that children be discouraged from specializing in a single sport before adolescence, that they never be encouraged to "work through" injuries such as "shin splints" or stress fractures, and that they receive regular care from a physician who can monitor health effects of intensive training, such as unmet nutritional needs and delays in sexual maturation (American Academy of Pediatrics Committee on Sports Medicine and Fitness, 2000).

Rest and Sleep

Sleeping and resting are essential to growth and health. Sleep actually helps young people to grow, because growth hormones are released at higher rates as children snooze. In addition to promoting growth, sleep may help the brain to maintain normal functioning and promote its development (N. R. Carlson, 1999).

Infancy The newborn baby spends a long time sleeping, 16 to 18 hours a day according to some estimates (Wolff, 1966). About half of this time is spent in *regular sleep:* the baby shows little body activity, a relaxed face, and slow, regular breathing. The other half is spent in *irregular sleep:* the baby gently moves her limbs, may contort her face into a grimace, and shows rapid eye movements. Irregular sleep, also called rapid-eye-movement sleep, may serve to stimulate infants' brains and oxygenate their eyes (Blumberg & Lucas, 1996; Roffwarg, Muzio, & Dement, 1966). Other states of arousal include *drowsiness,* a state in which the body is relatively quiet, the eyes open and shut, and the infant appears dazed; *quiet alertness,* when infants' eyes are open and attentive, their bodies are still, and breathing is even; *waking activity,* when infants show bursts of uncoordinated activity and breathe irregularly; and *crying,* accompanied by vigorous movements (Wolff, 1966).

Gradually, infants develop a sleep-wake cycle that corresponds to adults' day-night cycles (St. James-Roberts & Plewis, 1996). They begin to sleep through the night when they are ready to, partly depending on sleeping arrangements and other factors. Teresa recalls that her sons as infants were oblivious to the pediatrician's guideline that they should be able to sleep through the night by 10 weeks of age and 10 pounds in weight. Besides individual differences in infants' sleeping habits, cultures vary in sleeping practices for infants, suggesting there is no single "best" way to put babies to sleep (Shweder, Goodnow, Hatano, LeVine, Markus, & Miller, 1998). (We will return to the topic of culture and sleeping practices in Chapter 14.)

Although there is no best way to put babies to sleep, there is one wrong way. Medical experts advise caregivers *not* to place babies on their stomachs for sleeping. This is a risk factor for **Sudden Infant Death Syndrome** (SIDS). SIDS is a leading cause of death among infants from 1 month through 1 year in age (American Academy of Pediatrics Task Force on Infant Sleep Position and Sudden Infant Death Syndrome [AAPTFISPSIDS], 2000; CJ Foundation for SIDS, 2002). When an infant dies without apparent cause, and nothing is revealed

Sudden Infant Death Syndrome
Death of infant in the first year of life, typically during sleep, that cannot be explained by a thorough medical examination; it peaks between 2 and 4 months.

in the follow-up autopsy and investigation, the death may considered as SIDS. SIDS is rare in the first month, peaks at 2–4 months, and declines after that (AAPTFISPSIDS, 2000). During the time that SIDS is most common, infants' brains are developing circuits that control arousal, breathing, heart rate, and other basic physiological functions. Small delays in this development may prove fatal if infants are under stress, for example, if they have a respiratory infection (F. M. Sullivan & Barlow, 2001). Perhaps infants who die suddenly do not wake when breathing becomes difficult or they may be unable to clear their throats, a reflex known to be less active when infants sleep on the stomach. In fact, it is quite possible that there are multiple causes of SIDS (Sullivan & Barlow, 2001).

Practitioners who work with infants must be well aware of current recommendations not only for reducing the risk of SIDS but for preventing suffocation more generally. These include placing babies on their backs to sleep, refraining from smoking near them, not letting them get too hot, using a firm mattress, and avoiding soft surfaces and loose bedding (AAPTFISPSIDS, 2000; CJ Foundation for SIDS, 2002). Parents who share a bed with an infant are advised to take particular precautions to avoid suffocation, to refrain from smoking and using alcohol and other substances that could impair their own arousal, and to place the infant face up for sleeping.

These recommendations regarding sleeping position do *not* rule out placing babies on their stomachs while awake. In fact, medical experts recommend that caregivers allow infants some supervised time on their stomachs. "Tummy time" can help infants to exercise neck and upper body muscles; it can also relieve pressure on the back part of the head and thereby help it to grow normally (AAPTFISPSIDS, 2000).

Early Childhood Through Adolescence   Time spent sleeping decreases steadily over the course of childhood and adolescence. Two-year-olds sleep 12 hours, 3- to 5-year olds sleep 11 hours, 10- to 13-year-olds sleep 10 hours, and 14- to 18-year-olds sleep 8½ hours (Roffwarg, Muzio, & Dement, 1966). These figures, of course, are averages. The number of hours of sleep children need at a particular age, and how rested they feel after sleeping a given number of hours, varies greatly.

Occasional sleep problems are normal occurrences in childhood. Nightmares are common between ages 3 and 6, and children may seek reassurance from adults to battle the demons of the night that seem so real. More seriously, one-fourth of all children have chronic problems sleeping (Durand, 1998). Pronounced sleep disturbances (e.g., waking repeatedly during the night) may be a symptom of serious health problems, chemical abuse, or excessive stress. For instance, repeated nightmares are especially common among children who have been victims of abuse or other traumatic incidents (Durand, 1998; Vignau et al., 1997). Also, children with certain disabilities (e.g., cerebral palsy, severe visual impairment, autism, attention-deficit hyperactivity disorder) often have difficulty sleeping (Durand, 1998).

When children and adolescents get insufficient sleep, they are likely to be irritable and have difficulty with changes in routine. Any aggressive tendencies they have may worsen (Durand, 1998). In a study with preschool children, the children's sleep patterns predicted their adjustment in school as perceived by their teachers (Bates, Viken, Alexander, Beyers, & Stockton, 2002). Adjustment was defined as a composite of variables, including children's compliance with the teacher's requests, enthusiasm for learning, and control of aggressive impulses. What seemed most damaging was a failure to establish regular sleep habits, with frequent changes in bedtime and in the number of hours they slept. The association between disrupted sleep and poor adjustment in school held up even when family stress and family management practices were controlled statistically. In another study, disrupted sleep in older children (7- to 12-year-olds) predicted impairment in simple tasks such as pressing digits on a keyboard to match symbols on screen (Sadeh, Gruber, & Raviv, 2002). Children with disrupted sleep were most impaired in the morning.

In our own experience, adolescents are less likely to get sufficient sleep than younger children. Although they require less sleep than they did in their earlier years, they are growing rapidly, and their bodies need considerable time to rest. However, out-of-school obligations—extracurricular activities, part-time jobs, social engagements, and homework assignments—may keep them up until the wee hours of the morning. In some cases, adolescents make up for lost sleep at school; for instance, it's not uncommon for high school teachers (and college professors as well) to find students napping during class time—a practice hardly conducive to classroom learning!

Accommodating Children's Needs for Rest and Sleep Adults who work with children and adolescents often have youngsters in their care who do not sleep easily and soundly, including some who are truly sleep-deprived. With this in mind, we offer the following suggestions:

■ *When appropriate, provide time for sleep during the day.* Infants and toddlers *must* sleep during the day. It is common practice, and most certainly good practice, to include an afternoon naptime in the schedule of preschoolers who attend school in the afternoon. A few older children and adolescents—for instance, those with brain injuries or other chronic health conditions—may need an hour or two of sleep as well, perhaps on a couch in the school nurse's office (Jackson & Ormrod, 1998).

■ *Include time for rest in the daily schedule.* Young children typically give up their afternoon nap sometime between ages 2 and 5, but for quite some time after that, they need to recharge their batteries with quiet and restful activities (e.g., listening to stories or music) in the afternoon. At any age level, children learn most effectively when they take an occasional, restful break from intense activity.

■ *Be alert concerning children who appear sleepy, irritable, or distractible.* Practitioners should certainly speak tactfully with family members when they think fatigue is causing children to have trouble concentrating, maintaining reasonably good spirits, and resisting aggressive impulses.

■ *Give youngsters enough time to complete assignments, and help them plan their time so that they don't leave assigned tasks until the last minute.* At the high school level, adolescents may have several hours of homework each night. Add to this workload extracurricular events, social activities, family commitments, and a part-time job, and you have adolescents who are seriously overcommitted. Lengthy last-minute homework assignments ("For tomorrow, write a five-page essay on the pros and cons of labor unions") make it virtually impossible for young people to plan ahead and budget their time, and when something has to be left out of the daily schedule, that "something" may very well be sleep.

Even when teachers and other practitioners give adequate time for homework and projects, many high school students underestimate how long it will take to finish assignments. Especially when an out-of-school task is lengthy and complex (a major project, a research paper, etc.), adults should encourage regular progress by giving deadlines for completing various *parts* of the task.

■ *Recognize that sleep problems can be sign of illness or emotional stress.* Words of acknowledgement and kindness ("You look tired today, Darragh. Did you sleep all right last night?") may give children permission to share their troubles and, as a result, take the first step toward resolving them.

Health-Compromising Behaviors

Especially as they grow older and gain increasing independence from adult supervision, children and adolescents face many choices about how to spend their leisure time. They often make decisions without adequate knowledge about how certain behaviors are likely to affect their health and physical well-being. Here we look at three health-compromising behaviors: cigarette smoking, alcohol and drug use, and sexual activity.

Cigarette Smoking An alarming number of young people smoke cigarettes. In 1998, 9% of 8th graders, 16% of 10th graders, and 22% of 12th graders were smokers (Interagency Forum on Child and Family Statistics, 1999). Boys and girls had similar patterns of smoking, but rates differed among ethnic groups. For example, 28% of White American students smoked daily, compared to 14% of Hispanic Americans and 7% of African Americans. Unfortunately, many smoking teens don't kick the habit and continue to smoke as adults.

Alcohol depresses the central nervous system and impairs coordination, perception, speech, and decision making; for instance, heavy drinkers may talk incoherently and walk with a staggering gait. Teens who drink excessively are more likely to have car accidents and commit rape. Among high school seniors, 80%–90% have tried alcohol and 25%–40% are frequent drinkers.

Inhalants are attractive to many adolescents because they cause an immediate "high" and are readily available in the form of such household substances as glue, paint thinner, aerosol paint cans, and nail polish remover. These very dangerous substances can cause brain damage and death. Approximately 1 in 5 adolescents has tried an inhalant at least once; its use is greatest among younger teenagers (e.g., eighth graders).

Marijuana delays reaction time, modifies perception, and instills a mild feeling of euphoria, but it can also heighten fears and anxieties. Teens who smoke marijuana may have red eyes, dry mouths, mood changes, loss of interest in former friends and hobbies, and impaired driving. It is the most widely used mind-altering drug taken by adolescents. More than one-third of high school seniors have tried it, as have 17% of eighth graders; 6% of high school students report smoking it almost every day.

Cocaine (including *crack,* a particularly potent form) overstimulates the central nervous system and gives users a brief sense of intense euphoria; it can also cause tremors, convulsions, vomiting, respiratory problems, and heart failure. Cocaine users may be energetic, talkative, argumentative, and boastful; long-time users may appear anxious and depressed. Crack users are prone to violence and crime. One out of six high school students has tried cocaine, and 2%–5% use it regularly.

Amphetamines ("speed") are stimulants that give their users a sense of energy, alertness, confidence, and well-being. Overdoses are possible, addiction frequently occurs, and changes to the brain and heart may occur. People who use speed regularly may combat psychiatric problems, such as believing that "everyone is out to get me." In the United States, 15% of the population has tried amphetamines or another stimulant at least once.

Lysergic acid diethylamide (LSD) is a psychedelic drug that gives its users the sensation of being on an exotic journey, or "trip." It is usually swallowed as a chemical on a piece of paper or as a drop of liquid placed on the tongue. It can impair judgment, provoke anxiety, trigger underlying mental problems and, in the case of "bad trips," cause serious distress. LSD has been tried by 10% of the American population.

Methylene dioxymethamphetamine (MDMA, or "ecstasy") gives its users a sense of euphoria and exuberance, sensory enhancements and distortions, and feelings of being at peace with the world and emotionally close to others (it is sometimes called the "hug drug"). However, the sense of euphoria often leads its users to ignore bodily distress signals, such as muscle cramping and dehydration; more serious effects include convulsions, impaired heart function, and occasionally death. It is often available at dance clubs ("raves"), where its effects are intensified with music and flashing lights. MDMA use appears to be on the increase among older adolescents. In a large-scale survey conducted in 1999 (Johnston, O'Malley, & Bachman, 2000), approximately 5% of 10th and 12th graders reported having used it in the previous 12 months.

FIGURE 3-21 Effects, symptoms, and trends in adolescent substance abuse

Sources: Adams, Gullotta, & Markstrom-Adams, 1994; Atwater, 1996; DanceSafe, 2000a, 2000b; Feldman & Wood, 1994; Johnston, O'Malley, & Bachman, 2000; Kulberg, 1986; Smith, 1994; J. M. Taylor, 1994.

Because the health risks are so well publicized, it is difficult for many adults to understand why adolescents choose to smoke. Undoubtedly "image" is a factor. Teens may smoke cigarettes as a way of looking older and affiliating with certain peer groups. Advertising plays a role as well. Only three cigarette brands account for almost all of teen smoking, perhaps reflecting the youthful, fun-loving images that certain tobacco companies cultivate in the media. Use of particular brand names varies by ethnic group, reflecting differing cultural norms for different groups (Johnston, O'Malley, Bachman, & Schulenberg, 1999). Regardless of the reasons they begin smoking, adolescents who continue to smoke may develop health problems that they might otherwise avoid.

Alcohol and Drug Use Alcohol and drugs are arguably the most serious threats to physical health that adolescents face today. With their judgment impaired while they are under the influence of alcohol or drugs, teenagers often engage in reckless behaviors. Occasionally a single episode with a particular drug leads to permanent brain damage or even death. (You will recall our introductory case study, in which three boys died in an attempt to get "high.") Losing judgment, adolescents may put themselves at risk in other ways, such as failing to take precautions during sexual activity. Those who are intravenous drug users may share needles, putting themselves at risk of contracting HIV (Thiede, Romero, Bordelon, Hagan, & Murrill, 2001). Figure 3–21 lists substances used by some adolescents. In addition, new substances and combinations of drugs are regularly introduced to vulnerable teens.

Given the hazards of alcohol and drugs, why do adolescents so frequently use them? For some, it's a matter of curiosity: Hearing about alcohol and drugs so often, not only from their peers but also from adults and the media, teens may simply want to experience their effects firsthand. Also, because adolescence is a time when young people seek self-definition (Who shall I be? How does it feel to be a certain kind of me?), experimentation with new roles and behaviors, including drug use, is common (Durkin, 1995; Shedler & Block, 1990).

Adult behaviors, too, influence substance abuse. Many adolescents who use drugs or alcohol have parents who do little to promote their self-confidence, willingness to abide by society's rules and conventions, or ability to delay immediate pleasures to achieve long-term gains (Botvin & Scheier, 1997; Jessor & Jessor, 1977). Furthermore, drug and alcohol use is more typical when people in the local community are relatively tolerant of such behavior (Poresky, Daniels, Mukerjee, & Gunnell, 1999).

Peer group norms and behaviors are yet another factor affecting substance abuse (J. A. Epstein, Botvin, Diaz, Toth, & Schinke, 1995; B. M. Segal & Stewart, 1996). To a great extent, use of alcohol and drugs is a social activity (Durkin, 1995), and teenagers may partake simply as a means of "fitting in." Or, teens inclined to violate social norms may actively seek out peer groups similarly disposed to trouble (A. M. Ryan, 2000).

A majority of teenagers try alcohol or drugs at one time or another. If these substances give them pleasure, satisfy a desire for thrills, alleviate anxieties, or deaden feelings of pain and depression, they may begin to use them regularly. Unfortunately, some eventually develop an **addiction** to, or biological and psychological dependence on, drugs or alcohol. They grow accustomed to using the substance and need increasing quantities to produce a desired effect. If use is stopped, addicts experience intense cravings and severe physiological and psychological reactions (Hussong, Chassin, & Hicks, 1999). Teenagers who are impulsive and disruptive, perform poorly in school, find little value in education, and have families where mental illness or substance abuse is present are at risk for becoming dependent on alcohol and drugs (A. L. Bryant & Zimmerman, 1999; Chassin, Curran, Hussong, & Colder, 1996; Flannery, Vazsonyi, Torquati, & Fridrich, 1994; T. A. Wills, McNamara, Vaccaro, & Hirky, 1996).

Sexual Activity   Teenagers get mixed messages about the acceptability of sexual activity. Social and religious norms often advocate abstinence, yet television and films depict explicit sexual behavior. Peers may urge participation in sexual activity, and teens themselves experience sexual desires. Schools and youth organizations usually do little to help teens sort out these messages and feelings. Although they often include information about male and female anatomy, procreation, and birth in their health or biology curricula, they rarely offer much guidance about how to make sense of one's emerging sexuality or how to behave in romantic relationships (Pipher, 1994).

On average, adolescents are more sexually active now than they were 30 years ago. For example, for females in the United States, the median age for a first sexual experience declined from age 19 in 1971 to age 15½ in 1990 (U.S. Department of Health and Human Services, 1994). Furthermore, about half of the adolescents who are sexually active either never use contraceptives or use them only occasionally (U.S. Department of Health and Human Services, 1997). From the perspective of physical health and well-being, early sexual activity is problematic because it can lead to a sexually transmitted infection (STI), pregnancy, or both.

Sexually transmitted infections.   Sexually transmitted infections vary in their severity. Syphilis, gonorrhea, and chlamydia can be treated with antibiotics, but teens do not always seek prompt medical help when they develop symptoms. Without treatment, serious problems can occur, including infertility and sterility, heart problems, and birth defects in future offspring. Although there is no known cure for genital herpes, medication can make the symptoms less severe.

Undoubtedly the most life-threatening STI is Acquired Immune Deficiency Syndrome (AIDS), a medical condition in which the immune system is weakened, permitting severe infections, pneumonias, and cancers to invade the body. AIDS is caused by a virus, human immunodeficiency virus (HIV), which can be transmitted through the exchange of bodily fluids, including blood and semen, during just a single contact. Half of all new HIV infections in the United States occur in young people between 13 and 24 years of age (Futter-

addiction
Physical and psychological dependence on a substance, such that increasing quantities must be taken to produce the desired effect and withdrawal produces adverse physiological and psychological effects.

man, Chabon, & Hoffman, 2000). Sexual transmission is the primary means of HIV transmission during adolescence (American Academy of Pediatrics Committee on Pediatric AIDS and Committee on Adolescence, 2001).

The only good news about this deadly disease is that it has spurred public awareness campaigns that have led to safer sex practices, such as less intimate contact with new acquaintances and more frequent use of condoms (Catania et al., 1992; J. A. Kelly, 1995). The bad news is that safe sexual practices are not universal. As noted earlier, many adolescents believe that they are invulnerable to normal dangers, and they may falsely believe that their partner is "safe" (J. D. Fisher & Fisher, 1992; J. A. Kelly, Murphy, Sikkema, & Kalichman, 1993; Moore & Rosenthal, 1991). In a study of 289 homeless youth in Seattle, it was the heterosexual youngsters who had the least knowledge of protective strategies (L. S. Wagner, Carlin, Cauce, & Tenner, 2001). Many young people believe that only members of "high risk groups" can spread HIV (Amirkhanian, Tiunov, & Kelly, 2001). Some people with disabilities are at especially high risk for acquiring HIV and AIDS because they tend to have limited knowledge of sex and contraception, are more likely to engage in high-risk sexual behavior, and are more vulnerable to sexual abuse by others (Mason & Jaskulski, 1994).

Pregnancy. Despite popular beliefs to the contrary, teenage pregnancy rates are now lower than they were throughout much of the 20th century (Coley & Chase-Lansdale, 1998). Nevertheless, in the United States, approximately 1 teenage girl out of 10 becomes pregnant every year (Durkin, 1995; M. P. Sadker & Sadker, 1994). More than half of these pregnancies end in abortion or miscarriage, but many others, of course, go to full term (Chase-Lansdale & Brooks-Gunn, 1994; Henshaw, 1997). In 1997, the birthrate for American girls ages 15 to 17 was 32 per 1,000, representing a slight drop from 1991, when the rate was 39 per 1,000 (Interagency Forum on Child and Family Statistics, 1999).

Most girls who become teenage mothers come from low-income families that are often headed by single parents with low educational attainment. They may believe that life offers them few if any educational or career options (Coley & Chase-Lansdale, 1998). Many look to sex and motherhood to supply the emotional closeness they don't find in other relationships (Coley & Chase-Lansdale, 1998). Some teenage girls believe their families want them to have babies (Stack & Burton, 1993). Thirteen-year-old Janice, who is pregnant, explains:

> I'm not having this baby for myself. The baby's grandmother wants to be a "mama" and my great-grandfather wants to see a grandchild before he goes blind from sugar. I'm just giving them something to make them happy. (Stack & Burton, 1993, p. 161)

When young mothers have not fully matured physically, and especially when they do not have access to adequate nutrition and health care, they are at greater risk for medical complications during pregnancy and delivery. Problems arise after delivery as well. On average, teenage mothers have more health problems, are less likely to complete school or keep a steady job, live in greater poverty, and have more impaired psychological functioning than their peers (Coley & Chase-Lansdale, 1998; Upchurch & McCarthy, 1990).

Addressing Health-Compromising Behaviors Schools, community and recreation centers, and boys' and girls' clubs can do a great deal to address behaviors that put children and adolescents at physical risk. Sometimes they are the only resource available to youngsters whose families either cannot or will not intervene. We offer a few thoughts on appropriate support:

■ *Prevent problems.* It is much easier to teach students to resist cigarettes, alcohol, and drugs then it is to treat dependence on these substances. One important approach is to establish a "no tolerance" policy on school grounds, in after-school programs, in community centers, and in recreation centers. Youngsters are less likely to smoke, drink, or take drugs if they think they might be caught (Voelkl & Frone, 2000). On the other hand, scare tactics, instruction about the detrimental effects of tobacco and drugs, and attempts to enhance students' self-esteem are relatively ineffective. What seem to work better are programs that strive to change *behaviors* of children and adolescents.

Children and adolescents are less likely to engage in health-compromising behaviors when they have constructive alternatives for their leisure time.

Such programs might ask them to make a public commitment to stay clean and sober, teach them how to resist peer pressure, and give them strategies for solving social problems, curbing impulsive behaviors, and coping with anxiety (Botvin & Scheier, 1997; Forgey, Schinke, & Cole, 1997).

The effects of intervention programs diminish over time. Therefore, youngsters' resistance to tobacco, alcohol, and drugs needs to be established *before* they face temptation and then boosted *along the way* as they confront peer pressure. Ideally, prevention programs should take into consideration the cultures in which youngsters have grown up.

Approaches to preventing pregnancy and transmission of STIs among adolescents are more controversial. Many parents, for example, object to schools' advocacy of the use of condoms and other forms of "safe sex." (And of course at the present time, condom use is no guarantee of protection against either infection or pregnancy.) Recent evidence suggests, however, that having condoms available in schools moderately increases condom use for those students who are already sexually active (and so may offer some protection against HIV infection) but does not necessarily increase rates of sexual activity (Guttmacher et al., 1997).

Adolescents' use of condoms is far from universal, in part because of interpersonal factors (e.g., reluctance to use a condom or to ask that a partner use one) and situational factors (e.g., impaired judgment due to alcohol or drugs; Manderson, Tye, & Rajanayagam, 1997). Programs that encourage sexual abstinence are a less-controversial alternative and can be effective in the short run, although they are less so over a long period (McKay, 1993).

■ *Encourage adolescents with infections to abstain or to use precaution.* Sadly, many adolescents already are infected with HIV. Obviously, they need medical treatment and care. They must also be encouraged to stop the spread of infection. When they remain sexually active, precautions are essential. Unfortunately, this is a message they may not be prepared to hear. A study of 13- to 18-year-old HIV-infected adolescent girls revealed, for example, that only 73% reported consistent partner condom use during the preceding three months (Belzer, Rogers, Camarca, Fuschs, Peralta, Tucker, & Durako, 2001). In another study, 43% of HIV-infected male and female adolescents receiving care through medical clinics reported unprotected sex at last intercourse (Murphy, Durako, Moscicki, Vermund, Ma, Schwarz, & Muenz, 2001).

■ *Provide healthy options for free time.* Children and adolescents are less likely to engage in health-compromising behaviors when they have better things to do with their time. For instance, in our opening case study, a softball league provided a more enticing and productive form of recreation than using drugs. Community leaders can advocate for after-school youth centers, community athletic leagues, and public service programs for young people. As an example, the *First Choice* program, which has been implemented at over 50 sites in the United States, is targeted especially at students who are at risk for dropping out of school or getting in serious trouble with the law (Collingwood, 1997). The program focuses on physical fitness and prevention of drug use and violence. Elements that appear to contribute to its success include educational and physical activity classes, a peer fitness leadership training program, parent support training, and use of existing community resources.

■ *Ask adolescents to keep their long-term goals continually in mind.* Youngsters need personally relevant reasons to stay away from illegal substances and to make wise choices about sexual activity. Having firm long-term goals and optimism about the future can help them to resist peer and media pressure. The adolescent therapist Mary Pipher often uses the North Star as a metaphor for the compelling sense of direction that positive self-knowledge can bestow:

> You are in a boat that is being tossed around by the winds of the world. The voices of your parents, your teachers, your friends and the media can blow you east, then west, then back again. To stay on course you must follow your own North Star, your sense of who you truly are. Only by orienting north can you chart a course and maintain it, only by orienting north can you keep from being blown all over the sea.

Student's Pledge

As a participant in the _____ High School Athletic Program, I agree to abide by all training rules regarding the use of alcohol, tobacco, and other drugs. Chemical dependency is a progressive but treatable disease, characterized by continued drinking or other drug use in spite of recurring problems resulting from that use. Therefore, I accept and pledge to abide by the training rules listed in the athletic handbook and others established by my coach.

To demonstrate my support, I pledge to:

1. Support my fellow students by setting an example and abstaining from the use of alcohol, tobacco, and other drugs.

2. Not enable my fellow students who use these substances. I will not cover up for them or lie for them if any rules are broken. I will hold my teammates responsible and accountable for their actions.

3. Seek information and assistance in dealing with my own or my fellow students' problems.

4. Be honest and open with my parents about my feelings, needs, and problems.

5. Be honest and open with my coach and other school personnel when the best interests of my fellow students are being jeopardized.

Student _____ Date _____

**PARENTS: We ask that you co-sign this pledge to show your support.

Sample Letter from Coach to Parent about a Drug or Alcohol Violation

Dear Parent:

Your daughter _____ has violated the _____ High School extra-curricular activities code of conduct. She voluntarily came forward on Thursday afternoon and admitted her violation of the code, specifically, drinking alcohol. The code is attached.

We respect her honesty and integrity and hope you do as well. Admitting a mistake such as this is very difficult for her. Not only does she have to deal with authorities such as us, she must face you, her parents, as well as her peers—which is probably the most difficult. We understand that no one is perfect and that people do make mistakes. Our code, and the resulting consequences of violating the code, is a nationally recognized model and is designed to encourage this type of self-reporting where the student can seek help and shelter from guilt without harsh initial penalties. She has admitted to making a mistake and is willing to work to alleviate the negative effects of the mistake.

As you can see in the enclosed code, we require that your daughter complete 10 hours of drug and alcohol in-service education and counseling. In addition, she must sit out 10 practice days of competition. She is still part of the team and must attend practices and competition; she is just not allowed to compete or participate in games for 10 days.

We hope you understand and support our effort to provide a healthy athletic program for the students. If you have any questions, please call either one of us at the high school.

Sincerely,

FIGURE 3–22 Team Up drug prevention materials for high school athletic coaches

Source: U.S. Drug Enforcement Administration (2002). *Team Up: A Drug Prevention Manual for High School Athletic Coaches.* Washington, DC: U.S. Department of Justice Drug Enforcement Administration.

True freedom has more to do with following the North Star than with going whichever way the wind blows. Sometimes it seems like freedom is blowing with the winds of the day, but that kind of freedom is really an illusion. It turns your boat in circles. Freedom is sailing toward your dreams. (Pipher, 1994, pp. 254–255)[5]

■ *Implement programs that have demonstrated success with the population of young people with whom you work.* Obviously, the programs you can implement will depend on your own job duties. One effective drug prevention program was developed by staff members in the Forest Hills School District in Cincinnati, Ohio, and was implemented by coaches there (see Figure 3–22). It has since been tried elsewhere, and featured by the U.S. Drug Enforcement Agency. This comprehensive program enlists participation by school coaches, principals, other school staff, team captains, parents, and the adolescents themselves (U.S. Drug Enforcement Administration, 2002). Coaches speak openly and often with athletes about substance use. Peer pressure is also used to discourage them from using alcohol and drugs. When athletes do break the rules, they are given defined consequences, but in a way that communicates hope that they will try harder next time. The pledges for students to sign and a sample letter from coaches to parents about a drug or alcohol violation in Figure 3–22 will give you the flavor of the program.

The four areas we've discussed in this section—eating habits, physical activity, rest and sleep, and health-compromising behaviors—all have a central bearing on youngsters' physical development. In the Observation Guidelines table "Assessing Health Behaviors of Children and Adolescents," we identify characteristics and behaviors that can be clues as to whether youngsters are on the right track toward physical fitness and good health (obviously, practitioners should not make inferences about health or provide treatment for which they are not trained). We turn now to children who have special physical needs and may require modified instructional materials or practices to help them achieve their full potential.

---

[5] From *Reviving Ophelia* by Mary Pipher, Ph.D., copyright 1994 by Mary Pipher, Ph.D. Used by permission of Putnam Berkley, a division of Penguin Putnam Inc.

OBSERVATION GUIDELINES

Assessing Health Behaviors of Children and Adolsecents

CHARACTERISTIC	LOOK FOR	EXAMPLE	IMPLICATION
Eating Habits	• Frequent consumption of junk food (candy, chips, carbonated beverages, etc.) • Unusual heaviness or thinness, especially if these characteristics become more pronounced over time • Lack of energy • Reluctance or inability to eat anything at lunchtime	Melissa is a good student, an avid runner, and a member of the student council. She is quite thin but wears baggy clothes that hide her figure, and she eats only a couple pieces of celery for lunch. Her teacher and principal suspect an eating disorder and meet with Melissa's parents to share their suspicion.	Observe what children eat and drink during the school day. Seek free or reduced-rate breakfasts and lunches for children from low-income families. Consult with specialists and parents when eating habits are seriously compromising children's health.
Physical Activity	• Improvements in speed, complexity, and agility of gross motor skills (e.g., running, skipping, jumping) • Proficiency in fine motor skills (e.g., tying shoes, using scissors, writing and drawing, building models, playing a musical instrument) • Restlessness and fidgeting (reflecting a need to release pent-up energy) • Bullying and other socially inappropriate behaviors during playtime • Cooperation and teamwork during organized sports activities • Overexertion (increasing the risk of injury)	During a class field day, a fifth-grade teacher organizes a soccer game with her students. Before beginning the game, she asks them to run up and down the field, individually accelerating and decelerating while kicking the ball. She then has them practice kicking the ball in ways that allow them to evade another player. Only after such practice does she begin the game (Logsdon, Alleman, Straits, Belka, & Clark, 1997).	Incorporate regular physical activity into the daily schedule. Choose tasks and activities that are enjoyable and allow for variability in skill levels. Make sure youngsters have mastered necessary prerequisite skills before teaching more complex skills.
Rest and Sleep	• Listlessness and lack of energy • Inability to concentrate • Irritability and overreaction to frustration • Sleeping in class	A teacher in an all-day kindergarten notices that some of his students become cranky during the last half-hour or so of school, and so he typically reserves this time for storybook reading and other quiet activities.	Provide regular opportunities for rest. When a youngster seems unusually tired day after day, talk with him or her (and perhaps with parents) about how lack of sleep can affect attention and behavior. Jointly seek possible solutions to the problem.
Health-Compromising Behaviors	• The smell of cigarettes on clothing • Physiological symptoms of drug use (e.g., red eyes, dilated pupils, tremors, convulsions, respiratory problems) • Distortions in speech (e.g., slurred pronunciation, fast talking, incoherence) • Poor coordination • Impaired decision making • Mood changes (e.g., anxiety, depression) • Dramatic changes in behavior (e.g., unusual energy, loss of interest in friends) • Signs of sensory distortions or hallucinations • Rapid weight gain, and a tendency to wear increasingly baggy clothes (in girls who may be pregnant)	A community counselor notices a dramatic change in James's personality. Whereas he used to be energetic and eager to engage in activities, he now begins to "zone out" during counseling sessions. He slumps in his chair, looking down or staring out the window. His limited speech is unintelligible. The counselor suspects drug use and asks him about his demeanor. James denies that anything is wrong, so the counselor confronts him directly about her suspicions, refers him to a drug treatment center, and consults with her supervisor about additional steps to take.	Educate children and adolescents about the dangers of substance abuse and unprotected sexual activity; teach behaviors that will enable youngsters to resist temptations, tailoring instruction to their cultural backgrounds. Encourage participation in enjoyable and productive leisure activities that will enable young people to socialize with health-conscious peers. Consult with a counselor, psychologist, or social worker when you suspect that a youngster is pregnant or abusing drugs or alcohol.

Special Physical Needs

Some children have long-term physical conditions that affect their school performance, friendships, and leisure activities. Here we look at chronic illness, serious injuries, and physical disabilities in children and adolescents; we then identify strategies for accommodating these conditions.

Chronic Illness

All children get sick now and then, but some have ongoing, long-term illnesses as a result of genetic legacies (e.g., cystic fibrosis), environmentally contracted illnesses (e.g., AIDS), or an interaction between the two (e.g., some forms of cancer). In the United States, two-thirds of chronically ill children and adolescents attend their neighborhood schools for part or all of the school day (A. Turnbull, Turnbull, Shank, & Leal, 1999). Some of them show few if any symptoms at school, but others have noticeable limitations in strength, vitality, or alertness.

When practitioners work with chronically ill children, they must learn as much as they can about the nature and potential effects of the illness. As children get older, many of them learn how to manage their symptoms; for instance, most children with diabetes can monitor blood sugar levels and take appropriate follow-up action. Yet children sometimes forget to take prescribed medication, and they are not always completely reliable in assessing their status. For example, children with asthma may not realize when they are having a severe reaction (D. J. Bearison, 1998). Accordingly, practitioners may need to keep an eye on children's symptoms and seek family help when conditions deteriorate or medical assistance in cases of emergency.

Some children who are ill feel so "different" that they are hesitant to approach peers (A. Turnbull et al., 1999). Furthermore, they may blame their physical condition (perhaps accurately, perhaps not) for any problems they have in social relationships (Kapp-Simon & Simon, 1991). As a result, they may become isolated, with few opportunities to develop interpersonal skills. We urge practitioners to be attentive to chronically ill youngsters who remain on the periphery of social interaction, as they may require some assistance in forming friendships. To illustrate, one program teaches adolescents with health problems such social skills as how to start conversations, listen empathetically, and resolve conflicts (Kapp-Simon & Simon, 1991).

Unfortunately, some healthy children actively avoid or reject peers who have serious illnesses. To some extent, such reactions reflect ignorance. Many children, young ones especially, have naïve notions about illness. For instance, preschoolers may believe that people catch colds from the sun or get cancer by being in the same room as someone with cancer (Bibace & Walsh, 1981). As children get older, their conceptions of illness gradually become more complex, they grow more attuned to their own internal body cues, and they can differentiate among types of illness (D. J. Bearison, 1998).

Professionals who work with children must intervene when peers exclude or ridicule a young person who has a chronic illness. Consider the experiences of Ryan White, an adolescent who contracted HIV from a blood transfusion. Many community members believed that Ryan's presence at school would jeopardize the health of other students, and school officials initially refused to allow him to attend school. After Ryan spent many months studying at home (sometimes "participating" in class through computer hook-up), a court order finally allowed him to go back to school. His return was not a happy one:

> [B]eing back at school was almost as lonely as being home. Heath was still my buddy, but he wasn't in my grade. Other kids backed up against their lockers when they saw me coming, or they threw themselves against the hallway walls, shouting, "Watch out! Watch out! There he is!" Maybe some were putting me on. I think most of them were acting like that just to get to me, to make me mad mainly. I worked hard at pretending I didn't see the kids who were making fun of me.
>
> But it hurt that no one wanted to get close to me. "It's okay for him to come to school, just as long as I don't sit by him," one boy said. Some kids were so afraid they wouldn't walk in the same hall with me. I wasn't even five feet and I weighed seventy-six pounds—quite chunky for me actually. But you'd think I was some big bruiser, the way kids ran when they saw me coming. When we had to team up in class, no one wanted to be my partner. One girl complained, "If people with measles and chicken pox can't come to school, why should Ryan?" I called Mom every day at lunchtime, just to have someone to talk to. (R. White & Cunningham, 1991, pp. 118–119)[6]

---

[6] From *Ryan White: My Own Story* by Ryan White and Ann Marie Cunningham, copyright © 1991 by Jeanne White and Ann Marie Cunningham. Used by permission of Dial Books for Young Readers, an imprint of Penguin Putnam Books for Young Readers, a division of Penguin Putnam Inc.

Community residents were, of course, misinformed about the nature of HIV and AIDS, which cannot be spread through typical day-to-day forms of human contact. In desperation, Ryan's family moved to a different school district, which undertook numerous initiatives to prepare the community and school for his presence. School administrators invited experts to come talk about AIDS to teachers and students, and students met individually with school staff members to air their concerns and get reassurance. Student government officers dropped by Ryan's house to say hello. When he arrived at school the first day,

> Wendy and Jill and some other student government officers met me right at the door, and helped me find all my classes. I'd kept to myself for so long, it was like being on another planet. When I walked into classrooms or the cafeteria, several kids called out at once, "Hey, Ryan! Sit with me!" . . .
>
> As I left after my first day, a reporter asked me, "How do you like *this* school?"
>
> "Oh, I think I'm going to like it here," I said. He must have noticed I was beaming. I'd been welcomed with open arms. I felt like I had hundreds of friends. It seemed like everyone said to themselves, "What if you were standing in *his* shoes? How would *you* feel?" (White & Cunningham, 1991, pp. 149–150)[7]

Serious Injuries and Health Hazards

Injuries represent a major threat to children and adolescents. Every year, more young people die from accidental injuries than from cancer. In fact, for children and adolescents between 1 and 19 years of age, injuries are the leading cause of death (Deal, Gomby, Zippiroli, & Behrman, 2000). As children get older, their increasing independence makes them particularly susceptible to certain kinds of injuries; for example, injuries from firearms and motor vehicle accidents increase throughout the adolescent years (U.S. Department of Health and Human Services, 1997).

Although some injuries quickly heal, others have lasting effects that must be accommodated. For instance, each year more than one million youngsters sustain brain injuries as a result of playground falls, bicycle mishaps, skiing accidents, and other traumatic events (Brain Injury Association, 1999). Depending on location and severity, brain injuries can have temporary or long-term effects on physical functioning (e.g., seizures, headaches, poor motor coordination, chronic fatigue) and psychological processes (e.g., impairments in perception, memory, concentration, language, decision making, or anger management). Thus, the assistance professionals provide for children with brain injuries must be tailored to each individual's unique needs. At school, such assistance for one child may mean minimizing distractions in the classroom, for another it may mean allowing extra time to complete assignments, and for yet another it may mean adjusting expectations for performance, at least for the first few weeks or months (A. Turnbull et al., 1999). Outside the classroom, a coach might need to give explicit instructions for athletic moves, a mental health therapist might teach a child to deal effectively with anger, or a supervisor of an after-school program might show sympathy to a child who has persistent headaches.

Many childhood injuries are avoidable, of course, and schools and other organizations serving children can play a key role in educating children about such preventive measures. Adults can teach children to use seat belts while riding in motor vehicles, wear helmets while biking and skating, and install smoke detectors at home (e.g., Klassen, MacKay, Moher, Walker, & Jones, 2000). Practitioners should also be aware of youngsters who are more vulnerable than others; for instance, children with Down syndrome are particularly susceptible to sprains and dislocations because of poor muscle tone and excessive mobility in their joints (P. L. Krebs, 1995). Unfortunately, some injuries are intentionally inflicted by others, perhaps as a result of abuse, and practitioners must keep a sharp eye out for signs of it. (See Chapter 12.)

---

[7] From *Ryan White: My Own Story* by Ryan White and Ann Marie Cunningham, copyright © 1991 by Jeanne White and Ann Marie Cunningham. Used by permission of Dial Books for Young Readers, an imprint of Penguin Putnam Books for Young Readers, a division of Penguin Putnam Inc.

Finally, professionals who work with children can learn about hazardous substances that may be present in their community. Because their brains and bodies are growing quickly, young children can be seriously affected by exposure to some substances. For example, children can come into contact with lead from a variety of sources: in the womb if their mothers have lead in their bodies; in dirt, dust, or sand if it is present in their play areas; and in paint chips in older homes (Agency for Toxic Substances and Disease Registry, 1999). Depending on the amount of lead they ingest, children may develop blood anemia, kidney damage, colic, muscle weakness, and brain damage. Some of these problems may go away if children are removed from the lead source, but there can be lasting declines in intelligence. Obviously, professionals who work with children will want to do all they can to protect children from all harmful substances in the environments they provide for them.

Physical Disabilities

Children with physical disabilities, such as cerebral palsy, muscular dystrophy, congenital heart problems, or blindness, have the same basic needs as other children, namely good diet, regular physical activity, and adequate rest and sleep. In addition, they may need specially adapted equipment (e.g., a wheelchair, a speech synthesizer, or a computer printer that prints in Braille) and a classroom layout that permits safe movement. Some children with physical disabilities, especially those with multiple handicaps, have cognitive as well as physical impairments, but many others have intellectual capabilities similar to those of their nondisabled peers (A. Turnbull et al., 1999).

Because physical activity and exercise are central to health, fitness, and mood, professionals must find ways to adapt physical activities for children with special physical needs. Basically, such adaptation involves giving as much support as necessary to enable successful performance in movement; for example, a teacher can assist students who are visually impaired by guiding their bodies into correct positions and inserting bells or other noise-makers inside playground balls (D. H. Craft, 1995). It is also essential to communicate expectations for success.

Accommodating Children's Special Physical Needs

Children with chronic illnesses, serious injuries, and physical disabilities are diverse in terms of the strengths on which they can build and the weaknesses that may impede their developmental progress. Yet there are some general guidelines that apply to *all* children with special physical needs:

■ *Help every child participate in all activities to the fullest extent possible.* In recent years, children with special physical needs have increasingly participated in general education classes. Many educators have found that when they keep an open mind about what their students can accomplish, and especially when they

Adults can help all children participate in physical activity to the fullest extent possible.

think creatively and collaboratively about how they can adapt regular classroom activities to accommodate students with special needs, almost all students can participate meaningfully in virtually all classroom activities (Logan, Alberto, Kana, & Waylor-Bowen, 1994; Salisbury, Evans, & Palombaro, 1997). Likewise, practitioners in the community can make accommodations that welcome the participation of children with special physical needs. For example, a recreation center can make it possible for a child with cerebral palsy to get into and out of the swimming pool safely by using a ramp. A boys' club can set up a buddy system so a child with limited fine motor control can participate in wood carving.

■ *Seek guidance from parents or guardians and from specialized organizations.* Parents and guardians often have helpful suggestions about adjustments that would enable their children to participate more fully in school, extracurricular activities, clubs, and community events. And professional organizations—most are easily found on the Internet—offer a wealth of ideas about adapting instruction and equipment for children with chronic physical conditions and disabilities. Two broadly focused organizations are the American Alliance for Health, Physical Education, Recreation and Dance (with a subspecialty organization, Adapted Physical Activity Council) and the National Consortium for Physical Education and Recreation for Individuals with Disabilities. Specific disabilities are the focus of other organizations such as the American Athletic Association for the Deaf, Wheelchair Sports USA, National Handicapped Sports, Special Olympics, United States Cerebral Palsy Athletic Association, Dwarf Athletic Association of America, and the U.S. Association for Blind Athletes.

■ *Know what to do in emergencies.* Some children have conditions that may result in occasional life-threatening situations. For example, a child with diabetes may go into insulin shock, a child with asthma may have trouble breathing, or a child with epilepsy may have a *grand mal* seizure. Practitioners should consult with parents and school medical personnel to learn ahead of time exactly how to respond to such emergencies.

■ *Educate peers about the disability.* As Ryan White's experiences illustrate, peers are more likely to show kindness to a child with a physical or health impairment if they understand the nature of the disability. Peers should know, for example, that AIDS cannot be spread through breathing the same air and that epileptic seizures, though frightening, are only temporary. Keep in mind, however, that a practitioner should talk about a child's physical condition *only* when the child and his or her parents have given permission for the practitioner to do so.

■ *Keep lines of communication open with children who are hospitalized or homebound.* Sometimes children's physical conditions keep them hospital-bound or homebound for lengthy periods of time. In such circumstances, they can often participate in classroom lessons, activities, and social events by telephone or computer hook-up. When they cannot, they may be especially appreciative of correspondence and photographs from classmates and other important people in their lives.

■ *Use precautions when caring for children who are sick or injured, or who have open cuts.* The majority of children who are infected with HIV will attend child care and school (American Academy of Pediatrics Committee on AIDS and Committee on Infectious Disease [AAPCAIDSCID], 1999). Parents are *not* required to inform school authorities if their children are HIV positive. It is extremely unlikely that casual contact would lead to this infection being spread. Instead, sexual contact, blood to blood contact, and perinatal contact (at or around birth) are most common modes of transmission (AAPCAIDSCID, 1999). The American Academy of Pediatric AIDS and Committee on Infectious Disease (1999) reports that no cases of HIV transmission in school settings have been reported. Nonetheless, appropriate barrier precautions for blood (e.g., latex gloves) are advisable when children skin their knees, have open wounds, and the like. Experts advise that razors and toothbrushes should not be shared and that caregivers wash their hands after changing diapers and wiping noses (AAPCAIDSCID, 1999). If you do touch blood, wash your hands and other body parts even if you used gloves. When disinfecting surfaces contaminated by blood and other bodily fluids (such as diaper changing tables), use gloves (AAPCAIDSCID, 1999). Practitioners also need to teach children basic safety precautions, such as staying away from a friend's bloody knee. Finally, seek advice from supervisors and medical authorities when you have questions.

The health of children and adolescents affects not only their physical development but also other domains. Brain development affects cognitive development, of course, and children's energy levels and endurance influence their ability to master challenging new intellectual tasks. Moreover, health and fitness indirectly affect social development, as our final case study illustrates.

CASE STUDY: LUCY

In her early teenage years, Lucy had leukemia. After a long hospitalization, plus radiation and chemotherapy treatments that resulted in temporary hair loss, Lucy's disease finally went into remission. Eventually Lucy was healthy enough to return to school, but her life at school was quite different from what it once had been. Her therapist Mary Pipher (1994) explains:

It had been hard for her to return to school. Everyone was nice to Lucy, almost too nice, like she was a visitor from another planet, but she was left out of so many things. Her old friends had boyfriends and were involved in new activities. When she was in the hospital they would visit with flowers and magazines, but now that she was better, they didn't seem to know what to do with her.

Frank [her father] said, "Lucy's personality has changed. She's quieter. She used to clown around. Now she is more serious. In some ways she seems older; she's suffered more and seen other children suffer. In some ways she's younger; she's missed a lot."

Lucy had missed a great deal: ninth-grade graduation, the beginning of high school, parties, dating, sports, school activities and even puberty (the leukemia had delayed her periods and physical development). She had lots of catching up to do. She'd been so vulnerable that her parents were protective. They didn't want her to become tired, to eat junk food, to forget to take her medicines or to take any chances. Her immune system was weak and she could be in trouble with the slightest injury. Lucy, unlike most teens, didn't grimace at her parents' worries. She associated them with staying alive. (Pipher, 1994, p. 84)

From *Reviving Ophelia* by Mary Pipher, Ph.D., copyright 1994 by Mary Pipher, Ph.D. Used by permission of Putnam Berkeley, a division of Penguin Putnam Inc.

Now go to our Companion Website to assess your understanding of chapter content with a Practice Quiz, apply what you've learned in Essay Questions, and broaden your knowledge with links to related Developmental Psychology Web sites. Go to www.prenhall.com/mcdevitt.

- Lucy's illness delayed the onset of puberty. What other effects might her illness have had on her development relative to peers? As you ponder this question, consider her cognitive and social development as well as her physical development.
- In some respects, Lucy probably developed more quickly than most adolescents her age. What particular strengths might Lucy have had as a result of having combated a life-threatening illness?
- As an adult working with this age group, what strategies might you use to ease Lucy's return to school?

SUMMARY

Nature and Nurture in Physical Development

All children have a unique set of genetic instructions that influence not only their characteristics at birth but also (through the process of *maturation*) many characteristics that emerge as they grow. Environmental conditions have a strong impact as well; for instance, nutrition and exposure to toxins affect brain development. Environmental factors frequently interact with genetic predispositions as they nurture physical and psychological traits; for instance, as children grow older and more independent, they are increasingly able to seek out experiences that are compatible with their inherited talents and tendencies. And ultimately, genes require environmental support to do their work.

Principles of Physical Development

Different systems of the body grow at different rates. Over time, physiological functioning becomes both increasingly differentiated (e.g., different cells take on different functions) and increasingly integrated (e.g., different body parts work more closely together). Children seem to have certain targets in physical growth that their bodies aim for, even if temporarily deterred by illness or inadequate nutrition. Overall, physical development is characterized by both quantitative and qualitative change.

Development of the Brain

The human brain is a complex organ that regulates basic physiological functions (e.g., respiration and heart rate), sensations of pleasure and pain, motor skills and coordination, emotional responses, and intellectual pursuits. The brain consists of millions of interconnected circuits of neurons that make up the distinct parts of the brain. During prenatal development, neurons are created and these cells migrate to places where they will do their work. During infancy, the brain creates many connections between neurons; areas of the brain that support perceptual learning show particularly rapid growth. During early and middle childhood, the brain protects those connections that are used most often and lets the others die out; particular refinements also solidify language skills and permit smooth communication between areas of the brain that must be integrated during academic learning. During adolescence, the brain grows in areas that reflect forethought and judgment. Throughout child development and adulthood, the brain changes with learning. In general, human brains are similar to one another in overall structure, but individual differences allow for variations in abilities, learning and experience, and temperament, and in some cases result in cognitive or psychiatric disabilities.

Physical Development Across Childhood

Predictable changes in physical functioning occur during childhood and adolescence. During infancy, survival mechanisms, such as reflexes, are implemented, crying time peaks then decreases, feeding moves from milk to a combination of milk and soft solids, and motor skills permit exploration and learning. Early childhood consists of vigorous physical activity and the acquisition of new motor skills. Middle childhood is a time of consolidation, when growth rate slows down and children put motor skills to purposeful use. Puberty begins in early adolescence and extends over several years' time; on average, girls begin and end this sequence about one and one-half years earlier than boys. Adult height and sexual maturation are attained in late adolescence.

Issues in Physical Well-Being

Health depends on several factors, including eating habits, physical activity, and rest and sleep. Some children and adolescents show patterns of behavior (e.g., eating disorders, choice of sedentary activities, overcommitments that result in insufficient sleep) that may seriously jeopardize their physical well-being. In adolescence, additional health-compromising behaviors may emerge as youths struggle with such temptations as cigarette smoking, alcohol, drugs, and unprotected sexual activity.

Special Physical Needs

Youngsters with chronic illness, serious injuries, and physical disabilities often need modifications in instruction, equipment, or the classroom environment. Ultimately, practitioners should strive to make experiences as "normal" as possible for these children.

KEY CONCEPTS

gene (p. 80)
chromosome (p. 80)
DNA (p. 80)
gamete (p. 80)
meiosis (p. 80)
zygote (p. 81)
monozygotic twins (p. 83)
dizygotic twins (p. 83)
alleles (p. 83)
dominant gene (p. 83)
recessive gene (p. 83)
codominance (p. 83)
polygenic inheritance (p. 83)

maturation (p. 87)
canalization (p. 87)
differentiation (p. 90)
integration (p. 92)
neuron (p. 93)
dendrite (p. 93)
axon (p. 93)
synapse (p. 93)
neurotransmitter (p. 93)
glial cell (p. 93)
hindbrain (p. 94)
midbrain (p. 94)
forebrain (p. 94)

cortex (p. 94)
executive functions (p. 94)
left hemisphere (p. 96)
right hemisphere (p. 96)
schizophrenia (p. 96)
synaptogenesis (p. 99)
synaptic pruning (p. 99)
myelination (p. 100)
reflex (p. 105)
cephalocaudal growth (p. 107)
proximodistal growth (p. 107)
colic (p. 108)
gross motor skills (p. 109)

fine motor skills (p. 109)
puberty (p. 111)
growth spurt (p. 111)
menarche (p. 113)
spermarche (p. 113)
personal fable (p. 114)
obesity (p. 117)
anorexia nervosa (p. 117)
bulimia (p. 117)
rough-and-tumble play (p. 119)
Sudden Infant Death Syndrome (p. 122)
addiction (p. 126)

Symoen, age 9

Melissa, age 12

Cognitive Development 1: Piaget and Vygotsky

CASE STUDY: WHALE WATCHING

Six-year-old Kerry and her mother are talking about their family's recent whale-watching expedition:

Mother: And we went with, who'd we go with?
Kerry: David.
Mother: David. Who else?
Kerry: And Nana and Papa.
Mother: And who else? Daddy went too, didn't he?
Kerry: Yeah.
Mother: Yeah. Who else?
Kerry: That's all.
Mother: Oh, and Auntie Karen and Uncle Pete, right?
Kerry: Yeah.
Mother: And David's two brothers.
Kerry: Mmhm.
Mother: We went whale watching and um I think it turned out to be a disaster because it was rough out there and we got kind of seasick. We did see whales, but not as good as we wanted to.
Kerry: I saw one.
Mother: Yeah, we saw them. They're big, huh?
Kerry: [Nods.]
Mother: How many were there?
Kerry: About thirteen.
Mother: About thirteen! There were only two or three!
Kerry: No, there wasn't, because they were runnin' back and forth like fifty times!
(Hemphill & Snow, 1996, p. 182)

Art by Ian, age 6.

Kerry has almost certainly learned something about the animal world from her whale-watching experience. By observing whales firsthand, she has probably acquired a better understanding of the characteristics and behaviors of whales than she could gain from a verbal description or picture book illustrations. At the same time, Kerry's interpretations of what she observed may not be entirely accurate. For instance, she and her mother disagree about the number of whales that the group saw, and one of them—perhaps both of them—counted incorrectly. Furthermore, Kerry can recall certain aspects of the expedition, such as the specific people who accompanied her, only with her mother's assistance.

The conversation between Kerry and her mother gives us a brief glimpse at how a young child thinks about a particular event. It is an example of cognition in action. **Cognition** encompasses all the mental activities in which a person engages, including perception, categorization, understanding, inference drawing, logical reasoning, problem solving, imagination, and memory. These processes evolve and change in many ways over the course of childhood and adolescence. As Kerry grows older, for example, she will acquire many new concepts that will help her interpret her experiences with the animal kingdom.

To some extent, cognitive development is a function of physiological maturation. As you discovered in Chapter 3, the brain undergoes a series of genetically controlled changes during infancy, childhood, and adolescence that allow increasingly sophisticated thinking processes. Environmental events—both informal experiences (e.g., play activities with age-mates and encounters with new, intriguing objects) and more formal, planned interventions (e.g., whale-watching trips and classroom lessons)—also play a key, in fact essential, role in the development of children's and adolescents' cognitive capabilities. In addition, as will become clear very shortly, much of children's cognitive development is the result of their own efforts to make sense of their world.

The nature and course of cognitive development are the focus of Chapters 4, 5, and 6. In this chapter, we consider two early theories—those of Jean Piaget and Lev Vygotsky—that have greatly enhanced our understanding of how children's thinking changes with age. In the following two chapters, we look more closely at the development of cognitive processes (Chapter 5) and the nature of intelligence (Chapter 6).

Piaget's Theory of Cognitive Development

Children of different ages often think and reason very differently about the situations they encounter and the phenomena they observe. Consider, for example, a 6-year-old and an 8-year-old in a study by Piaget (1952a). The experimenter (Exp) shows the children a box that contains about a dozen wooden beads; two of them are white and the rest are brown. The 6-year-old, whom we'll call Brian,[1] responds to the experimenter's questions as follows:

Exp:	Are there more wooden beads or more brown beads?
Brian:	More brown ones, because there are two white ones.
Exp:	Are the white ones made of wood?
Brian:	Yes.
Exp:	And the brown ones?
Brian:	Yes.
Exp:	Then are there more brown ones or more wooden ones?
Brian:	More brown ones.
Exp:	What color would a necklace made of the wooden beads be?
Brian:	Brown and white. (Here [Brian] shows that he understands that all the beads are wooden.)
Exp:	And what color would a necklace made with the brown beads be?
Brian:	Brown.
Exp:	Then which would be longer, the one made with the wooden beads or the one made with the brown beads?
Brian:	The one with the brown beads.
Exp:	Draw the necklaces for me.

cognition
The various mental activities in which a person engages.

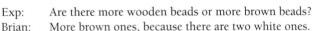

[1]Piaget identified individuals in his studies by abbreviations. We've substituted names throughout the text to allow for easier discussion.

Brian draws a series of black rings for the necklace of brown beads; he then draws a series of black rings plus two white rings for the necklace of wooden beads.

Exp: Good. Now which will be longer, the one with the brown beads or the one with the wooden beads?
Brian: The one with the brown beads. (dialogue from Piaget, 1952a, pp. 163–164)

The experimenter gives 8-year-old "Natalie" the same problem:

Exp: Are there more wooden beads or more brown beads?
Natalie: More wooden ones.
Exp: Why?
Natalie: Because the two white ones are made of wood as well.
Exp: Suppose we made two necklaces, one with all the wooden beads and one with all the brown ones. Which one would be longer?
Natalie: Well, the wooden ones and the brown ones are the same, and it would be longer with the wooden ones because there are two white ones as well. (dialogue from Piaget, 1952a, p. 176)

Brian has difficulty with a question that, to us, seems ridiculously simple. Even though all the beads are wooden and only some (albeit the majority) are brown, he concludes that there are more brown beads than wooden ones. Natalie, who is two years older, answers the question easily: Logically there must be more wooden beads than brown beads. Natalie exhibits **class inclusion**, the recognition that an object can belong both to a particular category and to one of its subcategories simultaneously.

In the early 1920s, the Swiss biologist Jean Piaget began studying children's responses to a wide variety of problems, including the class inclusion problem just described (e.g., Piaget, 1928, 1952a, 1959, 1970; Piaget & Inhelder, 1969). He was particularly curious about the nature of knowledge and how children acquire it. To determine where knowledge comes from and the forms that it takes at different age levels, he observed the everyday actions of infants and children and drew inferences about the logic that seemed to be influencing their behavior. He also pioneered the use of a procedure he called the **clinical method**, whereby he gave children a variety of tasks and problems (among them the "wooden beads" problem just illustrated) and asked a series of questions about each one. Piaget tailored his interviews to the particular responses that children gave, with follow-up questions varying from one child to the next. This approach enabled him to probe the specific reasoning processes that the children were using. The results of his studies provide many unique insights about how children think and learn about the world around them.

Key Ideas in Piaget's Theory

From his observations of children in problem-solving situations, Piaget derived numerous concepts and principles related to the nature of cognitive development. Among the most central ones are the following:

■ *Children are active and motivated learners.*   Piaget believed that children do not just passively observe and remember the things they see and hear. Instead, they are naturally curious about their world and actively seek out information to help them understand and make sense of it (e.g., Piaget, 1952b). They continually experiment with the objects they encounter, manipulating them and observing the effects of their actions. For example, we authors think back (without much nostalgia) to the days when our children were in high chairs, experimenting with their food (picking it up, and squishing, pushing, rolling, dropping, and throwing it) as readily as they would eat it.

■ *Children organize what they learn from their experiences.*   Children don't just assemble the things they learn into a collection of isolated facts. Instead, they pull their experiences together into an integrated view of how the world operates. For example, by observing that food, toys, and other objects always fall down (never up) when released, children begin to construct a rudimentary understanding of gravity. As they interact with family pets, visit zoos, look at picture books, and so on, they develop an increasingly complex understanding of animals. Piaget depicted learning as a very *constructive* process: Children actively create their understandings of the world rather than just passively absorbing their experiences.

class inclusion
Recognition that something simultaneously belongs to a particular category and to one of its subcategories.

clinical method
Procedure whereby a researcher probes a child's reasoning about a task or problem, tailoring questions to follow up on what the child has previously said or done.

In Piaget's terminology, the things that children learn and can do are organized as **schemes,** groups of similar thoughts or actions. Initially, children's schemes are largely behavioral in nature, but over time they become increasingly mental and, eventually, abstract. For example, an infant may have a scheme for putting things in her mouth, a scheme that she uses in dealing with a variety of objects, including her thumb, her toys, and her blanket. A 7-year-old may have a scheme for identifying snakes, one that includes their long, thin bodies, their lack of legs, and their slithery nature. As a 13-year-old, Jeanne's daughter Tina had her own opinion about what constitutes fashion, a scheme that allowed her to classify various articles of clothing on display at the mall as being either "totally awesome" or "really stupid."

Piaget proposed that children use newly acquired schemes over and over in both familiar and novel situations. For example, in the Cognitive Development/Infancy clip on the Observation CD, you can observe 16-month-old Corwin repeatedly taking a toy out of a paper bag and then putting it back in. In the process of repeating their schemes, children refine them and begin to use them in combination with one another. Eventually, they integrate schemes into larger systems of mental processes called **operations.** This integration allows them to think in increasingly sophisticated and logical ways. For instance, 8-year-old Natalie's reasoning about the "beads" problem shows greater integration than 6-year-old Brian's: Although both children understand that some beads are both brown and wooden, only Natalie takes both characteristics into account simultaneously to conclude that there must be more wooden beads than brown beads. Brian apparently can consider only one characteristic at a time; as a result, he compares the brown beads only with the remaining wooden beads (the white ones) and thereby concludes that there are more brown ones than wooden ones.

Observe Corwin repeating "putting-in" and "taking-out" schemes in the Cognitive Development/Infancy clip.

■ *Children adapt to their environment through the processes of assimilation and accommodation.* According to Piaget, children's developing schemes allow them to respond in ever more successful ways to their environment through a developmental process called **adaptation.** Adaptation occurs as a result of two complementary processes: assimilation and accommodation.

Assimilation entails dealing with an object or event in a way that is consistent with an existing scheme. For example, an infant may assimilate a ball into her putting-things-in-the-mouth scheme. A 7-year-old may quickly identify a new slithery object in the backyard as a snake. A 13-year-old may readily label a schoolmate's clothing as being either quite fashionable or "soooo *yesterday.*"

Sometimes children cannot easily interpret a new object or event using their existing schemes. In these situations, one of two forms of **accommodation** will occur. Children will either modify an existing scheme to account for the new object or event or form an entirely new scheme to deal with it. For example, an infant may have to open her mouth wider than usual to accommodate a large plastic ball or teddy bear's paw. The 13-year-old may have to revise her existing scheme of fashion according to changes in what's hot and what's not. The 7-year-old may find a long, thin, slithery thing that can't possibly be a snake because it has four legs. After some research, he will develop a new scheme—*salamander*—for this creature.

Although children's schemes change over time, the two processes through which their schemes are acquired and modified—assimilation and accommodation—remain the same throughout the course of development. Assimilation and accommodation typically work hand in hand as children develop knowledge and understanding of the world. Children interpret each new event within the context of their existing knowledge (assimilation) but at the same time may modify their knowledge as a result of the new event (accommodation). Accommodation rarely happens without assimilation. People of any age can benefit from (accommodate to) new experiences only when they can relate those experiences to their current knowledge and beliefs.

■ *Interaction with one's physical environment is critical for cognitive development.* New experiences are essential for cognitive development; without them, the modification of schemes through accommodation cannot take place. By exploring and manipulating the world around them—by conducting many little "experiments" with various objects and

scheme
In Piaget's theory, an organized group of similar actions or thoughts.

operation
In Piaget's theory, an organized and integrated system of thought processes.

adaptation
Developmental process of responding to the environment in an increasingly effective manner.

assimilation
Dealing with a new event in a way that is consistent with an existing scheme.

accommodation
Dealing with a new event by either modifying an existing scheme or forming a new one.

substances—children learn the nature of such physical characteristics as volume and weight, discover principles related to force and gravity, acquire a better understanding of cause-effect relationships, and so on. Activities such as "fiddling" with sand and water, playing games with balls and bats, and experimenting in a science laboratory help children construct a more complete and accurate understanding of how the physical world operates. The following anecdote from preschool teacher Frances Hawkins illustrates this process:

> Tommy . . . had built a tower on a base of three regular blocks on end, with a round, flat piece of Masonite on top. Then on top of this were three more blocks and Masonite, supporting in turn a third story. Each story was defined by round, flat pieces of Masonite in the structure. The tower was already taller than Tommy, and he had a piece of triangular Masonite in hand and was gently testing the tower's steadiness against his taps. Small taps and the tower would lean, settle, and become still. Again and again he varied the strength and place of the taps; watched, waited, tapped again, and finally—on purpose—did hit hard enough to topple the structure. Then the entire process of building the tower and testing it was repeated. (Hawkins, 1997, p. 200)

■ *Interaction with other people is equally critical.* As you will soon discover, young children often have difficulty seeing the world from anyone's perspective but their own. By conversing, exchanging ideas, and arguing with others, they gradually begin to realize that different individuals see things differently and that their own view of the world is not necessarily a completely accurate or logical one. Elementary school children may begin to recognize logical inconsistencies in what they say and do (e.g., recall Brian's insistence that there were more brown beads than wooden beads) when someone else points out those inconsistencies. Through discussions with peers or adults about social and political issues, high school students may slowly modify their newly emerging idealism about how the world "should" be.

■ *The process of equilibration promotes progression toward increasingly complex forms of thought.* Piaget proposed that children are sometimes in a state of **equilibrium:** They can comfortably explain new events in terms of existing schemes. But equilibrium doesn't continue indefinitely. As children grow, they frequently encounter situations that they cannot adequately explain in terms of their current understanding of the world. These situations create **disequilibrium**, a sort of mental "discomfort" that spurs them to try to make sense of what they observe. By replacing, reorganizing, or better integrating their schemes (in other words, through accommodation), children eventually are able to understand and explain previously puzzling events. The movement from equilibrium to disequilibrium and back to equilibrium again is known as **equilibration.** Equilibration and children's intrinsic desire to achieve equilibrium promote the development of more complex levels of thought and knowledge.

Let's return to the case of Brian and the "beads" problem presented earlier. The experimenter asks Brian to draw two necklaces, one made with the wooden beads and one made with the brown beads. The experimenter hopes that after Brian draws a brown-and-white necklace that is longer than an all-brown necklace, he will notice that his drawings are inconsistent with his statement that there are more brown beads. The inconsistency might lead Brian to experience disequilibrium, perhaps to the point where he would reevaluate his conclusion and realize that the number of all the brown beads plus two white ones must necessarily be greater than the number of brown beads alone. In this case, however, Brian apparently is oblivious to the inconsistency, remains in equilibrium, and so has no need to revise his thinking.

■ *Children think in qualitatively different ways at different age levels.* Piaget was a *stage theorist:* He proposed that children proceed through four stages of cognitive development and that their thinking and reasoning processes are qualitatively different at each one. These qualitative changes in children's thinking are the result of both neurological maturation and the increasing integration of their knowledge and thought processes. Let's examine the characteristics of each stage.

Children and adolescents benefit from opportunities, either informal or structured, to explore and manipulate physical objects. As Curtis and Kyle play basketball (see the Physical Activity/Middle Childhood clip, what laws of physics might they be observing in action?

When children encounter mathematical results that they cannot explain using existing mathematical concepts, they may experience disequilibrium—a mental "discomfort" that may motivate them to acquire more advanced understandings.

equilibrium
State of being able to explain new events in terms of existing schemes.

disequilibrium
State of being unable to explain new events in terms of existing schemes.

equilibration
Movement from equilibrium to disequilibrium and back to equilibrium; a process that promotes the development of increasingly complex forms of thought and knowledge.

FIGURE 4-1 Piaget's stages of cognitive development

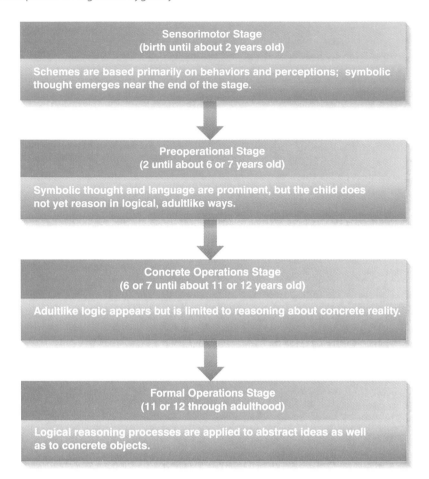

Sensorimotor Stage
(birth until about 2 years old)

Schemes are based primarily on behaviors and perceptions; symbolic thought emerges near the end of the stage.

Preoperational Stage
(2 until about 6 or 7 years old)

Symbolic thought and language are prominent, but the child does not yet reason in logical, adultlike ways.

Concrete Operations Stage
(6 or 7 until about 11 or 12 years old)

Adultlike logic appears but is limited to reasoning about concrete reality.

Formal Operations Stage
(11 or 12 through adulthood)

Logical reasoning processes are applied to abstract ideas as well as to concrete objects.

Piaget's Stages of Cognitive Development

Piaget's four stages of cognitive development are as follows:

1. Sensorimotor stage (birth until about 2 years)
2. Preoperational stage (2 years until about 6 or 7 years)
3. Concrete operations stage (6 or 7 years until about 11 or 12 years)
4. Formal operations stage (11 or 12 years through adulthood)

These stages are briefly summarized in Figure 4–1.

Piaget believed that each stage builds on the accomplishments of any preceding stages, so that children must progress through the four stages in an invariant sequence. Furthermore, he suggested that the stages are *universal*—that they describe the cognitive development of children throughout the world.

As you will discover later in the chapter, many psychologists question the notion that cognitive development is either as stagelike or as universal as Piaget believed. Nevertheless, Piaget's stages provide insights into the nature of children's thinking at different age levels, and we will therefore look at them in depth. Note that the ages associated with each stage are averages; some children may reach a stage at a slightly younger or older age than average. Furthermore, some children may be *transitional* from one stage to the next and so for a short time display characteristics of two adjacent stages simultaneously.

Sensorimotor Stage (Birth Until Age 2) Imagine this situation:

We show a colorful stuffed clown to 6-month-old Elena. Elena reaches for the clown in much the same way that she reaches for her teddy bear and her stacking blocks. She then drops it and squeals in delight as it falls to the floor. We pick up the clown and, as Elena watches, put it inside a box so that it is no longer visible. At this point, Elena seems to forget about her new toy and turns to play with something else.

Elena readily applies several schemes to the clown, including reaching-and-grasping, letting-go, and visually-following-a-moving-object. Yet she acts as if she cannot think about a clown she cannot actually see: it is out of sight and therefore out of mind. Piaget proposed that infants' early schemes are based primarily on perceptions (e.g., visual tracking) and behaviors (e.g., grabbing, dropping)—hence the term *sensorimotor*. Only gradually do infants become capable of developing *mental* schemes that enable them to think about objects beyond their immediate view.

After extensive observations of infants and toddlers, especially his own three children, Piaget described the first two years of life as a series of six substages:

1. Reflexes (birth to 1 month)
2. Primary circular reactions (1–4 months)
3. Secondary circular reactions (4–8 months)
4. Coordination of secondary circular reactions (8–12 months)
5. Tertiary circular reactions (12–18 months)
6. Mental representation (18–24 months)

From her actions as well as her age, we can conclude that 6-month-old Elena is presently in the third substage. Let's look back in time and then follow Elena as she progresses through the six substages of the sensorimotor stage:

Substage 1: Reflexes (birth to 1 month).   In the first month of life, infants' behaviors reflect innate and automatic responses to particular stimuli. For instance, if you put something in or near Elena's mouth at this substage, she will suck on it. If you put something against the palm of her hand, her fingers will close around it. Initially, Elena's actions are automatic, reflexive behaviors (like breathing and coughing) that keep her alive. Yet she soon begins to modify some reflexes to better accommodate to her environment. For instance, she quickly learns to distinguish between a nipple and the surrounding areas of a breast or bottle. And other reflexes, such as the tendency to grab onto something placed in her hand, fade away over time.

Substage 2: Primary circular reactions (1–4 months).   In the first few months of life, infants' behaviors are focused almost exclusively on their own bodies (in Piaget's terminology, the behaviors are *primary*) and are repeated over and over again (i.e., they are *circular*). By the time Elena is 3 months old, she has repeated her innate reflexes countless times. She has also begun to refine them and to combine them into more complex actions. For example, she now opens and closes her hand and then puts it in her mouth. Although she is more focused on her own body than on the world around her, she is beginning to anticipate things that will happen based on clues in her environment. For instance, she may cry when hungry, but when her mother appears, she may quiet down as if she knows that she is about to be fed.

Substage 3: Secondary circular reactions (4–8 months).   Sometime around 4 months, infants become more aware of, and more responsive to, the outside world (in Piaget's terminology, their behaviors become *secondary*), and they begin to notice that their behaviors can have interesting effects on the objects around them. For instance, as we saw earlier, at 6 months Elena picks up and then drops the clown; each time her caregiver gives the clown back to her, she may drop it again yet fret that she no longer has it. Elena seems fascinated by the effects of her actions, although at this point she is not necessarily making a conscious connection between the particular things she does and the resulting consequences. If you watch 7-month-old Madison explore a variety of objects in the Emotional Development/Infancy clip on the Observation CD, you will notice that her explorations seem similarly spontaneous and unplanned. More purposeful behaviors will appear in Substage 4.

Substage 4: Coordination of secondary circular reactions (8–12 months).   After repeatedly observing that certain actions lead to certain consequences, infants gradually acquire knowledge of cause-effect relationships. Accordingly, they begin to engage in **goal-directed behavior**: They behave in ways that they know will bring about desired results. For example, as a 9- or 10-month-old, Elena might drop the clown *intentionally*, knowing in advance that it will fall to the floor and waiting eagerly to see this happen.

Infants in the fourth substage also begin to combine behaviors in new ways to accomplish their goals. For example, when Elena sees the string of a pull-toy near her, rather than

Observe Madison's explorations of objects in the Emotional Development/Infancy clip.

goal-directed behavior
Intentional behavior aimed at bringing about an anticipated outcome.

Observe Corwin's understanding of object permanence in the Cognitive Development/Infancy clip.

crawling over to the toy, she may instead reach out and grab the string. She will purposely pull it and will not be surprised that the toy comes to her so she can pick it up. At Substage 4, infants also acquire **object permanence**, the realization that physical objects continue to exist even when they are removed from view. Whereas at 6 months, Elena forgot about the toy clown once it was put in a box, at 10 months she knows where the clown is and may search its hiding place to retrieve it. In the Cognitive Development/Infancy clip on the Observation CD, 16-month-old Corwin shows object permanence when he looks for the toy elephant that his mother repeatedly hides.

Substage 5: Tertiary circular reactions (12–18 months). Beginning sometime around their first birthday, infants show increasing flexibility and creativity in their behaviors, and their experimentation with objects often leads to new outcomes (the term *tertiary* reflects this new versatility in previously acquired responses). For instance, imagine that at age 15 months, Elena is given a tennis ball and a coffee can. She'll explore the two objects thoroughly, rolling them, dropping them, throwing them, putting the ball inside the can, and so on. Her creative explorations now are quite deliberate.

Piaget illustrated tertiary circular reactions with a description of his daughter Jacqueline, then 14 months old:

> Jacqueline holds in her hands an object which is new to her; a round, flat box which she turns all over, shakes, rubs against the bassinet, etc. She lets it go and tries to pick it up. But she only succeeds in touching it with her index finger, without grasping it. She nevertheless makes an attempt and presses on the edge. The box then tilts up and falls again. Jacqueline, very much interested in this fortuitous result, immediately applies herself to studying it. . . .
>
> Jacqueline immediately rests the box on the ground and pushes it as far as possible (it is noteworthy that care is taken to push the box far away in order to reproduce the same conditions as the first attempt, as though this were a necessary condition for obtaining the result). Afterward Jacqueline puts her finger on the box and presses it. But as she places her finger on the center of the box she simply displaces it and makes it slide instead of tilting it up. She amuses herself with this game and keeps it up (resumes it after intervals, etc.) for several minutes. Then, changing the point of contact, she finally again places her finger on the edge of the box, which tilts it up. She repeats this many times, varying the conditions, but keeping track of her discovery: now she only presses on the edge! (Piaget, 1952b, p. 272)

Substage 6: Mental representation (18–24 months). Piaget proposed that in the latter half of the second year, young children develop **symbolic thought**, the ability to represent and think about objects and events in terms of internal, mental entities, or *symbols*. They may "experiment" with objects in their minds, first predicting what will happen if they do something to an object, then transforming their plans into action. To some degree, mental prediction and planning replace overt trial-and-error as growing toddlers experiment and attempt to solve problems. By the time Elena is 2 years old, she is forming mental images of objects and events; in essence, she now has an imagination. She's also becoming more efficient at solving problems. Although she still uses her body to explore and experiment, her mind is an important part of the process as well.

The capacity for mental representation is seen in the emergence of **deferred imitation**, the ability to recall and copy another person's behaviors hours or days after their behaviors have been observed. Although infants show some ability to imitate others' actions quite early in life (beginning in the second substage, as Piaget noted), up until now they have imitated only the behaviors they see someone else demonstrating on the spot. Their newly acquired ability to recall and imitate other people's *past* actions enables them to engage in make-believe and pretend play. Thus, we may see Elena "talking" on a toy telephone or "driving" with the toy steering wheel attached to her carseat, even when the people around her are preoccupied with other matters. As you will discover shortly, such pretend play serves an important function in Piaget's preoperational stage.

The acquisitions of the sensorimotor stage are basic building blocks on which later cognitive development depends. The Observation Guidelines table "Assessing Cognitive Advances in Infants and Toddlers" presents some of the behaviors you might look for as you work with infants and toddlers. As children move into more advanced stages of development, they don't entirely discard sensorimotor ways of interacting with the environment. Even as adults, we continue to use the behavioral and perceptual schemes we acquired as in-

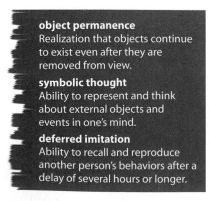

object permanence
Realization that objects continue to exist even after they are removed from view.

symbolic thought
Ability to represent and think about external objects and events in one's mind.

deferred imitation
Ability to recall and reproduce another person's behaviors after a delay of several hours or longer.

OBSERVATION GUIDELINES

Assessing Cognitive Advancements in Infants and Toddlers

CHARACTERISTIC	LOOK FOR	EXAMPLE	IMPLICATION
Repetition of Gratifying Actions	• Repetition of actions involving the child's own body • Repetition of actions on outside objects • Evidence that the child repeats an action because he or she notices and enjoys it	Myra waves her arms, stops, and waves her arms again. She makes a sound and repeats it, almost as if she enjoys hearing the sound of her own voice.	Provide a variety of visual, auditory, and tactile stimuli; for instance, play "This little piggy" with an infant's toes, hang a mobile over the crib, and provide age-appropriate objects (e.g., rattles, plastic cups). Be patient and responsive when seemingly "pointless" actions (e.g., dropping favorite objects) are repeated.
Exploration of Objects	• Apparent curiosity about the effects that different behaviors have on objects • Use of multiple behaviors (feeling, poking, dropping, shaking, etc.) to explore an object's properties • Use of several sensory modalities (e.g., seeing, listening, feeling, tasting)	Paco reaches for his caregiver's large, shiny earring. The caregiver quickly removes the earring from her ear and holds its sharp end between her fingers while Paco manipulates the silver loop and multicolored glass beads that hang from it.	Provide objects that infants can explore using multiple senses, making sure the objects are free of dirt and toxic substances and are large enough to prevent swallowing.
Experimentation	• Creativity and flexibility in the behaviors the child uses to discover how things work • Specific problems that the child tackles and the approaches he or she uses to solve them	Jillian drags a stepstool to her dresser so that she can reach the toys on top of it. One by one, she drops the toys, watching how each one lands and listening to the sound it makes on impact.	Child-proof the environment so that experiments and problem solving are safe. Provide objects that require a sequence of actions (e.g., stacking cups, building blocks, pull toys). Closely supervise toddlers' activities.
Imitation and Pretending	• Imitation of actions modeled by another person • Imitation of actions when the model is no longer present (deferred imitation) • Using one object to stand for another	Darius holds a doll and sings to it the way his mother sings to him. He combs the doll's hair with a spoon and uses an empty plastic vitamin bottle to feed the doll.	Engage children in reciprocal, imitative games (e.g., peekaboo, hide-and-seek). Provide props that encourage pretend play (miniature shopping carts, plastic carpentry tools, dolls, etc.).

fants (reaching and grasping, following a moving object with our eyes, etc.), and sometimes trial-and-error experimentation is the only way to interact with a new and puzzling object.

Preoperational Stage (Age 2 Until Age 6 or 7)   The ability to represent objects and events mentally (i.e., symbolic thought) gives children in the preoperational stage a more extended "world view" than they had during the sensorimotor stage. They can now recall past events and envision future ones and therefore can begin to tie their experiences together into an increasingly complex understanding of the world.

Language skills virtually explode during the early part of the preoperational stage. The words in children's rapidly increasing vocabularies provide labels for newly developed mental schemes and serve as symbols that enable children to think about objects and events even when they are not directly in sight. Furthermore, language provides the basis for a new form of social interaction, verbal communication. Children can express their thoughts and receive information from other people in a way that was not possible during the sensorimotor stage.

The emergence of symbolic thought is reflected not only in rapidly expanding language skills but also in the changing nature of children's play. Young children often engage in fantasy and make-believe, using realistic objects or reasonable substitutes to act out the roles and behaviors of the people they see around them. Piaget proposed that such pretend play enables children to practice using newly acquired symbolic schemes and familiarize themselves with the various roles they see others assume in society. This idea is illustrated in the following scenario, in which 5-year-olds Jeff and Scott construct and operate a "restaurant":

In a corner of Jeff's basement, the boys make a dining area from several child-sized tables and chairs. They construct a restaurant "kitchen" with a toy sink and stove and stock it with plastic dishes and "food" items. They create menus for their restaurant, often asking a parent how to spell the words but sometimes using their knowledge of letter-sound relationships to guess how a particular word might be spelled.

Jeff and Scott invite their mothers and fathers to come to the new restaurant for lunch. After seating their "customers," the boys pretend to write their meal orders on paper tablets and then scurry to the kitchen to assemble the requested lunch items. Eventually they return to serve the meals (hamburgers, French fries, and cookies—all of them plastic—plus glasses of imaginary milk), which the adults "eat" and "drink" with gusto. After the young waiters return with the final bills, the adults pay for their "meals" with nickels and leave a few pennies on the tables as tips.

TABLE 4-1   Preoperational Versus Concrete Operational Thought

PREOPERATIONAL THOUGHT	CONCRETE OPERATIONAL THOUGHT
Egocentrism Inability to see things from someone else's perspective; thinking that one's own perspective is the only one possible. *Example:* A child tells a story without considering what prior knowledge the listener is likely to have.	**Differentiation of one's own perspective from the perspectives of others** Recognition that different people see the same things differently; realization that one's own perspective may be incorrect. *Example:* A child asks for validation of his own thoughts (e.g., "Did I get that right?").
Confusion between physical and psychological events Confusion of external, physical objects with internal thoughts; thinking that thoughts have physical reality and that objects think and feel. *Example:* A child is afraid of the "monsters" in a dark closet and worries that a doll will feel lonely if left alone at home.	**Distinction between physical and psychological events** Recognition that thoughts do not have physical reality and that physical objects don't have psychological characteristics such as "feelings." *Example:* A child realizes that imagined monsters don't exist and that dolls have no thoughts or feelings.
Lack of conservation Belief that amount changes when a substance is reshaped or rearranged, even though nothing has been added or taken away. *Example:* A child asserts that two rows of five pennies similarly spaced have equal amounts; however, when one row is spread out so that it is longer than the other, she says that it has more pennies.	**Conservation** Recognition that amount stays the same if nothing has been added or taken away, even when the substance is reshaped or rearranged. *Example:* A child asserts that two rows of five pennies are the same number of pennies regardless of their spacing.
Irreversibility Lack of awareness that certain processes can be undone, or reversed. *Example:* A child doesn't realize that a row of five pennies previously made longer by extra spacing can be shortened back to its original length.	**Reversibility** Ability to envision how certain processes can be reversed. *Example:* A child moves the five pennies in the longer row close together again to demonstrate that both rows have the same amount.
Reliance on perception over logic Dependence on how things appear when drawing conclusions. *Example:* A child hears a story about a girl whose uncle gives her a baby rattle as a gift. Though sad about the age-inappropriate gift, the girl in the story smiles so that she won't hurt her uncle's feelings. When looking at a picture of the smiling girl, the child concludes that the girl feels happy (Friend & Davis, 1993).	**Reliance on logic over perception** Dependence on conceptual understandings when drawing conclusions. *Example:* A child hearing the same story and seeing the picture of the smiling girl concludes that the girl *looks* happy but actually feels sad (Friend & Davis, 1993).
Single classification Ability to classify objects in only one way at any given point in time. *Example:* A child denies that a mother can also be a doctor.	**Multiple classification** Recognition that objects may belong to several categories simultaneously (includes *class inclusion*). *Example:* A child acknowledges that a mother can also be a doctor, a jogger, and a spouse.
Transductive reasoning Reasoning that involves combining unrelated facts (e.g., inferring a cause-effect relationship simply because two events occur close together in time and space). *Example:* A child believes that clouds make the moon grow (Piaget, 1928).	**Deductive reasoning** Drawing an appropriate logical inference from two or more pieces of information. *Example:* A child deduces that if Jane is taller than Mary, and if Mary is taller than Carol, then Jane must be taller than Carol.

With the emergence of symbolic thought, young children are no longer restricted to the here-and-now and so can think and act far more flexibly than previously. At the same time, preoperational thinking has some definite limitations, especially as compared to the concrete operational thinking that emerges later (see Table 4–1). For example, Piaget described young children as exhibiting **egocentrism**, the inability to view situations from another person's perspective.[2] Young children may have trouble understanding why they must share school supplies with a classmate or why they must be careful not to hurt someone else's feelings. They may play games together without ever checking to be sure that they are all playing according to the same rules. They may also exhibit **egocentric speech**, saying things without considering the perspective of the listener. They may leave out critical details as they tell a story, giving a fragmented version that a listener cannot possibly understand. As an illustration, an adult in Piaget's laboratory once told a story and asked a child whom we'll call Giovanna to retell it:

The original:

Once upon a time, there was a lady who was called Niobe, and who had 12 sons and 12 daughters. She met a fairy who had only one son and no daughter. Then the lady laughed at the fairy because the fairy only had one boy. Then the fairy was very angry and fastened the lady to a rock. The lady cried for ten years. In the end she turned into a rock, and her tears made a stream which still runs today. (Piaget, 1959, p. 82)

Giovanna's version:

Once upon a time there was a lady who had twelve boys and twelve girls, and then a fairy [had] a boy and a girl. And then Niobe wanted to have some more sons. Then she was angry. She fastened her to a stone. He turned into a rock, and then his tears made a stream which is still running today. (Piaget, 1959, p. 102)

Notice that Giovanna never explained who "she," "her," and "he" were—things that couldn't possibly have been obvious to a listener. (She also remembered parts of the story incorrectly. We'll look at the nature of memory in Chapter 5.)

In Giovanna's rendition of the story we find one reason why, from Piaget's perspective, social interaction is so important for cognitive development. Someone listening to the child's story might express confusion about who was angry and who turned into a rock. Repeated feedback from other people helps children learn that their thoughts and feelings are unique to them—that their perception of the world is not always shared by others and, in some cases, may not even reflect the true state of affairs.

Preoperational thinking is also *illogical* (at least from an adult's point of view), especially during the preschool years. For example, a child may draw inaccurate inferences about cause and effect, perhaps saying that clouds make the moon grow (Piaget, 1928). As another example, recall Brian's insistence that there were more brown beads than wooden beads, an error that reflects *single classification,* an inability to categorize an object in more than one way at a time. Following is a third example of the "logic" of children exhibiting preoperational thought:

We show 4-year-old Lucy the three glasses in Figure 4–2. Glasses A and B are identical in size and shape and contain an equal amount of water. We ask Lucy if the two glasses of water contain the same amount, and she replies confidently that they do. We then pour the water in Glass B into Glass C. We ask her if the two glasses of water (A and C) still have the same amount. "No," Lucy replies. She points to glass A: "That glass has more because it's taller."

Lucy's response illustrates a lack of **conservation:** She does not realize that because no water has been added or taken away, the amount of water in the two glasses must be equivalent. Young children often confuse changes in appearance with actual changes in amount. Piaget suggested that such confusion occurs, in general, because children in the preoperational stage depend more on perception than on logic when they reason. In the Cognitive Development/Early Childhood clip of the Observation CD, notice how 2-year-old Maddie

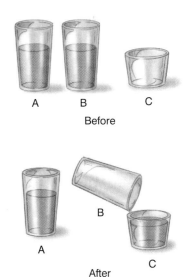

A B C
Before

A B C
After

FIGURE 4–2 Conservation of liquid: Do glasses A and C contain the same amount of water after the water in B is poured into C?

egocentrism
Inability of a child in Piaget's preoperational stage to view situations from another person's perspective.

egocentric speech
Speaking without taking the perspective and knowledge of the listener into account.

conservation
Realization that if nothing is added or taken away, amount stays the same regardless of any alterations in shape or arrangement.

---

[2]Bjorklund and Green (1992) have suggested that young children's egocentrism, rather than being a limitation, may actually have an adaptive function. A common finding in studies of human learning is that people can remember information more easily when they see its relevance to their own lives.

Observe Maddie's age-typical lack of conservation of number in the Cognitive Development/Early Childhood clip.

is easily swayed by appearance when the "fishy crackers" in one row are spaced farther apart than in the other row.

As children approach the later part of the preoperational stage, perhaps at around 4 or 5 years of age, they show early signs of being logical. For example, they sometimes draw correct conclusions about conservation problems (e.g., the water glasses) or classification problems (e.g., the wooden beads). They cannot yet explain *why* their conclusions are correct, however; they base their reasoning on hunches and intuition rather than on any conscious awareness of underlying logical principles. When children move into the concrete operations stage, they become increasingly able both to make logical inferences and to explain the reasoning behind their conclusions.

Concrete Operations Stage (Age 6 or 7 Years Until Age 11 or 12)   At about age 6 or 7, children's thinking processes become integrated into *operations* that allow them to pull their thoughts and ideas together more effectively than they have before. As a result, concrete operational thought is more advanced than preoperational thought in a number of ways (see Table 4–1). For example, children now realize that their own thoughts and feelings are not necessarily shared by others and may reflect personal opinions rather than reality. Accordingly, they know that they can sometimes be wrong and begin to seek out external validation for their ideas, asking such questions as "What do you think?" and "Did I get that problem right?"

Children in the concrete operations stage are capable of many forms of logical thought. For instance, they show conservation: They readily understand that if nothing is added or taken away, amount stays the same despite any changes in shape or arrangement. (As an example, see 10-year-old Kent's response to the M&Ms task in the Cognitive Development/Middle Childhood clip on the Observation CD.) They can readily classify objects into two categories simultaneously. (Recall 8-year-old Natalie's ease in solving the wooden beads versus brown beads problem.) And they demonstrate deductive reasoning: They can draw logical inferences from the facts they are given.

Observe how Kent conserves number but has difficulty with proverbs in the Cognitive Development/Middle Childhood clip.

Children continue to develop their newly acquired logical thinking capabilities throughout the elementary school years. For instance, over time they become capable of dealing with increasingly complex conservation tasks. Some forms of conservation, such as conservation of liquid and conservation of number (the latter illustrated by the M&Ms problem in the Cognitive Development/Middle Childhood clip and the "pennies" problem in Table 4–1), appear at age 6 or 7, but other forms may not appear until several years later. Consider the task involving conservation of weight depicted in Figure 4–3. Using a balance scale, an adult shows a child that two balls of clay have the same weight. One ball is removed from the scale and smashed into a pancake shape. The child is then asked if the pancake weighs the same as the unsmashed ball, or if the two pieces of clay weigh different amounts. Children typically do not achieve conservation of weight—that is, they do not realize that the flattened pancake weighs the same as the round ball—until sometime around age 9–12 (Sund, 1976).

Although children displaying concrete operational thought show many signs of logical thinking, their cognitive development is not yet complete (see Table 4–2). They have difficulty thinking about proportions and ratios, formulating and testing hypotheses, and separating and controlling variables—processes central to adult forms of mathematical and

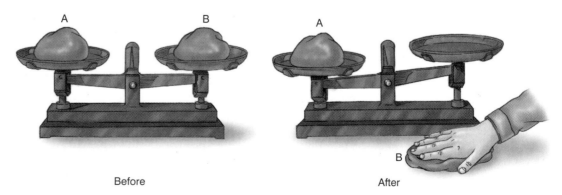

Before   After

FIGURE 4–3   Conservation of weight: Balls A and B initially weigh the same. When Ball B is flattened into a pancake shape, how does its weight now compare with that of Ball A?

TABLE 4-2 **Concrete Operational Versus Formal Operational Thought**

CONCRETE OPERATIONAL THOUGHT	FORMAL OPERATIONAL THOUGHT
Dependence on concrete reality Logical reasoning only about concrete objects that are readily observed. *Example:* A child has difficulty with the concept of negative numbers, wondering how something can possibly be less than zero.	***Ability to reason about abstract, hypothetical, and contrary-to-fact ideas*** Logical reasoning about things that are not tied directly to concrete, observable reality. *Example:* A child understands negative numbers and is able to use them effectively in mathematical procedures and problems.
Inability to formulate and test multiple hypotheses Identifying and testing only one hypothesis when seeking an explanation for a scientific phenomenon. *Example:* When asked what makes a pendulum swing faster or more slowly, a child states that the weight of the pendulum is the determining factor and disregards any observations she has made that contradict her hypothesis.	***Formulation and testing of multiple hypotheses*** Developing and testing several hypotheses about cause-effect relationships related to a particular phenomenon. *Example:* When asked what makes a pendulum swing faster or more slowly, a child proposes that weight, length, and strength of initial push are all possible explanations and then tests the effects of each variable.
Inability to separate and control variables Confounding two or more variables when attempting to confirm or disprove a particular hypothesis about a cause-effect relationship. *Example:* In testing possible factors influencing the oscillation rate of a pendulum, a child adds more weight to the pendulum while at the same time also shortening the length of the pendulum string.	***Separation and control of variables*** Testing one variable at a time while holding all others constant, in an attempt to confirm or disprove a particular hypothesis about a cause-effect relationship. *Example:* In testing factors that influence a pendulum's oscillation rate, a child tests the effect of weight while keeping string length and strength of push constant and then tests the effect of length while keeping weight and push constant.
Lack of proportional reasoning Lack of understanding about the nature of proportions. *Example:* A child cannot make sense of the procedure his teacher demonstrates for converting fractions to ratios.	***Proportional reasoning*** Understanding proportions and using them effectively in mathematical problem solving. *Example:* A child works easily with proportions, fractions, decimals, and ratios.

scientific reasoning. They also have trouble understanding and reasoning about abstract ideas. In language, this weakness may be reflected in their difficulty interpreting proverbs (observe 10-year-old Kent's difficulty in the Cognitive Development/Middle Childhood clip on the Observation CD). In mathematics, it may be reflected in their confusion about such concepts as *pi* (π), *infinity,* and *negative numbers.* In social studies, it may limit their comprehension of such abstract notions as *democracy, communism,* and *human rights.* Finally, children who show concrete operational thought are likely to have difficulty reasoning about ideas that involve hypothetical situations or that contradict reality, as a study with children of various ages (Piaget, 1928) illustrates. An adult presented this problem: *Someone said, "If ever I kill myself from despair I won't choose a Friday, because Friday is a bad day and would bring me ill luck." What's silly about that?* Several children responded as follows:

9-year-old: People can kill themselves every day; they don't need to kill themselves on a Friday.
9-year-old: Friday is not unlucky.
10-year-old: Perhaps Friday will bring him good luck.
11-year-old: He doesn't know if it will bring him ill luck. (responses from Piaget, 1928, pp. 63, 65)

The true "silliness" of the situation is, of course, that people who commit suicide don't have to worry about any subsequent bad luck. Yet many elementary school children fail to make the connection; instead, they deny that Friday is a bad day or reject the idea that people can or might kill themselves (Copeland, 1979).

Formal Operations Stage (Age 11 or 12 Through Adulthood) Take a moment to consider the following task:

An object suspended by a rope or string—a pendulum—swings indefinitely at a constant rate. Some pendulums swing back and forth very quickly, whereas others swing more slowly. One or more of four variables might affect how fast a pendulum

swings (i.e., its oscillation rate): the weight of the suspended object, the force with which the object is pushed, the height from which the object is initially released, and the length of the string that holds the object. Design an experiment that can help you determine which of these factors affect(s) a pendulum's oscillation rate.

To identify the one or more factors that influence oscillation rate, you must separate and control variables: You must test one factor at a time while holding all others constant. For instance, to test the hypothesis that weight makes a difference, you should try different weights while keeping constant the force with which you push each weight, the height from which you drop it, and the length of the string. Similarly, if you hypothesize that the length of the string is a critical factor, you should vary the length of the string while continuing to use the same weight and starting the pendulum in motion in the same manner. If you carefully separate and control the variables, your observations should lead you to conclude that only length affects a pendulum's oscillation rate.

Piaget and his colleague Bärbel Inhelder asked children of many ages to tackle the pendulum problem. The following two examples, with children we'll call Craig and Emily, illustrate how children of different ages responded to the problem.

Craig, age 10, begins his experimentation with a long string and a 100-gram weight. He then shortens the string and changes to a 200-gram weight, which he drops from a higher point.

> Exp: Did you find out anything?
> Craig: The little one goes more slowly and the higher it is the faster it goes.

He puts the 50-gram weight on the same short string.

> Craig: The little weight goes even faster.

He then ignores what he just observed.

> Craig: To go faster, you have to pull up [shorten] the string, and the little one goes less fast because it is less heavy.
> Exp: Do you still wonder what you have to do to make it go faster?
> Craig: The little weight goes faster.
> Exp: How can you prove it?
> Craig: You have to pull up the string. (dialogue from Inhelder & Piaget, 1958, p. 71)

Emily, age 15, at first believes that each of the four factors is influential. She studies different weights with the same string length (medium) and does not notice any appreciable change.

> Emily: That doesn't change the rhythm.

She then varies the string length, using the same 200-gram weight.

> Emily: When the string is small, the swing is faster.

Finally, she varies the dropping point and then the strength of the push, each time using the same medium length string and the same 200-gram weight.

> Emily: Nothing has changed. (dialogue from Inhelder & Piaget, 1958, pp. 75–76)

Notice how Craig changes weight and length simultaneously when he experiments, and he has difficulty separating the two variables even when he draws his conclusions (e.g., to prove that weight makes a difference, he says that "You have to pull up the string"). In contrast, Emily systematically tests each of the four variables in isolation from the other three, and she correctly concludes that only length makes a difference.

According to Piaget, several abilities essential for sophisticated scientific and mathematical reasoning emerge in formal operations (see Table 4–2). Three of these—reasoning logically about hypothetical ideas, formulating and testing hypotheses, and separating and controlling variables—together allow adolescents to use a *scientific method,* in which several possible explanations for an observed phenomenon are proposed and tested in a systematic manner. Only with formal operational thinking can people address and answer questions about cause-effect relationships in a truly scientific fashion.

More advanced verbal and mathematical problem solving also appears once formal operational thinking develops. Formal operational thinking makes abstract problems, such as interpreting proverbs and solving mathematical word problems, easier to deal with (notice how easily 14-year-old Alicia interprets proverbs in the Cognitive Development/Late Adolescence clip on the Observation CD). Adolescents generally become better able to understand such concepts as *negative numbers* and *infinity* because they can now comprehend how numbers can be below zero and how two parallel lines will never touch even if they go on forever. And because they can now use proportions in their reasoning, they can make sense of fractions, ratios, and decimals, and they can use proportions to solve problems.

Observe Alicia interpret proverbs in the Cognitive Development/Late Adolescence clip.

Because adolescents capable of formal operational reasoning can deal with hypothetical and contrary-to-fact ideas, they can envision how the world might be different from, and possibly better than, the way it actually is. As a result, they may be idealistic about social, political, religious, and ethical issues. For example, high school students often argue that they should be allowed to wear anything they want to school, no matter how skimpy or suggestive their fashion choices might be. They may reject their parents' political or religious affiliations and seek out alternative belief systems. Many adolescents begin to show concern about world problems and devote some of their energy to worthy causes such as the environment, world hunger, or animal rights. Curiously, however, their devotion may sometimes be more evident in their talk than in their actions (Elkind, 1984).

As adolescents become increasingly able to reason about abstract, hypothetical, and contrary-to-fact ideas, they also become increasingly idealistic about how the world should be.

Idealistic adolescents often offer recommendations for change that seem logical but aren't practical in today's world. For example, they may argue that racism would disappear overnight if people would just begin to "love one another," or they may propose that a nation should disband its armed forces and eliminate all its weaponry as a way of moving toward world peace. Piaget suggested that adolescent idealism reflects an inability to separate one's own logical abstractions from the perspectives of others and from practical considerations. It is only through experience that adolescents eventually begin to temper their optimism with some realism about what is possible in a given time frame and with limited resources.

Current Perspectives on Piaget's Theory

Piaget's theory has inspired hundreds of research studies concerning the nature of children's cognitive development. In general, research supports Piaget's proposed sequence in which different abilities emerge (Flavell, 1996; Siegler & Richards, 1982). For example, the ability to reason about abstract ideas emerges only after children are already capable of reasoning about concrete objects and events (e.g., see Figure 4–4), and the order in which various conservation tasks are mastered is much as Piaget proposed. Researchers have discovered, however, that Piaget was not always accurate regarding the ages at which various abilities appear. They have found, too, that children's logical reasoning capabilities may vary considerably from one occasion to another and are, in part, a function of previous knowledge and experiences, education, and culture. Also, many researchers question the stagelike nature of cognitive development that Piaget proposed. We turn now to these issues; we'll then identify some of Piaget's enduring contributions to the field of child development.

Capabilities of Infants A growing body of research indicates that Piaget probably underestimated the thinking capabilities of young infants. By 4 or 5 months of age (sometimes as early as 3½ months), infants look surprised when objects vanish unexpectedly, supporting the idea that they have some understanding of object permanence earlier than Piaget believed (Baillargeon, 1994). Mental representation of observed events (i.e., symbolic thinking) also emerges sooner than Piaget proposed. Infants as young as 9 months can remember actions that adults perform (e.g., shaking a plastic egg, pushing a button on a box) long enough to imitate them 24 hours later, and in fact babies only 6 weeks old may imitate facial expressions they have seen the day before (Meltzoff, 1988; Meltzoff & Moore, 1994).

FIGURE 4–4 Although Piaget did not always get the ages right, research indicates that, by and large, abilities appear in the general sequence that Piaget suggested. When 4-year-old Isabelle is asked "How were lakes made?" she willingly offers a cause-effect explanation but never questions its accuracy ("You get a bucket and you fill it up with water. You get lots and lots of buckets," left). Older children are more apt to offer plausible explanations and to seek feedback about their responses, but they have difficulty with abstract ideas, as 8-year-old Jeff's literal interpretation of a common figure of speech indicates (center). Adolescents, such as 14-year-old Brady, can more easily think abstractly, and as a result they can envision alternatives to reality, such as fish rowing upside-down at the water's surface (right).

nativism
Theoretical perspective that some knowledge is biologically built in and present at birth.

Furthermore, Piaget overlooked one important distinction that infants begin to make very early in their lives—the distinction between human beings and inanimate objects—and respond to people and objects in distinctly different ways (Trevarthen & Hubley, 1978).

Piaget's theory leads us to believe that infants learn even the most fundamental principles of the physical world by exploring and experimenting with their environment. In contrast, some developmental theorists argue that infants' brains are "preprogrammed" to a certain degree, that infants are born already possessing some basic knowledge, or at least some preliminary intuitions, about their world (e.g., Baillargeon, 1994; Spelke, 1994). For instance, even very young infants seem to know that an object maintains its existence and shape as it moves, that one object can influence another only when the two come into contact, and that two objects cannot occupy the same space at the same time (Spelke, 1994). This idea that some knowledge and inclinations are biologically preprogrammed and therefore present at birth is known as **nativism**. Nativism is prevalent in contemporary views of infant cognition and language development; hence, we will encounter it again in Chapters 5 and 7.

Capabilities of Preschoolers Preschool children are probably more competent than Piaget's description of the preoperational stage would indicate. Children as young as 3 or 4 years old are not completely egocentric; in many situations, they can take another person's perspective. For example, they recognize that an object looks different when viewed from different angles, and they can identify such emotions as sadness or anger in others (Lennon, Eisenberg, & Carroll, 1983; Newcombe & Huttenlocher, 1992).

Preschoolers also think more logically than Piaget suggested. For instance, they often make appropriate inferences when they listen to stories (M. Donaldson, 1978; Gelman & Baillargeon, 1983). Children as young as 4 sometimes show conservation; they are more likely to answer a conservation problem correctly if the transformation occurs out of sight, so that they are not misled by appearances (M. Donaldson, 1978; Rosser, 1994). And many supposedly preoperational children can correctly solve multiple classification problems if words are used to draw attention to the entire group; for example, many 4- and 5-year-olds realize that, in a *forest* of eight pine trees and two oak trees, there must, of course, be more trees than pine trees (Gelman & Baillargeon, 1983; Resnick, 1989; Rosser, 1994).

Why have Piaget and more recent researchers sometimes found conflicting results? Theorists have offered several explanations. One possibility is that the children in Piaget's studies sometimes misinterpreted the wording of his problems (Reyna, 1996; Rosser, 1994). For example, when water is poured from a short, fat glass into a tall, skinny one, children might say that the tall one has more water because they misconstrue the word *more* to mean "higher." Sometimes, too, a question or problem may have more parts (e.g., too many pieces of information in a perspective-taking task, too many candies in a conservation-of-number task) than a child can reasonably keep track of and remember (Gelman, 1972; Newcombe & Huttenlocher, 1992). Also, on some occasions, children may simply say what they think an adult expects them to say (Winer, Craig, & Weinbaum, 1992). For instance, when a researcher asks the same question twice (e.g., "Do the two glasses have the same amount of water?" and later, "Do they still have the same amount?"), children may conclude that a change must have occurred; otherwise, the researcher would not have repeated the question.

Capabilities of Elementary School Children Piaget may have underestimated the capabilities of elementary-age children as well. Children in this age group occasionally show evidence of abstract and hypothetical thought (Carey, 1985b; Metz, 1995). As an illustration, consider this hypothetical situation:

> All of Joan's friends are going to the museum today.

> Pat is a friend of Joan.

Children as young as 9 can correctly deduce that "Pat is going to the museum today" even though the situation involves people they don't know and so has no basis in their own concrete reality (Roberge, 1970). Also, elementary school children can occasionally separate and control variables, especially when the tasks are simplified and they are given hints about the importance of controlling all variables except the one they are testing (Danner & Day, 1977; Metz, 1995; Ruffman, Perner, Olson, & Doherty, 1993). And even first graders can understand simple proportions (e.g., fractions such as ½, ⅓, and ¼) if they can relate them to everyday objects (Empson, 1999).

Capabilities of Adolescents Formal operational thought processes probably emerge much more gradually than Piaget originally proposed. High school and college students often have difficulty with tasks involving such formal operational thinking abilities as separation and control of variables (Flieller, 1999; Kuhn, Amsel, & O'Loughlin, 1988; Pascarella & Terenzini, 1991; Schauble, 1996; Siegler & Richards, 1982). Furthermore, adolescents may demonstrate formal operational thought in one situation or content domain while thinking less logically and more concretely in another (Klaczynski, 2001; Lovell, 1979; Tamburrini, 1982). Evidence of formal operations typically emerges in the physical sciences earlier than in such subjects as history and geography; adolescents often have difficulty thinking about abstract and hypothetical ideas in history and geography until well into the high school years.

A related issue that arises here is whether formal operations is really the final stage of cognitive development, as Piaget suggested. For instance, some theorists have proposed that many adults progress to a fifth, post-formal stage in which they can envision multiple approaches to the same problem and recognize that each approach may be valid from a particular perspective (Commons, Richards, & Armon, 1984; Sinnott, 1998). Other theorists disagree, arguing that adult life simply poses different kinds of problems than the academically oriented ones that adolescents encounter at school (Schaie & Willis, 2000).

Effects of Prior Knowledge and Experience Piaget believed that once children acquire a particular reasoning skill, they can apply it in virtually any context. It is becoming increasingly apparent, however, that for people of all ages, the ability to think logically in a particular situation depends on knowledge and background experiences relative to that situation. Preschoolers are less likely to make incorrect inferences about cause and effect (e.g., to say that clouds make the moon grow) when they have accurate information about cause-effect relationships (Carey, 1985a). Children as young as 4 may begin to show conservation after having experience with conservation tasks, especially if they can actively manipulate the materials of the tasks and are asked to discuss their reasoning with someone who already exhibits conservation (D. Field, 1987; Mayer, 1992; F. B. Murray, 1978).

FIGURE 4–5 What are some possible reasons why Herb is catching more fish than the others?

Based on Pulos & Linn, 1981.

And in general, young children are more likely to think in a concrete operational rather than preoperational fashion if they are familiar with the objects they are dealing with (Ceci & Roazzi, 1994).

Formal operational thought, too, is affected by the specific knowledge and experiences that children and adolescents have acquired. Ten-year-olds can learn to solve logical problems involving hypothetical ideas if they are taught particular strategies for solving such problems (S. Lee, 1985). Children in the upper elementary and middle school grades are better able to separate and control variables in laboratory experiments when they have practice and guidance in doing so (Kuhn & Phelps, 1982; J. A. Ross, 1988; Schauble, 1990). Junior high and high school students, and adults as well, often apply formal operational thought to topics about which they have a great deal of knowledge yet think "concrete operationally" about topics with which they are unfamiliar (Linn, Clement, Pulos, & Sullivan, 1989; Metz, 1995; Schliemann & Carraher, 1993).

As an illustration of how knowledge affects formal operational thinking, consider the fishing pond in Figure 4–5. In a study by Pulos and Linn (1981), 13-year-olds were shown a similar picture and told, "These four children go fishing every week, and one child, Herb, always catches the most fish. The other children wonder why." If you look at the picture, it is obvious that Herb is different from the three other children in several ways, including the kind of bait he uses, the length of his fishing rod, and the place where he is standing. Children who were experienced fishermen more effectively separated and controlled variables for this situation than they did for the pendulum problem described earlier, whereas the reverse was true for nonfishermen (Pulos & Linn, 1981). In the Cognitive Development/Middle Childhood and Late Adolescence clips on the Observation CD, 10-year-old Kent and 14-year-old Alicia both consider this problem, which is presented in Figure 4–5. Notice how Kent, who appears to have some experience with fishing, considers several possible variables, whereas Alicia, admittedly a nonfisherman, considers only two:

Kent: He has live, live worms, I think. Fish like live worms more, I guess 'cause they're live and they'd rather have that than the lures, plastic worms. . . . Because he might be more patient or that might be a good side of the place.

Maybe, since Bill has a boombox thing [referring to the radio], I don't think they would really like that because . . . and he doesn't really have anything that's extra like them all. But he's the standing one. I don't get that. But Bill, that could scare the fish away to Herb because he's closer kind of, I guess.

Alicia: Because of the spot he's standing in probably. . . . I don't know anything about fishing. Oh, okay! He actually has live worms for bait. The other girl's using saltine crackers. . . . She's using plastic worms, he's using lures, and she's using crackers and he's actually using live worms. So, obviously, the fish like the live worms the best.

Observe how experience with fishing affects Kent's and Alicia's ability to identify variables in the Cognitive Development/Middle Childhood and Late Adolescence clips.

One general experience that promotes more advanced reasoning is formal education. Going to school and the specific nature of one's schooling are associated with mastery of concrete operational and formal operational tasks (Artman & Cahan, 1993; Flieller, 1999). For instance, you may be happy to learn that taking college courses in a particular area (in child development, perhaps?) leads to improvements in formal reasoning skills related to that area (Lehman & Nisbett, 1990).

Effects of Culture   Piaget proposed that his stages were universal, that they applied to children and adolescents around the globe. Yet research indicates that the course of cognitive development differs somewhat from one culture to another (Glick, 1975). For example, Mexican children whose families make pottery for a living acquire conservation skills much earlier than Piaget indicated (Price-Williams, Gordon, & Ramirez, 1969). Apparently, making pottery requires children to make frequent judgments about needed quantities of clay and water—judgments that must be fairly accurate regardless of the specific shape or form of the clay or water container. In other cultures, especially in some where children don't attend school, conservation appears several years later than it does in Western cultures, and formal operational reasoning may never appear at all (N. S. Cole, 1990; Fahrmeier, 1978). In such contexts, some logical reasoning skills may simply have little relevance to people's daily activities (J. G. Miller, 1997).

Does Cognitive Development Occur in Stages?   As you have seen, Piaget was not completely on target about when certain abilities develop and, in some cases, whether they develop at all. He also overestimated the extent to which children generalize newly acquired reasoning skills to a broad range of tasks and contexts.

In light of all the evidence, does it then still make sense to talk about discrete stages of cognitive development? A few theorists say yes. In particular, *neo-Piagetian* theorists have proposed stage theories that may more adequately account for current findings about children's logical thinking. However, most contemporary developmentalists believe that cognitive development is not as stagelike as Piaget proposed—that a child does not reason in consistently logical or illogical ways at any particular time period (Flavell, 1994; Kuhn, 2001b; Siegler, 1998). Although children exhibit certain developmental *trends* in their thinking (e.g., a trend toward increasingly abstract thought), their knowledge and experience in particular domains will influence the sophistication of their reasoning.

A perspective known as *information processing theory* characterizes some of the general trends in cognitive processes that we are likely to see as children develop. We describe both information processing theory and neo-Piagetian theories (which draw from information processing theory as well as from Piaget's ideas) in Chapter 5.

Piaget's Enduring Contributions   Despite the concerns we have raised, Piaget's theory has had a profound influence on contemporary theories of cognitive development. His lasting contributions to our understanding of children's thinking include the following insights:

■ *Cognitive development is, to a considerable degree, propelled by intrinsic motivation.*   As you have seen, Piaget believed that children are naturally curious about their environment and therefore actively explore it to learn as much as they can. They are especially motivated when they encounter surprising or puzzling events (those that create disequilibrium). Many contemporary theories of cognition and cognitive development retain such notions of intrinsic motivation: Growing children want to learn more about the people, objects, and

Piaget's belief that children construct rather than absorb knowledge has stood the test of time. This drawing reflects 6-year-old Laura's conception of underwater ocean life.

events around them and naturally engage in the kinds of behaviors and activities that bring about learning and development.

■ *Children actively construct their own knowledge and understandings.* Piaget proposed that through their interactions with their physical and social environments, children construct an increasingly complex view of the world. The idea that children don't just "absorb" their experiences—that they actively try to interpret and make sense of them, and then integrate what they've learned into more general, personally constructed understandings—figures prominently in many contemporary views of learning and cognition.[3] The view that people construct rather than absorb knowledge is generally known as **constructivism**. More specifically, because it focuses on constructive processes within a single person, it is sometimes called **individual constructivism**.

■ *Children benefit only from experiences that they can relate to what they already know.* In Piaget's view, accommodation typically occurs only when it is accompanied by some degree of assimilation. New knowledge, understandings, and reasoning processes (new schemes) are typically derived from previously acquired knowledge and processes (existing schemes). Although Piaget was frustratingly vague about how assimilation and accommodation might actually work (e.g., Klahr, 1982), contemporary developmentalists embrace the idea of new acquisitions being based on earlier ones almost without exception. Developmentally speaking, new knowledge, skills, and cognitive processes don't just appear out of thin air.

■ *The nature of thinking and reasoning changes qualitatively with age.* Whether we talk about discrete stages or more gradual trends, it is clear that children's cognitive processes change qualitatively over time, enabling them to think in increasingly sophisticated ways (e.g., Halford, 1989). Piaget explained developmental change in terms of such concepts as *schemes* (which increase in number and are modified with experience) and *operations* (which become increasingly sophisticated over time). As you will discover in Chapter 5, contemporary theorists also focus on qualitative developmental change, although they are more apt to speak of changes in working memory, long-term memory, cognitive strategies, metacognitive knowledge, and personal "theories" about the nature of living beings and inanimate objects.

Adults can help children learn new information more effectively by building on children's previous knowledge and experiences.

■ *Piaget's stages provide a rough idea of when new abilities are likely to emerge.* Piaget identified and documented many characteristics of children's thinking that researchers continue to study today. We list several of them in the Observation Guidelines table "Assessing Reasoning Skills," where we also give suggestions for working with children and adolescents.

Although we have, we hope, dissuaded you from taking Piaget's stages at face value, we urge you to keep them in mind when considering the kinds of tasks that children and adolescents probably can and cannot do at different ages. Some abilities and *in*abilities may be a function of knowledge and experience (or lack thereof) and therefore subject to change under the right circumstances, whereas others (perhaps because of neurological factors) may be more dependent on time and maturation (Metz, 1997). It is important to remember, too, that children don't necessarily discard their earlier ways of thinking when they acquire more sophisticated ones. For instance, even when children acquire the ability to think abstractly, they may continue to think concretely, and occasionally in a "sensorimotor" fashion, about many of the situations they encounter.

constructivism
Theoretical perspective proposing that learners construct a body of knowledge from their experiences, rather than absorbing information at face value.

individual constructivism
Theoretical perspective that focuses on how people construct meaning from events without the assistance of others.

---

[3]Contemporary theorists have tweaked Piaget's ideas a bit, however. For one thing, they have found that perception of the physical world may be more important than actual physical manipulation of it; for example, even children with significant physical disabilities make major cognitive advancements (Bebko, Burke, Craven, & Sarlo, 1992). Furthermore, whereas Piaget stressed the importance of interaction with peers, contemporary theorists acknowledge that interaction with adults is equally important, albeit for different reasons (Flavell, Miller, & Miller, 1993; Gauvain, 2001). Vygotsky's theory better addresses the importance of interaction with adults.

OBSERVATION GUIDELINES

Assessing Reasoning Skills

CHARACTERISTIC	LOOK FOR	EXAMPLE	IMPLICATION
Egocentrism*	• Describing events without giving listeners sufficient information to understand them • Playing group games without initially agreeing about rules • Difficulty understanding others' perspectives	In her attempt to show Jeremy how to play a computer game, Luisa continually leaves out critical details in her instructions. Yet she doesn't seem to understand why Jeremy is confused.	Let children know when you don't understand what they are telling you. Ask them to share their ideas and opinions with one another.
Concrete Thought	• Dependence on concrete manipulatives to understand concepts and principles • Difficulty understanding abstract ideas	Tobey solves arithmetic word problems more easily when he can draw pictures of them.	Use concrete objects and examples to illustrate abstract situations and problems.
Abstract Thought	• Ability to understand strictly verbal explanations of abstract concepts and principles • Ability to reason about hypothetical or contrary-to-fact situations	Ilsa can imagine how two parallel lines might go on forever without ever coming together.	When working with adolescents, occasionally use verbal explanations (e.g., short lectures) to present information, but assess their understanding frequently to make sure they understand.
Idealism	• Idealistic notions about how the world should be • Inability to take other people's needs and perspectives into account when offering ideas for change • Inability to adjust ideals in light of what can realistically be accomplished	Martin advocates a system of government in which all citizens contribute their earnings to a common "pool" and then withdraw money only as they need it.	Engage adolescents in discussions about challenging political and social issues.
Scientific Reasoning Skills	• Identifying multiple hypotheses for a particular phenomenon • Separation and control of variables	Serena proposes three possible explanations for a result she has obtained in her physics lab.	Have middle school and high school students design and conduct simple experiments. Include experiments about issues related to their backgrounds and interests.
Mathematical Reasoning Skills	• Understanding and using abstract mathematical symbols (e.g., π, the variable x in algebraic equations) • Understanding and using proportions in mathematical problem solving	Giorgio uses a 1:240 scale when drawing a floor plan of his school building.	Initially, introduce abstract mathematical concepts and tasks (e.g., proportional reasoning) using simple examples (e.g., fractions such as $\frac{1}{3}$ and $\frac{1}{4}$). Progress to more complex examples only when young people appear ready to handle them.

*Consistent with common practice, our use of the term *egocentrism* here refers to the egocentric thinking that characterizes preoperational thought. Piaget actually talked about different forms of egocentrism at each of the four stages of development. For instance, in Piaget's mind, the idealism of adolescence is another form of egocentrism. More specifically, it reflects an inability to distinguish one's own logical conclusions from the perspectives of others and from constraints of the real world.

■ *Piaget's clinical method reveals a great deal about children's thinking processes.* The many tasks that Piaget developed to study children's reasoning abilities—tasks dealing with conservation, classification, separation and control of variables, for example—and the kinds of probing follow-up questions that he pioneered yield invaluable insights about the logic that children and adolescents use when they think about their world. Researchers and practitioners alike frequently use Piaget's tasks and method in their efforts to uncover how children and adolescents think and learn.

Implications of Piaget's Theory and Post-Piagetian Research

Piaget's theory and the body of research it has inspired have numerous practical implications for educators, caregivers, and other professionals. These include the following:

See examples of age-appropriate objects for exploration in the Emotional Development/ Infancy clip.

■ *Provide opportunities for children to experiment with physical objects and natural phenomena.*   Children of all ages can learn a great deal by exploring the natural world in a hands-on fashion. In infancy this might involve having regular access to objects with visual and auditory appeal, such as mobiles, rattles, stacking cups, and pull toys (note the plastic tower, books, and musical octopus in the Emotional Development/Infancy clip on the Observation CD). At the preschool level, this might involve playing with water, sand, wooden blocks, and age-appropriate manipulative toys. During the elementary school years, hands-on exploration might entail throwing and catching balls, going on nature walks, working with clay and watercolor paints, or constructing Popsicle-stick structures.

Despite their increased capabilities for abstract thought in adolescence, teenagers also benefit from opportunities to manipulate and experiment with concrete materials—perhaps equipment in a science lab, cameras and film, food and cooking utensils, or wood and woodworking tools. Such opportunities allow them to discover laws of the natural world firsthand and to tie their newly emerging abstract ideas to the physical, concrete world.

■ *Explore children's reasoning with problem-solving tasks and probing questions.*   By presenting a variety of Piagetian tasks involving either concrete or formal operational thinking skills—tasks involving conservation, multiple classification, separation and control of variables, proportional reasoning, and so on—and observing children's responses to such tasks, adults can gain valuable insights into how the children think and reason. They can then tailor activities and instructional materials accordingly. Figure 4–6 presents an example of a Piagetian task that one might use to probe children's reasoning processes about the concept of *area.*

Observe the use of probing questions in the Research/Early Adolescence clip.

To probe children's reasoning in novel situations, teachers and other practitioners need not stick to traditional Piagetian tasks. On the contrary, Piaget's clinical method is applicable to a wide variety of content domains and subject matter. For example, in the Research/Early Adolescence clip on the Observation CD, an interviewer asks 12-year-old Claudia a series of questions to probe her reasoning in a categorization task. Using a similar approach, Liben and Downs (1989) showed young children (kindergartners, first graders, and second graders) various kinds of maps (e.g., a road map of Pennsylvania, an aerial map of Chicago, a three-dimensional relief map of a mountainous area) and asked the children to interpret what they saw. The children interpreted many of the symbols in a concrete fashion. For example, some correctly recognized some of the roads "because they are gray" but thought that the roads marked in red were actually painted red. The children also had trouble understanding the scales of the maps (a finding consistent with Piaget's belief that proportional reasoning doesn't emerge until considerably later). For example, one child rejected the idea that a road could be a road because it was "too skinny for two cars to fit on," and another denied that mountains on a relief map were mountains because "they aren't high enough."

■ *Keep Piaget's stages in mind when interpreting children's behavior and planning activities, but don't take the stages too literally.*   Piaget's four stages are not always accurate descriptions of children's and adolescents' thinking capabilities. Nevertheless, you might think of the stages as providing a rough idea about the cognitive processes you are apt to see at various age levels (Kuhn, 1997; Metz, 1997). For example, infant caregivers should remember that repetitive behaviors, even those that make a mess or cause inconvenience (dropping food, throwing toys), are one important means through which infants master basic motor skills and learn cause-effect relationships. Preschool teachers should not be surprised to hear young children arguing that the three pieces of a broken candy bar constitute more candy than a similar, unbroken bar (a belief that reflects lack of conservation). Elementary school teachers should recognize that their students are likely to have trouble with proportions (e.g., fractions, decimals) and with such abstract concepts as *historical time* in history, and *place value, negative numbers,* and *pi* in mathematics (Barton & Levstik, 1996; Byrnes, 1996; Tourniaire & Pulos, 1985). And educators and other professionals who work with adolescents should expect to hear passionate arguments that reflect idealistic yet unrealistic notions about how society should operate.

Materials:
2 sheets of 8½" by 11" green construction paper
2 small toy cows
24 sugar cubes or equal-size small wooden blocks

Procedure:

In Piaget's clinical method, the interviewer tailors questions to the particular things that a child has previously said and done, but such flexibility often comes only with considerable experience. Here we present a procedure that a novice interviewer might use in presenting a conservation-of-area task.

1. Lay the 2 sheets of construction paper side by side, and place a cow on each sheet. Say, *These two cows are grazing in their pastures. Do they each have the same amount of grass to eat?* The child will probably say yes. Place a cube on each sheet and say, *A farmer builds a barn in each pasture. Do the two cows still have the same amount of grass to eat, or does one cow have more than the other?* The child will probably say that the cows each have the same amount.
2. Add 3 more cubes to each sheet. On the first sheet, place the cubes next to the first cube so that they form a square. On the second sheet, scatter 3 additional cubes around the pasture. Ask, *The farmer builds three more barns in each pasture, like this. Do the cows still have the same amount of grass to eat, or does one have more?*

3. Place 8 more cubes on the first sheet, placing them next to the square so that the 12 cubes form a rectangle. Place 8 more cubes on the second sheet, scattering them around the pasture. Ask, *The farmer builds eight more barns in each pasture, like this. Do the cows still have the same amount of grass to eat, or does one have more?* After the child responds, ask, *How do you know?*
4. If the child says that both cows have the same amount, say, *The other day, someone told me that this cow has more to eat* (point to the cow on the second sheet). *What could you do or say to convince that person that the two cows have the same amount?*

Interpretation:

Children who have fully achieved conservation of area realize that the amount of grass is the same if the same number of barns are placed in each pasture, despite the different arrangements of the barns. To justify a "same" response, children might (a) explain that the same number of barns cover the same amount of grass regardless of their arrangement or (b) move the scattered barns in the second pasture into a rectangular shape similar to that of the barns in the first pasture. In Piaget's theory, conservation of area appears early in the concrete operations stage.

FIGURE 4–6 Conservation of area: An example of how one might probe children's reasoning processes with Piaget's clinical method

Piaget's stages also provide guidance about strategies that are likely to be effective in teaching children at different age levels. For instance, given the abstract nature of historical time, elementary school teachers planning history lessons should probably minimize the extent to which they talk about specific dates before the recent past (Barton & Levstik, 1996). Also, particularly in the elementary grades (and to a lesser degree in middle and high school), instructors should find ways to make abstract ideas more concrete for their students. As one simple example, a third-grade teacher, realizing that *place value* might be a

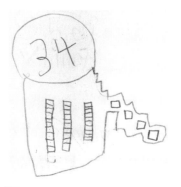

FIGURE 4-7 Noah's depiction of the number 34

difficult concept for her students to comprehend, showed them how to depict 2-digit numbers with blocks, using 10-block rows for the number in the 10s column and single blocks for the number in the 1s column. In Figure 4–7, one of her students, 8-year-old Noah, depicts the number "34" using this approach.

■ *Present situations and ideas that children cannot easily explain using their existing knowledge and beliefs.* Events and information that conflict with youngsters' current understandings create disequilibrium that may motivate them to reevaluate and perhaps modify what they "know" to be true. For instance, if they believe that "light objects float and heavy objects sink" or that "wood floats and metal sinks," an instructor might present a common counterexample: a metal battleship (floating, of course) that weighs many tons.

■ *Plan group activities in which young people share their beliefs and perspectives with one another.* As noted earlier, Piaget proposed that interaction with peers helps children realize that others often view the world very differently than they do and that their own ideas are not always completely logical or accurate. Interactions with age-mates, especially those that involve conflicts or differences of opinion, are likely to create disequilibrium and thus may spur children to reevaluate their current perspectives.

Many contemporary psychologists share Piaget's belief in the importance of such **sociocognitive conflict** (e.g., Damon, 1984; De Lisi & Golbeck, 1999; N. M. Webb & Palincsar, 1996). They have offered several reasons why interactions with peers may help promote cognitive growth:

- Peers speak at a level that children can understand.
- Whereas children may accept an adult's ideas without argument, they are more willing to challenge and contest the ideas of their peers.
- When children hear competing views held by peers—individuals who presumably have knowledge and abilities similar to their own—they may be motivated to reconcile the contradictions.
  (Champagne & Bunce, 1991; Damon, 1984; Hatano & Inagaki, 1991)

A study by N. Bell, Grossen, and Perret-Clermont (1985) illustrates the effect that sociocognitive conflict can have on young children's logical reasoning capabilities. Young children who did not yet demonstrate conservation of liquid (i.e., they stated that two differently shaped glasses contained different amounts of water) were each paired with a same-age partner and asked to play a "game" in which the two had to share equal amounts of juice. The experimenter gave the nonconserving children two glasses, one taller and thinner than the other, and asked them to pour the same amount of juice into each one. In most cases, the children poured juice to equal heights in the two glasses, which provoked disagreement from their partners. The "game" ended only after the children and their partners both agreed that they had the same amount of juice to drink. On a conservation posttest a week later, the children showed greater gains in their ability to conserve liquid than a control group who had worked with the same materials alone.

Research by Kuhn, Shaw, and Felton (1997) illustrates similar effects of peer interaction and conflict for adolescents. For five successive weeks, seventh and eighth graders met in pairs to discuss capital punishment, a topic about which many of them had strong yet varying opinions. Students were paired with different partners each week so that, over the course of the experiment, they were exposed to opinions both consistent and discrepant with their own. During the paired discussions, the students were observed asking questions that clearly challenged one another's reasoning (e.g., "What do you mean by 'justifiable'?"; "Do you think that [capital punishment] is going to stop them from doing that?"). After the fifth discussion, the researchers found that the students' reasoning about capital punishment had changed in several important ways:

- The students had a better understanding of both the pros and cons of capital punishment.
- Although few students completely reversed their positions on capital punishment, many took a less extreme stance on the issue.
- The students identified more reasons for believing as they did than they had before the discussions.

sociocognitive conflict
Encountering and having to wrestle with ideas and viewpoints different from one's own.

DEVELOPMENT AND PRACTICE

Applying Piaget's Theory

■ Provide hands-on experiences with physical objects. Allow and encourage children to explore and manipulate things.

A child care provider collects many objects that the toddlers in her care can play with. These include not only age-appropriate objects from reputable toy companies but also common household objects (pots and pans, cardboard boxes, old issues of *National Geographic*, etc.) that are unbreakable and have no sharp edges.

■ Provide opportunities for children to share their ideas and perspectives with one another.

A community youth leader has the teenagers in his group discuss various strategies for addressing the growing problem of gang violence in their community. Together, the group identifies several realistic things it can do to dissuade neighborhood children from becoming involved in gang activities.

■ Present puzzling phenomena.

A second-grade teacher crumples a paper towel and places it inside an otherwise empty glass. She asks her students to predict what will happen to the towel when she places the glass upside-down in a bowl of water. Many children predict that the paper towel will get wet. The teacher performs the experiment; when she removes the glass from the water, the children discover that the paper towel is completely dry. She follows this experiment with other activities to help the children learn more about the nature and properties of air.

■ Relate abstract and hypothetical ideas to concrete objects and observable events.

A middle school science teacher illustrates the idea that heavy and light objects fall at the same speed by having students drop objects of various weights from a second-story window.

- The students showed greater awareness that multiple and possibly equally legitimate perspectives could exist about the issue.

When using group interaction to help children and adolescents acquire more sophisticated understandings, keep in mind that they can also acquire misinformation from one another (Good, McCaslin, & Reys, 1992). It is essential, then, that instructors closely monitor discussions and correct for any misconceptions or misinterpretations that young people may pass on to their peers.

■ *Use familiar content and tasks when asking children to reason in sophisticated ways.* Earlier we presented evidence to indicate that children and adolescents display more advanced reasoning skills when they work with topics they know well. With such evidence in mind, teachers and other practitioners might ask the youngsters they are working with to

- Conserve liquid within the context of a juice-sharing task (as Bell and her colleagues did).
- Separate and control variables within the context of a familiar activity (perhaps fishing, playing sports, or riding a bicycle).
- Consider abstract ideas about subject matter that have already been studied in depth in a concrete fashion.

In Piaget's theory, cognitive development is largely an individual enterprise: By assimilating and accommodating to new experiences, children develop increasingly more advanced and integrated schemes over time. Thus, Piaget's perspective depicts children as doing most of the mental "work" themselves. In contrast, another early developmental theory—that of the Russian psychologist Lev Vygotsky—places much of the responsibility for children's development on the adults in their society and culture. From Vygotsky's perspective, children's interactions with adults play a critical role in fostering the development of skills and thinking capabilities essential for success in the adult world. We turn now to this very different, yet equally influential, theory of cognitive development.

Vygotsky's Theory of Cognitive Development

In the "Whale Watching" case at the beginning of the chapter, a mother helps her daughter Kerry understand and interpret what might otherwise have been a very confusing event for a 6-year-old. In particular, Mother helps Kerry recall the family members who were present, attaches labels to aspects of the experience (e.g., "disaster," "seasick"), and questions Kerry's assessment of the number of whales encountered on the trip.

Vygotsky proposed that adults, like Kerry's mother, promote children's cognitive development by engaging them in meaningful and challenging activities, helping them perform those activities successfully, and talking with them about their experiences. Because he emphasized the importance of society and culture for promoting cognitive growth, his theory is sometimes called a **sociocultural perspective**.

Vygotsky conducted numerous studies of children's thinking from the 1920s until his premature death from tuberculosis in 1934 at the age of 37. Many Western psychologists did not fully appreciate the usefulness of his work until several decades later, when his major writings were translated into English (Vygotsky, 1962, 1978, 1987a, 1997). Although Vygotsky never had the chance to develop his theory fully, his ideas are clearly evident in our views of child development, learning, and instructional practices today.

Key Ideas in Vygotsky's Theory

Vygotsky acknowledged that biological factors play a role in development: Children bring certain characteristics and dispositions to the situations they encounter, and their responses to those situations vary accordingly. Furthermore, children's behaviors, which are influenced in part by inherited traits, affect the particular experiences that they have (Vygotsky, 1997). However, Vygotsky's primary focus was on the role of nurture, and especially on the ways in which a child's social and cultural environments foster cognitive growth. Following are central ideas and concepts in Vygotsky's theory:

■ *Through both informal interactions and formal schooling, adults convey to children the ways in which their culture interprets and responds to the world.* In their interactions with children, adults share the *meanings* that they attach to objects, events, and, more generally, human experience. In the process, they transform, or *mediate,* the situations that children encounter. Meanings are conveyed through a variety of mechanisms, including language (spoken words, writing, etc.), symbols, mathematics, art, music, literature, and so on.

As one simple example, imagine yourself as a 2-year-old. It seems to be an especially busy day in the household. Your mother is doing things—blowing up balloons, wrapping boxes in brightly colored paper and ribbon, and so on—that are not part of her normal routine. Your older brother seems especially excited about something, and after lunch several other children his age arrive at your home in an equally energetic state. They all play games for a while, then your brother opens the packages that your mother and the other children give him. Later, your mother brings in a large frosted cake with several lighted candles on top, and your brother blows the candles out. Fortunately, Mom occasionally stops to tell you what is going on. It is your brother's birthday, she says (although she won't explain much about what a *birthday* is until you are older), and his family and friends want to help him celebrate by playing with him and giving him presents. By blowing out the candles on his cake, she says, your brother is trying to make a wish come true. Mom's explanations are essential to your making sense of the occasion, because a birthday celebration and the various rituals it includes are such culture-specific phenomena.

Informal conversations are one common method by which adults pass along culturally appropriate ways of interpreting situations. No less important in Vygotsky's eyes is formal education, where teachers systematically impart the ideas, concepts, and terminology used in various academic disciplines (Vygotsky, 1962). Although Vygotsky, like Piaget, saw value in allowing children to make some discoveries themselves, he also saw value in having adults describe the discoveries of previous generations (Karpov & Haywood, 1998).

■ *Thought and language become increasingly interdependent in the first few years of life.* For adults, thought and language are closely interconnected: We adults often think in terms of the specific words that our language provides. For example, when we think about household pets, our thoughts contain words such as *cat* and *dog*. In addition, we usually express our thoughts when we converse with others; as we sometimes put it, we "speak our minds."

From Vygotsky's perspective, parents and other adults promote children's cognitive development in part by conveying how their culture interprets the world.

sociocultural perspective
Theoretical perspective emphasizing the importance of society and culture for promoting cognitive development.

In contrast, according to Vygotsky, thought and language are separate functions for infants and young toddlers. In the early years, thinking occurs independently of language, and when language appears, it is first used primarily as a means of communication rather than as a mechanism of thought. But sometime around age 2, thought and language become intertwined: Children express their thoughts when they speak, and they think at least partially in terms of words (see Figure 4–8).

When thought and language merge, we begin to see **self-talk** (also known as *private speech*), whereby children talk to themselves out loud. Vygotsky suggested that self-talk has a specific purpose: By talking to themselves, children learn to guide and direct their own behaviors through difficult tasks and complex maneuvers in much the same way that adults have previously guided them.[4] Self-talk eventually evolves into **inner speech**, whereby children "talk" to themselves mentally rather than aloud. They continue to direct themselves verbally through tasks and activities, but others can no longer see and hear the means by which they do it.

Recent research has supported Vygotsky's views regarding the progression and role of self-talk and inner speech. The frequency of children's audible self-talk decreases during the preschool years, but this decrease is accompanied by an increase in whispered mumbling and silent lip movements, presumably reflecting a transition to inner speech (Bivens & Berk, 1990; R. E. Owens, 1996). Furthermore, self-talk increases when children are performing more challenging tasks, those at which they must work harder to be successful (Berk, 1994; Schimmoeller, 1998).

■ *Complex mental processes begin as social activities; as children develop, they gradually internalize the processes they use in social contexts and begin to use them independently.* Vygotsky proposed that many thinking processes have their roots in children's social interactions with other people. As children discuss objects and events with adults and other knowledgeable individuals, they gradually incorporate into their own thinking the ways in which the people around them talk about and interpret the world, and they begin to use the words, concepts, symbols, and other representations that are typical for their culture.[5] In essence, they are acquiring *conceptual tools* that enable them to interpret, organize, and respond to tasks and problems more effectively.

The process through which social activities evolve into internal mental activities is called **internalization**. Taken together, self-talk and inner speech illustrate the internalization process. Over time, children gradually internalize the directions that they have initially received from those around them so that they are eventually giving *themselves* directions.

Some mental processes develop from children's interactions with peers rather than adults. For example, children frequently argue with one another about a variety of matters: how best to carry out an activity, what games to play, who did what to whom, and so on. According to Vygotsky, childhood arguments help children discover that there are often several points of view about any single situation. Eventually, he suggested, children internalize the "arguing" process, developing the ability to look at a situation from several different angles on their own.

To the extent that specific cultures pass along unique concepts, ideas, and belief systems, children of different cultural backgrounds will acquire somewhat different knowledge, skills, and ways of thinking. Thus, Vygotsky's theory leads us to expect greater diversity among children than Piaget's theory does. For instance, recall a point made earlier: Children acquire conservation skills earlier if conservation of clay and water is important for their family's pottery business. Similarly, children are more likely to acquire map-reading skills if maps (perhaps of roads, subway systems, and shopping malls) are a prominent part of their community and family life (Trawick-Smith, 2003; B. B. Whiting & Edwards, 1988).

In infancy, thought is nonverbal in nature, and language is used primarily as a means of communication.

At about 2 years of age, thought becomes verbal in nature, and language becomes a means of expressing thoughts.

With time, children begin to use *self-talk* to guide their own thoughts and behaviors.

Self-talk gradually evolves into *inner speech*, whereby children guide themselves silently (mentally) rather than aloud.

FIGURE 4–8 Vygotsky proposed that thought and language initially emerge as separate functions but eventually become intertwined.

self-talk
Talking to oneself as a way of guiding oneself through a task.

inner speech
"Talking" to oneself mentally rather than aloud.

internalization
In Vygotsky's theory, the gradual evolution of external, social activities into internal, mental activities.

---

[4] Recall Piaget's notion of egocentric speech, based on his observation that young children often say things without taking into account the listener's perspective. Vygotsky proposed that such speech is better understood as talking to oneself than as talking to someone else and that it is most likely to appear when children are engaged in challenging tasks that they must talk themselves through.

[5] This process of internalizing the meanings and understandings of one's culture is sometimes called *appropriation*, a term suggested by Leont'ev (e.g., 1981), a Russian contemporary of Vygotsky.

■ *Children can perform more challenging tasks when assisted by more advanced and competent individuals.* Vygotsky distinguished between two kinds of abilities that children are likely to have at any particular point in their development. A child's **actual developmental level** is the upper limit of tasks that he or she can perform independently, without help from anyone else. A child's **level of potential development** is the upper limit of tasks that he or she can perform with the assistance of a more competent individual. To get a true sense of children's cognitive development, Vygotsky proposed, we should assess their capabilities both when performing alone *and* when performing with assistance.

Children can typically do more difficult things in collaboration with adults than they can do on their own. For example, they may be able to read more complex prose with the assistance of a parent or teacher than they are likely to read independently. They can play more difficult piano pieces when an adult helps them locate some of the notes on the keyboard or provides suggestions about what fingers to use. And notice how a student who cannot independently solve division problems with remainders begins to learn the correct procedure through an interaction with her teacher:

Teacher:	[writes 6)$\overline{44}$ on the board] 44 divided by 6. What number times 6 is close to 44?
Child:	6.
Teacher:	What's 6 times 6? [Writes 6]
Child:	36.
Teacher:	36. Can you get one that's any closer? [erasing the 6]
Child:	8.
Teacher:	What's 6 times 8?
Child:	64 . . . 48.
Teacher:	48. Too big. Can you think of something . . .
Child:	6 times 7 is 42. (Pettito, 1985, p. 251)

■ *Challenging tasks promote maximum cognitive growth.* The range of tasks that children cannot yet perform independently but can perform with the help and guidance of others is known as the **zone of proximal development (ZPD)**. A child's zone of proximal development includes learning and problem-solving abilities that are just beginning to emerge. Naturally, any child's ZPD will change over time. As some tasks are mastered, other, more complex ones take their place.

Vygotsky proposed that children learn very little from performing tasks they can already do independently. Instead, they develop primarily by attempting tasks they can accomplish only in collaboration with a more competent individual—that is, when they attempt tasks within their zone of proximal development. In a nutshell, it is the challenges in life, not the easy successes, that promote cognitive development.

Whereas challenging tasks are beneficial, impossible tasks, which children cannot do even with considerable structure and assistance, are of no benefit whatsoever (Vygotsky, 1987b). (Obviously, for example, it is pointless to ask a typical kindergartner to solve for *x* in an algebraic equation.) A child's ZPD therefore sets a limit on what he is cognitively capable of learning.

■ *Play allows children to stretch themselves cognitively.* Recall the scenario of Jeff and Scott playing "restaurant" presented earlier in the chapter. The two boys take on several adult roles (restaurant manager, waiter, cook) and practice a variety of adultlike behaviors: assembling the necessary materials for a restaurant, creating menus, keeping track of customers' orders, and tallying final bills. In real life, such a scenario would, of course, be impossible: Very few 5-year-old children have the cooking, reading, writing, mathematical, or organizational skills necessary to run a restaurant. Yet the element of make-believe brings these tasks within the boys' reach (e.g., Lillard, 1993). In Vygotsky's words:

> In play a child is always above his average age, above his daily behavior, in play it is as though he were a head taller than himself. (Vygotsky, 1978, p. 102)

In play activities, children rely on their imagination as much as on real objects; in the process, they learn to use their thoughts to guide their behaviors. As they substitute one object for another (e.g., pretending that a cardboard box is the family car), they begin to

actual developmental level
Upper limit of tasks that a child can successfully perform independently.

level of potential development
Upper limit of tasks that a child can successfully perform with the assistance of a more competent individual.

zone of proximal development (ZPD)
Range of tasks that one cannot yet perform independently but can perform with the help and guidance of others.

distinguish between objects and their meanings and to respond to internal representations (e.g., to the concept of *car*) as much as to external objects.

Furthermore, even when children play, their behaviors must conform to certain standards or expectations. For instance, children in the preschool and early elementary school years often act in accordance with how a "daddy," "teacher," or "waiter" would behave. In the organized group games and sports that come later, children must follow a specific set of rules. By adhering to such restrictions on their behavior, children learn to plan ahead, to think before they act, and to engage in self-restraint, skills critical for successful participation in the adult world.

Especially within the last 20 years, many Western theorists and practitioners have embraced and extended Vygotsky's ideas. We turn now to modern Vygotskian perspectives about how children can learn and develop effectively.

Current Perspectives on Vygotsky's Theory

Vygotsky focused primarily on the processes through which children develop, rather than on the characteristics that children of particular ages are likely to exhibit. He did identify stages of development but portrayed them in only the most general terms. From our perspective, the stages are not terribly informative (we refer you to Vygotsky, 1997, pp. 214–216, if you would like to learn more about them). For these reasons, Vygotsky's theory has been more difficult for researchers to test and either verify or disprove than has Piaget's theory. In fact, the most frequent criticisms of Vygotsky's ideas are his lack of precision and his inattention to details (Gauvain, 2001; Haenan, 1996; E. Hunt, 1997; Wertsch, 1984).

Despite such weaknesses, many contemporary theorists and practitioners have found Vygotsky's theory both insightful and helpful. Although they have taken Vygotsky's notions in many different directions, we can discuss much of their work within the context of several general ideas: the cultural context of development, social construction of meaning, scaffolding, participation in adult activities, acquisition of teaching skills, dynamic assessment, and the value of play.

The Cultural Context of Development   Increasingly, many contemporary developmentalists are recognizing the many ways in which culture shapes children's cognitive development (e.g., Gauvain, 2001; Guberman, Rahm, & Menk, 1998; Siegler, 1998). Culture ensures that each new generation benefits from the wisdom that preceding generations have accumulated. It also guides children in certain directions by encouraging them to pay attention to particular stimuli (and not to others) and to engage in particular activities (and not in others). Furthermore, it provides a lens through which children come to construct culturally appropriate interpretations of their experiences.

We see the effects of culture in many of children's everyday activities both in and out of school—for instance, in the books they read, the jokes they tell, the roles they enact in pretend play, and the extracurricular activities they pursue. As one example, consider the game of Monopoly. Through this popular board game, children learn about buying and mortgaging real estate, paying rent and taxes, and making business decisions within a capitalistic society; furthermore, they practice skills in mathematics (e.g., making change, calculating percentages) and negotiation (e.g., selling and exchanging properties). Happily, children seem able to adapt the game to fit their own ability levels; for example, 14-year-olds use more complicated mathematical procedures when playing the game than 8-year-olds do (Guberman et al., 1998).

Social Construction of Meaning   As mentioned earlier, Vygotsky proposed that adults help children attach meaning to the objects and events around them. More recently, theorists have elaborated on this idea. They point out that an adult such as a parent or teacher often helps a child make sense of the world through joint discussion of a phenomenon or

Vygotsky suggested that make-believe play allows children to practice adult roles. And when they use one object to stand for another (e.g., when they use plastic crates for train cars), they become increasingly able to distinguish between objects and their meanings.

Playing Monopoly provides an opportunity to practice mathematical skills and such adult activities as buying and mortgaging real estate, paying rent and taxes, and negotiating trades with other business people.

event they have mutually experienced (Eacott, 1999; Feuerstein, 1990; Feuerstein, Klein, & Tannenbaum, 1991; John-Steiner & Mahn, 1996). Such an interaction, sometimes called a **mediated learning experience**, encourages the child to think about the phenomenon or event in particular ways: to attach labels to it, recognize principles that underlie it, draw certain conclusions from it, and so on. For instance, in the opening case study, Kerry's mother helps her to understand the whale-watching expedition in several ways: by prompting her to recall the people who were present, interpreting the trip as a "disaster," describing the whales as "big," and counting the number of whales sighted. In such a conversation, the adult must, of course, consider the prior knowledge and perspectives of the child and tailor the discussion accordingly (Newson & Newson, 1975).[6]

In addition to co-constructing meanings with adults, children often talk among themselves to derive meaning from their experiences. As we reflect back on our own childhood and adolescent years, we recall having numerous conversations with friends in our joint efforts to make sense of our world, perhaps within the context of identifying the optimal food and water conditions for raising tadpoles, deciding how best to carry out an assigned school project, or figuring out why certain teenage boys were so elusive.

School is one obvious place where children and adolescents can toss around ideas about a particular issue and perhaps reach consensus about how best to interpret and understand the topic in question. As an example of how members of a classroom might work together to construct meaning, let's consider an interaction that takes place in Keisha Coleman's third-grade class (P. L. Peterson, 1992). The students are discussing how they might solve the problem $-10 + 10 = ?$. They are using a number line like the one below to facilitate their discussion.

Several students, including Tessa, agree that the solution is "zero" but disagree about how to use the number line to arrive at that answer. Excerpts from a discussion between Tessa and her classmate Chang (as facilitated by Ms. Coleman) follow:

Tessa:	You have to count numbers to the right. If you count numbers to the right, then you couldn't get to zero. You'd have to count to the left.
[Ms. Coleman]:	Could you explain a little bit more about what you mean by that? I'm not quite sure I follow you. . . .
Tessa:	Because if you went that way [points to the right] then it would have to be a higher number.
Chang:	I disagree with what she's trying to say. . . . Tessa says if you're counting right, then the number is—I don't really understand. She said, "If you count right, then the number has to go smaller." I don't know what she's talking about. Negative ten plus negative ten is zero. . . . What do you mean by counting to the right?
Tessa:	If you count from ten up, you can't get zero. If you count from ten left, you can get zero.
Chang:	Well, negative ten is a negative number—smaller than zero.
Tessa:	I know.
Chang:	Then why do you say you can't get to zero when you're adding to negative ten, which is smaller than zero?
Tessa:	OHHHH! NOW I GET IT! This is positive. . . . You have to count right.
[Ms. Coleman]:	You're saying in order to get to zero, you have to count to the right? From where, Tessa?
Tessa:	Negative 10. (P. L. Peterson, 1992, pp. 165–166)

The class continues in its efforts to pin down precisely how to use the number line to solve the problem. Eventually, Tessa offers a revised and more complete explanation. Point-

mediated learning experience
Discussion between an adult and a child in which the adult helps the child make sense of an event they have mutually experienced.

---

[6]During the conversation, the adult and child must, of course, both be aware that they are attending to and discussing the same things. We will talk about such *intersubjectivity* in Chapter 5.

ing to the appropriate location on the number line, she says, "You start at negative 10. Then you add 1, 2, 3, 4, 5, 6, 7, 8, 9, 10." She moves her finger one number to the right for each number that she counts. She reaches the zero point on the number line when she counts "10" and concludes, "That equals zero."

Notice that at no time does Ms. Coleman impose her own interpretations on either the problem itself or on what Tessa and Chang have to say about the problem. Instead, she lets the two children struggle to make sense of the problem and, eventually, to agree on how best to solve it.

In recent years, many theorists have become convinced of the value of joint meaning-making discussions in helping children acquire more complex understandings of their physical, social, and academic worlds (e.g., Hatano & Inagaki, 1993; Hiebert et al., 1997; Lampert, 1990; Sosniak & Stodolsky, 1994). This perspective, generally known as **social constructivism**, is reflected in increased advocacy for instructional practices involving student interaction—class discussions, cooperative learning activities, peer tutoring, and so on—in elementary and secondary classrooms.

Scaffolding   Theorists have given considerable thought to the kinds of assistance that can help children complete challenging tasks and activities. The term **scaffolding** is often used to describe the guidance or structure provided by more competent individuals that enables children to perform tasks within their zone of proximal development. To understand this concept, think of the scaffolding used in the construction of a new building. The *scaffold* is an external structure that provides support for the workers (e.g., a place where they can stand) until the building itself is strong enough to support them. As the building gains substance and stability, the scaffold becomes less necessary and is gradually removed.

In much the same way, an adult guiding a child through a new task may provide an initial scaffold to support her early efforts. In the teacher-student dialogue about division cited earlier, the teacher provided clues about how to proceed, such as searching for the multiple of 6 closest to, but still less than, 44. Similarly, adults provide scaffolding when they illustrate the use of particular tools or procedures, give hints about how to approach a difficult problem, or break down a complex task into smaller, easier steps (Rosenshine & Meister, 1992; D. Wood, Bruner, & Ross, 1976). In the example that follows, notice how a mother helps her 4-year-old daughter Sadie assemble a toy from Duplo blocks (larger versions of Legos) by following a set of instructions:

Appropriate scaffolding often enables children to perform tasks they cannot otherwise do.

Mother:	Now you need another one like this on the other side. Mmmmmm . . . there you go, just like that.
Sadie:	Then I need this one to go like this? Hold on, hold on. Let it go. There. Get that out. Oops!
Mother:	I'll hold it while you turn it. (*Watches Sadie work on toy.*) Now you make the end.
Sadie:	This one?
Mother:	No, look at the picture. Right here (*points to plan*). That piece.
Sadie:	Like this?
Mother:	Yeah. (Gauvain, 2001, p. 32)

As children become more adept at performing new tasks, scaffolding like that provided by Sadie's mother can be gradually phased out, and the children eventually perform the tasks on their own.

Participation in Adult Activities   Virtually all cultures allow—and in fact usually require—children to be involved in adult activities to some degree. Children's early experiences are often at the fringe of an activity (Lave & Wenger, 1991). As the children acquire greater competence, they gradually take a more central role in the activity until, eventually, they are full-fledged participants.

In most cases, children's early involvement in adult activities is carefully scaffolded and supervised through what is sometimes known as **guided participation** (e.g., Rogoff, 1995,

social constructivism
Theoretical perspective that focuses on people's collective efforts to impose meaning on the world.

scaffolding
Support mechanism, provided by a more competent individual, that helps a child successfully perform a task within his or her zone of proximal development.

guided participation
Active engagement in adult activities, typically with considerable direction and structure from an adult or other more advanced individual; children are given increasing responsibility and independence as they gain experience and proficiency.

1996). For example, when our own children were preschoolers, we often let them help us bake cookies by asking them to pour the ingredients we'd measured into the mixing bowl, and we occasionally let them do some preliminary mixing as well, but we stood by their side and offered suggestions about how to get the measurements right, minimize spilling, and so on. Similarly, when taking them to the office with us, we had them press the appropriate buttons in the elevator, check our mailboxes, open envelopes, or deliver documents to the department secretary, but we kept a close eye on what they were doing and offered guidance as necessary. In later years, we gave them increasing responsibility and independence. For example, by the time Jeanne's son Jeff reached high school, he was baking and decorating his own cakes and cookies, and he ran errands around the community—for example, he made trips to the library and post office—to help Jeanne as she worked on her books.

Through their annual cookie drives, Girl Scouts are introduced to adult business practices in marketing, salesmanship, accounting, and taking inventory.

Parents are not the only ones who engage children in adult activities. For example, schools sometimes invite students to be members of faculty decision-making committees, and parent-teacher organizations ask students to help with school fund-raising efforts. Girl Scout troops introduce girls to salesmanship, accounting, and other adult business practices during annual cookie drives (Rogoff, 1995). Many local newspapers take on high school students as cub reporters, movie reviewers, and editorial writers, especially during the summer months.

In some instances, adults work with children and adolescents in formal or informal **apprenticeships**, one-on-one relationships in which the adults teach the young people new skills, guide their initial efforts, and present increasingly difficult tasks as proficiency improves and the zone of proximal development changes (Rogoff, 1990, 1991). Many cultures use apprenticeships as a way of gradually introducing children to particular skills and trades in the adult community—perhaps weaving, tailoring, or midwifery (Lave & Wenger, 1991; Rogoff, 1990). Apprenticeships are also common in teaching a child how to play a musical instrument (D. J. Elliott, 1995).

In an apprenticeship, children learn both the skills and the language associated with a particular activity.

In apprenticeships, children learn not only the behaviors but also the language of a skill or trade (Lave & Wenger, 1991). For example, when master weavers teach apprentices their art, they use such terms as *warp, weft, shuttle,* and *harness* to focus attention on a particular aspect of the process. Similarly, when teachers guide students through scientific experiments, they use words like *hypothesis, evidence,* and *theory* to help the students evaluate their procedures and results (D. Perkins, 1992). Furthermore, an apprenticeship can show children how adults typically think about a task or activity; such a situation is sometimes called a **cognitive apprenticeship** (J. S. Brown, Collins, & Duguid, 1989; Rogoff, 1990; W. Roth & Bowen, 1995). For instance, an adult and child might work together to accomplish a challenging task or solve a difficult problem (perhaps sewing a patchwork quilt, designing a treehouse, or collecting data samples in biology fieldwork). In the process of talking about various aspects of the task or problem, the adult and child together analyze the situation and develop the best approach to take, and the adult models effective ways of thinking about and mentally processing the situation.

Although apprenticeships can differ widely from one context to another, they typically have some or all of the following features (A. Collins, Brown, & Newman, 1989):

- *Modeling.* The adult carries out the task, simultaneously thinking aloud about the process, while the child observes and listens.
- *Coaching.* As the child performs the task, the adult gives frequent suggestions, hints, and feedback.
- *Scaffolding.* The adult provides various forms of support for the child, perhaps by simplifying the task, breaking it into smaller and more manageable components, or providing less complicated equipment.

apprenticeship
Situation in which a novice works intensively with an expert to learn how to accomplish complex tasks.

cognitive apprenticeship
Mentorship in which an expert and a novice work together on a challenging task and the expert suggests ways to think about the task.

- *Articulation.* The child explains what he or she is doing and why, allowing the adult to examine the child's knowledge, reasoning, and problem-solving strategies.
- *Reflection.* The adult asks the child to compare his or her performance with that of experts, or perhaps with an ideal model of how the task should be done.
- *Increasing complexity and diversity of tasks.* As the child gains greater proficiency, the adult presents more complex, challenging, and varied tasks to complete.
- *Exploration.* The adult encourages the child to frame questions and problems on his or her own and thereby to expand and refine acquired skills.

From a Vygotskian perspective, gradual entry into adult activities increases the probability that children will engage in behaviors and thinking skills that are within their zone of proximal development. Some theorists believe that participation in everyday adult activities has an additional advantage: It helps children tie their newly acquired skills and thinking abilities to the specific contexts in which they are likely to need them later on (Carraher, Carraher, & Schliemann, 1985; Light & Butterworth, 1993).[7]

Acquisition of Teaching Skills As children learn new skills from more experienced members of their community, they may also learn how to teach those skills to someone else (Gauvain, 2001). With age and experience, they become increasingly adept at teaching others what they have learned. For example, in a study in rural Mexico, Mayan children were observed as they worked with younger siblings in such everyday activities as preparing food and washing clothes (Maynard, 2002). Their earliest form of "instruction" (perhaps around age 4 or 5) was simply to let a younger brother or sister join in and help them. At age 6 or 7, they tended to be directive and controlling, giving commands and taking over if something wasn't done correctly. By the time they were 8, however, they were proficient teachers, using a combination of demonstrations, explanations, physical guidance, and feedback to scaffold their siblings' efforts.

For another example of how skillfully children can teach one another, let's return to the game of Monopoly. Four 8-year-old girls are playing the game while a researcher videotapes their interactions (Guberman et al., 1998). One girl, Carla, has limited math skills and little experience playing the game. On her first turn, she lands on Connecticut Avenue:

Nancy:	Do you want to buy it?
Carla:	Hmmmm . . . [There is a long pause and some unrelated discussion among the players.] How much is it again? Twelve hundred . . .
Nancy:	A hundred and twenty dollars.
Carla:	A hundred and twenty [She starts to count her money] . . . a hundred [She is referring to a $10 bill] . . .
Sarah:	You give her one of these and one of these. [She holds up first a $100 bill and then a $20 bill of her own money.] (Guberman et al., 1998, p. 436; format adapted)

Notice how Nancy and Sarah scaffold Carla's initial purchase. Nancy asks her to consider buying the property and tells her the purchase price. When it is clear that Carla is having trouble counting out $120 (e.g., she thinks that a $10 bill is worth $100), Sarah gives her sufficient guidance that she can identify the needed bills by color alone. Later in the game, as Carla becomes more competent, the other girls reduce their support. For instance, at one point Carla lands on Virginia Avenue, with a purchase price of $160:

Carla hesitates making the payment, looking through her money. Eventually, she takes a $100 bill from her money and appears unsure how to continue.

Nancy: Just a fifty and a ten.

Carla gives a $50 bill and a $10 bill to the banker. (Guberman et al., 1998, p. 437; format adapted)

When children teach others, the "teachers" often benefit as much as the "students" do (Fuchs, Fuchs, Mathes, & Simmons, 1997; Inglis & Biemiller, 1997; N. M. Webb &

---

[7]This second advantage reflects what theorists call a *situative perspective* of cognition and cognitive development: Thinking is described as being associated with, or situated in, the specific tasks in which people are engaged.

Palincsar, 1996). For instance, when young people study something with the expectation that they will be teaching it to someone else, they are more motivated to learn it, find it more interesting, and learn it more effectively (Benware & Deci, 1984; Semb, Ellis, & Araujo, 1993). Furthermore, when children who are relatively weak in a particular skill (compared to their age-mates) have the opportunity to guide younger children in that skill, they develop greater ability to guide themselves as well, presumably because they internalize the directions they have been giving another (Biemiller, Shany, Inglis, & Meichenbaum, 1998). Peer tutoring also has social benefits: Cooperation and other social skills improve, classroom behavior problems diminish, and friendships develop among children of different ethnic groups and between children with and without disabilities (DuPaul, Ervin, Hook, & McGoey, 1998; Greenwood, Carta, & Hall, 1988).

Dynamic Assessment   As noted earlier, Vygotsky believed that we can get a more complete picture of children's cognitive development when we assess both their *actual developmental level* (the upper limit of tasks they can successfully accomplish on their own) and their *level of potential development* (the upper limit of tasks they can accomplish when they have the assistance of more competent individuals). When assessing children's cognitive abilities, however, most teachers and clinicians focus almost exclusively on *actual* developmental level: They ask children to take tests, complete assignments, and so on, without help from anyone else. To assess children's level of potential development, some theorists have suggested an alternative known as **dynamic assessment**, which involves (a) identifying tasks that children cannot initially do independently, (b) providing in-depth instruction and practice in behaviors and cognitive processes related to the task, and then (c) determining the extent to which each child has benefited from the instruction (Feuerstein, 1979, 1980; Kozulin & Falik, 1995; Lidz, 1997; Tzuriel, 2000). This approach often yields more optimistic evaluations of children's cognitive capabilities than traditional measures of cognitive ability and may be especially useful in assessing the abilities of children from diverse cultural backgrounds (Feuerstein, 1979; Tzuriel, 2000).

Keep in mind that we currently have little hard data about the validity and reliability of dynamic assessment techniques (Anastasi & Urbina, 1997; Tzuriel, 2000). However, one advantage of these techniques is the rich body of qualitative information they can yield about children's strategies, motivations, and dispositions. For example, Figure 4–9 presents a checklist that one clinician has used during a dynamic assessment of children's learning and problem-solving skills. Although a few of the items on the checklist are specific to the tasks the clinician presented, most of them are sufficiently generic that they might be applied in a wide variety of circumstances.

Value of Play   Many contemporary theorists share Vygotsky's and Piaget's belief that play provides an arena in which youngsters can practice the skills they will need in later life. They have observed play in many species, especially those species that are relatively flexible in their behaviors (e.g., monkeys, chimpanzees, bears, dogs, cats), and suspect that it has one or more adaptive functions (Bjorklund & Green, 1992; Vandenberg, 1978). Psychologists have long been aware of the value of play for children's social development (i.e., for developing cooperation and conflict resolution skills), but increasingly they are acknowledging its importance for children's cognitive development as well. For instance, they suggest that play helps children experiment with new combinations of objects, identify cause-effect relationships, and learn more about other people's perspectives (Chafel, 1991; Lillard, 1998; K. Rubin, Fein, & Vandenberg, 1983; Zervigon-Hakes, 1984).

To some degree, play probably serves different purposes for different age groups. For infants, one primary goal of play activities seems to be to discover what objects are like and what they can do, as well as what people can do to and with them. Through such discoveries, infants learn many basic properties of the physical world (e.g., Morris, 1977). Through more social games, such as peek-a-boo and pat-a-cake, infants practice imitation and acquire rudimentary skills in cooperation and turn-taking (e.g., Bruner & Sherwood, 1976). When play takes on an element of make-believe somewhere around age 2, children begin to substitute one object for another and eventually perform behaviors involving imaginary objects—for instance, "eating" imaginary food with an imaginary fork (O'Reilly, 1995; Pederson, Rook-Green, & Elder, 1981). As Vygotsky suggested, such pretense prob-

dynamic assessment
Systematic examination of how a child's knowledge or reasoning may change as a result of learning or performing a specific task.

Learning Strategies Checklist

	None of the time	Some of the time	Most of the time
Attention/Discrimination			
▪ initiates focus with minimum cues	0	1	2
▪ maintains focus with minimum cues	0	1	2
▪ responds to relevant cues, ignores irrelevant cues	0	1	2
Comparative Behavior			
▪ comments on features of task	0	1	2
▪ uses comparative behavior to select item	0	1	2
▪ talks about same/different	0	1	2
Planning			
▪ talks about overall goal	0	1	2
▪ talks about plan	0	1	2
Self-Regulation/Awareness			
▪ waits for instructions	0	1	2
▪ seeks help when difficult	0	1	2
▪ corrects self	0	1	2
▪ rewards self	0	1	2
Transfer			
▪ applies strategies within tasks	0	1	2
▪ applies strategies between tasks	0	1	2
Motivation			
▪ persists even when frustrated	0	1	2
▪ shows enthusiasm	0	1	2

FIGURE 4–9 Example of a checklist for evaluating a child's approach to learning during a dynamic assessment

Copyright 1993 by E. Peña. Reprinted by permission.

ably helps children begin to distinguish between external objects and internal representations (Chafel, 1991). When, in the preschool years, children expand their pretend play into elaborate scenarios—sometimes called **sociodramatic play**—they can also practice roles such as "parent," "teacher," or "waiter," and they gain a greater appreciation of what other people might be thinking and feeling[8] (Göncü, 1993; Haight & Miller, 1993; Lillard, 1998; Lyytinen, 1991). Examples of things to look for are presented in the Observation Guidelines table "Observing Young Children's Play Activities."

As children reach school age, role-playing activities gradually diminish, and other forms of play take their place. For instance, elementary school children often spend time playing cards and board games, constructing things from cardboard boxes or Legos, and engaging in team sports. Many of these activities continue into adolescence. Although such forms of play do not mimic adult roles in as obvious a manner as "house" and "restaurant," they, too, serve a purpose. In particular, they help children and adolescents develop skills in planning, communication, cooperation, and problem solving that will be important for their later success in the adult world (Bornstein, Haynes, Pascual, Painter, & Galperin, 1999; Christie & Johnsen, 1983; Sutton-Smith, 1979).

Implications of Vygotsky's Ideas

Vygotsky's work and the recent theoretical advances it has inspired have numerous implications for teaching and working with children and adolescents:

▪ *Present challenging tasks, perhaps within the context of cooperative activities.* To promote cognitive development, adults should present some tasks and assignments that children can perform successfully only with assistance—that is, tasks within the children's

sociodramatic play
Play in which children take on assumed roles and act out a scenario of events.

---

[8]Understanding what other people might be thinking and feeling is sometimes referred to as *theory of mind*. We examine this concept in Chapters 5 and 10.

OBSERVATION GUIDELINES

Observing Young Children's Play Activities

CHARACTERISTIC	LOOK FOR	EXAMPLE	IMPLICATION
Exploratory Play with Objects	• Interest in exploring objects in the environment • Ability to manipulate objects • Use of multiple senses in exploratory play	When Tyler sees a new jack-in-the-box among the supply of toys in the playroom, he picks it up, inspects it on all sides, and begins to turn the crank (although not enough to make "Jack" pop out). After Tyler leaves it to play with something else, Sarah picks it up. Rather than visually inspecting it, however, she sniffs it, then puts the crank in her mouth and begins to suck and chew on it.	Provide a wide variety of toys and other objects for infants and toddlers to explore and experiment with, making sure that all are safe, clean, and nontoxic. Anticipate that children may use these things in creative ways (and not necessarily in the ways they were intended to be used) and that they will move frequently from one object to another.
Group Play	• Extent to which children play with one another • Extent to which children in a play group coordinate their play activities	Lamarr and Matthew are playing with trucks in the sandbox, but each boy seems to be in his own little world.	Give children opportunities to play together, and provide toys that require a cooperative effort.
Use of Symbolic Thought and Imagination	• Extent to which children use one object to stand for another • Extent to which children incorporate imaginary objects into their play	Julia tells her friend she is going to the grocery store, then opens an imaginary car door, sits on a chair inside her "car," steers an imaginary steering wheel, and says, "Beep, beep" as she blows an imaginary horn.	When equipping a play area, include objects (e.g., wooden blocks, cardboard boxes) that children can use for a variety of purposes.
Role Taking	• Extent to which children display behaviors that reflect a particular role • Extent to which children use language (e.g., tone of voice, specific words and phrases) associated with a particular person or role • Extent to which children coordinate and act out multiple roles within the context of a complex play scenario	Mark and Alisa are playing doctor. Alisa brings her teddy bear to Mark's "office" and politely says, "Good morning, Doctor. My baby has a sore throat." Mark holds a Popsicle stick against the bear's mouth and instructs the "baby" to say "aaahhh."	Provide toys and equipment associated with particular roles (e.g., toy medical kit, cooking utensils, play money).

FIGURE 4–10 In this simple worksheet, a preschool teacher scaffolds 4-year-old Hannah's efforts to draw the numerals 1 to 5.

zone of proximal development. In group situations, such as in the classroom, children with different zones of proximal development may need different tasks and assignments, a point that makes a strong case for providing as much individualized instruction as possible.

In some instances, success at a challenging task may require the assistance of a more skilled individual, such as an adult or older child. But at other times, a group of children of equal ability might jointly accomplish a task that none of its members could do independently. In such situations, group members essentially provide scaffolding for one another's efforts. Cooperative learning groups and other activities in which children work collaboratively can be highly effective in promoting cognitive development and academic achievement (A. L. Brown & Palincsar, 1989; Lou et al., 1996; Stevens & Slavin, 1995).

■ *Scaffold children's efforts.* When adults provide the challenging tasks so important for cognitive development, they should also provide sufficient scaffolding to enable children to accomplish those tasks successfully. Following are some examples of how an adult might scaffold a new and difficult task:

• Demonstrate the proper performance of the task in a way that children can easily imitate
• Divide the task into several smaller, simpler parts
• Provide a structure, set of steps, or guidelines for performing the task (e.g., see Figure 4–10)

- Ask questions that get children thinking in appropriate ways about the task
- Keep children's attention focused on the relevant aspects of the task
- Give frequent feedback about how the children are progressing
  (Gallimore & Tharp, 1990; Good et al., 1992; Rogoff, 1990; Rosenshine & Meister, 1992; D. Wood et al., 1976)

As children develop increasing competence, adults can gradually withdraw these support mechanisms and eventually allow the children to perform the task independently—in other words, to stand on their own two feet.

As an example of such scaffolding, Katie Powers, a student in one of Jeanne's classes, once described how she taught an 8-year-old girl how to play the middle C scale on the piano. To make the task easier, Katie labeled the eight piano keys with small Post-it notes. She began to model playing the scale and offered hints about fingering, and then coached the girl as she played it herself:

> As she watched my hands play the scale, I asked her to watch how I am using only one hand with only five fingers to play eight keys. After I played it three times she chimed in that I was using my thumb to start over again. I asked her to try to explain more. She said that after I used a few fingers, I put my thumb under to start over with my fingers again. . . . She understood that the thumb is going under the hand. It then did not take us long to figure out what fingers go on which keys. She really understood the concept of tucking the thumb under, it just took her a few tries to figure out and remember when the thumb tucks under. The hint I told her about, which was how if we only use five fingers, how many additional fingers would we need to finish playing all eight keys. It's three, so therefore you tuck the thumb under after the middle finger. Once we figured out where each finger would go, she practiced playing the scale for a few minutes. She did it very slowly, thinking about what she was doing, which was very important. She messed up a few times, getting mixed up about where to tuck her thumb, but she kept saying to herself "after middle finger . . . after middle finger". . . When she played the scale correctly three or four times in a row, I noticed that she was not speaking out loud about when to tuck her thumb. She was also playing the scale a little faster and smoother. Then when we took the Post-it notes off, she began to think harder again. She was speaking out loud again about when to tuck her thumb. At first she had trouble, getting a little confused, but once she started saying it out loud again, then it seemed to help her a lot. She could play the scale slowly, but correctly, and still repeating to herself about tucking her thumb. (Courtesy of Katie Powers)

■ *Promote self-regulation by teaching children to talk themselves through difficult situations.* Did you notice how the girl learning to play the middle C scale reminded herself when to tuck her thumb by repeating, "after middle finger . . . after middle finger"? Through self-talk and inner speech, children begin to direct and control their own behaviors—in other words, they engage in **self-regulation**—in much the same way that adults have previously directed them. Children who talk themselves through challenging tasks pay more attention to what they are doing and are more likely to show improvement in their performance (Berk & Spuhl, 1995).

Meichenbaum (1977, 1985) has successfully used five steps to teach children how to give themselves instructions and thereby guide themselves through a new task:

1. *Cognitive modeling.* An adult model performs the desired task while verbalizing instructions that guide performance.
2. *Overt, external guidance.* The child performs the task while listening to the adult verbalize the instructions.
3. *Overt self-guidance.* The child repeats the instructions aloud (*self-talk*) while performing the task.
4. *Faded, overt self-guidance.* The child whispers the instructions while performing the task.
5. *Covert self-instruction.* The child silently thinks about the instructions (*inner speech*) while performing the task.

In this sequence of steps, depicted in Figure 4–11, the adult initially serves as a model both for the behavior itself and for the process of self-guidance. Responsibility for performing

	TASK PERFORMANCE	TASK INSTRUCTIONS
Step 1	The adult performs the task, modeling it for the child.	The adult verbalizes instructions.
Step 2	The child performs the task.	The adult verbalizes instructions.
Step 3	The child performs the task.	The child repeats the instructions aloud.
Step 4	The child performs the task.	The child whispers the instructions.
Step 5	The child performs the task.	The child thinks silently about the instructions.

FIGURE 4–11 Meichenbaum's five steps for promoting self-regulation

self-regulation
Directing and controlling one's own actions.

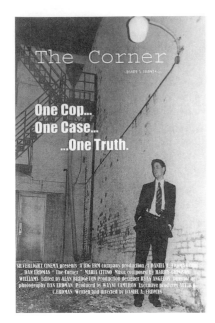

Authentic activities involve tasks similar to ones that growing children and adolescents will eventually encounter in the outside world. For his senior project, 18-year-old Daniel wrote a story and screenplay, selected a cast, and directed, produced, and promoted his own film.

Observe the variety of play areas for infants and young children in the Environments module of the Observation CD.

authentic activity
Instructional activity similar to one that a child might eventually encounter in the outside world.

the task is soon turned over to the child; eventually, responsibility for directing the performance is turned over as well.

■ *Assess children's abilities under a variety of work conditions.*   Teachers and others who foster children's cognitive development need to know not only what the children can and cannot do, but also under what conditions they are most likely to accomplish various tasks successfully (Calfee & Masuda, 1997). By asking children to work under varying conditions—sometimes independently, sometimes in collaboration with one or more peers, and sometimes with adult instruction and support—one can get a better sense of the tasks that are in each child's zone of proximal development.

■ *Provide opportunities to engage in authentic activities.*   As we've already seen, children's participation in adult activities plays a critical role in their cognitive development. Many theorists have suggested that adults can better promote learning and cognitive development by having children engage in **authentic activities**—activities similar to those that the children may eventually encounter in the adult world—rather than in more traditional academic tasks (e.g., D. T. Hickey, 1997; Hiebert & Fisher, 1992; Lave, 1993). Following are some examples:

Writing an editorial	Performing in a concert
Participating in a debate	Planning a family budget
Designing an electrical circuit	Conversing in a foreign language
Conducting an experiment	Making a videotape
Writing a computer program	Constructing a museum display
Creating and distributing a class newsletter	Developing a home page for the Internet

Researchers have only begun to study the effects of authentic activities on learning and cognitive development, but preliminary results are encouraging. For example, children may show greater improvement in writing skills when they practice writing stories, essays, and letters to real people, rather than completing short, artificial writing exercises (Hiebert & Fisher, 1992). Likewise, they may gain a more complete understanding of how to use and interpret maps when they construct their own maps than when they engage in workbook exercises involving map interpretation (Gregg & Leinhardt, 1994).

■ *Help children acquire the basic conceptual tools of various activities and academic disciplines.*   Virtually every adult activity involves certain concepts and ways of thinking, and mastering them enables children to engage more successfully in the activity. For instance, children can become better musicians when they can read music and understand what *keys, chords,* and *thirds* are. They develop their carpentry skills when they know how to interpret blueprints and understand terms such as *plumb* and *soffit.* Furthermore, through such disciplines as science, mathematics, and social studies, our culture passes along key concepts (e.g., *molecule, negative numbers, democracy*), symbols (e.g., H_2O, π, ∞), and visual representations (e.g., graphs, maps) that can help growing children organize and interpret the physical and social worlds in which they live. Literature, poetry, music, and fine arts help children impose meaning on the world as well—for example, by capturing the thoughts and feelings that characterize human experience.

■ *Give children the chance to play.*   So far, all of our suggestions—presenting difficult tasks, engaging children in authentic activities, teaching concepts and symbols, and so on—imply that children's cognitive development depends largely on formal instruction and involves some amount of "work." Yet, as we have seen, informal play activities have value as well, and many theorists advocate including them as an integral part of children's daily schedules, especially at the preschool level (Chafel, 1991; Hirsh-Pasek, Hyson, & Rescorla, 1990; Van Hoorn, Nourot, Scales, & Alward, 1999). Following are several suggestions for promoting preschoolers' play:

- Partition the classroom into small areas (e.g., a corner for blocks, a "housekeeping" area, an art table) that give children numerous options. (See, for example, the environments for infants and young children in the Environments module of the Observation CD.)

DEVELOPMENT AND PRACTICE

Applying Vygotsky's Theory

- Present some tasks that children can perform successfully only with assistance, and have them work in small groups to accomplish complex tasks.

  When a youth group leader takes 12-year-olds on their first camping trip, he has the children work in threesomes to pitch their tents. Although he has previously shown the children how to set up their tents, this is the first time they've actually done it themselves, and so he provides written instructions that they can follow. In addition, he circulates from campsite to campsite to check on each group's progress and provide assistance as necessary.

- Provide sufficient scaffolding to enable children to perform challenging tasks successfully; gradually withdraw the support as they become more proficient.

  A child care provider has the 2-year-olds in her care take turns distributing the crackers, fruit, and napkins at snack time, and she asks all of them to bring their dishes and trash to the kitchen after they have finished eating. Initially, she must show the children how to carry the food so that it doesn't spill, and she must remind them to make sure that every child gets a helping; she must also remind them to clean up when they are done. As the year progresses, such explicit guidance and reminders are no longer necessary, although she must occasionally say, "I think two of you have forgotten to bring your cups to the kitchen. I'm missing the one with Big Bird on it and the one with Cookie Monster."

- Encourage children to talk themselves through difficult tasks.

  A physical education teacher shows beginning tennis players how to use self instructions to remember correct form when swinging the racket:

1. Say *ball* to remind yourself to look at the ball.
2. Say *bounce* to remind yourself to follow the ball with your eyes as it approaches you.
3. Say *hit* to remind yourself to focus on contacting the ball with the racket.
4. Say *ready* to get yourself into position for the next ball to come your way. (Ziegler, 1987)

- Ask children to engage in authentic adult activities.

  A third-grade teacher has his students create a school newspaper that includes news articles, a schedule of upcoming events, a couple of political cartoons, and some classified advertisements. The students assume varying roles (reporters, cartoonists, editors, proofreaders, photocopiers, and distributors) during the project.

- Demonstrate and encourage adultlike ways of thinking about situations.

  A high school chemistry teacher places two equal-size inflated balloons into two beakers of water, one heated to 25° C and the other heated to 50° C. The students all agree that the balloon placed in the warmer water expands more. "Now how much more did the 50-degree balloon expand?" the teacher asks. "Let's use Charles's Law to figure it out."

- Give young children numerous opportunities to practice adult roles and behaviors in play activities.

  A preschool teacher equips his classroom with many household items (dress-up clothes, cooking utensils, a toy telephone, etc.) so that his students can play "house" during free-play time.

- Provide realistic toys (e.g., dolls, dress-up clothes, plastic dishes and food) that suggest certain activities and functions, as well as more versatile objects (e.g., Legos, wooden blocks, cardboard boxes) that allow children to engage in fantasy and imagination.
- Provide enough toys and equipment to minimize potential conflicts, but keep them limited enough in number that children must share and cooperate.
  (Frost, Shin, & Jacobs, 1998)

Comparing Piaget and Vygotsky

Together, Piaget's and Vygotsky's theories give us a more complete picture of cognitive development than either one provides alone. The Developmental Trends table "Thinking and Reasoning Skills at Different Age Levels" draws on elements of both theories to describe characteristics of children and adolescents in different age ranges.

The two theories share some common themes that continue to appear in more contemporary theories of cognitive development. At the same time, they have important differences that have led modern researchers to probe more deeply into the mechanisms through which children's thinking processes develop.

Common Themes

If we look beyond the very different vocabulary Piaget and Vygotsky often used to describe the phenomena they observed, we notice three themes that their theories share: challenge, readiness, and the importance of social interaction.

DEVELOPMENTAL TRENDS

Thinking and Reasoning Skills at Different Age Levels

AGE	WHAT YOU MIGHT OBSERVE	DIVERSITY	IMPLICATIONS
Infancy (Birth–2) 	• Physical exploration of the environment, with experimentation becoming increasingly complex and flexible over time • Growing awareness of simple cause-effect relationships • Emergence of ability to represent the world mentally (e.g., as reflected in deferred imitation and make-believe play)	• Temperamental differences (e.g., the extent to which infants are adventuresome vs. more timid and anxious) influence exploratory behavior. • Infants and toddlers who are closely attached to their caregivers are more willing to venture out and explore their environment (see Chapter 9). • In some cultures, adults encourage infants to focus more on people than on the physical environment. When people rather than objects are the priority, children may be less inclined to touch and explore their physical surroundings.	• Set up a varied, safe, age-appropriate environment for exploration. • Provide objects that stimulate different senses—for instance, things that babies can look at, listen to, feel, and smell. • Suggest age-appropriate toys and activities that parents can provide at home.
Early Childhood (2–6) 	• Rapidly developing language skills • Thinking that, by adult standards, is illogical • Limited perspective-taking ability • Frequent self-talk • Sociodramatic play • Little understanding of how adults typically interpret events	• Shyness may reduce children's willingness to talk with adults and peers and to engage in cooperative sociodramatic play. • Adultlike logic is more common when children have accurate information about the world (e.g., about cause-effect relationships). • Children learn to interpret events in culture-specific ways.	• Provide numerous opportunities for children to interact with one another during play and other cooperative activities. • Introduce children to a variety of real-world environments and situations through field trips and picture books. • Talk with children about their experiences and possible interpretations of them.
Middle Childhood (6–10) 	• Conservation, multiple classification, and other forms of adult logic • Limited ability to reason about abstract or hypothetical ideas • Emergence of group games and team sports that involve coordinating multiple perspectives • Ability to participate in many adult activities (perhaps only peripherally)	• Development of logical thinking skills is affected by the importance of those skills in a child's culture. • Formal operational reasoning may occasionally appear for simple tasks and familiar contexts, especially in 9- and 10-year-olds. • Physical maturation and psychomotor skills affect willingness to play some games and team sports.	• Use concrete manipulatives and experiences to illustrate concepts and ideas. • Supplement verbal explanations with concrete examples, pictures, and hands-on activities. • Allow time for organized play activities. • Introduce children to various adult professions, and provide opportunities to practice authentic adult tasks.
Early Adolescence (10–14) 	• Emerging ability to reason about abstract ideas • Increasing scientific reasoning abilities (e.g., separating and controlling variables, formulating and testing hypotheses) • Emerging ability to reason about mathematical proportions • Emerging idealism about political and social issues, but often without taking real-world constraints into consideration • Increasing ability to engage in adult tasks	• Adolescents can think more abstractly when they have considerable knowledge about a topic. • Adolescents are more likely to separate and control variables for situations with which they are familiar. • Development of formal operational reasoning skills is affected by the importance of those skills in an individual's culture. • The ideals that young people espouse may reflect their religious, cultural, or socioeconomic backgrounds.	• Present abstract concepts and principles central to various academic disciplines, but tie them to concrete examples. • Have students engage in scientific investigations, focusing on familiar objects and phenomena. • Assign mathematics problems that require use of simple fractions, ratios, or decimals. • While demonstrating how to do a new task, also show how you think about the task.
Late Adolescence (14–18) 	• Abstract thought and scientific reasoning skills more prevalent, especially for topics about which adolescents have a substantial knowledge base • Idealistic notions tempered by more realistic considerations • Ability to perform many tasks in an adultlike manner	• Abstract thinking is more common in some content areas (e.g., mathematics, science) than in others (e.g., history, geography). • Formal operational reasoning skills are less likely to appear in cultures that don't require those skills. • Teenagers' proficiency in particular adult tasks varies considerably from individual to individual and from task to task.	• Study particular disciplines in depth; introduce complex and abstract explanations and theories. • Encourage discussions about social, political, and ethical issues; elicit multiple perspectives regarding these issues. • Involve adolescents in activities that are similar or identical to the things they will eventually do as adults. • Show how experts in a field think about the tasks they perform.

Challenge We see the importance of challenge most clearly in Vygotsky's concept of the *zone of proximal development:* Children benefit most from tasks that they can perform only with the assistance of more competent individuals. Challenge appears in a more disguised form in Piaget's theory, but it plays a critical role nonetheless: Children develop more sophisticated knowledge and thought processes only when they encounter phenomena they cannot adequately understand using existing schemes—in other words, phenomena that create *disequilibrium.*

Readiness According to both theories, growing children may be cognitively ready for some experiences yet not be ready for others. From Piaget's perspective, children can accommodate to new objects and events only when they can also assimilate them into existing schemes; there must be some overlap between the "new" and the "old." In addition, Piaget argued that children cannot learn from an experience until they have begun the transition into a stage that allows them to deal with and conceptualize that experience appropriately (e.g., they cannot benefit from hearing abstract ideas until they have begun the transition into formal operations).

Vygotsky, too, proposed that there are limits on the tasks that children can reasonably handle at any particular time. As children acquire some capabilities, other, slightly more advanced ones emerge in an embryonic form. They fall within the child's ZPD and can be fostered through adult assistance and guidance.

Teachers and other professionals who work with children must be very careful when considering the concept of *readiness,* however. Historically, many practitioners have assumed that biological maturation and background experiences (or the lack thereof) put an upper limit on what children can do and that some children may not be "ready" for formal instructional settings (e.g., kindergarten) or for instruction about particular topics. However, all children are ready to learn *something.* The issue is not whether a child is ready, but what a child is ready for and how best to facilitate his or her cognitive development in academic and nonacademic settings (Stipek, 2002; R. Watson, 1996).[9]

Importance of Social Interaction In Piaget's eyes, the people in a child's life can present information and arguments that create disequilibrium and foster greater perspective taking. For instance, when young children disagree with one another, they gradually come to realize that different people may have different yet equally valid viewpoints, and they begin to shed their preoperational egocentrism.

In Vygotsky's view, social interactions provide the very foundation for thought processes: Children internalize the processes they use when they converse with others until, ultimately, they can use them independently. Furthermore, tasks within the ZPD can, by definition, be accomplished only when others assist in children's efforts.

Theoretical Differences

Following are four questions that capture key differences between Piaget's and Vygotsky's theories of cognitive development.

To What Extent Is Language Essential for Cognitive Development? According to Piaget, language provides verbal labels for many of the schemes that children have previously developed; it is also the primary means through which children interact with others and so can begin to incorporate multiple perspectives into their thinking. In Piaget's view, however, much of cognitive development occurs independently of language.

For Vygotsky, language is absolutely critical for cognitive development. Children's thought processes are internalized versions of social interactions that are largely verbal in nature. For instance, through self-talk and inner speech, children begin to guide their own

---

[9]Some school districts use the results of so-called "readiness" tests to suggest that some children wait an extra year before beginning kindergarten or first grade. As you will discover in Chapter 6, such tests are fairly limited in scope (they focus primarily on cognitive skills while overlooking social and emotional skills that may be equally important) and are not necessarily accurate predictors of children's later classroom performance. Accordingly, educators who use them should consider their results only in conjunction with other information about children.

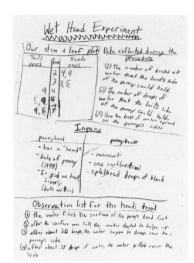

behaviors in ways that others have previously guided them. Furthermore, in their conversations with adults, children learn the meanings that their culture ascribes to particular events and gradually begin to interpret the world in "culturally appropriate" ways.

To what extent does cognitive development depend on language? Perhaps the truth lies somewhere between Piaget's and Vygotsky's theories. Piaget probably underestimated the importance of language: Children acquire more complex understandings of phenomena and events not only through their own interactions with the world but also (as Vygotsky suggested) by learning how others interpret those phenomena and events. On the other hand, Vygotsky may have overstated the case for language: Verbal exchanges may be less important for cognitive development in some cultures than in others. For instance, in a study by Rogoff, Mistry, Göncü, and Mosier (1993), adults in four cultures—middle-class communities in the United States and Turkey, a Native American community in Guatemala, and a tribal village in India—were asked to help toddlers with the difficult tasks of getting dressed and manipulating strange new toys. Adults in the United States and Turkey provided a great deal of verbal guidance as they helped the children. The Guatemalan and Indian adults conversed less with the children; instead, much of their guidance took the form of gestures and demonstrations.

What Kinds of Experiences Promote Development? Piaget maintained that children's independent, self-motivated explorations of the physical world form the basis for many developing schemes, and children often construct these schemes with little guidance from others. In contrast, Vygotsky argued for activities that are facilitated and interpreted by more competent individuals. The distinction, then, is one of self-exploration versus guided exploration and instruction. Ideally, children almost certainly need both kinds of experiences—opportunities to manipulate and experiment with physical phenomena on their own and opportunities to draw upon the wisdom of prior generations (Karpov & Haywood, 1998). In the "Wet Head Experiment" depicted in Figure 4–12, 10-year-old Amaryth documents her experimentation with water and a penny (she is trying to answer the question *Which side of a penny can hold more water on its surface?*). Yet she uses strategies that her teacher has taught her (careful measurement, observation, and record-keeping, plus reflection on how she could make her experiment better) to enhance what she gains from the process.

What Kinds of Social Interactions Are Most Valuable? Both theorists saw value in interacting with people of all ages. However, Piaget emphasized the benefits of interactions with peers (who could create conflict), whereas Vygotsky placed greater importance on interactions with adults and other more advanced individuals (who could support children in challenging tasks and help them make appropriate interpretations).

Some contemporary theorists have proposed that interactions with peers and interactions with adults play different roles in children's cognitive development (W. Damon, 1984; Rogoff, 1991; N. M. Webb & Palincsar, 1996). When children's development requires that they abandon old perspectives in favor of new, more complex ones, the sociocultural conflict that often occurs among age-mates (and the multiple perspectives that emerge from it) may be optimal for bringing about such change. But when children's development instead requires that they learn new skills, the thoughtful, patient guidance of a competent adult may be more beneficial (e.g., Radziszewska & Rogoff, 1991).

How Influential Is Culture? In Piaget's mind, the nature of children's logical thinking skills and the progression of these skills over time are largely independent of the specific cultural context in which children are raised. In Vygotsky's view, however, culture is of paramount importance in determining the specific thinking skills that children acquire.

Vygotsky was probably more on target here. Earlier in the chapter, we presented evidence to indicate that children's reasoning skills do not necessarily appear at the same ages in different countries; in fact, some reasoning skills (especially those involving formal operational thought) may never appear at all.

In the Basic Developmental Issues table "Contrasting Piaget and Vygotsky" we compare the two perspectives in terms of our three general themes: nature and nurture, universality and diversity, and qualitative and quantitative changes. Keep in mind that neither theorist was completely "right" or completely "wrong": Both offered groundbreaking insights into the na-

BASIC DEVELOPMENTAL ISSUES

Contrasting Piaget and Vygotsky

ISSUE	PIAGET	VYGOTSKY
Nature and Nurture	Piaget believed that biological maturation probably constrains the rate at which children acquire new thinking capabilities. However, he focused on how interactions with both the physical environment (e.g., manipulation of concrete objects) and the social environment (e.g., discussions with peers) promote cognitive development.	Vygotsky acknowledged that children's inherited traits and talents affect the ways in which they deal with the environment and hence affect the experiences that they have. But his theory primarily addresses the environmental conditions (e.g., engagement in challenging activities, guidance of more competent individuals, exposure to cultural interpretations) that influence cognitive growth.
Universality and Diversity	According to Piaget, the progression of children's reasoning capabilities is similar across cultures. Once children have mastered certain reasoning processes, they can apply those processes to a wide range of tasks. Children differ somewhat in the ages at which they acquire new abilities.	From Vygotsky's perspective, the specific cognitive abilities that children acquire depend on the cultural contexts in which the children are raised and the specific activities in which they are asked and encouraged to engage.
Qualitative and Quantitative Change	Piaget proposed that children's logical reasoning skills progress through four, qualitatively different stages. Any particular reasoning capability continues to improve in a gradual (quantitative) fashion throughout the stage in which it first appears.	Vygotsky acknowledged that children undergo qualitative changes in their thinking but did not elaborate on the nature of these changes. Much of his theory points to gradual and presumably quantitative improvements in skills. For instance, a child may initially find a particular task impossible, later be able to execute it with adult assistance, and eventually perform it independently.

ture of children's learning and thinking, and, as you will discover in the next chapter, both have influenced more recent theories of cognitive development. In fact, Piaget's and Vygotsky's theories complement each other to some extent, with the former helping us understand how children often reason on their own and the latter providing ideas about how adults can help them reason more effectively. The final case study describes how four young adolescents reason about a classic Piagetian task—the pendulum problem—and illustrates the scaffolding that a teacher can provide to help them reason in a more "formal operational" fashion.

CASE STUDY: ADOLESCENT SCIENTISTS

Scott Sowell has just introduced the concept of *pendulum* in his seventh-grade science class. When he asks his students to identify variables that might influence the frequency with which a pendulum swings, they suggest three possibilities: the amount of weight at the bottom, the length of the pendulum, and the "angle" from which the weight is initially dropped.

Mr. Sowell divides his students into groups of four and gives each group a pendulum composed of a long string with a paperclip attached to the bottom (Figure A). He also provides extra paperclips that the students can use to increase the weight at the bottom. He gives his students the following assignment: *Design your own experiment. Think of a way to test how each one of these affects the frequency of swing. Then carry out your experiment.*

Jon, Marina, Paige, and Wensley are coming to grips with their task as Mr. Sowell approaches their table.

Marina:	We'll time the frequency as the seconds and the . . . um . . . what? (*She looks questioningly at Mr. Sowell.*)
Mr. S.:	The frequency is the number of swings within a certain time limit.

Figure A

The group agrees to count the number of swings during a 15-second period. After Jon determines the current length of the string, Wensley positions the pendulum 25 degrees from vertical. When Jon says "Go" and starts a stopwatch, Wensley releases the pendulum. Marina counts the number of swings until, 15 seconds later, Jon says, "Stop." Jon records the data from the first experiment: length = 49 cm, weight = 1 paperclip, angle = 25°, frequency = 22.

The group shortens the string and adds a second paperclip onto the bottom of the first clip. They repeat their experiment and record their data: length = 36 cm, weight = 2 paperclips, angle = 45°, frequency = 25.

Wensley: What does the weight do to it?
Marina: We found out that the shorter it is and the heavier it is, the faster it goes.

Mr. Sowell joins the group and reviews its results from the first two tests.

Mr. S.:   What did you change between Test 1 and Test 2?
Marina: Number of paperclips.
Mr. S.:   OK, so you changed the weight. What else did you change?
Wensley: The length.
Marina: And the angle.
Mr. S.:   OK, so you changed all three between the two tests. So what caused the higher frequency?
Wensley: The length.
Marina: No, I think it was the weight.
Jon: I think the weight.
Paige: The length.
Mr. S.:   Why can't you look at your data and decide? (*The students look at him blankly.*) Take a look at the two tests. The first one had one paperclip, and the second had two. The first test had one length, and the second test had a shorter length. Why can't you come to a conclusion by looking at the two frequencies?
Marina: All of the variables changed.

Mr. Sowell nods in agreement and then moves on to another group. The four students decide to change only the weight for the next test, so they add a third paperclip to the bottom of the second. Their pendulum now looks like Figure B. They continue to perform experiments but are careful to change only one variable at a time, or so they think. In reality, each time the group adds another paperclip, the pendulum grows longer. Mr. Sowell visits the students once again.

Mr. S.:   One thing you're testing is length, right? And another thing is weight. Look at your system. Look at how you might be making a slight mistake with weight and length. (*He takes two paperclips off and then puts one back on, hanging it, as the students have done, at the bottom of the first paperclip.*)
Marina: It's heavier *and* longer.
Mr. S.:   Can you think of a way to redesign your experiments so that you're changing only weight? How can you do things differently so that your pendulum doesn't get longer when you add paperclips?
Jon: Hang the second paperclip from the bottom of the string instead of from the first paperclip.

When Mr. Sowell leaves, the students add another paperclip to the pendulum, making sure that the overall length of the pendulum stays the same. They perform another test and find that the pendulum's frequency is identical to what they obtained in the preceding test. Ignoring what she has just seen, Marina concludes, "So if it's heavier, the frequency is higher."

- In what ways does Mr. Sowell scaffold the students' efforts during the lab activity?
- With which one of Piaget's stages is the students' reasoning most consistent, and why?
- Use one or more of Piaget's ideas to explain why Marina persists in her belief that weight affects a pendulum's frequency, despite evidence to the contrary.
- Drawing on post-Piagetian research findings, identify a task for which the students might be better able to separate and control variables.

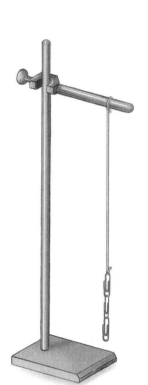

Figure B

Now go to our Companion Website to assess your understanding of chapter content with a Practice Quiz, apply what you've learned in Essay Questions, and broaden your knowledge with links to related Developmental Psychology Web sites. Go to: www.prenhall.com/mcdevitt.

SUMMARY

Piaget's Theory

Piaget portrayed children as active and motivated learners who, through numerous interactions with their physical and social environments, construct an increasingly complex understanding of the world around them. He proposed that cognitive development proceeds through four stages: (1) the sensorimotor stage (when cognitive functioning is based primarily on behaviors and perceptions); (2) the preoperational stage (when symbolic thought and language become prevalent, but reasoning is "illogical" by adult standards); (3) the concrete operations stage (when logical reasoning capabilities emerge but are limited to concrete objects and events); and (4) the formal operations stage (when thinking about abstract, hypothetical, and contrary-to-fact ideas becomes possible).

Developmental researchers have found that Piaget probably underestimated the capabilities of infants, preschoolers, and elementary school children, and overestimated the capabilities of adolescents. Researchers have found, too, that children's reasoning on particular tasks depends somewhat on their prior knowledge, experience, and formal schooling relative to those tasks. Most contemporary developmentalists doubt that cognitive development is as stagelike as Piaget proposed, but they acknowledge the value of his research methods and his views about motivation, the construction of knowledge, and the appearance of qualitative changes in cognitive development.

Vygotsky's Theory

Vygotsky proposed that social activities are precursors to, and form the basis for, complex mental processes (e.g., children gradually internalize the arguing process, enabling them to consider multiple perspectives when they think and reason); self-talk and inner speech reflect this internalization process. Adults promote cognitive development both by passing along the meanings that their culture assigns to objects and events and by assisting children with challenging tasks. Often, children first experiment with adult tasks and ways of thinking within the context of their early play activities.

Contemporary theorists have extended Vygotsky's theory in several directions. For instance, some recommend that adults frequently engage children and adolescents in authentic, adultlike tasks, initially providing the scaffolding necessary to accomplish those tasks successfully and gradually withdrawing the scaffolding as youngsters become more proficient. Other theorists suggest that adults can help children benefit from their experiences through joint construction of meanings, guided participation, and cognitive apprenticeships. And most developmentalists believe that children's play activities prepare them for adult life by allowing them to practice a variety of adultlike behaviors and to develop skills in planning, communication, cooperation, and problem solving.

Comparing Piaget and Vygotsky

Challenge, readiness, and social interaction are central to the theories of both Piaget and Vygotsky. However, the two perspectives differ on the role of language in cognitive development, the relative value of self-exploration versus more guided activities, the relative importance of interactions with peers versus adults, and the influence of culture.

KEY CONCEPTS

cognition (p. 140)
class inclusion (p. 141)
clinical method (p. 141)
scheme (p. 142)
operation (p. 142)
adaptation (p. 142)
assimilation (p. 142)
accommodation (p. 142)
equilibrium (p. 143)
disequilibrium (p. 143)
equilibration (p. 143)
goal-directed behavior (p. 145)

object permanence (p. 146)
symbolic thought (p. 146)
deferred imitation (p. 146)
egocentrism (p. 149)
egocentric speech (p. 149)
conservation (p. 149)
nativism (p. 154)
constructivism (p. 158)
individual constructivism (p. 158)
sociocognitive conflict (p. 162)

sociocultural perspective (p. 164)
self-talk (p. 165)
inner speech (p. 165)
internalization (p. 165)
actual developmental level (p. 166)
level of potential development (p. 166)
zone of proximal development (ZPD) (p. 166)

mediated learning experience (p. 168)
social constructivism (p. 169)
scaffolding (p. 169)
guided participation (p. 169)
apprenticeship (p. 170)
cognitive apprenticeship (p. 170)
dynamic assessment (p. 172)
sociodramatic play (p. 173)
self-regulation (p. 175)
authentic activity (p. 176)

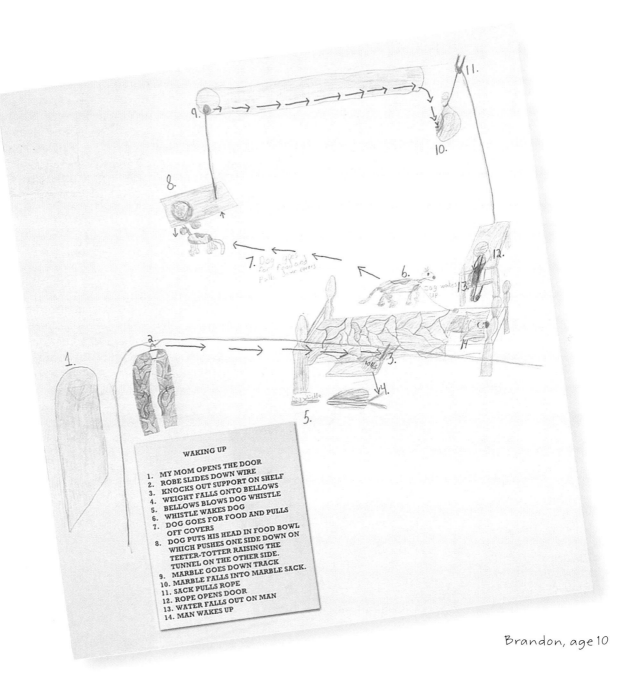

WAKING UP

1. MY MOM OPENS THE DOOR
2. ROBE SLIDES DOWN WIRE
3. KNOCKS OUT SUPPORT ON SHELF
4. WEIGHT FALLS ONTO BELLOWS
5. BELLOWS BLOWS DOG WHISTLE
6. WHISTLE WAKES DOG
7. DOG GOES FOR FOOD AND PULLS OFF COVERS
8. DOG PUTS HIS HEAD IN FOOD BOWL WHICH PUSHES ONE SIDE DOWN ON TEETER-TOTTER RAISING THE TUNNEL ON THE OTHER SIDE.
9. MARBLE GOES DOWN TRACK
10. MARBLE FALLS INTO MARBLE SACK.
11. SACK PULLS ROPE
12. ROPE OPENS DOOR
13. WATER FALLS OUT ON MAN
14. MAN WAKES UP

Brandon, age 10

Cognitive Development 2: Cognitive Processes

CASE STUDY: HOW THE UNITED STATES BECAME A COUNTRY

Our colleague Dinah Jackson once asked students in grades 2 through 8 to write essays addressing the following question: *The land we live on has been here for a very long time, but the United States has only been a country for a little more than 200 years. How did the United States become a country?* Here are some of their responses:

Second grader:

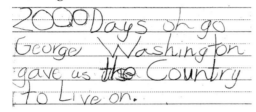

2000 Days oh go George Washington gave us the Country To Live on.

Third grader:

The pilgrams came over in 17 hundred, when they came over they bilt houses. The Idiuns tifout they were mean. Then they came friends, and tot them stuff. Then winter came, and alot died. Then some had babies. So thats how we got here.

Sixth grader:

The U.S.A. became a contry by some of the British wanting to be under a different rule than of the kings. So, they sailed to the "new world" and became a new country. The only problem was that the kings from Britin still ruled the "new world". Then they had the revolutionary war. They beat Britin, and became an independent country.

Eighth grader:

We became a country through different processes. Technology around the world finally caught up with the British. There were boats to travel with, navigating tools, and the hearts of men had a desire to expand. Many men had gone on expeditions across the sea. A very famous journey was that of Christopher Columbus. He discovered this land that we live. More and more people poured in, expecting instant wealth, freedom, and a right to share their opinions. Some immigrants were satisfied, others were displeased. Problems in other countries forced people to move on to this New World, such as potato famins and no freedom of religions. Stories that drifted through people grew about this country. Stories of golden roads and free land coaxed other families who were living in the slums. Unfortunately, there were slums in America. The people helped this country grow in industry, cultures, religions, and government. Inventions and books were now better than the Europeans. Dime-novels were invented, and the young people could read about heroes of this time. May the curiosity and eagerness of the children continue.

Responses courtesy of Dinah Jackson.

185

These four compositions illustrate important changes in children's knowing and thinking as they grow older. Not surprising, of course, is an increase in knowledge: The sixth and eighth graders know considerably more—not only about the origins of their country but also about correct spelling and rules of punctuation and capitalization—than the second and third graders do. Furthermore, whereas the third grader describes the nation's history as a list of seemingly unrelated facts, the sixth and eighth graders have pulled what they have learned into an integrated whole that "hangs together." In addition, the younger children's descriptions reflect very simplistic and concrete understandings (e.g., the country was a gift from George Washington, the Pilgrims came over and built houses); in contrast, the eighth grader uses abstract concepts (e.g., technological progress, freedom of religion, overly optimistic expectations for wealth) to explain immigration to the United States.

In this chapter, we will look at contemporary theories of cognition and cognitive development that focus on changes in children's thinking, learning processes, and knowledge. Most of our early discussion will revolve around *information processing theory,* a perspective that underlies much of the current research in cognitive development. Later, in our discussion of *theory theory,* we will discover how children construct increasingly complex understandings (theories) about various topics and subject matter. Eventually, we will draw from Piaget's and Vygotsky's theories as well as information processing concepts to explore *neo-Piagetian* approaches to cognitive development and *sociocultural* influences on information processing. Finally, we will consider exceptionalities in information processing, including learning disabilities, attention-deficit hyperactivity disorder, and autism.

Information Processing Theory

Do children become better able to pay attention as they grow older? Do they learn and remember things more effectively as they move through the school grades? How does the nature of their knowledge change over time? Such questions reflect the approach of **information processing theory**, a group of theoretical frameworks that address how human beings receive, think about, mentally modify, and remember information, and on how such cognitive processes change over the course of development.

Information processing theory emerged in the late 1950s and early 1960s and has continued to evolve in the decades that have followed. Initially, many information processing theorists believed that human beings might think in ways similar to how computers operate, and they borrowed computer terminology to describe human thought processes. For example, they described people as *storing* (i.e., putting) information in memory and then *retrieving* it from memory (i.e., finding it) when they need it at a later time. In recent years, however, theorists have found that people often think in distinctly non-computer-like ways. Much of information processing theory now has a *constructivist* flavor similar to that of Piaget's theory (Derry, 1996; Mayer, 1996). In other words, theorists recognize that human beings actively construct their own unique understandings of the world, rather than simply receiving and absorbing knowledge from the outside world in the relatively "mindless" way that a computer does. As an example of such construction, consider once again the second grader's explanation in the opening case study:

> 2000 Days oh go George Washington gave us the Country to Live on.

Almost certainly, no one ever told her that Washington gave people the United States. Instead, she uses something she has been told, probably that Washington was a key figure in the country's early history, to construct what is, to her, a reasonable explanation of her country's origin. Similarly, the student has probably never seen the word *ago* spelled as "oh go," yet she uses two words she has seen to construct a reasonable (albeit incorrect) spelling.

Key Ideas in Information Processing Theory

Information processing theorists don't always agree about the specific mechanisms involved in learning and remembering information. Nevertheless, many of them do agree on the following points:

information processing theory
Theoretical perspective that focuses on the specific ways in which people mentally think about ("process") the information they receive.

■ *Input from the environment provides the raw material for cognitive processing.* People receive input from the environment through the senses—sight, hearing, smell, taste, touch—and subsequently translate that raw input into more meaningful information. The first part of this process, detecting stimuli in the environment, is **sensation.** The second part, interpreting those stimuli, is **perception.**

Because even the simplest interpretation of an environmental event takes time, many theorists believe that human memory includes a mechanism that allows people to remember raw sensory data for a very short time (perhaps 2 to 3 seconds for auditory information, and probably less than a second for visual information). This mechanism goes by a variety of names; we will refer to it as the **sensory register.**

■ *In addition to a sensory register, human memory includes two other storage mechanisms: working memory and long-term memory.* **Working memory** is the component of memory where people hold new information as they mentally process it. Working memory is where most thinking, or cognitive processing, occurs. For instance, it is where people try to solve a problem or make sense of what they are reading. **Long-term memory** is the component that allows people to keep the many things they learn from their experiences over the years, including such knowledge as where cookies are stored in the kitchen and how much 2 and 2 equal, as well as such skills as how to ride a bicycle and how to use a microscope.

Working memory keeps information for only a very short time (perhaps 20 to 30 seconds unless the individual continues to think about and actively process it); hence, it is sometimes called *short-term memory.* Working memory also appears to have a limited capacity: It has only a small amount of "space" in which people can hold and think about events or ideas. As an illustration, try computing the following division problem in your head:

$$59\overline{)49,383}$$

Did you find yourself having trouble remembering some parts of the problem while you were dealing with other parts? Did you ever arrive at the correct answer of 837? Most people cannot solve a division problem with this many numbers unless they can write the problem on paper. There simply isn't "room" in working memory to hold all the numbers you need to remember in order to solve the problem in your head.

In contrast to working memory, long-term memory lasts indefinitely. Some theorists propose that anything stored in long-term memory remains there for a lifetime, but others believe that information may slowly fade away over time, especially if it isn't used much after it is stored. Long-term memory is assumed to have an unlimited capacity: It can "hold" as much information as a person needs to save.

To think about information previously stored in long-term memory, people must retrieve it and examine it in working memory. Thus, although people's capacity to store information in long-term memory may be boundless, their ability to think about what they've stored is limited to whatever they can hold in working memory at any one time.

■ *Attention is essential to the learning process.* Most information processing theorists believe that attention plays a key role in the interpretation of information and its storage in memory. Attention is the primary process through which information moves from the sensory register into working memory. Many theorists argue that when people don't pay attention to something, they essentially lose it from memory and so cannot possibly remember it later on. In the Memory/Middle Childhood clip on the Observation CD, you can see what happens when a child isn't paying attention. Ten-year-old David remembers 3 of the 12 words that the interviewer reads to him. He sees his lapse in attention as the reason he did not recall more words: "My brain was turned off right now."

■ *A variety of cognitive processes are involved in moving information from working memory to long-term memory.* Whereas attention is instrumental in moving information from the sensory register to working memory, other, more complex processes are needed if people are to remember information for longer than a minute or so. Some theorists suggest that repeating information over and over (*rehearsing* it) is sufficient for its long-term storage. Others propose that people store information effectively only when they connect it to concepts and ideas that already exist in long-term memory—for instance, when they use what

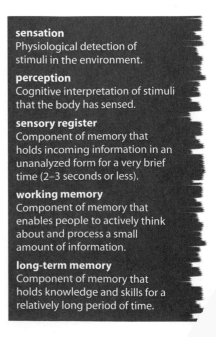

In the Memory/ Middle Childhood clip, observe David's realization that attention affects his memory of a word list.

sensation
Physiological detection of stimuli in the environment.

perception
Cognitive interpretation of stimuli that the body has sensed.

sensory register
Component of memory that holds incoming information in an unanalyzed form for a very brief time (2–3 seconds or less).

working memory
Component of memory that enables people to actively think about and process a small amount of information.

long-term memory
Component of memory that holds knowledge and skills for a relatively long period of time.

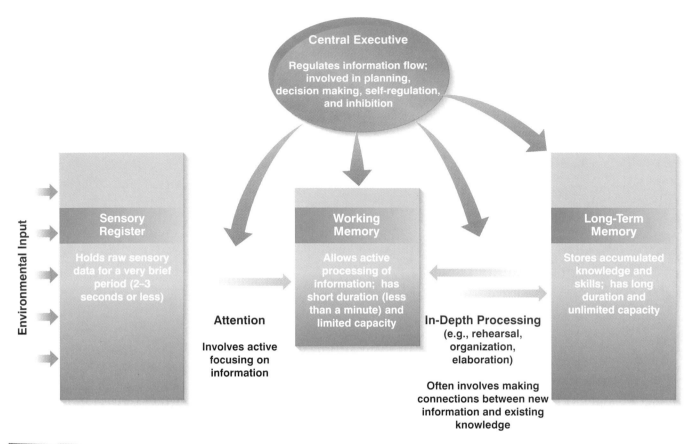

FIGURE 5–1 A model of the human information processing system

they already know either to *organize* or expand (i.e., *elaborate*) on the new information. The three processes just listed, rehearsal, organization, and elaboration, are examples of the *executive functions* described in Chapter 3. We will look at their development more closely later in the chapter.

■ *People control how they process information.* Some sort of cognitive "supervisor" is almost certainly necessary to ensure that a person's learning and memory processes work effectively. This mechanism, sometimes called the **central executive**, oversees the flow of information throughout the memory system, and is critical for planning, decision making, self-regulation, and inhibition of unproductive thoughts and behaviors. Although the central executive is probably closely connected to working memory (e.g., Kimberg, D'Esposito, & Farah, 1997), information processing theorists haven't yet pinned down its exact nature.

Figure 5–1 presents a model of how the mechanisms and processes just described fit together into an overall human information processing system.

■ *Cognitive development involves gradual changes in various components of the information processing system.* Information processing theorists reject Piaget's notion of discrete developmental stages. Instead, they believe that children's cognitive processes and abilities develop through steady and gradual *trends*. In the following sections, we look at developmental trends in sensation and perception, attention, working memory, long-term memory, and thinking and reasoning.

Sensation and Perception

Children's ability to learn about their environment—including the objects they encounter and the people with whom they interact—depends on their ability to *perceive* their environment. Most sensory and perceptual development occurs in infancy. But because infants cannot describe what they are seeing and hearing, researchers have had to resort to roundabout methods to study infant capabilities.

central executive
Component of the human information processing system that oversees the flow of information throughout the system.

One common strategy in infancy research involves observing what infants prefer to look at. Two visual stimuli are presented side by side (perhaps on a screen above an infant's crib), and the infant's eye movements are carefully monitored; in subsequent presentations, the positions of the two stimuli are varied. If the infant looks more at one stimulus than the other, regardless of its position, then we know that the child (a) can tell the two stimuli apart and (b) has a definite preference for one over the other.

A second widely used strategy relies on the phenomenon of **habituation**, the tendency of human beings and many other species to "get used to" and lose interest in (i.e., to *habituate* to) stimuli that are in their environment for an extended period. When a stimulus is first presented, infants may respond to it in a variety of ways: They look at it, they may suck harder on a pacifier placed in their mouths, and their heart rate and blood pressure change. As the novelty wears off, their gaze wanders, they suck less intensively, and physiological functions return to earlier levels. Once a different stimulus is presented, however, researchers may again observe intensive gazing and sucking and heightened physiological responses. To *dishabituate* in this way, infants must be able to distinguish between the stimulus they are currently perceiving and the one they perceived previously.

Research methodologies such as those just described have enabled researchers to determine many things about the development of sensation and perception, including the following:

■ *Some sensory and perceptual capabilities are present at birth; others emerge within the first few weeks or months of life.* Even newborns can discriminate among different tastes, smells, sounds, and sound sequences; in fact, newborns hear sounds almost as clearly as adults do (Bijeljac-Babic, Bertoncini, & Mehler, 1993; Flavell et al., 1993; Rosenstein & Oster, 1988; Steiner, 1979). Some elements of perception, the *interpretation* of sensed stimuli, appear early as well. For instance, newborns have some ability to determine the direction from which a sound is coming, and within the first week they seem to understand that objects maintain the same shape and size even when they are rotated or moved farther away and so look different (Morrongiello, Fenwick, Hillier, & Chance, 1994; Slater, Mattock, & Brown, 1990; Slater & Morison, 1985).

Many sensory and perceptual capabilities, such as visual acuity, visual focusing, color discrimination, and the ability to locate the source of sounds, continue to improve during the first few months—and in some cases, the first year or two—of life (R. J. Adams, 1987; Ashmead, Davis, Whalen, & Odom, 1991; Aslin, 1993; Hillier, Hewitt, & Morrongiello, 1992). Visual acuity changes markedly during the first year; at birth, it is less than 20/600, but by 8 months of age it is around 20/80 (Courage & Adams, 1990). Infants can nevertheless do a great deal with their limited eyesight. For instance, within the first few days of life, they can recognize the contours of their mothers' faces and can imitate facial expressions depicting happiness, sadness, and surprise (T. Field et al., 1982; M. H. Johnson & de Haan, 2001; Walton, Bower, & Bower, 1992). However, visual perception is probably not fully developed until the preschool years, when the visual cortex of the brain becomes similar in structure to that of an adult (T. L. Hickey & Peduzzi, 1987).

■ *Cross-modality associations appear very early.* Quite early in life, infants seem to have some awareness of relationships among the pieces of information they get from different sensory modalities. In one classic study (Meltzoff & Borton, 1979), 1-month-old babies sucked on either a smooth or bumpy pacifier that they couldn't see. When they were later shown pictures of both a smooth pacifier and a bumpy one, they spent more time looking at the one they had previously sucked. By 4 months of age, infants have considerable awareness of both sight-touch and sight-sound relationships; for instance, they have some knowledge of what visual events (e.g., seeing a woman playing peek-a-boo, or a stick striking a block of wood) are associated with particular sounds (Bahrick, 2002; Spelke, 1976; Streri & Spelke, 1988).

■ *Infants show consistent preferences for certain types of stimuli.* As early as the first week of life, infants are drawn to new and interesting stimuli and events (Haith, 1980, 1990). For instance, they prefer a complex design over a solid color or single stripe, and a three-dimensional mask or human face over a two dimensional picture of a face. As a

habituation
Changes in children's physiological responses to repeated displays of the same stimulus; it reflects loss of interest.

FIGURE 5–2 By refusing to crawl to the "deep" side of this glass-covered table (an apparatus known as a *visual cliff*), infants show a fear of heights.

general rule, infants prefer stimuli of moderate (rather than very weak or very strong) intensity (Lewkowicz & Turkewitz, 1981; Maurer & Maurer, 1988).

Key among infants' preferences are social stimuli. For instance, within 3 days of birth, they recognize their mother's voice and will suck more vigorously if doing so enables them to hear it (DeCasper & Fifer, 1980). By 1 month, they prefer looking at faces over other objects, and by 3 months, this preference exists even when the other objects are similar in other perceptual characteristics, such as symmetry and contrast (Dannemiller & Stephens, 1988; M. H. Johnson & Morton, 1991). By 4 months, infants also seem to prefer looking at human forms of movement (e.g., walking) over other movements (Bertenthal, 1993; Bertenthal & Pinto, 1993). This early inclination to focus on social stimuli is, of course, highly beneficial, as infants must depend on others not only for their survival but also for learning language and other essential aspects of their culture.

■ *Perceptual development is the result of both biological maturation and experience.* At what age do infants acquire depth perception? To address this question, researchers often use a *visual cliff,* a large glass table with a patterned cloth immediately beneath the glass on one side and the same pattern on the floor under the other side (e.g., see Figure 5–2). In a classic study by E. J. Gibson & Walk (1960), 36 infants 6 to 14 months old were placed on a narrow platform between the "shallow" and "deep" sides of a visual cliff. Their mothers stood at one end of the table and actively coaxed them to crawl across the glass. Although 27 of the infants willingly crawled off the platform to the "shallow" side, only 3 ventured onto the "deep" side; most instead either cried or crawled in the opposite direction despite their mothers' encouragement. By age 6 months, then, infants can apparently perceive depth and know that sharp drop-offs are potentially dangerous.

Is a crawling infant's fear of heights the result of biology or experience? Unfortunately, Gibson and Walk's results don't answer this question: The infants in their study might have had some biologically built-in aversion to heights or they may have learned through previous crawling experience that drop-offs should be avoided. Certainly, neurological maturation is involved in depth perception to some degree: Visual acuity must be sufficiently sharp and the visual cortex must be sufficiently developed that infants can perceive edges and inclines. Some species that can walk almost immediately after birth (e.g., chicks, lambs, baby goats) show avoidance and fear of the deep side of the visual cliff when they are less than 24 hours old (E. J. Gibson & Walk, 1960), suggesting that an inborn fear of heights is fairly common in the animal kingdom. But researchers have found that experience is also important: Infants who have had experience with self-locomotion, either crawling or using a walker, show greater fear of drop-offs (as evidenced in both avoidance behaviors and accelerated heartrates) than infants without such experience (Bertenthal, Campos, & Kermoian, 1994; Campos, Bertenthal, & Kermoian, 1992).

Generally, theorists believe that both neurological maturation and experience are essential for perceptual development (e.g., Held, 1993; M. H. Johnson, 1998). Furthermore, neurological changes may actually depend on experience to some degree. For example, research with cats indicates the possible existence of sensitive periods in the development of visual sensation: Kittens deprived of normal sight during only the first 2 to 3 months of life have limited visual capabilities later on (Bruer, 1999; Wiesel & Hubel, 1965). This is not to say, however, that parents and other caregivers should give infants as much stimulation as possible: The kinds of experiences that ensure optimal perceptual development are those that children with normal visual and auditory abilities are apt to encounter in any reasonably nurturing environment (Bruer, 1999).

From an evolutionary perspective, it makes sense that both heredity and environment should play a role in perceptual development. Because perception of one's surroundings is essential for survival, the human species has undoubtedly evolved some biologically built-in perceptual mechanisms. At the same time, the specific environments to which humans

DEVELOPMENT AND PRACTICE

Providing Appropriate Stimulation for Infants

■ Give infants some choice and control in their sensory experiences.

A home child care provider offers a variety of simple toys and other objects for the infants in her care to explore and play with. She often places several items within reach, and she respects infants' occasional rejection and apparent dislike of certain items.

■ Be aware of the dangers of too much stimulation.

A teacher in an infant child care center realizes that the center is often busy and noisy. Knowing that too much stimulation may be unsettling, he constantly monitors the sights, sounds, textures, and even smells that are present at any one time. He tries to tone down the environment a bit when introducing a new stimulus for an infant to experience or explore.

■ Read cues.

A father helps his daughter's child care provider understand the signals she typically gives. "She often turns away when she's had enough of something," he explains. "But at other times, she just acts sleepy. You know she's overstimulated if you put her in a quiet place and she perks up. If she's truly tired, then she quickly goes to sleep."

■ Avoid the "better baby" trap.

A child care provider recently attended a workshop on the latest "brain research," where several presenters made a strong pitch for certain new products, claiming that the products are "indispensable" for maximizing intellectual growth. Fortunately, she knows enough about cognitive development to realize that children benefit equally from a wide variety of toys and that an intensive "sensory stimulation" approach is probably not in the children's best interest.

■ Recognize that temperamental and cultural differences determine the optimum amount of stimulation for each child.

A teacher in a child care center has noticed that some of the toddlers in her group seem to respond to a good deal of sensory input by getting excited and animated, whereas others fuss, go to sleep, or in some other way indicate that they are on overload. Although she herself prefers a quiet, peaceful room, one of her coworkers enjoys lively salsa music and often plays it while the children are awake. The two teachers respect their own differences and often compare notes about how different children respond to quiet versus more active environments.

must adapt vary from place to place, and so the human brain has evolved to be responsive to local circumstances (J. J. Gibson, 1979; Greenough & Black, 1992; Thelen & Smith, 1998).

Attention

The development of attention is due, in part, to brain maturation, and, in particular, to the continuing development of the cortex in the first few years of life (Ridderinkhof & van der Molen, 1995; Ruff & Rothbart, 1996). The increasing involvement of the cortex contributes to the following developmental trends:

■ *Initially, attention is largely a function of the physical characteristics of stimuli and events; later, it also depends on children's prior knowledge.* Earlier we mentioned the tendency of infants to look at a new stimulus and react to it in some way (e.g., with a change in sucking or heart rate). Human beings, infants included, often focus attention and show physiological changes when a new stimulus is presented. In some cases, their attention is captured by a particularly intense stimulus (e.g., a loud noise, flash of light, or sudden movement). In other cases, a novel object or event will attract their attention. For instance, in the Cognitive Development/Infancy clip, 16-month-old Corwin quickly becomes engrossed in the multicolored geometric toy that he finds in a paper bag.

Observe how Corwin's attention is drawn to a novel object in the Cognitive Development/Infancy clip.

Although children's attention may initially be captured by intense or unusual stimuli, what holds their attention soon becomes a function of their existing knowledge about the world. In particular, infants tend to focus more on objects and events that are moderately different, but not too different, from those they are familiar with (Greenberg & O'Donnell, 1972; McCall, Kennedy, & Applebaum, 1977). This tendency is consistent with Piaget's belief that children can accommodate to (and so benefit from) new stimuli only to the extent that they can also assimilate those stimuli to their existing schemes.

■ *Children attend differently to people than to inanimate objects.* By the time they are 4 weeks old, infants show distinct ways of attending to their primary caregivers: They attend longer and may engage in a repetitive cycle of paying attention and then withdrawing it. Undoubtedly their attention is influenced by the fact that the person who is the focus of their attention responds to them, for instance by moving, showing emotion, and coordinating actions with the infants' own behaviors (Brazelton, Koslowski, & Main, 1974). In fact, adults often work hard to engage the attention of infants, and as you will discover later in the chapter, the attention-sharing sessions of infants and adults play an important role in cognitive development.

Observe Maddie's age-typical shifts in attention in the Cognitive Development/Early Childhood clip.

■ *With age, distractibility decreases and sustained attention increases.* Once they are captivated by an object or event, infants as young as 6 months are less distractible than they would be otherwise (Richards & Turner, 2001). How long young children can sustain their attention is to some extent a function of their temperament: Some toddlers can become quite engrossed in an activity when the task is self-chosen, intriguing, and free from interference by others. By and large, however, young children's attention tends to move quickly from one thing to another. Preschool and kindergarten children in free-play situations typically spend only a few minutes engaged in one activity before they move on to another (Dempster & Corkill, 1999; Ruff & Lawson, 1990; Stodolsky, 1974). (As an example, notice how quickly 2½-year-old Maddie loses interest in the conservation task in the Cognitive Development/Early Childhood clip.) Such distractibility isn't necessarily a bad thing, as it may draw young children to other potentially valuable learning activities and so, in some circumstances, may be beneficial. But it can be frustrating for adults who have particular agendas in mind.

Over time, children become better able to focus and sustain their attention on a particular task, and they are less distracted by irrelevant stimuli (Higgins & Turnure, 1984; Lane & Pearson, 1982; Ruff & Lawson, 1990). For example, in one experiment (Higgins & Turnure, 1984), children in three age groups (preschool, second grade, and sixth grade) were given age-appropriate visual discrimination tasks. Some children worked on the tasks in a quiet room, others worked in a room with a little background noise, and still others worked with a great deal of background noise. Preschool and second-grade children performed most effectively under the quiet conditions and least effectively under the very noisy conditions. But the sixth graders performed just as well in a noisy room as in a quiet room. Apparently the older children could ignore the noise, whereas the younger children could not.

As children grow older, they become better able to keep their attention on a particular task.

■ *Attention becomes increasingly purposeful.* By the time they are 3 or 4 months old, children show some ability to anticipate where an object of interest will be and then focus their attention in that direction (Haith, Hazen, & Goodman, 1988). In the preschool years, they begin to use attention specifically to help learn and remember something, and their ability to use it effectively continues to improve during the elementary and middle school years (DeMarie-Dreblow & Miller, 1988; Hagen & Stanovich, 1977; P. Miller & Seier, 1994). Indeed, their learning becomes increasingly a function of what they think they need to remember. To illustrate, imagine that you have six cards in front of you on a table. Each card has a different background color and a picture of a different object, much like the cards in Figure 5–3. You are told to remember only the colors of those cards. Now the cards are flipped over, and you are asked where the green card is, where the purple card is, and so on. You are then asked to name the picture that appeared on each card. Do you think you would remember the colors of the cards (the information that you needed to learn)? Do you think you would remember the objects (information that you did *not* need to learn and so may not have paid attention to)?

FIGURE 5–3 Imagine that you are told to remember the colors of each of these cards. After the cards are flipped over, do you think you would remember where each color appeared? Would you also remember what object appeared on each card, even though you were not asked to remember the objects?

Modeled after stimuli used by Maccoby & [Hage]n, 1965.

In a study by Maccoby and Hagen (1965), children in grades 1 through 7 were asked to perform a series of tasks similar to the one just described. The older children remembered the background colors more accurately than the younger children did. Yet the older children were no better than younger ones at remembering the objects pictured on the cards; in fact, the oldest group in the study remembered the *fewest* objects. These results suggest that older children are better at paying attention to and learning the things they need to know; they are not necessarily better at learning information irrelevant to their needs.

Working Memory

As you will recall, working memory is the component of the human information processing system where active, conscious thinking occurs. As children grow older, they become capable of thinking about a greater number of things at once and performing more complex cognitive tasks. This developmental trend in working memory is probably the combined result of three more specific trends:

■ *Processing speed increases.* Children execute many cognitive processes more quickly and efficiently as they get older (Fry & Hale, 1996; Gathercole & Hitch, 1993; Kail, 1991). For example, older children can make comparisons among similar stimuli, retrieve information from long-term memory, and solve simple problems more quickly than younger children (Cerella & Hale, 1994). Processing speed continues to increase, and thus the time required to execute many mental tasks continues to decrease, until early adulthood (R. Kail, 1993).

With time and practice, some of the things that children know and can do become **automatized.** In other words, children are able to perform certain mental and physical tasks very quickly and with little or no conscious effort. Once these activities become automatized, they take up very little "space" in working memory; as a result, children can devote more working memory capacity to other, potentially more complex tasks and problems. As one simple example of automatization, consider how children's reading ability improves over time. When children first begin to read, they often devote considerable mental effort to identifying the words on the page—remembering what the letter configuration *f-r-i-e-n-d* spells, sounding out an unfamiliar word such as *elementary,* and so on—and so may remember little about the meaning of what they've read. But with increasing exposure to a variety of reading materials, word identification gradually becomes an automatized process, such that children immediately recognize most of the words they encounter. At this point, children can concentrate on (i.e., devote most of their working memory capacity to) what is ultimately the most important part of the reading process: understanding the ideas that an author is trying to communicate. (This is not to say, however, that teachers should postpone teaching reading comprehension until word recognition is automatized; we will return to this point in Chapter 8.)

Automatization increases the likelihood that a child will respond to a particular situation in a particular way. In many instances, the child will have practiced and automatized the best response for that situation—"best," at least, for that child's environment and culture. Because different environments and cultures sometimes require very different responses, children need to learn the most effective ways of responding within the contexts in which they are growing up. Thus, the *non*automatized cognitive processes of young children may, to some degree, be a blessing rather than a curse, allowing them to practice and ultimately to automatize the processes that are most likely to serve them well in their own circumstances (Bjorklund & Green, 1992).[1]

■ *Children acquire more effective cognitive processes.* Not only do children process information more quickly, but they also acquire new and better cognitive strategies as they grow older (Kail & Park, 1994). For example, when preschoolers are asked to add 3 blocks to 5 blocks, they are likely to count all the blocks to arrive at the answer, 8. In contrast, third graders given the same problem are likely to retrieve the number fact "3 + 5 = 8" from long-term memory—a strategy that involves considerably less working memory capacity. Later in the chapter, we describe some of the learning and problem-solving strategies that emerge over time.

■ *The physical capacity of working memory may increase somewhat.* Much of the apparent increase in children's working memory capacity is probably due to the increased

---

[1] In Chapter 3, we considered the same idea from the standpoint of brain physiology. In the early years, many new synapses spring up among neurons (through the process of *synaptogenesis*), allowing the possibility of adaptation to a variety of environmental conditions. Soon thereafter, the frequently used synapses are strengthened and the little-used synapses wither away (through the process of *synaptic pruning*), resulting in a system that is especially suited for a particular environment.

automatization
Process of becoming able to respond quickly and efficiently while mentally processing or physically performing certain tasks.

speed and efficiency of their cognitive processes, rather than to an increase in their memory "space" (Fry & Hale, 1996; Gathercole & Hitch, 1993). Theorists disagree as to whether the actual "hardware" of working memory increases and becomes more efficient with development, but some evidence suggests that it does. For instance, older children perform cognitive tasks more quickly than younger children, and adults perform them still more quickly, even when all groups have had extensive practice with the tasks and so presumably have automatized them (R. Kail, 1993).

Long-Term Memory

Whereas working memory is an active processing center, long-term memory is a repository for the information and skills that people gather over the years. Some knowledge in long-term memory is almost certainly universal; for instance, children all over the globe soon learn that people typically have two legs but cats and dogs have four. Other knowledge is, of course, more dependent on children's unique experiences and on the cultural contexts in which they grow up. For example, in the four children's compositions in the opening case study, we consistently see a European American perspective on the early days of the United States: The focus is on immigration and early European colonization. Were we to ask Native American children how the United States came into being, we might get a very different perspective, perhaps one based on invasion, confiscation, or demolition.

Several developmental phenomena related to long-term memory enhance children's ability to understand and respond to their world:

■ *The capacity to store information in long-term memory appears very early in life.* Children appear to have some capacity to learn and remember even before they are born. In one study (DeCasper & Spence, 1986), pregnant women read aloud a passage from a children's book (e.g., Dr. Seuss's *The Cat and the Hat*) twice a day for the final 6 weeks of their pregnancy. Later, their newborn babies were given pacifiers, and the babies' sucking rates (either fast or slow) influenced whether they heard a recording of their mother reading the pre-birth story or a different one. Even though the infants were only 2 or 3 days old, they began to adjust their sucking rate so that they could hear the familiar one, which they had previously heard only while still in the womb!

The capacity for long-term memory storage manifests itself in a variety of ways in infancy and the toddler years. For instance, when a ribbon connected to a mobile is tied to a baby's foot, even a 2-month-old easily learns that kicking makes the mobile move and remembers the connection over a period of several days—or even longer if he or she is given an occasional reminder (Rovee-Collier, 1999). Infants age 3 to 6 months show evidence that they remember the order in which they've seen a sequence of three mobiles (Gulya, Rovee-Collier, Galluccio, & Wilk, 1998). At age 6 months, they can also recall and imitate actions they have seen 24 hours earlier; their memory for such actions increases in duration in the months that follow (Bauer, 1995; Collie & Hayne, 1999). By the time children are 2 years old, they are highly accurate in identifying pictures they have seen previously (A. L. Brown & Scott, 1971; Perlmutter & Lange, 1978).

■ *Talking about objects and events facilitates memory for them.* Despite the findings just described, children typically have little if any *conscious* recall of specific events that occurred during their first two years—a phenomenon known as **infantile amnesia**—and for several years after that, recall of past events continues to be rather sketchy. Early experiences have not necessarily faded from memory altogether; rather, they may simply be in a form that children cannot easily retrieve (C. A. Nelson, 1995; Newcombe, Drummey, Fox, Lie, & Ottinger-Albergs, 2000; Rovee-Collier, 1999). Talking about experiences enables children to store them in a verbal (language-based) form and so enhances the extent to which they can recall them verbally later on (Haden, Ornstein, Eckerman, & Didow, 2001; K. Nelson, 1996; E. Reese & Fivush, 1993; Simcock & Hayne, 2002; Tessler & Nelson, 1994).

■ *The amount of knowledge stored in long-term memory increases many times over.* This trend is an obvious one, and the four essays in the opening case study illustrate it clearly. Yet the obviousness of the trend does not diminish its importance in cognitive development. Long-term memory is the repository for children's accumulating body of information

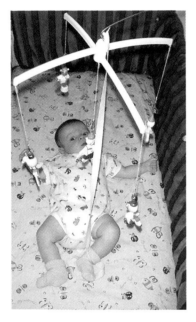

Infants have some ability to learn and remember things at birth (perhaps even sooner). This infant has learned that by kicking her left foot, she can make the mobile move. Chances are, she will still remember how to move the mobile when she sees it again several days later.

infantile amnesia
General inability to recall events that occurred in the early years of life.

and skills; thus, it provides the **knowledge base** from which children draw as they encounter, interpret, and respond to new events. As their knowledge base grows, children can interpret new events with increasing sophistication and respond to them more effectively (Flavell et al., 1993). Children vary considerably in the specific experiences they have, of course, and this diversity leads to the development of unique knowledge bases on which children build while learning new things. For example, in Figure 5–4, 10-year-old Amaryth describes a day when her family visited a national monument that was once a Hopi village. Travel opportunities such as this will undoubtedly enhance Amaryth's ability to learn about Native American civilizations in her history and social studies classes.

■ *Children's knowledge about the world becomes increasingly integrated.* Children begin categorizing their experiences as early as 3 months of age (we will return to this point in the upcoming section on learning strategies). Even so, much of what young children know about the world consists of separate, isolated categories and facts. In contrast, older children's knowledge includes many associations and interrelationships among concepts and ideas (Bjorklund, 1987; Flavell et al., 1993). This developmental change is undoubtedly one reason why older children can think more logically and draw inferences more readily: They have a more cohesive understanding of the world around them.

As an example, let's return once again to the essays in the opening case study. Notice how the third grader presents a chronological list of events without any attempt at tying them together:

The Idiuns thout they were mean. Then they came friends, and tot them stuff. Then winter came, and alot died. Then some had babies.

In contrast, the eighth grader frequently identifies cause-effect relationships among events:

More and more people poured in, expecting instant wealth, freedom, and a right to share their opinions. Some immigrants were satisfied, others were displeased. Problems in other countries forced people to move on to this New World, such as potato famins and no freedom of religions. Stories that drifted through people grew about this country. Stories of golden roads and free land coaxed other families who were living in the slums.

Another example of increasing integration is seen in children's knowledge of their local communities (Forbes, Ormrod, Bernardi, Taylor, & Jackson, 1999). In Figure 5–5 we present maps that three children drew of their hometown. The first grader's map includes only a few features of her town (her house, her school, nearby mountains) that she knows well, and the spatial relationships among the features are inaccurate. The third grader's map shows many features of his immediate neighborhood and their proximity to one another. The seventh grader's map encompasses numerous town landmarks and their relative locations on major streets; it also makes greater use of symbols (e.g., single lines for roads, squares for buildings, and distinctive letter *M*s to indicate McDonald's restaurants).

Children and adults alike sometimes organize their knowledge into what psychologists call *schemas* and *scripts*. **Schemas** (similar, but not identical, to Piaget's *schemes*[2]) are tightly integrated sets of ideas about specific objects or situations; for example, you might have a schema for what a typical horse looks like (it's a certain height, and it has an elongated head, a mane, four legs, etc.) and a schema for what a typical office contains (it probably has a desk, chair, bookshelves, books, manila folders, etc.). **Scripts** encompass knowledge about the predictable sequence of events related to particular activities; for example, you

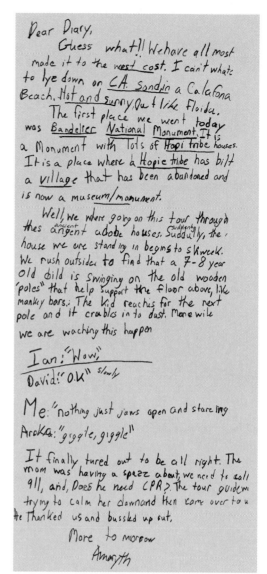

FIGURE 5–4 Children who have had diverse experiences (museum trips, travel to distant locations, etc.) have a broader knowledge base on which to build when they study classroom subject matter.

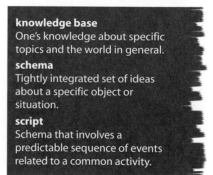

knowledge base
One's knowledge about specific topics and the world in general.

schema
Tightly integrated set of ideas about a specific object or situation.

script
Schema that involves a predictable sequence of events related to a common activity.

---

[2] Piaget suggested that *schemes* can be either mental or behavioral in nature (recall the example of an infant's putting-things-in-the-mouth scheme in Chapter 4), whereas contemporary theorists typically use the term *schema* to refer to mental rather than behavioral entities.

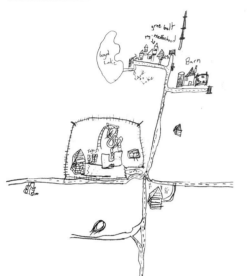

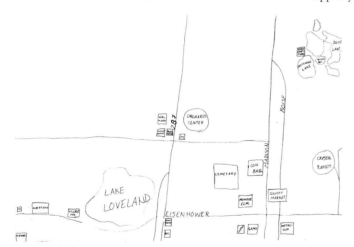

probably have scripts related to how weddings typically proceed, and what usually happens when you go to a fast-food restaurant. Schemas and scripts help children to make sense of their experiences more readily and to predict what is likely to happen in familiar contexts on future occasions.

Schemas and scripts increase in both number and complexity as children grow older (Farrar & Goodman, 1992; Flavell et al., 1993). Like Piaget's schemes, children's earliest schemas and scripts may be behavioral and perceptual in nature; for instance, toddlers can act out typical scenarios (scripts) with toys long before they have the verbal skills to describe what they are doing (Bauer & Dow, 1994). As children get older, these mental structures presumably become less tied to physical actions and perceptual qualities.

Schemas and scripts often differ somewhat from one culture to another. Therefore, cultural differences may influence the ease with which children can understand and remember the information they encounter (Lipson, 1983; Pritchard, 1990; R. E. Reynolds, Taylor, Steffensen, Shirey, & Anderson, 1982). For example, in one study (Lipson, 1983), elementary school children read stories called "First Communion" and "Bar Mitzvah," which described coming-of-age celebrations within the Catholic and Jewish religions respectively. Children with Catholic backgrounds remembered more from "First Communion," whereas children with Jewish backgrounds remembered more from "Bar Mitzvah." In another study (R. E. Reynolds et al., 1982), eighth graders read a letter written by a young teenager, Sam, to his friend Joe. In it, Sam describes an incident in the school cafeteria earlier in the day:

> I got in line behind Bubba. As usual the line was moving pretty slow and we were all getting pretty restless. For a little action Bubba turned around and said, "Hey Sam! What you doin' man? You so ugly that when the doctor delivered you he slapped your face!" Everyone laughed, but they laughed even harder when I shot back, "Oh yeah? Well, you so ugly the doctor turned around and slapped your momma!" It got even wilder when Bubba said, "Well man, at least my daddy ain't no girl scout!" We really got into it then. After a while more people got involved—4, 5, then 6. It was a riot! People helping out anyone who seemed to be getting the worst of the deal. (R. E. Reynolds et al., 1982, p. 358, italics omitted)

Many European American children incorrectly interpreted the story as one that described physical aggression, but African American children saw it for what it really was: a description of a friendly exchange of insults common among male youths in some African American communities.

■ *Children's growing knowledge base facilitates more effective learning.* As a general rule, older children and adults learn new information and skills more easily than younger children. A key reason for their facility is that they have more existing knowledge (including more schemas and scripts) that they can use to help them understand and organize what they encounter (Eacott, 1999; Halford, 1989; R. Kail, 1990). When the tables are turned—for instance, when children know more about a particular topic than adults do—the children are often the more effective learners (Chi, 1978; Lindberg, 1991; Schneider, Korkel & Weinert, 1989). For example, when Jeanne's son Alex was about 5 or 6, the two of them used to read books about lizards together. Alex always remembered more from the books than Jeanne did, because he was a self-proclaimed "lizard expert," and Jeanne knew very little about reptiles of any sort.

Thinking and Reasoning

From an information processing perspective, many developmental changes in thought processes reflect qualitative changes in the mental *strategies* that children use to learn and problem-solve; we will discuss the nature of such strategies later in the chapter. For now, we look at a few general developmental trends in thinking and reasoning:

■ *Thought becomes increasingly symbolic in nature.* As you will recall from Chapter 4, Piaget proposed that infants' and toddlers' schemes are predominantly sensorimotor in nature; that is, they are based on behaviors and perceptions. Near the end of the sensorimotor stage (at about 18 months, Piaget suggested), children begin to think in terms of **symbols**, mental entities (e.g., words) that do not necessarily reflect the perceptual and behavioral qualities of the objects or events they represent.

Piaget was probably correct in believing that sensorimotor representations of objects and events precede symbolic representations. However, the shift from one to the other is apparently more gradual than Piaget thought. Long before children reach school age, they begin to use such symbols as words, numbers, pictures, and miniature models to represent and think about real-life objects and events (De-Loache, Miller, & Rosengren, 1997; Flavell et al., 1993; J. Huttenlocher, New-combe, & Vasilyeva, 1999). Symbolic thought is also reflected in their pretend play—for example, when they use a doll as a real baby or a banana as a telephone receiver (Fein, 1979). But when children begin elementary school, they may initially have limited success in dealing with the wide variety of symbols they encounter. For instance, elementary school teachers often use blocks and other concrete objects to represent numbers or mathematical operations, but not all kindergartners and first graders make the connection between the objects and the concepts they stand for (DeLoache et al., 1997; Uttal et al., 1998). Maps, too, are largely symbolic in nature, and as noted in the preceding chapter, children in the early grades often interpret them too literally, for example thinking that a road that is red on a map is actually painted red (Liben & Downs, 1989). As children grow older, their use of symbols to think, remember, and solve problems grows in frequency and sophistication.

As these children play "store," they show that they already have a well-developed script for what typically happens at the checkout counter.

■ *Logical thinking abilities improve with age.* Although most information processing theorists reject Piaget's idea of discrete stages in logical thinking, they do agree that logical thinking improves, and often changes qualitatively, over time. Piaget proposed that deductive reasoning appears at the beginning of the concrete operations stage, but in reality even preschoolers sometimes draw logical inferences from the facts they are given (see Chapter 4). Preschoolers and elementary school children do not always draw correct inferences, however, and they have difficulty distinguishing between what *must* be true versus what *might* be true, given the evidence they have (Galotti, Komatsu, & Voelz, 1997; Pillow, 2002).[3] Even adolescents have difficulty evaluating the quality of their evidence (e.g., recall the discussion of separation and control of variables in Chapter 4), and their reasoning is often influenced by personal biases (Klaczynski, 2001; Kuhn, 2001a). Although the trend is toward more logical thinking with age, any given child or adolescent is apt to reason more logically on some occasions than others, even about similar problems (Klaczynski, 2001; Kuhn, 2001a).

■ *Gestures sometimes foreshadow the emergence of more sophisticated thinking and reasoning.* Early symbol use is not entirely dependable. For example, when 3-year-old and 5-year-old children are asked to recall what happened during a recent visit to a pediatrician's office, they can do so more completely when they act out the visit than when they describe it verbally (Greenhoot, Ornstein, Gordon, & Baker-Ward, 1999). Furthermore, as children make the transition to more advanced forms of reasoning about Piagetian tasks or mathematical problems, they often show such

Although they are eager investigators, children often have trouble evaluating the quality of their evidence.

---

[3] More specifically, they have trouble distinguishing between *deductive inferences*—those that logically must be true if the information from which they're derived is true—and *inductive inferences*—conclusions, based on a few observations, that may or may not be true. They also confuse evidence that something is true with possible explanations of why it might be true.

symbol
Mental entity that represents an external object or event, often without reflecting its perceptual and behavioral qualities.

reasoning in their gestures before they show it in their speech (Goldin-Meadow, 1997, 2001). The following scenario illustrates this trend:

> [A] 6-year-old child [is] attempting to justify her belief that the amount of water changed when it was poured from a tall, skinny glass into a short, wide dish. The child says, "It's different because this one's tall and that one's short," thus making it clear that she has focused on the heights of the two containers. However, in the very same utterance, the child indicates with her hand shaped like a C first the diameter of the glass and then, with a wider C, the larger diameter of the dish. The child speaks about the heights but has also noticed—not necessarily consciously—that the containers differ in width as well. (Goldin-Meadow, 1997, p. 13)

Gestures, like the 6-year-old's C-shaped hand gestures, appear to provide a way for children to "experiment" (cognitively) with new ideas. They may also alleviate the strain on working memory as children first begin to wrestle with more complex ways of thinking (Goldin-Meadow, 2001; Goldin-Meadow, Nusbaum, Kelly, & Wagner, 2001).

Implications of Information Processing Theory

Our discussion of information processing theory thus far leads to several implications for working with children and adolescents:

Environments for young children should be set up for safe movement and exploration. (See the Environments/ Infancy and Early Childhood clips for additional examples.)

■ *Provide a variety of choices for infants and young children.* In the first few years of life, children learn many things about the physical world through direct contact—by looking, listening, feeling, tasting, and smelling. Thus, infants, toddlers, and preschoolers should have a wide variety of toys and other objects to manipulate and play with, and their environment should be set up for safe movement and exploration. Children need enough options that they can identify activities and playthings that are within their current abilities yet also encourage cognitive growth. Choices have implications for motivation as well as cognitive development, as you'll discover in Chapter 11.

Because learning occurs largely through play rather than work in the early years, most preschool programs do not include recesses in the daily schedule. Young children do need considerable variety in their day, however, including a balance between active and quiet activities and between large-group activities and small-group or solitary play. The pace of activities must, of course, depend on the length of time children are away from home each day; for instance, naps are typically incorporated into all-day programs but rarely into two-hour morning programs.

■ *Talk with children about their experiences.* Children begin to talk about their experiences almost as soon as they begin to speak, and by age 2 they do it fairly often (van den Broek, Bauer, & Bourg, 1997). Adults should join in: As we have seen, talking with children about joint experiences can enhance their memories of what they are seeing and doing. As you will recall from Chapter 4, such discussions may also help children to interpret their experiences in culturally appropriate ways. Furthermore, they may enhance children's *sense of self,* as you will discover in Chapter 9.

In the Intrinsic Motivation/Early Childhood clip, hear Joey describe a challenge that he and most children face: keeping attention on academic tasks.

■ *During the school years, keep unnecessary distractions to a minimum.* As you have seen, attention is a critical factor in learning: Many information processing theorists believe that attention is essential for moving information from the sensory register into working memory. Yet many children, young ones especially, are easily distracted by the sounds and sights around them. For example, in the Intrinsic Motivation/Early Childhood clip, 6-year-old Joey gives a plausible explanation for why it is sometimes hard to pay attention at school: "The noise." In classroom lessons and other situations in which they must concentrate, children can more readily focus on the task at hand if conversations among others in the room are relatively quiet, small-group activities take place as far from one another as possible, and attractive but irrelevant objects remain out of view.

Despite adults' best efforts, children and adolescents—even highly motivated high school students—cannot keep their minds on a single task forever. Furthermore, some youngsters (perhaps because of a seemingly boundless supply of physical energy or perhaps because of a cognitive, emotional, or behavioral disability) have a more difficult time paying attention than others. With these facts in mind, adults should offer regular breaks from any intensive sedentary activities (Pellegrini & Bjorklund, 1997). At school, some breaks are built into the daily schedule in such forms as recess, passing periods, and lunch, but teachers may want to provide additional mental "breathers" as well, perhaps by alternating relatively sedentary cognitive activities with more physical, active ones.

◼ *Remember that human beings can think about only a small amount of information at any one time.* Although working memory capacity increases somewhat during childhood and adolescence, young and older people alike can mentally manipulate only a very limited amount of material in their heads at once. Thus, teachers and others who instruct children should pace any presentation of new information slowly enough that their students have time to "process" it all. They might also write complex directions or problems on a chalkboard or ask children to write them on paper. And they can teach more effective strategies for learning and solving problems (we'll say more about such strategies shortly).

◼ *Give children ongoing practice in using basic information and skills.* Some information and skills are so fundamental that growing children must become able to retrieve and use them quickly and effortlessly. For instance, to read well, children must be able to recognize most of the words on the page without having to sound them out or look them up in the dictionary. To solve mathematical word problems, they should have such number facts as "2 + 4 = 6" and "5 × 9 = 45" on the tips of their tongues. And to write well, they should be able to form letters and words without having to stop and think about how to make an uppercase *G* or spell the word *the*.

Ultimately, children and adolescents can automatize basic information and skills only by using and practicing them repeatedly (J. C. Anderson, 1983; W. Schneider & Shiffrin, 1977). This is definitely *not* to say that instructors should fill each day with endless drill-and-practice exercises involving isolated facts and procedures. Automatization can occur just as readily when the basics are embedded in a variety of stimulating, challenging (and perhaps authentic) activities.

DEVELOPMENT AND PRACTICE

Applying Information Processing Theory

◼ Minimize unnecessary distractions, especially when working with young children.

A psychologist is administering a battery of tests to a 6-year-old boy who is suspected of having a significant learning disability. Before the testing session, the psychologist puts away the kachina doll and Russian nesting dolls that decorate her office shelves. She also removes all of the testing materials from sight, putting items in front of the boy only as it is time to use them.

◼ Help children automatize essential basic skills.

Students in a fourth-grade class always have a high-interest, age-appropriate children's novel tucked in their desks. Their teacher encourages them to pull out the novel whenever they have free time (e.g., when they've finished an assignment early), partly as a way of helping them automatize basic reading skills.

◼ Begin at a level consistent with children's existing knowledge base.

At the beginning of a session on good eating habits, a health educator asks a few questions about the food pyramid. When it is clear that the teenagers in his group recall little of what they've learned about the pyramid, he reviews its components until everyone knows them well. At that point, he describes how one might use the pyramid as a guide for developing a balanced meal and asks the teens to use it as they choose a nutritious meal from the menu at a fast-food restaurant.

◼ Take children's cultural backgrounds into account when considering what they probably do and do not know.

A middle school social studies class includes students who have recently immigrated from either Mexico or the Far East. When the teacher begins a lesson on courtship and wedding traditions around the world, he asks students from various ethnic backgrounds to describe the typical dating practices and wedding ceremonies in their homelands.

◼ Ask children to apply new material to familiar contexts.

A third-grade teacher asks her students to write word problems that show how they might use addition in their own lives. Noah writes a problem involving himself and his sister:

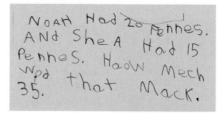

NoAH HaD 20 Pennes. ANd SheA HaD 15 PenneS. HaoW Mech 35. that Mack.

■ *Consider not only what children say, but also what they do, when determining what they know or are ready to learn.* Earlier we described a 6-year-old who said that a tall, thin glass had more water than a short, wide dish because of the height difference between the two containers. At the same time, she showed through her gestures that the tall container had a smaller diameter than the short one. Such discrepancies in what children say and do suggest a possible readiness for developing new ideas and logical reasoning skills—for instance, a readiness for acquiring conservation of liquid (Goldin-Meadow, 1997).

In some instances, adults might assess children's current knowledge by asking them to draw rather than describe what they have learned. For example, Figure 5–6 shows 8-year-old Noah's knowledge of how a seed becomes a plant. His picture clearly reflects his understanding that roots typically go down before a stalk grows up and that leaves gradually increase in size and number.

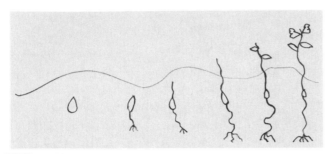

FIGURE 5–6 Noah's picture of how a seed becomes a plant

■ *Relate new information to children's existing knowledge.* Numerous research studies support the idea that people of all ages learn new information more effectively when they can relate it to what they already know (e.g., Dole, Duffy, Roehler, & Pearson, 1991; McKeown & Beck, 1994). Yet children and adolescents don't always make meaningful connections on their own. For instance, they may not realize that subtraction is simply the reverse of addition or that Shakespeare's *Romeo and Juliet* foreshadows modern-day racism in the United States and ethnic clashes in Eastern Europe. By pointing out such connections, adults can foster not only more effective learning but also the development of a more integrated knowledge base. In the Memory/Late Adolescence clip of the Observation CD, 16-year-old Hilary explains how she makes some connections on her own and how her teacher helps her make additional ones:

In the Memory/Late Adolescence clip, observe how Hilary connects new information to what she already knows.

> When I'm trying to study for a test, I try to associate the things that I'm trying to learn with familiar things. If I have a Spanish vocabulary test, I'll try to, with the Spanish words, I'll try to think of the English word that it sounds like because sometimes it does sound like the English word. And the our Government teacher is teaching us the amendments and we're trying to memorize them. He taught us one trick for memorizing Amendment Two, which is the right to bear arms. He said bears have two arms, so that's Amendment Two.

The Developmental Trends table "Basic Information Processing Abilities at Different Age Levels" summarizes the information processing capabilities of children and adolescents. Up to this point, however, we have said very little about the *central executive,* the cognitive supervisor of the information processing system. Although theorists have not carefully formulated the nature of the central executive, they have learned a great deal about two of its manifestations: metacognition and cognitive strategies.

Development of Metacognition and Cognitive Strategies

metacognition
Knowledge and beliefs about one's own cognitive processes, as well as efforts to regulate those cognitive processes to maximize learning and memory.

cognitive strategy
Specific mental process that people use to acquire or manipulate information.

As an adult with many years of formal education behind you, you have probably learned a great deal about how you think and learn. For example, you may have learned that you cannot absorb everything in a textbook the first time you read it. You may also have learned that you remember information better when you try to make sense of it based on what you already know rather than when you simply repeat it over and over again in a rote, verbatim fashion. The term **metacognition** refers both to the knowledge that people have about their own cognitive processes and to their intentional use of certain cognitive processes to improve learning and memory.

As children develop, the specific mental processes they use to learn information and solve problems—their **cognitive strategies**—become increasingly sophisticated and effective.

DEVELOPMENTAL TRENDS

Basic Information Processing Abilities at Different Age Levels

AGE	WHAT YOU MIGHT OBSERVE	DIVERSITY	IMPLICATIONS
Infancy (Birth–2) 	• Some ability to learn evident from birth • Adultlike hearing acuity within hours after birth • Considerable improvement in visual acuity over the first year • Preference for moderately complex stimuli • Attention easily drawn to intense or novel stimuli • Emerging classification skills (e.g., toddlers learn that different kinds of toys are stored in different places in the playroom)	• Attention spans are partly due to differences in temperament, but persistent inability to focus on any one object may signal a cognitive disability. • Exploration tendencies vary considerably: Some children may constantly seek new experiences, whereas others may be more comfortable with familiar objects.	• Change some toys and materials regularly to capture infants' interests and provide new experiences. • Provide objects that can be easily categorized (e.g., colored blocks, toy farm animals). • Allow for differences in interest, attention span, and exploratory behavior; offer choices of toys and activities.
Early Childhood (2–6) 	• Short attention span • Distractibility • Some understanding and use of symbols • Limited knowledge base with which to interpret new experiences	• Pronounced disabilities in information processing (e.g., ADHD, dyslexia) begin to reveal themselves in children's behavior. • Children's prior knowledge differs markedly depending on their cultural and socioeconomic backgrounds.	• Change activities often. • Keep unnecessary distractions to a minimum. • Provide a variety of experiences (field trips to the library, fire department, etc.) that enrich children's knowledge base.
Middle Childhood (6–10) 	• Increasing ability to attend to important stimuli and ignore irrelevant stimuli • Increasingly symbolic nature of thought and knowledge • Gradual automatization of basic skills • Increasing exposure to environments beyond the home and family, leading to an expanding knowledge base • Knowledge of academic subject matter relatively unintegrated, especially in science and social studies	• Many children with learning disabilities or ADHD have short attention spans and are easily distracted. • Some children with learning disabilities have a smaller working memory capacity than their peers. • Mild cognitive disabilities may not become evident until the middle or upper elementary grades.	• Intersperse sedentary activities with more physically active ones to help children maintain attention. • Provide many opportunities to practice basic knowledge and skills (e.g., number facts, word recognition), often through authentic, motivating, and challenging tasks. • Begin to explore hierarchies, cause and effect, and other interrelationships among ideas in various disciplines. • Consult experts when learning or behavior problems might reflect a cognitive disability.
Early Adolescence (10–14) 	• Ability to attend to a single task for an hour or more • Basic skills in reading, writing, and mathematics (e.g., word identification, common word spellings, basic math facts) largely automatized • Growing (though not necessarily well-organized) knowledge base relative to various topics and academic disciplines	• Many adolescents with information processing difficulties have trouble paying attention for a typical class period. • Many adolescents with sensory or physical disabilities (e.g., those who are blind or in a wheelchair) have a more limited knowledge base than their peers, due to fewer opportunities to explore the local community.	• Provide variety in learning tasks as a way of keeping learners' attention. • Frequently point out how concepts and ideas are related to one another, both within and across content domains. • Provide extra guidance and support for those with diagnosed or suspected information processing difficulties.
Late Adolescence (14–18) 	• Ability to attend to a single task for lengthy periods • Extensive and somewhat integrated knowledge in some content domains	• High school students have choices in course selection, leading to differences in the extent of their knowledge base in various content areas.	• Occasionally give assignments that require adolescents to focus on a particular task for a long period. • Consistently encourage adolescents to think about the "hows" and "whys" of what they are learning. • Assess learning in ways that require adolescents to depict relationships among ideas.

Their awareness of their own thinking, their ability to direct and regulate their own learning, and their beliefs about the nature of knowledge and learning also change in significant ways. In the following sections we describe development in each of these areas; we then identify additional implications for working with children and adolescents.

Learning Strategies

Toddlers as young as 18 months show some conscious attempts to remember something. For example, when asked to remember where a Big Bird doll has been hidden in their home, they may stare or point at its location until they are able to retrieve it (DeLoache, Cassidy, & Brown, 1985). Yet overall, young children rarely make a point of trying to learn and remember something. For instance, 4- and 5-year-olds can remember a set of objects more successfully by playing with them (affording occasions to talk about or categorize the objects) than by intentionally trying to remember them (L. S. Newman, 1990).

As they progress through the elementary and secondary grades, children and adolescents develop **learning strategies**—specific methods of learning information—that help them remember things more effectively. Here we describe three learning strategies that appear during the school years: rehearsal, organization, and elaboration.

Rehearsal What do you do if you need to remember a telephone number for a few minutes? Do you repeat it to yourself over and over as a way of keeping it in your working memory until you can dial it? This process of **rehearsal** is rare in preschoolers but increases in frequency and effectiveness throughout the elementary school years (Bjorklund & Coyle, 1995; Gathercole & Hitch, 1993; R. Kail, 1990).

Rehearsal takes different forms at different ages, as the following examples show:

- When preschoolers are asked to remember a particular set of toys, they tend to look at, name, and handle the toys more than they would otherwise; however, such actions have little effect on their memory for the toys (Baker-Ward, Ornstein, & Holden, 1984).
- At age 6, children can be trained to repeat a list of items as a way of helping them remember those items, but even after such training they seldom use rehearsal unless specifically told to do so (Keeney, Canizzo, & Flavell, 1967).
- By age 7 or 8, children often rehearse information spontaneously, as evidenced by lip movements and whispering during a learning task. However, they tend to repeat each item they need to remember in isolation from the others (Gathercole & Hitch, 1993; Kunzinger, 1985).
- By age 9 or 10, children combine items into a single list as they rehearse (Gathercole & Hitch, 1993; Kunzinger, 1985). As an example, if they hear the list "cat . . . dog . . . horse," they might repeat "cat" after the first item, say "cat, dog" after the second, and say "cat, dog, horse" after the third. Combining the separate items during rehearsal helps children remember them more effectively.

Keep in mind, of course, that the ages we've just presented are averages; some children develop various forms of rehearsal sooner than others.

Organization Take a minute to study and remember the following 12 words, then cover them up and try to recall as many as you can.

shirt	table	hat	chair
carrot	bed	squash	shoe
pants	potato	stool	bean

In what order did you remember the words? Did you recall them in their original order, or did you rearrange them somehow? If you are like most people, you grouped the words into three semantic categories—clothing, furniture, and vegetables—and recalled them category by category. In other words, you used **organization** to help you learn and remember the information. Research consistently shows that organized information is learned more easily and remembered more completely than unorganized information (e.g., Fabricius & Hagen, 1984). In the Memory module of the Observation CD, you can observe Brent, Colin, and Hilary organizing these 12 words into categories. For example, 6-year-old Brent recalls vegeta-

Observe how Brent, Colin, and Hilary organize a word list in the Memory/Early Childhood, Early Adolescence, and Late Adolescence clips.

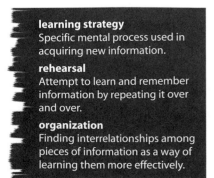

learning strategy
Specific mental process used in acquiring new information.

rehearsal
Attempt to learn and remember information by repeating it over and over.

organization
Finding interrelationships among pieces of information as a way of learning them more effectively.

bles first, then a type of furniture, then 3 items of clothing: "Beans, squash, stool, shirt, pants, hat . . . I forget."

Habituation studies tell us that children have some ability to categorize their experiences as early as 3 months of age (Behl-Chadha, 1996; Eimas & Quinn, 1994; Quinn, 2002). As they approach their first birthday, they begin to show classification in the way they touch objects. For instance, they may touch in sequence perceptually similar objects, such as balls or blocks or dolls (Sugarman, 1983). By age 2, they may physically pick up objects and group them by theme or function, perhaps using categories such as "things for the feet" or "kitchen things" (Fenson, Vella & Kennedy, 1989; Mandler, Fivush, & Reznick, 1987).

More consistent and intentional use of organization to facilitate learning and memory appears a bit later. Under certain circumstances, preschoolers intentionally organize information to help them remember it. For instance, imagine that an experimenter shows you 12 identical containers, several small pieces of candy, and several wooden pegs (see Figure 5–7). The experimenter places either a piece of candy or a wooden peg in each one and then closes it so that you cannot see its contents. How can you remember what each container holds? An easy yet effective strategy is to divide the containers into two groups, one with candy and one with pegs, as the experimenter fills them. Many 4-year-old children spontaneously use this strategy (DeLoache & Todd, 1988).

As children move through the late elementary, middle school, and secondary grades, they increasingly organize information to help learn it. Furthermore, their organizational patterns become more sophisticated, reflecting semantic, hierarchical, and often fairly abstract categories (e.g., *furniture, animals*) (Bjorklund & Jacobs, 1985; Bjorklund, Schneider, Cassel, & Ashley, 1994; DeLoache & Todd, 1988; Lucariello, Kyratzis, & Nelson, 1992; Plumert, 1994). They can also be more flexible in their organizational schemes. For example, consider the alternatives that 17-year-old Paul identifies for organizing the shells in the Intelligence/Late Adolescence clip:

> Yeah, I could do them by color, smoothness. Some are rough, some got little jagged edges on them. Some are just smooth. And these big ones they could do like patterns and stuff.

Elaboration   If we authors tell you that we've both spent many years living in Colorado, you will probably conclude that we either live or have lived in or near the Rocky Mountains. You might also infer that we have, perhaps, done a lot of skiing, hiking, or camping. In this situation, you are learning more than the information we actually gave you; you are also learning some information that you, yourself, supplied. This process of **elaboration**— adding additional ideas to new information based on what you already know—typically facilitates learning and memory, sometimes quite dramatically.

Children begin to elaborate on their experiences as early as the preschool years (Fivush, Haden, & Adam, 1995). As a strategy that they *intentionally* use to help them learn, however, elaboration appears relatively late in development (usually around puberty) and gradually increases throughout the teenage years (Flavell et al., 1993; W. Schneider & Pressley, 1989). Even in high school, it is primarily students with high academic achievement who use their existing knowledge to help them learn new information. Low-achieving high school students are much less likely to use elaboration strategies as an aid to learning, and many students of all ability levels resort to rehearsal for difficult, hard-to-understand material (Barnett, 2001; Pressley, 1982; E. Wood, Motz, & Willoughby, 1997; E. Wood, Willoughby, Reilley, Elliott, & DuCharme, 1994). The following interview with 15-year-old "Beth," who earns mostly As in her classes but works very hard for every one of them, illustrates:

> Adult: Once you have some information that you think you need to know, what types of things do you do so that you will remember it?

FIGURE 5–7   While you watch, an experimenter randomly places either a small candy or a wooden peg into each of 12 containers and closes its lid. What simple strategy could you use to help you remember which containers hold candy?

Modeled after DeLoache & Todd, 1988.

Notice Paul's ability to consider multiple organizational structures for sorting shells in the Intelligence/ Late Adolescence clip.

elaboration
Using prior knowledge to expand on new information and thereby learn it more effectively.

Beth: I take notes . . . (pause).
Adult: Is that all you do?
Beth: Usually. Sometimes I make flashcards.
Adult: What types of things do you usually put on flashcards?
Beth: I put words I need to know. Like spelling words. I put dates and what happened then.
Adult: How would you normally study flashcards or your notes?
Beth: My notes, I read them over a few times. Flashcards I look at once and try to remember what's on the other side and what follows it. (Interview courtesy of Evie Greene)

It is noteworthy that Beth, a high achiever, emphasizes taking notes and studying flash-cards, approaches that require little or no elaboration. In fact, using flashcards is nothing more than rehearsal.

Environmental and Cultural Influences on Learning Strategy Development   Environment appears to play a major role in determining the kinds of strategies children develop. For ex-ample, children are more likely to use effective learning strategies when teachers and other adults teach and encourage their use (e.g., Fletcher & Bray, 1996; Kurtz, Schneider, Carr, Borkowski, & Rellinger, 1990; E. B. Ryan, Ledger, & Weed, 1987). They are also more likely to use effective strategies when they discover that using them enhances learning suc-cess (Fabricius & Hagen, 1984; Starr & Lovett, 2000). In contrast, when young people find that assigned learning tasks are quite easy for them, they have little reason to acquire more effective strategies.

Culture, too, makes a difference. Children in African schools have better strategies for remembering orally transmitted stories than children in American schools (E. F. Dube, 1982). Children in China and Japan rely more heavily on rehearsal than their counter-parts in Western schools, perhaps because their schools place a greater emphasis on rote memorization and drill-and-practice (Ho, 1994; Purdie & Hattie, 1996). Children in typ-ical Western schools appear to have better strategies for learning lists of words (e.g., re-hearsal, organization) than unschooled children in developing nations, probably because list-learning tasks are more common in school settings (M. Cole & Schribner, 1977; Flavell et al., 1993).

This is not to say that schooling aids the development of all learning strategies, however. For instance, in a study by Kearins (1981), unschooled children in Australian aborigine communities more effectively remembered the spatial arrangements of objects than chil-dren who attended Australian schools. The aborigine children lived in a harsh desert envi-ronment with little rainfall, and so their families moved frequently from place to place in search of new food sources. With each move, the children had to learn quickly the spatial arrangements of subtle landmarks in the local vicinity so that they could find their way home from any direction (Kearins, 1981).

Problem-Solving Strategies

By the time children are 12 months old, they have some ability to solve problems, as well as some ability to think about how to solve them. For example, imagine that an infant sees an attractive toy beyond her reach. A string is attached to the toy; its other end is attached to a cloth closer at hand. But between the cloth and the infant is a foam rubber barrier. The infant puts two and two together, realizing that to accomplish her goal (getting the toy), she has to do several things: She removes the barrier, pulls the cloth toward her, grabs the string, and reels in the toy (Willatts, 1990). This ability to break a problem into two or more subgoals and work toward each one in turn continues to develop during the preschool and elementary school years (e.g., Klahr & Robinson, 1981; Welsh, 1991).

Another early problem-solving strategy is the use of one object (in essence, a *tool*) to ob-tain another object. For instance, when 1½- and 2-year-olds watch an adult use a rake to pull a desirable toy toward them, the toddlers may follow suit, using a variety of long, rigid objects (e.g., canes) to attain something they want (A. L. Brown, 1989).

As children get older, their problem-solving strategies become increasingly mental rather than behavioral; they also become more powerful and effective. Consider the fol-lowing problem: *If I have 2 apples and you give me 4 more apples, how many apples do I have altogether?* Young children can often solve such problems even if they have not yet had specific instruction in addition at school. A strategy that emerges early in development is simply to put up two fingers and then four additional fingers and count all the fingers to reach the solution, "6 apples." Somewhat later, children may begin to use a *min* strategy, whereby they start with the larger number (for the apple problem, they would start with 4) and then add on, one by one, the smaller number (e.g., counting "four apples . . . then five, six . . . six apples altogether") (Siegler & Jenkins, 1989). Still later, of course, children learn the basic addition facts (e.g., "2 + 4 = 6") that enable them to bypass the relatively inefficient counting strategies they've used earlier.

Children's problem solving sometimes involves applying certain *rules* to a particular type of problem, with more complex and effective rules evolving over time. As an example, consider the balancing task depicted in Figure 5–8. The first picture in the figure shows a wooden beam resting on a fulcrum. Because the fulcrum is located at the exact middle of the beam, the beam balances, with neither side falling down. Imagine that, while holding the beam horizontal, we hang a 6-pound weight on the fourth peg to the right of the fulcrum and a 3-pound weight on the ninth peg to the left of the fulcrum. Will the beam continue to be balanced when we let go of it, or will one side fall?

Long before receiving formal instruction in addition at school, young children often develop addition strategies on their own by building on their finger-counting skills.

Children acquire a series of increasingly complex rules to solve such a problem (Siegler, 1976, 1978, 1998). Initially (perhaps at age 5), they consider only the amount of weight on each side of the beam; comparing 6 pounds to 3 pounds, they would predict that the right side of the beam will fall. Later (perhaps at age 9), they begin to consider distance as well as weight, recognizing that weights located farther from the fulcrum have a greater effect, but their reasoning is not precise enough to ensure correct solutions. In the balance problem in Figure 5–8, they would merely guess at how greater distance compensates for greater weight. Eventually (perhaps in high school), they may develop a rule that reflects a multiplicative relationship between weight and distance:

The equipment: Balance and weights

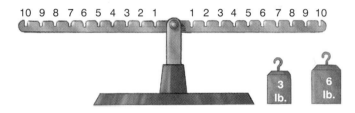

For the beam to balance, the product of weight and distance on one side must equal the product of weight and distance on the other side. In cases where the two products are unequal, the side with the larger product will fall.

The problem:

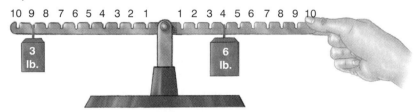

Applying this rule to the problem in Figure 5–8, they would determine that the product on the left side (3 × 9 = 27) is greater than the product on the right side (6 × 4 = 24) and so would correctly predict that the left side will fall.

FIGURE 5–8 A beam without weights balances on a fulcrum located at its center. After weights are hung from the beam in the manner shown here, will the beam continue to balance? If not, which side of the beam will drop?

Strategy Development as "Overlapping Waves"

Information processing theorists have found that a cognitive strategy doesn't necessarily appear all at once; instead, it emerges gradually over time. For instance, children first use learning strategies (e.g., organization and elaboration) somewhat accidentally; only later do they recognize the effectiveness of these strategies and intentionally use them to remember new information (DeLoache & Todd, 1988; Flavell et al., 1993). Children initially use newly acquired strategies infrequently and often ineffectively, but, with time and practice, they become more adept at applying the strategies successfully, efficiently, and flexibly as they tackle challenging tasks (P. A. Alexander, Graham, & Harris, 1998; Flavell et al., 1993; Siegler, 1998).

By the time children reach elementary school, they often have several strategies to choose from when dealing with a particular learning or problem-solving task, and so they may vary from one day to the next in their use of these strategies. Some strategies may be

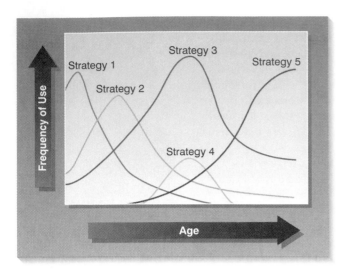

FIGURE 5-9 Strategic development as overlapping waves: Children gradually replace simple cognitive strategies with more advanced and effective ones. Here we see how five different strategies for dealing with the same task might change in frequency over time.

From *Children's Thinking* (3rd ed., p. 92), by R. Siegler, 1998, Upper Saddle River, NJ: Prentice Hall. Copyright 1998 by Prentice Hall. Adapted with permission of Prentice-Hall, Inc., Upper Saddle River, NJ.

developmentally more advanced than others, yet because children initially have trouble using them effectively, they may resort to less efficient but more dependable "backup" strategies. For example, when children first learn basic number facts, they cannot always retrieve those facts quickly and easily and so may instead count on their fingers—a strategy that they know will yield a correct answer—when dealing with simple problems. Eventually, however, they acquire sufficient proficiency with their new strategies that they can comfortably leave their less efficient ones behind (Alexander et al., 1998; Flavell et al., 1993; Siegler, 1998).

From an information processing perspective, then, strategic development does not occur in discrete, one-step-at-a-time stages. Instead, each strategy develops slowly and increases in frequency and effectiveness over a lengthy period, perhaps over several months or years. Later, it may gradually disappear if a better strategy emerges to take its place. Siegler (1996b, 1998) has used the analogy of *overlapping waves*, depicted in Figure 5–9, to describe this process.

Just as there is variability in the strategies that each child uses from one occasion to the next, so, too, is there variability in the strategies that different children of the same age use for a particular situation. For instance, in any high school classroom, some students may use organization and elaboration to study for a test while others resort to rote rehearsal. Such individual differences are due, in part, to the fact that some children and adolescents acquire competence with particular strategies sooner than others do. Other factors make a difference as well: Familiarity with the subject matter fosters more advanced strategies, as does personal interest in the task at hand (Alexander et al., 1998; Bergin, 1996; Folds, Footo, Guttentag, & Ornstein, 1990; Woody-Ramsey & Miller, 1988).

Metacognitive Awareness

In addition to acquiring new cognitive strategies, children acquire increasingly sophisticated knowledge about the nature of thinking. This **metacognitive awareness** includes (a) awareness of the existence of thought and then, later, awareness about (b) one's own thought processes, (c) the limitations of memory, and (d) effective learning and memory strategies.

Awareness of the Existence of Thought   By the time children reach the age of 3, they are aware of thinking as an entity in its own right (Flavell, Green, & Flavell, 1995). Their initial understanding of thought is quite simplistic, however. They are likely to say that a person is "thinking" only when he or she is actively engaged in a challenging task and has a thoughtful or puzzled facial expression. They also view thought and learning as relatively passive activities (e.g., the mind acquires and holds information but doesn't do much with it), rather than as the active, constructive processes that they really are (Flavell et al., 1995; Wellman, 1990).

Awareness of One's Own Thought Processes   Young children have only a limited ability to look inward at their own thinking and knowledge (Flavell, Green, & Flavell, 2000). Although many preschoolers have the words *know, remember,* and *forget* in their vocabularies, they don't fully grasp the nature of these mental phenomena. For instance, 3-year-olds use the term *forget* simply to mean "not knowing" something, regardless of whether they knew the information at an earlier time (Lyon & Flavell, 1994). When 4- and 5-year-old children are taught a new piece of information, they may say that they've known it for quite some time (M. Taylor, Esbensen, & Bennett, 1994). The following interview, which a kindergarten teacher aide conducted with a bright 5-year-old whom we'll call "Ethan," illustrates the relatively superficial awareness that young children have of their own thought processes:

Aide: When you learn a new song, like "The Horne Street School Song," how do you remember the words?

Ethan: I just remember. I didn't know how to sing it for a while until I listened to the words enough to remember them.

metacognitive awareness Extent to which one is able to reflect on the nature of one's own thinking processes.

Aide:	When I ask you during group time to "put on your thinking caps," what do I mean?
Ethan:	It means think. You think hard until you know what you are trying to think about. . . . I don't really know how you think, you just do.
Aide:	Where does thinking take place? Where do you think?
Ethan:	In your brain.
Aide:	How do you keep stuff in your brain so it doesn't disappear?
Ethan:	I have a great memory, that's how it stays in my head. I even can remember my dreams!
Aide:	How do you remember to give Mommy and Papa papers that we send home?
Ethan:	My good memory.
Aide:	Why do you have a good memory?
Ethan:	It's just good. It started when I turned three. I still had it when I was four, and now when I am five.
Aide:	For how long will you have your memory?
Ethan:	I don't think it is going to go away. I think it is going to get better as I get older.

(Interview courtesy of Betsy Hopkins)

Listen to Brent, David, Colin, and Hilary reflect on their thought processes in the Memory module of the Observation CD.

During the elementary and secondary school years, children and adolescents become better able to reflect on their own thought processes and so are increasingly aware of the nature of their thinking and learning (Flavell et al., 1993; Wellman & Hickling, 1994). (You can observe this progression firsthand by listening to the four children in the Memory module of the Observation CD.) To some extent, adults may foster such development by talking about the mind's activities—for instance, by referring to "thinking caps" or describing someone's mind as "wandering" (Wellman & Hickling, 1994). Possibly beneficial, too, is specifically asking children to reflect on what they're thinking. As an example, Figure 5–10 shows 8-year-old Noah's explanation of how he solved the problem 354 − 298.

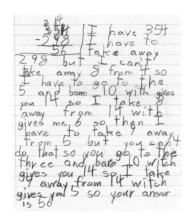

FIGURE 5–10 Noah's explanation of what he did when he solved the problem 354 − 298

Awareness of Memory Limitations Young children tend to be overly optimistic about how much they can remember. As they grow older and encounter a greater variety of learning tasks, they discover that some things are more difficult to learn than others (Bjorklund & Green, 1992; Flavell et al., 1993). They also begin to realize that their memories are not perfect and that they cannot possibly remember everything they see or hear. As an example of the latter trend, let's consider a study by Flavell, Friedrichs, & Hoyt (1970). Children in four age groups (ranging from preschool to fourth grade) were shown strips of paper with pictures of 1 to 10 objects. The children were asked to predict how many of the objects they could remember over a short period of time. The average predictions of each age group, and the average number of objects the children actually did remember, were as follows:

Age Group	Predicted Number	Actual Number
Preschool	7.2	3.5
Kindergarten	8.0	3.6
Grade 2	6.0	4.4
Grade 4	6.1	5.5

Notice that all four age groups predicted that they would remember more objects than they actually did. But the older children were more realistic about the limitations of their memory than the younger ones. The kindergartners predicted they would remember 8 objects, when they actually remembered fewer than 4!

In the Memory module of the Observation CD, you can observe similar overestimations by 6-year-old Brent and 10-year-old David: Both predict they will recall all 12 words presented, but Brent remembers just 6 and David recalls only 3. In contrast, 12-year-old Colin and 16-year-old Hilary predict their performance quite accurately.

Children's overly optimistic assessment of their own learning and memory capabilities may actually be beneficial for their cognitive development. In particular, it may give them the confidence to try new and difficult tasks—challenges that, from Vygotsky's perspective,

In the Memory module of the Observation CD, observe how older children are more realistic in predicting how many words they will be able to remember.

promote cognitive growth—that they would probably avoid if they were more realistic about their abilities (Bjorklund & Green, 1992). Too often we have seen older children and adolescents not take on challenging tasks simply because they were aware of their limitations and so had doubts that they could succeed.

Knowledge About Effective Learning and Memory Strategies   Imagine this: It is January, and you live in a cold climate. Just before you go to bed, some friends ask you to go ice skating with them right after class tomorrow. What might you do to be sure that you remember to take your ice skates to class with you? Older children typically generate more strategies than younger children for remembering to take a pair of skates to school. Yet even 5- and 6-year-olds can often identify one or more effective strategies—perhaps writing a note to themselves, recording a reminder on a tape recorder, or leaving their skates next to their school bag. One creative first grader suggested wearing the skates to bed as a sure-fire way of remembering them the following morning (Kreutzer, Leonard, & Flavell, 1975).

As mentioned earlier, children show greater use of such internal learning and memory strategies as rehearsal, organization, and elaboration as they grow older. With experience, they also become increasingly aware of what strategies are effective in different situations (Lovett & Flavell, 1990; Short, Schatschneider, & Friebert, 1993; Wellman, 1985). For example, consider the simple idea that, when you don't learn something the first time you try, you need to study it again. This is a strategy that 8-year-olds use, but 6-year-olds do not (Masur, McIntyre, & Flavell, 1973). Similarly, 10th graders are more aware than 8th graders of the advantages of using elaboration to learn new information (H. S. Waters, 1982). Even so, many children and adolescents seem relatively uninformed about which learning strategies work most effectively in different situations (Kuhn, Garcia-Mila, Zohar, & Andersen, 1995; J. W. Thomas, 1993). The following interview with "Amy," a 16-year-old with a history of low school achievement, illustrates how metacognitively naïve some adolescents are:

Adult:	What is thinking?
Amy:	I never really thought about it. I would say it is something you need to do to find an answer.
Adult:	What is learning?
Amy:	Something you do to get knowledge.
Adult:	What is knowledge?
Amy:	Any information that I don't know.
Adult:	What about the things you already know?
Amy:	That doesn't count.
Adult:	Doesn't count?
Amy:	As knowledge, because I already know it.
Adult:	How do you know when you have learned something?
Amy:	When I can repeat it, and it is the same as what the teacher said or what I read, and I can remember it forever or a really long time.

(Interview courtesy of Jennifer Glynn)

Notice how Amy thinks she has learned something when she can repeat what a teacher or textbook has told her; she says nothing about *understanding* classroom subject matter. And curiously, she thinks of knowledge as things that she *doesn't* know.

Self-Regulated Learning

As children and adolescents grow more aware of their learning and memory processes, they become more capable of **self-regulated learning**—of controlling and directing their own learning. Following are some important aspects of self-regulated learning (Schunk & Zimmerman, 1997; Winne, 1995a):

self-regulated learning
Directing and regulating one's own cognitive processes in order to learn successfully.

- Setting goals for a learning activity
- Planning an effective use of learning and study time
- Maintaining attention on the subject matter to be learned

- Identifying and using appropriate learning strategies
- Monitoring progress toward goals, evaluating the effectiveness of learning strategies, and adjusting goals or learning strategies as necessary
- Evaluating the final knowledge gained from the learning activity

As you can see, self-regulated learning is a complex, multifaceted process. In its "mature" form, it is virtually nonexistent in elementary school students. Even in the secondary grades, few students can effectively regulate their own learning; those who do tend to be the most academically successful (M. B. Bronson, 2000; Schunk & Zimmerman, 1997; Zimmerman & Risemberg, 1997).

Three theoretical perspectives have contributed to developmentalists' current understanding of self-regulated learning. First is information processing theorists' work regarding the nature of learning and memory. Second is social cognitive theorists' research on self-regulated behavior (this topic is discussed in Chapter 11). Third is Vygotsky's proposal that, through such mechanisms as self-talk and inner speech, growing children gradually transform social interactions into mental processes (see Chapter 4).

Here we look briefly at three key aspects of self-regulated learning: attention control, monitoring progress toward goals, and evaluating the effectiveness of learning strategies. We then consider how the process of *co-regulation* can foster the development of self-regulation.

Two aspects of self-regulation are planning effective use of study time and evaluating knowledge gained from a learning activity. This student planned to read one chapter during study hour and ask himself questions about it afterward.

Attention Control   As a college student, you probably do several things to keep your attention focused on the subject matter you want to learn. Perhaps you identify a time when you know you will be alert and ready to concentrate, locate a quiet place to read, and then, as you study, try to keep your mind clear of irrelevant thoughts. Such efforts to control your own attentional processes are critical to effective self-regulated learning (Rothbart & Ahadi, 1994).

As noted earlier, many children, younger ones especially, are easily distracted by the sights and sounds around them and so have difficulty paying attention for any length of time. Yet children can learn to better control their attention through self-talk, perhaps through the five steps presented in Chapter 4 (see Figure 4–11 on p. 175). Through this process, impulsive and distractible elementary school children can effectively learn to slow themselves down and think through what they are doing (Meichenbaum & Goodman, 1971). For example, notice how one formerly impulsive child learned to talk himself through matching tasks in which he needed to find two identical pictures among several very similar ones:

> I have to remember to go slowly to get it right. Look carefully at this one, now look at these carefully. Is this one different? Yes, it has an extra leaf. Good, I can eliminate this one. Now, let's look at this one. I think it's this one, but let me first check the others. Good, I'm going slow and carefully. Okay, I think it's this one. (Meichenbaum & Goodman, 1971, p. 121)

Monitoring Progress Toward Goals   When you study, what do you do to make sure you're learning the subject matter? Perhaps you ask yourself questions about the material and then try to answer them. Perhaps you study with friends, reviewing the material as a group and contrasting different interpretations of the material. Such activities are examples of **comprehension monitoring**, the process of checking one's understanding regularly while learning.

Children's ability to monitor their own comprehension improves throughout the school years; therefore, children and adolescents become increasingly aware of when they actually know something. Young children (e.g., those in the early elementary grades) often think they know or understand something before they actually do. As a result, they don't study things they need to learn as much as they should, and they often don't ask questions when they receive incomplete or confusing information (Dufresne & Kobasigawa, 1989; Markman, 1977; McDevitt, Spivey, Sheehan, Lennon, & Story, 1990). Even high school and college students sometimes have difficulty assessing their own knowledge accurately; for example, they often overestimate how well they will perform on an exam (e.g., Hacker, Bol, Horgan, & Rakow, 2000).

comprehension monitoring
Process of checking oneself to make sure one understands what one is learning.

Evaluating the Effectiveness of Learning Strategies   Not only do children and adolescents often misjudge the degree to which they have learned something, but they may also fail to evaluate the effectiveness of the learning strategies they are using. As a result, they don't always choose the most effective learning strategies at their disposal. When adults encourage them to reflect on the differing success rates of various approaches, they are more inclined to use better strategies (Pressley, Levin, & Ghatala, 1984; Pressley, Ross, Levin, & Ghatala, 1984).

Co-Regulation and the Transition to Self-Regulation   Using Vygotsky's perspective, we might reasonably suspect that self-regulated learning has its roots in, and so must be preceded by, socially regulated learning. At first, other people (e.g., parents, teachers) might help children learn by setting goals for a learning activity, keeping children's attention focused on the learning task, suggesting effective learning strategies, monitoring learning progress, and so on. Over time, children assume increasing responsibility for these processes: They begin to set their own learning goals, stay on task with little prodding from others, identify potentially effective strategies, and evaluate their own learning.

Developmentally speaking, a reasonable bridge between other-regulated learning and self-regulated learning is **co-regulated learning,** in which an adult and one or more children share responsibility for directing the various aspects of the learning process (McCaslin & Good, 1996). For instance, the adult and children might mutually agree on the specific goals of a learning endeavor, or the adult might describe the criteria that indicate successful learning and then have children evaluate their own performance in light of those criteria. Initially, the adult might provide considerable structure, or scaffolding, for the children's learning efforts; then, in a true Vygotskian fashion, such scaffolding can be gradually removed as children become more effectively self-regulating.

Epistemological Beliefs

As people who learn new things every day, we all have ideas about what "knowledge" and "learning" are—ideas that are collectively known as **epistemological beliefs.** Included in people's epistemological beliefs are their views about

- The certainty of knowledge
- The simplicity and structure of knowledge
- The source of knowledge
- The speed of learning
- The nature of learning ability

As children and adolescents develop, many (though not all) of them change their beliefs in each of these areas; typical changes are shown in Table 5–1. For example, children in the elementary grades typically believe in the certainty of knowledge; they think that the absolute truth about any topic is somewhere "out there" waiting to be discovered (Astington & Pelletier, 1996). As they reach the high school and college years, some begin to realize that knowledge is a subjective entity and that different perspectives on a topic may be equally valid (Perry, 1968; Schommer, 1994b, 1997). Additional changes may also occur in high school; for example, 12th graders are more likely than 9th graders to believe that knowledge consists of complex interrelationships (rather than discrete facts), that learning happens slowly (rather than quickly), and that learning ability can improve with practice (rather than being fixed at birth) (Schommer, 1997). Some high school students continue to have very superficial views of knowledge and learning, however: Recall how 16-year-old Amy defined *learning* simply as "something you do to get knowledge" and *knowledge* as "any information that I don't know."

Students' epistemological beliefs influence the ways in which they study and learn (Hofer & Pintrich, 1997; Purdie, Hattie, & Douglas, 1996; Schommer, 1997). For example, when students believe that knowledge consists of discrete facts that are indisputably either right or wrong, that one either has that knowledge or doesn't, and that learning is a relatively rapid process, they may focus on rote memorization of the subject matter and give up quickly if they find themselves struggling to understand it (e.g., see Figure 5–11). In contrast, when students believe that knowledge is a complex body of information that is learned gradually with time and effort, they are likely to use a wide variety of learning

co-regulated learning
Process through which an adult and child share responsibility for directing various aspects of the child's learning.

epistemological beliefs
Beliefs regarding the nature of knowledge and knowledge acquisition.

TABLE 5-1 Developmental Changes in Epistemological Beliefs

WITH REGARD TO...	CHILDREN INITIALLY BELIEVE THAT...	AS THEY DEVELOP, THEY MAY EVENTUALLY BEGIN TO REALIZE THAT...
The certainty of knowledge	Knowledge about a topic is a fixed, unchanging, absolute "truth."	Knowledge about a topic (even that of experts) is tentative and dynamic; it continues to evolve as ongoing inquiry and research add new insights and ideas.
The simplicity and structure of knowledge	Knowledge is a collection of discrete and isolated facts.	Knowledge is a set of complex and interrelated ideas.
The source of knowledge	Knowledge comes from outside the learner; that is, it comes from a teacher or "authority" of some kind.	Knowledge is derived and constructed by learners themselves.
The speed of learning	Knowledge is acquired quickly, and in an all-or-nothing fashion, or else not at all. As a result, people either know something or they don't.	Knowledge is acquired gradually over time. Thus, people can have greater or lesser degrees of knowledge about a topic.
The nature of learning ability	People's ability to learn is fixed at birth (it is inherited).	People's ability to learn can improve over time with practice and the use of better strategies.

Sources: Astington & Pelletier, 1996; Hammer, 1994; Hofer & Pintrich, 1997; Hogan, 1997; Linn, Songer, & Eylon, 1996; W. G. Perry, 1968; Schommer, 1994a, 1994b, 1997.

strategies, and they persist until they have made sense of the ideas they are studying (Butler & Winne, 1995; Kardash & Howell, 1996; Schommer, 1994a, 1994b). Not surprisingly, then, students with more advanced epistemological beliefs achieve at higher levels in the classroom (Schommer, 1994a).

More advanced levels of achievement may, in turn, bring about more advanced views about knowledge and learning (Schommer, 1994b; Strike & Posner, 1992). The more that learners get beyond the "basics" and explore the far reaches of a discipline—whether science, mathematics, history, literature, or some other content domain—the more they discover that learning involves acquiring an integrated and cohesive set of ideas, that even the experts don't know everything about a topic, and that truly complete and accurate "knowledge" of how the world operates may ultimately be an unattainable goal.

We speculate, however, that less sophisticated epistemological beliefs may have some benefits for young children. Children may initially be more motivated to learn about a topic if they think there are absolute, unchanging facts (and sometimes there are!) that they can easily learn and remember. And it is often very efficient to rely on parents, teachers, and the library as authoritative sources for desired information.

> Definitions: Assn #5
> Physical environment - things in the environment that are not living: rocks, water, etc.
> Limiting factors - factors of the nonliving physical environment that limit where organisms live.
> biological environment - an environment which consists of other plants + animals.
> habitat - where an organism lives.
> niche - the way an organism fits into its environment.
> dispersal - a spreading out of animals from their habitat.

FIGURE 5-11 This flashcard, which 12-year-old Jennie constructed to study for a science test, reflects her belief that knowledge consists of discrete facts that should be memorized.

Interdependence of Cognitive and Metacognitive Processes

Developmental changes in the various areas we've described—attention, memory, knowledge base, cognitive strategies, metacognitive awareness, self-regulated learning, and epistemological beliefs—are clearly interdependent. For instance, children's improving ability to pay attention and their increasing self-regulatory efforts to control their attention enable them to benefit more from learning activities. Their growing knowledge base, in turn, enhances their ability to use such learning strategies as organization and elaboration while reading and studying. As learning and problem-solving strategies become more effective and efficient, these strategies require less working memory capacity and so enable children to deal with more complex tasks and problems.

As adolescents' beliefs about the nature of knowledge become more sophisticated, so, too, are their learning strategies apt to change in light of those beliefs. For example, if high school students conceptualize "knowledge" about a topic as a unified body of facts and interrelations, they are more likely to use such strategies as organization and elaboration, rather than simple rehearsal, to master that topic. Furthermore, their growing comprehension-monitoring abilities give them feedback about what they are and are not learning and so may enhance their awareness of which learning strategies are effective and which are not.

The Developmental Trends table "Cognitive Strategies and Metacognitive Awareness at Different Age Levels" summarizes developmental changes in children's cognitive strategies, metacognitive awareness, self-regulated learning, and epistemological beliefs. We now identify some implications of these changes for teachers and other practitioners.

DEVELOPMENTAL TRENDS

Cognitive Strategies and Metacognitive Awareness at Different Age Levels

AGE	WHAT YOU MIGHT OBSERVE	DIVERSITY	IMPLICATIONS
Infancy (Birth–2)	• Use of one object to attain another (in the second year) • Emerging ability to plan a sequence of actions to accomplish a goal (appearing sometime around age 1) • General absence of intentional learning strategies; however, toddlers may look or point at a location to remember where a desired object is hidden • Little awareness and knowledge of thought processes (may have some awareness that other people have intentions, however; see Chapter 10)	• Emergence of early problem-solving strategies is somewhat dependent on experimentation with physical objects. • Willingness to engage in trial-and-error and other exploratory behavior is partly a function of temperamental differences. • Children with significant physical disabilities may have limited opportunities to explore and experiment.	• Model tool use and other simple problem-solving strategies. • Pose simple problems for infants and toddlers to solve (e.g., place desired objects slightly out of reach), but monitor children's reactions to make sure they are not unnecessarily frustrated in their efforts to solve problems.
Early Childhood (2–6)	• Some evidence of rehearsal in the preschool years, but with little effect on learning and memory • Occasional use of organization with concrete objects • Some ability to learn simple strategies modeled by others • Awareness of thought in oneself and others, albeit in a simplistic form; limited ability to reflect on the specific *nature* of one's own thought processes • Belief that learning is a relatively passive activity • Overestimation of how much a person can typically remember	• Children's awareness of the mind and mental events varies to the extent that the adults in their lives talk with them about thinking processes. • Many young children with autism have little conscious awareness of the existence of thought, particularly in other people.	• Model strategies for simple memory tasks (e.g., pinning permission slips on jackets to remind children to get their parents' signatures). • Talk often about thinking processes (e.g., "I *wonder* if…" "Do you *remember* when…?").
Middle Childhood (6–10)	• Use of rehearsal as the predominant learning strategy • Gradual increase in organization as an intentional learning strategy • Emerging ability to reflect on the nature of one's own thought processes • Frequent overestimation of one's own memory capabilities • Little if any self-regulated learning	• Chinese and Japanese children rely more heavily on rehearsal than their peers in Western schools; this difference continues into adolescence. • Children with information processing difficulties are less likely to organize material as they learn it. • A few high-achieving children are capable of sustained self-regulated learning, particularly in the upper elementary grades.	• Encourage children to repeat and practice the things they need to learn. • Ask children to study information that is easy to categorize, as a way of promoting organization as a learning strategy (Best & Ornstein, 1986). • Ask children to engage in simple, self-regulated learning tasks (e.g., small-group learning activities); give them suggestions about how to accomplish those tasks successfully.

DEVELOPMENTAL TRENDS

Cognitive Strategies and Metacognitive Awareness at Different Age Levels *(continued)*

AGE	WHAT YOU MIGHT OBSERVE	DIVERSITY	IMPLICATIONS
Early Adolescence (10–14) 	• Emergence of elaboration as an intentional learning strategy • Few and relatively ineffective study strategies (e.g., poor note-taking skills, little if any comprehension monitoring) • Increasing flexibility in the use of learning strategies • Emerging ability to regulate one's own learning • Belief that "knowledge" about a topic is merely a collection of discrete facts	• Adolescents differ considerably in their use of effective learning strategies (e.g., organization, elaboration). • Some adolescents, including many with information processing difficulties, have insufficient strategies for engaging effectively in self-regulated learning.	• Ask questions that encourage learners to elaborate on new information. • Teach and model effective strategies within the context of various subject areas. • Assign homework and other tasks that require independent learning; provide sufficient structure to guide learners' efforts. • Give adolescents frequent opportunities to assess their own learning.
Late Adolescence (14–18) 	• Increase in elaboration • Growing awareness of what cognitive strategies are most effective in different situations • Increasing self-regulatory learning strategies (e.g., comprehension monitoring) • Increasing recognition that knowledge involves understanding interrelationships among ideas	• Only high-achieving teenagers use sophisticated learning strategies (e.g., elaboration); others typically resort to simpler, less effective strategies (e.g., rehearsal). • Many teenagers with information processing difficulties have insufficient reading skills to learn successfully from typical high school textbooks; furthermore, their study skills tend to be unsophisticated and relatively ineffective.	• Continue to teach and model effective learning strategies both in and out of school. • Assign more complex independent learning tasks, giving the necessary structure and guidance for those who are not yet self-regulated learners. • Present various subject areas as dynamic entities that continue to evolve with new discoveries and theories.

Implications of Metacognitive and Strategic Development

Metacognition is at the very heart of cognition, and metacognitive development is therefore central to cognitive development: Children are more likely to acquire and use effective strategies when they are aware of the strategies they use and monitor how well each one helps them reach their goals (Kuhn, 2001b). Following are suggestions for fostering the development of cognitive strategies and metacognition.

■ *Model and teach effective problem-solving and learning strategies.* Adults can foster more effective problem-solving and learning strategies by modeling them for children. Infants as young as 10 months can overcome obstacles to obtain an attractive toy if an adult shows them how to do it (Chen, Sanchez, & Campbell, 1997; Want & Harris, 2001). Engaging television programs in which young children are encouraged to join on-screen characters in solving various problems (e.g., Nickelodeon's *Blue's Clues*) also help young children acquire new problem-solving strategies (Crawley, Anderson, Wilder, Williams, & Santomero, 1999).

Learning strategies, too, can clearly be modeled and taught. For instance, 4- and 5-year-olds can be taught to organize objects into categories as a way of helping them remember the objects (Carr & Schneider, 1991; Lange & Pierce, 1992). As children encounter increasingly challenging learning tasks at school and elsewhere, simple categorization alone is, of course, not enough. By the time they reach high school, adolescents will need to learn—and must often be explicitly taught—strategies such as elaboration, comprehension monitoring, goal setting, note taking, and time management. Explicit instruction about how to use these strategies fosters better learning and higher academic achievement (Hattie, Biggs, & Purdie, 1996). Such instruction is most effective when:

- Strategies are taught within the context of specific academic subject matter, rather than in isolation from actual learning tasks.
- Students learn many different strategies and the situations in which each one is appropriate.
- Students practice new strategies frequently with a wide variety of learning and problem-solving tasks. (Hattie et al., 1996; Pressley, El-Dinary, Marks, Brown, & Stein, 1992)

Hear Hilary express her view of rehearsal in the Memory/Late Adolescence clip.

Once adolescents become proficient in more advanced strategies, they are apt to find them more rewarding than less sophisticated ones such as rehearsal. In the Memory module of the Observation CD, 16-year-old Hilary describes her feelings about rehearsal this way:

> Just felt like I was trying to memorize for a test or something. . . . Sometimes it's kind of boring or repetitious, [just] going over it.

Small-group learning and problem-solving activities, especially when structured to encourage particular cognitive processes, can also promote more sophisticated strategies (e.g., King, 1999; Palincsar & Herrenkohl, 1999). One approach for fostering more effective learning is to teach children how to ask one another thought-provoking questions about the material they are studying. The following exchange shows two fifth graders using such questions as they study material about tide pools and tidal zones:

Janelle: What do you think would happen if there weren't certain zones for certain animals in the tide pools?
Katie: They would all be, like, mixed up—and all the predators would kill all the animals that shouldn't be there and then they just wouldn't survive. 'Cause the food chain wouldn't work—'cause the top of the chain would eat all the others and there would be no place for the bottom ones to hide and be protected. And nothing left for them to eat.
Janelle: O.K. But what about the ones that had camouflage to hide them? (King, 1999, p. 95)

Notice how Janelle's questions don't ask Katie to repeat what she has already learned. Instead, Katie must use what she's learned to speculate and draw inferences; in other words, she must engage in elaboration. Questioning like Janelle's appears to promote both better recall of facts and increased integration of ideas, undoubtedly because it encourages more sophisticated learning strategies (Kahl & Woloshyn, 1994; King, 1999; E. Wood et al., 1999).

These students are asking each other thought-provoking questions about the chapter they are studying. This technique promotes better recall of facts and increased integration of ideas.

Why are collaborative learning and problem-solving activities so beneficial? For one thing, group members scaffold one another's efforts, providing assistance on difficult tasks and monitoring one another's progress toward a particular goal. Second, group members must describe and explain their strategies, thereby allowing others to observe and possibly model them. Third, in a Vygotskian fashion, group members may eventually internalize their group-based strategies; for example, when they engage in mutual question-asking, they may eventually ask *themselves*, and then answer, equally challenging questions as they read and study.

■ *Give children frequent feedback about their progress, and help them see the relationship between their strategies and their learning and problem-solving success.* Children are likely to acquire and use new and more effective strategies only if they realize that their prior strategies have been ineffective. For example, a teacher might ask students to study similar sets of information in two different ways—perhaps to study one using rehearsal and another using elaboration. The teacher might then assess students' recollection of both sets of information: Presumably the more effective strategy will have promoted better learning and memory. With repeated, concrete comparisons of the effectiveness of different strategies, children will gradually discard the less effective ones for those that will serve them well as they encounter more challenging learning tasks in the years to come.

■ *Provide opportunities for children to evaluate their own learning, and help them develop mechanisms for doing so effectively.* As noted earlier, self-regulated learners monitor their progress throughout a learning task and then evaluate their ultimate success in mastering the material they have been studying. Theorists have offered several recommendations for promoting self-monitoring and self-evaluation:

- Teach children to ask themselves, and then answer, questions about the material they are studying (Rosenshine, Meiser, & Chapman, 1996).
- Have children set specific goals for each learning session and then describe how they've met them (Morgan, 1985).
- Provide specific criteria that children can use to judge their performance (Winne, 1995b).
- On some occasions, delay feedback, so that children first have the opportunity to evaluate their own performance (Butler & Winne, 1995; Schroth, 1992).
- Encourage children to evaluate their performance realistically, and then reinforce them (e.g., with praise or extra-credit points) when their evaluations match an adult's evaluation or some other external standard (McCaslin & Good, 1996; Schraw, Potenza, & Nebelsick-Gullet, 1993; Zuckerman, 1994).
- Have children compile portfolios that include samples of their work, along with a written reflection on the quality and significance of each sample (Paris & Ayres, 1994; N. E. Perry, 1998; Silver & Kenney, 1995).

By engaging in ongoing self-monitoring and self-evaluation of their performance, children should eventually develop appropriate standards for their performance and apply those standards regularly to their accomplishments—true hallmarks of a self-regulated learner.

◾ *Expect and encourage increasingly independent learning over time.*   As you have seen, self-regulated learning is a complex endeavor that involves many abilities (goal setting, attention control, flexible use of cognitive strategies, comprehension monitoring, etc.) and takes many years to master. Throughout the elementary and secondary school years, teachers and other adults must encourage and scaffold it in age-appropriate ways. For instance, they might provide examples of questions that children can use to monitor their comprehension as they read (e.g., "Explain how . . . ," "What is a new example of . . . ?"). They might provide a general organizational framework that children can follow while taking notes. They might provide guidance about how to develop a good summary (e.g., "Identify or invent a topic sentence," "Find supporting information for each main idea"). Such scaffolding is most likely to be helpful when children are studying subject matter they find difficult to comprehend yet can comprehend if they apply appropriate metacognitive strategies—in other words, when the subject matter is within their zone of proximal development (Pressley et al., 1992). As children develop increasing proficiency with each self-regulating strategy, the scaffolds can gradually be withdrawn.

◾ *Promote more sophisticated epistemological beliefs.*   For maximal learning and achievement, especially in the secondary and post-secondary school years, young people must be aware that knowledge is not a cut-and-dried set of facts and that effective learning is not simply a process of repeating those facts over and over again. One possible way to foster more advanced epistemological beliefs is to talk specifically about the nature of knowledge and learning—for example, to describe learning as an active, ongoing process of finding interconnections among ideas and eventually constructing one's own understanding of the world (Schommer, 1994b). But probably an even more effective approach is to provide experiences that lead children and adolescents to discover that knowledge is dynamic rather than static and that successful learning sometimes occurs only through effort and persistence. For example, teachers might give their students complex problems that have no clear-cut right or wrong answers, have students read conflicting accounts and interpretations of historical events, or ask students to compare several, possibly equally valid explanations of a particular phenomenon or event (Britt, Rouet, Georgi, & Perfetti, 1994; Leinhardt, 1994; Linn, Songer, & Eylon, 1996; Schommer, 1994b).

Having children interact with one another may also influence their views of the nature of knowledge and learning (e.g., C. L. Smith, Maclin, Houghton, & Hennessey, 2000). Heated discussions about controversial topics (e.g., pros and cons of capital punishment, interpretation of classic works of literature, or theoretical explanations of scientific phenomena)

DEVELOPMENT AND PRACTICE

Promoting Metacognitive and Strategic Development

■ Encourage learning strategies appropriate for the age group.

An elementary teacher encourages his students to study their spelling words through rehearsal—for instance, by writing the words over and over. In contrast, a high school teacher asks her students to think about why certain historical events may have happened as they did, encouraging them to speculate about the personal motives, economic circumstances, and political and social issues that may have influenced people's decision making at the time.

■ Model effective learning and problem-solving strategies and encourage children to use such strategies themselves.

A preschool teacher asks children to bring in empty egg cartons for a crafts project the following week. "Let's write ourselves little reminder notes and tape them to our jackets," she suggests. "That way, we'll be sure to remember the cartons when we leave for school tomorrow morning."

■ Identify situations in which various strategies are likely to be useful.

The leader of an after-school community center for teenagers says, "We've brainstormed a number of things we might do to improve the physical appearance of our building. Let's put them into categories according to the kind of work each one involves—painting, carpentry, sewing, and so on—and then find out which of you have interest and skills in each of those categories."

■ Give children opportunities to practice learning with little or no help; provide the scaffolding necessary to ensure their success.

A middle school social studies teacher distributes various magazine articles related to current events in the Middle East, making sure that each student receives an article appropriate for his or her reading level. She asks her students to read their articles over the weekend and prepare a one-paragraph summary to share with other class members. She also provides guidelines about what information students should include in their summaries.

■ Give children numerous opportunities to assess their own learning efforts and find out what they do and don't know.

A first aid instructor has his students read a chapter from their first aid manual at home that night. The following day, he gives them a nongraded quiz to help them identify parts of the chapter that they haven't yet mastered.

■ Talk with children about the nature of knowledge and learning in various disciplines.

A school librarian has sixth graders read three different accounts of a particular historical event as a way of helping them discover that history is not necessarily all clear-cut facts—that there are sometimes varying perspectives on what occurred and why.

should help children gain an increased understanding that there is not always a simple "right" answer to a question or issue. Furthermore, by wrestling and struggling as a group with difficult subject matter, children may begin to understand that one's knowledge about a topic is likely to evolve and improve gradually over time. Finally, adults must remember that group methods of inquiry are a critical feature of how the adult world tackles challenging issues and problems (Good, McCaslin, & Reys, 1992; Greeno, 1997; Pogrow & Londer, 1994). By providing opportunities for children to formulate questions and problems, discuss and critique one another's explanations and analyses, and compare and evaluate potential solutions, adults give children practice in these all-important adult strategies.

As a brief aside, we should note that, although some children have frequent opportunities to exchange ideas with adults at home (e.g., at the family dinner table), other children, including many who are at risk for academic failure and dropping out of school, rarely have opportunities to discuss academic subject matter at home. Discussions about puzzling phenomena or controversial topics at school and in after-school activities may fill a significant void in the cognitive experiences of these children (Pogrow & Londer, 1994).

Children's Construction of Theories

Growing children develop beliefs not only about the nature of knowledge and learning but also about many other aspects of their world. Some psychologists have proposed that children eventually combine their understandings into integrated belief systems, or *theories*, about particular topics (e.g., Hatano & Inagaki, 1996; Keil, 1989; Wellman & Gelman, 1998). This perspective, sometimes called **theory theory**,[4] is illustrated by the following di-

theory theory
Theoretical perspective proposing that children construct increasingly integrated and complex understandings of physical and mental phenomena.

---

[4] No, you're not seeing double. Although the term *theory theory* may seem rather odd, to us it suggests that many psychologists, "dry" as their academic writings might sometimes be, do indeed have a sense of humor.

alogue in Keil (1989) between an experimenter (E) and a child (C), whose responses reveal an integrated belief system regarding the nature of living things:

> [E:] These fruits are red and shiny, and they're used to make pies and cider, and everybody calls these things apples. But some scientists went into an orchard where some of these grow and they decided to study them really carefully. They looked way deep inside them with microscopes and found out these weren't like most apples. These things had the inside parts of pears. They had all the cells of pears and everything like that, and when they looked to see where they came from they found that these came off of pear trees. And, when the seeds from this fruit were planted, pear trees grew. So what are these: apples or pears? (pp. 305–306)
>
> C: Pears.
> E: How do you know?
> C: Because the seeds, when you plant the seeds a pear tree would grow, and if it were an apple, an apple tree would grow. They've got the insides of a pear and an apple wouldn't have the insides of a pear if it wasn't a pear.
> E: Then how come it looks like this?
> C: It's been sitting out for a long time and it turned red.
> E: And it doesn't have a pear shape? . . . How did that happen?
> C: (Shrug) (p. 171)[5]

This child, like many elementary school children, clearly recognizes that the essential nature of living things is determined by their internal makeup (e.g., their cells) rather than by their outward appearance. His responses indicate that he has developed an integrated belief system—a theory—about the topic. Children have a very different understanding of nonliving things, as another dialogue from Keil (1989) illustrates:

> [E:] These things are used for holding hot liquids like coffee and tea and cocoa or milk to drink, and everybody calls these things cups. Some scientists went to the factory where some of these are made . . . to study them. They looked way deep inside with microscopes and found out these weren't like most cups. The ones made at this factory had the inside parts of bowling balls. And when they looked to see how they were made, they found out that bowling balls were ground up to make them. So what do you think these things really are: cups or bowling balls? (p. 306)
>
> C: They're used for the same purpose as cups and they look like cups and you can drink from them and you can't bowl with them, they're definitely cups!
> E: Can they still be cups if they're made out of the same stuff as bowling balls?
> C: Yeah . . . and if you could melt down a glass and make it into a bowling ball without breaking it to bits, it would still be a bowling ball and not a cup. (p. 174)[6]

In this situation, the child realizes that the internal makeup of cups and bowling balls is irrelevant; instead, the *function* of the object is paramount.

In their theories about the world, children as young as 8 or 9 seem to make a basic distinction between biological entities (e.g., apples, pears) and human-made objects (e.g., cups, bowling balls). Furthermore, as the two dialogues suggest, children seem to conceptualize the two categories in fundamentally different ways (Keil, 1987, 1989). Biological entities are defined primarily by their origins (e.g., their DNA, the parents who brought them into being). Even preschoolers will tell you that you can't change a yellow finch into a bluebird by giving it a coat of blue paint or dressing it in a "bluebird" costume (Keil, 1989). In contrast, children understand that human-made objects are defined largely by the functions they serve (e.g., holding coffee, knocking down bowling pins). Thus, if cups are melted and reshaped into bowling balls, their function changes and so they become entirely different entities.

It appears that within the first three years of life, children begin to form theories about the physical world, the biological world, the social world, and the nature of thinking (Flavell et al., 1993; Wellman, Cross, & Watson, 2001; Wellman & Gelman, 1992). As they

---

[5,6] From Frank Keil, *Concepts, Kinds, and Cognitive Development*, 1989, The MIT Press.

grow older, they expand on and refine their theories, integrating many of the facts, concepts, and beliefs they acquire and incorporating numerous hierarchical and cause-effect relationships (Keil, 1994; McCauley, 1987; Wellman & Gelman, 1998).

In our discussion of metacognitive awareness earlier in the chapter, we got a glimpse of children's understanding of the nature of thinking—something that many developmentalists refer to as *theory of mind*. Children's theories about people's thought processes, as well as their theories about social institutions, play important roles in their overall social understanding; accordingly, we will explore these topics in Chapter 10. For now, we look at the nature of children's theories about the physical world.

Children's Theories of the Physical World

Young infants are amazingly knowledgeable about the physical world. For example, by age 3 or 4 months, they show signs of surprise when one solid object passes directly through another one, when an object seems to be suspended in midair, or when an object appears to move immediately from one place to another without traveling across the intervening space to get there (Baillargeon, 1994; Spelke, 1994; Spelke, Breinlinger, Macomber, & Jacobson, 1992). Such findings suggest that young infants know that objects are substantive entities with definite boundaries, that they will fall unless something holds them up, and that their movements across space are continuous. These findings also suggest to some theorists (e.g., Flavell et al., 1993; Spelke, 2000) that infants have some basic knowledge about the physical world that is biologically built in at birth, reflecting the *nativism* perspective mentioned in Chapter 4. Such knowledge would have an evolutionary advantage, of course—it would give infants a head start in learning about their environment—and evidence for it has been observed in other species as well (Spelke, 2000). Nevertheless, the extent to which the human brain is hard-wired with certain knowledge, or perhaps with predispositions to acquire that knowledge, is, at present, an unresolved issue.

Children's early conceptions of objects, whatever their origins may be, provide a foundation for constructing an integrated and increasingly elaborate theory of the physical world. But especially in the preschool and early elementary years, children's theories develop with little or no direct instruction from other, more knowledgeable individuals, and so they often include naïve beliefs and misconceptions[7] about how the world operates. Consider the following conversation with a 7-year-old whom we'll call Rob:

Adult: How were the mountains made?
Rob: Some dirt was taken from outside and it was put on the mountain and then mountains were made with it.
Adult: Who did that?
Rob: It takes a lot of men to make mountains, there must have been at least four. They gave them the dirt and then they made themselves all alone. [sic]
Adult: But if they wanted to make another mountain?
Rob: They pull one mountain down and then they could make a prettier one. (dialogue from Piaget, 1929, p. 348; format adapted)

The belief that people play a significant role in influencing physical phenomena (e.g., making clouds move, causing hurricanes) is common in the early elementary years (Piaget, 1960a), and some cultures actually promote it (Lee, 1999). Children in the elementary grades may also believe that natural objects and phenomena have a particular purpose; for instance, pointy rocks exist so that animals can scratch themselves when they have an itch, and snow stops falling in the spring so that fruit can grow (Kelemen, 1999; Piaget, 1929).

Children typically have many other erroneous beliefs about the world. For instance, they may believe that the sun revolves around the earth, that the Great Lakes contain salt water, and that rivers can run from north to south but not from south to north. Some misconceptions persist well into adolescence. For example, many high school and college students

---

[7] Theorists use a variety of terms when referring to such beliefs, including *naïve beliefs, misconceptions, alternative frameworks, lay conceptions,* and *children's science* (Duit, 1991; Magnusson, Boyle, & Templin, 1994).

believe that an object continues to move only if a force continues to act on it and that an object dropped from a moving train or airplane will fall straight down (diSessa, 1996; McCloskey, 1983). In reality, of course, an object continues to move at the same speed in a particular direction unless a force acts to change its speed or direction (reflecting the law of inertia), and an object dropped from a moving train or plane not only falls but also continues to move forward (reflecting the laws of gravity and inertia).

Several factors probably contribute to the inaccuracies in children's theories about the world. Sometimes misconceptions result from how things appear to be (Byrnes, 1996; diSessa, 1996; Duit, 1991). For example, from our perspective living here on the earth's surface, the sun looks as if it moves around the earth, rather than vice versa. Sometimes misconceptions are encouraged by common expressions in language; for instance, we often talk about the sun "rising" and "setting" (Duit, 1991; Mintzes, Trowbridge, Arnaudin, & Wandersee, 1991). Sometimes children infer incorrect cause-effect relationships between two events simply because those events often occur at the same time[8] (Byrnes, 1996; Keil, 1991). Perhaps even fairy tales and television cartoon shows play a role in promoting misconceptions (Glynn, Yeany, & Britton, 1991). For example, after cartoon "bad guys" run off the edge of a cliff, they usually remain suspended in air until they realize that there's nothing solid holding them up. Sometimes children acquire erroneous ideas from others; in some cases, teachers and textbooks provide misinformation (Begg, Anas, & Farinacci, 1992; Duit, 1991).

Earlier in the chapter, we presented the principle that *children's growing knowledge base facilitates more effective learning.* This principle holds true only when that knowledge is an accurate representation of reality. When children's "knowledge" is inaccurate, it often has a counterproductive effect, in that *children's erroneous beliefs about a topic interfere with their understanding of new information related to that topic.* For example, many children in the early elementary grades believe that the earth is flat rather than round. When adults tell them that the earth is actually round, they may interpret that information within the context of what they already "know" and so think of the earth as being both flat and round—in other words, shaped like a pancake (Vosniadou, 1994).

Implications of Theory Theory

Given the nature of children's and adolescents' theories about the world, there are several practical implications for adults to bear in mind:

■ *Encourage and answer children's "why" and "how" questions.* As you may know from your own experience, young children ask many *why* and *how* questions: Why is the sky blue? How does the telephone call know which house to go to? Such questions often pop up within the context of shared activities with adults (Callanan & Oakes, 1992, p. 214). Although adults may find them bothersome, they typically reflect children's genuine desire to make sense of their world and enhance their theories about what causes what and why things are the way they are.

■ *When teaching a new topic, determine what children already know and believe about it.* Adults can more successfully address children's misconceptions when they know what those misconceptions are (Roth & Anderson, 1988; C. Smith, Maclin, Grosslight, & Davis, 1997; Vosniadou & Brewer, 1987). For example, when beginning a new curriculum unit, teachers should probably assess students' existing beliefs about the topic, perhaps simply by asking a few informal questions that probe what students know and *mis*know.

■ *When children have misconceptions about a topic, work actively to help them acquire more accurate understandings.* Even as children encounter more accurate and adultlike perspectives about the world, their existing misconceptions do not necessarily disappear. In fact, because early "knowledge" influences the interpretation of subsequent experiences, misconceptions are often quite resistant to change even in the face of blatantly contradictory information (Chambliss, 1994; Chinn & Brewer, 1993; Kuhn, 2001b; Shuell, 1996). Thus, teachers and other adults must make a concerted effort to help students modify their

---

[8] Such thinking reflects the *transductive reasoning* of which Piaget spoke (see Table 4–1).

early, inaccurate theories to incorporate more accurate and productive world views—in other words, to undergo **conceptual change**. Theorists and researchers have offered several strategies for promoting conceptual change:

- Ask questions that challenge children's current beliefs.
- Present phenomena that children cannot adequately explain within their existing perspectives.
- Engage children in discussions of the pros and cons of various explanations of observed phenomena.
- Explicitly point out what the differences between children's beliefs and "reality" are.
- Show how the correct explanation of an event or phenomenon makes more sense than any alternative explanation children themselves can offer.
- Have children study a topic for an extended period of time so that accurate explanations are mastered rather than learned at a superficial level. (Chan, Burtis, & Bereiter, 1997; Chinn & Brewer, 1993; diSessa, 1996; Posner, Strike, Hewson, & Gertzog, 1982; Prawat, 1989; K. J. Roth, 1990; Slusher & Anderson, 1996; Vosniadou & Brewer, 1987)

In our discussions thus far, we have often drawn from Piaget's theory and research to better understand the nature and development of children's cognitive processes; for example, the interview with Rob about where mountains come from was conducted in Piaget's laboratory. Some contemporary theories of cognitive development rely even more heavily on Piaget's work. We turn to these *neo-Piagetian* approaches now.

Neo-Piagetian Approaches to Cognitive Development

For reasons we considered in the preceding chapter, many contemporary developmentalists have largely abandoned Piaget's early notions regarding children's cognitive development. Yet some psychologists believe that, by rejecting Piaget's theory, we may be throwing the baby out with the bathwater. These psychologists have combined some of Piaget's ideas with concepts from information processing theory to construct **neo-Piagetian theories** of how children's learning and reasoning capabilities change over time (e.g., Case, 1985; Case & Okamoto, 1996; Fischer, Knight, & Van Parys, 1993).

Key Ideas in Neo-Piagetian Theories

Neo-Piagetian theorists do not always agree about the exact nature of children's thinking at different age levels or about the exact mechanisms that promote cognitive development. Nevertheless, several ideas are central to neo-Piagetian approaches:

■ *Children acquire general structures that pervade their thinking in particular content domains.* Piaget proposed that over time, children develop increasingly integrated systems of mental processes (operations) that they can apply with equal effectiveness to a wide variety of tasks and content domains. However, as noted in Chapter 4, recent research indicates that children's ability to think logically depends considerably on their specific knowledge, experiences, and instruction related to the task at hand. Thus, the sophistication of children's reasoning is far more variable from one situation to the next than Piaget predicted.

To address such variability, neo-Piagetians propose that children do not develop a single system of logical operations; instead, they develop more specific systems, or **structures**, of concepts and thinking skills that influence thinking and reasoning capabilities within particular content domains.

■ *Cognitive development is constrained by the maturation of information processing mechanisms.* As noted earlier, children's working memory capacity increases over time; accordingly, children acquire an increasing ability to think about several things simultaneously. Neo-Piagetians believe that the changing capacity of working memory is,

conceptual change
Revising one's knowledge and understanding of a topic in response to new information about the topic.

neo-Piagetian theory
Theoretical perspective that combines elements of both Piaget's theory and information processing theory and portrays cognitive development as involving a series of distinct stages.

structure
In neo-Piagetian theory, a specific system of concepts and thinking skills that influence thinking and reasoning in a particular content domain.

in large part, a function of neurological maturation. They further propose that children's limited working memory capacity at younger ages restricts their ability to acquire complex thinking and reasoning skills; in a sense, it places a "ceiling" on what they can accomplish at any particular age (Case & Okamoto, 1996; K. W. Fischer & Bidell, 1991; Lautrey, 1993).

■ *Formal schooling has a greater influence on cognitive development than Piaget believed.* Within the limits set by neurological maturation, formal schooling plays a critical role in children's cognitive development. One prominent neo-Piagetian, Robbie Case, has proposed that cognitive development results from both active attempts at learning (e.g., paying attention, thinking about how ideas are interrelated) and subconscious "associative" learning (e.g., learning gradually and unintentionally that certain stimuli are often encountered together in one's experiences). In Case's view, both forms of learning can promote the acquisition of knowledge about specific situations and the development of more general cognitive structures. Subsequently, specific knowledge and general structures each contribute to the development of the other in a reciprocal fashion (Case & Okamoto, 1996).

■ *Development in specific content domains can be characterized as a series of stages.* Although neo-Piagetians reject Piaget's notion that a single series of stages characterizes all cognitive development, they speculate that cognitive development in specific content domains may have a stagelike nature (e.g., Case, 1985; Case & Okamoto, 1996; K. W. Fischer & Bidell, 1991). Children's entry into a particular stage is marked by the acquisition of new abilities, which the children practice and gradually master over time. Eventually, they integrate these abilities into more complex structures that mark their entry into a subsequent stage.

Recently, however, some neo-Piagetians have suggested that even in a particular content domain, cognitive development is not necessarily a single series of stages through which children progress as if they were climbing rungs on a ladder. Instead, it might be better characterized as progression along "multiple strands" of skills that interconnect in a web-like fashion (K. W. Fischer et al., 1993). From this perspective, children may acquire more advanced levels of competence in a particular area through any one of several pathways. For instance, as they become increasingly proficient in reading, they may gradually develop their word decoding skills, their comprehension skills, and so on, but the relative rates at which they master each of these skills will vary from one child to the next.

To give you a better understanding of the nature of cognitive development from a neo-Piagetian perspective, we now look at a theory proposed by Robbie Case, a developmental psychologist at the University of Toronto until his untimely death in 2000.

Development of Central Conceptual Structures: Case's Theory

From Case's perspective, integrated networks of concepts and cognitive processes—**central conceptual structures**—form the basis for much of children's thinking, reasoning, and learning in specific content domains (Case & Okamoto, 1996; Case, Okamoto, Henderson, & McKeough, 1993). Over time, these structures undergo several major transformations, each of which marks a child's entry to the next higher stage of development.

Case speculated about the nature of children's central conceptual structures in three specific areas: social thought, spatial relationships, and number. A central conceptual structure related to *social thought* underlies children's reasoning about interpersonal relationships, their knowledge of common scripts related to human interaction, and their comprehension of short stories and other works of fiction; this structure includes children's general beliefs about human beings' mental states, intentions, and behaviors. A central conceptual structure related to *spatial relationships* underlies children's performance in such areas as drawing, construction and use of maps, replication of geometric patterns, and psychomotor activities (e.g., writing in cursive, hitting a ball with a racket); this structure enables children to align objects in space in accordance with one or more reference points (e.g., the x- and y-axes used in graphing). A central conceptual structure related to *number* underlies children's ability to reason about and manipulate mathematical quantities; this structure reflects an integrated understanding of how such mathematical concepts and operations as numbers, counting, addition, and subtraction are interrelated (Case & Okamoto, 1996).

central conceptual structure
Integrated network of concepts and cognitive processes that forms the basis for much of one's thinking, reasoning, and learning in specific content domains.

According to Robbie Case's neo-Piagetian perspective, children develop central conceptual structures in social thought, spatial relationships, and number (and perhaps in other areas as well). These structures affect children's reasoning and performance on a variety of relevant tasks.

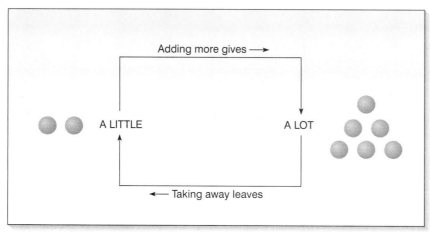

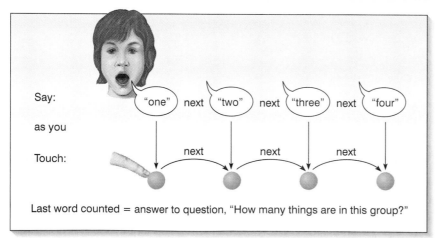

FIGURE 5–12 Hypothetical numerical structures at age 4

From "The Role of Central Conceptual Structures in the Development of Children's Thought" by R. Case, Y. Okamoto, in collaboration with S. Griffin, A. McKeough, C. Bleiker, B. Henderson, & K. M. Stephenson, 1996, *Monographs of the Society for Research in Child Development, 61*(1, Serial No. 246), p. 6. Copyright 1996 by the Society for Research in Child Development. Adapted with permission from the Society for Research in Child Development.

Case proposed that, from ages 4 to 10, parallel changes occur in children's central conceptual structures in each of the three areas, with such changes reflecting increasing integration and multidimensional reasoning over time (Case & Okamoto, 1996). We describe the development of children's understanding of number as an example.

Development of a Central Conceptual Structure for Number Case and his colleagues (Case & Mueller, 2001; Case & Okamoto, 1996; Case et al., 1993; Griffin, Case, & Siegler, 1994) have developed a relatively precise model of the nature of children's knowledge about quantities and numbers during the preschool and elementary years. At age 4, children understand the difference between "a little" and "a lot" and recognize that addition leads to more objects and subtraction leads to fewer objects; such knowledge might take the form depicted in the top half of Figure 5–12. Furthermore, 4-year-olds can accurately count a small set of objects and conclude that the final number they reach equals the total number of objects in the set; this process is depicted in the bottom half of Figure 5–12. For example, 4-year-olds can visually compare a group of 5 objects with a group of 6 objects and tell you that the latter group contains more objects. They can also count accurately to either 5 or 6. Yet they cannot answer a question such as, "Which is more, 5 or 6?"—a question that involves knowledge of both more-versus-less and counting. It appears that they have not yet integrated their two understandings of number into a single conceptual framework.

By the time children are 6, they can easily answer simple "Which is more?" questions. Case proposed that at the age of 6, the two structures in Figure 5–12 have become integrated into the more comprehensive structure depicted in Figure 5–13 (Case & Mueller, 2001). As illustrated in the figure, children's knowledge and reasoning about numbers now includes several key elements:

• Children understand and can say the verbal numbers "one," "two," "three," etc.

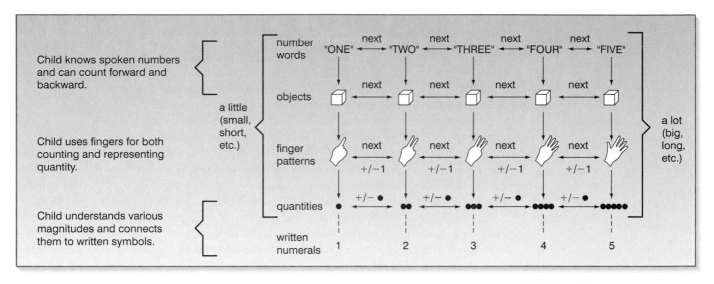

FIGURE 5-13 Hypothetical central conceptual structure at age 6

Source: From "Differentiation, Integration, and Covariance Mapping as Fundamental Processes in Cognitive and Neurological Growth" by R. Case & M. P. Mueller, 2001, *Mechanisms of Cognitive Development: Behavioral and Neural Perspectives* (J. L. McClelland & R. S. Siegler, Eds.), p. 201. Mahwah, NJ: Erlbaum. Adapted with permission from Lawrence Erlbaum Associates.

- They recognize the written numerals 1, 2, 3, etc.
- They have a systematic process for counting objects: They say each successive number as they touch each successive object in a group. Eventually, children count by mentally "tagging" (rather than physically touching) each object.
- They also use their fingers for representing small quantities (e.g., 3 fingers equals 3 objects). Their use of fingers for both counting objects and representing quantities may be a key means through which they integrate the two processes into a single conceptual structure.
- They equate movement toward higher numbers with such concepts as "a lot," "more," and "bigger." Similarly, they equate movement toward lower numbers with such concepts as "a little," "less," and "smaller."
- They understand that movement from one number to the next is equivalent to either adding one unit to the set or subtracting one unit from it, depending on the direction of movement.
- They realize that any change in one dimension (e.g., from 3 to 4) must be accompanied by an equivalent change along other dimensions (e.g., from "three" to "four," and from ••• to ••••).

In essence, the more comprehensive conceptual structure at age 6 forms a mental "number line" that children can use to facilitate their understanding and execution of such processes as addition, subtraction, and comparisons of various quantities.

At age 8, Case proposed, children have sufficiently mastered this central conceptual structure that they can begin using two number lines simultaneously to solve mathematical problems. For instance, they can now answer such questions as, "Which number is bigger, 32 or 28?" and "Which number is closer to 25, 21 or 18?" Such questions require them to compare digits in both the 1s column and 10s column, with each comparison taking place along a separate number line. In addition, 8-year-olds presumably have a better understanding of operations that require transformations across columns, such as "carrying 1" to the 10s column during addition or "borrowing 1" from the 10s column during subtraction.

Finally, at about age 10, children become capable of generalizing the relationships of two number lines to the entire number system. They now understand how the various columns (1s, 10s, 100s, etc.) relate to one another and can expertly move back and forth among the columns. They can also treat the answers to mathematical problems as mental entities in and of themselves and so can answer such questions as "Which number is bigger, the difference between 6 and 9 or the difference between 8 and 3?"

Case tracked the development of children's central conceptual structure for number only until age 10. He acknowledged, however, that children's understanding of numbers continues to develop well into adolescence. For instance, he pointed out that teenagers often have trouble with questions such as "What is a half of a third?" and suggested that their difficulty results from an incomplete conceptual understanding of division and the results (i.e., fractions) that it yields.

Effects of Instruction and Culture on Central Conceptual Structures   Whereas Piaget downplayed the importance of education in the development of children's logical reasoning capabilities, Case proposed that, within the limits of children's neurological maturation and working memory capacity, formal instruction can definitely promote the development of their central conceptual structures (Case & Okamoto, 1996; Case et al., 1993; Griffin, Case, & Capodilupo, 1995). For instance, explicit training in such activities as counting, connecting specific number words (e.g., "three," "five") with specific quantities of objects, and making judgments about relative number (e.g., "Since this set [•••] has more than this set [••], we can say that 'three' has more than 'two'") leads to improved performance not only in these tasks but in other quantitative tasks as well (Case & Okamoto, 1996; Griffin et al., 1995).

In several studies of children from diverse cultural backgrounds, Case found no significant cross-cultural differences in abilities that he suggested are related to children's central conceptual structures for number, social thought, and spatial relations. For instance, when the drawings of Chinese and Japanese children (who receive a great deal of training in drawing skills beginning in preschool) are compared with those of Canadian and American children (who are given numerous opportunities to draw but little if any explicit instruction in how to draw), differences are found in the content and complexity of the pictures but not in the spatial relationships among the figures that the drawings contain. Similarly, Japanese and American children differ in the content of the stories they tell (reflecting cultural differences in the events they experience) but not in their storytelling skills per se (reflecting similar abilities in social thought) (Case & Okamoto, 1996). Such findings suggest that the conceptual structures Case described may develop within the context of a wide variety of educational and cultural experiences.

Implications of Neo-Piagetian Theories

Neo-Piagetian theories yield some of the same practical implications that we have derived from other theories. For example, like information processing theory and theory-theory approaches, neo-Piagetian approaches lead to the conclusions that parents, teachers, and other adults should relate new information to children's existing knowledge base and that they should accommodate children's limited working memory capacities. But neo-Piagetian theories also have two additional implications:

■ *Don't predict children's performance in one domain based on their performance in a very different domain.*   From a neo-Piagetian perspective, children may develop at different rates in different content areas. For example, some children may be more advanced in social reasoning than in spatial relations, whereas the reverse may be true for other children. In Chapter 6, we will see a similar idea reflected in Gardner's theory of multiple intelligences.

■ *Identify and teach concepts and skills central to children's understanding of a particular content area.*   Some subject matter may provide the foundation on which a great deal of subsequent learning depends; examples include knowledge and skills related to counting, interpretation of people's motives and actions, and the ability to locate objects accurately in two-dimensional space. If Case and his colleagues are correct, training in such essential knowledge and skills should be a high priority for teachers and other adults who work regularly with children and adolescents.

The Basic Developmental Issues table "Contrasting Three Theories of Cognitive Development" contrasts information processing theory, theory theory, and neo-Piagetian theory with respect to the three themes: nature and nurture, universality and diversity, and qualitative and quantitative changes. However, even as you think about the contrasts, keep in mind that various theoretical perspectives of cognitive development aren't necessarily mutually exclusive. For example, neo-Piagetians draw on information processing theorists' concept of working memory. In the following section, we consider how some theorists have combined ideas from the sociocultural perspective (described in Chapter 4) with information processing theory.

BASIC DEVELOPMENTAL ISSUES

Contrasting Three Theories of Cognitive Development

ISSUE	INFORMATION PROCESSING THEORY	THEORY THEORY	NEO-PIAGETIAN THEORY
Nature and Nurture	Focus is on how environmental input is interpreted, stored, integrated, and remembered and on how formal instruction can best facilitate more effective learning and cognitive development. Information processing difficulties (learning disabilities, ADHD, autism) often have biological origins.	From interactions with their physical and social environments, children construct integrated understandings and beliefs about various physical and mental phenomena.	Both informal experiences and formal schooling promote cognitive development. However, biological maturation places an upper limit on the complexity of knowledge and skills that children can acquire at a particular age level.
Universality and Diversity	The components of the information processing system (e.g., working memory, long-term memory, central executive) are universal. However, some people use their information processing capabilities more effectively than others. People's prior knowledge and their mastery of various cognitive strategies influence the degree to which they can learn new information and skills effectively.	The specific theories that children construct are influenced by informal experiences, formal schooling, and cultural practices and beliefs.	Children develop systems of integrated concepts and thinking skills (structures) that influence much of their thinking and learning within particular content domains. In the preschool and elementary years, these structures are likely to be similar across diverse cultures; in the secondary years, they become more culture-specific.
Qualitative and Quantitative Change	With development, children and adolescents acquire numerous cognitive strategies that are qualitatively different from one another. Each strategy evolves gradually over a lengthy period and becomes increasingly flexible, efficient, and effective. Theorists disagree about whether the physical capacity of working memory increases quantitatively with age.	As children gain more information about their world, they may add to and embellish upon their theories; such changes reflect quantitative increases. Under certain conditions, however, new and compelling experiences spur children to overhaul their theories in a way that reflects qualitative change.	Structures increase in complexity in a stagelike fashion; at each successive stage, they become more complex and integrated and so are qualitatively different from preceding stages. Within each stage, children develop increasing proficiency in using newly acquired concepts and skills.

Adding a Sociocultural Element to Information Processing Theory

At many points in our discussion of information processing theory, we've touched on the importance of children's social and cultural environments. For instance, we've noted that

- Talking with children about an event can enhance their memory of it.
- Different cultures may foster different schemas, scripts, and learning strategies.
- Co-regulated learning can pave the way for self-regulated learning.
- Small-group learning and problem-solving activities can promote strategy development.

Furthermore, young children seem to have a predisposition for social stimuli and social interaction from the very early days of life. As evidence for this idea, let's revisit a few findings mentioned in the earlier sections on perception and attention:

- Infants only 3 days old suck a pacifier more vigorously in order to hear their mother's voice.
- At 1 month of age, infants prefer looking at pictures of faces over those of other objects.
- Also at 1 month, infants attend longer to caregivers than to inanimate objects.

With such findings in mind, some theorists have suggested that a combination of information processing and sociocultural perspectives provides a better explanation of how cognitive development occurs than either perspective can provide alone. In particular, information processing theory may tell us a great deal about *what* changes over time, and sociocultural views (e.g., notions about co-construction of meaning, guided participation, and the like) may help us explain *how* those changes occur (Gauvain, 2001; Ornstein & Haden, 2001).

This blend of information processing and sociocultural approaches is still in its infancy. Nevertheless, researchers have made considerable progress in three areas: intersubjectivity, social construction of memory, and joint use of cognitive strategies.

Intersubjectivity

For two people to interact and communicate, they must have some shared understanding on which to build; for instance, each should have some awareness of what the other sees, knows, thinks, and feels. Such mutual understanding is known as **intersubjectivity** (Newson & Newson, 1975; Rommetveit, 1985; Trevarthen, 1980). The beginnings of intersubjectivity are seen at about 2 months of age, when infants and their caregivers focus on and interact with each other, exchanging smiles, taking turns vocalizing, and so on (Adamson & McArthur, 1995).

Sometime around 9 or 10 months of age, intersubjectivity becomes more complex, taking the form of **joint attention**. At this point, an infant and caregiver can focus on a single object, with both members of the pair monitoring the *other's* attention to the object and coordinating their behaviors toward the object (Adamson & McArthur, 1995; Carpenter, Nagell, & Tomasello, 1998; Trevarthen & Hubley, 1978). The following observation of 9-month-old Tracey and her mother illustrates this phenomenon:

> Tracey repeatedly looked up at her mother's face when receiving an object, pausing as if to acknowledge receipt. She also looked up to her mother at breaks in her play, giving the indication of willingness to share experiences as she had never done before. . . . When her mother showed her how to make the wheels of the inverted trolley turn and squeak, Tracey watched closely and touched the wheels. When her mother eagerly said, "Pull it!", Tracey made a move to draw the trolley towards her, but failed because the string was not taut, at the same time, expecting success, she looked up and smiled eagerly at her mother. This was clearly a learned anticipation of the pleasure they usually shared when she did the trick of pulling in the trolley correctly. (Trevarthen & Hubley, 1978, pp. 201, 204)

Observe joint attention in the Literacy/Infancy clip.

You can also see joint attention in action in the Literacy/Infancy clip on the Observation CD as 16-month-old Corwin and his mother read a book together.

Early in the second year, infants also begin to show **social referencing,** looking at someone else for clues about how to respond to or feel about a particular object or event (Feinman, 1992; Klinnert, Emde, Butterfield, & Campos, 1986). Children are most likely to engage in social referencing when they encounter a new and uncertain situation. For example, in one study (Klinnert, 1984), 1- and 1½-year-old infants were shown three new toys to which their mothers had been instructed to respond with a happy, fearful, or neutral expression. Upon seeing each new toy, most infants looked at their mother and chose actions consistent with her response: They typically moved toward the toy if Mom showed pleasure but moved away from it if she showed fear.

As information processing theorists tell us, attention is critical to learning and cognitive development. As we bring the sociocultural perspective into the picture, we see that awareness of a *partner's* attention is critical as well (Baldwin, 2000; Gauvain, 2001). For instance, when an adult uses a word that an 18-month-old toddler has never heard before, the toddler will often look immediately at the speaker's face and follow the speaker's line of vision to the object being referenced; in this way, children probably learn many object labels (Baldwin, 2000). More generally, we find that a child can learn from a person with more experience only if both people are focusing on the same thing and *know* that they are sharing their focus. Because intersubjectivity is so critical for children's ability to learn from more experienced members of their community, it appears to be a universal phenomenon across cultures (Adamson & Bakeman, 1991).

Social Construction of Memory

In Chapter 4, we described how adults often help children construct meaning from events (see "Social Construction of Meaning," p. 167). Adults also help children reconstruct events they have previously stored in long-term memory. Almost as soon as children are old

intersubjectivity
Shared understandings that provide the foundation for social interaction and communication.

joint attention
Phenomenon in which two people (e.g., a child and caregiver) simultaneously focus on the same object or event, monitor each other's attention, and coordinate their responses.

social referencing
Looking at someone else (e.g., a caregiver) for clues about how to respond to a particular object or event.

enough to talk, their parents begin to engage them in frequent conversations about past events (Fivush, Haden, & Reese, 1996; Gauvain, 2001; Ratner, 1984). Initially, the parents do most of the work, reminiscing, asking questions, prompting recall, and so on, but by time children are 3, they, too, are active participants in the conversations (Fivush et al., 1996).

Discussions about past events have several benefits (Gauvain, 2001). First, as noted earlier in the chapter, children are more likely to remember the experiences they talk about. Second, because adults focus on certain aspects of events and not others, children learn what things are important to remember. Third, because adults are apt to interpret events in particular ways (e.g., finding some things amusing and others distasteful), children acquire perspectives and values appropriate for their culture. For example, when European American mothers recall past events with their 3-year-olds, they often refer to the thoughts and feelings of the participants; in contrast, Korean mothers are more likely to talk about social norms and expectations, such as what someone should have done. Such differences are consistent with the priorities and values of these two cultures (Mullen & Yi, 1995).

Yet another benefit of reminiscing about past events is that children learn to use a narrative structure for telling stories: They recall events in a temporal sequence, and they include information about particular people's intentions and actions (Gauvain, 2001). Many children acquire a rudimentary narrative structure before they are 2, and this structure enhances their memory of what they have experienced (Bauer & Mandler, 1990). As you will discover in Chapter 7, children's narratives become increasingly sophisticated as they get older.

Talking about events occasionally has a downside, however, especially for young children (Bruck & Ceci, 1997; Leichtman & Ceci, 1995). Imagine that a man identified as "Sam Stone" briefly visits a preschool classroom; he comments on the story the teacher is reading to the children, strolls around the perimeter of the room, waves good-bye, and leaves. Later, an adult asks, "When Sam Stone got that bear dirty, did he do it on purpose or was it an accident?" and "Was Sam Stone happy or sad that he got the bear dirty?" When asked such questions, children may recall that Sam soiled a teddy bear, even though he never touched a stuffed animal during his visit (Leichtman & Ceci, 1995, p. 571). Such susceptibility to leading questions is more common in 3- and 4-year-olds than in 5- and 6-year-olds; the older children are less likely to be swayed by the power of suggestion (Leichtman & Ceci, 1995). We urge professionals who use young children's testimonies in legal matters to be careful to ask questions that do not communicate any foregone conclusions about what children may have experienced or witnessed. For instance, one might simply say, "Tell me what happened, as best as you can remember it." Furthermore, professionals should, whenever possible, seek additional evidence that might either corroborate or cast doubt on young children's recollections.

Joint Use of Cognitive Strategies

Using a narrative structure to recall an event is, in essence, a cognitive strategy that facilitates learning and recall. Earlier in the chapter we indicated that children acquire more sophisticated learning and problem-solving strategies when adults model and teach those strategies. A sociocultural perspective suggests that adults should go a step further, engaging children in activities that require collaborative use of particular strategies. Through joint use and discussion of strategies—typically with considerable adult guidance and scaffolding at first—children gradually internalize those strategies and begin using them independently (Freund, 1990; Gauvain, 2001). The following example illustrates such internalization:

> Ben, age 4, shuffles into the family room with a jar of pennies that he has been saving. He announces to his mother that he wants to count them to see how much money he has. With mother looking on, Ben dumps the coins on the coffeetable and begins to count the pennies, one by one. All is going well until he counts some pennies a second time. Mother interrupts and suggests that he put the pennies in rows so that he doesn't count any twice. Ben agrees to do this, but he aligns his rows poorly. Mother shows him how to straighten them by making a few sample rows herself. She also tells him that it is important to put 10 coins in each row and no more. They finish building the rows together and then they count the pennies: there are 47. A few days later Ben tells his mother that his father gave him some more pennies so he needs to count them again. Mother looks on as Ben dumps the pennies on the coffeetable and begins, on his own, to set up rows of 10. (Gauvain, 2001, p. 140)

When interviewing children who have witnessed a crime, professionals must be very careful not to ask leading questions that may influence what children "remember."

As another example, imagine that you have several errands to complete at various locations around town: Perhaps you want to register to vote, purchase a flashlight and a package of spaghetti for an upcoming camping trip, get a cake for a friend's birthday celebration tomorrow, renew your driver's license, and pick up a can of paint to refinish an old table. How will you plan your trip? If you want to use your time efficiently, you will group the errands according to tasks you can accomplish simultaneously (a hardware store will have flashlights and paint, a grocery store will have spaghetti and cake, and perhaps you can register to vote and renew your license in the same government complex). You might also think about destinations that are near one another (perhaps a local shopping center has both a grocery store and a hardware store) and plan to go to one immediately after the other. When children engage in such planning activities with an adult, they acquire more efficient planning strategies—grouping errands by location and planning an efficient route—than they develop on their own (Gauvain, 1992; Radziszewska & Rogoff, 1988).

Often, adult-child partnerships are more effective than child-child partnerships in fostering new strategies. Children, young ones especially, can be fairly oblivious to what their partner is thinking or doing, and they may simply take over if their partner is struggling. Adults are more likely to actively engage their partners in an activity, verbalize and model appropriate strategies, monitor what their partners are doing, and scaffold effective strategy use with suggestions and questions (Gauvain, 2001; Radziszewska & Rogoff, 1988).

Implications of a Sociocultural Approach to Information Processing

In this and the preceding chapter, we have identified numerous implications of the sociocultural and information processing perspectives. Following are two additional implications that emerge when we consider both perspectives simultaneously.

■ *Regularly engage infants in social interaction.*   In the early months, such interactions may simply involve making eye contact, smiling and talking, extending a finger to be grabbed, and so on. Later, such interactions are more likely to involve jointly looking at, manipulating, experimenting with, and talking about objects. Such activities, simple though they may be, foster the mutual awareness (intersubjectivity) so essential for later information sharing and perspective taking.

■ *Involve children and adolescents in joint activities that require new strategies.*   Vygotsky suggested that growing children are most likely to benefit from challenging tasks when they have the guidance and support of more experienced individuals. Information processing theorists point out that cognitive development involves the acquisition of increasingly effective and efficient cognitive strategies. Taken together, the two perspectives highlight the importance of having adults work closely with youngsters to scaffold the use and eventual mastery of sophisticated approaches to learning and problem solving.

Critique of Contemporary Approaches to Cognitive Development

Contemporary theories have extended our understanding of cognitive development far beyond Piaget's and Vygotsky's early ideas. Information processing theory has made significant inroads into the question of how human beings mentally process and learn new information and how cognitive processes change over the course of childhood and adolescence. Theory theory helps us understand why children's naïve beliefs (e.g., "The world is flat") may persist even in the face of contradictory evidence. Neo-Piagetian perspectives have provided food for thought about the precise nature of children's knowledge in certain content areas. Together such approaches lead us to conclude that cognitive development involves more gradual changes, and that the evolution of children's reasoning capabilities is more domain-specific, than Piaget suggested. And developmentalists now agree almost without exception that children's knowledge becomes increasingly integrated over time. This integration may, depending on one's theoretical perspective, take the form of *schemas*, *scripts, theories,* or *central conceptual structures.*

Much work remains to be done on the nature and course of cognitive development. For instance, we do not yet know whether we can better characterize cognitive development in terms of stages or trends. While Case has proposed that the integration of knowledge central to children's thinking in certain content domains occurs in a series of discrete stages, many other theorists (e.g., Keating, 1996a; Siegler, 1996a) remain unconvinced.

Nor have developmentalists completely resolved the issue of general versus domain-specific changes. General changes seem to occur in attention, working memory capacity, learning strategies, and metacognitive awareness, and these changes probably influence children's thinking and learning across a broad range of contexts and subject areas. But to what extent do children acquire general knowledge structures (e.g., *theories* or *central conceptual structures*) that underlie much of their thinking and reasoning in particular content areas? Researchers have only recently begun to study this critical developmental question, and so a firm answer (if one is possible) is probably many years away.

Perhaps the biggest challenge for today's theorists is to explain in precise terms how and why cognitive development occurs (Gauvain, 2001; Siegler, 1998). Theorists have made some progress on this front, to be sure—for instance, children appear to have an innate need to adapt to their environment, and they almost certainly acquire more complex strategies as adults nurture such strategies—but we do not yet have a detailed understanding of how various aspects of heredity and environment work in concert to transform newborn infants into cognitively sophisticated adults. To arrive at such an understanding, developmentalists must eventually pull together the concepts and research findings of multiple theoretical perspectives and research methodologies. The integration of sociocultural and information processing perspectives described earlier is a step in this direction.

Although we do not yet have a complete picture of cognitive development, existing theories and research findings tell us a great deal about what to look for in children's development (e.g., see the Observation Guidelines table "Assessing Cognitive Processing and Metacognitive Skills"), and they give caregivers, teachers, and others who work with children and adolescents considerable guidance about appropriate activities and instructional strategies for various age groups. What we have learned about cognitive development also helps us identify children who may be having difficulties in processing certain kinds of information. We turn now to exceptionalities in information processing.

Exceptionalities in Information Processing

All human beings learn and process information in a somewhat unique, idiosyncratic manner. But the information processing capabilities of some individuals are different enough that they require the use of specially adapted instructional practices and materials. Here we consider three kinds of exceptionalities in information processing: learning disabilities, attention-deficit hyperactivity disorder, and autism.

Learning Disabilities

Children and adolescents with **learning disabilities** comprise the largest single category of individuals who receive special educational services (U.S. Department of Education, 1996). Although experts have not reached complete agreement about how best to define learning disabilities, most apply the following criteria when classifying a child as having a learning disability (Mercer, Jordan, Allsopp, & Mercer, 1996; National Joint Committee on Learning Disabilities, 1994):

■ *The child has significant difficulties in one or more specific cognitive processes.* For instance, the child may have difficulties in certain aspects of perception, language, memory, metacognition, or interpretation of social cues. Such difficulties are typically present throughout the individual's life and are assumed to result from a specific, possibly inherited neurological dysfunction (Light & Defries, 1995; Manis, 1996).

■ *The child's difficulties cannot be attributed to other disabilities, such as mental retardation, an emotional or behavioral disorder, hearing loss, or a visual impairment.* Many children with

learning disability
Significant deficit in one or more cognitive processes, to the point where special educational services are required.

OBSERVATION GUIDELINES

Assessing Cognitive Processing and Metacognitive Skills

CHARACTERISTIC	LOOK FOR	EXAMPLE	IMPLICATION
Intersubjectivity	• Reciprocal interaction with caregivers • Attempts to coordinate one's own actions toward an object with the actions of another person • Social referencing (i.e., responding to an object or event based on how an adult responds to it)	A child care provider is obviously frightened when a large dog appears just outside the fenced-in play yard, and she yells at him to go away. Fifteen-month-old Owen observes her reaction and begins to cry.	Regularly engage young infants in affectionate and playful interactions (smiles, coos, etc.). Remember that your own actions and reactions toward objects and events will communicate messages about the value, appeal, and safety of those objects and events.
Attention	• Sustained attention to both objects and human beings • Ability to stay on task for an age-appropriate period • On-task behavior when distracting stimuli are present	During after-lunch story time, a second-grade teacher has been reading Roald Dahl's *Charlie and the Chocolate Factory*. Most of the children are quiet and attentive the entire time, but Ben fidgets and squirms, and soon he finds a new form of entertainment: making silly faces at classmates sitting nearby.	Monitor children's ability to pay attention in an age-appropriate fashion. If children have exceptional difficulty staying on task, minimize distractions, teach them strategies for focusing their attention more effectively, and, if appropriate, encourage them to release pent-up energy in productive ways.
Automatization of Basic Skills	• Retrieval of simple facts in a rapid, effortless fashion • Ability to use simple problem-solving strategies quickly and efficiently	Elena easily solves the problem $\frac{4}{12} = \frac{x}{36}$ because she immediately reduces 4/12 to 1/3.	Give children numerous opportunities to use and practice essential facts and skills; do so within the context of interesting and motivating activities.
Learning Strategies	• Use of rehearsal in the elementary grades • Use of more integrative strategies (e.g., organization, elaboration) in the secondary grades • Flexible use of strategies for different learning tasks	Terry studies each new concept in her high school physics class by repeating the textbook definition aloud three or four times in a row. Later, she can barely remember the definitions she has studied, and she is unable to apply the concepts when trying to solve physics problems.	Show struggling learners that their difficulties may be due to ineffective strategies, and teach them strategies that can help them learn more successfully.
Self-Regulated Learning Capabilities	• Initiative in identifying and seeking out needed information • Intentional efforts to keep attention focused on an assigned task • Effective planning and time management • Realistic appraisal of what has and has not been learned	At wrestling practice one day, John tells his coach that he has just read several articles about the pros and cons of using steroids to increase muscle mass. "I'm a little confused about why most experts advise against them," he says. "Can you help me understand their logic?"	When youngsters fail to complete independent assignments in a timely or thorough manner, provide more structure for subsequent tasks. Gradually remove the structure over time as they become better able to regulate their own learning and performance.
Beliefs about Knowledge and Learning	• Optimism that knowledge and ability improve with practice and persistence • Striving to understand interrelationships among ideas • Comparing and evaluating various perspectives and theories	Several middle school students are studying for a test on westward migration in North America during the 1800s. Some students focus on cause-effect relationships among events. Others make a list of facts from the textbook and study them in a piecemeal fashion.	Convey the message that mastering a topic is an ongoing, lifelong enterprise that requires effort and persistence. Especially when working with adolescents, communicate that knowledge about a topic includes an understanding of how different ideas interrelate and a recognition that competing perspectives are not necessarily right or wrong.

learning disabilities have average or above-average intelligence. For example, they may obtain average scores on an intelligence test, or at least on some of its subtests.

■ *The child's difficulties interfere with academic achievement to such a degree that special educational services are warranted.* Children with learning disabilities invariably show poor performance in one or more specific areas of the academic curriculum; their achievement in those areas is much lower than would be expected based on their overall intelligence level. At the same time, they may exhibit achievement consistent with their intelligence in other subjects.

Several lines of research converge to indicate that learning disabilities often have a biological basis. Some children with learning abilities have minor abnormalities in parts of the brain involved in language processing (Manis, 1996). Some are prone to "interference" from signals in the brain that are irrelevant to the task at hand (Dempster & Corkill, 1999). Furthermore, learning disabilities often run in families (Light & Defries, 1995; Oliver, Cole, & Hollingsworth, 1991).

Children identified as having a learning disability are a particularly heterogeneous group: They are far more different than they are similar (Bassett et al., 1996; Chalfant, 1989; National Joint Committee on Learning Disabilities, 1994). Yet teachers and other practitioners are likely to see several characteristics in many of them. Children with learning disabilities may take a "passive" approach to learning rather than actively involving themselves in a learning task; for instance, they may stare at a textbook without thinking about the meaning of the words printed on the page. They are less likely to be aware of and use effective learning and problem-solving strategies. Some of them appear to have less working memory capacity than their age-mates, and so they have difficulty engaging in several cognitive processes simultaneously (Brownell, Mellard, & Deshler, 1993; Mercer, 1997; Swanson, 1993; A. Turnbull et al., 2002; Wong, 1991).

Children with learning disabilities typically have less effective learning and memory skills than their classmates and so may need extra structure and guidance to help them study effectively.

Learning disabilities may manifest themselves somewhat differently in elementary and secondary school (J. W. Lerner, 1985). At the elementary level, students with learning disabilities are likely to exhibit poor attention and motor skills and often have trouble acquiring one or more basic skills. As they reach the upper elementary grades, they may also begin to show emotional problems, due at least partly to frustration about their repeated academic failures. In the secondary school grades, difficulties with attention and motor skills may diminish. But at this level, students with learning disabilities may be particularly susceptible to emotional problems. Besides dealing with the usual emotional issues of adolescence (e.g., dating, peer pressure), they must also deal with the more stringent demands of the junior high and high school curriculum. Learning in secondary schools is highly dependent on reading and learning from relatively sophisticated textbooks, yet the average high school student with a learning disability reads at a third- to fifth-grade level and has acquired few if any effective study strategies (Alley & Deshler, 1979; Ellis & Friend, 1991; Heward, 1996). Perhaps for these reasons, adolescents with learning disabilities are often among those students most at risk for failure and dropping out of school (Barga, 1996).

Attention-Deficit Hyperactivity Disorder

Children with **attention-deficit hyperactivity disorder (ADHD)** have either or both of the following characteristics (American Psychiatric Association, 1994; Barkley, 1998; Landau & McAninch, 1993):

- *Inattention.* Children with ADHD may have considerable difficulty focusing and maintaining attention on the task before them; they are easily distracted either by external stimuli or by internal thought processes. Inattentiveness may manifest itself in behaviors such as daydreaming, difficulty listening to and following directions, and an inability to persist at tasks that require sustained mental effort.
- *Hyperactivity and impulsivity.* Children with ADHD may seem to have an excess amount of energy; for instance, they are likely to be fidgety, move around at inappropriate times, talk excessively, and have difficulty working or playing quietly. They may also show such impulsive behaviors as blurting out answers, interrupting others, making careless mistakes, and acting without thinking about the potential consequences of behaviors.

In addition to inattentiveness, hyperactivity, and impulsivity, children identified as having ADHD may have difficulties with cognitive processing, academic achievement, interpersonal skills, or classroom behavior (Barkley, 1998; Claude & Firestone, 1995; Gresham & MacMillan, 1997; Grodzinsky & Diamond, 1992; Lorch et al., 1999). In adolescence, attention span and impulse control improve somewhat, and hyperactivity diminishes (Hart,

attention-deficit hyperactivity disorder (ADHD) Disability (probably biological in origin) characterized by inattention and/or hyperactivity and impulsive behavior.

Lahey, Loeber, Applegate, & Frick, 1995). Even so, adolescents with ADHD have more difficulty than their peers in successfully meeting the challenges of the teenage years—the physical changes of puberty, more complex classroom assignments, increasing demands for independent and responsible behavior, and so on—and they are more prone to tobacco and alcohol use, traffic accidents, and dropping out (Barkley, 1998; Whalen, Jamner, Henker, Delfino, & Lozano, 2002).

Regardless of the specific nature of a child's or adolescent's difficulties, a deficit in executive functioning (the elusive *central executive* we spoke of earlier)—and more specifically in the inhibition of inappropriate responses—may be at the heart of ADHD (Barkley, 1998; B. J. Casey, 2001). The condition is assumed to have a biological and possibly genetic origin (Barkley, 1998; Landau & McAninch, 1993). It seems to run in families, is three times as likely to be identified in boys as in girls, and is more frequently shared by identical twins than by fraternal twins (Conte, 1991; Faraone et al., 1995; Gillis, Gilger, Pennington, & DeFries, 1992). Once children have been identified as having ADHD, many of them can be helped to control their symptoms through a combination of medication (e.g., Ritalin) and specific instruction to promote more appropriate behavior (Barkley, 1998; Carlson, Pelham, Milich, & Dixon, 1992).

Autism

On the surface, **autism** appears to be more of a disability in social and emotional functioning than in cognitive processing. Probably its most central characteristic is a marked impairment in social interaction: Many children with autism form weak if any emotional attachments to other people and prefer to be alone (Denkla, 1986; Schreibman, 1988). They also show deficits in intersubjectivity (e.g., they seldom make eye contact or engage in joint attention) and theory of mind (e.g., they seem to have little awareness of their own thought processes and rarely if ever consider what others might be thinking) (Baron-Cohen, 1991; Gauvain, 2001; Ornstein, 1997). Several other characteristics are also common, including communication impairments (e.g., absent or delayed speech), repetitive behaviors (e.g., continually rocking or waving fingers in front of one's face), narrowly focused and odd interests (e.g., an unusual fascination with watches), and a strong need for a predictable environment (American Psychiatric Association, 1994; E. G. Carr et al., 1994; Dalrymple, 1995; Turnbull et al., 2002).

In recent years, theorists have begun to conceptualize autism as a *spectrum* of disorders, with some instances of the condition being more severe than others. For instance, children with *Asperger syndrome* share some features of autism—especially difficulties in thinking about and responding to social situations—but they develop language and do not display the repetitive behaviors associated with more extreme forms of the condition.

Autism is almost certainly caused by a brain abnormality (Dawson, Munson, et al., 2002; Gillberg & Coleman, 1996). Its origins are often genetic, and it is more commonly seen in males than females (Bristol et al., 1996; Bryson, 1997). Despite its apparent "social" nature, an information processing abnormality may be at its root. In many instances, areas of the brain that play a key role in thinking about social information are impaired (Dawson, Carver, et al., 2002; Leslie, 1991). Furthermore, some children with autism appear to have either an undersensitivity or an oversensitivity to sensory stimulation (R. C. Sullivan, 1994; Williams, 1996). Temple Grandin, a woman who has gained international prominence as a designer of livestock facilities, reflects on her childhood experiences with autism:

> From as far back as I can remember, I always hated to be hugged. I wanted to experience the good feeling of being hugged, but it was just too overwhelming. It was like a great, all-engulfing tidal wave of stimulation, and I reacted like a wild animal. . . .
>
> Shampooing actually hurt my scalp. It was as if the fingers rubbing my head had sewing thimbles on them. Scratchy petticoats were like sandpaper scraping away at raw nerve endings. . . .
>
> When I was little, loud noises were also a problem, often feeling like a dentist's drill hitting a nerve. They actually caused pain. I was scared to death of balloons popping, because the sound was like an explosion in my ear. Minor noises that most people can tune out drove me to distraction. (Grandin, 1995, pp. 63, 66, 67)

autism
Disability (probably biological in origin) characterized by infrequent social interaction, little awareness of one's own and others' thoughts, communication impairments, repetitive behaviors, narrowly focused interests, and a strong need for a predictable environment.

Grandin's reflections suggest that the abnormal behaviors so commonly associated with extreme forms of autism may reflect a child's attempts to make the environment more tolerable (E. G. Carr et al., 1994; Grandin, 1995). Social withdrawal and the desire for a predictable environment both help keep environmental stimulation at a comfortable level. Rocking behaviors, too, can help moderate stimulation, as Grandin explains:

> Rocking made me feel calm. It was like taking an addictive drug. The more I did it, the more I wanted to do it. (Grandin, 1995, p. 45)

Children and adolescents with autism often show great variability in their cognitive abilities (American Psychiatric Association, 1994). Some have exceptional strengths in visual-spatial skills (Grandin, 1995; Williams, 1996). In a few instances, children and adolescents with autism possess an extraordinary ability, such as exceptional musical talent, that is quite remarkable in contrast to other aspects of their mental functioning (Cheatham, Smith, Rucker, Polloway, & Lewis, 1995; Treffert, 1989; Winner, 2000b).

Working with Children Who Have Information Processing Difficulties

Learning disabilities, ADHD, and autism are each fairly heterogeneous categories. Hence, teachers and other practitioners who work with children in any single category must consider the unique needs of every child. For example, some children with learning disabilities may need intensive instruction in reading, others may require assistance with writing, and still others may benefit from training in specific learning strategies. Here we offer a few general suggestions applicable to many children with information processing difficulties:

■ *Help children keep their attention on the task at hand.* Many children with information processing difficulties are easily distracted. Thus, adults who work with them should minimize the presence of other stimuli likely to compete for their attention, perhaps by finding a quiet room for tasks requiring considerable concentration or pulling down window shades when appealing alternatives lurk outside. Many children also benefit from specific training in attention-focusing strategies, such as keeping one's eyes directed toward a speaker or moving to a new location if the current one presents too many distracting sights and sounds (Buchoff, 1990).

■ *Teach strategies for controlling hyperactivity and impulsivity.* All children, but especially those with information processing difficulties, need regular opportunities to release pent-up energy, perhaps in the form of recess, sports, or hands-on activities (Barkley, 1998; Panksepp, 1998). In addition, after a period of high activity, adults might give children a "settling-in" time that allows them to calm down gradually (Pellegrini & Horvat, 1995); as an example, when children return from lunch, many elementary teachers begin the afternoon by reading a chapter from a high-interest storybook. Teaching children to use self-talk can also help them resist the tendency to respond too quickly and impulsively to situations and problems (Meichenbaum & Goodman, 1971).

■ *Provide extra scaffolding for studying, doing homework, and completing other learning tasks.* Children with information processing difficulties often need considerable support for learning tasks, especially those they complete on their own (e.g., Bryan, Burstein, & Bryan, 2001). Such support might take a variety of forms—suggestions for taking notes, handouts that enumerate major ideas, memory tricks for remembering particular tidbits of information (e.g., using HOMES to remember the five Great Lakes: Huron, Ontario, Michigan, Erie, and Superior), to-do lists for checking off when specific tasks have been completed, and so on.

When children have information processing difficulties, adults should minimize the presence of distracting stimuli that may compete for their attention. This girl, who has autism, works best in a classroom that is not crowded or noisy.

■ *Keep the daily schedule and physical environment relatively predictable.* Some novelty in activities does wonders for maintaining children's interest and motivation (Renninger, Hidi, & Krapp, 1992). But a day that has surprises around every corner may arouse excessive anxiety in some children, and such anxiety interferes with effective information processing (Eysenck, 1992; Lazarus, 1991). Furthermore, many children with autism find comfort and security in the predictability of their surroundings. To maintain some sense of predictability, teachers and others who work with children who have disabilities might schedule certain activities at the same time each day or on a particular day of each week (Dalrymple, 1995). When there is a change in the schedule (perhaps because of a fire drill or field trip), they should give children advance warning of the change and indicate when the schedule will be back to normal (Dalrymple, 1995). And if the group includes one or more children with autism, furniture and equipment should be rearranged infrequently, if at all.

■ *Teach social skills.* Some children with learning disabilities have difficulty processing social information, some with ADHD behave so impulsively that they alienate their peers, and as a general rule children with autism have significant impairments in social interaction. These children stand to benefit from specific training in social skills, which can enhance their interpersonal effectiveness (e.g., Cunningham & Cunningham, 1998; Williams, Donley, & Keller, 2000). In Chapter 13, we identify a variety of strategies for promoting effective interaction with others.

Children with learning disabilities, ADHD, and autism are not the only ones who have trouble processing and learning information. As a general rule, *children and adolescents process information less effectively than adults do.* The final case study provides a clear example.

CASE STUDY: THE LIBRARY PROJECT

In the final year of her teacher education program, Jessica Jensen is a teacher intern in four eighth-grade social studies classes. She has recently assigned a month-long group project that involves considerable library research. Midway through the project, Jess writes the following entry in her journal:

> Within each group, one student is studying culture of the region, one has religion, one has economy, and one government. The point is for the students to become "experts" on their topic in their region. There are a lot of requirements to this assignment. I'm collecting things as we go along because I think a project this long will be difficult for them to organize. . . .
>
> So we spent all week in the library. I collected a minimum of two pages of notes yesterday, which will be a small part of their grade. The one thing that surprised me in our work in the library was their lack of skills. They had such difficulty researching, finding the information they needed, deciding what was important, and organizing and taking notes. As they worked, I walked around helping and was shocked. The librarian had already gotten out all of the appropriate resources. Even after they had the books in front of them, most did not know what to do. For instance, if they were assigned "economy," most looked in the index for that particular word. If they didn't find it, they gave up on the book. After realizing this, I had to start the next day with a brief lesson on researching and cross-referencing. I explained how they could look up *commerce, imports, exports,* and how these would all help them. I was also shocked at how poor their note-taking skills were. I saw a few kids copying paragraphs word for word. Almost none of them understood that notes don't need to be in full sentences. So, it was a long week at the library.
>
> Next week is devoted to group work and time to help them work on their rough drafts. With the difficulty they had researching, I can imagine the problems that will arise out of turning their notes into papers. (Courtesy of Jessica Jensen)

- Initially, the intern realizes that her students will need some structure to complete the project successfully. In what ways do she and the librarian structure the assignment for the students?
- What specific strategies do the students use as they engage in their library research? In what ways are their strategies less effective than an adult's might be?
- How does the students' prior knowledge (or lack thereof) influence the effectiveness of their strategies?

Now go to our Companion Website to assess your understanding of chapter content with a Practice Quiz, apply what you've learned in Essay Questions, and broaden your knowledge with links to related Developmental Psychology Web sites. Go to www.prenhall.com/mcdevitt.

SUMMARY

Information Processing Theory

Information processing theory focuses on how children receive, think about, mentally modify, and remember information, and on how these cognitive processes change over the course of development. Information processing theorists propose that cognitive capabilities improve with age and experience; such improvements take the form of gradual trends rather than discrete stages. Young infants have many sensory and perceptual capabilities at birth or soon thereafter. In general, however, children are less efficient learners than adults are; for instance, they have shorter attention spans, a smaller working memory capacity, and a smaller and less integrated knowledge base to which they can relate new information.

Development of Metacognition and Cognitive Strategies

The term *metacognition* encompasses both the knowledge that people have about their own cognitive processes and their intentional use of certain cognitive processes to facilitate learning and memory. Children's metacognitive knowledge and cognitive strategies improve throughout the school years. For instance, children become more proficient in such learning strategies as rehearsal, organization, and elaboration, and they acquire increasingly powerful and effective ways of solving problems. With age, they become more aware of the nature of thinking, learning, and knowledge, and they develop strategies for regulating their own learning.

Theory Theory

Some theorists propose that children gradually construct integrated belief systems (theories) about the physical world, the biological world, the social world, and mental events. Such theories are not always accurate; for instance, children's theories about the physical world may include erroneous beliefs about the solar system and laws of motion. To the extent that children's theories include misconceptions, they may interfere with children's ability to acquire more sophisticated understandings.

Neo-Piagetian Theories

Neo-Piagetian theories combine elements of Piaget's theory with concepts from information processing theory. Neo-Piagetians reject Piaget's proposal that children acquire a single system of logical operations. Instead, they suggest that children acquire several more specific systems of concepts and thinking skills relevant to particular content domains (e.g., Robbie Case proposed that specific systems develop for social thought, spatial relationships, and number). Many neo-Piagetians also suggest that these systems develop in a stagelike manner, with slowly maturing information processing mechanisms (e.g., working memory capacity) setting an upper limit on the complexity of thinking and reasoning skills that can emerge at a particular age.

Combining Theoretical Perspectives

Each of the theories we've examined in Chapters 4 and 5 provides helpful insights into the nature of cognitive development. Although these theories are sometimes incompatible (e.g., neo-Piagetian theorists propose discrete stages, whereas information processing theorists propose more gradual trends), in many instances elements of two or more theories can effectively be combined to give us a better understanding of how and why children's cognitive abilities improve with age. For instance, when we draw from both sociocultural theory and information processing theory, we discover some of the mechanisms through which adults can help children acquire more effective cognitive strategies.

Exceptionalities in Information Processing

The information processing capabilities of some children are different enough that they require the use of specially adapted instructional practices and materials. Children with learning disabilities have significant difficulties in one or more specific cognitive processes. Children with attention-deficit hyperactivity disorder (ADHD) have difficulty focusing attention on assigned tasks and/or are unusually hyperactive and impulsive for their age group. Children with autism exhibit a marked impairment in social interaction, perhaps as a result of deficits in certain areas of the brain or of extreme undersensitivity or oversensitivity to sensory stimulation.

KEY CONCEPTS

information processing theory (p. 186)
sensation (p. 187)
perception (p. 187)
sensory register (p. 187)
working memory (p. 187)
long-term memory (p. 187)
central executive (p. 188)
habituation (p. 189)
automatization (p. 193)
infantile amnesia (p. 194)

knowledge base (p. 195)
schema (p. 195)
script (p. 195)
symbol (p. 197)
metacognition (p. 200)
cognitive strategy (p. 200)
learning strategy (p. 202)
rehearsal (p. 202)
organization (p. 202)
elaboration (p. 203)
metacognitive awareness (p. 206)

self-regulated learning (p. 208)
comprehension monitoring (p. 209)
co-regulated learning (p. 210)
epistemological beliefs (p. 210)
theory theory (p. 216)
conceptual change (p. 220)
neo-Piagetian theory (p. 220)
structure (in neo-Piagetian theory) (p. 220)

central conceptual structure (p. 221)
intersubjectivity (p. 226)
joint attention (p. 226)
social referencing (p. 226)
learning disability (p. 229)
attention-deficit hyperactivity disorder (ADHD) (p. 231)
autism (p. 232)

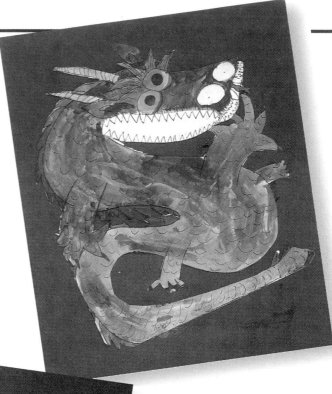

Aftyn, age 9

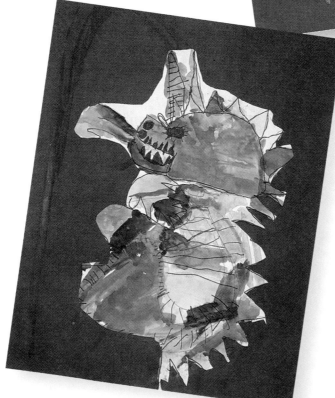

Amber, age 9

Intelligence

CASE STUDY: GINA

Seventeen-year-old Gina has always been a good student. In elementary school, she consistently achieved straight As on her report cards until finally, in sixth grade, she broke the pattern by getting a B in history. Since then, she has earned a few more Bs, but As continue to dominate her record. Her performance has been highest in her advanced mathematics courses, where she easily grasps the abstract concepts and principles that many of her classmates find difficult to understand.

Gina has other talents as well. She won her high school's creative writing contest two years in a row. She has landed challenging roles in her school's drama productions. And as the president of the National Honor Society in her senior year, she has masterfully coordinated a schoolwide peer tutoring program to assist struggling students.

Gina's teachers describe her as a "bright" young woman. Her friends affectionately call her a "brainiac." Test results in her school file bear out their assessments: An intelligence test that she took in junior high school yielded a score of 140, and this year she performed at the 99th percentile on college aptitude tests.

This is not to say that Gina is strong in every arena. She shows little artistic ability in her paintings or clay sculptures. Her piano playing is mediocre despite five years of weekly lessons. In athletic events, she has little stamina, strength, or flexibility. She is shy and unsure of herself at social events. And she hasn't earned an A in history since fifth grade, in large part because she studies ineffectively by simply memorizing people, places, and dates.

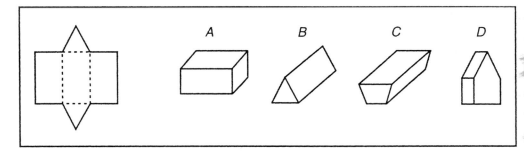

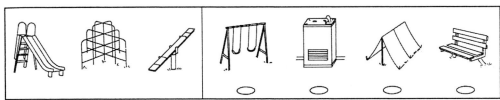

See the slide, the jungle gym and the teeter-totter. Which one belongs with them?

Some school districts, like Gina's, administer general or specific measures of cognitive ability periodically throughout the school years. Such tests typically focus on reasoning and problem-solving skills, perhaps about verbal, mathematical, or spatial material. The top item involves spatial reasoning and might be appropriate for older children and adolescents. The lower item requires children to identify similarities among objects and would be read to children in the primary grades.

Drawings from *Measurement and Evaluation in Psychology and Education,* 6th edition (pp. 243, 251), by R. M. Thorndike, 1997, Upper Saddle River, NJ: Merrill/Prentice Hall. Reprinted by permission of Pearson Education, Inc., Upper Saddle River, NJ 07458.

As we examined cognitive development in Chapters 4 and 5, we focused primarily on what cognitive abilities and processes are typical for children of various ages. As we address the topic of *intelligence* in this chapter, we focus more on the differences among children in any single age group.

Psychologists don't all agree about what intelligence is. However, many use the term when they are talking about consistently high performance across time and across a variety of tasks. Gina's performance reflects both kinds of consistency: She has earned high marks throughout her school career, and she achieves at high levels in many areas. Yet intelligence is not necessarily a permanent, set-in-concrete characteristic that people either do or do not have. Children's intelligence can, and often does, change with age and experience. Furthermore, children can behave more or less "intelligently" depending on the circumstances.

In this chapter, we consider the nature of intelligence from diverse theoretical perspectives. We look at how intelligence is often measured and how IQ scores are derived. We devote much of the remainder of the chapter to the **psychometric approach** to cognitive development, an approach that focuses on how children's performance on intelligence tests changes over time and how IQ scores are related to other characteristics and behaviors that children exhibit. In the process, we explore controversies about the relative effects of heredity and environment and the origins of group differences in IQ scores. Finally, we consider the two ends of the intelligence continuum: giftedness and mental retardation.

Defining Intelligence

Theorists define and conceptualize intelligence in many different ways, but most agree that it has several distinctive qualities:

- It is *adaptive*, such that it can be used flexibly to respond to a variety of situations and problems.
- It involves *learning ability*: People who are intelligent in particular domains learn new information and behaviors more quickly and easily than people who are less intelligent in those domains.
- It involves the *use of prior knowledge* to analyze and understand new situations effectively.
- It involves the complex interaction and coordination of *many different mental processes*.
- It is *culture-specific*. What is "intelligent" behavior in one culture is not necessarily intelligent behavior in another culture.
  (Greenfield, 1998; Laboratory of Human Cognition, 1982; Neisser et al., 1996; Sternberg, 1997; Sternberg & Detterman, 1986)

With these qualities in mind, we offer one possible (but intentionally broad) definition of **intelligence:** the ability to benefit from experiences and thereby modify future behaviors to accomplish new tasks successfully.

For most theorists, intelligence is somewhat distinct from what an individual has actually learned (e.g., as reflected in school achievement). At the same time, intelligent thinking and intelligent behavior inevitably *depend* on prior learning to some degree. The more people know about their environment and about the tasks they need to perform, the more intelligently they can behave.

psychometric approach
Approach to cognitive development that focuses on children's performance on intelligence tests.

intelligence
Ability to modify and adjust one's behaviors in order to accomplish new tasks successfully.

Theoretical Perspectives of Intelligence

Some theorists have suggested that intelligence is a single, general ability that affects performance on many different tasks. Historically, considerable evidence has supported this idea (McGrew, Flanagan, Zeith, & Vanderwood, 1997; Neisser et al., 1996; Spearman, 1927). Although different measures of intelligence yield somewhat different scores, they all correlate with one another: People who score high on one measure tend to score high on others as well. Even tests with two different kinds of content (e.g., a verbal test based on knowledge of vocabulary and a nonverbal test based on ability to find patterns in geometric designs) tend to correlate with one another (N. Brody, 1985; Carroll, 1992; Spearman, 1904).

However, the correlations are not perfect: People who get the highest scores on one test do not always get the highest scores on another test. For instance, children and adolescents who demonstrate exceptional ability in some areas of the school curriculum may exhibit only average performance in others (e.g., remember Gina's high performance in mathematics and writing but average performance in art and music). Therefore, not all psychologists believe that intelligence is a single entity that people "have" in varying amounts; instead, some propose that people may be more or less intelligent in different situations and on different kinds of tasks. In this section, we present five theoretical perspectives on the single-entity versus multiple-abilities nature of intelligence.

Spearman's *g*

In the early 1900s, Charles Spearman (1904, 1927) proposed that intelligence comprises both a single, pervasive reasoning ability (a *general factor*) that is used on a wide variety of tasks and a number of narrow abilities (*specific factors*) involved in executing particular tasks. From Spearman's perspective, people's performance on any given task depends both on the general factor and on any specific factors that the task may involve. To the extent that two tasks or tests tap into the general factor and the same specific factor(s), people's performance on the two will be highly intercorrelated. To the extent that two tasks or tests reflect one or more dissimilar specific factors, the correlation between them will be somewhat lower. For example, measures of various language skills (vocabulary, word recognition, reading comprehension, etc.) are all highly correlated, presumably because they all reflect both general intelligence and verbal ability (a specific factor). A particular measure of verbal ability (e.g., a vocabulary test) will correlate less highly with a measure of mathematical problem solving: The two measures both reflect general intelligence but tap into different specific abilities.

Many contemporary psychologists believe that sufficient evidence supports Spearman's concept of a general factor—often known simply as Spearman's **g**—in intelligence and that the ability to process information quickly may be at its root. Researchers often find substantial correlations between measures of information processing speed (e.g., reaction times to familiar stimuli) and IQ scores (Brody, 1992; Fry & Hale, 1996; Vernon, 1993). For example, children who, as infants, habituate very quickly to new visual stimuli (recall our discussion of *habituation* in Chapters 2 and 5) tend to have substantially higher IQ scores in childhood and adolescence (Dougherty & Haith, 1997; McCall & Mash, 1995; S. A. Rose & Feldman, 1995; L. A. Thompson, Fagan, & Fulker, 1991). Not all theorists agree that a g factor exists, however: Whether researchers find evidence for a single general factor in cognitive abilities depends on the specific abilities measured and on the statistical methods used to analyze the data (Neisser, 1998a; R. J. Sternberg & Grigorenko, 2000).

Spearman's concept of g reflects the idea that intelligence may involve a general ability to think and reason about a wide variety of tasks. Some evidence indicates that an ability to process information quickly may be at its core.

Cattell's Fluid and Crystallized Intelligence

Cattell (1963, 1987) has found evidence for two distinctly different components of general intelligence (*g*). First, people differ in **fluid intelligence** (g_f), their ability to acquire knowledge quickly and thereby to adapt to new situations. Second, people differ in **crystallized intelligence** (g_c), the knowledge and skills they have accumulated from their experiences and schooling. These two components may be more or less relevant to different kinds of tasks. Fluid intelligence relates more to novel tasks, especially those that require rapid decision making and are largely nonverbal in nature. Crystallized intelligence is more important for familiar tasks, especially those that are heavily dependent on language and prior knowledge.

According to Cattell, fluid intelligence is largely the result of inherited biological factors, whereas crystallized intelligence depends on both fluid intelligence and experience and so is influenced by both heredity and environment (Cattell, 1980, 1987). Fluid intelligence peaks in late adolescence and begins to decline in the early 20s. In contrast, crystallized intelligence continues to increase throughout childhood, adolescence, and most of adulthood (Cattell, 1963).

g
General factor in intelligence that influences performance in a wide variety of tasks and content domains.

fluid intelligence
Ability to acquire knowledge quickly and thereby adapt readily to new situations.

crystallized intelligence
Knowledge and skills accumulated from prior experience and schooling.

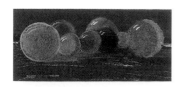

In Gardner's theory of multiple intelligences, the ability to draw lifelike renditions of three-dimensional objects falls in the domain of spatial intelligence. Art by Oscar, seventh grade (top) and Daniela, eighth grade (bottom).

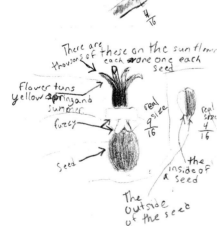

As she documents what she observes on a sunflower, 10-year-old Amaryth reveals her naturalist intelligence.

Yet most psychologists (including Spearman and Cattell themselves) have acknowledged that neither a single *g* factor nor a distinction between g_f and g_c can account for all aspects of intelligent behavior—that more domain-specific abilities play a role as well. Furthermore, Spearman's and Cattell's approaches were almost entirely statistical in nature: Both theorists mathematically analyzed the interrelationships among people's scores on a variety of tests of cognitive ability. The two theorists we consider next, while not discounting the value of a statistical approach, have considered other evidence as well, and they have reached somewhat different conclusions about the nature of intelligence.

Gardner's Multiple Intelligences

Howard Gardner acknowledges that a general factor may very well exist in intelligence, but he questions its usefulness in explaining people's performance in particular situations (Gardner, 1995). He proposes that people have several more specific abilities, or *multiple intelligences*, that are relatively independent of one another. Initially, Gardner identified seven distinct intelligences: linguistic, logical-mathematical, spatial, musical, bodily-kinesthetic, interpersonal, and intrapersonal (Gardner, 1983, 1993; Gardner & Hatch, 1990). More recently, he has found evidence for an eighth intelligence: naturalist (Gardner, 1999). Gardner's eight intelligences are described and illustrated in Table 6–1.[1]

Gardner presents some evidence to support the existence of multiple intelligences. For instance, he describes people who are quite skilled in one area (perhaps in composing music) and yet have seemingly average abilities in the other areas. He also points out that people who suffer brain damage sometimes lose abilities that are restricted primarily to one intelligence; for instance, one person might show deficits primarily in language, whereas another might have difficulty with tasks that require spatial reasoning.

According to Gardner, intelligence is reflected somewhat differently in different cultures, depending on how each culture shapes and molds the raw talents of its growing children. For example, in Western culture, spatial intelligence might be reflected in painting, sculpture, or geometry. But among the Gikwe bushmen of the Kalahari Desert, it might be reflected in the ability to recognize and remember many specific locations over a large area (perhaps over several hundred square miles), identifying each location by the rocks, bushes, and other landmarks found there (Gardner, 1983).

Gardner's perspective offers the possibility that the great majority of children are intelligent in one way or another. Many educators have wholeheartedly embraced such an optimistic view of human potential and propose that all students can successfully master classroom subject matter when instructional methods capitalize on each student's particular intellectual strengths (e.g., Armstrong, 1994; L. Campbell, Campbell, & Dickinson, 1998).

In psychological circles, however, reviews of Gardner's theory are mixed. Some psychologists do not believe that Gardner's evidence is sufficiently compelling to support the notion of eight distinctly different abilities (Brody, 1992; Kail, 1998). Others agree that people may have a variety of relatively independent abilities but argue for intelligences other than the ones Gardner has described (e.g., Horn & Noll, 1997; R. J. Sternberg et al., 2000). Still others reject the idea that abilities in specific domains, such as in music or bodily movement, are really "intelligence" per se (Bracken, McCallum, & Shaughnessy, 1999; Sattler, 2001).

Sternberg's Triarchic Theory

Whereas Gardner focuses on different kinds of intelligence, Robert Sternberg (1984, 1985, 1997, 1998) focuses more on the nature of intelligence itself. Drawing on findings from research on human information processing, Sternberg proposes that intelligent behavior involves an interplay of three factors, all of which may vary from one occasion to the next: (1) the environmental *context* in which the behavior occurs, (2) the way in which one's prior *experiences* are brought to bear on

---

[1]Gardner (1999) has also suggested the possibility of a ninth intelligence, *existential intelligence,* but acknowledges that evidence for it is relatively weak.

TABLE 6-1 Gardner's Eight Intelligences

TYPE OF INTELLIGENCE	EXAMPLES OF RELEVANT BEHAVIORS
Linguistic intelligence The ability to use language effectively	• Making persuasive arguments • Writing poetry • Identifying subtle nuances in word meanings
Logical-mathematical intelligence The ability to reason logically, especially in mathematics and science	• Solving mathematical problems quickly • Generating mathematical proofs • Formulating and testing hypotheses about observed phenomena[1]
Spatial intelligence The ability to notice details of what one sees and to imagine and "manipulate" visual objects in one's mind	• Conjuring up mental images in one's mind • Drawing a visual likeness of an object • Making fine discriminations among very similar objects
Musical intelligence The ability to create, comprehend, and appreciate music	• Playing a musical instrument • Composing a musical work • Having a keen awareness of the underlying structure of music
Bodily-kinesthetic intelligence The ability to use one's body skillfully	• Dancing • Playing basketball • Performing pantomime
Interpersonal intelligence The ability to notice subtle aspects of other people's behaviors	• Reading another's mood • Detecting another's underlying intentions and desires • Using knowledge of others to influence their thoughts and behaviors
Intrapersonal intelligence Awareness of one's own feelings, motives, and desires	• Discriminating among such similar emotions as sadness and regret • Identifying the motives guiding one's own behavior • Using self-knowledge to relate more effectively with others
Naturalist intelligence The ability to recognize patterns in nature and differences among natural objects and life-forms	• Identifying members of various species • Classifying natural forms (e.g., rocks, types of mountains) • Applying one's knowledge of nature in such activities as farming, landscaping, or hunting

[1]This example may remind you of Piaget's theory of cognitive development. Many of the stage-relevant characteristics that Piaget described fall within the realm of logical-mathematical intelligence.

a particular task, and (3) the *cognitive processes* required by that task. These three dimensions are summarized in Figure 6–1.

Role of Environmental Context Sternberg proposes that intelligent behavior involves adaptation: People must modify their responses to deal successfully with specific environmental conditions, modify the environment to better fit their own needs, or select an alternative environment more conducive to success. He also proposes that behavior may be more or less intelligent in different cultural contexts. For example, learning to read is an adaptive response in some cultures yet may be an irrelevant skill in others.

Sternberg has identified three general skills that are particularly adaptive in Western culture. One is *practical problem-solving ability*, such as the ability to identify exactly what the problem is in a particular situation, reason logically about the problem, and generate a multitude of possible problem solutions. A second skill is *verbal ability*, such as the ability to speak and write clearly, develop and use a large vocabulary, and understand and learn from what one reads. A third skill is *social competence*, such as the ability to relate effectively to other human beings, be sensitive to others' needs and wishes, and provide leadership.

Role of Prior Experiences Sternberg proposes that intelligent behavior sometimes involves the ability to deal successfully with a brand-new situation; at other times, it involves the ability to deal with familiar situations rapidly and efficiently. In both cases, an individual's prior

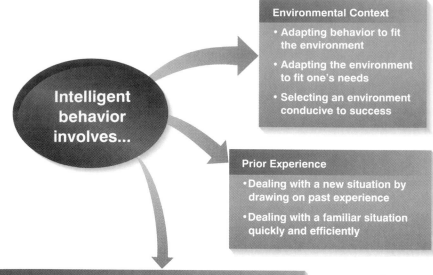

experiences play a critical role. When people encounter a new task or problem, they must draw on past experience and consider the kinds of responses that have been effective in similar circumstances. When they deal with more familiar tasks, basic knowledge and skills related to the task must be sufficiently *automatized* that the task can be completed quickly and effortlessly. As noted in Chapter 5, automatization results from experience—from retrieving certain information and using certain skills over and over again.

Role of Cognitive Processes   In addition to considering how context and prior experience affect behavior, we must also consider how a person thinks about (mentally processes) a particular task or situation. Sternberg proposes that numerous cognitive processes are involved in intelligent behavior: interpreting a new situation in ways that promote successful adaptation, sustaining concentration on a task, separating important and relevant information from unimportant and irrelevant details, identifying possible strategies for solving a problem, finding relationships among seemingly different ideas, making effective use of external feedback about one's performance, and so on. Different cognitive processes are likely to be relevant to different situations, and thus an individual may behave more or less "intelligently" depending on the specific cognitive processes needed at the time.

FIGURE 6-1   Sternberg's triarchic model of intelligence

To date, research neither supports nor refutes the notion that intelligence has the triarchic nature Sternberg describes. In fact, certain aspects of Sternberg's theory (e.g., how the three factors work together, what specific roles metacognition plays) are described in such general terms that they are difficult to test empirically (Sattler, 2001; Siegler, 1998).

Nevertheless, Sternberg's theory helps us understand intelligence in terms of the specific information processing mechanisms that may underlie it. Furthermore, it reminds us that a child's ability to behave intelligently may vary considerably, depending on the particular context and specific knowledge, skills, and cognitive processes that a task requires. Some theorists believe that context makes all the difference in the world—a belief that is clearly evident in the concept of distributed intelligence.

Distributed Intelligence

Implicit in our discussion so far has been the assumption that intelligent behavior is something that individuals engage in with little if any help from the objects or people around them. But some psychologists point out that people are far more likely to behave intelligently when they have the support of their physical, social, and cultural environments (Pea, 1993; D. N. Perkins, 1995; Sternberg & Wagner, 1994). For example, it's easier for many people to solve for *x* in the equation

$$\frac{7}{25} = \frac{x}{375}$$

if they have pencil and paper, or perhaps even a calculator, with which to work out the problem. They are also more likely to write a convincing persuasive essay if they brainstorm with their peers about arguments to make in support of a particular opinion. As we noted in Chapter 4, virtually anyone can perform more difficult tasks when he or she has the support structure, or *scaffolding,* to do so.

This idea that intelligent behavior depends on people's physical, social, and cultural support systems is sometimes referred to as **distributed intelligence**. People can "distribute" their thinking (and therefore think more intelligently) in at least three ways (Pea, 1993; D. N. Perkins, 1992, 1995). First, they can use physical objects, and especially technology (e.g., calculators, computers), to handle and manipulate large amounts of information. Second, they can work with other people to explore ideas and solve problems. Third, they can represent and think about the situations they encounter using the various symbolic systems that their culture provides—for instance, the words, diagrams, charts, mathematical equations, and so on that help them simplify or summarize complex topics and problems.

From this perspective, intelligence is not a characteristic that resides "inside" people, nor is it something that can be easily measured and then summarized with a single test score. Instead, it is a highly variable and context-specific ability that virtually anyone can possess when the appropriate support system is available. The concept of distributed intelligence is still in its infancy, however. Much work remains to be done, both in delineating the specific ways in which the environment supports intelligent behavior and in determining how great an effect such support is likely to have.

The five perspectives just presented provide widely diverging views of the nature of human intelligence. Their differences with respect to the three themes—nature and nurture, universality and diversity, and qualitative and quantitative change—are presented in the Basic Developmental Issues table "Contrasting Theories of Intelligence." We turn now to a related topic: how various theorists have attempted to measure intelligence.

The concept of distributed intelligence reminds us that children and adolescents often perform more intelligently when they work with others to tackle problems, have symbolic systems such as charts and equations to represent and transform information, and use computers to organize and manipulate data.

Measuring Intelligence

Although psychologists have not been able to agree on what intelligence is, they have been trying to measure it for almost a century. In the early 1900s, school officials in France asked the psychologist Alfred Binet to develop a way of identifying students who were unlikely to benefit from regular school instruction and would therefore be in need of special education. To accomplish the task, Binet devised a test that measured general knowledge, vocabulary, perception, memory, and abstract thought. He found that students who performed poorly on his test tended to have difficulty performing successfully in the classroom as well. Binet's test was the earliest version of what we now call an **intelligence test**. Today, intelligence tests are widely used to assess children's cognitive functioning and predict academic achievement, especially when a child may possibly have special needs.

Tests of General Intelligence

Most intelligence tests in use today have been developed to do the same thing that Alfred Binet's first test was intended to do: identify people with special needs. In many cases, intelligence tests are used as part of a diagnostic battery of tests to determine why certain children are showing developmental delays or academic difficulties and whether they require special interventions or educational services. In other instances, intelligence tests are used to identify children with exceptionally high ability who are probably not being challenged by the regular school curriculum and may require more in-depth instruction or advanced classwork for their cognitive growth.

Intelligence tests typically include a wide variety of questions and problems for children to tackle. The focus is not on what children have specifically been taught at school, but rather on what they have learned and deduced from their general, everyday experiences. Most intelligence tests include measures of deductive reasoning and problem solving. Many include questions involving general knowledge and vocabulary that most children have presumably encountered in everyday life at one time or another. Some tests include analogies that tap the ability to recognize similarities among well-known relationships. And some ask children to manipulate concrete objects and analyze pictures and spatial relationships.

Examples of General Intelligence Tests To give you a feel for the nature of general intelligence tests, we briefly describe three of them.

distributed intelligence
Thinking facilitated by physical objects and technology, social support, and concepts and symbols of one's culture.

intelligence test
General measure of current cognitive functioning, used primarily to predict academic achievement over the short run.

BASIC DEVELOPMENTAL ISSUES

Contrasting Theories of Intelligence

ISSUE	SPEARMAN'S GENERAL FACTOR (g)	CATTELL'S FLUID AND CRYSTALLIZED INTELLIGENCE	GARDNER'S MULTIPLE INTELLIGENCES	STERNBERG'S TRIARCHIC THEORY	DISTRIBUTED INTELLIGENCE
Nature and Nurture	Spearman did not specifically address the issue of nature versus nurture. Subsequent researchers have found evidence that g is probably influenced by both heredity and environment.	Cattell proposed that fluid intelligence is largely the result of inherited factors. Crystallized intelligence is influenced by both heredity (because it depends partly on fluid intelligence) and environmental experiences.	Gardner believes that heredity provides some basis for individual differences in the eight intelligences. However, culture influences the form that each intelligence takes, and formal schooling influences the extent to which each intelligence flourishes.	Sternberg emphasizes the roles of environmental context (e.g., culture) and prior experience in intelligent behavior; thus, his focus is on nurture.	Environmental support mechanisms (physical tools, social interaction, and the symbolic representations of one's culture) influence a person's ability to behave intelligently.
Universality and Diversity	Spearman assumed that the existence of g is universal across cultures. However, people vary both in their general intellectual ability and in more specific abilities.	The distinction between fluid and crystallized intelligence is applicable across cultures. People within a particular culture differ in their fluid and crystallized abilities. In addition, the nature of crystallized intelligence (i.e., what specific knowledge and skills are important) varies from one cultural setting to another.	According to Gardner, the eight intelligences are products of human evolution and so are seen worldwide. However, any particular intelligence will manifest itself differently in different environments and cultures.	The three factors of the triarchy (context, experience, cognitive processes) are universal. Different cultures may value and require different skills, however, so intelligence may take particular forms in each culture.	The physical, social, and symbolic support mechanisms at one's disposal vary widely from situation to situation and from one cultural group to another.
Qualitative and Quantitative Change	Spearman derived his theory from various tests of cognitive abilities. Implicit in such tests is the assumption that abilities change quantitatively over time.	Cattell, too, based his theory on numerical measures of various abilities. Thus, his emphasis was on quantitative changes in both fluid and crystallized intelligence.	Growth in each intelligence has both quantitative and qualitative elements. For example, in logical-mathematical intelligence, children gain skills in increments (quantitatively) but also acquire increasingly complex (and qualitatively different) abilities.	The effects of relevant prior experiences, more automatized knowledge and skills, and more efficient cognitive processes involve quantitative change. The acquisition of new strategies over time involves qualitative change.	Intelligent behavior is situation-specific and dependent on qualitative differences in context from one occasion to the next.

Wechsler Intelligence Scale for Children. One widely used intelligence test for children and adolescents is the third edition of the *Wechsler Intelligence Scale for Children*, or *WISC-III* (Wechsler, 1991), which is designed for children and adolescents ages 6 to 16. The WISC-III consists of 13 subtests, each involving either verbal responses or object manipulation. Examples of items like those on the WISC-III are presented in Figure 6–2. Some subtest scores are combined to obtain a *Verbal IQ* score; others are combined to obtain a *Performance* (i.e., nonverbal) *IQ* score. From the Verbal and Performance scores, a *Full-Scale IQ* score can also be derived.[2]

---

[2]You can learn more about the WISC-III and other published intelligence tests by visiting the Companion Website accompanying this text. Go to www.prenhall.com/mcdevitt and then to "Web Links."

What do intelligence tests look like? Here are items similar to those found on the verbal and performance portions of the WISC.

Items Similar to Those on Verbal Subtests
• How many wings does a bird have?
• What is the advantage of keeping money in a bank?
• If two buttons cost 15¢, what will be the cost of a dozen buttons?
• In what way are a saw and a hammer alike?

Items Similar to Those on Performance Subtests
• What's missing in this picture?

• Put these pictures in order so they tell a story that makes sense.

• Put these pieces together to make a duck.

FIGURE 6–2 Items similar to those found on the *Wechsler Intelligence Scale for Children: Third Edition (WISC-III)*.

Copyright © 1991 by The Psychological Corporation, a Harcourt Assessment Company. Reproduced by permission. All rights reserved. "Wechsler Intelligence Scale for Children" and "WISC-III" are trademarks of the Psychological Corporation.

Stanford-Binet Intelligence Scales. A second commonly used instrument is the *Stanford-Binet Intelligence Scales* (Roid, 2003; Thorndike, Hagen, & Sattler, 1986). The Stanford-Binet can be used with people ages 2 through adulthood. The individual being assessed is asked to perform a wide variety of tasks, some involving verbal material and responses (e.g., defining vocabulary words, finding logical inconsistencies in a story, or interpreting proverbs) and others involving concrete objects or pictures (e.g., remembering a sequence of objects, copying geometric figures, or identifying absurdities in pictures). The Stanford-Binet yields an overall IQ score; its most recent edition (Roid, 2003) also yields Verbal and Nonverbal IQs, plus more specific scores in Fluid Reasoning, Knowledge, Working Memory, Visual-Spatial Processing, and Quantitative Reasoning.

Universal Nonverbal Intelligence Test. The WISC-III and Stanford-Binet depend heavily on language; even when tasks involve reasoning about strictly nonverbal, visual material (e.g., see the Performance items in Figure 6–2), the child is given verbal instructions about how to complete the tasks. One recently published instrument, the *Universal Nonverbal Intelligence Test*, or *UNIT* (Bracken & McCallum, 1998), involves no language whatsoever. Designed for children and adolescents ages 5 to 17, the UNIT consists of six subtests involving memory or reasoning regarding visual stimuli (Figure 6–3). Its content (e.g., people, mice, cheese) was chosen from objects and symbols presumed to be universal across all industrialized cultures. Instructions are given entirely through gestures, pantomime, and modeling, and the child responds by either pointing or manipulating objects.

Nonverbal tests such as the UNIT are especially useful for children who have hearing impairments or language-related learning disabilities, as well as for children for whom English is a second language. For instance, children who are deaf and children who have been raised speaking a language other than English perform better on the UNIT than on more traditional language-based intelligence tests (Maller, 2000; McCallum 1999).

IQ Scores   In the early 20th century, some psychologists began to calculate scores for intelligence tests by comparing a child's *mental age* (i.e., referring to the age group whose performance was most similar to the child's performance) with his or her chronological age (W. Stern, 1912; Terman, 1916). The mathematical formula used involved division, and so the resulting score was called an *intelligence quotient,* or **IQ,** score.[3] Even though we still use the term *IQ,* intelligence test scores are no longer based on the old formula. Instead, they are determined by comparing a person's performance on the test with the performance of others in the same age group. Scores near 100 indicate average performance: People with a score of 100 have performed better than half of their age-mates on the test and not as well as the other half. Scores well below 100 indicate below-average performance on the test; scores well above 100 indicate above-average performance.

Figure 6–4 shows the percentage of people getting scores at different points along the scale (e.g., 12.9% get scores between 100 and 105). Notice how the curve is high in the middle and low at both ends. This shape tells us that many more people obtain scores close to 100 than scores very much higher or lower than 100. For example, if we add up the percentages in different parts of Figure 6–4, we find that approximately two-thirds (68%) of individuals in any particular age group score within 15 points of 100 (i.e., between 85 and 115). In contrast, only 2% score as low as 70, and only 2% score as high as 130. This symmetrical and predictable distribution of scores happens by design rather than by chance; psychologists have created a method of scoring intelligence test performance that intentionally yields such a distribution.[4]

Figure 6–4 does not include scores below 70 or above 130. Such scores are certainly possible but are relatively rare. For instance, Gina, from the opening case study, once obtained a score of 140 on an intelligence test. A score of 140 is equivalent to a percentile rank of 99.4; in other words, only 6 people out of every 1,000 would earn a score this high or higher.

Validity and Reliability of General Intelligence Tests   In Chapter 2, we introduced you to the concepts of validity and reliability. In general, the *validity* of an intelligence test is the extent to which it measures what it is designed to measure. The *reliability* of an intelligence test is the extent to which it yields consistent, dependable scores.

To determine the validity of intelligence tests, researchers have focused primarily on predictive validity and construct validity. When they consider the *predictive validity* of an intelligence test, they are concerned with how well test scores correlate with (and so predict) future performance, perhaps school achievement or job proficiency. When they consider the *construct validity* of an intelligence test, they are concerned with whether or not the test actually measures intelligence. Because the concept of "intelligence" is hard to pin down

---

IQ score
Score on an intelligence test determined by comparing one's performance with the performance of same-age peers.

[3]Alfred Binet himself objected to the use of intelligence quotients, believing that his tests were too imprecise to warrant such scores. Lewis Terman, an American psychologist, was largely responsible for popularizing the term *IQ* (Montagu, 1999a).

[4]If you have some knowledge of descriptive statistics, you probably recognize Figure 6–4 as a normal distribution. IQ scores are based on a normal distribution with a mean of 100 and, for most tests, a standard deviation of 15. (Prior to the fifth edition, the Stanford-Binet had a standard deviation of 16.)

Symbolic Memory is primarily a measure of short-term visual memory and complex sequential memory for meaningful material. The task is to view a sequence of universal symbols for 5 seconds and then recreate it from memory using the Symbolic Memory Cards.

Spatial Memory is primarily a measure of short-term visual memory for abstract material. The task is to view a pattern of green and/or black dots on a 3 × 3- or 4 × 4-cell grid for 5 seconds and then recreate the pattern from memory using green and black chips on a blank Response Grid.

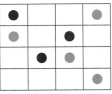

Object Memory is primarily a measure of short-term recognition and recall of meaningful symbolic material. The examinee is presented a randomly arranged pictorial array of common objects for 5 seconds, after which the stimulus page is removed, and a second pictorial array is presented containing all of the previously presented objects and additional objects to serve as foils. The task requires the examinee to identify objects presented in the first pictorial array by placing a response chip on the appropriate pictures.

Cube Design is primarily a measure of visual-spatial reasoning. The task requires the examinee to use two-colored cubes to construct a three-dimensional design that matches a stimulus picture.

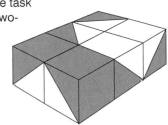

Analogic Reasoning is primarily a measure of symbolic reasoning. The task requires the examinee to complete matrix analogies that employ both common objects and novel geometric figures by pointing to one of four multiple choice options.

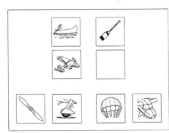

Mazes is primarily a measure of reasoning and planful behavior. The examinee uses paper and pencil to navigate and exit mazes by tracing a path from the center starting point of each maze to the correct exit, without making incorrect decisions en route. A series of increasingly complex mazes is presented.

FIGURE 6-3 Items similar to those on the Universal Nonverbal Intelligence Test (UNIT)

FIGURE 6-4 Percentage of IQ scores in different ranges

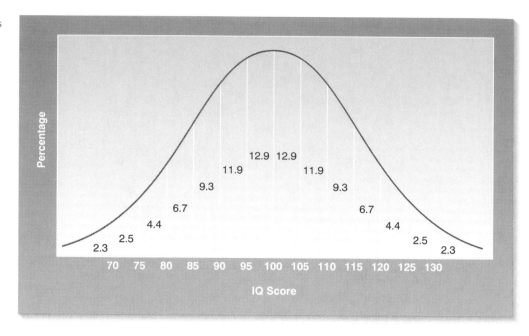

and, in any case, cannot be directly observed, researchers have used roundabout ways to address construct validity. For instance, they look at how well various intelligence tests correlate with one another; when the correlations are high, they know that the tests are measuring the same thing and assume that the "thing" is intelligence. They also look for evidence that older children perform better on the test items than younger children—a result consistent with the assumption that children become more intelligent with age. (Note, however, that children's *IQ scores* do *not* necessarily increase with age; more on this point later.) As an example of such age differences, observe how the three children define the word *freedom* in the Middle Childhood, Early Adolescence, and Late Adolescence clips in the Intelligence module of the Observation CD:

Kate (age 8): You want to be free. Or you want to play something . . . and you got caught and they have to keep you like in jail or something like in a game and you want to get free.

Ryan (age 13): It means that you can, like, do stuff that you want.

Paul (age 17): Basically something that everyone has these days or should have. It's the right to be able to make your own decisions and choose for yourself what you want to do or want to be.

Notice how, with age, the responses get increasingly abstract and complex. Kate limits her definition to a specific behavior, getting out of "jail" in a game. Ryan defines the term more abstractly and broadly, implying that it has relevance to a wide variety of situations. Paul offers an abstract definition as well, but his is more specific and precise than Ryan's.

Innumerable research studies have shown that traditional measures of general intelligence, such as the WISC-III and the Stanford-Binet, have both predictive and construct validity. On average, children and adolescents who get higher scores on these tests do better on standardized achievement tests, have higher school grades, and complete more years of education (Brody, 1997; Gustafsson & Undheim, 1996; Neisser et al., 1996). To a lesser extent, IQ scores also predict later performance in the adult workplace (Sattler, 2001; Sternberg, 1996). In addition, children's scores on different tests tend to be quite similar, and their performance on many test items improves with age. Because the UNIT has only recently arrived on the scene, we do not yet have data about its long-term predictive powers, but preliminary evidence indicates that it, too, has construct validity, as well as predictive validity for the short run (Farrell & Phelps, 2000; McCallum & Bracken, 1997; Young & Assing, 2000).

To determine the reliability of intelligence tests, researchers look at various indications of consistency, especially the extent to which different items and subtests within a particular test yield similar results for a particular individual (*internal consistency reliability*), the ex-

Notice how children's word definitions become increasingly sophisticated with age in the Middle Childhood, Early Adolescence, and Late Adolescence clips in the Intelligence module of the Observation CD.

tent to which two different examiners score a child's performance in the same way (*interrater reliability*), and the extent to which the same test yields similar scores on two different occasions (*test-retest reliability*). The WISC-III, Stanford-Binet, and UNIT are highly reliable in these respects (Anastasi & Urbina, 1997; Sattler, 2001; Young & Assing, 2000).

Whenever we use a general intelligence test to estimate a child's cognitive ability and then summarize the child's performance with a single IQ score, we are to some degree buying into Spearman's concept of g. An alternative approach, using specific ability tests, allows assessment of a child's cognitive capabilities without necessarily assuming that intelligence is a single entity.

Specific Ability Tests

Although intelligence tests sometimes yield subscores related to various aspects of reasoning or memory, their primary purpose is to assess overall cognitive functioning. In contrast, **specific ability tests** have been developed to assess particular cognitive abilities. Some of these tests, called *aptitude tests*, are designed to assess a person's potential to learn in particular content domains, such as mathematics or auto mechanics. Others focus on specific aspects of cognitive processing (e.g., memory for auditory information, ability to think and reason about spatial relationships) and are often used in identifying learning disabilities.

Specific ability tests are more consistent with a multidimensional view of intelligence, such as Spearman's concept of specific abilities or Gardner's concept of multiple intelligences. They typically have high reliability and a reasonable degree of predictive and construct validity (Anastasi & Urbina, 1997; R. J. Cohen & Swerdlik, 1999). However, they get mixed reviews on whether they predict performance on particular tasks more accurately than general measures of intelligence (Anastasi & Urbina, 1997; McGrew et al., 1997; Neisser et al., 1996).

Dynamic Assessment

In recent years, some theorists have suggested an approach that focuses not on assessing existing cognitive abilities but instead on assessing children's ability to learn in new situations (Feuerstein, 1979; Feuerstein, Feuerstein, & Gross, 1997; Lidz, 1997; Tzuriel, 2000). This approach, called **dynamic assessment** (some variations are called *assessment of learning potential*), typically involves having a child perform particular tasks, then offering instruction and guidance relative to the task, and finally determining how much the child has gained from the assistance. Such an approach is consistent with several theoretical frameworks, including Vygotsky's view that adult assistance is essential for maximal cognitive development (see Chapter 4), Sternberg's contention that intelligence involves adaptation to new situations, and distributed intelligence theorists' suggestion that intelligent behavior is heavily context-dependent. (Figure 4–9 on page 173 presents an example of a checklist one clinician has used when conducting dynamic assessments.)

Dynamic assessment is still in its infancy, but preliminary evidence indicates that it can sometimes provide a more optimistic view of children's abilities than traditional intelligence tests; it can also provide a wealth of qualitative information about children's approaches to learning and cognitive strategies (Feuerstein, 1979; Hamers & Ruijssenaars, 1997; Tzuriel, 2000). At the same time, dynamic assessment often involves considerable training before it can be used appropriately, and it typically requires a great deal of time to administer (Anastasi & Urbina, 1997; Tzuriel, 2000). Furthermore, questions have been raised about how best to determine the validity and reliability of the instruments, and those instruments that have been evaluated have fared poorly in comparison to more traditional approaches (Lidz, 1997; Reschly, 1997; Tzuriel, 2000). Accordingly, when practitioners use dynamic assessment to assess children's capabilities, they should do so cautiously and always within the context of other data.

Assessing the Abilities of Infants and Young Children

If an examiner is to assess a child's cognitive abilities accurately, the child must, of course, be a cooperative participant in the process—for instance, by staying alert, paying attention, and maintaining interest in the assessment tasks. Unfortunately, infants and young children

specific ability test
Test designed to assess a specific cognitive skill or the potential to learn and perform in a specific content domain.

dynamic assessment
Systematic examination of how a child's knowledge or reasoning may change as a result of learning or performing a specific task.

are not always cooperative. Infants may be sleepy, fussy, or afraid of the stranger conducting the assessment. Young children may have short attention spans, lose interest in the test questions and materials, or misinterpret instructions. Because of such factors, which can vary considerably from one occasion to the next, test scores for infants and young children tend to have lower reliability than those of older children and adolescents (Anastasi & Urbina, 1997; Bracken & Walker, 1997; Fleege, Charlesworth, & Burts, 1992; Wodtke, Harper, & Schommer, 1989).

Nevertheless, practitioners sometimes need to monitor the cognitive development of infants and young children, perhaps to identify significant developmental delays that require intervention or perhaps to determine readiness for formal education. Accordingly, we briefly describe the nature of tests available for infants, toddlers, and preschoolers.

Tests for infants and toddlers. Infants born in hospital settings are typically assessed as soon as they are born. At both 1 minute and 5 minutes after birth, a doctor or nurse evaluates their color, heart rate, reflexes, muscle tone and respiration, giving each characteristic a rating between 0 and 2. A perfect score on this *Apgar Scale* is 10 (the Apgar Scale is described in more detail in Chapter 2). A more in-depth assessment for newborns from birth until 2 months is the *Neonatal Behavioral Assessment Scale* (Brazelton Institute, 2000); often used to identify significant neurological abnormalities, it assesses alertness and attention, the quality of visual and auditory processing, and a variety of reflexes and behaviors.

Perhaps the most widely used test for older infants and toddlers is the *Bayley Scales of Infant Development* (Bayley, 1993). Designed for children ages 1 month to 3½ years, it includes a *Mental Scale* (assessing such things as habituation, memory, problem solving, language, and number concepts) as well as measures of behavior and motor skills. A photograph of the Bayley Scales being administered appears on page 51 of Chapter 2.

Tests of cognitive abilities for infants and toddlers might better be called *developmental assessments* than intelligence tests per se. They appear to assess current cognitive functioning reasonably well and can be helpful in identifying significant cognitive disabilities if they are used in combination with other information (Sattler, 2001). However, measures of cognitive growth in the first few years of life often have little or no relationship to intelligence in later years (Hayslip, 1994; McCall, 1993; Neisser et al., 1996). "Bright" babies do not necessarily become the brightest fourth graders, and "slow" toddlers may eventually catch up to, or even surpass, their peers (more about this point later in the chapter).

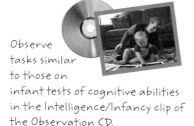

Observe tasks similar to those on infant tests of cognitive abilities in the Intelligence/Infancy clip of the Observation CD.

In the Intelligence/Infancy clip of the Observation CD, you can observe 16-month-old Corwin stacking blocks and identifying pictures of various objects and animals. Such tasks are typical of developmental tests for toddlers. An examiner administering such a test might also rate Corwin on such characteristics as attention, engagement in the test activities, and emotional regulation.

Tests for preschoolers. As noted earlier, the Stanford-Binet Intelligence Scales can be used for children as young as 2. Another commonly used test for young children is a 1989 revision of the *Wechsler Preschool and Primary Scale of Intelligence,* or WPPSI-R (Wechsler, 1989). Suitable for children ages 3 to 7, the WPPSI-R has items similar in format to those on the WISC-III; also like the WISC-R, it yields *Verbal* and *Performance* IQs as well as an overall IQ score.[5] As measures of intelligence for young children, both the Stanford-Binet and WPPSI-R have some construct validity (e.g., they correlate with other measures of intelligence) and sufficient internal consistency reliability and test-retest reliability that they provide reasonable estimates of children's current cognitive functioning (Gyurke, 1991; McCallum, 1991; Sattler, 2001). Although young children's IQ scores correlate somewhat with their scores in later years, the correlations are modest at best—no doubt because many young children have high energy levels, short attention spans, and little interest in sitting still for more than a few minutes. Thus, measures of IQ obtained in the preschool years have

---

[5]A third edition of the WPPSI, which will be suitable for children as young as 2½, is scheduled for publication as this book goes to press.

limited predictive validity and should not be used to make predictions about children's academic performance over the long run (Bracken & Walker, 1997).

Other tests for preschoolers, known as *school readiness tests,* are designed to determine whether children have acquired cognitive skills—for instance, knowledge of colors, shapes, and letters—essential for success in kindergarten or first grade. Although widely used in school districts, such tests have come under fire in recent years, for several reasons. First, the scores they yield correlate only moderately at best with children's academic performance even a year or so later (Lidz, 1991; Powers, 1974; Stipek, 2002). Second, they typically assess only cognitive development, whereas social and emotional development should also be considerations in determining a child's readiness for formal education (Miller-Jones, 1989; Pellegrini, 1998). Finally, by age 5, most children are probably ready for some sort of structured educational program. Rather than determining whether they can adapt to a particular educational curriculum and environment, it is probably more beneficial to determine how the school curriculum and environment can be adapted to fit the particular needs of individual children (Lidz, 1991; Stipek, 2002).

As you can see, we must be careful how we interpret and use the results of intelligence tests and other measures of cognitive abilities. As a general rule, and especially when test results are used to make decisions about young children, practitioners should use test scores only in combination with other information—observations of the children in a variety of settings, interviews with parents and teachers, and so on. Practitioners should also reserve judgment about whether IQ scores reflect children's inherited abilities, on the one hand, or their environments and background experiences, on the other. In the next section, we sift through the data concerning the relative effects of heredity and environment.

Hereditary and Environmental Influences on Intelligence

It is often difficult to separate the relative influences of heredity and environment on human characteristics. People who have similar genetic makeup (e.g., brothers and sisters, parents and their children) typically live in similar environments as well. So when we see similarities in IQ among members of the same family, it is hard to know whether those similarities are due to the genes or to the environments that family members share. Nevertheless, a significant body of research tells us that both heredity and environment affect intelligence, at least as it is reflected in IQ scores.

Evidence for Hereditary Influences

Earlier we mentioned that measures of information processing speed correlate with IQ scores. Speed of processing depends on neurological efficiency and maturation, which are genetically controlled. From this standpoint, then, we have some support for a hereditary basis for intelligence (D. N. Perkins, 1995). We find additional evidence in the general observation that children with certain genetic defects (e.g., Down syndrome) have, on average, significantly lower IQ scores than their nondisabled peers (Keogh & MacMillan, 1996). Two additional sources of evidence, twin studies and adoption studies, also indicate that intelligence has a genetic component.

Twin Studies Numerous studies have used monozygotic (identical) twins and dizygotic (fraternal) twins to get a sense of how strongly heredity affects IQ. Because monozygotic twins begin as a single fertilized egg which then separates, they are genetically equivalent human beings. In contrast, dizygotic (fraternal) twins are conceived as two separate fertilized eggs; they share about 50% of their genetic makeup, with the other 50% being unique to each twin. If identical twins have more similar IQ scores than fraternal twins, then we can reasonably suspect that heredity influences intelligence.

Most twins are raised together by the same parent(s) and in the same home; thus, they share similar environments as well as similar genes. Yet even when twins are raised separately (perhaps because they have been adopted and raised by different parents), they typically have

Even when identical twins are raised by different families, they typically have similar IQ scores, indicating that intelligence has a biological component. However, twins raised in different homes are somewhat less similar than twins raised in the same home, indicating that environment affects intelligence as well.

similar IQ scores (Bouchard & McGue, 1981; Brody, 1992; Mackintosh, 1998; Plomin & Petrill, 1997). In a review of twin studies, Bouchard and McGue (1981) found these average (median) correlations:

	Correlations of Twins' IQs
Identical twins raised in the same home	.86
Identical twins raised in different homes	.72
Fraternal twins raised in the same home	.60

The correlation of .72 indicates that identical twins raised in different environments nevertheless tend to have very similar IQ scores. In fact, these twins are more similar to each other than are fraternal twins raised in the same home.[6]

Adoption Studies   Another way to separate the effects of heredity and environment is to compare adopted children with both their adoptive and biological parents. Adopted children share a similar environment with their adoptive parents; they share a similar genetic makeup with their biological parents. When researchers obtain IQ scores for adopted children and for both their biological and adoptive parents, they typically find that the children's IQ scores are more highly correlated with the scores of their biological parents than with the scores of their adoptive parents. In other words, in a group of people who place their infants up for adoption, those with the highest IQs tend to have offspring who, despite being raised by other people, also have the highest IQs. Furthermore, the IQ correlations between adopted children and their biological parents become stronger, and those between the children and their adoptive parents become weaker, as the children grow older, especially during late adolescence (Bouchard, 1997; McGue, Bouchard, Iacono, & Lykken, 1993; Plomin, Fulker, Corley, & DeFries, 1997; Plomin & Petrill, 1997). (If you find this last finding puzzling, we will offer an explanation shortly.)

Keep in mind that twin studies and adoption studies do not completely separate the effects of heredity and environment (Collins, Maccoby, Steinberg, Hetherington, & Bornstein, 2000; Wahlsten & Gottlieb, 1997). For example, adopted children have shared a common environment for at least 9 months—the 9 months of prenatal development—with their biological mothers. Likewise, monozygotic twins who are raised in separate homes have shared a common prenatal environment and often have similar, if not identical, postnatal environments as well. Furthermore, twin studies and adoption studies do not allow researchers to examine the ways in which heredity and environment might interact in their effects on measured intelligence; such interactive effects are often added to the "heredity" side of the scoreboard (Collins et al., 2000; Turkheimer, 2000). Despite such glitches, twin and adoption studies point convincingly to a genetic component in intelligence (Bouchard, 1997; Brody, 1992; E. Hunt, 1997; Neisser, 1998a; Petrill & Wilkerson, 2000).

This is not to say that children are predestined to have an intelligence level similar to that of their biological parents. In fact, most children with high intelligence are conceived by parents of average intelligence rather than by parents with high IQ scores (Plomin & Petrill, 1997). Children's genetic ancestry, then, is hardly a surefire predictor of what their own potential is likely to be. Environment also makes an appreciable difference, as we shall now see.

Evidence for Environmental Influences

Numerous sources of evidence converge to indicate that environment has a significant impact on IQ scores. We find some of this evidence in twin studies and adoption studies. Studies of the effects of home environment, early nutrition, toxic substances, early intervention,

---

[6]In our teaching experiences, we have found that some students erroneously interpret the higher correlations as indicating that identical twins have higher intelligence. This is of course not the case; the size of the correlations indicates the *strength of the relationship,* not the level of intelligence.

and formal schooling provide additional support for the influence of environment. Also, a steady increase in performance on intelligence tests over the past several decades—known as the Flynn effect—is almost certainly attributable to environmental factors.

Twin Studies and Adoption Studies Revisited   Look once again at the IQ correlations for identical twins raised in the same home versus in different homes. The median correlation for twins raised in different homes is .72; that for twins raised in the same home is .86. In other words, twins raised in different homes have less similar IQs than twins raised in the same home. The distinct environments that different families provide do have some influence on intellectual development.

Adoption studies, too, indicate that intelligence is not determined entirely by heredity (Capron & Duyme, 1989; Devlin, Fienberg, Resnick, & Roeder, 1995; Waldman, Weinberg, & Scarr, 1994). For instance, in a study by Scarr and Weinberg (1976), some children of poor parents (with unknown IQs) were adopted by middle-class parents with IQs averaging 118–121. Others remained with their biological parents. IQ averages of the children in the two groups were as follows:

	Average IQs
Adopted children	105
Nonadopted children	90

Although the adopted children's IQ scores were, on average, lower than those of their adoptive parents, they were about 15 points higher than those in the control group raised by their biological parents.

Effects of Home Environment   One likely explanation for the beneficial effects of adoption is that adoptive parents, who typically have more financial resources and higher levels of education, can provide a more stimulating home environment than the biological parents might have been able to offer. In fact, stimulating home environments—those in which parents interact frequently with their children, make numerous learning and reading materials available, encourage the development of new skills, use complex sentence structures in conversation, and so on—are associated with higher IQ scores in children (Bradley & Caldwell, 1984; Brooks-Gunn, Klebanov, & Duncan, 1996; McGowan & Johnson, 1984). Studies of home environment are typically correlational in nature, however, and so do not show conclusively that home environment *causes* any observed differences in intelligence. An alternative explanation for the same results is that more intelligent parents provide more stimulating environments *and,* through heredity, produce more intelligent children.

Recently, N. L. Segal (2000) took a somewhat different approach in studying the possible effects of home environment on intelligence. She identified 90 sets of "virtual twins": pairs of unrelated children of about the same age (no more than 9 months apart) living in the same home. Some of these "twins" consisted of two adopted children, and others consisted of one adopted and one biological child, but in every case they had shared the same home since their first birthday. Segal found a small positive correlation (.26) between the IQs of these pairs; such a correlation, small as it was, could be attributed only to a common environment (N. L. Segal, 2000).

Effects of Early Nutrition   Severe malnutrition, either before birth or during the early years of life, can limit neurological development and thereby have a long-term influence on cognitive development, especially abstract reasoning and other advanced cognitive processes (D'Amato, Chitooran, & Whitten, 1992; Sigman & Whaley, 1998). In infancy, poor nutrition is associated with slower habituation rates (S. A. Rose, 1994). Later on, it is associated with lower IQ scores, poorer attention and memory, and lower school achievement (Eysenck & Schoenthaler, 1997; Lozoff, 1989; L. S. Miller, 1995; Ricciuti, 1993; Scott-Jones, 1984). Children sometimes recover from short periods of poor nourishment (due, perhaps, to war or illness), but the effects of long-term deprivation are more enduring (Sigman & Whaley, 1998).

Effects of Toxic Substances   A variety of toxic substances in children's prenatal or early postnatal environments—for instance, alcohol, drugs, radiation, lead (e.g., in the lead-based paints used in many older buildings)—affect neurological development and thus also affect children's later IQ scores (e.g., Michel, 1989; Neisser et al., 1996; Streissguth, Barr, Sampson, & Bookstein, 1994; Vogel, 1997; Vorhees & Mollnow, 1987). An example of such effects is **fetal alcohol syndrome (FAS)**, in which children whose mothers consumed large amounts of alcohol during pregnancy are born with distinctive facial features (e.g., wide-set eyes and a thin upper lip) and soon show poor motor coordination, delayed language, and mental retardation (Dorris, 1989).

Effects of Early Intervention   Some research studies have examined the effects of providing food supplements and vitamins to infants and young children who would not otherwise have adequate nutrition. Such interventions are most likely to enhance children's motor development; in some instances, cognitive development is enhanced as well (Pollitt & Oh, 1994; Sigman & Whaley, 1998).

When children live in impoverished home environments, enriching preschool programs and other forms of early intervention can make an appreciable difference. For instance, Head Start and other preschool programs frequently lead to short-term gains in IQ scores (Bronfenbrenner, 1999a; Ramey, 1992; Seitz, Rosenbaum, & Apfel, 1985; Zigler & Finn-Stevenson, 1987). The effects of such programs don't continue indefinitely, however; without follow-up interventions during the elementary school years, any advantages in terms of IQ scores diminish over time and may disappear altogether (Bronfenbrenner, 1999a; F. A. Campbell & Ramey, 1995; Gustafsson & Undheim, 1996).

We must not be disheartened by such results. For one thing, publicly funded preschool programs such as Head Start often enroll the most economically disadvantaged children in the community. To study the long-term effects of these programs, researchers sometimes have difficulty finding an appropriate control group; for instance, they may compare children who attended the programs with children who, though not attending preschool, grew up in more advantaged circumstances (Schnur, Brooks-Gunn, & Shipman, 1992). Furthermore, early intervention often leads to long-term improvements in areas not reflected in IQ test scores; for instance, in one series of studies, children who attended an intensive child care program from 3 months until 5 years of age were achieving at higher levels in reading, writing, and mathematics even at ages 12 and 15 (F. A. Campbell & Ramey, 1994, 1995). In addition, children who attend intensive, developmentally appropriate academic preschool programs are, later on, more likely to have high achievement motivation and self-esteem, less likely to need special education services, and more likely to graduate from high school (F. A. Campbell & Ramey, 1995; Royce, Darlington, & Murray, 1983; Spencer, Noll, Stoltzfus, & Harpalani, 2001; Washington & Bailey, 1995).

Practitioners should keep in mind that early intervention does not mean bombarding infants and small children with constant or intense stimulation. As we have seen in Chapters 4 and 5, children have a natural desire to learn about their environment, and most eagerly explore their surroundings. But they can handle only so much information—and certainly only so much new information—at any one time. Furthermore, a secure, supportive relationship with one or more caregivers is just as important as age-appropriate toys and activities (Gonzalez-Mena, 2002). The Development and Practice feature "Offering Effective Interventions in the Early Years" provides several suggestions for caregivers who work with young children.

Effects of Formal Schooling   The very act of attending school leads to small increases in IQ. Children who begin their educational careers early and attend school regularly have higher IQ scores than children who do not. When children must start school later than they would otherwise for reasons beyond their families' control, their IQs are about 5 points lower for every year of delay. Furthermore, children's IQ scores decline slightly over the course of the summer months, when they are not attending school. And other things being equal, children who drop out have lower IQ scores than children who remain in school. For every year of high school not completed, IQ drops an average of 1.8 points (Ceci & Williams, 1997).

The Flynn Effect   The last few decades have seen a slow, steady increase in people's average performance on IQ tests throughout the industrialized world; this trend is commonly known as the **Flynn effect** (Flynn, 1987, 1999; Neisser, 1998b). A similar change has been observed in children's performance on traditional Piagetian tasks (Flieller, 1999). Such improvement is difficult to attribute to heredity because the same gene pool (albeit with an

Research indicates that stimulating preschool experiences often increase IQ, at least over the short run.

fetal alcohol syndrome (FAS)
Condition in which a child is born with distinctive facial features, delayed motor and language development, and mental retardation; results from excessive alcohol consumption throughout pregnancy.

Flynn effect
Gradual increase in intelligence test performance observed worldwide over the past several decades.

DEVELOPMENT AND PRACTICE

Offering Effective Interventions in the Early Years

■ Remember that development begins at conception.

A nurse at a health clinic in a low-income neighborhood consults regularly with the pregnant women in his care, making sure that they are eating well, taking appropriate vitamin supplements, and exercising regularly.

■ Provide an enriching environment.

A child care provider makes a variety of manipulative toys available to the toddlers who come to her home every day, and she sometimes shows age-appropriate television shows designed to stimulate thinking and language skills. Furthermore, her meals and snacks are healthful and well-balanced.

■ Create partnerships with families.

A Head Start program director hires several parents to work as teachers in the program two or three days a week. Through their involvement, the parents learn effective teaching strategies that they can use when interacting with their children at home.

■ Look at model programs for ideas about effective approaches.

A social worker has acquired funding to develop an early intervention program in her community. To learn more about the type of program that might best meet the community's needs, she visits several successful preschools in nearby cities. She also signs up for a training program that focuses on the implications of research in infant and toddler care for community practice.

occasional mutation) is passed along from one generation to the next; thus, its cause is almost certainly environmental. Theorists disagree as to the likely explanation, however: Better nutrition, high quality home environments, better schooling (for parents as well as children), and more enriching and informative stimulation (increased access to television, reading materials, etc.) are all possibilities (Flieller, 1999; Flynn, 1987; Neisser, 1998b).

How Nature and Nurture Interact in Their Influence

Clearly, both nature and nurture play a role in the development of intelligence. Some theorists have asked the question, "How much does each of these factors influence IQ?" and have estimated the relative contribution of genetics (the *heritability* of IQ) from the correlations obtained in twin and adoption studies (e.g., McGue et al., 1993; Plomin et al., 1997). Such heritability estimates typically attribute at least 40% of intelligence, and often more, to inherited factors (Petrill & Wilkerson, 2000). But other theorists point out that such estimates are derived from populations with limited environmental variability (e.g., the research sample may be comprised largely of middle-income families living in a single culture) and so probably underestimate the role that environmental differences play in intellectual development (Biesheuvel, 1999; Bronfenbrenner, 1999b; Ceci, Rosenblum, de Bruyn, & Lee, 1997).

Many psychologists believe that it may ultimately be impossible to separate the relative effects of heredity and environment. They suggest that the two combine to influence children's cognitive development and measured IQ in ways that we can probably never disentangle (Collins et al., 2000; Halpern & LaMay, 2000; Plomin, 1994; Turkheimer, 2000). Theorists have made the following general points about how nature and nurture interact as they affect intellectual development:

■ *Genetic expression is influenced by environmental conditions.* Genes require environmental support (e.g., adequate nutrition) to do their work (see Chapter 3). Thus, they are not entirely self-contained, independent "carriers" of developmental instructions; the particular instructions they transmit are influenced by the environments in which they operate (Bidell & Fischer, 1997). In an extremely impoverished environment—one with a lack of adequate nutrition and little if any stimulation—heredity may have little to say about the extent to which children develop intellectually (Plomin & Petrill, 1997). In an ideal environment—one in which nutrition, parenting practices, and educational opportunities are optimal and age-appropriate—heredity is more likely to have a significant influence on children's IQ scores (Rowe, Jacobson, & Van den Oord, 1999).

In addition, intelligence is almost certainly the result of many genes, each contributing a small amount to measured IQ (Sattler, 2001). The effects of these genes may appear at different points in development, and each gene's expression may be influenced by particular environmental conditions at those times. Thus, we do not have a single heredity-environment interaction, but rather a number of heredity-environment interactions all contributing to intellectual growth (Simonton, 2001).

■ *Heredity establishes a range rather than a precise figure.* Heredity does not dictate that a child will have a particular IQ score. Instead, it appears to set a range of abilities within which children will eventually fall, with the specific level of ability each one achieves depending on his or her specific environmental experiences (Weinberg, 1989). Heredity may also affect how susceptible or impervious a child is to particular environmental influences (Rutter, 1997).

■ *Especially as they get older, children choose their environments and experiences.* Children may actively seek out environmental conditions that match their inherited abilities—a phenomenon known as **niche-picking** (Halpern & LaMay, 2000; Petrill & Wilkerson, 2000; Scarr & McCartney, 1983). For example, children who, genetically speaking, have exceptional quantitative reasoning ability may enroll in advanced mathematics courses, delight in tackling mathematical brainteasers, and in other ways nurture their inherited talents. Children with average quantitative ability are less likely to take on such challenges and so have fewer opportunities to develop their mathematical skills. In such circumstances, the relative effects of heredity and environment are difficult to tease apart.

Earlier we mentioned that the IQ correlations between adopted children and their biological parents become stronger over time. We now have a possible explanation for this finding. Children gain increasing independence as they get older. Particularly as they reach adolescence, they spend less time in their home environments, and they make more of their own decisions about the kinds of opportunities to pursue—decisions undoubtedly based, in part, on their natural talents and tendencies (McGue et al., 1993; Petrill & Wilkerson, 2000).

You might think of intelligence as being the result of four factors (Gottlieb, 1992). *Genetic activity* affects *neural activity,* which in turn affects *behavior,* which in turn affects the *environment.* But influence moves in the opposite direction as well: The environment affects behavior, and these two (through stimulation, nutritional intake, physical activity, etc.) affect neural activity and genetic expression. The continuing interplay of genetics, neural activity, behavior, and environment is depicted in Figure 6–5.

Theorists continue to debate the relative influences of heredity and environment on intelligence. From the standpoint of research evidence, the effects of both nature and nurture are well established. Probably a more fruitful course of action for researchers is to examine more closely the specific ways in which the two work together to direct and foster intellectual growth (Bidell & Fischer, 1997; E. Hunt, 1997; Turkheimer, 2000; Wahlsten & Gottlieb, 1997).

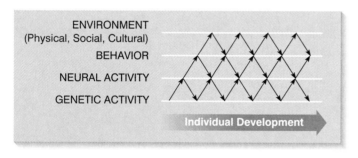

FIGURE 6–5 Bidirectional influences among genetic activity, neural activity, behavior, and environment

From *Individual Development and Evolution: The Genesis of Novel Behavior* (p. 186), by G. Gottlieb, copyright © 1991 by Oxford University Press, Inc. Used by permission of Oxford University Press, Inc.

Developmental Trends in IQ Scores

In one sense, children definitely become more "intelligent" as they develop: They know more, can think in more complex ways, and can solve problems more effectively. However, IQ scores are not based on how much children develop over a period of years; instead, they are based on how well children perform in comparison with their age-mates. On average, then, IQ does not increase with age; by definition, the average IQ score for any age group is 100.

Yet IQ scores do change in two ways over the course of development:

■ *IQ scores become increasingly stable.* In our discussion of Spearman's g, we mentioned that habituation rates in infancy are correlated with later intelligence. Infants' performance on traditional measures of cognitive growth, however, is not terribly predictive of their later IQ scores (Hayslip, 1994; McCall, 1993; Neisser et al., 1996). Furthermore, very young children can show considerable variability in their test scores from one occasion to the next.

niche-picking
Tendency to actively seek out environments that match one's inherited abilities.

There are at least three possible reasons for the instability of IQ scores in infancy and early childhood. First, as noted earlier in the chapter, young children's test performance is often influenced by a variety of unstable and irrelevant factors, including short attention span, lack of motivation to complete assessment tasks, misinterpretation of instructions, and so on. Second, some of the genetic factors that influence intellectual development may not "kick in" immediately after birth; rather, their influence may emerge only gradually over time (Sattler, 2001; Simonton, 2001). And third, the types of items on intelligence tests change considerably as children grow older. The Developmental Trends table "Intelligence at Different Age Levels" identifies some commonly used indicators of intelligence at different age levels plus additional considerations to keep in mind at each level.

As children progress through the school years, their IQ scores become increasingly stable. Although children continue to develop cognitively, each one's relative intelligence in comparison with peers changes less over time (Brody, 1992; Neisser et al., 1996; Sattler, 2001). As an example, look once again at the chapter's opening case study. Gina obtained an IQ score of 140 (equivalent to the 99th percentile) in junior high school and performed at a similar level on college aptitude tests several years later.

Despite this increasing stability, we must remember that IQ scores simply reflect an individual's performance on a particular test at a particular time; longitudinal studies indicate that some change (sometimes as much as 10 to 20 points' worth, and occasionally even more) can reasonably be expected over the years. In fact, the longer the time interval between two administrations of an IQ test, the greater the change in IQ we are likely to see, especially when young children are involved (Bloom, 1964; Humphreys, 1992; McCall, 1993; Sattler, 2001). IQ scores and other measures of cognitive ability often increase over time when children are highly motivated and independent learners and when parents and other adults provide stimulating activities and a variety of reading materials (Echols, West, Stanovich, & Kehr, 1996; Sameroff, Seifer, Baldwin, & Baldwin, 1993; Stanovich, West, & Harrison, 1995).

■ *IQ scores become increasingly better predictors of future achievement.* As noted earlier, IQ scores predict academic achievement, and, to a lesser degree, occupational performance as well. But intelligence tests have greater predictive validity as children get older. Tests given in the preschool and early elementary years are often relatively inaccurate estimates of how well children will do in school several years later (Pellegrini, 1998; Wodtke et al., 1989). Accordingly, tests administered in the early years should not be used to make long-term predictions about school achievement; they are more appropriately used for screening children for significant developmental delays that require immediate intervention.

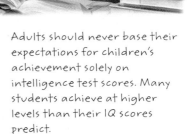

Teachers, clinicians, and other practitioners should remember two additional things about the relationship between intelligence test scores and school achievement. First, intelligence does not necessarily cause achievement. Even though children with high IQs typically perform well in school, we cannot say conclusively that their high achievement is actually the result of their intelligence. Intelligence probably does play an important role in school achievement, but many other factors— motivation, quality of instruction, parental support, family income, peer group norms, and so on—are also involved. Second, the relationship between IQ scores and achievement is not a perfect one; there are many exceptions to the rule. For a variety of reasons, some children with high IQ scores do not perform well in the classroom. And other children achieve at higher levels than would be predicted from their IQ scores alone. Adults should never base their expectations for children's achievement solely on intelligence test scores.

Adults should never base their expectations for children's achievement solely on intelligence test scores. Many students achieve at higher levels than their IQ scores predict.

Group Differences in Intelligence

By design, intelligence tests reveal individual differences in children's general cognitive ability. But what do these tests reveal about group differences? Here we examine research findings related to possible socioeconomic, gender, ethnic, and racial differences in intelligence test performance.

AGE	WHAT YOU MIGHT OBSERVE	DIVERSITY	IMPLICATIONS
Infancy (Birth–2) 	• Success on test items that involve early developmental accomplishments (e.g., recognition memory, visual preferences, eye-hand coordination) • Distractibility and short attention span • Variability in performance from one assessment to the next • Performance dependent on examiner's ability to establish a positive relationship with the infant	• Temperamental differences affect infants' willingness to interact with the examiner and test materials (e.g., shy or cautious infants may be reluctant to interact with examiner). • Prematurity may depress test scores (practitioners should consider date of conception as well as date of birth when interpreting performance). • Exposure to drugs or alcohol before birth may adversely affect test performance.	• Create a secure and comfortable examiner-child relationship before beginning an assessment. • Use results only to identify significant developmental delays requiring immediate intervention; refrain from making long-term predictions about intellectual growth. • Communicate honestly with parents about their child's test performance, while also describing the test's strengths and weaknesses as an assessment tool.
Early Childhood (2–6) 	• Success on test items that involve naming objects, stacking blocks, drawing circles and squares, remembering short lists, and following simple directions • Short attention span, influencing test performance • Variability in test scores from one occasion to the next	• Significant developmental delays in the early years may indicate mental retardation or other disabilities. • On average, children from lower-income families perform at lower levels on measures of cognitive development than children from middle-income families; however, enriching preschool experiences can decrease and occasionally eliminate this difference.	• Use IQ tests primarily to identify significant delays in cognitive development; follow up by seeking intervention programs for children with such delays. • Provide preschool experiences that foster children's language skills, knowledge of numbers and counting, and visual-spatial thinking.
Middle Childhood (6–10) 	• Success on test items that involve defining concrete words, remembering sentences and short sequences of digits, understanding concrete analogies, recognizing similarities among objects, and identifying absurdities in illogical statements • Some consistency in test scores from one occasion to the next • Noticeable differences among children in mastery of classroom subject matter	• Children with learning disabilities may perform poorly on some parts of an intelligence test. • For this age range, many intelligence tests become increasingly verbal in nature; thus, proficiency with the English language can significantly affect test performance. • Children from some ethnic minority groups may perform poorly in situations where the test-giver has not established rapport.	• Individualize instruction to match children's varying abilities to learn in particular content domains. • Do *not* assume that poor performance in some domains necessarily indicates limited ability to learn in other areas. • Take children's cultural and linguistic backgrounds into account when interpreting IQ scores.
Early Adolescence (10–14) 	• Success on test items that involve defining commonly used abstract words, drawing logical inferences from verbal descriptions, and identifying similarities between opposite concepts • Considerable individual differences in the ability to understand abstract material	• Adolescents from some ethnic minority groups may associate high test performance with "acting White" and so intentionally perform poorly. • Some adolescents who are gifted may try to hide their talents; cultures that stress traditional male and female roles may actively discourage females from achieving at high levels.	• Expect considerable diversity in adolescents' ability to master abstract classroom material, and individualize instruction accordingly. • Make sure that school enrichment programs include students from ethnic minority groups; do not rely exclusively on IQ scores to identify students as gifted (see Observation Guidelines on p. 266).
Late Adolescence (14–18) 	• Success on test items that involve defining infrequently encountered vocabulary, identifying differences between similar abstract words, interpreting proverbs, and breaking down complex geometric figures into their component parts • Relative stability in most adolescents' IQ scores • Increasing independence to seek out opportunities consistent with existing ability levels (niche-picking)	• Fears of "acting White" or in other ways appearing "too smart" may continue into the high school years.	• Provide challenging activities for teenagers who are gifted. • Encourage bright adolescents from lower-income families to pursue a college education, and help them with the logistics of college applications (e.g., applying for financial aid).

Sources: Bayley, 1993; Brooks-Gunn et al., 1996; Colombo, 1993; Davis & Rimm, 1998; Greenspan & Meisels, 1996; Luckasson et al., 1992; Mayes & Bornstein, 1997; McLoyd, 1998b; Ogbu, 1994; Terman & Merrill, 1972; Thomas & Chess, 1977; Thorndike et al., 1986; Wechsler, 1991.

As you read this section, please keep two principles in mind. First, *there is a great deal of individual variability within any group.* We will describe how children of different groups perform on average, yet some children are very different from that "average" description. Second, *there is almost always a great deal of overlap between any two groups.* As an example, consider gender differences in verbal ability. Research studies often find that girls have slightly higher verbal performance than boys (Halpern & LaMay, 2000; Lueptow, 1984; Maccoby & Jacklin, 1974). Yet the difference is typically quite small, with a great deal of overlap between the two groups. Figure 6–6 shows the typical overlap between girls and boys on measures of verbal ability: Notice that many of the boys perform at higher levels than some of the girls despite the average advantage for girls. Obviously, we could not use such data to make predictions about how particular girls and boys would perform in classrooms and other settings.

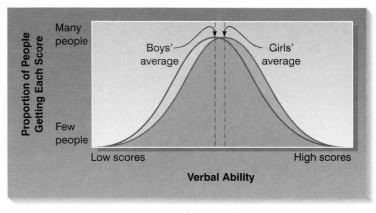

FIGURE 6–6 Typical "difference" between girls and boys in verbal ability

Socioeconomic Differences

A person's **socioeconomic status** (often abbreviated as **SES**) encompasses such variables as family income, occupation, and level of education—variables that reflect the individual's general social and economic standing in society. On average, children from low-SES families earn lower IQ scores than children from middle-SES families; they also perform at lower levels on achievement tests, are more likely to be placed in special education programs, and are less likely to graduate from high school (Brooks-Gunn et al., 1996; McLoyd, 1998b; Neisser et al., 1996). Children who grow up in persistently impoverished conditions are at greatest risk for poor performance in these respects, but even children who endure only short-term poverty suffer to some degree (McLoyd, 1998b).

Several factors probably contribute to differences in IQ and school achievement among socioeconomic groups (McLoyd, 1998b; L. S. Miller, 1995). Poor nutrition and health care, both before and after birth, can interfere with maximal neurological development. On average, children of poor families have less cognitive stimulation at home, for many possible reasons. Parents who work long hours (especially single parents) may have little time to spend with their children and may be unable to find or afford high-quality child care; some parents with limited educational backgrounds have never learned much about children's developmental needs (Edwards & Garcia, 1994; Portes, 1996); and the family may, in general, be preoccupied with its survival and physical well-being. Once children begin school, they may lack essential knowledge and skills (e.g., familiarity with letters and numbers) upon which more advanced learning depends. Their lower school attendance rates, due to frequent health problems, family crises, and changes of residence, further decrease their opportunities for cognitive growth.

In addition, teachers—especially those who have grown up in middle-income families—often have lower academic expectations for children from lower-income homes; as a result, they may give these children less time and attention, fewer opportunities to learn, and less challenging assignments (K. Alexander, Entwisle, & Thompson, 1987; McLoyd, 1998b; R. Rosenthal, 1994). Unwittingly, then, teachers may exacerbate any socioeconomic differences in cognitive ability that already exist.

As we have already seen, enriching preschool experiences can boost IQ scores (at least over the short run) and enhance school achievement for children from lower-income families. Programs that teach parents how to provide stimulating activities for their growing children also appear to make a difference (F. A. Campbell & Ramey, 1994). And when teachers have high expectations for students from lower-income backgrounds, the students are more likely to perform at high levels (Midgley, Feldlaufer, & Eccles, 1989; Phillips, 1997).

socioeconomic status (SES)
One's general social and economic standing in society, encompassing such variables as family income, occupation, and education level.

Gender Differences

Males and females are, on average, equivalent in general intellectual ability. Apart from a greater frequency of mental retardation in boys than girls, there are rarely any significant gender differences in IQ scores (Halpern, 1997; Neisser et al., 1996). This finding is at least partly a function of how intelligence tests are developed: As a general rule, test constructors eliminate any test items on which one gender performs better than the other.

Average differences in more specific cognitive abilities are sometimes found but are usually small. For example, females are often slightly better at such verbal tasks as reading and writing (Halpern, 1997; Hedges & Nowell, 1995; Maccoby & Jacklin, 1974). Particularly after puberty, males perform somewhat better on some tasks involving visual-spatial thinking (which require people to imagine two- or three-dimensional figures and mentally manipulate them), and adolescents with extremely high mathematical ability are more likely to be male than female (Benbow, Lubinski, Shea, & Eftekhari-Sanjani, 2000; Eisenberg, Martin, & Fabes, 1996; Halpern, 1997; Hegarty & Kozhevnikov, 1999). In such domains, however, there is typically a great deal of overlap between the two genders.

Some gender differences in specific intellectual abilities may be partly due to subtle biological differences in the brain (Halpern & LaMay, 2000; Neisser et al., 1996; O'Boyle & Gill, 1998). Environmental factors appear to play a role as well. In our society, boys and girls often have distinctly different experiences growing up. For instance, boys are more likely to have toys that require physical manipulation in space (building blocks, model airplanes, footballs, etc.), and such items can foster the development of visual-spatial skills. In contrast, girls are more likely to have dolls, housekeeping items (e.g., dishes, plastic food), and board games—items that are apt to encourage verbal communication with peers (Halpern, 1992; Liss, 1983; Sprafkin, Serbin, Denier, & Connor, 1983). In addition, researchers occasionally observe other patterns of gender differences in particular ethnic groups—for instance, Hispanic girls may demonstrate better visual-spatial ability than Hispanic boys—and such findings weaken the argument for biological differences (Huston, 1983; Schratz, 1978).

In recent years, perhaps because of the push for more equitable educational opportunities, males and females have become increasingly similar in the abilities that they demonstrate (Eisenberg et al., 1996; Gustafsson & Undheim, 1996; Jacklin, 1989). For all intents and purposes, teachers and other practitioners should expect boys and girls to have similar aptitudes for virtually all subject areas.

Ethnic and Racial Differences

Some measures of early cognitive functioning in infants reveal no differences among ethnic groups (Fagan & Singer, 1983). However, ethnic and racial differences in intelligence and more specific cognitive abilities appear in the preschool years and persist throughout childhood and adolescence. On average, Asian Americans and European Americans outperform African Americans and Hispanic Americans (Brody, 1992; Bruer, 1997; McCallum, 1999; Neisser et al., 1996). In some studies, Asian Americans score at the highest levels of all, outscoring European Americans by 1 to 5 points (Brody, 1992; Flynn, 1991).

Speculations about the source of such differences have prompted considerable debate. In the 1994 book *The Bell Curve,* Richard Herrnstein and Charles Murray used three consistently observed group differences—European American families have higher incomes than African American families, children from upper- and middle-income families have higher IQ scores than children from lower-income families, and European American children have higher IQ scores than African American children—to conclude that European Americans have a genetic advantage over African Americans. As you might suspect, the book generated considerable controversy and a great deal of outrage.

Scholars have poked many holes in *The Bell Curve* (Jacoby & Glauberman, 1995; Marks, 1995; Montagu, 1999b). For instance, they find numerous weaknesses in the research studies and statistical analyses that Herrnstein and Murray described; as one simple example, they remind us that we can never draw conclusions about causation by looking only at correlational studies. They argue that any innate differences in intelligence have not had sufficient time to evolve, nor does it seem logical that some groups would evolve to be less adaptive (i.e., less intelligent) than others. They point out, too, that the very concept of *race,* though widely used to categorize people in our society, has no basis in biology: It is virtually impossible to identify a person's "race" by analyzing his or her DNA.

In past years, some theorists have suggested that cultural bias in intelligence tests explains ethnic and racial differences in IQ scores. Today, however, most theorists believe that cultural bias is not the primary culprit and suggest that other environmentally based factors—perhaps including socioeconomic status, discrimination, and motivation—are to blame. Let's look at each of these possible explanations.

Cultural bias. A test has **cultural bias** when one or more of its items either offend or unfairly penalize people of a particular ethnic background, gender, or socioeconomic status, to the point that the test has less predictive and construct validity for those individuals. Some characteristics of intelligence tests may lead some children to attain scores that do not accurately reflect either their intelligence or their ability to achieve long-term academic or professional success. For instance, many contemporary intelligence tests focus on aspects of cognition (e.g., abstract thinking) that enable people to succeed in Western, industrialized society; these tests may be less relevant to the demands of other cultures (J. G. Miller, 1997; Ogbu, 1994). Lack of familiarity with a test's questions and tasks may also hamper children's performance (Heath, 1989; Neisser et al., 1996). Facility with the English language is a factor as well: Children for whom English is a second language perform relatively poorly on test items that are primarily verbal in nature (Lopez, 1997).

Despite such considerations, cultural bias does not appear to be the primary factor accounting for group differences in IQ scores. IQ scores have similar reliability, construct validity, and predictive validity (e.g., they predict academic performance equally well) for different ethnic and racial groups, at least for children whose native language is English (R. T. Brown, Reynolds, & Whitaker, 1999; Neisser et al., 1996; Sattler, 2001). Furthermore, publishers of intelligence tests routinely employ individuals from diverse backgrounds to ensure that test content is fair and appropriate for students of all races and ethnicities (Linn & Gronlund, 2000). Even when tests are intentionally designed to minimize culture-specific content, group differences are observed (Linn & Gronlund, 2000; Neisser, 1998a). For example, the nonverbal UNIT test described earlier was created specifically to minimize cultural influences on test performance: The UNIT's authors consulted with people from African American, Hispanic American, Asian American, and Native American backgrounds to ensure that the tasks and content were not culturally or racially biased (McCallum, 1999). Ethnic and racial group differences on the UNIT are considerably smaller than the differences seen on more traditional intelligence tests, but there are group differences on the test nonetheless (McCallum, 1999).

Socioeconomic status. One likely reason for the lower IQ scores of African American and Hispanic American children is that, on average, these children live in families and neighborhoods with lower incomes than do European American children. Socioeconomic status affects the quality of prenatal and postnatal nutrition, availability of stimulating books and toys, access to educational opportunities, and other environmental factors that are likely to affect intellectual development and test performance (Brooks-Gunn et al., 1996; McLoyd, 1998b).

Discriminatory practices. Even if different ethnic and racial groups have similar economic resources, systematic and long-term discrimination (e.g., exclusion from better schools and jobs, lower expectations for classroom performance) can limit minority children's opportunities for intellectual growth (Ogbu, 1994). Widespread discrimination may cause heredity to have an indirect effect on intelligence, in that inherited skin color or other physical characteristics (rather than inherited intellectual potential per se) elicit responses from society that affect intellectual development. Block (1999) offers a helpful analogy:

> Consider a culture in which red-haired children are beaten over the head regularly, but all other children are treated well. This effect will increase the measured heritability of IQ because red-haired identical twins will tend to resemble one another in IQ (because they will both have low IQs) no matter what the social class of the family in which they are raised. The effect of a red-hair gene on red hair is a "direct" genetic effect because the gene affects the color via an internal biochemical process. By contrast . . . the red hair genes affect IQ *indirectly.* (Block, 1999, pp. 466–467, emphasis added)

cultural bias
Extent to which an assessment instrument offends or unfairly penalizes some individuals because of their ethnicity, gender, or socioeconomic status.

Motivation to do well on an intelligence test increases the IQ scores that children earn, especially on group-administered paper-pencil tests.

Motivation. Many children put forth maximum effort on assigned school tasks, including intelligence tests (Flynn, 1991; Ogbu, 1994). But others, including some African American and Hispanic American youngsters, may have little motivation to perform well on an intelligence test. Some may give minimal answers (e.g., "I don't know") as a way of shortening a testing session that they find confusing and unsettling (Zigler & Finn-Stevenson, 1992). Others may view school achievement of any sort as a form of "acting White" and therefore as something that interferes with their own sense of cultural identity (Ogbu, 1994). Still others may exhibit a phenomenon known as **stereotype threat:** They perform more poorly, unintentionally and perhaps as a result of excessive anxiety, if they believe that members of their group typically do not do well on the test (Osborne & Simmons, 2002; Steele, 1997).

Undoubtedly, the factors just described have different influences (and in some cases, no influence at all) on how individual children perform on an intelligence test. An encouraging trend is that various ethnic and racial groups have, in recent years, become increasingly similar in IQ scores and other measures of cognitive ability. Such a trend can be attributed only to more equitable environmental conditions across society (Ceci, Rosenblum, & Kumpf, 1998; Huang & Hauser, 1998; Neisser et al., 1996).

Critique of Current Perspectives on Intelligence

At present, the psychological study of intelligence is a virtual minefield of explosive issues: What is intelligence? How should we measure it? How much is it influenced by hereditary (and so presumably immutable) factors? Can enriching experiences significantly improve it? The answers to such questions have major implications for educational and clinical practice, political decision making, and social policy, but they have not yet been answered definitively. In addition, several fundamental concerns about contemporary research and practice related to intelligence and intelligence tests must be raised:

■ *Research has relied too heavily on traditional intelligence tests.* Existing intelligence tests have been designed primarily to identify individuals who may require special interventions or educational services, and in this context they can be quite helpful. Yet researchers have used them in other ways as well—for instance, to make cross-group comparisons, draw conclusions about the relative effects of heredity and environment in intellectual development, and evaluate the effectiveness of preschool programs for low-income children—without due consideration of the appropriateness of IQ tests for such purposes.

By and large, published intelligence tests are atheoretical in nature: They are comprised of tasks that have been found to predict school achievement rather than tasks that, from a theoretical perspective, reflect the essence of what intelligence might actually be. We do not fault intelligence test authors for this state of affairs. After all, their primary goal has been to assist clinicians and educators in monitoring children's intellectual progress, not to help researchers explore the underlying nature of intelligence.

Traditional intelligence tests are probably too limited to help researchers completely answer broad theoretical questions about the origins and development of intelligence. And they certainly don't reflect contemporary views of intelligence—views that portray intelligence as an entity that involves complex cognitive and metacognitive processes and perhaps several relatively independent abilities (Gardner, 1995; D. N. Perkins, 1995; Sternberg, 1996). As Robert Sternberg has put it, "there is more to intelligence than IQ" (1996, p. 15).

■ *IQ scores are too often interpreted out of context.* Over the years, the use of intelligence tests has been quite controversial. In earlier decades (as recently as the 1970s), IQ scores were frequently used as the sole criterion for identifying children as having mental retar-

stereotype threat
Reduction in performance (often unintentional) as a result of a belief that one's group typically performs poorly.

dation. In part as a result of this practice, children from racial and ethnic minority groups were disproportionately represented in special education classes, where it was easy to "write them off" as not having much potential for academic achievement.

Most counselors, clinical and school psychologists, and other specialists now have sufficient training in psychoeducational assessment to understand that a single IQ score should never warrant a diagnosis of "mental retardation" or any other condition. Decisions about special educational placement and services must always be based on multiple sources of information about a child. Yet many other people (including many teachers) seem to view IQ scores as precise measures of permanent characteristics. For instance, we often hear remarks such as "She has an IQ of such-and-such" spoken in much the same matter-of-fact manner as someone might say, "She has brown eyes."

For most children, IQ scores are reasonably accurate reflections of their current cognitive development and learning potential. But for a few children, IQs may be poor summaries of what they can do at present or are likely to do in the future. Teachers and other practitioners must be extremely careful not to put too much stock in any single IQ score, particularly when working with children from diverse backgrounds.

■ *Assessment of intelligence focuses almost exclusively on skills that are valued in mainstream Western culture.* The items found on traditional intelligence tests focus on a limited set of cognitive skills that are valued in mainstream Western, middle-class culture, and particularly in school settings (Sternberg, 1996). Such a bias enhances the tests' predictive validity, because our schools, too, place heavy emphasis on the skills valued in mainstream Western culture.

Yet other cultural and socioeconomic groups value and nurture other abilities that may be equally beneficial for children's long-term academic and professional success. For example, Mexican American children may show exceptional skill in cooperating with their peers; cooperation is a valued skill among many Mexican Americans (Abi-Nader, 1993; Okagaki & Sternberg, 1993; Vasquez, 1990). African American children may show particular talent in oral language—more specifically in colorful speech, creative storytelling, or humor (Torrance, 1989). In Navajo culture, intelligence may be reflected in a child's ability to help the family and tribe, to perform cultural rituals, or to demonstrate expert craftsmanship (Kirschenbaum, 1989). In parts of Polynesia, it might be reflected in art, music, or dance (Reid, 1989). Ultimately, we can gain a better understanding of children's intellectual abilities only when we broaden the ways in which we assess those abilities.

Some cultures value and nurture abilities that are not reflected in traditional intelligence tests.

■ *Intelligence tests overlook dispositions and metacognitive strategies as important contributors to intellectual functioning.* Most descriptions and measures of intelligence focus on specific things that a child *can* do (abilities), with little consideration of what a child is *likely* to do (dispositions) (Kuhn, 2001a; D. N. Perkins, 1995; D. Perkins, Tishman, Ritchhart, Donis, & Andrade, 2000). For instance, intelligence tests don't evaluate the extent to which children view a situation from multiple perspectives, examine data with a critical eye, and metacognitively reflect on what they are doing as they tackle everyday tasks and problems, nor do they assess how effectively children engage in self-regulated learning. Yet such qualities are often just as important as intellectual ability in determining success in academic and real-world tasks (D. Perkins et al., 2000).

■ *Many theorists have placed higher priority on assessing current intelligence than on developing future intelligence.* Implicit in the practice of intelligence testing is the assumption that intelligence is a relatively fixed, and perhaps largely inherited, ability. In our minds, there has been entirely too much focus on sorting children and entirely too little on fostering their development. Fortunately, some psychologists and educators are now calling for a shift in focus from the *assessment* of intelligence to the *development* of intelligence (Boykin, 1994; Council for Exceptional Children, 1995; Nichols & Mittelholtz, 1997; Resnick, 1995; Sternberg et al., 2000). As theorists and researchers gain a better understanding of the nature of intelligence and the environmental factors that promote it, society and schools can, we hope, shift to a more proactive approach, one in which all children are given the opportunities they need to maximize their intellectual growth.

Implications of Theories and Research on Intelligence

Given existing knowledge about the nature and development of intelligence, as well as our concerns about shortcomings in the field, we offer the following suggestions to teachers and other practitioners who work with infants, children, and adolescents:

■ *Maintain a healthy skepticism about the accuracy of IQ scores.* Intelligent tests can, in many cases, provide a general idea of children's current cognitive functioning. Yet IQ scores are rarely dead-on measures of what children can do. As we have seen, the scores of young children may vary considerably from one testing to the next and have limited predictive validity. And the scores of children from diverse ethnic and linguistic backgrounds are often affected by background experiences, motivation, and proficiency in English. We cannot stress this point enough: IQ scores should never be used as the sole criterion in making diagnoses and decisions about children.

■ *Remain optimistic about every child's potential.* As you have learned, the environments in which children grow—at home, in school, and elsewhere—have a significant effect on their intellectual development. IQ scores are hardly set in concrete in the early years; they can and often do improve over time. Furthermore, if intelligence is as multifaceted as theorists such as Gardner and Sternberg propose, then different children are apt to be intelligent in different ways. Finally, many factors in addition to intelligence— learning strategies, motivation, adult guidance, availability of educational resources, and so on—also play critical roles in children's ability to succeed in school and in the outside world.

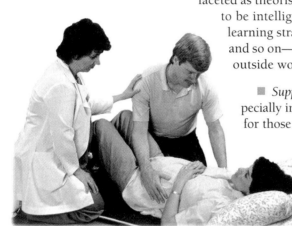

Public agencies can most effectively promote children's intellectual development when they provide support services during the prenatal period as well as during infancy and early childhood.

■ *Support early intervention programs in your community.* Early intervention is especially important for infants and toddlers with developmental disabilities, as well as for those from low-income neighborhoods or disruptive family circumstances. Such intervention can take the form of regular checkups and nutritional support for pregnant women, stimulating infant care and preschool programs, or suggestions and materials for helping inexperienced mothers nurture their children's cognitive growth at home. Ideally, interventions should integrate a variety of services into a single support network and should consider children's social and emotional needs as well as their cognitive development (Gonzalez-Mena, 2002; Shonkoff & Phillips, 2000).

■ *Capitalize on children's unique strengths and abilities to teach new topics and skills.* Gardner's theory in particular encourages instructors to use a variety of approaches in instruction, building on the diverse abilities that different children may have (Armstrong, 1994; F. A. Campbell et al., 1998; Gardner, 1999, 2000). For instance, the following scenario illustrates how some children may learn more effectively when they can use their visual-spatial skills:

> In third grade, Jason loved to build with blocks, legos, toothpicks, popsicle sticks, anything that fit together. During a unit on ancient history, Jason built an object for every culture studied. He fashioned Babylonian ziggurats out of legos, Egyptian pyramids with toothpicks and small marshmallows, the Great Wall of China from miniature clay bricks which he made, the Greek Parthenon from styrofoam computer-packing, Roman bridges out of popsicle sticks and brads, and Mayan temples with molded plastic strips resurrected from an old science kit. While appearing apathetic during most classroom activities, Jason was highly animated during his building projects. History came alive for Jason when he could build the structures of each era and culture studied. (F. A. Campbell et al., 1998, p. 79)

Educators should consider children's multiple abilities not only when they plan lessons but also when they assess achievement. For instance, one of Jeanne's teaching interns, Dan Moulis, gave students in his middle school social studies class several options to demon-

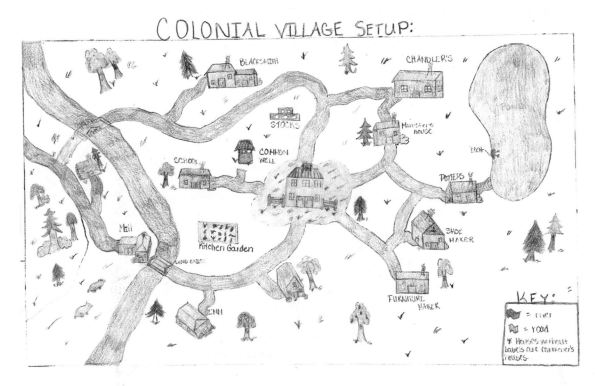

COLONIAL VILLAGE SETUP:

FIGURE 6-7 Jenna, a middle school student, used her artistic talents to show her knowledge of colonial life in America

strate their knowledge of settlers' life in colonial America. Several used their artistic talents to depict typical colonial villages; Figure 6–7 presents one student's creation.

■ *Be open-minded about the ways in which children might demonstrate intelligence.* To the extent that intelligence is culture-dependent, intelligent behavior is likely to take different forms in children from different cultural backgrounds (Gardner, 1995; Neisser et al., 1996; Perkins, 1995; Sternberg, 1985). We must not limit our conception of intelligence to children's ability to succeed at traditional school tasks. The Observation Guidelines table "Seeing Intelligence in Children's Daily Behavior" presents a variety of behaviors that may reflect higher intelligence than children's IQ scores reveal.

■ *Promote more "intelligent" cognitive strategies.* Look back once again at the chapter's opening case study. Gina's relative weakness in history is due largely to her ineffective study strategies. In fact, teachers, parents, and other adults can promote more effective learning, studying, and problem solving—and thereby promote more intelligent behavior—by teaching children more sophisticated and effective cognitive and metacognitive strategies (Perkins, 1995; Perkins & Grotzer, 1997).

■ *Give children the support they need to think more intelligently.* The notion of distributed intelligence tells us that intelligent behavior should be relatively commonplace when children have the right tools, social groups, and symbolic systems with which to work (Pea, 1993). Rather than asking the question, "How intelligent are these children?" adults should instead ask themselves, "How can I help these children think as intelligently as possible? What tools, social networks, and symbolic systems can I provide?"

Children and adolescents often differ considerably in the extent to which they display intelligent thinking and behavior. For the most part, educators and other practitioners can easily accommodate such variability within the context of normal instructional practices. In some cases, however, young learners have ability levels so different from those of peers that they require special educational services to help them reach their full potential. We turn now to exceptionalities in intelligence.

OBSERVATION GUIDELINES

Seeing Intelligence in Children's Daily Behavior

CHARACTERISTIC	LOOK FOR	EXAMPLE	IMPLICATION
Oral Language Skills	• Sophisticated vocabulary • Colorful speech • Creative storytelling • Clever jokes and puns	LaMarr entertains his friends with clever "Your momma's so fat . . ." jokes.	Look for unusual creativity or advanced language development in children's everyday speech.
Learning Ability	• Ability to learn new information quickly • Ability to find relationships among diverse ideas • Excellent memory	Four-year-old Gina teaches herself to read using several reading primers she finds at home. Initially, she asks her mother to read a few of the words in the books. Once she knows these words, she deduces many letter-sound correspondences on her own and applies them to decipher additional words.	Make note of situations in which children learn and comprehend new material more quickly than their peers. Look for creative analogies and interconnections.
Problem-Solving Skills	• Ability to solve challenging problems • Flexibility in applying previously learned strategies to novel situations • Ability to improvise with commonplace objects and materials	A fourth-grade class plans to perform a skit during an upcoming open house. When the children puzzle about how to hang a sheet from the ceiling (to serve as a stage curtain), Jeff suggests that they turn their desks to face the side of the classroom rather than the front. This way, the sheet can be hung from a light fixture that runs the length of the room.	Present unusual tasks and problems for which children have no ready-made strategies.
Cognitive and Metacognitive Strategies	• Use of sophisticated learning strategies • Desire to understand rather than memorize • Effective comprehension monitoring	Shannon, a sixth grader, explains that she learned the countries on South America's west coast (Colombia, Ecuador, Peru, Chile) by creating the sentence, "*Co*lin *e*ats *pe*as and *ch*ocolate."	Ask children to explain how they think about the things they are trying to learn and remember.
Curiosity and Inquisitiveness	• Voracious appetite for knowledge • Tendency to ask a lot of questions • Intrinsic motivation to master challenging subject matter	Alfredo reads every book and article he can find about outer space; he has a particular interest in black holes.	Find out what children like to do in their free time.
Leadership and Social Skills	• Ability to persuade and motivate others • Exceptional sensitivity to other people's feelings and body language • Ability to mediate disagreements and help others reach reasonable compromises	As a high school student, Gina organizes a school-wide peer tutoring program.	Observe how children interact with their peers at play, in cooperative group work, and in extracurricular activities.

Sources: B. Clark, 1997; Gottfried, Gottfried, Bathurst, & Guerin, 1994; Lupart, 1995; Maker, 1993; Maker & Schiever, 1989; D. N. Perkins, 1995; Torrance, 1989, 1995; Turnbull et al., 1999; Winner, 1997.

Exceptionalities in Intelligence

No matter how we define or measure intelligence, we find that some children and adolescents show exceptional talent and others show significant cognitive delays relative to their peers. The two ends of the intelligence continuum are commonly known as *giftedness* and *mental retardation.*[7]

---

[7]Note that, in the United States, different states may establish somewhat different criteria for these two categories, especially with regard to determining eligibility for special services.

Giftedness

Gina, described in the opening case study and revisited in the Observation Guidelines table, is an example of someone who is gifted. More generally, **giftedness** is unusually high ability or aptitude in one or more areas, to the point where special educational services are necessary to help a young learner meet his or her full potential. Children and adolescents who are gifted (sometimes called *gifted and talented*) show exceptional achievement or promise in one or more of the following areas:

- General intellectual ability
- Aptitude in a specific academic field
- Creativity
- Visual or performing arts
- Leadership
  (U.S. Department of Education, 1993)

When we try to pin down giftedness more precisely, we find considerable disagreement about how to do so (K. R. Carter, 1991; Keogh & MacMillan, 1996). Many school districts identify students as gifted primarily on the basis of general IQ scores, often using 125 or 130 as a minimum cutoff point (Keogh & MacMillan, 1996; Webb, Meckstroth, & Tolan, 1982), but some experts argue that multiple criteria should be applied when determining children's eligibility for special services (Council for Exceptional Children, 1995; Renzulli & Reis, 1986; Sternberg & Zhang, 1995). For instance, one theorist has argued that creativity and task commitment should be considered in addition to IQ scores (Renzulli, 1978). Furthermore, scores on general intelligence tests may be largely irrelevant when identifying children who show exceptional promise in specific academic fields, creativity, the arts, or leadership.

A further complication is that giftedness is likely to take different forms in different cultures. The tendency to rely heavily on traditional intelligence tests for identifying giftedness is probably a key reason that many minority populations are underrepresented in gifted education programs (C. R. Harris, 1991; Maker & Schiever, 1989; U.S. Department of Education, Office of Civil Rights, 1993).

Possible Roots of Giftedness   Giftedness may be partly an inherited characteristic: Some individuals who are gifted show unusual brain development, perhaps advanced development in the right hemisphere or greater involvement of both hemispheres in performing certain kinds of tasks (Winner, 2000b). Correlational studies suggest (though do not necessarily prove) that environmental factors play a significant role as well (B. Clark, 1997; A. W. Gottfried et al., 1994). For instance, children who are gifted are more likely to be first-born or only-born children, who generally have more attention and stimulation from their parents than other children do. They often have many opportunities to practice and enhance their talents from a very early age, long before they have been identified as being gifted. Children who are gifted are also more likely to seek out enriching opportunities—an example of the *niche-picking* phenomenon described earlier.

In one longitudinal study (A. W. Gottfried et al., 1994), many gifted children showed signs of advanced cognitive and linguistic development beginning at 18 months of age. As is true for Gina in the opening case study, a child's giftedness is often evident throughout childhood and adolescence. Yet some children may be "late bloomers": Their talents become evident relatively late in the game, perhaps as environmental conditions bring such talents to fruition.

Common Characteristics of Children Who Are Gifted   Although children who are gifted are typically very different from one another in their particular strengths and talents, in general they learn more quickly and easily, exhibit greater flexibility in ideas and approaches to tasks, engage in abstract thinking at an earlier age, and have advanced metacognitive skills (Candler-Lotven, Tallent-Runnels, Olivárez, & Hildreth, 1994; K. R. Carter & Ormrod, 1982; Lupart, 1995; Winner, 1997, 2000b). Often they have an exceptional drive to learn, seek out challenging endeavors, make their own discoveries, and master tasks with little instruction from others (Winner, 2000a, 2000b). Most have high self-esteem, good social skills, and above-average emotional adjustment (Cornell et al., 1990; A. W. Gottfried et al., 1994). However, a few extremely gifted children may have

giftedness
Unusually high ability in one or more areas, to the point where children require special educational services to help them meet their full potential.

social or emotional difficulties because they are so very different from their peers (Keogh & MacMillan, 1996; Winner, 1997).

Many youngsters who are gifted become bored or frustrated when school experiences and organized outside activities don't provide tasks that challenge them and help them develop their unique abilities; they may find instruction slow and repetitive of things they already know (Friedel, 1993; Winner, 1997). One junior high school student expressed her feelings this way:

> They won't let us learn. . . . What I mean is, they seem to think they have to keep us all together all the time. That means in the subjects I'm good at I can't learn more because I'm always waiting for others to catch up. I guess if I get too far ahead I'll be doing the next year's work, but I can't understand what's wrong with that if that's what I'm ready for. (Feldhusen, Van Winkel, & Ehle, 1996, p. 48)

Recalling Lev Vygotsky's theory of cognitive development from Chapter 4, we could say that children who are gifted are unlikely to be working within their zone of proximal development if they are limited to the same tasks assigned to their peers, diminishing their opportunities to develop more advanced cognitive skills.

As a result of frequent boredom and frustration, some students who are gifted lose interest in school tasks and put in only the minimum effort they need to get by in the classroom (Feldhusen, 1989); as an example, see Figure 6–8. In fact, gifted children are among our schools' greatest underachievers: When required to progress at the same rate as their nongifted peers, they achieve at levels far short of their capabilities (K. R. Carter, 1991; Gallagher, 1991; Reis, 1989). Such underachievement may especially be an issue for females and children from minority groups (Ford, 1996; Nichols & Ganschow, 1992).

Some children and adolescents try to hide their exceptional talents. They may fear that peers will ridicule them for their high academic abilities and enthusiasm for academic topics, especially at the secondary school level (Covington, 1992; DeLisle, 1984). Girls in particular

FIGURE 6–8 Many students who are gifted lose interest in school when not sufficiently challenged by classroom activities. These excerpts are from a letter written by Geoff, an eleventh grader, to request permission to graduate early. School officials found his rationale convincing and complied with his request.

Dear Mr. P——:

I have found in recent months that it is time for me to make the next step in my life. This step is graduation. I would like to graduate a year early in May, this year, with the class of 2002.

This is a step I have chosen as the best for me for several reasons. The first reason is that I would like to spend a semester studying abroad in Austria. I have chosen Austria because it is a country where German is spoken and this is the language I have been learning for four years....

I have also decided to graduate because several people have suggested that this is my best option, as they believe that I am at a maturity level that indicates I should move on. These people, among others, are primarily my parents, my advisor, and the school counselor. They suggest that I am ready to graduate, but perhaps not ready for college, which is why I've chosen to do a foreign exchange and give myself time to further mature and prepare for college.

Besides these reasons, I personally believe that I would have extreme difficulty attending school next year and succeeding. I have been told that this same thing is seen every year, when seniors become tired of attending, as they lack the motivation to succeed. I am afraid that this would happen to me, but on a higher level, as I already feel that I am losing motivation. Attending school next year could mean dire consequences for my transcript, my G.P.A., and my life.

When speaking with [the school counselor], we decided that I need to finish an internship and one job shadow, and I will have the credits necessary to graduate by the end of the school year. I plan to set up several internships over a period of five days in five different fields of engineering, so I can get an idea of what each field is like....

I hope you understand my reasons for leaving and I am sure that you will support me in my decision to graduate early. It will be difficult to change in such a gigantic way, but it will be very beneficial for me in the end.

Sincerely,
Geoff A——

are likely to hide their talents, especially if they have been raised in cultures that do not value high achievement in females (Covington, 1992; Davis & Rimm, 1998; Nichols & Ganschow, 1992). Gifted Asian Americans, because of cultural traditions of obedience, conformity, and respect for authority, may be reluctant to engage in creative activities and may willingly comply when asked to perform unchallenging assignments (Maker & Schiever, 1989).

Fostering the Development of Children Who Are Gifted   Teachers and other practitioners can use a variety of strategies to meet the needs of children and adolescents who are gifted. Following are several suggestions that experts have offered:

■ *Provide individualized tasks and activities.*   Even though children who are gifted are a very heterogeneous group, many schools provide the same curriculum and materials for all of the students they've identified as being gifted. In fact, no single academic program can meet the specific needs of each and every gifted child. Different youngsters may need special services in very different areas—for example, in mathematics, creative writing, or studio art.

■ *Form study groups of individuals who have similar interests and abilities.*   In any single location, there are likely to be several young people who have common interests and abilities, and it may sometimes be helpful to pull them together into study groups where they can cooperatively pursue a particular topic or task (Fiedler, Lange, & Winebrenner, 1993; Stanley, 1980). In some instances, a school-based study group may explore a topic with greater depth and more sophisticated analysis than other students in the classroom do (an *enrichment* approach). In other cases, such a group may simply move through the standard curriculum at a more rapid pace (an *acceleration* approach).

Forming homogeneous study groups has several advantages. First, a single instructor can meet the needs of several individuals simultaneously. Second, like their nongifted peers, most gifted learners yearn for social interaction and benefit from increased contact with others who have similar interests (McGinn, Viernstein, & Hogan, 1980; Winner, 2000b). And third, youngsters are less likely to try to hide their talent and enthusiasm for the subject matter when they work with peers who have similar ability and motivation (Feldhusen, 1989).

■ *Teach complex cognitive skills within the context of specific subject areas.*   Some programs for the gifted have tried to teach complex thought processes (e.g., problem solving and logical reasoning) as skills totally separate from academic subject matter. But this approach tends to have minimal impact on the development of giftedness, and in fact it often focuses on skills that many students have already acquired. Instead, educators are better advised to teach complex thinking skills within the context of specific topics—for example, reasoning and problem-solving skills in science, or creativity in writing (Linn et al., 1989; Moon, Feldhusen, & Dillon, 1994; Pulos & Linn, 1981; Stanley, 1980).

■ *Provide opportunities for independent study.*   As we have seen, many children and adolescents who are gifted have advanced learning and metacognitive skills and a strong motivation to learn about and master challenging topics and tasks. Therefore, independent study in areas of interest may be quite appropriate. When teachers and other adults provide opportunities for independent study, however, they should teach the study habits and research skills necessary to use time and resources effectively.

■ *Encourage high goals.*   Because gifted youngsters are capable of higher performance in specific areas, they should ideally set higher goals for themselves in those areas. Adults should encourage them to aim high, while at the same time reminding them not to expect perfection for themselves (W. D. Parker, 1997; Sanborn, 1979). For instance, some high school students may have given little or no thought to attending college, perhaps because their families have never expected them to pursue higher education; under such circumstances, their teachers and counselors might give them the opportunity to visit a college campus and explore possible means of funding a college education (Spicker, 1992).

■ *Seek resources outside of school.*   Any single school district is likely to have students with exceptional potential in so many different areas that no single teacher—not even a specialist in gifted education—can reasonably meet all of their needs (L. H. Fox, 1979; Stanley, 1980). It is therefore sometimes appropriate to identify suitable *mentors,* individuals

DEVELOPMENT AND PRACTICE

Providing Challenging Activities for Gifted Children and Adolescents

- Individualize instruction in accordance with learners' specific talents.

  A mathematically gifted junior high school student studies calculus via computer-assisted instruction, while a classmate with exceptional reading skills is assigned novels appropriate to his reading level.

- Form study groups of gifted learners with similar abilities and interests.

  The director of an after-school community center—himself a talented musician—creates and then provides semiweekly instruction and practice sessions for a quintet of musically talented 10- and 11-year-olds. As the group gains skill and camaraderie, it begins meeting daily, even though the director cannot always be there to provide assistance.

- Teach complex cognitive skills within the context of specific school topics rather than separately from the standard school curriculum.

  A teacher has an advanced science study group conduct a series of experiments related to a single topic. To promote critical thinking, she gives the students several questions they should ask themselves as they conduct these experiments.

- Seek outside resources to help students develop their exceptional talents.

  A high school student with a high aptitude for learning foreign languages studies Russian at a local university.

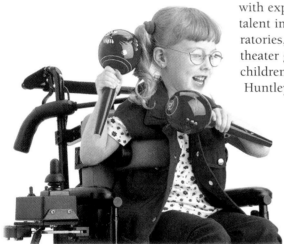

with expertise in a particular area who can help young people develop their own talent in that area. In other circumstances, outside agencies—for example, laboratories, government offices, private businesses, volunteer community groups, theater groups, and art and videotaping studios—may provide opportunities for children and adolescents to develop their unique talents (Ambrose, Allen, & Huntley, 1994; Piirto, 1999; Seeley, 1989).

Keep in mind that a child can be gifted and also have a disability. For example, some gifted children have learning disabilities, ADHD, emotional disorders, or physical or sensory challenges (e.g., Hettinger & Knapp, 2001). In such situations, teachers and other practitioners must address the disabilities as well as the areas of giftedness when planning instruction and activities. A few gifted children—for example, those with a limited English background or those who have specific learning disabilities—may even need some training in basic skills (Brown-Mizuno, 1990; C. R. Harris, 1991; Udall, 1989).

Some children who are gifted also have disabilities—possibly learning disabilities, emotional disorders, or physical challenges. This girl's teacher must take both her giftedness and her physical disability into account when planning instruction.

mental retardation
Condition marked by significantly below-average general intelligence and deficits in adaptive behavior.

adaptive behavior
Behavior related to daily living skills and appropriate conduct in social situations.

Mental Retardation

Children with **mental retardation** show developmental delays in most aspects of their academic and social functioning. A child must exhibit two characteristics before a diagnosis of mental retardation is appropriate (American Association on Mental Retardation, 1992):

- *Significantly below-average general intelligence.* Children with mental retardation perform poorly on traditional intelligence tests; their IQ scores are usually no higher than 65 or 70, reflecting performance in the bottom 2 percent of their age group (Keogh & MacMillan, 1996; Turnbull et al., 2002). They show other signs of below-average intelligence as well; for instance, they learn slowly and perform quite poorly on school tasks in comparison with their age-mates, and they show consistently poor achievement across virtually all academic subject areas.

- *Deficits in adaptive behavior.* Low intelligence test scores and poor academic performance are insufficient evidence to classify children as having mental retardation. An additional criterion is a deficit in **adaptive behavior**, which includes *practical intelligence* (management of the ordinary activities of daily living) and *social intelligence* (appropriate conduct in social situations). In these areas, children and adolescents with mental retardation often exhibit behaviors typical of individuals much younger than themselves (American Association on Mental Retardation, 1992).

Possible Roots of Mental Retardation   Mental retardation is often caused by abnormal genetic conditions; for example, most children with Down syndrome have delayed cognitive development. Sometimes mental retardation runs in families, such that many family members' abilities fall at the lower end of the normal distribution of intelligence (Kail, 1998).

Yet heredity is not always to blame. Some instances of mental retardation are due to non-inherited biological causes, such as severe malnutrition or substance abuse during the mother's pregnancy (recall our discussion of fetal alcohol syndrome), oxygen deprivation associated with a difficult birth, or ingestion of lead paint in early childhood (Keogh & MacMillan, 1996; McLoyd, 1998b; Streissguth et al., 1994; Vogel, 1997). Conditions in the home, such as parental neglect or an extremely impoverished and unstimulating home life, may also be at fault (Batshaw & Shapiro, 1997; Feuerstein, 1979; M. M. Wagner, 1995a). Undoubtedly as a result of such factors as malnutrition, ingestion of lead, and other environmental hazards, children from poor, inner-city neighborhoods are overrepresented among school children who are identified as having mental retardation (U.S. Department of Education, Office of Civil Rights, 1993).

Common Characteristics of Children with Mental Retardation   Children and adolescents with mental retardation show impairments in many aspects of information processing, including attention, working memory, and learning strategies (Butterfield & Ferretti, 1987; Dempster & Corkill, 1999; Turnbull et al., 2002). They have little metacognitive awareness of how they think and learn, have trouble generalizing the things they learn to new situations, and often exhibit a sense of helplessness about their ability to learn new things (Butterfield & Ferretti, 1987; Seligman, 1975; Turnbull et al., 2002). Their play activities are typical of children much younger than themselves (F. P. Hughes, 1998; Malone, Stoneham, & Langone, 1995).

Yet adults must remember that children with mental retardation also have many strengths and that they are more likely to master new knowledge and skills when instruction builds on what they know and do well. In *Expecting Adam,* Martha Beck (1999) describes how her son Adam, who has Down syndrome, learned the alphabet. Soon after Adam turned 3, Beck and her husband began regular drills on alphabet letters, but they made little progress until they stumbled on a different instructional approach three years later:

> [F]rom the time he started preschool at three, we kept running Adam through the alphabet, repeating the name of each letter, along with its major sound, thousands and thousands of times in the strained voices of tourists who believe they can overcome any language barrier by sheer volume.
>
> It didn't work. When quizzed without prompting, Adam never recognized the letters on his own. By the time he was six I was ready to give up.
>
> Then one day John [Adam's father] was holding up a plastic letter and making its sound, which happened to be "EEEEEEE," when Adam suddenly perked up and said, "Wizbef!" This is the way he pronounces his sister Elizabeth's name. . . . During that day, we discovered that Adam's learning capacity went way beyond anything we expected—as long as everything he learned related directly to someone he cared about. He had absolutely no interest in, for example, "E is for egg." But E for Elizabeth—now *that* was crucial information.
>
> In the end we all learned the alphabet this way. The symbols we had been trying to link to abstract sounds ended up as a parade of personalities: Adam first, of course, and then Billy, Caleb, Diane, Elizabeth, Francine, Grandpa . . . As we figured out how he learned, the landscape of our son's mind began to reveal itself to us. Instead of a rationally constructed structure of empirical observations, logical conclusions, and arbitrary symbols, Adam's mental world seems to be more like a huge family reunion. It is a gathering of people, all linked by Adam's affection into a complex universe of relationships and characteristics. In this world, Adam learned as fast as anyone I know. Long before he could read or write even the most basic words (or so I thought), Adam came home to tell me, in his garbled tongue, about the new boy who had just moved into his class, and who had become Adam's friend. When I couldn't understand his pronunciation of the boy's name, Adam grabbed a pencil in his stubby, grubby little-boy fingers, and wrote "Miguel Fernando de la Hoya" on a piece of paper—a piece of paper, needless to say, which I intend to frame.

From *Expecting Adam* (pp. 314–315) by Martha Beck, copyright © 1999 by Martha Beck. Used by permission of Times Books, a division of Random House, Inc.

Fostering the Development of Children with Mental Retardation   The great majority of children and adolescents with mental retardation attend school, and many of them are capable of mastering a wide variety of academic and vocational skills. Following are several strategies that experts recommend for teachers and other practitioners:

■ *Pace instruction to ensure a high rate of success.*   When working in classrooms with students who have mental retardation, teachers should pace instruction at a rate commensurate with students' abilities; for example, they might move through topics more slowly, repeat important ideas frequently, and provide numerous opportunities to practice new tasks. Students with mental retardation typically have a long history of failure at academic tasks; hence, they need frequent success experiences to learn that they can succeed in school and elsewhere.

■ *Use instructional materials appropriate to children's cognitive abilities.*   In many cases, the standard instructional materials for a particular age level are not appropriate for young people with mental retardation. Instead, instructors should find reading materials, workbooks, concrete manipulatives, and so on, that are suitable for the learning and reasoning capabilities that each individual currently demonstrates. Materials commonly used for children at lower grade levels are sometimes appropriate, provided that such materials do not appear too "babyish." In other cases, a special educator may be able to recommend appropriate materials.

■ *Provide considerable scaffolding to facilitate effective cognitive processing.*   Children and adolescents with mental retardation typically have little awareness of how to direct and regulate their own learning. So it is often helpful to provide explicit guidance about how to think about topics and learning materials. For instance, classroom teachers can help students focus their attention by using such phrases as "get ready," "look," or "listen" (Turnbull et al., 2002). They can provide simple, structured study guides that indicate

---

DEVELOPMENT AND PRACTICE

Maximizing the Development of Children and Adolescents with Mental Retardation

■ Encourage infants to use the strengths they have, and offer opportunities and support for acquiring new knowledge and skills.

An 18-month-old who has mental retardation and physical disabilities has recently begun attending an infant child care center. His caregiver thinks creatively about how to help him interact with his physical environment. For example, she glues Popsicle sticks to the pages of cardboard books so that he can easily grab them and turn the pages. To help him feel secure in his infant chair, she puts skid-proof material on the seat of the chair and cushions at the sides to keep him upright.

■ Introduce new material at a slower pace, and provide many opportunities for practice.

A fourth-grade teacher gives a student only two new addition facts a week, primarily because any more than two seem to overwhelm him. Every day, the teacher has the student practice writing the new facts and review addition facts learned in previous weeks.

■ Explain tasks concretely and in very specific terms.

An art instructor gives a student explicit training in the steps she needs to take at the end of each painting session: (1) Rinse the paintbrush out at the sink, (2) put the brush and watercolor paints on the shelf in the back room, and (3) put the painting on the counter by the window to dry. Initially the instructor needs to remind her of every step in the process. Eventually, with time and practice, she carries out the process independently.

■ Give explicit guidance about how to study.

A child-specific teacher's aide tells a student, "When you study a new spelling word, it helps if you repeat the letters out loud while you practice writing the word. Let's try it with *house,* the word you are learning this morning. Watch how I repeat the letters—H . . . O . . . U . . . S . . . E—as I write the word. Now you try doing what I just did."

■ Give feedback about specific behaviors rather than about general areas of performance.

A vocational educator tells a student, "You did a good job in wood shop this week. You followed my instructions correctly, and you put away the equipment when I asked you to do so."

■ Encourage independence.

A life skills instructor shows a student how to use her calculator to figure out how much she needs to pay for lunch every day. The teacher also gives the student considerable practice in identifying the correct bills and coins to use when paying various amounts.

quite specifically what to focus on when studying (Mastropieri & Scruggs, 1992). They also can teach a few simple, concrete memory strategies, such as repeating instructions over and over (rehearsal) or physically rearranging a group of items that must be remembered (organization) (Fletcher & Bray, 1995; Turnbull, 1974). When children with mental retardation acquire such strategies, their learning and academic performance improve (Perkins, 1995).

■ *Teach vocational and general life skills.*   Many young adults with mental retardation live somewhat independently and join the adult work force in some capacity. Accordingly, an important part of their education, often within the high school curriculum, is training in general life and work skills. Because of their limited ability to generalize what they have learned from one situation to another, it is especially important to teach life and work skills in realistic settings—those that closely resemble the situations in which they will find themselves once they leave school (Turnbull et al., 2002).

Although usually a long-term condition, mental retardation is not necessarily a lifelong disability, especially when the presumed cause is environmental rather than genetic (Beirne-Smith, Ittenbach, & Patton, 1998; Landesman & Ramey, 1989). Our final case study illustrates just how much of a difference environment can make.

CASE STUDY: FRESH VEGETABLES

Twelve-year-old Steven had no known genetic or other organic problems but had been officially labeled as having mental retardation based on his low scores on a series of intelligence tests. His prior schooling had been limited to just part of one year in a first-grade classroom in inner-city Chicago. His mother had withdrawn him after a bullet grazed his leg while he was walking to school one morning. Fearing for her son's safety, she would not let him outside the apartment after that, not even to play, and certainly not to walk the six blocks to the local elementary school.

When a truant officer finally appeared at the door one evening five years later, Steven and his mother quickly packed their bags and moved to a small town in northern Colorado. They found residence with Steven's aunt, who persuaded Steven to go back to school. After considering Steven's intelligence and achievement test scores, the school psychologist recommended that he attend a summer school class for students with special needs.

Steven's summer school teacher soon began to suspect that Steven's main problem might simply be a lack of the background experiences necessary for academic success. One incident in particular stands out in her mind. The class had been studying nutrition, and so she had asked her students to bring in some fresh vegetables to make a large salad for their morning snack. Steven brought in a can of green beans. When a classmate objected that the beans weren't fresh, Steven replied, "The hell they ain't! Me and Momma got them off the shelf this morning!"

If Steven didn't know what *fresh* meant, the teacher reasoned, then he might also be lacking many of the other facts and skills on which any academic curriculum is invariably based. She and the teachers who followed her worked hard to help Steven make up for all those years in Chicago during which he had experienced and learned so little. By the time Steven reached high school, he was enrolling in regular classes and maintaining a 3.5 grade-point-average.

Adapted from D. L. Jackson & Ormrod (1998).

• Does Steven have mental retardation? Why or why not?
• The school psychologist recommended that Steven be placed in a special class for students with special needs. Was such a class the most appropriate placement for Steven? Why or why not?

Now go to our Companion Website to assess your understanding of chapter content with a Practice Quiz, apply what you've learned in Essay Questions, and broaden your knowledge with links to related Developmental Psychology Web sites . Go to www.prenhall.com/mcdevitt.

SUMMARY

Characterizing Intelligence

Intelligence involves adaptive behavior and may manifest itself differently in different cultures. Some theorists believe that intelligence is a single entity (a general factor, or *g*) that influences children's learning and performance across a wide variety of tasks and subject areas; this belief is reflected in the widespread use of IQ scores as general estimates of academic ability. But other theorists (e.g., Gardner, Sternberg) propose that intelligence consists of many, somewhat independent abilities and therefore cannot be accurately reflected in a single IQ score. There is growing recognition that children are more likely to behave "intelligently" when they have physical, social, and symbolic support systems to help them in their efforts.

Measuring Intelligence

Most intelligence tests have been developed primarily to identify children and adults with special needs (e.g., those who are gifted or have mental retardation). Contemporary intelligence tests include a variety of tasks designed to assess what people have learned and deduced from their everyday experiences. Performance on these tests is usually summarized by one or more IQ scores, which are determined by comparing an individual's performance with the performance of others of the same age. In some instances, specific ability tests or dynamic assessment may be more useful for evaluating children's capabilities in specific areas or their ability to benefit from certain kinds of instruction. Tests for infants and young children are often helpful in identifying those who have significant developmental delays; however, results of these tests should not be used to make long-term predictions about children's cognitive development.

Hereditary and Environmental Influences

Studies with twins and adopted children indicate that intelligence may be partly an inherited characteristic. But environmental conditions, including home environment, nutrition, toxic substances, enriching preschool programs, and formal schooling, can also have a significant impact on IQ scores. Heredity and environment interact in their influence to the point where it may be virtually impossible to separate the relative effects of each on children's intellectual development.

Developmental Trends and Group Differences

Performance on intelligence tests predicts school achievement to some degree, with IQ scores becoming increasingly stable and having greater predictive validity as children grow older. However, individual children's IQ scores may change considerably over time, especially during the early years.

On average, children from low-income families earn lower IQ scores than children from middle-income families. Males and females perform similarly on general tests of intelligence, although slight gender differences are sometimes observed on tests of specific cognitive abilities. Average differences in IQ scores are frequently found among various ethnic and racial groups; environmental factors are probably the primary root of these differences.

Critique of Current Perspectives

Research on intelligence has relied heavily on traditional intelligence tests, which are largely atheoretical in nature, emphasize skills valued in Western culture, and overlook dispositions and metacognitive strategies as important contributors to intellectual performance. Some theorists are now calling for a shift in focus from the assessment of children's present intelligence levels to the development of their future intelligence.

Implications of Theory and Research on Intelligence

Used within the context of other information, intelligence tests can often provide a general idea of children's current cognitive functioning. Yet educators and other practitioners should remain optimistic about every child's potential for intellectual growth. They should anticipate that different children will be intelligent in different ways and should capitalize on children's unique strengths and abilities to promote learning and achievement. And they should give children the social support and the physical and symbolic tools they need to think more intelligently.

Exceptionalities in Intelligence

Children and adolescents identified as being gifted show exceptional achievement or promise in general intellectual ability, aptitude in a specific academic field, creativity, leadership, or visual and performing arts. Giftedness may reflect itself differently in different cultures; in general, however, gifted individuals frequently demonstrate rapid learning, flexibility of ideas, and facility in abstract thinking. Strategies for promoting the achievement of gifted children include forming study groups of individuals with similar abilities, teaching complex cognitive skills within the context of various academic subject areas, providing opportunities for independent study, and seeking appropriate mentors in the community.

Mental retardation is characterized by low general intellectual functioning and deficits in adaptive behavior. Strategies for working effectively with children who have mental retardation include pacing instruction more slowly than usual, scaffolding cognitive processing, and teaching vocational and general life skills.

KEY CONCEPTS

psychometric approach (p. 238)
intelligence (p. 238)
g (general factor in intelligence) (p. 239)
fluid intelligence (p. 239)
crystallized intelligence (p. 239)

distributed intelligence (p.243)
intelligence test (p. 243)
IQ score (p. 246)
specific ability test (p. 249)
dynamic assessment (p. 249)

fetal alcohol syndrome (FAS) (p. 254)
Flynn effect (p. 254)
niche-picking (p. 256)
socioeconomic status (SES) (p. 259)

cultural bias (p. 261)
stereotype threat (p. 262)
giftedness (p. 267)
mental retardation (p. 270)
adaptive behavior (p. 270)

ME LLAMO ANA. ♡♡♡♥♡♡♡

Ana, age 5

El Exam de Hablar

En el verano, hace mucho calor y este es porque llevo una minifalda de mezclilla azul. También, llevo una camiseta rosada con sandalias rosadas de rayas. Típicalmente, voy a la piscina con mis amigos durante el verano. Cuando la voy, llevo un traje de baño azul. Porque hay mucho sol en el verano, siempre llevo los lentes de sol y son pardos y negros. El verano pasado, viajé a la playa con mi familia y pienso ir este verano. Cuando voy, siempre trayer una bolsa de rayas para la playa. Me encanta el verano porque no hay escuela y paso el rato con mis amigos toda el día a la piscina. También, hace buen tiempo, hace sol, y es muy divertido!

Tori, age 14

Language Development

CASE STUDY: MARIO

Mario's parents were fluent in both English and Spanish. The family lived in rural Vermont but spoke Spanish almost exclusively at home, in part because Mario's mother found English harsh and unpleasant to the ear. Most of Mario's early exposure to English was in the English-speaking child care centers and preschools he attended off and on from the time he was 2.

When Mario was 5, his dominant language was Spanish, but he was proficient in English as well. After his first 2 months in kindergarten, his teacher wrote the following in a report to Mario's parents:

> [Mario is] extremely sociable. He gets along fine with all the children, and enjoys school. He is quite vocal. He does not seem at all conscious of his speech. His slight accent has had no effect on his relations with the others. Whenever I ask the class a question, he is always one of the ones with his hand up.
>
> His greatest problem seems to be in the give and take of conversation. Since he always has something to say, he often finds it difficult to wait his turn when others are talking. When he talks, there are moments when you can see his little mind thinking through language—for he sometimes has to stop to recall a certain word in English which he might not have at his finger tips. (Fantini, 1985, p. 28)

The following school year, a speech therapist misperceived Mario's accent to be an articulation problem and so recommended him for speech therapy (Mario's parents refused to give their consent). By the time Mario was 8, any trace of an accent had disappeared from his speech, and his third-grade teacher was quite surprised to learn that he spoke a language other than English at home.

Standardized tests administered over the years attested to Mario's proficiency in English. Before he began kindergarten, his score on a standardized vocabulary test was at the 29th percentile, reflecting performance that, though a little on the low side, was well within an average range. Later, when he took the California Achievement Test in the fourth, sixth, and eighth grades, he obtained scores at the 80th percentile or higher (and mostly above the 90th percentile) on the reading, writing, and spelling subtests. When Mario spent a semester of fifth grade at a Spanish-speaking school in Bolivia, he earned high marks in Spanish as well, with grades of 5 on a 7-point scale in reading, writing, and language usage.

As Mario grew older, however, his vocabulary and written language skills developed more rapidly in English than in Spanish, in large part because his school instruction took place almost exclusively in English. His father described the situation this way:

> [B]y about fifth grade (age ten), he had entered into realms of experience for which he had no counterpart in Spanish. A clear example was an attempt to prepare for a fifth grade test on the topic of "The Industrial Revolution in England and France." It soon became clear that it was an impossibility to try to constrain the child to review materials read and discussed at school—in English—through Spanish. With this incident, [use of English at home] became a fairly well established procedure when discussing other school topics, including science, mathematics, and the like. (Fantini, 1985, p. 73)

Excerpts from *Language Acquisition of a Bilingual Child: A Sociolinguistic Perspective,* by A. E. Fantini, 1985. Clevedon, England: Multilingual Matters. (Available from the SIT Bookstore, School for International Training, Kipling Road, Brattleboro, VT 05302.) Reprinted with permission.

Learning a language is a remarkable accomplishment. At a minimum, it includes acquiring (a) an understanding of what various words mean (and most adults understand many tens of thousands of them), (b) oral-motor skills that enable precise pronunciation, (c) knowledge of innumerable rules for putting words together into meaningful sequences, and (d) awareness of how to speak with others in ways that are considered polite and socially acceptable. Mario's language development was all the more remarkable because he mastered two languages instead of one.

In this chapter, we often revisit Mario as we explore the multifaceted nature of human language and its development. We begin our discussion by looking at several theoretical perspectives on how children acquire their first language—that is, their **native language**.

Theoretical Perspectives of Language Development

To understand and use their native language effectively, children must master four basic components of the language: **phonology**, how words sound and are produced; **semantics**, what words mean; **syntax**, how words are combined to form understandable phrases and sentences; and **pragmatics**, how to engage in effective and socially acceptable communication with others. Mastering any one of these components is, from an objective standpoint, an extremely complex and challenging undertaking. Yet within the first 3 or 4 years of life, most children acquire sufficient proficiency in all four areas to carry on productive conversations with those around them. How they accomplish this monumental task in such a short time is one of the great mysteries of child development.

Theorists have offered numerous explanations for how children learn their native language. Here we describe early theories based on modeling and reinforcement plus four more contemporary perspectives: nativism, information processing theory, sociocultural theory, and functionalism.

Early Theories: Modeling and Reinforcement

Some early theorists suggested that language development comes about largely through modeling: A child imitates the speech that he or she hears other people produce. Imitation must certainly be involved in language development to some extent; otherwise, it would not be possible for all members of a particular social group to pronounce words in the same ways and to use similar grammatical structures. Infants occasionally imitate the sounds that parents and other caregivers make (Tronick, Cohn, & Shea, 1986). Older children, too, sometimes pick up other people's words, expressions, rhymes, and song lyrics (R. E. Owens, 1996; Peters, 1983). For example, when Mario began attending an English-speaking preschool, he came home using such expressions as "Shut up!" and "Don't do dat!" which he had apparently acquired by listening to his classmates (Fantini, 1985, p. 97).

The behaviorist B. F. Skinner (1957) offered another early explanation of language development: Parents and other adults in a child's environment reinforce increasingly more complex language use. Skinner proposed that initially, when infants are uttering a wide variety of speech sounds in a seemingly random fashion, parents respond favorably only to sounds that are used in the family's native language; for example, an English-speaking family is likely to reinforce an "r" sound (which occurs in English speech) but not a rolling "r" (which occurs in Spanish and French but not in English). As the child grows older, the parents begin to reinforce the use of single words, then the use of multiword combinations, and eventually only word combinations that are, from an adult's perspective, grammatically correct.

Skinner's explanation of language acquisition has not held up under the scrutiny of either research or individual case studies. The speech of young children includes many phrases that the people around them neither say nor reinforce (N. Chomsky, 1959; V. Cook & Newson, 1996; D. Lightfoot, 1999). For instance, a child may say "Allgone milk" or "I goed to Grandma's house." Moreover, parents usually reinforce their children's statements on the basis of what is factually accurate rather than what is grammat-

native language
The first language a child learns.

phonology
The sound system of a language; how words sound and are produced.

semantics
The meanings of words and word combinations.

syntax
Rules used to put words together into sentences.

pragmatics
Strategies and rules for effective and socially acceptable verbal interaction.

ically correct (O'Grady, 1997). For example, in one study, researchers observed parents reinforcing statements such as "Her curl my hair" and "Mama isn't boy, he a girl" (which were true) but not statements such as "There's the animal farmhouse" and "And Walt Disney comes on Tuesday" (which were false) (R. Brown & Hanlon, 1970, p. 49).

Even in the elementary and secondary school years, the great majority of grammatical errors in children's speech go uncorrected (Bohannon, MacWhinney, & Snow, 1990). Furthermore, children may continue to produce grammatically incorrect sentences despite feedback that the sentences need revision, as the following dialogue illustrates:

Child: Nobody don't like me.
Mother: No, say "nobody likes me."
Child: Nobody don't like me.

   [Eight repetitions of this dialogue]

Mother: No, now listen carefully; say "nobody likes me."
Child: Oh! Nobody don't likes me. (McNeill, 1966, p. 68)

Yet in other situations, children may learn to use correct grammatical structures even when they receive no feedback that they are using these structures correctly (Cromer, 1993).

Clearly, neither modeling nor reinforcement sufficiently explains how children eventually acquire an adultlike form of their native language. As an alternative, many theorists have turned to biology to explain language development, as we will now see.

Nativism

Noam Chomsky (1964, 1965, 1972, 1976) has proposed that growing children have a built-in, biological mechanism—a **language acquisition device**—that enables them to learn many complex aspects of language in a very short time. This mechanism provides a certain amount of "preknowledge" about the nature of language that makes the task of learning language much simpler than it would be if children had to start from scratch. Numerous other theorists share Chomsky's belief that human beings, though certainly not born knowing any particular language, nevertheless inherit some predispositions that assist them in acquiring linguistic knowledge and skills (e.g., H. S. Cairns, 1996; Gopnik, 1997; Hirsh-Pasek & Golinkoff, 1996; Lenneberg, 1967; D. Lightfoot, 1999). Such an approach to language development is generally known as **nativism**.

Nativists have used three major arguments to support their contention that language development has a biological basis:

1. The language used in everyday speech is inadequate to allow children to acquire the complex, adultlike language that they eventually acquire. In typical day-to-day conversations, adults often use incomplete sentences, are lax in their adherence to grammatical rules and, when talking to very young children, may use artificially short and simple language (V. Cook & Newson, 1996; M. Harris, 1992; D. Lightfoot, 1999).
2. To communicate effectively, children must derive a myriad of unspoken, underlying rules that govern how words are put together and then use these rules to generate sentences they have never heard before (N. Chomsky, 1959, 1972; Littlewood, 1984; Pinker, 1993).
3. All children in a particular language community learn essentially the same language despite widely differing early childhood experiences and a general lack of systematic instruction in appropriate language use (Cromer, 1993; Littlewood, 1984; D. Lightfoot, 1999).

If human beings do indeed have a built-in language acquisition device, what might such a device include? Many nativists propose that it includes a **Universal Grammar**, a set of parameters that allow some grammatical structures but exclude other possibilities; thus, children essentially pick from a limited number of options when they learn syntactic rules (H. S. Cairns, 1996; N. Chomsky, 1976; D. Lightfoot, 1999; O'Grady, 1997). For instance, most (and possibly all) languages seem to have some words that function as nouns and others that function as verbs (O'Grady, 1997; Pinker, 1984; Strozer, 1994).

Children's exposure to language influences their language development; for instance, watching Sesame Street increases children's vocabularies (Rice, Huston, Truglio, & Wright, 1990). But children's early linguistic experiences are haphazard and incomplete, leading many developmentalists to propose that human beings have some biologically built-in knowledge about the nature of language.

language acquisition device
Biologically built-in mechanism hypothesized to facilitate language learning.

nativism
Theoretical perspective that some knowledge is biologically built in and present at birth.

Universal Grammar
Hypothesized set of parameters within the language acquisition device that allow some grammatical structures but exclude others.

Also, many languages, including those with historically different origins, have similar rules for forming negatives and asking questions (N. Chomsky, 1965).

Some nativists suggest that infants may have additional predispositions that help them learn their native language. For instance, young infants tune in to certain kinds of speech (especially shorter and louder utterances) and show early abilities to distinguish among very similar speech sounds, to divide a stream of sound into small segments (e.g., syllables), and to identify common patterns in what they hear (P. K. Kuhl & Meltzoff, 1997; O'Grady, 1997; Pettito, 1997; Werker & Lalonde, 1988). They may also have some built-in concepts (e.g., colors such as red, pink, and yellow) that predispose them to categorize their experiences in certain ways; learning the labels for preexisting concepts is almost certainly easier than learning the concepts themselves (Bornstein, 1978; Strozer, 1994). And at the most basic level, infants seem to know, from a very early age, that there is meaning in speech—that spoken language corresponds directly with specific world events (Hirsh-Pasek & Golinkoff, 1996).

Nativists have not yet come to consensus about the exact nature of the language acquisition device or the precise ways in which it contributes to language development (Hirsh-Pasek & Golinkoff, 1996; O'Grady, 1997). However, several lines of research converge to support their belief that language has its roots in biology:

■ *Children from diverse cultural and linguistic backgrounds tend to reach milestones in language development at similar ages.*   For example, all children, even those who are congenitally deaf and have never heard a human voice, begin to produce speechlike syllables—**babbling**—at about 6 or 7 months of age on average (Kuhl & Meltzoff, 1997; J. L. Locke, 1993). In general, children who have regular exposure to a language make similar progress in language development, regardless of which language they are learning and regardless of whether it is spoken or manually signed (Crago, Allen, & Hough-Eyamie, 1997; Pettito, 1997).

■ *Language disabilities often run in families.*   Just as the ability to learn language may be inherited, so too might an impaired ability to learn language be passed from parents to their children (H. S. Cairns, 1996; Gopnik, 1997). For example, a person who, when listening to speech, has difficulty breaking up the series of sounds into meaningful parts may have children who face the same challenge.

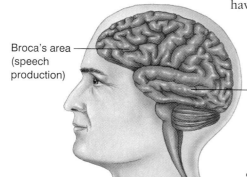

Broca's area (speech production)

Wernicke's area (language comprehension)

FIGURE 7–1 Language specialization centers in the brain. Broca's area (in the left frontal lobe) is involved in speech production. Wernicke's area (in the left temporal lobe) is involved in language comprehension.

babbling
Universal tendency for human beings to produce speechlike sounds in infancy.

■ *Certain areas of the brain appear to specialize in language functions.*   Some language disorders are associated with congenital brain abnormalities or with injuries in specific parts of the brain (Aitchison, 1996; J. L. Locke, 1993; Strozer, 1994). People who can comprehend language but do not speak often have damage in *Broca's area,* located in the left frontal cortex. People who cannot comprehend language but produce meaningless, nonsensical speech often have damage in *Wernicke's area,* a region in the left temporal lobe (see Figure 7–1).

For most people, the left hemisphere of the brain dominates in speech and language comprehension. But remember a point we made in Chapter 3: No single mental activity—language included—is exclusively the domain of one hemisphere or the other. For example, the right hemisphere is actively involved in sifting through multiple possible meanings of an ambiguous comment and in going beyond literal interpretations to find humor, sarcasm, or irony (Beeman & Chiarello, 1998; Ornstein, 1997). It also plays a sizable role in enabling children who are deaf to understand American Sign Language (Neville & Bavelier, 2001). In fact, the right hemisphere predominates in language activities for a sizable minority of left-handers. Moreover, if the left hemisphere incurs injury prior to age 1, the right hemisphere will often take over what are ordinarily the left hemisphere's "responsibilities" (Kolb & Whishaw, 1996; Ornstein, 1997; Stiles & Thal, 1993).

■ *There appear to be sensitive periods in some aspects of language development.* Children who have little or no exposure to language in the early years often have trouble acquiring language later on, even with adequate or enriched language experiences (e.g., Curtiss, 1977; Newport, 1990). A frequently cited example is Genie, a girl who was confined to a small, dark room and had little meaningful contact with others until she was

14. Genie subsequently had intensive training in language; although she learned to say and understand many words, her grammar never matured beyond that of a typical 2½-year-old (Curtiss, 1977).

Additional evidence comes from people who learn a second language. Typically, people learn how to pronounce a second language flawlessly only if they study it before mid-adolescence or, even better, in the preschool or early elementary years (Bialystok, 1994a; Collier, 1989; Flege, Munro, & MacKay, 1995). Children may also have an easier time mastering a language's various verb tenses and complex aspects of syntax when they are immersed in the language within the first 5 to 10 years of life (Bialystok, 1994a, 1994b; J. S. Johnson & Newport, 1989). The effects of age are particularly evident when the second language is syntactically and phonetically very different from the first (Bialystok, 1994a; Strozer, 1994).

Not all research studies yield evidence in support of sensitive periods in language development, however, and some of those that do are methodologically flawed (Bialystok, 1994a). Studies comparing the relative success of various age groups learning a second language yield mixed results; the more sophisticated cognitive abilities of older children and adults may sometimes counterbalance any biological advantage that younger children have (Bialystok, 1994b; M. Long, 1995; Snow & Hoefnagel-Höhle, 1978). It may be, too, that what appears to be a predetermined "best" time for learning language is simply the result of the brain's tendency to adapt fairly quickly to the specific environment in which it finds itself (recall our discussion of synaptogenesis and synaptic pruning in Chapter 3). "Specializing" in one's native language early on—attending to and practicing particular speech sounds, zeroing in on certain syntactic formats, and so on—may enhance automatization in the use of that language, but perhaps at the expense of learning a second language (Merzenich, 2001).

Because language acquisition involves learning a complex body of knowledge and skills that are perceptual, psychomotor, and cognitive in nature, there are probably different sensitive periods for different aspects of language development (Bruer, 1999; J. L. Locke, 1993). Furthermore, people can learn the vocabulary of a particular language at virtually any age (Bruer, 1999). Thus, it may be difficult, perhaps even impossible, to pinpoint a single, specific age range when language is most effectively learned.

Although the evidence for a biological basis for language development is compelling, researchers have yet to obtain indisputable evidence that human beings are prewired to acquire language. Furthermore, even if they were able to prove that a language acquisition device exists, such information would not necessarily tell us *how* human beings learn language (Pinker, 1987). The theoretical perspectives that follow better address this issue.

Information Processing Theory

Some theorists, while not necessarily denying the role of biology, focus more on the specific cognitive processes that children use as they acquire language and on the environmental events that promote language acquisition. The ideas that these theorists offer vary considerably but are all consistent with the general framework of information processing theory. We can summarize the information processing perspective of language development with the following key principles:

■ *General developmental changes in cognitive processes account for many trends observed in children's use and understanding of language.* Information processing theorists propose that children's language development is both propelled and limited by the same mechanisms—attention, working memory, an organized knowledge base, and so on—that influence learning and cognition in general (E. Bates & MacWhinney, 1987; G. F. Marcus, 1996; T. M. McDevitt & Ford, 1987; J. L. Morgan & Demuth, 1996).

Communicating one's thoughts to others is a complex task indeed. It involves knowledge not only about spoken language but also about appropriate eye contact, gestures, and tone of voice (T. M. McDevitt & Ford, 1987). Given the limited capacity of working memory, the simple act of conversing with others might involve coordinating so many skills that it would be virtually impossible. Fortunately, some of those skills (e.g., word pronunciation, syntactic rules, retrieval of word meanings) are automatized and so make minimal demands on working memory. In many situations, effective communication is also facilitated

Even in the first few weeks of life, most infants enjoy listening to the human voice, and they will expend considerable effort to hear a familiar one.

by previously developed schemas and scripts (e.g., "Hi, how are you?" "Fine, thanks. How are you?") that occur frequently in social interaction and can be used with little thought or effort.

From an information processing standpoint, attention is essential for language learning (M. Harris, 1992; Hirsh-Pasek & Golinkoff, 1996). Infants pay attention to human speech and speech-related events from a very early age. For instance, within a few days after birth, infants show a preference for human voices over other sounds, can distinguish between familiar and unfamiliar voices, and will expend considerable effort to hear a familiar one (DeCasper & Fifer, 1980; Fifer & Moon, 1995; J. L. Locke, 1993). They are also more likely to look at speakers who use the short, simple, rhythmic language that adults frequently use when talking to young children (R. P. Cooper & Aslin, 1990; Fernald, 1992; Kaplan, Goldstein, Huckeby, & Cooper, 1995). Adults seem to know (perhaps unconsciously) that attention is critical for language learning. Adults in Western cultures often point to the people or objects under discussion when talking with their young children, thereby directing their children's attention (M. Harris, 1992). And the mother of a young deaf child is most likely to sign to her child when she knows that the child can simultaneously see both her signs and the objects or events she is talking about (M. Harris, 1992).

■ *Language learning involves hypothesis testing, deductive reasoning, and active construction of a language system.* In the process of acquiring knowledge of their native language, growing children may form hypotheses about the meanings of words and the ways in which words can legitimately be combined into sentences. They test these hypotheses against what they hear and eventually pull seemingly correct hypotheses into an integrated set of rules. These rules then regulate their understanding and use of language (M. Atkinson, 1992; H. S. Cairns, 1996; Cromer, 1993; Karmiloff-Smith, 1993).

Perhaps as a result of the biologically built-in knowledge about language that nativists describe, children's hypotheses about their language are probably limited to a manageable number of possibilities (e.g., Akhtar, Carpenter, & Tomasello, 1996; Golinkoff, Hirsh-Pasek, Bailey, & Wenger, 1992; Markman, 1989). Children seem to use deductive reasoning to further limit their hypotheses. We find an example of such deductive reasoning in a study by T. K. Au and Glusman (1990). The researchers showed preschoolers a stuffed monkeylike animal with pink horns and consistently referred to the animal as a *mido*. Later, they presented a collection of stuffed animals that included several midos and asked the children to find a *theri* in the set. Although the children had no information to guide their selection, they always chose an animal other than a mido. Apparently they deduced that because the monkeylike animals already had a name, a theri had to be a different kind of animal.

Reasoning also comes into play when children use their knowledge of word meanings to derive syntactic categories—a process known as **semantic bootstrapping** (E. Bates & MacWhinney, 1987; Pinker, 1984, 1987). The ability to produce syntactically correct sentences requires knowing that different words are used in different ways (as nouns, verbs, adjectives, etc.); thus, young children must have an intuitive sense of various word categories long before they study those categories in school. The meanings of words can provide a basis for categorizing words according to their syntactic functions: People and concrete objects are nouns (and so serve similar functions in sentences), actions are verbs, physical properties and characteristics are adjectives, spatial relationships and directions are prepositions, and so on (Pinker, 1984).

Whereas information processing theorists consider the cognitive processes involved in language development, sociocultural theorists look more at the kinds of social interactions that foster it, as you will now see.

Sociocultural Theory

As we have seen, modeling and reinforcement do not fully explain how children acquire advanced language capabilities. Yet in some way, language development *must* depend on social interaction: By its very nature, language is a legacy of one's culture, and until children are able to read and write, they encounter it almost exclusively in social contexts.

semantic bootstrapping
Using knowledge of word meanings to derive knowledge about syntactic categories and structures.

The sociocultural approach to language development (e.g., John-Steiner, Panofsky, & Smith, 1994) is still in its infancy. But findings such as the following are consistent with a sociocultural perspective:

■ *Interactions with caregivers play a significant role in semantic development.* To date, research on the social mechanisms promoting language development has focused largely on how children learn specific words from their parents and other caregivers. As you might expect, children are more likely to learn words that they hear frequently. For instance, in a longitudinal study by M. Harris (1992), children and their mothers were videotaped in free-play situations from the time the children were 6 months old until they reached 2. Harris discovered that the children were more apt to say words that their mothers used often, and the children typically first used the words in the same contexts as their mothers had.

Sometimes, adults and older children in a child's life provide direct instruction in words and their meanings. In the following dialogue, 5-year-old Kris is playing with her 23-month-old cousin Amy. Kris holds up a stuffed dog:

Kris:	What is it?
Amy:	Doggie.
Kris:	What?
Amy:	Doggie.
Kris:	A doggie, yeah. (Picks up elephant.) What is this?
Amy:	Doggie.
Kris:	What?
Amy:	Baby.
Kris:	(Prompts Amy.) No. Uh—. Uh—.
Amy:	Pig.
Kris:	Uh—. Elephant.
Amy:	Elephant.
Kris:	Yeah elephant. (dialogue from P. J. Miller, 1982, p. 74; format adapted)

■ *Intersubjectivity is an important element in adult-child conversations.* As you may recall from Chapter 5, **intersubjectivity** is a phenomenon in which two people (e.g., a child and caregiver) have shared understandings and each has some awareness of what the other might be looking at or thinking. Some degree of intersubjectivity is probably critical if children are to learn new words (Baldwin, 2000; Gauvain, 2001). For example, imagine that you and a friend are in the produce section of the local supermarket. "Oh goody," your friend exclaims, "a carambola. I love carambolas!" If you have never heard the word *carambola* before, how might you figure out what your friend is referring to? The easiest thing, of course, would be to look at your friend's face and then follow his or her gaze to the object in question (in this case, a star-shaped, yellow-green tropical fruit). But you are apt to do this only if you realize that your friend is probably looking at what he or she is talking about.

As early as the second year, children use what they know or can surmise about other people's thoughts to assist them in learning word meanings.[1] For example, in a study by Baldwin (1993), 18-month-olds were looking at one new toy while an adult looked at another. When the adult exclaimed, "A modi!" the children typically turned their attention to see what the adult was looking at. A short time later, when the children were asked to get the modi, they were most likely to choose the toy the adult had been looking at, even though they themselves had been looking at something different when they heard the word *modi*.

Another important question relating to language development involves motivation: Why do children *want* to learn the language of their society? Functionalism offers one possible explanation.

intersubjectivity
Shared understandings that provide the foundation for social interaction and communication.

---

[1] As you may recall from Chapter 5, children with autism typically have deficits in intersubjectivity. Not surprisingly, then, they often show delays in vocabulary development (Baldwin, 2000).

Functionalism

Like sociocultural theory, **functionalism** is just emerging as a way of looking at language development. Following are two key elements of a functionalist perspective:

■ *Children learn language because it makes them more effective within their social group.* Some theorists argue that human beings' language skills have evolved because language serves several useful functions (hence the term *functionalism*) for the human species. Not only does language enable children to communicate, but it also helps them acquire knowledge, establish beneficial interpersonal relationships, regulate their own behavior, and influence others' behaviors; accordingly, it enables them to satisfy their own needs and desires (E. Bates & MacWhinney, 1987; L. Bloom & Tinker, 2001; Budwig, 1995; Pinker, 1997).

From a very early age, children seem to be aware of the power of language in controlling the actions of others (e.g., Bloom & Tinker, 2001). For instance, when Mario attended preschool as a 3-year-old, he quickly learned such expressions as "No do dat no more!" and "Get auto here!" (Fantini, 1985, pp. 97–98). We can reasonably guess that such language enabled Mario to control his classmates' behaviors in ways that more gentle speech might not have.

■ *The development of language is closely related to development in other domains.* Information processing theorists tie language development to trends in cognitive development. Sociocultural theorists pull the development of perspective-taking and social relationships into the picture as well. Functionalists are adamant in insisting that language development is inextricably intertwined with all other developmental domains—including cognitive, social, and emotional development—and so cannot be studied independently of other domains (Bloom & Tinker, 2001; Langacker, 1986).

Cognitive development is, of course, critical for the development of language: Although young children occasionally use words without understanding their meaning (we'll say more about this point shortly), in most instances children can talk only about things that they can first think about. Yet language is equally important for children's cognitive development: It provides a symbolic system by which they can mentally represent and remember external events, enables them to exchange information and perspectives with the people around them, helps them make associations among the various pieces of information they acquire, and (from Vygotsky's perspective) helps them internalize processes that they first experience in a social context.

Language is interconnected with social and moral development as well. Social interaction provides the primary means through which children acquire language. Furthermore, through conversations and confrontations with adults and peers, children learn socially acceptable ways of behaving toward others (see Chapter 13) and, in most cases, eventually establish a set of principles that guide their moral decision making (see Chapter 10).

Emotional development, too, affects and is affected by language development and competencies. We see an example in the case of Alice, who immigrated from China to the United States at the age of 8 (she took the name Alice after her arrival). When she first began attending an American school, Alice feared that her awkward attempts at English would lead to peer rejection. A few years later, she described the situation this way:

> I thought if I tried to speak I would say something wrong and pronounce a word wrong. They would laugh at me, tease me, whatever. So it took me a while before I could really use the language, just speak it, but then I overcame that. (Igoa, 1995, p. 83)

After Alice gained proficiency in English as well as Chinese, her use of the two languages was closely tied to family expectations and her sense of identity. She explained her feelings as follows:

> I see myself as somewhere in between. I'm caught in between. Because at home my parents expect me to be not a traditional Chinese daughter . . . but they expect things because I was born in China and I am Chinese. And at school, that's a totally different story because you're expected to behave as an American. You know, you speak English in your school; all your friends speak English. You try to be as much of an American as you can. So I feel I'm caught somewhere in between. . . . I feel I can no longer be fully Chinese or fully American anymore. (Igoa, 1995, p. 85)

As the functionalist perspective reminds us, language development affects and is affected by development in the cognitive, social, and emotional domains.

functionalism
Theoretical perspective of language development that emphasizes the purposes language serves for human beings.

Critiquing Theories of Language Development

The Basic Developmental Issues table "Contrasting Contemporary Theories of Language Development" summarizes how nativism, information processing theory, sociocultural theory, and functionalism differ with respect to the broad themes of nature and nurture, universality and diversity, and qualitative and quantitative change. Another important difference among different theoretical perspectives is one of focus: Nativism focuses on syntactic development, information processing and sociocultural theories look more closely at semantic development, and functionalism considers how motivation fits into the overall picture. Therefore, theorists often shift from one perspective to another or combine elements of two or more perspectives, depending on the particular aspect of language development they are discussing.

BASIC DEVELOPMENTAL ISSUES

Contrasting Contemporary Theories of Language Development

ISSUE	NATIVISM	INFORMATION PROCESSING THEORY	SOCIOCULTURAL THEORY	FUNCTIONALISM
Nature and Nurture	Children develop language only when they are exposed to the language of others; thus, environmental input is essential. But children also appear to rely on a biological mechanism that includes predetermined "knowledge" about the nature of language and possibly also includes skills that help them decipher the linguistic code.	Most information processing theorists assume that language learning involves a complex interplay between inherited inclinations and abilities, on the one hand, and experiences that facilitate effective language learning (e.g., attention-getting actions by parents, frequent use of words in simplified contexts), on the other.	Sociocultural theorists don't necessarily discount the role of heredity, but they focus on the social contexts that promote development and the cultural legacy (culture-specific interpretations of words and phrases, world views that underlie linguistic exchanges, etc.) that a society passes along from one generation to the next.	As their needs and desires become increasingly ambitious and complex, children propel their own language development through their efforts to communicate more effectively. Their needs and desires are probably the result of both heredity and environment.
Universality and Diversity	Although human languages differ in many respects, most languages have certain things in common (e.g., the use of nouns and verbs). Furthermore, children in different language communities reach milestones in language development at similar ages. Diversity exists primarily in the specific phonological, semantic, and syntactic features of various languages.	Information processing mechanisms that affect language acquisition (e.g., attention, working memory) are universally relevant across cultures. Children's unique language experiences, which differ among and within cultures, lead both to differences in the language(s) that children speak and to differences in children's knowledge of a particular language (e.g., the precise meanings they assign to specific words).	Some mechanisms that promote language development (e.g., intersubjectivity) may be universal across cultures. At the same time, different societies cultivate many culture-specific linguistic practices.	The drive to understand and be understood by others is universal. Different cultural groups may be more responsive to, and so nurture, some ways of communicating more than others.
Qualitative and Quantitative Change	Children often acquire specific syntactic structures in a predictable sequence, with noticeable, stagelike changes in linguistic constructions after each new acquisition (e.g., Dale 1976; O'Grady, 1997).	Many changes in language development—for instance, children's ever-enlarging vocabularies, ongoing refinement of word meanings, increasing automaticity in pronunciation and other skills, and expanding working memory capacities (enabling production of longer and more complex sentences)—come about in a trendlike, quantitative fashion.	The nature of adult-child relationships that nurture language development may change both quantitatively and qualitatively over time. As an example of qualitative change, intersubjectivity initially involves only an adult and child; later, it involves a mutual focus on, as well as shared understandings of, an object (see Chapter 5).	With development, children's needs and desires change in both quality and intensity. Thus, both qualitative and quantitative change is to be expected.

A key source of controversy remains, however. Most nativists propose that children inherit a mechanism whose sole function is to facilitate the acquisition of language, whereas other theorists (especially those who take an information processing or functionalist approach) believe that language development arises out of more general cognitive abilities that promote learning and development across a wide variety of domains. In fact, considerable evidence points to a language-specific developmental mechanism of some sort (Maratsos, 1998; Siegler, 1998). Children of all cultures learn language very quickly, and they acquire complex grammatical structures even when those structures are not necessary for effective communication. In addition, children with mental retardation show marked differences in language development depending on their particular disability. (N. G. S. Harris, Bellugi, Bates, Jones, & Rossen, 1997). To illustrate, let's compare children who have Down syndrome with children who have *Williams syndrome,* a genetic disorder characterized by distinctive facial features, poor muscle tone, and abnormalities in the circulatory system. Children with both conditions typically have low measured IQ scores (often between 50 and 70), putting them in the bottom 2% of their peer group. Yet children with Down syndrome typically have delayed language development (consistent with their intellectual development), whereas children with Williams syndrome have such good language skills that they are often initially perceived as having normal intellectual abilities. This difference in language skills between two groups who in other respects have similar intelligence makes sense only if a language-specific mechanism guides language development somewhat independently of other areas of intellectual development.

Other theoretical issues related to language development also remain unanswered. Two that have potential implications for caregivers, teachers, and other practitioners are the following:

■ *Which comes first, language comprehension or language production?* Psychologists studying language development frequently make a distinction between expressive and receptive language skills. **Receptive language** is the ability to understand what one hears and reads; in other words, it involves language *comprehension.* **Expressive language** is the ability to communicate effectively either orally or on paper; in other words, it involves language *production.*

A widely held assumption is that receptive language skills must precede expressive language skills; after all, it seems reasonable that children must understand what words and sentences mean before they use them in their own speech and writing. Yet many theorists don't believe the relationship between receptive and expressive language is actually so clear-cut (R. E. Owens, 1996). Children sometimes use words and expressions whose meanings they don't completely understand. Teresa recalls, for example, a 3-year-old girl in her preschool class who talked about the "accoutrements" in her purse, presumably after hearing others use the word in a similar context. Although the girl used the word appropriately in this situation, she did not understand all its connotations; in other words, her production exceeded her comprehension. Ultimately, receptive and expressive language skills probably develop hand in hand, with language comprehension facilitating language production and language production also enhancing language comprehension.

■ *What role does infant-directed speech play in language development?* Earlier we mentioned that infants seem to prefer the short, simple, rhythmic speech that adults often use when they talk to young children. Such **infant-directed speech** (also called *motherese* or *caregiver speech*) is different from normal adult speech in several ways: It is spoken more slowly and distinctly and at a higher pitch, consists of sentences with few words and simple grammatical structures, has exaggerated shifts in tone that help convey a speaker's message, uses a limited vocabulary, involves frequent repetition, and is generally concerned with objects and events that take place in close temporal and physical proximity to the child (P. K. Kuhl & Meltzoff, 1997; Littlewood, 1984). Adults frequently use such speech when they converse with young children, and they adapt their use of it to the age of the children; for example, preschool teachers use simpler speech with their students than first-grade teachers do (Rondal, 1985). You can hear examples of a mother using infant-directed speech with 16-month-old Corwin in the Infancy clips of the Cognitive Development, Intelligence, and Literacy modules of the Observation CD.

Hear Corwin's mother use infant-directed speech in the Infancy clips of the Cognitive Development, Intelligence, and Literacy modules of the Observation CD.

receptive language
Ability to understand the language that one hears or reads.

expressive language
Ability to communicate effectively through speaking and writing.

infant-directed speech
Short, simple, high-pitched speech often used when talking to young children.

Logically, infant-directed speech should facilitate language development: Its clear pauses between words, simple vocabulary and syntax, exaggerated intonations, and frequent repetition should make it easier for children to decipher what they hear. The problem with this hypothesis is that infant-directed speech is not a universal phenomenon. In some cultures, adults do not think of young children as suitable conversation partners and so speak to them only rarely, if at all; despite these circumstances, the children successfully acquire the language of their community (Heath, 1983; Ochs & Schieffelin, 1995; O'Grady, 1997).

If infant-directed speech isn't essential for language development, what, then, is its purpose? One possibility is simply that it enhances adults' ability to communicate effectively with young children (O'Grady, 1997). After all, many parents interact frequently with their infants and toddlers and undoubtedly want to be understood (e.g., M. Harris, 1992). Infant-directed speech may also be part of parents' and other adults' attempts to establish and maintain affectionate relationships with children—relationships that should have social and emotional benefits down the road (Trainor, Austin, & Desjardins, 2000).

Trends in Language Development

Children's first form of communication is crying. Soon thereafter, they also begin to communicate by smiling, cooing, and pointing. On average, they begin using recognizable words sometime around their first birthday, and they are putting these words together by their second birthday. During the preschool years they become capable of forming increasingly longer and more complex sentences. By the time they enroll in elementary school, at age 5 or 6, they use language that seems adultlike in many respects. Yet throughout the elementary and secondary school years, children and adolescents learn thousands of new words, and they become capable of comprehending and producing increasingly more complex sentences. They also continue to develop skills for conversing appropriately with others, and they acquire a better understanding of the nature of language.

In the following sections we explore the development of semantics, syntax, listening, speaking, sociolinguistic behavior, and metalinguistic awareness over the course of infancy, childhood, and adolescence.

Semantic Development

Young children appear to understand some words as early as 8 months of age, and they typically say their first word at about 12 months (Fenson et al., 1994; M. Harris, 1992; O'Grady, 1997; Tincoff & Jusczyk, 1999). In the Literacy/Infancy clip of the Observation CD, you can hear 16-month-old Corwin say several words, including "mooo," "boon" (for *balloon*), "two," and "bye." By the time they are 18 months old, many children have 50 words in their expressive vocabularies (O'Grady, 1997). There is considerable variability from child to child, however; for example, Mario did not say his first Spanish word until he was 16 months old, and by his second birthday he was using only 21 words (Fantini, 1985). Figure 7–2 lists the words in the speaking vocabulary of Teresa's son Connor at 18 months.

At some point during the end of the second year or beginning of the third year, a virtual explosion in speaking vocabulary occurs, with children learning 30 to 50 words a month and, later, as many as 20 new words each day. Mario, for example, was using more than 500 words by the time he was 3 (Fantini, 1985; M. Harris, 1992; O'Grady, 1997). In the preschool years, children also begin to organize their knowledge of various words into categories, hierarchies (e.g., *dogs* and *cats* are both *animals*), and other interword relationships (M. Harris, 1992).

Words:	
ball	bowl
mo (for *more*)	hot
no	boy
do (for *dog*)	eye
at (for *cat*)	toes
moo (for *cow* or *moon*)	balloo (for *balloon*)
duck (for *truck, duck, stuck*)	bubble
bus	E, O (for the letters on signs)
Mama	woo-woo (for a dog barking)
Dada	knock-knock
my	doll
bye-bye	uh-oh!
hi	uice (for *juice*)
night-night	bath
book	hole
ah-dooo (for *cock-a-doodle-doo*)	up
birdie	bike
ho-ho (for *Santa Claus*)	pie
dowel (for *towel*)	bock (for *block*)
tea	
milk	**Two-Word Combinations:**
nana (for *banana*)	bye-bye duck
boat	bye-bye Dada
	my nana

FIGURE 7–2 At 18 months, Connor had 43 words in his speaking vocabulary and was beginning to combine them into 2-word "sentences."

Hear Corwin's early words in the Literacy/Infancy clip of the Observation CD.

When children are 6, their knowledge of words in their language—their **lexicon**—includes 8,000 to 14,000 words, of which they use about 2,600 in their own speech (Carey, 1978). By the sixth grade, children's receptive vocabulary includes, on average, 50,000 words; by high school, it includes approximately 80,000 words (G. A. Miller & Gildea, 1987; Nippold, 1988; R. E. Owens, 1996). Thus, children learn several thousand new words each year (W. E. Nagy, Herman, & Anderson, 1985). The rapid increase in vocabulary throughout childhood and adolescence is especially remarkable when we consider what word knowledge includes: Children must know not only what each word means but also how to pronounce it and how to use it in appropriate contexts (H. S. Cairns, 1996).

The dramatic increase in the number of words that children can use and understand is the most obvious aspect of semantic development. Yet several other principles characterize semantic development as well:

■ *Children initially focus on lexical words; grammatical words come a bit later.* All languages have two main categories of words (Shi & Werker, 2001). **Lexical words** have some connection, either concrete or abstract, to objects or events in people's physical, social, and psychological worlds; they include nouns (e.g., *horse, freedom*), verbs (e.g., *swim, think*), adjectives (e.g., *handsome, ambiguous*), and adverbs (e.g., *quickly, intentionally*). **Grammatical words** (also known as *function words*) have little meaning by themselves but affect meanings of other words or interrelationships among words or phrases; they include articles (e.g., *a, the*), auxiliary verbs (e.g., the *have* in *I have swum*), prepositions (e.g., *before, after*), and conjunctions (e.g., *however, unless*).

By the time they are 6 months old, children can distinguish between lexical words and grammatical words and show a distinct preference for lexical words (Shi & Werker, 2001). Furthermore, when they begin to combine words into 2- and 3-word "sentences," they use lexical words almost exclusively.

■ *Over time, children continue to refine their understandings of lexical words.* Children's initial understandings of lexical words are often fuzzy: Children have a general idea of what certain words mean but define them imprecisely and may use them incorrectly. One common error is **undergeneralization**, in which children attach overly restricted meanings to words, leaving out some situations to which the words apply. For example, Jeanne once asked her son Jeff, then 6, to tell her what an *animal* is. He gave her this definition:

It has a head, tail, feet, paws, eyes, nose, ears, lots of hair.

Like Jeff, young elementary school children often restrict their meaning of *animal* primarily to nonhuman mammals, such as dogs and horses, and insist that fish, birds, insects, and people are *not* animals (Carey, 1985b; Saltz, 1971).

Another frequent error is **overgeneralization**: Words are given meanings that are too broad and so are applied to situations in which they're not appropriate. The following examples illustrate this phenomenon:

- Can't you see? I'm barefoot all over!
- I'll get up so early that it will still be late.
- Isn't there something to eat in the cupboard? There's only a small piece of cake, but it's middle-aged.

(Chukovsky, 1968, p. 3)

In addition to undergeneralizing and overgeneralizing, children sometimes confuse the meanings of similar words. The following conversation illustrates 5-year-old Christine's confusion between *ask* and *tell*:

Adult:	Ask Eric his last name. [Eric Handel is a classmate of Christine's.]
Christine:	Handel.
Adult:	Ask Eric this doll's name.
Christine:	I don't know.
Adult:	Ask Eric what time it is.
Christine:	I don't know how to tell time.
Adult:	Tell Eric what class is in the library.
Christine:	Kindergarten.

Preschoolers are, in many respects, quite proficient in using their native language. Yet they still have much to learn; for instance, they may exhibit undergeneralization or overgeneralization in their initial understandings of words.

lexicon
The words one knows in a particular language.

lexical word
Word that in some way represents an aspect of one's physical, social, or psychological world.

grammatical word
Word that affects the meanings of other words or the interrelationships among words in a sentence.

undergeneralization
Overly restricted meaning for a word, excluding some situations to which the word applies.

overgeneralization
Too broad a meaning for a word, such that it is used in situations to which it doesn't apply.

Adult: Ask Eric who his teacher is.
Christine: Miss Turner. (dialogue from C. S. Chomsky, 1969, p. 55; format adapted)

In a similar manner, young children often confuse comparative words, sometimes interpreting *less* as "more" or thinking that *shorter* means "longer" (R. E. Owens, 1996; Palermo, 1974).

■ *Children have difficulty with grammatical words throughout the elementary and middle school years.* Children's mastery of a particular grammatical word typically evolves slowly over a period of several years. For instance, although 3-year-olds can distinguish between the articles *a* and *the,* children as old as 9 are occasionally confused about when to use each one (R. E. Owens, 1996; Reich, 1986). Children in the upper elementary and middle school grades have trouble with many conjunctions, such as *but, although, yet, however,* and *unless* (Nippold, 1988; R. E. Owens, 1996). As an illustration, consider the following two pairs of sentences:

Jimmie went to school, but he felt sick.
Jimmie went to school, but he felt fine.

The meal was good, although the pie was bad.
The meal was good, although the pie was good.

Even 12-year-olds have trouble identifying the correct sentence in pairs like these, reflecting only a vague understanding of the connectives *but* and *although* (E. W. Katz & Brent, 1968). (The first sentence is correct in both cases.)

■ *Understanding of abstract words emerges later than understanding of concrete words.* Words like *but* and *although* may be particularly difficult for elementary school children because their meanings are fairly abstract. If we consider Piaget's proposal that abstract thought doesn't emerge until early adolescence, we realize that children may not fully understand abstract words until the junior high or high school years. Young children in particular are apt to define words (even fairly abstract ones) in terms of the obvious, concrete aspects of their world (Anglin, 1977; Ausubel, Novak, & Hanesian, 1978). For example, when Jeanne's son Jeff was 4, he defined *summer* as the time of year when school is out and it's hot outside; by the time he was 12, he knew that adults define summer in terms of the earth's tilt relative to the sun—a much more abstract notion.

How Children Learn Word Meanings Many words encompass *categories* of objects, events, or relationships (proper nouns are an obvious exception), and so an ability to categorize experiences is probably an essential prerequisite for learning them. Infants begin to categorize the animate and inanimate objects in their world as early as 3 months of age (Behl-Chadha, 1996; Eimas & Quinn, 1994; Quinn, 2002). Sometime between 3 and 10 months, they can categorize spatial relationships that provide the basis for certain prepositions and directional words (e.g., *above* vs. *below, between, left* vs. *right*) (Quinn, 2003). By 10 to 12 months, they also distinguish between greater and lesser quantities of something, providing a foundation for learning words such as *more* and *less* (Feigenson, Carey, & Hauser, 2002).

An additional challenge in learning word meanings, and in acquiring syntax as well, is that children must mentally divide the continuous stream of speech they hear into the individual "pieces" that are words. Even in the simplified infant-directed speech mentioned earlier, adults rarely stop between words; rather, one word flows directly into the next (Jusczyk, 1997). Despite such nonstop verbal action, infants begin to identify the specific words in speech by 7 or 8 months of age (Aslin, Saffran, & Newport, 1998; Jusczyk, 1997). Exactly how they do it remains a mystery, but they probably rely on numerous clues, including the characteristic rhythm, stress patterns, and consistencies in word sequences that they hear in their native language (Jusczyk, 2002).

Once children have such basics down, how do they zero in on the meanings of specific words? In some cases, adults provide direct instruction at home and at school, perhaps by labeling objects or by asking questions ("Where is the _____?") while looking at picture books with children (Dunham, Dunham, & Curwin, 1993; Fukkink & de Glopper, 1998; Sénéchal, Thomas, & Monker, 1995). More often than not, however, caregivers, teachers, and other individuals do not explicitly identify what they are referring to when they use new words. As a result, youngsters probably learn most words by inferring their meaning from the context in which they encounter them (Akhtar, Jipson, & Callanan, 2001; Pinker, 1987; Waxman, 1990). Toddlers sometimes need numerous repetitions of a particular word before they understand and use it (M. Harris, 1992; Peters, 1983; Woodward, Markman, & Fitzsimmons, 1994). But by the time they are 2 or 3, children can often infer a word's general meaning after only one exposure—a process known as **fast mapping** (Heibeck & Markman, 1987; Pinker, 1982).

Young children seem to use a number of general "rules" to fast-map word meanings. Following are some examples:

- If I see several objects and know labels for all of them except one, a new word is probably the name of the unlabeled object.
- If someone uses a word while pointing to a particular object, the word probably refers to the *whole* object rather than to just a part of it.
- Generally speaking, when a word is used to refer to a particular object or action, it refers to *similar* objects or actions as well.
- If a word is preceded by an article (e.g., "This is a _____"), it refers to a category of objects; if it has no article in front of it (e.g., "This is _____"), it is the name of a *particular* object (i.e., it is a proper noun).
- Words for particular things (i.e., proper nouns) are more likely to refer to animate objects (e.g., people, pets) than inanimate ones.

(Akhtar et al., 1996; T. K. Au & Glusman, 1990; Gelman & Taylor, 1984; Golinkoff et al., 1992; Golinkoff, Hirsh-Pasek, Mervis, Frawley, & Parillo, 1995; Jaswal & Markman, 2001; Markman, 1989, 1992)

As children get older, they continue to use such rules to draw inferences about word meanings. They also refine their understandings of words through repeated encounters with the words in different contexts and sometimes through direct feedback when they use the words incorrectly (Carey & Bartlett, 1978). In many cases, learning a word's precise meaning involves identifying the **defining features** of the concept that the word represents—that is, identifying the characteristics that a particular object or event must exhibit in order to be classified as an instance of that concept. For example, a *circle* must be both round and two-dimensional. People who *walk* are people who stand upright, move their bodies by moving their feet, and have at least one foot on the ground at all times.

Words are most easily learned when they have defining features that are concrete and obvious. Words are harder to learn when their defining features are abstract, subtle, or difficult to pin down. Children, younger ones especially, are often misled by **correlational features**—attributes that are nonessential but frequently present—that are more readily observable than the defining features (Keil, 1989; Mervis, 1987). Consider how children at three different age levels define *plant*:

Andrew (age 7):   Something that people plant in a garden or somewhere.
Amaryth (age 10):   A growing thing that's sometimes beautiful.
Tony (age 13):   A life form that uses sunlight and carbon dioxide to live.

Andrew focuses on a feature that is true for some but not all plants: their location in a garden. In contrast, Amaryth mentions one defining feature (growth) that is true of, but not unique to, plants, along with a correlational feature (beauty). Tony mentions characteristics that a biologist might identify; presumably he has learned these defining features in one of his science classes at school.

Fostering Semantic Development   Researchers have identified several strategies that caregivers, teachers, and other adults can use to help children learn word meanings:

■ *Talk regularly to, with, and around infants and toddlers.*   Even when they cannot yet speak themselves, very young children nevertheless learn a great deal from hearing their native language. Initially, they learn its basic characteristics—for instance, its typical rhythms and stress patterns and the specific sounds (phonemes) that it does and does not include. Later, as they begin to divide speech into individual words, they also begin to draw inferences about what

fast mapping
Inferring a word's general meaning after a single exposure.

defining feature
Characteristic that must be present in all instances of a concept.

correlational feature
Characteristic present in many instances of a concept but not essential for concept membership.

some of those words mean. The richer the language that young children hear—the greater the variety of words, and the greater the complexity of syntactic structures, that people around them use—the faster their vocabulary will develop (Hoff & Naigles, 2002).

■ *Give definitions.*　People of all ages learn words more easily when they are told what the defining features are—in other words, when they are given definitions (Merrill & Tennyson, 1977; Tennyson & Cocchiarella, 1986). Definitions are particularly valuable when defining features are abstract or otherwise not obvious. Children can usually learn what a *circle* is and what *red* means even without definitions, because roundness and redness are characteristics that are easily noticed. But the defining features of such words as *polygon* and *fragile* are more subtle; for words like these, definitions can be very helpful. Ideally, children should be encouraged to define new vocabulary in their own words and use this vocabulary in a variety of contexts.

■ *Provide examples and nonexamples.*　People often acquire a more accurate understanding of a word when they are shown several examples (Barringer & Gholson, 1979; Tennyson & Cocchiarella, 1986). Ideally, such examples should be as different from one another as possible so that they illustrate a word's entire range. To illustrate, if adults limit their examples of *animal* to dogs, cats, cows, and horses, children will understandably draw the conclusion that all animals have four legs and fur (a case of undergeneralization). But if adults also present goldfish, robins, beetles, earthworms, and people as examples of *animal,* children are more likely to recognize that animals can look very different from one another and that not all of them have legs or fur.

Children acquire more accurate understandings of words when they see concrete examples.

In addition to having examples, children benefit from having nonexamples of a word, especially those examples that are "near misses" to the word's meaning (Winston, 1973). For instance, to learn what a *salamander* is, a child might be shown such similar animals as snakes and lizards and told that they are "not salamanders." By presenting nonexamples, including the near misses, adults minimize the extent to which children are likely to overgeneralize in their use of words.

■ *Give feedback when children use words incorrectly.*　Misconceptions about word meanings (e.g., under- and overgeneralizations) sometimes reveal themselves in children's speech and writing. Astute caregivers and teachers listen closely not only to what children say but also to how they say it, and they also look at how children use words in their writing. For instance, a preschooler might mistakenly refer to a rhinoceros as a "hippo," an elementary school student might deny that a square is a rectangle, and a high school student might use the term *atom* when she is really talking about molecules. In such situations, adults should gently correct the misconceptions, for instance by saying something along these lines: "A lot of people get hippos and rhinoceroses confused, because both of them are large and gray. This animal has a large horn growing out from its nose, so it's a rhinoceros. Let's find a picture of a hippo and look at how the two animals are different."

■ *Encourage children to read as much as possible.*　As noted earlier, young people probably acquire many more new words through their informal encounters with those words than through formal vocabulary instruction. One way for them to encounter new words is by reading fiction and nonfiction. Avid readers learn many more new words and so have larger vocabularies than do children who read infrequently (Allen, Cipielewski, & Stanovich, 1992; Fukkink & de Glopper, 1998; Stanovich, 2000; Swanborn & de Glopper, 1999).

What dose worrisome mean?
What is and dose prevaricate mean?
Sobrvect 1?

Regular reading promotes vocabulary development. On this page of her fifth-grade journal, 10-year-old Amaryth has jotted down unknown words in a book she is reading.

Syntactic Development

Which of the following sentences are grammatically correct?

- Growing children need nutritious food and lots of exercise.
- Experience students find to be many junior high school an unsettling.
- Allow class discussions to exchange ideas and perspectives students.
- Schizophrenia often does not appear until adolescence or adulthood.

You undoubtedly realized that the first and last sentences are grammatically correct and that the two middle ones are not. But *how* were you able to tell the difference? Can you describe the specific grammatical rules you used to make your decision?

Rules of syntax—the rules that we use to combine words together into meaningful sentences that express the interrelationships among the words—are incredibly complex (Chomsky, 1972). Much of our knowledge about syntax is at an unconscious level: Although we can produce acceptable sentences and can readily understand the sentences of others, we cannot put our finger on exactly what it is that we know about language that allows us to do these things (Aitchison, 1996).

Despite the complexity of syntactic rules, and despite experts' inability to pin down their exact nature, children seem to pick up on them rather quickly. By the time they reach school age, children have mastered many of the basics of sentence construction (McNeill, 1970; Reich, 1986). Nevertheless, we continue to see some gaps in their syntactic knowledge throughout the elementary school years and often into the secondary school years as well.

Following are noteworthy aspects of syntactic development over the course of childhood and adolescence:

■ *Some syntax appears in children's earliest sentences.* Initially, children use a single word to express a complete thought. For instance, Jeanne's daughter Tina used to say "Diddin" when asking for her favorite teddy bear (who eventually assumed the name Diddin even when Tina could pronounce *teddy* quite well), and, like many toddlers, Tina would stretch out her arms and plead "Up!" when she wanted to be carried or cuddled. Developmentalists sometimes use the word **holophrase** to refer to such one-word "sentences."

When children first begin combining words into two- and three-word sentences, they typically use lexical words (rather than grammatical words) almost exclusively. For instance, they might say "Give doggie" to mean *Give it to the doggie* or "Mommy pumpkin" to mean *Mommy is cutting a pumpkin* (R. Brown, 1973, p. 205). By using such **telegraphic speech**, children maximize the meaning their short "sentences" convey, just as adults used to do when they sent telegrams and did not want to pay extra for long messages.

Yet children show evidence that they are using simple syntactic rules even when their sentences are only two words long (R. Brown, 1973; H. S. Cairns, 1996; O'Grady, 1997). For example, their two-word combinations might reflect description ("Pillow dirty"), location ("Baby table"), or possession ("Adam hat"). As children's sentences increase in length, they also increase in syntactic complexity—for instance, including a subject, verb, and object (e.g., "I ride horsie") or describing both an action and a location ("Put truck window," "Adam put it box") (R. Brown, 1973, pp. 141, 205).

■ *Young children rely heavily on word order when they interpret sentences.* By the time they are 1½, children have some understanding that, at least in English, word order affects meaning; for instance, they know that "Big Bird is washing Cookie Monster" means something different from "Cookie Monster is washing Big Bird" (Hirsh-Pasek & Golinkoff, 1996). At the same time, young children can be misled by the order in which words appear (O'Grady, 1997). For instance, many preschoolers seem to apply a general rule that a pronoun refers to the noun that immediately precedes it. Consider the sentence "John said that Peter washed him." Many 4-year-olds think that *him* refers to *Peter* and so conclude that Peter washed himself. Similarly, kindergartners are likely to have trouble with the sentence "Because she was tired, Mommy was sleeping" because no noun appears before *she*.

■ *Children tend to learn general rules for word endings before they learn exceptions.* Knowledge of syntax includes knowledge about when to use word endings (suffixes) such as *-s*, *-er*, and *-ed*. When children first learn the rules for using suffixes (e.g., that *-s* indicates plural, *-er* indicates a comparison, and *-ed* indicates past tense), they often apply these rules indiscriminately, without regard for exceptions. Thus, a child might say "I have two *foots*," "Chocolate ice cream is *gooder* than vanilla," or "I *goed* to Grandma's house." This phenomenon, known as **overregularization**, is especially common during the preschool and early elementary years. It gradually diminishes as children master the irregular forms of various words—for instance, as they learn that the plural of *foot* is *feet*, the comparative form of *good* is *better*, and the past tense of *go* is *went* (Cazden, 1968; G. F. Marcus, 1996; Siegler, 1994).

holophrase
A single word used to express a complete thought; commonly observed in children's earliest speech.

telegraphic speech
Short, grammatically incomplete sentences that include lexical (rather than grammatical) words almost exclusively; common in toddlers.

overregularization
Applying a syntactical rule in situations where exceptions to the rule apply.

Yet most high school students (and, in fact, many adults as well) haven't completely mastered the irregularities of the English language (G. F. Marcus, 1996). For instance, throughout his high school years, Jeanne's son Jeff consistently said "I have *broughten* . . . " despite Jeanne's constant reminders that he should say "I have *brought*. . . . "

■ *Children's questions increasingly incorporate adult syntactic rules.* In some languages, it's very easy to ask questions. In Chinese, one can change a statement into a question simply by adding *ma* to the end of the sentence. In English, however, asking questions is more difficult. At a minimum, it requires switching the order of the subject and verb ("Are you hungry?"). When the past tense is involved, asking a question requires putting the auxiliary verb but *not* the main verb first ("Have you eaten yet?"). And when something other than a yes or no answer is called for, a question word (e.g., *who, what, where, how*) must also appear at the beginning ("What did you eat?").

English-speaking children often seem to master these question-asking rules one step at a time. Initially, their questions may be nothing more than telegraphic sentences with a rise in pitch at the end (e.g., "Kitty go home?" R. Brown, 1973, p. 141). At about 2½ years, they attach question words to the beginning, and sometime in their third year, they add an auxiliary verb such as *is* or *does*. However, preschoolers often neglect one or more of the rules for asking questions; for instance, they may ask "What you want?" (forgetting to add the auxiliary verb) or "What you will do?" (forgetting to put the auxiliary verb before the subject) (de Villiers, 1995, pp. 516, 518). By the time they are 5, most children have mastered the correct syntax for questions (de Villiers, 1995).

■ *The ability to comprehend passive sentences evolves gradually during the preschool and elementary school years.* Passive sentences frequently confuse young children, who may incorrectly attribute the action reflected in the verb to the subject of the sentence—someone who is actually the *recipient* of the action. Consider these two sentences:

The boy is pushed by the girl.

The cup is washed by the girl.

Preschoolers are more likely to be confused by the first sentence—that is, to think that the boy is the one doing the pushing—than by the second sentence (Karmiloff-Smith, 1979). The first sentence has two possible "actors," but the second sentence has only one: Both boys and girls can push someone else, but cups can't wash girls. Complete understanding of passive sentences doesn't appear until sometime around fourth grade (O'Grady, 1997; R. E. Owens, 1996; Tager-Flusberg, 1993).

■ *Children can be confused by sentences with multiple clauses.* Word order sometimes leads young children to misinterpret multiple-clause sentences (E. V. Clark, 1971; Sheldon, 1974). Consider the sentence "The horse kicked the pig after he jumped over the fence." Children as old as 6 often say that the horse kicked the pig *before* it jumped over the fence, even though the word *after* clearly communicates the opposite sequence (E. V. Clark, 1971).

Children begin to produce simple subordinate clauses, such as those that follow and modify nouns (e.g., "This is the toy *that I want*") at about age 4 (R. E. Owens, 1996). Sentences with one clause embedded in the middle of another clause are more difficult, particularly if the noun tying the clauses together has a different function in each clause. Consider the sentence "The dog *that was chased by the boy* is angry" (R. E. Owens, 1996, p. 382). The dog is the subject of the main clause ("The dog . . . is angry") but the recipient of the action in the embedded clause (". . . [dog] was chased by the boy"). Seventh graders easily understand such sentences, but younger children overrely on word order to interpret them and so may conclude that the boy, rather than the dog, is angry (R. E. Owens, 1996).

■ *Knowledge of syntactic rules continues to develop at the secondary level.* In middle school and high school, adolescents learn more subtle aspects of syntax, such as subject-verb and noun-pronoun agreement, correct uses of *that* versus *which* to introduce subordinate clauses, functions of punctuation marks such as colons and semicolons, and so on. They rarely develop such knowledge on their own; instead, most of their syntactic development probably occurs as the result of formal instruction, especially through courses in language arts, English composition, and foreign languages.

■ *Multilingual children readily distinguish among the syntactic structures used in different languages.* As Mario simultaneously learned Spanish and English, he also learned which syntactic rules applied to each language. Intrusions from one language to the other occurred infrequently even in the preschool years (he once pluralized the English word *balloon* with the Spanish suffix *-es,* saying "balloones") and disappeared altogether soon after (Fantini, 1985).

How Children Acquire Syntactic Knowledge Even infants have some awareness of patterns in speech. For example, in one study, 7-month-olds heard a series of "sentences" each comprised of three nonsense syllables (e.g., *ga, na, ti, li*). Infants in Group 1 consistently heard them in a predictable "ABA" pattern (e.g., "Ga ti ga," "Li na li"), whereas infants in Group 2 consistently heard them in an "ABB" pattern (e.g., "Ga ti ti," "Li na na"). After habituating to these sentences, they heard another series of "sentences" with new nonsense syllables; some followed the ABA pattern (e.g., "Wo fe wo") and others followed the ABB pattern (e.g., "Wo fe fe"). The infants paid greater attention when listening to the pattern that was new for them, showing that the pattern they had heard before was "the same old thing," even though new sounds were involved (G. F. Marcus, Vijayan, Bandi Rao, & Vishton, 1999).

Theorists do not yet have a clear understanding of how children learn syntactic rules. To some extent, this learning might be a matter of using word meanings to draw conclusions about syntactic categories (e.g., nouns, verbs) and appropriate relationships among them—the process of *semantic bootstrapping* mentioned earlier (Bates & MacWhinney, 1987; Pinker, 1984, 1987). It may also involve discovering the probabilities with which various word combinations appear in sentences (MacWhinney & Chang, 1995; Saffran, Aslin, & Newport, 1996). As one simple example, children may notice that *the* is usually followed by names of objects or events or by "describing" words (e.g., they might hear *the dog, the picnic,* or *the pretty hat*). In contrast, it is rarely followed by words that identify specific actions (e.g., they never hear *the do* or *the went*).

Despite such uncertainty, most theorists believe that syntactic development is largely a constructive and unconscious process, especially in the early years (Aitchison, 1996; H. S. Cairns, 1996; Karmiloff-Smith, 1993). Young children typically receive little if any direct instruction about how to form sentences. Instead, they apparently develop their own set of rules through their observations of other people's speech. Corrective feedback from others may sometimes be helpful in the process, yet, as noted earlier, children acquire increasingly sophisticated syntactic structures even without such feedback.

As children develop new rules, they may initially misapply them. The overregularization phenomenon described earlier is a case in point. When children first learn the *-ed* rule for the past tense of verbs, they sometimes let the rule override the irregular verb forms they already know. Thus, a child who has previously said *I went* may begin to say *I goed.* Eventually, the child refines the rule to allow for exceptions and applies it only when appropriate (Dale, 1976; G. F. Marcus, 1996).

Formal language arts instruction brings some syntactic knowledge to a conscious level. Beginning in the upper elementary and middle school grades, children often learn to identify the various parts of a sentence (e.g., subject, direct object, prepositional phrase, subordinate clause) about which they acquired intuitive knowledge many years earlier. They also study various verb tenses (e.g., present, past, present progressive) even though they have been using these tenses in their everyday speech for quite some time.

Fostering Syntactic Development Particularly as they are learning the more complex and subtle aspects of syntax, children and adolescents often benefit from ongoing instruction and practice in the grammatical aspects of the English language. Following are several examples of how caregivers and teachers can promote children's syntactic development:

■ *Expand on young children's telegraphic speech.* When young children speak in telegraphic sentences, caregivers can engage in **expansion**, repeating the sentences in a more mature form; for example, when a toddler says, "Mommy lunch," mother might respond by saying, "Mommy is eating her lunch" (R. E. Owens, 1996, p. 224). Expansion gives children gentle feedback about the incompleteness of their own utterances and possibly encourages them to imitate more complex syntactic structures (R. E. Owens, 1996; Scherer & Olswang, 1984).

expansion
Repeating a child's short utterances in a more complete and grammatically correct form.

■ *Teach irregular forms of verbs and comparative adjectives.* Children do not always hear the standard irregular forms of verbs and adjectives in the everyday speech of people around them. For example, their young playmates may talk about what's *badder* or *worser,* and many adults confuse the past tenses of the verbs *lay* and *lie* (*laid* and *lay,* respectively). Some formal instruction in irregular forms may therefore be the only way that children discover which terms are correct and which are not.

■ *Describe various sentence structures and give children considerable practice in their use.* Having children examine and practice common syntactic structures (active and passive voice, independent and dependent clauses, etc.) has at least two benefits. First, children should be better able to vary their sentence structure as they write—a strategy associated with more sophisticated writing (Byrnes, 1996; Spivey, 1997). Second, learning the labels for such structures (e.g., *passive voice*) in English should help them acquire analogous structures in other languages that they study at a later time.

■ *Provide ample opportunities for children to express their ideas in a relatively "formal" way, both orally and on paper, and give feedback about appropriate syntax in those contexts.* As nativists have pointed out, people do not always adhere to syntactic rules in their everyday speech. What's common in casual speech, such as using the plural pronoun *they* to refer to a single individual of either gender, may be frowned upon in writing. In formal and public situations (e.g., a presentation to a large group, or a letter to the editor of a local newspaper), correct grammar is, in many people's minds, an indication that the speaker or writer is educated and well-informed and is therefore someone to take seriously (R. E. Owens, 1996; Purcell-Gates, 1995; H. L. Smith, 1998).

Especially in adolescence and adulthood, many advances in language development probably occur as a result of formal instruction rather than informal experiences.

Development of Listening Skills

As you might guess, children's ability to understand what they hear is closely related to their semantic and syntactic development. In addition, the development of listening skills is characterized by the following trends:

■ *In the first year, infants learn to focus primarily on sounds important in their native language.* The basic elements of spoken language—the sounds designated as consonants and vowels—are collectively known as **phonemes.** Phonemes are the smallest units of spoken language that indicate differences in meaning in a particular language. For instance, the word *bite* has three phonemes: a "buh" sound, an "eye" sound, and a "tuh" sound. If we change any one of these sounds—for instance, if we change *b* to *f* (*fight*), long *i* to long *a* (*bait*), or *t* to *k* (*bike*)—we get a new word with a different meaning.

In the first few months of life, infants can discriminate among a wide variety of phonemes, including many that they don't hear in the speech around them (Jusczyk, 1995; Werker & Lalonde, 1988). Before long, they show a noticeable preference for sounds and words they hear frequently; for instance, 5-month-olds pay more attention to their own name than to other, similar-sounding words (Mandel, Jusczyk, & Pisoni, 1995). When they reach 8 or 9 months, they also seem to prefer listening to the sounds and rhythms of their native language. For instance, Mario showed an early preference for Spanish rather than English (Fantini, 1985; Jusczyk & Aslin, 1995; Saffran et al., 1996).

This early tuning-in to a particular language gradually alters what infants "hear" and "don't hear" in the speech around them. By the time infants are a year old, they primarily hear the differences that are important in their own language (Kuhl, Williams, Lacerda, Stevens, & Lindblom, 1992; Werker & Lalonde, 1988). For example, 1-year-old babies in English-speaking countries continue to hear the difference between "L" and "R" sounds; this distinction is critical for making such discriminations as *lap* versus *rap* and *lice* versus *rice.* In contrast, Japanese children gradually lose the ability to tell the difference, presumably because Japanese treats the two sounds as a single phoneme. On the other hand, English-speaking babies lose the ability to distinguish among various "S" sounds that comprise two or more different phonemes in certain other languages.

phonemes
Smallest units of a spoken language that signify differences in meaning.

Although there appears to be an early sensitive period in the ability to distinguish among various speech sounds, the window of opportunity doesn't slam shut at age 1. Children continue to fine-tune their discriminative powers in the early years. For instance, they may have some difficulty distinguishing between words that differ by only one phoneme until they are 5 (Gerken, 1994; Rayner, Foorman, Perfetti, Pesetsky, & Seidenberg, 2001). Furthermore, they may continue to hear some sound differences not important in their own language until they are 8 to 10 years old (Siegler, 1998).

■ *Young children rely more heavily on context than older children do.*   Children do not necessarily need to focus on every word, or even every sound, when they listen to what other people say; for instance, 18-month-olds often know from the context what word a speaker is going to say after hearing only the first two phonemes (Fernald, Swingley, & Pinto, 2001). Furthermore, using various nonverbal contextual clues, children often realize that what a speaker says is different from what the speaker actually means (Donaldson, 1978; Flavell et al., 1993; Paul, 1990). For example, kindergartners may correctly conclude that a teacher who asks "Whose jacket do I see lying on the floor?" is actually requesting the jacket's owner to pick it up and put it where it belongs. Not all children are used to such indirect requests, however. In certain communities in the southeast United States, parents seldom use them; in such communities, young children are more likely to adhere to classroom rules when their teachers specifically tell them what needs to be done (Heath, 1983).

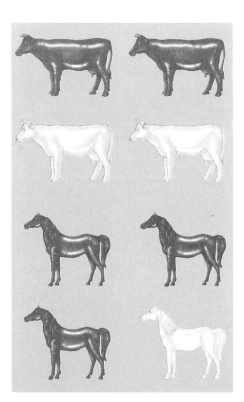

Young children are sometimes too dependent on context for determining the meaning of language, to the point where they don't listen carefully enough to understand a spoken message accurately. They may "hear" what they think the speaker means, based on their beliefs about the speaker's intentions, rather than discerning what was actually said. A study by McGarrigle (cited in Donaldson, 1978) illustrates such misinterpretation. Six-year-olds were shown four cows (two black, two white) and four horses (three black, one white) and asked, "Are there more *cows* or more *black horses*?" (see Figure 7–3). Only 14% correctly answered that there were more cows; most said that there were more black horses. Follow-up questions indicated that the children were interpreting the question as a request to compare only the black cows with the black horses. For example, one child defended his incorrect answer this way: "There's more black horses 'cos there's only two black cows" (p. 44).

Older children and adolescents consider the context in a somewhat different way, in that they compare a message to the reality of the situation. Such a comparison enables them to detect sarcasm—to realize that the speaker actually means the exact opposite of what he or she is saying (Capelli, Nakagawa, & Madden, 1990). For instance, they understand that someone who says "Oh, that's just great!" in the face of dire circumstances doesn't think the situation is "great" at all.

FIGURE 7–3 Are there more cows or more black horses?

After McGarrigle (cited in Donaldson, 1978).

■ *Young children have an overly simplistic view of what "good listening" is.*   Children in the early elementary grades believe that they are good listeners if they simply sit quietly without interrupting the person speaking. Older children (e.g., 11-year-olds) are more likely to recognize that good listening also requires an understanding of what is being said (T. M. McDevitt, Spivey, Sheehan, Lennon, & Story, 1990).

■ *Elementary school children do not always know what to do when they don't understand what they hear.*   In studies by T. M. McDevitt (1990; T. M. McDevitt et al., 1990), children in grades 1, 3, and 5 were given the following dilemma:

> This is a story about a girl named Mary. Mary is at school listening to her teacher, Ms. Brown. Ms. Brown explains how to use a new computer that she just got for their classroom. She tells the children in the classroom how to use the computer. Mary doesn't understand the teacher's directions. She's confused. What should Mary do? (T. M. McDevitt, 1990, p. 570)

Some children responded that Mary should ask the teacher for further explanation. But others said that Mary should either listen more carefully or seek clarification of the procedure from other children. Many children, especially younger ones, apparently believe that it is inappropriate to ask their teacher for help, perhaps because they have previously been discouraged from asking questions in school or at home (T. M. McDevitt, 1990; T. M. McDevitt et al., 1990). Cultural background plays a role here as well: Many children growing up in Asian and Mexican American communities are reluctant to ask questions because they've been taught that initiating a conversation with an adult is disrespectful (Delgado-Gaitan, 1994; Grant & Gomez, 2001; Trawick-Smith, 2003).

■ *Older children and adolescents become increasingly able to find multiple meanings in messages.* As children move into the middle and secondary grades, they become aware that messages may be ambiguous and so have two or more possible meanings (Bearison & Levey, 1977; Nippold, 1988; R. E. Owens, 1996). They also become better able to understand **figurative speech**, speech that communicates meaning beyond a literal interpretation of its words. For instance, they understand that idioms are not to be taken at face value— that a person who "hits the roof" doesn't really hit the roof and that someone who is "tied up" isn't necessarily bound with rope. They become increasingly adept at interpreting similes and metaphors (e.g., "Her hands are like ice," "That man is the Rock of Gibraltar"). And in the late elementary years, they begin to draw generalizations from proverbs such as "Look before you leap" or "Don't put the cart before the horse." In the Middle Childhood and Late Adolescence clips of the Cognitive Development module of the Observation CD, you can observe how children's ability to understand proverbs improves with age. For example, whereas 10-year-old Kent seems baffled by the old adage "A rolling stone gathers no moss," 14-year-old Alicia offers a reasonable explanation: "Maybe when you go through things too fast, you don't collect anything from it." Adolescents' ability to interpret proverbs in a generalized, abstract fashion continues to develop throughout the secondary school years (R. E. Owens, 1996).

Observe the progression in understanding figurative speech as you listen to 10-year-old Kent and 14-year-old Alicia interpret proverbs in the Middle Childhood and Late Adolescence clips of the Cognitive Development module of the Observation CD.

Although children's ability to understand figurative language depends to some degree on their cognitive maturity, it may also depend on how much they have been exposed to such language. Many inner-city African American communities make heavy use of figurative language, such as similes, metaphors, and hyperbole (intentional exaggeration), in their day-to-day conversations, jokes, and stories (Hale-Benson, 1986; Ortony, Turner, and Larson-Shapiro, 1985; H. L. Smith, 1998). The following anecdote illustrates:

> I once asked my mother, upon her arrival from church, "Mom, was it a good sermon?" To which she replied, "Son, by the time the minister finished preaching, the men were crying and the women had passed out on the floor." (H. L. Smith, 1998, p. 202)

With such a rich oral tradition, it is not surprising that inner-city African American youth are especially advanced in their ability to comprehend figurative language (Ortony et al., 1985).

Cognitive Factors Influencing the Development of Listening Comprehension Not only does children's ability to understand what they hear depend on their knowledge of word meanings and syntax, but it also depends on their general knowledge about the world. For instance, children can better understand a peer's description of a newly purchased Volkswagen Beetle if they have a schema of what Volkswagen Beetles look like. They can better understand a friend's story about a trip to a fast-food restaurant if they have a script of what such visits typically entail. Children's schemas, scripts, and other knowledge about the world enable them to draw inferences from the things they hear, thus filling gaps in the information presented.

Working memory—that part of memory where human beings first hold new information while they mentally process it—also influences listening comprehension (Anthony, Lonigan, & Dyer, 1996; L. French & Brown, 1977). Children's ability to understand the things they hear is limited to what they can reasonably hold in working memory. A message that presents too much information in too short a time will be difficult, perhaps even impossible, to understand; in such circumstances, what children hear may, as the saying goes, go in one ear and out the other. Because young children tend to have a smaller working memory capacity than older children and adults (see Chapter 5), they will be especially limited in their ability to understand and remember what they hear. Preschoolers, for instance, often have trouble remembering and following directions with multiple steps (L. French & Brown, 1977).

Children's general cognitive abilities play a role as well. Interpreting messages in nonliteral ways requires abstract thinking and an ability to draw analogies across diverse situations

figurative speech
Speech that communicates meaning beyond a literal interpretation of its words.

DEVELOPMENT AND PRACTICE
Promoting Listening Skills in Young Children

- Discuss the components of good listening.

   A first-grade teacher explains to her students that "good listening" involves more than just sitting quietly, that it also involves paying attention and trying to understand what the speaker is saying.

- Discuss courses of action that children should take when they don't understand a speaker.

   When a 7-year-old girl has exceptional difficulty learning to read, a school psychologist administers a series of tests to determine where the problem lies. As he presents each new assessment task, he encourages the girl to ask questions whenever she doesn't understand what he is asking her to do.

- Expect children to listen attentively for only short periods of time.

   A kindergarten teacher has learned that most of his students can listen quietly to a storybook for no more than 10 or 15 minutes at a stretch, and he plans his daily schedule accordingly.

- Present only small amounts of information at once.

   A home child care provider helps the 3- and 4-year-olds in her care make "counting books" to take home. She has previously prepared nine sheets of paper (each with a different number from 1 to 9) for each child. She has also assembled a variety of objects that the children can paste on the pages to depict the numbers (two buttons for the "2" page, five pieces of macaroni for the "5" page, etc.). As she engages the children in the project, she describes only one or two steps of the process at a time.

(R. E. Owens, 1996; Winner, 1988). Given what we know about when abstract thinking develops, it is hardly surprising that children have difficulty understanding metaphors and proverbs in the preschool and early elementary years.

Promoting Listening Comprehension   Caregivers, teachers, and other practitioners who work with toddlers, preschoolers, and children in the lower elementary grades must take into account the limited listening comprehension skills that young children are likely to have (see the Development and Practice feature "Promoting Listening Skills in Young Children"). Following are three more general suggestions for adults who work with children and adolescents at all age levels:

   Take children's semantic and syntactic development into account when speaking to them, and check frequently to be sure that they understand.   Using vocabulary and syntactic structures appropriate to the age group is, of course, essential if adults want children to understand what they say. Furthermore, rather than assuming that their messages have been understood, adults should in some way assess children's understanding, perhaps by asking questions, having children restate ideas in their words, or having them demonstrate what they've learned through actions or pictures.

   Adjust the length of verbal presentations to the attention span of the age group, and avoid information overload.   As information processing theory tells us, people of all ages can understand a message only when they are paying attention, and they can handle only a limited amount of information at a time. Given such limitations, children and adolescents alike often benefit from hearing something more than once (e.g., Wasik, Karweit, Burns, & Brodsky, 1998).

   Encourage critical listening.   Sometime around age 4 to 6, children begin to realize that what people say is not necessarily what is true (Flavell et al., 1993). Yet throughout the elementary and secondary school years, children and adolescents sometimes have difficulty separating fact from fiction in the messages they hear. Children who are taught not to believe everything they hear are more likely to evaluate messages for errors, falsehoods, and ambiguities. For example, when children are reminded that television commercials are designed to persuade them to buy something, they are less likely to be influenced by those commercials (T. M. McDevitt, 1990; Roberts, Christenson, Gibson, Mooser, & Goldberg, 1980).

Development of Speaking Skills

As children become more proficient in understanding what other people say, they also become more proficient at expressing their own thoughts, ideas, and wishes. When children first begin to speak, their objective is often to control someone else's behavior. For example, a toddler who yells "Elmo!" may very well be asking a parent to purchase the Elmo doll she sees on a shelf at the toy store. Over the next 2 or 3 years, however, children increasingly use speech to exchange information with others. By age 4, exchanging information appears to be the primary function of oral language (R. E. Owens, 1996).

Children begin to develop their speaking skills long before they utter their first word, however. Following are several trends that characterize the development of speaking skills in infancy, childhood, and adolescence:

■ *In the first year of life, children become increasingly adept at making speech sounds and increasingly language-specific in their vocalizations.* Between 1 and 2 months of age, infants typically begin **cooing**, making vowel sounds in an almost "singing" manner (e.g., "aaaaaaa," "oooooo"). Sometime around 6 months, they begin *babbling,* combining consonant and vowel sounds into syllables that they may repeat over and over (e.g., "mama-mamama," "doodoodoo"). Over time, babbling becomes increasingly speechlike in nature, as infants combine different syllables into language-like utterances.

Initially, babbling includes a wide variety of speechlike sounds, but infants soon drop the sounds they don't hear in the speech around them (J. L. Locke, 1993). In essence, infants first babble in a universal "language" and then later babble only in their native tongue.

As noted earlier, babbling is not restricted to children who can hear: Infants who are deaf begin to babble at about the same age that hearing infants do. Furthermore, babbling is not necessarily limited to spoken language: Deaf children exposed to sign language often begin to "babble" manually at 7 to 10 months of age (Pettito, 1997).

■ *Pronunciation continues to develop through the early elementary years.* Children typically do not master all the phonemes of the English language until they are about 8 years old (R. E. Owens, 1996). During the preschool years, they are likely to have difficulty pronouncing *r* and *th;* for instance, they might say "wabbit" instead of "rabbit" and "dat" instead of "that." Most children have acquired these sounds by the time they are 6, but at this age they may still have trouble with such diphthongs as *str, sl,* and *dr* (R. E. Owens, 1996).

Recall the kindergarten teacher's reference to Mario's "slight accent." Mario mastered Spanish pronunciation by the time he was 3; a few months later, he could produce many of the additional phonemes required for English. Nevertheless, Spanish sounds occasionally crept into Mario's English for several years thereafter (Fantini, 1985).

■ *As children grow older, their conversations with others increase in length and depth.* Early conversations tend to be short. Most young children are quite willing and able to introduce new topics into a conversation, but they have difficulty maintaining a sustained interchange about any single topic (R. E. Owens, 1996). As a result, the focus of discussion is likely to change frequently; for instance, a 5-year-old may talk about 50 different topics within a 15-minute period (Brinton & Fujiki, 1984). As children grow older, they can carry on lengthier discussions about a single issue or event, and, as they reach adolescence, the content of their conversations becomes increasingly abstract (R. E. Owens, 1996).

■ *Children become increasingly able to adapt their speech to the characteristics of their listeners.* As early as age 3, preschoolers use simpler language with toddlers than they do with adults and peers (T. M. McDevitt & Ford, 1987; Shatz & Gelman, 1973). Yet preschoolers and elementary school children don't always take their listeners' visual perspectives and prior knowledge into account and so may provide insufficient information for their listeners to understand what they are saying (Glucksberg & Krauss, 1967; T. M. McDevitt & Ford, 1987). We can recall numerous occasions when our own children have yelled "What's this?" from another room, apparently unaware that we could not possibly see what they were looking at. To some extent, such speech may reflect preoperational egocentrism (Piaget, 1959). However, it may also be the result of young children's lack of proficiency in describing precisely the objects and events that they are currently experiencing or have previously witnessed (T. M. McDevitt & Ford, 1987). (We will identify another explanation for egocentric speech in the discussion of theory of mind in Chapter 10.)

As children grow older, they become capable of carrying on lengthy conversations about a single topic.

cooing
Making and repeating vowel sounds (e.g., "oooooo"); common in early infancy.

As children grow older, they become increasingly able to take other people's knowledge and perspectives into consideration and so are better able to make their meanings clear; for instance, they give more elaborate explanations to people who they know are unfamiliar with what they are talking about (Sonnenschein, 1988). They also become better able to read the subtle nonverbal signals (e.g., the puzzled brows, the lengthy silences) that indicate that others don't understand what they are saying (T. M. McDevitt & Ford, 1987).

■ *Over time, children become more skillful at narratives.* Beginning in the preschool years, children can tell a story, or **narrative**—a sequence of events, either real or fictional, that are logically interconnected (McKeough, 1995; Sutton-Smith, 1986).[2] The following narrative, told by 4-year-old Lucy, is typical of children's early fiction:

> Once upon a time there was a girl who lived on a farm with a very good horse and she always rode to the country on the horse and they had a picnic together. (McKeough, 1995, p. 156)

Kindergartners and first graders can typically describe a sequence that reflects appropriate ordering of events and includes cause-effect relationships (Kemper, 1984; Kemper & Edwards, 1986; McKeough, 1995). Narratives become increasingly complex during the elementary years. Definite plot lines begin to emerge, as do descriptions of people's thoughts, motives, and emotions (Kemper, 1984; R. E. Owens, 1996).

The exact nature of children's narratives varies somewhat from culture to culture. For example, in some African American communities, narratives may include several events that, on the surface, appear to be unrelated yet all contribute to a single underlying message—perhaps providing strategies for helping a baby brother (Hale-Benson, 1986; R. E. Owens, 1996; Trawick-Smith, 2003). Children from some backgrounds may have little or no exposure to certain kinds of narratives before beginning school (Heath, 1986). For instance, in some working-class Southern communities, children have few if any opportunities to describe events that they alone have experienced; they are more likely to describe events that they have shared with their listeners (Heath, 1986).

■ *Creative and figurative expressions emerge during the elementary years and continue into adolescence.* Children become increasingly creative in their language use. Elementary school children have widely shared expressions that they use to make choices ("Eenie, meenie, minie, mo"), challenge one another ("I double-dare you"), and establish standards for behavior ("Finders keepers, losers weepers") (R. E. Owens, 1996). In inner-city African American communities, creative word play may also appear in the form of **playing the dozens**,[3] playful teasing of one another through exaggerated insults (e.g., "Your momma is so dumb that she climbed over a pane of glass to see what was on the other side"). (Additional examples of playing the dozens appear in the story of Sam, p. 196, in Chapter 5.) Exaggeration (hyperbole) is evident in African American storytelling as well. In the following exchange, 12-year-old Terry and his neighbor Tony begin with a kernel of truth (a cat fight in the neighborhood) and then let their imaginations run wild:

Terry:	Didja hear 'bout Aunt Bess' cat las' night?
Tony:	No, what 'bout dat ol' cat?
Terry:	Dat cat get in a fight.
Tony:	A fight?
Terry:	Yeah, it kilt a dog.
Tony:	Ain't no cat can kill no dog.
Terry:	Dis cat, he kilt a big dog, dat ol' German shepherd stay down by ol' man Oak's place.
Tony:	What'd you do?
Terry:	Me? I kilt a horse.
Tony:	You ain't kilt no horse, (pause) more'n likely a mouse. Where?
Terry:	On Main Street. Yesterday.
Tony:	And you kilt one, for sure?

narrative
A temporal sequence of events that are logically interconnected; a story.

playing the dozens
Friendly, playful exchange of insults, common in some African American communities. Also called *joaning* or *sounding*.

---

[2] As you should recall from Chapter 5, narratives of actual events often enhance children's ability to recall their experiences.

[3] You may also see the terms *joaning* and *sounding*.

Terry: Yea, me 'n dat ol' cat, we built a big fire, stirred it aroun', threw oil in it, got it goin' good, and I rod [*sic*] dat horse right in.

Tony: Ya did?

Terry: Yup.

Tony: I know, it took a while to git de cat outta de fire, 'bout (pause) maybe a week or so, 'n Mr. Rowe [who owns a bicycle shop on Main Street] give us a bicycle, 'n we ride de horse, 'n my friend, Steve, he ride de horse, too, 'n we come back and foun' dat ol' cat done kilt dat big dog.

Terry: Why?

Tony: 'Cause dat cat say "Wow, I'm de greates', ain't no dog kin git me," (pause) like ain't no fire gonna git *me* (pause) 'n my horse (pause) 'n my bicycle. (Heath, 1983, pp. 183–184; reprinted with the permission of Cambridge University Press)

The use of figurative language in children's speech emerges during the elementary years and increases in frequency and sophistication during the secondary school years. Adolescents often use metaphors, similes, and phrases with double meanings; they are also likely to use sarcasm to communicate a message opposite from what their words mean literally (R. E. Owens, 1996).

■ *Adolescents sometimes use their own teen "dialect" in conversing with one another.* Many adolescents express themselves in ways that are unique to their age group, or perhaps to a small group of friends (R. E. Owens, 1996). For example, over the years, teenagers have used a variety of adjectives—*cool, boss, radical, awesome,* and so on—to describe something they really like. And at age 16, Jeanne's son Alex insisted on addressing everyone (including his mother) as "Dude." Such expressions help adolescents establish themselves as belonging to a particular peer group in much the same way that their clothing and hairstyles do (J. R. Harris, 1995).

How Children Develop Speaking Skills   Although young children occasionally talk to themselves (perhaps, as Vygotsky has suggested, providing a means for more effectively guiding their own behavior), most oral language during the preschool years occurs during conversations with other individuals (R. E. Owens, 1996). Frequently, preschoolers' conversational partners are adults, who typically guide and control the discussions (R. E. Owens, 1996). In their interactions with peers, children can converse more as equal partners. Furthermore, when children assume the roles of "mommy," "teacher," "doctor," or "storekeeper" in play activities, they can experiment with the variety of linguistic styles and jargon that they associate with such roles (Christie & Johnsen, 1983; K. E. Nelson, 1986), and they may use narratives to develop a story line for their play:

> You're the daddy. And you pretend to get dressed. You're going to take the baby to the zoo. (R. E. Owens, 1996, p. 347)

During the elementary and secondary school years, experience—in the form of both structured activities (e.g., oral presentations at school) and unstructured interactions (e.g., conversations with friends)—almost certainly continues to play a key role in the development of speaking skills. For instance, the prevalence of word play and figurative language in inner-city African American communities is probably largely responsible for the especially creative speech of the children who grow up in these communities (Ortony et al., 1985; H. L. Smith, 1998).

Promoting Speaking Skills   To help children and adolescents develop their speaking skills, adults should, of course, give them many and varied opportunities to speak in both structured and unstructured contexts. The following strategies may also be helpful:

■ *Regularly engage infants in "conversation."*   By the time infants are 3 or 4 months old, most readily engage in verbal interactions with adults (Siegler, 1998). For instance, they have some knowledge of turn taking, quietly listening when an adult speaks to them and vocalizing when the adult stops (Ginsburg & Kilbourne, 1988). They also tend to mimic the intonations (e.g., changes in pitch and stress) that a caregiver uses (Masataka, 1992). When a caregiver mimics *their* vocalizations, infants' speechlike sounds increase in frequency (Bloom, Russell, & Wassnberg, 1987). It appears, then, that verbal interaction has benefits

The classroom provides an excellent context in which children and adolescents can develop their speaking skills.

Observe Corwin's conversations with his mother in the Infancy clips of the Cognitive Development, Intelligence, and Literacy modules of the Observation CD.

even for children who do not yet understand the bulk of what they hear. In the Infancy clips of the Cognitive Development, Intelligence, and Literacy modules of the Observation CD, you can observe the "conversations" that 16-month-old Corwin has with his mother. Although Corwin says few words distinctly enough to be understood, he certainly knows how to take turns in the dialogue and to respond in some way to his mother's questions.

■ *Let children know when something they say is difficult to understand.* People of all ages occasionally have trouble communicating their thoughts clearly to others; young children may have particular difficulty because of their limited ability to consider the knowledge and perspectives of their listeners. Asking questions or expressing confusion when children describe events and ideas ambiguously or incompletely should gradually help them express their thoughts more precisely and take into account what their listeners already do and do not know.

■ *Ask children to tell stories.* Adults often ask questions that encourage children to respond in narrative form (Hemphill & Snow, 1996); for instance, a teacher might ask, "What did you do this weekend?" or "Do you remember what happened the last time someone brought a pet to show-and-tell?" Giving children opportunities to narrate events—either actual incidents or fictional creations—provides a context in which they can practice speaking for sustained periods of time and build on the rich oral traditions of many cultural groups (Hale-Benson, 1986; Hemphill & Snow, 1996; McCarty & Watahomigie, 1998).

Storytelling ability can be enhanced by specific training and practice (McKeough, 1995). Consider how 6-year-old Leanne's ability to tell a story improved over a 2-month period as a result of specific instruction about how to conceptualize and tell stories:

Before instruction:

A girl—and a boy—and a kind old horse. They got mad at each other. That the end. (McKeough, 1995, p. 170)

After instruction:

Once upon a time there was a girl. She was playing with her toys and—um—she asked her mom if she could go outside—to play in the snow. But her mom said no. And then she was very sad. And—and she had to play. So she she [sic] asked her mom if she could go outside and she said yes. She jumped in the snow and she was having fun and she had an idea and she jumped in the snow and she felt happy. (McKeough, 1995, p. 170)

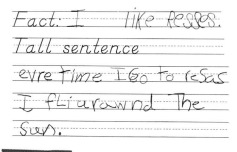

FIGURE 7-4 Morris (age 6) shows that he knows the difference between a fact ("I like recess") and a "tall sentence" ("Every time I go to recess I fly around the sun").

■ *Encourage creativity in oral language.* Linguistic creativity can be expressed in many ways—for example, through stories, poems, songs, rap, jokes, and puns. Such forms of language not only may encourage creative language use but also help children identify parallels between seemingly dissimilar objects or events—parallels that enable them to construct similes, metaphors, and other analogies. Hyperbole can be encouraged as well, as long as children realize that they are intentionally stretching the truth. For instance, for the assignment depicted in Figure 7–4, 6-year-old Morris has been instructed to write a fact and then a "tall sentence" in which he should fantasize or exaggerate.

The playful use of language can have an additional benefit, as an event in Mario's childhood illustrates:

Seven-year-old Mario tells his parents a joke that he has heard at school earlier in the day. He relates the joke in English: "What did the bird say when his cage got broken?" His parents have no idea what the bird said, so he tells them, "Cheap, cheap!"

Mario's parents find the joke amusing, so he later translates it for the family's Spanish-speaking nanny: "*¿Qué dijo el pájaro cuando se le rompió la jaula?*" He follows up with the bird's answer: "*Barato, barato.*" Mario is surprised to discover that the nanny finds no humor in the joke. He knows that he has somehow failed to convey the point of the joke but cannot figure out where he went wrong. (Fantini, 1985, p. 72)

The joke, of course, gets lost in translation. The Spanish word *barato* means "cheap" but has no resemblance to the sound that a bird makes. Only several years later did Mario understand that humor that depended on word play would not necessarily translate from one language to another (Fantini, 1985). His eventual understanding of this principle was an aspect of his growing *metalinguistic awareness,* a characteristic you will learn more about shortly.

Proficiency in listening to and speaking with others includes knowledge not only about various aspects of language itself, but also about the nonverbal behaviors that one's society deems acceptable for social interaction—behaviors that are often quite different for different cultures. We turn now to an examination of such *sociolinguistic behaviors*.

Development of Sociolinguistic Behaviors

Let's return to a comment Mario's kindergarten teacher made in her report to Mario's parents:

> His greatest problem seems to be in the give and take of conversation. Since he always has something to say, he often finds it difficult to wait his turn when others are talking. (Fantini, 1985, p. 28)

Children's ability to converse successfully with others depends partly on knowledge and skills that have little or nothing to do with language per se. For instance, in mainstream Western culture, most children learn to take turns with other people involved in a conversation; in many situations, it's neither productive nor polite for everyone to talk at once or to interrupt one another. Children may discover that behaviors such as looking a speaker in the eye, smiling, and nodding in agreement are effective ways to show that they are listening and understand what the speaker is saying. They may learn to greet others (e.g., "Hello") and to end a conversation with some form of sign-off (e.g., "Good-bye"). They may learn, too, that ways that they might speak to their peers (e.g., "Shut up!" "Get outa here!") are unacceptable when talking to adults. Instead, as children get older, most begin to realize that they should temper requests to authority figures with qualifications ("I'm not sure, Mrs. Brown, but I think it's my turn") and appropriate signs of deference ("Mr. Suarez, can I go outside now?").

The social conventions that govern appropriate verbal interaction are called **sociolinguistic behaviors.** Sociolinguistic behaviors fall within the broader domain of *pragmatics,* which includes not only rules of conversational etiquette—taking turns in conversations, saying goodbye when leaving, and so on—but also strategies for initiating conversations, changing the subject, telling stories, and arguing persuasively.

Children continue to refine their knowledge of pragmatics and sociolinguistic conventions throughout the preschool years and elementary grades (Garvey & Berninger, 1981; R. E. Owens, 1996; Warren-Leubecker & Bohannon, 1989); our own observations indicate that this process continues into the middle and high school years as well. However, children from different cultures often learn different conventions, particularly in matters of etiquette, as you will see now.

Cultural Differences in Sociolinguistic Behaviors Experts have identified numerous cross-cultural differences in sociolinguistic behaviors. Such differences may lead to misunderstandings when adults who have been raised in one culture work with children who have been raised in another. For example, some Native American communities believe it unnecessary to say hello or good-bye (Sisk, 1989); when children from those communities fail to extend greetings, adults who are working with them might erroneously conclude that they are being rude. In other Native American communities, children learn that they should rarely express their feelings through facial expressions (Montgomery, 1989); an adult from another culture might easily misinterpret a child's lack of facial expression as an indication of boredom or disinterest. Following are additional cultural differences that may lead to misunderstandings in classrooms and other group settings. (These differences are summarized in the Observation Guidelines table "Identifying Cultural Differences in Sociolinguistic Conventions.")

■ *Being silent.* Relatively speaking, mainstream Western culture is a chatty one. People often say things to one another even when they have very little to communicate; they make small talk as a way of maintaining interpersonal relationships and filling awkward silences (Irujo, 1988; Trawick-Smith, 2003). But in some cultures, silence is golden; for instance, Brazilians and Peruvians often greet their guests silently, Arabs stop speaking as a way of signaling that they want privacy, and Apaches generally value silence (Basso, 1972; Menyuk & Menyuk, 1988; Trawick-Smith, 2003). Children and adolescents who come from such backgrounds are, of course, likely to behave consistently with their upbringing by saying little in the classroom and other group settings. Unfortunately, adults and peers may react to their silence by thinking that they are "rude" or "strange" (Menyuk & Menyuk, 1988).

sociolinguistic behaviors
Social and culturally specific conventions that govern appropriate verbal interaction.

OBSERVATION GUIDELINES

Identifying Cultural Differences in Sociolinguistic Conventions

CHARACTERISTIC	LOOK FOR	EXAMPLE	IMPLICATION
Talkativeness	• Frequent talking, even about trivial matters, *or* • Silence unless something important needs to be said	When Muhammed abruptly stops talking to his peers and turns to read his book, the other children think his action is rude.	Don't interpret a child's sudden or lengthy silence as necessarily reflecting apathy or intentional rudeness.
Style of Interacting with Adults	• Willingness to initiate conversations with adults, *or* • Speaking to adults only when spoken to	Elena is exceptionally quiet in class, and she answers questions only when her teacher directs them specifically at her. At lunch and on the playground, however, she readily talks and laughs with her friends.	Keep in mind that some children won't tell you when they are confused. If you think they may not understand, take them aside and ask specific questions that assess what they have learned. Provide additional instruction to address any gaps in their understanding.
Eye Contact	• Looking others in the eye when speaking or listening to them, *or* • Looking down or away in the presence of adults	Herman always looks at his feet when an adult speaks to him.	Don't assume that children aren't paying attention just because they don't look you in the eye.
Personal Space	• Standing quite close to a conversation partner, perhaps touching that person frequently, *or* • Keeping distance between oneself and others when talking with them	Michelle is noticeably uncomfortable when other people touch her.	Give children some personal space during one-on-one interactions. So that they might more effectively interact with others, teach them that what constitutes personal space differs from culture to culture.
Responses to Questions	• Answering questions readily, *or* • Failure to answer very easy questions	Leah never responds to "What is this?" questions, even when she knows the answers.	Be aware that some children are not used to answering the types of questions that adults frequently ask during instruction. Respect children's privacy when they are reluctant to answer questions about home and family life.
Wait Time	• Waiting several seconds before answering questions, *or* • Not waiting at all, and perhaps even interrupting others	Mario often interrupts his classmates during class discussions.	When addressing a question to an entire group, give children several seconds to think before calling on one child for an answer. When some children interrupt regularly, establish a procedure (e.g., hand-raising and waiting to be called on) that ensures that everyone has a chance to be heard.

■ *Interacting with adults.* In most Western communities, the expectation is that children will speak up when they have comments or questions. Yet children raised in the Yup'ik culture of Alaska are expected to learn primarily by close, quiet observation of adults; they rarely ask questions or otherwise interrupt what adults are doing (E. E. Garcia, 1994). In other cultures, children learn very early that they should engage in conversation with adults only when their participation has been directly solicited; this is the case in many Mexican American and Southeast Asian communities, as well as in some African American communities in the southeastern United States (Delgado-Gaitan, 1994; Grant & Gomez, 2001; Ochs, 1982). In fact, children from some backgrounds, including many Puerto Ricans, Mexican Americans, and Native Americans, have been taught that speaking directly and assertively to adults is rude, perhaps even rebellious (Delgado-Gaitan, 1994; Hidalgo, Siu, Bright, Swap, & Epstein, 1995; Lomawaima, 1995).

■ *Making eye contact.* For many people, looking someone in the eye is a way of indicating that they are trying to communicate or are listening intently. But in many African American, Puerto Rican, Mexican American, and Native American cultures, a child who looks an adult in the eye is showing disrespect. Children in such cultures are taught to look down in the presence of adults (Gilliland, 1988; Torres-Guzmán, 1998; Trawick-Smith, 2003). The following anecdote shows how accommodation to this culturally learned behavior can make a difference:

> A teacher [described a Native American] student who would never say a word, nor even answer when she greeted him. Then one day when he came in she looked in the other direction and said, "Hello, Jimmy." He answered enthusiastically, "Why hello Miss Jacobs." She found that he would always talk if she looked at a book or at the wall, but when she looked at him, he appeared frightened. (Gilliland, 1988, p. 26)

■ *Maintaining personal space.* In some cultures, such as in some African American and Hispanic communities, people stand close together when they talk and may touch one another frequently (Hale-Benson, 1986; Slonim, 1991; D. W. Sue, 1990). In contrast, European Americans and Japanese Americans tend to keep a fair distance from one another—they maintain some **personal space**—especially if they don't know one another very well (Irujo, 1988; Trawick-Smith, 2003). Adults who work regularly with children must be sensitive to the personal space that children from various cultural backgrounds need in order to feel comfortable in interactions with others.

In some cultures, looking an adult in the eye is a sign of respect; in other cultures, it is interpreted as disrespect.

■ *Responding to questions.* A common interaction pattern in many Western classrooms is the **IRE cycle:** A teacher *initiates* an interaction by asking a question, a student *responds* to the question, and the teacher *evaluates* the response (Mehan, 1979). Similar cycles are frequently found in parent-child interactions in middle-class European American homes; for instance, as we reflect back on our interactions with our own children as toddlers and preschoolers, we can recall many occasions when we asked questions such as "How old are you?" and "What does a cow say?" and praised our children when they answered correctly. But children raised in other environments—for instance, many of those raised in lower-income homes, as well as those raised in some Mexican American, Native American, or Hawaiian communities—are unfamiliar with such question-answer sessions when they first come to school (Losey, 1995). Furthermore, children in some of these cultures, such as those in many Navajo and Hawaiian communities, may feel more comfortable responding to adults' questions as a group rather than interacting with adults one-on-one (K. H. Au, 1980; L. S. Miller, 1995).

■ *Answering different kinds of questions.* Consider the following questions:

- What's this a picture of?
- What color is this?
- What's your sister's name?

These questions seem simple enough to answer. But in fact, different cultures teach children to answer different kinds of questions. European American parents frequently ask their children to identify objects and their characteristics (notice the kinds of questions that Mother asks Corwin in the Literacy/Infancy clip of the Observation CD). Yet in certain other cultures, parents rarely ask their children questions that they themselves know the answers to (Crago, Annahatak, & Ningiuruvik, 1993; Heath, 1980; Rogoff & Morelli, 1989). For example, parents in some African American communities in the southeastern United States are more likely to ask questions involving comparisons and analogies; rather than asking "What's that?" they may instead ask "What's that like?" (Heath, 1980). Furthermore, children in these same communities are specifically taught *not* to answer questions that strangers may ask about personal and home life (e.g., "What's your name?" "Where do you live?"). Teachers' comments about these children reflect their lack of understanding about the culture from which the children come:

Hear the kinds of questions that European American mothers ask their young children in the Literacy/Infancy clip of the Observation CD.

> "I would almost think some of them have a hearing problem; it is as though they don't hear me ask a question. I get blank stares to my questions. Yet when I am making statements or telling stories which interest them, they always seem to hear me."

> "The simplest questions are the ones they can't answer in the classroom; yet on the playground, they can explain a rule for a ballgame or describe a particular kind of bait with no problem. Therefore, I know they can't be as dumb as they seem in my class." (Heath, 1980, pp. 107–108)

personal space
Personally and culturally preferred distance between two people during social interaction.
IRE cycle
Adult-child interaction pattern marked by adult initiation, child response, and adult evaluation; in Western cultures, such a pattern is often seen in instructional settings.

Meanwhile, parents describe the confusion their children are experiencing:

"My kid, he too scared to talk, 'cause nobody play by the rules he know. At home I can't shut him up."

"Miss Davis, she complain 'bout Ned not answerin' back. He says she asks dumb questions she already know about." (Heath, 1980, p. 107)

■ *Waiting and interrupting.* Teachers frequently ask their students questions and then wait for an answer. But exactly how long do they wait? The typical **wait time** for many teachers is a second or even less; at that point, they either answer a question themselves or call on another student (M. B. Rowe, 1974, 1987). Yet people from some cultures leave lengthy pauses before responding as a way of indicating respect, as this statement by a Northern Cheyenne illustrates:

Even if I had a quick answer to your question, I would never answer immediately. That would be saying that your question was not worth thinking about. (Gilliland, 1988, p. 27)

For many cultural groups, then, students are more likely to participate in class and answer questions when given several seconds to respond (Grant & Gomez, 2001; Mohatt & Erickson, 1981; Tharp, 1989).

In contrast, children from certain other backgrounds, rather than pausing as a way to show respect, may interrupt adults or peers who haven't finished speaking—behavior that many of us might interpret as rudeness. For instance, in some African American, Puerto Rican, and Jewish families, family discourse often consists of several people talking at once; in fact, people who wait for their turn might find themselves being excluded from the discussion altogether (Condon & Yousef, 1975; Farber, Mindel, & Lazerwitz, 1988; Hale-Benson, 1986; Slonim, 1991). And in some Hawaiian communities, an interruption is taken as a sign of personal involvement in the conversation (Tharp, 1989).

How Sociolinguistic Behaviors Develop As we have seen, even young infants show turn taking in their "conversations" with others, in that they tend to remain quiet when an adult is talking. This tendency may be essential to language development (J. L. Locke, 1993) and so may reflect a biological predisposition. By and large, however, conversational etiquette and other sociolinguistic behaviors are almost certainly culturally transmitted. Sometimes parents and other family members teach these behaviors directly. In the following interaction between 20-month-old Amy and her mother, Amy burps, and her mother pats her chest:

Mother:	Oh, what do you say?
Amy:	(Touches her throat.) Thank you.
Mother:	No, excuse me.
Amy:	(Touches her throat again.) Excuse me.
Mother:	Excuse me. Yeah. (dialogue from P. J. Miller, 1982, p. 100; format adapted)

Teachers and other adults often instruct children in desired sociolinguistic behaviors as well. For instance, Mario once explained to his parents how his kindergarten teacher encouraged students to take turns when speaking in class (we present an English translation):

[A]t school, I have to raise my hand . . . and then wait a long, long time. And then the teacher says: "Now you can speak, Mario," and she makes the other children shut up, and she says, "Mario's speaking now." (Fantini, 1985, p. 83)

Children probably learn many conventions not so much through direct instruction as through imitating the behaviors of others—perhaps modeling how their parents answer the telephone, greet people on the street, and converse with friends and relatives. The feedback they receive from others (sometimes blatant, sometimes more subtle) may also encourage them to conform to sociolinguistic conventions. For instance, most young children eventually learn that they get along better with their peers when they ask for something nicely ("Can I please have that?") rather than make demands ("Gimme that!"). Older children and adolescents may discover that when they stand too close to others, their conversational partners act uneasy and may even back up to create a more comfortable distance.

wait time
The length of time a teacher pauses, after either asking a question or hearing a student's comment, before saying something else.

Taking Sociolinguistic Differences into Account   When the sociolinguistic behaviors expected at home differ significantly from those expected at school and in other group settings, a sense of confusion, or **culture shock,** can result. Such culture shock can interfere with children's adjustment to the group setting and, ultimately, with their behavior and achievement as well (Garcia, 1995; C. D. Lee & Slaughter-Defoe, 1995; Ogbu, 1992; Phelan, Yu, & Davidson, 1994). Adults further compound the problem when, interpreting children's behaviors as being unacceptable or otherwise "odd," they jump too quickly to the conclusion that certain youngsters are unable or unwilling to make productive contributions to the group (Bowman, 1989; Hilliard & Vaughn-Scott, 1982).

Clearly, teachers and other practitioners must educate themselves about the diverse sociolinguistic patterns they are likely to find in their day-to-day interactions with children so that they don't read unintended messages into children's behaviors. Furthermore, adults must keep children's varying conversational styles in mind as they design group lessons and activities. For instance, teachers might check their students' understanding of classroom material by calling for group rather than individual responses or perhaps by having students write their responses on paper. They might also vary the nature of their questions to include the kinds of questions that different students are accustomed to answering at home. And they should allow sufficient wait time—perhaps several seconds—for all students to think about and respond to the questions they pose.

Some children lack the pragmatic skills that are desirable in any culture; for instance, we have known children who seemed so insistent on dominating a conversation that no one else could get a word in. When children haven't mastered the basic conventions of conversational etiquette, their peers may find their behavior irritating or strange. Such a lack of pragmatic skills can seriously interfere with children's relationships with age-mates. It is important for practitioners to observe children's pragmatic skills as they interact both with adults and with peers and to provide guided practice in any skills that may be missing. Practitioners may also want to talk with parents or other family members to learn what conversational rules are followed at home. If difficulties with pragmatics persist despite ongoing efforts to address them, children should be evaluated by a speech-language pathologist or other appropriate clinician.

Development of Metalinguistic Awareness

Children's **metalinguistic awareness** is their ability to think about the nature of language and reflect on the functions that it serves. For instance, it includes conscious awareness that speech is comprised of smaller units (words, phonemes, etc.), that printed words have one-to-one correspondences to spoken words, and that language is an entity separate from its meaning. It also includes the ability to distinguish between what a person says and what he or she actually means (Yaden & Templeton, 1986).

In the late preschool or early elementary years, children become consciously aware that words are the basic units of language, that spoken words are comprised of phonemes, and that different phonemes tend to be associated with different letters or letter combinations (Tunmer, Pratt, & Herriman, 1984). In the elementary grades, children gradually become capable of determining when sentences are grammatically acceptable and when they are not (Bowey, 1986; Hakes, 1980). As they move into upper elementary and middle school, they begin to understand the component parts of speech (nouns, verbs, adjectives, etc.); such growth is almost certainly due, at least in part, to the formal instruction they receive about parts of speech. More sophisticated aspects of metalinguistic awareness, such as recognizing that a word or phrase has multiple meanings, don't emerge until the middle school years and continue to develop throughout adolescence. The Developmental Trends table "Language Skills at Different Age Levels" summarizes some of the characteristics you are likely to see in children's linguistic knowledge and skills at various age levels.

How Children Develop Metalinguistic Awareness   Theoretical accounts of metalinguistic development focus almost exclusively on the effects of experience. One factor that probably promotes metalinguistic awareness is "playing" with language. Children play with

culture shock
Sense of confusion that occurs when one encounters an environment with expectations for behavior very different from those in one's home environment.

metalinguistic awareness
Extent to which one is able to think about the nature of language.

DEVELOPMENTAL TRENDS

Language Skills at Different Age Levels

AGE	WHAT YOU MIGHT OBSERVE	DIVERSITY	IMPLICATIONS
Infancy (Birth–2) 	• Interest in listening to the human voice and in exchanging vocalizations with adults • Repetition of vowel sounds (cooing) at age 1–2 months and consonant-vowel syllables (babbling) at about 6 months • Understanding of some common words at about 8 months • Use of single words at about 12 months • Use of two-word combinations at about 18 months • Rapid increase in vocabulary in second year	• In the latter half of the first year, babbling increasingly reflects the specific phonemes of the native language. • Temperament may influence the rate of language development somewhat; more cautious children may wait a bit before beginning to speak. • Chronic ear infections can interfere with early language development. • Infants with severe hearing difficulties babble, but the quality of their babbling changes little over time. Spoken language progresses no further unless intensive training is provided.	• Engage young infants in "conversations," using simplified and animated (i.e., infant-directed speech), and responding when they vocalize. • Label and describe the objects and events that children see. • Ask simple questions (e.g., "Is your diaper wet?" "What does a cow say?"). • Repeat and expand on children's early "sentences" (e.g., follow "Kitty eat" with "Yes, the kitty is eating").
Early Childhood (2–6) 	• Rapid advances in vocabulary and syntax • Incomplete understandings of many simple words (e.g., undergeneralization, overgeneralization, confusion between simple comparatives such as *more* vs. *less*) • Overregularization (e.g., *goed, gooder, foots*) • Overdependence on word order and context (instead of syntax) when interpreting messages • Superficial understanding of what "good listening" is • Difficulty pronouncing some phonemes (e.g., *r, th, sl, dr*) • Increasing ability to construct narratives	• Children raised in bilingual environments may show slight delays in language development, but any delays are short-lived and usually not a cause for concern. • Major speech and communication disorders (e.g., abnormal syntactic constructions) reveal themselves in the preschool years.	• Give children corrective feedback when their use of words indicates inaccurate understanding. • Work on simple listening skills (e.g., sitting quietly, paying attention). • Ask follow-up questions to make sure that children accurately understand important messages. • Ask children to construct narratives about recent events (e.g., "Tell me about your camping trip last weekend"). • Read age-appropriate storybooks as a way of enhancing vocabulary.
Middle Childhood (6–10) 	• Increasing understanding of temporal words (e.g., *before, after*) and comparatives (e.g., *bigger, as big as*) • Incomplete knowledge of irregular word forms • Literal interpretation of messages (especially before age 9) • Pronunciation mastered by age 8 • Consideration of a listener's knowledge and perspective when speaking • Sustained conversations about concrete topics • Construction of narratives with plots and cause-effect relationships • Linguistic creativity and word play (e.g., rhymes, word games)	• Minor speech and communication disorders (e.g., persistent articulation problems) become evident. • African Americans often show advanced ability to use figurative language (e.g., metaphor, hyperbole). • Bilingual children are apt to show advanced metalinguistic awareness.	• Teach irregular word forms (e.g., the past tense of *ring* is *rang,* the past tense of *bring* is *brought*). • Use group discussions as a way to explore academic subject matter. • Have children develop short stories that they present orally or in writing. • Encourage jokes and rhymes that capitalize on double meanings and homonyms (i.e., sound-alike words). • When articulation problems are evident in the upper elementary grades, consult with a speech-language pathologist.

language in many ways—through rhymes, chants, jokes, puns, and so on (Christie & Johnsen, 1983; R. E. Owens, 1996). Such word play is almost certainly beneficial; for instance, rhymes help children discover the relationships between sounds and letters, and jokes and puns help children discover that words and phrases can have more than one meaning (Bradley & Bryant, 1991; Cazden, 1976; Christie & Johnsen, 1983).

DEVELOPMENTAL TRENDS

Language Skills at Different Age Levels *(continued)*

AGE	WHAT YOU MIGHT OBSERVE	DIVERSITY	IMPLICATIONS
Early Adolescence (10–14) 	• Increasing awareness of the terminology used in various academic disciplines • Ability to understand complex, multiclause sentences • Emerging ability to look beyond literal interpretations; comprehension of simple proverbs • Emerging ability to carry on lengthy conversations about abstract topics • Significant growth in metalinguistic awareness	• Girls are more likely than boys to converse about intimate and confidential matters. • African American teens may bandy insults back and forth in a playful manner. • Adolescents may prefer to use their native dialects even if they have mastered Standard English.	• Begin to use the terminology used by experts in various academic disciplines (e.g., *simile* in language arts, *molecule* in science). • Use classroom debates to explore controversial issues. • Present proverbs and ask children to consider their underlying meanings. • Explore the nature of words and language as entities in and of themselves.
Late Adolescence (14–18)	• Acquisition of many vocabulary words specifically related to various academic disciplines • Subtle refinements in grammar, mostly as a result of formal instruction • Mastery of a wide variety of connectives (e.g., *although, however, nevertheless*) • General ability to understand figurative language (e.g., metaphors, proverbs, hyperbole)	• Boys are apt to communicate their thoughts in a direct and straightforward manner; girls are more likely to be indirect and tactful. • A preference for one's native dialect over Standard English continues into the high school years.	• Consistently use the terminology associated with various academic disciplines. • Distinguish between similar abstract words (e.g., *weather* vs. *climate, velocity* vs. *acceleration*) • Explore complex syntactic structures (e.g., multiple embedded clauses). • Consider the underlying meanings and messages in poetry and fiction. • When teenagers have a native dialect other than Standard English, encourage them to use it in informal conversations and creative writing; encourage Standard English for more formal situations.

Sources: C. Baker, 1993; Bruer, 1999; Bruner, 1983; Chomsky, 1972; Eilers & Oller, 1994; Elias & Broerse, 1996; Fantini, 1985; Fenson et al., 1994; Fifer & Moon, 1995; Hale-Benson, 1986; J. L. Locke, 1993; McDevitt, 1990; K. Nelson, 1973; O'Grady, 1997; Ortony et al., 1985; R. E. Owens, 1996; H. L. Smith, 1998.

Children's early experiences with books also promote metalinguistic awareness (Yaden & Templeton, 1986). The very process of reading to children helps them realize that printed language is related to spoken language. In addition, some children's books playfully address the nature of language. An example is *Amelia Bedelia Goes Camping* (Parish, 1985), one in a series of books featuring a rather obtuse maid who takes quite literally everything her employers say. For example, Amelia hits the road with a stick when they say it's time to "hit the road."

Formal language arts instruction further fosters metalinguistic awareness. By exploring parts of speech, various sentence structures, and the like, children and adolescents develop a better understanding of the underlying structure of language. By reading and analyzing poetry and classic literature, they discover a variety of mechanisms—similes, metaphors, symbolism, and so on—that one might use to convey multiple layers of meanings.

Finally, research consistently indicates that knowledge of two or more languages (bilingualism) promotes greater metalinguistic awareness (Diaz & Klingler, 1991; E. E. Garcia, 1994; Moran & Hakuta, 1995). By the time Mario was 5, for example, he showed considerable awareness of the nature of language:

> Mario was well aware that things were called in one of several possible ways, that the same story could be retold in another language (he was capable of doing this himself), and he knew that thoughts were convertible or translatable through other forms of expression. He was aware of a variety of codes [languages], not only of Spanish, English and Italian, but also of others like Aymara, French, German, Twi, Japanese, and Quechua. He knew that a code could be varied so as to make it sound funny or to render its messages less transparent, such as in Pig Spanish. . . .

[As Mario grew older,] he became increasingly analytical about the medium which so many take for granted as their sole form of expression. He demonstrated interest, for example, in the multiple meaning of some words ("'right' means three things"); and in peculiar usages ("Why do you call the car 'she'?"); as well as intuitions about the origins of words ("'soufflé' sounds French"). (Fantini, 1985, pp. 53–54)

Promoting Metalinguistic Development   The factors that promote metalinguistic awareness—language play, reading experiences, formal instruction, and bilingualism—have obvious implications for teaching and working with children. Three implications are the following:

■ *Explore multiple meanings through ambiguities, jokes, riddles, and the like.*   Having fun with language can be educational as well as entertaining. For example, teachers and other practitioners can ask children to identify the double meanings of such sentences as these (Wiig, Gilbert, & Christian, 1978):

He is drawing a gun.

This restaurant even serves crabs.

Jokes and riddles provide another vehicle for exploring multiple meanings (Shultz, 1974; Shultz & Horibe, 1974):

Call me a cab.
Okay, you're a cab.

Tell me how long cows should be milked.
They should be milked the same as short ones, of course.

■ *Read literature that plays on the nature of language.*   Many children's books capitalize on the idiosyncrasies of language. One of our favorites is *The Phantom Tollbooth* (Juster, 1961), which has considerable fun with word meanings and common expressions. In one scene, the main character (Milo) asks for a square meal and is served (you guessed it) a plate "heaped high with steaming squares of all sizes and colors." Among the all-time classics in English word play are Lewis Carroll's *Alice's Adventures in Wonderland* and *Through the Looking Glass*. These books are packed with whimsical uses of double word meanings, homonyms, and idioms. The following excerpt from *Through the Looking Glass* illustrates:

"But what could [a tree] do, if any danger came?" Alice asked.
"It could bark," said the Rose.
"It says, 'Boughwough!'" cried a Daisy. "That's why its branches are called boughs."

■ *Encourage children to learn a second language.*   Promoting metalinguistic awareness is just one of several benefits of learning a second language. In the next section we look more closely at second language learning and bilingualism.

Development of a Second Language

As the adult workplace becomes increasingly international in scope, there is greater need than ever before for children to learn one or more languages in addition to their native tongue. Here we address three issues related to the development of a second language: the optimal timing for second-language learning, the nature of bilingualism, and approaches to teaching a second language.

The Timing of Second-Language Learning

As noted earlier, there may be one or more sensitive periods for learning language, thus making exposure to a language in the first few years of life ideal. Yet research evidence regarding the best time to learn a *second* language is mixed and often tainted by methodological problems (Bialystok, 1994b; Hakuta & McLaughlin, 1996; Long, 1995; Newport, 1993). In general, early exposure to a second language is more critical if the second language is very different from the first; for instance, a native English speaker benefits more from an early start in Japanese or Arabic than from an early start in French or German (Bialystok, 1994a; Strozer, 1994). Early exposure also seems to be especially important for mastering flawless pronunciation and complex grammatical constructions (Bialystok, 1994a, 1994b; Bruer, 1999; J. S. Johnson & Newport, 1989). However, any advantage young children may have because of biological "readiness" is probably counterbalanced by the greater cognitive maturity, world knowledge, and metalinguistic sophistication on which adolescents and adults can build as they study a new language (Bialystok, 1994b; V. Collier, 1989; M. Long, 1995). People of all ages can acquire proficiency in a second language; there is probably no definitive "best" time to begin.

Although there may be no hard-and-fast sensitive period for learning a second language, beginning second-language instruction in the early years definitely has benefits. For one thing, it appears that learning a second language leads to higher achievement in reading, vocabulary, and grammar (Cunningham & Graham, 2000; Diaz, 1983; Reich, 1986). Instruction in a foreign language also sensitizes young children to the international and multicultural nature of the world in which they live. Children who learn a second language during the elementary school years express more positive attitudes toward people who speak that language, and they are more likely to enroll in foreign language classes in high school (Reich, 1986). Learning a second language can have immediate social benefits as well: In classrooms in which children speak only one of two different languages (perhaps some speaking only English and others speaking only Spanish), instruction in the second language promotes cross-communication and peer interaction (A. Doyle, 1982).

Bilingualism

Bilingualism is the ability to speak two languages fluently. Bilingual children, like Mario, can switch easily from one language to the other, and they readily distinguish the contexts in which they should use each one (Fantini, 1985).

Some bilingual children have been raised in families in which two languages are spoken regularly. Others have lived for a time in a community where one language is spoken and then moved to a community where a different language is spoken. Still others live in a bilingual society—for example, in Canada (where English and French are spoken), Wales (where English and Welsh are spoken), and certain ethnic neighborhoods in the United States (where a language such as Spanish or Chinese is spoken along with English).

Several decades ago, many theorists believed that bilingual environments were detrimental to children's linguistic and cognitive development. Researchers frequently found bilingual children to have substantially lower IQ scores than monolingual English-speaking children (G. E. García, Jiménez, & Pearson, 1998). Unfortunately, their studies typically used, as their "bilingual" samples, children who had recently immigrated to the United States. Thus, the children were not yet proficient in English (they were not truly bilingual) and so performed poorly on intelligence tests administered in English (G. E. García et al., 1998).

Recent research has been far more complimentary. Children raised in bilingual environments from birth or soon thereafter may show some initial delays in language development, and, as we discovered earlier, they may occasionally mix the two languages in their early speech. However, by elementary school they have caught up to their monolingual peers and have learned to keep the two languages separate (C. Baker, 1993; Bialystok, 2001; Lanza, 1992). Furthermore, as we have seen, bilingual children show greater metalinguistic sophistication than their monolingual peers. And when they are truly fluent in both languages, they tend to perform better in situations requiring complex cognitive functioning—for instance, on intelligence tests and on tasks requiring creativity (Diaz & Klingler, 1991; E. E. Garcia, 1994; Moran & Hakuta, 1995).

Being bilingual may also be advantageous from cultural and personal standpoints. In many Native American groups, the ancestral language is important for communicating oral history and cultural heritage and for conducting business within the group; at the same time, adults in the community realize that mastery of spoken and written English is essential for children's long-term success (McCarty & Watahomigie, 1998). Most Puerto Rican children, who will have more educational and professional opportunities if they

bilingualism
Knowing and speaking two languages fluently.

know English, speak Spanish at home, partly as a way of showing respect to their parents and partly as a way of maintaining a sense of cultural identity (Nieto, 1995a; Torres-Guzmán, 1998). A high school girl named Marisol put it this way:

> I'm proud of [being Puerto Rican]. I guess I speak Spanish whenever I can. . . . I used to have a lot of problems with one of my teachers 'cause she didn't want us to talk Spanish in class and I thought that was like an insult to us, you know? Just telling us not to talk Spanish, 'cause they were Puerto Ricans and, you know, we're free to talk whatever we want. . . . I could never stay quiet and talk only English, 'cause sometimes, you know, words slip in Spanish. You know, I think they should understand that. (Nieto, 1995a, p. 127)

Observe a bilingual teacher as she both talks and signs in the Language/Classroom clip of the Observation CD.

In some cases, being bilingual is the only way children can maintain personal relationships with important people in their lives; for instance, some children are bilingual in English and American Sign Language as a way of communicating effectively with one parent who can hear and another who is deaf (L. A. Pettito, 1997). The teacher in the Language/Classroom clip of the Observation CD is clearly bilingual: She consistently uses both spoken English and sign language as she talks.

Approaches to Teaching a Second Language

Just as children typically learn their native language through the informal and haphazard daily exposure they have to the language, so, too, may they learn two languages simultaneously if, like Mario, they are raised in a consistently bilingual environment. When children begin a second language at an older age, perhaps in the elementary years or even later, they often learn it more quickly if their language-learning experiences are fairly structured (Strozer, 1994). But as you may have learned from your own experience, studying a foreign language for one 45-minute period several times a week hardly promotes rapid mastery.

Two more intensive approaches—immersion and bilingual education—have been shown to be effective in promoting second-language proficiency. Each approach is useful in particular situations. To simplify our discussion, let's assume that students are living in an English-speaking country. For English-speaking students who are learning a second language while still living in their native country, total **immersion** in the second language—hearing and speaking it almost exclusively in the classroom throughout the day—is often the method of choice. Total immersion helps students become proficient in a second language relatively quickly, and any adverse effects on achievement in other academic areas appear to be short-lived (V. P. Collier, 1992; Cunningham & Graham, 2000; Genesee, 1985; Thomas, Collier, & Abbott, 1993). But for non-English speaking students learning English (e.g., children who have recently immigrated to the United States), total immersion in English may actually be detrimental. These students do best when instruction in academic subject areas is given in their native language while they are simultaneously taught to speak and write in English. Such **bilingual education** leads to higher overall academic achievement, continuing development of the native language, greater self-esteem, and a better attitude toward school (E. E. Garcia, 1995; C. E. Snow, 1990; Willig, 1985; S. Wright & Taylor, 1995; S. C. Wright, Taylor, & Macarthur, 2000). Ideally, students in a bilingual education program gradually move into English-based classes as their English proficiency improves (Krashen, 1996).

Why does immersion work better for some students whereas bilingual education is more effective for others? The relative effectiveness of the two approaches depends on students' proficiency in their native language when they begin second-language instruction; it also depends on whether students have ongoing opportunities to continue developing their first language while they study the second. Remember, language plays many important roles in cognitive development; for instance, it provides a symbolic means for mentally representing and thinking about the world, promotes social interactions through which children can encounter new information and divergent perspectives, and is the vehicle through which social interactions become internalized into mental processes. Thus, if instruction in a second language somehow undermines children's de-

Bilingual education programs are especially effective when they encourage skills in students' native language as well as in English.

immersion
Approach to second-language instruction in which students hear and speak that language almost exclusively in the classroom.

bilingual education
Approach to second-language instruction in which students are instructed in academic subject areas in their native language while simultaneously being taught to speak and write in the second language.

velopment in the first language, it is likely to have deleterious effects on their cognitive development.

Immersion programs are typically effective only when children already have a solid foundation in their first language and have regular opportunities to use and enhance their skills in that language; in such circumstances, learning a second language doesn't interfere with cognitive development (V. Collier, 1989; Krashen, 1996). English-speaking children in this country who are immersed in a second language at school still have many opportunities— at home, with their friends, and in the local community and culture—to continue using and developing their English. In contrast, recent immigrants may have few opportunities outside of their homes to use their native language. If they are taught exclusively in English, they may very well lose proficiency in their native language before developing adequate proficiency in English, and their cognitive development and academic achievement will suffer in the process. In such cases, bilingual education, which is designed to foster growth in *both* languages, is more likely to promote cognitive as well as linguistic growth (Krashen, 1996; Pérez, 1998; Winsler, Díaz, Espinosa, & Rodriguez, 1999).

Given the many advantages of second-language learning and bilingualism, perhaps educators should begin to think about promoting bilingualism in *all* students (Navarro, 1985; NCSS Task Force on Ethnic Studies Curriculum Guidelines, 1992; Pérez, 1998). Widespread bilingualism would not only promote children's cognitive and linguistic development but also enhance communication, interaction, and interpersonal understanding among children with diverse linguistic and cultural backgrounds (Minami & Ovando, 1995).

Diversity in Language Development

As is true in other developmental domains, children do not all achieve milestones in language development at exactly the same age. For instance, children say their first word, on average, at 12 months of age, but Mario didn't say his first word until 16 months; his first English word appeared considerably later, at age 2½ (Fantini, 1985). To some degree, temperament may influence the rate at which speech emerges: Shy or reserved children may wait until they understand a good portion of what they hear before attempting to speak themselves (Nelson, 1973). In addition to idiosyncratic individual differences, we also see some differences based on children's gender, socioeconomic status, and ethnicity.

Gender Differences

As infants and toddlers, girls are, in general, more verbally active than boys; they also begin to speak about a month earlier, form longer sentences sooner, and have a larger vocabulary (Halpern & LaMay, 2000; J. S. Reznick & Goldfield, 1992). Once they reach the school years, girls outperform boys on tests of verbal ability (see Chapter 6). This difference is quite small, however, and there is considerable overlap between the two groups (see Figure 6–6 on page 259).

Some research indicates that there are qualitative differences in the language that boys and girls use and that these differences persist into adulthood. On average, males, who see themselves as information providers, speak more directly and bluntly. In contrast, females, who seek to establish and deepen relationships through their conversations, are more likely to be indirect, tactful, and polite when trying to get their point across (R. E. Owens, 1996; Tannen, 1990).

Socioeconomic Differences

In the 1960s and early 1970s, many developmental psychologists proposed that children from lower-income families had an impoverished linguistic environment—that parents of low socioeconomic status (SES) spoke less frequently to their children, used syntactically less complex sentences, and in other ways did less to promote language development than middle-SES parents did. As a result, these psychologists suggested, children growing up in low-SES circumstances acquired less sophisticated language skills than their middle-SES peers (e.g., Bernstein, 1971; M. P. Deutsch, 1963; J. M. V. Hunt, 1969).

Females are more likely than males to use conversation as a way of establishing and maintaining interpersonal relationships.

In recent years, many theorists have called this *language deficit* idea into question (e.g., P. J. Miller, 1982; Portes, 1996). For instance, children growing up in extremely impoverished living conditions have often been observed to speak quite eloquently about their circumstances (Coles, 1967, 1971a, 1971b, 1977). However, they often speak in dialects other than the **Standard English** that is used in the media and most school systems, and such dialects are sometimes misinterpreted as reflecting incomplete language development. (We will look at the nature of dialects shortly.)

There do appear to be socioeconomic differences in semantic development, however; children from higher-income homes have larger vocabularies than children from lower-income homes (e.g., Hart & Risley, 1995; B. A. Wasik & Bond, 2001). In one recent longitudinal study (Hart & Risley, 1995), researchers observed mother-infant interactions in three socioeconomic groups: upper-middle-class families (in which at least one parent had a professional occupation), lower-middle-class families (in which parents had primarily blue-collar occupations), and lower-class families (who were on welfare). Mothers in all three groups interacted frequently with their infants, expressing affection, providing toys, and so on. But there were noticeable differences in the quantity and quality of language: Mothers from higher-SES families talked with their babies more, used a greater variety of words, asked more questions, and elaborated more on topics. Although the children in all three groups began to talk at the same age, noticeable differences in their vocabularies were observed by age 3, and the sizes of their vocabularies were correlated with the amount of mother talk in their earlier years.

Ethnic Differences

We have already described some of the sociolinguistic behaviors that vary from one ethnic group to another. We have also described the unique narrative styles and creative use of figurative language that are frequently observed in African American communities. Children from various ethnic backgrounds show other language differences as well. Differences in word usage are common. For instance, in the United States and Canada, *corn* refers to a particular kind of grain, whereas in Great Britain and Ireland *corn* is often used to refer to grains in general and therefore includes wheat, oats, and so on.

Some languages, especially those spoken by people who are spread over a large geographic area, include grammatical structures used only in particular regions. A **dialect** is a version of a language that shares many syntactic rules with its parent language but also has some syntactic rules unique to itself. Consider the following sentences (Milroy, 1994, p. 157):

> It would take you to get there early.
>
> I'm just after my dinner.

If you have been raised in North America, you may not be able to make much sense of them, because they reflect a dialect of English spoken in Northern Ireland. (The two sentences mean, "It's advisable to arrive early" and "I've just finished my dinner," respectively.)

Dialects often include unique ways of pronouncing words as well as unique grammatical structures. For instance, a dialect of English spoken in Jamaica (sometimes called a *patois*) involves pronunciations so different from those of Standard English that residents of North America may understand little of what a native Jamaican says. In China, the same written words usually have the same or similar meanings throughout the country, but their pronunciations may be as different as night and day in various regions (Chang, 1998).

Some dialects are associated with particular ethnic and cultural groups. For example, Figure 7–5 shows a writing sample for an English-speaking fifth-grader who resides in the Northern Mariana Islands of the Pacific Ocean. Notice how he mixes present and past tenses in his description of a past event. Perhaps the most widely studied ethnic dialect is **African American English** (also known as *Black English Vernacular,* or simply *Black English*). This dialect, which is actually a group of similar dialects, is used in many African American communities throughout the United States and is characterized by sentences such as these:

> He got ten dollar.
>
> Momma she mad.

Standard English
Form of English generally considered acceptable in school (as reflected in textbooks, grammar instruction, etc.) and in the media.

dialect
Form of a language characteristic of a particular geographic region or ethnic group.

African American English
Dialect of some African American communities that includes some pronunciations, grammatical constructions, and idioms different from those of Standard English.

Nobody don't never like me.

I be going to dance tonight.

(R. E. Owens, 1995, p. A–8)

At one time, researchers believed that the African American dialect represented a less complex form of speech than Standard English and so urged educators to teach students to speak "properly" as quickly as possible. But they now realize that it is, in fact, a very complex language system with its own predictable grammatical rules and its own unique idioms and proverbs, and that it promotes communication and complex thought as readily as Standard English (R. E. Owens, 1995; DeLain, Pearson, & Anderson, 1985; Fairchild & Edwards-Evans, 1990).

Many children and adolescents view their native dialect as an integral part of their cultural identity (Garrison, 1989; McAlpine, 1992; Ogbu, 1999). Furthermore, when a local dialect is the language most preferred by residents of a community, it is often the means through which people can most effectively connect with one another in their day-to-day interactions. At the same time, however, many members of society at large associate higher social status with people who speak Standard English, and they perceive speakers of other dialects in a lesser light (Gollnick & Chinn, 2002; Purcell-Gates, 1995; H. L. Smith, 1998). As an example, people who speak African American English are less often hired by employers and, when hired, are offered lower-paying positions (Terrell & Terrell, 1983).

Most experts recommend that all children develop proficiency in Standard English because success in mainstream adult society will be difficult to achieve without such proficiency (e.g., Casanova, 1987; M. Craft, 1984). At the same time, practitioners should recognize that other languages and dialects are very effective means of communication in many situations (Fairchild & Edward-Evans, 1990; E. E. Garcia, 1995; C. D. Lee & Slaughter-Defoe, 1995). For example, although classroom teachers may wish to encourage Standard English in most written work and in formal oral presentations, they might find other dialects quite appropriate in creative writing or informal class discussions.

Ideally, children and adolescents from diverse dialectic backgrounds probably function most effectively when they can use both their local dialect and Standard English in appropriate settings (Gollnick & Chinn, 2002; Ogbu, 1999; Warren & McCloskey, 1993). One teacher of African American children has explained it this way:

> I don't want them to be ashamed of what they know but I also want them to know and be comfortable with what school and the rest of the society require. When I put it in the context of "translation" they get excited. They see it is possible to go from one to the other. It's not that they are not familiar with Standard English. . . . They hear Standard English all the time on TV. It's certainly what I use in the classroom. But there is rarely any connection made between the way they speak and Standard English. I think that when they can see the connections and know that they can make the shifts, they become better at both. They're bilingual! (Ladson-Billings, 1994, p. 84)

The group differences we've just described all reflect normal variability in children's oral language skills. We now look at exceptionalities in language development.

FIGURE 7–5 A local dialect is evident in this writing sample from a fifth grader who lives in the Northern Mariana Islands of the Pacific Ocean.

Writing sample courtesy of the Commonwealth of the Northern Mariana Islands Public School System and of the Pacific Resources for Education and Learning (PREL).

Exceptionalities in Language Development

In Chapter 5, we mentioned that some children with learning disabilities have difficulty understanding or remembering what other people say. We mentioned, too, that children with autism may have delayed speech or may not even speak at all. Here we describe possible language difficulties for two additional groups of children: those with speech and communication disorders and those with sensory impairments.

Speech and Communication Disorders

Some children seem to develop normally in all respects except for language. Children with **speech and communication disorders** (sometimes known as *specific language impairments*) have abnormalities in spoken language or in language comprehension that

speech and communication disorders Category of special needs characterized by abnormalities in spoken language that significantly interfere with children's performance and achievement.

significantly interfere with their performance at school and elsewhere. Such disorders may involve problems in one or more of the following areas:

- Articulation (e.g., mispronunciations or omissions of certain sounds)
- Fluency (e.g., stuttering, or an atypical rhythm in speech)
- Syntax (e.g., abnormal syntactic patterns, or incorrect word order)
- Semantics (e.g., difficulty interpreting words that have two or more distinctly different word meanings; consistent use of words with imprecise meanings, such as *thing* or *that*)
- Pragmatics (e.g., talking for a long time without letting anyone else speak)
- Receptive language (e.g., inability to distinguish between different phonemes in other people's speech; difficulty understanding or remembering directions) (American Speech-Language-Hearing Association, 1993; R. E. Owens, 1996; Turnbull et al., 2002)

Speech and communication disorders are also suspected when children fail to demonstrate age-appropriate language (e.g., a kindergartner who communicates only by pointing and gesturing or a third grader who says, "Him go," instead of, "He's gone"). However, speech patterns that are due to a regional or ethnic dialect and those that are due to a bilingual background do *not* fall within the realm of speech and communication disorders (recall the speech therapist who inappropriately recommended that Mario have speech therapy).

Children with speech and communication disorders sometimes have problems with reading and writing as well as with spoken language (Fey, Catts, & Larrivee, 1995; J. R. Johnston, 1997). They may also have personal or social problems as a result of their disability. For instance, they may feel self-conscious and embarrassed when they speak, or they may be reluctant to speak at all (Patton, Blackbourn, & Fad, 1996). Furthermore, if they sound "odd" or are difficult to understand, they may have difficulty making friends, and thoughtless peers may ridicule them (LaBlance, Steckol, & Smith, 1994; Rice, Hadley, & Alexander, 1993).

Sometimes language disorders are inherited; for instance, they often run in families, and if one identical twin has a disorder, the other is highly likely to have it as well (Gopnik, 1997; Tomblin, 1997). Sometimes the disorders are associated with specific brain abnormalities (J. L. Locke, 1993). But in many cases, the exact cause of a speech or communication disorder is unknown (Wang & Baron, 1997).

Working with Children Who Have Speech and Communication Disorders   Typically, trained specialists work with children who have impaired communication skills. Nevertheless, parents, teachers, and other adults can do several things to help these children:

■ *Encourage regular oral communication.*   Because children with speech and communication disorders need as much practice in public speaking as anyone else, adults should encourage them to talk at school and in other group settings, provided that doing so does not cause exceptional anxiety and that their peers know how to respond to them with care and compassion.

■ *Listen patiently.*   When children have difficulty expressing themselves, adults may be tempted to assist them—for example, by finishing their sentences. But children with speech and communication disorders are more likely to make progress when others allow them to complete their own thoughts, no matter how long it takes them to do so. Adults must learn to listen patiently to children with speech problems, and they must encourage friends and classmates to do likewise.

■ *Ask for clarification when a message is unclear.*   When adults have trouble understanding what a child is saying, they should repeat what they do understand and ask the child to clarify the rest. Honest feedback helps children learn how well they are communicating (Patton et al., 1996).

■ *Provide guidance about how to converse appropriately with others.*   When children lack basic pragmatic skills—for instance, when they dominate a conversation to the point where no one else can participate—they benefit from guided practice and explicit feedback about their conversational skills (Bloom & Lahey, 1978).

Sensory Impairments and Language Development

When children do not have the same access to sensory information that their peers have, they may show delays in language development. For instance, children who have severe visual impairments (e.g., those who are blind) cannot relate what they hear to objects and events around them unless they can perceive those objects and events through sound, touch, or other senses. As a result, they may have more limited semantic knowledge: They simply haven't had as many opportunities to make connections between words and their meanings as sighted children have (M. Harris, 1992). In contrast, their syntactic development is more likely to be on target; for instance, they progress from one-word to two-word "sentences" at about the same time that their age-mates do (M. Harris, 1992).

Children with hearing impairments are at risk for delays in both the semantic and syntactic aspects of language development, especially if their hearing impairment has been present since birth or appeared early in life (M. Harris, 1992). Furthermore, children who have been completely deaf from birth or soon thereafter typically need special training to develop proficiency in speaking.

Most children who use a visual language system as their primary mode of communication follow a normal pattern of language development (M. Harris, 1992; Newport, 1990; L. A. Pettito, 1997). As noted earlier in the chapter, even infants who are deaf produce speechlike sounds at about the same age as hearing infants, and those who are regularly exposed to sign language often "babble" with their hands before they actually communicate with signs (J. L. Locke, 1993; L. A. Pettito, 1997). When their parents regularly use sign language to communicate with them, children sign their first word at around 18 to 22 months, with multiword phrases following soon thereafter (L. A. Pettito, 1997).[4] Like hearing children, children who use sign language appear to construct rules that guide their language use, and they refine these rules over time; for instance, the overregularization phenomenon frequently observed in young children's speech is seen in children's sign language as well (Goldin-Meadow & Mylander, 1993; L. A. Pettito, 1997).

A case study of BoMee (Wilcox, 1994) illustrates just how much is possible when parents provide a linguistically rich environment through sign language. BoMee was born in Korea 8 weeks prematurely. Although she could hear at birth, early illnesses or medications apparently caused profound hearing loss shortly thereafter. At age 2½, BoMee was adopted by American parents, who communicated with her regularly in sign language. Within a few weeks after BoMee's arrival, they also began to sign their self-talk as a way of "thinking aloud." For instance, BoMee's mother might sign "What goes next in this recipe?" or "Where are my shoes?" Within a week, BoMee began signing her own self-talk, such as "Where my shoes are?" Soon, self-talk was a regular feature in BoMee's problem-solving activities. On one occasion, BoMee was trying to put a dress on her doll, but the dress was too small. She signed to herself:

> Hmmm, wrong me. This dress fit here? Think not. Hmmm. For other doll here. (Translation: *Hmmm, I'm wrong. Does this dress go on this doll? I don't think so. Hmmm. It goes on this other doll.*) (Wilcox, 1994, p. 119)

BoMee showed other normal linguistic behaviors as well. She simplified her language when she signed to her baby brother. And just as hearing children typically read aloud in the early stages of reading, BoMee signed "out loud" when she began to read.

Like Mario, BoMee may have had an advantage in the development of metalinguistic awareness. She was exposed to both English-based signs and American Sign Language (which has different vocabulary and syntax) and quickly became bilingual in her knowledge of the two language systems. She understood very early that some people talked and others used sign language. Furthermore, shortly after her third birthday, she appropriately signed

---

[4] Keep in mind that the age at which children sign their first word is likely to vary considerably from child to child, depending on parents' proficiency with, and frequency in using, sign language.

Happy Mother's Day!

Children with hearing loss can interact more effectively with their peers when everyone knows sign language. Here, Marianne, a hearing child, has created a Mother's Day card using the sign for "I love you."

"This Little Piggy" in two different ways—in English-based signs and in American Sign Language—to people who understood only one of the two languages. Obviously, children with hearing loss can have very normal cognitive and linguistic development as long as their language environment is appropriate for them.

Working with Children Who Have Sensory Impairments   When children are blind, specialists teach them to read and write in Braille; when they are deaf, specialists provide training in such communication skills as American Sign Language, finger spelling (alphabetic hand signs), and speechreading (reading lips). Yet many children with significant sensory impairments are members of regular classrooms and participate in the same extracurricular activities that their nondisabled peers do. Following are several strategies that practitioners should keep in mind when working with these children:

■ *Communicate the same message through multiple modalities.*   Children with normal hearing and vision rely on both auditory information and visual cues (body language, nearby objects and events, etc.) to interpret other people's spoken messages. Children with impaired vision and those with significant hearing loss get only part of the story, and their ability to understand what is happening around them is often hampered as a result. Thus, adults must be especially careful to transmit *complete* messages to children with sensory impairments. For instance, teachers might provide opportunities for visually impaired children to feel objects or in other ways experience topics of discussion—perhaps by having them explore three-dimensional relief maps or globes of various parts of the world (in geography), conduct hands-on experiments (in science), or role-play important historical events (in history). Similarly, adults should present visual equivalents of spoken messages for children with hearing loss—perhaps by writing important points on paper or a chalkboard or illustrating key ideas with pictures and other graphics.

■ *Learn elements of American Sign Language and finger spelling, and teach them to children's peers.*   Some children with hearing loss, because of their reduced ability to communicate, may feel socially isolated from the adults and peers around them. When important people in children's lives gain competence in American Sign Language and finger spelling, they open the lines of communication. Parents, of course, should learn and use manual language as early in a child's life as possible. Children can best master the syntax of American Sign Language when they learn it before age 4, indicating that one or more sensitive periods characterize the development of manual language as well as spoken language (Newport, 1990).

Observe the use of sign language in the classroom in the Language/ Individuals clip.

When children with hearing loss are members of general education classrooms, their teachers and classmates should learn some sign language as well. For example, Jeanne once taught at a middle school where every student—those with hearing loss and those without—received some instruction in signing. One girl who was totally deaf was quite popular with her classmates, and she and her friends could communicate rather easily during class. In the Language/Individuals clip of the Observation CD, you can see both hearing children and children with hearing loss practicing sign language and using it to converse with their teacher and one another.

■ *Intervene as early as possible to address any correctable hearing impairments.*   Even temporary hearing difficulties, such as chronic ear infections, can adversely affect language development and should be addressed as quickly as possible (Bruer, 1999). In some cases, cochlear implants improve hearing in children with congenital ear abnormalities, and language development often proceeds normally once these devices are inserted (Svirsky, Robbins, Kirk, Pisoni, & Miyamoto, 2000).

■ *Identify and address deficiencies in language skills that may be the result of children's sensory impairments.*   Teachers and other practitioners must be on the lookout for any developmental delays in language that students may have as a result of their sensory impairments. Many of the strategies presented throughout the chapter are as appropriate for children with limited vision or hearing as they are for nondisabled children. In some cases, special educators or other specialists can also provide suggestions and guidance.

In some situations, mild hearing loss is not identified until children reach school age. In other situations, it does not even *appear* until school age or even later; for instance, a child may suffer some hearing loss as a result of a very high fever or chronic ear infections. When practitioners observe language delays in children who appear to be "normal" in other respects, referral to an audiologist is in order.

Mastery of the basic underpinnings of language (i.e., semantics and syntax) and proficiency in the receptive and expressive aspects of spoken language (i.e., listening and speaking) are, of course, important in their own right. But they also provide the foundation for receptive and expressive skills in written language (i.e., reading and writing). We turn to the development of children's literacy skills in the next chapter.

CASE STUDY: BOARDING SCHOOL

Some parts of Alaska are so sparsely settled that building local high schools makes little economic sense. So in some Native American communities, older students are sent to boarding school for their high school education. A high priority for boarding school teachers is to help students master the English language. With this information in mind, consider the following incident:

> Many of the students at the school spoke English with a native dialect and seemed unable to utter certain essential sounds in the English language. A new group of speech teachers was sent in to correct the problem. The teachers worked consistently with the students in an attempt to improve speech patterns and intonation, but found that their efforts were in vain.
>
> One night, the boys in the dormitory were seeming to have too much fun, and peals of laughter were rolling out from under the door. An investigating counselor approached cautiously and listened quietly outside the door to see if he could discover the source of the laughter. From behind the door he heard a voice, speaking in perfect English, giving instructions to the rest of the crowd. The others were finding the situation very amusing. When the counselor entered the room he found that one of the students was speaking. "Joseph," he said, "You've been cured! Your English is perfect." "No," said Joseph returning to his familiar dialect, "I was just doing an imitation of you." "But if you can speak in Standard English, why don't you do it all of the time?" the counselor queried. "I can," responded Joseph, "but it sounds funny, and I feel dumb doing it." (Garrison, 1989, p. 121)

- Why might Joseph prefer his native dialect to Standard English?
- Is Joseph bilingual? Why or why not?
- The counselor told Joseph that he had "been cured." What beliefs about Joseph's native dialect does this statement reflect?

 Now go to our Companion Website to assess your understanding of chapter content with a Practice Quiz, apply what you've learned in Essay Questions, and broaden your knowledge with links to related Developmental Psychology Web sites. Go to www.prenhall.com/mcdevitt.

SUMMARY

Theoretical Perspectives

Although modeling, reinforcement, and feedback almost certainly play some role in language development, early theories based on such processes could not adequately account for the fact that most children acquire a very complex language system in a very short period of time. Several more recent theoretical perspectives have emerged, each focusing on somewhat different aspects of language development. *Nativists* propose that young children have a built-in mechanism that facilitates their acquisition of language; this mechanism allows toddlers and preschoolers to construct a complex set of grammatical rules even when the language spoken around them is haphazard and imperfect. *Information processing theorists* apply general concepts and principles of cognition (e.g., the importance of attention, the limited capacity of working memory) to explain how some aspects of language may develop. *Socio-cultural theorists* emphasize the role that social interaction and cultural practices play in language learning. *Functionalists* propose that children develop language primarily because it enhances their effectiveness in their social group and increases their ability to satisfy their own needs. Many theorists draw from elements of two or more of these perspectives when explaining how language develops. Nevertheless, some areas of incompatibility among the theories (e.g., whether people inherit some "preprogramming" to learn language) remain unresolved.

Trends in Language Development

Children and adolescents continue to develop their linguistic knowledge and skills throughout the preschool and school years. For instance, school-age children add several thousand new words to their vocabulary each year. Over time, they rely less on word order and more on syntax to interpret other people's messages, and they can comprehend and produce sentences with increasingly complex syntactic structures. Their conversations with others increase in length, they become better able to adapt the content of their speech to the characteristics of their listeners, and they become more aware of the unspoken social conventions that govern verbal interactions in their culture. They also acquire a growing understanding of the nature of language as an entity in and of itself.

Learning a Second Language

Although research results are mixed with regard to the "best" time to learn a second language, recent research is consistent in indicating that knowing two or more languages enhances achievement in reading and language arts, promotes greater metalinguistic awareness, and fosters multicultural sensitivity. An *immersion* approach to teaching a second language is effective only when children have ample opportunity to con-

tinue developing their native language outside of school; in other situations, *bilingual education* is usually preferable.

Diversity and Exceptionalities in Language Development

Subtle qualitative differences have been observed in the conversational styles of males and females. Various ethnic groups may show differences in sociolinguistic behaviors, storytelling traditions, use of figurative language, and dialects.

Some children have disabilities that affect their language development. Children with *speech and communication disorders* have abnormalities in articulation, fluency, syntax, receptive language, or other aspects of receptive and expressive language that significantly interfere with their performance and accomplishments in and out of school. Children with hearing impairments and (to a lesser extent) those with visual impairments may have more limited language proficiency because of reduced exposure to language or reduced awareness of the meaningful contexts in which it occurs.

KEY CONCEPTS

native language (p. 278)
phonology (p. 278)
semantics (p. 278)
syntax (p. 278)
pragmatics (p. 278)
language acquisition device (p. 279)
nativism (p. 279)
Universal Grammar (p. 279)
babbling (p. 280)
semantic bootstrapping (p. 282)
intersubjectivity (p. 283)
functionalism (p. 284)

receptive language (p. 286)
expressive language (p. 286)
infant-directed speech (p. 286)
lexicon (p. 288)
lexical word (p. 288)
grammatical word (p. 288)
undergeneralization (p. 288)
overgeneralization (p. 288)
fast mapping (p. 290)
defining feature (p. 290)
correlational feature (p. 290)
holophrase (p. 292)
telegraphic speech (p. 292)

overregularization (p. 292)
expansion (p. 294)
phonemes (p. 295)
figurative speech (p. 297)
cooing (p. 299)
narrative (p. 300)
playing the dozens (p. 300)
sociolinguistic behaviors (p. 303)
personal space (p. 305)
IRE cycle (p. 305)
wait time (p. 306)
culture shock (p. 307)

metalinguistic awareness (p. 307)
bilingualism (p. 311)
immersion (p. 312)
bilingual education (p. 312)
Standard English (p. 314)
dialect (p. 314)
African American English (p. 314)
speech and communication disorders (p. 315)

Kayla, age 4

2 22222² | | || (| |) | (3 33333 3|

5

5

5

5

Claire, age 5

Suddenly swerving,
seven small swans
swam silently
southward, seeing six
swift sailboats
sail slowly seaward.

Laura, age 8

yg13 —

Hi! Thanks for the
letter! I am terrible at
keeping in touch lately!!
Well the big question on my
mind was how was Ani!
From what you said it sounds
like the concert was awsome!
I wish I could have gone!
My birthday came and went!
I have been SO busy!
Prom was
                        alright! My dress,
kicked some unbelievable ass.
the night was long → but
I had fun!

Tina, age 17

Development of Literacy: Reading and Writing

CASE STUDY: PHYLLIS AND BENJAMIN JONES

Phyllis Jones and her son Benjamin live in a low-income, inner-city, African American neighborhood. Here is their story:

[Phyllis] finished high school and two years of college, and regrets that she did not go farther. She wishes she had "listened to her grandmother" who was "always pushing" her to study; instead, "I did enough just to get by." She is deeply concerned about her son's education, and determined that he will go farther than she did. She is particularly concerned about his learning to read, noting that "without reading, you can't do anything," and that "readers are leaders—I want Benjamin to read and read and read." She has little trust in the local public schools, and is acutely aware of the large numbers of poor black children who fail to learn to read well and who drop out of school: "I guess black people have a tendency to just say 'Oh, I can't do it, I can't do it, I can't do it.'"

Mrs. Jones decided that the only way to be certain that Benjamin would learn to read was to teach him herself. She began buying books for him when he was an infant, and she asked friends and relatives to give him books as Christmas and birthday presents. Before he turned 3, she bought him a set of phonics tapes and workbooks, which she used to conduct regular lessons, helping Benjamin learn to recognize the forms and sounds of letters, combinations of letters, and eventually entire words. She also gave him lessons in letter formation, hand-writing, and spelling. When Benjamin was 3, he began attending a Head Start program, while his mother continued to teach him at home. She tried to make these activities "fun for Benjamin." She was pleased with his interest in reading and writing, and sometimes frustrated that he did not learn as quickly as she wanted him to.

Benjamin sometimes pretended to read magazines, newspapers, and books. His mother was gratified by his enthusiasm, commenting on his "reading" of *The Gingerbread Man,* "you can hear the laughter and joy in his voice." But she also told Benjamin he was "not really reading." On one occasion, she pointed to the print in the book Benjamin was pretending to read and said "these are what you read. Someday you will learn to read." Another time she commented, "Benjamin thinks he can read. What he'll do is recite some words from a story and exclaim with great joy 'I can read! I can read!' I explained to him that he isn't reading. Reading is looking at a book and saying the words that are written there. But I say one day he will read—soon, just like Tony [an older friend of Benjamin's]." By the time Benjamin was 4, his mother noted that he knew "all of his alphabet by sight. Praise God!"

When Benjamin turned 4, Mrs. Jones began taking him to a reading program at the store-front church she attended. This program was designed for older children, but she thought he would "pick up something." She also continued to work on reading and writing at home, using index cards to make a card game to teach Benjamin how to write his name. When he was about 4½, Benjamin began sounding out words that he noticed around him, such as "off" and "on." His mother commented, "now he wants to know what everything spells and wants to guess at some of them. He asked me on the bus if E-M-E-R-G-E-N-C-Y spelled 'emergency'." On another occasion, when she picked Benjamin up at Head Start, "he said, 'Guess what we did today? I'll give you a hint—it begins with J. Then he said the word was J-E-M, which was supposed to be 'gym'." His mother was delighted with his interest in reading: "Hurrah! I hope it carries through the rest of his life." By the end of his second year in Head Start, when he had just turned 5, Benjamin could read a number of simple words by sounding them out and had a small sight vocabulary. His mother took great pride in these achievements: "Hallelujah! He can read!"

Reprinted by permission of the publisher from *Early Literacy* by Joan Brooks McLane and Gillian Dowley McNamee, pp. 103–105, Cambridge, MA: Harvard University Press. Copyright © 1990 by Joan Brooks McLane and Gillian Dowley McNamee.

Phyllis knows how important reading and writing are for success in the adult world, and so she has provided a foundation that should facilitate Benjamin's reading and writing development in the years to come. Other children are not so fortunate. Many students in our public schools never attain the level of literacy they need to participate fully in adult society (Hiebert & Raphael, 1996).

To some extent, children's literacy skills build on their oral language skills. The thousands of words and innumerable syntactic structures that children master in spoken language are basic elements of written language as well. However, written language differs from spoken language in two important ways: It involves a second-order symbol system, and it takes place in a relatively context-free situation.

As noted in Chapter 4, spoken words serve as symbols that enable children to represent objects and events mentally and to think about them more efficiently. Written words, too, are symbols, but they comprise a *second-order symbol system:* They are symbols that stand for *other* symbols (i.e., they stand for spoken words). To learn to read and write, children must learn the relationships between how words sound and are produced in speech, on the one hand, and how they look and are written on paper, on the other. They must also master nuances of the written symbol system that have no counterparts in spoken language, such as punctuation marks and appropriate uses of upper- and lowercase letters (Dyson, 1986; Liberman, 1998; Paris & Cunningham, 1996).

Spoken language typically occurs in an information-rich context that facilitates communication. People of all ages (and especially young children) often rely on the context to help them understand what they hear, and they frequently use nonverbal cues (gestures, facial expressions, pauses, etc.) to help them convey their meanings when they speak. In contrast, written language is relatively context-free: One person writes something at one time and someone else reads it at a later time, often in a different location. Writers cannot always anticipate what their readers are likely to know and not know, and readers cannot ask questions if something doesn't make sense. Thus, writers must express themselves more clearly and completely, and readers must rely more heavily on the content of the message itself, than would be necessary in everyday conversation (Byrnes, 1996; Cameron, Hunt, & Linton, 1996; Nuthall, 1996).

In this chapter, we explore the development of reading and writing throughout childhood and adolescence. We begin by examining three theoretical perspectives of how and why literacy skills develop.

Theories of Literacy Development

Theorists have proposed a variety of explanations for how reading and writing develop. Many reflect one of three general viewpoints: an information processing perspective, a whole-language perspective, or a sociocultural perspective.

The Information Processing Perspective

Information processing theorists believe that reading and writing involve the same general mechanisms (working memory, prior knowledge, cognitive and metacognitive strategies, etc.) that other forms of cognition involve. In addition, most information processing theorists believe that reading and writing are *constructive* processes. Reading is constructive in the sense that people combine what they see on the printed page with their existing knowledge and beliefs as they derive meaning from text (Weaver & Kintsch, 1991). Writing is constructive in that good writers must organize their thoughts into a logical sequence and communicate their message in a way that their audience is likely to understand (Bereiter & Scardamalia, 1987; Cameron et al., 1996; S. Greene & Ackerman, 1995). As children grow older, their ability to construct meaning in both reading and writing improves considerably, in large part because they have an increasing knowledge base—both about the world in general and about the structures and conventions of written language—on which they can draw (Beck, McKeown, Sinatra, & Loxterman, 1991; Benton, 1997; Byrnes, 1996).

From an information processing view, reading and writing can place a considerable strain on people's limited working memory capacities (Benton, 1997; W. S. Hall, 1989; McCutchen, 1996; Stanovich, 2000). Reading involves thinking about many things simultaneously, including words and their meanings, syntactic structures, and general knowledge about the subject matter. Writing involves thinking about all of these *plus* thinking about how to communicate effectively and remembering correct spellings, punctuation rules, and other conventions of written language. Until some of these cognitive processes become automatized (i.e., until they occur quickly, efficiently, and with little conscious effort), mature forms of reading and writing are virtually impossible.

Reading and writing skills improve as children acquire certain cognitive and metacognitive strategies. For instance, as children grow older, they are more likely to engage in comprehension monitoring—that is, to evaluate regularly their understanding of the author's message—as they read (see Chapter 5). They are also more likely to consider their future audience as they write and then tailor their words, sentence structures, and general message accordingly (R. T. Kellogg, 1994; Knudson, 1992; Perfetti & McCutchen, 1987). And in both reading and writing, children become increasingly able to set goals for themselves and to direct their efforts toward achieving those goals (Scardamalia & Bereiter, 1986; N. M. Webb & Palincsar, 1996).

You will see the influence of information processing theory throughout the chapter. For example, you will see it in our description of the roles that *phonological awareness* and *automatization* play in word recognition. You will see it in our discussion of *story schemas* in reading comprehension. And it will underlie our discussion of how spelling, composition skills, and metacognitive processes in writing develop.

Writing involves many things: considering what the reader is likely to know, expressing thoughts coherently, spelling words correctly, adhering to conventions of grammar and punctuation, and so on. Most children and adolescents don't have the working memory capacity to handle all of these tasks simultaneously.

The Whole-Language Perspective

As noted in Chapter 7, children master the basic components of their native language within the first few years of life. What's especially remarkable about this accomplishment is that they do so with little if any explicit instruction. Daily immersion in the language seems to be sufficient for acquiring a sizable vocabulary and learning many of the complexities of syntax. In essence, learning a language is a very natural human process.

Some theorists propose that written language is a natural extension of speech, and so learning to read and write is, and should be, just as natural a process as learning to understand and communicate in spoken language (e.g., Edelsky, Altwerger, & Flores, 1991; K. S. Goodman, 1989; K. S. Goodman & Goodman, 1979; C. Weaver, 1990). They argue that children learn reading and writing most effectively by being immersed in a *literate environment*—one with many books, magazines, newspapers, and writing tools—and by engaging in real-life literacy tasks. This view is generally known as the **whole-language perspective**.

Whole-language theorists focus more on the kinds of home and school environments in which literacy can most effectively develop than on the internal, cognitive mechanisms that propel literacy development per se. Within the past two decades, these theorists have been visible and highly influential advocates for teaching reading and writing through authentic activities, such as reading stories and magazine articles, writing letters to relatives, and so on. We summarize research findings about the effectiveness of this approach later in the chapter.

The Sociocultural Perspective

Building on Vygotsky's theory of cognitive development (see Chapter 4), some theorists propose that literacy, like any other cognitive activity, is largely a product of children's social and cultural environments (J. Green & Dixon, 1996; John-Steiner, Panofsky, & Smith, 1994; Pérez, 1998). When children learn to read and write, they also learn culturally appropriate ways of achieving their goals through reading and writing (Pérez, 1998). Children learn the purposes of reading by watching their parents and other caregivers engage in such ordinary activities as reading the newspaper, sorting the mail, and consulting the telephone book. They learn the multiple functions of writing when they observe adults

whole-language perspective Theoretical perspective that proposes that children develop literacy skills most effectively within the context of authentic reading and writing tasks.

Observe Corwin's early attempts at scribbling in the Literacy/Infancy clip of the Observation CD.

making grocery lists, filling out application forms, and communicating with friends by e-mail. You can see a simple example of the power of observation in the Literacy module of the Observation CD: 16-month-old Corwin watches his mother scribbling with a crayon and eventually begins to scribble himself.

As children grow, they may converse frequently with adults and peers about literacy tasks (Panofsky, 1994; Pérez, 1998). At home, they may read bedtime storybooks with their parents and occasionally pause to talk about characters and events in the stories. In the elementary grades, they often work with classmates to compose short stories. In high school language arts classes, they discuss possible interpretations of poetry and novels with their teachers and peers. From a Vygotskian perspective, children gradually *internalize* these social processes, transforming them into their own ways of understanding and producing written language.

In this chapter, the sociocultural perspective will be particularly evident in two places. First, as we discuss early literacy, we describe how parents, caregivers, and teachers can promote literacy development through the environments they create for children and their interactions with children about written language. Second, as we describe *reciprocal teaching*, we show how classroom teachers can help children and adolescents practice and internalize metacognitive strategies for understanding what they read.

Critiquing Theories of Literacy Development

The three perspectives we've just examined focus on different aspects of literacy development: Information processing theorists address the cognitive processes involved in reading and writing, whole-language theorists describe the kinds of environments in which they believe reading and writing can most effectively emerge, and sociocultural theorists emphasize the social practices that promote literate behavior and thought processes. In one sense, then, the three theories are not necessarily incompatible; in fact, some whole-language theorists believe that their ideas are very much in line with sociocultural ideas (Y. M. Goodman & Goodman, 1990).

Yet people from different theoretical camps (and, to a lesser extent, people within theoretical camps) sometimes disagree about the best ways to teach reading and writing. Virtually all theorists believe that authentic reading activities (e.g., reading books, magazines, and newspapers) and authentic writing activities (e.g., writing stories, poems, and personal and business letters) are essential for promoting optimal literacy development. However, whole-language theorists advocate using authentic activities almost exclusively, whereas many information processing theorists suggest that systematic training in basic knowledge and skills (letter-sound relationships, common spelling patterns, etc.) provides fundamental building blocks on which more complex reading and writing processes depend. The bulk of the research sides with information processing theory here: Although authentic reading and writing activities play an important role in literacy development, children develop greater competency in reading and writing when they also have specific instruction in the basic elements of written language (see the upcoming sections on phonological awareness and reading instruction).[1]

The Basic Developmental Issues table "Contrasting Perspectives of Literacy Development" contrasts the three theoretical perspectives in terms of nature and nurture, universality and diversity, and qualitative and quantitative change. We turn our attention now to trends in the development of literacy, beginning with literacy in the early years.

---

[1] The ongoing debate between information processing theorists and whole-language theorists has been quite heated and is sometimes referred to as the "Reading Wars" (Rayner, Foorman, Perfetti, Pesetsky, & Seidenberg, 2001; Stanovich, 2000). Information processing theorists maintain that reading and writing are not the "natural" processes that spoken language is: As human beings evolved over tens of thousands of years, their ability to communicate through speech gradually emerged, but reading and writing are fairly recent acquisitions and do not appear in all cultures. Whole-language theorists counter that instruction in basic skills (e.g., phonics) often involves boring, drill-and-practice exercises that take the joy and meaning out of reading and writing.

BASIC DEVELOPMENTAL ISSUES

Contrasting Perspectives of Literacy Development

ISSUE	INFORMATION PROCESSING PERSPECTIVE	WHOLE-LANGUAGE PERSPECTIVE	SOCIOCULTURAL PERSPECTIVE
Nature and Nurture	The "hardware" of the information processing system (the brain) is, of course, inherited, but systematic instruction promotes the cognitive processes essential for reading and writing. Some difficulties with literacy tasks (e.g., dyslexia) may have genetic origins.	Learning to read and write is as natural a process as learning to understand and produce spoken language and so presumably has some biological underpinnings. Authentic literacy activities (e.g., reading books and magazines, writing letters to friends and relatives) optimize literacy development.	The focus is on the social and cultural environments in which children observe and engage in reading and writing. Children learn the purposes of literacy by watching others engage in everyday reading and writing tasks, and their social interactions related to reading and writing become internalized cognitive processes.
Universality and Diversity	Some characteristics of the information processing system (e.g., the limited capacity of working memory) are universal across different environments and cultures. Yet other characteristics (e.g., the specific knowledge stored in long-term memory) vary considerably from one child to another.	The context in which literacy most effectively develops—an environment in which authentic printed materials and writing implements are prominent and easily available—is universal. However, children's access to a literate environment varies across cultures; it may also vary across families *within* a culture.	Different cultures use reading and writing for different purposes (and some cultures don't use reading or writing at all), and children's literacy skills vary accordingly.
Qualitative and Quantitative Change	Many information processing theorists describe general trends in children's reading and writing capabilities over time. But a few (e.g., P. Bryant, Nunes, & Aidinis, 1999; Chall, 1996; Ehri, 1991; Juel, 1991) propose that certain aspects of reading and writing development may proceed through discernible stages (revealing qualitative change).	Children's proficiency in reading and writing develops in a gradual, continuous fashion.	Children's reading and writing skills emerge gradually over time. Adults initially provide considerable scaffolding for children's efforts and then slowly withdraw this scaffolding as the children become able to read and write independently.

Literacy in the Early Years

Like Phyllis Jones, many parents place a high priority on reading and writing. These parents promote their children's literacy skills in numerous ways—by providing easy access to reading and writing materials, modeling reading and writing behavior, making frequent trips to the library, talking about the things they've read and written, and, more generally, demonstrating that reading and writing are enjoyable activities (McLane & McNamee, 1990; Teale, 1978). But perhaps most importantly, they read to their children regularly (L. Baker, Scher, & Mackler, 1997; Sulzby & Teale, 1991).

Some parents introduce children to books well before their first birthdays, pointing at pictures and labeling the objects they see (C. Snow & Ninio, 1986). We think back to the books we bought for our own children long before they were walking or talking. Some consisted of nothing more than a few cloth, plastic, or otherwise indestructible pages that depicted a simple item (perhaps a doll, toy truck, cat, or dog) on each page. Although these books hardly had spellbinding plots, they often captured our infants' attention, at least temporarily. In the Emotional Development/Infancy clip of the Observation CD, you can see 7-month-old Madison manipulate two simple books, one made of cloth and the other made of stiff cardboard pages containing family photographs.

Reading to children may be particularly valuable when parents and other caregivers talk with children about what they are reading together (Panofsky, 1994). Consider the following scenario, in which a mother and her 4-year-old son are reading H. A. Rey's *Curious George Flies a Kite*:

Observe appropriate books for infants in the Emotional Development/Infancy clip of the Observation CD.

Mother: *George looked into the water. . . . He was so near, maybe he could get it with his hands. George got down as low as he could, and put out his hand.*

FIGURE 8–1 Two examples of preschoolers' pseudowriting. A 4-year-old boy wrote the letter at top to his mother and told his teacher it said, "Dear Mommy, from Tommy." A 5-year-old girl wrote the lengthy piece at bottom without explaining its meaning.

Writing samples courtesy of Cathy Zocchi.

Observe Carrie's emergent literacy in the Literacy/Early Childhood clip of the Observation CD.

emergent literacy
Knowledge and skills that lay a foundation for reading and writing; typically develops in the preschool years from early experiences with written language.

Child:	Will he fall in dere?
Mother:	What?
Child:	Will he fall in dere?
Mother:	Will he fall in there? I don't know, let's see [turns page]. Oh, you were right! *Splash, into the lake he went. The water was cold and George was cold and wet too. This was no fun at all.*
Child:	He shoulda just got his two hands down dere, den put his feet on dere [pointing].
Mother:	Yeah, he could have hung on to the dock with his feet, 'cause his feet are like hands, aren't they? (dialogue from Panofsky, 1994, pp. 236–237; format adapted)

Like this mother, adults often make comments and ask questions that help young children make better sense of a story. For instance, they may label or interpret pictures ("That's a butterfly," "See the tear? He's crying"), identify feelings ("Oh, no!" "He's happy, huh?"), or encourage speculation ("Do you think the fish will like the cake?" "I bet he's scared") (Panofsky, 1994). By doing so, adults engage children in the *social construction of meaning* that we discussed in Chapter 4.

Emergent Literacy

Through their early exposure to reading and writing, children learn many things about written language (Paris & Cunningham, 1996; Pérez, 1998; Weiss & Hagen, 1988). For instance, they learn that

- Print has meaning and conveys information
- Different kinds of printed matter (storybooks, newspapers, telephone books, grocery lists, etc.) serve different purposes
- Spoken language is represented in a consistent way in written language (e.g., particular letters of the alphabet are associated with particular sounds in spoken language, words are always spelled the same way)
- Written language includes some predictable elements and conventions (e.g., fairytales often begin with "Once upon a time," and in the English language, writing proceeds from left to right and from the top of the page to the bottom)

Such basic knowledge about written language, which lays a foundation for reading and writing skills, is known as **emergent literacy.**

Many behaviors of preschool children reflect emergent literacy. Like Benjamin, young children may pretend to read storybooks, speaking in a "storytelling" fashion, turning the pages regularly and, in some cases, recalling part or all of a story from memory (McLane & McNamee, 1990; Sulzby, 1985). They may recognize some letters of the alphabet, as 4-year-old Carrie does in the Literacy/Early Childhood clip of the Observation CD. They also may correctly identify words that appear in familiar contexts, such as on a stop sign, a cereal box, a soft drink can, or the sign for a fast-food restaurant (Dickinson, Wolf, & Stotsky, 1993; Share & Gur, 1999).

Emergent literacy appears in preschoolers' writing activities as well (Dyson, 1986; McLane & McNamee, 1990; Pérez, 1998). Initially, their attempts at writing may be nothing more than random scribbles. Eventually they may be wavy lines or squiggles written from left to right across the page, perhaps with occasional spaces to indicate where one "word" ends and another begins. Increasingly, their writing assumes letterlike shapes that reflect characteristics of their own language; for example, preschoolers who speak Arabic include many dots in their early pseudowriting, reflecting the prominence of dots in written Arabic (D. W. Rowe & Harste, 1986). Figure 8–1 shows two examples of American children's pseudowriting; notice how the older child's writing more closely resembles English letter forms.

Many preschoolers do not yet realize that writing must take a *particular* form to have meaning, and even those who have learned this important idea are often unable to distinguish between true writing and meaningless marks on a page. For instance, children may scribble something and ask an adult, "What did I write?" (McLane & McNamee, 1990). After a 5-year-old boy named Ashley had written several letterlike shapes on a sheet of paper, an adult asked him, "Tell me about your letters." In a very matter-of-fact manner, Ashley responded, "I don't read 'em; I just write 'em" (Dyson, 1986, p. 205).

Effects of Early Literacy Experiences

Researchers consistently find that young children who are read to frequently during the preschool years have more advanced language development (e.g., larger vocabularies), are more interested in reading, have greater awareness of word sounds (phonemes) and letter-sound relationships, and learn to read more easily once they reach elementary school (Frijters, Barron, & Brunello, 2000; Sénéchal & LeFevre, 2002; Sulzby & Teale, 1991; Whitehurst et al., 1994). Associating literacy activities with pleasure may be especially important; for instance, children who enjoy their early reading experiences are more likely to read frequently on their own later on (L. Baker et al., 1997). In this respect, authentic literacy activities (e.g., reading children's stories) are more beneficial than activities involving drill and practice of isolated skills (e.g., the workbooks Phyllis Jones provided for Benjamin). A heavy focus on drill and practice may lead young children to conclude that reading and writing are tedious, joyless tasks (L. Baker et al., 1997).

By the time they reach school age, some children have more than a thousand hours of reading and writing experience behind them (M. J. Adams, 1990; Teale, 1986). Yet for a variety of reasons, other children may have encountered few if any books or other written materials before they begin school (Pérez, 1998). By observing young children as they interact with books and writing materials, adults can learn a great deal about what the children have and have not learned about the nature of written language. The Observation Guidelines table "Assessing Emergent Literacy in Young Children" offers several ideas about what to look for.

When children's home environments do not give them a preliminary understanding of the nature and purposes of reading and writing, child care providers and preschool teachers play a critical role in laying the foundation for later literacy development. The "Implication" column of the Observation Guidelines table lists several strategies caregivers, teachers, and other adults can use to foster the knowledge and skills of emergent literacy.

Storybook reading in the early years promotes the development of emergent literacy—basic knowledge about written language and literature that provides the foundation for learning how to read and write.

Development in Reading

Reading is a complex, multifaceted process that continues to develop throughout the childhood and adolescent years. In kindergarten and first grade (if not before), children begin to identify the specific words they see in print; shortly thereafter, they begin to derive meaning from the printed page. As they get older, they become capable of reading and comprehending increasingly sophisticated and challenging text, and by high school much of their learning both in and out of school depends on their ability to understand and remember what they read. In the following pages, we explore the development of three important aspects of learning to read—phonological awareness, word recognition, and reading comprehension—and consider how reading processes may change qualitatively over time.

Development of Phonological Awareness

Before Benjamin Jones was 3, his mother began teaching him to recognize the shapes and sounds of letters. Letter recognition is a clear prerequisite for learning to read (M. J. Adams, 1990; M. Harris & Giannouli, 1999). Yet learning to recognize all 26 letters of the alphabet in both uppercase and lowercase forms poses a challenge for many children, in part because some letters differ from one another only in their orientation. For instance, young children often have trouble distinguishing between *M* and *W*, and among *b, d, p,* and *q*.

In addition to knowing the letters, children also need to associate those letters with the particular sounds that make up spoken language. A growing body of research indicates that **phonological awareness**[2]—hearing the distinct sounds of which words are comprised—is

phonological awareness
Ability to hear the distinct sounds within words.

---

[2] You may sometimes see the term *phonemic awareness.*

OBSERVATION GUIDELINES

Assessing Emergent Literacy in Young Children

CHARACTERISTIC	LOOK FOR	EXAMPLE	IMPLICATION
Attitudes toward Books	• Frequent manipulation and perusal of books • Attentiveness and interest when adults read storybooks • Eagerness to talk about the stories that are read	Martina often mentions the Berenstain Bears books that her father reads to her at home.	Devote a regular time to storybook reading, choose books with colorful pictures and imaginative story lines, and occasionally stop to discuss and interpret characters and events in a story. Make regular trips to the library.
Behaviors with Books	• Correct handling of books (e.g., holding them right side up, turning pages in the appropriate direction) • Pretend reading • Use of picture content or memory of the story to construct a logical sequence of events when pretending to read • Asking "What does this say?" about particular sections of text	Rusty doesn't seem to know what to do with the books in his preschool classroom. He opens them haphazardly and apparently sees nothing wrong with ripping out pages.	If children have had only limited experience with books, occasionally read one-on-one with them. Let them hold the books and turn the pages. Ask them to make predictions about what might happen next in a story.
Word Recognition	• Recognition of product names when they appear in logos and other familiar contexts • Recognition of own name in print	Katherine sees a take-out bag from a local fast-food restaurant and correctly asserts that it says "Burger King."	Prominently label any coat hooks, storage boxes, and other items that belong to individual children. Write children's names in large letters on paper and encourage them to trace or copy the letters. When children are ready, ask them to put their first name (or first initial) on their artwork.
Writing Behaviors	• Production of letterlike shapes • Writing in a left-to-right sequence • Ability to write some letters correctly or almost correctly • Ability to write own name	Hank can write his name, but he frequently reverses the N and sometimes leaves it out altogether (Rowe & Harste, 1986).	Give children numerous opportunities to experiment with writing implements (paper, crayons, markers, pencils, etc.) in both structured tasks and unstructured situations. Guide letter and word formation when children show an interest.
Knowledge about the Nature and Purposes of Written Language	• Awareness that specific words are always spelled in the same way • Correct identification of telephone books, calendars, and other reference materials • Pretend writing for particular purposes	When Shakira and Lucie pretend to grocery shop, they write several lines of squiggles on a piece of paper. They say that this is a list of items they need at the store.	Encourage play activities that involve pretend writing (e.g., writing and delivering "letters" to friends or classmates; Hawkins, 1997). Let children see you engaging in a wide variety of reading and writing activities.

an important element of successful reading (M. Harris & Hatano, 1999; Stanovich, 2000; R. K. Wagner, Torgesen, & Rashotte, 1994). Phonological awareness includes such abilities as these:

- Hearing the specific syllables within words (e.g., hearing "can" and "dee" as separate parts of *candy*)
- Dividing words into discrete phonemes (e.g., hearing the sounds "guh," "ay," and "tuh" in *gate*)
- Blending separate phonemes into meaningful words (e.g., recognizing that, when put together, the sounds "wuh," "eye," and "duh" make *wide*)
- Identifying words that rhyme (e.g., realizing that *cat* and *hat* end with the same sounds)

Phonological awareness evolves gradually in the preschool and early elementary years (Barron, 1998; Goswami, 1999; Lonigan, Burgess, Anthony, & Barker, 1998). Typically it follows this sequence:

DEVELOPMENT AND PRACTICE

Promoting Phonological Awareness and Letter Recognition in Young Children

■ Read alphabet books that use colorful pictures, amusing poems, or entertaining stories to teach letters and letter sounds.

A home child care provider shares *The Alphabet Book* (Holtz, 1997) with her group of 4-year-olds. The book has many colorful photographs, each devoted to a different letter. As the children look at the picture for the letter *B,* they delight in identifying the many *B* words they find there—*baby, bottle, block,* and so on.

■ Have children think of words that rhyme.

A kindergarten teacher challenges his students to think of at least five words that rhyme with *break.*

■ Ask children to identify words that begin (or end) with a particular sound or group of sounds.

A first-grade teacher asks, "Who can think of a word that begins with a 'str' sound? For example, *string* begins with a 'str' sound. What are some other words that begin with 'str'?"

■ Say several words and ask children which one begins (or ends) in a different sound.

A second-grade teacher asks, "Listen carefully to these four words: *bend, end, dent,* and *mend.* Which one ends in a different sound than the others? Listen to them again before you decide: *bend, end, dent,* and *mend.*"

■ Show pictures of several objects and ask children to choose the one that begins (or ends) with a different sound from the others.

A kindergarten teacher shows his class pictures of a dog, a door, a wagon, and a dragon. "Three of these things start with the same sound. Which one starts with a *different* sound?"

■ Have children practice writing alphabet letters on paper and representing letters in other ways.

A first-grade teacher has children make letters with their bodies. For example, one child stands with his arms outstretched like a *Y,* and two others bend over and clasp hands to form an *M.*

■ Ask children to create and spell nonsense words using letter-sound relationships.

A music teacher has second graders sing several verses of the song, "I Know an Old Lady Who Swallowed a Fly," substituting a different nonsense word for the word *fly* in each verse. For instance, one verse goes like this:

> *I know an old lady who swallowed a zwing.*
> *I don't why*
> *She swallowed the zwing.*
> *I guess she'll die* (Reutzel & Cooter, 1999, p. 146)

---

1. *Awareness of syllables.* Most children can detect the discrete syllables within words by age 4, well before they begin school and start learning to read (Goswami, 1999; M. Harris & Giannouli, 1999).

2. *Awareness of parts of syllables.* Soon after they become aware of the individual syllables in multisyllabic words, children begin to realize that many syllables can be divided into two parts: an *onset* (one or more consonants that precede the vowel sound) and a *rime* (the vowel sound and any consonants that follow it). For example, they can separate *bend* into "buh" and "end" and *spray* into "spruh" and "ay." Most 4- and 5-year-olds show some ability to hear the onsets and rimes that make up word syllables (Goswami, 1998, 1999).

3. *Awareness of individual phonemes.* By the time they are 6 or 7, many children can identify the individual phonemes in spoken words (Goswami, 1999; R. E. Owens, 1996). This ability seems to emerge hand in hand with learning to read (Goswami, 1999; M. Harris & Giannouli, 1999; Perfetti, 1992). Apparently, seeing individual phonemes represented as letters in printed words helps children listen for those phonemes and then hear them as distinct sounds (L. C. Ehri & Wilce, 1986).

Specifically teaching children to hear the onsets, rimes, and individual phonemes in words enhances their later reading ability (L. Bradley & Bryant, 1991; Bus & van IJzendoorn, 1999; Byrne, Fielding-Barnsley, & Ashley, 2000; Stanovich, 2000; Torgesen et al., 1999). Phyllis Jones helped Benjamin develop this ability by using phonics workbooks and audiotapes. But it is often more effective to promote phonological awareness within the context of energetic and enjoyable listening, reading, and spelling activities (Muter, 1998). The Development and Practice feature "Promoting Phonological Awareness and Letter Recognition in Young Children" presents several useful strategies.

Development of Word Recognition

At age 4, Benjamin could use what he knew about letter-sound relationships to sound out some of the words he saw in his everyday environment. The English language isn't completely dependable when it comes to letter-sound correspondences; for example, the letters *ough* are pronounced quite differently in the words *through, though, bough,* and *rough.* Despite such occasional anomalies, letter-sound correspondences in English are fairly predictable if we consider common letter patterns rather than individual letters (Stanovich, 2000). For instance, the letters *ight* are always pronounced with a long *i* sound and silent *g* and *h* (e.g., *light, might, right*), and the letters *tion* are always pronounced "shun" (e.g., *motion, vacation, intuition*).

When developing readers encounter a word they have never seen before, they may use a variety of **word decoding** skills to determine what the word probably is. They may

- Identify the sounds associated with each of the word's letters and then blend the sounds together.
- Think of words they know that are spelled similarly to the unknown word. For instance, a child may notice a similarity between *peak,* a word she doesn't know, and *beak,* a word she has already learned, and simply replace the "buh" sound with "puh." Initially, children make such analogies based on rimes, such as *beak–peak* and *cat–hat.* Later, they can draw analogies that cross onset-rime boundaries, such as *beak–bean* and *cat–can* (Goswami, 1999).
- Identify clusters of letters that are typically pronounced in certain ways. For instance, in the common word ending *-ology,* the *g* is always pronounced "juh," never "guh."
- Use semantic and syntactic context to make an educated guess as to what the word might be. For instance, the word *pint* is pronounced differently than other *–int* words (*hint, mint, squint,* etc.), but a sentence such as *The recipe called for a pint of milk* provides clues as to its identity.

After encountering a word in print enough times, children no longer need to decode it when they see it; instead, they recognize it immediately and automatically (M. J. Adams, 1990; L. C. Ehri, 1998).

In the preschool and early elementary years, word recognition abilities typically emerge in the following sequence:

1. Initially (perhaps at age 4), children rely almost entirely on context clues to identify words (L. Ehri, 1994; Juel, 1991; Share & Gur, 1999). For example, many preschoolers correctly identify the word *stop* when it appears on a red, octagonal sign at the side of the road. They can "read" the word *Cheerios* on a cereal box. They know that a word at a fast-food restaurant is *McDonalds* when the *M* takes the form of the well-known golden arches.

2. Sometime around age 5, children begin to look at one or more features of the word itself; however, they do not yet make connections between how a word is spelled and how it sounds. Often, they focus on one or two visually distinctive features of a word, using a strategy known as *logographic* or *visual-cue* reading (L. Ehri, 1991, 1994; Share & Gur, 1999). For example, they see the "tail" hanging down at the end of *dog* or the two "ears" sticking up in the middle of *rabbit* (L. Ehri, 1991, 1994). Some children remember certain words (such as the various names posted on children's school lockers) by their overall shapes—a strategy known as *visuographic* reading (Share & Gur, 1999).

3. Soon after, children begin to use some of a word's letters for phonetic clues about what the word must be. For example, they might read *box* by looking at the *b* and *x* but ignoring the *o* (L. Ehri, 1991, 1994).

4. Once children have mastered typical letter-sound relationships, they rely heavily on such relationships as they read (L. Ehri, 1991, 1994). Doing so allows them to decode such simple words as *cat, bed, Dick,* and *Jane.* However, they have difficulty when they encounter words that violate general pronunciation rules. For instance, using the rule that *ea* is pronounced "ee," they might read *head* as "heed" or *sweater* as "sweeter."

5. As children gain more experience with written language, they develop a reasonable **sight vocabulary**; that is, they recognize a sizable number of words immediately and no longer need to decode them. At this point, they use not only letter-sound relationships but also word analogies, common spelling patterns, and context to decipher new words (L. C. Ehri & Robbins, 1992; Juel, 1991; R. E. Owens, 1996;

word decoding
Identifying an unknown word by using letter-sound relationships, analogies, common letter patterns, and/or semantic and syntactic context.

sight vocabulary
Words that a child can recognize immediately while reading.

M. E. Peterson & Haines, 1992). Most children in the middle elementary grades use multiple strategies to decode unknown words (R. E. Owens, 1996).

6. As children continue to read, their recognition of most common words becomes automatized (M. J. Adams, 1990; L. C. Ehri, 1998; Juel, 1991). Although they do not lose their word decoding skills, they depend on them only infrequently once they reach the middle school and high school grades (Goldsmith-Phillips, 1989; Gough & Wren, 1998).

From an information processing perspective, the mental processes that occur during reading take place in working memory. If children must use their limited working memory capacity to decode individual words, they have little "room" left to understand the overall meaning of what they are reading. It is essential, then, that children eventually automatize their recognition of most words (M. J. Adams, 1990; B. A. Greene & Royer, 1994; Stanovich, 2000). As you should recall from Chapter 5, automatization develops primarily through practice, practice, and more practice. In some instances—perhaps with young beginning readers or with older children who have particular difficulty learning to read (e.g., those with certain learning disabilities)—teachers and other adults can sometimes promote automatization by using flashcards of individual words. But it is probably more effective (and certainly more motivating!) simply to encourage children to read as often as possible (L. C. Ehri, 1998; Share, 1995).

Development of Reading Comprehension

At its most basic level, the term *reading comprehension* means understanding the words and sentences on the page. But for advanced readers, it also means going beyond the page itself: making inferences and predictions, identifying main ideas, detecting an author's assumptions and biases, and so on (Perfetti, 1985).

Children's ability to comprehend what they read is related to, and almost certainly dependent on, their overall language development (Rayner, Foorman, Perfetti, Pesetsky, & Seidenberg, 2001). For instance, children with larger vocabularies perform better on tests of reading comprehension (R. G. Anderson & Freebody, 1981). Their metalinguistic awareness—their knowledge about the nature of language itself—is also a factor in successful reading (Downing, 1986; Tunmer & Bowey, 1984).

Abilities associated with effective reading comprehension emerge and improve throughout the elementary and secondary school years (and, for many people, into adulthood as well). Several general trends characterize the development of reading comprehension in childhood and adolescence:

■ *Children's growing knowledge base facilitates better reading comprehension.* As they grow older, children become better able to understand what they read, in part because they know more about the topics about which they are reading (Byrnes, 1996; Rayner et al., 2001). In fact, children's reading comprehension ability at *any* age is influenced by topic knowledge (Lipson, 1983; Pearson, Hansen, & Gordon, 1979). In one study, for example, second graders were asked to read a passage about spiders; children who knew a lot about spiders remembered more and drew inferences more readily than their less knowledgeable peers (Pearson et al., 1979).

■ *Children acquire more knowledge about common structures in fictional and nonfictional texts.* Most 5- and 6-year-olds can distinguish between books that tell stories and books that provide information (S. L. Field, Labbo, & Ash, 1999). As children get older, they also learn how various kinds of text are typically organized, and such knowledge helps them make better sense of what they read. For instance, they gradually acquire a **story schema**[3] that represents the typical components of fictional narratives: They learn that stories usually have a particular *setting* (time and place), one or more *characters* with personalities and motives that influence their actions and reactions, a *plot* that reflects a logical sequence of events, and a *resolution* of a problem or conflict that arises (Graesser, Golding, & Long, 1991; N. L. Stein & Glenn, 1979). When a work of fiction is organized in an unusual way

Young readers often rely heavily on context clues and word shapes to help them identify words. As they learn various letter-sound relationships, they become increasingly proficient at sounding out new words. With time and practice, they develop a sizeable sight vocabulary and can recognize many words quickly and easily.

story schema
Knowledge of the typical elements and sequence of a narrative.

---

[3] Some theorists instead use the term *story grammar.*

(e.g., when it consists of a series of flashbacks), older children may use a story schema to rearrange the text's elements into a structure that makes sense (Byrnes, 1996; N. L. Stein, 1982; Zwaan, Langston, & Graesser, 1995).

As children grow older, they also begin to use common structures in nonfiction to enhance their comprehension (Byrnes, 1996). For instance, when reading a textbook, they may rely on headings and subheadings to help them identify key ideas and organize what they are studying. And when reading a persuasive essay, they may anticipate that the author will first present a particular point of view and then offer evidence to support it.

◾ *Children become increasingly able to draw inferences from what they read.* Particularly as children reach the upper elementary grades, they become more adept at drawing inferences and so more effectively learn new information from what they read (Chall, 1996; Paris & Upton, 1976). Yet, at this level, they (like younger children) tend to take the things they read at face value, with little attempt to evaluate them critically and little sensitivity to obvious contradictions (Chall, 1996; P. Johnston & Afflerbach, 1985; Markman, 1979).

As children reach adolescence and move into the secondary grades, they read written material with a more critical eye (Chall, 1996; R. E. Owens, 1996). They begin to recognize that different authors sometimes present different viewpoints on a single issue. They also become more aware of the subtle aspects of fiction—for example, the underlying theme and symbolism of a novel.

The ability to draw inferences seems to be a key factor in children's reading comprehension: Poor readers are less likely to make inferences when they read (Cain & Oakhill, 1998; Oakhill, Cain, & Yuill, 1998). Some poor readers appear to have less working memory capacity, which limits their ability to consider and integrate multiple pieces of information at the same time (Oakhill et al., 1998). In addition, many poor readers don't relate what they read to what they already know about a topic; thus, they are less likely to fill in the missing details they need to make sense of text (Cain & Oakhill, 1998).

◾ *Metacognitive strategies increase in number and sophistication, especially in adolescence.* As children gain more experience with reading, and particularly with reading textbooks and other informational text, they develop a variety of strategies for comprehending written material. For instance, adolescents are better able to identify main ideas than elementary school children are (Byrnes, 1996). High school students are more likely to monitor their comprehension as they read, and also to backtrack (i.e., reread) when they don't understand something the first time, than children in the upper elementary and middle school grades (Garner, 1987; Hacker, 1995). However, not all adolescents use effective metacognitive reading strategies—identifying main ideas, monitoring comprehension, rereading, and so forth—and those who do not often have considerable difficulty understanding and remembering what they read (Alvermann & Moore, 1991; Hacker, 1995).

Numerous research studies indicate that, with proper instruction and support, children and adolescents can learn to use effective metacognitive strategies and improve their reading comprehension as a result. One effective approach is *reciprocal teaching*, to be described shortly. The Development and Practice feature "Promoting Use of Effective Reading Comprehension Strategies" presents several additional suggestions.

As you have discovered, reading is a complex activity that encompasses numerous skills and abilities. One prominent reading theorist, Jeanne Chall, has synthesized some of the trends in reading development into a series of stages, which we consider now.

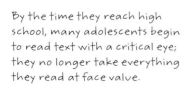

By the time they reach high school, many adolescents begin to read text with a critical eye; they no longer take everything they read at face value.

Chall's Stages of Reading Development

Drawing on research findings in psychology, linguistics, and neurology, Chall (1996) has proposed that reading development involves six qualitatively distinct stages. At each stage, children and adolescents acquire new knowledge and skills that provide a foundation for any stages that follow. As we describe the stages, we also list ages and approximate grade levels at which they appear. These ages and grade levels typify reading development in many Western, English-speaking schools at the present time; they do not necessarily apply to other cultural contexts or other historical periods (Chall, 1996).

DEVELOPMENT AND PRACTICE

Promoting Use of Effective Reading Comprehension Strategies

■ Teach reading comprehension skills in all subject areas and content domains.

When a first aid instructor tells his students to read a section of their manual, he also suggests several strategies they might use to help them remember what they read. For example, as they begin each section, they should use the heading to make a prediction as to what the section will be about. At the end of the section, they should stop and consider whether their prediction was accurate (Pressley et al., 1994).

■ Model effective reading strategies.

A girl in a seventh-grade history class reads aloud a passage describing how, during Columbus's first voyage across the Atlantic, many members of the crew wanted to turn around and return to Spain. Her teacher says, "Let's think of some reasons why the crew might have wanted to go home." One student responds, "Some of them might have been homesick." Another suggests, "Maybe they thought they'd never find their way back if they went too far."

■ Encourage children to relate what they are reading to things they already know about the topic.

Children in a third-grade classroom are each reading several books on a particular topic (e.g., dinosaurs, insects, outer space). Before they begin reading a book, their teacher asks them to write answers to three questions: (a) What do you already know about your topic? (b) What do you hope to learn about your topic? and (c) Do you think

what you learn by reading your books will change what you already know about your topic? (H. Thompson & Carr, 1995).

■ Ask children to identify key elements of the stories they read.

A fourth-grade teacher instructs his students to ask themselves five questions as they read stories: (a) Who is the main character? (b) Where and when did the story take place? (c) What did the main characters do? (d) How did the story end? and (e) How did the main character feel? (Short & Ryan, 1984).

■ Suggest that children create mental images that capture what they are reading (Gambrell & Bales, 1986).

When an after-school literature group reads Nathaniel Hawthorne's *The Scarlet Letter*, the librarian asks group members to close their eyes and imagine what the two main characters, Arthur Dimsdale and Hester Prynne, might look like. He then asks for volunteers to describe their mental images.

■ Scaffold children's early efforts to use complex strategies.

A middle school science teacher asks her students to write summaries of short textbook passages. She gives them four rules to use as they develop their summaries: (1) Identify the most important ideas, (2) delete trivial details, (3) eliminate redundant information, and (4) identify relationships among the main ideas (Rinehart, Stahl, & Erickson, 1986).

Stage 0: Prereading (to age 6). Children develop some awareness of word sounds and learn to recognize most letters of the alphabet. They can pretend to read a book and know enough to hold the book right-side up and turn the pages one at a time. However, these pre-reading activities depend little, if at all, on actual print. (Chall's Stage 0 encompasses the *emergent literacy* described earlier.)

Stage 1: Initial reading, or decoding (ages 6–7, grades 1–2). Children focus on learning letter-sound relationships and gain increasing insight into the nature of English spelling. They depend almost entirely on the printed page as they read; in Chall's words, they are "glued to the print."

Stage 2: Confirmation, fluency, ungluing from print (ages 7–8, grades 2–3). Children solidify the letter-sound relationships they learned in Stage 1 and automatize their recognition of many common words. They are beginning to take advantage of the redundancies in language, as well as their general knowledge about the world, and so they are less dependent on each and every letter and word on the page (in Chall's words, they are "ungluing from print"). They become increasingly fluent in their reading and can read silently. Although children now read for meaning, most of what they read confirms what they already know; for instance, they read familiar books and stories but do not yet read textbooks that introduce new ideas.

Stage 3: Reading for learning the new (ages 9–14, grades 4–8 or 9). Children can now learn new information from the things they read; by the end of Stage 3, reading surpasses listening as a means of acquiring information. Children begin to study the traditional academic content areas (science, history, geography) in earnest and gain much of their knowledge about these subjects from textbooks. They also begin to develop strategies for finding information in chapters, books, and reference materials (looking at headings, consulting indexes, etc.).

Reading materials become increasingly complex, abstract, and unfamiliar during Stage 3, and success at reading and understanding them increasingly relies on children's prior understandings of word meanings and the subject matter. Accordingly, children whose language

DEVELOPMENTAL TRENDS

Reading at Different Age Levels

AGE	WHAT YOU MIGHT OBSERVE	DIVERSITY	IMPLICATIONS
Infancy (Birth–2) 	• Physical manipulation and exploration of simple cloth and cardboard books • Increasing enjoyment of storybooks; initially, toddlers focus more on pictures than on story lines • Attention to and enjoyment of rhythm and rhymes	• Temperamental differences influence infants' and toddlers' ability to sit still and attend to books.	• Provide small, durable picture books of cloth, cardboard, or plastic. • Read books with catchy rhythms and rhymes to capture and maintain attention. • During story time, label and talk about the pictures in books. Recognize that toddlers may not be able to sit still for a lengthy story.
Early Childhood (2–6) 	• Use of reading materials in play activities • Increasing knowledge of letters and letter-sound correspondences • Identification of a few words in well-known contexts (e.g., words on commercial products) • Use of a word's distinctive features (e.g., a single letter or overall shape) to read or misread it	• Children who have had little exposure to books and reading before they begin school may have less knowledge about the nature of reading. Some cultures emphasize oral language more than written language. • When parents speak a language other than English, they may have provided early literacy experiences in their native tongue; such experiences provide a good foundation for reading and writing in English. • Lower-income parents are less likely to read either for information or for pleasure. • Some children begin school knowing the alphabet and may have a small sight vocabulary as well. Others may need to start from scratch when learning letters and letter sounds.	• Read to young children using colorful books with high-interest content. • Teach letters of the alphabet through engaging, hands-on activities. • Teach letter-sound correspondences through storybooks, games, rhymes, and enjoyable writing activities. • Encourage children to read words that can easily be deciphered from the contexts in which they appear. • Encourage parents to read regularly to children either in English or in another native language.
Middle Childhood (6–10) 	• Ability to hear individual phonemes within words • Increasing proficiency in word decoding skills • Growing sight-word vocabulary, leading to greater reading fluency • Beginning of silent reading (at age 7 or 8) • Increasing ability to draw inferences • Tendency to take things in print at face value	• Children with deficits in phonological awareness have a more difficult time learning to read; this correlation is especially strong in languages where writing involves a phonetic alphabet. • Children with hearing impairments are less likely to master letter-sound correspondences. • On average, girls develop reading skills earlier than boys. • Children vary widely in their comprehension strategies; some strategies are far more effective than others.	• Explore "families" of words that are spelled similarly. • Assign well-written trade books (e.g., children's paperback novels) as soon as children are able to read and understand them. • Engage children in small- or large-group reading discussions. Focus on interpretation, drawing inferences, and speculation. • For children who struggle with reading, explicitly teach phonological awareness and word decoding skills, especially within the context of meaningful reading activities.

fourth-grade slump
Tendency for some children (especially those from low-income backgrounds) to experience greater difficulty with reading tasks as they encounter more challenging material in the upper elementary grades.

skills and general world knowledge are relatively limited begin to struggle with reading and learning. This **fourth-grade slump** is often seen in children from low socioeconomic backgrounds, perhaps because they have had less access to reading materials and enriching educational opportunities (museum visits, family travel, etc.) than their more economically privileged peers (Chall, 1996).

Early in Stage 3, children learn best from reading material that presents a single viewpoint in a clear, straightforward manner, and they typically take what they read at face value. As they reach grades 7 and 8, however, they begin to analyze and think critically about what they read.

DEVELOPMENTAL TRENDS

Reading at Different Age Levels *(continued)*

AGE	WHAT YOU MIGHT OBSERVE	DIVERSITY	IMPLICATIONS
Early Adolescence (10–14) 	• Automatized recognition of most common words • Ability to learn new information through reading • Emerging ability to go beyond the literal meaning of text • Emerging metacognitive processes that aid comprehension (e.g., comprehension monitoring, backtracking)	• Adolescents with deficits in phonological awareness continue to lag behind their peers in reading development. • Individuals who were poor readers in elementary school often continue to be poor readers in adolescence. • Some individuals (e.g., some with mental retardation) may have excellent decoding skills yet not understand what they read. • Individuals with sensory challenges may have less general world knowledge that they can use to interpret what they read.	• Assign age-appropriate reading materials in various content areas; give youngsters some scaffolding (e.g., questions to answer) to guide their thinking and learning as they read. • Begin to explore classic works of poetry and literature. • Use reciprocal teaching to promote the reading comprehension skills of poor readers. • Seek the advice and assistance of specialists to help promote the reading skills of low-ability readers.
Late Adolescence (14–18)	• Automatized recognition of many abstract and discipline-specific words • Ability to consider multiple viewpoints about a single topic • Ability to evaluate critically what is read • More sophisticated metacognitive reading strategies	• Poor readers draw few if any inferences from what they read and use few if any effective metacognitive processes. • As classroom learning becomes more dependent on reading textbooks and other written materials, adolescents with reading disabilities may become increasingly frustrated in their attempts to achieve academic success. • Girls are more likely than boys to enroll in advanced language and literature classes.	• Expect that many teenagers can learn effectively from textbooks and other reading materials, but continue to scaffold reading assignments, especially for poor readers. • Encourage adolescents to draw inferences and make predictions from what they read. • Critically analyze classic works of poetry and literature. • Modify reading materials and paper-pencil assessments for individuals with poor reading skills.

Sources: Cain & Oakhill, 1998; Chall, 1996; Dryden & Jefferson, 1994; L. Ehri, 1994; Felton, 1998; M. Harris & Hatano, 1999; Hedges & Nowell, 1995; Hulme & Joshi, 1998; P. Johnston & Afflerbach, 1985; McLane & McNamee, 1990; R. E. Owens, 1996; L. Reese, Garnier, Gallimore, & Goldenberg, 2000; Share & Gur, 1999; Trawick-Smith, 2003; Trelease, 1982; Turnbull et al., 2002; Wigfield et al., 1996; Yaden & Templeton, 1986.

Stage 4: Multiple viewpoints (age 14 on, high school). In high school, teenagers become more skilled readers of textbooks, reference materials, and sophisticated works of fiction. They can now handle reading materials that present multiple points of view, and they can integrate the new ideas they encounter in text with their previous knowledge about a topic.

Stage 5: Construction and reconstruction (age 18 on, college). Particularly if young people go on to college, they may begin to construct their *own* knowledge and opinions (often at a high level of abstraction) by analyzing, synthesizing, and evaluating what others have written. They also read more purposefully; that is, they may read certain parts of a text but skip other parts to accomplish their goals for reading the text as efficiently as possible. Chall has estimated that fewer than 40% of college students develop their reading skills to a Stage 5 level.

In general, then, as young people move through the elementary and secondary grades, they read with greater fluency and flexibility and become able to read increasingly complex, unfamiliar, and abstract material. As they acquire the skills of new stages, however, they do not necessarily lose previously learned skills. For example, even college students proficient at Stage 5 reading may occasionally relax with a mystery novel that they read in a Stage 2 or Stage 3 fashion (Chall, 1996). The Developmental Trends table "Reading at Different Age Levels" traces the development of reading over the course of childhood and adolescence.

Chall's stages of reading make it clear that different types of reading materials and different instructional techniques are appropriate at different age levels. We look now at general approaches and strategies for promoting children's and adolescents' reading development.

10/10 ⭐

Meggie

1. rode	6. pole
2. note	7. mole
3. nose	8. woke
4. bone	9. code
5. rose	10. stove

FIGURE 8-2 In this assignment, 7-year-old Meggie, a first grader, practices words with a long *o* sound and silent *e*. Instruction in specific letter-sound relationships and common spelling patterns helps children with both reading and spelling. However, too much focus on such drill and practice may lead children to conclude that reading and writing are meaningless, joyless activities.

Approaches to Reading Instruction

In the early elementary years, reading instruction focuses on both word recognition and basic comprehension skills, often within the context of reading simple stories (Chall, 1996; R. E. Owens, 1996). In the upper elementary and middle school grades, most children have acquired sufficient linguistic knowledge and reading skills to concentrate almost exclusively on reading comprehension. In the secondary grades, reading instruction is, unfortunately, typically found only in study skills classes (which focus on learning from textbooks and other nonfiction), English and American literature classes (which focus on interpreting fiction), and "remedial" or "developmental" reading classes (which are limited to students who have significant delays in reading proficiency).

Throughout most of the twentieth century, a *basic-skills* approach to reading instruction predominated in the early grades of most schools. Within the past 20 years, some teachers have adopted a *whole-language* alternative to reading instruction. In the following sections, we look at specific teaching practices and research findings related to each of these approaches. We then consider *reciprocal teaching* as a strategy for promoting reading comprehension, as well as several more general strategies for fostering reading development in children and adolescents.

Teaching Basic Skills   Many theorists argue that children learn to read most effectively when teachers teach word decoding and reading comprehension skills in a direct, systematic fashion. For instance, to teach letter-sound relationships, teachers might use phonics exercises (practice in identifying onsets and rimes, blending sounds together to form words, etc.; as an example, see Figure 8–2), or they might use basal reading series and other books that emphasize simple words, common letter patterns, and considerable repetition. To teach reading comprehension, teachers might give children instruction and practice in such skills as identifying main ideas and creating summaries (e.g., Oakhill et al., 1998; Rinehart et al., 1986).

Explicit training in basic reading skills appears to facilitate reading development, especially for poor readers (L. Bradley & Bryant, 1991; Bus & van IJzendoorn, 1999; S. M. Ross, Smith, Casey, & Slavin, 1995; Rayner et al., 2001; W. Schneider, Roth, & Ennemoser, 2000; Stanovich, 2000). Unfortunately, such training sometimes takes the form of tedious exercises that children find dull and boring (Hiebert & Raphael, 1996; Turner, 1995). It does not *have* to be dull and boring, however; with a little creativity, it can be quite engaging and motivating. For example, Dr. Seuss was a master at writing and illustrating stories that young children find highly entertaining. The following excerpt from his book *One Fish Two Fish Red Fish Blue Fish* helps children learn the *-ook* pattern:

> We took a look.
> We saw a Nook.
> On his head
> he had a hook.
> On his hook
> he had a book.
> On his book
> was "How to Cook."
> (Seuss, 1960, p. 30)

Whole Language Instruction   As noted earlier, whole-language theorists propose that learning to read is as natural a process as learning to speak. Accordingly, they suggest that children learn to read most effectively by reading authentic materials (children's books, novels, magazines, newspapers, etc.) and especially by reading things they have chosen for themselves (K. S. Goodman, 1989; K. S. Goodman & Goodman, 1979; C. Weaver, 1990). Letter-sound relationships, word decoding, and other basic skills are taught solely within the context of real-world reading tasks, and far less time is devoted to them than is true in basic-skills approaches. Instead, children spend a great deal of time writing and talking with their peers about the things that they have read.

Whole-language instruction[4] has the advantage of engaging children in authentic literacy activities from the very beginning; thus, this approach may be particularly valuable for chil-

---

[4] You may also see the term *literature-based instruction*.

dren who have had little or no experience with books and other written materials at home (Purcell-Gates, McIntyre, & Freppon, 1995). It may also be more motivating; for instance, in a study with third graders, using children's novels and other trade books and giving students choices about which books to read led to greater interest and persistence in reading (Sheveland, 1994). On the downside, however, phonological awareness is often short-changed in whole-language classrooms (Juel, 1998; Liberman, 1998; Rayner et al., 2001).

Comparing Basic Skills and Whole Language Approaches   Numerous research studies have been conducted comparing the effectiveness of basic-skills and whole-language approaches to reading instruction. Studies with kindergartners and first graders find that whole-language approaches are often more effective in promoting emergent literacy—familiarity with the nature and purposes of books, pretend reading, and so on (Purcell-Gates et al., 1995; Sacks & Mergendoller, 1997; Stahl & Miller, 1989). However, basic-skills approaches—in particular, those that focus on developing phonological awareness and knowledge of letter-sound relationships—typically yield better results in teaching students to read, especially with children from low-socioeconomic backgrounds and with children who show early signs of a reading disability (M. J. Adams, 1990; Rayner et al., 2001; Stahl & Miller, 1989; Stanovich, 2000). Considering such research, many theorists now urge that teachers strike a balance between whole-language activities and basic-skills instruction (Biemiller, 1994; Pressley, 1994; Rayner et al., 2001).

Reciprocal Teaching: Helping Children Read for Learning   As you may recall from our discussion of metacognition in Chapter 5, children and adolescents typically know relatively little about how they can best learn and remember information. As illustrations, here are three high school students' descriptions of how they study a textbook (A. L. Brown & Palincsar, 1987, p. 83):

> ". . . I stare real hard at the page, blink my eyes and then open them—and cross my fingers that it will be right here." [Student points at head.]

> "It's easy, if she [the teacher] says study, I read it twice. If she says read, it's just once through."

> "I just read the first line in each paragraph—it's usually all there."

None of these students mentions any attempt to understand the information, relate it to prior knowledge, or otherwise think about it in any way. We might guess that they are not using effective learning strategies—cognitive processes that should help them store and retain information in long-term memory.

Not only must children learn to read, but they must also read to learn, that is, they must acquire new information from what they read. When we examine the cognitive processes that good readers (successful learners) often use, especially when reading challenging material, we find strategies such as these (A. L. Brown & Palincsar, 1987):

- *Summarizing.* Good readers identify the main ideas—the gist—of what they read.
- *Questioning.* Good readers ask themselves questions to make sure they understand what they are reading; in other words, they monitor their comprehension as they proceed through reading material.
- *Clarifying.* When good readers discover that they don't comprehend something— for example, when a sentence is confusing or ambiguous—they take steps to clarify what they are reading, perhaps by rereading it or making logical inferences.
- *Predicting.* Good readers anticipate what they are likely to read next, making predictions about the ideas to come.

In contrast, poor readers—those who learn little from textbooks and other reading materials— rarely summarize, question, clarify, or predict. For example, many students cannot adequately summarize a typical *fifth*-grade textbook until high school or even junior college (A. L. Brown & Palincsar, 1987; Palincsar & Brown, 1984). Clearly, then, many children do not easily acquire the ability to read for learning.

Reciprocal teaching (A. L. Brown & Palincsar, 1987; Palincsar & Brown, 1984, 1989; Palincsar & Herrenkohl, 1999) is an approach to teaching reading through which students learn effective reading-to-learn strategies by observing and imitating what their teacher and

reciprocal teaching
Approach to teaching reading whereby students take turns asking teacherlike questions of their classmates.

In reciprocal teaching, children help one another make sense of what they are reading.

classmates do. The teacher and several students meet in a group to read a piece of text, occasionally stopping to discuss and process the text aloud. Initially, the teacher leads the discussion, asking questions about the text to promote summarizing, questioning, clarifying, and predicting. Gradually, he or she turns this role over to different students, who then take charge of the discussion and ask one another the same kinds of questions that their teacher has modeled. Eventually, the students can read and discuss a text almost independently of the teacher; they work together to construct its meaning and check one another for comprehension and possible misunderstandings.

As an illustration, consider the following reciprocal teaching session for a group of six first graders reading a passage about snowshoe rabbits. In this particular case, the teacher reads the text in small segments (at higher grade levels, the children themselves take turns reading). After each segment, the teacher pauses while the children discuss and process the segment. As you read the dialogue, look for examples of summarizing, questioning, clarifying, and predicting (there is at least one instance of each).

The children were reading about the snowshoe rabbit, and it was the 16th day of dialogue. The teacher had just read a segment of text describing the season in which baby rabbits are born and the ways in which the mother rabbit cares for her babies. A student named Kam is the dialogue leader.

Kam: When was the babies born?
Teacher: That's a good question to ask. Call on someone to answer that question.
Kam: Robby? Milly?
Milly: Summer.
Teacher: What would happen if the babies were born in the winter? Let's think.

Several children make a number of responses, including: "The baby would be very cold." "They would need food." "They don't have no fur when they are just born."

Kam: I have another question. How does she get the babies safe?
Kris: She hides them.
Kam: That's right but something else. . . .
Teacher: There is something very unusual about how she hides them that surprised me. I didn't know this.
Travis: They are all in a different place.
Teacher: Why do you think she does this?
Milly: Probably because I heard another story, and when they're babies they usually eat each other or fight with each other.
Teacher: That could be! And what about when that lynx comes?

Several children comment that that would be the end of all the babies.

Travis: If I was the mother, I would hide mine, I would keep them all together.
Kris: If the babies are hidden and the mom wants to go and look at them, how can she remember where they are?
Teacher: Good question. Because she does have to find them again. Why? What does she bring them?
Milly: She needs to bring food. She probably leaves a twig or something.
Teacher: Do you think she puts out a twig like we mark a trail?

Several children disagree and suggest that she uses her sense of smell. One child, recalling that the snowshoe rabbit is not all white in the winter, suggests that the mother might be able to tell her babies apart by their coloring.

Teacher:	So we agree that the mother rabbit uses her senses to find her babies after she hides them. Kam, can you summarize for us now?
Kam:	The babies are born in the summer. . . .
Teacher:	The mother . . .
Kam:	The mother hides the babies in different places.
Teacher:	And she visits them . . .
Kam:	To bring them food.
Travis:	She keeps them safe.
Teacher:	Any predictions?
Milly:	What she teaches her babies . . . like how to hop.
Kris:	They know how to hop already.
Teacher:	Well, let's read and see. (dialogue courtesy of A. Palincsar)

Reciprocal teaching provides a mechanism through which both the teacher and students can model effective reading and learning strategies. Vygotsky's theory of cognitive development is also at work here: Children should eventually *internalize* (and thus use independently) the processes that they first use in their discussions with others. Furthermore, the structured nature of a reciprocal teaching session scaffolds children's efforts to make sense of the things they read and hear. For example, if you look back at the previous dialogue, you may notice how the teacher models elaborative questions and connections to prior knowledge ("What would happen if the babies were born in the winter?" "Do you think she puts out a twig like we mark a trail?") and provides general guidance and occasional hints about how children should process the passage about snowshoe rabbits ("Kam, can you summarize for us now?" "And she visits them . . . "). Also notice in the dialogue how the children support one another in their efforts to process what they are reading. Consider this exchange as an example:

Kam:	I have another question. How does she get the babies safe?
Kris:	She hides them.
Kam:	That's right but something else . . .

Reciprocal teaching has been used successfully with a wide variety of students, ranging from first graders to college students, to teach effective reading and listening comprehension skills (Alfassi, 1998; Campione, Shapiro, & Brown, 1995; McGee, Knight, & Boudah, 2001; Palincsar & Brown, 1989; Rosenshine & Meister, 1994). For example, in an early study of reciprocal teaching (Palincsar & Brown, 1984), six seventh-grade students with a history of poor reading comprehension participated in 20 reciprocal teaching sessions, each lasting about 30 minutes. Despite this relatively short intervention, students showed remarkable improvement in their reading comprehension skills. They became increasingly able to process reading material in an effective manner and to do so independently of their classroom teacher. Furthermore, they generalized their new reading strategies to other classes, sometimes even surpassing the achievement of their peers (A. L. Brown & Palincsar, 1987; Palincsar & Brown, 1984).

General Strategies for Promoting Reading Development

Traditionally, reading is taught primarily in elementary school. Many teachers and other adults assume that middle school and high school students read well enough to learn successfully from textbooks and other printed materials. As you have seen, however, such an assumption is not always warranted; even at the high school level, many adolescents have not yet mastered all of the skills involved in reading effectively. Furthermore, children who are poor readers in elementary school often continue to be poor readers in the secondary grades (Felton, 1998) and so may be in particular need of ongoing instruction and support in reading. We offer the following general strategies for promoting reading development throughout childhood and adolescence:

■ *Help parents of young children acquire effective storybook reading skills.* As we have seen, early experiences with books provide basic knowledge about written language upon which later reading skills build. They can also enhance children's cognitive development more generally. For example, in the Literacy/Infancy clip of the Observation CD, Corwin's mother enthusiastically engages her son in a discussion about the book they are looking at:

Mother:	Do you wanna see the cow? Would you like to read with Mama? You ready for the cow? Where is he? (turns the page) Huh! The cow says . . .
Corwin:	Mooo!
Mother:	What's that? (points to something in the book)
Corwin:	Boon.
Mother:	Balloon! We can count! One . . .
Corwin:	Two.
Mother:	Two! (reading book) This is my nose. Where's your nose?
Corwin:	(touches his nose)
Mother:	Nose! Where's your toes?
Corwin:	(grabs his toes)
Mother:	There's your toes!

Observe the strategies that Corwin's mother uses during book reading in the Literacy/Infancy clip of the Observation CD.

Notice how the mother models enthusiasm for the book and uses its content to review object labels (*balloon, nose,* and *toes*) and general world knowledge (numbers, what a cow says) with Corwin.

Yet some parents have little awareness of how to read to young children, perhaps because they themselves were rarely if ever read to when they were young. For such parents, explicit instruction in reading, as well as in strategies for reading to young children (labeling and describing pictures, asking questions that encourage inferences and predictions, inviting children to make comments, etc.) can make an appreciable difference in their ability to foster knowledge of written language and appreciation for literature (Edwards & Garcia, 1994; Gallimore & Goldenberg, 2001; Ho, Hinckley, Fox, Brown, & Dixon, 2001).

■ *Use meaningful contexts to teach basic reading skills, and encourage parents to do likewise.* With a little thought, teachers, parents, and other adults can develop enjoyable, meaningful activities to teach almost any basic reading skill. For instance, to promote phonological awareness in young children, adults might conduct a game of "Twenty Questions" (e.g., "I'm thinking of something in the room that begins with the letter *B*"), or they might ask children to locate three objects that begin with the letter *T* and three more that end with *T*. To foster greater automaticity in word recognition, they might simply engage children in a variety of authentic reading activities (L. C. Ehri, 1998).

■ *Promote vocabulary development.* As mentioned earlier, children's reading development is somewhat dependent on their general language development. One especially critical factor is the extent of their vocabulary, or *lexicon:* Reading comprehension depends on children's understanding of the words they encounter in books and other printed materials (Chall, 1996; M. S. Jones, Levin, Levin, & Beitzel, 2000). Systematic vocabulary instruction can begin well before the school years. For example, in one study (Wasik & Bond, 2001), an approach called *interactive book reading* was used to enhance the vocabulary of 4-year-olds from low-income families. Preschool teachers used concrete objects to illustrate new words that children encountered in storybooks; they also provided numerous opportunities for the children to use the words in various contexts. At the end of the school year, the children performed significantly higher than a control group on several measures of receptive and expressive language.

■ *Use high-interest works of literature.* Research consistently indicates that young people read more energetically and persistently, use more sophisticated metacognitive strategies, and remember more content when they are interested in what they are reading (R. C. Anderson, Shirey, Wilson, & Fielding, 1987; J. T. Guthrie et al., 1998; Sheveland, 1994). For example, in the Literacy/Late Adolescence clip of the Observation CD, 14-year-old Alicia describes the importance of being able to choose what she reads:

I really don't like it when the reading is required. I can't read books if they're required. I just avoid reading them because they don't seem very interesting. And even after you read them, even though they might be interesting, they're not as interesting as if you picked them up by yourself.

Observe Alicia's preference for self-chosen literature in the Literacy/Late Adolescence clip of the Observation CD.

As much as possible, then, whether teachers are using a whole-language approach or not, they should choose reading materials that are likely to be relevant to students' own lives and concerns, and they should give students some choices as to what they read.

■ *Have children work in pairs to help one another with reading.* Children often make considerable gains in reading when they work in pairs in structured reading or prereading activities (Fuchs, Fuchs, Mathes, & Simmons, 1997; Fuchs et al., 2001). In one study (Fuchs et al., 1997), 20 second- through sixth-grade classrooms participated in a project called Peer-Assisted Learning Strategies (PALS), designed to foster more effective reading comprehension skills. In each classroom, students who were paired together had moderate but not extreme differences in their reading levels. Each pair read material at the level of the weaker reader and engaged in these activities:

- *Partner reading with retell.* The stronger reader read aloud for 5 minutes, then the weaker reader read the same passage aloud. Reading something that had previously been read presumably enabled the weaker reader to read the material easily. After the double reading, the weaker reader described the material just read.
- *Paragraph summary.* The students both read a passage one paragraph at a time. Then, with help from the stronger reader, the weaker reader tried to identify the subject and main idea of each paragraph.
- *Prediction relay.* Both students read a page of text, and then, with help from the stronger reader, the weaker reader would summarize the text and also make a prediction about what the next page would say. The students would read the following page, then the weaker reader would confirm or disconfirm the prediction, summarize the new page, make a new prediction, and so on.

This procedure enabled stronger and weaker readers alike to make significantly greater progress in reading than children who had more traditional reading instruction, even though the amount of class time devoted to reading instruction was similar for both groups. Quite possibly, the PALS children performed better because they had more opportunities to talk about what they were reading, received more frequent feedback about their performance and, in general, were more often encouraged to use effective reading strategies (Fuchs et al., 1997).

■ *Conduct group discussions about stories and novels.* Children and adolescents often construct meaning more effectively when they discuss what they read with their peers. For instance, adults can form "book clubs" in which children lead small groups of peers in discussions about specific books (Alvermann, Young, Green, & Wisenbaker, 1999; McMahon, 1992). They can hold "grand conversations" about a particular work of literature, asking children to share their responses to questions with no single right answers—perhaps questions related to interpretations or critiques of various aspects of a text (Eeds & Wells, 1989; Hiebert & Raphael, 1996). They can also encourage children to think about a piece of literature from the author's perspective, posing such questions as "What's the author's message here?" or "Why do you think the author wants us to know about this?" (Beck, McKeown, Worthy, Sandora, & Kucan, 1996). By tossing around possible interpretations of what they are reading, children often model effective reading and listening comprehension strategies for one another (R. C. Anderson et al., 2001).

■ *Assign activities that encourage children to interpret what they read through a variety of media.* Group discussions are hardly the only mechanisms for fostering interpretation of reading materials. As alternatives, children might perform skits to illustrate stories, write personal letters that one character in a story might send to another character, or create works of art that illustrate the setting or characters of a novel or the underlying meaning of a poem. For example, Figure 8–3 shows how 16-year-old Jeff illustrated Paul Laurence Dunbar's poem *We Wear the Mask* as an assignment for his American literature class.

■ *Encourage reading outside of school.* Reading beyond school walls—for instance, reading during the summer months—probably accounts for a significant portion of young

We Wear the Mask
by Paul Laurence Dunbar

We wear the mask that grins and lies,
It hides our cheeks and shades our eyes,—
This debt we pay to human guile;
With torn and bleeding hearts we smile,
And mouth with myriad subtleties.

Why should the world be overwise,
In counting all our tears and sighs?
Nay, let them only see us, while
We wear the mask.

We smile, but, O great Christ, our cries
To thee from tortured souls arise.
We sing, but oh the clay is vile
Beneath our feet, and long the mile;
But let the world dream otherwise,
We wear the mask!

FIGURE 8–3 Interpreting poetry through art. Jeff's brightly colored painting is the cheerful face ("mask") that its African American owner presents in public. The black face is the flip side of the mask, as viewed by the person wearing it. Depicted in the holes of the mask are a lynching (left eye); a whipping (right eye); an African American woman and a white baby (nostrils), reflecting white owners' rape of slaves; and a slave ship with someone being thrown overboard (mouth).

people's growth in reading (D. P. Hayes & Grether, 1983; Stanovich, 2000). Providing books that children can take home to read or reread (perhaps accompanied by audiotapes) encourages outside reading and can significantly enhance reading comprehension skills (Koskinen et al., 2000). Visits to the local library can also encourage outside reading. In fact, when planning a library visit, teachers and child care providers might extend an invitation for parents to accompany the group; in some cases, this may be the first time the parents have ever been to a library (Heath, 1983).

Youngsters develop additional insights about both reading and writing when they become authors themselves and when their peers read what they have written. We turn our attention now to the nature and development of writing and to strategies for helping children and adolescents become more proficient writers.

Development in Writing

Children exhibit rudimentary forms of writing long before they reach school age, especially if they see those around them writing frequently. Consider what happened when 2½-year-old Rachel first saw her older brother Joshua writing thank-you letters after his sixth birthday:

> Rachel made a series of wavy lines on a piece of paper and told her mother it was a "thank-you letter to Grandma." About six months later, Rachel made letterlike marks on a piece of lined paper and told her mother it said "Dear Grandma and Grandpa. Thank you for the lots of presents. Love, Rachel." She then asked her mother to "get the stuff to mail it to them." A year and a half after this, when Rachel was 4½ and Joshua had recently turned 8, Rachel took a piece of her brother's lined stationery and made neat rows of letters and letterlike shapes (in no apparent order). Then she said to her mother, "I want to write a letter. I have to write a thank-you note to Grandma." She asked, "How do you spell 'Dear Grandma I love my presents'?" Her mother wrote this out for her. Rachel copied "Dear Grandma," then stopped, saying "This is boring," and asked her mother to write the rest. Her mother did, and the finished letter was mailed to her grandmother.[5]

When children grow up in literacy-rich environments, they begin to engage in pre-writing activities quite early.

[5] Reprinted by permission of the publisher from *Early Literacy* by Joan Brooks McLane and Gillian Dowley McNamee, pp. 42–43, Cambridge, Mass.: Harvard University Press. Copyright © 1990 by Joan Brooks McLane and Gillian Dowley McNamee.

Rachel's early "letters" to her grandparents demonstrated her growing awareness of what writing involves. Even at 2½, she knew that writing progresses from left to right and from the top of the page to the bottom; she also knew that writing conveys a message to someone else. A few months later, she replaced wavy lines with letterlike shapes, reflecting increasing knowledge about the general forms that letters take and, we suspect, maturing psychomotor skills. By the time she was 4½, she could produce the letters of the alphabet and knew that words must be spelled in particular ways.

For adults, writing is, of course, much more than simply putting letters on paper and spelling words correctly. To become skillful writers, growing children must not only master handwriting and spelling but also discover how to communicate their thoughts clearly, learn conventions of capitalization and punctuation, and metacognitively regulate the entire writing effort. In the next few pages, we examine the development of handwriting, spelling, composition skills, written grammar, and metacognitive processes in writing.

FIGURE 8–4 At age 4, Sam clearly differentiates between drawing and writing.

Development of Handwriting

As early as 18 months of age, many toddlers can hold a pencil or crayon and scribble randomly on paper (McLane & McNamee, 1990); in fact, in the Literacy/Infancy clip of the Observation CD, young Corwin begins to do so even sooner when his mother encourages him. Children's early efforts with pencil and paper are largely exploratory, as they experiment with the kinds of marks they can produce. They "write" by producing scribbles, wavy lines, and pictures; thus, they make little or no distinction between writing and drawing (Graham & Weintraub, 1996; Sulzby, 1986).

With the increasing psychomotor coordination that emerges during the preschool years, children become better able to control their hand movements and can produce recognizable shapes. By age 4, their writing is clearly different from drawing; for instance, it may consist of wavy lines or connected loops that loosely resemble adults' cursive writing (look once again at Figure 8–1). By the time they are 5, children frequently incorporate actual letters and other letterlike forms in the things they write (Graham & Weintraub, 1996). In Figure 8–4, 4-year-old Sam clearly differentiates between writing and drawing, and his writing is almost exclusively letters. Notice how he spells his own name sideways going up the page; this "signature" appears frequently in his work at age 4.

During the elementary school years, children's handwriting gradually becomes smaller, smoother, and more regular (Graham & Weintraub, 1996). In the upper elementary grades, children also develop their own unique handwriting styles (Graham & Weintraub, 1996). As an illustration, contrast the cursive writing samples of Tina, Alex, and Jeff in Figure 8–5.

Little if any improvement in handwriting occurs after elementary school, and for some youngsters handwriting quality actually declines during adolescence (Graham & Weintraub, 1996). Some legibility may be lost because adolescents write more quickly than younger children. In fact, rapid, automatized handwriting (or, as an alternative, automatized keyboarding) is an important factor in effective writing (Graham, Harris, & Fink, 2000; D. Jones & Christensen, 1999).

Tina *All of a sudden the air became cool and the sky was dark. Sue looked at Paul, Paul looked at Sue.*

Alex *Henry delivers newspapers so he doesn't have much time to work on the clubhouse*

Jeff *Have a good Mothers day* *Sincerely* *Jeffrey*

FIGURE 8–5 By the upper elementary grades, children have begun to develop their own unique handwriting styles. Notice the stylistic differences in these three samples of cursive writing, all written by 9-year-olds.

Development of Spelling

As you might guess, phonological awareness is as important in spelling as it is in reading (P. Bryant et al., 1999; Griffith, 1991; Lennox & Siegel, 1998). Benjamin Jones showed phonological awareness when, as a 4-year-old, he spelled *gym* as "JEM," thereby representing both the "juh" and "mm" sounds in the word. As children gain greater familiarity with written English, they also take into account common word endings (e.g., most past tense verbs end in -*ed*) and other common letter patterns as they spell (P. Bryant et al., 1999; Leong, 1998).

Children learn the correct spellings of a few words (such as their names) almost as soon as they learn how to write letters of the alphabet. But they also acquire several general spelling strategies, which typically appear in the following sequence:

1. *Prephonemic spelling.* Beginning writers, including most kindergarten and first graders, often create and use **invented spellings** that may only vaguely resemble actual words. Consider the invented spellings in this kindergartner's creation entitled "My Garden" (note that "HWS" is *house*):

THIS IS A HWS
THE SUN
WL SHIN
ND MI
GRDN
WL GRO (Hemphill & Snow, 1996, p. 192)

Invented spellings typically reflect some but not all of the phonemes in a word; for instance, a child might spell *rabbit* as "RT" (Ferreiro, 1990; Gentry, 1982; Treiman, 1998). Sometimes children use a letter's name for clues about when to use it in a word. As an example, a child might spell *work* as "YRK" because both Y (pronounced "why") and *work* begin with a "wuh" sound (Treiman, 1998).

2. *Phonemic spelling.* As children develop greater phonological awareness, they try to represent all of a word's phonemes in their spelling (Beers, 1980; Frith, 1985; Gentry, 1982). For example, "My Garden" includes phonemic spellings of *shine* ("SHIN") and *grow* ("GRO").

3. *Orthographic spelling.* Eventually (perhaps in first or second grade), children begin to consider conventional spelling patterns (Beers, 1980; P. Bryant et al., 1999; Gentry, 1982). At this point, they use analogies between similar-sounding words—for instance, drawing a parallel between *went* and *sent* or between *nation* and *vacation* (Frith, 1985; Nation & Hulme, 1998). They also apply their increasing knowledge of general spelling rules, such as adding the suffix *-ed* for past tense (P. Bryant et al., 1999). Thus, they spell the past tense of *pour* as "POURED" (or perhaps "PORED") rather than "POURD." Curiously, many children initially apply the *-ed* rule to irregular verbs (e.g., spelling *felt* as "FELED") and sometimes even to nonverbs (e.g., spelling *soft* as "SOFED"), thus showing the *overregularization* phenomenon described in Chapter 7 (P. Bryant et al., 1999).

4. *Automatized spelling.* With increasing practice in reading and writing, children learn how various words are actually spelled and can ultimately retrieve many correct spellings quickly and accurately (Rittle-Johnson & Siegler, 1999). Children differ considerably in the extent to which they automatize spelling. Some have mastered most commonly used words by the time they reach the upper elementary grades; others continue to make numerous spelling errors throughout adolescence and into adulthood.

We caution you not to interpret the preceding sequence as a series of discrete stages in spelling development. Instead, children may use a variety of spelling strategies at any single age, and their use of different strategies over time probably resembles the *overlapping waves* phenomenon described in Chapter 5 (Rittle-Johnson & Siegler, 1999). For instance, 6-year-olds and 12-year-olds may both use a sounding-out procedure for words they don't know and automatic retrieval for words they *do* know, but sounding out is a more frequent strategy at age 6 and retrieval is more common at age 12. The Development and Practice feature "Helping Children and Adolescents Learn Word Spellings" describes several strategies for promoting spelling development.

To write effectively and become credible authors, growing children and adolescents must eventually learn the correct spellings of the words they use frequently. (Alternatively, those who have difficulty with spelling, perhaps because of a learning disability, must learn to make regular use of dictionaries and computer spell-check options.) This is not to say, however, that authentic writing tasks should be postponed until after children have learned to spell the words they want to write. On the contrary, many experts urge educators, care-

invented spelling Children's early, self-constructed word spellings, which may reflect only some of a word's phonemes.

DEVELOPMENT AND PRACTICE

Helping Children and Adolescents Learn Word Spellings

- When engaging young children in authentic writing activities, write a few important words out for them, and give them the correct spellings of any other words they ask for.

  When children at a child care center make valentine cards to take home, the teacher shows the children how *valentine* and *I love you* are spelled.

- Teach common spelling patterns.

  A second-grade teacher asks children to study a list of words that end in an "uff" sound. The list, which includes *puff, muff, stuff, rough, tough,* and *enough,* illustrates two common ways of spelling the sound.

- Teach general spelling rules.

  A fourth-grade teacher teaches his students the rule "*I* before *e* except after *c,* or when pronounced 'ay,' as in *neighbor* and *weigh.*" But he cautions them that the rule is not completely reliable; for example, the words *either* and *height* are exceptions.

- Encourage older children and adolescents to use dictionaries and computer spell checking programs when they are unsure of how words are spelled.

  As middle school students complete articles for the school newspaper, their faculty advisor shows them how to use the spell check function in the word processing software. She explains that a spell checker is not completely trustworthy; for example, it won't identify situations in which *they're* has been incorrectly used in place of *there* or *their.*

- Stress the importance of correct spelling for a writer's credibility.

  A career counselor points out several obvious spelling errors in a story in the local newspaper. He then asks the high school students with whom he is working to reflect on the impressions that such errors convey about the reporter who wrote the story.

givers, and other adults to engage children in authentic writing tasks even when the children must rely largely on invented spellings to get their thoughts on paper (e.g., Clarke, 1988; Treiman, 1993). Ultimately, the development of children's composition skills—not their knowledge of word spellings—lies at the heart of their ability to write effectively.

Development of Composition Skills

When preschool children engage in early writing activities at home, they often do so with a particular purpose in mind, perhaps to write a letter or label a possession. Only when children enter kindergarten or first grade do most of them begin to write for writing's sake.

Children's earliest compositions are usually narratives: Children write about their personal experiences and create short, fictional stories (Hemphill & Snow, 1996). Expository writing—research reports, persuasive and argumentative essays, and so on—emerges considerably later (R. E. Owens, 1996), possibly because teachers typically don't ask for such writing until the upper elementary grades.

The nature and quality of children's and adolescents' writing change in many ways throughout the elementary and secondary school years. Following are four general trends in the development of composition skills:

- *Children increasingly take their audience into account when they write.* In our discussion of language development in the preceding chapter, we mentioned that children become increasingly able to adapt their speech to the characteristics of their listeners. The same is true for writing: With age and experience, children become better able to envision the audience to whom they are writing and tailor their text accordingly (R. T. Kellogg, 1994; Knudson, 1992; Perfetti & McCutchen, 1987).

- *Children and adolescents develop their topics in greater depth as they grow older.* When children of various ages are asked to write about a particular topic, older ones tend to include more ideas than younger ones do (Donovan, 1999; Scardamalia & Bereiter, 1986). Such growth continues throughout the school years; for instance, when writing persuasive essays, high school students include more arguments than elementary and middle school students do, and 12th graders include more arguments than 9th graders (Knudson, 1992; McCann, 1989).

- *With age comes an increasing ability to write a cohesive composition.* In the elementary grades, children use few if any devices to tie their compositions together. For instance, they may write a story by beginning with "Once upon a time," listing a sequence of events that lead only loosely to one another, and then ending with "They lived happily ever after" (McLane & McNamee, 1990). Their nonfiction, too, may be little more than a list of facts or events.

Older children, and especially adolescents, are more capable of analyzing and synthesizing their thoughts when they write, and so they compose more cohesive, integrated texts (McCutchen, 1987; R. E. Owens, 1996; Spivey, 1997). As an example, Spivey (1997) gave 6th, 8th, and 10th graders three texts about rodeos (each written by a different author) and asked them to integrate what they learned into a single written description of rodeos. The younger students tended to write in a disconnected, piecemeal fashion, often borrowing phrases or entire sentences from each of the three texts they had read. In contrast, the older students wrote more integrated discussions of what they had learned from the reading materials and made frequent connections among the ideas they had acquired from each resource.

■ *Especially in adolescence, a knowledge-telling approach gradually evolves into a knowledge-transforming approach.* Young writers often compose a narrative or essay simply by writing ideas down in the order in which they think of them. Such an approach is known as **knowledge telling** (Bereiter & Scardamalia, 1987; McCutchen, 1996). As an example, we refer back to Chapter 5's opening case study. In response to the question *How did the United States become a country?*, one third grader wrote:

> The pilgruns came over in 17 hundreds, when they came over they bilt houses. The Idiuns thout they were mean. Then they came friends, and tot them stuff. Then winter came, and alot died. Then some had babies. So thats how we got here.

With age, experience, and an increasing ability to take the characteristics of potential readers into account, some adolescents (and a few younger children as well) begin to conceptualize writing not as a process of putting ideas on paper but instead as a process of presenting ideas in a way that enables their readers to *understand* the ideas. This approach, known as **knowledge transforming**, is illustrated by an eighth grader's response to the question *How did the United States become a country?* (we've left her spelling errors intact):

> We became a country by way of common sense. The inhabitants on American soil thought it rather silly and ridiculus to be loyal to, follow rules and pay taxes to a ruler who has never seen where they live. King George III had never set foot (as far as I know) on American soil, but he got taxes and other things from those who lived here. When America decied to unit and dishonnor past laws and rules, England got angry. There was a war. When we won, drew up rules, and accepted states America was born.
>
> In a more poetic sense, we became a country because of who lived here and what they did. They actions of heros, heroines, leaders, followers, and everyday people made America famous, an ideal place to live. The different cultures and lifestyles made America unique and unlike any other place in the world. If you think about it, it's like visiting the worlds at Epcot in Florida. You can go from country to country without leaving home. (courtesy of Dinah Jackson)

The analogy between the United States and Disney World's Epcot Center is knowledge transforming at its finest.

One reason for knowledge telling (rather than knowledge transforming) in the early years is that most young children, and many adolescents as well, rarely think ahead about what they are going to write (Berninger, Fuller, & Whitaker, 1996; Pianko, 1979). The limited capacity of working memory may also be a factor: Young writers must consider so many different things (the content, the audience, spelling, grammar, punctuation, handwriting, etc.) when they write that they have little "room" available for thinking creatively about how they can effectively communicate their message (Benton, 1997; Flower & Hayes, 1981; McCutchen, 1996). Adults can free up some of this capacity by suggesting that children address only one aspect of the writing process at a time; for instance, teachers might ask their students to plan and organize their thoughts before they begin writing and ignore the mechanics of writing until after they have written their first draft (K. R. Harris & Graham, 1992; Treiman, 1993). To encourage younger children (e.g., first graders) to focus exclusively on the composition process, teachers might ask them to dictate rather than write their stories (McLane & McNamee, 1990; Scardamalia, Bereiter, & Goelman, 1982).

knowledge telling
Writing down ideas in whatever order they come to mind, with little regard for communicating the ideas effectively.

knowledge transforming
Writing ideas in such a way as to intentionally help the reader understand them.

Adults can also promote knowledge transforming by brainstorming with children about strategies for communicating ideas effectively (e.g., using examples, analogies, graphics, similes, and rhetorical questions) to a particular audience (Chambliss, 1998). Figure 8–6 shows how, as a sixth grader, 11-year-old Charlotte practiced using similes. An additional strategy is to provide examples of how expert writers translate their ideas into a form that readers can easily understand (Byrnes, 1996; Englert, Raphael, Anderson, Anthony, & Stevens, 1991).

Development of Syntax and Grammatical Rules

As children grow older, they use increasingly longer sentences in their writing (Byrnes, 1996). By the time they are 12 or 13, the syntactic structures they use in written work are considerably more complex than those that they use in speech (Gillam & Johnston, 1992). With age, too, comes increasing automatization of punctuation and capitalization rules (Byrnes, 1996).

Providing extensive grammar instruction outside of authentic writing tasks appears to have little effect on the overall quality of students' writing (Berninger et al., 1996; Hillocks, 1989). Nevertheless, a certain amount of systematic instruction in grammatical rules is probably essential. In Western society, we are much fussier about adherence to correct grammar in writing than in speaking. The same errors that are readily forgiven in speech—incomplete sentences, lack of agreement between subjects and verbs, and so on—are often interpreted as signs of carelessness or ignorance when they appear in writing.

Development of Metacognitive Processes in Writing

In addition to developing handwriting, spelling, composition skills, and knowledge of grammatical rules, children and adolescents must also learn how to focus and regulate their writing efforts. They must consider the nature of the audience for whom they are writing. They must determine the goals they want to achieve in a composition and plan their writing accordingly. They must critically evaluate their work, looking not only for grammatical and spelling errors but also for omissions, ambiguities, logical flaws, and contradictions in meaning. Finally, of course, they must revise their writing to address each of the problems they've identified. All of these mental activities are aspects of the *metacognitive* component of writing.

As noted earlier, youngsters become increasingly capable of taking their audience into account as they write. All too often, however, children and adolescents write without giving much thought to who their audience might be, perhaps because the only person who actually reads their work is their teacher (Benton, 1997). They are more likely to write effectively when they are asked to adapt their writing to a particular audience (Burnett & Kastman, 1997; Cameron et al., 1996; Sperling, 1996). For instance, teachers might ask their students to write a letter to children the same age who live in environments very different from their own—perhaps in a large city or in rural farm country (Benton, 1997; Kroll, 1984). Alternatively, teachers might ask students to imagine themselves in particular roles—perhaps as reporters investigating a news story or travelers hoping to spread peace throughout the world (J. J. Schneider, 1998). Children as young as 7 or 8 can adapt their writing to different audiences when they understand who those audiences are (J. J. Schneider, 1998).

Most children and adolescents also have much to learn about *planning* what and how they are going to write: They rarely set goals for a piece of writing or organize their thoughts before they put pencil to paper (Benton, 1997; Berninger et al., 1996; Pianko, 1979). Here, too, teachers can make a difference by encouraging, or even insisting, that students develop a concrete plan and perhaps one or more goals for writing a short story, essay, research paper, or other composition. In one study, for example, seventh and eighth graders who were studying persuasive writing techniques were taught how to set specific goals for themselves (e.g., to include a certain number of reasons in support of their argument, or to address a particular number of counterarguments). Students who received such training wrote longer and qualitatively better essays than students in a control group (Page-Voth & Graham, 1999).

FIGURE 8–6 Teachers and other practitioners can promote children's composition skills by teaching them strategies for effectively communicating ideas. Here 11-year-old Charlotte gives a definition of *simile* and lists several examples at the top of the page. She then practices her new skill in a description of sadness.

DEVELOPMENTAL TRENDS

Writing at Different Age Levels

AGE	WHAT YOU MIGHT OBSERVE	DIVERSITY	IMPLICATIONS
Infancy (Birth–2) 	• Beginnings of eye-hand coordination, with intentional reaching, grabbing, and holding on to objects by 6 months of age • Development of the *pincer grasp,* use of the thumb and forefinger to pick up and hold objects • Appearance of scribbling at 18 to 24 months • Interest in mimicking "writing"; gradual emergence of understanding that some objects are used for writing	• Individual differences appear in the development of fine motor skills. • Infants can imitate only what they see, so those who never see anyone writing are unlikely to mimic writing or understand that some objects are used for writing.	• Allow toddlers to manipulate small objects that do not present choking hazards. • Have a variety of tools available for scribbling and coloring (e.g., fat crayons or washable, non-toxic markers). • Tape writing paper to the table or floor to permit easier writing.
Early Childhood (2–6) 	• Increasing muscular control in writing and drawing • Pseudowriting (e.g., wavy lines, connected loops) in preschool play activities • Ability to write own name (perhaps at age 4) • Ability to write most letters of the alphabet (at age 4 or later) • Invented spellings (at ages 5–6)	• Some children have little if any exposure to written materials at home and so have less knowledge of letters. • Some cultures place greater emphasis on writing than others. • Children who are visually impaired gain less awareness of print conventions (left-to-right progression, use of punctuation, etc.) in pre-literacy activities.	• Make writing implements (pencils, pens, markers, paper) easily available. • Give children opportunities to write their names and a few other meaningful words. • Have children act out stories they have orally composed.

Children often write more effectively when adults suggest a particular structure to follow.

Finally, children of all ages have considerable difficulty identifying problems in their own writing, particularly those related to clarity and cohesiveness (Beal, 1996; Berninger et al., 1996; Fitzgerald, 1987). Many young people, especially those in the elementary grades, have trouble reading their own writing as another person might read it and so believe they are expressing themselves more clearly than they actually are (Bartlett, 1982; Beal, 1996). As a result, they often don't revise their work unless a teacher or other adult specifically urges them to do so; when they do rewrite, they tend to make only small, superficial changes (Beal, 1996; Cameron et al., 1996; Francis & McCutchen, 1994).

Experts have identified several strategies through which adults can help children revise what they've written:

- Schedule time for revising so that children can get assistance as they need it.
- Before youngsters begin rewriting, ask them to list five things they can do to make their writing better.
- Provide questions children should ask themselves as they rewrite (e.g., "Is this confusing?" "Do I need another example here?" "Who am I writing this for?").
- Explicitly teach revision strategies, including adding, deleting, moving, and rewriting text.
- Occasionally have children work in pairs or small groups to help one another revise. (Benton, 1997; Bereiter & Scardamalia, 1987; Cameron et al., 1996; Fitzgerald & Markman, 1987; Graham, MacArthur, & Schwartz, 1995; Graves, 1983; Kish, Zimmer, & Henning, 1994; N. M. Webb & Palincsar, 1996)

As you have seen, writing skills change in numerous ways throughout childhood and adolescence. The Developmental Trends table "Writing at Different Age Levels" summarizes the changes in writing seen during infancy and the preschool, elementary school, and secondary school years.

DEVELOPMENTAL TRENDS

Writing at Different Age Levels *(continued)*

AGE	WHAT YOU MIGHT OBSERVE	DIVERSITY	IMPLICATIONS
Middle Childhood (6–10) 	• Gradual increase in smoothness of handwriting; gradual decrease in handwriting size • Increasing use of letter-sound relationships and common letter patterns in spelling • Predominance of narratives in writing • Difficulty identifying problems (especially problems of clarity) in own writing	• Children who are better readers also tend to be better writers, presumably because general language ability provides a foundation for both reading and writing. • Children with deficits in phonological awareness have a more difficult time learning to spell, especially when their language uses a phonetic alphabet. • Girls show higher achievement in writing and spelling beginning in the elementary years. • Children with dyslexia often have poor handwriting skills.	• Engage children in authentic writing activities (e.g., writing letters, creating a newsletter). • Explore various ways in which particular phonemes and phoneme combinations are spelled in the English language. • Introduce expository forms of writing (e.g., descriptions, lab reports). • Build opportunities for revision into the schedule; provide suggestions about how children can revise and improve their work.
Early Adolescence (10–14) 	• Automatized spelling of most common words • Increasing use of expository forms of writing • Use of longer and more complex syntactic structures • Reluctance to revise unless strongly encouraged to do so	• Some older children and adolescents (e.g., those with learning disabilities) may have exceptional difficulty with spelling and sentence structure.	• When applicable, encourage adolescents to use local dialects in creative writing projects. • Introduce persuasive and argumentative forms of writing. • Give feedback on first drafts, including suggestions on how to improve clarity and cohesiveness. • Indicate a specific audience for whom to write.
Late Adolescence (14–18) 	• Ability to write about a particular topic in depth • More organized and cohesive essays • Increasing tendency to knowledge-transform rather than knowledge-tell • More revisions than at younger ages, but with a focus on superficial rather than substantive problems	• Individuals with learning disabilities may overemphasize the role of mechanics (spelling, grammatical rules, etc.) in the writing process. • Individuals from some cultural backgrounds (e.g., those from some East Asian countries) may be reluctant to put their thoughts on paper unless they are confident that they are correct.	• Assign lengthy writing projects; provide considerable guidance about how to accomplish them effectively. • Teach specific strategies for organizing and synthesizing ideas. • Show examples of effective writing (e.g., writing that knowledge-transforms rather than knowledge-tells). • For those who have language-based learning disabilities, downplay the importance of correct spelling and grammar when evaluating written work; teach strategies for overcoming or compensating for weaknesses.

Sources: Beal, 1996; Berninger et al., 1996; Byrnes, 1996; Cameron et al., 1996; Dickinson et al., 1993; Dien, 1998; Gentry, 1982; Graham & Weintraub, 1996; M. Harris & Hatano, 1999; Hedges & Nowell, 1995; Hemphill & Snow, 1996; R. Kellogg, 1967; MacArthur & Graham, 1987; McLane & McNamee, 1990; Rittle-Johnson & Siegler, 1999; Robin, Berthier, & Clifton, 1996; Rochat & Bullinger, 1994; Rochat & Goubet, 1995; Shanahan & Tierney, 1990; Smitherman, 1994; Spivey, 1997; Trawick-Smith, 2003; Turnbull et al., 2002; Yaden & Templeton, 1986.

General Strategies for Promoting Writing Development

Theorists and practitioners have offered several suggestions for promoting children's and adolescents' writing development:

■ *Provide tools for drawing and writing as soon as children are old enough to use them.* Quite early in life, children can begin to explore—and thereby discover what they can do with—painting, drawing, and writing implements (e.g., see Figure 8–7; also see Figure 3–12 on p. 110). As fine motor skills, cognitive abilities, and knowledge of symbols continue to improve during the preschool years, children will increasingly be able to produce recognizable shapes and letters. The Environments/Early Childhood clip of the Observation CD shows an area of a preschool classroom equipped with numerous drawing and writing implements.

Observe a preschool drawing and writing center in the Environments/Early Childhood clip of the Observation CD.

FIGURE 8-7 Once infants are old enough to sit up on their own, they can begin to explore the properties of paper and paint, as 5-month-old Lauryn did in this early finger painting. Such activities should be closely supervised, of course, and only nontoxic substances used.

Observe students' preference for self-chosen writing topics in the Middle Childhood, Early Adolescence, and Late Adolescence clips of the Literacy module of the Observation CD.

■ *Present authentic writing tasks.* By presenting authentic, personally meaningful writing tasks—writing letters to relatives, e-mail messages to people in distant locations, short stories for classmates, editorials for the local newspaper, and so on—teachers, caregivers, and other adults can encourage children to consider the language abilities and prior knowledge of their audience (Benton, 1997; Hiebert & Fisher, 1992; Sugar & Bonk, 1998). Such tasks can also prompt children to set specific goals for writing and to acquire the writing skills they need to achieve those goals.

■ *Offer choices about writing topics.* Young people write more frequently, and in a more organized and cohesive fashion, when they are interested in their topic (Benton, 1997; Garner, 1998). For instance, one high school English teacher, who noticed that several very capable students were failing his class because they weren't completing assigned writing tasks, began having his students write about their personal experiences and share them on the Internet with students in other classrooms; the teacher monitored their compositions for vulgar language but imposed no other restrictions. The students suddenly began writing regularly, presumably because they could write for a real audience and could now choose what they wrote about (Garner, 1998). In the Middle Childhood, Early Adolescence, and Late Adolescence clips of the Literacy module of the Observation CD, Daniel, Brendan, and Alicia all mention that they like to choose their writing topics. Daniel responds this way to the interviewer's question "Do you like to write?":

> Sort of. . . . It depends on the kind of story and writing. I mean, I don't want it to be, like, an assignment that the teacher tells me to do, like a certain type of story she wants me to write. I want it to be from my ideas.

■ *Scaffold the complex processes involved in writing.* When children and adolescents initially engage in a particular genre of writing (e.g., creating a summary, writing a persuasive essay), they often benefit from having an explicit structure to follow as they write (Ferretti, MacArthur, & Dowdy, 2000; R. T. Kellogg, 1994; MacArthur & Ferretti, 1997). Later, adults can provide *prompts,* short written reminders that help youngsters think about a writing task in the ways that experts do (Englert et al., 1991; Graham & Harris, 1992; Kish et al., 1994). For example, Scardamalia and Bereiter (1985) have used prompts such as the following to help young writers think more like experts when they write:

> "My main point . . . "
> "An example of this . . . "
> "The reason I think so . . . "
> "To liven this up, I'll . . . "
> "I can tie this together by . . . "

Scaffolding in self-evaluation and revision processes may also be helpful (De La Paz, Swanson, & Graham, 1998; McCormick, Busching, & Potter, 1992; Sitko, 1998). In a study by De La Paz, Swanson, & Graham (1998), eighth graders with a history of writing difficulties were given a series of questions to consider as they evaluated and revised a persuasive essay. The first questions asked students to focus on the overall essay and determine whether it presented sufficient ideas to make its case, organized ideas logically, and addressed obvious counterarguments that a reader might make. Later questions encouraged students to focus on individual paragraphs and sentences, looking for places where ideas were incomplete, unclear, or misrepresented. Students who learned and used the series of questions revised their work more frequently and effectively and improved the overall quality of their writing (De La Paz et al., 1998).

■ *Encourage an initial focus on communicating a message clearly; postpone attention to writing mechanics until final drafts.* Unfortunately, the feedback that classroom teachers give students about their writing often focuses more on spelling, grammar, and punctuation than on matters of style, clarity, and cohesiveness (Byrnes, 1996; Covill, 1997), and such feedback may unintentionally give students the message that writing mechanics are the most important ingredient in good writing. Instead, we urge teachers to focus their initial feedback on the overall quality of students' writing and to delay feedback about mechanical errors until relatively late in the game, perhaps as students are polishing up their final drafts.

■ *Use peer groups to promote effective writing skills.* When children and adolescents collaborate on writing projects, they produce longer and more complex texts, revise more, and enhance one another's writing skills (Sperling, 1996; M. N. Webb & Palincsar, 1996). Adults can also ask youngsters to read and respond to one another's work; in the process, youngsters may become better able to examine their own writing from the perspective of potential readers (Benton, 1997; Cameron et al., 1996; Sperling, 1996).

■ *Encourage use of word processing programs.* Word processing programs encourage young writers to revise; after all, it is much easier to change words and move sentences when one is working on a computer rather than on paper (Cochran-Smith, 1991; R. T. Kellogg, 1994). Word processing may also lessen working memory load by taking over some of the mechanical aspects of writing (e.g., checking spelling), thus allowing children to concentrate on the overall quality of writing (I. Jones & Pellegrini, 1996; Sitko, 1998). As an illustration, consider what the same first grader wrote by hand and by computer (I. Jones & Pellegrini, 1996):

By hand:

Some busy wut to play boll But thay cnat play Boll Be cus the Big Busys and the grul wit to tale on them (p. 711)

By computer:

The man cooks some soup and he cooks carrots in the soup and the king gives the man a big hat, and the man goes to the house and the man shows the hat cap to the children. (p. 711)

■ *Include writing assignments in all areas of the curriculum.* Writing shouldn't be a skill that only elementary teachers and secondary English teachers teach. In fact, writing takes different forms in different disciplines; for instance, writing fiction is very different from writing a science laboratory report, which in turn is very different from writing an analysis of historical documents. Ideally, all teachers should teach writing to some degree, and especially at the secondary level, they should teach the writing skills specific to their own academic disciplines (Burnett & Kastman, 1997; Sperling, 1996).

Developing Literacy in a Second Language

To some extent, children can apply the reading and writing skills they've learned in one language to literacy tasks in a second language (Comeau, Cormier, Grandmaison, & Lacroix, 1999; Krashen, 1996; Pérez, 1998). Children's knowledge of letter-sound relationships in English certainly facilitates their reading and writing in other languages that use the same alphabet and represent many sounds in the same way. In addition, the strategies children use for deriving meaning from texts written in one language are often equally applicable to texts in another language (García, Jiménez, & Pearson, 1998).

Yet certain aspects of literacy may be somewhat language-specific (Pérez, 1998). Not all languages use the same left-to-right, top-to-bottom directions that many Western languages do. For instance, writing in most Semitic languages (e.g., Hebrew, Arabic) goes from right to left, and Chinese characters are written in vertical, top-to-bottom columns that begin on the right side of the page and proceed leftward. Word spellings in Semitic languages represent some but not all vowel sounds (e.g., soft "uh" sounds are often omitted), so children raised in Semitic countries may have to fine-tune their phonological awareness to read and spell in English.

When children first learn to read and write a second language, they may sometimes get the two languages confused, and their knowledge of one language may lead them to misinterpret what they read in the other language (García et al., 1998). But being able to read and write *well* in two languages—**biliteracy**—has definite advantages. One benefit, of

Young writers can more effectively revise their writing when they collaborate on a writing project and when they have access to a word processing program.

biliteracy
Ability to read and write well in two languages.

course, is that children can communicate with diverse linguistic groups on paper as well as in speech. Second, when the two languages have similar roots, children can use their knowledge of words in one language to speculate about the likely meaning of words in the other (García et al., 1998). A third advantage is that children acquire greater metalinguistic awareness—for instance, understanding that writing symbols are arbitrary in nature and that similar strategies are applicable in comprehending text in any language (García et al., 1998). Finally, biliteracy can be a source of pride for children and in some instances is an important part of their identities (Jiménez, 2000).

Adults should never assume that when children are learning English as a second language, literacy will follow quickly or easily. Particularly if children have been raised in a culture that depends less heavily on reading and writing than mainstream Western culture does, their literacy skills—perhaps even their knowledge of the potential value and uses of reading and writing—may take several years and considerable experience and guidance to develop (Pérez, 1998).

Diversity in Literacy Development

We often see differences in children's literacy development as a function of their gender, socioeconomic status, and ethnicity. We also see differences in literacy development across languages.

Gender Differences

On average, girls read, write, and spell somewhat better than boys (Feingold, 1993; Hedges & Nowell, 1995). Girls are also more confident than boys about their writing abilities, even when no differences in the actual writing performance of the two groups exist (Pajares & Valiante, 1999). At the high school level, girls are more likely than boys to enroll in advanced language and literature classes (Wigfield, Eccles, & Pintrich, 1996). Reasons for such differences have not been actively explored, but we suspect that they are at least partly the result of girls' slightly higher verbal abilities during the school years (see Chapter 6).

Socioeconomic Differences

In general, children from lower-income families come to school with fewer literacy skills than children from middle- and upper-income families; the difference not only persists, but in fact *increases*, over the course of the elementary and secondary school years (Chall, 1996; Jimerson, Egeland, & Teo, 1999; Portes, 1996). Thus, as children from low-income families get older, they fall further and further behind their more economically advantaged peers in reading and writing. To some extent, these socioeconomic differences occur because, on average, children from lower-income families have less access to reading materials (fewer books and magazines, fewer trips to the library, etc.) than children from middle-income families. As children reach the upper elementary grades, their more limited opportunities for enriching educational experiences (travel, trips to zoos and museums, etc.) and less extensive vocabularies may also play a role (recall our earlier discussion of the *fourth-grade slump*).

Socioeconomic status is also a predictor of immigrant children's ability to develop literacy in English as a second language, probably for several reasons: Children from middle- and upper-income immigrant families typically have a more solid foundation in reading and writing in their native language, greater access to printed materials in English, and parents and other caregivers who can help them with their schoolwork (Krashen, 1996).

This is not to say that all children from low-income backgrounds are at a disadvantage. As the opening case study illustrates, many low-income parents are fully aware of the importance of reading and writing and so read to their children regularly and in other ways foster literacy development (Jimerson et al, 1999; McLane & McNamee, 1990). Yet many others have little knowledge of how to promote literacy through home reading activities and often benefit from explicit instruction in the story-reading skills described earlier in the chapter.

Ethnic Differences

Ethnic and cultural groups differ considerably in their emphasis on engaging young children in reading activities. Some African American groups focus more on oral storytelling than on book reading (Trawick-Smith, 2003). Some Native American communities stress art, dance, and oral histories that carry on the group's cultural traditions (Trawick-Smith, 2003). Immigrant Hispanic parents often place higher priority on promoting their children's moral development (e.g., teaching them right from wrong) than early literacy skills (Gallimore & Goldenberg, 2001).

Even when children have been regularly immersed in books and writing implements, their cultural backgrounds influence their interpretations of what they read (recall our discussion of *schemas* and *scripts* in Chapter 5). As an example, Rosenna Bakari, a colleague of ours who specializes in African-centered education, describes an incident involving her 7-year-old daughter Nailah:

> [An event] that always stands out in my mind is a reading comprehension question that Nailah had in a workbook. The question asked why two brothers drew a line down the middle of a messy room to clean it. The answer was pretty obvious: The boys were dividing the room in half so that they could each clean their part. However, Nailah could not get to that answer no matter how I scaffolded her. When I told her the answer, she replied, "Why would they divide the room up? They should just both clean it together." I immediately realized that in her African-centered world, division rarely takes place. Most things in our house are communal. Each child is responsible for the other. So for her to get to that answer would have taken something beyond reasonable reading comprehension. She would have had to understand that there are people in the world who operate under different views about sharing and responsibility. That's a more difficult task for a seven-year-old. (R. Bakari, personal communication, 2002)

Writing practices also differ from one group to another. For instance, Vietnamese children may be reluctant to commit their ideas to paper unless they are confident that their ideas are correct and will not be misinterpreted (Dien, 1998). The Yup'ik peoples of northern North America frequently engage in *storyknifing*, whereby they carve symbols and pictures in the mud while simultaneously telling tales about the family's or community's history (deMarrais, Nelson, & Baker, 1994).

People from most ethnic groups in Western society value literacy and see it as essential for children's eventual success in the adult world (Gallimore & Goldenberg, 2001; Pérez, 1998). Educators must be sensitive to what children's early language and literacy experiences have been and use them as the foundation for instruction in reading and writing. For example, reading instruction is more effective for native Hawaiian children when they can engage in *overlapping talk* (in which they frequently interrupt one another) as they discuss the stories they are reading; such a conversational style is consistent with their speaking practices at home (K. H. Au & Mason, 1981). African American children who use African American English at home and with friends write more imaginative narratives when they incorporate this dialect into their writing at school (Smitherman, 1994). And children and adolescents from all backgrounds will respond more favorably to literature and textbooks that reflect their own culture's ways of living and thinking (Gollnick & Chinn, 2002).

Cross-Linguistic Differences

Languages differ considerably in the extent to which spelling accurately captures how words are pronounced. Spanish, Portuguese, Italian, German, and Finnish have highly regular and predictable spelling patterns, such that a word's spelling usually tells a reader exactly how the word is pronounced and its pronunciation tells a writer exactly how it is spelled. English, French, and Greek are less regular, in that some sounds can be represented by two or more different letters or letter combinations. Some languages do not use an alphabet at all, so that predictable relationships between the forms of spoken and written language are few and far between. For instance, Chinese and Japanese are written as *characters* that represent entire syllables rather than individual phonemes.[6]

The more regular and predictable a language's letter-sound relationships are, the more easily children learn to read and spell; for instance, Italian and German children learn to read more quickly and easily than English-speaking children do (M. Harris & Hatano, 1999). In highly regular languages, knowledge of letter-sound correspondences may be all that children need to decode and spell words accurately. In less regular languages, such as English and French, knowledge of common spelling patterns plays an important role as well (M. Harris & Hatano, 1999). In nonalphabetic languages such as Chinese, children may learn a few words because they resemble the objects or events they represent (e.g., the Chinese word for *ascend* or *on top of* is written 上, the word for *descend* or *below* is written 下), but they probably learn most simply through repeated exposure and practice.

Curiously, phonological awareness seems to be an important factor in reading even in nonalphabetic languages (McBride-Chang & Ho, 2000; Ziegler, Tan, Perry, & Montant, 2000). The underlying cause of this relationship has not been pinned down, but it may in some way be related to the fact that when people read, they mentally retrieve how the words are pronounced as one way of determining the meanings of words on the page (Rayner et al., 2001; Ziegler et al., 2000).

Exceptionalities in Reading and Writing Development

To some extent, development of literacy skills goes hand in hand with overall intellectual development. Many (but not all) children who are later identified as intellectually gifted begin to read earlier than their peers, and some read frequently and voraciously (Piirto, 1999; Turnbull et al., 2002). Children with mental retardation learn to read more slowly than their age-mates, and they acquire fewer effective reading strategies. In some instances, they may develop excellent word decoding skills yet understand little or nothing of what they read (Cossu, 1999). Writing development, too, is correlated with general measures of intelligence. Some children who are gifted exhibit extraordinary writing talent, and most children with mental retardation show general delays in their writing skills.

Children with visual or hearing impairments may also be at a disadvantage when learning to read and write. To the extent that their general language development is delayed (see Chapter 7), reading and writing will certainly be affected. In addition, children who are visually impaired cannot see the printed page when caregivers read to them in the early years, and so they know less about the conventions of written language (the left-to-right progression of words, the use of punctuation, etc.) when they begin school (Tompkins & McGee, 1986). Children with hearing impairments who have learned a manual language (e.g., American Sign Language) rather than spoken language cannot take advantage of letter-sound relationships when they learn to read and spell, and they may have limited knowledge of the idioms and other irregularities of day-to-day speech (Andrews & Mason, 1986; Chall, 1996). Although some of these children may have some phonological knowledge (Alegria, 1998), they nevertheless face a greater challenge than hearing children when, in the process of learning to read and write, they must make connections between the words they use in conversation and the forms that those words take in written language. Often, graduating high school students who are deaf read only at a fourth- or fifth-grade level (Chall, 1996).

General intellectual development and sensory disabilities do not account for all the exceptionalities observed in reading and writing development. Here we look briefly at dyslexia and writing disabilities.

---

[6] Children in China, Taiwan, and Japan are often taught one or more alphabetic, phonetic systems for representing their language in writing before they are taught more traditional characters, and such training increases their phonological awareness (e.g., Hanley, Tzeng, & Huang, 1999).

Dyslexia

Some children with learning disabilities have considerable difficulty learning to read; they may have trouble recognizing printed words or have little comprehension of what they read. In their extreme form, such difficulties are known as **dyslexia**. Many theorists believe that dyslexia has biological roots; for instance, some people with dyslexia show abnormalities in parts of the brain that handle visual information (Galaburda & Rosen, 2001). Other theorists propose that some instances of dyslexia may simply reflect the lower end of a normal distribution of specific cognitive abilities (Shaywitz, Escobar, Shaywitz, Fletcher, & Makuch, 1992).

Contrary to popular belief, dyslexia is typically *not* a problem of visual perception, such as reading words or letters backwards (Stanovich, 2000). Instead, most children with reading disabilities have deficits in phonological awareness (Chiappe & Siegel, 1999; Hulme & Joshi, 1998; Morris et al., 1998; Stanovich, 2000; Swanson, Mink, & Bocian, 1999). Others appear to have deficits in the ability to identify visual stimuli quickly; in reading, such deficits translate into difficulty automatizing connections between printed words and their meanings (Stanovich, 2000; Wimmer, Mayringer, & Landerl, 2000; Wolf & Bowers, 1999). Some children with reading disabilities may also have general information processing difficulties, such as a smaller working memory capacity or a tendency to process information at a slower-than-average rate (Wimmer, Landerl, & Frith, 1999; Wolf & Bowers, 1999).

Writing Disabilities

Some children with learning disabilities have problems in handwriting, spelling, or expressing themselves coherently on paper; for instance, children with **dysgraphia** have exceptional difficulty with handwriting. Children with writing disabilities typically focus their writing efforts on addressing mechanical issues (spelling, grammar, etc.), and their ability to communicate effectively in their writing suffers as a result (Graham, Schwartz, & MacArthur, 1993). The quality of their writing improves considerably when the mechanical aspects of writing are minimized (e.g., when they can dictate their stories and other compositions) and when they are given a specific series of steps to follow as they write (Hallenbeck, 1996; MacArthur & Graham, 1987; Sawyer, Graham, & Harris, 1992).

Reading disabilities and writing disabilities are frequently found together. Curiously, however, some children can write words quite accurately yet cannot read the very same words. Cossu (1999) has described several children in Italy who could spell with almost 100% accuracy yet were completely unable to read. On one occasion, a 9-year-old girl correctly wrote a list of 30 two-syllable words but then, when asked to read them immediately afterward, misread every one. For instance, she read *riva* (shore) as *ruota* (wheel), *naso* (nose) as *ago* (needle), and *rospo* (toad) as *fiore* (flower). Apparently, she relied strictly on letter-sound correspondences to spell the words (Italian is a phonetically regular and predictable language) but then could not take advantage of those correspondences to convert printed letters back into speech.

Helping Children and Adolescents with Reading and Writing Disabilities

Ideally, youngsters with reading and writing disabilities receive assistance in reading and writing from specialists who have been trained to address their unique needs. Nonetheless, most of them attend general education classrooms for most or all of the school day, and they participate in the extracurricular activities (sports, scout troops, etc.) typical for their age group. In such contexts, they often encounter reading and writing tasks that their peers have little trouble with and invariably find themselves coming up short. Tom, a second grader, describes how he felt when trying to learn how to read in first grade:

> I falt like a losr. Like nobad likde me. I was afrad then kais wod tec me. Becacz I wased larning wale . . . I dan not whet to raed. I whoe whte to troe a book it my mom.
> (*I felt like a loser. Like nobody liked me. I was afraid that kids would tease me. Because I wasn't learning well . . . I did not want to read. I would want to throw a book at my mom.*)
> (N. F. Knapp, 1995, p. 9)

dyslexia
Inability to master basic reading skills in a developmentally typical time frame.

dysgraphia
Exceptional difficulty acquiring handwriting skills.

Following are several strategies that classroom teachers and other practitioners may find helpful in working with children and adolescents who have difficulties in reading and writing:

■ *Identify and address reading and writing problems as early as possible.* If children initially struggle with literacy tasks, they engage in such tasks as little as possible and so limit their opportunities for practice, improvement, and automatization of basic skills. As a result, the gap between them and their peers widens over time (Stanovich, 2000).[7] To minimize the damage, then, children should make up their deficits early in the game, ideally in first grade if not earlier (e.g., Cunningham & Stanovich, 1997; Morris, Tyner, & Perney, 2000).

The typical criterion for identifying children with disabilities in reading or writing is a significant discrepancy between general intelligence level (e.g., as indicated by an IQ score) and performance on reading or writing tasks. Unfortunately, appreciable discrepancies may not appear until the upper elementary grades, at which point the children are so far behind their peers that it is virtually impossible to catch up (M. S. Meyer, 2000; Reschly, 1997). Furthermore, to the extent that reading contributes to world knowledge, which in turn affects performance on many intelligence tests (see Chapter 6), then large discrepancies between reading and IQ may never appear (M. S. Meyer, 2000).

We urge teachers and other practitioners who work with children in the early elementary grades to be on the lookout for signs of reading or writing disabilities. Perhaps the most telling sign will be considerable difficulty in learning letter-sound relationships and applying them effectively in reading and writing tasks. In Figure 8–8, we present a writing sample that suggests a need for extra assistance in acquiring phonological awareness.

■ *Provide explicit and intensive training in basic skills.* Although many children learn to read and write quite effectively in whole-language classrooms, children with reading and writing disabilities rarely do so. Instead, children with reading and writing difficulties benefit from deliberate and intensive training in letter recognition, phonological awareness, word identification strategies, and handwriting fluency (Graham, Harris, & Fink, 2000; Lovett et al., 2000; W. Schneider et al., 2000; Stanovich, 2000).

■ *Provide technological scaffolding.* Numerous computer programs are available to facilitate reading and writing. For example, some reading software provides assistance when children encounter words that they can't decode and identify; when a child touches an unknown word with a light pen or clicks on it with a mouse, the computer reads the word for the child. And most word processing programs provide assistance with spelling and grammar.

Ideally, children and adolescents at all grade levels should have whatever scaffolding they need to succeed at reading and writing tasks. Success is far and away the most effective motivator for encouraging young people to develop their literacy skills.

FIGURE 8–8 This writing sample suggests that 7-year-old Nathan has difficulty identifying each sound he hears in speech, as his writing omits some sounds and misrepresents others. His teacher translated what he wrote: "I drew this pumpkin" and "A bat."

Reading and Writing as Facilitators of Cognitive Development

Reading and writing are, of course, valuable in their own right. But in addition, reading and writing activities can promote cognitive development more generally. When children and adolescents read regularly, they add to the knowledge base that is so important for helping them interpret and respond to new experiences effectively. Reading also exposes young people to more sophisticated vocabulary than they typically encounter while conversing with others or watching television (Stanovich, 2000).

Writing, too, promotes learning and cognition. For instance, writing about a particular topic enhances learners' understanding of the topic (Benton, 1997; Klein, 1999; Konopak, Martin, & Martin, 1990). In addition, various kinds of writing activities may encourage learners to engage in and thereby further develop specific cognitive skills, including organization, elaboration, analysis, and critical thinking (Baron, 1987; Greene & Ackerman, 1995; R. T. Kellogg, 1994). By assigning writing activities in all areas of the school curriculum—in science, mathematics, social studies, and so on, as well as in language arts—and in

---

[7] In reading, this phenomenon is sometimes called the *Matthew effect* (Stanovich, 1986).

activities outside of school as well, teachers and others who work with children and adolescents promote development in specific content domains as well as in writing per se.

Our society has a significantly higher literacy rate than it did 50 or 100 years ago (Chall, 1996). Yet even today, many children and adolescents—perhaps because of inherited disabilities or perhaps because of insufficient opportunities and instruction—do not have the reading and writing skills they need to learn effectively in school or to participate fully in adult society. Researchers and practitioners are making great strides in discovering how best to promote literacy development in people of all ages. The final case study illustrates one possible approach.

CASE STUDY: THE TEXAS TUTORING PROGRAM

A group of college students with poor reading skills (their comprehension skills are, on average, similar to those of a typical ninth grader) are tutoring first and second graders who are struggling with reading. The college students meet with their young partners in 45-minute sessions twice a week. They also meet one evening a week to discuss how literacy develops and exchange ideas about possible tutoring activities. At the end of the school year, the college students are reading better than a control group who have attended a regular developmental reading course at the same college, and the first and second graders in the tutoring program are reading better than their untutored classmates (Juel, 1998).

A researcher has videotaped the tutoring sessions. When she analyzes the tapes, she finds several qualities that characterize the most effective tutors. For one thing, they model and scaffold basic reading skills, as the following dialogue illustrates:[8]

Tutor:	So whenever you see those two letters together, it sounds like "aaaaattt, aaaaaatttt." So what is that?
Child:	"Aaaaattt."
Tutor:	Right, so what word is that?
Child:	At.
Tutor:	Right. So you've got the "at." Let's put a sound on the front of it, okay? What's one of your favorite sounds? I know, it's "ssss."
Child:	"S."
Tutor:	Right. (Puts the letter *s* in front of *at*.) So you go, "ssss"—"at," and put them together. What have you got? You see? You see how that works? "Ssss" plus "at" gives you "sat." What about "m" plus "at"? What does that give you? (Replaces the letter *s* with *m*.)
Child:	"m."
Tutor:	And what is the other part?
Child:	"At."
Tutor:	Put them together. What do you get? You got the "at." You got the "mmmmm" sound. You put them together and what do you get? "Mmmmmaaaaaaat."
Child:	Mat.
Tutor:	Good. (Replaces *m* with *f*.) So you got "f" and "at." Gives you what?
Child:	(Laughs.) Fat.
Tutor:	Right. They come together. You have this word "fffffaaaat." Fat. What do you hear when you say that word *fat*?
Child:	"Ffff."
Tutor:	Right. And the last two?
Child:	"At."
Tutor:	Right. All we did was change the letters, and you change the sound. (Puts up appropriate letters.) "At," then "sssat," then "mmmat," "fat." See? What about "b" plus the "at"?
Child:	Buh. Bat.
Tutor:	Right. You got it. (Juel, 1998, pp. 461–462)

---

[8] Excerpts from "What Kind of One-on-One Tutoring Helps a Poor Reader?" by C. Juel. In *Reading and Spelling: Development and Disorders*, by C. Hulme & R. M. Joshi (Eds.), 1998, Mahwah, NJ: Erlbaum. Reprinted with permission.

Effective tutors also develop supportive, affectionate relationships with their partners and continually point out that the youngsters are making progress. The following exchange is a typical example:

Tutor: Hum, so your teacher tells me that you be reading a lot. Is that true? Can you tell? Can you see the improvement in yourself?

Child: Yeah.

Tutor: How? How can you see that you've improved? Do you read faster now? Can you sound out words a little bit better than you did before?

Child: I can sound out words.

Tutor: I mean you just spelled *tape*. It wasn't up on the board and you could spell it. You spelled it in your head. That's the hardest way to spell things. So that's improvement right there. You could do it without looking. You know all your sounds now . . . so, you're getting better and better every day. Have you been practicing? (Child nods.) See, that's why you're getting better and faster. The more you practice the faster you get. (Juel, 1998, p. 459)

The researcher speculates that because the college students themselves have had difficulty learning to read, they are more aware of specific strategies that their partners can use. One tutor explains it this way:

I had a lot of difficulty in school. My parents were told I was learning disabled. I carry this with me to this day. I found early on that I could learn okay, but usually not in the classroom. I learned early on that my best teachers were my peers, the ones who had just been through the same stuff. They could always explain things better to me than anyone else. I even find this to be true in college. (Juel, 1998, p. 463)

Now go to our Companion Website to assess your understanding of chapter content with a Practice Quiz, apply what you've learned in Essay Questions, and broaden your knowledge with links to related Developmental Psychology Web sites. Go to www.prenhall.com/mcdevitt.

- In this situation, elementary school children who are poor readers benefit from working with older students who are also poor readers. Might children benefit just as much from being tutored by children their own age who are good readers? Why or why not?
- The tutors themselves have improved their reading skills, more so than students who have taken a remedial college reading course. How might you explain this finding?
- The Texas Tutoring Program uses college students as tutors. Might low-reading high school students also be effective tutors in such a program? Why or why not?

SUMMARY

Theories of Literacy Development

Information processing theorists propose that reading and writing involve the same mechanisms (attention, working memory, metacognitive strategies, etc.) that are involved in cognition more generally. Whole-language theorists draw parallels between literacy development and oral language development and suggest that children learn to read and write most effectively within the context of authentic literacy activities. Sociocultural theorists apply Vygotsky's ideas to the development of reading and writing and so emphasize culture-specific literacy practices, the importance of conversations with adults, and the gradual internalization of such practices and conversations. The three theoretical perspectives sometimes yield different implications about how children can most effectively learn to read and write.

Early Literacy

When toddlers and preschoolers have multiple and varied experiences with reading and writing materials and activities, they learn a great deal about the nature of written language; for instance, they learn that spoken language is represented in a consistent fashion in written language and that different kinds of printed materials serve different purposes. Such knowledge, known as *emergent literacy*, provides an important foundation for the reading and writing skills that children acquire once they begin school.

Reading Development

Skilled reading involves knowing letter-sound correspondences, recognizing individual letters and entire words quickly and automatically, using context clues to facilitate decoding, constructing meaning from the words on the page, and metacognitively regulating the reading process. Phonological awareness (hearing the distinct sounds within spoken words), word decoding skills, and the automatic recognition of many common words typically develop in the early and middle elementary school years. Reading comprehension and metacognitive strategies continue to develop throughout childhood and adolescence. Strategies for fostering reading development include teaching parents strategies for effective storybook reading, promoting children's phonological awareness, providing many opportunities to read authentic literature, and engaging children and adolescents in discussions about what they read.

Writing Development

To become skillful writers, children and adolescents must not only master handwriting and spelling but must also discover how to communicate their thoughts clearly; learn conventions of capitalization, punctuation, and syntax; and metacognitively regulate the entire writing effort. Handwriting is usually mastered in the elementary grades, but other aspects of writing continue to develop throughout the school years. Educators can promote writing development by asking youngsters to clarify their goals for writing and the audience for whom they are writing, organize their thoughts before they begin to write, and focus more on clear communication than on writing mechanics in early drafts. Teachers and other practitioners should assign authentic writing tasks in all areas of the curriculum, scaffold youngsters' initial efforts in various genres of writing, and provide sufficient criteria and feedback to guide youngsters as they revise their written work.

Literacy in a Second Language

To some extent, children can apply the reading and writing skills they've learned in one language to literacy tasks in a second language as well. However, certain aspects of literacy (e.g., the particular sounds that letters represent or the direction in which writing proceeds) may be somewhat language-specific.

Diversity and Exceptionalities in Reading and Writing

On average, girls read and write slightly better than boys, and children from middle- and upper-income families have better developed literacy skills than children from lower-income families. Different ethnic groups place greater or less emphasis on literacy activities, and young children's preliteracy knowledge and skills may vary accordingly. Children who speak languages with phonetically regular and predictable spelling patterns (e.g., Italian or German) learn to read and spell more easily than children who speak less regular languages.

Some children who are intellectually gifted have superior reading and writing skills; children with mental retardation typically show delays in reading and writing. Children with visual or hearing impairments may show delays as well, due either to little familiarity with the conventions of written language (in the case of visual impairments) or less ability to capitalize on letter-sound relationships (in the case of hearing impairments). Yet some children have reading or writing disabilities despite average or above average intelligence and normal vision and hearing; such disabilities should be identified and addressed as early as possible, ideally no later than first grade.

Reading and Writing as Facilitators of Cognitive Development

Reading and writing development can promote cognitive development more generally. When children and adolescents read regularly, they add to the knowledge base (including knowledge of vocabulary) that helps them interpret and respond to their experiences. Various writing activities encourage youngsters to develop such cognitive skills as elaboration, analysis, and critical thinking.

KEY CONCEPTS

whole-language perspective (p. 325)
emergent literacy (p. 328)
phonological awareness (p. 329)

word decoding (p. 332)
sight vocabulary (p. 332)
story schema (p. 333)
fourth-grade slump (p. 336)
reciprocal teaching (p. 339)

invented spelling (p. 346)
knowledge telling (p. 348)
knowledge transforming (p. 348)

biliteracy (p. 353)
dyslexia (p. 357)
dysgraphia (p. 357)

CHAPTER 9

The airplane is flying and it is almost about to crash.

Isabelle, age 4

September 11, 2001

Dear President Bush,

You know what happend today? About those terrorists? Well, I want them to stop just as much as you do. I mean, it is pretty scary. But what I want to know is what we can do. And don't ask me what you should do. Your the président, anyway.

Sincerly,

Samuel

Samuel, age 10

I thought, "How could this happen?" . . . At first I didn't quite understand how, or why, or what. I was scared. I was in awe. I couldn't believe that something this big, this terrible had happened in our wonderful country. . . . I feel so bad for all the people involved with this, and all the children in New York who don't know about their parents. . . . The pictures on the news were awful. Horrifying? Amazing? I don't know. . . . I almost cried. I knew I believed it when I got a really bad feeling in my stomach. . . . I am not sure why, but for some reason I felt a special closeness to all my classmates at the time, and I hope that this event will not destroy us, but bring us together.

Sarah, age 14

Eric, age 17

Personal and Emotional Development

CASE STUDY: MARY

In 1954, Dr. Emmy Werner and her colleagues began a longitudinal study of children born on the island of Kauai, Hawaii. Children in the study faced numerous problems in their early years: They lived in poverty, had parents with mental health problems, received inadequate care, and so on. Despite exposure to numerous risk factors, the majority of these children developed no serious learning or behavior problems during childhood or adolescence.

Mary was one of these resilient children. Her father was a plantation laborer with only 4 years of formal education. Her mother was seriously overweight and had suffered from a variety of medical problems while pregnant with Mary. Nevertheless, Mary's parents were happy about her birth and gave her good care as a baby.

At 12 months of age, Mary was described as "easy to deal with," "very active," and a "healthy, alert child who is apparently given much attention." At 22 months, she was an "active, cheerful, energetic, and determined child who showed independence, perseverance, and feminine characteristics, but who also seemed somewhat excitable, distractible, and nervous" (E. E. Werner & Smith, 1982, p. 141).

As Mary entered middle childhood, her family environment deteriorated. Her mother had mood swings, suffered from several major illnesses, and was hospitalized twice for emotional disturbance. Mary, too, had her troubles. Her mother reported that, at age 10, Mary had "crying spells and headaches, temper tantrums, and stubborn, contrary behavior" (E. E. Werner & Smith, 1982, p. 142).

Later, Mary showed some understanding of her mother's behavior. She saw her as:

> . . . very grumpy—well, she's going through change of life early—every little thing bothers her. She's lonely. My father leaves her a lot and we have our own life. When they're that age, they do get lonely. . . . I used to be blamed for every little thing that my sister did when my parents went out, and when my father went to work, my mother used to hit me and beat me. That's how come I'm not very close to my mother. In a way I used to hate her, but as I got older I understood her better, how she was going through that change of life—but we're not really close. (p. 142)[1]

Her description of her father was more positive and affectionate:

> . . . soft-hearted, very soft-hearted—he cares for our happiness and has always been like that. He's generous, not selfish. I feel very close to him. (p. 142)

Somehow, Mary learned to manage her negative emotions. As an adolescent, she was outgoing, sociable, and concerned with how others perceived her. She believed that she controlled her own destiny—she was not at the mercy of forces beyond her control—and

---

[1] Excerpts from *Vulnerable but Not Invincible: A Longitudinal Study of Resilient Children*, by E. E. Werner and R. S. Smith, 1982, New York: McGraw-Hill. Reprinted 1989, 1998. New York: Adams, Bannister, Cox. Reprinted with permission.

she approached new situations cautiously, seeking information before acting. However, she disliked tension in her interpersonal relationships and avoided conflict:

> Me, I don't start fights too much. My mother, she'll go around the house grumbling, until I finally get up to a point where I can't stand it. I can't stand to see a family fighting. Parents shouldn't fight, they should be able to talk things out. (p. 143)

Mary was a good student who scored in the top 25% on achievement tests in high school. Thus, while her family life was often troubled, school was an arena in which she could succeed.

When Mary met with the researchers for the last time, she was 18 and planning to enroll in a community college to prepare for a career in medical or legal secretarial work. She described herself:

> If I say how I am, it sounds like bragging—I have a good personality and people like me. I'm not the greedy type—I'm jealous a lot of times, yes. And I don't like it when people think they can run my own life—I like to be my own judge. I know right and wrong, but I feel I have a lot more to learn and go through. Generally, I hope I can make it—I hope. (p. 140)

Mary's case underscores the significance of children's early relationships with caregivers. During her infancy, and before her mother's emotional breakdowns, observers found both parents affectionate. It seems likely, then, that Mary initially formed a close bond with her mother but later learned to keep her distance as she encountered instability, irritability, and criticism. As an adolescent, Mary remained close to her father. In this chapter, we learn about early *attachments* children form with parents, siblings, and other caregivers. We find that these relationships, when warm and nurturing, give children a secure base from which to explore the world and relate to other people. However, we also see that healthy attachments do not ensure good outcomes, nor do weak attachments guarantee bad ones.

A second theme in Mary's case, and throughout this chapter, is that emotions give meaning to children's experience. Mary's parents were happy when she was born, and as a young child Mary thrived on their affection. Yet there were indications of negative emotions as well: Mary had crying spells and temper tantrums, and she disliked being blamed for everything. In studying the emotional lives of children, we find that children begin life with simple emotions and gradually add complex feelings. Children also learn to deal with negative emotions more effectively as they grow older. For instance, Mary's temper tantrums gradually diminished as she learned to channel her anger into more productive modes of expression.

Finally, Mary showed a sense of *self*, reflecting on who she was as an individual. She was concerned not to appear conceited, but she perceived herself to have a good personality, to know right from wrong, to be jealous (though not greedy), and to be receptive to learning opportunities. In this chapter, we examine how children think and feel about themselves and their own worth as human beings.

This chapter gives us a chance to probe the very core of children's social-emotional functioning—their attachments, emotional expression, and sense of self. We start at the very beginning, with children's first attachments to caregivers.

Early Attachments

By **attachment**, we mean an enduring emotional tie that unites one person to another (Ainsworth, 1973). During infancy and early childhood, attachments to parents and other caregivers protect children (Ainsworth, 1963; Bowlby, 1958). These bonds keep infants in close proximity to their caregivers, whose foremost priorities are to keep them safe, nourished, reasonably happy, and feeling loved.

In the last few decades, the dominant theoretical perspective on caregiver-infant relationships has been **ethological attachment theory**, a perspective originally suggested by John Bowlby (1951, 1958), fleshed out by Mary Ainsworth (1963, 1973; Ainsworth, Blehar, Waters, & Wall, 1978), and tested and refined by many contemporary psycholo-

attachment
An enduring emotional tie uniting one person to another.

ethological attachment theory
Theoretical perspective that emphasizes the functional importance of caregiver-child bonds in protecting children and giving them a secure base from which to explore their surroundings.

gists. Ethological attachment theory describes children's social-emotional bonds with parents in terms of evolutionary function; this theory is therefore an example of the *evolutionary perspectives* introduced in Chapter 1. Attachment theorists speculate that severe environmental conditions made it necessary for our ancestors' children to stay close to parents and to learn all they could from them. Children who had the capacity for bonding survived and learned to relate to kin as well as to hunt, gather, use tools, and communicate. Eventually, they found mates and raised their own children.

Because of evolutionary pressures, infants still depend on parents for feeding, love, and protection from harm. Parents are biologically predisposed to care for their infants, and infants are biologically programmed to stay close to their parents, especially in times of danger. Infants maintain proximity by crying, clinging, and crawling when distressed; under less stressful conditions, they show affection with snuggles, smiles, and cooing. Infants' inherited capacity to bond to parents and other caregivers is translated into a real attachment only when these adults are reasonably warm and attentive (R. A. Thompson, 1998). As we shall see, this happens most of the time, but not always.

Attachments themselves change as children mature and caregivers introduce lessons that let children practice responsibility. Let's see exactly how these attachments unfold.

Developmental Course of Attachments

To some extent, infants begin life indiscriminately social—they watch and listen to all people in their vicinity and allow themselves to be comforted by anyone with the right touch (Schaffer, 1996). Through repeated experiences, though, infants learn they cannot count on just anyone to be affectionate and attentive, but, rather, on a few wonderful people who regularly care for them. By about the second month, infants recognize familiar people—the faces of parents and other caregivers, their voices, and their smells. By the third month, they smile selectively at people they know best (Camras, Malatesta, & Izard, 1991).

The attachments that infants form with their parents and other primary caregivers provide a foundation for later relationships.

Full-fledged attachments are evident beginning at about 7 months. Now, the infant is truly bonded to a small number of people, possibly a mother, father, grandparent, professional caregiver, or some combination of these or other individuals. Attachments can be seen when infants reach out to be picked up by caregivers; protest when separated from them; and wriggle, coo, and show unmistakable looks of recognition when a caregiver walks into the room. Attachments are also evident when infants sense danger, pain, and uncertainty (Bowlby, 1988). In the latter half of the first year of life and well into the second year, an unfamiliar adult often incites fear—**stranger anxiety**—in infants (Mangelsdorf, Shapiro, & Marzolf, 1995). This fear often escalates into a red-faced, tearful, arm-flapping demand for safe haven—contact with a familiar caregiver. Of course, not all strangers will provoke this kind of reaction, but infants tend to become wary of unfamiliar people during the second half of their first year. Their desire for reassurance from familiar caregivers protects them from wandering off just when they are able to crawl and motivated to explore.

Early on, caregivers do most of the initiating in the infant-caregiver relationship. Few parents, for example, can resist the chance to cuddle their young babies, and most drop everything to respond to their infants' urgent cries. While lovingly addressing infants' physical needs, parents and other caregivers solidify attachments with them.

With time, the relationship changes. Caregivers increasingly hear subtle nuances in cries and vocalizations. Infants change as well. Within their first two years, infants show understandings that they can influence caregivers ("If I cry, Daddy comes"; "When I smile, Mommy smiles back"). They begin to take turns in a conversation, as you can see in 16-month-old Corwin's interchanges with his mother in the Literacy/Infancy clip of the Observation CD. Corwin's vocalizations are simple, but they serve nicely as interjections into the conversation.

Observe 16-month-old Corwin taking turns in a conversation with his mother in the Literacy/Infancy clip of the Observation CD.

Gradually, infants begin to form expectations about caregivers. For example, two-year-olds may realize that parents who leave them briefly will return; toddlers thus find separations less traumatic than previously (Schaffer, 1996). Gaining some common sense, young children can safely spend less time in physical contact with attachment figures—and they insist on doing just that. Particularly when they have loving relationships with parents, children are happy to play with peers in parents' absence (Howes, 1999). Many children go off

stranger anxiety
Fear of unfamiliar adults in the latter half of the first year and into the second year of life.

to child care happily and then enthusiastically reunite with parents at the end of the day, talking exuberantly about their day and hugging parents (Main & Cassidy, 1988).

In middle childhood, youngsters venture farther away but still depend on close ties with family members and other caregivers. They expect parents and caregivers to keep tabs on them, to celebrate their successes, and to be there when they need them. When parents are not present, perhaps because of divorce, travel, or death, children may become angry, aggressive, or physically ill, and may withdraw from their customary activities (Pribilsky, 2001).

In adolescence, family relationships change as young people assert their independence. Adolescents become less emotionally dependent on approval from parents, construct a firmer sense of their own values (as we discover later in this chapter), manage spending money and other affairs, and take it in stride when they fail to meet parents' standards (J. A. Hoffman, 1984). Most independent-minded adolescents remain attached to parents, however.

The developmental course of attachments we have outlined is one that assumes a trusting relationship with parents. Unfortunately, this kind of relationship does not always occur. We now look at individual differences in attachment.

Attachments to family members continue to be important throughout childhood and adolescence.

Individual Differences in Infants' Attachments

If you look around at young children you know, you may notice variations in how they respond to caregivers. Some run to caregivers when upset; others have trouble receiving comfort even when it's offered. To study such differences in the laboratory, Ainsworth created a mildly stressful situation for 1-year-old infants. First, a mother and her infant were brought to a playroom and left alone. A stranger (a research assistant) soon entered the room and attempted to play with the baby. After 3 minutes, the mother left the room, leaving the baby alone with the stranger. Subsequently, the mother returned and the stranger departed, leaving mother and baby together. Next, mother departed, and baby was alone; the stranger returned at this point. Finally, the mother returned and the stranger departed (Ainsworth et al., 1978). This sequence, commonly known as the *Strange Situation*, has become a classic research tool for assessing attachment in young children.

In the Strange Situation, attention is focused primarily on the child's behavior. Observers rate the child's attempts to seek contact with caregiver, the physical proximity of the child to the caregiver, the child's resistance to or avoidance of the caregiver, and the child's level of distress. From such ratings, the child is given one of four classifications:

- Infants who exhibit **secure attachment** seem to use caregivers as a secure base. When caregivers are present, infants actively explore new toys and surroundings. When caregivers return after leaving the room, infants smile at or talk to them, move over to greet them, or in other ways seek proximity to them. About 65% of infants from typical middle-class backgrounds are classified as securely attached (R. A. Thompson, 1998).
- Infants who exhibit **insecure-avoidant attachment** fail to greet caregivers when they come back into the room and perhaps even look away upon their return. Even before their caregivers' departure, these children appear indifferent to their presence: they go about their business independently, and they are somewhat superficial in their interactions with toys. About 20% of children participating in Strange Situation studies are classified as insecure-avoidant (R. A. Thompson, 1998).
- Infants who exhibit **insecure-resistant attachment** seem preoccupied with their caregivers, but they are not easily comforted during reunions. Even when caregivers return, these infants remain distressed and angry; they may rush to parents and other caregivers yet quickly struggle to be released. Insecure-resistant infants comprise about 15% of participants in Strange Situation studies (R. A. Thompson, 1998).
- More serious problems in attachment that were not part of Ainsworth's original classification have subsequently been identified. For example, a **disorganized and disoriented attachment** style has been documented (Main & Solomon, 1986, 1990). Infants in this group lack a coherent way of responding to stressful events. These

secure attachment
Attachment classification in which children use attachment figures as a secure base from which to explore and as a source of comfort in times of distress.

insecure-avoidant attachment
Attachment classification in which children appear somewhat indifferent to attachment figures.

insecure-resistant attachment
Attachment classification in which children are preoccupied with their attachment figures but gain little comfort from them when distressed.

disorganized and disoriented attachment
Attachment classification in which children lack a single coherent way of responding to attachment figures.

infants may be calm and contented one minute yet, without provocation, become angry the next minute. They may interrupt their own actions midstream, for example by crawling toward caregivers and then suddenly freezing with apprehension. It is difficult to estimate the percentage of children in this recently identified category, but it seems likely that only a small minority of children would be classified as having a disorganized and disoriented attachment. A very few children show *no* attachment behaviors or exhibit other extremely serious problems, such as displaying fear of caregivers rather than being comforted by them. Such extremely serious problems frequently call for intervention by trained professionals.

Infant practitioners may occasionally wonder about the quality of children's attachments to family members and to themselves. Also, mental health professionals may be asked by social service agencies to assess children's relationships with caregivers. Practitioners can observe how children and caregivers typically behave toward one another, recognizing, of course, that "bad days" and unusual events temporarily disrupt normal interactions in all families and child care settings. The Observation Guidelines table "Assessing Young Children's Attachment Security" summarizes how children with particular kinds of attachments might act. These guidelines are a place to start; practitioners who inform high-stakes decisions for children, such as custody placements, will obviously need intensive observational training and appropriate credentials.

Origins of Attachment Security

What factors lead to different patterns of attachment? Research has shown that the quality of the caregiver-child relationship, the cultural setting, and the child's own behavior each play a role.

Quality of Caregiver-Child Relationship   The relationship between caregivers and children appears to be the most powerful factor in attachment security. When caregivers are sensitive and responsive to young children, protect them, and provide for their needs, children are inclined to develop secure attachments (Chisholm, 1996; NICHD Early Child Care Research Network, 1997). Caregivers who are sensitive and responsive may show these qualities:

1. *They consistently respond to infants' needs.* Caregivers establish routines for feeding, diapering, and holding infants. They do not run to every whimper, but they are faithfully available when infants express genuine needs (Cassidy & Berlin, 1994). Caregivers who fail to show this quality may be neglectful or available only occasionally; others are callous to infants' feelings.
2. *They regularly express affection.* Caregivers dote on babies, caressing them, looking into their eyes, talking to them, and expressing tenderness and warmth. Caregivers who fail to show this quality may be withdrawn or even hostile and rejecting.
3. *They permit babies to influence the pace and direction of their mutual interactions.* Caregivers let infants take the lead on occasion. They carefully note where infants are looking, notice their body posture, and recognize when infants invite them to interact (Isabella & Belsky, 1991; Stern, 1977). They learn to act in synchrony with individual infants, letting them take a turn in an interaction by smiling, moving their hands, or babbling. Caregivers who fail to show this quality may be overly intrusive, perhaps to the point that babies look away from them, cry, or try to go to sleep. Other caregivers may fail to notice or respond to infants' bids for affection, for example, ignoring infants' attempts to make eye contact.

Children with insecure attachments often have caregivers who have difficulty caring for them or are unwilling to invest energy in them (R. A. Thompson, 1998). These caregivers may struggle with serious emotional issues, limited financial resources, and the stresses of many responsibilities—caring for children, maintaining a household, holding down a job, and so on. Some children—those who are insecure-avoidant—become independent early on and find creative ways to obtain needed care. Other children—those who are insecure-resistant—cling tenaciously to caregivers to increase chances of gaining needed resources.

OBSERVATION GUIDELINES

Assessing Young Children's Attachment Security

CHARACTERISTIC	LOOK FOR	EXAMPLE	IMPLICATION
Secure Attachment to Caregivers	• Active, intentional exploration of the environment in the presence of the caregiver • Protest at being separated from a caregiver; ability to be soothed when the caregiver returns • Initial wariness of strangers, with subsequent acceptance if reassured by the caregiver	Luis cries when his father drops him off at the child care center in the morning. After a few minutes, he settles down and crawls to a familiar and affectionate caregiver who is becoming the target of his attachment as well.	It is natural for young children to resist separation from family members. Help them establish a routine of saying good-bye in the morning, and give them extra attention during this time. Reassure parents and other family members by describing children's daily activities and behaviors, and inform them of how long it takes their children to settle into a relaxed routine after their departure.
Insecure-Avoidant Attachment to Caregivers	• Superficial exploration of the environment • Indifference to a caregiver's departure; failure to seek comfort upon the caregiver's return • Apparent discomfort around strangers, but without an active resistance to their overtures	Jennifer walks around her new preschool with a frown on her face. She parts easily with her mother, and after a short time she seems to settle into her new environment. She glances up when her mother comes at the end of the day, but she doesn't seem overjoyed about her mother's return.	Independence from parents is often a sign of children's familiarity with child care or preschool settings. For children who seem at ease with separation, support them throughout the day. Offer support to children who appear indifferent to family members; some parents have difficulty fulfilling children's emotional needs due to stresses in their own lives. Form your own affectionate relationships with children, as such support can lead to secure attachments.
Insecure-Resistant Attachment	• Exceptional clinginess and anxiety with caregiver • Agitation and distress at the caregiver's departure; continued crying or fussing after the caregiver returns • Apparent fear of strangers; tendency to stay close to caregiver in new situation	Irene tightly clutches her mother as the two enter the preschool building, and she stays close by as mother signs her in for the morning. She is quite upset when her mother leaves yet finds little comfort in mother's return a few hours later.	If insecure-resistant children appear anxious when they enter a new child care or preschool setting, give them extra time to part with their parents. Sometimes a "comfort" object from home (a teddy bear or blanket) can help. Be patient and reassuring as you interact with these children, knowing that they can eventually form a secure attachment to you.
Disorganized and Disoriented Attachment, and Other Serious Attachment Problems	• Unpredictable emotional responses • Cautious approaches to caregiver • By end of first year, failure to contact caregiver when distressed • Reckless exploration and no use of caregiver as secure base • Reversed roles, with excessive concern about caregiver • No signs of attachment to family members or other familiar caregivers, or fear of them	Myles seems lost at school. He arrives hungry, walks aimlessly for some time, and eventually sits to play with blocks. He is aggressive with his peers, and his teacher sees bruises on his arms.	Provide special attention and monitoring to children who seem disorganized and disoriented in their attachment. Be on the lookout for signs of abuse, and be ready to seek advice from authorities. Remember that these children are *not* doomed to serious lifelong problems, but you must work hard to establish positive, trusting relationships with them.

In many cases, children with disorganized and disoriented attachments live with people whose behaviors are unpredictable; often these children are victims of abuse or maltreatment. Consequently, they typically approach caregivers slowly and cautiously, unsure if they will receive affection or punishment.

Although insecure attachment patterns are somewhat adaptive over the short run, they are counterproductive over the long run. For instance, children who become demanding and clingy may end up with adequate nourishment under extremely impoverished conditions (M. W. DeVries & Sameroff, 1984). Yet these children may remain excessively dependent on caregivers long after they should be establishing some independence, or they may become overly demanding and competitive with other children (R. A. Thompson, 1998).

Cultural Setting   A second factor affecting children's attachments is the cultural setting (Rothbaum, Weisz, Pott, Miyake, & Morelli, 2000). Cultures differ appreciably in emphasis on a close, exclusive relationship between parents and infants. Here are two examples:

- In some studies with Japanese children, a high proportion of children displayed behaviors that researchers interpret as insecure-resistant attachment. Many infants became quite upset when mothers left the room, perhaps because Japanese people emphasize physical closeness, intimacy, and strong mother-child bonds (Miyake, Chen, & Campos, 1985; Takahashi, 1990). Infants' separation from mother is not common, baby-sitters are rare, and when mothers leave their children, they often seek assistance from grandparents (Saarni, Mumme, & Campos, 1998).
- In northern Germany, many infants display behaviors that, on the surface, indicate insecure-avoidant attachment (Grossmann, Grossmann, Huber, & Wartner, 1991). These babies do not fret much when their mothers leave the playroom, nor do they move frantically toward mothers when they return. In northern Germany, infants are regularly left at home alone or outside supermarkets as mothers do brief errands. The time alone is not lengthy, but it happens often enough to be routine. These children seem to grow accustomed to getting along on their own, at least for brief periods of time.

These cultural examples suggest that children adjust to their experiences (or lack thereof) of parents' coming and going. When separation is rare, infants may expect parents to be present, always. When parents must leave, infants may be overwhelmed with distress, a state fueled by parents' own anxiety over the separation. In contrast, when parents leave infants routinely, infants learn to get on by themselves, at least for brief periods. Thus, different cultural groups help infants to develop trusting relationships in ways that are not always validly assessed by the Strange Situation. In other words, the child who protests excessively or minimally may nevertheless have a secure, loving relationship with parents. These normal cultural variations can be distinguished from circumstances *within* cultures when parents are harsh, abusive, apathetic, or neglectful, and when children learn to withdraw, to fear primary caregivers, or to let negative emotions intensify into uncontrolled outcries.

Children's Contributions   A third factor affecting the security of children's attachment is the children themselves. Children make known their needs to parents and other caregivers, allow themselves to be comforted, and reciprocate with affection. Children therefore actively participate in their relationships with caregivers.

Children's dispositions may also play a small part in the types of attachments they form. Through their unique ways of handling stress and relating to others, children influence the manner in which caregivers respond to them. Whereas some fuss when scared, others protest less adamantly. Perhaps those who are prone to be fearful and irritable are more difficult to care for, and those who are even-tempered and sociable invite positive interactions. However, available research suggests that differences in infants' behaviors play only a minor role in attachment security. Parents and other caregivers are generally able to be sensitive to a wide range of dispositions in children. Babies who are premature, delayed in their development, and unusually fussy can easily develop secure attachments when their individual needs are met sensitively (van IJzendoorn, Goldberg, Kroonenberg, & Frenkel, 1992).

Multiple Attachments

Early research examined *mothers* as primary attachment figures (Ainsworth, Blehar, Waters, & Wall, 1978; Bowlby 1969/1982). Because women physically bear children and often do most of the feeding, bathing, and diapering, this emphasis is understandable. But as we will see in Chapter 12, fathers can be equally passionate parents, waking in the night to feed children, cheering when they first walk and talk, and advocating for them when the rest of the world lets them down. Often, extended family members also form loving ties with children. Contemporary research on attachment examines the nurturing bonds that infants form with many caregivers, including fathers, grandparents, aunts, uncles, brothers and sisters, adoptive and foster families, and professional caregivers (Howes, 1999).

Observe 7-month-old Madison and her father interact playfully and affectionately in the Emotional Development/Infancy clip of the Observation CD.

When two parents are present in the home, infants may develop strong attachments to both. Both parents are likely to instill secure attachments when they sensitively respond to children's needs and are present in children's lives for an extended time (Howes, 1999). However, there is some evidence that fathers and mothers form attachments in slightly different ways. For example, in a study comparing styles of parents with infants between 12 and 26 months, mothers spent more time caring for infants while fathers spent more time with infants in pretend play (Kazura, 2000). You can observe a father's tender and playful style with his baby daughter in the Emotional Development/Infancy clip of the Observation CD.

Because a child's two parents inevitably have different styles, the child may form somewhat different relationships with each. However, there tends to be a modest association between how secure infants feel with mothers and with fathers (DelCarmen-Wiggins, Huffman, Pedersen, & Bryan, 2000; N. A. Fox, Kimmerly, & Schafer, 1991). Those who are securely attached to mothers are likely to be securely attached to fathers as well. Nonetheless, many infants show strong preferences on different occasions for one parent over the other. And sadly, there are some infants who do not form secure attachments with either parent.

Children also form close bonds with other people besides parents. In many cultures, other people besides parents care for infants. Children in Kenya, for instance, are cared for extensively by older siblings and protest loudly when separated from them (Weisner, 1997). In other cultures, including the Israeli kibbutzim, children spend considerable time in settings with adults who are not members of their families (J. F. Jackson, 1986, 1993; van IJzendoorn, Sagi, & Lambermon, 1992). Such networks of nurturing adults have important benefits for children, who can rely on many trustworthy individuals (Howes, 1999). Also, as children's needs change, access to multiple caregivers provides options for different kinds of support (C. B. Fisher, Jackson, & Villarruel, 1998). For example, it is perfectly healthy for a 1-year-old to crawl to Grandma when a stranger enters the family home; at 6, to seek advice from his uncle as he faces bullies on the playground; and at 14, to have heart-to-heart talks with Dad about career options.

Infants also routinely form attachments to employed professionals in child care centers, classrooms, and other settings. Secure attachment with these figures, as with parents, depends upon sensitive care, sustained relationships, and emotional investment (Howes, 1999). Unfortunately, long-term relationships sometimes are not possible in child care centers. In circumstances of high turnover, children must form new relationships with caregivers yearly, sometimes more frequently. In a study with toddlers, children directed more attachment behaviors to adults who worked in a center 3 months or more compared to adults who were newly employed (Barnas & Cummings, 1994). Under conditions of employee change, new caregivers must be patient as children slowly become convinced that they can be trusted.

Children often form strong attachments to caregivers who sensitively care for them over a period of time.

Multiple attachments can be cast in the same evolutionary perspective as attachments in general. Throughout human history, many children have lost parents to contagious diseases and other uncontrollable circumstances. Thus, the human race evolved in such a way that children had to reach out to multiple adults (Meindl, 1992). In contemporary times, exposure to multiple caregivers provides a pool of caring adults from which children can draw and that, when primary attachments are weak, serves as an important back-up system.

Attachment Security and Later Development

As children gain experience with primary caregivers, they begin to form an understanding, or *mental representation*, of what relationships with other people are like (Bowlby, 1969/1982, 1973; R. M. Ryan, Stiller, & Lynch, 1994). Their understanding of "typical" relationships in turn influences the relationships they form with other individuals—particularly with other adults, such as teachers (R. M. Ryan et al., 1994). If you've ever visited a preschool, perhaps you know what we're talking about. Some children, curious and affectionate, flock to you with books and puzzles in hand, assuming you will want to join them in their chosen activities (we certainly urge you to do so!). In making these social overtures, children convey their expectations: "Unfamiliar adults find me likeable." Such positive expectations are not universal, however, as you might expect from our previous discussion of individual differences in attachment security. A few children may look at you suspiciously, not because they're shy, but because they wonder, "What harm might you cause me?"

Generally speaking, early attachment security is associated with positive long-term outcomes. In Western cultures, children who were securely attached as infants tend to become relatively independent, empathic, socially competent preschoolers, especially in comparison with children who were insecurely attached (Kestenbaum, Farber, & Sroufe, 1989; Sroufe, 1983; Vaughn, Egeland, Sroufe, & Waters, 1979). In middle childhood and adolescence, they tend to be self-confident, adjust easily to school environments, establish productive relationships with teachers and peers, and do well at classroom tasks (Elicker, Englund, & Sroufe, 1992; Sroufe, Carlson, & Schulman, 1993; Urban, Carlson, Egeland, & Sroufe, 1991). It is important to note that not all of these findings apply to children in non-Western cultures. For instance, in Japan, caregivers encourage infants to rely on familiar caregivers and be reserved with strangers. Thus, for Japanese children, close and affectionate relationships with caregivers are not as likely to lead to independence and sociability (Rothbaum et al., 2000).

At least two factors may be at the root of the positive outcomes of secure attachment. First, sensitive parents and other caregivers usually continue to be responsive as children grow; in other words, secure attachments evolve into solid, loving, two-sided relationships. Second, children with secure attachments form positive, self-fulfilling expectations about other people, and they take these expectations into new relationships. They expect other people to be trustworthy, and they give second chances to those who initially let them down—actions that feed and sustain healthy emotional ties. The same principles may be at work in creating negative outcomes with insecure attachment: Parents or caregivers may continue to be rejecting, and children form mental representations—and expectations—of other people as untrustworthy (Main, 1995).

Initially, attachment theorists suggested that an infant's early attachments to primary caregivers (especially the mother) set the tone for all future relationships (e.g., Bowlby, 1973). This turns out to be inaccurate. The kinds of bonds children form with their mothers do not firmly dictate the kinds of bonds they make with other caregivers. Furthermore, as youngsters grow older, their attachments to peers—perhaps to best friends and, eventually, to romantic partners—may be significantly different from those they have previously formed with parents (Baldwin, Keelan, Fehr, Enns, & Koh-Rangarajoo, 1996; La Guardia, Ryan, Couchman, & Deci, 2000). This makes sense when we consider that young people continue to be affected by how others, not just their parents, treat them. Apparently, growing children and adolescents form not one mental representation (based solely on the early attachment to the primary caregiver), but several mental representations of what interpersonal relationships are like (Baldwin et al., 1996).

Social bonds may also change as a result of stressful events. For instance, children who initially form secure attachments but later live through one or more traumatic events (perhaps the parents get divorced, a family member dies or suffers a debilitating illness, or they are physically or sexually abused by another family member) may have difficulty forming attachments as adolescents or adults (Lewis, Feiring, & Rosenthal, 2000; Waters, Merrick, Treboux, Crowell, & Albersheim, 2000; Weinfield, Sroufe, & Egeland, 2000). In our opening case study, Mary formed a secure attachment to both of her parents when she was an infant. A few years later, when her mother's behavior became erratic and occasionally abusive, apparently the result of an emerging mental illness, Mary's attachment to her mother waned. Her attachment to her father, however, remained strong, and she enthusiastically made friends and achieved in school.

In summary, early ties are vital but they are not always a permanent determinant of later social-emotional health. We now look at what practitioners can do to support children's attachments.

Professional Implications of Attachment Research

As we have seen, infant attachments provide the foundation for later relationships. This foundation can be rebuilt if it's shaky, and it must occasionally be bolstered if, despite a solid beginning, it later disintegrates in the face of adverse circumstances (R. A. Thompson, 1998). In essence, secure attachment is like a multivitamin: It increases the chances of, but does not guarantee, good health. Conversely, a child with an early insecure attachment may, with love and guidance, become a happy, productive adult. Based on attachment literature, we formulate these recommendations for adults who work with young people:

■ *Cultivate strong relationships with young children.* Although family members are usually the recipients of children's first attachments, young children often form close bonds with employed caregivers. Furthermore, high-quality attachments in child care can compensate for poor parenting to some extent (Howes & Ritchie, 1998; NICHD Early Child Care Research Network, 1997). Thus, the recipe for good bonding—sensitive, responsive, reliable care—is applicable beyond the home: in child care, schools, after-school programs, clubs, religious communities, and foster care.

■ *Acknowledge and encourage multiple attachments.* At school, children may talk about a variety of people in their lives—brothers and sisters, aunts and uncles, grandparents, neighbors. Teachers can encourage children to invite these individuals to concerts, school performances, and orientation meetings. To counselors and social workers, children may mention the support they receive from people outside the home—perhaps a friend's parent. Professionals can validate the place these people have in children's hearts. Likewise, community organizers can let children know that they are free to invite family and other friends to musical recitals, award nights, and other occasions for recognition.

■ *Encourage sympathetic dispositions in children.* Some children who have had few affectionate relationships have poorly developed social skills and so may, in many people's eyes, be difficult children to like. They may appear uncaring to others' distress, for example, hitting a child who has gotten hurt rather than offering sympathy (Volling, 2001). To help these children, model helpful reactions when other people are hurt, talk about your feelings, and encourage them to show sympathy.

■ *Encourage parents to watch their children's play.* Practitioners can encourage parents to watch their children carefully and notice what they attend to and what gives them pleasure. You can point out how babies learn when they look at their fingers, suck on their toes, and listen to voices. Marveling at this incredible, spontaneous learning can be a good first step toward affirming and extending it ("Look at that mirror, Abigail! Is it shiny? Do you see yourself?").

■ *Model affectionate, thoughtful caregiving for family members.* Parents who maltreat their children were often maltreated themselves as children (Egami, Ford, & Crum, 1996). They may not know what it feels like to have affectionate relationships with children. Infant caregivers can show parents how positively infants respond to affection, especially during routine games, such as peek-a-boo and tickling. They also can point out the significance of infants' gestures such as smiling, looking away, or cooing. Some parents may not understand that these gestures are how babies communicate. Professionals can demonstrate how they return a baby's smiles, vocalizations, and eye contact and hold the baby tenderly. They can point out as well the signals infants give that they are not ready to play (e.g., averting a gaze) or have had enough (e.g., pouting). Family educators might also ask parents to practice relaxing together on the couch or carrying small infants in snuggly carriers close to their chest (Anisfeld, Casper, Nosyce, & Cunningham, 1990; Lieberman, Weston, & Pawl, 1991).

■ *Help parents understand how infants and children think and feel.* Infants can be mysterious—even exasperating—creatures. Parents do not always understand what makes their babies "tick" ("Why does Mike keep jumping out of his crib? Every time he does it, he gets hurt. What is he thinking?"). Professionals can casually share ideas about infants' motives, feelings, and understandings to help parents appreciate how babies view the world ("Mike is one determined little guy, isn't he? He really wants to explore his environment!"). When parents are thoughtful and concerned about how infants feel and construe events, attachments tend to be more secure (Koren-Karie, Oppenheim, Dolev, Sher, & Etzion-Carasso, 2002).

■ *Support families when parents experience distress.* Discord between parents and other family stresses can increase the likelihood that parents will be inattentive to infants' needs.

To help avert the serious attachment problems that may result (M. Rutter & O'Connor, 1999), professionals can inform families of agencies and resources in their area that might provide assistance. For example, parents who have been out of work for a long time may appreciate hearing about employment agencies and charitable organizations. Also, if you have appropriate training and credentials, you may be able to offer counseling to parents.

■ *When parents divorce, help children remain attached to both parents.* Often parents share custody of children, making it likely that children will maintain attachments to both parents. Teachers can help by sending home duplicate copies of newsletters and correspondence to both parents' homes. Social workers can help by advising parents on practical issues arising from children's moving back and forth between two households. For example, they can talk with parents about ways in which children of different ages handle rotations between two households (J. B. Kelly & Lamb, 2000).

■ *Promote social bonds in all ages.* Developmental researchers tend to emphasize attachments in infancy, but close social bonds are a lifelong human need. During middle childhood and adolescence, youngsters want to *belong* to the various communities in which they spend time—families, classrooms, clubs, and sports teams, for example. Adults can consciously foster ties that young people are forming to one another and also to them. They can give them chances to become involved, plan trips, work together in projects, and design menus.

Adults can promote social bonds in young people of all ages.

■ *Seek professional guidance when attachment problems are serious.* We have learned that infants may fail to develop healthy attachments and that there are many things practitioners can do informally to help insecure infants and their families. However, some attachment problems are so serious that families require a therapist and formal intervention (Booth & Koller, 1998; V. A. Brown, 2002; T. M. Levy & Orlans, 2000). Thus, it is important for practitioners to be alert for signs of deeply troubled infant-family relationships. You will want to seek professional guidance if you notice one or more of the following situations:

- An infant shows *no* attachment behaviors by the end of the first year (e.g., he or she does not seek primary caregivers when distressed and may be indiscriminately friendly with all adults).
- An infant is extremely inhibited, clinging to the caregiver rather than venturing at all to explore the environment.
- An infant is reckless in exploration of the environment, throwing toys and destroying objects, and failing to seek contact with the caregiver.
- An infant shows a role reversal, displaying excessive concern over the status of the attachment figure, rather than the caregiver showing concern for the infant.
- An infant fails to develop a coherent way of responding to stressful events but sometimes shows fear of the caregiver.
- An infant under the age of 3 years has lost a primary attachment figure and appears to be devastated with grief (Greenberg, 1999; Main & Solomon 1986, 1990; Zeanah, 2000).

Serious attachment problems in children often arise when parents face major mental health problems. For example, when mothers are emotionally depressed, they may be detached and unresponsive with their infants, or hostile and intrusive (Teti, Gelfand, Messinger, & Isabella, 1995). In turn, infants may become chronically sad and withdrawn. Professional intervention that guides these mothers to address their own unresolved emotional needs may be a necessary step before professionals can successfully engender an involved, affectionate parenting style (Benoit & Parker, 1994; Main, Kaplan, & Cassidy, 1985). If one parent has serious mental health problems but will not seek treatment, the other parent or another family member may be able to pick up the slack and provide the children with loving attention.

■ *Offer a range of services when children are placed with new families.* When children are taken out of families, children frequently form healthy bonds with their new caregivers (K. Chisholm, Carter, Ames, & Morison, 1995; Howes & Segal, 1993; Marcovitch et al., 1997). However, professionals who work with children and their new families should not leave this adjustment to chance. Instead, they can prepare the new families to recognize and meet the children's individual needs. For example, a foster family may be taught to expect temper tantrums from an 8-year-old child who has recently joined their family. Social workers may encourage family members to communicate their expectations for controlled behavior, to follow through with appropriate consequences when the child does cause property damage, and to persist in showing love even though the child has not yet learned to reciprocate with affection.

Having bonded with family members and other caregivers, children are ready to take on other social-emotional tasks, such as becoming friends with peers and learning to treat other people fairly and compassionately. Effective social relationships require children to "read" other people's emotional cues and to express their own emotions authentically and appropriately. Sound relationships also require children to know themselves—where they fit into family and social groups, what is distinctive about them as individuals, and where their strengths and limitations lie. Children's emotional development and formation of a sense of self are our focus for the remainder of this chapter.

Emotional Development

Emotions (sometimes referred to as *affect*) are the feelings, both physiological and psychological, that people have in response to events that are personally relevant to their needs and goals. Emotional states energize thinking and acting in ways that are often adaptive to the circumstances (Goleman, 1995; Saarni et al., 1998). Happiness, anger, fear, anxiety, and other emotional responses focus children's attention on important aspects of their lives; they also help children develop new ideas, goals, and plans. Emotions are not just a means for venting excess energy; rather, they help youngsters redirect their actions and relationships.

We find illustrations of emotion in the everyday lives of children. An infant looks expectantly at his mother's face, sees a preoccupied expression, and averts his gaze, showing sadness because he is unlikely to obtain attention. *Sadness* occurs when people cannot achieve a desired goal or experience a loss. A young boy playing with Grandma's computer becomes angered when she tells him it is her turn. *Anger* is a common response when a goal is thwarted. A ten-year-old girl who has seen televised accounts of terrorist acts is fearful when she hears a loud noise, afraid it might be an explosion. *Fear* occurs when people feel threatened and believe that their safety may be at stake. Of course, positive emotions occur regularly and serve important functions as well. *Happiness* helps children to enjoy life and repeat pleasurable experiences. *Pride* leads children to commit themselves to continued good behavior (Saarni et al., 1998). The Observation Guidelines table "Assessing the Emotions of Children and Adolescents" presents yet other occasions when children's emotions are natural, immediate responses to personally meaningful events.

The ways in which children express deeply held emotions—and to some degree the emotions themselves—change with development. Let's examine how emotional expression unfolds with age and experience.

Developmental Changes in Emotions

As children grow older, they acquire a broadening range of emotions and become increasingly aware of their own and others' feelings. Their emotional development is characterized by the following trends:

■ *Infants begin life with a few basic emotions and gradually add new feelings.* *Contentment, interest,* and *distress* are shown within the first six months of life (Emde, Gaensbauer, & Harmon, 1976; Hiatt, Campos, & Emde, 1979; M. Lewis, 2000; Stenberg & Campos, 1990). Hungry babies who begin to feed most certainly feel pleasure (M. Lewis, 2000). A small smile may occur when infants are relaxed, happy, or enchanted with animated people. Small babies show interest by watching objects carefully, inspecting their own body parts, mouthing fingers and toes, and tilting their head to listen closely to the fine points of speech and music. Newborns exposed to a loud and sudden noise express distress; they do the same when hunger and fatigue mount.

As they mature, infants add to these basic emotions. Simple distress can become true *anger* when infants' desires are obstructed: Daddy does not come immediately to pick baby

emotion
Affective response to an event that is personally relevant to one's needs and goals.

OBSERVATION GUIDELINES

Assessing the Emotions of Children and Adolescents

CHARACTERISTIC	LOOK FOR	EXAMPLE	IMPLICATION
Happiness	• Smiles • Laughter • Spontaneity	Paul, age 17, chatters with his friends during his school's end-of-the-year athletic field day. He is happy about having schoolwork over and looks forward to his summer job and paychecks.	Happiness helps people to enjoy life and to seek similar pleasurable experiences. Help children and adolescents to find appropriate outlets to express their joy and celebrate with them. Encourage them to talk about things they are happy about. Celebrate with them.
Anger	• Frowns and angry expressions • Possible retaliation toward the target of anger	Aranya, age 14, is furious that she wasn't admitted into an elective course, whereas her two closest friends *were*. Aranya is angry with her teacher, who she thinks dislikes her.	Anger helps people deal with obstacles to their goals, often spurring them to try new tactics. Help youngsters to express their anger appropriately and to determine how they can redirect their energy toward new solutions.
Fear	• Scared face • Withdrawal from circumstances • Physiological responses, such as sweating	Tony, age 2½, sits on his mat, eyes wide, body tense. He stares at a poster of a clown in his preschool classroom. On this particular day, he becomes downright scared; he runs to his teacher and buries his head in her lap.	Fear occurs when people feel threatened and believe that their physical safety and psychological well-being are potentially at stake. Fear motivates people to flee, escape from harm, seek reassurance, and perhaps fight back. Help children to articulate their fears. Offer reassurance.
Sadness	• Sad expression • Crying • Pouting • Being quiet • Possible withdrawal from circumstances	Greta, age 15, sits quietly on a bench near her locker. With her head hung low, she rereads the letter from a cheerleading organization. She has not been admitted to the prestigious cheerleading summer camp.	People are sad when they realize that they cannot attain a desired goal or when they experience a loss, such as a friend moving to a distant city. Sadness causes some people to reassess their goals, and it prompts others to offer nurturance. Help youngsters to express their sadness and to think of ways to deal with their feelings.
Disgust	• Wrinkled nose • Remarks such as "Phew!" • Withdrawal from the source of displeasure	Norton, age 8, peers at the lunch he has just purchased in the school cafeteria. He wrinkles his nose and averts his gaze from the "tuna melt" on his plate.	Disgust occurs when people encounter food, smells, and sights that they sense are unhealthful for them. Disgust is nature's way of getting people to be wary of something that is potentially troublesome. Respect children's feeling of disgust, but also help them to reason through why they might have this reaction.
Anxiety	• Frequent worrying • Avoidance of source of anxiety	Tanesha, age 16, has to give an oral presentation to a community group. She feels prepared but is worried that, when she is standing all by herself in front of the group, she might get so nervous that she will forget everything she wants to say.	As long as they are not excessive, worries can cause people to take steps to avoid the problem. These steps can make them more successful in achieving their standards. Help youngsters to take steps to contain their worries and to take proactive measures to achieve reasonable standards of performance in areas of most significant concern to them.
Shame	• Signs of embarrassment • Attempts to withdraw from situation • Looking down and away from other people	Luke, age 7, is stunned. He's just had an accident, urinating on the floor. He had felt a bit antsy beforehand, but wasn't aware that he needed to go to the bathroom. Now 20 pairs of eyes are glued on him.	When children feel ashamed, they are aware of other people's standards for behavior and know they are not meeting these standards. Shame motivates children to try harder. Shame works only when it comes from within; adults should never ridicule students to shame them. Hurtful comments don't motivate more responsible behavior; they provoke anger, withdrawal, and escape. Help children to redirect their behavior so that they can meet their own standards.
Guilt	• Sad expression • May appear self-conscious • May show concern for a person the child has harmed	A.J., age 12, regrets bad-mouthing his friend Pete to other classmates. A.J. sinks down low in his chair, feeling guilty for what he said behind Pete's back and for Pete's sadness.	Guilt occurs when people do something—in this case, betraying a friend—that violates their own standards. It leads people to right the wrong. More generally, it causes people to behave in socially appropriate ways that protect others from harm. Help children to express their feelings and to realize that they can try harder next time.
Pride	• Happy expression • Desire to show off work and accomplishments to other people	Jacinda, age 5, is beaming. For the last 20 minutes, she's painstakingly pasted sequins, stars, and feathers onto a mask. Her final product is a colorful, delicately adorned creation. She is happy with her work, as is evident from her ear-to-ear grin.	People are proud when they earn others' respect and meet their own goals. Pride fosters continued commitment to behaving appropriately and achieving high standards. Pride motivates people to share their accomplishments with others. Encourage children to describe things that make them proud. Share in their joy when they accomplish something meaningful for them.

Adaptive functions of emotions based on material in Saarni et al. (1998).

ALEX5

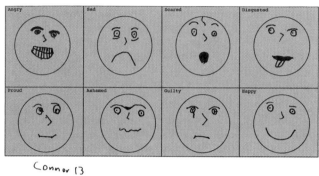

Connor 13

FIGURE 9–1 Drawings of basic emotional expressions by Alex (age 5) and Connor (age 13)

up, and Mommy does not indulge baby's desire to press the buttons on the DVD player. Infants show their anger vividly: They cry, thrash, and look directly, with accusation, at caregivers. Infants tend to show *fear* during the second half of the first year. This new emotion is evident in the stranger anxiety we examined earlier as a sign of attachment. Animals and objects that move in unexpected ways also often scare infants.

■ *Infants respond to other people's emotions.* A basic ability to detect emotions in others is present in infancy (Caron, Caron, & MacLean, 1988; Haviland & Lelwica, 1987; Schwarz, Izard, & Ansul, 1985). If you've ever visited an infant child care center, you may have noticed the **emotional contagion** of babies: When one starts crying, others soon join in (Eisenberg, 1992; Hatfield, Cacioppo, & Rapson, 1994). By 3 months, infants imitate the happy, sad, and angry faces their mothers make (Haviland & Lelwica, 1987). At about the same time, infants react to the emotional expressions of caregivers in meaningful ways. For example, researchers once used particular facial expressions with 4-month-old infants in a peek-a-boo game (Montague & Walker-Andrews, 2001). All infants were familiar with the game from playing it with parents, but the researchers changed it, displaying either angry, sad, or fearful expressions along with the expected happy expressions. Infants who watched *sad* expressions progressively looked away, as if they wanted to shield themselves from this emotion. Infants who watched *fearful* expressions increased attention to the adult's face and then gradually looked less, as if they wanted to learn more but then had enough. Infants who watched *angry* expressions increased their looking and maintained this interest, as if they were organizing internal processes needed for self-defense (Montague & Walker-Andrews, 2001). When caregivers violate infants' expectations for a particular emotional expression, for example, showing no smiles after a period of social play, infants also react. Between 3 and 9 months, they may respond to a parent's deadpan face by smiling, crying, looking away, and using self-soothing behaviors such as sucking their thumbs (T. Field, Vega-Lahr, Scafidi, & Goldstein, 1986; G. A. Moore, Cohn, & Campbell, 2001; Tronick, Als, Adamson, Wise, & Brazelton, 1978).

■ *Children learn to guide their actions on the basis of other people's emotional expressions.* In the first year or two of life, children also show the ability to monitor the emotions of others, particularly parents and trusted caregivers. You may recall our discussion of *social referencing* in Chapter 5: Children who engage in social referencing watch their parents' faces, especially in the presence of a novel or puzzling phenomenon (Boccia & Campos, 1989; Sorce, Emde, Campos, & Klinnert, 1985). A toddler may glance at Mommy's face when a new babysitter enters the house: Is Mommy smiling or frowning?

■ *Children learn to reflect on emotions.* As children grow older, they become thoughtful about emotions. As early as age 2 or 3, they talk about emotions that they and others experience ("Daniel got mad and pushed me"), and they realize that emotions are connected to people's desires ("I'm angry that Kurt ate the last cookie") (Bretherton, Fritz, Zahn-Waxler, & Ridgeway, 1986; Dunn, Bretherton, & Munn, 1987; Wellman, Harris, Banerjee, & Sinclair, 1995). By middle childhood, they realize that their interpretations determine how they feel about a particular situation and that other people have different interpretations and, as a result, different feelings ("Arlene feels bad because she thinks I don't like her") (P. L. Harris, 1989). Children also learn to connect labels of emotions with particular facial expressions and conditions under which these emotions may be elicited. Drawings in Figure 9–1, by two boys at ages 5 and 13, reveal differentiation among anger, sadness, fear, disgust, and guilt.

By the upper elementary grades, children begin to realize that emotional expressions do not always reflect people's true feelings (Selman, 1980). For instance, a 9-year-old may observe his teacher's cheerful demeanor yet realize she just lost her brother to cancer and is probably sad. During the end of middle childhood and the beginning of adolescence,

emotional contagion
Tendency for infants to cry spontaneously when they hear other infants crying.

children also understand that people can have ambivalent feelings (S. K. Donaldson & Westerman, 1986; Harter & Whitesell, 1989). For instance, a 12-year-old girl may love her father but be angry with him for moving out of the house; she may like going to see him during custodial visits but not like the feelings of turmoil these visits provoke in her.

■ *Children expand their repertoire of basic emotions to include self-conscious emotions.* Simple emotions of fear, anger, and happiness in infancy make room for **self-conscious emotions** in early childhood. These are affective states that reflect awareness of social standards and other people's concerns about these standards (M. Lewis, 1993, 1995). Self-conscious emotions include guilt, shame, embarrassment, and pride. Teresa recalls early displays of guilt and shame in both of her sons. As toddlers and preschoolers, the boys would often respond angrily when misbehavior resulted in their being sent to their room or having a privilege taken away. Occasionally they'd swat at her or stomp out of the room. However, they'd often return a few minutes later, looking at her face for signs of sadness and affectionately rubbing her arm as they apologized.

■ *Children and adolescents gradually learn to regulate their emotions.* **Emotional regulation** (also called *coping*) refers to strategies children use to manage stressful situations (E. M. Brenner & Salovey, 1997). In the opening case study, Mary had several strategies for coping with troubling events. She entered new situations cautiously, trying to gather information before committing herself to a course of action. She shied away from open conflicts, and she kept her distance from her overly critical and punitive mother.

As newborns, infants need help when they feel hungry, tormented, or fearful. Most can count on caregivers to help them relieve distress. Soon, infants also learn to soothe themselves to some extent: They may suck on a thumb, avert their gaze from a stranger, or crawl away (Mangelsdorf et al., 1995). Of course, they continue to depend as well on caregivers to help them manage uncomfortable feelings. Without such support, infants may develop unhealthy emotional habits. For example, when parents habitually leave crying babies alone for extended periods, the babies may grow increasingly agitated when they cry, a pattern that makes it difficult later for parents to calm them down (Eisenberg, Cumberland, & Spinrad, 1988).

As children grow older, experience a range of emotionally significant events, and observe role models, they acquire more coping strategies (Saarni et al., 1998). They may observe their parents controlling anger physically yet expressing it verbally: "I'm angry that you said you were going to make dinner and didn't keep your commitment!" They may then use a similar strategy in dealing with peer conflicts: "You said you would meet me at four o'clock but you never showed up. Where were you?!" In Figure 9–2, you can see 7-year-old Miguel's drawing and comments about being angry. He wrote, "I try not to hit and shout," indicating he is learning to control his temper. Youngsters who appropriately control and express their emotions are those most likely to be popular with peers (Fabes et al., 1999). In the Emotional Development/Middle Childhood clip of the Observation CD, it is apparent that 10-year-old Daniel has learned the value of expressing anger in socially appropriate ways:

Interviewer:	What kinds of things make kids your age angry?
Daniel:	Not getting what you want, even though it's, there's no real good explanation for not getting it. At school, I guess reading some sorts of books that I don't like. They don't like teachers yelling at 'em. Or they don't like listening sometimes.
Interviewer:	What are some things kids do when they're angry?
Daniel:	Frowning, maybe crying, pouting, back talking.
Interviewer:	What things are hard for kids when they get angry?
Daniel:	Calming themselves down. Of course, then you can go back to reading comic books and playing video games.

Children also become better able to appraise advantages and disadvantages of particular coping strategies. For instance, a 14-year-old may observe a best friend becoming entangled in a fight or an intoxicated neighbor heading for her car with keys in hand; in such circumstances, the teenager quickly identifies a range of possible solutions and considers the potential benefits and disadvantages of each one. Sometimes children's appraisals of

FIGURE 9–2 Seven-year-old Miguel drew and commented on his efforts to express anger appropriately. He wrote, "I try not to hit and shout."

Listen to 10-year-old Daniel describe how children deal with anger in the Emotional Development/ Middle Childhood clip of the Observation CD.

self-conscious emotion
Affective state that reflects awareness of a community's social standards (e.g., pride, guilt, shame).

emotional regulation
Strategies to manage responses to stressful events (also called *coping*).

emotionally charged events enable them to deal directly with a problem—for instance, by confronting a peer. At other times, when they cannot change the situation, they instead try to deal with their emotions. For example, a child might alleviate anxiety about an upcoming test by reminding himself that he has done well in the past on such examinations.

Children also change developmentally in their choices of whom they go to for reassurance when they are sad or angry. In general, younger children are more inclined to go to adults (especially parents, other family members, and teachers) whereas older children and adolescents are more likely to seek support of peers (Rossman, 1992). You can see this developmental difference in the comments of 4-year-old Zoe and 13-year-old Crystal about how children deal with sadness in the Early Childhood and Early Adolescence clips of the Emotional Development module of the Observation CD:

Listen to 4-year-old Zoe and 13-year-old Crystal talk about being consoled by other people in the Early Childhood and Early Adolescence clips of the Emotional Development module of the Observation CD.

Zoe: They're angry sometimes. . . . I cry. . . . I don't know. . . . Have something to eat. . . . Tell the teacher. Have something to drink.

Crystal: Cry on somebody's shoulder or lean, like lean on somebody. For someone to comfort them. The counselor, or their friend, or a teacher [could help] . . . They could calm 'em down or to let them tell what's wrong. . . .

Zoe believes that her teacher will provide the necessary comfort. Crystal shares the opinion that social support is desirable, but mentions both adults and peers as people who can be helpful.

A final component of emotional regulation is determining when to express emotions publicly. Children gradually learn to curb their emotional reactions in order to protect themselves and other people (Cole, 1986). For example, many preschoolers understand that they should not reveal their true feelings when disappointed by a gift from a well-meaning relative. Many youngsters, especially some boys, believe they should not show sadness, as 15-year-old Greg explains in the Emotional Development/Late Adolescence clip of the Observation CD:

Listen to 15-year-old Greg explain how adolescents cope with sadness in the Emotional Development/Late Adolescence clip of the Observation CD.

Interviewer: What are some things that kids do when they're sad?

Greg: Cry, or like if you're a guy, you don't show it. . . . Eat, or just go with their really good friends and have them talk to them.

■ *Concern for others' feelings is an important emotional response that develops with age, especially when encouraged by adults.* **Empathy** is the capacity to experience the same feelings as another person, who perhaps may be in pain or distress (Damon, 1988; Eisenberg, 1982; M. L. Hoffman, 1991). Empathic concern for the welfare of other people is an important moral characteristic that we will examine in Chapter 10, and in Chapter 13, we will examine how children use empathic feelings when they take care of other people. You can hear 14-year-old Brendan express empathic concern as he talks about caring for injured birds in the Neighborhood/Early Adolescence clip in the Observation CD. When asked by the interviewer how he would improve his neighborhood if he could, Brendan replies that he would clean up the trash and "take all the birds that can't fly into your houses and take care of 'em until they're nursed back to health."

Listen to 14-year-old Brendan express empathic concern for injured birds in the Neighborhood/Early Adolescence clip of the Observation CD.

As an illustration of the research on children's empathy, consider a longitudinal study conducted when children were in second to fifth grade and again two years later (Zhou et al., 2002). Children who were empathic to the distress of others at the first phase of data collection (they showed emotional distress when they watched slides of people in distressing situations, such as a crying child in a war scene) showed higher social competence (being well-behaved and having friends) and fewer negative social behaviors (e.g., arguing, lying, physically harming others) two years later. Children tended to be empathic when they had mothers who were warm and expressive, a finding that is consistent with other research studies indicating that caregivers can cultivate empathy in children.

■ *Adolescence brings new anxieties and pressures.* Adolescents tend to be more emotionally volatile than younger children: They more often report feeling lonely, embarrassed, or anxious, and they have more extreme mood swings (Arnett, 1999). The hormonal changes that accompany puberty may account for some of this volatility. As young teenagers undergo rapid, uncontrollable physical changes, they may feel self-conscious and awkward, perhaps even alienated from their own bodies (Rudlin, 1993).

empathy
Capacity to experience the same feelings as another person, especially in pain or distress.

Environmental factors are probably even more influential (Arnett, 1999). Adolescence ushers in new situations and problems that young people haven't encountered before. As they grow more independent, they may find their needs and desires conflicting with those of parents and other authority figures (Arnett, 1999). Conflicts with peers become an increasing source of inner turmoil. School provides additional pressures: Worries about completing homework, achieving good grades, and "fitting in" with classmates are common concerns for adolescents (Phelan, Yu, & Davidson, 1994). All of these factors come into play for even the most "normal" adolescents, but some have additional challenges—perhaps living in poverty, experiencing ongoing family conflict, or being abused by a family member—that they must deal with (Cicchetti & Toth, 1998; Rutter & Garmezy, 1983).

Not surprisingly, many (though by no means all) adolescents perceive their lives as being quite stressful, particularly in industrialized Western countries (Arnett, 1999; Masten, Neemann, & Andenas, 1994). Some adolescents believe that the problems they face exceed their capabilities to cope effectively, but most find the resources they need to confront pressures in their lives (Masten et al., 1994). Adolescents may turn to their peers for understanding, or perhaps for distraction from their troubles. They may also express their frustrations through poetry and art. For example, early in his senior year of high school, 17-year-old Jeff felt "locked in" by the combined pressures of a demanding course load, impending due dates for college applications, and his role as confidant for several troubled friends. Late one night, he put his schoolwork aside to create the picture shown in Figure 9–3. Because he had trouble drawing human figures, he combined two favorite things—a soft drink and black-and-white cowhide—to represent himself. As you can see, a cage and gigantic boulder hold him in, and so he cannot join in as his peers (represented by other soft drink cans) frolic freely in the distance.

FIGURE 9–3 Drawing himself as a cow-patterned soda can, 17-year-old Jeff dramatically depicts how the pressures in his life prevent him from doing the things he would like to do.

Individual Differences in Temperament and Personality

Emotionally, children are different from one another even in early infancy. Some infants are fussy and demanding; others, like Mary in our opening case, are cheerful and easy to care for. Some are fearful and anxious; others actively seek novelty and adventure. Some are quiet and shy; others are sociable and outgoing. Such differences reflect **temperament**—ways of responding to events and novel stimulation, and of regulating impulses (J. Kagan, 1998a; Rothbart & Bates, 1998). Temperament has a genetic basis, as we shall see, but it also is very much affected by social experiences.

As children grow older, they also develop distinctive ways of behaving, thinking, and feeling. That is, they develop unique **personalities**. Temperament surely affects personality: a child who is timid relates to people and events differently than one who is socially confident. Yet a child can respond to any temperamental characteristic in countless ways. For example, an anxious child might learn to respond in one of these ways: withdrawing from other people; exploding with anger when others irritate him or her; becoming rigid and fussy; managing unpleasant worry through exercise, prayer, or meditation. But personality includes more than temperament. Personality is affected by children's intellectual interests and the many habits they learn while growing up—for example, traditions for fulfilling family obligations, strategies for dealing with stressful situations, styles of managing belongings, and preferences for spending leisure time. Think back to our introductory case: Mary's adolescent personality was more complex than could have been predicted from her cheerful temperament as an infant. She grew into an adolescent who was concerned with how others perceived her, believed she controlled her own destiny, avoided conflict, experienced jealousy, performed at high levels academically, and was optimistic about her future.

Both temperament and personality help us to understand how children respond to emotions, form relationships, and get on with their lives. Temperament may be especially helpful to consider when children are infants and toddlers; personality may be more useful as youngsters move through their childhood and adolescent years. We look at each in turn.

Temperament Many aspects of temperament, such as cheerfulness, outgoingness, moodiness, and anxiety, probably have a genetic basis; for example, identical twins reared in different homes often have similar temperaments (Henderson, 1982; Rothbart & Bates, 1998;

Despite gains in emotional regulation, adolescents can be emotionally volatile on occasion.

temperament
Constitutional ways of responding to emotional events and novel stimulation, and of regulating impulses.

personality
Characteristic way an individual person behaves, thinks, and feels.

Researchers suspect that cultural differences in temperament result partly from differing approaches to parenting. Many Japanese mothers comfort infants in a peaceful and soothing manner—an approach that may partly explain a tendency for Japanese children to be quiet and subdued.

Tellegren, Lykken, Bouchard, & Wilcox, 1988). Yet the genetic basis for temperament is best thought of as only a *predisposition* to behave in a certain way. That predisposition is then modified by experience (Kagan, 1998a; R. A. Thompson, 1998). For example, shy children have more opportunities to interact with other children—and thus they may overcome shyness—if they attend preschool rather than remain at home until kindergarten or first grade.

In addition, parents, teachers, and peers may intentionally cultivate certain ways of responding. In other words, children's emotional responses are the targets of **socialization**—systematic efforts by adults, other children, and institutions (e.g., schools and churches) to prepare youngsters to act in appropriate ways in their society (Harwood, Miller, & Irizarry, 1995). For instance, Japanese parents do much to keep their babies pacified and quiet, in part out of regard for a cultural ideal of harmony and in part out of consideration for neighbors who live on the other side of thin walls. Japanese mothers therefore talk infrequently, speak softly, and gently stroke their babies (Miyake, Campos, Kagan, & Bradshaw, 1986). In contrast, American mothers talk to infants frequently, often in an expressive and evocative manner, perhaps in an effort to stimulate cognitive development or strengthen the caregiver-infant relationship (e.g., Trainor, Austin, & Desjardins, 2000).

Research on temperamental characteristics suggests some stability over time. We therefore can, to some degree, predict children's later social behaviors from their temperament (Caspi, 1998; Kagan, 1998a; Rothbart & Bates, 1998; A. Thomas & Chess, 1977). For example, children who are inhibited and fearful as young children tend to become fairly anxious adolescents and adults (Caspi, 1998). Children who freely show negative affect (e.g., fussiness, frequent anger) in the early years are more likely to show negative affect (e.g., depression, anxiety) later in life (Caspi, 1998). Such stability is undoubtedly due both to genetic factors and to persistent characteristics of children's environments; that is, affectionate families continue to express confidence in their children, and unstable neighborhoods persist in attracting short-term residents with no regard for the children living there.

Professionals who work with groups of young children are often impressed with the remarkably different temperaments these children have. For example, infant caregivers often see particularly active babies who love to crawl around their environment, sway to music, and squirm in their high chairs (Thomas & Chess, 1977; Zero to Three: National Center for Infants, Toddlers, and Families, 2003). To meet their needs, caregivers may permit them to explore and move often. In contrast, infants who show a lower activity level may sit contently and let the world come to them. Caregivers may sit quietly with them, talk softly about pictures in a book, and acknowledge their focus on toys. Levels of adaptability also vary among infants and toddlers, with some moving easily between feeding, napping, and playing, and others resisting transitions. Caregivers can make the environment interesting for both groups of children, but for those who do not adapt smoothly to changes, they can explain routines, point out imminent changes, and reassure them when customary schedules must be altered.

Sensitive caregivers also strive to complement children's natural inclinations; they may reserve some quiet one-on-one time for highly mobile little tykes and model active movements for infants normally content to stay in one place. Additional specific examples of temperament and the implications for practitioners are provided in the Observation Guidelines table, "Noticing Temperament in Infants and Toddlers."

Personality Over time, a child integrates biologically based social-emotional tendencies with his or her experiences, relationships, and intellectual interests. The result is a distinctive and somewhat stable personality. For example, a child may be passionate about finding order in the material world. As a 4-year-old, he has an insatiable appetite for learning about dinosaurs; as an 8-year-old, he is fascinated with space and aeronautics; as a 12-year-old, he learns all he can about bridges and buildings; as a 16-year-old, he becomes an expert in computers; and as a young man, he prepares for a career in civil engineering. However, some children do change their personalities in rather substantial ways. Thus, a 6-year-old girl may be highly sociable, talking frequently, smiling at others, and befriending many peers, but evolve into a 14-year-old who prefers to spend time with just one close friend with whom she discloses her innermost feelings. Nor do children always act in the

socialization
Systematic efforts by other people and by institutions to prepare youngsters to act in ways deemed by society to be appropriate and responsible.

OBSERVATION GUIDELINES

Noticing Temperament in Infants and Toddlers

CHARACTERISTIC	LOOK FOR	EXAMPLE	IMPLICATION
Activity Level	*High activity level:* • squirms a lot • as infant, wiggles while getting diaper changed • as toddler, loves to run, climb, jump and explore *Low activity level:* • sits in high chair contentedly and watches the world go by • sits quietly on own and plays with toys	2-year-old Brenda is constantly on the move. Her caregiver finds he can more easily change her diaper if he cleans her bottom and then lets her stand, allowing her to help fasten the tabs on the new diaper.	For infants and toddlers with *high activity level*, provide many opportunities for safe exploration of the environment. Create challenges in the environment, such as a safe obstacle course with a favorite toy at the end. Encourage children to dance to music. Incorporate movement into quiet activities, such as reading a book, by encouraging children to flip and touch the pages. For children with *low activity level*, slow down to their pace and then invite more active play.
Sensitivity to Physical Input	*High sensitivity:* • withdraws from bright lights • cries when music is loud *Low sensitivity:* • doesn't mind new stimulation • doesn't pay much attention until stimulation is extreme	Angela reacts strongly to sudden changes, so her caregiver puts a new mobile in her lap and lets her get used to it before showing her how the mobile can be turned on to play music and rotate.	For *highly sensitive* children, keep the environment calm—dim the lights, play music quietly, and shield them from chaotic social events. For *less sensitive* children, watch for the kind of stimulation they crave. For example, if they like active social games, engage them in peek-a-boo, or roll a ball on your head and give them a turn.
Emotional Intensity	*High emotional intensity:* • fearful, cautious with new people and experiences • dramatic displays of anger, sadness *Low emotional intensity:* • quiet and does not fuss much • shows more interest when emotional exchanges are more intense	Raj is a very outgoing, passionate toddler—he laughs hard, cries hard, and has dramatic temper tantrums. His caregiver is patient with him and helps him to verbalize his negative feelings when they seem to get out of control.	For children who are *emotionally intense*, empathize with their strong feelings, and suggest appropriate ways to express them ("I can see you're angry. Remember: no biting. Can you come help me set the table?"). Help children who are *less emotionally intense* to articulate their feelings ("You look sad, can you tell me how you're feeling?").
Sociability	*High sociability:* • smiles at new people • enjoys playing in large groups • is somewhat independent of caregivers *Low sociability:* • doesn't interact with new people unless feels safe • prefers to play with one other child • stays close to familiar adult in new social situation	Tony is shy around other people, especially adults not in his immediate family. He would rather sit and play alone than join in an active group of toddlers climbing outside. His caregiver occasionally helps him to join in on fun interactions with other children.	For children who show *high sociability*, encourage this disposition. Also encourage them to sit and do quiet activities on their own. For children who show *low sociability*, let them warm up to new people slowly. For example, hold the child in your arms when meeting a new person; sit near the child when he or she ventures to play with an unfamiliar peer; and offer reassurance in new settings ("Let's go visit the preschool room and see what they do in there—they have an awesome slide").
Adaptability	*Ease with change:* • has an easy time with transitions, such as moving inside after outdoor play • notices changes in environment, such as new furniture, with interest but no concern *Difficulty with change:* • resists new objects and experiences, such as new cups with a different kind of lid • acts out during transitions between activities • is suspicious with new people	Thomas frets when going to bed at night. He acts out whenever there is a change of routine at school. When going to a new place, he demands continual attention from his father. His caregiver gives him plenty of warning when there is a change in routine and talks to him about novel events before they happen.	When children show *ease with change*, continue to make their world challenging, but also predictable. With children who have *difficulty with change*, establish routines so that children know what to expect from day to day, advise them when there is a departure from a regular routine ("We usually have nap time after lunch, but today we have a visitor first"), give them warning about a change ("When I turn off the light, it will be time to pick up toys"), and give choices when possible ("Would you prefer to build blocks or go to dramatic play?").

(continued)

OBSERVATION GUIDELINES

Noticing Temperament in Infants and Toddlers (continued)

CHARACTERISTIC	LOOK FOR	EXAMPLE	IMPLICATION
Persistence	*High persistence*: • can wait patiently while bottle is being heated in the microwave • shows tolerance for frustration *Low persistence*: • wants comfort immediately • gets frustrated easily	Rosemary shows no tolerance for frustration. When she is hungry, she wants her meal *now!* When completing puzzles, she gets angry when pieces don't fit immediately into the proper slots.	For *highly persistent* children, explain what you are doing to meet their needs ("I'm slicing up these apples for a healthy snack") and comment on their progress toward goals ("You are working hard on that puzzle!"). For children who show *little persistence*, offer comfort when they are frustrated ("Can I sit with you while you do that?"), help them to consider other ways to reach their desired goal ("What if you turned the puzzle piece around like this?"), and encourage them to break up difficult tasks into smaller, more manageable parts.

Based on observational indicators of temperament and recommendations for dealing with them in Zero to Three: National Center for Infants, Toddlers, and Families (2003). For basic distinctions in temperaments, see Thomas and Chess (1977).

same way across all settings. A child may be spontaneous and cheerful on the playground, yet be distracted and agitated in the classroom.

Recognizing that personality changes somewhat over time and across situations, psychologists have nevertheless found five dimensions of personality to be notably stable: *extraversion* (being socially outgoing), *agreeableness* (being warm and sympathetic), *conscientiousness* (being persistent and organized), *neuroticism* (being anxious and fearful), and *openness* (being curious and imaginative). These five dimensions were originally identified from research with adults, but they also characterize children (Caspi, 1998; Digman, 1989; John, 1990; John, Caspi, Robins, Moffitt, & Stouthamer-Loeber, 1994; McCrae, Costa, & Busch, 1986). The stability of these dimensions is due partly to genetics. Not quite half of individual differences in personality traits may be genetically determined; biological influences are strongest with extraversion and neuroticism (Loehlin, 1992).

Professionals who work with children often find it useful to consider children's personalities when determining how best to support them. Let's take a look at each of these five dimensions and consider how professionals might take them into account.

Extraversion. Extraverted children are active, assertive, emotionally expressive, talkative, enthusiastic, and socially outgoing. Extraverted children often appreciate opportunities to work on projects with peers. In addition, practitioners can intersperse opportunities for physical movement between quiet activities to give these children needed exercise, and perhaps provide a public forum, such as a dramatic performance, for expression. In contrast, children who are shy may benefit from explicit invitations from others to join them on the playground. Teachers and other professionals may need to help them ease into groups when other youngsters ignore them. Furthermore, practitioners are advised to keep shy children on their radar screen, since these children may not have the confidence to say what they feel, think, or need.

Agreeableness. Agreeable children are warm, responsive, generous, kind, sympathetic, and trusting. Children who are agreeable may be pleased to have validation that adults and other children appreciate their cooperative spirit. Practitioners may work to cultivate agreeableness in children who are less prone to be pleasant, coaching them to compliment other children, share toys, offer comfort to others in distress, and voice opinions without putting people down.

Conscientiousness. Conscientious children are attentive, persistent in activities, organized, and responsible. Practitioners can admire the persistence and organization shown by these children and point out how their style pays off in well-designed work products. Children who set lower standards and fail to complete tasks can be taught to set appropriate goals, to resist counterproductive urges, and to monitor their own progress toward goals; we will examine these strategies in discussions of self-regulation in Chapter 11.

Neuroticism. Neurotic children are anxious, fearful, lacking in confidence, and self-pitying. Children who are overly anxious and fearful may need support in dealing with negative feelings. They also need encouragement to try challenging tasks they would otherwise avoid because such difficult tasks trigger apprehension. Later in this chapter we will address tactics professionals can take to support children who worry excessively. Children who are relaxed and confident thrive when given continuous support from adults. No one is self-assured all the time, however, and adults can express extra support when normally confident children face momentous losses, personal failures, or traumatic events.

Openness. Children who are open are curious, artistic, exploring, and imaginative. Children who are particularly open intellectually need to exercise their budding skills in many contexts. Those who are less driven to explore art, literature, history, and the scientific world may need to be shown the intrigue and beauty of these and other fields.

We have examined these five personality dimensions separately. In fact, individual children combine the five dimensions in creative ways that can both delight and tax practitioners. For example, an after-school program supervisor may have one child who is socially outgoing but a bit anxious and not terribly agreeable; another child who is self-confident and conscientious, but somewhat conforming and slow to exercise her imagination; another who worries constantly and craves approval from adults but is quietly curious and thoughtful. Each child is truly one of a kind.

To respond constructively to such an array of personalities, professionals can reflect on how their activities lend themselves to varied profiles. For example, a first-grade teacher plans a Halloween activity of making "dirt" cake, knowing she can count on one boy to be methodical in measuring cocoa and other ingredients. She pairs him with another boy who will attack the project enthusiastically, but without restraint; together, they might make a good pair. She goes through her class, assigning partners who will similarly complement each other in terms of strengths and limitations. Permitting children to choose from among a few specified options is another way to respect their individuality. For instance, children might be asked to report on a book they have read, choosing from an array of defined options—a written analysis, poster, or oral presentation. Because children are naturally inclined to play to their strengths, it is also good practice to coach them on other occasions to use their less developed talents.

Temperament and personality draw our attention to important individual differences in how children express themselves. Other differences in emotional expression may be partly a result of membership in particular groups, as we will now see.

Group Differences in Emotions

All children progress developmentally in their expression and control of emotions. To some degree, their developmental pathways are influenced by group membership—by gender, family and culture, and socioeconomic status.

Gender Differences On average, male and female babies are similar in temperament; any gender differences are subtle and situation-dependent (Eisenberg, Martin, & Fabes, 1996). After the age of 2, however, consistent gender differences emerge. For instance, boys show more anger than girls beginning in the preschool years, and girls more often report feeling sad, fearful, and guilty beginning in the elementary grades (Eisenberg et al., 1996). Girls also respond more negatively to failures, to such an extent that their subsequent performance may suffer (Dweck, 1986). As early as elementary school, boys begin to put on a self-confident front when they feel vulnerable (Eisenberg et al., 1996; Sadker & Sadker, 1994).

Biology may be a source of some gender differences in emotions; for instance, rising hormonal levels at puberty are associated with increases in moodiness and depression in girls, but with aggressiveness and rebelliousness in boys (Buchanan, Eccles, & Becker, 1992; Susman, Inoff-Germain, et al., 1987). Yet many theorists suspect that differences in socialization are a more significant cause of gender differences in emotional responding (Durkin, 1995; Eisenberg et al., 1996; Sadker & Sadker, 1994). For instance, parents are more likely to discourage overt anger in daughters than in sons (Birnbaum & Croll, 1984; Malatesta & Haviland, 1982). Parents are apt to discourage sons from expressing emotions yet may encourage daughters to talk about their feelings (J. H. Block, 1979; Eisenberg et al., 1996). At school, many teachers prefer the passive, compliant nature that girls are more likely to exhibit (Bennett, Gottesman, Rock, & Cerullo, 1993; Pollack, 1998). Consider, for example, Pollack's (1998) observations of a fourth-grade classroom:[2]

> [O]n several occasions I had observed the fourth-grade class of Ms. Callahan. She was particularly skillful, modern, and warm in her approach, universally beloved by her students. I have every reason to believe that Ms. Callahan was a teacher who would want both boys and girls to derive all they could from the classroom experience.
>
> On this visit, some boys and girls who had been organized into "teams" were working together on a writing project about friendship. Adult volunteers were consultants for these teams and were helping them with their computer skills. I was surprised to see that instead of focusing on the writing project, Ms. Callahan's attention was almost entirely taken up by disciplining the boys. Several lively boys were making a commotion in one corner near the computer. Ms. Callahan cautioned them about making too much noise, and told them to return to their desks and wait their turns. With long faces, the boys meandered across the room and slumped into their seats. A moment later one of the boys could not resist calling out about something. Ms. Callahan gave him a stern second warning. "I don't want to have to caution you again," Ms. Callahan said. "If I do, you're heading for the principal's office."
>
> I had observed the class before, and now I noticed that two of the more creative male students—Robert and Shawn—were not in evidence. I asked Ms. Callahan if they were sick that day.
>
> "No," she explained. "Robert is too excitable for the group process. He's working on an entirely different project." She pointed him out—sitting alone on the floor, tucked out of view, banished from the team endeavor.
>
> "And where's Shawn?" I inquired.
>
> "He was telling inappropriate jokes about Albert Einstein earlier in the day and distracting the entire class. So, he's sitting outside working on his spelling," Ms. Callahan sighed. "Some kids just seem unable to fit into this more quiet team-based teaching."
>
> I wish I had asked her what those jokes about Albert Einstein were, but I was too concerned about her attitude toward these boys. She clearly felt that they could not "fit in" and that they were "unable" to participate appropriately, when I knew (as she did) that these were bright boys with a lot to offer. Although I doubt that Ms. Callahan would agree, I think the prevailing method in class that day was structured around the way girl students prefer to work, and that boys were at a disadvantage. (pp. 240–241)

Family and Cultural Differences   Earlier we suggested that temperamental differences in infants occur partly because of how parents in different cultures care for their babies. Cultural differences in socialization practices continue throughout childhood, resulting in noticeable differences in emotional responding. For instance, in China and Japan, many children are raised to be shy and restrained, whereas in Zambia, smiling and sociability are apt to be the norm (Chen, Rubin, & Sun, 1992; Hale-Benson, 1986; Ho, 1986, 1994; Rothbaum et al., 2000). Girls in India are more likely than British girls to be deferential and controlled, and to hide negative feelings such as anger and sadness, especially in the presence of adults (Joshi & MacLean, 1994).

Cultures also differ in how they deal with specific emotions, such as anger (Saarni, 2000). For example, some Kung! families in Botswana accept children's tantrums toward parents but discourage aggression toward peers; some working class families in Baltimore encourage aggression toward peers who themselves have caused injury. Many families in Japan ask children to focus on how others feel when they break social rules (Conroy, Hess, Azuma, & Kashiwagi, 1980; Konner, 1972; P. Miller & Sperry, 1987).

Families do not blindly carry out patterns in their culture and, in fact, families within a culture can differ markedly from one another in socializing emotional expression. In one study, for example, researchers listened to conversations among family members with 3-year-old children; some children *never* mentioned emotions during an hour-long conversation at home whereas one child mentioned emotions

Families within a culture or ethnic group can differ markedly from one another in emotional expression.

[2] From *Real Boys: Rescuing Our Sons from the Myths of Boyhood* by William Pollack, copyright © 1998 by William Pollack. Used by permission of Random House, Inc.

more than 27 times (Dunn, Brown, & Beardsall, 1991). When they occur, family "lessons" about emotions may help children to understand how emotions operate. For example, a longitudinal study examined 6-year-old children's understanding of complex emotions such as feeling happy about having more time to play when the school year ends, but also being sad because of missing one's teacher (J. R. Brown & Dunn, 1996). Children explained complex emotions more effectively when their parents had talked with them at age 3 about why people behave as they do, when they had older siblings who interacted positively with them, and when they possessed advanced language skills.

Socioeconomic Differences Children from low-income families are slightly more prone to emotional difficulties than children from middle-income families (Caspi, Taylor, Moffitt, & Plomin, 2000; McLoyd, 1998a). Environmental factors are almost certainly to blame for the majority of these differences. Children living in impoverished circumstances have more than their share of reasons to feel sad, fearful, and angry. For instance, they may not know where their next meal is coming from, and they are more likely to encounter violence and drug addiction in their neighborhoods. Their parents have limited resources (and sometimes limited energy) to address their needs and may discipline inconsistently (McLoyd, 1998a). Furthermore, many children from low-income backgrounds, particularly those with histories of learning problems, have few positive interactions with teachers at school (R. M. Clark, 1983). (We learn more about children's experiences in low-income environments in Chapter 14.)

The emotional stresses of middle- and high-income backgrounds can also be substantial, however. For example, some middle-income parents project their own aspirations onto their children. They may expect children to follow unrealistic developmental timetables such as cooperatively sharing toys with peers at 18 months and reading at three years. When children do not measure up, parents may become critical, overly directive, and controlling (Hyson, Hirsh-Pasek, Rescorla, Cone, & Martell-Boinske, 1991). Youngsters of all ages may worry about parental expectations, particularly when they think they are far from meeting them.

Professionals who work with children are in a strategic position to ensure that much goes right, rather than wrong, in children's lives. We now consider some strategies that adults can use to promote children's emotional development.

Promoting Children's Emotional Development

Emotions are an important part of children's everyday lives, yet many adults are uneasy in dealing with them (Sylvester, 1995). We propose that practitioners can promote emotional development if they consider emotions as *competencies*—that is, as valuable skills that can improve over time. Indeed, some theorists have argued that the ability to interpret and use emotions effectively is a kind of "intelligence" (Bodine & Crawford, 1999; Goleman, 1995; J. D. Mayer, 2001). This may be appropriate: In Chapter 6, we defined intelligence as "the ability to benefit from experiences and thereby modify future behaviors to accomplish new tasks successfully." This definition has a practical ring: It is action-oriented and conveys the importance of learning from everyday experience. Emotions, like other forms of intelligence, are action-oriented, as we've previously noted, and guide behavior toward personally relevant needs and goals.

How can emotional competencies be cultivated in work with infants, children, and adolescents? We offer these suggestions:

■ *Help crying infants find comfort.* Caregivers can do several things to help infants in distress. First, they can strive to give timely reassurance—not always immediately, as they are likely to have other demands—but avoid delaying to such an extent that crying escalates into turbulent agitation. Second, caregivers can permit the actions infants use to reduce their own stress. Searching for a favorite blanket, putting a finger in the mouth, tugging at an ear with a gentle hand—these are positive signs that infants are learning to soothe themselves. Third, caregivers can consciously invite a baby to join them in a calm state—showing baby a smiling face, holding baby close to the chest, rubbing baby gently, and trying to breathe in a shared rhythm (Gonzalez-Mena, 2002). Fourth, caregivers can investigate why the infant is crying and try to meet the unfilled need or remove the painful stimulus, as suggested in Chapter 3. Finally, caregivers should try to stay calm and not take it personally—infants sometimes cry despite the most sensitive care.

■ *Create an atmosphere of warmth, acceptance, and trust.* Children learn and perform more successfully when they have positive emotions—for instance, when they feel secure, happy, and excited about an activity (Boekaert, 1993; Isen, Daubman, & Gorgoglione, 1987; Oatley & Nundy, 1996). And they are more likely to confide in an adult about troublesome issues if they know that the adult will continue to like and respect them no matter what they may reveal about themselves in heart-to-heart conversations.

■ *Encourage young people to express their feelings.* Children and adolescents can better deal with their feelings when they are aware of what their feelings are. Some teachers successfully incorporate discussions about feelings into everyday classroom routines. For example, when Teresa's son Connor was in first grade, his teacher ended each day with "circle time." She asked the children to hold hands and communicate how they felt about their day: one squeeze for happy, two squeezes for sad, three squeezes for bored, and so on. They took turns, and, without words, communicated how they felt; all eyes were glued on the single hand doing the squeezing. This simple exercise gave the children a chance to reflect on, and then communicate, their basic emotional states.

To have a significant impact on children's emotional expression, adults need to support emotional expression systematically and repeatedly (Raver, 2002). One illustration of a comprehensive emotional education program is the Promoting Alternative Thinking Strategies (PATHS) curriculum (Greenberg, Kusche, Cook, & Quamma, 1995). Sixty lessons in second- and third-grade classrooms focus on self-control, emotions, and problem solving. Children are taught that emotional feelings are okay, some feelings are comfortable and others uncomfortable, feelings can help them learn what to do in certain situations, and some ways of dealing with feelings are better than others. Children keep a record of their feelings and use a poster showing a traffic signal as a guide to regulating their responses to feelings. Teachers encourage children to refer to the poster—to stop and calm down (red), to slow down and consider their options (yellow), and to try their plan (green). This program has been implemented with children from a range of ability levels; it has been shown to increase emotional understanding and to decrease problem behaviors (Greenberg, Domitrovich, & Bumbarger, 2000).

Some children are reluctant to share their feelings publicly. When they are young, they can find safe outlets for emotional expression in play. Through fantasy play with peers, children often work out their fears and anger (Kohlberg & Fein, 1987). For older children, writing about feelings, perhaps in essays or journals shared only with a teacher or counselor, can provide a confidential outlet. In the essay in Figure 9–4, 10-year-old Shea describes her growing awareness of the various emotions she experiences. In the journal entry in Figure 9–5, 8-year-old Noah—ordinarily a happy, energetic student—reveals how upset he is about his parents' divorce.

■ *Discuss emotions experienced by characters you study in literature and history.* Stories provide many opportunities to talk about emotional states. We have found in our own experience that children in the elementary grades are able to make sensible guesses about how characters' emotional states lead them to particular courses of action. For instance, in *Frog and Toad Are Friends* (Lobel, 1979), a book suitable for 4- to 8-year-olds, Frog waits impatiently to play with his hibernating friend, Toad, and plays a trick on him to get him up early. The story provides a forum for discussions about feelings one can have with friends, such as anger at being teased (Solomon, Watson, Battistich, Schaps, & Delucchi, 1992). After reading Judith Viorst's (1972) *Alexander and the Terrible, Horrible, No Good, Very Bad Day*, children can relate their own memories of feeling angry, disappointed, or frustrated. Older children and adolescents can read firsthand historical accounts for tales of inequities and hostilities—good groundwork for discussions about how people deal with feelings.

■ *Ask children to guess what emotions people may feel in particular scenarios.* Children can practice analyzing situations and considering how those involved might feel. In Figure 9–6, you can see the kinds of situations an elementary school counselor asks children to pretend they face. Adults can guide children to see that anger, fear, guilt,

What Hits Me

Feeling excitment bubble inside know something great is waiting to happen to you. Feeling scared or nervous, want to dive under the covers and go back to sleep even though it is 8:30 and it is almost time to go to school. Feeling sad because your parents got divorced and you dad just moved out of the house. Feeling scared and excited at same time because you have discovered something that's mysterious and you are determind to figur it out.

FIGURE 9–4 In this "What Hits Me" essay, 10-year-old Shea describes her experiences with various emotions.

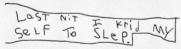

FIGURE 9–5 In this journal entry, 8-year-old Noah reveals his sadness about his parents' recent divorce.

Marissa and Wendy Sue have been good friends for a long time. Marissa told Lucy about Wendy Sue's family. Wendy Sue had asked her not to tell anyone.

FIGURE 9–6 Counselors can ask children to pretend they are characters in particular situations, such as this one, and help them talk about how they might feel and respond. Idea courtesy of Sally Tossey, Columbus, Ohio.

and other feelings are reasonable reactions to particular circumstances. In addition, they can ask children to think about how they might act when they have such uncomfortable feelings.

■ *Take cultural differences into account.* As we have seen, some cultures encourage open expression of feelings, whereas others actively discourage such expressiveness. Adults working with children from diverse cultures must continually be mindful of such differences when interpreting children's emotional expressions (or lack thereof).

■ *Help children keep anxiety at a manageable level.* **Anxiety** is an emotional state characterized by worry and apprehension, often about future events with unknown outcomes. When we are anxious, we may experience such physiological symptoms as muscle tension and headaches, and we may have trouble concentrating. In Figure 9–7, you can see an excerpt from 10-year-old Andy's expression of dread prior to leaving for summer camp.

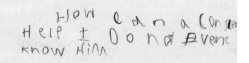

FIGURE 9–7 Ten-year-old Andy was anxious about going to summer camp and explained his feelings in a series of yellow sticky notes. Andy was especially concerned about sleeping away from home and missing his family. He also commented that the rules "stink." In this excerpt, Andy wonders "How can a counselor help? I do not even know him."

Practitioners can do a variety of things to help keep anxiety at a manageable level. For instance, when teachers assign oral reports, they can encourage students to create index cards or other memory "crutches." Before giving an important test (such as the standardized tests that many school districts require), they can administer a practice test that gives students a general idea of what to expect. And in general, professionals should make sure that in classrooms and other learning environments, no single assessment is so important that a child's ultimate success or failure depends on it.

■ *Pay attention to your own emotions.* Professionals often find themselves angered, saddened, and frustrated by the people they serve. Consider this description by Beverly Davis (2001), a practitioner and clinical supervisor in child protective services:

> Each working day, child protective service workers' emotions reflect the intensity of human trauma, safety and danger in their midst. . . . Not only are they vulnerable to the personal responses that these experiences evoke, but there is the potential for being flooded with these induced feelings, resulting in unmanageable anxiety. . . . This is particularly true when working with children and adults who have limited control over their emotions and behavior. Their heightened impulsivity and direct emotional expressions place more pressure on child protective service staff for control. Hence a great deal of staff energy is directed to managing and containing their reactions to the families' emotional needs. This may lead to their emotional depletion, a major occupational hazard. (p. 446)

Davis recommends that professionals in child protective services talk honestly with one another about their feelings. They can also speculate on what their emotions might signify. For example, a social worker may feel angry toward a mother who is not cooperating with his recommendations. Further reflection may lead him to realize that this mother does have the best interest of her children at heart but perceives him to be intrusive and out of touch with *her* reality.

We also urge you to attend to uncomfortable feelings children and families may elicit in you. Otherwise, for example, children who are irritable and hostile might provoke you to become coercive—not a style that will help them develop a sunnier disposition or greater self-control.

Adults can model staying calm in stressful situations, and they can help relieve children's anxiety by talking through problems in a warm, supportive manner.

■ *Model appropriate ways of dealing with negative emotions.* Youngsters often struggle with how to deal with anger, fear, and sadness; they can benefit from seeing adults express these emotions appropriately. Teresa vividly remembers how her fifth-grade teacher expressed anger: Rather than raising her voice, she lowered it to a whisper. Her approach worked well: Students sensed her disappointment, responded with concern and guilt, and tried to make amends. Practitioners can enhance the benefits of modeling controlled, honest emotional reactions by offering an explanation: "I'm really angry now. Let's talk this out when we've both calmed down."

Some children have such strong emotions that simply talking about feelings and modeling appropriate ways of coping will have limited effect. We now look at serious emotional problems that some youngsters have, as well as at strategies that practitioners can use with them.

anxiety
Emotional state characterized by worry and apprehension.

Emotional Problems in Children and Adolescents

In the opening case study, Mary's mother suffered from an "emotional disturbance." Adults and children alike experience fluctuations in mood. However, some people have more than their share of negative emotional experiences, to the point where their quality of life and ability to tackle everyday problems are disrupted.

Some emotional problems are manifested in *externalizing behaviors*, actions that affect other people; examples are aggression, destructiveness, lying, stealing, defiance, and lack of self-control. Others are manifested in *internalizing behaviors*, actions that typically affect only the individual who has the problem; examples are depression, anxiety, withdrawal from social interaction, eating disorders, and suicidal tendencies. When distressed, boys are more likely to display externalizing behaviors; girls are more likely to develop internalizing disorders (Rutter & Garmezy, 1983). Although youngsters with externalizing behaviors are more likely to be referred for evaluation and special services (Kerr & Nelson, 1989), those with internalizing behaviors are often at just as much risk for school failure and social problems.

Emotional problems are affected by both nature and nurture. Many emotional problems are believed to result from environmental factors, such as child abuse, inconsistent parenting practices, stressful living conditions, exposure to violence, and family drug or alcohol abuse (H. C. Johnson & Friesen, 1993; G. R. Patterson, DeBaryshe, & Ramsey, 1989; Shaffer, 1988). We got a sense of the impact of environmental problems earlier when we examined attachment. If children are not comforted by caregivers when they are distressed, they eventually give up, pretending they are fine when they are really deeply troubled. Or they may explode with anger, not having been coached in self-control and not caring what other people think. At the same time, biological causes, such as heredity, chemical imbalances, brain injuries, and illnesses, can also contribute to these problems (Hallowell, 1996; Johnson & Friesen, 1993). Overall, it appears that no single factor—biological, psychological, or environmental—entirely accounts for serious emotional difficulties, except in extreme conditions (Cicchetti & Toth, 1998).

Three emotional-behavioral disorders are fairly common in children and adolescents: depression, anxiety disorder, and conduct disorder. We look at each of these conditions and then formulate some recommendations for working with youngsters who have ongoing emotional problems.

Depression People with **depression** feel exceptionally sad, discouraged, and hopeless; they may also feel restless, sluggish, helpless, worthless, or guilty (American Psychiatric Association, 1994; Seligman, 1991). Seriously depressed individuals may have trouble concentrating, lose interest in their usual activities, have little appetite, and have difficulty sleeping (American Psychiatric Association, 1994; Hertel, 1994). In children and adolescents, irritability may be more evident than sadness. Other common characteristics of depression in young people include complaints about physical pain, withdrawal from social relationships, significant substance abuse, and talk of suicide. In a variation of depression, *bipolar disorder* (also known as *manic-depression*), occurs when individuals experience periods of extreme elation (*mania*) as well as periods of deep depression.

The specific symptoms of depression vary somewhat from culture to culture. The American Psychiatric Association provides several examples of how depression might manifest itself in different cultures:

> Complaints of "nerves" and headaches (in Latino and Mediterranean cultures), of weakness, tiredness, or "imbalance" (in Chinese and Asian cultures), of problems of the "heart" (in Middle Eastern cultures), or of being "heartbroken" (among Hopi). (American Psychiatric Association, 1994, p. 324)

Many instances of depression and bipolar disorder probably have biological, and possibly genetic, roots (Cicchetti, Rogosch, & Toth, 1997; Griswold & Pessar, 2000). These conditions tend to run in families, are often foreshadowed by temperamental moodiness and insecure attachment, and may reflect chemical imbalances (Cicchetti et al., 1997; Griswold & Pessar, 2000). Yet environmental factors often play a role as well; for instance, the death of a loved one, mental illness or marital conflict in parents, child maltreatment, poverty, and inadequate schools may bring about or worsen depressive symptoms (Cicchetti et al., 1997). When in-

depression
Emotional condition characterized by significant sadness, discouragement, and hopelessness.

dividuals yield to extreme stress with a depressive episode, the event may alter their neurological chemistry, making it more likely that they will suffer another depressive episode in the future (Akiskal & McKinney, 1973; Antelman & Caggiula, 1977; Siever & Davis, 1985).

Before adolescence, depression and bipolar disorder are rare. Their prevalence increases during adolescence; for instance, 5% to 10% of teenagers have one or more major depressive episodes (Cicchetti et al., 1997). During childhood, depression rates are approximately equal for boys and girls, but by age 16, rates are considerably higher for girls than for boys, perhaps because girls are more likely to dwell on their problems (Cicchetti et al., 1997; Eisenberg et al., 1996; Nolen-Hoeksema, 1987).

How might depression emerge in the life of a child? Let's consider Billy, a 5-year-old boy who's just entered kindergarten. His single mother suffers from depression and gives him little attention. She occasionally gives in to his persistent demands, but at other times she vacillates between indifference and explosive anger. When Billy first comes to school, he clings anxiously to his mother. When she leaves, he is irritable and tired, and he has trouble focusing on activities and interacting with peers. He is not diagnosed with depression for another 10 years, when he now shows classic symptoms—missing school, sleeping irregularly, abusing alcohol, and feeling sad a lot of the time. Billy exemplifies two of the vulnerability factors for depression: a possible genetic predisposition to a moody temperament (inherited from his mother) and an insecure attachment to his mother (the outcome of harsh parenting).

Suicide. Suicide is an ever-present risk for youth with serious depression or bipolar disorder. Depressed individuals who contemplate suicide often believe that they face problems they cannot solve or have extreme emotional pain they wish to end (D. Miller, 1994). Approximately 15% of individuals with a major depressive disorder die by their own hand (American Psychiatric Association, 1994).

The overwhelming despair and high frequency of suicide that characterize depression make it a condition professionals must take seriously. Through their daily contact with youngsters, teachers and other practitioners have numerous opportunities to observe fluctuations in mood and performance and so may spot cases of possible depression in children. (Friends and family, though they may have closer ties to youngsters, may not comprehend how serious a problem is or may possibly deny its existence.) Professionals will want to offer emotional reassurance to young people who appear troubled, but they should consult with supervisors and counselors if they suspect depression or another serious emotional disturbance.

Anxiety Disorders In its milder forms, anxiety is a common and very "normal" emotion. But some people, including some children and adolescents, worry excessively and find it difficult to control their worrisome thoughts and feelings; in other words, they have an **anxiety disorder** (American Psychiatric Association, 1994). Children with a *generalized anxiety disorder* tend to worry excessively about a wide variety of things—perhaps including their academic achievement, their performance in sports, and potential catastrophic events such as wars or hurricanes. Some individuals have more specific anxiety disorders—perhaps worrying excessively about gaining weight, having a serious illness, being away from family and home, or feeling embarrassed in public (American Psychiatric Association, 1994).

Anxiety as a trait tends to run in families, and individuals with anxiety disorders also tend to have biological relatives with other affective disorders, such as major depression (American Psychiatric Association, 1994; Last, Hersen, Kazdin, Francis, & Grubb, 1987). Furthermore, children with anxiety disorders are more susceptible to other emotional difficulties, such as serious depression (Mattison, 1992). There are hints in the research that family environment may play a role in the onset of anxiety disorders, but more investigation is needed (Famularo, Kinscherff, & Fenton, 1992; Mattison, 1992).

Conduct Disorder When children and adolescents display a chronic pattern of externalizing behaviors, they are sometimes identified as having a **conduct disorder.** Youngsters who display a conduct disorder ignore the rights of others in ways that are unusual for their age. Common symptoms include aggression to people and animals (e.g., initiating physical fights, forcing someone into sexual activity, torturing animals), destruction of property (e.g., setting fires, painting graffiti), theft and deceitfulness (e.g., breaking into cars, lying

anxiety disorder
Chronic emotional condition characterized by excessive, debilitating worry.

conduct disorder
Chronic emotional condition characterized by lack of concern for the rights of others.

about shoplifting so as not to be caught), and serious violations of rules (e.g., ignoring reasonable curfews, being truant from school) (American Psychiatric Association, 1994).

One or two antisocial acts do not necessarily indicate a serious emotional problem. Conduct disorders are more than a matter of "kids being kids" or "sowing wild oats." Instead, they represent deep-seated and persistent disregard for the rights and feelings of others, as reflected in a *consistent* pattern of antisocial behavior, often beginning in the early elementary years. Youths with conduct disorder tend to see the world through conflict-colored glasses, for example by always assuming that others have hostile intentions toward them (Crick & Dodge, 1994).

Approximately 2% to 6% of school-age youths could be classified as conduct disordered, with rates being three or four times higher for boys than for girls (Kazdin, 1997). Particular manifestations of conduct disorder vary by gender: Boys are more likely to engage in theft and aggression; girls are apt to engage in sexual misbehavior. When boys and girls exhibit conduct disorders in childhood and adolescence, they are likely to have problems in adulthood, including antisocial and criminal behavior, frequent changes in employment, high divorce rates, little participation in families and community groups, and early death (Kazdin, 1997).

As is true for the emotional disorders we've previously considered, biology may be *partly* to blame for conduct disorders; for instance, children and adolescents with conduct disorders may have difficulty inhibiting aggressive impulses, perhaps as a result of brain damage or other neurological abnormalities (Dempster & Corkill, 1999; Gladwell, 1997; Kazdin, 1997). Family environments may be influential as well: Conduct disorders are more common when children's parents provide little affection, are highly critical, and unpredictably administer harsh physical punishment (Blackson et al., 1999; DeKlynen, Speltz, & Greenberg, 1998; Kazdin, 1997; G. R. Patterson et al., 1989; Webster-Stratton & Hammond, 1999). Tragically, some school environments contribute to the problem. Conduct disorders are more frequently observed in situations where teachers have low expectations for students, provide little encouragement or praise for schoolwork, and put little effort into planning lessons (Kazdin, 1997).

Working with Young People Who Have Serious Emotional Problems   Effective programs for youngsters with emotional disorders are usually individualized. Without such adaptations, schools, social programs, and recreational settings are difficult places for youths with serious emotional problems. As a telling statistic, less than half of students with serious emotional problems graduate from high school (Bassett et al., 1996; Koyanagi & Gaines, 1993). Teachers, psychologists, and special education professionals can collaboratively design support systems. Professionals such as camp counselors who work with youths in other capacities may wish to consult with mental health specialists to determine kinds of accommodations they can make. In addition, practitioners can consider these strategies:

■ *Show an interest in the well-being of all children and adolescents.*   Many youngsters with emotional disorders have few positive and productive ties with individuals outside of school, and so their relationships with caring professionals may become all the more important (S. C. Diamond, 1991). The many "little things" professionals do each day—greeting youngsters warmly, expressing concern when they seem worried, and lending a ready ear when they want to share their ideas or frustrations—can make a world of difference (S. C. Diamond, 1991).

■ *Teach social skills.*   Many children and adolescents with emotional problems have difficulty maintaining friendships (Asher & Coie, 1990; Cartledge & Milburn, 1995; Schonert-Reichl, 1993). Practicing effective social skills, such as saying something friendly to a peer, seems to improve peer relationships in these youngsters (e.g., Gillham, Reivich, Jaycox, & Seligman, 1995). (We will look at specific strategies for teaching social skills in our discussion of peer relationships in Chapter 13.)

■ *Provide extra structure for youngsters who have high levels of anxiety.*   Communicate expectations for performance in clear and concrete terms. Highly anxious youngsters perform better in well-structured environments, such as classrooms with explicit expectations for academic achievement and social behavior (Hembree, 1988; Stipek, 1993; Tobias,

1977). If you can find out what's bothering these youngsters, you may be able to help. For instance, a preschool teacher might initiate a morning routine for a child to stand at the window to wave good-bye to parents. A coach might set specific goals for athletes rather than allowing them to worry about outrageously high standards.

■ *Be alert for signs that a child or adolescent may be contemplating suicide.*   Seriously depressed youngsters often give signs that they may be thinking about taking their own lives. Such warning signs include the following (Kerns & Lieberman, 1993):

- Sudden withdrawal from social relationships
- Disregard for personal appearance
- A dramatic personality change
- A sudden elevation in mood
- A preoccupation with death and morbid themes
- Overt or veiled threats (e.g., "I won't be around much longer")
- Actions that indicate "putting one's affairs in order" (e.g., giving away prized possessions)

Adults must take any of these behaviors seriously. They should show genuine caring and concern for potentially suicidal youngsters, and they should also seek trained help, for example, from a school psychologist or counselor, *immediately* (McCoy, 1994).

Adults must always be alert for signs that a youngster is seriously depressed. If they suspect that a young person is contemplating suicide, they should seek trained help immediately.

■ *Set reasonable limits for behavior.*   All children need to learn that certain actions— aggression, destructiveness, stealing, and so on—are unacceptable. Establishing rules for appropriate behavior and giving consequences (e.g., loss of privileges) for infractions provide the structure and guidance many children need to keep undesirable behaviors in check (Turnbull et al., 2002).

■ *Give children and adolescents a sense that they have some control.*   Some young people, especially those who consistently defy authority figures, often behave even less appropriately when people try to control them. With such youngsters, it is important that practitioners not get into power struggles, situations where only one person "wins" and the other inevitably loses. Instead, adults might create situations in which children conform to expectations yet also know they have some control over what happens to them. For instance, students in a classroom can learn techniques for observing and monitoring their own actions (Kern, Dunlap, Childs, & Clark, 1994). They can also be given choices (within reasonable limits) about how to proceed in particular situations (Knowlton, 1995).

To some extent, children's emotional well-being is related to how they perceive themselves— for instance, whether they see themselves as capable or incapable of handling life's daily challenges, whether they compare favorably or unfavorably with those around them, and whether they like or dislike the person they see in the mirror. We turn our attention now to children's knowledge, beliefs, and feelings about themselves as human beings.

Development of a Sense of Self

Let's look once again at 18-year-old Mary's description of herself:

> If I say how I am, it sounds like bragging—I have a good personality and people like me. I'm not the greedy type—I'm jealous a lot of times, yes. And I don't like it when people think they can run my own life—I like to be my own judge. I know right and wrong, but I feel I have a lot more to learn and go through. Generally, I hope I can make it—I hope. (Werner & Smith, 1982, p. 140)

Like Mary, youngsters often have definite beliefs about themselves, their personal attributes, and their strengths and weaknesses; these beliefs constitute their **self-concept.** Mary's self-concept includes her reflection that she is likeable, independent, and prone to jealousy. **Self-esteem,** on the other hand, refers to the feelings people have about their capabilities and worth. Mary seems to have positive feelings about herself—so much so that

self-concept
Beliefs that people have about themselves, their characteristics, and their abilities.

self-esteem
Feelings that people have about their own capabilities and self-worth.

she thinks she might come across as "bragging." Children's self-perceptions include their self-concept, self-esteem, and other specific beliefs about themselves.[3]

Factors Influencing Self-Perceptions

Several factors affect children's self-concept and self-esteem. From the very beginning of life and extending into adulthood, the behaviors of other people—family members, other adults, siblings, and peers—play a crucial role in the development of individuals' self-concepts (Durkin, 1995; Harter, 1983b, 1988, 1998; Hartup, 1989). When we examined attachment, we suggested that children use their experiences with caregivers for ideas on how to act in relationships. Children also learn about *themselves* from their history of interactions with caregivers (Bretherton, 1991). Thus, a child may learn not only that his caregiver treats him lovingly, but also that he is lovable.

Caregivers continue to send messages as children grow and develop. For example, parents who accept their children as they are and treat children's concerns as important are likely to have children with high self-esteem. Parents who punish children for the things they cannot do, without also praising them for things done well, are likely to have children with low self-esteem (Harter, 1983b).

The behaviors of adults outside the family have an impact as well; for example, the relative proportion of positive and negative feedback that teachers give influences youngsters' expectations for future academic success (e.g., T. D. Little, Oettingen, Stetsenko, & Baltes, 1995). Peers also communicate information about youngsters' social competence through a variety of behaviors—for example, by seeking out their companionship or by ridiculing them in front of others. Some adolescents are especially preoccupied with peers' approval, basing their own sense of self-worth largely on what peers think of them (Harter, Stocker, & Robinson, 1996).

Children's own past behaviors and performance are also influential. To some extent, their self-concepts and self-esteem depend on how successfully they have behaved in the past (Damon, 1991; H. W. Marsh, 1990a). Children are more likely to believe they have an aptitude for mathematics if they have been successful in previous math classes, and to believe that they are likable individuals if they have been able to establish and maintain friendly peer relationships.

So far our discussion has focused primarily on the effects of children's experiences—that is, of environment—in self-perceptions. Biology also has an impact, although indirectly. Inherited temperamental tendencies, physical skills, and intellectual capabilities contribute to children's successes in social, athletic, and academic pursuits. Furthermore, physical appearance is a highly influential factor in the self-esteem of people of all ages (Harter, 1998); for instance, adults respond differently to children depending on their perceived physical attractiveness (Langlois, 1981; E. Maccoby & Martin, 1983). And children with disabilities—conditions that often have biological roots—report less positive self-concepts, on average, than their nondisabled peers (e.g., Harter, Whitesell, & Junkin, 1998).

Developmental Trends in Children's Self-Perceptions

The physical, cognitive, and social capabilities of children change with age, and their perceptions of themselves shift accordingly:

■ *Self-perceptions become increasingly abstract.* Young children tend to define themselves in terms of external and concrete characteristics. As they grow older, they begin to define themselves more in terms of internal and abstract characteristics (Harter, 1983a, 1988; Livesley & Bromley, 1973; M. Rosenberg, 1986). For example, Jeanne once asked her three children to describe themselves. Their responses were as follows:

Adults can help young people develop positive views about themselves by helping them to succeed and by treating them kindly.

---

[3] Theorists often have difficulty distinguishing between *self-concept* and *self-esteem*, as the two constructs clearly overlap (Hart, 1988; Marsh & Craven, 1997; Wigfield & Karpathian, 1991). In general, they tend to use *self-concept* to refer to *cognition* (beliefs, theories) about the self and *self-esteem* to refer to *affect* (emotions). Another distinction emerges as children grow: self-concept becomes a complex hierarchy of beliefs whereas self-esteem remains a single global feeling about oneself.

Jeff (age 6): I like animals. I like making things. I do good in school. I'm happy. Blue eyes. Yellow hair. Light skin.

Alex (age 9): I have brown hair, brown eyes. I like wearing short-sleeved shirts. My hair is curly. I was adopted. I was born in Denver. I like all sorts of critters. The major sport I like is baseball. I do fairly well in school. I have a lizard, and I'm going to get a second one.

Tina (age 12): I'm cool. I'm awesome. I'm way cool. I'm twelve. I'm boy crazy. I go to Brentwood Middle School. I'm popular with my fans. I play viola. My best friend is Lindsay. I have a gerbil named Taj. I'm adopted. I'm beautiful.

Notice how Jeff and Alex mostly talked about how they looked, how they behaved, and what they liked. In contrast, Tina described more abstract qualities—cool, awesome, boy crazy, popular, beautiful—that she had apparently derived from many specific, concrete experiences over time. (Appropriately, her list did not include "modest.")

■ *Self-perceptions become increasingly differentiated.* As children grow older, they develop more differentiated beliefs about themselves (Harter, 1983a; M. Rosenberg, 1986). For example, they come to see themselves as good at some things and not so good at others: A child may perceive herself to be proficient at running but clumsy at gymnastics. When we talk about people's self-beliefs at this level, we are often talking about their **self-efficacy**—their beliefs about whether they are capable of achieving certain goals or outcomes (e.g., Bandura, 1982, 1997).

Children and adolescents tend to behave in ways that are consistent with their beliefs about themselves and their expectations for future success or failure (Pintrich & Garcia, 1994; Yu, Elder, & Urdan, 1995). Children who have positive beliefs about themselves in particular domains are those most likely to succeed in these areas (Assor & Connell, 1992; Ma & Kishor, 1997; H. W. Marsh & Yeung, 1998; F. Pajares, 1996). For instance, those who believe that they are capable of high academic achievement are more likely to pay attention in class, use effective learning strategies, seek out challenges, and persist in the face of difficulty (Eccles, Wigfield, & Schiefele, 1998; D. K. Meyer, Turner, & Spencer, 1994; Zimmerman & Bandura, 1994). In contrast, those who believe they are "poor students" are more likely to misbehave in class, study infrequently or not at all, ignore homework assignments, and avoid taking difficult subjects.

■ *Self-perceptions also become more integrated.* Eventually, children pull the distinctions they make about themselves into an integrated conception of who they are (Harter, 1988). Around age 15, they identify aspects of their self-definitions that are potentially contradictory and then develop higher-level understandings that resolve these contradictions (Harter, 1988). For instance, they may resolve their perceptions of being both "cheerful" and "depressed" into a realization that they are "moody," or they may explain their inconsistent behaviors in different situations by concluding that they are "flexible" or "open-minded" (Harter, 1988).

■ *Children gradually base self-assessments on comparisons with peers.* Young children (e.g., first graders) tend to base self-evaluations largely on their own improvement over time. Older children (e.g., sixth graders) are more likely to consider how well classmates perform when they evaluate their own capabilities (H. W. Marsh, 1990b; J. G. Nicholls, 1984; Pintrich & Schunk, 1996). Adolescents who think they do better than others are likely to develop positive views of their abilities, whereas those who think they perform less well may develop negative self-perceptions.

■ *With age, self-concepts become more stable.* Children with positive self-perceptions in the early years also tend to have positive self-perceptions in later years. Conversely, children who think poorly of themselves in elementary school also tend to have lower self-esteem in high school (H. W. Marsh & Craven, 1997; O'Malley & Bachman, 1983; Savin-Williams & Demo, 1984). As children get older, their self-perceptions become increasingly stable, probably for several reasons:

1. People usually behave in ways that are consistent with what they believe about themselves, and their behaviors are likely to produce reactions from others that confirm their self-concepts.

self-efficacy
Belief that one is capable of executing certain behaviors or reaching certain goals in a particular task or domain.

2. People tend to seek out information that confirms what they already believe: Those with positive self-perceptions are more likely to seek out positive feedback, whereas those with negative self-perceptions may actually look for information about their weaknesses (S. Epstein & Morling, 1995; Swann, 1997).

3. People seldom put themselves in situations where they believe they won't succeed, thereby eliminating any possibility of discovering that they *can* succeed. For example, if a teenager believes he is a poor athlete and so refuses to go out for the baseball team, he may never learn that, in fact, he has the potential to become a good player.

4. Factors that contribute to one's self-esteem—for example, parents' behaviors, socioeconomic circumstances, and one's physical attractiveness—usually remain relatively stable throughout childhood (O'Malley & Bachman, 1983).

This is not to say that once children acquire unfavorable self-concepts, they will always think poorly of themselves. Quite the contrary can be true, particularly when circumstances change significantly—for instance, when, after a history of failures, children begin experiencing regular success (H. W. Marsh & Craven, 1997). We will look at specific strategies for enhancing self-perceptions a bit later in the chapter.

Development of the Self During Childhood and Adolescence

The developmental trends just listed reflect gradual changes in the nature of self-concepts over time. We also see qualitative differences as children grow. We now look at unique aspects of self-perceptions at five age levels: infancy, early childhood, middle childhood, early adolescence, and late adolescence.

Infancy (Birth–2)   Self-concept first appears in infancy. As part of an emerging self-concept, infants develop an impression that they are unique physical beings. Through repeated physical experiences, infants learn they have bodies that bring them discomfort—through hunger, injury, and fatigue—and pleasure—through feeding, mouthing fingers and toes, and relaxing in contact with caregivers. Infants' ability to imitate other people's facial expressions also nourishes their emerging sense of self (Meltzoff, 1990). An infant detects similarities between his own facial expressions and those of people he imitates—older brother with his mouth open wide, Aunt Mei Lin smiling broadly at him, and Daddy playfully sticking out his tongue. Through such everyday imitative acts, infants begin to see that they are separate beings who can rearrange their faces and bodies to resemble those of other people.

Social relationships contribute to the emerging sense of self. Infants have daily experiences with people that affect their developing ideas about who they are and what they are like ("My family likes me—I am worthy of their love") (Bretherton, 1991; Durkin, 1995; M. Lewis & Brooks-Gunn, 1979). The mental representations infants create of relationships with caregivers, which, as we noted earlier, are products of attachment, are a case in point. Possibly, infants' protests at separation from caregivers reflect a new and uneasy insight that they exist separately from caregivers. Focusing with another person on the same object or person also adds to the growing sense of self. For example, when Mommy and baby examine a toy together, baby shifts her gaze between toy and Mommy's face. The baby begins to learn that she has a sense of "we-ness" with her mother and at other times has her own separate focus (Emde & Buchsbaum, 1990).

Toward the second half of the second year, infants show that they recognize themselves when they look in the mirror. In a clever study of self-recognition, babies 9 to 24 months were placed in front of a mirror (M. Lewis & Brooks-Gunn, 1979). Next, their mothers wiped their faces and surreptitiously left a red mark on their noses. Finally, the researchers watched the infants to see how they responded to their image. Infants less than a year old did not touch their nose, although some touched the mirror. By 15 to 18 months, many infants touched their own nose when they saw their reflection, as if they understood that the image in the reflection belonged to them.

Children show other signs of self-recognition during the second and third years. For example, toddlers begin to refer to themselves by "me" and "I" (M. Lewis & Brooks-Gunn, 1979). At 2 and 3, exclamations of "Mine!" are common (L. Levine, 1983). Learning about oneself, including what is *mine*, is a natural part of development and may even be a pre-

DEVELOPMENT AND PRACTICE

Helping Infants and Toddlers to Develop Healthy Self-Concepts

■ Structure group infant care such that infants can form and maintain stable relationships with caregivers.

An infant-toddler program is arranged into separate rooms so that each caregiver has a small number of infants with whom to form close relationships. Toddler teachers make a point to visit in the infant room occasionally, so that they get to know children who will soon be moving to their rooms. In another center, caregivers arrange groups of children to be consistent over time; as the infants outgrow the "Infant Room," for example, they "graduate" together to the "Toddler Room," and their caregiver goes with them.

■ Give warm and responsive care, meeting infants' needs in a timely fashion.

An infant program has one caregiver for every three infants so that no child has to be left unattended for very long. When it is impossible to tend immediately to a child's needs, the caregiver reassures the child that his or her needs are important and that she will provide care as soon as possible.

■ Respond positively to newly developed abilities.

Caregivers in one center celebrate milestones as they notice them, including new teeth, advances in crawling, first steps, and first words. They share their admiration with family members, but are sensitive to the desire of parents and other family members to witness the accomplishment first: "Raj is getting ready to walk, isn't he!"

■ Demonstrate healthy attitudes toward infants' bodies and physiological functions.

The director of an infant program trains staff members to use neutral terms for body functions. For example, she asks a new teacher not to use the term "stinky baby," but instead to make a simple statement that an infant's diaper needs to be changed.

■ Help parents to see their children's normal social-emotional development in positive terms.

A staff member in a toddler room talks with a father about his concern that his daughter has started to grab toys from her baby brother. The teacher empathizes with the father, saying that it is hard to watch the tugging but also comments, "She is a kind little girl—Reesha will learn to share."

■ Set limits and redirect unacceptable behavior in a firm, but gentle way.

An infant-toddler program director helps his teachers think about their role in teaching children: they are wise teachers who help children to learn self-control; they are not authority figures doling out punishments. Concretely, he suggests that teachers tell the children what they *can* do instead of telling them what they cannot do ("Walk inside, please. Run outside.").

---

cursor to sharing. Caregivers who remain patient during inevitable skirmishes ("My ball," "No, my ball," "No, mine!") can help young children assert themselves and become good playmates with others. In the Development and Practice feature "Helping Infants and Toddlers to Develop Healthy Self-Concepts" we suggest actions caregivers can take to enhance small children's self-perceptions.

Early Childhood (Ages 2–6)   The self-concepts of early childhood are simple, concrete, and categorical (Damon & Hart, 1988). Children see themselves in terms of obvious physical characteristics and simple psychological traits (recall that 6-year-old Jeff had "blue eyes" and was "happy").

During this phase, cognitive improvements and language make possible advances in self-concept. For example, children learn what is right and wrong from caregivers and apply these standards to themselves, often feeling badly when they cannot get it right (J. Kagan, 1981). Thus, a 5-year-old boy becomes agitated when he cannot slather the jelly neatly on the bread like his father does. Another development that depends on cognitive advances is the *autobiographical self*, a representation of the important events in one's life (Harter, 1998). Recall the introductory case in Chapter 5 when 6-year-old Kerry and her mother talked about watching whales. Such retelling of shared events strengthens social bonds and children's sense of who they are, what they know, and what they contributed to events (K. Nelson, 1993). Knowledge of self seems to be an important feature in children's memories (Howe & Courage, 1993).

Most young children have positive self-concepts, to the point where they may believe they are more capable than they actually are (Flavell et al., 1993; Paris & Cunningham, 1996). They probably make such overestimations because they base their self-assessments on their improvement in various activities over time, rather than on a comparison to age-mates. Overconfidence is probably beneficial for children's development, in that it motivates them to try and persist at challenging tasks (Bjorklund & Green, 1992; Pintrich & Schunk, 1996).

When young children develop a firm sense of themselves, they find it easier to share with others.

Song of Myself

I am Shea
Above me are the bright colored leaves on the trees
Below me are seeds waiting to become flowers next spring
Before me are years to come full of new things to be learned
Behind me are memories I've forgotten
All around me are my friends lending me a helping hand
I see children having fun
I smell the sweet scent of flowers
I hear the birds talking to each other
I feel the fur of a helpless baby bunny
I move like wind as I run through the grass
I am old like the planets who have been here from the beginning
I am young like a seed waiting to sprout
I am the black of a panda's patches
I am the gold of the sun
I am the green of a cat's eye
I am the many colors of the sunset
I am a parrot, kangaroo, tiger, turtle
I am kind, responsible, pretty, smart
I think, plan, help, research
I give ideas to people that need them
I fear lightning
I believe that we all are equal
I remember my dreams
I dream of bad things as well as the good
I do not understand why some people pollute the Earth
I am Shea, a child of honesty
May I walk in peace

FIGURE 9–8 Shea's *Song of Myself.* Shea and her classmates were given "stems" to guide their writing (e.g., "Above me . . .," "I feel . . .," "I am . . .," "I dream . . .").

Listen to 10-year-old David express a healthy, self-enhancing interpretation of why he did not recall as many words as he originally expected he would in the Memory/Middle Childhood module of the Observation CD.

Some young children are less optimistic, however. For instance, in a series of studies by Carol Dweck and her colleagues, preschoolers, kindergartners, and first graders worked on several picture puzzles that were either unsolvable (the pieces didn't fit together) or too difficult to complete in the time provided. Later, when the children were given a second opportunity to work on these puzzles, some chose to do so, but others preferred to work on puzzles they had already completed successfully. Of these "nonpersisting" youngsters, many showed signs of *learned helplessness*—a belief that their efforts would simply not pay off for them (Burhans & Dweck, 1995). (We will revisit the phenomenon of learned helplessness in Chapter 11.)

Middle Childhood (Ages 6–10) During middle childhood, children tend to see themselves in more complex physical and psychological terms. Recall, for example, Jeanne's son Alex, who at the age of 9 described his physical characteristics, his family origins and city of birth, his interests in baseball and animals, and his good performance in school. Consider as well 9-year-old Shea's *Song of Myself*, presented in Figure 9–8, and the multiplicity of domains that are addressed; for instance, she says, "I am kind, responsible, pretty, smart; I think, plan, help, research. . . . " In middle childhood, children are usually aware also that they have both strengths and weaknesses, that they do some things well and other things poorly (Harter, Whitesell, & Junkin, 1998; H. W. Marsh & Craven, 1997; Wigfield, 1994). Self-perceptions regarding skills are no longer simply good or bad, all-or-nothing; they include variations within domains. A child might see herself as good at math and poor at history within academic domains, and good at gymnastics and poor at basketball within athletic domains (Harter, 1998).

Countless experiences lead children to develop a generally positive—or negative—sense of their worth as human beings: They believe either that they are good, capable individuals or that they are somehow inept and unworthy (Harter, 1990a; H. W. Marsh & Craven, 1997). Research indicates that children's self-esteem sometimes drops soon after they begin elementary school (Harter, 1990a; Stipek, 1981), probably as a result of the many new academic and social challenges that school presents. Elementary school gives children many occasions to compare their performance with that of peers, and their self-assessments gradually become more realistic (D. Hart, 1988; Paris & Cunningham, 1996; Wigfield, 1994). However, this comparative approach inevitably creates "winners" and "losers." Children who routinely find themselves at the bottom of the heap must do some fancy footwork to keep their self-esteem intact. Often, they focus on areas in which they excel (e.g., sports, social relationships, or hobbies) and discount areas that give them trouble (e.g., "Reading is dumb").

Outside academic settings, children also endeavor to protect their sense of self-worth (S. E. Taylor & Brown, 1988). For example, they may overestimate what they individually add to a group's accomplishments and believe that their skills are better than they actually are. Accordingly, 7-year-old Gloria believes her butterfly stroke will land her a gold medal in the Olympics—a charming expectation, but very unlikely. Children also minimize the mistakes they make, explaining their performance in ways that enhance their sense of self. You can see 10-year-old David give a healthy, upbeat spin on why he did not recall as many words as he expected he might in the Memory/Middle Childhood clip of the Observation CD. He predicted that he might recall 12 out of 12 words, and actually recalled 3. Here is David's positive interpretation:

David:	Okay, shirt, carrot, bed . . . I'm sorry, I can't remember the rest of it.
Interviewer:	It's okay.
David:	Yeah. It's just, I don't know. My brain was turned off right now. I use it a lot during school hours so then I just like to relax. . . .
Interviewer:	What did you do to remember the ones that you remembered?
David:	Even though I said 12, I was just trying to challenge myself a little.

Of course, some children hear critical words often or find themselves failing in many domains. When this happens, it is difficult for them to protect their self-esteem. Generally, however—perhaps because they have so many domains to consider as they look for strengths—most children maintain fairly high self-esteem during the elementary school years (Wigfield & Eccles, 1994).

Early Adolescence (Ages 10–14) By the time they reach adolescence, young people have distinct beliefs about themselves in at least eight domains: cognitive competence, behavioral conduct, physical appearance, romantic appeal, regard from peers, relationships with close friends, athletic competence, and job performance (Harter, Whitesell, & Junkin, 1998). They view some of these domains as being more important than others, and their proficiency in domains that they think are important has a big influence on their overall sense of self-worth (Bender, 1997; Harter, Whitesell, & Junkin, 1998; H. W. Marsh & Craven, 1997). In Figure 9–9, you can see the many domains that 11½-year-old Grace mentions as being part of her self-concept. She reveals positive feelings about several distinct facets of herself, including her relationship with her sister, her athletic skills, and her interest in drama.

A drop in self-esteem often occurs at about the time that youngsters move from elementary school to junior high school; this drop can be especially pronounced for some girls (Eccles & Midgley, 1989; H. W. Marsh, 1990b; Sadker & Sadker, 1994; Simmons & Blyth, 1987; Wigfield & Eccles, 1994). The physiological changes of puberty may be a factor: self-perceptions depend increasingly on beliefs about appearance and popularity, and boys and girls alike tend to think of themselves as being somewhat less attractive once they reach adolescence (Cornell et al., 1990; D. Hart, 1988; Harter, 1990a; Harter, Whitesell, & Junkin, 1998). The changing school environment probably also has a negative impact. Traditional junior high schools often differ from elementary schools in several ways (Eccles & Midgley, 1989). Students don't have the opportunity to form close relationships with teachers that many of them had in elementary school. They may also discover that grades are based more on competitive criteria—that is, on how well they perform in comparison with classmates. Furthermore, at a time when they probably have an increased need for close friendships, they may find themselves in classes with unfamiliar peers.

With all of these unsettling changes occurring simultaneously, it is not surprising that we see a temporary drop in young adolescents' self-esteem. Fortunately, many school districts take great pains to ease students' transition into a more socially complex and academically challenging secondary school environment. For instance, large schools may split up the student body into "clusters" of perhaps 60–90 students, and many schools provide explicit guidance in the skills and habits necessary for learning on one's own. Once adolescents have successfully adjusted to their new school environment, most enjoy positive self-concepts and general mental health (Durkin, 1995; Nottelmann, 1987; S. I. Powers, Hauser, & Kilner, 1989; Wigfield & Eccles, 1994).

In early adolescence, two new phenomena appear. First, many young adolescents believe that, in any social situation, everyone else's attention is focused squarely on them

FIGURE 9–9 Grace's description of herself

My name is Grace. I'm 11½ years old . . . I have blue eyes and brown hair. My birthplace was Hinsdale, Illinois and we moved here when I was about ten or eleven months old. I have a three-year-old sister named Isabelle. She has blond hair and blue eyes. We are pretty close, not in age, but sometimes (like all sisters do) we fight. She always gets into my stuff and says, "Dace, why tant I pway wif dat?" However, you have to love her! What else would you like to know about me?

I really like sports! Tennis is one of my favorites. I plan to make the tennis team, but we'll just have to see about that. I like lacrosse too, but I'm not as good at that as tennis. I'm in a four-year jazz and ballet dance class at the St. Michelle School of Ballet. I take drama classes when I can and I want to be an actress. Football is fun to watch. I baby sit, listen to CD's and the radio, and hang out with my friends. That's all about me!

© Zits Partnership. Reprinted with special permission of King Features Syndicate.

A frequently observed phenomenon in early adolescence is the personal fable: Young teenagers often believe that they are completely unique, to the point where no one else can possibly understand their thoughts and feelings.

(Elkind, 1981a; Lapsley, 1993; R. M. Ryan & Kuczkowski, 1994). This self-centered aspect of the adolescent self-concept is sometimes called the **imaginary audience**. Because they believe they are the center of attention, teenagers (girls especially) are often preoccupied with their physical appearance and are quite critical of themselves, assuming that everyone else is going to be equally observant and critical. Extreme sensitivity to embarrassment, when coupled with inadequate social skills, leads some adolescents to respond to insults with undue violence (Lowry, Sleet, Duncan, Powell, & Kolbe, 1995).

A second noteworthy phenomenon in early adolescence is the **personal fable**. You may recall from Chapter 3 that young teenagers often believe they are completely unlike anyone else (Elkind, 1981a; Lapsley, 1993). For instance, they often think their own feelings are unique—that those around them have never experienced such emotions. Hence, they may insist that no one else, least of all parents, can possibly know how they feel. Furthermore, they may feel invulnerable and immortal, believing that they are not susceptible to the normal dangers of life. Thus, many adolescents take seemingly foolish risks, such as driving at high speeds, experimenting with drugs, or having unprotected sexual intercourse (J. Arnett, 1995; DeRidder, 1993; Packard, 1983; Thomas, Groër, & Droppleman, 1993).

When teenagers act dangerously, adults have an obligation to put a stop to their behavior. When adolescents' risk taking is less serious, adults can keep in mind that these behaviors serve a purpose. The personal fable—in particular, the sense of invulnerability—may encourage young people to venture out into the world and try new things (Bjorklund & Green, 1992; Lapsley, 1993). At the same time, the imaginary audience keeps them "connected" to their larger social context, so that they are continually considering how others might judge their actions (Lapsley, 1993; Ryan & Kuczkowski, 1994). Both of these phenomena appear to peak in early adolescence and then slowly decline (Lapsley, 1993; Lapsley, Jackson, Rice, & Shadid, 1988).

Late Adolescence (Ages 14–18)   As their worlds broaden, teenagers have a greater variety of social experiences and so are apt to get conflicting messages from different people (D. Hart, 1988). The result is that their self-concepts may include contradictory views (Harter, 1990b; Wigfield, Eccles, & Pintrich, 1996). As they reach high school age, they begin to wrestle with these contradictions and, with luck, eventually establish a sense of **identity**—a self-constructed definition of who they are, what they find important, what they truly believe, and what they want to do in life.

Before adolescents achieve a true sense of their adult identity, most need considerable time to explore options for careers, political stands, religious affiliations, and so on. Marcia (1980) has observed four distinct patterns of behavior that may characterize an adolescent's search for identity:

- *Identity diffusion*: The adolescent has made no commitment to a particular career path or ideological belief system. Possibly there has been some haphazard experimentation with particular roles or beliefs, but the individual has not yet embarked on a serious exploration of issues related to self-definition.

imaginary audience
Belief that one is the center of attention in any social situation.

personal fable
Tendency for adolescents to think of themselves as unique beings invulnerable to normal risks and dangers.

identity
People's self-constructed definition of who they are, what they find important, what they believe, and what goals they want to accomplish in life.

- *Foreclosure*: The adolescent has made a firm commitment to an occupation and a particular set of beliefs. The choices have been based largely on what others (especially parents) have prescribed, without an earnest exploration of other possibilities.
- *Moratorium*: The adolescent is undergoing an **identity crisis**: he or she has no strong commitment to a particular career or set of beliefs, but is actively exploring and considering a variety of professions and ideologies.
- *Identity achievement*: The adolescent has previously gone through a period of moratorium and emerged with a clear choice regarding occupation and commitment to political and religious beliefs.

Foreclosure—identity choice without prior exploration—rules out potentially more productive alternatives, and identity diffusion leaves youth without a clear sense of direction. Perhaps the ideal situation is to proceed through moratorium, a period of exploration that may continue into early adulthood, before finally settling on a clear identity (Berzonsky, 1988; Marcia, 1988). This valuable search for one's true commitments can involve considerable effort. An interview in the Observation CD give us a glimpse into the hard work involved in defining one's own beliefs. Fifteen-year-old Greg faces the developmentally appropriate challenge of determining whether doing well in school reflects his own or his parents' values. Here is his reasoning in the Intrinsic Motivation/Late Adolescence clip:

Adolescents often experiment with different identities before they develop a firm sense of their own values.

Interviewer:	What are the things that make you want to do well in school?
Greg:	My parents. [*Both laugh.*]
Interviewer:	Okay.
Greg:	My parents mostly.
Interviewer:	Okay.
Greg:	And myself . . . sometimes.
Interviewer:	Okay. How do your parents influence you wanting to do well in school?
Greg:	I don't know. They did well so they want me to. . . .
Interviewer:	You said that sometimes you also want to do well for you. Can you tell me more about that?
Greg:	'Cause, I mean, you feel better if you get all As than Cs or Fs.

Even as high school students move rapidly toward independence, their attachment to family members—especially parents—continues to play a significant role in their personal development. Adolescents who have strong emotional bonds with parents tend to have higher self-esteem and function at more mature levels (Josselson, 1988; R. M. Ryan & Lynch, 1989). Such bonds are not overly restrictive or protective, however; parents best foster adolescents' personal growth by gradually releasing the apron strings (Lapsley, 1993; Ryan & Lynch, 1989). Adolescents who feel alienated from their parents are susceptible to the opinions of others for a longer period of time; the imaginary audience persists. They also have more difficulty establishing a sense of identity (i.e., they are identity-diffused) (Josselson, 1988; Marcia, 1988; R. M. Ryan & Kuczkowski, 1994).

Listen to 15-year-old Greg talk about his personal desire to do well in school and the values his parents hold in the Intrinsic Motivation/ Late Adolescence clip of the Observation CD.

Membership in groups—perhaps informal cliques at school, organized clubs or teams, ethnic neighborhoods, and the community at large—often plays a key role in adolescents' establishment of a sense of identity (Durkin, 1995; Lave & Wenger, 1991; Wigfield et al., 1996). Not only do such groups help teenagers define who they are, but they also endorse values and goals that teenagers may adopt for themselves.

An emerging concern for being true to oneself is evident in adolescents' annoyance when other teenagers are perceived as "phony" (Harter & Monsour, 1992). Adolescents often realize that they take on different "selves" depending on who they are with: parents, friends, romantic partners, teachers, or relatives, for example. Over time and through a lot of soul-searching, they eventually construct a mature self that is organized, reasonably coherent, and committed to particular moral standards (Damon & Hart, 1988). This mature self, based on a stronger sense of individual identity, is more consistent—it is less dependent on others and their wishes.

In the Developmental Trends table "Emotional and Personal Development at Different Age Levels," we summarize the course of emotional growth and self-perceptions across

identity crisis
Period during which an individual actively struggles to choose a course in life.

DEVELOPMENTAL TRENDS

Emotional and Personal Development at Different Age Levels

AGE	WHAT YOU MIGHT OBSERVE	DIVERSITY	IMPLICATIONS
Infancy (Birth–2) 	• Attachment behaviors (seeking contact with caregiver when afraid, hurt, and hungry) • Distress at separation from caregiver • Increasing repertoire of ways to communicate feelings; crying and smiling are gradually supplemented with laughter, hand gestures, and words • Beginning ability to soothe self by sucking thumb, hugging favorite blankets, pulling on ear, etc. • Possessive behavior toward toys • Increasing recognition of self in mirror, and use of "I" and "me"	• Some children have multiple attachments and move easily from one caregiver to another, whereas other children may have one strong attachment and strongly protest separation from the attachment figure. • Cultures that stress individualism encourage small children to express all their feelings, including anger and sadness. Collectivist cultures that place harmony above self-expression discourage infants and toddlers from expressing feelings; instead, they teach restraint (Camras, Oster, Campos, Campos, Ujiie, Miyake, Wang, & Meng, 1998).	• Model appropriate emotions and remain calm when infants and toddlers cry and shout. • Be responsive and sensitive to the needs of infants—they are learning to trust you when you help them satisfy their needs. • Seek professional guidance when you encounter infants who appear to have serious attachment problems. • Take infants' separation distress seriously. It may take time for infants to form attachments to you and other caregivers outside the home. Give them plenty of reassurance. • Help parents and other family members to cope with their infants' separation distress. Explain to them how long it takes for them to regain their composure. Encourage them to watch their infants through one-way mirrors, if available.
Early Childhood (2–6) 	• Desire to be close to parents when afraid, hurt, or uncertain • Wide variety of emotions (e.g., happiness, sadness, fear, anger, disgust) • Emergence of self-conscious emotions (e.g., pride, shame, guilt) • Rudimentary sense of one's unique characteristics, talents, and weaknesses • Optimism about what academic and physical tasks can be accomplished	• Children vary in the number of close attachments they form, the extent to which they find reassurance in these attachment figures, and their responses to strangers. Some cling tightly to caregivers, others venture confidently to explore new environments and check out strangers. • Children vary in how they express their emotions. Some are very controlled, especially in masking anger and sadness. Others are more expressive.	• Realize that young children may initially be cautious or fearful in a new classroom or other group situation; they will become more confident as they begin to form attachments to their teachers or group leaders. • Be patient in establishing relationships with young children; some may form attachments quickly, but others may take several weeks or months before trusting adults outside the home. • Teach appropriate ways of handling negative emotions. Encourage children to "use their words" rather than pushing or hitting when angry.
Middle Childhood (6–10) 	• Increasing number of bonds with people outside the family, including peers, teachers, and other adults • Increasing ability to regulate emotions • Increasing tendency to base self-perceptions of ability on how others perform • Generally good self-esteem in most children	• Children are affected by major family disruptions (e.g., divorce of parents, death or illness). Such risk factors may provide opportunities for social-emotional growth but often undermine children's security, at least temporarily. • Some children have strong role models for emotional regulation (e.g., a parent may work out negative feelings and conflicts in productive ways). • Individual children derive their sense of self-worth from different arenas—social relationships, academic performance, athletic accomplishments. • Children who are treated warmly by others tend to develop positive feelings about their self-worth. Those who are rejected, ridiculed, or ignored have a harder time feeling good about themselves.	• Incorporate discussions of emotional states into the curriculum; for example, address the feelings of characters in literature and history. • Model appropriate ways of expressing feelings. • Praise children for their talents and accomplishments in numerous areas (e.g., in physical activities, social relationships, and specific academic subjects). • Respect cultural differences in regulating emotions.

DEVELOPMENTAL TRENDS

Emotional and Personal Development at Different Age Levels *(continued)*

AGE	WHAT YOU MIGHT OBSERVE	DIVERSITY	IMPLICATIONS
Early Adolescence (10–14) 	• Frequent fluctuations in mood, partly as a result of hormonal changes • Careful regulation of emotions (e.g., hiding joy about a good grade in order to appear "cool" to peers) • Possible temporary drop in self-esteem after the transition to middle school or junior high • Preoccupation with appearance (often reflected in conformity in dress, behavior, etc.) • Increased risk taking, accompanied by a sense of invulnerability	• Adolescents differ in the extent to which they strive to conform to gender stereotypes. • Drops in self-esteem, when sizable and not followed by a rebound, can signal a serious problem. • Some serious emotional problems, such as depression and bipolar disorder, first appear during adolescence. • Some adolescents tend to internalize their stresses (e.g., experiencing depression or anxiety); other respond with externalizing behaviors (e.g., being violent, breaking the law).	• Be a supportive "ear" when young people want to share anxieties. • Keep in mind that some moodiness is normal in the middle school grades. However, talk with parents or the school counselor about your concerns for the emotional well-being of youngsters who seem especially troubled. • To help adolescents discover that not everyone views the world as they do, plan activities in which many if not all adolescents in the group readily and candidly express their opinions.
Late Adolescence (14–18)	• Seeking of intimacy with same-sex and opposite-sex peers • Decrease in the self-consciousness evident in early adolescence • Wrestling with identity issues: Who am I? What do I believe? How do I fit into society?	• Adolescents differ in the extent to which they focus on dating and intimacy. • Some adolescents willingly accept the professional goals and ideologies that their parents offer. Others engage in more soul-searching and exploration as they strive to develop their identity. • Minority youth are more likely than European American youth to reflect on how their ethnic status plays a role in their identity.	• Provide opportunities for adolescents to work closely together on projects and assignments. • Explore diverse belief systems. • Provide service learning and mentoring opportunities that allow adolescents to try on a variety of occupational "hats."

the five age ranges. Keep in mind, however, that such development is characterized by considerable diversity. We now look at group differences in youngsters' sense of self.

Group Differences in Self-Perceptions

We have already seen examples of diversity in children's self-perceptions. For instance, some preschoolers are more optimistic about their own capabilities than others, and adolescents with close attachments to their parents have higher self-esteem than do adolescents without these bonds. To some extent, group differences are also reflected in young people's self-perceptions. Here we consider research findings related to gender, ethnicity, and cultural background.

Gender Differences   As children grow older, their understandings of gender become increasingly sophisticated, and this trend has implications for both self-concept and behavior. During early childhood, children show a rudimentary understanding of gender. For instance, they realize that there are two sexes, can label them, and know that they personally are either a girl or a boy (Etaugh, Grinnell, & Etaugh, 1989; Fagot & Leinbach, 1989). But it takes several years for them to appreciate that this state is permanent—in other words, that boys do not become girls if they grow their hair long and wear ribbons, and that girls do not become boys if they cut their hair short and wear boys' clothes (Bem, 1989; DeLisi & Gallagher, 1991; Emmerich, Goldman, Kirsh, & Sharabany, 1977; Slaby & Frey, 1975). With this developing concept of gender, young children watch the world around them for further clues about what is "male" and what is "female." They are especially attentive to role models of their own gender.

During middle childhood, friendships are largely dictated by gender: Although boys may have friends who are girls, and vice versa, children usually prefer same-sex companions. Furthermore, by defining themselves as "boy" or "girl," children tend to choose activities that society deems to be "gender-appropriate." For example, girls are more concerned about their appearance, but also less satisfied with it, beginning in middle childhood (Maloney, McGuire, & Daniels, 1988; R. Stein, 1996). Of course, there are individual differences in how strictly children adhere to sex-role stereotypes. **Androgynous** individuals show both feminine and masculine attributes; for instance, they might be nurturing with friends (a stereotypically "feminine" characteristic) yet assertive in classroom activities (a stereotypically "masculine" characteristic) (Bem, 1977). Children, adolescents, and adults who relax sex-role boundaries are fairly well adjusted, perhaps because they have more choices in standards by which they evaluate themselves and because others respond favorably to their wide range of skills and dispositions (Piche & Plante, 1991; D. E. Williams & D'Alessandro, 1994).

With the onset of puberty, being "male" or "female" takes on new meaning. Many young adolescents show an upsurge in gender-specific interests (Galambos, Almeida, & Petersen, 1990). For example, at age 13, Teresa's son Connor displayed a newfound interest in American football—definitely a rough and "manly" sport—and joined the middle school football team. Also during adolescence, earlier interests may begin to dwindle, particularly if they are emblematic of the opposite sex. For example, both of us recall having mixed feelings about mathematics in adolescence. Although math was something we were good at, we thought of it as a "masculine" domain that would somehow make us look less feminine. (Fortunately, our interest rekindled in college, where we felt freer to "be ourselves" and not conform to sex-role stereotypes.) However, even girls who have grown up in more recent, "open-minded" decades tend to have less interest and self-confidence in subject areas that are traditionally "masculine"—notably mathematics, science, and sports (Binns, Steinberg, Amorosi, & Cuevas, 1997; Chandler & Goldberg, 1990; M. J. Middleton, 1999; E. Rowe, 1999; Wigfield et al., 1996).

As young people grow, they integrate their ideas about gender into their core concepts of self. For instance, they determine how well they match ideal gender roles. If their characteristics approximate these ideals, they feel good about themselves, especially if they strongly value being a "manly" man or a "womanly" woman. If the match isn't a good one, their self-perceptions may suffer (Harter, 1998).

Children and adolescents learn about and adhere to gender roles through several mechanisms. Biology clearly has some influence. The brain is permanently marked "male" or "female" during prenatal development; for example, a part of the forebrain known as the *hypothalamus* is shaped somewhat differently in boys and girls (Arnold & Gorski, 1984). Gender differences in the brain become more prominent during adolescence because circulating hormones activate gender-specific structures that previously were quiet (Ruble & Martin, 1998). As noted earlier, in boys these rising hormones are associated with increased aggression—a stereotypically "male" characteristic (Susman, Inoff-Germain et al., 1987).

But perhaps more importantly, children and adolescents are socialized to conform to gender roles: Family, peers, and the broader community reinforce them for "staying within bounds" and punish them (e.g., by ridicule or exclusion) when they violate accepted gender roles (Pipher, 1994; Ruble & Martin, 1998). For example, a boy who cries after breaking his arm may be called a "sissy," and a girl who excels in mathematics might be teased for being a "math geek." Other people affect children's concepts of typical gender roles ("Nurses are almost always women"), provide possible self-perceptions ("Like most girls, I'm no good at auto mechanics"), state preferences ("I'm a boy, so I like trucks"), and model behaviors ("How does my lipstick look?") (Ruble & Martin, 1998). Some influences may be more subtle, such as communicating specific values that differentiate males and females ("We need some time for girl talk," from a mother or, "Let's shoot hoops and blow off steam," from a father) (Tennenbaum & Leaper, 2002).

Gender roles are also intensified by children's own thinking and desire to fit into society's structure (Ruble & Martin, 1998). Children help to socialize themselves by constructing an understanding of gender as a stable attribute: It doesn't change from day to day, and it doesn't depend on clothing or hairstyle. They develop mental representations, or schemas, for what boys do and what girls do (Bem, 1981; C. L. Martin, 1991; C. L. Martin & Halverson, 1981). With such understandings in place, children are mo-

androgyny
Tendency to have some characteristics that are stereotypically "female" (e.g., nurturance) and others that are stereotypically "male" (e.g., assertiveness).

As long as I can remember, I always felt a little different when it came to having crushes on other people. When I was in elementary school I never had crushes on girls, and when I look back on that time now, I was probably most attracted to my male friends. I participated in some of the typical "boy" activities, like trading baseball cards and playing video games, but I was never very interested in rough sports. I often preferred to play with the girls in more role-playing and cooperative games. Of course, I didn't understand much about sex or gender roles at the time. I just figured I would become more masculine and develop feelings for the opposite sex after going through puberty.

To my dismay, middle school and the onset of puberty only brought more attention to my lack of interest in girls. The first time I thought about being gay was when I was in 6th grade, so I was probably 11 or 12 years old at the time. But in my mind, being gay was not an option and I began to expend an incredible amount of energy repressing my developing homosexual urges. In 7th grade, I had my first experience with major depression. Looking back on it, I am almost positive that being gay was the immediate cause of the depression....When I finally recovered from the episode a few months later, I did my best to move on with my life and forget about my problems with sexuality. I continued to repress my feelings through high school, a task that became more and more difficult as the years went by. I never really dated any girls and my group of friends in high school was highly female. When I was 16, a junior in high school, I had another more severe bout of depression....I continued to be ashamed of my feelings and refused to even tell my psychologist about concerns over my sexuality. After finally emerging from my depression, I came to somewhat of an agreement with myself. I decided that I would simply put my conflict on hold, hoping it would resolve itself. Unfortunately, I still held on to the hope that it would resolve itself in heterosexuality and I remained distraught by my feelings. I finally came out during my freshmen year at [college] with the support of my friends and an extremely accepting social environment.

Having exposure to the homosexual lifestyle in college is what finally made me realize that I could have a normal life and that I would not have to compromise my dreams because of it. Even though my high school was relatively liberal and very supportive of different backgrounds, there was very little discussion about homosexuality, even in health class. We had visibly gay teachers, but it was rarely openly talked about. I think the reason it took me so long to accept my sexuality was simply because I had no exposure to it while growing up. It angers me that people refer to homosexuality as a lifestyle choice because I had no choice over my sexuality. I spent seven years of my life denying my homosexuality, and believe me, if there had ever been a choice between gay or straight during that time, I would have chosen straight in a second. Today I can't imagine my life without being gay and I would never choose to be straight....

FIGURE 9–10 A gay youth's search for identity—Michael's experience

Personal communication to J. Ormrod (June 2002). Used by permission.

tivated to interpret the world through the lens of gender-related roles, as Benita Balegh's recollection illustrates:

[In our home] it was OK, even feminine, not to be good in math. It was even cute. And so I locked myself out of a very important part of what it is to be a human being, and that is to know all of oneself. I just locked that part out because I didn't think that was an appropriate thing for me to do. . . . [But] it was not OK for the men to not do well in math. It was *not* OK for them to not take calculus. It was not manly. . . .

Another thing that affected me greatly happened when I went to a foreign country. One day I decided that I was going to build a sandbox for my little boy. I went in to get the wood and they told me, "Oh, no! You cannot buy wood. You have to have your husband's permission before you can purchase wood." That was a very big shock to me. But it was a shock that helped me see the insidiousness of what had happened to me in the beginning. And it helped me to open my eyes. When I came back to my country I was very intolerant of what I had swallowed hook, line, and sinker. (Benita Balegh, in Weissglass, 1998, p. 160)

As happens to many young people, Benita's desire to fit society's definitions of gender roles changed as she grew. As a child, and in the contexts of family and school, she learned and accepted sex-role stereotypes. Later, she rejected aspects of traditional gender roles that seemed inequitable.

Finally, as we consider gender and self-representations, it is essential to recognize the unique dilemmas faced by youngsters who are homosexual or bisexual in orientation. These young people face the challenge of forming an integrated self-concept and maintaining high self-esteem even as they face rampant rejection in society at large and, sadly, occasional rejection by family and peers. Gay and lesbian youngsters who have close relationships with their parents and families tend to have a more positive sense of their own identity and to disclose their orientation ("come out") sooner than those with poor relationships (L. A. Beaty, 1999). In Figure 9–10, Mike, a college student, looks back at the difficulty he had in forming an identity as a gay person. Had there been more open and accepting discussion about homosexuals in his community, his search for identity might have been less painful. We explore the topic of sexual orientation in greater detail in Chapter 13.

Ethnic and Cultural Differences   Many children from ethnic minority groups have positive self-concepts and high self-esteem. In fact, researchers often find that, on average, minority youth have more favorable self-perceptions than European American youth (Cooper & Dorr, 1995; Spencer & Markstrom-Adams, 1990; Stevenson, Chen, & Uttal, 1990; van Laar, 2000). Given that members of minority groups are often the victims of prejudice, this finding seems quite puzzling, but theorists have offered possible explanations. First, widespread discrimination—while deplorable—may, in a backhanded way, actually enhance the self-concepts of some youngsters, who take credit for their successes (they worked hard for them and have exceptional talent) but blame outside factors for their failures (others are biased against them and are preventing them from getting ahead) (van Laar, 2000).

A second explanation is that some ethnic groups encourage children to take pride in the accomplishments of their families and communities, rather than in their own, individual achievements (Harrison, Wilson, Pine, Chan, & Buriel, 1990; Olneck, 1995; Pang, 1995; Trawick-Smith, 2003). Such groups often encourage a strong **ethnic identity**, an awareness of one's membership in the group and a willingness to adopt its characteristic behaviors. A strong ethnic identity often helps youth from minority groups deal with racist behaviors of others (McAdoo, 1985; Spencer & Markstrom-Adams, 1990). Consider this statement by Eva, an African American high school student:

> I'm proud to be black and everything. But, um, I'm aware of, you know, racist acts and racist things that are happening in the world, but I use that as no excuse, you know. I feel as though I can succeed. . . . I just know that I'm not gonna let [racism] stop me. . . . Being black is good. I'm proud to be black but you also gotta face reality. And what's going on, you know, black people are not really getting anywhere in life, but I know I will and I don't know—I just know I will. Well, I'm determined to . . . and with God's help, you can't go wrong. (Way, 1998, p. 257)

Not all minority youth identify strongly with their ethnic backgrounds, however (Phinney, 1989). The strength of their ethnic identity will inevitably depend, in part, on the extent to which their families and society nurture it (Dien, 1998; Thornton, Chatters, Taylor, & Allen, 1990).

Another important factor affecting the self-perceptions of children from ethnic minority groups is the treatment they receive in classrooms. Consider Rogelio López del Bosque's recollection of his schooling:

> During my years of school, I experienced low expectations and hostile attitudes on the part of some teachers, administrators, and other students. I had difficulty assimilating into this unfamiliar environment. Continuously, I was made aware that speaking Spanish had bad consequences. I was also told many times that I should not speak Spanish because I used an incorrect form. Was the language I learned at home inferior? I had learned to express my love, desires, and fears in that language. Of course, my parents must have been a very bad influence by teaching me such language, this Tex-Mex. . . .
>
> Like all children, there were so many qualities that I brought with me to school that were valuable. I was eager to learn, eager to please, and eager to do a good job and feel right just like everyone. Instead, like so many other students with similar backgrounds, I was made to feel wrong, unintelligent, and inferior. My whole person was in jeopardy. (López del Bosque, 2000, pp. 3–4)

Although most professionals today are aware of the need to respect young people's ethnic and cultural backgrounds, they do not always know how to show their regard. Certainly they can do all they can to learn about the values of young people with whom they work. They can also recognize the natural desires of children to speak their first language. Even more concretely, professionals can ask children what names they wish to be called. In Figure 9–11, you can see the reaction of a refugee child in Canada when he was not called by his proper name. Finally, professionals must help children of all backgrounds acquire the knowledge, skills, and abilities they need to achieve genuine successes both in the classroom and in the outside world. By helping children to *be* successful, practitioners thereby help them to *feel* successful.

At this point, let's step back and reconsider what we've learned relative to the three basic themes of nature and nurture, universality and diversity, and qualitative and quantitative change. The Basic Developmental Issues table "Emotional and Personal Characteristics

Many youngsters have positive self-concepts as well as strong ethnic identities.

ethnic identity
Awareness of one's membership in a particular ethnic or cultural group, and willingness to adopt certain behaviors characteristic of that group.

I had lots of friends back home, and I remember all of them, we used to play soccer together. I have also friends here now, well…mostly classmates.

School is OK but there is one thing that bothers me. My name is Mohammed, no other. Here, my teacher calls me Mo, because there are five other kids with the same name: My friends sometimes call me M. J., which is not too bad, but I wish they will call me by my real name. I like what my grandma called me: "Mamet." I like how she used to say it. One thing makes me really mad. I have a pen pal called Rudy. He lives in Toronto. Once I showed his letter to my teacher and she said: "That is nice name." Now, all my friends call me Rudy. I hate it, because that's not me, that's not my name. My name is "MO-HA-MMED." Do you understand me?

FIGURE 9–11 Identity in a refugee child in Canada

Excerpt from "Refugee Children in Canada: Searching for Identity" by A. M. Fantino and A. Colak (2001) in *Child Welfare 80 (5)*, pp. 591–592, a publication of the Child Welfare League of America.

of Children and Adolescents" summarizes how these themes surface not only in the development of the self but also in the formation of attachments and emotional development. We turn now to strategies for enhancing children's sense of self.

Enhancing Children's Sense of Self

The interplay between self-esteem and behavior can create a vicious downward spiral: Poor self-esteem leads to less productive behavior, which leads to fewer successes, which perpetuates poor self-esteem. Yet simply telling young people that they are "good" or "smart" or "popular" is unlikely to make a dent in poor self-perceptions (Damon, 1991; H. W. Marsh & Craven, 1997; Pajares, 1996). Furthermore, vague, abstract comments such as "nice job" have little meaning in the concrete realities of children (McMillan, Singh, & Simonetta, 1994). For an effective impact, try these strategies:

■ *First and foremost, be kind to children.* Children soak up words they hear from adults and adults' actions toward them. As they listen and watch, they wonder, "What does this mean about me?" Youngsters can interpret harsh words and careless actions as indications that adults do not like them, possibly because they are not worthy of loving care.

■ *Promote success on academic, social, and physical tasks.* Success experiences are powerful catalysts for the development of positive self-concepts and high self-esteem (Damon, 1991; H. W. Marsh & Craven, 1997). Thus, teachers, coaches, and other professionals who work with youngsters should gear assignments to their capabilities—for instance, by making sure that they have already mastered any necessary prerequisite knowledge and skills.

Yet success at very easy activities is unlikely to have much of an impact. Mastering the significant challenges in life—earning the hard-won successes that come only with effort and persistence—brings more enduring and resilient self-perceptions (Dweck, 1986; B. Lerner, 1985). Thus, teachers and other practitioners are most likely to bolster youngsters' self-perceptions when they assign challenging tasks and provide the structure and support (the scaffolding) youngsters need to accomplish those tasks successfully. They should also help young people keep the little "failures" along the way in perspective: Mistakes are an inevitable part of learning anything new (Clifford, 1990; Eccles & Wigfield, 1985).

■ *Focus children's attention on their own improvement rather than on how others perform.* Youngsters are likely to be optimistic about their chances of success if they see that they are making progress. They are unlikely to be optimistic if they see that their own performance doesn't measure up to that of peers (Deci & Ryan, 1992; Krampen, 1987; Stipek, 1996). To help young people develop positive self-concepts, adults can encourage them to focus on their own performance and how it improves with practice, feedback, and renewed effort—*not* on how they compare to peers.

■ *Give constructive and encouraging feedback; at the same time, communicate high but realistic expectations.* In part because of the frequent feedback children get from others, their self-perceptions are usually similar to the perceptions others have of them (Harter, 1990a; Shaffer, 1988). For example, children's beliefs about their academic ability are similar to their classroom teachers' beliefs about their aptitude. Their beliefs about their

BASIC DEVELOPMENTAL ISSUES

Emotional and Personal Characteristics of Children and Adolescents

ISSUE	ATTACHMENT TO CAREGIVERS	EMOTIONAL STATES AND REGULATION	DEVELOPMENT OF THE SELF
Nature and Nurture	Young human beings are biologically predisposed to form close social-emotional bonds with their parents and other primary caregivers, but they are more likely to form attachments to such individuals when they are treated in a socially sensitive and responsible fashion. Parents, in turn, are by nature predisposed to care for their offspring, but they learn specific ways of caring for their children from other family members and from the community and culture in which they live.	The full range of emotions is made possible by human genetic instructions; the brain is wired to experience anger, joy, fear, and so on. Genetic factors also affect individual differences in temperament (e.g., activity level, irritability, and ways of responding to new stimuli). Nurture affects ways in which emotions are expressed. Children learn to control expression of negative emotional responses by observing other people and from practicing various ways of dealing with emotional experiences. Some children who are maltreated or have parents who are emotionally depressed cope in counterproductive ways, yet other children show considerable resilience to negative emotional experiences.	The capacities to reflect on oneself as a social agent and to think about how other people view oneself are species-specific and so seem to have a genetic basis. These capacities are not fully functioning at birth. Rather, they develop with experience and social input. Temperamental tendencies interact with experience and feedback from others to become the fodder for self-reflection (e.g., "I'm always getting in trouble at school") and influence self-concept and self-esteem.
Universality and Diversity	The predisposition to form close social-emotional bonds is universal. Moreover, socially sensitive care is the universal trigger for forming emotional attachments. However, not all children form secure attachments to their caregivers, and different environments place distinct demands on children. For example, being clingy and demanding may help infants who live in an environment with scarce resources. Similarly, being able to negotiate multiple relationships may enhance adjustment when numerous caregivers are present during the early years.	All children experience such basic emotions as happiness, sadness, anger, and fear. The tendency for emotional states to energize particular kinds of responses (e.g., fleeing in response to fear) is also universal. But substantial diversity is present in how children regulate their emotions (e.g., when trying to conceal their true feelings). Some children are more likely than others to respond to situations in a positive, "upbeat" fashion.	Self-concept seems to be universal as a multidimensional construct; that is, all children see themselves as good at some things and not so good at other things. The trend toward increasing self-reflection also appears to be universal. But children differ in the particular domains in which they think they are strong and weak, as well as in the importance that they attach to each domain. Gender differences and cultural differences are seen in self-concepts and self-esteem, but there is also considerable variability *within* populations of boys and girls and cultural groups.
Qualitative and Quantitative Change	The development of attachments largely reflects quantitative change: Children gradually become more active in guiding interactions with their parents, initiating conversations and other exchanges, taking "turns" to keep interactions going, and so on. Qualitative change occurs when young children, who have previously met strangers with no protest, suddenly display "stranger anxiety." During this phase, they are anxious around people they do not know and show a clear preference for attachment figures.	Children gradually gain knowledge and skills for assessing others' emotions. By watching facial expressions, listening to voice tones, and drawing inferences from behaviors, children learn how others express and control emotions. They also reflect on their own emotional states. However, the emergence of self-conscious emotions (pride, shame, guilt, etc.) represents a qualitative change in development. As children become more aware of societal standards, they learn how they apply to themselves, are motivated (usually) to adhere to them, and feel ashamed or guilty when they violate them.	Quantitative changes occur in self-concept, with children gaining more experiences in different domains of life and reflecting on their talents and skills in each. The result of these many experiences and self-reflections is that children's self-concept becomes increasingly complex and multifaceted. In the early years, children use self-improvement as a gauge for evaluating their performance, but beginning in middle childhood they begin to compare their performance to that of their peers—a shift that reflects qualitative change.

physical ability are correlated with the perceptions of their physical education teachers. And their sense of their own competence in social situations is likely to be a reflection of their actual popularity with peers.

Obviously, practitioners promote more positive self-concepts if they acknowledge and praise children's accomplishments. At the same time, adults' feedback should reflect fairly accurate assessments of what children currently can and cannot do; thus, it must inevitably include criticism as well as praise (H. W. Marsh, 1990b; Parsons, Kaczala, & Meece, 1982; Stipek, 1996). If adults provide only praise—and particularly if they provide inflated evaluations of children's performance—children will be unaware of areas that need improvement (T. D. Little et al., 1995; Paris & Cunningham, 1996). When adults praise children for successes on easy tasks, children may conclude that they are not capable of handling anything more difficult. Conversely, when adults constructively criticize children's performance on difficult tasks, they may, in the process, communicate an expectation that the children can do better (Pintrich & Schunk, 1996). The key factor appears to be the expectations that adults communicate through their statements and actions. When adults communicate high expectations and offer support for attaining challenging goals, children construct positive views of themselves (Eccles, Jacobs, Harold-Goldsmith, Jayaratne, & Yee, 1989; M. J. Harris & Rosenthal, 1985).

■ *Consider the unique needs of girls and boys.* Many youngsters place little value on characteristics and abilities that they think are more "appropriate" for members of the opposite sex. In addition, they may place too much value on qualities they think they need to be "feminine" or "manly." Thus, some teenage girls may strive for impossible standards of physical beauty; some teenage boys may worry that they are maturing too slowly and lack the height and build of some of their classmates.

With these points in mind, adults should probably use somewhat different tactics in nurturing self-concepts of girls and boys. For example, they might help girls identify realistic standards by which to judge themselves and (given girls' propensity to react more negatively to failures) encourage them to pat themselves on the back for their many successes, even those (and perhaps especially those) in traditionally "male" domains such as science and mathematics. But boys, too, have special needs. (It's our opinion, in fact, there is entirely too little literature on the needs of boys.) Many boys are often brought up to believe they should be manly and "tough," and that they should hide self-doubt and feelings of inadequacy. Accordingly, practitioners may want to take special pains to acknowledge boys' "softer" sides—their compassion and skill in interacting with small children, for example.

We have seen that adults can do many things to promote positive, healthy self-perceptions in children. We provide some additional recommendations in the Development and Practice feature, "Enhancing Children's Emotional Development and Sense of Self." What seems to be particularly critical is that youngsters succeed in areas that are important to them and have people they care about treat them well. We should note, however, that the popular educational literature often overrates positive self-esteem as a target (Harter, 1998). Certainly we want students to feel good about who they are, but we also want them to study hard, learn a lot, and get along with peers.

As we've explored the topics of attachment, emotions, and self-perceptions, we've found that different age groups have different priorities. For instance, forming attachments is a major focus in infancy, whereas establishing a personal identity takes precedence during adolescence. Erik Erikson has synthesized some of these age-specific issues into a life-span perspective of development. His theory is the final topic of the chapter.

A Life-Span Approach to Personal and Emotional Development: Erikson's Theory

Erikson (1963, 1972) outlined eight developmental periods, or **psychosocial stages**, to characterize the course of personal and emotional development. He proposed that human beings tackle a different developmental task at each stage and that their achievements at

psychosocial stages
In Erikson's theory, eight periods of life that involve age-related tasks or dilemmas.

DEVELOPMENT AND PRACTICE

Enhancing Children's Emotional Development and Sense of Self

■ Communicate a genuine interest in children's welfare.

When a student is visibly teary-eyed during class, her teacher invites her to take a walk during lunchtime. The student describes the trouble she is having making friends at her new school, and she and her teacher develop a plan to address the problem.

■ Promote success on tasks, athletic events, and hobbies.

A scout leader provides written instructions and diagrams (scaffolding) for surviving in subzero temperatures. He makes sure that the boys are familiar with all rules and guidelines before taking them to the January campout.

■ Hold reasonably high expectations for children's performance.

A swimming coach encourages children to come out for the swim team regardless of past experience. She works as closely with newcomers as with experienced swimmers so that all team members can improve.

■ Give positive feedback for children's accomplishments. Accompany negative feedback with the message that children can improve.

The swimming coach tells a child, "Your crawl stroke has really improved. Your timing on the butterfly is a bit off; let's work on that today."

■ Give children opportunities to examine and try out a variety of "adult" roles.

A first-grade teacher develops a list of classroom chores, such as getting a hot-lunch count, delivering messages to the main office, and feeding the class goldfish and rabbit. He assigns these chores to students on a rotating basis.

■ Learn about the domains of performance most important to individual students.

A fifth-grade teacher asks his students to write an essay about the school activities that they like most and least. He makes sure his students have frequent opportunities to engage in their favorite activities and compliments them when they do especially well in their areas of interest.

---

that stage have lifelong implications. Here we describe his eight stages and relate them to concepts we have previously considered.

Trust Versus Mistrust (Infancy)   According to Erikson, infants' primary developmental task is to learn whether or not they can trust other people. When caregivers can be depended on to feed a hungry stomach, change an uncomfortable diaper, and provide affection at regular intervals, an infant learns *trust*—that others are consistently dependable. When caregivers ignore the infant's needs, are inconsistent in their attention, or are abusive, the infant learns *mistrust*—that the world is an unpredictable and dangerous place. Erikson's notion of trust aligns closely with the secure attachment we spoke of earlier. His notion of mistrust reflects insecure attachment and, even more, serious attachment problems.

Professionals who work with young children—or, indeed, with young people of any age—must earn their trust by being affectionate, sensitive, and reliable. Professionals must often give extra attention to youngsters who have not previously developed secure relationships with caregivers. To survive, these insecure children have learned ways of getting by that shield themselves from further indignity and harm; it is up to new caregivers to show them that they can, in fact, be trusted.

Autonomy Versus Shame and Doubt (Toddler Years)   As toddlers gain muscular coordination, neurological connections, and time for practice, they become capable of satisfying some of their own needs. They learn to feed themselves, wash and dress themselves, and use the bathroom. When parents and other caregivers encourage self-sufficient behavior, toddlers develop *autonomy*, a sense of being able to handle many problems on their own. But when caregivers demand too much too soon, refuse to let children perform tasks of which they are capable, or ridicule early attempts at self-sufficiency, children may instead develop *shame and doubt* about their ability to conduct themselves appropriately.

Erikson's concept of autonomy is reminiscent of an idea we considered earlier—that securely attached children are more willing to venture out on their own and explore their environment. His concepts of shame and doubt suggest the beginnings of self-conscious emotions and poor self-esteem.

Initiative Versus Guilt (Preschool Years)   If all goes well, children spend their infancy and toddler years learning to trust others and to construct a sense of autonomy: The world is a good place, people love them, and they can make things happen. With these important lessons inscribed in their hearts, children are ready to face Erikson's third psychosocial stage. With a growing drive for independence, preschoolers begin to have their own ideas about activities they want to pursue; for example, they may undertake simple art projects, make houses and roadways in the sandbox, or play "house" with other children. When adults encourage such efforts, children develop *initiative*, independence in planning and undertaking activities. When adults discourage such activities, children may instead develop *guilt* about their needs and desires.

Drawing on a concept we considered earlier, we could say that children with high self-esteem—those who feel good about themselves—are more likely to initiate challenging tasks that will benefit their long-term development. Adults, through the messages they communicate about children's capabilities, play a key role in fostering positive self-perceptions.

Industry Versus Inferiority (Elementary School Years) When they reach elementary school, children are expected to master many new skills, and they soon learn that they can gain recognition of adults through their academic assignments, athletic accomplishments, artistic performances, religious participation, and so on. When children do things and when they are praised for their accomplishments, they begin to demonstrate *industry*, a pattern of working hard, persisting at lengthy tasks, and putting work before pleasure. But when children are ridiculed or punished for their efforts or when they find that they cannot meet adults' expectations for performance, they may develop feelings of *inferiority* about their own abilities.

Earlier we discovered that children in the lower elementary grades define themselves largely in terms of concrete, observable characteristics, such as physical appearance. In Chapter 4, we learned that children often have difficulty with abstract ideas. It makes sense, then, that children in this age range should derive satisfaction from concrete, observable accomplishments.

Children derive satisfaction from their success on concrete tasks.

Identity Versus Role Confusion (Adolescence) As they make the transition from childhood to adulthood, adolescents wrestle with the questions of who they are and how they fit into the adult world. Initially, they experience *role confusion*—mixed ideas and feelings about the specific ways in which they will fit into society—and may experiment with a variety of things (e.g., tinkering with cars, baby-sitting for neighbors, engaging in extracurricular activities at school, affiliating with political groups). According to Erikson, most adolescents eventually achieve a sense of *identity* regarding who they are and where their lives are headed.

As you may have noticed, Erikson's concept of identity is very similar to Marcia's concept of identity achievement, and his concept of role confusion should remind you of Marcia's concepts of identity diffusion and moratorium. This is not a coincidence: Marcia used Erikson's theory of psychosocial development as a springboard for his own work on adolescent identity.

Intimacy Versus Isolation (Young Adulthood) Once people have established their identities, they are ready to make commitments to one or more other individuals. They become capable of *intimacy*—that is, they form close, reciprocal relationships with others (e.g., through marriage or close friendships) and willingly make the sacrifices and compromises that such relationships require. When people cannot form intimate relationships (perhaps because of their reluctance or inability to forego the satisfaction of their own needs), a sense of *isolation* may result.

Generativity Versus Stagnation (Middle Age) During middle age, the primary developmental tasks are contributing to society and guiding future generations. When an individual makes a contribution, perhaps by raising a family or by working toward the betterment of society, *generativity*—a sense of productivity and accomplishment—results. In contrast, an individual who is self-centered and unable or unwilling to help society move forward develops a feeling of *stagnation*—a dissatisfaction with lack of production.

Integrity Versus Despair (Retirement Years) According to Erikson, the final developmental task is a retrospective one. Individuals look back on their lives. They develop feelings of contentment and *integrity* if they believe that they have led a happy, productive life.

Alternatively, they may develop a sense of *despair* if they look back on a life of disappointments and unachieved goals.

Critiquing Erikson's Theory

Erikson's stages nicely summarize some of the ideas we've presented in this chapter. Yet the stages are probably not completely accurate descriptions of what happens at each age period, in part because they ignore the very important role that culture plays in development. For example, many cultures intentionally discourage self-assertiveness in young children, sometimes as a way of protecting them from the very real dangers of their environments (Chen et al., 1992; Harwood et al., 1995; Powell, 1983). Furthermore, Erikson believed that most people achieve a sense of identity by the end of adolescence. But more recent evidence indicates that, even by the high school years, only a small minority of students in mainstream Western cultures have begun to think seriously about the eventual role they will play in society and the lifelong goals they wish to pursue (S. L. Archer, 1982; Durkin, 1995; Marcia, 1988). Also problematic is the fact that Erikson based his stages on observations of *men*. For many women, a focus on intimacy occurs simultaneously with, and in some cases may even precede, a focus on identity (Josselson, 1988).

Perhaps it is useful to take a perspective on Erikson's theory similar to the perspective we advocated for Piaget's theory in Chapter 4: The eight psychosocial stages provide a general idea of the ages at which various issues are likely to emerge. Nevertheless, considerable flexibility and diversity are present in these timelines.

The importance of children's emotions and self-perceptions will continue to be evident as we explore the development of social understanding and morality in Chapter 10 and motivation in Chapter 11. For now, however, we use our closing case study to consider how emotions and self-perceptions influence classroom behavior.

CASE STUDY: THE GIRLY SHIRT

Eight-year-old Tim caused quite a disruption in class this morning. His teacher, Amy Fox, isn't quite sure why things got out of control, so she is meeting with Tim while the rest of the class is at lunch in order to understand what happened.

Ms. Fox:	Things got out of control in class this morning, didn't they, Tim?
Tim:	I guess they did.
Ms. Fox:	Tell me what happened.
Tim:	John and Steven were teasing me about my shirt. They really made me mad.
Ms. Fox:	They were teasing you about your shirt? What did they say?
Tim:	That it's too pink. That it's a "girly" color.
Ms. Fox:	Really? I don't think it's too "girly" at all. In fact, I rather like that color on you. But anyway, you say the boys teased you about it. What did you do then?
Tim:	I yelled at them. Then when you gave me that dirty look, they kept on laughing, and so I kept on yelling.
Ms. Fox:	I see. John and Steven were certainly wrong to tease you about your clothes. I'll speak to them later. But right now I'm concerned about how you reacted to the situation. You were so loud that the class couldn't possibly continue with the lesson.
Tim:	I know. I'm sorry.
Ms. Fox:	I appreciate your apology, Tim. And I'd like to make sure that the next time someone hurts your feelings—maybe intentionally, maybe not—you don't blow up the way you did today. Let's come up with a plan for how you might keep your temper under better control.

- In what way does John's and Steven's behavior reflect the process of *socialization*? What effect might their behavior have on Tim's self-concept?
- Considering what you have learned about trends in emotional development, is Tim's reaction typical for his age?
- What kind of plan might be effective in helping Tim control his anger?

Now go to our Companion Website to assess your understanding of chapter content with a Practice Quiz, apply what you've learned in Essay Questions, and broaden your knowledge with links to related Developmental Psychology Web sites. Go to www.prenhall.com/mcdevitt.

SUMMARY

Early Attachments

Early attachments are close and enduring social-emotional bonds that form between infants and their caregivers. Sensitive and responsive attention provides the necessary catalyst for the formation of attachments, but children also contribute by returning affection. Secure attachments in the early years predict positive social-emotional outcomes later on. However, attachments manifest themselves somewhat differently in different cultures, and the nature of people's attachments can and often does change over time.

Emotional Development

Emotions have adaptive functions for children—they help them decide how to act. Emotions develop in several ways; for instance, children and adolescents become increasingly able to regulate their emotions in ways that are both socially acceptable and personally effective. Individual differences in emotional functioning are the result of both biology (e.g., temperament and gender-specific hormones) and environment (e.g., socialization by parents, peers, and culture). Dealing with youngsters' emotions is an important activity for adults who work with them, and practitioners can do many things to promote emotional development. Adults need to be especially alert to the needs of youngsters with serious emotional needs (e.g., depression, anxiety disorders, conduct disorders).

Development of the Self

Children develop beliefs about themselves (self-concept) and they have feelings about their worthiness (self-esteem). Infants develop simple understandings about their physical self as well as how they relate to primary caregivers. In childhood, the focus is largely on learning what one can and cannot do; in adolescence, the focus shifts to the formation of an identity—a sense of who one is and what course one's life will take. Adults can most effectively foster positive self-concepts by helping young people succeed at challenging academic, social, and physical tasks and by treating them affectionately and respectfully.

Erikson's Theory

Erikson proposed that eight stages (the first beginning in infancy and the last occurring in old age) describe the evolution of people's personal and emotional tasks. There are similarities between how Erikson described the stages and what other theorists have learned about attachment, self-concept, and identity. However, some psychologists argue that Erikson's theory does not accurately describe emotional development in some cultures, nor does it adequately account for the interplay of identity and intimacy.

KEY CONCEPTS

attachment (p. 364)
ethological attachment theory (p. 364)
stranger anxiety (p. 365)
secure attachment (p. 366)
insecure-avoidant attachment (p. 366)
insecure-resistant attachment (p. 366)

disorganized and disoriented attachment (p. 366)
emotion (p. 374)
emotional contagion (p. 376)
self-conscious emotion (p. 377)
emotional regulation (p. 377)
empathy (p. 378)
temperament (p. 379)
personality (p. 379)

socialization (p. 380)
anxiety (p. 387)
depression (p. 388)
anxiety disorder (p. 389)
conduct disorder (p. 389)
self-concept (p. 391)
self-esteem (p. 391)
self-efficacy (p. 393)
imaginary audience (p. 398)

personal fable (p. 398)
identity (p. 398)
identity crisis (p. 399)
androgyny (p. 402)
ethnic identity (p. 404)
psychosocial stages (p. 407)

CHAPTER 10

Brianna, age 4

Emilee and Shir-Lisa, age 12

Joey, age 17

Social Understanding and Moral Development

CASE STUDY: TOM

For a 13-year-old, Tom is remarkably insightful about social problems within his society. Although members of his immediate family have advocated and modeled tolerance for people from all walks of life, he is frustrated by the racial and religious prejudice he sees in his extended family and among his peers:

> My father told me to make all kinds of friends. If you don't get friends—it's the same with adults—you are always cranky and mad.
>
> . . . [My father] made a love-match to a Catholic [my mother] against his parents' will. My grandmother, she's still mad. My father is different from all his other brothers. Maybe it came from the time he went for my mother.
>
> . . . My uncle thinks prejudice against Russians is unfair, but he makes my cousins prejudiced. My cousins keep talking against Jews, and Catholics, too. But my father tells them they should save up and be so smart. Once he made them scramble for pennies to tease them out of it! That's what kids do to Jews! Prejudice, it's really painful. People can really just hate. I can't believe how people hate others, and I don't understand it. . . .
>
> I think the main problem causing racism is people just don't want to associate. . . . They don't care that much. We put people together in the schools, and it's a lot better than white and black separate, but still nobody really tries. Especially in the high school; my brother tells me about that. I've seen here in junior high that more kids don't like black kids than before, and they don't try to make them feel better any more. They used to, in sixth grade. Now they go off, the blacks by themselves, so what can you do? Well, I get models and make them with Tim because we were friends in sixth. You got to care. Some Indians are starving, and people don't care. Even right here in the U.S. We gotta put money in that. I read the paper, and I see nobody knows what's going on. You gotta change the system of forgetting poor people, first of everything. (F. H. Davidson & Davidson, 1994, pp. 88–90)[1]

Yet Tom has considerable optimism that a democratic society has the means to make societal conditions more equitable for people from diverse backgrounds:

> It's important to consider what laws should be made. It is laws that make a nation, because people would otherwise go by their own thoughts, and there could be no cooperation, no society, no progress. Cooperation makes progress. It would be better if the whole world could work on laws, but the way it is, nations do. If you don't have taxes, you can't have good education. You have to have money provided. If you put something in, you get something out. Then educated people can work on the laws, to make them more fair, and to see why they have to pay taxes. It's the main thing not to be rich, as an ideal, not to beat out the other guys, but just to live, and to preserve all life.
>
> . . . It gets more selfish as you get older. Maybe you get a job and you're busy. Then you kind of forget the things you wanted to do for somebody. That's why I want to be a politician—to do all the projects I want to do, to change things. (F. H. Davidson & Davidson, 1994, p. 90)

[1] Excerpts from *Changing Childhood Prejudice: The Caring Work of the Schools* by Florence H. Davidson and Miriam M. Davidson. Copyright © 1994 by Florence H. Davidson and Miriam M. Davidson. Reproduced with permission of Greenwood Publishing Group, Inc., Westport, CT.

om is deeply concerned about the rights and welfare of his fellow human beings. He voices disdain for unjustified prejudices and for the widespread indifference to those in need, but he tries to understand how people might acquire their biases and self-centeredness: "Maybe you get a job and you're busy. Then you kind of forget the things you wanted to do for somebody" (F. H. Davidson & Davidson, 1994, p. 90). He believes that society has an obligation to care for those who live in poverty and expresses optimism that by becoming a politician, he can "do all the projects I want to do, to change things" (p. 90).

Tom's advanced social understandings and desire to make the world a better place provide us with a positive, hopeful context in which to introduce the topics of this chapter: children's beliefs about other people, their conceptions of society (social conventions, communities, government, etc.), and their moral development (their sense of right and wrong, concern for the rights of others, and commitment to helping those less fortunate than themselves). We begin by exploring a multifaceted phenomenon known as social cognition.

Social Cognition

SOCIAL COGNITION

Beliefs About Self

Sense of self (Chapter 9)
• Self-concept
• Self-esteem
• Self-efficacy
• Identity

Beliefs about abilities and control (Chapter 11)
• Sense of competence
• Self-determination
• Attributions

Beliefs About Others

Beliefs about relationships
• Attachments (Chapter 9)
• Friendships (Chapter 13)

Theory of mind (Chapter 10)
• Person perception
• Social perspective taking
• Social information processing

Beliefs about society (Chapter 10)
• Social conventions
• Conceptions of communities
• Conceptions of political and economic systems
• Stereotypes

Beliefs about children
• Parents' beliefs about children and education (Chapter 12)
• Professionals' beliefs about child development (Chapter 2)

FIGURE 10–1 Social cognition—thinking about people and society—takes a variety of forms.

social cognition
Thinking about people, self, and society.

As someone who is currently studying child development, you may find children and adolescents to be fascinating creatures. Youngsters share this fascination about others. While you're wondering about them, they're wondering about you and, perhaps even more intently, about one another. Children and adolescents spend much of their mental energy engaged in **social cognition**, thinking about people (including themselves) and society. Children and adolescents think a lot about social matters, and they use the fruits of their social thinking to fine-tune their interpersonal skills and relationships (Fiske & Taylor, 1991).

Social cognition is such an important topic that we've integrated it into several chapters of the book, albeit under different labels (see Figure 10–1). In Chapter 9, we discussed children's developing beliefs about themselves—about who they are, what they stand for, and where they hope to go in life. This is social cognition turned inward, applied to the self. In Chapter 11, we will show that children's beliefs about their skill levels and about their ability to control important aspects of their lives are influential in their activity choices, persistence, and other aspects of motivation.

Turned outward, social cognition helps people make sense of social relationships and institutions. For example, in Chapter 9, you learned that secure attachments predispose children to see other people as potentially trustworthy, whereas insecure attachments lead them to view other people with uneasiness or suspicion. As you will see in Chapter 13, children also develop understandings about other close relationships, such as friendships. And in Chapter 12, we will examine an aspect of parents' social cognition—in particular, their beliefs about children and about the purposes that schools and education should serve. Professionals, too, have varying beliefs about children, as reflected in the metaphors we considered in Chapter 2.

Social cognition, then, is a robust theme that can be found in many developmental "places." In this chapter, we put social cognition itself under the microscope, focusing on how children and adolescents think about people. We begin by examining children's *theory of mind*, their growing awareness of human beings' intentions, thoughts, beliefs, and feelings.

Theory of Mind

Just as children construct theories about the physical and biological worlds (recall the discussion of *theory theory* in Chapter 5), so, too, do they construct theories about the psychological world. More specifically, they develop a **theory of mind** that encompasses increasingly complex understandings of people's mental states—thoughts, beliefs, feelings, motives, and so on. Their theory of mind enables them to interpret and predict the behaviors of the important people in their lives and, as a result, to interact with those individuals more effectively (e.g., Flavell, 2000; Gopnik & Meltzoff, 1997; Wellman & Gelman, 1998). Here we trace the development of theory of mind over the course of infancy, childhood, and adolescence.

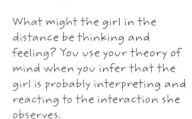

Infancy (Birth–Age 2)   Infants quickly discover that people are different from inanimate objects: Unlike objects, people are active, expressive, and responsive (Poulin-Dubois, 1999). In fact, infants may look away or become upset when adults remain motionless in front of them (see Chapter 9). In the latter part of their first year, infants also begin to realize that people have an "inner life" that objects do not. For instance, by about 9 months, they seem to know that a caregiver is looking at the same thing that they themselves are looking at (recall our discussion of *intersubjectivity* in Chapter 5). At about the same time, they acquire a rudimentary awareness of **intentionality**: They know that other people behave in order to accomplish certain goals, and they begin to draw inferences about people's intentions from such actions as reaching for, pointing at, and gazing at objects (Baldwin, 2000; Flavell, 2000; Woodward, 1998; Woodward & Sommerville, 2000).

What might the girl in the distance be thinking and feeling? You use your theory of mind when you infer that the girl is probably interpreting and reacting to the interaction she observes.

In the second year, infants become increasingly cognizant of other people's mental states. As an example, recall the phenomenon of *social referencing* introduced in Chapter 5: Infants as young as 12 months will look to see how an adult responds to an object or event—perhaps with pleasure or disgust, perhaps by approaching or backing off—and then respond in a similar manner. At this point, then, they clearly have some awareness of other people's attentional focus and emotions (Moses, Baldwin, Rosicky, & Tidball, 2001).

By 18 months, children clearly know that their own actions influence other people's emotions and behavior. For instance, they are more likely to offer an adult a food item that the adult has reacted favorably to before, even though they themselves dislike that particular food (Repacholi & Gopnik, 1997).[2] In some cases, they may even behave in ways that they know will annoy or upset an adult (Dunn & Munn, 1987; Flavell et al., 1993). For example, as a toddler, Jeanne's daughter Tina occasionally ran into the street in front of the house and then looked tauntingly back at Mom as if to say, "Look what I'm doing! I know this upsets you! Catch me if you can!"

Early Childhood (Ages 2–6)   Even 2-year-olds have some implicit understanding of what others know: If an adult talks about a person named "Jessie," they conclude that Jessie must be someone the adult knows rather than someone he or she doesn't know (Birch & Bloom, 2002).[3] In the preschool years, children become increasingly aware of people's mental states. Beginning at age 2 (sometimes even earlier), they spontaneously use words that refer to people's desires and emotions (e.g., *want, feel sad*), and by age 2½ or 3, words such as *think* and *know* appear in their speech (Astington & Pelletier, 1996; Bartsch & Wellman, 1995; Bretherton & Beeghly, 1982; Flavell, Green, & Flavell, 1995). This statement by Ross, age 2 years and 10 months, illustrates an awareness of his mother's mental state:

> Mommy can't sing it. She doesn't know it. She doesn't understand. (Bartsch & Wellman, 1995, p. 41)

By the time children are 3, they realize that the mind is distinct from the physical world—that thoughts, memories, and dreams are not physical entities (Wellman & Estes,

theory of mind
Awareness that people have an inner, psychological life (thoughts, beliefs, feelings, etc.).
intentionality
Engaging in an action congruent with one's purpose or goal.

---

[2] In Chapter 4, we saw evidence that 3- and 4-year-olds are not as egocentric as Piaget said they were. Here, we see evidence that even toddlers can occasionally take another person's perspective.
[3] Based on such findings, Birch and Bloom (2002) have suggested that theory of mind must be an important element in children's ability to learn word meanings from other people.

FIGURE 10–2 Which boy wants to swing? Astington (1991) used such drawings to assess young children's understanding of intention.

From "Intention in the Child's Theory of Mind" by J. W. Astington. In *Children's Theories of Mind* (p. 168), by C. Moore & D. Frye, 1991, Hillsdale, NJ: Erlbaum, p. 168. Reprinted with permission of Lawrence Erlbaum Associates.

1986; Woolley, 1995). Yet preschoolers often have trouble looking inward and describing the nature of their own thinking and knowledge (see Chapter 5). Furthermore, they may mistakenly assume that what they know is what other people know as well. Consider the following situation:

> Max puts a piece of chocolate in the kitchen cupboard and then goes out to play. While he is gone, his mother discovers the chocolate and moves it to a drawer. When Max returns later, where will he look for his chocolate?
> (based on Wimmer & Perner, 1983)

Max will look in the cupboard, of course, because that's where he thinks the chocolate will be. However, 3-year-olds are quite certain that he will look in the drawer, where the chocolate is actually located. Not until age 4 or 5 do children appreciate a *false belief:* They realize that circumstances may reasonably lead people to believe something different from what they themselves know to be true (Avis & Harris, 1991; Gopnik & Astington, 1988; Wellman, Cross, & Watson, 2001; Wimmer & Perner, 1983).

Within this context, we find another possible explanation of the *egocentric speech* that Piaget described. As you will recall from Chapter 4, young children often describe objects and events without providing the details necessary for their listeners to understand. Piaget proposed that egocentric speech reflects preoperational egocentrism, an inability to view a situation from another person's perspective, whereas Vygotsky suggested that it might instead represent self-talk. In Chapter 7, we indicated that egocentric speech may sometimes be due to insufficient language skills to describe something precisely. A theory-of-mind framework puts yet another spin on the phenomenon: Egocentric speech may reflect young children's ignorance about how the mind works; in particular, they don't yet realize that people to whom they are talking can make sense of new information only to the extent that they have sufficient knowledge to do so (Perner, 1991).

Preschoolers are often eager to learn why people do the things they do, as this conversation between 2½-year-old Adam and his mother illustrates:

Adam:	Why she write dat name?
Mother:	Because she wanted to.
Adam:	Why she wanted to?
Mother:	Because she thought you'd like it.
Adam:	I don't want to like it. (Wellman, Phillips, & Rodriquez, 2000, p. 908)

Inherent in Adam's question *Why she write dat name?* is an additional advancement in theory of mind: Preschoolers become increasingly aware of the relationship between people's mental state and their behavior. They understand that people's perceptions, emotions, and desires influence their actions, and they become increasingly adept at inferring people's mental states from behaviors and other events (Astington & Pelletier, 1996; Flavell, 2000; Wellman et al., 2000). As an illustration, Astington (1991) showed 3- to 5-year-old children a series of pairs of pictures (e.g., see Figure 10–2) and then asked questions such as "Which boy thinks he'll swing?" and "Which boy would like to swing?" (p. 167). The majority of the 5-year-old children pointed to the child preparing to engage in the behavior in question; few of the 3-year-olds answered correctly.

With age, children also acquire a more sophisticated understanding of intentionality. Whereas 3-year-olds often think that people intentionally cause their mistakes and accidents, 4- and 5-year-olds are better able to distinguish between intentional and unintentional behaviors (Astington, 1991, 1993).

Middle Childhood (Ages 6–10)   As they reach the elementary grades, children become capable of drawing more sophisticated inferences about people's mental states. For instance, they are more tuned in to the subtle nuances of other people's behavior, and they realize that people's actions do not always reflect their thoughts and feelings—for instance, that people who appear happy may actually feel sad (Flavell et al., 1993; Gnepp, 1989). They know, too, that people can have mixed, conflicting feelings about a situation (Selman, 1980).

Middle childhood heralds more complex understandings of the nature of thinking as well. Whereas 4- and 5-year-olds believe that thoughts result primarily from external events that trigger them, older children know that thinking is an ongoing process—in essence, a stream of consciousness—and that people are thinking even when they are sitting quietly, seemingly doing nothing at all (Flavell et al., 1995).

At this point, too, children begin to realize that people interpret what they see and hear, rather than just "recording" it verbatim, and so children realize that people may occasionally misconstrue an event they have witnessed (M. Chandler & Boyes, 1982; Flavell et al., 1993). They are now starting to understand that thinking and learning are active, constructive processes rather than passive duplications of external events (Flavell et al., 1995; Wellman, 1990). Furthermore, they increasingly take people's preexisting expectations and biases into account when interpreting what people say and do (Pillow & Henrichon, 1996).

Finally, children now recognize that thoughts and feelings may be closely intertwined. As they move through middle childhood, they gradually come to realize that their own interpretations determine how they feel about a particular situation and that other people have different interpretations and, as a result, different feelings ("Arlene feels bad because she thinks I don't like her") (Flavell, Flavell, & Green, 2001; P. L. Harris, 1989).

Early Adolescence (Ages 10–14)   As children move into early adolescence, they begin to appreciate that people can have ambivalent feelings about events and other individuals (Donaldson & Westerman, 1986; Flavell & Miller, 1998; Harter & Whitesell, 1989). They also become aware that people may simultaneously have multiple, and possibly conflicting, intentions (Chandler, 1987). Consider the following situation:

> Kenny and Mark are co-captains of the soccer team. They have one person left to choose for the team. Without saying anything, Mark winks at Kenny and looks at Tom, who is one of the remaining children left to be chosen for the team. Mark looks back at Kenny and smiles. Kenny nods and chooses Tom to be on their team. Tom sees Mark and Kenny winking and smiling at each other. Tom, who is usually one of the last to be picked for team sports, wonders why Kenny wants him to be on his team. . . .

- Why did Mark smile at Kenny?
- Why did Kenny nod?
- Why did Kenny choose Tom to be on the team? How do you know this?
- Do you think that Tom has any idea of why Kenny chose him to be on the team? How do you know this? . . .
- How do you think Tom feels? (Bosacki, 2000, p. 711; format adapted)[4]

Quite possibly, Tom has mixed feelings about being chosen for the team. He may think that he's a poor athlete (he's often one of the last picked) and so may wonder why Mark and Kenny chose him. He may also wonder what Mark's smile means: It could mean that Mark is delighted to find a decent player still available to be picked, yet it might instead signal a

---

[4] From "Theory of Mind and Self-Concept in Preadolescents: Links with Gender and Language," by S. L. Bosacki, 2000, *Journal of Educational Psychology, 92,* pp. 709–717. Copyright © 2000 by the American Psychological Association. Adapted with permission.

malicious intention to make Tom look foolish on the soccer field. Despite his misgivings, Tom may be happy that he will have a chance to play one of his favorite games. Young adolescents become increasingly thoughtful about such matters, and their ability to recognize the complexity of thoughts and emotions in themselves is correlated with their ability to recognize them in others (Bosacki, 2000).

Courtesy of their expanding cognitive abilities, memory capacity, and social awareness, young adolescents increasingly engage in **recursive thinking** (Oppenheimer, 1986; Perner & Wimmer, 1985): They can think about what other people might be thinking about them and eventually can reflect on other people's thoughts about themselves through multiple iterations (e.g., "You think that I think that you think. . . "). This is not to say that adolescents (or adults, for that matter) always use this capacity. In fact, thinking only about one's own perspective, without regard for the perspective of others, is a common phenomenon in the early adolescent years (recall our discussion of the *imaginary audience* in Chapter 9). Thus, adults may often need to remind young teens to consider why others might reasonably think and behave as they do.

Late Adolescence (Ages 14–18)   As they move into the high school grades, many adolescents gain a more sophisticated understanding of knowledge and thinking. For instance, they may increasingly conceptualize knowledge as an integrated body of ideas (rather than a collection of discrete facts) that continues to evolve over time, and they may begin to discover that how people think about information affects their ability to learn it (see the discussion of *epistemological beliefs* in Chapter 5).

Older adolescents can draw on a rich knowledge base derived from numerous social experiences, and so they become ever more skillful at drawing inferences about people's psychological characteristics, intentions, and needs (Eisenberg, Carlo, Murphy, & Van Court, 1995; Paget, Kritt, & Bergemann, 1984). In addition, they are more attuned to the complex dynamics—not only thoughts, feelings, and present circumstances, but also past experiences—that influence behavior (A. A. Flanagan & Tucker, 1999; Selman, 1980). And they realize that other people are not always aware of why they act as they do (Selman, 1980). What we see emerging in the high school years, then, is a budding psychologist: an individual who can be quite astute in deciphering and explaining the motives and actions of others. Yet adults must remember that throughout childhood and adolescence, some youngsters are more perceptive than others, and their perceptiveness plays a significant role in their ability to interact effectively with other people (Astington & Pelletier, 1996).

Factors Promoting Development of a Theory of Mind   To some degree, development of a theory of mind probably depends on maturational processes in the frontal cortex of the brain (Carlson & Moses, 2001; Perner, Lang, & Kloo, 2002). Yet environmental factors almost certainly play a role as well. Discussions with adults and other children about thoughts, feelings, motives, needs, and so forth promote greater awareness about the existence of mental events and emotional states as entities separate from physical reality (Dunn, Bretherton, & Munn, 1987; Jenkins & Astington, 1996; Ruffman, Slade, & Crowe, 2002; Woolfe, Want, & Siegal, 2002). For instance, parents who openly consider differing points of view during family discussions may help children realize that different points of view can legitimately exist (Astington & Pelletier, 1996). In the early years, sociodramatic play activities, in which children assume the roles of parents, teachers, doctors, and so on, may help children to imagine what people might think and feel in different contexts (P. L. Harris, 1989; Lillard, 1998; Rubin & Pepler, 1995).

Culture probably makes a difference as well. Whereas some cultures frequently explain people's behaviors in terms of their states of mind, others are more likely to interpret behaviors in terms of situational circumstances, without reference to people's thoughts or feelings per se (Lillard, 1999). In the United States, children who live in urban areas often refer to people's psychological states when explaining good and bad behaviors; for example, a child might say, "He helped me to catch bugs, because he and I like to catch bugs." In contrast, children who live in rural areas are more likely to attribute people's behaviors to situational factors; for example, a child might say, "She helped me pick up my books, because if she didn't I would have missed the bus." The latter approach is evident not only in rural American cultures but also in many Asian cultures (Lillard, 1999).

recursive thinking
Thinking about what other people may be thinking about oneself, possibly through multiple iterations.

Youngsters' growing theories of mind have implications for three other acquisitions during childhood and adolescence: *person perception, social perspective taking,* and *social information processing.* We now consider each of these phenomena.

Person Perception

By **person perception**, we mean the ability to recognize and interpret others' physical features, behaviors, and internal psychological states. How do children and adolescents perceive the people around them? To make this question meaningful, we ask you to imagine a simple event:

> A man walks into a room with a sad look on his face. He stumbles a bit, then sits at a table beside a young boy, smiles, picks up a cookie, takes a bite, drinks from a glass of milk, and puts the half-filled glass on the table.

Given some of the things we've learned about the development of theory of mind, and drawing from what we've learned about cognitive development as well, we can speculate about how youngsters of various ages might respond to such an event.

Infancy (Birth–Age 2)   How an infant responds to the man would depend a great deal on age. In the first few months, a baby's attention would be drawn to movement and novel stimuli; furthermore, given the particular attraction to other human beings typical of early infancy, the baby would focus more on the man and the boy than on the furniture or glass of milk (see Chapter 5). A slightly older baby might show fear if the man and boy are people whom he or she doesn't know; such *stranger anxiety* is common in the latter half of the first year and first part of the second year (see Chapter 9). In the second year, the baby might begin to perceive the predictable and intentional nature of the man's actions—for instance, anticipating that when the man picks up the cookie, he will put it in his mouth, and that when he picks up the glass of milk, he will take a sip.

Early Childhood (Ages 2–6)   We would expect a preschooler to perceive the man as engaging in a series of intentional, goal-driven actions (although the child would not use such words) and to make some superficial inferences about the man's feelings and desires. For instance, a child might say that the man is "hungry" or that he "wants" to sit near the boy.

Middle Childhood (Ages 6–10)   In the elementary school years, children recognize that people have psychological qualities but tend to zero in on concrete, observable features (D. Hart & Damon, 1986; Livesley & Bromley, 1973; L. S. Newman, 1991; Oppenheimer & De Groot, 1981). Thus, a 6- or 7-year-old might mention that the man sits down and eats a cookie and that the boy is wearing a soccer uniform. As children get older, they increasingly address psychological characteristics, such as being friendly, grouchy, or bossy (Barenboim, 1981), and they realize that people sometimes hide their true emotions (see Chapter 9). A 9-year-old might therefore suggest that the man is a father who is sad and tired after a hard day at work, but he is trying to be happy and upbeat for the benefit of his son.

Early Adolescence (Ages 10–14)   Young adolescents turn to person perception with a passion. When describing people, they continue to offer information about appearance and general background information, such as a person's age, gender, religion, or school affiliation (Livesley & Bromley, 1973). Thus, we might learn that the man, who appears to be a father, sits down with a young boy, who may be his son. Their interpretation might include multiple motivations: Perhaps the father has missed his son during the day and is hungry because it has been a long time since lunch. Especially notable during early adolescence is the dramatic increase in inferences about psychological states: As a result, we may hear about a boy who is lonely and hungry and a father who is frustrated with his job but finds comfort in his family.

Late Adolescence (Ages 14–18)   In the later teenage years, we see increased awareness of the complex factors, both present and past, that influence behavior. For instance, an older teen might speculate that the man had been troubled by other interpersonal relationships (perhaps with his wife or boss), tried to drown his sorrows at a local bar (his

person perception
Recognition and interpretation of people's basic characteristics, including their physical features, behaviors, and internal psychological states.

drunken state explains his stumble upon entering the room), and now wants to hide his despair and inebriation from his son.

Social Perspective Taking

To truly understand and get along with other people, children must apply their growing theory of mind and understanding of human psychology by stepping occasionally into other people's shoes and looking at the world from other viewpoints. In the opening case, Tom tries to understand why, in his mind, people become increasingly selfish as they get older: "Maybe you get a job and you're busy. Then you kind of forget the things you wanted to do for somebody" (F. H. Davidson & Davidson, 1994, p. 90). Such **social perspective taking** helps children to make sense of actions that might otherwise be puzzling and to choose responses that are most likely to achieve desired results and maintain positive interpersonal relationships.

Here we describe Robert Selman's description of how social perspective taking develops over time. We then look at how empathy may also enter into the equation.

By learning to appreciate the perspectives of others, children and adolescents become increasingly effective in interpersonal situations.

Selman's Theory   Consider the following situation:

Holly is an 8-year-old girl who likes to climb trees. She is the best tree climber in the neighborhood. One day while climbing down from a tall tree she falls off the bottom branch but does not hurt herself. Her father sees her fall. He is upset and asks her to promise not to climb the trees any more. Holly promises.

Later that day, Holly and her friends meet Sean. Sean's kitten is caught up in a tree and cannot get down. Something has to be done right away or the kitten may fall. Holly is the only one who climbs trees well enough to reach the kitten and get it down, but she remembers her promise to her father. . . .

- Does Holly know how Sean feels about the kitten?
- Does Sean know why Holly cannot decide whether or not to climb the tree? . . .
- What does Holly think her father will think of her if he finds out?
- Does Holly think her father will understand why she climbed the tree? (Selman & Byrne, 1974, p. 805)

To answer these questions, you must look at the situation from the perspectives of three different people: Sean, Holly, and Holly's father.

By presenting situations like this one and asking children to view them from various perspectives, Selman (1980; Selman & Schultz, 1990) found that with age, children show an increasing ability to take the perspective of others. He described a series of five levels that characterize the development of perspective taking:

- *Level 0: Egocentric perspective taking.*   Children are aware of physical differences among people but have little awareness of psychological differences. They are incapable of looking at a situation from anyone's perspective but their own (hence the reference to Level 0).
- *Level 1: Subjective perspective taking.*   Children realize that people have different thoughts and feelings as well as different physical features. However, they view someone else's perspective in a relatively simplistic, one-dimensional fashion (e.g., a person is simply happy, sad, or angry) and tend to equate behavior with feelings (e.g., a happy person will smile, and a sad person will pout or cry).
- *Level 2: Second-person, reciprocal perspective taking.*   Children realize that people occasionally have mixed feelings about an event—for instance, that Holly might feel both compassion for the kitten and uneasiness about breaking her promise to her father. At this level, children also understand that people may feel differently than their behaviors indicate and that people may sometimes do things they didn't really want or intend to do.
- *Level 3: Third-person, mutual perspective taking.*   Children can take an "outsider's" perspective of interpersonal relationships: They can look at their own interactions with another person as a third individual might. They appreciate the need to satisfy

social perspective taking
Imagining what someone else is thinking or feeling.

both oneself and another simultaneously and therefore understand the advantages of cooperation, compromise, and trust.

- *Level 4: Societal, symbolic perspective taking.* Children realize that people are a product of the many factors in their environments and, furthermore, that people are not always aware of why they act as they do.

Echoing Piaget's description of preoperational egocentrism, Selman proposed that most preschoolers engage in little or no perspective taking and so are at Level 0. However, young children actually do appear able to consider how other people think and feel about things, even if they do not always exercise this ability; thus, they are not as egocentric as Piaget and Selman proposed. For example, even young preschoolers realize that another person can see an object only if he or she is looking in the object's direction and has a clear, unobstructed view. Older preschoolers also realize that the same object may look different to people viewing it from different angles—for example, that a book that is right-side-up to one person will be upside-down to someone sitting across the table (Flavell, 1992, 2000). Furthermore, in their daily communication, children appear to be truly other-oriented most of the time; that is, they listen to what other people say, respond appropriately, and take into account how their listeners might be thinking and feeling (Garvey & Horgan, 1973; Mueller, 1972; Rubin & Pepler, 1995).

Although Selman may not have accurately pinned down when early perspective taking emerges, his five levels nevertheless provide a helpful framework for evaluating individual children's social perspective-taking skills. Accordingly, we describe and illustrate them in the Observation Guidelines table "Using Selman's Levels to Assess Social Perspective Taking."

Role of Empathy Emotions sometimes complement cognitive processes in social perspective taking (Eisenberg, Losoya, & Guthrie, 1997; Feshbach, 1997; M. L. Hoffman, 1998; Zahn-Waxler & Smith, 1992). As you should recall from Chapter 9, *empathy* involves experiencing the same feelings as someone else, perhaps someone in pain or distress. Empathy seems to play a central role in children's desire to "do the right thing," that is to behave morally, as we shall discover later in the chapter. It is also a key factor in children's prosocial behaviors (see Chapter 13).

Children show some signs of empathy by age 2 or 3: They may look concerned when someone else is in distress and try to give comfort and assistance (S. Lamb & Feeny, 1995; Lennon & Eisenberg, 1987; Zahn-Waxler & Radke-Yarrow, 1982; Zahn-Waxler, Radke-Yarrow, Wagner, & Chapman, 1992). Empathy continues to develop throughout childhood, and often into adolescence as well (Eisenberg, 1982). In early childhood, children are empathic primarily toward people that they know, such as friends and classmates. But by the late elementary school years, children may also begin to feel empathy for complete strangers—perhaps for the poor, the homeless, or those living in war-torn nations (Damon, 1988; M. L. Hoffman, 1991). (We examine empathy's role in helping behaviors in Chapter 13.)

To summarize our discussion thus far, we might say that children show an early disposition to take into account how others perceive, interpret, and respond emotionally to events. Initially, this disposition is superficial, fragile, and undependable. Over time, it becomes increasingly complex and insightful, and in adolescence, it includes the ability to consider numerous viewpoints simultaneously and recursively. The growing capacity for social perspective taking does not ensure that young people will always apply it, however, as even older adolescents (and adults as well, in fact) do not necessarily consider other people's perspectives and feelings in particular social settings.

Social Information Processing

As you have seen, children have a lot to think about when they consider what other people are thinking, feeling, and doing. Such **social information processing**—the mental processes involved in understanding and responding to social events—is in many respects similar to the more general information processing we described in Chapter 5: It involves selecting and paying *attention* to certain stimuli, making sense of those stimuli through *elaboration*, *storing* and *organizing* what has been learned in long-term memory, and *retrieving* previously acquired information and beliefs on relevant occasions. Dodge (1986)

social information processing Series of cognitive steps applied to understanding of, and responding to, social events.

OBSERVATION GUIDELINES

Using Selman's Levels to Assess Social Perspective Taking

CHARACTERISTIC	LOOK FOR	EXAMPLE	IMPLICATION
Level 0: Egocentric Perspective Taking	• Awareness that people are different in physical ways (e.g., gender, appearance) • Little if any awareness that people are also different in psychological ways (e.g., thoughts, feelings); assumption that other people share one's thoughts and feelings • Indignant responses when other people express differing views	Three-year-old Andrea assumes that her preschool classmates know about her fear of heights. So she expresses surprise and indignation when Rose and Molly ask her to join them in going down the slide.	Encourage children to share their unique perspectives about simple topics. For example, read a story to preschoolers and then ask them to describe how they each felt about various story characters' actions. Point out the variability in the children's opinions ("Isn't it wonderful how much we can learn from hearing all these different ideas?").
Level 1: Subjective Perspective Taking	• Realization that other people have thoughts and feelings different from one's own • Overly simplistic perceptions of others' perspectives • Tendency to equate people's outward expressions (e.g., smiles) with their internal feelings	Eight-year-old Li-Wen realizes that her friend Tony is sad about his grandfather's death. However, she does not fully appreciate the depth of his sorrow, nor does she understand his simultaneous relief that the grandfather's physical suffering has ended.	Acknowledge children's perceptiveness in detecting the unique perspectives of others. Extend their understanding by pointing out the complex feelings that people sometimes have.
Level 2: Second-Person, Reciprocal Perspective Taking	• Realization that others may have mixed and possibly contradictory feelings about a situation • Understanding that people may feel differently from what their behaviors indicate and that people sometimes do things they didn't intend to do	Eleven-year-old Pablo understands that his friend Mark may have misgivings about his decisions to experiment with inhalants at a friend's house. Pablo hears Mark bragging but senses some reservations in Mark's tone of voice and body language.	Help children to make sense of the complex motivations that guide people's actions. Communicate the legitimacy of mixed feelings ("I bet you're both excited and sad about your move to a new town").
Level 3: Third-Person, Mutual Perspective Taking	• Ability not only to see a situation from one's own and another's perspectives but also to look at a two-person relationship from a distance (i.e., as an outsider might) • Appreciation of the need to satisfy both oneself and another simultaneously • Understanding of the advantages of cooperation, compromise, and trust	Two high school freshmen, Jasmine and Alethea, discover that they've both arranged a homecoming party for the same night. They learn that they've sent invitations to numerous mutual friends as well as to each other. Since they were both looking forward to hosting a party, they discuss options for rescheduling one or both of the parties.	Acknowledge children's respect for the rights of others as they pursue their own needs and goals. Help children brainstorm alternative strategies when they have trouble identifying ways for everyone to "win" in certain situations.
Level 4: Societal, Symbolic Perspective Taking	• Recognition that people are a product of their environment—that past events and present circumstances contribute to personality and behavior • Understanding that people are not always aware of why they act as they do • Emerging comprehension of the true complexity of human behaviors, thoughts, and emotions	In their high school psychology course, Keith and Jerome are preparing a joint oral report on strategies of social persuasion. They find magazine advertisements that are geared toward adolescents and discuss possible images and feelings that advertisers are trying to invoke.	Initiate discussions of psychological motives, perhaps within the context of studying historical events in a history class or works of poetry and fiction in a literature group. For example, encourage adolescents to identify the varying motives that may have converged to affect a character's decisions in a classic work of literature.

Sources: Based on Selman, 1980; Selman & Schultz, 1990.

has proposed that people go through five steps when they encounter, interpret, and respond to specific social situations. To give life to Dodge's model, let's imagine an extension of our earlier vignette with the man, the boy, and the glass of milk. This time we'll include a third person, a girl whom we'll call Audrey:

A man walks into a room with a sad look on his face. He stumbles a bit, then sits at a table beside a young boy, who is sitting next to his friend Audrey. The man smiles, picks up a cookie, takes a bite, drinks from a glass of milk, and puts the half-filled glass on the table. The boy looks up at the man, smiles, and knocks over the milk. The milk spills and splashes onto Audrey's shirt.

From Dodge's perspective, Audrey would engage in the following cognitive processes in her efforts to understand and respond to the situation (we describe these processes within the context of concepts presented in Chapter 5):

1. *Encoding.* Audrey would focus on certain aspects of the situation, including other people's appearance and behavior, and store this information in working memory. We suspect that she would be especially attentive to the spilling of the milk, as this event would be fast-moving and attention-getting.

2. *Mental representation.* Audrey would interpret what she's observed, elaborating on the information she's obtained in light of what she already knows about human nature. Considering her preliminary ideas of what's going on, she might search for other relevant information that might confirm or contradict her interpretations. For instance, she might wonder: Why did the man stumble? Was spilling the milk an accident, or did the boy do it on purpose? What will the boy do now? Using the social cues in the situation, as well as her own knowledge and beliefs about how people typically behave, she might formulate some tentative answers to such questions.

3. *Response search.* Audrey would draw on her past experiences to decide how to handle the situation; she would search for and retrieve potentially useful responses from long-term memory. To deal with the spilled milk, she might consider a variety of possibilities—perhaps patiently cleaning up the spill, or, contrariwise, retaliating against the "aggressor"— depending on her prior social experiences.

4. *Response decision.* Once she has retrieved alternative responses, Audrey will weigh the benefits and drawbacks of each one. What would she gain and lose from cleaning up the mess? What would she gain and lose from retaliating? Perhaps she would ponder various alternatives for quite some time, or perhaps she would reach her conclusion quickly, with very little forethought.

5. *Enactment.* Once she has settled on a course of action, she would make her response and observe its effects. For example, if she cleans up the mess (and perhaps asks the boy to be more careful), she might find that she maintains a productive relationship with him. If, instead, she retaliates, she might find herself embroiled in an escalating argument.

As you can see, Dodge's model of social information processing is not confined to perception of and response to immediate social stimuli; it also draws on memories of past social events and actions and incorporates deliberation and decision making. Furthermore, Dodge suggests that children's emotional states (e.g., whether they are happy, sad, or angry) affect their interpretations at each of the five steps, and their interpretations, in turn, affect their emotional reactions (Dodge, 1991).

The social information processing model has spawned much research and has been an especially useful perspective for describing exceptionally aggressive children (Crick & Dodge, 1996; Lochman & Dodge, 1994, 1998; D. Schwartz et al., 1998; Zelli, Dodge, Lochman, & Laird, 1999). Children who are overly aggressive tend to attribute aggressive intentions to others, often mistakenly. For instance, they would quickly conclude that the boy in our vignette spilled the milk as a premeditated, hostile act. Aggressive children's thinking may be different in other ways as well. They may have, for example, a bigger arsenal of aggressive actions to pull from their behavioral repertoire, and they are likely to perceive their aggressive behaviors as justified and effective (e.g., the boy should be "taught a lesson"). We will look at the nature and possible roots of aggression more closely in Chapter 13.

Fostering the Development of Social Cognition

The theories and research findings just reviewed have numerous implications for those who work with children and adolescents. We offer the following suggestions for fostering greater understanding of other people:

When adults understand how children and adolescents think about social situations—in other words, when they understand the development of social cognition—they can better help youngsters interact effectively with peers.

■ *Talk about psychological phenomena and other people's perspectives in age-appropriate ways.* Adults frequently talk about their own thoughts and feelings and speculate about what other people (e.g., peers, parents, figures in historical and current events, or fictional characters) might be thinking and feeling. In doing so, they almost certainly enhance children's and adolescents' understanding of the complex internal lives of others. Adults should, of course, try to gear their comments to children's cognitive and linguistic capabilities. For instance, preschoolers understand such straightforward feelings as *sad, disappointed,* and *angry* (Chalmers & Townsend, 1990; Wittmer & Honig, 1994). Adolescents have sufficient cognitive and social reasoning capabilities to consider abstract and complex psychological qualities (e.g., being *passive aggressive* or having an inner *moral compass*) and to speculate about people's feelings in catastrophic circumstances (e.g., the bombing of Hiroshima and Nagasaki in World War II) (Yeager et al., 1997).

At the same time, adults can gradually nudge young people toward thinking in slightly more advanced ways about the people around them—perhaps "one level up" in terms of Selman's levels of perspective taking. For example, preschool teachers might point out how classmates' feelings may differ from children's own feelings (Level 1). Adults who work with children in the elementary grades can discuss situations in which people may have mixed feelings or want to hide their feelings—situations such as going to a new school, trying a difficult but enjoyable sport for the first time, or celebrating a holiday without a favorite family member present (Level 2). Adults who work with adolescents might, either informally (e.g., in free-flowing conversations) or formally (e.g., in a high school psychology class) explore the many ways in which people are affected by their past experiences and present understandings (Level 4).

■ *Provide opportunities for youngsters to encounter multiple, and often equally legitimate, perspectives.* The sociodramatic play of early childhood has benefits not only for cognitive development (see Chapter 4) but for social cognition as well: Children who engage in pretend play must work hard to determine how their play partners are conceiving various pretend roles and activities. Later, during the elementary and secondary school years, teachers and other professionals can engage young people in group discussions about complex or controversial topics and in group projects that require coordination of varying skills and talents. Such activities inevitably expose youngsters to diverse perspectives, perhaps including those of different genders, races, cultures, religions, and political belief systems. And adults who work with children and adolescents at all age levels can elicit varying perspectives on the unplanned incidents and conflicts—the accidental spilled milk, the disputes about playground equipment, the derogatory ethnic jokes, and so on—that arise.

■ *Be especially attuned to the interpretations and misinterpretations of children with cognitive and social-emotional disabilities.* Children with certain disabilities (e.g., ADHD, autism, mental retardation) often have particular difficulty drawing accurate inferences from others' behaviors and body language (Gray & Garaud, 1993; Leffert, Siperstein, & Millikan, 1999; Milch-Reich, Campbell, Pelham, Connelly, & Geva, 1999). For example, children with autism less frequently share a focus of attention with other people: They are less apt to notice where a parent is looking and follow the parent's gaze toward an object (Charman et al., 1997; Sigman, Kasari, Kwon, & Yirmiya, 1992). Children with autism also do not often engage in sociodramatic play and appear to have little understanding of other people's thoughts and emotions; in other words, they show deficits in development of a theory of mind (Baron-Cohen, Tager-Flusberg, & Cohen, 1993; Hobson, 1993; F. P. Hughes, 1998). Children with some disabilities, therefore, may need considerable adult guidance and support in their efforts to make sense of others' thoughts, feelings, and intentions.

Children's and adolescents' ability to interact effectively in their social world depends not only on their understanding of the people around them but also on their understanding of society more generally. We look now at young people's conceptions of social institutions and social groups.

DEVELOPMENT AND PRACTICE

Helping Children and Adolescents Understand Other People

■ Regularly include references to thoughts, feelings, and interpretations in daily conversations with children.

As a teacher in a child care center reads a story to a group of young children, she occasionally stops to ask questions about what the characters in the story might be thinking and feeling. For instance, while reading *The Berenstain Bears' Trouble with Pets* (Berenstain & Berenstain, 1990), she asks, "Why does the Bear family let Little Bird fly away?" and "How do you think Mama and Papa Bear feel when Lady makes a mess in the living room?"

■ Ask children to share their perceptions and interpretations with one another.

A kindergarten teacher finds several children arguing over how Serena tripped and fell during their game of tag. Meanwhile,

Serena is crying. The teacher comforts Serena and then asks the children for their varying perspectives on what happened. She suggests that each of them may be partly right. She also urges them to be more careful when they play running games, as it is easy for children to bump one another accidentally in such activities.

■ Ask children to consider the perspectives of people they don't know.

During a discussion of a recent earthquake in South America, a sixth-grade teacher asks his students to imagine how people must feel when they lose their home and possessions so quickly and don't know whether their loved ones are dead or alive.

Conceptions of Society and Social Groups

Individual people are objects of children's analysis, but so are groups of people—families, peer-group cliques, ethnic and racial groups, community associations, corporate organizations, governments, and so on. Children gradually develop **conceptions of society**, beliefs about the nature, structure, and operation of social institutions (Furth, 1980). As with many conceptual developments, children first apply personalized and concrete notions to the task of understanding various parts of society and then gradually transform their ideas into more comprehensive, integrated, and abstract belief systems, or *theories* (Furth, 1980; Slonim & Case, 2002; Turiel, 1983). Notice the parallel to our earlier descriptions of developmental trends in person perception and social perspective taking: There is a common shift from concrete to abstract representations.

We now look more closely at children's conceptions about several aspects of their society, including social conventions, neighborhoods and communities, political systems, and economic systems, as well as the ways in which children's experiences mold such conceptions. We then consider how children's views of particular social groups may be subject to *social-cognitive biases* that result in counterproductive prejudices and stereotypes.

Awareness of Social Conventions

By the time children are 6 or 7, they are aware that society has certain rules and conventions regarding acceptable and unacceptable behaviors (Turiel, 1983). For instance, they know that in mainstream Western culture, people are expected to wear clothes in public and that children should show deference to adult authority figures. They know, too, that certain actions, such as picking one's nose or using obscene language in the classroom, are frowned upon and often lead to social sanctions.

In the early elementary grades, children believe that social conventions should be followed for their own sake. As they grow older, however, they become more aware of the importance of social conventions for maintaining a cohesive society (Turiel, 1983). As an example, imagine that a boy named Peter calls his teacher by her first name. Children and adolescents almost invariably say that such behavior is inappropriate, but they offer differing explanations about why it is inappropriate. Let's consider how three boys analyzed the situation (Turiel, 1983):

John (age 6):

[He shouldn't have called the teacher by her first name] because what the teacher tells you, you have to obey and it is being nice to call someone what they want to be called. . . . Because he or she is pretty important.

conceptions of society
Beliefs about the nature, structure, and operations of social institutions.

Art by Zoe, age 4

Art by Elena, age 9

Art by Brendan, age 14

Art by Robin, age 15

For examples of how children depict the social and physical characteristics of their neighborhoods, view the Early Childhood, Middle Childhood, Early Adolescence, and Late Adolescence clips of the Neighborhood module of the Observation CD.

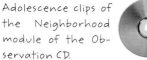

Bruce (age 11):

Wrong, because the principal told him not to. Because it was a rule. It was one of the rules of the school. . . . Because you should follow the rules. . . . [I]f there wasn't a rule, it wouldn't matter. . . . It wouldn't matter what they called her if there wasn't a rule.

Richard (age 17):

I think he was wrong, because you have to realize that you should have respect for your elders and that respect is shown by addressing them by their last names. . . . Informally, you just call any of your friends by their first names, but you really don't have that relation with a teacher. Whereas with parents too, you call them Mom and Dad and it's a different relation than the other two. . . . I think he'd have to realize that you have to go along with the ways of other people in your society. . . . (Turiel, 1983, pp. 107, 108, 110; format adapted)

Generally speaking, 6- and 7-year-olds (like John) believe that people should follow rules and conventions in large part because authority figures tell them they must do so. In contrast, 10- and 11-year-olds (like Bruce) believe that one should follow rules and conventions simply because they exist, even though they recognize that rules and conventions are somewhat arbitrary. By late adolescence (e.g., at ages 14 to 16), young people realize that conventions help society function more smoothly; for instance, Richard says that "you have to go along with the ways of other people in your society" (Kurtines, Berman, Ittel, & Williamson, 1995; Turiel, 1983).

Conceptions of Neighborhoods and Communities

For children, "society" is initially what they see close to home in their neighborhoods and communities. As they get older, their knowledge of their local surroundings increases in scope and detail (e.g., see the three maps of a Colorado community in Figure 5–5 on p. 196).

Although parents define neighborhoods in terms of physical blocks and boundaries that children can safely navigate, children conceptualize their neighborhoods more as social networks with friends and other neighbors (B. K. Bryant, 1985; L. M. Burton & Price-Spratlen, 1999). For example, in the Early Childhood, Middle Childhood, Early Adolescence, and Late Adolescence clips of the Neighborhood module of the Observation CD, Zoe, Elena, Brendan, and Robin depict their neighborhoods in both pictures and words. Although 4-year-old Zoe includes only one person ("my friend") in her picture, the older three focus on the social nature of the neighborhood as much as on its physical characteristics. Fourteen-year-old Brendan, for example, describes his neighborhood this way:

There's a lot of people. Nice people. And there's fun stuff to do around here. . . . We play football or sports in the backyards, and we have playgrounds and a basketball court. . . . Races and stay over at friends' houses.

Children's perceptions of their neighborhoods and communities seem to affect some aspects of their social-emotional development, such as how fearful they become (Garbarino, Kostelny, & Dubrow, 1991a; van Andel, 1990). Neighborhoods and communities vary considerably in how supportive they are as environments for young people, and children quickly become attuned to potential dangers to their physical and psychological safety (B. K. Bryant, 1985; Gephart, 1997). For instance, in the Neighborhood/Middle Childhood clip of the Observation CD, 9-year-old Elena mentions that her neighbor Joe is "a sweet guy," but says that in earlier days "some people just came zipping right through fast and fast and not going to the speed limit." Consider, too, the story of Candida, who grew up in a region of Nicaragua where guerilla fighters posed a constant danger:

One day, when Candida was nine years old, she went out with her father and mother to milk the cows. A group of Contras ambushed and kidnapped all three of them. Candida was separated from her parents and taken away by the Contras. She was held for five months during which time she learned the Contra life: stealing food from houses and carrying supplies while the Contras moved about.

She shuddered as she told us about being forced to watch as the Contras stripped a kidnapped man naked, and then slit his throat with a knife. Afterward, she was given his clothes to wear.

Some of the Contras tried to rape her. An older Contra intervened, claiming that she already belonged to him. He kept her as his "mascot" and protected her from the others. Candida stated that two other kidnapped girls with her had not been so lucky. One was chosen to be the "wife" of the leader, and the other girl was continually raped. (Garbarino, Kostelny, & Dubrow, 1991b, pp. 92–93)[5]

Listen to the children's descriptions of the support systems and potential dangers in their neighborhoods in the Middle Childhood, Early Adolescence, and Late Adolescence clips of the Neighborhood module of the Observation CD.

Candida finally escaped from the Contras. She learned that her parents had been killed, but she reunited with surviving members of her extended family. She did not speak for a year after being adopted by her father's cousin, and she had frequent nightmares. Eventually, she gathered her resolve and learned to cope, in part by laboring for a better world:

Sixteen now, she is known as the *solidad,* the one who is not yet married. She told us she had more important things on her agenda. Sure, she has boyfriends, but she plans to become a civil engineer. She excels in school, especially at math, and has finished six grades in less than three years. . . . She is very active in politics and is very proud that she could vote in the elections. While she hopes there won't be more war, she will join the struggle if necessary. (Garbarino et al., 1991b, p. 93; see footnote 5)

Candida has firsthand knowledge of a brutal and ruthless society. Her interest in politics has grown naturally out of her desire to embrace higher values and work toward a better society (Garbarino et al., 1991b). Candida is hardly alone in her experience with dangerous social environments; we will see other examples in our discussions of abusive families in Chapter 12, aggressive relationships in Chapter 13, and poverty in Chapter 14. For now, however, let's pick up on Candida's interest in political participation.

Conceptions of Political Systems

Although most children and adolescents do not encounter an immediate social environment as terrifying as Candida's, many still yearn for a more humane world, and this longing may feed an interest in political systems. Recall Tom's concerns about the plight of poor people in our introductory case: He is determined to improve the living conditions of those around him and envisions a political career that would enable him to do so. Many young people are, like Tom and Candida, naturally motivated to learn about the structure of government and political participation.

Children's understanding of the nature of government and political systems changes with age (Slonim, 2001; Slonim & Case, 2002).[6] At age 6 or 7, children typically have little understanding of what government involves or how it facilitates society's functioning; some think of "government" as being a single individual (e.g., a benevolent president or other prominent leader) who essentially takes care of the world. By the time they are 11 or 12, they understand that a government consists of a group of people, each of whom has a particular function to play in moving society forward and helping it run smoothly, as one 11-year-old's definition of *government* illustrates:

Many young people envision and yearn for a more humane world.

[P]eople that are in charge of what they do with the money, with the wages of the police officer, the doctor and the teacher, they enforce laws . . . taxes . . . they're the head of the community, they run things. (Slonim, 2001, pp. 93–94)

As young people reach the later high school years at ages 16 to 18, they realize that a government also reflects and maintains the structure and values of the society it serves. Consider this definition of *government* from an 18-year-old:

I would say an elected body . . . at least in our society it's elected, it doesn't have to be elected, it's a body that . . . deals essentially with issues that are greater than the individual level, cause

---

[5] From *No Place to Be a Child: Growing Up in a War Zone,* by J. Garbarino, K. Kostelny, & N. Dubrow, 1991, Lexington, MA: Lexington Books. Copyright © 1991 by Lexington Books. This material is used by permission of John Wiley & Sons, Inc.

[6] Slonim and Case have suggested that children's understanding of society and government may reflect an underlying *central conceptual structure* (see the discussion of this concept in Chapter 5).

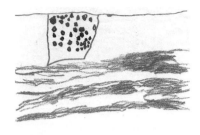

Young children's conceptions of their country and government are fairly concrete, perhaps centering around important symbols (e.g., flags, national monuments) and prominent leaders (e.g., kings, presidents). Art by Louie, age 5.

you and I can only see so far but . . . we won't be able to agree in terms of a nation, what society thinks they need for each other . . . so they represent your values and beliefs as a collective whole, it won't be individualized but it will be similar, they don't represent you but they represent a group of people. (Slonim, 2001, p. 95)

Family discussions about controversial political issues enhance young people's understanding of government and politics and can sometimes foster a commitment to civic causes (Chaffee & Yang, 1990). Adults outside the family can be influential as well—for instance, by conducting discussions about current events and providing opportunities for participation in student government or community service (Chapman, Nolin, & Kline, 1997; Niemi & Junn, 1998). More generally, parents, teachers, and other adults can promote an appreciation for democracy and equal opportunity by treating all youngsters fairly and equitably, genuinely listening to their ideas and opinions, and insisting that they treat one another in a similar manner (C. A. Flanagan & Faison, 2001).

How favorably young people view their country and government is, in part, a function of their group membership. For instance, in the United States, adolescents of European American descent tend to think that their country has, since its beginning, consistently been dedicated to principles of democracy, freedom, and individual rights; many overlook the fact that the majority of citizens (e.g., women and African Americans) were not full-fledged participants until well into the twentieth century. In contrast, teens of African American descent, who are more attuned to injustices their ancestors suffered and perhaps have themselves been targets of inequitable treatment, are more apt to view government institutions and policies as being racist and discriminatory (Epstein, 2000).

Conceptions of Economic Systems

We get a sense of children's conceptions of the world of industry and commerce from a study by Berti and Bombi (1988). These researchers interviewed 120 Italian children, ages 4 to 13, who lived in Marghera, an industrialized city near Venice. In the following excerpts (translated from Italian), an interviewer asks children about work and industry. We begin with Mara (age 4½):

Adult:	What work does your father do?
Mara:	He goes to Venice.
Adult:	And when he gets there what does he do?
Mara:	Works with his friends.
Adult:	What does he do when he works?
Mara:	My mother gives him money.
Adult:	Does he need money to work?
Mara:	Yes.
Adult:	What does he do with it?
Mara:	Because then there is water and he goes fishing. (dialogue from Berti & Bombi, 1988, p. 139; reprinted with the permission of Cambridge University Press)

Mara's ignorance of the nature of adult work is typical of the youngest children (ages 4 and 5) that Berti and Bombi interviewed. In contrast, children ages 6 to 10 were generally able to describe some of the activities that occur in the workplace. In the following interview, Mauro (age 8½) shows some understanding of the employment hierarchy but struggles with issues related to ownership of property:

Adult:	Whose are the toys which they make in the factory?
Mauro:	They take them to the shops and sell them.
Adult:	Who takes them?
Mauro:	The workers.
Adult:	But do the dolls belong to the workers or to the boss?
Mauro:	The boss, I think.
Adult:	You don't seem very convinced?
Mauro:	I'm not really.
Adult:	Why not?
Mauro:	Because it's the workers who make them.
Adult:	Why don't the workers keep them?
Mauro:	Because they have to sell them. (dialogue from Berti & Bombi, 1988, p. 143; reprinted with the permission of Cambridge University Press)

The oldest children, ages 12 and 13, differentiated between bosses, who supervised the workers, and owners, who owned property in the business. In the final interview, we hear from Alessandro (age 12½):

Adult:	Does the factory belong to someone?
Alessandro:	Of course, small factories though: Montedison for instance doesn't belong to a single person. I think it belongs to a lot of people.
Adult:	Why do you think that?
Alessandro:	Because it's impossible that one man could have such a big industry. There would have to be lots of people. On the other hand a small factory which makes furniture or shoes has a single owner.
Adult:	Why couldn't there be just a single owner for the big factory?
Alessandro:	Because he would have to have an enormous amount of money to keep all those workers.
Adult:	What do the owners do?
Alessandro:	They have to maintain contacts with the middlemen, so that if someone wanted a certain type of shoe they would send their representatives around to show them theirs. . . . I think they would sit in an office with lots of telephones.
Adult:	They wouldn't supervise the workers?
Alessandro:	No.
Adult:	Whose are the things which they make in the factory?
Alessandro:	They must belong to the owner, who sells them to someone, who then sells them to someone else who has a shop.
Adult:	How come these things belong to the owner?
Alessandro:	Because he pays the workers who do this particular job. (dialogue from Berti & Bombi, 1988, pp. 143–144; reprinted with the permission of Cambridge University Press)

Berti's and Bombi's interviews reveal a developmental progression toward more complete and systematic understandings of factories, production, and trade. To some extent, developmental changes in children's conceptions of economic systems (and, in fact, of conceptions of society more generally) are the result of advancements in cognitive abilities, such as their increasing capacity for abstract thought. Furthermore, children may uncover anomalies in their own thinking, which motivate them to seek more information (recall Piaget's concept of *disequilibrium,* described in Chapter 4). Children who start to question parts of the system may then learn more about complex operations (e.g., What do banks do with the money that people deposit? Is it fair that some people get paid more than others?) (Furth, 1980; Jahoda, 1979).

Social experiences play a role as well. When children have direct contact with the world of work, they become knowledgeable about commerce and trade at an earlier age. For example, in a series of studies by Jahoda (1979, 1982, 1983), children in Zimbabwe, Africa, had a better understanding of the need for profit in business than their peers in European countries, apparently because many of the Zimbabwean children were actively involved in family farms and retail shops.

In Western countries, many children have little if any involvement in the worlds of business and finance and therefore have limited opportunities to learn about them directly. Instead, they make reasonable guesses about these worlds by applying their developing reasoning skills to the knowledge they *do* have. For instance, at about age 4, Teresa's son Connor asked for a credit card for his birthday (he didn't get one). At age 5, her son Alex watched his father paying bills and spontaneously observed, "I get it! The money goes round and round!" But despite Alex's perceptive deduction about how the system works, he had little awareness of the value of money (see Figure 10–3).

FIGURE 10–3 At age 6, Alex had little appreciation for the value of money. For Christmas, he asked for two videogame systems, a model boat, a Harry Potter Lego set, and $50,000. (In lines 4 and 5, he says, "I want to see your Rudolph [reindeer] fly.")

Social-Cognitive Bias and Prejudice

Although young people acquire advanced social cognitive processes and considerable knowledge about their social world, they do not always make use of such acquisitions, in part because they frequently lack the time and inclination to engage in careful, rational, and methodical thinking (Cialdini, 2001; Kahneman, 2000; Thaler, 2000). In fact, people of all ages regularly use mental shortcuts, or **social-cognitive biases,** to make their dealings with their complex social world more efficient and manageable (Brenner, Koehler, Liberman, &

social-cognitive bias
Mental shortcut in thinking about social phenomena.

Tversky, 1996; Tversky & Kahneman, 1990). For example, people may uncritically accept what an authority figure says, assume that expensive items are invariably of higher quality than inexpensive ones, or believe that a single action reflects a person's typical behavior and personality. To illustrate, let's return to our earlier scenario involving the man, the boy, and Audrey. If Audrey is predisposed to think that a single behavior indicates how a person typically acts, she might assume that the man (who has a sad look) is a generally unhappy guy and that the boy (who spills the milk) is perpetually clumsy or inconsiderate.

Many social-cognitive biases are a minor nuisance—they lead to small distortions in thinking—but don't cause grave harm. Some social biases, however, have serious consequences. For instance, people occasionally make hasty judgments about others based on group membership (e.g., gender, ethnicity, sexual orientation, religious affiliation). In other words, they respond on the basis of a **stereotype**, a rigid, simplistic, and erroneous characterization of a particular group. Often, people have stereotypes that encompass a host of negative attributes (e.g., "stingy," "lazy," "promiscuous") and lead them to exhibit negative attitudes, feelings, and behaviors—that is, **prejudice**—toward a particular group. Recall our introductory case: Tom's uncle and cousins made derogatory remarks about Jewish and Catholic people, and classmates shunned Tim because he was African American.

The roots of stereotypes and prejudice lie in the natural tendency of human beings to categorize their experiences. In their first few years, children learn that people belong to different groups, such as boys, girls, "blacks," and "whites," and many preschoolers can identify members of various ethnic groups (Aboud, 1988, 1993). As children are forming these social categories, they tend to favor their own group and to expect undesirable characteristics and behaviors from members of other groups, especially if the different groups are in competition with one another (Black-Gutman & Hickson, 1996; J. R. Harris, 1995; Powlishta, 1995; Wilder & Shapiro, 1989).

Productive interactions with peers of diverse backgrounds and races help children discover that every individual has unique qualities and that ethnic and racial stereotypes are rarely accurate.

stereotype
Rigid, simplistic, and erroneous characterization of a particular group.

prejudice
Exhibiting negative attitudes, feelings, and behaviors toward particular individuals because of their membership in a specific group.

To some degree, stereotypes and prejudice decrease as children move through the elementary school grades (D. E. Carter, Detine-Carter, & Benson, 1995; F. H. Davidson, 1976; C. L. Martin, 1989; Powlishta, Serbin, Doyle, & White, 1994). This decline is probably due to children's increasing ability to see the limits of social categories; for instance, they begin to realize that people who share membership in a category (e.g., "girls") may be similar in some ways but very different in others.

Although advancements in cognitive abilities work to reduce stereotypes and prejudice, other factors may work to maintain or strengthen them, and some children show an increase in prejudice as they reach early adolescence (Black-Gutman & Hickson, 1996). Children whose parents make racist jokes within earshot or restrict playmates to peers of similar backgrounds are more likely to exhibit prejudice against certain ethnic groups (Ashmore & DelBoca, 1976). Stereotypical images in the media may contribute as well. For example, children who watch a lot of television are more likely to have stereotypical views of males and females, perhaps because television programs more often than not depict males as strong and aggressive and females as weak and passive (Huston et al., 1992; Kimball, 1986; Signorielli & Lears, 1992).

Stereotypes and prejudice are of concern to many adults who work with children and adolescents, in part because of their potentially harmful effects on youngsters' self-esteem and social interactions. By adolescence, and probably before, children who are victims of prejudice are aware that they are treated unfairly (Phinney & Tarver, 1988; R. D. Taylor, Casten, Flickinger, Roberts, & Fulmore, 1994). Over time they acquire a variety of strategies for coping with prejudice and discrimination; for instance, they may become more assertive, try harder in social situations, withdraw from competition, or seek the social support of family and friends (Major & Schmader, 1998; C. T. Miller & Myers, 1998; Swim, Cohen, & Hyers, 1998). Such strategies may or may not be effective, however, as people who are daily victims of prejudice are more likely to become ill or depressed (Allison, 1998).

Clearly, the detrimental effects of prejudice make it an important target for intervention in schools and through other social agencies. We look now at strategies for enhancing children's and adolescents' conceptions of society and promoting accurate perceptions of various social groups.

Enhancing Children's Conceptions of Society and Social Groups

Teachers and other professionals who work regularly with children and adolescents are in a prime position to foster more accurate and productive understandings of society and social groups. We suggest several strategies:

■ *Bring children to the world of work, commerce, and government.* Children gain considerable knowledge about how their society functions from field trips to the post office, bank, police station, local government offices, and so on, particularly when such trips involve a behind-the-scenes view of the daily activities of such institutions. Field trips have an additional benefit in that they provide a mechanism for involving parents and other family members in children's activities at school and elsewhere (we address the importance of family involvement in Chapter 12).

■ *Bring society's institutions into the classroom.* In preschool and kindergarten settings, teachers and other caregivers can bring assorted props (e.g., supplies from a pizza restaurant, hardware store, hair salon, or veterinary clinic) to extend children's fantasies in pretend play (Ferguson, 1999). In the elementary and secondary grades, teachers might ask students to set up a market economy (e.g., producing, selling, and buying goods), create a student government to make classroom decisions, or establish a classroom courthouse to try mock cases. Furthermore, students of all ages can learn from community members who visit the classroom to describe their day-to-day activities in the workforce.

One activity that's easy to bring into classroom settings is the process of voting. For example, Teresa recalls how, during a presidential election, 5-year-old Alex's kindergarten teacher demonstrated the voting process by having the children mark ballots about their preferred type of cookie, chocolate chip or oatmeal. (Chocolate chip cookies won, hands down.) A systematic introduction to the democratic process can be found in a curriculum called "Kids Voting USA," designed for students in kindergarten through grade 12 (M. McDevitt & Chaffee, 1998). In this curriculum, students have age-appropriate lessons about voting, political parties, and political issues, and they relate what they learn to local election campaigns. For instance, they might conduct their own mock elections, analyze candidates' attacks of opponents, or give speeches in class about particular propositions on the ballot. Participants in the program are more likely to focus regularly on media reports about an election, initiate discussions about the election with friends and family members, and be knowledgeable about candidates and election results. The effects are particularly striking for students from low-income families, who traditionally are less aware of and less involved in local politics than wealthier families: The program narrows the "political awareness" gap among different socioeconomic groups. Curiously, the students' involvement in the program has an impact on their parents as well; accordingly, we will revisit the program in our discussion of families in Chapter 12.

In the "Kids Voting USA" curriculum, students in grades K–12 learn about the democratic process while following the course of a local campaign and election. This poster by Danielle, age 18, was the winning entry in a contest conducted in connection with the program.

■ *Examine society's inequities.* Older children and adolescents, especially those from low-income families, may struggle with inequities in income, living conditions, and educational opportunities. Teachers and other adults can help young people from all backgrounds become aware of inequities in their society, identify possible causes of such inequities, and develop solutions for overcoming them. As Flanagan and Faison (2001) put it, "to promote democracy youth need to know the full story, not just the 'good parts' of history. If they appreciate that history and politics are controversial, they may see the importance of taking a stand and of adding their voice to the debate" (Flanagan & Faison, 2001, p. 3).

■ *Provide opportunities and support that enable children and adolescents to make a difference in their community.* Both in school and out, young people should discover that their efforts can, in fact, have an impact. As an example, a mathematics teacher at an inner-city middle school consistently encouraged her students to identify problems in their community and

DEVELOPMENT AND PRACTICE

Fostering a Better Understanding of Society and Social Groups

- Bring representatives and artifacts from social institutions to the classroom.

    A fourth-grade teacher invites people in a variety of professions (e.g., in industry, retail, social service, government) to talk about what they do in their jobs and how they contribute to the community's productivity and well-being.

- Identify important causes in which young people can become actively involved and make a difference.

    Members of a Girl Scout troop visit a local nursing home the first Wednesday afternoon of every month. Each girl "adopts" one or more "grandparents" to whom she sends a card or small gift on major holidays.

- Encourage youngsters to look for the individual differences that exist within groups of people who share a particular attribute, such as ethnic heritage, gender, or religious affiliation.

The leader of a high school book club suggests that the group read *Nine Parts of Desire,* journalist Geraldine Brooks's (1995) description of the diverse religious beliefs and practices of Muslim women in Middle Eastern countries.

- Combat prejudice.

    When a preschool teacher hears a girl deriding a classmate for being "too brown," he takes her aside and points out that good people come in many colors and that he personally thinks brown skin is very beautiful. The teacher also insists that the girl apologize to the classmate and try to make amends by inviting the classmate to join her in putting together a picture puzzle.

work to solve them (Tate, 1995). One of her classes expressed concern about the 13 liquor stores located within 1000 feet of their school, in part because of the alcoholics and drug dealers that the stores attracted. The students calculated the distance of each store from the school, gathered information about zoning restrictions and other regulations, identified potential violations, met with a local newspaper editor (who published an editorial describing the situation), and eventually met with state legislators and the city council. As a result of their efforts, city police monitored the liquor stores more closely, major violations were identified (leading to the closing of two stores), and the city council made it illegal to consume alcohol within 600 feet of the school (Tate, 1995).

■ *Work to break down stereotypes and prejudice.* Adults can address negative stereotypes and prejudice in a variety of ways. One effective strategy is to encourage children to see people as *individuals*—as human beings with their own unique strengths and weaknesses—rather than as members of particular groups. For instance, adults might point out how dramatic the differences among members of any single group usually are (García, 1994; Lee & Slaughter-Defoe, 1995; Spencer & Markstrom-Adams, 1990). It is even more effective to increase interpersonal contacts among people from diverse groups (and ideally to create a sense that "we are all in this together"), perhaps through cooperative group activities, multischool community service projects, or pen pal relationships with children in distant locations (Devine, 1995; D. W. Johnson & Johnson, 2000; Koeppel & Mulrooney, 1992; Oskamp, 2000; Ramsey, 1995).

Second, adults should challenge stereotypes and prejudicial attitudes whenever they encounter them. For example, if a teenager talks about "lazy migrant workers," an adult might respond by saying, "I occasionally hear students express that view. I wonder where that stereotype came from. Migrant workers are often up working before dawn and picking produce until dusk. And many of them take up other demanding jobs when the growing season is over." Notice how the adult confronts the "lazy migrant worker" stereotype tactfully and matter-of-factly and does not assume that Bill's remark has malicious intent. Youngsters often thoughtlessly repeat the prejudicial remarks of others; playing on their interests in appearing tolerant and open-minded may be more effective than chastising them for attitudes they have not carefully thought through (Dovidio & Gaertner, 1999).

Finally, in instructional settings, educators should use curriculum materials that portray all groups in a positive light—for example, selecting textbooks, works of fiction, and videotapes that portray people of diverse ethnic backgrounds as legitimate participants in mainstream society rather than as exotic "curiosities" that live in a strange and separate world. Educators should be particularly vigilant in screening out materials that portray members of minority groups in an overly simplistic, romanticized, exaggerated, or otherwise stereo-typical way (Banks, 1994; Boutte & McCormick, 1992; Ladson-Billings, 1994; Pang, 1995).

Children's understandings of other people and the broader social world support their growing ability to consider others' rights and needs—in other words, their growing sense of morality. We turn to the nature of moral development now.

Moral Development

The term **morality** refers to a general set of standards about right and wrong and encom-passes such traits as honesty, compassion, and respect for other people's rights and needs. Immoral behaviors involve actions that are unfair, cause physical or emotional harm, or vi-olate the rights of others. In the opening case, we met Tom, a young adolescent with a strong sense of what is morally right—an internal compass that he uses to direct his own course of action and judge other people's conduct. Tom expresses an abhorrence for preju-dice against people of other religions and races and shows a commitment to working for a more compassionate society.

Families, schools, and social relationships are highly influential in young people's moral development. Tom's strong moral convictions developed, at least in part, out of the lessons he received at home. Some lessons were positive ones: His father taught him to "make all kinds of friends" and modeled religious tolerance by marrying a Catholic despite other fam-ily members' objections. Curiously, less exemplary models fostered Tom's moral develop-ment as well: The bigotry he observed in his extended family and classmates has only strengthened his determination to combat intolerance and injustice.

In some instances, however, the negative influences may overpower the positive ones. Consider the case of Lun Cheung, who at age 4 emigrated from Hong Kong to New York with his family. Unable to find employment commensurate with his advanced education, Lun's father worked as a cook in a Chinese restaurant, but his frustration led to major de-pression and several lengthy stays at a psychiatric hospital. Lun's mother was a seamstress at a garment factory, leaving Lun in the care of three overbearing brothers who insisted that Lun do all the household chores. In seventh grade, Lun, searching for more supportive re-lationships, joined a gang in New York's Chinatown and was soon embroiled in a world of extortion, violence, and murder:

> He had a friend in seventh grade who served alongside his father in the Ghost Shadows, one of Chinatown's two dominant gangs. First inducted a year earlier at age twelve, Lun's friend drove his own Pontiac Firebird and carried $800 in cash instead of lunch money. When the boy in-vited Lun to join the Ghost Shadows, Lun felt honored and pleased. There were no oaths or rit-uals, Lun would later remember, only the warning, "Join another gang and we'll kill you. . . . "
>
> Lun started his career as the junior partner in a three-man extortion firm. The ring was re-sponsible for Mott Street, a few bustling blocks of curio shops, restaurants, and herbal medi-cine shops, the place any guidebook would direct a tourist to experience "the real Chinatown." Lun stood rear guard as the leader demanded money, cursing each shopkeeper's ancestors. A small business was assessed $150 a month, a large one $400. Owners who refused to pay were beaten, and for those who persisted, the leader packed a .38. Lun also served as a watchman outside basement gambling parlors, and one night while he was on duty, he saw several Ghost Shadows attack a rival gangster, bludgeoning him with a lead pipe until his head cracked like a melon. (S. G. Freedman, 1990, pp. 303–304)[7]

By the time English teacher Jessica Siegel had Lun in her high school journalism class, he was, fortunately, no longer a member of the gang. In an autobiography that Ms. Siegel asked her students to write, Lun explained why and how he was finally able to break free from gang life:

> [I]n the tenth grade, as he told Jessica in his autobiography, he was jumped and beaten sense-less and his best friend Steve was killed. Another friend, this one a gang member, accidentally killed himself while cleaning his gun. Lun's parents sent him to Hong Kong that summer, where

---

[7] Pages 303–304 from *Small Victories* by Samuel G. Freedman. Copyright © 1990 by Samuel G. Freed-man. Reprinted by permission of HarperCollins Publishers, Inc.

morality
General set of standards about right and wrong.

he boarded with cousins and vowed to straighten his ways. He returned in the fall to a hard, dull, legitimate life, doing his homework, working as a cashier, and choosing new friends. . . . He watched from the sidelines as the police splintered the Ghost Shadows with dozens of arrests, and he was relieved to see temptation sent to prisons far away. (Freedman, 1990, p. 304)[8]

At last report, Lun was a second-semester freshman at Brooklyn College, off to a good start toward making a more productive contribution to society.

What circumstances influence young people's ability to behave in a respectful, compassionate, and in other ways *moral* manner toward their fellow human beings? In Lun Cheung's case, a traumatic incident—the murder of his best friend—was an important turning point. In most cases, however, moral development is nurtured by an accumulation of many seemingly minor experiences: observing moral behavior (such as that Tom saw in his father), bickering with siblings and peers about what's "fair," being chastised by a parent for hurting someone's feelings, seeing sadness on another's face, wrestling with moral issues in the classroom, and so on.

In the pages that follow, we consider the multidimensional nature of moral development. We first look at how various researchers have approached the study of moral development and at general trends in moral reasoning and behavior. We then consider Lawrence Kohlberg's theory of moral reasoning and the factors that affect moral development.

Approaches to the Study of Moral Development

Developmentalists have approached moral development from several angles. Some have focused on how families and communities socialize children to behave in morally acceptable ways. Others have focused instead on children's interpretations and reasoning (i.e., their cognition) about moral issues. Still others have emphasized the emotions (e.g., empathy, shame) that accompany morally "right" and "wrong" behaviors. Let's look more closely at each of these approaches.

Focus on Socialization   Conceivably, moral development has a genetic basis. Some evolutionary theorists have speculated that moral behaviors—helping people in need, showing respect for other people's possessions, and so on—hold social groups together and so increase the likelihood that the human species will survive and reproduce (Cosmides & Tooby, 1989; R. Wright, 1994). Most psychologists assume that environmental factors likewise play a significant role in moral development. For example, numerous aspects of Lun Cheung's environment (overbearing siblings, regular contact with gang members, monetary rewards for illicit activities) almost certainly contributed to his immoral behaviors in early adolescence.

Some theorists have proposed that moral development is primarily a process of **internalization**: Growing children increasingly adopt and take ownership of their society's rules and values regarding acceptable behavior. In this view, internalization occurs largely as a result of socialization, whereby parents and other members of the society model appropriate behaviors, reward children for behaving in a similarly appropriate manner, and punish behaviors deemed to be harmful, inconsiderate, or in other ways morally wrong.

One early theorist who stressed the importance of early experiences on moral development was Sigmund Freud (e.g., 1959). Freud proposed that, at birth, children are motivated primarily to satisfy their own instinctual urges, especially urges related to sex and aggression (recall our description of psychodynamic perspectives in Chapter 1). Parents and other members of society soon insist that the children follow certain expectations for behavior, which are often in conflict with what children instinctually want to do. Sometime

Over time, children increasingly internalize their society's rules and conventions for behavior. What rules and conventions does this artist have in mind? Art by Jessica, sixth grade.

internalization
In moral development, adopting society's rules and values about acceptable behavior as one's own.

_____

[8] Page 304 from *Small Victories* by Samuel G. Freedman. Copyright © 1990 by Samuel G. Freedman. Reprinted by permission of HarperCollins Publishers, Inc.

between ages 3 and 6, Freud suggested, children develop a conscience, or *superego,* that enables them to resist their biological impulses. They do so in large part by *identifying* with the same-sex parent and assuming that parent's values regarding appropriate behavior.

More recently, other theorists have, like Freud, described moral development as a process of being socialized by parents and other caregivers and eventually taking on the moral behaviors and values that the preceding generation espouses (e.g., Blasi, 1995; R. V. Burton & Kunce, 1995; Peláez-Nogueras & Gewirtz, 1995; Skinner, 1971). We will see the influence of this approach later in the chapter as we consider *induction* and *modeling* as factors affecting moral development.

Focus on Cognition The processes of socialization and internalization do not fully account for the phenomena observed in moral development. Children and adolescents don't always take adults' standards for behavior at face value (J. R. Harris, 1998; Turiel, 1998). In fact, some are quite critical of how the preceding generation behaves and insist on behaving differently; recall Tom's disdain for his grandmother's and uncle's attitudes about Catholics and Jews. Furthermore, young people acquire considerable flexibility in their moral decision making: They apply varying moral standards in different circumstances, depending on their interpretation of each situation and the likely outcomes of their actions (Grusec & Goodnow, 1994). Theorists who take a cognitive approach therefore place much of the responsibility for moral development on children themselves, rather than on the adults in children's lives.

Many developmentalists who focus on cognitive processes have suggested that, through interactions with adults and peers, children gradually construct their own moral beliefs and values. One early theorist taking this approach was Jean Piaget, whose theory of cognitive development is described in Chapter 4. Piaget proposed that, over time, children construct increasingly complex and flexible understandings of "good" and "bad" behavior. For instance, in the early elementary years, children believe that behaviors that are "bad" or "naughty" are those that cause serious damage or harm. By the upper elementary grades, however, children consider people's motives and intentions when evaluating behaviors. As an illustration of this change, consider the following situations:

A. A little boy who is called John is in his room. He is called to dinner. He goes into the dining room. But behind the door there was a chair, and on the chair there was a tray with fifteen cups on it. John couldn't have known that there was all this behind the door. He goes in, the door knocks against the tray, bang go the fifteen cups, and they all get broken!

B. Once there was a little boy whose name was Henry. One day when his mother was out he tried to get some jam out of the cupboard. He climbed up on to a chair and stretched out his arm. But the jam was too high up and he couldn't reach it and have any. But while he was trying to get it he knocked over a cup. The cup fell down and broke. (Piaget, 1932/1960b, p. 118)

A 6-year-old child, whom we'll call "Susan," evaluates the two boys' misdeeds this way (she initially refers to the 15 cups as "plates"):

Adult: Are those children both naughty, or is one not so naughty as the other?
Susan: Both just as naughty.
Adult: Would you punish them the same?
Susan: No. The one who broke fifteen plates.
Adult: And would you punish the other one more, or less?
Susan: The first broke lots of things, the other one fewer.
Adult: How would you punish them?
Susan: The one who broke the fifteen cups: two slaps. The other one: one slap. (dialogue from Piaget, 1932/1960b, p. 121; format adapted)

In contrast, 9-year-old "Greta" takes the boys' motives into account:

Adult: Which of these two silly things was naughtiest, do you think?
Greta: The one where he tried to take hold of a cup was [the silliest] because the other boy didn't see [that there were some cups behind the door]. He saw what he was doing.
Adult: How many did he break?
Greta: One cup.
Adult: And the other one?

Many developmental theorists suggest that children construct their own beliefs about right and wrong, rather than simply adopting adults' moral values. What beliefs might lead these boys to think that shoplifting is morally acceptable?

Greta: Fifteen.
Adult: Then which one would you punish most?
Greta: The one who broke one cup.
Adult: Why?
Greta: He did it on purpose. If he hadn't taken the jam, it wouldn't have happened.
          (dialogue from Piaget, 1932/1960b, p. 125; format adapted)

After interviewing children about a variety of situations—causing damage, telling lies, stealing someone else's possessions, playing games, and so on—Piaget proposed that children's moral reasoning undergoes qualitative changes over time. For preschoolers, "good" behavior consists of obeying adults and other authority figures. Around age 5, children begin to judge what is good and appropriate based on established *rules* for behavior. At this point, they see rules as firm and inflexible, as dictates to be obeyed without question (Piaget called this rule-based morality **moral realism**). Sometime around age 8 or 9, children begin to recognize that rules are created primarily to help people get along and can be changed if everyone agrees to the change.

Researchers have found that Piaget was not always accurate about when various aspects of moral reasoning emerge; for instance, many preschoolers recognize that certain behaviors (e.g., pushing others or damaging their property) are wrong even if an adult assures them that such behaviors are acceptable (Nucci & Turiel, 1978; Tisak, 1993; Turiel, 1983). However, many developmentalists find value in Piaget's notion that children construct their own standards for moral behavior—often as a result of having discussions with adults and peers—rather than simply adopting the moral guidelines of those around them (Davidson & Youniss, 1995; Kohlberg, 1984; Kurtines et al., 1995; Turiel, 1998). Furthermore, theorists acknowledge that development of children's moral understandings depends considerably on advancing cognitive capabilities, such as perspective taking and abstract thought (Eisenberg, 1995; Kohlberg, 1969; Kurtines et al., 1995). You will find an example of a constructivist approach to moral development in Lawrence Kohlberg's theory of moral reasoning, to be described shortly.

Focus on Emotions   Some theorists have focused not on the cognitions but on the emotions involved in moral reasoning and behavior. Sigmund Freud and several other early theorists (Aronfreed, 1976; Parke & Walters, 1967) argued that children tend to behave in a morally appropriate manner primarily because behaving otherwise elicits considerable *anxiety*. More recently, theorists have proposed that several "feel-good" emotions—especially *love, attachment, sympathy,* and *empathy*—entice children to engage in moral behaviors, and "feel-bad" emotions—*shame* and *guilt* as well as anxiety—discourage them from indulging in immoral ones (Damon, 1988; M. L. Hoffman, 1991; J. Kagan, 1984; Turiel, 1998). For example, children are more likely to engage in **prosocial behavior**—that is, to behave more for another's benefit than for one's own—if they feel empathy for the person in need (Eisenberg, 1995; Eisenberg, Zhou, & Koller, 2001). They also are more likely to repair any damage that their thoughtless actions have caused if they feel guilty about what they have done (Eisenberg, 1995; Narváez & Rest, 1995).

Combining Theoretical Perspectives   Increasingly, developmentalists are including both cognition and emotion in their explanations of moral development and behavior (e.g., J. C. Gibbs, 1995; Narváez & Rest, 1995; Turiel, 1998). For example, Nancy Eisenberg's theory of prosocial reasoning proposes that children's judgments about prosocial behavior are dependent on their ability to empathize with other people (we describe Eisenberg's theory in Chapter 13). Developmentalists also acknowledge that, to some extent, children base their moral standards on those of their families, communities, and cultures. For instance, as you will see shortly, people of different cultures acquire somewhat different ideas about morality—a finding that can be explained only if one acknowledges the role of socialization in moral development.

Clearly, then, all three of the approaches just considered make a contribution to our understanding of moral development. We summarize and contrast the three approaches in the Basic Developmental Issues table "Contrasting Approaches to the Study of Moral Development." We turn now to general trends in the development of morality.

moral realism
Viewing rules for behavior as firm and inflexible, as having a life of their own separate from the purposes they serve.

prosocial behavior
Action intended to benefit another, without regard for one's own needs.

BASIC DEVELOPMENTAL ISSUES

Contrasting Approaches to the Study of Moral Development

ISSUE	FOCUS ON SOCIALIZATION	FOCUS ON COGNITION	FOCUS ON EMOTIONS
Nature and Nurture	Emphasis is on nurture: Theorists consider the ways in which members of society (especially parents) model and encourage moral behavior and values, as well as the strategies people use to discourage immoral activities.	Specific experiences (e.g., conflicts with peers, encounters with moral dilemmas) influence the views of morality that children construct. Children's ability to think abstractly about moral issues depends on their cognitive development, which may be partly constrained by biological maturation.	The various emotions that underlie moral behavior have a biological basis, but the extent to which children associate them with particular moral actions is determined largely by experience and learning.
Universality and Diversity	The process of socialization is universal, as are many of the techniques (e.g., modeling, rewards, punishments) that adults use to socialize children. However, different cultures, and to some extent different families within each culture, socialize different moral beliefs and behaviors.	The general sequence through which children progress as they acquire moral reasoning capabilities is presumed to be universal across cultures. Not all individuals progress through the entire sequence, however, and the specific moral ideals that children construct may be somewhat culture-specific.	Love, empathy, shame, guilt, and other emotions associated with moral behavior are universal across cultures. However, children's feelings about various behaviors differ, depending on their prior experiences. Some children (e.g., many of those identified as having conduct disorders) show deficits in the emotions typically associated with immoral actions.
Qualitative and Quantitative Change	Children's increasing conformity to society's standards for behavior is presumed to be predominantly quantitative in nature.	Children and adolescents progress through a series of qualitatively different stages in moral reasoning.	Emotions such as shame, guilt, and empathy increase in a quantitative fashion in the early years. Empathy also shows qualitative change, progressing from a superficial understanding of other people's needs in the preschool and early elementary years to a true appreciation for the plights of others in adolescence. Some adolescents move to yet another level, showing empathy for entire groups of people, including many people whom they do not know.

Developmental Trends in Morality

Researchers have uncovered several developmental trends that characterize children's moral reasoning and behavior.

■ *Children begin using internal standards to evaluate behavior at a very early age.* Many children begin to distinguish between what's "good" and "bad" and what's "nice" and "naughty" well before their second birthday; for instance, they may look at a broken object and say "uh-oh!" (J. Kagan, 1984; S. Lamb & Feeny, 1995). In the Intelligence/Infancy clip of the Observation CD, 16-month-old Corwin shows concern ("uh-oh!") when his block tower falls down.

See evidence that Corwin has emerging internal standards in the Intelligence/Infancy clip of the Observation CD.

Some early theorists, including Freud and Piaget, believed that young children base their decisions about right and wrong exclusively on what adults tell them to do and not do and on which behaviors adults reward and punish. Young children certainly do try out a wide variety of behaviors to see how their parents and other caregivers will respond, but they begin to apply their own standards for behavior by age 2, and probably even earlier (Dunn, 1988; Kim & Turiel, 1996; Kochanska, Casey, & Fukumoto, 1995; S. Lamb, 1991). For instance, infants and toddlers may wince, cover their eyes or ears, or cry when they witness an aggressive interaction. Sometime around age 3, children also know that causing *psychological* harm, such as fear or embarrassment, is inappropriate (Helwig, Zelazo, & Wilson, 2001). By age 4, most children understand that causing harm to another person is wrong even if an authority figure tells them otherwise (Laupa, 1994).

■ *Children increasingly distinguish between moral transgressions and conventional transgressions.* Society discourages some actions because they cause damage or harm, violate human rights, or run counter to basic principles of equality, freedom, or justice. Such actions are **moral transgressions**. Society discourages other actions because, although not unethical, they violate widely held understandings about how one should behave (e.g., you should never talk back to your parents or burp at the dinner table). These actions are **conventional transgressions** that interfere with society's ability to run smoothly (recall our earlier discussion of social conventions). Conventional transgressions are usually culturally defined; for instance, although burping is frowned upon in mainstream Western culture, people in some cultures burp at the table to compliment their host. In contrast, many moral transgressions are universal across cultures.

Children learn about the "wrongness" of moral and conventional transgressions in different ways. Consider the following scenarios (Laupa & Turiel, 1995):

- A number of nursery school children are playing outdoors. There are some swings in the yard, all of which are being used. One of the children decides that he now wants to use a swing. Seeing that they are all occupied, he goes to one of the swings, where he pushes the other child off, at the same time hitting him. The child who has been pushed is hurt and begins to cry. (p. 461)
- Children are greeting a teacher who has just come into the nursery school. A number of children go up to her and say "Good morning, Mrs. Jones." One of the children says, "Good morning, Mary." (p. 461)

In the first scenario, the child who pushes his peer gets immediate feedback that he has caused harm and distress: The child cries and is clearly injured. In the second scenario, the child who calls a teacher by her first name may get verbal feedback that such behavior is unacceptable but will not see any concrete evidence of harm. Sometimes children get no feedback that they have violated social conventions, in part because some conventions are situation-specific (e.g., some adults prefer that children call them by their first names). When adults do respond to conventional transgressions, they typically respond differently than they do to moral transgressions. For instance, they are more likely to use physical punishment (e.g., a spanking) for moral infringements than for conventional ones (Catron & Masters, 1993). And when adults explain what children have done wrong, they focus on other people's needs and rights for moral transgressions ("You've really hurt Megan's feelings by your unkind remark") but emphasize rules and the need for social order for conventional violations ("We always use our 'indoor' voices when speaking in class") (Chilamkurti & Milner, 1993; Nucci & Nucci, 1982b; Nucci & Turiel, 1978; Smetana, 1989).

Children show a similar distinction in their reactions to their peers' transgressions (Nucci & Nucci, 1982a, 1982b; Turiel, 1983). They talk about possible injury or injustice in the case of moral transgressions, as the following observation on a playground illustrates:

> Two boys have forcibly taken a sled away from a younger boy and are playing with it. A girl who was watching says to the boys, "Hey, give it back, assholes. That's really even odds, the two of you against one little kid." The girl pulls the sled away from one of the older boys, pushes him to the ground, and hands the sled back to the younger boy. He takes the sled and the incident ends. (Nucci & Nucci, 1982a, p. 1339)

In contrast, children talk about the importance of rules and norms in the case of conventional transgressions. For instance, if a 7-year-old boy sees another child spitting on the grass, he might admonish the child, "You're not supposed to spit" (Nucci & Nucci, 1982a, p. 1339).

Even preschoolers have some understanding that not all actions are wrong in the same way, and that some misbehaviors—those that violate moral conventions—are more serious than others (Nucci & Weber, 1995; Smetana, 1981; Smetana & Braeges, 1990; Turiel, 1983). Their sensitivity to violations of social conventions is minimal in early childhood but increases throughout the elementary school years (Nucci & Nucci, 1982b; Nucci & Turiel, 1978; Turiel, 1983). Initially, children distinguish between moral and conventional transgressions only for situations with which they have had personal experience (e.g., a boy bullying children on the playground vs. a girl eating dinner with her fingers). By the time they are 6, they make the distinction for less familiar situations as well (Davidson, Turiel, & Black, 1983; Helwig & Jasiobedzka, 2001; Laupa & Turiel, 1995).

moral transgression
Action that causes damage or harm or in some other way infringes on the needs and rights of others.

conventional transgression
Action that violates society's general guidelines (often unspoken) for socially acceptable behavior.

Children and adults do not always agree about which behaviors constitute moral transgressions, which ones fall into the conventional domain, and which ones fall into a third category of personal choice. For instance, adolescents typically think of their friends as being a matter of personal choice, whereas their parents may view their selection of friends as having potential moral implications (Smetana & Asquith, 1994). For instance, friends influence teenagers' choices about whether to spend leisure time productively or inappropriately (recall Lun Cheung's moral decline once he started hanging out with the wrong crowd). Furthermore, whereas adults typically view drug use as a moral transgression, teenagers often think it is acceptable as long as it doesn't harm other people (Berkowitz, Guerra, & Nucci, 1991).

■ *Children's understanding of fairness evolves throughout early and middle childhood.* The ability to share with others depends on children's sense of **distributive justice**, their beliefs about what constitutes people's fair share of a valued commodity (food, toys, recreational time, etc.). Children's notions of distributive justice change over time (Damon, 1977, 1980). In the preschool years, their beliefs about what's fair are based on their own needs and desires; for instance, it would be perfectly "fair" to give oneself a large handful of candy and give others smaller amounts. In the early elementary grades, children base their judgments about fairness on strict equality: A desired commodity is divided into equal portions. Sometimes around age 8, children begin to take merit and special needs into account; for instance, children who contribute more to a group's efforts should reap a greater portion of the group's rewards, and people who are exceptionally poor might be given more resources than others.

■ *Emotions related to moral behavior develop in early and middle childhood.* As you have learned, certain emotions accompany and may spur moral behavior, and these emotions emerge gradually as children grow older. Children begin to show signs of **guilt**—a feeling of discomfort when they know that they have inflicted damage or caused someone else pain or distress—as early as 22 months, and those who show it at a young age are less likely to misbehave later on (Kochanska, Gross, Lin, & Nichols, 2002). By the time children reach the middle elementary grades, most of them occasionally feel **shame**: They feel embarrassed or humiliated when they fail to meet the standards for moral behavior that parents, teachers, and other adults have set for them (Damon, 1988; M. L. Hoffman, 1991). Both guilt and shame, though unpleasant in nature, are thought to be important motivators for moral and prosocial actions (you may recall our description of guilt and shame as *self-conscious emotions* in Chapter 9).

Guilt and shame emerge when children believe they have done something wrong. In contrast, *empathy* motivates moral and prosocial behavior even in the absence of wrongdoing; as you have learned, empathy emerges in early childhood but continues to develop through middle childhood and adolescence. Empathy is especially likely to promote moral and prosocial behavior when it leads to **sympathy**, whereby children not only assume another person's feelings but also have concerns about the individual's well-being (Eisenberg & Fabes, 1991; Turiel, 1998).

■ *Children increasingly take circumstances into account in their evaluation of behavior.* Earlier, we described how 6-year-old Susan and 9-year-old Greta judged two boys who broke cups. Susan equated naughtiness with the number of cups broken, whereas Greta believed that the boy who broke many cups was less naughty because he was not intentionally misbehaving. As children get older, they are more likely to take motives, intentions, and other situational factors into account in their moral judgments and decision making (Helwig et al., 2001; Piaget, 1932/1960b; Thorkildsen, 1995; Turiel, 1998). For example, children and adolescents are more likely to think of lying as immoral if it causes someone else harm than if it has no adverse effect—that is, if it is just a "white lie" (Turiel, Smetana, & Killen, 1991). And although most American adolescents endorse such civil liberties as freedom of speech and freedom of religion in principle, they recognize that such liberties must sometimes be restricted to protect others from harm (Helwig, 1995).

In general, children and adolescents become increasingly able to reason flexibly and abstractly about moral issues as they grow older. Lawrence Kohlberg has proposed a series of stages that capture some of the changes in their moral reasoning over time. We look at his theory now.

distributive justice
Beliefs about what constitutes people's fair share of a valued commodity.

guilt
Feeling of discomfort when one inflicts damage or causes someone else pain or distress.

shame
Feeling of embarrassment or humiliation after failing to meet the standards for moral behavior that others have set.

sympathy
Feeling of sorrow or concern about another's problems or distress.

Development of Moral Reasoning: Kohlberg's Theory

Consider the following situation:

> In Europe, a woman was near death from a rare form of cancer. There was one drug that the doctors thought might save her, a form of radium that a druggist in the same town had recently discovered. The druggist was charging $2,000, ten times what the drug cost him to make. The sick woman's husband, Heinz, went to everyone he knew to borrow the money, but he could only get together about half of what the drug cost. He told the druggist that his wife was dying and asked him to sell it cheaper or let him pay later. But the druggist said no. So Heinz got desperate and broke into the man's store to steal the drug for his wife. (Kohlberg, 1984, p. 186)

Should Heinz have stolen the drug? What would you have done if you were Heinz? Which is worse, stealing something that belongs to someone else or letting another person die a preventable death, and why?

The story of Heinz and his dying wife is an example of a **moral dilemma**—a situation for which there is no clear-cut right or wrong solution. Kohlberg presented a number of moral dilemmas to people of various ages and asked them to propose solutions for each one. Following are three boys' solutions to Heinz's dilemma (we have given the boys fictitious names so that we can refer to them again):

Andrew (a fifth grader):

Maybe his wife is an important person and runs a store, and the man buys stuff from her and can't get it any other place. The police would blame the owner that he didn't save the wife. He didn't save an important person, and that's just like killing with a gun or a knife. You can get the electric chair for that. (Kohlberg, 1981, pp. 265–266)

Blake (a high school student):

If he cares enough for her to steal for her, he should steal it. If not he should let her die. It's up to him. (Kohlberg, 1981, p. 132)

Charlie (a high school student):

> In that particular situation Heinz was right to do it. In the eyes of the law he would not be doing the right thing, but in the eyes of the moral law he would. If he had exhausted every other alternative I think it would be worth it to save a life. (Kohlberg, 1984, pp. 446–447)

Each boy offers a different reason to justify why Heinz should steal the lifesaving drug. Andrew bases his decision on the possible advantages and disadvantages of stealing or not stealing the drug for Heinz alone; he does not consider the perspective of the dying woman at all. Likewise, Blake takes a very self-serving view, proposing that the decision to either steal or not steal the drug depends on how much Heinz loves his wife. Only Charlie considers the value of human life in justifying why Heinz should break the law.

After obtaining hundreds of responses to moral dilemmas, Kohlberg proposed that the development of moral reasoning is characterized by a series of stages (e.g., Colby, Kohlberg, Gibbs, & Lieberman, 1983; Kohlberg, 1963, 1984). These stages, as in any stage theory, form an invariant sequence: An individual progresses through them in order, without skipping any. Each stage builds upon the foundation laid by earlier stages but reflects a more integrated and logically consistent set of moral beliefs than those before it. Kohlberg grouped his stages into three *levels* of morality—the preconventional, conventional, and postconventional levels. These three levels and the two stages within each one are described in Table 10–1.

As you can see, **preconventional morality** is the earliest and least mature form of morality, in that the child has not yet adopted or internalized society's conventions regarding what is right or wrong. The preconventional child's judgments about the morality of behavior are determined primarily by physical consequences: Behaviors that lead to rewards and pleasure are "right," and behaviors that lead to punishment are "wrong." Andrew's response to the Heinz dilemma is a good example of preconventional (Stage 1) thinking: He considers the consequences of Heinz's actions only for Heinz himself. Kohlberg also classified Blake's response as a preconventional (in particular, a Stage 2) response. Blake is beginning to recognize the importance of saving someone else's life, but the decision to do so ultimately depends on whether or not Heinz loves his wife; in other words, it depends on *his* feelings alone.

In Kohlberg's early stages of moral development, rewards and punishments are important for children's emerging sense of right and wrong.

moral dilemma
Situation in which there is no clear-cut answer regarding the morally correct thing to do.

preconventional morality
A lack of internalized standards about right and wrong; making decisions based on what is best for oneself, without regard for others' needs and feelings.

TABLE 10-1		**Kohlberg's Three Levels and Six Stages of Moral Reasoning**	
LEVEL	**AGE RANGE**	**STAGE**	**NATURE OF MORAL REASONING**
Level I: Preconventional morality	Seen in preschool children, most elementary school students, some junior high school students, and a few high school students	Stage 1: Punishment-avoidance and obedience	People make decisions based on what is best for themselves, without regard for the others' needs or feelings. They obey rules only if established by more powerful individuals; they disobey when they can do so without getting caught. The only "wrong" behaviors are ones that will be punished.
		Stage 2: Exchange of favors	People begin to recognize that others also have needs. They may try to satisfy others' needs if their own needs are also met ("you scratch my back, I'll scratch yours"). They continue to define right and wrong primarily in terms of consequences to themselves.
Level II: Conventional morality	Seen in a few older elementary school students, some junior high school students, and many high school students (Stage 4 typically does not appear until the high school years)	Stage 3: Good boy/good girl	People make decisions based on what actions will please others, especially authority figures (e.g., parents, teachers, popular peers). They are concerned about maintaining interpersonal relationships through sharing, trust, and loyalty, and they take other people's perspectives and intentions into account in their decision making.
		Stage 4: Law and order	People look to society as a whole for guidelines concerning what is right or wrong. They know that rules are necessary for keeping society running smoothly and believe it is their "duty" to obey them. However, they perceive rules to be inflexible; they don't necessarily recognize that as society's needs change, rules should change as well.
Level III: Postconventional morality	Rarely seen before college (Stage 6 is extremely rare even in adults)	Stage 5: Social contract	People recognize that rules represent an agreement among many individuals about appropriate behavior. They think of such rules as useful mechanisms that maintain the general social order and protect individual human rights, rather than as absolute dictates that must be obeyed simply because they are "the law." They also recognize the flexibility of rules; rules that no longer serve society's best interests can and should be changed.
		Stage 6: Universal ethical principle	People adhere to a few abstract, universal principles (e.g., equality of all people, respect for human dignity and rights, commitment to justice) that transcend specific norms and rules for behavior. They answer to a strong inner conscience and willingly disobey laws that violate their own ethical principles. Stage 6 is an "ideal" stage that few people ever reach.

Sources: Colby & Kohlberg, 1984; Colby et al., 1983; Kohlberg, 1976, 1984, 1986; Reimer, Paolitto, & Hersh, 1983; Snarey, 1995.

Conventional morality is characterized by an acceptance of society's conventions concerning right and wrong: The individual obeys rules and follows society's norms even when there is no reward for obedience and no punishment for disobedience. Adherence to rules and conventions is somewhat rigid; a rule's appropriateness or fairness is seldom questioned. Conventional individuals believe in the Golden Rule ("Treat others as you would have them treat you") and in the importance of keeping promises and commitments.

People who exhibit **postconventional morality** have developed their own abstract principles to define what actions are morally right and wrong—principles that typically include such basic human rights as life, liberty, and justice. They view rules as useful mechanisms that maintain the general social order and protect human rights, rather than as absolute dictates that must be obeyed without question. They also recognize that rules that no longer serve society's best interests can and should be changed (recall how, in the opening case, Tom says that "You gotta change the system"). Postconventional thinkers tend to obey rules consistent with their own principles, and they may disobey rules inconsistent with those principles, as we see in Charlie's (Stage 5) response to the Heinz dilemma:

conventional morality
Acceptance of society's conventions regarding right and wrong; behaving to please others or to live up to society's expectations for appropriate behavior.

postconventional morality
Behaving in accordance with self-developed, fairly abstract principles regarding right and wrong.

In the eyes of the law he would not be doing the right thing, but in the eyes of the moral law he would. If he had exhausted every other alternative I think it would be worth it to save a life. (Kohlberg, 1984, pp. 446–447)

Factors Influencing Progression Through Kohlberg's Stages   Kohlberg proposed that moral reasoning is somewhat dependent on Piaget's stages of cognitive development (Kohlberg, 1976). Postconventional morality, because it involves reasoning with abstract principles, cannot occur until an individual has acquired formal operational thought. Even the second stage of conventional morality requires an understanding of the interplay between the rather abstract ideas of *law* and *order*. Thus, conventional and postconventional levels of moral reasoning do not usually appear until adolescence. At the same time, progression to an advanced stage of cognitive development does not guarantee equivalent moral development; for example, it is quite possible to be formal operational in logical reasoning but preconventional in moral reasoning. In other words, cognitive development is a necessary but insufficient condition for moral development to occur.

To explain why children progress from one stage to the next, Kohlberg used Piaget's concept of *disequilibrium*. As you will recall from Chapter 4, Piaget proposed that children progress to a higher stage of cognitive development when they realize that their knowledge and schemes do not adequately explain the events around them. Because this disequilibrium is an uncomfortable feeling, children are motivated to reorganize their thoughts and ideas into a more complex and integrated system, one that better accounts for their experiences. Kohlberg proposed that a similar process promotes moral development. Individuals become increasingly aware of the weaknesses of a particular stage of moral reasoning, especially when their moral judgments are challenged by people reasoning at the next higher stage (e.g., a Stage 3 individual who agrees to let a popular cheerleader copy his homework may begin to question his decision if a Stage 4 individual argues that the cheerleader would learn more by doing her own homework). By struggling with such challenges and with moral dilemmas, children and adolescents must often restructure their thoughts about morality and so gradually move from one stage to the next.

What Research Tells Us About Kohlberg's Theory   Many research studies of moral development have followed on the heels of Kohlberg's theory. Some research confirms Kohlberg's sequence of stages: Generally speaking, people seem to progress through various forms of moral reasoning in the order that Kohlberg proposed, and they don't regress (i.e., go backwards) to lower forms (Boom, Brugman, & van der Heijden, 2001; Colby & Kohlberg, 1984; Reimer et al., 1983; L. J. Walker & Taylor, 1991). Nonetheless, although young people clearly exhibit more sophisticated moral reasoning as they grow older, theorists have pointed out several difficulties with Kohlberg's theory:

■ *Kohlberg's theory confuses the moral and social-conventional domains.*   Some elements of Kohlberg's theory, such as the disregard for other people's needs at Stage 1, reflect moral issues. Other elements, such as the recognition at Stage 5 that rules help society run more smoothly, better characterize social conventions. As we have seen, even preschoolers discriminate between these two kinds of "right" and "wrong," and society imposes different kinds of sanctions for different kinds of transgressions. It may therefore be inappropriate to combine both domains into a single theory (Rest, Narváez, Bebeau, & Thoma, 1999; Turiel, 1983).

■ *Most children are more advanced than Kohlberg thought.*   On the basis of his own research, Kohlberg concluded that children in the preschool and early elementary school years are typically at Stages 1 and 2, reflecting preconventional morality: They have little regard for the needs of others and make decisions that are in their own best interest. He proposed that most older children and adolescents are at Stages 3 and 4, reflecting conventional morality: They look to authority figures and society's rules for guidance about how to behave. Yet as you learned in our discussion of developmental trends, children have their own, internal standards for right and wrong—in particular, with regard to actions that cause physical or psychological harm—as early as age 2 or 3. Furthermore, many preschoolers are concerned about fairness for all parties (they have a sense of distributive justice), and they know that it is wrong to fight and hurt someone else even if an authority tells them otherwise. Also, well before puberty, children may recognize that laws are useful mechanisms that can be changed if necessary, rather than absolute dictates that are set in stone. The following interview with 9-year-old Elena in the Neighborhood /Middle Childhood clip of the Observation CD shows her understanding that laws serve a purpose: They help to keep people safe.

Interviewer: Neighborhoods and cities have lots of different laws. Why do you think people make these laws?

Elena: For example, they closed this road because a lot of children were playing around here and some people just came zipping right through fast and fast and not going to the speed limit.

Interviewer: What would it be like if we didn't have laws?

Elena: If we didn't have these laws, by the time I step out of the door probably I would have a broken leg.

In the Neighborhood/Middle Childhood clip of the Observation CD, observe Elena's understanding that some laws are created to keep people safe.

■ *Kohlberg's theory focuses on moral thinking rather than moral behavior.* Generally speaking, people who exhibit higher stages of moral reasoning behave more morally as well (Bear & Richards, 1981; Blasi, 1980; Reimer et al., 1983). For example, individuals at the higher stages are less likely to cheat or make prejudicial remarks about others, more likely to help people in need, and more likely to disobey orders that would cause harm to another individual (F. H. Davidson, 1976; Kohlberg, 1975; Kohlberg & Candee, 1984; P. A. Miller, Eisenberg, Fabes, & Shell, 1996). However, researchers typically find only moderate relationships between moral reasoning and moral behavior, probably because nonmoral considerations (e.g., "How much will I be inconvenienced if I help someone in need?" "Will other people like me better if I participate in this public service project?") often enter into moral decision making (M. L. Arnold, 2000; Eisenberg, 1987; Rest et al., 1999; Turiel, 1983).

■ *Moral development may not be as stagelike as Kohlberg believed.* If youngsters truly go through discrete stages in their moral reasoning, then in any limited time period we should see considerable consistency in the nature of their reasoning. Then, after a fairly brief transitional period, they should begin to show reasoning at the next higher stage. Yet people of all ages behave and reason in ways that are much less consistent than a stage theory would indicate, and Kohlberg himself acknowledged that youngsters may, at any single age, show reasoning across a three-stage span.

Perhaps, then, moral development is better characterized as a series of *trends* rather than a sequence of stages (e.g., recall the trends in morality described earlier). Perhaps, too, children and adolescents gradually acquire several different standards that guide their moral decision making to a greater or lesser degree in different situations; such standards might include the need to address one's own personal interests, a desire to abide by society's rules and conventions, and, eventually, an appreciation for abstract ideals related to human rights and the betterment of human society (Rest et al., 1999). With age, youngsters increasingly apply more advanced standards, but even the earliest one—the need to address one's own needs—may pop up on occasion (Rest et al., 1999).

Kohlberg ventured into an aspect of development that had been almost ignored prior to his time. His research offers many insights into how young people think about moral matters, and his theory has inspired many of the studies of moral development that have followed. As you can see, however, Kohlberg's theory is not a completely accurate picture of how morality develops; furthermore, it ignores the very critical roles that emotions, motives, and personal goals play in moral behavior (M. L. Arnold, 2000; Narváez & Rest, 1995). Developmental psychology still awaits a comprehensive theory of moral development that adequately addresses all the issues we have raised.

The Developmental Trends table "Social Understanding and Morality at Different Age Levels" summarizes much of what we have learned about social cognition and moral development. We now consider factors that appear to promote moral development.

DEVELOPMENTAL TRENDS

Social Understanding and Morality at Different Age Levels

AGE	WHAT YOU MIGHT OBSERVE	DIVERSITY	IMPLICATIONS
Infancy (Birth–2) 	• Emerging awareness that other people have desires, goals, and intentions different from one's own • Looking at others for clues about how to respond to objects and events (social referencing) • Acquisition of some standards for behavior (e.g., saying "uh-oh!" when an object falls and breaks) • Reactions of distress to aggressive behavior	• In the second year, children begin to label objects and events in ways that reflect culture-specific standards (e.g., *good, bad, dirty, boo boo*). • Some toddlers begin to show guilt about certain behaviors (e.g., damaging a valuable object) late in the second year.	• Use words such as *like, want,* and *think* regularly in descriptions of yourself and children. • Acknowledge undesirable events (e.g., spilled milk or a broken object), but don't communicate that children are somehow inadequate for causing them. • Provide protection from aggression and other distressing events, as such events may confuse children about appropriate standards for behavior.
Early Childhood (2–6) 	• Emerging awareness of other people's mental and emotional states • Growing ability to take others' perspectives, with some signs of empathy for people in distress • Growing realization that the mind does not always represent events accurately (e.g., that a person may have a *false belief*) • Little or no knowledge of social institutions • Some awareness that behaviors causing physical or psychological harm are morally wrong • Guilt for some misbehaviors (e.g., damaging a valuable object) • Greater concern for one's own needs than for the needs of others	• Children whose parents talk frequently about thoughts and feelings tend to have a more advanced theory of mind. • Children with siblings tend to have greater awareness that other people's perspectives may be different from their own. • Experiences with the outside world (e.g., with parents' places of business) affect children's knowledge of social institutions. • Some cultures emphasize early training in moral values; for example, in many Hispanic communities, a child who is *bien educado* (literally, "well educated") knows right from wrong and behaves appropriately. • Children who show greater evidence of guilt about transgressions are more likely to adhere to rules for classroom conduct. • At ages 2 and 3, girls are more likely to show guilt than boys.	• Talk frequently about various people's thoughts, feelings, perspectives, and needs. • Bring social institutions into the playroom, for instance, by providing props that enable children to role-play numerous professions in their sociodramatic play. • Make standards for behavior very clear. • When children misbehave, give reasons why such behaviors are not acceptable, focusing on the harm and distress they have caused for others (i.e., use *induction*).
Middle Childhood (6–10) 	• Increasing awareness of other people's psychological characteristics, but with a tendency to oversimplify the nature of others' mental states • Growing recognition that others interpret experiences rather than taking them at face value • Increasing empathy for unknown individuals who are suffering or needy • Knowledge of social conventions for appropriate behavior • Naïve understandings of government and economic systems • Ability to distinguish between behaviors that violate human rights and dignity versus those that violate social conventions • Recognition that one should strive to meet others' needs as well as one's own; growing appreciation for cooperation and compromise • Feelings of shame for moral wrongdoings	• Some children consistently misinterpret peers' thoughts and motives (e.g., by interpreting accidents as deliberate attempts to hurt them). • Some cultures place greater emphasis on ensuring individuals' rights and needs, whereas others place greater value on the welfare of the community as a whole. • Children whose parents explain why certain behaviors are unacceptable show more advanced moral development. • Children with certain disabilities (e.g., ADHD, autism, mental retardation) tend to have difficulty making accurate inferences about people's motives and intentions.	• Assist children in their attempts to resolve interpersonal conflicts by asking them to consider one another's perspectives and to develop a solution that addresses everyone's needs. • Introduce children to the political and economic activities of their country (e.g., have them vote on candidates and issues, give them opportunities to buy and sell goods) • Talk about how rules enable classrooms and other group environments to run more smoothly. • Explain how children can often meet their own needs while helping others (e.g., when asking children to be "reading buddies" for younger children, explain that doing so will help them become better readers).

DEVELOPMENTAL TRENDS

Social Understanding and Morality at Different Age Levels *(continued)*

AGE	WHAT YOU MIGHT OBSERVE	DIVERSITY	IMPLICATIONS
Early Adolescence (10–14) 	• Interest in other people's internal mental states and feelings; recognition that people may have multiple and possibly conflicting motives and emotions • Growing knowledge of government and economic systems • Some tendency to think of rules and conventions as standards that should be followed for their own sake • Interest in pleasing others	• Some adolescents with social-emotional problems (e.g., those with conduct disorders) show deficits in empathy for others. • Children's religious beliefs (e.g., their beliefs in an afterlife) influence their judgments about morality. • Violence-prone children and adolescents often believe that hitting another person is reasonable retribution for unjust actions.	• Conduct discussions that require adolescents to look at controversial issues from multiple perspectives. • When imposing discipline for moral transgressions, remember that induction may be especially important for youngsters who have deficits in empathy and moral reasoning. • Involve adolescents in group projects that will benefit their school or community.
Late Adolescence (14–18)	• Recognition that people are products of their environment and that past events and present circumstances influence personality and behavior • Ability to think recursively about one's own and others' thoughts • Understanding that rules and conventions help society run more smoothly • More abstract understanding of government and economic systems • Increasing concern about doing one's duty and abiding by the rules of society as a whole rather than simply pleasing certain people	• Adolescents who have less advanced moral reasoning—especially those who focus on their own needs almost exclusively (i.e., preconventional reasoners)—are more likely to engage in antisocial activities. • For some young people, high moral values are a central part of their overall identity; these individuals often show a strong commitment to helping those less fortunate than themselves.	• Do not tolerate ethnic jokes or other remarks that show prejudice toward a particular group. • Talk about other people's complex (and sometimes conflicting) motivations, perhaps while discussing current issues, historical events, or works of fiction. • Give teenagers a political voice in decision-making at school and elsewhere.

Sources: American Psychiatric Association, 1994; Astor, 1994; D. A. Baldwin, 2000; Barenboim, 1981; Baron-Cohen, Tager-Flusberg, & Cohen, 1993; Berti & Bombi, 1988; Chandler & Moran, 1990; Damon, 1988; Dunn, 1988; C. A. Flanagan & Faison, 2001; Flavell, 2000; Gallimore & Goldenberg, 2001; J. C. Gibbs, 1995; Gray & Garaud, 1993; D. Hart & Fegley, 1995; Helwig & Jasiobedzka, 2001; Helwig, Zelazo, & Wilson, 2001; Hoffman, 1975, 1991; Juvonen, 1991; J. Kagan, 1984, 1998b; Kochanska, Casey, & Fukumoto, 1995; Kochanska, Gross, Lin, & Nichols, 2002; Kohlberg, 1984; Kurtines et al., 1995; S. Lamb & Feeny, 1995; Leffert et al., 1999; Livesley & Bromley, 1973; Milch-Reich et al., 1999; Moses, Baldwin, Rosicky, & Tidball, 2001; Oppenheimer, 1986; Perner & Wimmer, 1985; Repacholi & Gopnik, 1997; Rushton, 1980; Schonert-Reichl, 1993; Selman, 1980; Selman & Schultz, 1990; Shweder, Mahapatra, & Miller, 1987; Siegler, 1998; Slonim & Case, 2002; Snell & Janney, 2000; Triandis, 1995; Turiel, 1983, 1998; Woolfe, Want, & Siegal, 2002; Zahn-Waxler, Radke-Yarrow, et al., 1992.

Factors Affecting Moral Development

It does little good to lecture young people about morally appropriate behavior (Damon, 1988), and attempts at "character education" are fraught with difficulties (A. Higgins, 1995; Turiel, 1998).[9] But several other conditions do seem to make a difference in the development of moral reasoning and behavior: use of reasons, interactions with peers, models of moral and prosocial behavior, moral issues and dilemmas, and self-perceptions. We look at each of these in turn.

---

[9] Some prominent members of our society (e.g., some politicians, religious leaders, and newspaper columnists) suggest that society is in a sharp moral decline and urge parents, educators, and youth leaders to impose appropriate moral traits (honesty, integrity, loyalty, responsibility, etc.) through lectures at home, in school, and elsewhere, as well as through firm control of children's behavior. Several problems arise with such an approach: (a) These traits are difficult to define precisely (e.g., at what point does integrity become stubbornness?); (b) people do not always agree about which traits are most important to nurture; and (c) there is little evidence to indicate that firm control of children's behavior is sufficient to inculcate a particular set of values (Higgins, 1995; Turiel, 1998). Furthermore, the assumption that previous generations were more morally righteous than the present generation of youth remains unsubstantiated (Turiel, 1998).

Use of Reasons   Although it is important to impose consequences for immoral or antisocial behaviors, punishment by itself often focuses children's attention primarily on their own hurt and distress (M. L. Hoffman, 1975). Adults are more likely to promote children's moral development when they focus children's attention on the hurt and distress that their behaviors have caused others. For example, an adult might describe how a behavior harms someone else either physically ("Having your hair pulled the way you just pulled Mai's can really be painful") or emotionally ("You probably hurt John's feelings when you call him names like that"). An adult might also show children how they have caused someone else inconvenience ("Because you ruined Marie's jacket, her parents are making her work around the house to earn the money for a new one"). Still another approach is to explain someone else's perspective, intention, or motive ("This science project you've just ridiculed may not be as fancy as yours, but I know that Michael spent many hours working on it and is quite proud of what he's done").

Giving children reasons about why specific rules are necessary and holding them accountable for their transgressions can help promote their moral development.

Giving children reasons why certain behaviors are unacceptable is known as **induction** (M. L. Hoffman, 1970, 1975). The consistent use of induction in disciplining children, particularly when accompanied by *mild* punishment for misbehavior, appears to promote compliance with rules as well as the development of such prosocial characteristics as empathy, compassion, and altruism (Baumrind, 1971; G. H. Brody & Shaffer, 1982; M. L. Hoffman, 1975; Maccoby & Martin, 1983; Rushton, 1980).

In our discussion of families in Chapter 12, we describe different parenting styles and their potential effects on children's social-emotional development. As you will discover when you read that chapter, induction is an integral aspect of *authoritative parenting*, a style characterized by emotional warmth and concern for children's needs and perspectives as well as high standards and expectations for behavior. Authoritative parenting appears to promote moral development by helping children to become sensitive to others' needs and willing to accept responsibility for their own wrongdoings (Damon, 1988; Eisenberg, 1995; M. L. Hoffman, 1975; Zhou et al., 2002). In contrast, power-assertive (*authoritarian*) parenting (e.g., "Do this because I say so!") is far less effective in promoting moral development (e.g., Kochanska et al., 2002).[10]

Interactions with Peers   Children learn many lessons about morality in their interactions, both congenial and conflict-ridden, with other children. Some lessons begin quite early, perhaps when adults allow infants and toddlers to interact at home or in child care settings. Such interactions should be monitored closely, as they are often physical in nature, and occasionally one child will hurt another. When adults admonish children about aggressive actions and suggest alternative ways to resolve conflicts, they begin to foster an awareness of appropriate and inappropriate ways to treat others.

Beginning in the preschool years and continuing through adolescence, group activities bring up issues related to sharing, cooperation, and negotiation (Damon, 1981, 1988; Turiel, 1998). Conflicts between siblings and playmates frequently arise as a result of physical harm, disregard for another's feelings, mistreatment of possessions, and so on (Dunn & Munn, 1987; Killen & Nucci, 1995). In order to learn to resolve interpersonal conflicts successfully, children must begin to look at situations from other children's perspectives, show consideration for other children's feelings and possessions, and attempt to satisfy other children's needs in addition to their own (Killen & Nucci, 1995).

Models of Moral and Prosocial Behavior   The behaviors that children observe around them affect the extent to which they exhibit moral and prosocial behaviors. For example, when parents are generous and show concern for others, their children tend to do likewise (Rushton, 1980). In contrast, when children see their peers cheating, they themselves are more likely to cheat (Sherrill, Horowitz, Friedman, & Salisbury, 1970). Children see both prosocial and antisocial models on television as well as in real life. When children watch

induction
Explaining why a certain behavior is unacceptable, often with a focus on the pain or distress that someone has caused another.

_____

[10] Although the two terms look very similar, there are important differences between authorit*ative* and authorit*arian* parenting (see Chapter 12).

television shows that emphasize prosocial behavior (e.g., *Barney and Friends* or *Mister Rogers' Neighborhood*), they are more likely to exhibit prosocial behavior themselves; conversely, when they see violence on television, they are more likely to display violent behavior (Eron, 1980; Hearold, 1986; Rushton, 1980). (We examine the effects of television in more detail in Chapter 14.)

Moral Issues and Dilemmas Kohlberg proposed that children develop morally when they are challenged by moral dilemmas they cannot adequately deal with at their current stage of moral reasoning. Research confirms his belief: Discussions of controversial topics and moral issues appear to promote the transition to more advanced moral reasoning and increased perspective taking, especially when children are exposed to a higher stage of moral reasoning than their own (Berkowitz & Gibbs, 1985; DeVries & Zan, 1996; Power, Higgins, & Kohlberg, 1989; Schlaefli, Rest, & Thoma, 1985).

Self-Perceptions Children are more likely to engage in moral behavior when they think they have the ability to help other people—in other words, when they have high *self-efficacy* about their ability to make a difference (Narváez & Rest, 1995). Furthermore, in adolescence, some youngsters begin to integrate a commitment to moral values into their overall sense of *identity* (Blasi, 1995; Damon, 1995; Youniss & Yates, 1999). They think of themselves as moral, caring individuals and place a high priority on acting in accordance with this self-perception. Their acts of altruism and compassion are not limited to their friends and acquaintances, but extend to the community at large. For example, in one study (D. Hart & Fegley, 1995), researchers conducted in-depth interviews with inner-city Hispanic and African American teenagers who demonstrated an exceptional commitment to helping others (for example, by volunteering many hours at Special Olympics, a neighborhood political organization, or a nursing home). These teens did not necessarily display more advanced moral reasoning (in terms of Kohlberg's stages) than their peers, but they were more likely to describe themselves in terms of moral traits and goals (e.g., helping others) and to mention certain ideals toward which they were striving.

Such self-perceptions don't appear out of the blue, of course. Children are more likely to have high self-efficacy for particular behaviors (including moral ones) when they have the guidance, support, and feedback they need to carry out those behaviors successfully (see Chapter 9). And they are more likely to integrate moral values into their overall sense of identity when they become actively involved in service to others even before they reach puberty (Youniss & Yates, 1999). Through ongoing community service activities—food and clothing drives, visits to homes for the elderly, community clean-up efforts, and so on—children and adolescents alike learn that they have the skills and the responsibility for helping those less fortunate than themselves and in other ways making the world a better place in which to live. In the process, they also begin to think of themselves as concerned, compassionate, and moral citizens (Youniss & Yates, 1999).

Diversity in Moral Development

The factors just described—use of reasons, interactions with peers, models of moral behavior, moral issues and dilemmas, and self-perceptions—can lead to considerable diversity in the moral values and behaviors that young people acquire. In addition, some theorists have suggested that moral development may be somewhat different for youngsters of different genders and cultural backgrounds, as we will see now.

Gender Differences As you have learned, Kohlberg developed his stages of moral reasoning after studying how people responded to hypothetical moral dilemmas. But consider this quirk in his research: Subjects in his early studies were exclusively males (Kohlberg, 1963). When he eventually began to interview young adults of both genders, he found that females reasoned, on average, at Stage 3, whereas males were more likely to reason at Stage 4 (Kohlberg & Kramer, 1969).

Carol Gilligan (1982, 1987; Gilligan & Attanucci, 1988) has raised concerns about Kohlberg's findings, proposing that Kohlberg's theory does not adequately describe female moral development: His stages emphasize issues of fairness and justice but omit other aspects of morality, especially compassion and caring for those in need, that Gilligan suggests are more characteristic of the moral reasoning and behavior of females. She argues that females are socialized to stress interpersonal relationships and to take responsibility for the well-being of others to a greater extent than males; therefore, females develop a morality that emphasizes a greater concern for others' welfare. The following dilemma can elicit either a **justice orientation** that Gilligan says characterizes male morality or a **care orientation** that characterizes female morality:

The Porcupine Dilemma

A group of industrious, prudent moles have spent the summer digging a burrow where they will spend the winter. A lazy, improvident porcupine who has not prepared a winter shelter approaches the moles and pleads to share their burrow. The moles take pity on the porcupine and agree to let him in. Unfortunately, the moles did not anticipate the problem the porcupine's sharp quills would pose in close quarters. Once the porcupine has moved in, the moles are constantly being stabbed. The question is, what should the moles do? (Meyers, 1987, p. 141, adapted from Gilligan, 1985)

According to Gilligan, males are more likely to look at this situation in terms of someone's rights being violated. For example, they might point out that the burrow belongs to the moles, and so the moles can legitimately throw the porcupine out. If the porcupine refuses to leave, some may argue that the moles are well within their rights to kill him. In contrast, females are more likely to show compassion and caring when dealing with the dilemma. For example, they may suggest that the moles simply cover the porcupine with a blanket; this way, his quills won't annoy anyone and everyone's needs will be met (Meyers, 1987).

Gilligan has suggested that a morality of care proceeds through three stages. At the first stage, children are concerned exclusively about their own needs, mostly to ensure their own survival. At the second stage, they show concern for people who are unable to care for themselves, including infants and the elderly. At the third and final stage, they recognize the interdependent nature of personal relationships and extend compassion and care to all human beings (Gilligan, 1977, 1982).

Gilligan raises a good point: Males and females are often socialized quite differently, as you discovered in Chapter 9. Furthermore, by including compassion for other human beings as well as consideration for their rights, she broadens our conception of what morality is (Durkin, 1995; L. J. Walker, 1995). Yet critics have found several shortcomings in Gilligan's theory. Gilligan provides only the most general explanation of how gender differences emerge (and has not empirically tested it) and offers no explanation at all about how children might move from one stage to the next (Turiel, 1998; L. J. Walker, 1995). Moreover, her early studies involved only small samples of college women discussing a single issue, abortion, which is clouded by women's views on whether an unborn fetus is a living human being (Turiel, 1998). An additional problem is that the women's responses were analyzed in an arguably superficial and subjective fashion; the absence of a systematic coding scheme raises concerns about the validity and reliability of Gilligan's findings (Turiel, 1998; L. J. Walker, 1995).

The essential point, however, is that most research studies do not find major gender differences in moral reasoning (Eisenberg et al., 1996; Nunner-Winkler, 1984; L. J. Walker, 1991). Minor differences (usually favoring females) sometimes emerge in early adolescence but disappear by late adolescence (Basinger, Gibbs, & Fuller, 1995; Eisenberg et al., 1996). Furthermore, males and females typically incorporate both justice and care into their moral reasoning, applying different orientations (sometimes one, sometimes the other, sometimes both) to different moral problems (D. K. Johnston, 1988; Rothbart, Hanley, & Albert, 1986; Smetana, Killen, & Turiel, 1991; L. J. Walker, 1995). Such findings are sufficiently compelling that Gilligan herself has acknowledged that both justice and care orientations are frequently seen in males and females alike (L. M. Brown, Tappan, & Gilligan, 1995; Gilligan & Attanucci, 1988).

Cultural Differences Different cultural groups have somewhat different standards about what constitute right and wrong behaviors. For example, some cultures emphasize the importance of being considerate of other people (e.g., "Please be quiet so that your

Are girls more likely than boys to be socialized to take care of others? Carol Gilligan suggests that they are, but other researchers have found no significant differences in the care orientations of males and females.

justice orientation
Focus on individual rights in moral decision making.

care orientation
Focus on nurturance and concern for others in moral decision making.

sister can study"), whereas others emphasize the importance of tolerating inconsiderate behavior (e.g., "Please try not to let your brother's radio bother you when you study") (Fuller, 2001; H. L. Grossman, 1994). In mainstream Western culture, lying to avoid punishment for inappropriate behavior is considered wrong, but it is a legitimate way of saving face in certain other cultures (Triandis, 1995). And whereas many European Americans argue that males and females should have equal rights and opportunities, many Hindu people in India believe that a woman's obedience to her husband is integral to the moral order, and so a husband is justified in beating his wife if she doesn't obey (Shweder et al., 1987).

Additional support for cultural differences comes from cross-cultural studies of Kohlberg's stages. Although progression through Kohlberg's Stages 1 through 4 appears to be universal across many cultures, Stage 5 is observed in modern, urbanized societies—which place high priority on justice and the rights of individuals—more often than in more traditional ones (Snarey, 1995).

Cultural differences almost certainly affect the degree to which children, boys and girls alike, acquire justice or care orientations toward morality (Markus & Kitayama, 1991; J. G. Miller, 1997; J. G. Miller & Bersoff, 1992; Shweder, Much, Mahapatra, & Park, 1997). At the same time, we must be careful not to overgeneralize about differences in moral reasoning across cultural groups. In fact, most cultures place value on both individual rights and concern for others (Turiel, 1998; Turiel, Killen, & Helwig, 1987). Furthermore, moral decision making within any culture is often situation-specific, calling for justice in some situations, compassion in other situations, and a balance between the two in still others (Turiel, 1998; Turiel et al., 1987).

Promoting Moral Development

Children's and adolescents' beliefs about moral and immoral behavior—about what's right and wrong—affect their actions at home, at school, and in the community at large. For example, we see fewer inappropriate behaviors when youngsters recognize the importance of following certain rules of conduct, fewer instances of theft or violence when they respect the property and safety of others, and fewer cases of cheating when they believe that cheating is morally unacceptable.

Young people's beliefs about morality also affect how they think about and understand the topics they study in school. For instance, their moral values are likely to influence their reactions when, in history, they read descriptions of the slave trade in pre-Civil War America or the Holocaust during World War II (see Figure 10–4). Their sense of human dignity may be affronted when they read the anti-Semitic statements that some characters in Shakespeare's *The Merchant of Venice* make about a Jewish moneylender. And the importance of fairness and respect for the rights of others certainly come into play in any discussions about good sportsmanship on the athletic field. Students simply cannot avoid moral issues as they study school subject matter and get involved in extracurricular activities.

Adults play a significant role in the moral development of the children and adolescents under their care and supervision (Pollard, Kurtines, Carlo, Dancs, & Mayock, 1991; Rushton, 1980). Consider the teacher who prepares a class for the arrival of a new student, first by discussing the feelings of uncertainty, apprehension, and loneliness that the student is likely to have, and then by helping the class identify steps it can take to make the student feel at home. This teacher is encouraging perspective taking and setting the stage for students to behave prosocially toward the newcomer. Now consider the teacher who ignores incidents of selfishness and aggression in class and on the playground, perhaps using the rationale that students should always work things out among themselves. This teacher is doing little to promote students' social and moral growth and in fact may inadvertently be sending students the message that antisocial behavior is quite acceptable.

FIGURE 10–4 Children's moral beliefs influence their interpretations of and reactions to school subject matter. Here Cody tries to imagine and capture the feelings of Jewish people during World War II in a seventh-grade unit on the Holocaust.

Drawing from the theories and research findings previously presented, we offer the following recommendations for adults who work regularly with children and adolescents:

■ *Clarify which behaviors are acceptable and which are not, and help children understand the reasons for various regulations and prohibitions.* Adults must make it clear that some behaviors (e.g., hitting, pushing, insulting, bringing weapons to school) will not be acceptable under any circumstances. Adults should also explain that some behaviors may be quite appropriate in certain situations yet inappropriate in others. For example, copying a classmate's work is permissible when a student is learning but is unacceptable (it constitutes fraud) during tests and other assessments of what a student has already learned (Thorkildsen, 1995).

Adults should accompany any disciplinary actions or discussions of rules with explanations about why certain behaviors cannot be tolerated, with a particular emphasis on potential or actual physical or psychological harm (recall our earlier discussion of *induction*). For example, a child care provider might say, "If we throw the blocks, someone may get hurt. Jane can come back to the block area when she is ready to use the blocks for building" (Bronson, 2000, p. 206). Similarly, an elementary school teacher might remind students, "We walk when we are in line so nobody gets bumped or tripped" (M. B. Bronson, 2000, p. 205). Adults might also ask children to describe to one another exactly how they feel about particular misbehaviors directed toward them or to speculate about how they would feel in a situation where someone else has been victimized (Doescher & Sugawara, 1989; M. L. Hoffman, 1991).

■ *Expose children to numerous models of moral behavior.* Adults teach by what they do as well as by what they say. When adults model compassion and consideration of the feelings of others, such behaviors are likely to rub off on children. When they are instead self-centered and place their own needs before those of others, children may follow suit.

Adults can expose children to other models of moral behavior as well. For instance, they might invite public servants or members of charitable organizations to talk with young people about the many intangible rewards of community service work. They can also make use

DEVELOPMENT AND PRACTICE

Promoting Moral Development

■ Be firm about what behaviors are and are not acceptable.

A home child care provider believes that toddlers must be able to make choices but knows that they sometimes don't differentiate between moral and immoral ones. When she sees a girl hitting the family cat with a plastic baseball bat, she gently but firmly grabs the girl's arm and says, "I can't let you hit the cat. That hurts him and may scare him away. But you can hit this cushion or go pound the punching bag."

■ Talk about reasons why some behaviors are inappropriate, emphasizing the harm or inconvenience that those behaviors have caused.

A second-grade teacher explains to Sarah that because she has thoughtlessly left her chewing gum on Margaret's chair, Margaret's mother must now pay to have Margaret's new pants professionally cleaned. The teacher, Sarah, and Margaret work out an arrangement through which Sarah can make amends for the inconvenience and expense to Margaret and her family.

■ Model appropriate moral and prosocial behavior.

A youth group leader mentions that he will be working in the annual canned food drive on Saturday and asks if any of the young adolescents in his group would like to help.

■ Incorporate moral issues and dilemmas into group discussions.

When discussing the Vietnam War, a high school history teacher mentions that many young men in the United States avoided the draft by going to Canada. She asks her students to decide whether they think such behavior was appropriate and to explain their reasoning.

■ Remember that standards for what is moral and immoral differ somewhat from one culture to another.

An after-school care provider sees a boy inadvertently knock a peer's jacket off its hook. The teacher mentions the incident to the boy, but he denies that he had anything to do with the fallen jacket. Remembering that in this child's culture, lying is an acceptable way of saving face, the adult doesn't chastise the student; instead, she asks him to do her the "favor" of returning the jacket to its hook. A short time later, she engages the group in a conversation about the importance of being careful around other people's belongings.

of models of moral behavior found in literature (Ellenwood & Ryan, 1991). For example, in Harper Lee's *To Kill a Mockingbird,* set in the highly segregated and racially charged Alabama of the 1930s, a lawyer defends an African American man falsely accused of raping a white woman and exemplifies a willingness to fight for social justice in the face of strong social pressure to convict the man.

■ *Engage children in discussions about social and moral issues.*   Social and moral issues often arise in conjunction with inappropriate behaviors (e.g., aggression, theft) that occur at school and in other group settings. Kohlberg and his colleagues have recommended a practice known as a *just community* whereby young people and adults hold regular "town meetings" to discuss issues of fairness and justice and establish rules for appropriate behavior (e.g., A. Higgins, 1995; Power, Higgins, & Kohlberg, 1989). Meetings are democratic, youngsters and adults have one vote apiece, and the will of the majority is binding.

Moral issues also appear in classroom subject matter. For instance, an English class might debate whether Hamlet was justified in killing Claudius to avenge the murder of his father. A social studies class might wrestle with how a capitalist society can encourage free enterprise while at the same time protecting the environment and the rights of citizens. A science class might discuss the ethical issues involved in using laboratory rats to study the effects of cancer-producing agents.

Adults can do several things to ensure that discussions about moral issues promote children's moral development (Reimer et al., 1983). First, they can provide a trusting and nonthreatening atmosphere in which children feel free to express their ideas without censure or embarrassment. Second, they can help children identify all aspects of a dilemma, including the needs and perspectives of the various individuals involved. Third, they can help children explore their reasons for thinking as they do—that is, to clarify and examine the principles that their moral judgments reflect.

■ *Challenge children's moral reasoning with slightly more advanced reasoning.*   Adults are more likely to create disequilibrium regarding moral issues (and thus to foster moral growth) when they present moral arguments one stage above that at which children are currently reasoning. For instance, they might present "law and order" logic (Stage 4) to a teenager who is concerned primarily about gaining the approval of others (Stage 3). If they present a moral argument that is too much higher than the child's current stage, the child is unlikely to understand and remember what is said and so is unlikely to experience disequilibrium (e.g., Boom et al., 2001; Narváez, 1998).

■ *Expose children to diverse viewpoints about moral issues.*   Children may get some inkling of varying cultural perspectives in their daily interactions with peers ("You're always telling lies," "You'll go to hell," "You dishonor your family"). Adults can build on these early lessons by including differing perspectives in discussions about moral issues. For example, teachers might introduce diverse viewpoints through the literature, folklore, and historical accounts of various countries. Adults can also encourage children to look at moral dilemmas from several different angles—to consider the extent to which care, justice, convention, or personal choice is involved (Nucci & Weber, 1991). For example, although classmates who deface their school building with graffiti might believe that they are engaging in creative self-expression (personal choice), they are also breaking a rule (convention), disregarding other students' rights to study and learn in a clean and attractive setting (justice), and thumbing their nose to the needs of those around them (care).

In the various perspectives of social understanding and moral reasoning we've considered in this chapter, we find a common thread: a gradual progression away from self-centeredness toward increased awareness of the perspectives and needs of others and an increased desire to address others' needs and rights as well as one's own. In Chapter 11 we'll consider some of the motives that underlie children's desires to interact with and help others, and in Chapter 13 we'll look more closely at the development of prosocial behavior.

CASE STUDY: JOAN

Researcher Hans Furth asks 6-year-old Joan for her views about obedience to authority figures:

Dr. Furth: If a teacher tells you to do something, do you have to do it?

Joan: Yes, that's part of learning. . . . If you didn't, like if the teacher said, "Get out your little red number book," and you didn't, you'd have to go in the corner. . . .

Dr. Furth: Do you have to do something if your mummy tells you to?

Joan: Yes, because it's part of, your mummy loves you, and a child has to love your mother, mummy and, if you don't do what you're told, get a smack, and then your mummy won't love you; well, she will love you, but she will have to be horrible to you for a day; like send you into the corner, and you'd get upset, and would do more horrible things.

Dr. Furth: Um, so what do you do about it? How can you stop doing more horrible things?

Joan: By forgetting . . . all about it the next day.

Dr. Furth: How do you know about that, and about mummy loving you?

Joan: 'Cos, it just comes in my mind. . . .

Dr. Furth: If a friend tells you to do something, do you have to do it?

Joan: No—yes, well, sometimes you have to do it, if you're—yes, you have to do it, because that's part of being friends.

Dr. Furth: What—tell me some more.

Joan: Part of being friends, and then, if you don't do what the child, your friend, wants you to do, then you lose friends. (dialogue from Furth, 1980, p. 119; format adapted)

- What beliefs does Joan have about why she should obey her teacher and mother? How might you use Kohlberg's theory to understand her thinking?
- Applying what you've read about moral development in the chapter, predict how Joan's beliefs might change over the school years.
- What kinds of social experiences might affect Joan's beliefs about authority and morality?

 Now go to our Companion Website to assess your understanding of chapter content with a Practice Quiz, apply what you've learned in Essay Questions, and broaden your knowledge with links to related Developmental Psychology Web sites. Go to www.prenhall.com/mcdevitt.

SUMMARY

Social Understanding

As children grow older, they become increasing attuned to and interested in the mental life of those around them. They gradually learn that people have thoughts, feelings, and motives different from their own and that these thoughts, feelings, and motives can be complex and at times contradictory. They also become increasingly skilled in taking the perspectives of those around them: They can imagine how other people must think and feel and begin to empathize with those who are suffering or in need. To some degree, such social cognition encompasses elements of cognition more generally; for instance, it involves storing information about social events in working memory, expanding (elaborating) on such events using one's existing knowledge base, and retrieving possible responses from long-term memory.

Young people's conceptions of their society reflect a similar progression toward more complex, comprehensive, and abstract views. With age, children and adolescents gain greater awareness of social conventions as a means of helping their society function smoothly and cohesively, and they become increasingly knowledgeable about their society's po-

litical and economic foundations. Unfortunately, nonproductive ways of thinking about others, such as stereotypes and prejudice, sometimes accompany such advancements.

Classrooms and other group settings are important contexts in which children and adolescents develop increasing awareness of other people's needs and perspectives, as well as increasing knowledge about the nature of social conventions and institutions. Adults can foster greater awareness and knowledge in numerous ways—for instance, by exposing youngsters to multiple and equally legitimate perspectives about controversial issues, conducting discussions about inequities in society's institutions, and confronting inaccurate and counterproductive stereotypes.

Moral Development

Moral reasoning encompasses a complex array of understandings and dispositions. From a young age, children make distinctions between moral transgressions (those that cause harm or infringe on others' rights) and social transgressions (those that violate culture-specific social norms). As children get older, they gain an increasing understanding of fairness and an increasing capacity to feel guilt and shame about moral wrongdoings. Lawrence Kohlberg has suggested that moral reasoning progresses from an initial preoccupation with addressing one's own needs to greater concern for pleasing others and obeying rules and then, possibly, to a commitment to abstract principles of right and wrong. Although Kohlberg probably underestimated the moral understandings of young children, his theory has inspired much of the moral development research that has followed.

To some degree, different cultures foster different moral values, but virtually all cultures recognize the importance of fairness, justice, and concern for others. Adults can promote young people's moral development by explaining why certain behaviors are unacceptable (in that they cause harm or distress to another or jeopardize another's rights and needs), providing numerous models of moral and prosocial behavior, engaging youngsters in discussions about moral issues and dilemmas, and exposing them to diverse and slightly more advanced moral perspectives.

KEY CONCEPTS

social cognition (p. 414)
theory of mind (p. 415)
intentionality (p. 415)
recursive thinking (p. 418)
person perception (p. 419)
social perspective taking (p. 420)
social information processing (p. 421)

conceptions of society (p. 425)
social-cognitive bias (p. 429)
stereotype (p. 430)
prejudice (p. 430)
morality (p. 433)
internalization (p. 434)
moral realism (p. 436)
prosocial behavior (p. 436)
moral transgression (p. 438)

conventional transgression (p. 438)
distributive justice (p. 439)
guilt (p. 439)
shame (p. 439)
sympathy (p. 439)
moral dilemma (p. 440)
preconventional morality (p. 440)

conventional morality (p. 441)
postconventional morality (p. 441)
induction (p. 446)
justice orientation (p. 448)
care orientation (p. 448)

Connor, age 6

William, age 7

Joey, age 17

Development of Motivation and Self-Regulation

CASE STUDY: MAKING KITES

Ms. Keany[1] teaches a mathematics class for fifth and sixth graders who have a history of poor performance in math. She has recently shown her class how concepts in geometry relate to aerodynamics, emphasizing that the size and shape of an object affect the ease with which it can fly. As a follow-up to the lesson, she asks her students to experiment with a variety of sizes and shapes of kites and then to design a kite using what they have learned.

The kite project lasts several days. A researcher observes the class throughout the project and interviews the children afterward. She finds that different children take very different approaches to the task and have widely varying perspectives about it. For instance, a girl named Sara approaches the task as a scientist might: She seems keenly interested in creating an aerodynamic kite design and realizes that doing so will take time and patience. She redesigns her kite three times to make it as aerodynamic as possible. After the project, she summarizes her results:

> . . . I wasn't completely successful, because I had a few problems. But I realized that most scientists, when they try experiments, well, they're not always right. . . . [I]f I can correct myself on [errors] then I don't really mind them that much. I mean, everybody learns from their mistakes. I know I do. . . . I think mistakes are actually good, to tell you the truth. . . .
>
> When I had my test flights, the shape flew really, really well, and I was going to stick with that shape. . . . I had no doubts because I knew that I could really do it; I knew I could put this together really well, 'cause I had a lot of confidence in myself. . . . (D. K. Meyer, Turner, & Spencer, 1997, pp. 511–512)

Unlike Sara, Amy sticks with a single kite design throughout the project even though she has trouble getting her kite to fly. Later, Amy tells the researcher:

> I knew from the start what shape I wanted. Once I had the materials it was very easy to make the kite. . . . [T]here wasn't enough wind for the kites to fly. (D. K. Meyer et al., 1997, pp. 510, 513)

The researcher asks Amy how important the project was to her and whether she ever takes risks at school. She responds:

> I feel lazy because I don't like to make challenges for myself, to make goals. I just like to do it as I go along, not make goals or challenges. . . . I like to do well for [the teacher] and my parents, and myself, I guess. . . . [I]f it doesn't affect my grade, whether I do this or not, if I totally fail and do everything wrong, if it doesn't affect my grade, then I'll [take risks].
> (pp. 510, 512)

Had her kite flown, how might Amy have explained it? Amy tells the researcher that it would probably have been "beginner's luck" (D. K. Meyer, Turner, & Spencer, 1994, 1997).

[1] Although the case is real, "Ms. Keany" is a pseudonym.

ara is willing to experiment and make mistakes so that she can construct the best kite possible, whereas Amy prefers an easier, though less successful, course of action. Sara finds satisfaction in her own accomplishments, whereas Amy seems more interested in pleasing her teacher and parents. Sara attributes her successful kite to her own effort and ability, whereas Amy concludes that her failure was due to poor weather conditions and suspects that any success on the task would have been a matter of luck. All of these differences illustrate aspects of *motivation* that we consider in this chapter.

In general, **motivation** energizes, directs, and sustains behavior; it gets people moving, points them in a particular direction, and keeps them going. We usually see motivation reflected in a certain amount of *personal investment* in particular activities, as exemplified by the time and effort that Sara put into creating her kite.

Virtually all children and adolescents are motivated in one way or another. One may be keenly interested in academic subject matter and seek out challenging coursework, participate actively in classroom discussions, complete assignments diligently, and earn high grades. Another may be more concerned about social affairs, interacting with peers frequently, participating in numerous extracurricular activities, and chatting incessantly with friends on the phone or Internet. Still another may be focused on athletics, excelling in physical education classes, playing or watching sports most afternoons and weekends, and working out daily in hopes of making the soccer team next year. And yet another, perhaps because of an undetected learning disability, poor social skills, or a seemingly uncoordinated body, may be interested primarily in *avoiding* academics, social situations, or athletic activities.

Sometimes children and adolescents are motivated **intrinsically**—by factors within themselves or inherent in the task they are performing. For example, they may engage in an activity because it gives them pleasure, helps them develop a skill they think is important, or seems the ethically and morally right thing to do. At other times, they are motivated **extrinsically**—by factors external to themselves and unrelated to the task they are performing. For example, they may want the good grades, money, or glory that particular activities and accomplishments bring. As a general rule, youngsters learn more effectively, and they achieve at higher levels in instructional settings, when they are intrinsically rather than extrinsically motivated (Flink, Boggiano, Main, Barrett, & Katz, 1992; A. E. Gottfried, 1990; Pintrich & Schrauben, 1992).

Over the years, psychologists have looked at motivation and its development from a variety of angles. In the upcoming sections, we consider four general approaches to the study of motivation: the behaviorist, social cognitive, trait, and cognitive perspectives.

Behaviorist Perspectives of Motivation

Behaviorism emphasizes the influence of environmental conditions on people's behaviors. In particular, a behaviorist looks at the specific *stimuli* people encounter and their *responses* to those stimuli. Hence, behaviorism is sometimes called *stimulus-response theory* or, more simply, *S-R theory*.

Without question, the best-known behaviorist theory is the late B. F. Skinner's theory of **operant conditioning** (e.g., 1953, 1968). Skinner proposed that people's behaviors are largely influenced by the consequences that result from those behaviors. In particular, he proposed that responses that are followed by certain kinds of consequences are more likely to be made again. Consequences that lead to an increase in behavior—consequences that are usually, but not always, pleasant—are known as **reinforcers**.

From Skinner's perspective, children behave primarily to obtain reinforcing outcomes, and many of the behaviors they exhibit are those that have been reinforced in the past. For instance, Miguel might practice the piano regularly if his parents continually praise him for his efforts. Brigita might throw frequent temper tantrums if she's learned that her tantrums are the only way she can get special toys or privileges. Peter might misbehave in class if doing so gains him the attention of his teacher and classmates. The last of these examples illustrates an important point: Reinforcers are not always what we would typically think of as "rewards." The attention Peter gets for his misbehavior may seemingly be unpleasant—Peter's teacher may scold him for acting out, or his classmates might shake their

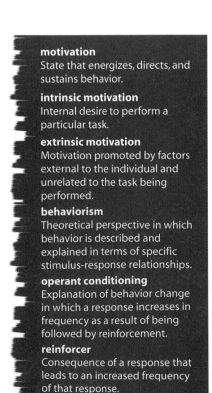

motivation
State that energizes, directs, and sustains behavior.

intrinsic motivation
Internal desire to perform a particular task.

extrinsic motivation
Motivation promoted by factors external to the individual and unrelated to the task being performed.

behaviorism
Theoretical perspective in which behavior is described and explained in terms of specific stimulus-response relationships.

operant conditioning
Explanation of behavior change in which a response increases in frequency as a result of being followed by reinforcement.

reinforcer
Consequence of a response that leads to an increased frequency of that response.

heads in disgust—but if Peter's misbehaviors increase as a result, then the attention is indeed a reinforcer.

So far, we have been talking about **positive reinforcement**, in which the consequence involves *getting* something—perhaps parental praise, a toy, or teacher attention. On some occasions, reinforcement instead involves *getting rid of* something: A child might misbehave, procrastinate, or complain of a stomachache to escape or avoid unpleasant stimuli or events. For instance, Jeanne confesses that as a junior high school student, she often stayed home "sick" as a way of avoiding tests she wasn't prepared for. The phenomenon in which a behavior increases because it enables a person to escape or avoid a particular event is known as **negative reinforcement**.

B. F. Skinner focused primarily on the effects of reinforcement. Many behaviorists believe, however, that a second kind of consequence—punishment—affects people's behavior as well. Behaviorist researchers have found that punishment of undesirable responses, especially when combined with reinforcement of desired responses, can produce lasting improvements in children's behavior (e.g., R. V. Hall et al., 1971; Walters & Grusec, 1977). For example, some teachers and therapists of children with serious behavioral problems award points (reinforcement) for desired behaviors and take away points (punishment) for inappropriate ones; at the end of the day, the children can exchange the points they've accumulated for small toys or privileges. Taking away previously earned points for unacceptable behavior (a strategy called *response cost*) can be quite effective in bringing about behavior change (O'Leary & O'Leary, 1972). Many other forms of punishment are ineffective, however, particularly those that model aggression or inflict physical or psychological harm (Davis & Thomas, 1989; M. A. Straus, 2000; J. E. Walker & Shea, 1999).

Trends in Children's Responses to Reinforcers

Behaviorists have observed developmental changes in children's responses to reinforcers:

■ *With age, secondary reinforcers become increasingly influential.* Young infants are concerned primarily with stimuli that satisfy built-in biological needs, such as food, drink, warmth, and physical affection.[2] Consequences that satisfy built-in needs are called **primary reinforcers**. Over time, children begin to associate certain other stimuli with primary reinforcers. For example, a child might learn that praise from mother often comes with a special candy treat or discover that a good grade frequently leads to a hug from father. Through such associations, consequences such as praise, good grades, money, trophies (see the Environments/Late Adolescence clip of the Observation CD), and attention (sometimes even in the form of a scolding) become reinforcing in their own right: They become **secondary reinforcers**.

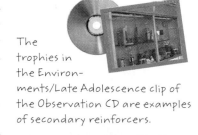

The trophies in the Environments/Late Adolescence clip of the Observation CD are examples of secondary reinforcers.

At home, parents often use both primary and secondary reinforcers to encourage desirable behaviors. At school, however, teachers and other school personnel use secondary reinforcers almost exclusively. When they do so, they must keep in mind that secondary reinforcers are learned reinforcers, and not all children and adolescents have learned to appreciate them. Although most youngsters will probably respond positively to such consequences as praise or a good grade, a few may not.

■ *Children soon learn that some responses are reinforced only occasionally.* With experience, children discover that reinforcers don't necessarily follow every response that they make. For example, a preschooler may learn that he has to ask his mother for a cookie several times before Mom relents and gives him one, and a teenager may learn that she has to practice a particular gymnastic skill over and over before she earns the praise of her coach. Whenever a response is reinforced only occasionally, with some occurrences of the response going unreinforced, *intermittent reinforcement* is at work. Children who are intermittently reinforced for their behaviors often learn to persist in the face of disappointment and failure.

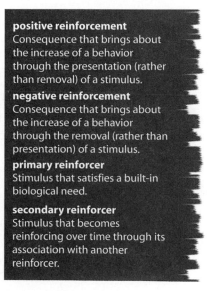

positive reinforcement
Consequence that brings about the increase of a behavior through the presentation (rather than removal) of a stimulus.

negative reinforcement
Consequence that brings about the increase of a behavior through the removal (rather than presentation) of a stimulus.

primary reinforcer
Stimulus that satisfies a built-in biological need.

secondary reinforcer
Stimulus that becomes reinforcing over time through its association with another reinforcer.

---

[2] To learn more about the need for physical affection, you may want to read about Harlow's classic research with rhesus monkeys (Harlow, 1959; Harlow & Harlow, 1962). Some of his research is described in the *Study Guide and Reader* that accompanies this book (see Reading 11–1).

Children are more likely to persist at difficult tasks when they discover that their responses do not always lead to success—in other words, when they are reinforced only intermittently.

■ *Children become increasingly able to delay gratification.* In his theory of operant conditioning, Skinner proposed that a reinforcer is most effective when it is presented immediately after a child has made a desired response. Consistent with Skinner's proposal, research indicates that immediate reinforcement is more effective than delayed reinforcement in instructional settings, at least in terms of helping children acquire new behaviors quickly (Kulik & Kulik, 1988).

As children get older, however, they become better able to **delay gratification**: They can forego small, immediate rewards for the larger rewards that their long-term efforts are likely to bring down the road (e.g., L. Green, Fry, & Myerson, 1994; Rotenberg & Mayer, 1990; Vaughn, Kopp, & Krakow, 1984). For example, a 3-year-old is apt to choose a small toy she can have now over a larger and more attractive toy she cannot have until tomorrow. An 8-year-old is more willing to wait a day or two for the more appealing item. Many adolescents can delay gratification for weeks at a time. For instance, as a 16-year-old, Jeanne's son Jeff worked long hours stocking shelves at the local grocery store (hardly a rewarding activity!) to earn enough money to pay half the cost of a $400-a-night limousine for the junior prom.

Some children and adolescents are better able to delay gratification than others, and those who do are less likely to yield to temptation, more carefully plan their future actions, and achieve at higher levels in academic settings (Durkin, 1995; Shoda, Mischel, & Peake, 1990; Veroff, McClelland, & Ruhland, 1975). However, even 4- and 5-year olds can learn to delay gratification for a few hours if their preschool teachers tell them that rewards for desired behaviors (e.g., sharing toys with other children) will be coming later in the day (S. A. Fowler & Baer, 1981). Teaching children effective waiting strategies also enhances their ability to delay gratification. For instance, in a study by Binder, Dixon, and Ghezzi (2000), three preschoolers with ADHD were asked to choose between a small immediate reward (half of a cookie) and a larger delayed one (a whole cookie). Initially, the three children were interested only in immediate gratification, always choosing the half cookie. But when they learned strategies for passing the time during a delay period (either by focusing their attention on another task or by reminding themselves, "If I wait a little longer, I will get the bigger one"), they became increasingly able to resist the immediate temptation of the half cookie and hold out for the whole one.

Although the study just described brings mental processes (e.g., reminding oneself, "If I wait a little longer . . . ") into the picture, behaviorists focus largely on children's behaviors and give little thought to cognition. As you will see now, another perspective of motivation—social cognitive theory—considers what children think as well as what they do.

Social Cognitive Perspectives of Motivation

Social cognitive theory (also called *social learning theory*) focuses on the role that observation and modeling play in children's learning and development and emphasizes the importance of self-perceptions and expectations as factors in motivation (Bandura, 1982, 1986; Schunk, 1989). By and large, social cognitive theorists focus more on general principles of learning and motivation than on how learning and motivation change over time. Thus, it is more helpful to talk about general principles that characterize social cognitive perspectives of motivation than about developmental trends per se:

■ *Children learn many new behaviors by watching those around them.* Almost from birth, infants seem motivated to imitate those around them. Infants as young as 1 or 2 days old may imitate an adult's facial expressions—perhaps pursing their lips, opening their mouths, or sticking out their tongues (T. Field, Woodson, Greenberg, & Cohen, 1982; Meltzoff & Moore, 1977; Reissland, 1988). Furthermore, as noted in Chapter 4, infants as young as 6 weeks old can remember and imitate things they've seen as much as 24 hours before (Meltzoff, 1988; Meltzoff & Moore, 1994). As children get older, they can recall and imitate increasingly complex patterns of behaviors; for instance, toddlers may pretend to drive a car or talk on a toy telephone, and preschoolers may imitate a variety of individuals (e.g., mommy, daddy, baby, the family dog) in their sociodramatic play.

delay of gratification
Foregoing small immediate rewards for larger, more delayed ones.

social cognitive theory
Theoretical perspective that focuses on the roles of observation and modeling in learning and motivation.

Social cognitive theorists have found some consistency in the types of models that children are apt to imitate (Bandura, 1986; T. L. Rosenthal & Bandura, 1978). Effective models typically exhibit one or more of the following characteristics:

- *Competence.* Children typically imitate people who do something well, not those who do it poorly. For instance, they will imitate the basketball skills of a professional basketball player rather than those of the class klutz.
- *Prestige and power.* Children often imitate people who are famous or powerful, such as a world leader, a renowned athlete, or a popular rock star—or, more locally, a head cheerleader, the captain of the high school hockey team, or a gang leader.
- *"Gender-appropriate" behavior.* Children are more likely to imitate models whom they believe are behaving appropriately for their own gender (with different children defining *gender appropriate* somewhat differently). For example, some girls may shy away from careers in mathematics, which they see as a "masculine" field, and some boys may not learn to cook because they perceive it to be a "woman's" skill. Exposure to numerous examples of people in nontraditional careers (e.g., female mathematicians and engineers, male chefs and nurses) can help broaden children's perceptions about what behaviors to imitate.

Infants show an ability to imitate others almost from birth.

■ *Children are more likely to behave in ways that they expect will bring about desirable consequences.* From a behaviorist perspective, the previous consequences of certain behaviors (previous reinforcements and, for some theorists, previous punishments as well) have a direct effect on children's present behavior. In contrast, social cognitive theorists argue that children's expectations of *future* consequences have a greater influence on their behavior choices. Past consequences obviously affect their expectations for future consequences, but present circumstances play a role as well. For example, 5-year-old Samuel may have learned that at home, whining and complaining have usually gotten him what he's wanted. When he begins kindergarten, however, he is likely to discover that whining and complaining are frowned upon at school and, in fact, may result in a lack of playmates at recess. Samuel may also discover, perhaps on his own or perhaps with his teacher's guidance, that other behaviors are more likely to lead to positive consequences such as teacher approval and attention from peers, and so he may intentionally choose actions that gain him the consequences he seeks.

■ *Children's expectations are influenced by what happens to others as well as by what happens to themselves.* Children are more motivated to engage in certain behaviors when they see other people reinforced for those behaviors; they are less likely to exhibit behaviors for which they have seen others punished. These phenomena are known as **vicarious reinforcement** and **vicarious punishment**, respectively. For example, by watching the consequences that their peers experience, children might learn that being elected to a student government office brings status and popularity, that acting out in class gets the teacher's attention, or that unsportsmanlike conduct on the playing field leads to being benched during the next game.

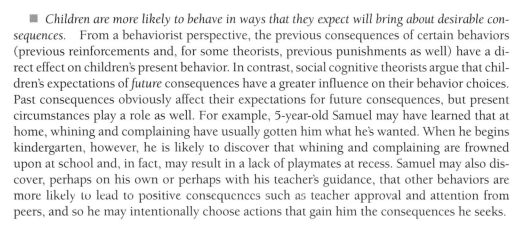

Hear Claudia describe her self-efficacy for math in the Intrinsic Motivation/Early Adolescence clip of the Observation CD.

■ *Children are more likely to undertake activities for which they have high self-efficacy.* In Chapter 9 we introduced the concept of *self-efficacy*: people's beliefs about their ability to achieve certain goals or outcomes. Children are more likely to choose an activity, exert considerable effort in performing it, and persist in the face of failure when they have high self-efficacy for that activity (Bandura, 1982, 1997). For example, in the Intrinsic Motivation/Early Adolescence clip of the Observation CD, 12-year-old Claudia reveals high self-efficacy for mathematics when she explains why math is her favorite subject: "I don't know, it just . . . I'm good at it and . . . it's just, I like it better than the other subjects." Similarly, in the opening case study, Sara reveals a high sense of self-efficacy about building a kite: "I had no doubts because I knew that I could really do it; I knew I could put this together really well" (D. K. Meyer et al., 1997, p. 512). Ideally, children's self-efficacy should be just a little bit higher than what they can *actually* do; under such circumstances, they will eagerly attack new challenges and so enhance their knowledge and skills (Bandura, 1997).

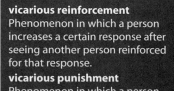

vicarious reinforcement
Phenomenon in which a person increases a certain response after seeing another person reinforced for that response.
vicarious punishment
Phenomenon in which a person decreases a certain response after seeing another person punished for that response.

To a considerable degree, children's self-efficacy beliefs are based on their past successes and failures with various tasks. But watching others, especially peers, has an effect as well (Schunk & Hanson, 1985; Schunk, Hanson, & Cox, 1987). When children see others of similar age and ability successfully accomplish a task, they are more likely to believe that they, too, can accomplish it. For instance, in one study (Schunk & Hanson, 1985), elementary school children having trouble with subtraction were given 25 subtraction problems to complete. Children who had seen another student successfully complete the problems got an average of 19 correct, whereas those who saw a teacher complete the problems got only 13 correct, and those who saw no model at all solved only 8.

Both behaviorists and social cognitive theorists focus largely on the kinds of experiences (reinforcement, punishment, observation of others, etc.) that influence children's motivation, and they assume that the principles and trends they've identified apply to most or all children. In contrast, trait theorists focus on ways in which children are often quite different from one another in motivation.

Trait Perspectives of Motivation

Trait theorists propose that people have a variety of motives and varying degrees of motivation. For example, children may differ in the extent to which they seek out friendly relationships with others (reflecting their *need for affiliation*), want others to praise them for what they do (reflecting their *need for approval*), and want to do well in school (reflecting their need for achievement, or *achievement motivation*). Let's briefly look at each of these needs.

Need for Affiliation

Observe the difference between Greg's and Claudia's need for affiliation in the Late Adolescence and Early Adolescence clips of the Intrinsic Motivation module of the Observation CD.

Some theorists have proposed that people of all ages have a fundamental need to feel socially connected and secure the love and respect of others; in other words, they have a **need for relatedness** (Connell, 1990; Connell & Wellborn, 1991; Honig, 2002). For infants and toddlers, this need is reflected in early efforts to engage other people through crying, smiling, eye contact, and imitation, as well as in the close attachments they form with one or more caregivers (see Chapter 9). For many school-age children and adolescents, this need may be reflected in the high priority they put on socializing with friends, sometimes at the expense of finishing chores, schoolwork, or other assigned tasks (W. Doyle, 1986; Wigfield, Eccles, Mac Iver, Reuman, & Midgley, 1991).

Children of all ages differ in the extent to which they desire and actively seek out friendly relationships with others, however (Kupersmidt, Buchele, Voegler, & Sedikides, 1996; Thomas & Chess, 1977). In other words, they differ in their **need for affiliation**. For example, in the Early Adolescence and Late Adolescence clips of the Intrinsic Motivation module of the Observation CD, 15-year-old Greg appears to have a higher need for affiliation than 12-year-old Claudia, although Claudia clearly enjoys some social interaction in the form of group work:

Greg

Interviewer:	What do you like best about school?
Greg:	Lunch.
Interviewer:	Lunch?
Greg:	All the social aspects. . . . Just friends and cliques. . . .

Claudia

Interviewer:	What do you like best about school?
Claudia:	Umm . . . I like to do projects. Like creative ones where you get to do, like, make models of things. And then if you are in a group, then you get to get more ideas, and sometimes the teacher will start you out a little, but then you get to do most of it.

Children's and adolescents' needs for affiliation are reflected in the kinds of choices they make at school and elsewhere (Boyatzis, 1973; E. G. French, 1956; Wigfield, Eccles, & Pintrich,

trait theory
Theoretical perspective focusing on stable individual differences in human behavior.

need for relatedness
Fundamental human need to feel socially connected and secure the love and respect of others.

need for affiliation
Consistent tendency in some individuals to seek out friendly relationships with others.

1996). For example, individuals with a low need for affiliation may prefer to work alone, whereas those with a high need for affiliation more often prefer to work in small groups. When choosing work partners at school, students with a low affiliation need are apt to choose classmates whom they believe to be competent at the assigned task; those with a high affiliation need are apt to choose friends (even relatively incompetent ones) over nonfriends. In high school, students with a low need for affiliation are likely to choose a class schedule that meets their own interests and ambitions, whereas those with a high need for affiliation are more likely to choose one that enables them to be with their friends.

Need for Approval

In the opening case study, Amy explains, "I like to do well for [the teacher] and my parents, and myself, I guess" (D. K. Meyer et al., 1997, p. 512). It appears that Amy works on classroom tasks primarily to please her teacher and parents. Pleasing *herself* (intrinsic motivation) is almost an afterthought.

The **need for approval** is a strong desire to gain the acceptance and positive judgments of other people (Igoe & Sullivan, 1991; Juvonen & Weiner, 1993; T. C. Urdan & Maehr, 1995). Children with a high need for approval are overly concerned with pleasing others and tend to give in easily to group pressure, for fear that they might otherwise be rejected (Crowne & Marlowe, 1964; Wentzel & Wigfield, 1998). Whereas their classmates might engage in a school task for the pleasure that success at the task brings, children with a high need for approval tend to engage in the task primarily to please their teacher and will persist at it only as long as their teacher praises them for doing so (Harter, 1975; S. C. Rose & Thornburg, 1984).

In the early years, children are most apt to seek the approval of adults, such as parents and teachers. As they get older, and especially as they move into adolescence, they are usually more interested in gaining the approval of their peers (Juvonen & Weiner, 1993; Urdan & Maehr, 1995). However, culture can influence the relative value that children and adolescents place on adult versus peer approval. For instance, many teenagers from Asian cultures highly value the approval of adult authority figures (e.g., Dien, 1998).

Adults cannot ignore (and they certainly can't eliminate) the high needs for affiliation and approval that many young people bring to the classroom and other group settings. On the contrary, children and adolescents are more successful when they feel that adults and their peers like and respect them and when they have a sense of belonging in the group (Goodenow, 1993; Ladd, 1990). The Development and Practice feature "Addressing Social Needs" suggests several ways in which adults can satisfy youngsters' needs for affiliation and approval in classrooms and other group settings.

Achievement Motivation

Of the various needs that children and adolescents might have, most researchers with a trait perspective have focused on the need for achievement, more often called **achievement motivation.** Achievement motivation is the need for excellence for its own sake, without regard for any external rewards that accomplishments might bring (e.g., Atkinson & Feather, 1966; McClelland, Atkinson, Clark, & Lowell, 1953; Veroff et al., 1975). Children with high achievement motivation seek out challenging tasks that they know they can accomplish with effort and persistence. They rarely rest on their laurels; instead, they set increasingly higher standards for excellence as their current standards are met (Eccles, Wigfield, & Schiefele, 1998; Veroff et al., 1975). In the Middle Childhood and Late Adolescence clips of the Intrinsic Motivation module of the Observation CD, 9-year-old Elena and 15-year-old Greg both express their desire for challenge at school:

Elena

Interviewer: What do you like best about school?

Elena: I like PEAK [a program for students identified as gifted]. It's this thing
                where you go to this program. It's for smart kids who have, like, good
                ideas for stuff you could do. And so they make it more challenging for
                you in school. So instead of third-grade math, you get fourth-grade math.

Most children and adolescents enjoy social contact. Quite possibly, this need for relatedness emerged early in the evolution of human beings: It kept social groups together and so enhanced their chances of survival against enemies.

Listen to Elena and Greg discuss their desire for challenge at school in the Middle Childhood and Late Adolescence clips of the Intrinsic Motivation module of the Observation CD.

need for approval
Consistent desire in some individuals to gain the acceptance and positive judgments of others.

achievement motivation
Need for excellence for its own sake, without regard for any external rewards that one's accomplishments might bring.

DEVELOPMENT AND PRACTICE

Addressing Social Needs

■ Give infants opportunities to interact with each other.

An infant child care center sets aside an area of the playroom where infants who are not yet crawling can sit or lie on blankets and watch one another. Adult caregivers put the children close enough that they can touch, but they closely monitor the children's interactions.

■ Plan learning tasks that involve social interaction.

A middle school history teacher incorporates classroom debates, small-group discussions, and cooperative learning tasks into lesson plans.

■ Continually communicate the message that you like and respect the young people with whom you are working.

A youth group leader tells a student that she saw his karate exhibition at the local mall over the weekend. "Wow, you were great!" she says. "How many years have you been studying karate?"

■ Give frequent praise to those who have a high need for approval.

Several children in a second-grade class have difficulty staying on task during independent assignments. Their teacher has found that they are more likely to stay on task when he praises them for doing so.

■ Give praise in private when being a high achiever is not socially acceptable among peers.

A high school English teacher reads a particularly creative story written by a young man who, she knows, is quite concerned about looking "cool" in front of his classmates. On the second page of his story (where the student's classmates won't be likely to see what she has written), she writes, "This is great work, Tony! I think it's good enough to enter into the state writing contest. Can we meet before or after school some day this week to talk more about the contest?"

■ Respect individual differences.

A child care provider notices that some of the young children in his care have a greater need for social contact than others. Some children really seem to enjoy sociodramatic play activities, while others are more interested in manipulating and experimenting with physical objects. Although he interacts with all of the children regularly, he is careful not to interrupt when children are deeply engaged in solitary play activities.

Greg

Interviewer:	What do teachers do that encourage you to do well at school?
Greg:	[S]ome of them kind of make it a competition, like class rank and stuff. . . . And that makes you want to. . . . And the challenge. If it's a really hard class, then I . . . will usually try harder in harder classes.

In its earliest conceptualization, achievement motivation was thought to be a general characteristic that youngsters exhibit consistently in a variety of tasks across many domains. More recently, however, many theorists have proposed that this need may instead be somewhat specific to particular tasks and occasions (e.g., Dweck & Elliott, 1983; Stipek, 1996; Wigfield, 1997). Theorists are also beginning to explain achievement motivation in terms of specific cognitive factors that influence the choices youngsters make and the tasks they pursue. Thus, explanations of achievement motivation have shifted away from a "trait" approach to a more cognitive approach. We now look at what contemporary cognitive perspectives of motivation encompass.

Cognitive Perspectives of Motivation

Within the last two or three decades, psychologists have radically changed their approach to the study of motivation and its development. The concrete, external reinforcers that many behaviorists have focused on now play less of a role in theoretical conceptions of how children behave. And interest in global traits that may vary from one child to another (achievement motivation, need for approval, etc.) is diminishing. Most theorists now describe human motivation as a function of human cognition—involving, for example, inquisitiveness, goal-setting, and development of interests in specific topics. From this perspective, motivation and cognitive development continually interact, with each one affecting the other. For example, interest in a topic and knowledge about that topic seem to feed into each other: Interest fuels a quest to learn more about something and encourages effective learning strategies, and the increasing knowledge that one gains in turn promotes greater interest (Alexander, 1997; Tobias, 1994; Voss & Schauble, 1992).

Some cognitive theorists further propose that motivation, rather than being a relatively permanent aspect of children's personalities, is largely a product of the particular context in which children find themselves (Graham & Weiner, 1996; Paris & Turner, 1994; Rueda

& Moll, 1994). For instance, in classroom settings, many factors influence motivation; these include the kinds of instructional materials that a teacher uses (whether they are interesting, challenging, relevant to students' needs, and so on), the extent to which students must compete with one another, and the ways in which students are evaluated (Boykin, 1994; Paris & Turner, 1994; Stipek, 1996). In the Intrinsic Motivation/Early Adolescence clip of the Observation CD, 12-year-old Claudia describes some of the factors that influence her motivation at school:

Interviewer:	What do teachers do that encourages you to do well?
Claudia:	Like, when they kind of sound enthusiastic. They don't just teach everything, they have a little fun with it, too.
Interviewer:	Why do you think that helps?
Claudia:	So they . . . we can stay focused.
Interviewer:	What kinds of things do you think make it hard for kids to pay attention at school?
Claudia:	If the teacher's not sure what they're doing, or they just keep playing movies over and over.

Hear Claudia describe environmental factors affecting her motivation in the Intrinsic Motivation/Early Adolescence clip of the Observation CD.

Cognitive theorists have gone in many directions in their explorations of human motivation. Here we focus on development in three areas: intrinsic motivation, goals, and attributions.

Development of Intrinsic Motivation

Cognitive theorists have offered a variety of theoretical explanations regarding the nature of intrinsic motivation, which may involve one or more of the following:

- *Curiosity.* Many developmentalists believe that children are naturally curious about their world and actively seek out information to help them make sense of it (e.g., Callanan & Oakes, 1992; Lieberman, 1993; Piaget, 1952b). Even as infants, children behave like "little scientists," experimenting constantly to discover the properties of various objects and the consequences of their own actions. Later, as they gain proficiency in their native language, their seemingly incessant questions (e.g., "How do they make statues?" "Why does it rain sometimes?" "What would happen if you cut someone's head off?") are an additional means through which they attempt to satisfy their curiosity (Callanan & Oakes, 1992, p. 218).

- *Need for cognitive consistency.* Jean Piaget suggested that another key factor driving a child's learning and development is *disequilibrium*, an inconsistency between new information and what the child already believes to be true. According to Piaget, disequilibrium causes mental discomfort and spurs the child to integrate, reorganize, or in some cases replace existing schemes to accommodate to the new information. Like Piaget, some contemporary developmental theorists believe that human beings have an innate need for consistency and coherence among the things they learn (e.g., M. B. Bronson, 2000).

- *Interest.* Theorists typically distinguish between two kinds of interest (Alexander & Jetton, 1996; Hidi & Anderson, 1992; Krapp, Hidi, & Renninger, 1992). *Situational interest* is evoked by something in the environment—something that is perhaps new, unusual, or surprising. In contrast, *personal interest* resides within the individual; people tend to have personal preferences about the topics they pursue and the activities in which they engage. Situational interests are transitory and highly dependent on environmental circumstances, whereas personal interests are relatively stable over time. As an example of the latter, look at Joey's series of drawings in Figure 11–1. Joey displayed an exceptional interest in art beginning at age 3. Throughout his childhood and adolescence, Joey had a strong interest in drawing the human form and, later, in fashion design. (Joey's self-portrait appears on the first page of Chapter 10.)

- *Value.* A task or activity has *value* when children believe that there are direct or indirect benefits in performing it (Dweck & Elliott, 1983; Feather, 1982; Wigfield & Eccles, 2000). Some activities are valued because they are associated with certain

Young children are "little scientists" who eagerly explore their environment in an effort to learn more about it.

Age 8   Age 11

Age 17

FIGURE 11–1 In these drawings, Joey shows his long-term personal interest in drawing the human form.

Observe Alicia's need for self-determination when she discusses required reading in the Literacy/Late Adolescence clip of the Observation CD.

sense of competence
Belief that one can deal effectively with a particular aspect of one's environment.
sense of self-determination
Belief that one has some choice and control regarding the future course of one's life.

personal qualities; for example, a boy who wants to be smart and thinks that smart people do well in school will place a premium on academic success. Other activities have high value because they are seen as means to a desired goal; for example, much as she detested mathematics, Jeanne's daughter Tina struggled through math classes throughout high school because many colleges require four years of math. Still other activities are valued simply because they bring pleasure and enjoyment (Eccles & Wigfield, 1985; Eccles [Parsons], 1983).

- *Competence.*   Some theorists propose that an important source of intrinsic motivation is an innate need to feel *competent*—to believe that one can deal effectively with one's environment (Deci & Ryan, 1992; Jacobs, Lanza, Osgood, Eccles, & Wigfield, 2002). The need for competence may have evolutionary significance: It pushes children to develop ways of dealing more effectively with environmental conditions and thus increases their chances of survival (R. White, 1959). Furthermore, children's beliefs about their competence at particular tasks and activities (referred to as *self-efficacy* by social cognitive theorists, but as **sense of competence** by some cognitive theorists) influence the choices that they make and their persistence in the face of difficulty.

- *Self-determination.*   Some theorists suggest that intrinsic motivation is more likely when children have a **sense of self-determination**, a belief that they have some choice and control regarding the things they do and the direction their lives take (Deci & Ryan, 1985, 1992). For instance, a child who thinks "I *want* to do this" or "I'd *find it valuable*" to do that has a high sense of self-determination. In contrast, a child who thinks "I *must* do this" or "*My teacher wants* me to do this" is thinking that someone or something else is directing the course of events. Consider 14-year-old Alicia's comment about required reading in the Literacy/Late Adolescence clip of the Observation CD:

> I really don't like it when the reading's required. I can't read books if they're required. I just avoid reading them because they don't seem very interesting. And even after you read them, even though they might be interesting, they're not as interesting as if you picked them up by yourself.

As you can see, intrinsic motivation may involve a variety of factors. The Observation Guidelines table "Identifying Aspects of Intrinsic Motivation" lists several common indicators and provides suggestions for promoting intrinsic motivation in classrooms and other settings.

Developmental Trends in Intrinsic Motivation   Researchers have identified several trends in intrinsic motivation over the course of childhood and adolescence:

■ *As children get older, they become less optimistic about their capabilities.*   As we have seen, one source of intrinsic motivation is a sense of competence: Children are more intrinsically motivated to perform tasks they think they can do well. Most 4- to 6-year-olds are actually *over*confident about their ability to perform various tasks; for instance, most first graders rank themselves as being one of the best readers in their class (Eccles et al., 1998; Nicholls, 1979). As they move through the elementary grades, however, they can better recall their past successes and failures, and they become increasingly aware of how their performance compares with that of their peers (Eccles et al., 1998; S. Feld, Ruhland, & Gold, 1979). Presumably as a result of these changes, they become less confident, though probably more realistic, about what they can and cannot do (e.g., Jacobs et al., 2002).

■ *As children grow older, their interests become increasingly stable and dependent on existing ability levels.*   In the early years, interests are largely situational in nature: Children are readily attracted to novel, attention-getting stimuli. By the middle to upper elementary grades, however, children acquire specific interests—perhaps in reptiles, ballet, or outer space—that persist over a period of time (Eccles et al., 1998; L. Nagy,

OBSERVATION GUIDELINES

Identifying Aspects of Intrinsic Motivation

CHARACTERISTIC	LOOK FOR	EXAMPLE	IMPLICATION
Inquisitiveness	• Eagerness to explore and learn • Fascination with objects and other people • Frequent and thoughtful questions • Lack of concern about external rewards for learning	Jamie often takes great interest in the new toys he finds at his infant care center. He is especially drawn to objects that come apart and can be reassembled in various ways.	Pique children's curiosity with puzzling situations, unusual phenomena, and opportunities to explore the physical world. Make sure their environment is safe for exploration.
Long-term Interests	• Consistent selection of a particular topic when choices are given • Frequent initiation of activities in a particular domain	Whenever his after-school group goes to the local library, Connor looks for books about military battleships or aircraft.	Relate instructional subject matter to children's interests and needs. Give them occasional choices about the topics they study and write about.
Sense of Competence	• Obvious pleasure in mastering tasks • Willingness to tackle challenging topics and activities • Willingness to take risks and make mistakes	Luana delights in trying to solve the brainteasers that her math teacher occasionally assigns for extra credit.	Give children the academic and social support they need to succeed at challenging tasks. Use evaluation procedures that encourage risk-taking and allow for occasional mistakes.
Effective Learning Strategies	• Focus on making sense of subject matter, rather than on rote memorization of facts • Persistence in trying to solve difficult problems and understand complex ideas	At home, Mark reads an assigned chapter about how mountains are formed. He finds the geography book's description of folded mountains confusing and asks his teacher about them in class the next day.	In both instruction and assessment activities, emphasize genuine understanding and integration of the subject matter, rather than rote memorization of isolated facts.

1912). By and large, children form interests in activities that they can do well and that are stereotypically associated with their gender and socioeconomic status (Gottfredson, 1981; Wigfield, 1994).

■ *Choices gradually shift from those based on personal interest to those based on personal competence and usefulness.* In the elementary grades, children primarily choose activities that they perceive to be interesting and enjoyable. As they reach adolescence and proceed through the secondary grades, however, they increasingly choose activities for which they have high self-efficacy or activities that will help them achieve their long-term goals (Eccles et al., 1998; Wigfield, 1994).

■ *Intrinsic motivation for learning school subjects declines during the school years.* Young children are often eager and excited to learn new things at school. But sometime between grades 3 and 9, children become less intrinsically motivated, and more *extrinsically* motivated, to learn and master school subject matter. Their intrinsic motivation may be especially low when they make the often anxiety-arousing transition from elementary to secondary school (Eccles & Midgley, 1989; Harter, 1992, 1996; J. M. T. Walker, 2001).

This decline in intrinsic motivation for academic subject matter is probably due to several factors. As children move through the grade levels, they are increasingly reminded of the importance of good grades (extrinsic motivators) for promotion, graduation, and college admission, and at the same time, evidence mounts to suggest that they are not necessarily "at the top of the heap" in comparison with their peers (Harter, 1992, 1996). Furthermore, they become more cognitively able to set and strive for long-term goals and begin to evaluate school subjects in terms of their relevance to such goals, rather than in terms of their intrinsic appeal. In addition, they may grow increasingly bored and impatient with overly structured, repetitive activities (Battistich, Solomon, Kim, Watson, &

FIGURE 11–2 Possible sequence in which internalized motivation develops.

Based on Deci & Ryan, 1995.

4. Integration: Children integrate certain behaviors into their overall system of motives and values. In essence, these behaviors become a central part of their sense of self.

3. Identification: Children begin to regard certain behaviors as being personally important or valuable to themselves.

2. Introjection: Children begin to behave in ways that gain the approval of others, partly as a way of protecting their self-esteem. They feel guilty when they violate certain standards for behavior but do not fully understand the rationale behind these standards.

1. External regulation: Children may initially be motivated to behave (or <u>not</u> to behave) in certain ways based primarily on the external consequences that will follow behaviors; that is, they are extrinsically motivated.

Schaps, 1995; Larson, 2000). The following interview with high school student Alfredo illustrates this last point:

Adult: Do you think your classes are interesting?
Alfredo: Some of them are. But some of them are boring. You go to the same class everyday and you just do the same type of work every day. Like biology, I like [this] class. She's about the only one I like. And last year I had the same problem. The only class I liked last year was science. . . . We used to do different things every day . . . but like classes like Reading, you go inside, read a story with the same person every day. That's boring.
Adult: That's boring? So will you just not show up?
Alfredo: No, I'll go but I won't do nothing sometimes. (dialogue from Way, 1998, p. 198)

■ *Over time, children internalize the motivation to perform some activities.* As youngsters get older, most begin to adopt some of the values of the people around them. Such **internalized motivation** typically develops gradually, perhaps in the sequence depicted in Figure 11–2 (Deci & Ryan, 1995). Thus, extrinsic and intrinsic motivation are not necessarily either/or phenomena; rather, in some situations, extrinsic motivation gradually evolves into internalized values.

Theorists have suggested that three conditions promote the development of internalized motivation (e.g., R. M. Ryan, Connell, & Grolnick, 1992). First, children should have a *warm and supportive environment,* one in which they feel a sense of relatedness to important adults (e.g., parents, teachers) in their lives. Second, children should have *some autonomy*: Adults exert no more control over their behavior than necessary, thus maximizing their sense of self-determination. Third, children should have *appropriate guidance and structure,* in the form of information about expected behaviors and why they're important, as well as about the consequences of inappropriate behaviors. When we consider the last two conditions, we realize that fostering internalized motivation involves a delicate balancing act between giving children sufficient opportunities for experiencing self-determination and providing some guidance about appropriate behavior. In a sense, parents, teachers, and other influential adults scaffold desired behaviors at first, gradually reducing their support as children exhibit desired behaviors more easily and frequently.

Development of Goals

As infants develop their motor skills (reaching, grabbing, crawling, etc.), they become increasingly capable of getting things they want, such as toys, food, or the family cat. Furthermore, they become increasingly capable of setting goals for themselves ("I want that toy, and I intend to get it!") and initiating behaviors that achieve those goals. As you may recall from Chapter 4, Piaget proposed that infants begin to engage in such *goal-directed be-*

internalized motivation
Adoption of behaviors that others value, even if those behaviors are not reinforced by environmental consequences.

havior sometime around 8 or 9 months of age. But in fact, they show some signs of goal directedness well before this. For example, as noted in Chapter 5, when one end of a string is attached to a 2-month-old baby's foot and the other end is attached to a mobile, at some point the baby realizes that foot motion makes the mobile move (Rovee-Collier, 1999). The infant typically begins to shake his or her foot more vigorously, apparently as a way to accomplish a particular goal: to gain a more interesting visual display.

Many contemporary psychologists believe that human beings are purposeful by nature: People set goals for themselves and choose courses of action that they think will help them achieve those goals (e.g., Dweck & Elliott, 1983; A. Kaplan, 1998; Locke & Latham, 1994). Some goals (e.g., "I want to finish reading my dinosaur book") are short-term and transitory; others (e.g., "I want to be a paleontologist") are long-term and relatively enduring. Children's goals influence both the extent to which they actively engage themselves in learning activities and the kinds of learning strategies they use as they read and study (Anderman & Maehr, 1994; Nolen, 1996; Winne & Marx, 1989).

Children and adolescents typically have a wide variety of goals: Being happy and healthy, doing well in school, bringing honor to the family, gaining popularity with peers, attaining recognition for accomplishments, defeating others in competitive events, earning money, finding a long-term mate, and having their own children are just a few of the many possibilities (M. E. Ford, 1996; Schutz, 1994). Among these many goals are certain *core goals* that drive much of what youngsters do (Schutz, 1994). For instance, those who attain high levels of academic achievement typically make classroom learning a high priority; those who achieve at lower levels are often more concerned with social relationships (Wentzel & Wigfield, 1998; Wigfield et al., 1996).

Here we look at research findings related to several kinds of goals: mastery and performance goals, social goals, and future aspirations. We then consider how children and adolescents often try to coordinate multiple goals.

Mastery Goals and Performance Goals   In the opening case study, both Sara and Amy want to do well in school but for different reasons. Sara has a **mastery goal:** She wants to acquire new knowledge and skills related to kites and their construction, and to do so she must inevitably make a few mistakes. Amy has a **performance goal:** She wants to look good and receive favorable judgments from others and so tries to avoid mistakes if at all possible (e.g., Ames, 1992; Dweck & Elliott, 1983; Nicholls, 1984).[3]

To the extent that children have mastery goals, they engage in the very activities that will help them learn: They pay attention at school, are more likely to process information in ways that promote long-term memory storage, and learn from their mistakes. Furthermore, they have a healthy perspective about learning, effort, and failure: They realize that learning is a process of trying hard and persevering even after temporary setbacks (Anderman & Maehr, 1994; Dweck & Elliott, 1983).

Children who have performance goals may be so concerned about how they appear to others that they stay away from challenging tasks that would help them master new skills (Dweck, 1986; Urdan, 1997). In some cases, they may exert only the minimal effort needed to achieve desired performance outcomes, and so they may learn only a fraction of what their instructors can offer them (Brophy, 1987; Dowson & McInerney, 2001).

Mastery and performance goals are not necessarily mutually exclusive; on many occasions, children are likely to have *both* kinds of goals at the same time (Anderman & Maehr, 1994; Hidi & Harackiewicz, 2000; Pintrich, 2000). However, we see a developmental trend in the relative prevalence of the two types of goals. Young children seem to be primarily concerned with mastery goals. By the time they reach second grade, however, they begin to show signs of having performance goals as well, and such goals become increasingly prominent as they move into middle and secondary school (Eccles & Midgley, 1989; Elliot & McGregor, 2000; Nicholls, Cobb, Yackel, Wood, & Wheatley,

mastery goal
Desire to acquire additional knowledge or master new skills.

performance goal
Desire to look good and receive favorable judgments from others.

---

[3] You may sometimes see the terms *learning goal* or *task involvement* used instead of *mastery goal,* and the term *ego involvement* used instead of *performance goal* (e.g., Dweck & Elliott, 1983; Nicholls, 1984).

Many young children are concerned with mastery goals, such as learning to read. Older children become increasingly concerned with performance goals, such as looking cool in front of peers.

1990). The greater emphasis on performance goals at older ages is probably due both to children's increasing awareness of how their performance compares with that of their peers and to the increasing emphasis that middle school and secondary school teachers place on grades and other forms of formal evaluation (Eccles et al., 1998; Nicholls et al., 1990).

Social Goals Earlier we noted that many children and adolescents make social relationships a high priority, and that in fact all human beings probably have some need for relatedness. In the school years, and especially during adolescence, youngsters are apt to have a variety of social goals, perhaps including the following:

- Forming and maintaining friendly or intimate relationships with others
- Becoming part of a cohesive, mutually supportive group
- Gaining other people's approval
- Achieving status and prestige among peers
- Meeting social obligations and keeping interpersonal commitments
- Assisting and supporting others, and ensuring their welfare
(Berndt & Keefe, 1996; Dowson & McInerney, 2001; M. E. Ford, 1996; Hicks, 1997; Schutz, 1994)

Young people's social goals affect their behavior and performance in the classroom and other group settings. For instance, if they are seeking friendly relationships with peers or are concerned about others' welfare, they may eagerly and actively engage in such activities as cooperative learning and peer tutoring (Dowson & McInerney, 2001). If they want to gain adults' attention and approval, they are apt to strive for good grades and in other ways shoot for performance goals (Hinkley, McInerney, & Marsh, 2001). A desire for peer approval also leads to a focus on performance goals rather than mastery goals (Anderman & Anderman, 1999). And if youngsters value the approval of *low-achieving* peers, they may exert little effort in their studies (Berndt, 1992; B. B. Brown, 1993; Steinberg, 1996). (Chapter 13 addresses the nature of peer influences in greater detail.)

Future Aspirations Children and adolescents often set long-term goals for themselves; for instance, they may want to go to college, get married, raise a family, or have a particular occupation. Young children set such goals with little thought and change them frequently; for instance, a 6-year-old may want to be a firefighter one week and a professional baseball player the next. By late adolescence, many (though by no means all) have reached some tentative and relatively stable decisions about the life and career paths they want to pursue (Marcia, 1980). To a considerable degree, the goals that adolescents set for themselves are a function of their self-efficacy for being successful in various roles and careers (Bandura, Barbaranelli, Caprara, & Pastorelli, 2001).

In general, boys set higher aspirations for themselves than girls do, especially in domains that are stereotypically masculine (Bandura et al., 2001; Deaux, 1984; Durkin, 1987; Lueptow, 1984). Even preschoolers are aware that men and women tend to hold different kinds of jobs: doctors, police officers, and truck drivers are usually men, whereas nurses, teachers, and secretaries are usually women. By the time children reach elementary school, they have formed definite stereotypes about the careers that are appropriate for males and females, and these gender stereotypes influence their own career aspirations (Deaux, 1984; Kelly & Smail, 1986; Liben, Bigler, & Krogh, 2002). As they move into the secondary school years, they are more likely to recognize that both males and females can hold virtually any job, but most continue to aspire to careers consistent with male and female stereotypes, and many girls further restrict themselves to careers that will not interfere with their future roles as wives and mothers (Eccles [Parsons], 1984; J. Smith & Russell, 1984). Girls are making some progress in this regard, however: Girls growing up now are more likely to have specific career plans than did their counterparts a generation or two ago (e.g., A. J. C. King, 1989). Nevertheless, many—especially within some ethnic groups—continue to aspire only to traditional female roles (Durkin, 1995; Olneck, 1995; S. M. Taylor, 1994).

Coordinating Multiple Goals   Most children and adolescents simultaneously have numerous goals toward which they are striving, and they take a variety of approaches in their attempts to juggle their goals. Sometimes they find activities that allow them to achieve several goals simultaneously; for instance, they may satisfy both academic and social goals by forming a study group to prepare for a test. But in other situations, they may believe they have to abandon one goal to satisfy another (McCaslin & Good, 1996; Phelan et al., 1994). For example, youngsters who want to do well in school may choose not to perform at their best so that they can maintain relationships with peers who don't value academic achievement. Students with mastery goals in particular subject areas may find that the multiple demands of school coerce them into focusing on performance goals (e.g., getting good grades) rather than studying the subject matter as thoroughly as they'd like. Brian, a junior high school student, expresses his ambivalence about striving for performance goals over mastery goals:

> I sit here and I say, "Hey, I did this assignment in five minutes and I still got an A+ on it." I still have a feeling that I could do better, and it was kind of cheap that I didn't do my best and I still got this A. . . . I think probably it might lower my standards eventually, which I'm not looking forward to at all. . . . I'll always know, though, that I have it in me. It's just that I won't express it that much. (S. Thomas & Oldfather, 1997, p. 119)

Teachers' instructional strategies and grading practices influence the extent to which their students have mastery goals at school and successfully juggle such goals with their social goals and performance goals. For example, students are more likely to strive for mastery goals when their assignments entice them to learn new skills (thus encouraging a focus on mastery), when they have occasional group projects (thus helping them meet their social goals), and when evaluation criteria allow for risk taking and mistakes (thus helping them meet their performance goals). Students are unlikely to strive for mastery goals when assignments ask little of them (consider Brian's concern about low standards), when their teachers insist that they compete with one another for resources or high test scores, and when any single failure has a significant impact on final grades.

Development of Attributions

In the opening case study, Amy has not gotten her kite to fly. Even though she has put little effort into designing and constructing the kite, she chalks up her failure to insufficient wind and speculates that a successful kite would have been a matter of luck. In contrast, Sara, who has created a more aerodynamic kite, takes ownership of both her success ("I knew that I could really do it") and her little failures along the way ("I mean, everybody learns from their mistakes. I know I do" [D. K. Meyer et al., 1997, pp. 511]).

The various causal explanations that people have for their successes and failures are **attributions** (e.g., Dweck, 1986; B. Weiner, 1986). Children form a variety of attributions about the causes of events in their lives; they draw conclusions (possibly accurate, possibly not) about why they do well or poorly on classroom tests and assignments, why they are popular with their peers or have trouble making friends, why they are skilled athletes or total klutzes, and so on. They may attribute their successes and failures to such factors as aptitude or ability (how smart or proficient they are), effort (how hard they tried), other people (how well an instructor taught or how much other children like them), task difficulty (how easy or hard something is), luck, mood, illness, fatigue, or physical appearance. Such attributions differ from one another in terms of at least three dimensions (B. Weiner, 1986, 2000):

- *Internal versus external.*   Children may attribute the causes of events to factors within themselves (*internal* things) or to factors outside themselves (*external* things). In the opening case study, Sara's attributions are clearly internal, whereas Amy's are external.
- *Stable versus unstable.*   Children may believe either that events are due to *stable* factors, which probably won't change much in the near future, or to *unstable* factors, which can vary from one occasion to the next. Sara attributes her success to

attribution
Belief about the cause of one's success or failure.

In the Environments/Late Adolescence clip of the Observation CD, observe in a high school corridor this description of responsibility, which suggests that students attribute their behaviors to internal and controllable causes.

her own, relatively stable ability ("I knew that I could really do it"). In contrast, Amy's explanations of "not enough wind" and "beginner's luck" are based on unstable factors that change unpredictably.

- *Controllable versus uncontrollable.* Children may attribute events to *controllable* factors, which they can influence and change, or to *uncontrollable* factors, which they cannot influence. Sara clearly sees herself in control of her success ("I knew I could put this together really well, 'cause I had a lot of confidence in myself"), whereas Amy of course has no control over bad weather conditions or a lucky break.

To some degree, the nature of a particular attribution—whether it is internal or external, stable or unstable, or controllable or uncontrollable—is in the eye of the beholder (B. Weiner, 2000). For example, what do we mean when we say that someone has high "ability" in a particular area? Some children have an **entity view** of ability: They believe that their ability to perform various tasks is inherited or in some other way beyond their control. Other children have an **incremental view**, thinking that, with effort and perseverance, they will almost certainly gain greater ability over time (Dweck & Leggett, 1988).

When children attribute their successes and failures to stable factors, they expect their future performance to be similar to their current performance: Successful children anticipate that they will continue to succeed, and unsuccessful children believe that they will always fail. In contrast, when children attribute their successes and failures to unstable factors, their current success rate has less influence on their expectations for future success (Dweck, 1978; B. Weiner, 1986). The most optimistic children—those who have the highest expectations for future success—are the ones who attribute their successes to stable factors such as innate ability and their failures to unstable but controllable factors such as lack of effort or inappropriate strategies (Schunk, 1990; B. Weiner, 1984).

When children believe that their failures are due to their own lack of effort and that they do have the ability to succeed if they work hard enough, they are likely to try harder and persist longer in future situations (Dweck, 1975; Feather, 1982; B. Weiner, 1984). But when they instead attribute failure to a lack of innate ability (they couldn't do it even if they tried), they give up easily and sometimes can't even perform tasks they have previously accomplished successfully (Dweck, 1978; Eccles [Parsons], 1983).

Children and adolescents are more likely to try hard and persist in the face of failure if they have an incremental view of ability—that is, if they believe that effort and practice will lead to significant improvement.

Developmental Trends in Attributions   Researchers have observed several trends in the development of attributions:

■ *Children are increasingly able to distinguish among various attributions.*   Up until age 5 or 6, children don't have a clear understanding of the differences among the possible causes—effort, ability, luck, task difficulty, and so on—of their successes and failures (Eccles et al., 1998; Nicholls, 1990). Especially troublesome is the distinction between effort and skill, which they gradually get a better handle on over time (Nicholls, 1990):

- At about age 6, children begin to recognize that effort and ability are separate qualities. At this point, they believe that people who try hardest are those who have the greatest ability, and that effort is the primary determiner of successful outcomes.
- At about age 9, children begin to understand that effort and ability often compensate for each other, that people with less ability may have to exert greater effort to achieve the same outcomes as their more able peers. They do not apply this distinction consistently, however.
- At about age 13, adolescents clearly differentiate between effort and ability. They realize that people differ both in their inherent ability to perform a task and in the amount of effort they exert on a task. They also realize that ability and effort can often compensate for each other but that a lack of ability sometimes precludes success no matter how much effort a person puts forth. In general, adolescents view effort as a sign of low ability: Someone who has to exert a great deal of effort to accomplish a task doesn't have "what it takes" to be successful.

entity view of ability
Belief that ability is a "thing" that is relatively permanent and unchangeable.

incremental view of ability
Belief that ability can and does improve with effort and practice.

■ *With age, children are more likely to attribute their own successes and failures to a stable ability rather than to effort.* In the elementary grades, children tend to attribute their successes to effort and hard work; therefore, they are usually relatively optimistic about their chances for success and so may work harder when they fail. By adolescence, however, they attribute success and failure more to a fairly stable ability that is beyond their control (Covington, 1992; Nicholls, 1990; Paris & Cunningham, 1996). To some degree, then, children move from an incremental view of ability in the elementary years to an entity view in adolescence (Dweck, 1999). Probably for this reason, adolescents in the secondary grades are more discouraged by their failures than children in the elementary grades (Eccles & Wigfield, 1985; Pressley, Borkowski, & Schneider, 1987).

Yet there are individual differences here: Some young people continue to hold an incremental view, and those who do are more likely to have mastery goals and seek out challenges to enhance their competence in various domains (Dweck & Leggett, 1988). Furthermore, the trend to attribute success and failure increasingly to ability rather than effort has been observed primarily in Western cultures. Adolescents from Asian backgrounds often attribute their academic achievement to effort, perhaps because many Asian parents actively nurture such a belief (Hess, Chang, & McDevitt, 1987; Lillard, 1997; Peak, 1993; Steinberg, 1996).

Some researchers have found gender differences in children's attributions for success and failure. They have observed that boys are more likely to attribute their successes to a fairly stable ability and their failures to lack of effort, thus displaying the attitude that *I know I can do this*. Girls show the reverse pattern: They attribute their successes to effort and their failures to lack of ability, believing that *I don't know whether I can keep on doing it, because I'm not very good at this type of thing*. Such differences, which can appear even when boys' and girls' previous levels of achievement are equivalent, are more frequently observed in stereotypically male domains such as mathematics and sports (Eccles & Jacobs, 1986; Fennema, 1987; Stipek, 1984; Vermeer, Boekaerts, & Seegers, 2000).

■ *As they get older, children and adolescents become more aware of the reactions that different attributions elicit.* Adults are often sympathetic and forgiving when children fail because of something beyond their control (illness, lack of ability, etc.) but frequently get angry when children fail simply because they didn't try very hard. By the time children reach fourth grade, most are aware of this fact and so may verbalize attributions that are likely to elicit a favorable reaction (Juvonen, 2000). For instance, a child who knows very well that she did poorly on a school assignment because she didn't put forth her best effort may distort the truth, telling her teacher that she "doesn't understand this stuff" or "wasn't feeling well."

Children also become more adept at tailoring their attributions for the ears of their peers. Generally speaking, fourth graders believe that their peers value diligence and hard work, and so they are likely to say that they did well on an assignment because they worked hard. In contrast, many eighth graders believe that their peers will disapprove of those who exert much effort on academic tasks, and so they often prefer to convey the impression that they aren't working very hard—for instance, that they "didn't study very much" for an important exam (Juvonen, 2000).

■ *Children gradually develop predictable patterns of attributions and expectations for their future performance.* Some children and adolescents develop a general sense of optimism that they can master new tasks and succeed in a variety of endeavors. They attribute their accomplishments to their own ability and effort and have an *I can do it* attitude known as a **mastery orientation**. Others, either unsure of their chances for success or else convinced that they cannot succeed, begin to display a sense of futility about their chances for future success. They have an *I can't do it* attitude known as **learned helplessness**.

Even though individuals with a mastery orientation and those with learned helplessness may have equal ability initially, those with a mastery orientation behave in ways that lead to higher achievement over the long run: They set ambitious goals, seek challenging situations, and persist in the face of failure. Individuals with learned helplessness behave very

mastery orientation
General belief that one is capable of accomplishing challenging tasks, accompanied by the intent to master such tasks.

learned helplessness
General belief that one is incapable of accomplishing tasks and has little or no control of the environment.

differently: Because they underestimate their own ability, they set goals they can easily accomplish, avoid the challenges that are likely to maximize their learning and growth, and respond to failure in counterproductive ways that almost guarantee future failure as well (Dweck, 1986; C. Peterson, 1990; Seligman, 1991).

Even 4- and 5-year-olds can develop learned helplessness about a particular task if they consistently encounter failure when attempting it (Burhans & Dweck, 1995; Ziegert, Kistner, Castro, & Robertson, 2001). But learned helplessness becomes more prevalent as children move through the elementary grades and middle school grades, perhaps because children are gradually abandoning their belief that anyone who tries hard can succeed (Eccles et al., 1998; Paris & Cunningham, 1996). By early adolescence, feelings of helplessness are relatively common: Some middle schoolers believe they cannot control what happens to them and are at a loss for strategies about how to avert future failures (Paris & Cunningham, 1996; C. Peterson, Maier, & Seligman, 1993).

Children and adolescents of color are more likely than their European American peers to develop a sense of learned helplessness about their ability to achieve success in academic settings (Graham, 1989; Holliday, 1985). Racial prejudice may be one factor here: Children begin to believe that, because of the color of their skin, they have little chance of success no matter *what* they do (Sue & Chin, 1983; van Laar, 2000). We suspect that such learned helplessness is probably limited to contexts in which young people believe that discrimination is a factor; it may diminish in contexts where other people clearly have no biases against particular groups.

Origins of Attributions   To some extent, children's attributions are the result of their previous success and failure experiences (Covington, 1987; Hong, Chiu, & Dweck, 1995). Those who usually succeed when they give a task their best shot are likely to believe that success is due to internal factors such as effort or high ability. Those who frequently fail despite their best efforts are likely to believe that success is due to something beyond their control—perhaps to a lack of ability or to such external factors as luck or an adult's arbitrary evaluations.

But children also pick up on other people's beliefs about why they have done well or poorly. Parents, teachers, and other adults communicate their interpretations of children's successes and failures in a variety of ways. Sometimes their attributions are directly expressed, as the following statements illustrate:

- "That's wonderful. Your hard work has really paid off, hasn't it?" (*effort*)
- "You did it! You're so smart!" (*fairly stable ability*)
- "Hmmm, maybe this just isn't something you're good at." (*ability, again*)
- "Maybe you're just having a bad day." (*luck*)

At other times, adults' messages are less explicit. For instance, frequent praise communicates the message that children's successes are due to effort, but by praising children for *easy* tasks, adults may simultaneously convey that success wasn't expected (Graham, 1990, 1991; Schunk, 1989; Stipek, 1996). When adults criticize and express anger about children's poor performance, they imply that children have the ability to master the task and simply aren't trying hard enough; when they express pity for the poor performance, they imply that low ability is the reason for the failure (Graham, 1997; Pintrich & Schunk, 1996; B. Weiner, 1984). Adults communicate low ability, too, when they provide unneeded assistance on easy tasks or encourage children to abandon challenging ones (Hokoda & Fincham, 1995; Stipek, 1996). As children get older, they become increasingly attuned to such subtle messages (Barker & Graham, 1987).

The Developmental Trends table "Motivation at Different Age Levels" summarizes developmental trends in motivation; it also describes some of the diversity that emerges at various age levels. We now step back and take a more critical look at each perspective.

DEVELOPMENTAL TRENDS

Motivation at Different Age Levels

AGE	WHAT YOU MIGHT OBSERVE	DIVERSITY	IMPLICATIONS
Infancy (Birth–2) 	• Curiosity about objects and people • Enthusiasm for exploring the environment • Some goal-directed behavior as early as 3 months • Little or no need for praise, especially in the first year; greater appreciation of praise after age 1	• Temperament and culture influence children's willingness to explore and experiment with their physical environment. • Attachment security influences children's willingness to explore (see Chapter 9). • Children with disabilities may show less interest in exploration than their nondisabled peers.	• Create a predictable, affectionate environment in which children feel comfortable exploring and trying new things. • Provide new and unusual objects that pique children's curiosity. • Identify objects and events that can capture the interest of children with disabilities.
Early Childhood (2–6) 	• Preference for small, immediate rewards over larger, delayed ones • Overconfidence about one's ability to perform novel tasks • Rapidly changing, situation-dependent interests • Focus on obtaining the approval of adults more than that of peers • Focus on mastery (rather than performance) goals • Little understanding of the reasons for successes and failures	• Differences in need for affiliation are evident as early as age 3 or 4. • Children who begin school without basic knowledge of colors, shapes, letters, or numbers may see obvious differences between their own abilities and those of peers, setting the stage for low self-perceptions. • Learned helplessness occasionally appears as early as age 4 or 5, especially after a history of failure.	• Praise (or in some other way reinforce) desired behaviors as soon as they occur. • Provide a wide variety of potentially interesting toys, puzzles, and equipment. • Make sure that children experience success more often than failure.
Middle Childhood (6–10) 	• Increasing ability to delay gratification • Increasing awareness of how one's performance compares with that of peers; more realistic assessment of abilities • Increasing prevalence of performance goals • Increasing distinction between effort and ability as possible causes of success and failure; tendency to attribute successes to hard work	• Children with a history of learning problems have less intrinsic motivation to learn academic subject matter. • Girls who are gifted may be reluctant to do their best because of concerns about appearing unfeminine or surpassing peers. • Children of color and children with disabilities are more likely to develop learned helplessness about their ability to achieve academic success.	• Communicate that *all* children can master basic knowledge and skills in academic subject matter. • Focus children's attention on the progress they are making, rather than on how their performance compares to that of their peers. • Stress the importance of learning for the intrinsic pleasure it brings; downplay the importance of grades and other external evaluations.
Early Adolescence (10–14) 	• Declining sense of competence, often accompanying the transition to middle school or junior high • Increasing interest in social activities; increasing concern about gaining approval of peers • Decline in intrinsic motivation to learn school subject matter • Increasing belief that ability is the result of stable factors (e.g., genetics) rather than effort and practice • Increasing motivation to learn and achieve in stereotypically gender-appropriate domains • Increasing focus on performance goals	• Girls are more likely than boys to have a high need for affiliation. • Some adolescents, girls especially, believe that demonstrating high achievement can interfere with popularity. • Adolescents from some ethnic groups (e.g., those from many Asian cultures) continue to place high value on adult approval. • On average, adolescents from lower socioeconomic backgrounds show lower achievement motivation than those from middle and upper socioeconomic backgrounds. • Some individuals develop a sense of learned helplessness about achieving academic success.	• Evaluate adolescents on the basis of how well they are achieving instructional objectives, not on how well their performance compares with that of their peers. • Assign cooperative group projects that allow adolescents to socialize, display their unique talents, and contribute to the success of the group. • When youngsters exhibit a pattern of failure, provide the support they need to begin achieving consistent success.

(continued)

DEVELOPMENTAL TRENDS

Motivation at Different Age Levels *(continued)*

AGE	WHAT YOU MIGHT OBSERVE	DIVERSITY	IMPLICATIONS
Late Adolescence (14–18) 	• Ability to postpone immediate pleasures in order to gain long-term rewards • Increasing stability of interests and priorities • Increasing focus on the utilitarian value of activities • Tendency to attribute successes and failures more to ability than to effort • Some tentative decisions about careers	• Girls work harder on school assignments, and are also more likely to graduate, than boys. • Adolescents from Asian cultures often attribute their successes and failures to effort rather than ability. • Many teens have career aspirations that are stereotypically gender appropriate. • Adolescents from low socioeconomic groups have lower academic aspirations and are at greater risk for failure and dropping out of school.	• Point out the relevance of school subject matter and other domains for adolescents' long-term goals. • Allow teens to pursue personal interests within the context of particular academic domains. • Provide opportunities for high school students to explore various careers and occupations.

Sources: Bandura et al., 2001; L. A. Bell, 1989; J. H. Block, 1983; Burhans & Dweck, 1995; H. Cooper & Dorr, 1995; Deaux, 1984; Deshler & Schumaker, 1988; Dien, 1998; Durkin, 1995; Dweck, 1986, 1999; J. S. Eccles & Midgley, 1989; J. S. Eccles et al., 1998; Fewell & Sandall, 1983; Graham, 1989; Green et al., 1994; Halpern, 1992; Harter, 1992, 1996; Jacobs et al., 2002; B. Jacobsen, Lowery, & DuCette, 1986; Juvonen, 2000; Lieberman, 1993; Lillard, 1997; Linder, 1993; McCall, 1994; J. G. Nicholls, 1990; F. Pajares & Valiante, 1999; Paris & Cunningham, 1996; Peak, 1993; C. Peterson, 1990; Portes, 1996; Rotenberg & Mayer, 1990; Rovee-Collier, 1990; M. P. Sadker & Sadker, 1994; Schultz & Switzky, 1990; Seligman, 1991; Vaughn et al., 1984; Wigfield et al., 1991; Ziegert et al., 2001.

Critiquing Theories of Motivation

Each of the theoretical perspectives we've considered in this chapter has merits and drawbacks. Behaviorism's most important contribution probably lies in its implications for changing children's behavior. Planned and systematic uses of reinforcement for desired responses, perhaps in conjunction with carefully chosen punishment for unacceptable behavior, are often highly effective in treating serious behavior problems; furthermore, they often work in situations where other approaches have failed (e.g., O'Leary & O'Leary, 1972; Rimm & Masters, 1974; M. A. Smith & Schloss, 1998). Yet by themselves, behaviorist views are too limited to explain all the nuances of human motivation. For example, they cannot explain why some children and adolescents seek out challenging situations (brainteasers, puzzling phenomena, etc.) that have no obvious external benefits and why others even put their lives in jeopardy for the thrill of riding a roller coaster or racing at lightning speed down the highway.

Trait theorists have made us aware of the variety of needs that children and adolescents have, and their research has yielded surveys and tests that are useful in assessing such needs. But, although they have pinned down some of the broad motivational differences that exist among children, they help us very little in explaining why and how those differences emerge as children develop.

Social cognitive and cognitive perspectives fill some of the voids in behaviorist and trait perspectives. For instance, they explain why people often seek out challenging situations: Successfully meeting a challenge enhances one's self-efficacy and sense of competence. They also explain why some children have higher levels of achievement motivation than others: Prior experiences influence children's self-efficacy, sense of competence, and attributions; and present circumstances can create disequilibrium, foster beliefs about an activity's value, and affect children's feelings of self-determination. However, cognitive approaches to motivation have been criticized for largely ignoring motivation's emotional components (Eccles et al., 1998). Furthermore, at the present time, they don't yet form a cohesive picture of the nature and development of motivation. Instead, they are like pieces of a jigsaw puzzle: They sometimes interlock and sometimes do not, and some of the pieces (for instance, in-depth explanations of how motivation and emotion interrelate) are missing.

The Basic Developmental Issues table "Contrasting Theories of Motivation" compares the four theoretical perspectives with regard to nature and nurture, universality and diversity, and qualitative and quantitative change. Despite their weaknesses and "missing pieces," they offer numerous strategies for practitioners who work with children and adolescents, as we will see now.

BASIC DEVELOPMENTAL ISSUES

Contrasting Theories of Motivation

ISSUE	BEHAVIORIST PERSPECTIVES	SOCIAL COGNITIVE PERSPECTIVES	TRAIT PERSPECTIVES	COGNITIVE PERSPECTIVES
Nature and Nurture	Behaviorists suggest that early reinforcers satisfy biological needs. However, they emphasize the environmental conditions that increase and decrease the frequencies of various responses.	Social cognitive theorists focus on experiences (e.g., past successes and failures) and environmental conditions (e.g., the presence of competent and prestigious models) that encourage and discourage certain behaviors.	Trait theorists focus on individual differences in people's needs and motives but with little concern about the origins of such differences. For the most part, then, they ignore the nature/nurture question.	Cognitive theorists propose that certain needs (e.g., needs for competence and self-determination) are shared by all human beings and so probably have a biological basis. The specific ways in which people address those needs are often influenced by environmental conditions (culture, parents' behaviors, etc.).
Universality and Diversity	Basic principles of reinforcement and punishment are universally shared. Furthermore, most of these principles apply not only to human beings but to other species as well. However, any particular consequence may have different effects on different individuals, largely as a result of differing learning histories.	Some phenomena (e.g., observing and imitating others' behaviors, developing beliefs about one's self-efficacy for various tasks) are universal. However, specific manifestations of these phenomena vary from one person to the next (e.g., different people imitate different models and have varying levels of self-efficacy for particular tasks).	By definition, trait theories focus on individual differences— that is, on the diversity that exists among people.	A few basic needs (e.g., the need for self-determination) are universal across the human race. However, their manifestations frequently vary across ages, genders, and ethnic groups.
Qualitative and Quantitative Change	Reinforcement and punishment influence the frequency (quantity) of the behaviors they follow; as the consequences for particular behaviors change over time, so, too, will the frequency of the behaviors change.	Self-efficacy increases or decreases in a quantitative fashion as a result of success and failure experiences.	Achievement motivation, need for affiliation, and other needs may either increase or decrease (in a quantitative fashion) with development.	Some developmental changes (e.g., the decrease in intrinsic motivation in academic domains, the increasing prevalence of performance goals) are quantitative. Other changes (e.g., the shift in focus from adult to peer approval, the evolving conception of how effort and ability are related) are qualitative.

Fostering Motivation in Children and Adolescents

Effective teachers, clinicians, and other practitioners motivate children and adolescents in a variety of ways. They create and conduct interesting activities, have reasonable expectations for performance, show a genuine concern for youngsters' learning and well-being in one-on-one and group interactions, and assess progress and achievement through meaningful assignments and evaluation. Following are additional recommendations:

■ *Focus on promoting intrinsic (rather than extrinsic) motivation.* As behaviorists have pointed out, extrinsic reinforcers—praise, money, points, good grades, and so on—often bring about desired changes in behavior. Yet such reinforcers have some disadvantages. Although they provide a source of extrinsic motivation, they can undermine children's *intrinsic* motivation, especially when children perceive them to be controlling, manipulative, or in some other way limiting to their freedom and sense of self-determination (Deci & Ryan, 1987). Furthermore, they may communicate the message that assigned tasks are unpleasant chores (why else would a reinforcer be necessary?), rather than activities to be carried out and enjoyed for their own sake (Hennessey, 1995; Stipek, 1993).

As we noted at the beginning of the chapter, children learn more effectively when they are intrinsically rather than extrinsically motivated. Ideally, then, adults should focus children's attention not on the external consequences of their efforts but on the internal pleasures—the feelings of enjoyment, satisfaction, and pride—that their accomplishments bring. Adults should also capitalize on factors that underlie intrinsic motivation; for instance, they might:

- Pique children's curiosity with new and intriguing objects
- Create disequilibrium by presenting puzzling phenomena
- Relate important skills and subject matter to children's interests and goals
- Enhance children's self-efficacy and sense of competence by identifying areas in which each child can be especially successful

Children learn more effectively when they are intrinsically rather than extrinsically motivated.

■ *Maintain children's sense of self-determination when describing rules and giving instructions.* Virtually any group situation needs a few rules and procedures to ensure that children act appropriately and activities run smoothly. Furthermore, adults must often impose guidelines and restrictions about how children carry out assigned tasks. The trick is to present these rules, procedures, guidelines, and restrictions without undermining children's sense of self-determination. Instead, adults should present them as *information*—for instance, as conditions that can help children accomplish important goals and objectives (Deci, 1992; Koestner, Ryan, Bernieri, & Holt, 1984).

An experiment by Koestner and colleagues (1984) illustrates how simple differences in wording can affect children's sense of self-determination and intrinsic motivation. First and second graders were asked to paint a picture of a house they would like to live in. The children were given the materials they needed—a paintbrush, a set of watercolor paints, two sheets of paper, and several paper towels—and then told some rules about how to proceed. For some children (the controlling-limits condition), restrictions described things that they could and couldn't do, as follows:

> Before you begin, I want to tell you some things that you will have to do. They are rules that we have about painting. You have to keep the paints clean. You can paint only on this small sheet of paper, so don't spill any paint on the big sheet. And you must wash out your brush and wipe it with a paper towel before you switch to a new color of paint, so that you don't get the colors all mixed up. In general, I want you to be a good boy (girl) and don't make a mess with the paints. (Koestner et al., 1984, p. 239)

For other children (the informational-limits condition), restrictions were presented as information, like this:

> Before you begin, I want to tell you some things about the way painting is done here. I know that sometimes it's really fun to just slop the paint around, but here the materials and room need to be kept nice for the other children who will use them. The smaller sheet is for you to paint on, the larger sheet is a border to be kept clean. Also, the paints need to be kept clean, so the brush is to be washed and wiped in the paper towel before switching colors. I know that some kids don't like to be neat all the time, but now is a time for being neat (Koestner et al., 1984, p. 239)

Each child was allowed 10 minutes of painting time. The experimenter then took the child's painting to another room, saying he would return in a few minutes. As he departed, he placed two more sheets of paper on the child's table, saying, "You can paint some more on this piece of paper, if you like, or if you want, you can play with the puzzles over on that table" (p. 239). In the experimenter's absence, the child was surreptitiously observed, and painting time was measured. Children in the informational-limits condition spent more time painting (so were apparently more intrinsically motivated to paint) than did their counterparts in the controlling-limits condition, and their paintings were judged to be more creative.

Following are additional examples of how adults might describe rules or give instructions in an informational rather than controlling manner:

- "We can make sure everyone has an equal chance to speak and be heard if we listen without interrupting and if we raise our hands when we want to contribute to the discussion."
- "I'm giving you a particular format to follow when you do your math homework. If you use this format, it will be easier for me to find your answers and figure out where and how you are running into difficulty."

■ *Minimize comparison and competition among children; instead, focus children's attention on their own improvement.* Inevitably, there are more losers than winners in competitive situations where children are pitted against one another, and many children lose even when they exert considerable effort. They quite logically reach the conclusion that effort is not enough, that some sort of natural ability is the critical ingredient for success (Ames, 1984; Nicholls, 1984; Stipek, 1993). They see themselves as lacking that elusive ability and become pessimistic about their prognosis for future success. Thus, adults should encourage children to focus more on their own improvement—improvement that indicates that hard work does make a difference—than on how well their performance compares with that of their peers (R. Butler, 1998; Deci & Ryan, 1992; Stipek, 1996).

■ *Expose children to successful models with characteristics and backgrounds similar to their own.* As social cognitive theorists have shown us, children are more likely to have high self-efficacy for a task if they have seen people similar to themselves achieve success at the task. Often, the most effective models are children of the same or a similar age (Schunk & Hanson, 1985; Schunk et al., 1987). But adults, too, can be effective models, especially if they have characteristics and backgrounds similar to children's own. For instance, young people from ethnic minority groups benefit from observing successful minority adults, and youngsters with disabilities become more optimistic about their own futures when they meet adults successfully coping with and overcoming disabilities (Pang, 1995; L. E. Powers, Sowers, & Stevens, 1995).

Children are more apt to be motivated when they focus on their own improvement rather than on how they compare to others. In this poem written for a school assignment, 12-year-old Janetta considers some of the ways in which she has improved over time.

■ *Use extrinsic reinforcers when necessary.* There may be occasions when, despite adults' best efforts, children will have little interest in acquiring certain knowledge or skills critical for their later success in life. In such situations, adults may have to provide extrinsic reinforcers—free time, grades, points, special privileges—to encourage learning. How can adults use such reinforcers without diminishing children's sense of self-determination? One thing they can do is use reinforcers such as praise to communicate information and enhance children's self-efficacy and sense of competence (Deci, 1992; R. M. Ryan, Mims, & Koestner, 1983); for example, a teacher might say:

- "Your description of the main character in your short story makes her come alive."
- "This poster clearly states the hypothesis, method, results, and conclusions of your science project. Your use of a bar graph makes the differences between your treatment and control groups easy to see and interpret."

When adults give reinforcement in a group situation, they should make sure that all children have a reasonable opportunity to earn it. For instance, they should be careful that in their attempts to improve the behavior of some children, they don't ignore other, equally deserving children. Furthermore, they should take into account the fact that a few children may have exceptional difficulty performing particular behaviors through no fault of their own. Consider the case of a young immigrant girl who had to adjust very quickly from a 10:00–5:00 school day in Vietnam to a 7:45–3:45 school day in the United States:

> [E]very week on Friday after school, the teacher would give little presents to kids that were good during the week. And if you were tardy, you wouldn't get a present. . . . I would never get

one because I would always come to school late, and that hurt at first. I had a terrible time. I didn't look forward to going to school. (Igoa, 1995, p. 95)

■ *Encourage children to shoot for specific goals.* Often children respond more favorably to goals that they set for themselves than to goals that others have set for them (Wentzel, 1999), possibly because self-chosen goals help them maintain a sense of self-determination. Yet many children (younger ones especially) often have trouble conceptualizing a "future" that is abstract and perhaps many years down the road (Bandura, 1997; Husman & Freeman, 1999). They may initially respond more favorably to short-term, concrete goals—perhaps learning a certain number of spelling words at school, getting the next highest belt in karate, or earning a merit badge in a scout troop (Bandura & Schunk, 1981; Good & Brophy, 1994; Schunk & Rice, 1989). By setting and working for a series of short-term goals, children get regular feedback about the progress they are making, develop a greater sense of self-efficacy that they can master important topics and skills, and achieve at higher levels (Bandura, 1981; Kluger & DeNisi, 1998; Page-Voth & Graham, 1999; Schunk, 1996). In Figure 11–3, 10-year-old Amaryth describes goals she set for herself in athletics and academics, as well as how she worked to achieve her goals. Her teacher awarded her a "Goal Medal" for successfully meeting her goals.

As children reach adolescence, their increasing capacity for abstract thought allows them to envision and work toward long-term goals—perhaps making a varsity sports team, gaining admission to a prestigious college, becoming a full-fledged contributor to the family business, or having a career in journalism. Some adolescents (e.g., many females, members of ethnic minority groups, and teenagers from low-income families) set their sights lower than they need to, curbing their long-term academic and career aspirations. Adults must not only encourage these young people to aim high but also convince them that high goals are achievable. For instance, when encouraging girls to consider stereotypically masculine career paths, adults might provide examples of women who have led successful and happy lives in those careers. When encouraging teens from low-income families to think about going on to college, they might assist with filling out scholarship applications and schedule appointments with college financial aid officers.

Adults who supervise voluntary (rather than involuntary) activities (e.g., youth group leaders, sports team coaches, and advisors of after-school extracurricular groups) are in an especially good position to encourage adolescents to pursue self-chosen goals (Heath, 1999; Larson, 2000). In such circumstances, adult supervisors can give teenagers major responsibility for group goal-setting and decision-making, pose dilemmas that stimulate teens to reflect on and experiment with a variety of strategies, and encourage teens to anticipate and plan for different outcomes.

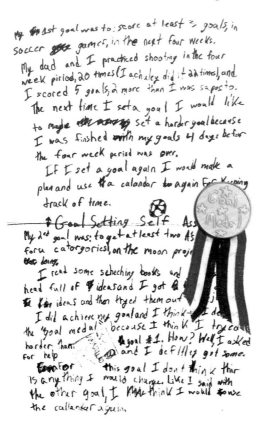

FIGURE 11–3 Children are often more motivated when they have specific goals to shoot for. Here 10-year-old Amaryth describes how she worked toward goals on the soccer field and in the classroom.

■ *Encourage mastery goals as well as (ideally even more than) performance goals.* To some degree, performance goals are inevitable in today's schools and in society at large (Butler, 1989; A. J. Elliot & McGregor, 2000). Children and adolescents will invariably look to their peers' performance as one means of evaluating their own performance, and many aspects of the adult world (gaining admission to college, seeking employment, working in private industry, playing professional sports, etc.) are inherently competitive in nature. Yet adults do youngsters a disservice when they focus attention on how youngsters appear to others and how often they do or do not surpass their peers. When adults instead explain how certain knowledge and skills will be useful in the future, point out the progress that has been made, and acknowledge that effective learning requires exerting effort and making mistakes, they are emphasizing mastery goals that will enhance learning and achievement over the long run (Anderman & Maehr, 1994; Bong, 2001; Graham & Weiner, 1996; Meece, 1994). Focusing learners' attention on mastery goals, especially when those goals relate to learners' own needs and lives, may especially benefit young people from diverse ethnic backgrounds and those at risk for academic failure (Alderman, 1990; E. E. Garcia, 1992; A. Kaplan & Maehr, 1999; Wlodkowski & Ginsberg, 1995).

■ *Take social goals into account.* For many children and adolescents, achieving social goals—for example, gaining the approval of adults and peers, becoming part of a supportive peer group, meeting social obligations, and helping others—is a high priority. Most young people will be more attentive to, and more successful at, important learning activities if they can address their social goals at the same time. Cooperative learning tasks, peer tutoring, group projects, team sports, field trips, and community service activities are just a few of the many mechanisms that enable youngsters to learn valuable new skills while also enhancing their social relationships.

Children and adolescents will more readily engage in learning activities if they can address their social goals at the same time.

■ *Downplay the seriousness of failures.* Children and adolescents are more apt to accept responsibility for their mistakes—and therefore to learn from them—if adults don't make a big deal of them (Katkovsky, Crandall, & Good, 1967). For instance, teachers might give students numerous opportunities to improve assignments and overall class grades (Ames, 1992). In some instances, adults may also find it appropriate to focus young learners' attention on the *processes* they use to tackle assigned tasks and solve problems, rather than on the final outcome of their efforts (Schunk & Swartz, 1993; Stipek & Kowalski, 1989). For example, a teacher may occasionally give an assignment with instructions like these:

> It doesn't matter at all how many you get right. In fact, these problems are kind of hard. I'm just interested in learning more about what [you] think about while [you're] working on problems like these. I want you to focus on the problem and just say out loud whatever you're thinking while you're working—whatever comes into your head. (Stipek & Kowalski, 1989, p. 387)

■ *Give encouraging messages about the causes of successes and failures.* Cognitive theorists often recommend that adults attribute children's past successes partly to a relatively stable ability and partly to such controllable factors as effort and learning strategies. In this way, adults provide assurance that children "have what it takes" to succeed but remind them that continued success also requires hard work. When identifying possible causes for failures, however, adults should focus primarily on effort and learning strategies—attributions that are internal, unstable, and controllable. Following are examples of what adults might say about children's successes and failures:

- "You've done very well. Obviously you're good at this, and you've been trying very hard to get better."
- "Your project shows a lot of talent and a lot of hard work."
- "The more you practice, the better you will get."
- "Perhaps you need to study a little bit more next time. Let's talk about how you might also need to study a little differently."

When children's failures are consistently attributed to lack of effort or ineffective strategies, rather than to low ability or uncontrollable external factors, and when new strategies or increased effort do in fact produce success, children often work harder, persist longer in the face of failure, and seek help when they need it (Dweck & Elliott, 1983; Eccles & Wigfield, 1985; Graham, 1991; Robertson, 2000).

■ *Help children learn that some successes come only with considerable effort and perseverance.* Once adults know that children have a high sense of competence about the topic or skill in question, they may occasionally want to assign tasks that children can accomplish successfully only if they exert considerable time and mental effort. In doing so, adults help children begin to realize that they can succeed at some tasks only with hard work, persistence, and well-chosen strategies (Eisenberger, 1992; Winne, 1995a).

■ *Tailor your motivational strategies to individual children's needs and motives.* As behaviorists point out, different reinforcers are more or less effective for different individuals. In addition, trait theorists remind us that children and adolescents vary considerably in their needs for affiliation and approval. Adults must take such diversity into account whenever they consider motivational strategies to use either with an entire group or with individual children. For example, public praise may be highly reinforcing to many children yet be the "kiss of death" to someone who wants to maintain high social status in a low-achieving peer group. The opportunity to study in small groups may be highly motivating for learners with a high need for affiliation yet have little appeal to those who cherish their time alone.

■ *Be especially attentive to the needs of students at risk.* **Students at risk** are those who have a high probability of failing to acquire the minimum academic skills necessary for success in the adult world. Many of them drop out before high school graduation; many others graduate without basic skills in reading or mathematics (National Assessment of Educational Progress, 1985; Slavin, 1989). Such individuals are often ill-equipped to make productive contributions to their families, communities, or society at large.

Some students at risk have special educational needs, such as learning disabilities. Others may have cultural backgrounds that don't mesh easily with the dominant culture at school. Still others may come from home environments in which academic success is neither supported nor encouraged.

Children and adolescents at risk come from all socioeconomic levels, but youngsters of poor, single-parent families are especially likely to leave school before high school graduation (Steinberg, Blinde, & Chan, 1984). Boys are more likely to drop out than girls, and African Americans, Hispanic Americans, and Native Americans are more likely to drop out than European American students (L. S. Miller, 1995; Roderick & Camburn, 1999). Students at greatest risk for dropping out are those whose families speak little or no English and whose own knowledge of English is also quite limited (Steinberg et al., 1984). In addition, students at risk often have a long history of low academic achievement, ineffective learning strategies, low self-esteem, and lack of psychological attachment to school (Belfiore & Hornyak, 1998; Finn, 1989; Garnier, Stein, & Jacobs, 1997).

Although students at risk for academic failure are a diverse group of individuals with a diverse set of needs, educators and other practitioners can do many things to help them succeed and stay in school:

- Identify them as early as possible, ideally in the elementary school grades, and begin to address their academic and social-emotional needs
- Make the curriculum relevant to their lives and needs
- Engage their interest with stimulating activities
- Communicate high expectations for academic success
- Acknowledge past learning problems but provide the time and resources necessary to help them overcome those problems
- Provide support for completing homework, perhaps in a structured after-school setting
- Encourage and facilitate participation in athletic programs, extracurricular activities, and student government
- Involve them in school policy and management decisions
  (Alderman, 1990; Belfiore & Hornyak, 1998; Cosden, Morrison, Albanese, & Macias, 2001; Finn, 1989; Garibaldi, 1992; Lee-Pearce, Plowman, & Touchstone, 1998; Murdock, 1999; Pogrow & Londer, 1994; Ramey & Ramey, 1998)

Most of these strategies can help to motivate almost *any* student, but they are especially critical for students at risk. As you will discover in our discussion of *resilience* in Chapter 14, adults' efforts can make a world of difference in the lives of such young people.

The strategies just presented focus on how adults can better address children's motives and needs. The topic we turn to now—self-regulation—focuses on how growing children can begin to address their *own* needs.

student at risk
Student who has a high probability of failing to acquire the minimal academic skills necessary for success in the adult world.

self-regulation
Directing and controlling one's own actions.

Development of Self-Regulation

People of all ages have a greater sense of self-determination (and so are more intrinsically motivated) when they can make choices about what they do and can, therefore, to some extent, direct the course of their lives. Making wise choices requires **self-regulation**, which includes capabilities such as the following:

- *Impulse control:*   Resisting sudden urges to engage in forbidden or counterproductive behaviors
- *Emotional control:*   Expressing emotions in a socially appropriate manner, and controlling them in ways that facilitate goal attainment
- *Delaying gratification:*   Putting off small, immediate rewards in anticipation of larger rewards at a later time
- *Goal setting:*   Identifying and striving for valued, self-chosen goals
- *Self-regulated learning:*   Directing and monitoring one's own attention and learning strategies in ways that promote effective cognitive processing

As you learned in Chapter 5, children who regulate their own learning are more academically successful than those who do not. Self-regulation is important in social relationships as well: Children who can control their emotions and behaviors have better social skills and are more popular among their peers (Bronson, 2000; Fabes et al., 1999; Patrick, 1997). In the upcoming pages, we look at the nature and development of self-regulation.

Theories of Self-Regulation

Theorists have taken a variety of approaches to studying self-regulation and its development. Their explanations fall into three of the perspectives we considered earlier: behaviorist, social cognitive, and cognitive.

Behaviorist Approaches   From a behaviorist perspective, behavior is initially controlled entirely by environmental stimuli (e.g., external reinforcement and punishment). Over time, and perhaps with explicit training, people learn strategies for changing and controlling their own behavior. For instance, Belfiore and Hornyak (1998) have proposed that to be self-regulating, children must learn two kinds of responses: *target responses* (the behaviors they need to be more successful) and *self-management responses* (behaviors they can use to control their target responses). For example, if a child wants to learn to keep appointments (a target response), he might learn to leave a reminder note on the kitchen counter the day of the appointment (a self-management response).

Belfiore and Hornyak applied this perspective to teaching adolescents how to regulate themselves in an after-school homework program; the target response in this case was *homework completion*. At the end of the regular school day, students reported to a particular classroom in the school building, where they would find their homework assignments on a shelf. They learned to follow the checklist depicted in Figure 11–4 and to check off steps that they had completed. They also learned to administer **self-reinforcement:** They gave themselves a reward (e.g., they allowed themselves to play a board game or spend time on the computer) whenever they had completed the steps on the checklist. Furthermore, they learned problem-solving strategies to use when they encountered difficulties (e.g., asking a teacher for assistance when they couldn't find the materials for an assignment). Initially, a teacher monitored whether the checklist reflected the homework completed; eventually, such monitoring was no longer necessary. Furthermore, the self-imposed extrinsic reinforcers became less critical; the sense of accomplishment the students felt about completing their homework became a sufficient reinforcer (Belfiore & Hornyak, 1998).

The checklist in Figure 11–4 might strike you as a set of steps that should be obvious to anyone. In fact, although many children and adolescents develop a similar list of steps on their own and so have little difficulty completing their homework, others need explicit guidance to acquire such a self-regulating system.

Social Cognitive Approaches   Social cognitive theorists (e.g., Schunk & Zimmerman, 1997; Zimmerman & Kitsantas, 1999) have suggested that the acquisition of self-regulation in any particular domain proceeds through four levels:

1. *Observational level.*   The child watches a behavior being performed. The person exhibiting the behavior (the model) explains what he or she is doing and encourages the child to learn the behavior.
2. *Imitative level.*   The child imitates the behavior, and the model provides guidance, feedback, and positive reinforcement. As the child becomes more proficient, guidance, feedback, and reinforcement are gradually phased out.

self-reinforcement
Self-imposed pleasurable consequence for a desired behavior.

FIGURE 11-4 Daily checklist for homework completion.

From "Operant Theory and Application to Self-Monitoring in Adolescents" by P. J. Belfiore and R. S. Hornyak, 1998. In *Self-Regulated Learning: From Teaching to Self-Reflective Practice* (p. 190), by D. H. Schunk & B. J. Zimmerman (Eds.), New York: Guilford Press. Copyright 1998 by Guilford Press. Reprinted with permission.

STUDENT: _____ DATE: _____

SUBJECT AREA: _____ GRADE: _____

TEACHER: _____

STEPS TO FOLLOW	YES	NO	NOTES
1. Did I turn in yesterday's homework?			
2. Did I write all homework assignments in my notebook?			
3. Is all homework in homework folder?			
4. Are all my materials to complete homework with me?			
5. BEGIN HOMEWORK?			
6. Are all homework papers completed?			
7. Did someone check homework to make sure it was completed?			
8. After checking, did I put all homework back in folder?			
9. Did I give this paper to teacher?			

3. *Self-controlled level.* The child can perform the behavior without the model present but relies largely on his or her memory for what the model did and tries to match it as closely as possible. The child now engages in self-reinforcement (perhaps self-praise, perhaps something more tangible) to sustain the activity.

4. *Self-regulated level.* The child can now perform the behavior flexibly and adapt it readily to changing circumstances. The child may occasionally seek out an expert's guidance to fine-tune the behavior but is in other respects working independently. The child now uses three strategies to guide performance:

   - *Self-observation:* Paying attention to specific aspects of the behavior being executed
   - *Self-judgment:* Comparing current performance against external standards
   - *Self-reaction:* Evaluating the performance as being acceptable or unacceptable

   At this point, motivation is entirely intrinsic: The enhanced feelings of self-efficacy are sufficient to sustain the behavior.

Many educators and clinicians have successfully applied ideas of social cognitive theory to help children and adolescents become more self-regulating. You will see the influence of social cognitive theory in our discussion of *self-monitoring* and *self-evaluation* a bit later in this section.

Cognitive Approaches As you learned in Chapter 4, Lev Vygotsky proposed that children gradually internalize social interactions into mental processes, often through a process of *self-talk.* By talking themselves through new and challenging situations, children begin to guide and direct their own behavior in much the same way that adults have previously guided them. At about age 6 or 7, such self-talk "goes underground" to become *inner speech*; in other words, children think (rather than talk) themselves through situations (Vygotsky, 1962). Many contemporary theorists believe that self-talk and its gradual internalization play a major role in the development of self-regulation (Berk, 1994; Biemiller, Shany, Inglis, & Meichenbaum, 1998; Schimmoeller, 1998; Schutz & Davis, 2000). You will see the influence of these concepts in our upcoming discussion of *self-instructions.*

Contemporary information processing theorists have described additional cognitive processes that enable people to direct and monitor their own learning and behavior (e.g., Kuhl, 1985; Menec & Schonwetter, 1994). Terms such as *metacognition* and *learning strate-*

gies (see Chapter 5) originated in information processing theory and clearly imply self-regulation in thinking, learning, and performance. More generally, cognitive theorists suggest that self-regulation encompasses processes such as these (Kuhl, 1985):

- Focusing attention on appropriate objects and events
- Selecting appropriate information to store in memory
- Identifying appropriate learning strategies to remember the information
- Controlling emotions (e.g., anxiety) so that they don't interfere with successful learning and performance
- Maintaining motivation to persist at an activity
- Choosing or creating an environment that facilitates all of the above (e.g., going to the library to study)

These processes emerge slowly throughout childhood and adolescence. For example, as you discovered in Chapter 5, young children are easily distracted by objects and events unrelated to the task at hand; thus, they seem to have little control over their own attention. Furthermore, children initially have few if any effective learning strategies. They acquire an increasing ability to direct their attention and increasingly sophisticated strategies as they proceed to higher levels of schooling and encounter more difficult tasks and subject matter.

Developmental Trends in Self-Regulation

Young children have considerable difficulty controlling their own behavior. For instance, parents often complain about the "terrible twos," the period between the second and third birthdays when children are mobile enough to get into almost anything and make quite a fuss when they don't get their own way.[4]

Self-regulation of actions, thoughts, and emotions requires several capabilities that are, in toddlers and other young children, only beginning to emerge. First, self-regulation requires an ability to inhibit certain behaviors and cognitions, and this ability is partly a function of neurological development (Blair, 2002; Dempster & Corkill, 1999; Schore, 1994). Second, to the extent that self-regulation involves self-talk, it requires sufficient language skills to accurately represent actions and events (Bronson, 2000). Third, self-regulation requires a number of cognitive mechanisms and processes—memory for past events, the ability to anticipate the consequences of future actions, an understanding of why various emotions have been aroused, and so on—that become increasingly effective and powerful with age (Bronson, 2000; Eccles et al., 1998).

Researchers have identified three ways in which children's self-regulatory capabilities change over time:

■ *External rules and restrictions gradually become internalized.* Children can comply with simple requests and restrictions by the time they are 12 to 18 months old (Kaler & Kopp, 1990; Kopp, 1982). As they become increasingly verbal, they begin to use self-talk to prevent themselves from engaging in prohibited behaviors even when caregivers are absent; for instance, a toddler may say "no" or "can't" to herself as she begins to reach for an electric outlet (Kochanska, 1993). By age 3 or 4, many children are acquiring flexible strategies for regulating their own behavior in accordance with adult rules and prohibitions. For example, if they are asked to wait for a short time (e.g., 15 minutes), they might invent games or sing to themselves to pass the time more quickly (Mischel & Ebbesen, 1970). If a playmate has an enticing toy, they may turn away and engage in an alternative activity as a way of lessening the temptation to grab the toy (Kopp, 1982). Children who have such strategies are better able to resist temptation than children who do not (Mischel, Shoda, & Rodriguez, 1989).

During the preschool, elementary, and secondary school years, children and adolescents increasingly take ownership of society's rules and regulations (Kochanska, Coy, & Murray, 2001; Deci & Ryan, 1995). Possibly this ownership proceeds through the process of internalization

---

[4] The "terrible twos" are to some extent a cultural phenomenon. When children are strongly encouraged to control their feelings even as toddlers, as is true in the Chinese and Japanese cultures, the "twos" don't necessarily stand out as a difficult period (Ho, 1994).

Over time, children become increasingly able to regulate their own behaviors and emotions. As a first grader, Brenda (top) expresses affection and other feelings in a spontaneous manner. As a seventh grader, Palet (bottom) shows a stronger inclination toward self-evaluation and emotional restraint.

authoritative parenting
Parenting style characterized by emotional warmth, high expectations and standards for behavior, consistent enforcement of rules, explanations regarding the reasons behind these rules, and the inclusion of children in decision making.

of motivation portrayed earlier in Figure 11–2 (Deci & Ryan, 1995). The first sign of internalization (the *introjection* phase) is evident when children feel some internal pressure (e.g., guilt) to comply with rules and regulations. Later (at the *identification* phase), children start to perceive rules and other desired behaviors to be important or valuable to them personally. Finally (at the *integration* phase), rules and regulations become an integral part of children's self-concepts. At this point, a teenage girl might define herself as being "generous" or "compassionate" and so strive to behave in ways consistent with her self-definition.

■ *Emotional reactions become more restrained.* As you may recall from Chapter 9, children show increasing *emotional regulation* as they grow older. Many toddlers have little control of their emotions; for instance, they may throw a temper tantrum if they don't get what they want or become physically aggressive if events make them frustrated or angry (Bronson, 2000; Kopp, 1992). In the preschool years, children's interactions with age-mates typically increase in frequency and duration, and so they must learn to control their emotions and behaviors sufficiently to get along with their peers (e.g., they must refrain from hitting and biting). By the early elementary grades, children become better able to view situations from other people's perspectives (see Chapter 10), and so they temper their emotional reactions in accordance with how they expect others to react (Bronson, 2000). As they move through the grade levels, they become increasingly able to vent their emotions appropriately, largely as a result of their experience in interacting with peers (Barkley, 1997).

■ *Self-evaluation becomes more frequent.* Infants and young toddlers do not seem to evaluate their own performance, nor do they show much concern about how others evaluate it. In contrast, 2-year-olds often seek adults' approval for their actions (Stipek, Recchia, & McClintic, 1992). Sometime around age 3, children show the first signs of self-evaluation; for instance, they look happy when they're successful and sad when they fail (Heckenhausen, 1984, 1987).

As children move through the preschool, elementary, and middle school years, they show a marked increase in self-awareness (Bronson, 2000; van Kraayenoord & Paris, 1997). Their parents may praise certain behaviors and criticize others, their teachers give them frequent information about their academic performance, and their peers often let them know in no uncertain terms about the effectiveness of their social skills. Such feedback allows them to develop criteria by which they can more accurately judge their own actions. As their ability for self-reflection grows and they become increasingly concerned about others' perceptions, especially in adolescence, they look more closely at their own behavior and evaluate it in terms of how they think others will judge it (Dacey & Kenny, 1994; Lapsley, 1993; R. M. Ryan & Kuczkowski, 1994).

Despite such improvements, many adolescents continue to lack the basic self-regulating behaviors they need for success in secondary school. Consider the case of Anna who, in her first semester of high school, earned mostly Ds and failed her science class. She explains her poor performance this way:

> In geography, "he said the reason why I got a lower grade is 'cause I missed one assignment and I had to do a report, and I forgot that one." In English, "I got a C . . . 'cause we were supposed to keep a journal, and I keep on forgetting it 'cause I don't have a locker. Well I do, but my locker partner she lets her cousins use it, and I lost my two books there. . . . I would forget to buy a notebook, and then I would have them on separate pieces of paper, and I would lose them." And, in biology, "the reason I failed was because I lost my folder . . . it had everything I needed, and I had to do it again, and, by the time I had to turn in the new folder, I did, but he said it was too late . . . 'cause I didn't have the folder, and the folder has everything, all the work . . . That's why I got an F." (Roderick & Camburn, 1999, p. 305)

Anna's constant absentmindedness indicates that she still has a long way to go in gaining control of her own behavior and academic performance.

Conditions That Foster Self-Regulation

In Chapter 12, we discuss *parenting styles*, general patterns of behavior that parents use to nurture and guide their children. We briefly describe one parenting style here, as it relates to our discussion of self-regulation. Through **authoritative parenting**, parents and other caregivers establish, justify, and consistently enforce standards for acceptable behavior while also showing emotional warmth, considering children's rights and needs, and including children in decision making. An authoritative environment—whether at home, school, a community center, or elsewhere—appears to promote intrinsic motivation and self-regulation (Baumrind, 1989; Bronson, 2000; Eccles et al., 1998; Reeve, Bolt, & Cai, 1999). In other words, when parents and teachers (and presumably other adults as well) have warm and supportive relationships with children, set reasonable boundaries for behavior, and take everyone's needs into consideration, they create the conditions in which children learn to make appropriate choices and work toward productive goals.

Adults promote self-regulation in another way as well: by modeling self-regulating behaviors (Bronson, 2000; Zimmerman, 1998). For example, in a classic study by Bandura and Mischel (1965), fourth and fifth graders watched adult models make a series of choices between small, immediate rewards and more valuable, delayed ones (e.g., plastic chess pieces available that day versus wooden ones that they could have in 2 weeks). Some models chose the immediate rewards (e.g., saying, "Chess figures are chess figures. I can get much use out of the plastic ones right away," p. 701). Others chose the delayed rewards (e.g., saying, "The wooden chess figures are of much better quality, more attractive, and will last longer. I'll wait two weeks for the better ones," p. 701). Immediately after they had observed the models, and also on a second occasion several weeks later, the children themselves were asked to choose between small, immediate rewards and larger, delayed ones (e.g., a small plastic ball now or a much larger one in 2 weeks). The children were more likely to delay gratification if they had seen the model do likewise.

Children and adolescents are also more likely to become self-regulating when they have age-appropriate opportunities for independence (Feldman & Wentzel, 1990; Silverman & Ragusa, 1990; Zimmerman, 1998). They are most likely to benefit from such opportunities when they are taught the skills they need to direct their own behaviors productively and successfully overcome any challenges they encounter (Belfiore & Hornyak, 1998).

Promoting Self-Regulation

Children and adolescents are more likely to engage in self-regulatory behaviors when they are intrinsically motivated to accomplish certain goals. To encourage self-regulation, then, adults must also encourage intrinsic motivation—for example, by creating conditions in which youngsters have high self-efficacy and can maintain their sense of self-determination (Bronson, 2000). With this caveat in mind, we offer the following recommendations:

■ *Create an orderly and somewhat predictable environment.* Children are in a better position to make wise choices and direct their activities appropriately when they have a reasonable structure to follow, know what to expect in the hours and days ahead, and can reasonably anticipate that certain behaviors will yield certain outcomes (e.g., Bronson, 2000). Communicating guidelines for behavior, establishing regular routines for completing tasks and assignments, identifying the locations of items that children may need during the day (glue, hole punches, dictionaries, atlases, etc.)—all of these strategies help children work productively with minimal guidance from adults.

■ *Provide age-appropriate opportunities for choice and independence.* Older children and adolescents need frequent opportunities to make their own decisions and direct their own activities. Independent assignments, computer-based instruction, group projects, homework, and the like are clearly beneficial for these age groups, particularly when the activities are structured so that children know how to proceed and understand the expectations for their performance (Cooper & Valentine, 2001; Zimmerman, 1998). When they make poor choices, adults should offer constructive feedback that will nurture, rather than dampen, their enthusiasm for independence on future occasions.

Although young children inevitably require some adult supervision to keep them safe, they, too, benefit from having some choice and independence. However, caregivers and teachers must anticipate problems that are likely to arise when children make their own decisions; the adults can then take steps to ensure that children make good choices. For instance, preschool and kindergarten teachers might create a few rules for taking turns and

This girl's willingness to delay gratification—to save the freshly baked cookies for the school picnic—reflects her emerging self-regulation.

sharing materials, designate certain areas of the classroom for messy activities (e.g., painting, working with clay), and put potentially dangerous objects out of reach (Bronson, 2000).

Children with mental and physical disabilities may be in particular need of opportunities for independence, as adults often monitor their behavior and well-being fairly closely (Sands & Wehmeyer, 1996). Such opportunities should, of course, be appropriate for the children's capabilities. For example, a teacher might ask a student with mental retardation to take the daily attendance sheet to the office but remind her that as soon as she has done so, she should return immediately to class (Patton et al., 1996). Or a teacher might give a student who is blind a chance to explore the classroom before other students have arrived, locating various objects in the classroom (wastebasket, pencil sharpener, etc.) and identifying distinctive sounds (e.g., the buzz of a wall clock) that will help the student get his bearings (Wood, 1998).

■ *Provide help and guidance when, but only when, children really need it.*   Being self-regulating doesn't necessarily always mean doing something independently; it also involves knowing when assistance is needed and seeking it out (Karabenick & Sharma, 1994). Adult assistance often provides the scaffolding that children need to succeed at new and challenging tasks. Accordingly, adults should welcome any reasonable requests for help or guidance and not convey the message that children are "dumb" or bothersome for asking (Newman & Schwager, 1992).

Sometimes, however, children—younger ones especially—ask for help when they actually just want company or attention. For instance, if a 4-year-old asks for help on a puzzle, an astute preschool teacher might, after watching the child work at the puzzle, say, "I don't think you need help with this. But I can keep you company for a few minutes if you'd like" (Bronson, 2000).

■ *To guide behavior, use suggestions and rationales more frequently than direct commands.* Young people are more likely to internalize guidelines for their behavior when adults make suggestions about how to accomplish goals successfully and provide a rationale for why some behaviors are unacceptable (Bronson, 2000; Hoffman, 1975). Figure 11–5 shows how Michael Gee, a fifth-grade teacher in Columbus, Ohio, encourages self-regulation by using a handout that explains his expectations for behavior. The handout, distributed during an open house at school, also gives parents important information about how Gee conducts his classroom.

Consistent with what we have learned about cognitive development, younger children respond more favorably to suggestions that are concrete rather than abstract. For example, to avoid incidents of bumping and pushing in the cafeteria, teachers at one school asked students to imagine that they had "magic bubbles" around them. They could keep their bubbles from popping if they kept a safe distance between themselves and others. This simple strategy resulted in fewer behavior problems at lunchtime (Sullivan-DeCarlo, DeFalco, & Roberts, 1998).

■ *Teach specific self-management skills.*   Many research studies indicate that children and adolescents become more self-regulating when they learn specific strategies for controlling and evaluating their own behavior. Such strategies include the following:

- **Self-monitoring:** Children aren't always aware of how frequently they do something wrong or how infrequently they do something right. To help them focus on these things, adults can ask them to observe and record their own behavior. Such self-focused observation and recording often brings about significant improvements in children's academic and social behaviors (K. R. Harris, 1986; Mace & Kratochwill, 1988; Webber, Scheuermann, McCall, & Coleman, 1993).
- **Self-instructions:** Sometimes children simply need a reminder about how to respond in particular situations. By teaching them how to talk themselves through these situations, adults give them a means through which they remind *themselves* about appropriate actions, thereby helping them to control their own behavior. Such a strategy is often effective in helping children with poor impulse control (Casey & Burton, 1982; Meichenbaum, 1985).
- **Self-evaluation:** At home, in school, and in public, children's behaviors are frequently judged by others—by their parents, teachers, peers, and so on. But to become self-regulating, children must eventually learn to judge their own behavior.

self-monitoring
Process of observing and recording one's own behavior.

self-instructions
Instructions that people give themselves as they perform a complex behavior.

self-evaluation
Judging one's own performance or behavior in accordance with predetermined criteria.

MY BROAD GOALS

- Plan and implement a balanced curriculum.

- Help students develop a repertoire of skills and styles of working (open-ended assignments/discrete assignments; collaboration/individual).

- Get students engaged in mental activity; emphasize learning and being a strategic thinker.

- Help students to be both organized and flexible, deal with a schedule, and set priorities for time and things done.

DISCIPLINE

Overarching Golden Rule
Treat others as you would like to be treated.

BASIC RULES

1. Be responsible for your own actions.
2. Use work time for school work; use recess time for play.
3. Appreciate other people; respect the rights of others.
4. Make your behavior appropriate for the situation.

I try to be fair and not play favorites. Everyone is valued and respected. I run the classroom to take care of everyone. The focus is on correcting the behaviors that need correcting so that we develop habit patterns of behavior that serve instructional goals.

My appeal: You've been taught at home for years how to behave. You have a good head—now use it.

Typical fifth-grade problems:

1. Cliques and excluding others—being angry at lunch, friends again after school. A problem especially with the girls.
2. Silliness and not setting boundaries for appropriate behavior, such as bringing recess into the classroom. A problem especially with the boys.
3. Too much undirected talk, talk across desks and across the room, especially during transition times.
4. Restroom problems—talking loudly in the hallways, messing around and loitering in the restrooms.
5. Whininess and sneakiness. Talk to me honestly and openly about problems.
6. "Romance" (going-with) talk or teasing. These are absolutely not allowed in the classroom.

FIGURE 11–5 A fifth-grade teacher's goals and expectations. In this handout, Michael Gee describes his expectations for *students'* behavior and encourages age-appropriate self-regulation.

Adapted with the permission of Michael Gee, Barrington Elementary School, Columbus, Ohio.

For instance, adults might have children complete self-assessment instruments that show them what to look for in their own performance (Paris & Ayres, 1994). At the secondary school level (and perhaps even sooner), young people might even play a role in identifying the criteria by which their performance should be evaluated.

The Development and Practice feature "Teaching Self-Management Skills" illustrates these and other self-management skills. Adults must, of course, monitor children's ability to use them and make adjustments accordingly. For instance, children with ADHD tend to have more success with self-monitoring and self-evaluation than with self-instructions. Even so, they often need adult monitoring and reinforcement to develop and maintain appropriate behaviors (Barkley, 1998).

One place in which motivation and self-regulation are especially important is school. For example, when judging children's readiness for kindergarten and first grade, teachers are more likely to consider their ability to pay attention and stay focused on classroom activities than their existing knowledge and cognitive skills (Blair, 2002). However, as you will recall from our earlier discussion of cognitive perspectives, motivation is often a product of the context in which children find themselves, rather than something they bring with them from home each day. We therefore now look at the effects of the school environment on children's and adolescents' motivation and behavior in the classroom.

Effects of the School Environment

Mary dropped out of school after the eleventh grade. In an interview, she explains why:

Mary: . . . These public schools are filled with violence and things. You know, people getting shot in the next classroom. It is not an environment for learning, you know what I mean. I just wasn't gonna risk my life to go to school. To me it wasn't that important.

DEVELOPMENT AND PRACTICE

Teaching Self-Management Skills

■ Have children observe and record their own behavior.

When a student has trouble staying on task during class activities, her teacher asks her to stop and reflect on her behavior every 10 minutes (with the aid of an egg timer) and determine whether she was doing what she was supposed to be doing during each interval. The student uses the checklist shown below to record her observations. Within a couple of weeks, the student's on-task behavior has noticeably improved.

Self-Observation Record for _____Karen_____

Every ten minutes, put a mark to show how well you have been staying on task.

    +   means you were almost always on task
    1/2 means you were on task about half the time
    −   means you were hardly ever on task

9:00-9:10	9:10-9:20	9:20-9:30	9:30-9:40	9:40-9:50	9:50-10:00
+	+	−	+	1/2	−
10:00-10:10	10:10-10:20	10:20-10:30	10:30-10:40	10:40-10:50	10:50-11:00
1/2	−	recess		+	1/2
11:00-11:10	11:10-11:20	11:20-11:30	11:30-11:40	11:40-11:50	11:50-12:00

■ Teach children instructions they can give themselves to remind them of what they need to do.

A school psychologist helps a student control his impulsive behavior on multiple-choice tests by having him mentally say to himself as he reads each question: "Read the entire question. Then look at each answer carefully and decide whether it is correct or incorrect. Then choose the answer that seems *most* correct."

■ Encourage children to evaluate their own performance.

Early in the season, the coach of a boys' baseball team videotapes each boy as he practices batting, pitching, and fielding ground balls. The coach then models good form for each of these activities and lists several things the boys should look for as they watch themselves on tape.

■ Teach children to reinforce themselves for appropriate behavior.

A teacher suggests that her students might develop more regular study habits by making a favorite activity—for example, shooting baskets, watching television, or calling a friend on the telephone—contingent on completing their homework first.

■ Provide strategies that children can use to solve interpersonal problems.

A school counselor teaches children a sequence to follow when they find themselves in a conflict with a classmate: *Identify* the source of the conflict, *listen* to each other's perspectives, *verbalize* each other's perspectives, and *develop* a solution that provides a reasonable compromise.

Interviewer:	What do you think about the actual education, putting aside the violence, what did you think about the actual school?
Mary:	In these public schools? Well, by the time they got the rowdy class to set down, the period was over.
Interviewer:	You just felt like it was pointless?
Mary:	Yeah. I was like going to school to take your life in hand, to set there and have them try to get the class together and once they did, it was time to leave. It was just like, this is wasting my time as well as the teacher's. . . . There was another thing—I knew a lot of people in this school, I had a lot of friends. I had friends who would just bring you down, I'll tell you that much. . . . You know it would be like, "Oh, well, we can cut this class today. We can always make it up tomorrow." But there's always—there's never a tomorrow. . . . "We'll cut class today. We'll go to class tomorrow. We'll cut class the next day." It's endless and it's useless 'cause you're just wasting the teacher's time and your own. (dialogue from Way, 1998, p. 200; format adapted)

Mary's remarks suggest three important characteristics of a productive classroom environment. First, students feel physically and psychologically safe. Second, teachers and students are focused on important instructional objectives, not on disruptive behavior. And third, students believe that their classmates are, like them, interested in learning and achieving and so do not, as Mary puts it, "bring you down."

In this section, we look at how adults can create classroom and school environments that effectively motivate children and adolescents to work hard and acquire new knowledge and skills. We first consider the role of schools in socializing children and adolescents to behave in acceptable ways in the adult world. We then examine the effects of classroom climate and teacher expectations on students' social-emotional well-being and academic achievement. Finally, we consider how teachers and students can create a *sense of community* in which they work together to maximize all students' learning and development.

The Role of Schools in Socialization

Beginning early in their lives, most children learn that there are certain things that they can or should do and other things that they definitely should not do. For example, many parents teach their toddlers not to hit other children, first-grade teachers ask their students to sit and listen quietly when someone else is speaking, and high school teachers expect their students to turn in homework assignments on time. As noted in Chapter 9, such efforts to teach children and adolescents how to behave appropriately in their society are collectively known as *socialization*.

Most children learn their earliest lessons about society's expectations from their parents, who teach them personal hygiene, table manners, rudimentary interpersonal skills (e.g., saying "please" and "thank you"), and so on. Yet teachers become equally important **socialization agents** once children reach preschool or elementary school. For example, teachers typically expect and encourage behaviors such as these:

- Behaving in an orderly fashion
- Showing respect for authority figures
- Controlling impulses
- Following instructions
- Completing assigned tasks in a timely manner
- Working independently
- Helping and cooperating with classmates
- Striving for academic excellence

When behaviors expected of students at school differ from those expected at home, children may become confused, nonproductive, and sometimes even resistant (Hess & Holloway, 1984). In other words, they may experience some **culture shock** when they first enter school.

Teachers' expectations for behavior—often unstated—are sometimes known as the *hidden curriculum* of the classroom (Anyon, 1988; Chafel, 1997; P. W. Jackson, 1988). An additional aspect of the hidden curriculum is the message that teachers communicate about the nature of academic learning and academic subject matter (Anyon, 1988; Chafel, 1997; Doyle, 1983). Unfortunately, this message often portrays schoolwork as memorizing facts, getting the right answer, doing tasks in a particular way and, in general, getting things done as quickly as possible. Understandably, students have little reason to feel intrinsically motivated under such circumstances and may passively or actively resist, as the following dialogue between a teacher and several students illustrates:

Educators should help students see their schoolwork as activities that enable them to achieve important knowledge and skills, not just as things to "get done."

Teacher:	I will put some problems on the board. You are to divide.
Child:	We got to divide?
Teacher:	Yes.
Several children:	(*Groan*) Not again, Mr. B., we done this yesterday.
Child:	Do we put the date?
Teacher:	Yes. I hope we remember we work in silence. You're supposed to do it on white paper. I'll explain it later.
Child:	Somebody broke my pencil. (*Crash*—a child falls out of his chair.)
Child:	(*repeats*) Mr. B., somebody broke my *pencil*!
Child:	Are we going to be here all morning? (Anyon, 1988, p. 367)

In this situation, the teacher presents math problems merely as "things that need to be done," and the children clearly have little interest in the assignment.

Effects of Classroom Climate

The dialogue just presented is troublesome in two additional ways as well. First, the teacher communicates a message of control ("You are to divide. . . . You're supposed to do it on white paper") that probably undermines students' sense of self-determination. Second, the teacher comes across as aloof and unconcerned about students' needs. More generally, the teacher's remarks seem to create a cold, nonnurturing classroom climate that is hardly conducive to students' learning.

socialization agent
Person who plays a key role in preparing youngsters to act in ways deemed by society to be appropriate and responsible.

culture shock
Sense of confusion that occurs when one encounters an environment with expectations for behavior very different than those in one's home environment.

By **classroom climate**, we mean the overall psychological atmosphere of the learning environment. From our earlier discussions of motivation and self-regulation, we can derive several general principles concerning the classroom climate in which students at all levels—preschool, elementary, and secondary alike—are most apt to thrive:

- Teachers communicate genuine caring, respect, and support for students.
- Students feel both physically and psychologically safe; for instance, they know that they can make mistakes without being ridiculed by their teacher or classmates, and that they can seek help from others when they need it.
- Teachers adopt an authoritative approach to instruction and classroom management, setting clear guidelines for behavior but, in the process, also considering students' needs and involving students in decision making.
- Teachers provide some order and structure to guide classroom assignments and procedures.
- Teachers give students opportunities to engage in appropriate self-chosen and self-directed activities.

Classrooms that reflect these principles are, in general, highly productive ones: Students have higher self-esteem and self-efficacy, are better behaved and more self-regulating, have a mastery orientation toward their schoolwork, and achieve at higher levels (Davis & Thomas, 1989; deCharms, 1984; Roderick & Camburn, 1999; A. M. Ryan & Patrick, 2001; Scott-Little & Holloway, 1992; Wentzel, 1999; Wentzel & Wigfield, 1998).

Such classrooms may be particularly beneficial for students growing up in impoverished home environments (S. C. Diamond, 1991; Levine & Lezotte, 1995; Werner & Smith, 1992). Many students from low-income neighborhoods are exposed to crime and violence nearly every day; their world may be one in which they can rarely control the course of events. A classroom that is dependable and predictable can engender a sense of self-determination that is difficult to come by elsewhere; hence, it can be a place to which they look forward to coming each day.

Comparing Elementary and Secondary Classroom Environments   Elementary school classrooms are typically warm, nurturing ones in which teachers get to know 20 or 30 students very well and so are in an ideal position to foster each student's cognitive, personal, and social development. Students also get to know one another quite well: They often work together on academic tasks and may even see themselves as members of a classroom "family." As students make the transition to secondary school, they simultaneously encounter many changes in their educational environment:

- The school is larger and has more students.
- Students have several teachers at a time, and each teacher has many students. Teacher-student relationships are therefore more superficial and less personal than they were in elementary school.
- There is more whole-class instruction, with less individualized instruction that takes into account each student's particular needs.
- Classes are less socially cohesive; students may not know their classmates very well and may be reluctant to call on peers for assistance.
- Competition among students (e.g., for popular classes and spots on an athletic team) is more common.
- Students have more independence and responsibility for their own learning; for instance, they sometimes have relatively unstructured assignments to be accomplished over a 2- or 3-week period, and they must take the initiative to seek help when they are struggling.
- Standards for assigning grades are more rigorous, so students may earn lower grades than they did in elementary school. Grades are often assigned on a comparative basis, with only the highest-achieving students getting As and Bs. (Eccles & Midgley, 1989; Harter, 1996; Hine & Fraser, 2002; Roderick & Camburn, 1999; Wentzel & Wigfield, 1998; Wigfield et al., 1996)

This poster in a middle school corridor (shown in the Environments/Early Adolescence clip of the Observation CD) illustrates one important element of an effective classroom climate: the feeling that one is physically and psychologically safe at school.

classroom climate
General psychological atmosphere of the classroom.

Furthermore, previously formed friendships can be disrupted as students move to new (and sometimes different) schools (Pellegrini & Bartini, 2000). And, of course, students are also dealing with the physiological changes that accompany puberty and adolescence.

For many students, these changes lead to decreased confidence, lower self-esteem, and considerable anxiety. Students develop less positive attitudes about school and academic subjects and show less intrinsic motivation to learn. Focus on social relationships increases, academic achievement drops, and some students become emotionally disengaged from the school environment—a disengagement that may eventually result in dropping out of school (Eccles & Midgley, 1989; Urdan & Maehr, 1995; Wigfield et al., 1996). Urban youth (especially males and minorities) are particularly at risk for making a rough transition from elementary to secondary school. For instance, in one recent study, 42% of students in the Chicago public schools failed at least one major course in the first semester of 9th grade. By 10th grade, 50% had failed at least one course (Roderick & Camburn, 1999).

Middle School as a Mechanism for Easing the Transition The concept of *middle school* was developed to ease the transition to secondary school (e.g., Kohut, 1988; Lounsbury, 1984). In principle, middle schools are designed to accommodate the unique needs of preadolescents and early adolescents, including their anxieties about more demanding academic expectations, the changing nature of their social relationships, and their own rapidly maturing bodies. Ideally, middle schools give attention to students' personal, emotional, and social development as well as to academic achievement and are attuned to students' individual differences and unique needs. They teach learning and study skills that help students move toward increasing independence as learners. At many middle schools, teams of four or five teachers work with a subset of the student population (perhaps 75 to 125 students per team), coordinating activities and exchanging information about how particular students are progressing. Such strategies often ease the transition to a secondary school format; even so, many young adolescents have considerable difficulty adjusting to a middle school setting (Eccles et al., 1998; Hine & Fraser, 2002; Roderick & Camburn, 1999; Rudolph, Lambert, Clark, & Kurlakowsky, 2001).

Students who make a smooth transition to a secondary school environment are more likely to be successful there and, as a result, are more likely to graduate from high school (Roderick & Camburn, 1999; Wigfield et al., 1996). The Development and Practice feature "Easing the Transition to Middle and Secondary School" suggests several strategies for educators at the middle school and high school levels.

Teacher Expectations: A Self-Fulfilling Prophecy?

As we have seen, teachers have expectations for how their students should behave and perform in the classroom; for instance, they expect students to follow instructions, complete assigned tasks, and treat adults and classmates with respect. But teachers also form expectations about how students *are likely* to perform. Teachers typically draw conclusions about their students relatively early in the school year, forming opinions about each one's strengths, weaknesses, and potential for academic success. In many instances, teachers size up their students fairly accurately: They know which ones need help with reading skills, which ones have short attention spans, which ones have trouble working together in the same cooperative group, and so on, and they can adapt their instruction and assistance accordingly (Goldenberg, 1992; Good & Brophy, 1994; Good & Nichols, 2001).

But even the best teachers occasionally make inaccurate assessments. For instance, teachers often underestimate the abilities of students who

- Are physically unattractive
- Misbehave frequently in class
- Speak in dialects other than Standard English
- Are members of ethnic minority groups

DEVELOPMENT AND PRACTICE

Easing the Transition to Middle and Secondary School

■ Provide a means through which every student can feel part of a small, close-knit group.

In September, a ninth-grade math teacher establishes *base groups* of three or four students who provide support and assistance for one another throughout the school year. At the beginning or end of every class period, the teacher gives the groups 5 minutes to help one another with questions and concerns about daily lessons and homework assignments.

■ Find time to meet one-on-one with every student.

Early in the school year, while his classes are working on a variety of cooperative learning activities, a middle school social studies teacher schedules individual appointments with each of his students. In these meetings, he searches for common interests that he and his students share and encourages the students to seek him out whenever they need help with academic or personal problems. Throughout the semester, he continues to touch base with individual students (often during lunch or before or after school) to see how they are doing.

■ Teach students the skills they need to be successful independent learners.

After discovering that many of her students have little idea of how to take effective notes in class, a high school science teacher distributes a daily "notes skeleton" that guides them through the note-taking process that day. For instance, before a lesson on the various diseases associated with poor nutrition, she distributes a sheet like the one shown at right. As the year progresses, she reduces the specific nature of these handouts; by the end of the school year, the handouts simply have four sections— "Topic of the Lesson," "Definitions," "Important Ideas," and "Examples"— that students fill in as they take notes.

■ Assign grades on the basis of mastery (not on comparisons with peers), and provide reasonable opportunities for improvement.

A junior high school language arts teacher requires students to submit two drafts of every essay and short story he assigns; he gives them the option of submitting additional drafts as well. He judges students' compositions on four criteria: cohesiveness, word usage, grammar, and spelling. He explains and illustrates each of these criteria and gives ample feedback on every draft that students turn in.

```
Topic: DIET AND DISEASES

Scurvy:
    Caused by: _____
    Symptoms:  _____

Rickets:
    Caused by: _____
    Symptoms:  _____

Beriberi:
    Caused by: _____
    Symptoms:  _____
    _____

Anemia:
    Caused by: _____
    Symptoms:  _____
    _____
```

- Are recent immigrants
- Come from low-income backgrounds
  (Banks & Banks, 1995; Bennett, Gottesman, Rock, & Cerullo, 1993; Knapp & Woolverton, 1995; McLoyd, 1998b; Oakes & Guiton, 1995; Ritts, Patterson, & Tubbs, 1992)

All too often, teachers attribute students' performance to ability levels that are relatively fixed and stable; in other words, they have an *entity view* of intelligence (Oakes & Guiton, 1995; Reyna, 2000). Their beliefs about these "stable" abilities affect their expectations for students' future performance, which in turn lead them to behave differently toward different students. For example, when teachers have high expectations for students, they create a warmer classroom climate, interact with students more frequently, provide more opportunities for students to respond, and give more positive feedback; they also present more course material and more challenging topics. In contrast, when teachers have low expectations for certain students, they offer fewer opportunities for speaking in class, ask easier questions, give less feedback about students' responses, and present few if any challenging assignments (Babad, 1993; Good & Brophy, 1994; Graham, 1990; Rosenthal, 1994).

Most children and adolescents are well aware of their teachers' differential treatment of individual students and use such treatment to draw logical inferences about their own and others' abilities (Butler, 1994; Good & Nichols, 2001; R. S. Weinstein, 1993). When their teachers repeatedly give them low-ability messages, they may begin to see themselves as their teachers see them. Furthermore, their behavior may mirror their self-perceptions; for example, they may exert little effort on academic tasks, or they may frequently misbehave in class (Marachi, Friedel, & Midgley, 2001; Murdock, 1999). In some cases, then, teachers' expectations and attributions may lead to a **self-fulfilling prophecy:** What teachers expect students to achieve becomes what students actually do achieve.

Certainly teacher expectations don't always lead to self-fulfilling prophecies. In some cases, teachers follow up on low expectations by offering the kinds of instruction and assistance that students need to improve, and students do improve (Goldenberg, 1992). In other cases, students may develop an "I'll show *you*" attitude that spurs them on to greater effort and achievement than a teacher anticipated (Good & Nichols, 2001). In still other cases, assertive parents may step in and offer evidence that their children are more capable than a teacher initially thought (Good & Nichols, 2001).

To what extent do teacher expectations affect students' classroom performance and overall academic growth? Research on this topic yields mixed results (Eccles et al., 1998; Goldenberg, 1992; R. Rosenthal, 1994). Some research indicates that girls, students from low-income families, and students from ethnic minority groups are more susceptible to teacher expectations than boys from middle-income, European American backgrounds (Graham, 1990; Jussim, Eccles, & Madon, 1996). Teacher expectations also appear to have a greater influence in the early elementary school years (grades 1 and 2), in the first year of secondary school, and, more generally, within the first few weeks of school—in other words, at times when students are entering new and unfamiliar school environments (Jussim et al., 1996; Kuklinski & Weinstein, 2001; Raudenbush, 1984; R. S. Weinstein, Madison, & Kuklinski, 1995).

Being Optimistic About Students' Performance A characteristic consistently found in effective schools is high expectations for student performance (Phillips, 1997; Roderick & Camburn, 1999). Even if students' initial academic performance is low, educators and other professionals must remember that cognitive abilities and skills can and do change over time, especially when environmental conditions are conducive to such change. We suggest three strategies to help adults maintain a realistic, yet also optimistic outlook on what young people can accomplish:

■ *Learn more about students' backgrounds and home environments.* Adults are most likely to develop low expectations for students' performance when they have rigid stereotypes about students from certain ethnic or socioeconomic groups (McLoyd, 1998b; Reyna, 2000). And such stereotypes are often the result of ignorance about students' home environments and cultures (Alexander, Entwisle, & Thompson, 1987). Education is the key here: Teachers and other school personnel must learn as much as they can about students' backgrounds and local communities. When they have a clear picture of students' families, activities, habits, and values, they are far more likely to think of students as *individuals*—each with a unique set of talents and skills—than as stereotypical members of a particular group.

■ *Collaborate with colleagues to maximize academic success on a schoolwide basis.* Educators are more likely to have high expectations for students when they are confident in their own ability to help students achieve academic and social success (Ashton, 1985; R. S. Weinstein et al., 1995). Consider the case of one inner-city high school. For many years, teachers at the school believed that their low-achieving students, most of whom were from low-income families, were simply unmotivated to learn. They also saw themselves, their colleagues, and school administrators as being ineffective and uninvested in helping these students succeed. To counteract such tendencies, the school faculty began holding regular 2-hour meetings in which they

- Read research related to low-achieving and at-risk students
- Explored various hypotheses as to why their students were having difficulty
- Developed, refined, and evaluated innovative strategies for helping their students succeed
- Established a collaborative atmosphere in which, working together, they could take positive action

self-fulfilling prophecy
Phenomenon in which an adult's expectations for a child's performance directly or indirectly bring about that level of performance.

Such meetings helped the teachers form higher expectations for students' achievement and a better understanding of what they themselves could do to help the students achieve (R. S. Weinstein et al., 1995).

■ *Be sure your attributions for students' successes and failures are accurate.* Young people can repeat their successes and address their failures only when they have accurate information about the causes of those outcomes. Yet all too often, youngsters get messages from adults—sometimes explicit, sometimes more subtle—that communicate inaccurate attributions. For instance, as we mentioned earlier, educators often attribute children's poor performance to low and stable ability levels, and such attributions may be revealed in pity, praise for easy accomplishments, or tendency to discourage pursuit of challenging tasks. Alternatively, teachers and other adults may attribute poor performance to low motivation: A student "isn't trying very hard" or "doesn't care." When children who exert a great deal of effort fail at a difficult task and are then told that they didn't try hard enough, they are likely to conclude that they simply don't have the ability to perform the task successfully (Graham, 1991; Stipek, 1996).

We should remind ourselves of two points made earlier in the chapter: Children like being successful (it gives them a *sense of competence*), and motivation is often a function of the particular learning environment rather than something that children carry around inside of them from place to place. We should remind ourselves, too, of points made in Chapters 4 and 5: Children learn and achieve more successfully when they have the scaffolding to accomplish challenging tasks and when they use effective cognitive strategies. Ideally, teachers and other professionals provide such scaffolding and teach such strategies.

In some cases, educators place the blame elsewhere, perhaps by pointing a finger at parents who are assumed to be shirking their parental responsibilities (e.g., Dorris, 1989). In fact, the great majority of parents want the best for their children and do many things to support their children's development and learning. Parenting children is a stressful job under even the best of circumstances. The stress is magnified several times over when children have significant disabilities, and parents of these children need support, not blame, from professionals.

Creating a Sense of Community in Classrooms and Schools

Earlier we suggested that teachers should minimize competitive situations. Competitions among *groups* of students can be effective motivators if all groups have equal ability and if the final outcome is determined more by student effort than by uncontrollable factors (Stipek, 1996). Under most circumstances, however, competitive events are counterproductive: They focus students' attention on performance (rather than mastery) goals, decrease students' self-efficacy and sense of competence, and increase the likelihood that students will attribute their failures to low ability (Ames, 1984; Deci & Ryan, 1992; Nicholls, 1984; Spaulding, 1992).

Cooperative classrooms, in which students work with and for one another, rather than against one another, are more motivating and productive learning environments, largely because they increase the likelihood that students will be successful (Ames, 1984; Deci & Ryan, 1985; A. M. Ryan & Patrick, 2001). Cooperative classrooms appear to be especially beneficial for girls (Eccles, 1989; Inglehart, Brown, & Vida, 1994) and for students from ethnic minority groups that value group achievements over individual accomplishments (Grant & Gomez, 2001; L. S. Miller, 1995; Suina & Smolkin, 1994).

Many experts encourage teachers to create a *sense of community* in the classroom—a sense that teachers and students have shared goals, respect and support one another's efforts, and believe that everyone makes an important contribution (Hom & Battistich, 1995; Kim, Solomon, & Roberts, 1995; Lickona, 1991; Osterman, 2000). Several strategies can help create a sense of classroom community:

- Using interactive instructional methods, such as class discussions and cooperative learning
- Soliciting students' ideas and opinions, and incorporating them into discussions and activities

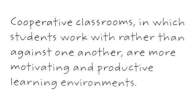

Cooperative classrooms, in which students work with rather than against one another, are more motivating and productive learning environments.

- Creating mechanisms through which students can help make the classroom run smoothly and efficiently (e.g., assigning various "helper" roles to students on a rotating basis)
- Emphasizing such prosocial values as sharing and cooperation
- Providing opportunities for students to help one another (e.g., by asking, "Who has a problem that someone else might be able to help you solve?")
- Providing public recognition of students' contributions to the overall success of the classroom

  (Emmer, Evertson, Clements, & Worsham, 1994; Kim et al., 1995; Lickona, 1991; Osterman, 2000)

When students share a sense of community, they are more likely to exhibit prosocial behavior, express positive attitudes about school, be intrinsically motivated to learn, and achieve at high levels. Furthermore, a sense of classroom community is associated with lower rates of disruptive classroom behavior, emotional distress, truancy, violence, drug use, and dropping out (Hom & Battistich, 1995; Kim et al., 1995; Osterman, 2000).

Ideally, educators should create a sense of community not only in individual classrooms but also in the school as a whole (Battistich et al., 1995; Battistich, Solomon, Watson, & Schaps, 1997; A. L. Brown & Campione, 1994). In schools that operate as true communities, students get the same message from all school personnel: that everyone is working together to help students become informed, successful, and productive citizens, and that students can and should help one another as well. When teachers and other school personnel communicate an overall sense of school community, students have more positive attitudes toward school, are more motivated to achieve at high levels, and exhibit more prosocial behavior, and students from diverse backgrounds are more likely to interact with one another. Furthermore, teachers have higher expectations for students' achievement and a greater sense of self-efficacy about their own teaching effectiveness (Battistich et al., 1995, 1997).

School environments clearly play a significant role in children's and adolescents' motivation to achieve academic success and to become productive, caring citizens. Schools are not the only environments that nurture (or in some cases stifle) motivation and appropriate behavior, however. Families, peers, and broader environmental contexts—cultural practices, socioeconomic conditions, neighborhood support, messages in the media, and so on—play equally important roles. We consider such influences in the next three chapters.

CASE STUDY: DERRIKA

In a study conducted in the Chicago public schools, Roderick and Camburn (1999) investigated the academic progress of students who had recently made the transition from relatively small elementary or middle schools to much larger high schools. Many students in their research sample experienced considerable difficulty making the transition from eighth to ninth grade, as the case of Derrika illustrates:

Derrika liked to be challenged and felt her eighth-grade teachers cared and made her work. Derrika entered high school with plans to go to college and felt that her strong sense of self would get her through: "Nobody stops me from doing good because I really wanna go to college . . . Nobody in my family's been to college . . . so I want to be the first person to go to college and finish."

Derrika began having problems in eighth grade. Despite average achievement scores and previously high grades, she ended eighth grade with a C average and failed science. In high school, her performance deteriorated further. At the end of the first semester, Derrika received Fs in all her major subjects, had 20 absences, almost 33 class cuts for the last two periods of the day, and had been suspended for a food fight. Derrika is vague in explaining her performance, except for biology, in which she admits, "I don't never get up on time." She feels that her elementary school teachers were better because, "If you don't want to learn, they are going to make you learn," while her current teachers think,

Now go to our Companion Website to assess your understanding of chapter content with a Practice Quiz, apply what you've learned in Essay Questions, and broaden your knowledge with links to related Developmental Psychology Web sites. Go to www.prenhall.com/mcdevitt.

"If you fail, you just fail. It ain't our fault. You're the one that's dumb." (Roderick & Camburn, 1999, p. 304)

- Given what you've learned about the development of motivation and self-regulation, how might you explain Derrika's sudden academic difficulties beginning in the eighth grade?
- To what factors did Derrika's elementary school teachers apparently attribute any academic failures that she had? To what factors do her high school teachers attribute her failures?
- What strategies might a teacher, counselor, or other practitioner use to help Derrika get back on the road to academic success?

SUMMARY

Motivation

Motivation energizes, directs, and sustains behavior. It can be either intrinsic (emanating from characteristics within a person or inherent in the task being performed) or extrinsic (emanating from factors external to both the person and the task). Children who are intrinsically motivated are more likely to pay attention and engage in effective learning strategies than children who are extrinsically motivated.

Behaviorists propose that the sources of motivation come largely from the consequences (e.g., rewards, punishments) that result from people's behaviors. As children develop, they work more for such reinforcers as praise, attention, and good grades than for reinforcers that satisfy basic physiological needs. They also learn that some behaviors are reinforced only occasionally, and they become increasingly able to delay gratification.

Social cognitive theorists propose that by observing the consequences of their own and others' behaviors, children form expectations about the future consequences that various responses are likely to bring. Children often imitate other people and are especially likely to imitate models whom they see as competent, prestigious, powerful, and "gender appropriate."

Trait theorists propose that some motives and needs vary considerably from one person to the next. For instance, some children have a high need for affiliation, in that they want to spend much of their time interacting with others (especially peers), whereas other children have a much lower need for affiliation. Children also differ in their needs for approval from adults and peers. With age comes an increasing need to gain the approval and affection of peers, often paired with a drop in the need for the approval and affection of adults.

Cognitive theorists focus on the nature of the mental phenomena (interests, goals, attributions, etc.) involved in motivation. They propose that intrinsic motivation is a multifaceted entity; for example, depending on the situation, it may involve curiosity, a need for cognitive consistency, interest in particular topics, or the perception that a particular skill has relevance for one's long-term goals. Cognitive theorists also suggest that children and adolescents have numerous goals (goals related to academic achievement, social relationships, future careers, etc.) and differing degrees of success in coordinating multiple goals. They argue, too, that children and adolescents attribute successes and failures to a variety of possible causes, and such explanations influence future behaviors.

Each of the four perspectives just described contributes to our understanding of children's motivation and its development. For instance, behaviorists suggest that extrinsic reinforcers (attention, praise, special privileges) are sometimes necessary to bring about desired behavior change. Social cognitive theorists emphasize the importance of exposing children to good role models who have characteristics and backgrounds similar to children's own. Trait theorists remind us that different children may require different motivational strategies; for example, some will enjoy and benefit from group projects more than others. Cognitive theorists suggest that adults encourage children to emphasize mastery goals (where the focus is on learning) rather than performance goals (where the focus is on creating a good impression). In addition, adults should communicate the belief that successes and failures are more a function of effort and learning strategies (temporary factors over which children have considerable control) than of natural ability (a more permanent entity over which children have very little influence).

Development of Self-Regulation

With age and experience, most children and adolescents become increasingly able to regulate and direct their own behavior and learning. They internalize the rules and restrictions that adults have imposed, more effectively control their emotional reactions, and can evaluate their own performance with increasing accuracy. Nevertheless, most high school students do not regulate their own behaviors as effectively as adults do. Adults promote self-regulation through authoritative parenting, in which they establish definite guidelines for behavior while also attending to children's needs, listening to children's ideas and perspectives, and providing a reasonable rationale for any requests. Adults can also model self-regulating behaviors, give children age-appropriate opportunities for independence, and teach specific self-management skills.

Effects of the School Environment

Schools play a major role in the socialization of children and adolescents: Teachers expect and encourage certain behaviors at school that parents and other caregivers may or may not require at home. Through their *own* behaviors (e.g., the extent to which they give guidelines for behavior, communicate caring and concern, and provide justifications for requests), teachers create a particular climate (psychological atmosphere) that may either foster or impede children's productivity. Furthermore, teachers form particular expectations about how individual students are likely to perform, and such expectations may, by affecting how teachers interact with students, lead to a self-fulfilling prophecy.

Classrooms and schools in which most students learn effectively are cooperative rather than competitive ones. Effective teachers create a sense of community in which teachers and students have shared goals, respect and support one another's efforts, and believe that everyone makes an important contribution. A sense of community may be especially important for students who are at risk for academic failure.

KEY CONCEPTS

motivation (p. 456)
intrinsic motivation (p. 456)
extrinsic motivation (p. 456)
behaviorism (p. 456)
operant conditioning (p. 456)
reinforcer (p. 456)
positive reinforcement (p. 457)
negative reinforcement (p. 457)
primary reinforcer (p. 457)
secondary reinforcer (p. 457)
delay of gratification (p. 458)

social cognitive theory (p. 458)
vicarious reinforcement (p. 459)
vicarious punishment (p. 459)
trait theory (p. 460)
need for relatedness (p. 460)
need for affiliation (p. 460)
need for approval (p. 461)
achievement motivation (p. 462)
sense of competence (p. 464)
sense of self-determination
    (p. 464)

internalized motivation (p. 466)
mastery goal (p. 467)
performance goal (p. 467)
attribution (p. 469)
entity view of ability (p. 470)
incremental view of ability
    (p. 470)
mastery orientation (p. 471)
learned helplessness (p. 471)
student at risk (p. 480)
self-regulation (p. 480)

self-reinforcement (p. 481)
authoritative parenting (p. 484)
self-monitoring (p. 486)
self-instructions (p. 486)
self-evaluation (p. 486)
socialization agent (p. 489)
culture shock (p. 489)
classroom climate (p. 490)
self-fulfilling prophecy (p. 493)

Sydney, age 5

Crystal, age 13

Robin, age 15

Families

CASE STUDY: CEDRIC AND BARBARA JENNINGS

Cedric Lavar Jennings is a senior at Ballou High School, an inner-city school in Washington, D.C. Throughout his school career, his grades have been exemplary, and he has recently learned that he has been accepted at Brown University for the following year.

Cedric and his mother Barbara are very close. They have been a family of two since Cedric was born. They live in a lower-income neighborhood on 16th Street, where crack cocaine dealers regularly do business at both ends of the block and gunshots are frequent background noise at night. Despite such an environment, Cedric has flourished, in large part because of his mother's support. Not only is he a high achiever, but he is also a very likeable young man with a strong moral code.

One night in January, Barbara and Cedric attend the Parent-Teacher-Student Association (PTSA) meeting at Ballou. After the meeting, they go to Cedric's homeroom, where Ms. Wingfield, the homeroom teacher, is handing out first-semester grade reports. Cedric is appalled to discover a B on his grade sheet. In *A Hope in the Unseen*, Suskind (1998) reports what happens next:

> "I got a B in physics! I can't believe it."
>
> He begins ranting about the cheating in his class, about how he thinks a lot of other kids cheated. . . . Barbara remembers that he mentioned something about this a week ago—but she dismissed the whole matter.
>
> Squeezed into a school desk next to him, she wants to tell Cedric that it doesn't matter. None of it. Some small hubbub about cheating and grades is meaningless now that he's been admitted to Brown, the top college acceptance of any Ballou student in years.
>
> But, of course, he knows all that, too. And the more dismissive her look, the more rabid he becomes. Then she gets it: it's about her watching over him, defending him, always being there. ". . . I mean, what are *we* going to do?!" he shouts at the end of his furious soliloquy about what's right and fair and just.
>
> She's up. "Well, Lavar [she usually calls him by his middle name], we'll just have to go have a word with that teacher." A second later, they're stomping together through the halls, headed for the physics classroom of an unsuspecting Mr. Momen. They find that he is alone. He turns and offers greetings as they enter, but Cedric launches right in—the whole diatribe, offered with added verve from his rehearsal with his mom.
>
> Mr. Momen, a wry, sometimes sarcastic man in his mid-forties, mournfully shakes his head, a helmet of gray-flecked hair. "Cedric, you got a B for the marking period," he says in precise, accented English. "The test for you is irrefutable. The curve says yours is a B, and that, for you, is a B for the marking period. So, okay. That's it, yes?"
>
> "But kids are cheating! You leave the room and they open the book. Lots of them. You don't know what goes on. You shouldn't leave the room, that's when it starts. It ends up that I get penalized 'cause I won't cheat."
>
> "Cedric, stop. I can't, myself, accuse all of them of cheating," says Mr. Momen, shrugging.
>
> Barbara watches the give-and-take, realizing that the teacher has artfully shoved Cedric into a rhetorical corner by placing her son's single voice against the silent majority—his word against theirs.
>
> Years of practice at this have taught her much: choose your words meticulously and then let them rumble up from some deep furnace of conviction. "My son doesn't lie," she says, like an oracle, "not about something like this."

The silent majority vanishes. She stands, straight and motionless, a block of granite. Momen looks back at her, eye to eye. Soon, the silence becomes unbearable. He's forced to move. "I guess he could take a retest I make for him," he says haltingly. "It will be a hard test, though, that I will make for you, Cedric."

"Fine," says Barbara, closing the deal. "Thank you, Mr. Momen. We can go now," she says. Once they're in the hallway, she whispers to Cedric, "You *will* be getting an A on that test, Lavar. You understand?" She doesn't expect an answer.

After a week of ferocious study, Cedric does get his A on the special test—scoring 100—and an A for the marking period. He brings home the paper and lays it on the dining room table, like a prize, a trophy.

Barbara looks at it for a moment. "On the next stop, you know you'll be on your own. I won't be there to come to the rescue," she says, feeling as though a clause of their partnership has expired.

"Well, then," he says a little tersely, tapping the paper once with his index finger, "I guess this paper is sort of your diploma." (pp. 113–115)

From *A Hope in the Unseen*, by Ron Suskind, copyright © 1998 by Ron Suskind. Used by permission of Broadway Books, a division of Random House, Inc.

Like Barbara Jennings, most parents give their children not only love but also supervision, encouragement, advocacy, and material resources. Families are structured environments with unequal distributions of power: By and large, parents call the shots. In the process, they teach children how to behave and what kind of people to become. As the opening case demonstrates, however, influence within families is a two-way street. Barbara's initial reaction to Cedric's B in physics is to let the matter drop, because the B will not affect her son's future. Yet Cedric, outraged by the unfairness of the situation, spurs her into action on his behalf.

A primary challenge parents face is to guide their children in safe and constructive directions while allowing increasing independence. In all cultures, most parents slowly loosen the apron strings, until eventually their offspring are making decisions and choosing their own courses of action. For example, Barbara Jennings comes to Cedric's assistance when his teacher grades him unfairly, but she also tells him, "On the next stop, you know you'll be on your own."

In this chapter we examine families, including their structures and influences. We explore diversity in how families express affection, discipline their children, and prepare them for school; we also consider how those who work with children can forge productive partnerships with families and thereby promote children's academic progress and social-emotional development.

Socialization in the Family

Families can take many forms, but generally they refer to an adult or group of adults (perhaps a single parent, a husband-and-wife pair, an unmarried couple, grandparents, or foster parents) caring for children for many years and guiding them in such a way that they can eventually take on adult roles and responsibilities (Reiss, 1980). Families are essentially the "headquarters" from which children get the support they need to tackle life's many tasks and challenges (Garbarino & Abramowitz, 1992a).

In Chapter 9, we introduced the concept of *socialization*, systematic efforts of adults, peers, and institutions to prepare children to act in ways society perceives to be appropriate. Parents and other family members play a major role in socializing children; in other words, they serve as **socialization agents**. They pass along the knowledge and values of society, encourage culturally approved ways of behaving, and insist that children assume increasing responsibility for their own (and perhaps others') welfare. Family members are, of course, not the only socialization agents in the community. Teachers, counselors, coaches, neighbors, and caregivers in youth organizations, religious groups, local community agencies, clubs, and recreation centers can also be important agents in the socialization of growing children.

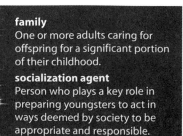

family
One or more adults caring for offspring for a significant portion of their childhood.

socialization agent
Person who plays a key role in preparing youngsters to act in ways deemed by society to be appropriate and responsible.

As socialization agents, parents and other adults have many strategies at their disposal (Damon, 1988). They describe, teach, and model proper ways of behaving in various situations. They reward certain behaviors and punish others. They arrange for children to gain certain kinds of experiences and steer them clear of less productive ones. And by nurturing close emotional bonds with children, they enhance children's motivation to comply with rules and requests.

Other socialization agents also have profound effects on children. Peers tell children what is acceptable and rebuke them when they stray too far from acceptable norms ("How weird!"). Other people (e.g., rock stars, sports figures) and the general media (e.g., films, television shows and commercials, magazines, computer games, Internet sites) transmit ideas that influence children's behaviors, attitudes, and lifestyle choices. Some of these messages are similar to those that families offer; others are in direct conflict with what caring adults think is best for children.

These assorted influences on children are not simple or direct. Children do not passively become what parents want them to be. Instead, children purposefully seek information about the social world and their place in it. They also filter advice they hear, choose role models to imitate, adjust standards for behavior, and reject actions inconsistent with their own ideas of who they are and should be. Thus, children are active participants in their own socialization (Deutsch, Ruble, Fleming, & Brooks-Gunn, 1988; Durkin, 1995; M. Lewis, 1991).

Children make decisions about which socialization agents to trust depending on their own developmental levels. Parents loom large in the lives of infants, toddlers, and preschoolers. Peers become increasingly important as children grow and develop, not necessarily replacing parents but certainly offering compelling models of how to dress, which music to listen to, and how to spend leisure time. Despite increasing influence of peers, parents typically remain strong sources of support and persuasion, especially in core values. Most young people continue to see their relationships with family members as important and valuable throughout adolescence (Cauce, Mason, Gonzales, Hiraga, & Liu, 1994; Furman & Buhrmester, 1992; Neubauer, Mansel, Avrahami, & Nathan, 1994).

Parents and other family members play a major role in socializing children.

Theoretical Perspectives

Developmental theorists have used five primary theoretical perspectives to explain how family members influence and socialize one another. These varying perspectives have emerged, in part, because different groups of theorists focus on distinct features of family systems: children's and parents' observable behaviors (behavioral learning perspectives), children's interpretations of parents' messages (cognitive-developmental perspectives), genetic foundations and evolutionary pressures (biological perspectives), and interactions among children, families, and community (developmental systems and sociocultural perspectives).

Behavioral Learning Perspectives   From behavioral learning perspectives (e.g., Bandura, 1986), family members serve as powerful role models, indirectly communicating messages about appropriate behaviors through their own actions. They also reward children for desirable responses and punish them for undesirable ones.

Children, in turn, closely attend to and remember what family members do and say. Children and adolescents have a remarkable capacity for observation and imitation, as you can see when an infant copies her father's exaggerated, playful facial expression; a 6-year-old sits and reads a book, just like her older sister is doing; and a 17-year-old adopts his mother's driving habits, complaining about and veering around slow drivers. To observe this capacity for observation and imitation, watch 16-month-old Corwin imitate his mother as she produces animal sounds in the Intelligence/Infancy clip of the Observation CD. Note that his mother warmly encourages him, and he cooperates by mimicking the sounds.

Through their experiences and observations, children also develop expectations about likely consequences of their behaviors. For example, a young child may hear a parent commending an older sibling for meeting a standard of moral action, academic performance, or

Observe Corwin imitate his mother's vocalizations in the Intelligence/Infancy clip of the Observation CD.

family obligation, and then follow suit without being asked. Recall the example of 2½ year-old Rachel in Chapter 8, who, after observing her 6-year-old brother write a thank-you letter to his grandparents, attempted to do the same.

Children and adolescents do not imitate everything they observe, however. From the behaviors they see other family members exhibit, as well as from the positive and negative consequences that result from their own and others' actions, children develop a growing sense of what actions are "right" and "wrong" and begin to abide by their *own* standards for behavior (Bandura, 1986). For example, in the opening case study, Cedric did not cheat on his physics exam even though his classmates did so. As an 18-year-old, Cedric has long since determined that cheating is wrong despite the possibility of desirable consequences (good grades).

Cognitive-Developmental Perspectives   From a cognitive-developmental perspective (e.g., see Piaget's theory of cognitive development in Chapter 4 and Kohlberg's theory of moral development in Chapter 10), children largely direct their own development. They energetically explore objects, tinker with ideas, acquire increasingly sophisticated ways of thinking, talk things over with other people, and combine various actions and procedures into complex forms of problem solving.

To some degree, cognitive developmentalists downplay the role of families, teachers, and other socialization agents. Piaget acknowledged that discussions and conflicts with peers are critical for helping children learn to see situations from other people's perspectives, and Kohlberg proposed that children may progress in moral reasoning when they encounter moral arguments at one stage above their own. By and large, however, cognitive developmentalists have devoted little attention to how families transmit particular behaviors, skills, ideas, and values. From a cognitive-developmental standpoint, when children show major developmental advances, *they* are largely responsible for the gains.

Some theorists have argued that cognitive-developmental perspectives give a lopsided view of children's development, neglecting the important influences of meaningful social interactions (e.g., M. Chandler, 1982; Durkin, 1995). However, the basic cognitive-developmental idea that children construct their own understandings and reasoning capabilities has withstood vigorous criticism (Brainerd, 1996; Flavell, 1996) and needs to be integrated into explanations about how families do and do not influence children. Specifically, there are limits to what parents and other family members can explicitly "teach" a child at any given time: Their efforts will have little or no effect on a child's thinking or behavior if the child is not cognitively ready for change. Teresa recalls a relevant example involving her son Alex, then 2. Teresa's husband and older son Connor taught Alex to answer "Two" to questions such as "How old are you?", "What's one plus one?", "What's the square root of four?", and "What's the cube root of eight?" Despite Alex's consistently correct responses, his understanding of mathematics certainly did not progress through this "training." You can observe a child operating within her own developmental level and resisting her father's gentle suggestions by watching 7-month-old Madison in the Emotional Development/Infancy clip of the Observation CD. Consistent with her age, she mouths a ball rather than carrying out her father's request to insert the ball in the slot of a toy.

The cognitive-developmental perspectives encourage us to distinguish areas of development that are and are not likely to benefit from family interactions. Basic logical reasoning capabilities—object permanence, conservation, classification, and so on—may undergo fairly predictable developmental changes in a wide variety of family experiences. Other developmental changes—including knowledge of specific subject areas, development of social skills, and acquisition of standards for acceptable behavior—may be more responsive to family influences.

On balance, then, this viewpoint offers valuable guidance about how family members can best foster children's development (Kohlberg, 1969; Maccoby, 1980). Ideally, families provide a rich physical, social, and intellectual environment in which children can explore physical phenomena, practice skills, exchange ideas, and encounter challenging concepts. On the other hand, families cannot support meaningful developmental change with intellectual "force-feeding," which is likely to promote only rote responses (e.g., "Two" to every question) or, worse, anxiety.

Biological Perspectives   From a biological perspective, families are highly influential agents in children's development. Parents of course give their children life. In the process,

Watch the Emotional Development/Infancy clip to see 7-month-old Madison acting within her existing developmental level (mouthing the ball) while interacting with her father.

they pass along common human traits, such as the ability to produce and understand language, manual dexterity with tools, a predisposition to form social relationships, and a tendency to observe and imitate others. Parents also give their children a unique genetic heritage. For instance, Teresa's older son Connor is in some respects like his father, in that he is good-humored and socially outgoing. From Teresa's side of the family, Connor has inherited a tendency to be tall. In other ways, Connor is like neither of his parents; he has, for example, a fascination with historical events that far exceeds that of either of his parents. Individual characteristics arise out of a complex interplay of genetics, exposure to hormones, and personal experiences (Bjorklund, 1997). Notice that in the Families/Middle Childhood clip of the Observation CD, 10-year-old Kent talks about the height of each family member, perhaps because he is aware that they all tend to be tall.

In the Families/ Middle Childhood clip, hear 10-year-old Kent describe members of his family in terms of height—a trait that has some genetic basis.

Biological perspectives also portray family life and children's development in terms of evolutionary pressures and adaptations. A species evolves when individuals who have certain characteristics adapt successfully to the environment and have families of their own, while those not possessing the characteristics do not survive to have offspring (Bjorklund, 1997; R. B. Cairns, 1983; Charlesworth, 1992; Dixon & Lerner, 1992). Like all living species, human beings organize their lives around physical survival and sexual reproduction—activities that ensure the long-term success of the species (Darwin, 1859).

Compared to the offspring of many other animal species, human children remain dependent on parents for a long time. A lengthy childhood gives children many opportunities to learn the ways of their culture: using tools, relating to others, and practicing adult roles (Bruner, 1972; Leaky, 1994). Evolutionary pressures are also evident in the emotional bonds that form between parents and children and in the moral conscience that motivates parents to meet their children's needs (see the discussion of attachment in Chapter 9). An evolutionary perspective even explains how parent-adolescent conflicts are ultimately beneficial. When adolescents regularly clash with their parents, they spend less time at home and more time with their peers; in the process, they develop increasing independence and self-reliance, thereby easing their transition to adulthood (Steinberg, 1993).

From an evolutionary perspective, parents' tendency to protect their children from danger enhances the likelihood that the species will survive, reproduce, and flourish. Art by Rachel, age 10.

Developmental Systems Perspectives Developmental systems perspectives contribute the insight that families are complex social units of people who interact regularly with one another and take on defined roles. You may recall from Chapter 1 that Bronfenbrenner's *ecological systems framework* is one type of developmental systems perspective; this framework suggests that family influences on children are strong and are part of broader environmental contexts affecting children's development (Bronfenbrenner, 1979, 1989, 1993).

Some family roles are defined by culture, generation, and gender. For instance, in most North American and European families with school-aged children, parents rather than children make decisions about many important family matters, such as where the family will live and what schools children will attend. Other roles emerge depending on family circumstances. For example, one child with athletic prowess might emerge as the family "star" and another might become a scapegoat blamed for the family's problems.

Two or more family members may form *subsystems*, perhaps in the form of longstanding alliances or animosities. For example, two brothers may occasionally rebel against their "unfair" parents, solidifying their connections to each another ("We don't like Mom, right?"), or a mother and daughter might unite against a physically punitive father. Alternatively, two parents might both be so consumed with the health of a chronically ill daughter that they neglect their relationship to one another (Bowen, 1978).

From Bronfenbrenner's perspective, the family is also a *nested system* within larger environmental and community systems. The *microsystem* consists of children's experiences in their immediate surroundings. In child care centers, schools, and the neighborhoods, children develop relationships with a variety of adults and peers. These relationships with people outside the family may be particularly important when parents work outside the home or have limited energy and resources (Garbarino & Abramowitz, 1992b). Extended family members are also increasingly recognized as important agents in children's microsystems. Extended family members take on varied roles, for example, as primary caregivers, cheerleaders when children reach important milestones, and affectionate playmates. You can see

Listen to 6-year-old Joey talk about activities he enjoys with family members in the Families/Early Childhood clip of the Observation CD.

this importance of extended family by listening to 6-year-old Joey in the Families/Early Childhood clip of the Observation CD.

Meanwhile, children influence the people around them by virtue of their personalities, interests, and behaviors. For instance, a boy fascinated with how automobiles work may assist neighbors who tinker with car engines. A girl who teaches foul language to other children may find herself restricted from future contact with those children.

The various microsystems in children's lives (their families, neighborhoods, schools, etc.) form a connected network known as the *mesosystem*. Children are more likely to thrive when families and schools maintain regular and productive communication. When links between important socialization agents are strong and positive, children perform better academically (Garbarino, 1981). Unfortunately, connections within the mesosystem are not always productive; for instance, the encounter between Barbara Jennings and Cedric's physics teacher could have led to a shouting match, or a less assertive mother might have been reluctant to confront the teacher about his unfair grading practices.

Another layer within Bronfenbrenner's hierarchy of systems is the *exosystem*, which includes individuals and institutions that influence children's microsystems even though their actual contact with children is minimal. Examples of entities within the exosystem include parents' work settings, public support systems (e.g., social service agencies), health and fitness clubs, and parents' extended families and friends. Exosystems can offer tremendous indirect support to children through the direct support they offer parents. When working parents can regularly relax in the company of friends, they are emotionally bolstered and as a result can interact with their children in a less stressed manner than they might otherwise.

At a still broader level, exosystems exist within contexts of cultural belief systems and behavior patterns, or *macrosystems*. Macrosystems include far-reaching events, such as war and social strife, general migration from inner-city settings into suburban and rural areas, and cultural values and practices (e.g., being self-reliant or racist). Children's moral development seems to depend somewhat on the form of government in their country: Children who grow up in democratic societies—where diverse viewpoints are acceptable and individual rights are legally protected—are more likely to listen to the viewpoints of others and less likely to conform to adult authority than children who grow up in totalitarian regimes (Garbarino & Bronfenbrenner, 1976).

The various systems just described are hardly static; they are *changing systems*. For instance, as children develop, a parent's role shifts. As infants and mobile toddlers, children must be watched constantly. As they grow older, they begin to internalize rules and guidelines for behavior and acquire a better understanding of what actions may threaten their well-being. By adolescence, they simply keep their parents informed about their activities and whereabouts (Maccoby, 1984). Parents, too, undergo developmental transformations and other changes across the lifespan. Changes in parents' occupational status, economic security, emotional well-being, and physical health all can affect children's day-to-day experiences.

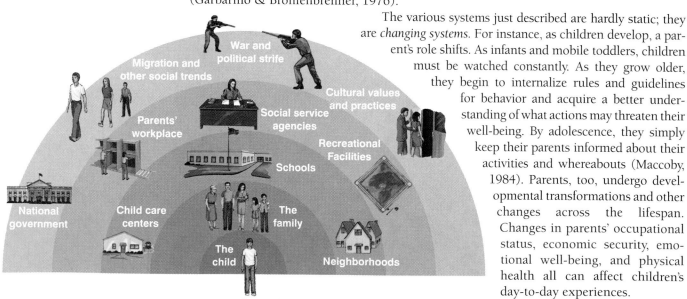

FIGURE 12-1 A developmental systems view of family socialization. Many systems affect children. The influences of some systems are direct and easily seen. The influences of others are more indirect and subtle, in that they affect the larger environment within which the family operates.

An ecological systems framework reminds us that families do not operate in isolation from the larger environmental context in which they exist. Neighborhoods, school systems, local communities, offices of government, and cultural milieus all have a significant influence, either direct or indirect, on family members' ability to function effectively. We illustrate the ecological systems theory in Figure 12–1.

Sociocultural Perspectives Sociocultural perspectives describe ways in which families help children to learn skills and concepts valued in their culture (Gauvain, 2001). In a (typically) nurturing way, parents carry out predictable routines, such as cooking and eating, taking trips to stores, and going to houses of worship; children are motivated to participate in these routines and to take on increasing levels of responsibility (Rogoff, 1990).

The lessons that parents arrange for their children have a profound influence. Throughout this book, we have included concrete illustrations of how interactions between parents and children facilitate development. For example, you may recall from Chapters 5 and 7 that parents and infants learn to focus on the same things at the same time in their shared physical environment; this development nourishes infants' cognitive development and language and communication skills. In Chapter 8, you learned that parents frequently read to children, helping them to decipher literate symbols and to learn story structures. In Chapter 9, you found that parents interact with children in ways that teach them about who they are and how they should relate to other people. Such intimate interchanges— and countless others—help children to think and act in culturally appropriate ways.

Children learn a lot from participating in routine activities with parents.

Parents also influence children through the experiences they arrange outside the home. Especially when their children are young, parents organize activities such as going to friends' houses to play (Gauvain, 1999, 2001). Through such repeated activities, parents often guide children to consider future events. When children are young, parents may ask them what they will do later in the day or what they might need ("It looks like it might rain. Did you pack a jacket?"). As they grow older, parents may help youngsters to think through complex tasks ("Does that assignment require you to turn in a rough draft as well as the final version? I wonder how long each will take to complete.").

A definite strength of sociocultural perspectives is that they acknowledge diversity in families. These perspectives emphasize that family activities vary by culture, income, community resources, and individual factors. A study with 7- to 10-year-old children from middle-class and low-income families illustrates such variations (Lareau, 2000). The study revealed that middle-class parents organized children's lives around acquiring competence in "leisure" pursuits. These families spent a lot of time carpooling children and managing busy schedules. In contrast, families from lower-income backgrounds had a more leisurely pace, though they faced other constraints, notably, a lack of money. Children in these families participated in activities that they largely controlled; they watched television, ate snacks, rode bicycles, played outside, and visited with members of their extended families. Their families spent more relaxed time together, talked aloud about making ends meet, and taught children (through example) the importance of maintaining connections with kin.

Integrating Perspectives of Family Socialization   In the Basic Developmental Issues table, "Contrasting Theories of Family Influences on Children," you can analyze the five theoretical perspectives in terms of their positions regarding nature and nurture, universality and diversity, and qualitative and quantitative change. Together, these viewpoints communicate powerful functions: families are the roots of a child's genetic instructions, role models for behavior, sources of rewards and punishments, brokers to society, and fountains of knowledge. But these theories indicate, as well, limits to family effects, as people outside the family are also influential and, within the family, children partly determine family dynamics and direct their own unfolding abilities and emotional responses.

Diversity in Socialization

Regardless of their theoretical perspective, most developmental scholars acknowledge that diversity exists in how families socialize their children. Here we describe three sources of diversity: children's gender, cultural environment, and family size.

Gender Differences   In most cultures, parents and other individuals in children's lives socialize girls and boys somewhat differently. For instance, European American parents are more likely to encourage their daughters to engage in stereotypically feminine behaviors (e.g., playing with dolls, helping other people) and to encourage their sons to undertake stereotypically masculine activities (e.g., playing with blocks, engaging in rough-and-tumble play) (Bornstein, Haynes, Pascual, Painter, & Galperin, 1999; Lytton

BASIC DEVELOPMENTAL ISSUES

Contrasting Theories of Family Influences on Children

ISSUE	BEHAVIORAL LEARNING PERSPECTIVES	COGNITIVE-DEVELOPMENTAL PERSPECTIVES	BIOLOGICAL PERSPECTIVES	DEVELOPMENTAL SYSTEMS PERSPECTIVES	SOCIOCULTURAL PERSPECTIVES
Nature and Nurture	Focus is on the experiences that parents arrange for children, including the behaviors they model and the consequences they impose for desirable and undesirable actions.	Children actively make sense of their experiences within their families. Children's conceptual understandings of physical and social phenomena, which are limited by their cognitive maturation, influence how they interpret parents' messages.	Significant biological foundations (nature) are present in our species, including intense emotional bonds between parents and their young. Families also care for dependent children over a lengthy period (nurture), a pattern that probably evolved to allow children time to learn the complex knowledge and skills of their society.	Focus is on environmental factors that affect family functioning. Families are support systems for children, and they are affected by broader community networks and regulations, such as neighborhoods, sick leave policies at work, and society's laws and norms. Children are active agents within the family, eliciting certain kinds of responses from others based on their own characteristics.	The primary emphasis is on nurture, though it is acknowledged that children inherit a common human capacity to learn cultural tools. Parents affectionately care for children and are motivated to help them master essential tools. Parents explain how things work in their culture, invite children to take part in goal-directed activities, and encourage them to take on increasing responsibility.
Universality and Diversity	Because families differ in the specific behaviors they model, reward, and punish, considerable diversity in children's behaviors is to be expected.	The sequences of many aspects of cognitive and moral development are assumed to be universal across societies and cultures. However, family interactions provide experiences and viewpoints that lead children to revise their thinking in particular directions.	Children usually form intense and enduring relationships with parents in the first years of life, learn the ways of the world from them during middle childhood, and begin to separate from them during adolescence. Yet families are composed of individuals with vastly different genetic dispositions.	Universality is present in a general sense, in that neighborhoods, communities, and broader societal conventions influence all children and families. Yet individual children grow within different family configurations and community networks. Children also contribute to their own family systems through their unique characteristics, interests, and demands.	Some aspects of family influence may be universal. For example, virtually all parents establish joint attention with children at some time or another. Probably most aspects of family life are diverse, depending on culture and the specific temperaments and personalities of family members.
Qualitative and Quantitative Change	Changes in children's lives tend to occur in trend-like, quantitative forms. Through training from parents and others, children gradually become more responsible for their own behavior.	Significant qualitative transformations occur in children's thinking, largely as a result of children's ongoing restructuring of their understandings of how physical and social environments operate.	Families support both qualitative and quantitative changes. For example, children's interest in sexual activity may increase in a slow, quantitative fashion during childhood, as reflected in questions children ask and answers they receive from parents and others. The nature of their interest may change qualitatively during adolescence, when they begin to think of themselves as sexual beings.	The systems in which a child grows up (the family, the neighborhood, various social agencies, etc.) and their interconnections may change in a qualitative fashion, such as when a community changes suddenly from high-employment to low-employment with the closure of a big company. Quantitative changes may also occur in the number of adults outside the family who support the child.	Quantitative change is emphasized. Children gradually take on responsibility for complex tasks, such as cleaning their room. They become increasingly competent with specific components of the tasks (e.g., making their beds, taking out trash, putting clothes away). Parents may foster some qualitative transformations in children, for example, asking a child to care for a younger sibling for the first time.

& Romney, 1991). Parents also tend to assign household chores based on traditional male and female roles; for example, they ask their daughters to wash dishes and clean the house and ask their sons to mow the lawn and take out the garbage (Eisenberg, Martin, & Fabes, 1996; McHale, Bartko, Crouter, & Perry-Jenkins, 1990). And parents are more likely to enroll their sons, rather than their daughters, in competitive sports leagues and programs for gifted students (Eccles, Wigfield, & Schiefele, 1998).

Children frequently choose activities they deem to be socially acceptable for their own gender.

Yet children themselves are often willing partners in gender socialization. In early childhood, children learn that the world is divided up into boys (males) and girls (females) and that they are members of one of these two groups. Soon after, they learn that gender is a permanent feature of their identity. Henceforth, they show great interest in the activities of boys and girls, men and women, daddies and mommies, inferring the "typical" characteristics of each gender. By the time children are 3, many of their play activities match traditional gender stereotypes (Langlois & Downs, 1980). Furthermore, their peers respond negatively (especially to boys) when they exhibit behaviors traditionally associated with the opposite sex (G. D. Levy, Taylor, & Gelman, 1995). Children also begin to view the world with gender-colored glasses, for example, by remembering a female physician as a "nurse" and a male nurse as a "doctor" (D. B. Carter & Levy, 1988; Liben & Signorella, 1993).

After developing a general sense of traits and activities that are "for girls" and "for boys," children focus more and more on activities they deem to be suitable for their gender (C. L. Martin, 1991; C. L. Martin & Halverson, 1987). For example, many boys can recite the names and functions of different kinds of trucks yet know little about kinds of dolls available at the toy store. As children soak up societal stereotypes, they may limit their own behavior so that it conforms to gender stereotypes. As they continue to grow, however, young people may relax these stereotypes somewhat. Compared to younger children, for example, adolescents become less rigid about jobs they consider appropriate for men and women; for example, many now admit that both sexes can be airplane pilots (Liben & Bigler, 2002).

Group and individual differences exist in how families socialize children to become men and women. For example, many lower-income African American parents socialize children toward an egalitarian model of sex-role status (P. T. Reid, 1985). African American mothers often encourage sons to be expressive emotionally; they serve as strong role models, and they communicate that both men and women can be powerful and helpful people. Within cultural groups, some parents are far more traditional than others; parents who endorse gender stereotypes tend to have children with similar beliefs (Tenenbaum & Leaper, 2002). Of course, children, too, possess their own predispositions, and these affect their responses to the traditional or egalitarian biases of their parents (Liben & Bigler, 2002).

Cultural Differences Families play a major role not only in gender socialization, but also in imparting their distinctive cultural beliefs and practices. For example, in some ethnic groups, including many Hispanic, Native American, and Asian communities, obligation to family is especially important. Children raised in these cultures are likely to feel responsibility for their family's well-being and a strong sense of loyalty to other family members; children go to great lengths to please their parents (Abi-Nader, 1993; E. E. Garcia, 1994; Hidalgo, Siu, Bright, Swap, & Epstein, 1995). Chinese families who immigrate to the United States strive to instill in their children honor of family, respect for elders, and eagerness to achieve academically (Chao, 2000). Cultures that emphasize family obligation often also place a high premium on cooperation within social groups and actively discourage competition (Hollins, 1996; Okagaki & Sternberg, 1993).

Within some ethnic traditions, families help children develop especially strong coping skills. African American families often show positive attributes that sustain children in difficult environmental conditions, such as high unemployment and poverty. For example, deep religious convictions fostered at home can help children deal with life's stresses (McCreary, Slavin, & Berry, 1996). Close bonds with extended family members may also help children resist negative peer pressure (Giordano, Cernkovich, & DeMaris, 1993).

Strict disciplinary strategies may communicate the importance of following family rules immediately so that harm is avoided (Kelley, Power, & Wimbush, 1992; Willis, 1992). Later in this chapter (in the section on families' influences on children), we examine cultural models of disciplining children in more detail.

In many Western cultures, parents value school achievement and encourage children to do well in school (Banks & Banks, 1995; Delgado-Gaitan, 1992; B. J. Duran & Weffer, 1992; Hossler & Stage, 1992; A. H. Yee, 1992). The specific form that such encouragement takes differs to some degree from one cultural group to another. Many Asian American parents transmit the belief that high academic achievement comes only with considerable effort and persistence (R. D. Hess, Chang, & McDevitt, 1987). In many Latino cultures, being well educated does not solely refer to having a good formal education, but also to being successful in social situations and showing respect to others (Okagaki & Sternberg, 1993; Parke & Buriel, 1998). In some traditional Native American and Polynesian communities, children are expected to excel in art, dance, and other cultural traditions more than in such academic pursuits as reading or mathematics (Kirschenbaum, 1989; N. Reid, 1989; Wise & Miller, 1983).

Cultural values are transmitted directly to children through adults' explanations and indirectly through participation in family rituals and styles of interacting. For example, children in many African American families experience high levels of stimulation at home; their households may be characterized as high-energy, fast-paced, socially rich, and in other ways exhilarating (C. T. Bailey & Boykin, 2001; Boykin, 1982). Accustomed to such a lively environment, these children may find settings dominated by European American adults (including many classrooms) to be uncomfortably slow and tedious.

Ideally, professionals who work with children try to understand the preferences, values, and practices children bring from home. Later in this chapter, we offer ideas about listening respectfully to families. We also re-examine more fully both culture and context and their implications in Chapter 14.

Effects of Family Size   Socialization processes play out somewhat differently depending on family size. In larger families, children have more role models to choose from, and subsystems within the family are more likely to develop. Children in large families often acquire altruistic behaviors (e.g., helping others, taking care of younger siblings), especially when it is clear that their contributions are essential to the welfare of the family (B. B. Whiting & Whiting, 1975). On the other hand, in smaller families (such as in Barbara and Cedric Jennings' family of two), family members often form close-knit and intimate relationships (Falbo, 1992).

Family size affects socialization, and so, too, does the way in which the family is structured. In the following section, we explore the issues children face in different kinds of households.

Family Structures

Children live with one or more adults who possess authority and are responsible for their education, health, and conduct. These adults are the heads of household. Oftentimes, heads of household have other responsibilities as well, including full- or part-time employment, home maintenance, volunteer work in the community, and so on.

As society has changed over time, so, too, has the nature of families changed. For instance, in 1830, almost 70% of children in the United States lived on farms in two-parent families (Hernandez, 1997). Children in farming families fed the chickens, milked the cows, harvested crops, and in other ways were vital contributors to their family's economic well-being. Today, fewer than 5% of children live on family farms (Hernandez, 1997). Most instead live in urban and suburban neighborhoods and have little involvement in parents' livelihoods. Furthermore, children are less likely to live in a traditional two-parent family than was true in the early 1800s. Consider these statistics compiled on American children by the U.S. Census Bureau (Fields, 2001):

One in 4 children grows up in a family headed by a single parent.

- 62% live with both biological parents
- 25% live in a one-parent family

- 7% live with a biological parent and a stepparent
- 4% live without a parent in their household (they may live with grandparents, other relatives, or foster parents, or have some other living arrangement)
- 2% live in a two-parent family in which one or both parents have adopted them[1]

These statistics indicate that the majority of children still live in two-parent families, but that a sizeable minority do not. And many other children live with single parents, with other relatives, and in other kinds of households. In the sections that follow, we take a look at children's experiences in families with different heads of household. In the Families module of the Observation CD, you can listen to four children describe families that differ in structure but are similarly portrayed with warmth and affection.

Mothers and Fathers

When mothers and fathers are both present in the home, they often play different and complementary roles in raising and caring for children. Mothers typically spend more time in physical caregiving responsibilities (feeding, bathing, scheduling doctors' appointments, etc.) and display more affection (e.g., kisses, hugs, smiles) toward their children (Belsky, Gilstrap, & Rovine, 1984; Hossain & Roopnarine, 1994; Parke & Tinsley, 1987). Mothers also spend more time engaging their children in visual games such as peek-a-boo, playing with toys with them, and reading to them (Parke & Tinsley, 1981). In a wide range of cultures, mothers overwhelmingly assume primary responsibility for the hands-on care of young children (Engle & Breaux, 1998).

As you may recall from Chapter 9, fathers are often more physically playful with children than mothers are. Fathers are more likely to engage their infants in active play, and they are often instrumental in helping children get along with people outside the family (Bridges et al., 1988; Engle & Breaux, 1998; Lamb, 1976; Pettit, Brown, Mize, & Lindsey, 1998). Nevertheless, fathers are not simply playmates; they spend substantial amounts of time caring for their children (Mackey, 2001). Although fathers typically defer to mothers in basic caregiving activities, they are quite competent and sensitive in feeding, bathing, and nurturing their children when they do take on these responsibilities (Endicott, 1992; Lamb, 1976; Lamb, Frodi, Hwang, Frodi, & Steinberg, 1982).

In many societies, fathers become more involved as children grow older; for instance, they may gradually take over the role of disciplinarian (Engle & Breaux, 1998). Fathers may also function as role models for boys during adolescence, helping sons expand their images of manhood to include subtle characteristics such as sensitivity and dependability in addition to stereotypical features such as strength and aggression (Munroe & Munroe, 1992). Overall, then, mothers and fathers are generally affectionate, but they care for children in slightly different ways; moreover, substantial diversity exists among mothers and among fathers in how they carry out parenting roles (Hosley & Montemayor, 1997; M. E. Lamb, 1997).

In addition to having direct effects on children by caring for their needs, mothers and fathers influence children through their relationship with each other. When children live with two parents, they may gain valuable lessons in cooperation and conflict resolution (J. P. McHale & Rasmussen, 1998). When parents have a healthy relationship, they tend to have good relationships with their children and shower them with signs of tenderness and love (Dube, Julien, Lebeau, & Gagnon, 2000; Ward & Spitze, 1998). Children of happily married couples tend to perceive their lives as enjoyable and satisfying, and when they reach adulthood, they are generally able to establish intimacy with their own partners

Listen to Joey, Kent, Crystal, and Robin, the children interviewed in the four clips of the Families module of the Observation CD, speak affectionately about their very different families.

---

[1] It is difficult to estimate percentages of adopted children, as some parents prefer to keep this information confidential. This estimate of 2% includes circumstances when neither parent is biologically related to the child as well as situations when a stepparent married to one of the children's two biological parents formally becomes a parent through adoption. Adopted children live in other family structures as well as in two-parent families. For example, approximately 16% of adopted children live in single-parent families (Fields, 2001).

A 5-year-old boy drew this picture of his traditional two-parent family: (clockwise, from right) his father, himself, his mother, and his older brother. Also included are the family goldfish and the family's house and driveway.

(Feldman, Gowen, & Fisher, 1998; Gohm, Oishi, Darlington, & Diener, 1998). In contrast, when parents are frequently embroiled in conflict, their interactions with their children are often tense, and they may lose their ability to discipline consistently (Almeida, Wethington, & Chandler, 1999; Belsky, 1981; Hetherington & Clingempeel, 1992). Marital conflict is associated with assorted problems in children and adolescents, including higher rates of externalizing behaviors (e.g., physical aggression) and internalizing behaviors (e.g., depression and anxiety), as well as long-term difficulties in trusting others and maintaining intimate relationships (Forehand, Biggar, & Kotchick, 1998; Hetherington et al., 1999; Tallman, Gray, Kullberg, & Henderson, 1999; Webster-Stratton & Hammond, 1999).

Attachment research indicates that children typically form strong emotional bonds with both of their parents (refer back to Chapter 9). On average, children who are securely attached to both parents show better social and emotional adjustment (e.g., they have better social skills, display greater empathy toward others, show fewer signs of depression, and are less likely to abuse alcohol and drugs) than children who are securely attached to one parent but insecurely attached to the other (Constantina, 1998; Lamb, 1976; Main & Weston, 1981; Rohner, 1998).

Children who begin life in two-parent families do not necessarily remain in that situation, however. We look now at how children fare during and following the divorce of their parents.

Divorced Parents

Once an infrequent occurrence, divorce is now fairly commonplace. The United States has the highest divorce rate in the world—marriages end in divorce for about half of all couples aged 25 to 40—but divorce rates in European countries have also soared since the mid-1960s (Cherlin & Furstenberg, 1988; Norton & Moorman, 1987).

For children, the divorce of parents is not a single event but instead a series of occurrences, each one requiring adjustment. Ongoing marital friction often precedes a divorce; couples who divorce rarely do so suddenly (Furstenberg & Cherlin, 1991). When parents have serious marital conflicts, they tend to be less available for their children, show less affection, and make demands inconsistently. Despite such warning signs, children are sometimes caught offguard when their parents decide to divorce (Wallerstein & Kelly, 1980). Earlier trial separations may have been accompanied by assurances that "Mommy still loves Daddy," or, "We're trying to work things out." Children may be left anxious and uncertain, unable to imagine a family structure that does not include both parents. Consumed with their own anger and bewilderment, parents may not be able to offer children adequate explanations or reassurance.

Children may gain firsthand experience with the courts as their parents legally divorce and determine custody of children. "No-fault" divorce, common in the United States, means that parents do not have to point fingers in the courts, but children may see parents do so privately (Hetherington & Stanley-Hagan, 1997). Sometimes, divorcing parents cannot reach agreement regarding custody of their children. Courts have historically favored mothers, but today, judges endeavor to determine what arrangement is truly in the children's best interests. Parents may also voluntarily—and sometimes by court mandate—go through mediation to determine custody and visitation rights. Joint custody is a growing trend in the United States (Hetherington & Stanley-Hagan, 1997).

The first year after divorce is particularly difficult for many parents and children (Hetherington, Cox, & Cox, 1978). Divorced couples may continue to squabble over finances and child-rearing responsibilities. As they try to cope with feelings of stress or depression, families may have difficulty managing all the tasks involved in maintaining an organized household, including shopping, cooking, cleaning, paying bills, and monitoring children's activities and homework (Wallerstein & Kelly, 1980). Financial setbacks can further complicate the picture. Women more often serve as the custodial parent but tend to earn lower wages than men. Parents who previously owned a house may have to sell it, and so, on top of everything else, children must move to new (and inevitably smaller) quarters and lose the proximity and support of many friends and neighbors (Furstenberg & Cherlin, 1991; J. R. Harris, 1998).

As divorcing parents begin to establish separate households, children learn where they will live and the circumstances under which they will see and talk with each parent. Such arrangements may change over time, however, especially if the parents have difficulty maintaining an amicable postmarital relationship. One parent may withdraw from the children and eventually invest, both emotionally and financially, in a new life and perhaps a new family. Thus, one unfortunate consequence of some divorces is that children lose intimate contact with one of their parents, in most cases their father (Furstenberg & Cherlin, 1991).

Although some divorced fathers gradually withdraw over time, this trend is by no means universal. Many fathers actively seek joint custody arrangements after their divorce (Thompson, 1994). Others continue to maintain contact with children through regular visits, particularly when they continue to live nearby, experience little conflict with mothers, and maintain a clear commitment to their role as father (Leite & McKenry, 2002; Thompson, 1994). Sometimes noncustodial fathers redefine their roles with their children, perhaps becoming fun-loving companions (e.g., taking regular trips to the movies, amusement parks, etc.) rather than nurturers and disciplinarians (Asmussen & Larson, 1991).

Every family experiencing divorce is unique, but some general factors appear to affect children's adjustment to the change. Divorce is sometimes more difficult for boys than girls, especially when mothers assume custody, do not remarry, and establish negative and coercive ways of interacting with their sons (Hetherington, 1988, 1989). Divorce can be particularly overwhelming for young children, who may erroneously believe that their own naughty behavior provoked their parents to separate and who may harbor unrealistic hopes for reconciliation (Fausel, 1986; Wallerstein, 1984). Although older children and adolescents usually find their parents' divorce quite painful, most cope reasonably well with the change, at least over the long run, especially if they have easygoing temperaments and age-appropriate social skills (Forehand et al., 1991; Hetherington, Bridges, & Insabella, 1998). Nevertheless, about 25% of adolescents from divorced families subsequently have some difficulty establishing social and emotional independence and intimate relationships with peers (Hetherington et al., 1998). Children's and adolescents' adjustment to divorce is especially difficult when conflicts between divorcing or divorced parents are drawn out and acrimonious (J. R. Johnston, 1994), when the parent assuming primary custody has difficulty meeting their needs (Hetherington, 1999a), or when they live through more than one marital breakup (Hetherington et al., 1998).

Some conditions help children in adjustments to a divorce. Children are more likely to adjust positively when parents and teachers maintain affectionate relationships with them, hold firm and consistent expectations for their behavior, and willingly listen to their concerns and opinions (Hetherington, 1988, 1989; Hetherington & Clingempeel 1992). Children who have support from family and friends weather a divorce more successfully than those who are socially isolated (Hetherington et al., 1998). And, of course, children are more likely to come out on top when divorced parents establish reasonably productive relationships with each other and agree on expectations and disciplinary measures (Hetherington et al., 1978).

In a few cases, divorce is actually beneficial for children's development. Some children rise to the occasion, comforting parents and siblings, filling in as needed around the house, and in other ways acquiring adultlike behaviors. Furthermore, a peaceful, single-parent home may be infinitely preferable to a household in which two parents engage in continual, intense bickering or in which one parent is abusive or irresponsible (Grych & Finchman, 1997).

Professionals can help children adjust to their parents' divorce by listening to them, focusing on their strengths, maintaining an interest in them, and helping their parents handle the practical demands of custody arrangements.

Single Parents

Single parents carry out the tasks of parenting with the realization that much responsibility falls on their shoulders. This realization often leads single parents to see their children's needs as a top priority.

Compared to two-parent families, though, single-parent families experience unique challenges. Many single parents have limited incomes that are fully stretched by family expenses. Approximately 90% of single parents are women (Fields, 2001). Single parents, mothers and fathers alike, express reservations about their ability to "do it all"—to juggle children, home, and work responsibilities (R. A. Thompson, 1994). Unless they have the support of extended family members, neighbors, or friends, single parents have difficulty coping when they are tired, sick, or emotionally taxed, and they may be unable to offer children the rich range of roles, activities, and relationships that are likely to maximize development (Garbarino & Abramowitz, 1992b).

Generally, though, single-parent families cope well, particularly if they have a reasonable standard of living and the support of a stable network of family and friends (J. R. Harris, 1998). In fact, the simpler structure of single-parent families provides some advantages: Children are shielded from intense conflict between parents, may observe their custodial parent show strong coping skills, and can enjoy the intimacy of a small family. Consider what Cedric Jennings wrote in his application to Brown University:

> [B]eing a black male in a single parent home is sometimes tough without that male figure to help in the growing process. But I thank God for my loving mother. I even see some of my peers that have a mother and father, but are heading in the wrong direction. Some of them are into drug-dealing and others try to be "cool" by not doing good in school and not going to classes. But my mother has instilled so many positive values in me it would be hard to even try to get on the wrong track. (Suskind, 1998, p. 107)[2]

Parents and Stepparents

The majority of divorced parents eventually remarry. When they do, they and their children become members of a **blended family**, a family in which an original parent-and-children family structure expands to include a new parent figure and any children for whom he or she has custody. Blended families are also formed when a remarried parent who already has a child has another child with the new spouse (these siblings are sometimes called "half-siblings," a term that is somewhat misleading because of its implication that these children cannot become fully integrated in the same family). Earlier we indicated that 7% of all children live with a stepparent; when we also include families with "half-siblings," a full 16.5% of all children in the U.S. are in blended families (Fields, 2001).

As is true for all family structures, children in blended families experience benefits and challenges. A new adult may bring additional income to the family and can help with household duties. Children can forge relationships with a new parent figure and, possibly, new brothers and sisters. Yet children may feel that they must now share their parent's time and affection with the new spouse. They may believe, too, that the new stepparent is interfering with a possible reunion of the divorced parents and that by showing affection to the stepparent, they are being disloyal to their nonresident parent (Papernow, 1988).

For a family to blend successfully, it must establish its own identity and traditions. It must decide how to spend money, divide household chores, prepare and serve meals, and celebrate holidays. It must also develop productive ways of expressing and resolving conflicts and agree upon rules and disciplinary techniques.

Although children from divorced and blended families are at somewhat higher risk for personal, social, and academic problems, most eventually adjust successfully to a blended family situation (Dawson, 1991; Furstenberg & Cherlin, 1991; Hetherington et al., 1998). In one survey of blended families, 91% of parents and 81% of children reported a large amount of sharing in their family; 78% of parents and 66% of children described family relationships as close; and 67% of parents and children stated that family life was relaxed (Furstenberg, Nord, Peterson, & Zill, 1983). Relationships between stepparents and stepchildren are not always as close and affectionate as those between biological parents and children, and stepparents may have greater difficulty disciplining their stepchildren (Furstenberg et al., 1983; Hetherington et al., 1999). Yet in many instances, stepparents soon become important parts of children's lives. Figure 12–2 shows a Mother's Day poem by 9½-year-old Shea for her stepmother Ann, who at that point had been a family member for about 3 years. It reveals clearly the close relationship that had developed between Shea and her stepmother.

blended family
Family created when one parent-child(ren) family structure combines with another parent figure and any children in his or her custody.

---

[2] From *A Hope in the Unseen,* by Ron Suskind, copyright © 1998 by Ron Suskind. Used by permission of Broadway Books, a division of Random House, Inc.

Extended Family

Many children have close relationships with relatives, including grandparents, aunts, uncles, and others. Grandparents play particularly central roles for many children. In the United States, 4.1 million children have one or both grandparents living with them and their parent or parents (Fields, 2001). An additional 1.3 million children live with one or both grandparents and do not have a parent present in the home. This means that in the United States 7.5% of all children have at least one grandparent present with them in their homes (Fields, 2001).

Grandparents aren't always able to choose their level of involvement in grandchildren's lives. When parents divorce, grandparents on the noncustodial parent's side of the family may be completely shut out of their grandchildren's lives. In yet other circumstances (e.g., when a child's parents are neglectful, imprisoned, or incapacitated by illness or substance abuse), grandparents become primary caregivers for their grandchildren (L. M. Burton, 1992; Minkler & Roe, 1992). Many children of poor, single teenage mothers live with their grandmothers either in addition to or instead of with their mothers. Grandmothers tend to be less punitive and more responsive to children's needs than teen mothers are, and children cared for by their grandmothers tend to have more economic stability, show greater self-reliance, and seem better able to avoid drug abuse and vandalism (Chase-Lansdale, Brooks-Gunn, & Zamsky, 1994; R. D. Taylor & Roberts, 1995; M. Wilson, 1989). Grandparents often take on the responsibility with mixed feelings: Although they are grateful for the close and intimate relationships they can have with their grandchildren, they may worry they do not have adequate energy and financial resources to raise another generation. Some regret the lifestyle changes that new parenting responsibilities require (Cox, 2000; Kornhaber, 1996).

In many cultural groups, grandparents and other extended family members (perhaps aunts and uncles) commonly assume central roles in the lives of children (Harrison, Wilson, Pine, Chan, & Buriel, 1990; Stack & Burton, 1993). In some cultures, male members of the extended family serve as primary father figures for children (Engle & Breaux, 1998). For example, in Botswana, the mother's brother may play the role of father, and in Vietnam, an older male relative, such as a grandfather, may assume fatherly responsibilities.

Many grandparents have the luxury of maintaining warm and loving relationships with their grandchildren while leaving discipline to the parents. Such nonjudgmental relationships can be quite beneficial for children. For example, child psychiatrist Arthur Kornhaber noticed that one of his patients, a boy named Billy, was typically hyperactive but was "more relaxed, less agitated, and less impulsive" with his grandmother (Kornhaber, 1996, p. 1). Dr. Kornhaber made some observations:

> What happened between Billy and his grandmother that transformed his behavior? Was Billy aware of how differently he behaved in the presence of his grandmother? I decided to find out. During our next session I asked him to draw a picture of his family and tell me about his drawing. Billy drew his family as a three-layered pyramid. He was on top, running after a football. His parents were underneath, in the center layer, watching him play, and "saying how well he played." On the bottom of the pyramid Billy placed his grandparents, looking up at him adoringly. "They are watching me play football and are happy that I am happy," Billy explained, "and my parents are happy because I am a good football player."
>
> Although he didn't know it, and I wasn't totally aware of it at the time, Billy had put his finger on an important difference in the way parents and grandparents love their children. His grandparents were happy that he was joyful; his parents were pleased because he was performing well. The former is love without condition, the latter is tinged with approval for performance. (Kornhaber, 1996, p. 2)

Not all children are as fortunate as Billy, however. Although some grandparents have close, meaningful relationships with their grandchildren, others are distant pen pals or even completely absent (Kornhaber, 1996).

MOM is WOW

She is great at hide-and-seek
She takes me to look at an antique
I get to see her three times a week

MOM is WOW

She helped teach me multiplication
She encourages my imagination
She is involved when it comes to participation

MOM is WOW

She's a great stepmom, I guarantee
She lets us watch Disney TV
She is an important part of the family tree

MOM is WOW

No matter what, she is never late
If I have a question, she will demonstrate
When it comes to stepmoms, she's great

MOM is WOW

FIGURE 12-2 In her fourth-grade class, 9½-year-old Shea wrote a Mother's Day poem for her stepmother. Shea's teacher provided the "Mom is wow" structure for the students to follow.

FIGURE 12–3 Seven-year-old Connor communicates his excitement about becoming a big brother. In his journal, Connor initially speculated that he might be getting a brother. When Alex joined their home at age 8 months, Connor found his brother to be cute. After a few days, Connor was aware of things that his baby brother liked (playing peek-a-boo and being carried by him).

In recent years, international adoptions have become increasingly common. Many adoptive parents encourage their children to learn about their native culture as well as the culture of their adoptive homeland.

Adoptive Parents

Approximately 2 out of every 100 children in the United States are adopted (Fields, 2001; Zill, 1985). Half of these adoptions involve a child's relatives or stepparents; the other half are arranged through social services agencies, adoption agencies, attorneys, and other intermediaries (Stolley, 1993). Birth mothers who place their infants up for adoption are often young, single women from middle- or upper-income two-parent families who support the decision; unmarried women who choose to keep and parent their infants are more likely to come from lower-income, single-parent families (Stolley, 1993).

Adoption can be a positive event for children, who can form ties with loving parents. It can also be a blessing for adoptive parents, who find themselves—sometimes overnight—with a child. In Figure 12–3, 7-year-old Connor conveys his excitement on becoming a big brother to 8-month-old Alex.

The last few decades have seen several changes in adoption practices (Center for the Future of Children, 1993). One growing practice is *open adoption*, in which the birth mother (and perhaps also the birth father) meet and choose the adopting family. Another is *international adoption*, whereby orphaned or relinquished children living in one country are adopted by families in another country. Many adoption agencies are now more flexible in evaluating potential adoptive parents; the result is an increasing number who are single, older, gay, lesbian, or from lower-income groups. The adoption of increasing numbers of older children is another trend. Often these children have special needs: they may have had poor care as infants or have physical or mental disabilities (Rutter & O'Connor, 1999).

Although adopted children are at slightly greater risk for emotional, behavioral, and academic problems than children raised by their biological parents, the great majority of adopted children thrive and grow up to be well-adjusted individuals (Brodzinsky, 1993). Adopted children seem to cope best when family members talk openly about the adoption yet provide the same love and nurturance that they would offer any biological offspring.

Occasionally, adoptive families need professional intervention if they are raising children who got off to a rough start before joining their families, or if the children resist forming attachments to adoptive parents. Children who have been abused or neglected or who have had several different placements before being adopted may have some difficulty forming positive relationships with new caregivers (Howe, 1995; Singer, Burkowski, & Waters, 1985).

Recall from Chapter 9 that children who experience early deprived conditions often form strong, stable ties with new parents and other caregivers, but specialized training for parents may increase chances that these children will embark on a new, healthy track.

Foster Care

In *foster care*, children are placed with families through a legal but temporary arrangement. Approximately 556,000 children in the United States are in foster care (U.S. Department of Health and Human Services, 2002). Tragically, parents' substance abuse is often a major factor in foster care placement. Approximately half of children enter foster care because their primary caregiver maltreated them (R. Collins, 1999).

Many children in foster care are available for adoption. However, because many adoptive parents prefer adopting newborn infants, foster children often become "the children who wait" (McKenzie, 1993). Thus, their living arrangements are interminably "temporary," often with frequent shifts from one family to another. Such a transitory existence is particularly detrimental when children have already faced challenges with birth parents—perhaps neglect, abuse, abandonment, or early exposure to drugs or HIV. Children in foster care exhibit higher rates of emotional and behavioral disturbance than do other children (Shealy, 1995).

Fortunately, many children in foster care are eventually adopted, often by their foster parents and sometimes by other adults who are willing or eager to adopt older children. If these children have not had a history of stable, consistent, and loving care, they may be angry or irritable and may have trouble forming close emotional ties with their adoptive parents. Furthermore, foster children, including those who are adopted later on, have a higher-than-average need for special services either within or outside of school. Many parents who adopt older children with special needs have had previous experience as foster parents and become skilled parents and effective advocates for their children (McKenzie, 1993).

Sadly, many children continue to wait for permanent homes, making it imperative that foster care be affectionate and developmentally appropriate. One study of foster mother-infant pairs showed that over half of the children formed secure attachments to foster parents (Dozier, Stovall, Albus, & Bates, 2001). Because foster families are not always prepared for the challenges foster children bring with them, special training may be needed. One promising tactic has been to train *therapeutic foster parents* to be professional caregivers; these parents care for only one or two children, are given ongoing emotional support themselves, have access to crisis intervention services, are encouraged to keep their focus on children's social and educational needs, and are advised by case managers who also have reasonably small loads (R. P. Hawkins, 1989). The expense of therapeutic foster care can pay off financially as well as morally; in one study, youths in therapeutic foster care showed a significant drop in criminal activity compared to youths in residential placement (Chamberlain & Reid, 1998). The success of therapeutic foster care certainly points to the need for ongoing support to foster parents. In particular, foster parents may benefit from education in the kinds of attachment problems we discussed in Chapter 9, as well as strategies to help children cope with anger and other troubling emotions.

Children in foster families may have periodic contact with social workers and other professionals outside their foster families. In one investigation of foster care and residential care, youngsters had definite ideas about how social workers could improve services for them (Munro, 2001). They wanted to have good ongoing relationships with social workers, and they complained when they did not have such relationships, or when there was high turnover in staff. They also objected when social workers did not permit them to see their birth parents as often as they would have liked. Finally, these youngsters sometimes felt betrayed when they talked to social workers, thinking their conversations were confidential but later discovering they were not. An important implication of this research is that children in foster care have viewpoints and rights that must be carefully considered by professionals. Discretion in telling others about children's family circumstances is also warranted.

Other Heads of Family

Our discussion of family configurations has not been exhaustive; some children experience variations on these configurations or live in other family configurations altogether. For instance, a growing number of children live with *gay and lesbian parents*. When Jeanne's daughter Tina was a teaching intern, 4 of the 15 first-grade students in her class had two gay or lesbian parents. Children who have gay and lesbian parents are as intelligent and well adjusted as other children, and the majority grow up to be heterosexual adults (Bailey, Bobrow, Wolfe, & Mikach, 1995; Faks, Filcher, Masterpasqua, & Joseph, 1995; Golombok & Tasker, 1996; Patterson, 1992). Children of homosexual parents may worry that their parents are stigmatized by society, but they usually learn to cope with this feeling without too much difficulty (C. J. Patterson & Chan, 1997).

Some children spend considerable time in a *cohabiting family,* in which a parent has an intimate nonmarital partner living in the home. About 5% of children in the U.S. live with parents who are cohabiting with partners (Fields, 2001). Cohabiting couples who have children are more likely to maintain a long-term relationship than couples without children (Wu, 1995). Little is known about the experiences of children with cohabiting parents, however. Like children in other family configurations, children with cohabiting parents probably adjust more favorably if their family circumstances are relatively stable and if both adults in the household maintain warm and consistent relationships with them.

Adolescent parents often need and receive support from government and social agencies. Many adolescent parents are sensitive and reliable caregivers to their children. However, some single adolescent mothers experience high stress; lack awareness of children's emotional, cognitive, and social needs; and are willing to conceive additional children despite financial problems (Borkowski et al., 2002). In the following excerpt, 17-year-old Margie shares her experience as an adolescent mother to a 1-year-old son. Margie recognizes her need to get through school, gives indications of her grave financial situation, and recognizes the pretentious ineffectuality of her baby's father.

> If I can get through school, and go to the beautician's school, learn that, I think I can do it: make enough money to pay my rent and buy us food. I get ten dollars sometimes from the baby's father, but it's not sure, from week to week, what he'll do—if he'll help us out. He gambles a lot, in cards, and if he really wins big, he'll come over and give me a ten (twice a twenty), and he feels like a real big shot, then. He'll tell me I should change the kid's diaper, when I've just done it—that way, he can show he's a father who cares for his son! (Coles, 1997, pp 73–74)[3]

Children of adolescent mothers tend to be at greater risk for developmental delays and problems of their own. In a comprehensive investigation of children of adolescent mothers, data were collected when children were 1, 3, 5, and 8 years of age (Borkowski et al., 2002). At age 1, only 37% of the children were securely attached to their mothers. At ages 3 and 5, many children showed intellectual delays, such as low vocabulary, visual motor integration problems, and poor skills in reading and mathematics; they also showed limited communication and daily living skills. At age 8, fewer than 30% of the children had performed satisfactorily at the end of second grade, and nearly 40% met criteria for being learning disabled or mentally retarded. Such delays are not inevitable, of course. Professionals can certainly better the odds if they educate and support adolescent parents and their children.

Because families can come in many different, yet effective forms, we urge that you not jump to conclusions about children based on the particular family structures in which they live. Two-parent families are easily overrated as the ideal situation (Furstenberg & Cherlin, 1991). In fact, there are many poorly functioning two-parent families, as well as many strong single-parent families who, like Barbara and Cedric Jennings, are sustained by friends, neighbors, extended family, and other community members. What undoubtedly matters most is not the structure of the family but the relationships that are formed within the family unit (Hetherington & Stanley-Hagan, 1999).

Implications of Diverse Family Structures

Following are recommendations for actions teachers and other practitioners can take to convey respect to children and families:

■ *When organizing activities that relate to children's families, make them flexible enough to be relevant to a wide variety of family circumstances.* School assignments, club activities, and community summer programs sometimes involve one or more family members. For instance, in the elementary grades, children sometimes make cards for Mother's Day and Father's Day. In high school biology classes, students may be asked to trace the occurrence of dominant and recessive traits (e.g., brown hair and blond hair) in several generations of their family. Such tasks, though well intentioned, may disenfranchise youngsters whose family configurations don't fit the traditional mold. With a little creativity, teachers and other professionals can easily broaden activities so that they accommodate diverse family structures. For instance, the biology teacher can be more inclusive by presenting data on several generations of a hypothetical biological family that all class members can analyze. As another example, recall Shea's Mother's Day poem to her stepmother (Figure 12–2). Shea's teacher gave Shea enough time to write two poems, one each for her mother and her stepmother.

■ *Model and encourage acceptance of diverse family structures.* Occasionally children taunt or tease classmates from nontraditional families; for instance, some gay and lesbian parents worry that their children will be ridiculed because of their parents' sexual orientation (Hare, 1994). At the preschool and elementary levels, teachers can counter-

---

[3] From *The Youngest Parents* by Robert Coles. Copyright © 1997 by Robert Coles. Used by permission of W. W. Norton & Company, Inc.

act such thoughtless behaviors by reading stories about children from a variety of family structures and by frequently expressing the view that families are formed in many ways. In the secondary grades, adolescents tend to be more informed and accepting about diverse family structures; nevertheless, teachers and other practitioners should keep an ear open for, and emphatically discourage, any derogatory comments about peers' family circumstances.

It is important, too, to acknowledge the very central roles that extended family members play in many children's lives. Whenever possible, they should be welcomed to open houses, plays and concerts, parent-teacher groups, and family conferences.

■ *Include fathers.* When children live in two-parent families, people outside the family often direct communication about children to mothers alone. Professionals can try to equalize communications to mothers and fathers when both are present in the home. By doing so, they can validate the incredibly influential roles that mothers and fathers alike play in children's lives.

Model, discuss, and encourage acceptance of all family structures.

■ *Be especially supportive when children undergo a major family transition.* Many events can change a child's family configuration, including divorce, remarriage, departure of a parent's nonmarital partner, death of a family member, or movement from one foster family to another. In each case, one or more old relationships may end, and one or more new relationships may begin. Adjustment to any major family transitions takes time, and children's feelings are likely to be ambivalent and somewhat changeable from one day to the next, underscoring the need for broad-based support from teachers and other caregivers for several months or perhaps even longer (Hetherington, 1999b). Other family members are likely to appreciate kind words and understanding as well, especially in the early weeks.

■ *Remain patient while children figure out how to solve practical problems related to new family structures.* Youngsters may find that they must learn to adapt to moving between two houses and following two sets of rules (Smart, Neale, & Wade, 2001). Consider 16-year-old Selina's articulation of the tensions that arise when she prepares to change households:

> It gets to about five o'clock on Sunday and I get like a really awful feeling and then . . . aah, packing up again . . . I don't complain about it. That's just the way it is. There's no *point* complaining about it, nothing's going to change. . . . [But] usually on a Sunday around that time . . . we're upset because we're having to move and everyone's temper's . . . you know, you get quite irritable. . . . (Smart et al., 2001, p. 128)[4]

In such circumstances, practitioners can express sympathy for children's frustration, but also encourage them to come up with a plan that will help them to organize belongings and adjust to different households.

■ *Let children say what they want to say; don't pry.* Children often prefer to keep family matters to themselves. They may feel that teachers, counselors, and other practitioners are inappropriately interested in their personal lives (Smart et al., 2001). It is desirable, therefore, for adults to offer reassurance without being too inquisitive. When children do bring up family problems, help them to consider options for dealing with them.

■ *Be proactive in reaching out to students who are living in foster care.* These children may be emotionally overburdened and have trouble asking for assistance and comfort. Furthermore, they may have profound academic and social needs and may sometimes engage in behaviors that challenge experienced professionals. Nevertheless, children in foster care almost invariably benefit when adults articulate clear and consistent expectations and offer ongoing personal support.

---

[4] From *The Changing Experiences of Childhood: Families and Divorce* (p. 128) by C. Smart, B. Neale and A. Wade, 2001, Malden, MA: Blackwell Publishers. Copyright 2001 by Carol Smart, Bren Neale and Amanda Wade. Reprinted by permission.

Influences Within Families

Parents and other family members affect children's lives in many ways. In this section we look at family caregivers' styles of raising children, their employment, and their strategies for guiding children's academic learning. We also examine children's influence on their families, and children's impact, as siblings, on one another. Finally, we identify risk factors in families and discuss maltreatment of children.

Families' Influences on Children

Among children's foremost needs are their requirements for love and discipline. Children eagerly soak up affection from parents, forming attachments as infants, thriving on tenderness during early and middle childhood, and benefiting from steady, rich, behind-the-scenes emotional support during adolescence. Disciplinary guidance is absolutely essential, but not always happily received, because parents' socialization goals frequently conflict with children's intentions. But whereas high levels of affection are most certainly beneficial, excessive control may hinder children's ability to make choices, learn from their mistakes, and develop self-confidence. Conversely, too little control may leave children without goals and unwilling to follow society's rules. Throughout the world, most parents manage to find acceptable, balanced ways to show their love and wield their authority (Rohner & Rohner, 1981). Yet there are individual differences. Parents vary in how they express warmth, affection, discipline, and guidance; that is, they develop characteristic **parenting styles**.

Parenting Styles   In a series of landmark studies, Diana Baumrind and her colleagues investigated parenting styles in American families with preschool-aged children (Baumrind, 1967, 1971, 1980, 1989, 1991). Through interviews and observations, Baumrind (1967) classified parents as exhibiting one of three styles: authoritarian, authoritative, or permissive. She found children's social-emotional adjustment to be related to parents' style of interacting with them. Her data do not furnish definitive information about causality but they are consistent with the interpretation that parents' expression of affection and authority plays some part in children's development.

Parents who use an **authoritarian style** expect complete and immediate compliance. They neither negotiate expectations nor provide reasons for their requests ("Clean your room because I told you to—and I mean *now*!"). Authoritarian parents also tend to be somewhat cool, aloof, and punitive with their children, and they expect children to act in a mature fashion at a fairly young age. Baumrind found that children of authoritarian parents often had social-emotional difficulties: they were withdrawn, mistrusting, and unhappy. Other researchers have found that these children have low self-esteem, little self-reliance, and poor social skills, and in some cases they are overly aggressive with others (Coopersmith, 1967; Lamborn, Mounts, Steinberg, & Dornbusch, 1991; Maccoby & Martin, 1983; Simons, Whitbeck, Conger, & Conger, 1991).

Parents who use an **authoritative style** also seek mature behavior from their children, but they do so in a warmer manner that incorporates give-and-take, explanations for why rules should be followed (recall our discussion of *induction* in Chapter 10), and respect for children's viewpoints ("OK, maybe you don't need to sort through your backpack every night, but we should come up with a schedule that prevents you from losing assignments. Can we both agree to every Wednesday and Saturday?"). Children of authoritative parents seemed to be the most well-adjusted children in Baumrind's studies. They appeared mature, friendly, energetic, confident in tackling new tasks, and able to resist distractions. Subsequent investigation has found that these children have high self-esteem, considerable self-reliance, and good social skills; furthermore, they achieve at high levels academically, are well-behaved at school, and adjust more successfully to family trauma (Coopersmith, 1967; Dekovic & Janssens, 1992; Dornbusch, Ritter, Leiderman, Roberts, & Fraleigh, 1987; Hetherington & Clingempeel, 1992; Lamborn et al., 1991; Loeb, Horst, & Horton, 1980; L. Steinberg, Elmen, & Mounts, 1989). Positive effects continue into the college years, where they show better adjustment, earn higher grades, and are more likely to persist at difficult tasks (Strage & Brandt, 1999).

parenting style
General pattern of behaviors that a parent uses to nurture and guide his or her children.

authoritarian style
Parenting style characterized by strict expectations for behavior and rigid rules that children are expected to obey without question.

authoritative style
Parenting style characterized by emotional warmth, high expectations and standards for behavior, consistent enforcement of rules, explanations regarding the reasons behind these rules, and the inclusion of children in decision making.

Parents who use a **permissive style** exercise little control over their children. Children act on their impulses with minimal parental restraint ("Fine. Just ignore what I said!"). In Baumrind's analysis, children of permissive parents appeared least competent overall. These children were immature, demanding and dependent on parents, and, not surprisingly, disobedient when parents asked them to do something they did not want to do. Permissive parents relinquish decisions to children (even fairly young ones) about when to go to bed, what chores (if any) to do around the house, and what curfews to abide by. Other investigators have found that these children tend to have difficulty in school, to be aggressive with peers, and to engage in delinquent acts as adolescents (Lamborn et al., 1991; Pulkkinen, 1982).

In Baumrind's classification, a single emotional orientation—warm or indifferent—did not emerge for the permissive style. Since her initial work, however, other researchers have distinguished two groups of parents who exert few demands for mature behavior: (a) those who are reasonably caring but lax in guiding and controlling children and (b) those who are inattentive or indifferent to their children's needs for affection (Maccoby & Martin, 1983). In Baumrind's original classification, permissive parents probably belonged to the first group, in that they were indulgent rather than indifferent.

Parents in the second group exhibit an **uninvolved style.** Uninvolved parents make few demands on their children, and they respond to children in an uncaring and rejecting manner. Children of uninvolved, indifferent parents show problems in school achievement, emotional control, tolerance for frustration, and delinquency (Lamborn et al., 1991; Simons, Robertson, & Downs, 1989). When neglect is extreme, it becomes a form of maltreatment, which we examine in more detail later in the chapter.

Overall, the research suggests that the authoritative style is particularly effective with many American children. Authoritative parents convey the message that children must live up to appropriate standards but at the same time are valued family members with meaningful viewpoints. By providing reasons behind rules, parents help children focus on the consequences of their actions for themselves and others and so help them understand and internalize society's rules and customs (Hess & McDevitt, 1984). In addition, by being caring and sensitive, authoritative parents create a peaceful, secure environment and instill in their children a desire to reciprocate with similar behaviors (C. Lewis, 1981; Sroufe & Fleeson, 1986). Finally, children may generalize the give-and-take of an authoritative household to negotiations with peers and other authority figures and so acquire good social skills. On the playground and in the community, children of authoritative parents know that rules exist for a reason, exceptions are sometimes possible, and everyone has a right to an opinion (Hinshaw, Zupan, Simmel, Nigg, & Melnick, 1997).

Parents find many ways to express affection and guide their children.

Factors Affecting Parenting Styles   As we have seen, an authoritative style appears to complement European American cultural values, producing children who seem to fit well with the ideal roles these cultures define: They listen respectfully to others, follow rules at a reasonably young age, try to be independent, and strive for academic achievement. With all the good news about authoritative parenting, why doesn't every parent adopt this style?

One answer is that other parenting styles are better suited to particular cultural and familial environments. For example, many Asian American families have somewhat different values. They make high demands for obedience within the context of a close, supportive mother-child relationship (Chao, 1994, 2000). The parenting style for some is bolstered by principles of Confucianism, which teach children that parents are right and that obedience and emotional restraint are essential for family harmony (Chao, 1994). In fact, some Chinese American children may feel badly when their parents fail to use an involved, directive style, which they see as an expression of love. Moreover, the children of very controlling (and apparently "authoritarian") Asian American parents often do quite well in school (Chao, 1994; Dornbusch et al., 1987; Lin & Fu, 1990).

Similarly, the authoritative style may not adequately capture the nuances of socialization in African American families. Some research suggests that authoritative parenting predicts good outcomes in African American children (D. Rowe, Vazsonyi, & Flannery, 1994; Steinberg, Lamborn, Darling, Mounts, & Dornbusch, 1994). However, other studies suggest that authoritarian parenting can be effective (Baumrind, 1982). In an investigation

permissive style
Parenting style characterized by emotional warmth but few expectations or standards for children's behavior.

uninvolved style
Parenting style characterized by a lack of emotional support and a lack of standards regarding appropriate behavior.

with both European American and African American families, strict parenting predicted problems in the former group but not in the latter (Deater-Deakard, Dodge, Bates, & Pettit, 1996). What is perhaps more significant, however, is that important family dimensions not identified by Baumrind may characterize many African American families. These include an emphasis on spirituality, extended family, resistance to oppression, and cultural pride (H. C. Stevenson, 1995; Taylor & Roberts, 1995).

Other aspects of families' lives may make the authoritative style ineffective. When parents live in dangerous neighborhoods, for example, they may better serve their children by being very strict and directive (Hale-Benson, 1986; McLoyd, 1998b). In addition, economic hardship, career pressures, marital discord, and other family stresses may seep into parents' interactions with children (Katz & Gottman, 1991; Russell & Russell, 1994). In some cases, the stresses of limited financial resources become so overwhelming that they reduce parents' ability to seek their children's ideas about family rules (Bronfenbrenner, Alvarez, & Henderson, 1984). Communicating high standards for behavior and negotiating rules with children take considerable resolve—perhaps more than some people under stress can manage.

Children's temperaments also affect parenting styles. Children with mild temperaments may elicit calm and reasoned behavior from parents, whereas more spirited, irritable, or rebellious children may provoke parents to clamp down firmly on frequent misbehavior (Eisenberg & Fabes, 1994; J. R. Harris, 1995, 1998; Scarr, 1993). Developmental psychologist Judith Harris (1998) has described her very different experiences—and parenting styles—with her two children:

> I . . . reared a pair of very different children. My older daughter hardly ever wanted to do anything that her father and I didn't want her to do. My younger daughter often did. Raising the first was easy; raising the second was, um, interesting. . . .
>
> How can you treat two children both the same when they *aren't* the same—when they do different things and say different things, have different abilities and different personalities?. . .
>
> I would have been pegged as a permissive parent with my first child, a bossy one with my second. . . .
>
> My husband and I seldom had hard-and-fast rules with our first child; generally we didn't need them. With our second child we had all sorts of rules and none of them worked. Reason with her? Give me a break. Often we ended up taking the shut-your-mouth-and-do-what-you're-told route. That didn't work either. In the end we pretty much gave up. Somehow we all made it through her teens. (J. R. Harris, 1998, pp. 26, 48)[5]

Parents also may be strict in some areas of development and lenient in others (Costanzo & Fraenkel, 1987). For instance, in raising their three children, Jeanne and her husband consistently held high expectations for academic performance and prosocial behavior; they were more lax about making sure children completed household chores or arrived home in time for dinner. In contrast, Teresa and her husband insisted that their children be present for dinner and complete their homework, but they cut them slack in many other areas of their lives.

Children's Influences on Families

In the preceding section, we suggested that children themselves have an impact on parenting styles. This idea contradicts the common belief that socialization is a one-way process—that children are influenced by parents but not vice versa. Such a misconception probably endures because children change in many ways as they grow older, and their parents are often their most visible teachers. Yet while children listen to parents' guidance, advice, and expectations, they also make their own wants and needs known, often quite emphatically (recall Cedric's outraged response to his B in physics: ". . . what are *we* going to do?!"). By requests, demands, and actions, children influence parents and other family members.

In fact, socialization of children involves *reciprocal influences,* whereby children and their parents simultaneously affect one another's behaviors and mutually create the envi-

---

[5] Reprinted with the permission of The Free Press, a Division of Simon & Schuster Adult Publishing Group, from *The Nurture Assumption: Why Children Turn Out the Way They Do* by Judith Rich Harris. Copyright © 1998 by Judith Rich Harris.

ronment in which they all live. Parents set the tone, to some degree, but children contribute immensely to relationships with parents. These reciprocal influences are evident in parent-child interactions from the very beginning (R. Q. Bell, 1988). Babies demand comfort and sustenance by crying, but they also coo, chatter, and lure their parents into contact in a most disarming manner. A father intent on sweeping the kitchen floor, for example, may find it hard to resist the antics of his 6-month-old who wriggles, chatters, and smiles at him. More generally, children respond in predictable ways, reward parents' attention with laughter or imitation, protest parents' absence, and in other ways tell parents that they matter.

Reciprocal influences continue as children grow. For example, children insert themselves into games and other social interactions, with preschoolers and parents taking turns imitating and responding to one another (Kohlberg, 1969). As children get older, they and their parents continue to respond to one another, taking cues from each other's actions. In Figure 12–4, 10-year-old Samuel thanks his mother for teaching him how to behave. Respecting his mother's intentions to help him, Samuel is more likely to listen to her requests, commands, and rules in the future. She, in turn, is likely to respond with pride and warmth to his gesture of appreciation. Children also influence parents and other family members through their unique talents and interests. For instance, Jeanne's son Alex encouraged her to take an undergraduate art history class with him when he was a high school senior; together they developed a more informed appreciation for a wide variety of art forms.

FIGURE 12–4 Ten-year-old Samuel thanks his mother for all she has taught him.

Children may also alter the emotional climate of families, sometimes for the better and sometimes not. Children who are successful at school, on the playing field, or in social situations often evoke feelings of joy and pride in other family members. Those who don't meet parents' expectations may cause disappointment, frustration, or anger. Some children are the source of emotional stress for parents; for instance, some parents (especially mothers) of children with serious disabilities report high levels of stress, especially if they have little help from their spouses in caring for the children's needs (L. Little, 2000a; Mahoney, O'Sullivan, & Robinson, 1992).

To some degree, children's influences on other family members arise out of dispositions and talents that they have inherited from their parents—a fact that complicates the question of who is influencing whom. For example, a father with an extensive vocabulary and a superior capacity for verbal reasoning may genetically endow his daughter with similar talents. As her verbal skills blossom, the young girl pleads with her parents to read to her, explain the meanings of challenging words, and discuss complex ideas. On the surface, her parents promote their daughter's verbal abilities through their actions, and undoubtedly they do. But their daughter also influences them, instigating her own opportunities for learning. An inborn, genetically supported talent prompts the requests she makes for verbal input (Scarr, 1992, 1993).

Some of children's influences on parents clearly have environmental origins. A compelling example comes from the field of political socialization (M. McDevitt & Chaffee, 1998). In a quasi-experimental study, approximately half of all classrooms in San Jose, California, participated in "Kids Voting USA," a program in citizenship education for students from kindergarten through grade 12 (you may recall our description of this program in Chapter 10), and the other half served as a control group. Apparently, children in the Kids Voting USA program brought their knowledge and excitement about politics home with them. Compared to students in the control group, they discussed politics more frequently, and possibly as a result, their parents began to pay more attention to the news, talked more often about politics, and gained greater knowledge and formed stronger opinions about candidates and political issues. Two years later, the 3-month program's effects on parents' interest in news and politics were still evident. In this case, interest "trickled up" from children to parents, with effects being particularly strong in families with limited incomes.

Many routine styles of interacting that parents and children jointly develop are positive. As we learned in Chapter 9, most parents are affectionate with their children; children respond by forming close ties to them and expressing their own affection. Figure 12–5, where 6-year-old Alex offers comfort to his father on the day his own father (Alex's grandfather) has died, illustrates this affection. But some routine styles of interacting are negative. Parents and

FIGURE 12–5 Six-year-old Alex wrote this sympathy card to his father the day Alex's grandfather (his father's father) died. Children reciprocate the affection their parents give them; this includes offering comfort when they see their parents distressed.

children can learn to accuse, mock, and ridicule one another. As they interact, they may intensify their demands and try to coerce each other, as shown in this interchange:

Mother:	I told you to clean your room. This is a *disaster.*
Daughter:	Get outta *my* room!
Mother:	[raises her voice] You clean up that mess or you're grounded! [stamps her foot]
Daughter:	Hah! You can't make me!
Mother:	For a month! [shouting now]
Daughter:	You stink! [stomps out of her room and marches to the front door]
Mother:	For two months! [shouting louder]
Daughter:	As if you'd notice I was gone! [slams door]

During this exchange, things go from bad to worse: both mother and daughter become angrier, the mother intensifies her demands, and her daughter is blatantly disobedient and accusatory. Such exchanges are common in some troubled families (Patterson & Reid, 1970). Familiar patterns of negative interaction tend to become somewhat fixed and habitual, making it difficult for family members to learn new ways of responding to one another. However, both parents and children can grow and change, often in response to people and events outside the family. We examine serious problems in families and ways to support families later in this chapter.

Siblings' Influences on One Another

Over the past 150 years, the size of American families has dropped considerably. For instance, in 1865, 82% of adolescents lived in families with five or more children; by 1930, 57% of adolescents lived in families with three or fewer children. Within that same 65-year period, the average (median) number of siblings for adolescents dropped from 7.3 to 2.6 children (Hernandez, 1997). Despite the drop in family size, having a sibling remains a common experience today; 79% of children in the U.S. live in a household with at least one sibling (Fields, 2001).

For many children, siblings are an important part of family life. Children are often deeply attached to their siblings and rely on them for comfort when anxious or upset (Bank, 1992; Stewart, 1983). The particular kinds of roles that siblings take on with one another depend partly on their relative ages. In our society, older siblings often assume caregiver responsibilities for young children when parents go shopping or do brief errands; in many other societies, older children are the primary caregivers for younger brothers and sisters for a significant part of the day (Parke & Buriel, 1998; Weisner & Gallimore, 1977). Older siblings also serve as role models (e.g., for asking parents to buy something) and playmates for younger children (Barr, 1999). In addition, they may teach young children new skills (e.g., tying shoes), although they are less likely than parents to be patient tutors (Perez-Granados & Callanan, 1997). To observe how the relative ages of siblings affect a young person, listen to 15-year-old Robin talk about her relationships with her siblings in the Families/Late Adolescence clip of the Observation CD:

Listen to 15-year-old Robin characterize her relationships with siblings in the Families/ Late Adolescence clip of the Observation CD.

> [My older brother] is kind of like my Dad. He's really nice to me. . . . With my brother, I usually like to play sports. With my little brother, I always play video games with him. My little sister, we like to argue with each other.

Sibling relationships are not always constructive, of course. Resentment may brew if one child feels slighted by a parent who appears to favor another (G. H. Brody, Stoneman, & McCoy, 1994). Children may also feel jealous or displaced when, with age, their siblings increasingly form friendships outside the family circle (Dunn, 1996). In addition, parents and other adults often compare children within a family, and some children may consistently come up short ("Why can't you get good grades like your sister?"). In response to such comparisons, children sometimes carve their own niches in the family and perhaps in the larger social sphere as well (e.g., "I'm the musician in the family; my brother is the athlete"; Huston, 1983).

Children's individual family experiences depend somewhat on their birth order—that is, on whether they were born first, second, or somewhere later down the line. Older children tend to have a slight advantage academically, perhaps because of the exclusive time they have had with their parents before any brothers or sisters came along (Zajonc & Mullally, 1997). Younger children show greater skill in interacting with peers, perhaps as a result of negotiating with older siblings and learning how to outmaneuver them to gain parental attention and family resources (Dunn, 1984; N. Miller & Maruyama, 1976). Even preschool-age siblings discuss their wants and desires with one another, and such discussions may help promote the social perspective taking we spoke of in Chapter 10 (Dunn, 1993; Perner, Ruffman, & Leekam, 1994; Ruffman, Perner, Naito, Parkin, & Clements, 1998).

At school and in other group settings, teachers and other professionals can take advantage of close-knit relationships among siblings. For instance, in times of family crisis (e.g., the death of a grandparent or a parent's going to prison), children may appreciate contact with siblings, perhaps on the playground, in the lunchroom, or in the nurse's office.

Twins and other children of multiple births have unique opportunities for steady companionship with siblings. Parents of identical (monozygotic) twins may favor keeping twins together, especially in the early grades (N. L. Segal & Russell, 1992). Rather than automatically separating twins (a practice followed by many educators), professionals may wish to make class assignments on an individual basis, with input from families. Many twins have little experience being separated prior to starting school, so being placed in different classrooms can be a big adjustment for them (Preedy, 1999). On the other hand, sometimes separate classrooms can help twins—for example, when (a) they have markedly different ability levels and one twin sees himself or herself as failing; (b) twins of differing talents intentionally stay at the same level so that one does not outshine the other; (c) twins are disruptive if they remain together; (d) they are overly dependent on each other and do not mix with other children; (e) they compete intensely or make reactive choices to each other's activities ("If he goes out, I stay in!"); or (f) one or both constantly tattle to parents about the other's actions (Preedy, 1999). As twins enter adolescence, they face the normal challenges of redefining relationships with parents; in addition, they sometimes have difficulty in forming unique identities and becoming somewhat autonomous from one another (D. A. Hay, 1999).

Sibling relationships are not essential for healthy development. *Only children*—children without brothers or sisters—are often stereotyped as spoiled and egotistical, but research patterns on their adjustment are complimentary. On average, only children perform well in school and enjoy particularly close relationships with their parents (Falbo, 1992; Falbo & Polit, 1986).

Parents' Employment

Parents' employment status can influence children in varied ways. Obviously, the income parents and other family members provide is essential for meeting children's basic needs for food, clothing, and shelter; when income is ample, it can also give children access to books and academic supplies, trips, home computers, recreation, and so forth. Parents' employment can also affect children indirectly through the arrangements parents provide for children while they are working, the skills and values parents bring home from the job, and the policies employers implement, (e.g., regarding extended parental leave or family sick leave).

The majority of parents with children are employed. In the United States, both parents are employed in about two-thirds of married couples with children under the age of 18 (U.S. Census Bureau, 2000a). Employment figures are also high for single-parent families. In one-parent family groups with children under the age of 18, 84% of fathers are employed and 73% of mothers are employed (U.S. Census Bureau, 2000b).

One implication of these high employment numbers is that many children are cared for by other people when parents are working. Employed American mothers of preschool-age children use the following primary care arrangements: 22% rely on the children's fathers or they look after the children themselves as they work; 29% ask relatives, particularly grandparents, to care for children; 22% place their children in an organized facility, such as a child care center or preschool; 20% use non-relative care, such as child care in a provider's home or in the child's own home; and 7% use some other arrangement (U.S. Census Bureau, 2003a).

Employed parents tend to use a combination of arrangements when their children reach middle childhood and early adolescence. The vast majority (84%) of working mothers of 5- to 14-year-olds report using school for child care while they are at work. Other care arrangements used by working mothers (nearly 18%) include enrichment activities (e.g., music, art, dance, language, computers), and, in descending order, the other parent, a grandparent, an older sibling, and sports programs. Moreover, nearly 16% rely on children's self-care after school. A much smaller percentage (about 4–6% each) use other relatives, organized care, a child-care center, or a non-relative in the home or in the provider's home.

The high numbers of children in *self-care* are of particular interest because children receive no adult supervision during this time. Self-care was often the only option for Barbara and Cedric Jennings:

> One day in late August, after Cedric and Barbara trolled a few thrift stores, they began walking the streets on all sides of the apartment. Barbara spoke to Cedric in careful, measured words. "You're gonna be a big kindergartner next week. And I got to be going back to get a job, when you're at school. Now, walking back from school, I don't want you to be talking to anyone, understand?"
>
> He nodded, picking up on her seriousness. Then she squatted next to him, so their faces were side by side, and she pointed across the street. "See that man over there?" she said firmly. "He's a drug dealer. He sometimes asks kids to do things. Don't ever talk to him. He's a friend of the devil." Block by block, corner by corner they went, until she'd pointed out every drug dealer for five blocks in either direction. Later that night, she slowly explained the daily drill. After school, he would walk by himself to the apartment, double lock the door, and immediately call her—the number would be taped by the phone. And, along the way, he would talk to no one.
>
> The first day of school arrived. She'd bought him an outfit specially for the day: blue slacks and a white shirt. She walked him over to Henry T. Blow Elementary, which was just behind their apartment.
>
> "Here, I got something for you." She took from her purse a fake gold chain with a key on one end and put it around his neck.
>
> "This, so you won't lose it."
>
> "Ma," he said, already conscious of his appearance, "can I wear it underneath?"
>
> She nodded, and he slipped it inside the crew neck of his white shirt. Years later, he would recall that dangling key—the metal cold against his smooth chest—and think ruefully about how exhilarating it felt: a first, cool breeze of freedom. (Suskind, 1998, p. 32)[6]

Many children come home to an empty house or apartment after school and tend to their own needs until their parents finish work.

Like Cedric, many children care for themselves after (and sometimes before) school while their parents are working. Many children in self-care (who are sometimes known as *latchkey children*) do well: They check in with parents by phone, make themselves a snack, do chores, and start their homework. Others become fearful and lonely (Long & Long, 1982) or may "care" for themselves unwisely, perhaps by participating in risky activities, partaking of alcohol and other mind-altering substances, or spending long hours playing video games or watching television. Self-care arrangements appear more effective when parents explain safety procedures, convey expectations for behavior when home alone, and monitor children's activities by phone (Galambos & Maggs, 1991a; Steinberg, 1986). (We will explore self-care in more depth in Chapter 14.)

Parents' employment influences children's development in other, very different ways as well. In the workplace, parents encounter certain kinds of decision-making practices—perhaps collaborative decisions that consider the needs of everyone, on the one hand, or top-down "Do what I tell you" mandates, on the other—and such practices filter down to the home front (Crouter, 1994; Kohn, 1977). Middle-income jobs often require extensive consultation with others, and people employed in such positions typically have a fair amount of autonomy and opportunity for decision making. Lower-income jobs more often place demands for punctuality and compliance to prespecified routines. Parents in both income groups seem to prepare their children to fit into existing income tracks, with middle-

---

[6] From *A Hope in the Unseen*, by Ron Suskind, copyright © 1998 by Ron Suskind. Used by permission of Broadway Books, a division of Random House, Inc.

income parents valuing self-direction in their children and lower-income parents preferring conformity to authority.

Through their employment, parents also serve as effective role models for their children, in that they are responsible, working citizens who are presumably contributing to the greater good of society. Girls whose mothers are employed outside the home are likely to perceive women as having numerous career options and rewarding lives (Williams & Radin, 1993). Daughters also seem to develop their own career aspirations in part from watching their mothers' professional accomplishments.

Work can interfere with effective parenting, however, especially when job pressures elevate stress levels at home and when parents must work excessively long hours (A. C. Crouter & Bumpus, 2001; MacDermid, Lee, & Smith, 2001; Moorehouse, 1991). Jobs that do not permit parents to take off time when they give birth, adopt children, or have sick children also can adversely affect parents and children (Kamerman, 2000; Ruhm 1998).

Families as Little Schoolhouses

In a sense, families are little "schoolhouses" for children. Through their families, children learn about people, the world, and future opportunities. These lessons color children's understandings of events, social relationships, tasks, and expectations at school. For example, should authority figures be feared, respected, or befriended? What are books used for? Is intellectual curiosity valued? Will I go to college? What careers might I consider?

Family Influences on Children's Achievement   Before they ever set foot in a classroom, children begin to acquire the foundations for school subjects at home; for instance, they learn basic purposes and patterns of language and may be exposed to reading materials, art, music, computer technology, and scientific and mathematical thinking (Hess & Holloway, 1984; Scott-Jones, 1991; also see the section "Emergent Literacy" in Chapter 8). When children do enter school, their parents, guardians, and siblings continue to offer ways to think about schooling—how to behave, what goals to strive for, how hard to try, what to do in the face of obstacles, and so on. Increasingly, parents also influence children by selecting a school for them from among many choices, including public schools, private schools, charter schools, home schooling, or schools that embody particular cultural values, such as African-centered education (Madhubuti & Madhubuti, 1994).

Many parents deliberately prepare their children for academic endeavors. Some, especially those who are well educated and financially comfortable, immerse their children in highly verbal and technologically rich environments that include sophisticated language, stimulating books and toys, and age-appropriate computer programs. They also encourage their children to manipulate complex objects and engage in exploratory play, and they take trips to museums and other educationally enriching sites. Numerous studies indicate that enriched home environments are associated with more advanced cognitive, linguistic, and academic skills (Bradley & Caldwell, 1984; Brooks-Gunn, Klebanov, & Duncan, 1996; Ericsson & Chalmers, 1994; Gottfried, Gottfried, Bathurst, & Guerin, 1994; B. Hart & Risley, 1995; Hess & Holloway, 1984; Jimerson, Egeland, & Teo, 1999; McGowan & Johnson, 1984). Keep in mind, however, that these studies are typically correlational and so do not show conclusively that home environments have a direct influence on children's cognitive development.

Parents also model particular ways of responding to academic material that children may try out at school (e.g., Bandura, 1986). (This idea should remind you of the behavioral learning perspective of socialization discussed earlier.) For example, children are more competent, enthusiastic readers when their parents read frequently at home (Hess & McDevitt, 1989). The composition in Figure 12–6 describes what Teresa's son, 13-year-old Connor, learned from his father about hard work and schooling. Connor had the assignment "Write an essay describing your idol" as part of an interdisciplinary unit on choices and responsibilities.

Family's Involvement in Children's Education   In the opening case study, Barbara Jennings intervened when Cedric unfairly received a B from his physics teacher. Barbara was involved in her son's education in other ways as well: She regularly attended parent-teacher-student meetings, made sure Cedric did his homework, and helped him with his

FIGURE 12-6 Parents influence their children partly by example, as 13-year-old Connor's essay illustrates.

MY FATHER

Choosing my idol was very easy for me. It was easy for me because of how successful he is now and where he came from. In Ireland in the mid Fifties my idol was born. He was born to a poor family. His father was a company sergeant in the Irish army. His father volunteered for the United Nations and went all the way to the Congo to maintain peace. He was injured in an attack on the Leopoldville airforce base in the Congo. . . .

My idol lived in a two-bedroom apartment on the military grounds. His Mom stayed home to look after him and his sister. My idol worked very hard in school. He made good choices. While some of his friends were playing soccer he was working hard and studying. Now after all that hard work he is a Dean of Education. He has two excellent children (especially the older one). He is my Father.

My dad got as far as he is in many ways. The one he thinks is the most important thing in getting him the furthest in life is the fact that his parents every night made him study and do homework. Sometimes he did not like having to do all the homework because he missed out on the fun. Now he says it is the education that got him so far. All of his friends would walk by his house and have a good time and ask him if he could come out. . . . He says that I should do my homework before friends and do it right because an education is very important. . . .

After working hard in secondary (high) school, he got a scholarship to go to college. Without the scholarship he could not have gone to college because his family could not afford to send him. Going to college was a big deal because not many Catholics at that time in that country went to college. College would be a big responsibility for him. He also made a choice to go to a predominately Protestant college, even though he was a Catholic. One consequence of this was that the Christian Brothers (teachers) in his high school were mad at him. He persevered and attended Trinity College Dublin.

In college he joined the rowing club. Rowing had many consequences for him. He made new friends, traveled the country, and became very fit. Another consequence for him was that he would be very tired after rowing. Sometimes he and his friends were so tired they couldn't ride their bikes home from practice. They would have to walk! He was very persistent. He also ran on the cross-country team. These sports could have affected him and his grades but he studied hard. He said that, "you have to have priorities." He had a responsibility to his grades. He got a degree in psychology.

What have I learned from my Dad's experiences? He came from a poor background to be very successful. From his background you could not have predicted his job or his success (or how wonderful his children are). What were the keys to his success? He studied hard, had goals and priorities, and was persistent. If I could do something similar I would probably study as hard as I could. Also I would try as hard as he did in school. He is trying to teach me the same values and work ethic. I would like to have his values. However, sometimes it's hard for me to devote time to studying. There's lots of distractions, especially friends, Nintendo, and sports. I'm trying my best.

assignments whenever she could. Parents and other family members are more likely to become involved in children's education when they believe that (a) their involvement is necessary or important, (b) they can exert a positive influence on their children's educational achievement, and (c) school personnel want their involvement (R. M. Clark, 1983; Hoover-Dempsey & Sandler, 1997; Lareau, 1989).

Generally speaking, family involvement in children's education and activities is a good thing (Hoover-Dempsey & Sandler, 1997). For instance, parents and other family members may enhance children's learning at school in a variety of ways: They might discuss school activities, assist with homework (or at least nag children to do it), lavish praise or give feedback about in-class projects and assignments, and confer with teachers about children's classroom progress. Some parents also contribute to school activities, perhaps by helping to chaperone field trips, participating in fund-raising activities, or serving on parent advisory boards. Students whose parents are involved in school activities have better attendance records, higher achievement, and more positive attitudes toward school than students whose parents are not actively involved; this difference exists even when the prior school performance of both groups of students has been the same (Chavkin, 1993; Eccles & Harold, 1993; J. L. Epstein, 1996; Hoover-Dempsey & Sandler, 1997; Jimerson et al., 1999). Students with actively involved parents are also more likely to graduate from high school (Rumberger, 1995).

Naturally, not all parent involvement is constructive (Hoover-Dempsey & Sandler, 1997). One can imagine assistance that is ill suited to children's developmental needs—when, for example, parents insist that their average-ability second grader do advanced algebra at home "for fun," or hover over a high school student while he completes his homework assignments, thereby preventing him from exercising self-regulatory skills. Nonetheless, in general, active parent involvement predicts good academic outcomes for children.

As teachers quickly discover, some parents eagerly and actively participate in their children's education whereas others seek little or no involvement. Numerous factors account for this difference, including parents' work schedules, child care responsibilities, health and energy levels, access to transportation, and emotional well-being. A few parents seem to have little interest in their children's welfare (see the earlier discussion of uninvolved parenting). Other parents believe that they are unwelcome at school or unlikely to make a difference in their children's academic progress (A. A. Carr, 1997; Hoover-Dempsey & Sandler, 1997). Later in the chapter, we consider strategies for encouraging such parents to become more involved in their children's schooling.

Taking Cultural Differences into Account   In Chapter 4, we introduced the idea of *apprenticeship* as a means by which adults gradually teach children new skills. Across all cultures, children serve as apprentices to their parents; they are slowly and steadily guided toward fuller participation in adult practices (Rogoff, 1990). Individual cultures and family legacies determine what tools and procedures children are exposed to, whether they are explicitly taught or instead learn from observation and eavesdropping, and how early they take on particular responsibilities.

When teachers and other practitioners are not familiar with a family's cultural values and practices, they may misconstrue the actions of the children. Consider the child who is taught at home to be docile, respectful, and conforming in interactions with adults. A teacher who expects a lot of talk from students may incorrectly interpret the child's behavior as reflecting a lack of motivation, intelligence, or social skills. Consider, too, the child who is taught at home that cooperation and helping others are more important than individual achievement. A teacher who expects all students to work independently on classroom assignments may, upon seeing the child help a classmate during "independent seatwork time," erroneously conclude that the child is cheating.

Youngsters are most likely to succeed at school and in the community when teaching strategies are compatible with, or at least respectful of, family practices. An example of instruction that builds on families' cultural practices is the Kamehameha Elementary Education Program (Au, 1997; Tharp & Gallimore, 1988). Designed to enhance the educational achievement of ethnic-minority Hawaiian children, teachers build on family values of cooperation and harmony by assembling small groups of children and encouraging them to work together on assignments (Jordan, 1981; Weisner, Gallimore, & Jordan, 1988).

Developing culturally compatible styles of interacting requires considerable familiarity with the cultural practices of children and their families. Professionals can learn a great deal about such practices by discussing local customs and values with parents and other family members, as well as by becoming active participants in (and open-minded observers of) the day-to-day activities of the local community.

Risk Factors in Families

As you have seen, "good" families—those that foster children's physical, cognitive, and social-emotional development—come in a wide variety of packages. Not all families provide optimal environments for children, however. Some have such limited financial resources that they cannot afford adequate food, housing, or medical care. Others are so overwhelmed by crises in their own lives (marital conflict, loss of employment, life-threatening illness, etc.) that they have little time or energy to devote to their children. Still others, including many uninvolved parents, suffer from serious psychological problems (e.g., depression or schizophrenia) or engage in a self-destructive lifestyle of alcohol or drug abuse.

Some children successfully rise above such environments to become productive, well-adjusted adults. For example, a child may cope with a parent's mental illness if other family members are affectionate and dependable (Mary, in the opening case study in Chapter 9, is one such instance). We will look at conditions that promote children's *resilience* in Chapter 14.

Unfortunately, many other children suffer long-term consequences of unhealthy family environments. For example, when parents have psychological problems, such as chronic mental illness, children show difficulties in adjustment and may themselves exhibit externalizing behaviors, such as aggression, or internalizing behaviors, such as anxiety or depression (McHale & Rasmussen, 1998; Zahn-Waxler, Mayfield, Radke-Yarrow, McKnew, Cytryn, & Davenport, 1988). The more family stresses children are exposed to, the more vulnerable they appear to become (Sameroff, Seifer, Barocas, Zax, & Greenspan, 1987). As Garbarino and Abramowitz (1992c) aptly put it, "Risk accumulates in the child's life like a poison" (p. 22).

The most serious consequence of an unhealthy family environment is, of course, *child maltreatment*. Maltreatment takes four major forms (English, 1998; R. A. Thompson & Wyatt, 1999). *Neglect* occurs when caregivers fail to provide food, clothing, shelter, health care, or basic affection and do not adequately supervise children's activities. Caregivers engage in *physical abuse* when they intentionally cause physical harm to children, perhaps by kicking, biting, shaking, or punching them. If spanking causes serious bruises or injuries, it, too, is considered physical abuse. Caregivers engage in *sexual abuse* when they seek sexual gratification from children through acts such as genital contact or pornography. They engage in *emotional abuse* when they consistently ignore, isolate, reject, denigrate, or terrorize children or when they corrupt children by encouraging them to engage in substance abuse or criminal activity. Sadly, some parents and other caregivers submit children to more than one form of abuse, as one woman's recollection illustrates:

> My father used to do the weirdest things to me. I hate him. He was in the navy, back in the war and stuff like that. I guess he picked up weird things like that. He used to put me in the corner and put a bag over my head and every time he'd walk by he'd kick me—just like a dog. My mom told me once he put a tick on my stomach and let the tick suck my blood. Things like that—really gross, things that a father would never do to their (sic) daughter. He'd stick toothpicks up my fingernails until it would bleed. [Did he sexually abuse you, too?] Oh, yeah. When I was six. Had to get me to the hospital. I had twenty stitches. I just can't talk about it. (Belenky, Clinchy, Goldberger, & Tarule, 1986, p. 159)

Dear Diary,
Father was home early from the bar. He was really drunk this time. I was just sitting down reading a book when he started hitting me. My mom tried to help me but it was no use. I finally went to a corner when he fainted. After that mom and I left for Aunt Mary's. Maybe we'll be safe there.

Like the father described in this child's diary entry, many family members who are abusive suffer from serious psychological problems.

Those who maltreat children are, in most cases, individuals who themselves suffer from serious psychological problems. They tend to have low self-esteem and to be anxious, depressed, aggressive, and impulsive (National Research Council, 1993b; Thompson & Wyatt, 1999). Some suffer from emotional illness; others have serious substance abuse problems (Bishop et al., 2001; Kienberger-Jaudes, Ekwo, & Van Voorhis, 1995; Thompson & Wyatt, 1999). Many have little or no contact with or support from family or friends and so are socially and emotionally isolated (Thompson & Wyatt). Some abusive parents are quite naïve about children's development and hold unrealistic expectations about what their children should be able to do (English, 1998). As an example, two staff members at a preschool reported the following incident:

> It was time to go to the yard, and . . . Donna B. made mud pies and puddles. I then saw her bringing Timmie over. He was crying. Donna later told the reason why he cried. . . . He was playing in some water and spilled it on his shirt. Sister Donna said he was crying because he was going to get another beating from his father for having his shirt wet.
>
> . . . I was trying to reassure and comfort Timmie who was sobbing quietly but convulsively when his sister Donna walked near and pulled up Timmie's shirt to show me his badly lacerated and still bloody-raw back. "He cry 'cause he father goin' give him 'nother beatin' for gettin' wet." (F. P. L. Hawkins, 1997, pp. 194–195)

The children most likely to be maltreated are those who are very young (premature infants are especially at risk), those who have disabilities, and those who are temperamentally difficult (English, 1998; L. Little, 2000b; P. Sullivan & Knutson, 1998; Thompson & Wyatt, 1999). In some cases, maltreated children suffer the ultimate consequence: death. More often, however, they survive but suffer long-lasting physical and psychological effects (English, 1998; Emery & Laumann-Billings, 1998; Leiter & Johnsen, 1997; Thompson & Wyatt, 1999). Infants without adequate nutrition may experience permanent retardation of their physical growth. Neglected toddlers have difficulty trusting others and forming healthy relationships with peers and adults (a finding consistent with our discussion of attachment in Chapter 9). When they reach school age, children who have been abused and neglected tend to do poorly in school and to be absent frequently; they are also more likely to experience emotional problems, commit crimes (e.g., shoplifting), and engage in alcohol and substance abuse. Children who endure sexual abuse may become infected with sexually transmitted diseases. Physically abused children are more likely than non-abused children to become aggressive themselves, to have poor social skills, and to show little or no empathy for the distress of others. Extreme forms of physical punishment are correlated with depression, failure to follow rules when parents are not watching, aggression with peers and, in adulthood, criminal and antisocial behavior (Gershoff, 2002).

In the United States, almost a million children are documented as being abused or neglected every year (Larner, Stevenson, & Behrman, 1998). The actual incidence of child maltreatment is certainly much higher, because many instances are never reported to authorities. Educators and others working with children and adolescents must, by law, contact proper authorities (e.g., Child Protective Services) when they suspect child abuse or neglect. Unfortunately, these reports do not always lead to provision of protective services for maltreated children. In many cases, authorities cannot find sufficient evidence to substantiate charges filed against the perpetrators, and in other cases work overload prevents authorities from giving immediate assistance (Larner et al., 1998; Wolock, Sherman, Feldman, & Metzger, 2001).

Our emphasis thus far has been largely on how *behaviors* of parents, children, and other family members influence family dynamics and children's developmental progress in positive and negative ways. *Cognitions*, the range of ideas parents hold about childhood, also affect family life, as you will discover in the next section.

How Parents Conceptualize Childhood

How parents act toward and socialize their children is, in part, a function of their beliefs about their children—as well as about children more generally—and the visions they have for their children's future. In this section, we examine a range of ideas that parents hold about childhood, consider how parents acquire these ideas, and identify situations in which parents' beliefs might be quite different from those of professionals who work with their children.

Diversity in Parents' Ideas

Some parents view childhood as a time of innocence to be cherished; others may instead view it as a period of selfish desires and uncivilized urges. Some see childhood as a useless period that should be grown out of as quickly as possible, whereas others may intentionally insulate their children from adult responsibilities (Goodnow & Collins, 1990). Such beliefs inevitably affect parents' approaches to childrearing.

Parents differ, too, in underlying goals they have for children. LeVine (1974, 1988) hypothesized that parents' goals are somewhat hierarchical (Figure 12–7). Their most basic goal is sheer survival. In harsh conditions (e.g., in times of war or famine), survival is parents' predominant concern; they place less priority on culturally defined ideals, such as being responsible, pious, polite, or tidy ("I don't talk nice to my kids when I'm worrying that they might get killed by some

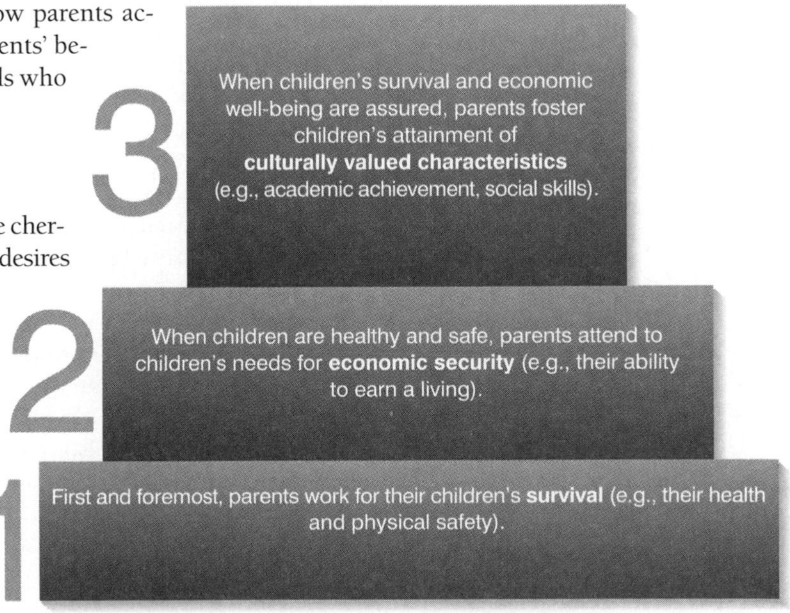

3 When children's survival and economic well-being are assured, parents foster children's attainment of **culturally valued characteristics** (e.g., academic achievement, social skills).

2 When children are healthy and safe, parents attend to children's needs for **economic security** (e.g., their ability to earn a living).

1 First and foremost, parents work for their children's **survival** (e.g., their health and physical safety).

FIGURE 12–7 Hierarchical nature of parents' goals for their children. After LeVine, 1974, 1988.

thug. I demand they come straight home from school!"). If parents feel certain their children are safe, they are freer to think about economic prospects ("He'll never get rich with his art, but he can always fall back on his computer skills"). With basic survival and economic needs assured, parents may attend to intellectual and social characteristics ("What a smart little guy my 3-year-old is. Ask him to name the planets!"). In reality, parents can probably juggle a range of concerns simultaneously, and lower- or higher-level concerns may float into consciousness at unpredictable times (Goodnow & Collins, 1990). To illustrate, parents in poor and distressed families, for whom we would predict concerns about survival and subsistence, may still frequently concentrate on their children's social and emotional needs (e.g., Richman, Miller, & Solomon, 1988). Conversely, parents whose children are usually healthy may still show concerns with survival, for instance, by having their children immunized against serious diseases and taking precautions to remove chemicals from drinking water.

Parents also differ in what they expect to gain from their children (Goodnow & Collins, 1990). Because you are reading this book, we are guessing that you have children in your life now or hope to have them in your life, perhaps as a parent, teacher, counselor, social worker, health professional, or community leader. Take a moment to consider your own reasons for wanting to have or work with children. We suspect you may want opportunities to cherish children, enjoy their companionship, delight in their antics and, by helping to nurture and guide the next generation, gain a sense of personal fulfillment. Most parents share such desires, but a few have self-centered motivations. Some people expect that bearing or fathering a child may give them "adult" status and, in some cultures, prestige. Others have children either as a matter of custom or under pressure from family and friends. Still others want a person in their lives who can give them unconditional love (Coley & Chase-Lansdale, 1998) or can care for them in later years (L. W. Hoffman, 1988). In some cases, a couple may hope that having a child will strengthen a faltering relationship, or they may conceive a child as an unintended consequence of sexual activity.

Origins of Parents' Ideas

The range of ideas that parents have about children leads us to wonder how these ideas are acquired. Mostly, parents' conceptions of childhood originate with the people around them—family, friends, people in the media, and so on—and from the specific culture in which they live (Goodnow & Collins, 1990; Hess, Chang, & McDevitt, 1987). A recent investigation by Okagaki and Frensch (1998) provides a concrete illustration of cultural influences on parents' beliefs. Okagaki and Frensch compared expectations of three groups of parents living in northern California: Asian Americans, Latino Americans, and European Americans. Of the three groups, Asian American parents held the highest expectations for their children's educational attainment; on average, these parents hoped their children would not only attend college but also obtain a graduate or professional degree. Asian American parents were also the least satisfied when their children earned grades lower than an A. Latino American parents were most likely to monitor their children's activities at school, and they placed high priority on the development of desired personal characteristics, such as conformity (e.g., showing respect to adults, obeying teachers) and autonomy (e.g., making decisions on one's own, working through problems by oneself). European American parents had the most confidence that they personally had the knowledge and skills necessary to help their children succeed in school.

Culture also influences parents' beliefs about the purposes of education. For some immigrant families, and particularly for parents of Mexican descent, education means not only academic achievement but also acquisition of the social and moral practices needed in one's journey along the *buen camino de la vida,* or "good path of life" (Dunbar, Azmitia, & Brown, 1999). Some parents from other cultural backgrounds, especially those from Southeast Asian countries, may think of education almost exclusively in terms of academic achievement and view less academic endeavors—sports, dramatic productions, field trips, and so on—as "play" activities that should be used primarily as rewards for hard work (Kang-Ning, 1981).

Personal experience is another, though probably less influential, source of parents' ideas about children (Goodnow & Collins, 1990). Parents may formulate hypotheses ("With all the attention I give my daughter, she's bound to become a superstar"), collect data ("No matter what I do or say, my daughter is mean to her brother"), and revise their expectations ("I guess children are less influenced by parents than I first thought, or maybe I've been too easy on her"). Some evidence indicates that parents do form and change beliefs in response to experience. For instance, Holden (1988) found that parents and nonparents differed in interpretations of an infant's crying and in how they went about determining causes of crying.

When parents use cultural messages and personal experiences in forming impressions, they do not necessarily do so systematically or rationally (Goodnow & Collins, 1990). Parents (like all human beings) may entertain two inconsistent beliefs without resolving the inconsistency. For example, a parent may believe that children should be responsible for their own "stuff" yet continually pick up after a son or daughter to minimize household clutter. Furthermore, parents (again, like all human beings) work hard to protect their own self-image. Most parents are fiercely invested in their children, are quite mindful of their own hard work in caring for them, and see their children's performance as a reflection of their own competence. Accordingly, they may blame others—often teachers and other professionals—when their children fail to live up to expectations.

Parents often take shortcuts in forming their beliefs and expectations. They sometimes use existing stereotypes to develop impressions of their children's abilities; for instance, the common (though erroneous) belief that "boys are better at math than girls" may color their assessment of the actual mathematical abilities of their sons and daughters (Dunton, McDevitt, & Hess, 1988; Parsons, Adler, & Kaczala, 1982). Parents are also selective in the advice they use from experts. For example, Cohen (1981) examined the beliefs of English mothers who had recently moved to a new housing development. These mothers formed a discussion group, reading and analyzing books that offered advice for nurturing children's development. They accepted advice to emphasize play and discovery while their children were small but in later years ignored experts' recommendations to avoid memorization, figuring that rote learning was needed to get into good schools.

Contrasting Perspectives of Parents and Professionals

In their views about children, parents and professionals can sometimes find themselves on opposite sides of the table. Consider these two situations and the contrasting viewpoints they reflect:

- Jane Schmidt is the single mother of 7-year-old Lawrence. In the mind of Lawrence's teacher, Rita, Jane is not very cooperative. Rita is concerned because Lawrence has not acquired basic skills in reading and mathematics. She suspects that Lawrence might catch up with the other children if he would only do the practice activities she sends home with him every night. But Jane rarely insists that Lawrence do his homework. From Rita's perspective, Jane is overindulgent and permissive. From Jane's perspective, Lawrence is working to his capacity and needs time after school for sports, play, and relaxation.
- Elliott, a high school art teacher, encourages his students to create original paintings, pottery, and sculptures. In an informal discussion at an orientation meeting, several parents ask why students are not getting direct instruction in artistic form and technique. One particularly vocal father argues that originality is not possible until students have mastered basic skills. Elliott explains that he tries to teach skills within the context of specific projects but wants the students to develop unique visions for their own creations. The parents don't buy it.

In these and many other situations, professionals and parents view children's needs differently, and it would be all too easy to fall into the trap of thinking "I'm right, so they must be wrong." Before jumping to such a conclusion, teachers and other professionals would do well to remember that many beliefs about childhood are just that—*beliefs*—and are not necessarily right or wrong but merely different.

Conflicting beliefs among parents and professionals sometimes arise out of differences in educational or cultural backgrounds. For instance, the father who argued with Elliott about the need for systematic instruction may himself have had considerable formal training in artistic techniques. Yet even when parents and practitioners share similar backgrounds, they may see the same children in different settings (home versus school or other setting) and draw on different knowledge bases as they interpret children's performance and behavior.

To some degree, parents and practitioners must have similar understandings about children if they are to work cooperatively (e.g., Churchill, 1999). Yet it is rarely productive for teachers or other professionals to try to convince parents to change their beliefs about children. (For one thing, parents are often right!) An alternative approach is for parents and practitioners to explain their ideas about development as well as their objectives for children. When professionals take the time to build rapport and credibility with parents, they may be in a good position to offer suggestions based on what they have learned through their experiences, coursework, and professional reading.

Partnerships with Families

When children begin some form of schooling—whether in an infant/toddler center, preschool, kindergarten, or first grade—effective teachers get parents and other family members (e.g., grandparents, older siblings) actively involved in children's learning (Davis & Thomas, 1989; J. L. Epstein, 1996; Levine & Lezotte, 1995). Ideally, relationships between family members and practitioners are *partnerships* in which everyone collaborates to promote children's learning (Hidalgo et al., 1995). Such relationships may be especially important when children come from diverse cultural backgrounds or when they have special educational needs (Hidalgo et al., 1995; Salend & Taylor, 1993; Turnbull et al., 2002). The same principle holds for many other settings as well, including clubs, religious education, and recreation centers: when communication between parents and professionals is good, parents can reinforce learning at home and professionals can learn from parents how to adjust programs to meet the needs of individual children.

Although most parents and other primary caregivers want what is best for their children, many do not participate actively in their schooling or activities outside the home. Some do not attend parent-teacher conferences, school open houses, community events, or other events specifically for family members. Other parents are actively involved when their children are in elementary school but increasingly withdraw as their children move to the middle and secondary school grade levels (J. L. Epstein, 1996; Finders & Lewis, 1994; Roderick & Camburn, 1999).

Before jumping too quickly to the conclusion that parents are uninterested in their children's lives, practitioners must realize that there are many possible reasons why parents are reluctant to become involved (Chavkin, 1993; Finders & Lewis, 1994; Hidalgo et al., 1995; Lareau, 1987; Salend & Taylor, 1993). Some may have an exhausting work schedule or lack adequate child care. Others may have difficulty communicating in English. Still others may believe that it is inappropriate to bother teachers and other professionals with questions about their children's progress or to offer information as to why their children are having difficulty. A few may avoid school because of their own painful memories. One father put it this way:

> They expect me to go to school so they can tell me my kid is stupid or crazy. They've been telling me that for three years, so why should I go and hear it again? They don't do anything. They just tell me my kid is bad.
>
> See, I've been there. I know. And it scares me. They called me a boy in trouble but I was a troubled boy. Nobody helped me because they liked it when I didn't show up. If I was gone for the semester, fine with them. I dropped out nine times. They wanted me gone. (Finders & Lewis, 1994, p. 51)

A good first step in getting families involved in children's education and activities is to get a sense of family structures, relationships, and neighborhoods. Professionals are more likely to establish productive partnerships when they accommodate family roles: If Grandma is the child's primary caregiver, for example, then she, possibly with the child's parent(s), should be invited to a parent-teacher conference. The Observation Guidelines table, "Identifying Family Conditions," lists characteristics of families that professionals can identify in their efforts to support children and their families.

Professionals should also consider a family's cultural background. For instance, although most Chinese American parents are deeply concerned about their children's education, they may be reluctant to seek out teachers because they're unfamiliar with procedures

OBSERVATION GUIDELINES

Identifying Family Conditions

CHARACTERISTIC	LOOK FOR	EXAMPLE	IMPLICATION
Family Structure	• Single versus multiple caregivers • Presence or absence of siblings • Extended family members living in the home • Nonrelatives living in the home • Children's attachments to and relationships with other family members	Alexis's chronic kidney disease flare-ups cause fatigue and irritability. At such times, she finds comfort in being with her sister at recess and at lunch. Alexis's teachers have observed the girls' close relationship and provide opportunities for them to be together when she's ill.	Accept all families as valued, legitimate caregivers of children, regardless of their form. Include extended family members (especially those who are regular caregivers) at school functions. Give children time to be with siblings in times of personal or family crisis.
Cultural Background	• Language(s) spoken at home • Children's loyalty to and sense of responsibility for other family members • Children's attitudes toward cooperation and competition • Children's and parents' communication styles (whether they make eye contact, ask a lot of questions, are open about their concerns, etc.)	Carlos is very reserved in class. He follows instructions and shows that he wants to do well in school. However, he rarely seeks his teacher's help. Instead, he often asks his cousin (a classmate) for assistance.	Remember that most children and parents are interested in academic achievement despite what their behaviors may make you think. Adapt instructional styles to children's preferred ways of interacting and communicating. Consider how families' cultural knowledge and skills might enrich the setting in which you work.
Family Livelihood	• Presence of a family business (e.g., farm, cottage industry) that requires children's involvement • Children in self-care for several hours after school • Older children and adolescents with part-time jobs (e.g., grocery store work, paper routes) • Parental unemployment	April completes several chores on the family farm before going to school each morning. She keeps ongoing records about the weight and general health of three calves born last year. She constructs charts to show their progress as a project for her seventh-grade science class.	Take young people's outside work commitments into account when assigning homework. For example, give students at least 2 days to complete short assignments and at least a week for longer ones. Be flexible about due dates when students contribute to family income.
Parenting Styles	• Parents' apparent warmth or coldness toward their children • Parents' expectations for their children's behavior and performance • Parents' concerns about their children's needs • Parents' willingness to discuss issues and negotiate solutions with their children • Possible effects of children's temperaments on parents' disciplinary styles	At a parent-teacher conference, Julia's parents express their exasperation about trying to get Julia to do her homework. "We've tried everything—reasoning with her, giving ultimatums, offering extra privileges for good grades, punishing her for bad grades—but nothing works. She'd rather hang out with her friends every night."	Acknowledge that most parents have their children's best interests at heart and use disciplinary methods they have seen others model. Recognize that parents often adapt their parenting styles to children's temperaments. Communicate high expectations, show sensitivity to childrens' needs, and give reasons for your requests.
Disruptive Influences	• Change in family membership (e.g., as a result of death, divorce, remarriage, or cohabitation) • Change of residence • Physical or mental illness in parents or other family members • Parental alcoholism or substance abuse	Justin has had trouble concentrating since his parents' divorce, and he no longer shows much enthusiasm for class activities.	Show compassion for children undergoing a family transition. Offer yourself as a listener. Realize that some families may quickly return to healthy functioning but others may be in turmoil for lengthy periods. Seek the assistance of a counselor when children have unusual difficulty.
Maltreatment	• Frequent injuries, attributed to "accidents" • Age-inappropriate sexual knowledge or behavior • Extreme withdrawal, anxiety, or depression • Untreated medical or dental needs • Chronic hunger • Poor hygiene and grooming • Lack of warm clothing in cold weather	Michael often has bruises on his arms and legs, which his mother says are the result of a "blood problem." He recently had a broken collar bone, and soon after, he has a broken arm and a black eye. "I fell down the stairs," he explains, but refuses to say more.	Immediately report any signs of child maltreatment to a school counselor or principal. Contact Child Protective Services for advice about additional courses of action.

for scheduling appointments or may think it inappropriate to question the judgment of school personnel (Hidalgo et al., 1995). Chinese American families may also prefer to support their children's schoolwork by helping them at home—teaching them basic academic skills, for example, and discouraging adolescents from working long hours in order to allow time for homework (Chao, 2000).

Communicating with Families

Effective communication is at the heart of any partnership. Accordingly, we urge professionals to keep in regular contact with families about their children's academic, social, and emotional progress. Families appreciate hearing about children's accomplishments, and they deserve to know about behaviors that consistently interfere with children's learning and adjustment. In fact, when lines of communication between professionals are regularly used, information can run both ways: from professional to family and from family to professional.

The particular forms of communication professionals use depend on their jobs and relationships with parents. They might include these common forms:

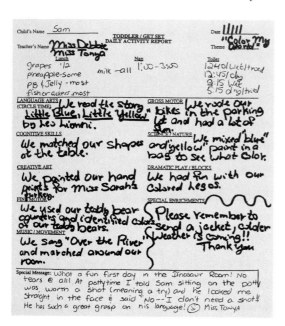

FIGURE 12–8 A structured toddler form completed for 2½-year-old Sam. Parents often appreciate information about what their children did during the day and also about the kinds of learning activities made available to them.

- *Meetings.* In most school districts, parent-teacher conferences are scheduled one or more times a year; additional meetings are scheduled if requested by either teacher or parent. In many schools, teachers invite students to join parent-teacher conferences. By doing so, they make it more likely that parents will attend the conference, encourage youngsters to reflect on their own academic progress, and help each participant leave the meeting with a shared understanding of progress and steps to be taken next. Social workers also meet periodically with parents, for example, conferring on the adjustment of a newly adopted child or determining whether children's needs are being met in a family referred for possible neglect.

- *Written communication.* Professionals can use structured forms to let parents know what their children are doing. Prepared forms that specify activities and leave space for individual comments can be helpful. In Figure 12–8, teachers describe 2½-year-old Sam's first day in the toddler room, including information about their program and how Sam fared. More formal newsletters communicate school- and community-wide events, resources, and policies. In addition to providing concrete information, these communications convey professionals' desire to stay in touch.

- *Telephone conversations.* Telephone calls are useful when issues require immediate attention. For example, teachers might call a parent to express their concern when a student's behavior deteriorates unexpectedly. But they might also call to express their excitement about an important step forward. Parents, too, should feel free to call teachers. Keep in mind that many parents are at work during the school day; hence, it is often helpful for teachers to take calls at home during the early evening hours.

- *E-mail and Web sites.* Increasingly, educators and other practitioners find that they can maintain regular contact with parents electronically—for instance, by sending e-mail messages and creating Web pages that list activities and assignments. In Figure 12–9, you can see an e-mail message sent by a school counselor to parents of middle school students about unkind remarks that had flared up among students. This message enabled the counselor to alert parents to events that were troubling some of the youngsters and to seek their support in encouraging proper behavior. Such electronic communication, of course, can only be used when parents have access to computers and e-mail.

- *Parent discussion groups.* In some instances, teachers, social workers, and other professionals may want to assemble a group of parents to discuss mutual concerns. For example, teachers might use such a group as a sounding board to choose among possible topics for the classroom curriculum, or perhaps to make decisions about assigning controversial yet potentially valuable works of literature.

Hello!

How much money would it take for you to agree to go back to your 7th grade year of school? You couldn't pay me enough!!!

Disrespect and thoughtless comments to peers seem to be on the upswing in the 7th grade at [our school]. Today we had a town meeting, and I had one of my serious chats with the class about the importance of treating others properly. I strongly encouraged students to step back and evaluate their own behavior. I asked them to think about whether their parents would be proud of how they treat others. I also asked if they personally were proud of how they treat others.

I think most of you know me well enough by now to know that I have a low tolerance for people who treat others poorly. If your child is having trouble with peers, please encourage him or her to talk with me. If s/he is struggling with taking that first step, I hope you would take the time to call me to discuss it. Unless I'm aware of concerns, I can't work on making things better.

It takes a village.

Nancy

Alternatively, they might want to use a discussion group as a mechanism through which all participants can share ideas about how best to promote students' academic, personal, and social development.

Whatever form the communication may take, several strategies enhance the likelihood of effectiveness:

■ *When two or more family members are primary caregivers, encourage them to stay in touch.* For example, when two parents are actively involved in a child's life—whether they live in the same household or not—practitioners should try to get to know both parents and show respect for the role that each plays in the child's development. All too often, fathers are left out of the picture when it comes to practitioner-parent communication, yet in today's society fathers tend to be more involved in children's lives than their own fathers were with them (Tamis-LeMonda & Cabrera, 1999).

■ *Take parents' work schedules and other commitments into account.* Some parents have considerable flexibility in their work schedules and may be able to come to a meeting or talk on the phone during the day. But many others are not so fortunate. If educators and other practitioners want to communicate with parents and other family members, they may sometimes have to schedule meetings or phone conversations in the early morning or evening hours.

■ *Establish rapport.* Although some parents feel confident and comfortable when they talk with teachers, counselors, health professionals, and other practitioners, others may be anxious, uncertain, or distrustful. Professionals can look for signs of discomfort, use friendly body language, display a sense of humor, and treat parents as authorities who can help them learn about their children.

■ *Be a listener as well as a talker.* Most parents want to be heard rather than just "talked at" (Hoover-Dempsey & Sandler, 1997), yet some may be reluctant to voice their perspectives without some encouragement. Professionals can often encourage input by asking specific questions ("What kinds of books does Jason like to read at home?", "What does Eri like to do in her free time?") and assuring them that they should feel free to call whenever they have questions or concerns.

■ *Step in their shoes.* Families often live very different lives than the professionals who work with them. By reading research on particular cultural groups and listening sympathetically, professionals can learn about parents' lives as they experience them. For example, by learning more about families who reside in temporary shelters for the homeless, professionals might discover that parents (a) actively monitor the whereabouts and activities of their children, in part because they do not trust neighbors and want to protect their children from gang activities, (b) appreciate caring concern from others, and (c) welcome safe activities for their children (Torquati, 2002).

■ *Remember that most parents view their children's behavior as a reflection of their own competence.* Parents typically feel proud when their children are successful in school and get along well with friends. In contrast, parents may respond to their children's academic failures or behavior problems with embarrassment, shame, or anger. Others deny that their "angels" could possibly be doing anything wrong and instead place blame on teachers and other professionals for any academic or social shortcomings. Practitioners are more likely to have productive discussions with parents if they place no blame and instead propose that they work as a team to find solutions.

■ *Be alert for possible philosophical and cultural differences.* As you have seen, parents have varying beliefs about their own children, the nature of childhood, and good educational practices; these beliefs are likely to color their interpretations of children's performance. Furthermore, their cultural backgrounds may influence whether they make eye contact, whether they are willing to speak their minds, and so on. Professionals are more likely to communicate effectively with parents if they are on the lookout for values, ideas, and customs that differ from their own. For instance, counselors can ask parents why they believe their child is unhappy at school.

When conferring with parents about problematic classroom behaviors, professionals should keep in mind that people from different cultural groups sometimes have distinct ideas about how children should be disciplined. For example, many Chinese American parents believe that Western schools are too lenient in correcting inappropriate behavior (Hidalgo et al., 1995). In some Native American and Asian cultures, a child's misbehaviors may be seen as bringing shame on the family or community; thus, a common disciplinary strategy is to ignore or ostracize the child for an extended period of time (Pang, 1995; Salend & Taylor, 1993). As teachers and other practitioners talk with parents from cultures different from their own, they can listen with an open mind and try to find common ground on which to develop strategies for helping children (Salend & Taylor).

When you suspect you have views that conflict with those of a member of a child's family, share your perspectives on the child's needs and ask the family member to share his or her own views.

■ *Accommodate language and literacy differences.* When a child's parents speak a language other than English, professionals will, of course, want to include in conversations someone who can converse fluently with the parents in their native tongue (and ideally, someone whom the parents trust). They should also have newsletters and other written messages translated.

■ *Curb your own biases.* Professionals may hold stereotypes relating to families and unconsciously pass these on to parents. For example, some caregivers in child care settings have negative views of low-income parents (Kontos, Raikes, & Woods, 1983; Kontos & Wells, 1986). In a study with poor single mothers, researchers found that mothers picked up on negative feelings from teachers (Holloway, Fuller, Rambaud, & Eggers-Péirola, 1997). One mother, for example, believed that teachers thought less of her because she had received assistance from the Department of Social Services.

■ *Support parents in their efforts to seek solutions to difficult problems.* Social workers often see families who face extremely challenging dilemmas. For example, one mother wanted to go back to school to improve her chances of getting a well-paying job that would benefit her children. The social worker had to explain that the welfare reform program she was in required her to work full-time (Berg & Kelly, 2000). She was frustrated, and responded "What do you want me to do?" (p. 127). For such problems, there are no easy answers. Rather than giving simple responses, a social worker may be better off showing understanding of how tough the problem is and encouraging the parent to think through options she might not have considered. In other words, the social worker can sometimes be more effective by validating parents' dilemmas rather than simply repeating program requirements.

■ *Inform parents of services available to them.* Families in trouble often value referrals to other agencies. For example, families who have been found to be seriously maltreating their children may be at risk for out-of-home placement of children. In such cases, therapists aim to protect children, but they can also help parents to increase their skills and to strengthen family bonds (Staudt, 2001). These families may appreciate information about

DEVELOPMENT AND PRACTICE

Making Institutions Family-Friendly

■ Help children and their families to feel that they are valued members of the group.

A caregiver of infants and toddlers provides cubbies for each child. On the outside, the child's name is posted and photographs of the child and his or her family are displayed. Children regularly point to their parents and other family members throughout the day.

■ Recognize the significance of families in children's lives.

A music teacher asks students to bring in photographs of their families to post on her bulletin board labeled "My Family and Me." She also includes the names of favorite family songs under each family.

■ Acknowledge the strengths of families' varying backgrounds.

When planning a lesson on the history of farming in Colorado, a middle school social studies teacher asks a mother if she would be willing to talk about her own childhood experiences as a member of an immigrant family that harvested crops every summer.

■ Use a variety of formats to communicate with parents.

A fourth-grade teacher works with the children in his class to produce a monthly newsletter for parents. Two versions of the newsletter are created, one in English and one in Spanish.

■ Tell parents about children's many strengths, even when communicating information about their shortcomings.

A school counselor talks on the phone with the parents of a student. She describes several areas in which the student has made considerable progress but also asks for advice about strategies that might help him stay on task and be more prosocial with peers.

■ Be sensitive to parents' concerns about their children.

A social worker talks with worried parents of a 16-year-old girl who has begun smoking and possibly experimenting with drugs. Thinking about the girl's interest in photography, the social worker seeks an opening in an after-school photography club, with hopes that the companionship of more academically oriented peers might get her back on the right track.

■ Encourage all parents and guardians to get involved in school activities.

A high school principal sends home a book of "coupons" with assorted activities that parents and other family members might do to help the school (e.g., tutoring in the classroom, baking goodies for a school open house, serving on the parent-teacher advisory group). She accompanies the book with a letter expressing her hope that all parents will return a coupon for at least one activity.

---

the range of services available to them, including financial assistance, counseling, parent education, juvenile court services, and recreation (Staudt, 2001).

■ *Let families admit their doubts.* Social workers, parent educators, and others who work closely with families find that all parents want to be treated with dignity. Once parents feel that professionals respect them, they are more inclined to disclose what's bothering them (Attride-Stirling, Davis, Markless, Sclare, & Day, 2001).

None of the communication strategies just described will, in and of itself, guarantee a successful working relationship with parents. Meetings with parents occur somewhat infrequently. Written communication is ineffective with parents who have limited literacy skills. And, of course, not everyone has a telephone, let alone e-mail. Despite the difficulty with staying in touch, effective professionals find ways to maintain connections with families (e.g., see the Development and Practice feature "Making Institutions Family-Friendly"). Ideally, practitioners want not only to communicate with parents, but to get them actively involved in children's activities.

Encouraging Family Involvement in Children's School Activities

Many students at both the elementary and secondary school levels report that they wish their families were more involved in school activities (J. L. Epstein, 1996). Furthermore, parents who believe their children's schools want them to be involved have more positive views about the schools (Dauber & Epstein, 1993). Ideally, family involvement should be important and meaningful, with a two-way communication of ideas and strategies (J. L. Epstein, 1996; Hoover-Dempsey & Sandler, 1997).

Effective practitioners get children's families actively involved in their activities. These mothers are helping out at a school-sponsored carnival.

Parents and other family members typically become involved in school activities only when they have a specific invitation to do so and when they know that school personnel genuinely want them to be involved (A. A. Carr, 1997; J. L. Epstein, 1996; Hoover-Dempsey & Sandler, 1997). For example, teachers might invite family members to a classroom skit in the evening or request parents' help with a school fund-raiser on a Saturday afternoon. Teachers might seek volunteers to help with field trips, special projects, or individual tutoring during the school day. And they can certainly use family members as resources to enrich the multicultural perspective of the community in which they work (Minami & Ovando, 1995).

However, some parents may believe that invitations are not directed specifically to them. Consider this parent's perspective:

> The thing of it is, had someone not walked up to me and asked me specifically, I would not hold out my hand and say, "I'll do it." Same thing here. You get parents here all the time, black parents that are willing, but maybe a little on the shy side and wouldn't say I really want to serve on this subject. You may send me the form, I may never fill the form out. Or I'll think about it and not send it back. But you know if that principal, that teacher, my son's math teacher called and asked if I would. . . . (A. A. Carr, 1997, p. 2)

Experts have offered numerous suggestions for getting families more involved in children's schooling. In particular, teachers and school leaders might

- Invite not only parents but also other important family members (e.g., grandparents, aunts, uncles) to participate in school activities, especially if a student's cultural background is one that places high value on the extended family (Hidalgo et al., 1995; Salend & Taylor, 1993)
- Find out what family members do exceptionally well (e.g., woodworking, cooking, calligraphy, storytelling) and ask them to share their talents with the class (Finders & Lewis, 1994)
- Identify individuals (e.g., bilingual parents) who can translate for those who speak little or no English (Finders & Lewis, 1994)
- Include parent advisory groups that offer suggestions and concerns about school curriculum and practices (J. L. Epstein, 1996)
- Use parents as liaisons with other community agencies and institutions (e.g., businesses, universities) that can support students' learning and development (J. L. Epstein, 1996)
- Provide opportunities for parents and other family members to volunteer for jobs that don't require them to leave home (e.g., to be someone whom students can call when unsure about homework assignments; M. G. Sanders, 1996)

Educators and other professionals wishing to involve parents must realize that parents have their own ideas about improving schools. In a study with African American and European American parents of children in an elementary school, researchers found that teachers wanted parents to be involved, particularly to help their children achieve (Lareau & Horvat, 1999). However, as the researchers interviewed parents and teachers, they learned also that teachers preferred parents to be deferential. When parents spotted problems in the school, their concerns were ignored. For example, Mrs. Mason, a beautician and associate pastor, was disturbed that the school ignored African American heroes:

> I've been over to the school all year, and there are certain holidays, I mean like Halloween . . . [when] witches and skeletons and what have you are hitting you all in the face as you walk down the hall. . . . There is a play on Washington's and Lincoln's birthday. But then Martin Luther King is the only black person that is really kind of recognized in America. And they don't really, most times they're saying that they might [recognize him], . . . but I still don't feel like they're giving as much effort as they should. (p. 43)

Moreover, school officials resisted the idea that racial injustice occurred in the school, even though many parents were convinced that African American children were singled out for disciplinary action. The principal found Mrs. Mason's accusations offensive:

> I just found her to be very upsetting . . . I think she is doing so much damage. She will not listen. You try to tell her about the volunteers and what is being done and the positive things and . . . that white children are getting detentions, too. . . . She's the kind of person who wakes me up in the middle of the night and I'm thinking, "What can I do, how can I reach this parent, what can be done to change her?" (p. 43)

Parents naturally get angry when they believe their children are not receiving good services and effective teaching: Recall from our introductory case that Barbara Jennings became indignant when Cedric was accused of lying to his teacher. Cedric's teacher, to his credit, gave Cedric another chance to show his knowledge. In Mrs. Mason's case, the principal interpreted her complaints as personal accusations, and communication came to a halt.

Practices to involve parents are not always successful. Unequal participation by family members from different educational and economic backgrounds is likely to be the case in many school districts unless school leaders effectively reach out to all families. School personnel can also continually encourage parents both to identify the inequities and problems they perceive and to suggest possible solutions (De Carvalho, 2001).

Supporting Families on the Home Front

As the ecological systems perspective reminds us, there are both direct and indirect routes to nurturing children's development. Undoubtedly, the most productive indirect route for professionals is through children's families.

Helping children sometimes means *helping parents help their children*. On average, teachers, clinicians, and other professionals who work with children have more training in child development than parents do, and parents often welcome information about developmental trends and effective childrearing strategies. Professionals should not preach to parents about such matters, but they can certainly provide suggestions about strategies that might work at home, perhaps at conferences or in regular newsletters and fliers sent home (see Figure 12–10 for an example of a flier for middle school parents). Issues of concern to parents change somewhat as children grow, as you can see in the Developmental Trends table, "Concerns Parents Have with Children of Different Ages."

Discipline is one skill in which parents often need guidance. Some parents routinely resort to physical punishment—spanking, slapping, and so on—to discipline their children. As noted earlier in the chapter, extreme forms of physical punishment are correlated with serious problems in children and adolescents, such as depression, aggression, failure to follow rules, and antisocial behavior. Such negative effects are not necessarily associated with light spanking or slapping, however (Baumrind, Larzelere, & Cowan, 2002). Although research results do not justify a blanket injunction against spanking, in some instances mild physical punishment can escalate into physical abuse (Baumrind et al., 2002). Some parents have trouble controlling their anger and seem to have little knowledge of alternative disciplinary strategies, such as time out, withdrawal of privileges, or explaining the reasons for rules. Thus, social workers, parent educators, and counselors may often find it helpful to teach a variety of effective techniques, and perhaps also to coach parents in practicing their expanded bag of disciplinary tricks in a clinic or other supervised setting (Baumrind et al., 2002).

Fostering children's cognitive development is a second area in which parents can often use assistance. Parents vary considerably in their own academic knowledge and skills, and accordingly in their ability to help their children with schoolwork (H. Cooper, 1989; Hernandez, 1997). Parents with limited education are often quite willing and able to help children master basic skills in such areas as reading, spelling, and mathematics, although they may want guidance in doing so (Edwards & Garcia, 1994; Portes, 1996). In one study, low-income mothers were shown several strategies for reading books to their young children, including pointing to and talking about the pictures in the books,

Adolescent Development

Eleven . . . is a time of breaking up, of discord and discomfort. Gone is the bland complaisance of the typical ten-year-old. Eleven is a time of loosening up, of snapping old bonds, of trial and error as the young child tests the limits of what authority will and will not permit.

Louise Bates Ames, Ph.D.
Your Ten- to Fourteen-Year-Old
Gesell Institute of Human Development

To understand your adolescent, you need to consider . . .
 . . . the child's basic individuality.
 . . . what is expected of anyone of his or her particular age level.
 . . . what environment your child finds himself or herself in.

Eleven-year-olds can be . . .
 egocentric,
 energetic,
 always "loving" or "hating";

 as well as . . .
  not as cooperative or accepting as in the past
  more angry than in the past
  inattentive
  hungry all the time
  more interested in the clothes they wear
   (but not in cleaning them!)
  uncertain
  more apt to cry
  fearful
  rebellious
  very interested and involved in family activities

FIGURE 12–10 Teachers can be valuable sources of information about child and adolescent development. In this flier for parents, middle school teacher Erin Miguel describes several common characteristics of young adolescents.

Reprinted with permission of Erin Miguel, Jones Middle School, Columbus, Ohio.

DEVELOPMENTAL TRENDS

Concerns Parents Have with Children of Different Ages

AGE	TOPICS	DIVERSITY	IMPLICATIONS FOR CAREGIVERS
Infancy (Birth–2) 	**Physical development** • Ensuring children's basic safety by structuring the environment so they cannot put themselves in danger (e.g., tumbling down stairs, swallowing cleaning supplies) • Meeting infants' physical needs (e.g., feeding on baby's schedule, diapering, and easing baby onto a sleep schedule that conforms to adults' patterns) • Giving proper nutrition to match physiological needs and pace of growth **Cognitive development** • Offering face-to-face interactions • Talking with infants and encouraging babbling • Encouraging infants to take turns in conversations and simple games • Providing appropriate sensory stimulation **Social-emotional development** • Watching for infants' preferences and abiding by these, for example, noticing when an infant watches a vehicle, saying "truck," and selecting picture books with trucks • Arranging for consistent, stable, responsive caregivers so that children become securely attached to these caregivers • Affirming infants' feelings so that they begin to understand emotions • Responding with reasonable promptness to infants' cries so that they learn to rely on parents	• Some parents may promote independence in children by encouraging them to try self-help actions, such as picking up bits of food and feeding themselves; others may prefer to do these things for children. • Nap time may depend on parents' beliefs about how much sleep children need and the proper way to help them fall asleep. • Parents may differ in how much they talk with infants. Some may verbalize frequently; others may soothe infants and focus on nonverbal gestures. • Families differ in beliefs about out-of-home care. Some parents resist commercial child care and will only leave infants for brief periods with familiar relatives. Other parents are comfortable with employed caregivers. • Concerns of parents depend partly on the temperament and health status of infants. When infants are difficult to soothe or are sick, parents may be quite concerned.	• Complete daily records of infants' physical care so that parents are aware of how their infants' needs were met and the kind of day they had. • Talk with parents about the developmental milestones you notice in infants. For example, point out when you notice a new tooth breaking through the gums. • Post a chart of typical developmental milestones so that parents can think about what their infants might be presently learning. Select a chart that emphasizes the variation in ages at which infants attain developmental milestones (e.g., rolling over, sitting up, crawling, walking, uttering their first word). • Ask parents about their concerns about their infants, and offer reassurance when appropriate.
Early Childhood (2–6)	**Physical development** • Ensuring children's basic safety (e.g., protecting them from street traffic and household chemicals) • Helping children with self-care routines (e.g., dressing, brushing teeth, bathing) • Finding appropriate outlets for physical energy **Cognitive development** • Responding to children's incessant questions • Channeling curiosity into constructive activities • Reading stories and in other ways promoting a foundation for literacy • Preparing for transition to formal schooling **Social-emotional development** • Curbing temper tantrums and in other ways dealing with temperamentally "difficult" children • Promoting sharing with siblings and peers • Addressing conflicts and aggressive behavior • Forming relationships with new caregivers in child care and preschool	• Some parents, worrying about their children's safety, are exceptionally reluctant to leave them in the care of others. • Low-income families have little or no discretionary income with which to purchase books and provide opportunities for cognitive enrichment. • Some kindergartners and first graders have had little or no prior experiences with other children; for instance, they may be only children or may not have previously attended child care or preschool. • Some parents (especially those from higher-income, professional backgrounds) may overdo efforts to maximize their children's cognitive development, giving children too many intellectually challenging activities and too few chances to relax or play.	• Suggest possible approaches to teaching young children about self-care habits, social skills, and impulse control. • Keep parents regularly informed about their children's progress in both academic and social skills. • Provide books and other stimulating materials that parents can check out and use at home. • When highly educated parents seem overly concerned about maximizing their children's cognitive development, suggest literature (e.g., John Bruer's *The Myth of the First Three Years*) that encourages a balance between stimulation and recreation.

DEVELOPMENTAL TRENDS

Concerns Parents Have with Children of Different Ages *(continued)*

AGE	TOPICS	DIVERSITY	IMPLICATIONS FOR CAREGIVERS
Middle Childhood (6–10)	**Physical development** • Fostering healthy eating habits • Using safety equipment (e.g., seatbelts in the car, helmets for cycling or skateboarding) • Establishing exercise routines and limiting television and video games **Cognitive development** • Helping children acquire habits and expectations for their academic work • Promoting mastery of basic academic skills • Enhancing children's education through family involvement and outings **Social-emotional development** • Giving children increasing independence and responsibility (e.g., waking up on time, doing homework) • Monitoring interactions with siblings, playmates • Instilling moral behaviors (e.g., honesty, fairness)	• Some parents may be overly stressed from work responsibilities. • Some neighborhoods have few if any playgrounds or other places where children can safely play. • Children's special talents and interests influence their choices of activities outside the home.	• Obtain and distribute literature about safety habits from local police, fire departments, and pediatricians' offices. • Provide resource materials (perhaps through a parent library in the classroom) that parents can use to assist their children with academic subject matter. • Encourage parents' involvement in school activities and parent-teacher groups. • Suggest facilities and programs in the community (e.g., youth soccer leagues, scout organizations) that provide free or inexpensive opportunities for after-school recreation and skill development.
Early Adolescence (10–14)	**Physical development** • Recognizing, dealing with early stages of puberty • Encouraging physical fitness • Affording basic clothing during periods of rapid growth **Cognitive development** • Supporting school-based changes in expectations for academic performance • Accepting that young adolescents envision a better world **Social-emotional development** • Showing sensitivity to self-consciousness about appearance • Accommodating requests for more leisure time with peers • Dealing with increased conflict as adolescents seek greater autonomy	• Children differ markedly in the age at which they begin puberty. • Different families have different decision-making styles. • Some parents may have considerable difficulty untying the apron strings to allow their children greater independence. • Parent-teenager conflicts are rare in some cultures, especially in those that cultivate respect for elders (e.g., many Asian cultures). • Some young teens may have little or no access to safe and appropriate recreational facilities. • Peer groups encourage varying behaviors and values.	• Identify and inform parents about age-appropriate athletic and social programs in the community. • Collaborate with colleagues and teachers to establish a homework hotline through which students can get ongoing support and guidance for home assignments. • Share with parents your impressions about reasonable expectations for independence and responsibility by young adolescents.
Late Adolescence (14–18)	**Physical development** • Keeping track of teenagers' whereabouts • Encouraging high school students to maintain realistic schedules that allow adequate sleep • Worrying about risky driving • Concern about possible alcohol, drug use **Cognitive development** • Encouraging youth to persist with increasingly challenging academic subject matter • Understanding adolescents' increasing capacity for logical, systematic thinking • Expanding adolescents' knowledge of employment prospects and college requirements **Social-emotional development** • Worrying about the loss of parental control over teenagers' social activities • Finding a reasonable balance between supervision and independence • Monitoring adolescents' part-time jobs	• Alcohol and drugs are readily available in any community, but their use is more frequent and socially acceptable in some neighborhoods and communities than in others. • Some parents refuse to believe that their children may be engaged in serious health-compromising behaviors, even when faced with evidence. • Families differ in their knowledge of, and experiences with, higher education; some may be unable to counsel their children about options in postsecondary education. • Parents differ in the extent to which they condone and encourage teenagers' part-time employment.	• Suggest ways in which young adolescents can maintain regular contact with their families when they are away from home for lengthy periods (e.g., by making regular phone calls home). • Provide information about possible careers and educational opportunities after high school; include numerous options, including part-time and full-time vocational programs, community colleges, and four-year colleges and universities.

Sources: W. A. Collins, 1990; Maccoby, 1980, 1984; Montemayor, 1982; Mortimer, Shanahan, & Ryu, 1994; Paikoff & Brooks-Gunn, 1991; Pipher, 1994; Warton & Goodnow, 1991; Youniss, 1983.

asking questions to improve and monitor the children's comprehension, and encouraging the children to draw inferences and make predictions (Edwards & Garcia, 1994). These strategies enabled the mothers to nurture their children's emergent literacy skills more effectively.

Professionals can further support children's development indirectly by *helping parents to help themselves*. In some cases, this might mean helping parents advance their own education or acquire new job skills. In others, it might mean connecting them with health care and social service agencies. In still others, it might involve helping them acquire such basic necessities as clothing, household furniture, or running water.

Home visits are a widely used way of supporting parents' efforts at home, especially with young children (Gomby, Culross, & Behrman, 1999). Existing home visiting programs have a variety of objectives, though typically they focus on educating parents about children's needs, providing information on supporting children's development, and preventing problems such as neglect or abuse. Home visiting programs work quite well with some parents but not so well with others. Some parents simply do not want strangers in their homes (Salend & Taylor, 1993). Others, though more willing, may frequently miss appointments (Gomby et al., 1999). To make home visits maximally effective, educators and child care professionals should present themselves as warm, friendly, and nonjudgmental; make an effort to establish rapport with parents and other family members; and offer concrete, practical suggestions about how to foster children's development and well-being. Possibly the most important function that home visits can serve is to open the door in forming relationships with families. A school district leader comments on the benefit of home visits in opening the door with migrant families:

> At the beginning of the school year, [Name] Elementary went house by house in their whole zone. . . . Everybody—the counselors, the librarian, the clerks, the paraprofessionals—went to visit families. Everybody's home was visited at least once by somebody in the school in a positive fashion. OK? They told [parents] *"Mire Señora, queremos que sepa que en la escuela nos importa su hija o hijo y queremos saber dónde vive y si le podemos ayudar en algo, estamos para servirle.* [Look, Miss, we want you to know that we care about your daughter or son and we want to know where you live and if we can help you in any way, we are here to serve you.]" And we began to get parents who said, "They care to come out here on an afternoon, when it's hot, you know, and visit? They really care about us!" (López, Scribner, & Mahitivanichcha, 2001, p. 264)

In the United States, Project Head Start offers one model of how educators can connect with and support low-income families (Seefeldt, Denton, Galper, & Younoszai, 1999; Sissel, 2000; Washington & Bailey, 1995). Although Head Start programs differ somewhat from one community to the next, parent involvement is typically encouraged in several ways:

- Parents are welcome at school at any time; they are given a specific place in which they can convene.
- Parents receive materials and suggestions for working with their children on educational tasks.
- Adult education classes are offered on such topics as parenting, nutrition, and health.
- Access to social services and adult literacy services is provided.
- Monthly family dinners are held at school.
- Parents are involved in planning for children's transition from the program to kindergarten or first grade.
- When employment opportunities within the program open up, parents are given preference for any positions for which they are qualified.

Such strategies appear to foster parents' views of themselves as important educators for their children and assure them that they can, in fact, enhance their children's academic abilities (Seefeldt et al., 1999; Washington & Bailey, 1995). Ongoing involvement in Head Start programs can also enhance parents' confidence about their own learning abilities and increase their employment options.

A common behavior displayed by preschoolers is asking a lot of *why* questions. Consider how two mothers of 4-year-old boys interpret their sons' incessant questioning. Elizabeth describes her son Charles as

> . . . mouthing off; just always mouthing off. Whenever I say anything to him, he asks me "Why?" Like I say we're going to the store and he says "Why?" Or I tell him "Don't touch the bug 'cuz it's dead" and he says "Why?" Like he's just trying to get me mad by never listening to me. He never accepts what I say. He mouths off all the time instead of believing me. It's like he just wants to tease me. You know, he tests me. (Belenky, Bond, & Weinstock, 1997, pp. 129–130)

In contrast, Joyce describes her son Peter this way:

> Well, you know, he's got such an active mind, always going; like he's never satisfied with just appearances—he's always trying to figure out how things tick, why they do. So if I ask him to do something or tell him to do something, he's always asking why. He really wants to understand what's the goal—what's the purpose—how come? He's really trying to piece the world all together . . . and understand it all. It's wonderful. Or if I say, "We're going to the store," he wants to know why. He's real interested in figuring out how one thing leads to another. It's great, because sometimes he helps me realize that I haven't really thought through why I'm saying what I am. And so we do think it through. (p. 130)

- How do the two mothers interpret their sons' questions differently? How might their beliefs about children prompt these different interpretations? How might their interpretations help us to predict their disciplinary styles?
- How might the lives of these women and their families differ more globally? In other words, what would you expect their educational backgrounds to be? What kinds of life stresses might each experience?
- What kinds of educational opportunities would these mothers create at home for their children? What might teachers do to encourage each mother's involvement at school?

Now go to our Companion Website to assess your understanding of chapter content with a Practice Quiz, apply what you've learned in Essay Questions, and broaden your knowledge with links to related Developmental Psychology Web sites. Go to www.prenhall.com/mcdevitt.

SUMMARY

Socialization in the Family

Families are complex social structures that have both immediate and long-term impacts on children and adolescents. Youngsters are not passive recipients of their families' socialization efforts, however; instead, they actively seek out and interpret the messages they get from others.

Five theoretical viewpoints help us to understand how families affect children's development. Behavioral learning perspectives consider specific experiences (modeling, giving consequences for behaviors, etc.) that family members provide for children. Cognitive-developmental perspectives describe ways in which children's ability to interpret family messages changes with age. Biological perspectives focus on parents' genetic influences on children and ways in which family relationships have survival value. Developmental systems perspectives, and particularly the ecological systems framework, look at families as complex systems of relationships that exist within larger social units. Sociocultural perspectives examine routine, intimate exchanges that family members have around culturally valued goals and activities. In some respects the five perspectives offer conflicting views of families, yet each contributes to an understanding of how families and children influence one another.

Family Structures

Families come in many forms, including two-parent families, single-parent families, blended families, adoptive families, foster families, cohabiting families, extended families, families with gay parents, families with adolescent parents, and numerous variations on these structures. Many young people experience one or more changes in family structure (e.g., as a result of divorce, remarriage, or death of a parent) at some point during their childhood or adolescence. Individual family configurations offer unique benefits and challenges for children, but ultimately the quality of family relationships is more important than family structure.

Family Influences

Parents influence children's development by showing affection, establishing rules and expectations, and disciplining children. Parents also affect children through the instruction, experiences, and resources they offer to promote growth. Parents may affect children's development through their employment outside the home; for instance, the children of working parents may care for themselves during after-school hours.

Children influence their families, in turn, by virtue of their temperaments, interests, and abilities. Children also influence families through the habitual styles of interacting that they set into motion. Children influence one another as siblings, but having a sibling is not vital to normal, healthy development.

Most families provide safe and nurturing environments for children. However, some families maltreat children, either by neglecting them or by subjecting them to physical, sexual, or emotional abuse. Such maltreatment may have long-term effects on children's physical, cognitive, and social-emotional development. Often, those who maltreat children suffer from serious emotional problems themselves.

Parents' Beliefs about Children

Parents' beliefs about their children's abilities, the nature of childhood, and the purposes of education affect their expectations, disciplinary practices, and approval or disapproval of the interventions of practitioners. Parents' beliefs arise in part out of cultural assumptions and in part out of their own personal experiences. Parents and professionals are more likely to work cooperatively toward common goals for children if they share similar beliefs or at least make serious efforts to understand one another's ideas.

Partnerships with Families

Effective partnerships with families rest squarely on good communication. Professionals have several methods of communication at their disposal but should also try to get parents actively involved in their children's education and activities. Professionals can be valuable sources of information to parents about how to support children's development more generally. Social workers and other professionals can listen to parents, encourage them to formulate solutions, and inform them about services available to them.

KEY CONCEPTS

family (p. 500)
socialization agents (p. 500)

blended family (p. 512)
parenting style (p. 518)

authoritarian style (p. 518)
authoritative style (p. 518)

permissive style (p. 519)
uninvolved style (p. 519)

Anik, age 5

Joe, age 9

Anna, age 17

Interpersonal Relationships

CASE STUDY: AQEELAH, KELLY, AND JOHANNA

Aqeelah, Kelly, and Johanna had been close friends since elementary school. The three came from diverse ethnic and religious backgrounds: Aqeelah was an African American Muslim, Kelly was an Irish Catholic, and Johanna was half Puerto Rican and half Jewish. The girls lived in a racially and ethnically mixed suburban New Jersey community that seemed proud of its cultural diversity and integrated school system.

Yet as Tamar Lewin (2000) reported in an article in *The New York Times,* other forces conspired to split the girls apart. In ninth grade, peers began pressuring them to declare loyalty to a single ethnic group:

> "[I]t's really confusing this year," [Aqeelah] said. "I'm too white to be black, and I'm too black to be white. If I'm talking to a white boy, a black kid walks by and says, 'Oh, there's Aqeelah, she likes white boys.' And in class, these Caucasian boys I've been friends with for years say hi, and then the next thing they say is, 'Yo, Aqeelah, what up?' as if I won't understand them unless they use that kind of slang. Or they'll tell me they really like 'Back That Thing Up' by Juvenile. I don't care if they like a rapper, but it seems like they think that's the only connection they have with me."
>
> "Last year this stuff didn't bother me, but now it does bother me, because some of the African-American kids, joking around, say I'm an Oreo."
>
> Johanna and Kelly were surprised by her pain; they had not heard this before. But they did sense her increasing distance from them.
>
> "It's like she got lost or something," Kelly said. "I never see her."
>
> Aqeelah had always been the strongest student of the three, the only one in a special math class, one rung above honors. But by winter, she was getting disappointing grades, especially in history, and beginning to worry about being moved down a level. Math was not going so well either, and so she dropped track to focus on homework. She was hoping to make the softball team, and disappointed that neither of her friends was trying out. "I'll never see you," she complained. (T. Lewin, 2000, p. 19)

Aqeelah did see less of Kelly and Johanna that year. Kelly and Johanna remained close, but Aqeelah spent more time with a family friend, another African American girl. Aqeelah was saddened by the growing distance between herself and her old friends:

> "I don't know why I don't call Johanna or Kelly," she said. "They'll always have the place in my heart, but not so much physically in my life these days. It seems like I have no real friends this year. You know how you can have a lot of friends, but you have no one? Everyone seems to be settled in their cliques and I'm just searching. And the more I get to know some people, the more I want to withdraw. I'm spending a lot more time with my family this year." (T. Lewin, 2000, pp. 19–20)

eers are powerful forces in the lives of children and adolescents. Close friends provide companionship and emotional support, and they acknowledge each other's individual strengths and talents. Friends and nonfriends alike also send regular messages about what behaviors are acceptable and what behaviors are not. Many of these messages are beneficial for long-term development; for instance, a child whose thoughtless remarks bring a peer to tears learns a basic lesson about tact. Other messages from peers are not necessarily in young people's best interests; for instance, the students who called Aqeelah an "Oreo" (someone who's "black" on the outside and "white" on the inside) were essentially telling her that it was inappropriate for her to associate with people outside her racial group.

In this chapter, we examine interpersonal behaviors, with a particular emphasis on relationships with age-mates. We explore theoretical perspectives and research findings regarding the development of interpersonal behaviors, then look more closely at the nature of peer relationships, and, finally, consider the nature and development of romantic relationships and sexuality. Throughout the chapter, we identify strategies that teachers and other professionals can use to promote social skills and productive peer relationships.

Development of Interpersonal Behaviors

As children grow older, they acquire a growing repertoire of **social skills**, strategies they use to interact effectively with others. Yet children vary considerably in their social competence. Some are courteous, know how to initiate and sustain conversations, and regularly cooperate and share with peers. Others are less skilled; they may be anxious and uncertain in social situations and keep to themselves, or they may shout, call names, use physical aggression, and in other ways alienate their age-mates. Not surprisingly, young people's social skills affect the number and quality of their friendships (Dishion, Andrews, & Crosby, 1995; Gottman, 1983; A. J. Rose & Asher, 1999).

Children develop social skills largely through experience and practice with peers and adults. For instance, when preschoolers engage in fantasy play, they must continually communicate, negotiate, and compromise regarding the course of events (Gottman, 1986b). When they cannot effectively resolve conflicts, their activities may quickly deteriorate. Consider what happens when two 4-year-old girls disagree as they begin to play house:

> D: I'm the mommy.
> J: Who am I?
> D: Um, the baby.
> J: Daddy.
> D: Sister.
> J: I wanna be the daddy.
> D: You're the sister.
> J: Daddy.
> D: You're the *big* sister! (Gottman, 1983, p. 57)
> J: Don't play house. I don't want to play house.

Children also learn social skills by observing the behaviors of those around them. For instance, children's parents may model a variety of interpersonal styles—upbeat, agreeable, and respectful of others' needs and rights, or, contrariwise, hostile and aggressive (Dodge, Pettit, Bates, & Valente, 1995; Nix et al., 1999; Putallaz & Heflin, 1986).

Cognitive factors, such as personal goals and interpretations of others' behaviors, affect children's social competence as well. For example, children respond differently to situations such as this one:

> You and your friend just finished playing a board game. You had fun playing the game because you got to pick the game and it is your favorite. You really want to play the same game again, but your friend doesn't want to and says it's her [or his] turn to pick. (A. Rose & Asher, 1999, p. 73)

Children who are most interested in preserving the friendship in such a situation (e.g., "I would be trying to stay friends," "I would be trying to be fair") tend to have more friends than children who are primarily concerned with addressing their own needs (e.g., "I would be trying to keep my friend from pushing me around," "I would be trying to get back at my friend"; J. Rose & Asher, 1999, p. 71). As another example, adolescents who interpret any unwilling-

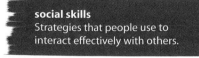

social skills
Strategies that people use to interact effectively with others.

ness or refusal on the part of another (e.g., "Do you want to go skating with me on Saturday?" "No, I can't. I'm busy on Saturday") as a sign of personal rejection are more likely to be aggressive in their interactions with others and have greater difficulty in their romantic relationships (G. Downey, Bonica, & Rincón, 1999; G. Downey, Lebolt, Rincón, & Freitas, 1998).

Our focus in the following pages is on two kinds of interpersonal behaviors—prosocial behavior and aggression—that have been the subject of considerable research.

Prosocial and Aggressive Behavior

As you may recall from Chapter 10, *prosocial behavior* is an action taken to benefit another person, such as helping, sharing, comforting, or showing empathy. **Aggressive behavior** is an action intentionally taken to hurt another person either physically (e.g., hitting, shoving, or fighting) or psychologically (e.g., embarrassing, insulting, or ostracizing). Curiosity about prosocial and aggressive tendencies in human beings, particularly in children, has spawned countless research studies and numerous theoretical explanations. Collectively, this body of work reveals that although prosocial behavior and aggression are at opposite ends of a helping-versus-hurting continuum, each has both hereditary and environmental origins. Here, we look at the effects of heredity and environment and at basic principles and trends that characterize the development of prosocial and aggressive behaviors.

Hereditary Influences From an evolutionary perspective, both prosocial and aggressive tendencies have enabled human beings to survive and flourish (Coie & Dodge, 1998; M. L. Hoffman, 1981; K. Lorenz, 1966). Prosocial behavior promotes group cohesion, is critical for childrearing, and helps people survive in harsh conditions. For example, if you help your younger cousin by dressing her wounds, offering her water, and carrying her back to camp, you may prolong her life. When she becomes an adult and has her own children, she will pass along some of the genes that the two of you share. Prosocial behavior may also have played a role in our ancestors' mate selection: Females may have overlooked the chest-pounding king of the jungle in favor of more socially sensitive males. Some kinds of aggression, though antisocial in nature, also increase chances of survival. Squabbling and warfare cause people to spread apart (thereby improving their chances of finding adequate food and other essential resources), and in times of battle the strongest members of the species are those most likely to survive and give birth to future generations.

An evolutionary perspective of the hereditary roots of prosocial and aggressive behaviors is, of course, speculative at best. Twin studies provide more convincing evidence that such behaviors have genetic origins: Monozygotic (identical) twins tend to be more similar than dizygotic (fraternal) twins with respect to altruistic behavior, empathy for others, and aggression (Ghodsian-Carpey & Baker, 1987; Matthews, Batson, Horn, & Rosenman, 1981; Plomin et al., 1993; Rushton, Fulkner, Neal, Nias, & Eysenck, 1986; Zahn-Waxler, Robinson, & Emde, 1992). Furthermore, children's aggressive behavior is partly determined by their temperaments, which tend to be fairly stable over time and often have a genetic basis (see Chapters 3 and 9). Some children, beginning in infancy, are more irritable, impulsive, angry, and fearful than other infants (Matheny, 1989). In one study, children's temperaments at 6 months predicted their mothers' reports of behavior problems at age 3 (Bates, Maslin, & Frankel, 1985).

Environmental Influences The environment also affects prosocial and aggressive behavior. One particularly influential factor is the presence of prosocial and aggressive models in children's lives. Children who observe sympathetic and generous models tend to be more helpful than those without such models (R. Elliott & Vasta, 1970; C. R. Owens & Ascione, 1991; C. C. Wilson, Piazza, & Nagle, 1990; Yarrow, Scott, & Waxler, 1973). People who are especially prosocial tend to have parents and other role models who have acted with compassion, often entailing personal sacrifice or risk (Oliner & Oliner, 1988; Rosenhan, 1970). For instance, rescuers of Jews in Nazi Europe before and during World War II perceived their parents as being people who regularly demonstrated strong moral convictions (London, 1970; Oliner & Oliner, 1988).

Just as prosocial models increase prosocial behavior, so, too, aggressive models—whether adults, peers, or fictional characters in the media—engender more aggressive behavior (Bandura, 1973; Eron, 1980; Kellam, 1990). In an experimental study we described in Chapter 2, preschool children were taken to a playroom where they observed one of four

aggressive behavior
Action intentionally taken to hurt another, either physically or psychologically.

In his drawing of a superhero holding a weapon, 6-year-old Myron shows his understanding that aggression can make characters powerful.

conditions: an adult model treating an inflated doll aggressively, a film of an adult acting aggressively, a televised cartoon character (a woman dressed in a cat costume) acting aggressively, or no model (Bandura, Ross, & Ross, 1963). Children who viewed the three aggressive models were more aggressive than children in the control condition. Furthermore, children who observed an adult acting aggressively in their presence were especially inclined to imitate specific acts, such as hitting the doll with a mallet, that they had personally witnessed.

Reinforcement plays a role in both prosocial and aggressive behavior. Over the short run, children engage in more prosocial behavior when they are reinforced (e.g., with candy or praise) for such behavior (Bryan, Redfield, & Mader, 1971; Eisenberg, Fabes, Carlo, & Karbon, 1992; Rushton & Teachman, 1978). However, such tangible rewards appear counterproductive over the long run, perhaps because children begin to perform prosocial actions to benefit themselves ("I gave her my candy because I knew Dad would give me an even bigger treat for sharing") rather than to express sympathy or genuine altruism (Eisenberg & Fabes, 1998; Fabes, Fultz, Eisenberg, May-Plumee, & Christopher, 1989; Szynal-Brown & Morgan, 1983). Aggressive behavior is often reinforced through its outcomes: It may enable children to gain desired objects or to get revenge (Coie & Dodge, 1998; Crick & Dodge, 1996; Lochman, Wayland, & White, 1993). Sadly, aggressive behavior in some children is reinforced by their victims' expressions of alarm and pain, perhaps because these children gain a sense of power when they see others squirm under their cruel treatment (Bandura, 1991).

The social and cultural contexts in which children are raised also affect their prosocial and aggressive tendencies. For instance, children are more likely to imitate their parents' prosocial behaviors when parents exhibit an authoritative parenting style—when they are warm and loving, hold high standards for behavior, and explain why certain behaviors are unacceptable (Eisenberg, 1995; Eisenberg & Fabes, 1998; M. L. Hoffman, 1988). Children also tend to be more prosocial when their parents (mothers as well as fathers) have work obligations outside the home and give them numerous responsibilities (e.g., taking care of younger siblings) to help keep the household going (B. B. Whiting & Whiting, 1975).

In contrast, some family environments are breeding grounds for aggression. For instance, frequent physical punishment at home appears to foster aggression and other antisocial behavior in children (M. A. Straus, 2000; also see Chapter 12). In some cultures, families may teach children that aggression is an appropriate means of resolving conflicts or maintaining one's honor (D. Cohen & Nisbett, 1994; E. Staub, 1995). Environments also increase the probability of aggression when they induce negative feelings, thoughts, and memories (L. Berkowitz, 1989, 1993). For instance, children who live in poverty tend to be more aggressive than their peers, perhaps because their parents live in more stressful conditions and may be more coercive and less effective with them as a result (Guerra, Huesmann, Tolan, Van Acker, & Eron, 1995).

Environmental settings, including schools, families, and the community, provide youngsters with many occasions to observe and try out aggressive and prosocial behaviors.

Schools and communities can provide firsthand experiences with prosocial and aggressive behavior as well. For example, teachers, religious leaders, community volunteers, and directors of youth organizations often recruit children to participate in charitable events and service initiatives. Sadly, children also experience aggression in their communities. For example, in the year 2000, 1.6% of American youths between 12 and 17 years of age were victims of violent crimes such as aggravated assault, rape, and robbery involving force or threat of violence (Federal Interagency Forum on Child and Family Statistics, 2002). Children who are victims of violent crimes are themselves at risk to commit serious acts of violence later on (Finkelhor & Dziuba-Leatherman, 1994; Lauritsen, Laub, & Sampson, 1992).

Development of Prosocial Behavior Even infants respond to the distress of others—they often begin to cry when they hear other infants crying—and toddlers attempt to comfort people who seem to be unhappy or in pain (Simner, 1971; Zahn-Waxler, Radke-Yarrow, Wagner, & Chapman, 1992). Young preschoolers occasionally exhibit such prosocial behaviors as helping, nurturing, and sharing, although their efforts are limited by minimal knowledge of what they can do specifically to help (Farver & Branstetter, 1994; S. Lamb, 1991). As a general rule, children behave more prosocially—for example, they become increasingly generous—as they grow older (Eisenberg, 1982; Rushton, 1980). This is evident in the Developmental Trends table "Prosocial Behavior at Different Age Levels."

DEVELOPMENTAL TRENDS

Prosocial Behavior at Different Age Levels

AGE	WHAT YOU MIGHT OBSERVE	DIVERSITY	IMPLICATIONS
Infancy (Birth–2) 	• Interest in other infants (e.g., watching actions of other infants, touching their faces and bodies, and vocalizing to them) • Positive emotional responses to other infants, such as smiling and reaching toward them • Imitation of one another's actions • Increasing preference for contact with familiar over unfamiliar peers • In the second year, exchange of roles such as hider and seeker	• Infants who are inclined by temperament to be fearful and inhibited may avoid unfamiliar peers. • Infants may be more inclined to show positive social behaviors when adult caregivers model these behaviors. • Infants may imitate the particular comforting gestures they see caregivers use with infants in distress.	• Express your sympathy for children in distress so infants watching the event begin to learn of your motivation to help others. • Allow infants to interact with one another under your guidance and protection. • When infants appear shy or uncomfortable around other infants, hold them tenderly as you interact with the other infants so they begin to feel safe being near them.
Early Childhood (2–6) 	• Attempts to comfort those in distress, especially people whom children know well • Some ineffective strategies for helping others in distress (e.g., crying, smiling, walking away, possibly even hitting a crying child) • Some sharing with others, especially familiar caregivers • Emerging concerns about possession and ownership that limit the inclination to share	• Children who have warm, sensitive parents more frequently comfort others. • Children from large families tend to be more prosocial than those from smaller ones. • Children who are encouraged to show kindness to other children in preschool and child care will eventually learn to do so spontaneously.	• Allow children to give comfort when they can. • Model sympathetic responses; explain what you are doing and why you are doing it. • Recognize that young children's selfish and territorial behaviors are part of normal development.
Middle Childhood (6–10) 	• Increasing ability to care for younger children (e.g., feeding, clothing, doctoring scraped knees) • Increasing ability to take another's perspective, enabling more appropriate care and comfort of those in distress • General increase in desire to help others as an objective in and of itself	• Children whose parents value prosocial behavior are more likely to value it as well and to have genuine concern for others. • Some children may act prosocially primarily to please adults or gain rewards.	• Alert children to needs of others, and encourage them to see such needs as a reason for providing assistance. • Draw attention to a comforted child's relief when another child helps ("Look how much better Sally feels now that you've shared your snack with her"). • Use prosocial adjectives (e.g., "kind," "helpful") when praising altruistic behavior.
Early Adolescence (10–14) 	• Growing ability to contribute to the maintenance of home and school environments • Emerging ability to serve as responsible caregivers of younger children • Tendency to believe that distressed individuals (e.g., the homeless) are entirely to blame for their own fate	• Some young adolescents are accustomed to sharing household responsibilities, whereas others are not. • Some young adolescents feel self-conscious about offering assistance even when concerned about others' welfare.	• Actively involve adolescents in helping to maintain their environment (e.g., picking up trash in the immediate vicinity). • Let adolescents know that giving, sharing, and caring for others are high priorities. • Encourage adolescents to think about how society's laws and practices affect people in need (e.g., the poor, the sick, the elderly).
Late Adolescence (14–18) 	• Growing ability to assess the psychological characteristics of others and to identify effective ways of providing comfort and assistance • Increasing ability to understand that people in any single category comprise a heterogeneous group (e.g., people may be homeless because they've lost their jobs or been the victims of natural disasters) • Belief that society has an obligation to help others in need	• Some teenagers are optimistic about what government and politicians can do to help people in need; others are cynical. • Despite the stereotype that females are more empathic than males, young men are sometimes more active in helping others than young women (Eagly & Crowley, 1986).	• Encourage community service work so as to engender a commitment to help others. Ask adolescents to reflect on their experiences through group discussions or written essays. • Assign autobiographies and other readings that depict individuals who have actively worked to help others.

Sources: Bar-Tal, Raviv, & Leiser, 1980; Burleson & Kunkel, 1995; Eagly & Crowley, 1986; Eckerman, 1993; Eisenberg & Fabes, 1998; Farver & Branstetter, 1994; Flanagan, 1995; Grusec & Redler, 1980; Hay, 1979; Hoffman, 1975; Howes, 1987; Krebs & Van Hesteren, 1994; H. N. Ross, Conant, Cheyne, & Alevizos, 1992; Torney-Purta, 1990; Vandell & Mueller, 1995; Vandell, Wilson, & Buchanan, 1980; West & Rheingold, 1978; B. B. Whiting & Whiting, 1975; Yates & Youniss, 1996; Youniss & Yates, 1999; Zahn-Waxler, Radke-Yarrow, Wagner, & Chapman, 1992.

Age, of course, is not the only variable that determines whether children and adolescents act prosocially. Youngsters who show higher stages of moral reasoning are more apt to exhibit moral and prosocial behavior (see the discussion of Kohlberg's theory in Chapter 10). Several other factors associated with prosocial behavior are reflected in the following general principles:

■ *Perspective-taking ability, empathy, and sympathy are associated with prosocial behavior.* Children and adolescents are more likely to help someone else when they can look at a situation from the other person's perspective and have empathy and sympathy[1] for the person's plight (Eisenberg, 1995; P. A. Miller, Eisenberg, Fabes, & Shell, 1996; Underwood & Moore, 1982). Sympathy, a genuine concern for the other person's well-being, is probably the most influential factor (Batson, 1991; Eisenberg & Fabes, 1998).

Early signs of perspective taking and empathy, in the form of concerned facial expressions, appear at age 2 or even earlier (Zahn-Waxler, Radke-Yarrow, et al., 1992), but a deep awareness of others' needs probably emerges only gradually over time. Nancy Eisenberg and her colleagues (Eisenberg, 1982; Eisenberg, Carlo, Murphy, & Van Court, 1995; Eisenberg, Lennon, & Pasternack, 1986) have identified five levels (orientations), reflecting varying degrees of empathy and sympathy, that can help us predict how children at different ages are likely to behave in situations that call for altruism and other prosocial behaviors:

1. *Hedonistic orientation.* Most preschoolers and many younger elementary school students show little or no interest in helping others unless they can meet their own needs in the process. They are most likely to behave prosocially toward another person when they like that person and believe they will probably get something in return.

2. *Superficial needs-of-others orientation.* Some preschoolers and many elementary school students show some concern for others' physical and emotional needs and may express willingness to help another person even at personal sacrifice to themselves. Yet their concern lacks full understanding of, or empathy for, the other person's perspective. For example, a child might simply say, "He's hungry," or, "She needs this," without further explanation.

3. *Stereotyped, approval-focused orientation.* Some elementary and secondary students advocate prosocial behavior on the grounds that they will be better liked or appreciated if they help. For example, they may explain, "She'll be my friend if I help her." Or, they may say that helping is the "right" thing to do, while holding limited and stereotypical views of what "good" and "bad" people do. They may simply state, for example, "It's nice to help out."

4. *Empathic orientation.* A few elementary students and many secondary students are able to express true empathy for another person's situation and consequently a willingness to help. They seem genuinely able to perceive a situation from another person's perspective. For instance, they might say, "I know just how she feels," or, "I'd feel badly if I didn't help him because then he'd be in pain."

5. *Internalized values orientation.* A small minority of high school students express internalized values about helping other people—values that reflect concern for equality, dignity, human rights, and the welfare of society as a whole. These individuals maintain their self-respect by behaving in accordance with such values. For instance, they might say, "I couldn't live with myself if I didn't help out," or, "It's the responsibility of all of us to help one another whenever we can."

These five orientations are not true *stages;* children and adolescents do not necessarily progress through them in a sequential or universal fashion. Instead, children's reasoning may reflect two or more different orientations during any particular time period (Eisenberg, Miller, Shell, McNalley, & Shea, 1991). Generally, however, as children and adolescents grow older,

Children tend to act more prosocially as they grow older; for example, they become increasingly empathic with age.

---

[1] As noted in Chapter 10, empathy involves experiencing the same emotion as someone else, perhaps someone in distress. Sympathy involves experiencing not only another person's emotions but also a feeling of sorrow or concern about his or her plight.

they reflect increasingly the upper-level orientations, and less frequently the lower-level orientations (Eisenberg et al., 1995).

■ *Children tend to behave more prosocially when they feel responsible for another's welfare.* Youngsters are more likely to help people they know well (e.g., siblings and friends) than strangers, apparently because they have a greater sense of responsibility for people they know (Costin & Jones, 1992). They are also more likely to help another person if that individual has previously helped them (L. Berkowitz, 1968; Dreman, 1976; Levitt, Weber, Clark, & McDonnell, 1985). Guilt is involved in feelings of responsibility as well: Children are more likely to be helpful when they feel guilty about having caused another person pain or distress (Eisenberg, 1995).

■ *Children are more likely to help those facing misfortunes that seem beyond their control.* In Chapter 11, we described the explanations, or *attributions,* that children often have for their own successes and failures. Children, like adults, tend to form attributions about others' successes and failures as well. When children believe that others have brought misfortunes upon themselves (perhaps because of carelessness or a lack of effort), they are often reluctant to help. Their willingness to act prosocially increases when they believe that a person's troubles have occurred as a result of an accident, disability, or other uncontrollable circumstance (Eisenberg & Fabes, 1998; Graham, 1997).

■ *Children weigh the costs and benefits of helping others.* Children are more likely to behave prosocially if the costs of doing so are inconsequential. For instance, they are more likely to share a snack if it's one that they don't particularly care for (Eisenberg & Shell, 1986). They are also more apt to be helpful if they believe that any significant costs involved are outweighed by the benefits of acting prosocially (Eisenberg et al., 1995; Eisenberg & Fabes, 1998). For instance, they are more likely to help if they believe the person will later return the favor (Eisenberg, Fabes, Schaller, Carlo, & Miller, 1991; L. Peterson, 1980). In some situations, of course, the benefits of prosocial actions are strictly internal: A feeling of personal satisfaction about helping someone else may more than make up for any loss of time or convenience.

Sometimes, of course, children believe that *aggression* yields more benefits than prosocial actions. Let's consider the trends and principles that characterize the development of aggressive behavior.

Development of Aggressive Behavior Aggression takes many forms. Sometimes it involves physical violence such as hitting, pushing, fighting, or using weapons (see Figure 13–1). At other times, the pain inflicted is psychological—when, for example, people insult, ridicule, or spread malicious gossip about others.

Aggression serves many functions. Sometimes it is simply a means to an end: A child whacks another child on the head, distracts her from a coveted toy, and, when she is defenseless, grabs the toy. Sometimes, aggression gives children a sense of power and control: A bully may feel stronger as he watches his victim cringe. Aggression can also serve social functions. For example, gossiping provides a means whereby children and adolescents alike can explore one another's beliefs and priorities; it may also help them establish an emotional bond—a sense of *we-ness*—that unites them against a common "enemy" (Gottman, 1986a, 1986b; Gottman & Mettetal, 1986). As an example, consider how two middle school students use gossip about their teachers to get to know each other better:

A: I have a dumb teacher. She goes, "Well, I'd like to try your muffins but I have no sense of taste." I'm going [*makes a disgusted face*].

B: [*Giggle.*]

A: I mean you could tell by her clothes that she had no sense of taste . . . [*Later.*] Yeah, my teacher she shows the dumbest movies. We, Friday we saw a movie about how bread gets moldy. She wants to teach us all about, um, calories and stuff and she's so fat you can tell she needs to learn more than us.

B: [*Giggle.*]

> Dear Diary,
> Today there was a tragedy at school. Two people are now no longer with us, all because one person decided to bring a gun to school. This isn't fair to the parents, friends, and relatives of those people who died. My best friend is now gone. How could this happen? Why?

FIGURE 13-1 Occasionally, physical aggression at school has tragic consequences such as those described in this child's diary entry.

A: There's not a fat person in the class, except for the teacher.
B: [*Giggle.*] About the most sophisticated foreign language teacher we have is our French teacher.
A: I can't stand it.
B: Oh, and she's always going, I say, "Hi, Miss Rickey" and she goes, "Bonjour" [giggles].
A: [*Giggle.*]
B: I was walking down steps and I almost fell. I was cracking up. I was going, "OK, whatever you say." (Gottman & Mettetal, 1986, p. 214; reprinted with permission of Cambridge University Press)

The capacity for aggression emerges early and takes a developmental course. Initially, infants show anger but they do not lash out to hurt others. In the first half of their first year, infants show angry expressions; in the second half of the first year, infants express anger to caregivers when caregivers prevent them from reaching their goals (C. R. Stenberg & Campos, 1990). For example, infants may cry angrily when a caregiver pulls them away from the television set because they want to push, pull, and lick the buttons. By the end of the first year, infants may swat another child who takes their toys (Caplan, Vespo, Pedersen, & Hay, 1991). During the preschool years, children continue to scuffle over possessions, and parents often become concerned about their children's hitting (Jenkins, Bax, & Hart, 1980).

Generally speaking, aggressive physical behaviors decline in frequency after early childhood; the decline may occur because youngsters learn to resist impulsive desires and to develop more effective ways of interacting with others and resolving conflicts (R. B. Cairns, Cairns, Neckerman, Ferguson, & Gariépy, 1989; Coie & Dodge, 1998; Loeber, 1982; Mischel, 1974). Additional developmental changes in aggression are described in the Developmental Trends table "Aggression at Different Age Levels."

Children gradually learn effective techniques to resolve conflicts.

The developmental decline in aggression over childhood is not universal, however. Some youngsters continue to use aggressive acts to get their way. Researchers have identified two distinct groups of aggressive children and adolescents (Crick & Dodge, 1996; Poulin & Boivin, 1999; Vitaro, Gendreau, Tremblay, & Oligny, 1998). Those who engage in *proactive aggression* are deliberately aggressive toward someone else as a means of obtaining desired goals. Those who engage in *reactive aggression* respond aggressively to frustration or provocation. As you will discover shortly, youngsters who display the two types of aggression have somewhat different characteristics. Those who exhibit proactive aggression are most likely to have difficulty maintaining friendships with others (Poulin & Boivin, 1999).

Earlier we indicated that aggressive tendencies are partly the result of genetics. In fact, the biological basis of aggression has been amply documented. For instance, high levels of the male hormone testosterone are correlated with high levels of aggression in adults (J. Archer, 1991). The causal nature of this relationship is somewhat unclear: Although different individuals have genetically influenced tendencies to produce greater or lesser amounts of testosterone, acting aggressively can also, in and of itself, lead to an increase in testosterone level (Coie & Dodge, 1998). The relative amounts of certain neurotransmitters (chemicals involved in transmitting messages from one neuron to another in the brain; see Chapter 3) also influence aggression: They influence whether children inhibit their initial impulses, on the one hand, or respond immediately to annoyance and provocation, on the other (Coie & Dodge, 1998). In some cases, individuals who display heightened aggression have neurological deficits, such as a head injury resulting in damage to the frontal lobe, an area of the cortex involved in the planning and control of behavior (Pennington & Bennetto, 1993; Raine & Scerbo, 1991).

Those children who are especially aggressive when they are young tend to be more aggressive in later years as well (Eron, 1980; Kupersmidt & Coie, 1990; Ladd & Burgess, 1999; Stattin & Magnusson, 1989). Furthermore, children who display proactive (but not reactive) aggression are at increased risk for engaging in delinquent activities later on (Vitaro et al., 1998). This stability does not mean that aggression is inevitable: Professionals can do much to help aggressive children curb their impulses, a point to which we will return in our later recommendations for fostering effective interpersonal skills.

Researchers have identified several general principles that can help us to understand the nature and causes of high levels of aggression in children and adolescents:

■ *Some aggressive children have deficits in perspective taking, empathy, and moral judgment.* Children and adolescents who are highly aggressive tend to get low scores on measures of perspective-taking ability, empathy, and moral reasoning (Chandler, 1973; Damon & Hart, 1988; Marcus, 1980). The ways in which aggressive youths often justify their aggression reveal their disengagement from the feelings and rights of others. For instance, they may

DEVELOPMENTAL TRENDS

Aggression at Different Age Levels

AGE	WHAT YOU MIGHT OBSERVE	DIVERSITY	IMPLICATIONS
Infancy (Birth–2) 	• Frustrations when not able to make own choices in the environment, especially beginning the middle of the first year; anger may be directed toward the person restricting the infant's choices or toward a familiar caregiver • By end of first year, possible hitting when another child takes toys • In second year, pushing and shoving to gain toys • Many conflicts over toys handled without aggression	• Some children have "difficult" temperaments (e.g., they are easily angered and distressed). • Some children are particularly contrary in the second year and may exhibit frequent temper tantrums. • When they are angered, some infants bite other children during their second year.	• Set up the environment to reduce frustration and aggressive behavior: make available duplicates of favorite toys, put up gates so that children can move freely within certain areas, set up separate areas for active movement. • When an aggressive incident occurs, remain calm and comfort the child who has been hit. • Explain to aggressive toddlers that hitting is not acceptable; it hurts other people. Help aggressors deal with angry feelings and redirect them to other activities. • Reinforce aggressive children when they play cooperatively with other children. • Consider reasons why a toddler might act out aggressively and what you might do to reduce frustrating circumstances. • If aggressive acts are a recurrent problem, respond by giving the child time out or removing the toy taken from a peer.
Early Childhood (2–6) 	• Displays of anger when desires are thwarted, especially in younger children; increasing ability to inhibit angry responses with age • Aggressive struggles with peers over possessions • Decrease in physical aggression and increase in verbal aggression (between ages 2 and 4) • Higher rates of aggression when children first get to know one another; eventually they work out their differences and establish dominance hierarchies (i.e., leaders and followers)	• Children with "difficult" temperaments are more likely to act aggressively toward peers. • Children with language delays are more likely to exhibit physical aggression (Richman, Stevenson, & Graham, 1982). • On average, boys are more physically aggressive than girls.	• Encourage young children to use their words rather than their fists. • Acknowledge any gentle, controlled, and constructive responses to frustration or provocation. • Comfort the victims of aggression, and administer appropriate consequences for the perpetrators. Explain why aggressive behavior cannot be tolerated. • Reassure parents that aggressive behavior is fairly common in preschoolers, but offer strategies for promoting prosocial behavior and discouraging aggression.
Middle Childhood (6–10)	• Decrease in overt physical aggression, but with an increase in more covert antisocial behaviors (e.g., cheating, lying, stealing) • Awareness of others' hostile intentions ("She meant to do that")	• Some children become highly aggressive in the elementary grades. • Some children gossip about others and exclude them from friendship groups. • Some children (more boys than girls) display ongoing conduct problems (defiance, aggression, temper tantrums). Children with conduct disorders may instigate fights, use weapons, vandalize buildings, or set fires.	• Do not tolerate physical aggression or bullying. Make sure children understand rules for behavior, and follow through with established procedures when children are aggressive. • Keep your eyes open for children who seem to be the frequent victims of others' aggression, and help them form productive relationships with peers. • Communicate with parents about effective disciplinary strategies (e.g., through newsletters or parent groups).

(continued)

DEVELOPMENTAL TRENDS

Aggression at Different Age Levels (continued)

AGE	WHAT YOU MIGHT OBSERVE	DIVERSITY	IMPLICATIONS
Early Adolescence (10–14) 	• Decline in physical aggression • Frequent teasing and taunting of peers • Occasional sexual harassment and hazing	• Some young adolescents engage in criminal behaviors, such as forced sex or other violent crimes. • Adolescents in some families and neighborhoods have easy access to weapons and regular exposure to violent role models. • Some adolescents may continue to gossip, ridicule others, and exclude them from social groups.	• Supervise students' between-class and after-school activities; make it clear that physical aggression is *not* acceptable on school grounds. • Enforce prohibitions against bringing weapons to school and other settings. • Initiate programs that have been shown to reduce aggression (e.g., peer mediation programs).
Late Adolescence (14–18)	• For many, less motivation to engage in aggressive behavior, often as a result of forming intimate relationships or securing stable employment • Possible increase in risky behaviors and aggressive activities, especially for some boys	• Boys are more likely to be arrested for criminal offenses than are girls (Snyder, Finnegan, Nimick, Sickmund, & Tierney, 1987). In late adolescence, serious crimes continue to increase for boys but level off for girls; boys' crimes decrease after age 18 (Elliott, 1994). • On average, youngsters who live in poor, violent neighborhoods are more apt to become aggressive. • Substance use and sexual activity increase the probability of aggression.	• Give adolescents reasons for optimism about making a living (e.g., arrange for internships with local business people or government officials). Expecting that they can get decent jobs, adolescents will have a reason to avoid criminal behavior. • Continually show adolescents how classroom subject matter relates to their personal goals and equips them to deal with demands of the outside world. • Work cooperatively with law enforcement and social service agencies in efforts to curtail aggression and crime in your community.

Sources: B. B. Brown, 1999; R. B. Cairns, 1979; Caplan, Vespo, Pedersen, & Hay, 1991; Coie & Dodge, 1998; Crick & Grotpeter, 1995; Dodge, 1980; D. S. Elliott, 1994; Gonzales-Mena & Widmeyer Eyer, 2001; Hartup, 1974; Hay & Ross, 1982; Jenkins, Bax, & Hart, 1980; Jersild & Markey, 1935; Jessor, Donovan, & Costa, 1991; Kagan, 1981; Ladd & Burgess, 1999; Lahey, Loeber, Quay, Frick, & Grimm, 1992; Loeber, 1982; Loeber & Hay, 1993; Loeber, Lahey, & Thomas, 1991; Loeber & Schmaling, 1985; Mischel, 1974; Ratcliff, 2001; Richman, Stevenson, & Graham, 1982; Rutter, 1989; Snyder, Finnegan, Nimick, Sickmund, & Tierney, 1987; Solomons & Elardo, 1989; Stenberg & Campos, 1990; Stenberg, Campos, & Emde, 1983; Strayer & Trudel, 1984; Thomas & Chess, 1977; Thomas, Chess, & Birch, 1968; Wenar, 1972.

rationalize violent acts by focusing on their own reputations ("I'm 'The Man'"), comparing their behaviors to more severe violations ("I never shot anyone with a gun"), describing what they're doing in euphemistic terms ("I gotta teach Billy a lesson"), deflecting personal responsibility ("I was just doing what Dad does"), or dehumanizing victims with derogatory labels ("She's a dumb-ass prude"; Coie & Dodge, 1998).

■ *Some aggressive children misinterpret social cues.*   Virtually every social situation provides clues about people's motives and intentions. Although some social cues are straightforward, others are not. For instance, if one child bumps into another, it is not always clear whether the child intended to cause harm. In such ambiguous situations, aggressive children and adolescents often perceive hostile intent in others' behaviors. This *hostile attributional bias* of aggressive children has been observed in numerous studies (Graham & Hudley, 1994; Graham, Hudley, & Williams, 1992; Guerra & Slaby, 1989; Juvonen, 1991; Katsurada & Sugawara, 1998; Lochman & Dodge, 1994). It is especially prevalent in children who are prone to *reactive* aggression (Crick & Dodge, 1996).

■ *Many aggressive children have poor social problem-solving skills.*   Imagine yourself in an 8-year-old's shoes encountering the following situation:

> Pretend one day that one of the adults came in with a plate of candy bars. There was just enough for each kid to have one candy bar and another kid in the group took two candy bars leaving none for you. (D. Schwartz et al., 1998, p. 440)

Aggressive children often have limited ability to generate effective solutions to such social dilemmas; for instance, they are apt to think that hitting, shoving, or barging into the middle of a game are perfectly acceptable behaviors (Lochman & Dodge, 1994; Neel, Jenkins, & Meadows, 1990; D. Schwartz et al., 1998; Shure & Spivack, 1980). And those who display high rates of *proactive* aggression are more likely than their nonaggressive peers to anticipate that aggressive action will yield positive results—for instance, that it will enhance their status (E. Anderson, 1990; Dodge, Lochman, Harnish, Bates, & Pettit, 1997; Hart, Ladd, & Burleson, 1990; Pellegrini & Bartini, 2000).

■ *Aggressive children may have different priorities than nonaggressive children.* Many people, children and adults alike, have a great need for affiliation; in other words, they actively seek out friendly relationships with others (see Chapter 11). For most young people, establishing and maintaining such relationships are high priorities. For aggressive youngsters, however, more self-centered goals—perhaps seeking revenge or gaining power and dominance—often take precedence (Crick & Dodge, 1996; Erdley & Asher, 1996; Lochman et al., 1993; Pellegrini, Bartini, & Brooks, 1999).

■ *Aggressive children may think aggression is appropriate behavior.* Many aggressive youngsters believe that violence and other forms of aggression are acceptable ways of resolving conflicts and retaliating for others' misdeeds (Astor, 1994; Boldizar, Perry, & Perry, 1989; Zelli, Dodge, Lochman, & Laird, 1999). For example, in a study by Astor (1994), children with a history of violent behavior (e.g., throwing rocks at others, hitting classmates with objects, engaging in fist fights, in one case beating up a substitute teacher) and nonaggressive children were given situations that described unprovoked and provoked acts of aggression. The following scenarios are examples:

Unprovoked Aggression

Josh and Mark are brothers. One day Mark was playing in the yard. He was running across the yard and fell down and hurt himself. He was really mad. He turned around and saw Josh. He hit Josh on the head. Josh looked upset and walked away. (Astor, 1994, p. 1057)

Provoked Aggression

Jack and Ron are brothers. One day after school, they were both playing in the backyard of their apartment. After a few minutes of playing Jack started teasing and calling Ron bad names. So Ron punched Jack in the stomach and face. Jack got hurt and cried a lot. (Astor, 1994, p. 1058)

In the Astor study, the children, aggressive and nonaggressive alike, believed that unprovoked acts of aggression were morally wrong. Furthermore, the nonaggressive children believed that physical aggression in response to psychological harm (e.g., teasing, name calling) was also morally unacceptable—that physical harm was a far more serious offense than psychological harm. In contrast, the violent children gave equal weight to the seriousness of physical and psychological aggression and believed that physical aggression was appropriate retaliation for psychological abuse. Astor speculated that the violent children may have been the recipients of considerable psychological aggression in their own lives and perceived it to be as painful as physical aggression.

■ *Some children show a pattern of bullying behavior, directing aggression to particular victims.* Researchers have found that some youngsters (*bullies*) direct considerable aggression toward particular children, or *victims* (Patterson, Littman, & Bricker, 1967; Pellegrini et al., 1999; D. Schwartz, Dodge, Pettit, & Bates, 1997). Some victims rarely retaliate or in other ways stand up for themselves; others are prone to reactive aggression (D. Schwartz et al., 1997; D. Schwartz et al., 1998). Children who are chronic bullies tend to be hyperactive, to overreact to accidents and other unfortunate incidents, to be relatively unpopular, and to believe that bullying behavior will enhance their status with peers (Pellegrini & Bartini, 2000; Pellegrini et al., 1999). In fact, many bullies feel powerful when other children watch them pester victims (Sutton, Smith, & Swettenham, 1999).

Why do children put up with bullying? Children victimized by bullies are often immature, anxious, socially withdrawn, and friendless (some also have disabilities) and so are relatively defenseless against more powerful aggressors (Hodges, Malone, & Perry, 1997; Juvonen, Nishina, & Graham, 2000; L. Little, 2000c; D. Schwartz, McFadyen-Ketchum,

Dodge, Pettit, & Bates, 1999). Those who respond with reactive aggression may experience aggression and abuse at home as well as at school (D. Schwartz et al., 1997). Obviously, professionals who become aware of bullying should take action to put an immediate stop to it.

■ *Some aggressive children use their theories of mind to bully or exclude other children.* In Chapter 10, we introduced the concept of *theory of mind* in reference to children's awareness of other human beings' intentions, thoughts, beliefs, and feelings. Some bullies are skilled at looking beneath the surface to other children's ideas and motivations and using this information to maximize the distress they cause (Sutton, Smith, & Swettenham, 1999). Their limitation is not with social perspective taking—these aggressors fully understand how victims feel. Instead, they simply do not care. That is, other children give them the chance to feel powerful and it matters little that other children are hurt in the process.

Another group of children use perspective taking and social skills to charm age-mates, gain their loyalty, and inflict psychological pain on children outside their in-group. They do this by gossiping, spreading rumors, and excluding other children (Sutton, Smith, & Swettenham, 1999). Some youngsters are painfully aware that they are targets of ridicule and exclusion. Twelve-year-old Cheri describes her experience:

> I was popular down in elementary school but now I'm out of the crowd, you know. No one likes me. I don't know what it is, they just don't like me. They would sit around in class and talk about me and stuff. It would really hurt my feelings. They write notes and stuff and they'd be passing it and I wouldn't be able to read it. And it would just tear my guts up. A lot of times I feel left out. Not like all of the time, but some of the time. Like when my friends, they go off. I feel like they know that I'm there, but it's just that they don't even notice me. I just feel like I'm left out. I only have one girlfriend and the rest of them are boys. Girls are, I don't know, they're not attracted to me. But I'm OK with it. It really doesn't bother me.[2]

Cheri ends her description with the disclaimer that being excluded no longer bothers her. Is she trying to cope with hurt feelings by denying them, or has she truly gotten over it? It is not possible to tell, but we do know that some children are especially sensitive to teasing, ridicule, and social exclusion (Crick, Casas, & Nelson, 2002). In Figure 13–2, 13-year-old Georgia expresses her dismay over Leslie's undue sensitivity. Real or imagined, perceptions that other children are having fun at their expense can be deeply painful for some youngsters. When children are victims of frequent acts of psychological aggression, they are more likely than other children to exhibit depression and delinquent actions (Crick et al., 2002).

In summary, aggression takes many forms, it serves several distinct functions, and some children are, for various reasons, more aggressive than others. In the Basic Developmental Issues table "Prosocial Behavior and Aggression," we examine these interpersonal behaviors in terms of the developmental themes of nature and nurture, universality and diversity, and qualitative and quantitative change. We now look at how children's interpersonal behaviors change over time and how they come to vary somewhat in different groups.

FIGURE 13–2 Reflecting back on an incident that occurred when she was in elementary school, 13-year-old Georgia expresses her dismay at Leslie's extreme sensitivity.

We were playing freeze tag one day at recess. Leslie got tagged and asked me to step on her shadow before anyone else. I stepped on Becca's shadow before I stepped on Leslie's and she got mad. I told Leslie to stop being so selfish and bratty. She took it extremely personally and stormed off, told a teacher, and called her mom.

I later apologized and we became friends again. I invited her to my birthday and she came but I could tell she felt uncomfortable. So, I decided to do makeovers. I was playing around with lipsticks and accidentally messed up on Leslie's makeover, but laughed because I knew it could be fixed. She ran to see the "damage" in the mirror, started to cry, and called her mom and left.

From then on, I've never really understood her and we've never been close. We see eachother and say "hi" in the halls, but that's it.

Interpersonal Behaviors at Different Ages

Throughout the life span, people continue to develop and refine strategies for interacting effectively with others, but most basic strategies are acquired in the first two decades of life. Each of the five developmental periods we've considered throughout the book—infancy, early childhood, middle childhood, early adolescence, and late adolescence—offers new lessons and new opportunities for practicing social skills.

Infancy (Birth–2) Interpersonal relationships begin with attachments to parents and other caregivers (see Chapter 9). Infants in child care settings or at home with other small children often extend their early social skills to other children; for example, they may look

---

[2] From *Girls in America: Their Stories, Their Words* (p. 70), by Carol Cassidy, 1999, New York: TV Books. Copyright 1999 by TV Books. Reprinted with permission of Carol Cassidy.

BASIC DEVELOPMENTAL ISSUES

Prosocial Behavior and Aggression

ISSUE	PROSOCIAL BEHAVIOR	AGGRESSION
Nature and Nurture	The capacity for prosocial behavior appears to be a natural, inborn human characteristic, but individual children have unique genetic endowments (e.g., temperaments) that affect prosocial behavior. Prosocial behavior is nurtured by role modeling, specific instruction and feedback, appeals to children to consider the needs of distressed people, evidence that people in need did not cause their own problems, and other environmental supports.	The capacity for aggression has a biological basis and is to some degree inherited. Aggressiveness in individual children is influenced by temperamental dispositions, hormone levels, and neurological structures in the brain. Yet the social environment powerfully influences how children express their aggressive impulses. Parents and other caregivers may treat children harshly and punitively and in other ways model or encourage aggressive behavior; such actions can lead to aggression and conduct problems.
Universality and Diversity	The capacity for prosocial behavior is universal in the human species; furthermore, people in most cultures become increasingly prosocial as they get older. Significant diversity exists in the extent to which various cultural groups encourage prosocial activities (e.g., sharing, nurturing), as well as in children's exposure to adults who model prosocial behavior and articulate a commitment to care for people in need.	Aggressive behavior is universal in human beings. Some general developmental sequences in aggressive expression, such as a gradual shift from physical aggression to verbal aggression, may also be universal. Substantial diversity is present in the ways that children and adolescents express aggression, in the amount of aggression young people encounter in their daily environments, and in the extent to which cultural groups condone aggression as a way of resolving conflict.
Qualitative and Quantitative Change	Qualitative changes may occur in children's understanding of why helping others is important and valuable; for instance, young children often give help primarily to gain rewards or approval, whereas older children and adolescents are more likely to have a genuine concern for those in need. Quantitative increases occur in children's knowledge of effective prosocial strategies and in their ability to carry out such strategies.	Qualitative change is seen in the shift from physical aggression to verbal aggression and in the transfer from accidental hurting when grabbing toys to deliberately hostile actions. The degree to which children and adolescents display aggressive behavior changes quantitatively with development. The frequency of aggression is often low in infancy, increases in early childhood, and decreases during middle childhood. For a minority, it increases again during adolescence, after which it usually decreases, especially as young adults take on conventional adult responsibilities and form intimate relationships with mates.

Sources: Coie & Dodge, 1998; Eisenberg & Fabes, 1998.

where another child points, babble in response to his or her sounds, and smile at him or her (Eckerman, 1979; Mueller & Silverman, 1989). As toddlers, they may offer one another toys and imitate one another, creating a shared focus (Howes, 1992; Howes & Matheson, 1992). Their developing language skills in the second year, as well as games with older children and adults (e.g., peek-a-boo, pat-a-cake), permit increasingly sustained and meaningful exchanges (Bronson, 1981).

Occasionally, infants display friendly expressions and gestures with each other.

Early Childhood (Ages 2–6) With the capacity for coordinating attention with others well underway by age 2, young children increasingly interact with age-mates, particularly within the context of play activities. In a classic study, Mildred Parten (1932) carefully observed the behaviors of 2- to 5-year-old children who attended a preschool at the University of Minnesota. From her observations, she identified six categories of behavior in preschoolers, five of which involve play:

- *Unoccupied behavior.* Children fail to engage in an activity or interact with another individual. They may wander around the room or simply sit and stare into space.
- *Solitary play.* Children sit absorbed with their own playthings. Other children are in the same room but might as well be on another planet: Children neither communicate with one another nor acknowledge one another's existence.
- *Onlooker behavior.* Children watch others who are engaged in play activities but make no social overtures. For instance, a child may quietly watch another child build a tower with wooden blocks.

- *Parallel play.* Children play quietly side by side. Although they may do similar things, they do not talk much to one another.
- *Associative play.* Children play together, sharing objects and talking a little. They may pass objects back and forth and make occasional comments on what they are doing.
- *Cooperative play.* Children actively coordinate their activities, swapping toys, taking on defined roles, and in other ways keeping an interaction going.

Parten concluded that children progress through a defined sequence of play—beginning with unoccupied behavior and solitary play, moving through the subsequent categories, and eventually developing cooperative play—all the while becoming more social in their exchanges.

To some extent, Parten was right: Children become increasingly interactive and cooperative in play activities as they grow older (Gottman, 1983; Howes & Matheson, 1992). However, younger and older preschoolers alike exhibit at different times all five categories of play; later forms do not completely replace earlier ones (Howes & Matheson, 1992). Furthermore, parallel play, though seemingly nonsocial, appears to have a definite social function: Children use it as a way to learn more about other children's interests and to initiate conversations (Bakeman & Brownlee, 1980; K. H. Rubin, Bukowski, & Parker, 1998). Moreover, remember that infants display some interest in peers and exhibit occasional friendly gestures toward them. Young children may play absorbed in their own private agendas but they do have a social side—from the beginning.

Such qualifications aside, Parten rightly elevated cooperative play to an advanced state. The imagination and social coordination that characterize cooperative play make it a stellar achievement of early childhood. In one form of cooperative play, **sociodramatic play**, children assume complementary imagined roles and carry out a logical sequence of actions. In the following scenario, we see Eric and Naomi, long-time friends, assuming roles of husband "Bob" and wife "Claudia." Naomi is making plans to go shopping:

N: I'm buying it at a toy store, to buy Eric Fisher a record 'cause he doesn't have a . . .
E: What happened to his old one?
N: It's all broken.
E: How did it get all broken?
N: Ah, a robber stealed it, I think. That's what he said, a robber stealed it.
E: Did he see what the action was? You know my gun is in here, so could you go get my gun? It's right over there, back there, back there, not paper . . . did you get it?
N: Yes, I found the robbers right in the closet.
E: Good, kill 'em.
N: I killed em.
E: Already?
N: Yes, so quick they can't believe it.
E: Well, Claudia, you can call me Bob everytime, Claudia . . . (Gottman, 1986b, p. 191; reprinted with permission of Cambridge University Press)

In Chapter 4, we considered the ways in which play, especially sociodramatic play, fosters cognitive development. Sociodramatic play and other forms of cooperative play also promote social development, requiring children to hone their social skills in the following ways:

■ *Children learn more about other people's perspectives.* For children to play successfully together, they must learn a great deal about one another's ideas, interests, and wishes (Göncü, 1993; Gottman, 1986b; Howes, 1992). They also get practice in establishing *intersubjectivity,* that is, in sharing understandings and finding common ground (Göncü, 1993; Gottman, 1983; Mueller & Brenner, 1977; we first introduced this concept in Chapter 5). Preschoolers exhibit a variety of strategies that show an appreciation for one another's perspectives. For instance, they may voice approval for one another's actions ("That's pretty"), express sympathy and support ("Don't worry about that, it'll come off"), and exchange witticisms ("How do you do this stupid thing?" "You do it in a stupid way?"; Gottman, 1983, p. 58).

sociodramatic play
Play in which children take on assumed roles and act out a scenario of events.

■ *Children learn how to coordinate their actions and perspectives.* When two children play together cooperatively, they must often take turns, share objects, and in other ways consider what their playmate is doing. They must also agree on individual roles ("I'll be the warrior"; "OK, I'll be the chief"), props ("The log can be our base"), and rules and guidelines that govern actions ("We'll let Frances play, but she has to be the horse"; Garvey, 1990; Howes & Matheson, 1992). And underneath it all, they must agree to share certain fantasies—a phenomenon known as **social pretense** (K. H. Rubin et al., 1998).

Young children often enter slowly and carefully into activities that require cooperation and coordination, particularly when they don't know one another very well (Gottman, 1983). Notice how two 4-year-olds, playing together for the first time, increasingly coordinate their activities with Play-Doh and eventually agree that they are making supper:

FIGURE 13-3 Alex (age 5) and Davis (age 6) shared fantasies that guided them in drawing this picture together.

J: You got white Play-Doh and this color and that color.
D: Every color. That's the colors we got. . . .
D: I'm putting pink in the blue.
J: Mix pink.
D: Pass the blue.
J: I think I'll pass the blue. . . .
D: And you make those for after we get it together, OK?
J: 'Kay.
D: Have to make these.
J: Pretend like those little roll cookies, too, OK?
D: And make, um, make a, um, pancake, too.
J: Oh rats. This is a little pancake.
D: OK. Make, make me, um, make two flat cookies. Cause I'm, I'm cutting any, I'm cutting this. My snake . . .
J: You want all my blue?
D: Yes. To make cookies. Just to make cookies, but we can't mess the cookies all up.
J: Nope. . . .
D: Put this the right way, OK? We're making supper, huh?
J: We're making supper. . . . (Gottman, 1983, pp. 56–57)

As children grow older, they more readily coordinate their play activities, particularly when they know one another well. In Figure 13–3, you can see the result of a coordinated effort between Alex (age 5) and his longtime friend Davis (age 6). As they worked on the picture, they continually listened to each other, built on each other's ideas, and drew from their many past experiences together.

■ *Children learn how to ask for what they want.* As children gain experience with their peers, they become increasingly skillful and polite in making requests of others (J. Parkhurst & Gottman, 1986). Directives are common among younger preschoolers (e.g., "Give me the red one"; "You hafta . . . "), whereas 5- and 6-year-olds are more likely to use hints and suggestions ("Have you got . . . ?" "Would you like . . . ?" "Let's . . . "; J. Parkhurst & Gottman, 1986, p. 329).

■ *Children develop strategies for resolving conflicts.* Cooperative play is a fertile training ground for developing social problem-solving and conflict-resolution skills (Göncü, 1993; Gottman, 1986b; Howes, 1992). For instance, children may haggle and eventually compromise about roles in sociodramatic play ("I want to be the Mommy, you're the baby"; "No, you were the Mommy last time; it's *my* turn"; "OK, but next time I get to be the Mommy"). In the Physical Activity/Early Childhood clip of the Observation CD, watch two 4-year-olds, Acadia and Cody, work diligently and skillfully at coordinating their activities. They use a variety of strategies to nourish their friendship and prevent differences from escalating: They make explicit reference to their friendship ("Let's go, Cody, my best friend"), encourage one another to climb ("This is gonna be cool!"), admit when they're wrong ("Silly me, I forget everything"), and eventually come to agreement about which slide to go down ("Yeah. Let's do it"). On the other hand, when children discover that they cannot reach agreement, they often return to an activity at which they have previously played more

Observe two young friends, Cody and Acadia, coordinating their activities and resolving their differences in the Physical Activity/Early Childhood clip of the Observation CD.

social pretense
Ability to share internal fantasies with a social partner.

harmoniously (Gottman, 1983). In some instances, preschoolers cooperate more successfully when adults help them iron out their difficulties (Mize, Pettit, & Brown, 1995; Parke & Bhavnagri, 1989).

Because cooperative play requires so many skills, children have to work hard at it. Fortunately cooperative play is so entertaining that they don't mind the effort. With time and practice, they become increasingly proficient; for example, they develop new strategies for finding common ground, engage in longer episodes of sociodramatic play, and construct increasingly elaborate roles and story lines (Göncü, 1993; K. H. Rubin et al., 1998). By the time they reach the early elementary grades, they are ready to take on new challenges in their interpersonal relationships.

Middle Childhood (Ages 6–10) Life becomes even more social in middle childhood. Any single day is filled with countless interactions with family members, teachers, classmates, and other individuals of all ages (Barker & Wright, 1951). This complex social world provides many opportunities to interact with age-mates. At ages 6 through 12, children spend about 40% of their waking hours with peers, approximately twice as much time as they did in early childhood (Zarbatany, Hartmann, & Rankin, 1990).

During middle childhood, children become attuned to other people's psychological characteristics—their personalities, emotions, and so on (see Chapter 10). They also become aware that, in the company of peers, certain ways of behaving are acceptable and others are not (Gottman & Mettetal, 1986; J. R. Harris, 1998). In a gossip session, for example, 8-year-old Erica and Mikaila reveal their shared belief that tattling on others is inappropriate:

E: Katie's just a . . .
M: Tattletale.
E: Yeah, she tells on everything.
M: Yeah. (Gottman & Mettetal, 1986, p. 206; reprinted with permission of Cambridge University Press)

FIGURE 13–4 Ten-year-old Jacob drew a child getting into an argument with a friend (left) and then coming to a mutually acceptable solution (right).

With their growing awareness of other people's opinions, children become eager and able to behave in socially acceptable ways; they also become more concerned about equitably resolving conflicts and preserving friendships (Hartup, 1996; Newcomb & Bagwell, 1995). In Figure 13–4, 10-year-old Jacob reveals his awareness that arguing with friends can be unpleasant, but that disputes often can be resolved to everyone's satisfaction. Not all attempts to resolve conflicts are successful, of course. Most children discover that such strategies as sulking ("I'm going home!"), threatening ("I'm never gonna play with you again!"), and hitting ("Take that!") rarely work. Through experimentation with a variety of strategies and through their growing capacity for social perspective taking and empathy, most children become proficient at maintaining amicable relationships with peers.

By the elementary school years, much of children's time is spent without the direct supervision of adults. When parents and teachers are not hovering nearby, children tend to sort things out for themselves, not only in dealing with disagreements but also in choosing and directing activities. Unlike younger children who get together in groups of two or three to engage in free-flowing fantasy, elementary school children often convene in larger groups and choose games and other activities that have established rules, such as verbal contests (e.g., "Twenty Questions" and "I Spy"), board games, team sports, and outdoor games played during recess (Corsaro, 1985; Hartup, 1984). In fact, rules take on a certain immutable quality: They are permanent fixtures that cannot be altered by whim, and failure to follow them constitutes cheating—a serious breach from what is good and civilized. In the following conversation with 10-year-old Ben, an adult asks if it would be possible to change the rules in a game of marbles. Ben agrees (somewhat unwillingly) that he could formulate new rules but has serious concerns about their legitimacy:

Ben: [I]t would be cheating.

Adult: But all your pals would like to [play with the new rule], wouldn't they?

Ben: Yes, they all would.

Adult: Then why would it be cheating?

Ben: Because I invented it: it isn't a rule! It's a wrong rule because it's outside of the rules. A fair rule is one that is in the game. (dialogue from Piaget, 1932/1960b, p. 55; format adapted).

In working through disagreements, children often make use of principles of fairness and familiar rules of games.

Children learn a great deal from participating in rule-governed games. For instance, they discover how to use rules to their own advantage ("If I put another house on Boardwalk, you have to pay me double next time you land on it"), how to form alliances with other children ("I'll run behind him, and then you pass me the ball over his head"), and how to deal with ambiguous situations ("It was *in!*" "Are you kidding? It was *out!*" "OK, it's out, but next time *I* get to decide!"). Occasional bickering aside, the predominance of rule-governed activities in middle childhood seems to reflect children's growing motivation to learn and abide by the rules of society (DeVries, 1997).

Early Adolescence (Ages 10–14)   Once children reach puberty, they rely increasingly on their peers for emotional support as well as recreation (Levitt, Guacci-Franco, & Levitt, 1993; R. M. Ryan, Stiller, & Lynch, 1994). Many young adolescents, girls especially, begin to reveal their innermost thoughts to others, and more often to peers rather than adults (Basinger, Gibbs, & Fuller, 1995; Levitt et al., 1993). Such self-disclosure is usually a key element of close friendships (Gottman, 1986a).

Even as their tendency for self-disclosure expands, young adolescents become increasingly self-conscious about what others might think of them. Recall our discussion of the *imaginary audience* in Chapter 9: Adolescents often overestimate other people's interest in their appearance and behavior. This heightened concern for how others evaluate them can lead them to be quite conforming—that is, to imitate rigidly their peers' choices in dress, music, slang, and behavior. By looking and sounding like others, they may feel that they better fit in with their age-mates (Hartup, 1983; R. E. Owens, 1996). Young adolescents encourage others to conform as well—exerting **peer pressure**—perhaps by teasing or insulting those who stand out as different. (Recall how some African American students called Aqeelah "Oreo" because of her friendships with European Americans.) Peer pressure, encouraging or discouraging certain behaviors, has its greatest impact during the junior high school years. Adolescents who have poor relationships with their families seem to be especially vulnerable (Berndt, Laychak, & Park, 1990; Erwin, 1993; Ryan & Lynch, 1989; Urdan & Maehr, 1995).

Teenagers' internal motivation to fit in probably is a more significant factor affecting their desire to conform than is peer pressure. (Recall our discussion of children contributing to their own socialization in Chapter 12.) One adolescent suggests that it is a desire to be part of the "in" crowd—rather than peer pressure, which is often the focus of adult concerns—that drives many to do foolish things:

> There's all this crap about being accepted into a group and struggling and making an effort to make friends and not being comfortable about your own self-worth as a human being. You're trying very hard to show everyone what a great person you are, and the best way to do that is if everyone else is drinking therefore they think that's the thing to do, then you might do the same thing to prove to them that you have the same values that they do and therefore you're okay. At the same time, the idea of peer pressure is a lot of bunk. What I heard about peer pressure all the way through school is that someone is going to walk up to me and say, "Here, drink this and you'll be cool." It wasn't like that at all. You go somewhere and everyone else would be doing it and you'd think, "Hey, everyone else is doing it and they seem to be having a good time—now why wouldn't I do this?" In that sense, the preparation of the powers that be, the lessons that they tried to drill into me, they were completely off. They had no idea what we are up against. (Lightfoot, 1992, p. 240)

Young adolescents also have a tendency to categorize other people. For instance, they may pigeon-hole their peers into such groups as "brains," "jocks," "skaters," and "geeks" (J. R. Harris, 1995; Pipher, 1994). Divisions along racial lines increase as well. Recall how

peer pressure
Tactics used to encourage some behaviors and discourage others in age-mates.

Aqeelah's long-time European American friends suddenly began using African American slang when they spoke to her ("Yo, Aqeelah, what up?") and assumed that, because she was African American, she would like rap music. With this trend toward racial categorization, young teens are also more likely to segregate into racial groups, much to the surprise of many, like Aqeelah, Kelly, and Johanna. For example, when Johanna had a birthday party in eighth grade, most of her friends spent the entire evening in two groups—blacks and whites—with one group hanging out and dancing in the basement and the other standing outside and talking (T. Lewin, 2000).

In their desire to fit in with peers, teenagers sometimes seem to lead double lives, displaying one set of behaviors with their families and an entirely different set of behaviors at school. For instance, if they believe that their classmates view high academic achievement as uncool, they might do their homework faithfully at home each night yet feign disinterest in classroom activities, disrupt class with jokes or goofy behaviors, and express surprise at receiving high grades (B. B. Brown, 1993; Covington, 1992). Many young adolescents have trouble reconciling these different sides and may feel as if they are continually hiding their true selves (L. M. Brown, Tappan, & Gilligan, 1995; Harter, Bresnick, Bouchey, & Whitesell, 1997; Harter, Waters, & Whitesell, 1997).

Late Adolescence (Ages 14–18)   Older adolescents spend almost half of their waking hours interacting with friends and classmates (Csikszentmihalyi, 1995). They spend relatively little time with adults and very little time exclusively with an adult, such as a parent or teacher (Csikszentmihalyi, 1995; Csikszentmihalyi & Larson, 1984).

Whereas young adolescents seem to split themselves into two or more separate selves, older adolescents strive to recombine those selves into an adult *identity* (see Chapter 9), and they often use their peers as a forum for self-exploration and self-understanding (Gottman & Mettetal, 1986). For example, the following dialogue shows two girls struggling with their beliefs about premarital sexual intercourse as they discuss one girl's recent breakup with her boyfriend Randy:

A: [*joking*] I think you should take Randy to court for statutory rape.
B: I don't. I'm to the point of wondering what "that kind of girl" . . . I don't know about the whole scene.
A: The thing is . . .
B: It depends on the reasoning. And how long you've been going out with somebody.
A: Yeah, I'm satisfied with my morals.
B: As long as you're satisfied with your morals, that's cool.
A: Yeah, but other people . . .
B: And I'm pretty, I'm pretty sturdy in mine.
A: Yeah [*giggle*], I know that. Mine tend to bend too easily. (Gottman & Mettetal, 1986, p. 218; reprinted with the permission of Cambridge University Press)

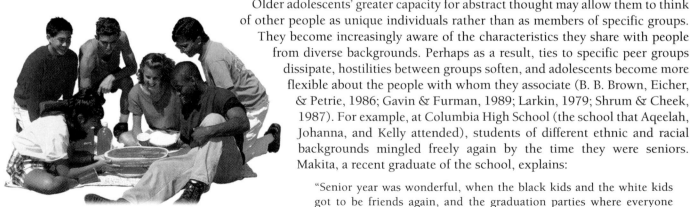

Older adolescents' greater capacity for abstract thought may allow them to think of other people as unique individuals rather than as members of specific groups. They become increasingly aware of the characteristics they share with people from diverse backgrounds. Perhaps as a result, ties to specific peer groups dissipate, hostilities between groups soften, and adolescents become more flexible about the people with whom they associate (B. B. Brown, Eicher, & Petrie, 1986; Gavin & Furman, 1989; Larkin, 1979; Shrum & Cheek, 1987). For example, at Columbia High School (the school that Aqeelah, Johanna, and Kelly attended), students of different ethnic and racial backgrounds mingled freely again by the time they were seniors. Makita, a recent graduate of the school, explains:

"Senior year was wonderful, when the black kids and the white kids got to be friends again, and the graduation parties where everyone mixed. . . . It was so much better." (T. Lewin, 2000, p. 20)

Gains in reasoning skills make it possible for older adolescents to feel comfortable in heterogeneous groups.

But social maturity is a long time in the making. Whereas high school seniors have far more sophisticated social skills than do preschoolers or fifth graders, most have not completely mastered the tact and courtesy so essential for resolving delicate interpersonal matters. For example, they may occasionally show intolerance for other people's weaknesses or yell crude or insulting remarks in a moment of anger. Furthermore, many older adolescents continue to engage in the high-risk behaviors that some peers endorse (Csikszentmihalyi & Larson, 1984).

Overall, what stands out about late adolescence is how vital peer relationships are. Parents and extended family members, teachers, counselors, coaches, and other adults continue to be important, but peers are the social partners of choice. As young people spend an increasing amount of time with their age-mates, they create the social experiences they need to launch themselves into the challenging world of adults. Soon they will need skills in inferring others' intentions, forming intimate relationships, raising the next generation, and dealing with people who are inclined to hurt or manipulate them. The social experiences of late adolescence prepare them for many of these later experiences, although new social challenges will, of course, continue to present themselves throughout adulthood.

Group Differences in Interpersonal Behaviors

We have just seen how interpersonal behaviors change with age. These behaviors may also differ to some extent at any given stage because of factors such as gender, cultural background, and special educational needs.

Gender Differences   Researchers and educators alike frequently see gender differences in children's play activities (Gallahue & Ozmun, 1998; Gottman, 1986b; Paley, 1984). In sociodramatic play, girls tend to enact scenarios that are relatively calm and sedate (e.g., playing house or school), whereas boys often introduce elements of adventure and danger (e.g., playing cops and robbers or fighting intergalactic battles). Boys are more active even in relatively sedentary activities; for instance, if their teachers ask them to sit down and draw, they may "animate . . . volcanoes and space wars with exploding noises, as if they have jumped inside the pictures" (Paley, 1984, p. 5). Boys' higher activity levels are also seen in their preference for large outdoor spaces, where they can run, throw balls, and chase one another (Frost, Shin, & Jacobs, 1998).

Preschoolers of both genders tend to relate to one another primarily through their activities. As they grow older, however, boys continue to place high priority on activities, whereas girls devote time to talking—for instance, sharing personal concerns, telling secrets, and seeking emotional support (Berndt, 1992; G. P. Jones & Dembo, 1989; McCallum & Bracken, 1993). In general, girls tend to form closer and more intimate relationships with others, and they are more sensitive to subtle, nonverbal messages (body language) (J. H. Block, 1983; Deaux, 1984). Girls may be slightly more kind and considerate, but in many situations boys are just as caring, affectionate, and sympathetic as girls (Eisenberg & Fabes, 1998).

The gender difference found most consistently in research studies is in *physical aggression:* Beginning in the preschool years, boys are more physically aggressive than girls (Collaer & Hines, 1995; Eagly, 1987; Loeber & Stouthamer-Loeber, 1998). This greater inclination toward physical aggression is probably the result of both biological factors (as noted earlier, testosterone has been linked with aggressive behavior) and socialization (parents are more likely to allow aggression in sons than in daughters) (Collaer & Hines, 1995; Condry & Ross, 1985; Eisenberg et al., 1996). However, girls are often just as aggressive as boys in subtle and less physical ways—for example, by tattling, gossiping, and snubbing their peers (Bjorkqvist, Osterman, & Kaukiainen, 1992; Brodzinsky, Messer, & Tew, 1979; Crick & Grotpeter, 1995; Loeber & Stouthamer-Loeber, 1998).

Boys also tend to be more assertive than girls. For example, in mixed-sex work groups, they are more likely to dominate activities and take charge of needed equipment, and they are more likely to get their way when group members disagree (Jovanovic & King, 1998). Such assertiveness may be nurtured in same-sex activity groups over the years, as boys' friendships typically involve more conflict and competition than girls' friendships do (Eisenberg et al., 1996). In contrast, girls are more likely to acquiesce to others' wishes, perhaps because they value group harmony more than boys do and so make frequent small concessions to keep the peace (P. M. Miller, Danaher, & Forbes, 1986).

Cultural Differences   Children may have more or fewer opportunities to interact with peers, depending on the culture in which they grow up. Unlike in North America, where most children come into frequent contact with age-mates at an early age, children in some cultures stay close to home and play primarily with parents and siblings, at least until they reach school age (Trawick-Smith, 2003; Whiting & Edwards, 1988). Children whose primary language is different from that of the larger society in which they live (e.g., as is true for non-English-speaking immigrants to an English-speaking country) also have limited opportunities to interact with age-mates (A. Doyle, 1982).

To some degree, different cultural groups also model and teach different interpersonal behaviors. For instance, children in China are encouraged to be shy; those in Israel are encouraged to be assertive (X. Chen, Rubin, & Li, 1995; Krispin, Sternberg, & Lamb, 1992). Smiling is a sign of agreement and friendliness in almost any cultural group, but in a few cultures (e.g., in some Japanese American families), it may also indicate embarrassment (Eckman, 1972). Sociolinguistic behaviors, or appropriate ways of acting when talking with others, also differ from culture to culture (see Chapter 7).

Cultures differ, too, in the degree to which they encourage competitive or cooperative behavior with others. In North America, many people see competition as desirable (e.g., parents may enter their children in dance contests, high school teachers sometimes grade on a curve), and children are more likely to be praised for their individual achievements than for group success. In contrast, many other cultures (e.g., most Asian and Hispanic societies) place a high premium on loyalty, trust, cooperation, and prosocial behavior (Greenfield, 1994a; P. B. Smith & Bond, 1994; Triandis, 1995).

Youngsters with Special Needs   On average, children and adolescents who have been identified as gifted have good social skills, although a few whose intellectual talents are highly advanced sometimes have difficulty in interpersonal relationships because they are so different from peers (A. E. Gottfried, Fleming, & Gottfried, 1994; Keogh & MacMillan, 1996; Winner, 1997). Those with mental retardation typically have social skills similar to those of much younger children (DuPaul & Eckert, 1994; Greenspan & Granfield, 1992). Youngsters with chronic emotional and behavioral problems (e.g., conduct disorders) often have difficulty making and keeping friends, usually because of deficits in social problem solving and other social skills (Asher & Coie, 1990; Cartledge & Milburn, 1995; DuPaul & Eckert, 1994). And some (but by no means all) youngsters with information processing difficulties, including most who have autism and some who have learning disabilities or ADHD, show less advanced social understanding and interpersonal skills than their nondisabled peers (e.g., Greenspan & Granfield, 1992; Milch-Reich, Campbell, Pelham, Connelly, & Geva, 1999). In the next section, we offer suggestions for helping such children—and in fact for helping all children—develop more effective interpersonal behaviors.

Fostering Effective Interpersonal Skills

Professionals who work with young people in social settings have many opportunities to encourage effective social skills and to discourage inappropriate behaviors such as hitting, gossiping, ridiculing, and affiliating with peers determined to follow destructive paths. Teachers working in child care centers and schools have daily opportunities to support friendly interactions among children. Counselors, community leaders, and other professionals can help children when they struggle with particular social skills, such as controlling aggressive impulses, resisting negative peer influences, and acting in ways that will gain them acceptance among peers (Elliott & Busse, 1991; McGill, 1997; Shechtman, 2001). Following are strategies for helping children and adolescents acquire effective interpersonal behaviors:

■ *Model empathic responses to others in distress.*   We saw earlier that some aggressive children, notably bullies and perpetrators of malicious gossip, may have little empathy for age-mates. To discourage children from becoming callous, professionals can talk about their own concern for how children feel. For example, an infant caregiver may verbalize her own feelings when a child is in distress ("Victor, I'm so sorry your gums are sore with those new teeth coming in; come, let me hold you"); doing so comforts the unhappy child and also models empathic responses to someone in need. When affectionate adults consistently demonstrate empathic styles, youngsters gradually can learn to respond in a similar manner.

■ *Establish firm rules for behavior.* Children must grasp the simple message that they are to be respectful, safe, and kind (Learning First Alliance, 2001). Teachers and other caregivers can reduce the likelihood of their hurting one another by establishing firm rules that prohibit physical aggression, weapon possession, and behaviors that cause psychological harm, including malicious gossip, prejudicial remarks, sexual harassment, intimidation, and ostracism (Juvonen et al., 2000). At the beginning of the school year (or when a club or other group is launched), school staff and other practitioners need to model and enforce these rules with absolute consistency—in the classroom, cafeteria, hallway, gym, and restrooms, and at athletic events, musical performances, and other extracurricular activities. Continued supervision is needed throughout the year, but it will be more effective when the message is loud and clear from the start (Learning First Alliance, 2001). By supervising children closely and putting a stop to aggressive acts before they grow ugly, adults can discourage bad habits and teach good social skills.

■ *Use more intensive strategies for young people who are chronically aggressive.* Unfortunately, simply establishing clear prohibitions against aggression and imposing appropriate consequences on those who violate such prohibitions are not always enough. Some children and adolescents have a history of aggressive behavior, perhaps as a result of neurological deficits or harsh and punitive parenting, and may require intervention. Strategies such as the following are often effective with chronically aggressive students:

* Teaching effective social skills
* Teaching more effective ways of resolving conflicts and solving interpersonal problems
* Teaching strategies for anger control (e.g., self-talk)
* Enhancing the ability to look at situations from others' perspectives
* Encouraging more advanced moral reasoning
* Fostering more accurate interpretations of others' behaviors, body language, and other nonverbal social cues (e.g., teaching students to distinguish between intentional and unintentional actions)
  (Crick & Dodge, 1996; Graham, 1997; Guerra & Slaby, 1990; Henrich, Brown, & Aber, 1999; J. N. Hughes, 1988; Iannotti, 1978; Sasso, Melloy, & Kavale, 1990)

■ *Teach specific social skills and social problem-solving strategies.* Through their frequent interactions with peers and adults, many young people acquire effective social behaviors on their own. Nevertheless, many others—perhaps because of limited opportunities to interact with age-mates, a disability, or poor role models at home—know little about how to initiate conversations, exchange compliments, offer emotional support, or in other ways establish and maintain rewarding interpersonal relationships (e.g., Patrick, 1997). Some also lack productive strategies for solving social problems; for example, they may barge into a game without asking or respond to any provocation with aggression.

Teachers, counselors, and other adults can teach many effective interpersonal behaviors both through explicit verbal instructions (see Figure 13–5) and through encouragement and modeling of desired behaviors. Such instruction is especially likely to be effective when students have opportunities to practice their newly learned skills (perhaps through role playing) and when they receive concrete feedback about how they are doing (S. N. Elliott & Busse, 1991; Schloss & Smith, 1994; S. Vaughn, 1991; Zirpoli & Melloy, 1993). The Development and Practice feature "Fostering Effective Interpersonal Skills" describes several strategies professionals might use.

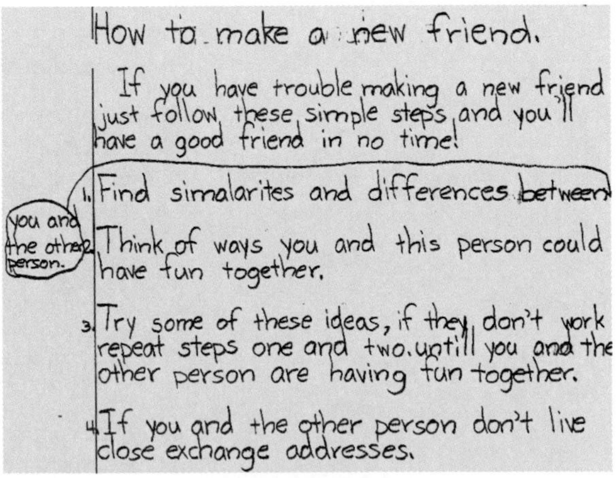

At the same time, adults must give children some leeway in their social lives. Children sometimes benefit from a trial and error approach with social strategies. Following is one

FIGURE 13–5 In this writing assignment, 9-year-old Mariel lists four strategies that her teacher has suggested for making a new friend.

DEVELOPMENT AND PRACTICE

Fostering Effective Interpersonal Skills

■ Create a safe and secure environment.

An infant teacher has fenced off one corner area of her room. The area is large enough for several infants who are not yet mobile to rest in baby seats or lie down on blankets where they can look in a mirror and interact with one another. The fence protects them from toddlers who are trotting around and speeding through the room with wheel toys. The babies and toddlers can see one another through the fence, and the toddlers often come over to hold up toys and talk to the babies. One or more teachers supervise interaction in both groups at all times.

■ Ask youngsters to role-play specific strategies.

A counselor who is working with several very shy and socially isolated high school students teaches them several ways to initiate and maintain conversations with others. "One thing you might do," he says, "is give a compliment about something you like about a person. Then you can follow up with a question to get the person talking. For example, you might say, 'I really liked what you said about protecting the rain forests in class the other day. I didn't realize how quickly the earth's rain forests were being destroyed. Have you read a lot about the topic?'" After describing several additional strategies, the counselor has the students work in pairs to practice each one.

■ Ask young people to brainstorm approaches to solving social dilemmas.

A middle school teacher presents this situation to his class: "Imagine that one of your classmates comes up to you and asks if she can copy your homework. You don't want to let her do it—after all, she won't learn what her teacher wanted her to learn by copying someone else's work—but you also don't want to make her angry or upset. How might you refuse her request while also keeping her friendship?"

■ Encourage children and adolescents to think carefully before acting in difficult social situations.

A soccer coach finds that several of her 9- and 10-year-old players react impulsively to any provocation; for instance, they might hit or yell at a teammate or opposing player who unintentionally bumps into them on the field. The coach teaches the athletes four steps to

follow in such situations: (a) *Think* about what just happened, (b) *list* three different ways to respond, (c) *predict* what might happen for each response, and (d) *choose* the best response.

■ Give concrete feedback about effective and ineffective interpersonal behaviors.

During a cooperative learning activity, a high school teacher notices that the members of one cooperative group are getting increasingly angry. After listening to their conversation for a minute or two, the teacher reminds them, "As we agreed yesterday, it's OK to criticize ideas, but it's not OK to criticize people."

■ Communicate your concern for children who are hurt, and enlist the support of other children in caring for them.

A preschool teacher sympathizes with a child who has skinned his knee. She brings out the first aid kit and asks another child to find a bandage as she applies the antiseptic.

■ Recognize children's good deeds.

When an after-school caregiver notices a child helping a classmate who doesn't understand an assignment, she comments, "Thank you for helping Amanda, Jack. You're always ready to lend a hand!"

■ Communicate the message that prosocial behavior is desirable.

A book club leader asks youngsters to look for prosocial and self-serving behaviors in the novels they are reading. He voices approval for characters who are altruistic and expresses disapproval for other characters who exploit or harm those around them.

■ Arrange for young people to participate in service activities in the school or community.

A high school requires all of its students to complete 25 hours of service to the school district each year. Students can meet this requirement in numerous ways, for instance by serving meals in the cafeteria, participating in a school fundraising drive, painting a mural on the gymnasium wall, or reading to "buddies" at the local elementary school.

elementary school teacher's perspective on the advantages of letting children learn some social lessons on their own:

> Before, when problems came up, I think I was very quick to intervene. Certainly, I asked the kids involved to express themselves "very briefly" about what had happened. But I was quick to judge, to comment, to advise, and to try to reconcile them, for instance, by saying, "Well, now you must be friends." Thus, the students themselves were not active in the problem solution. It was usually I who found the solutions and I who controlled the situation. Now I am not as quick to intervene. I ask the children to stop and think, and to express themselves about what happened, and I withdraw more and listen to them. Certainly it is more effective if they themselves face and solve the problems. Then the solution and the whole experience are more likely to stay with them. (Adalbjarnardottir & Selman, 1997, p. 421)

■ *Plan cooperative activities.* When youngsters participate in cooperative games rather than in competitive ones, aggressive behaviors tend to decrease (Bay-Hinitz, Peterson, & Quilitch, 1994). In cooperative learning activities, youngsters can learn and practice help-giving, help-seeking, and conflict-resolution skills while developing a better sense of justice and fairness (Damon, 1988; Lickona, 1991; Webb & Farivar, 1994). Furthermore, cooperative tasks that require a number of different skills and abilities foster an appreciation for the various strengths that children with diverse backgrounds are likely to contribute (E. G. Cohen, 1994; E. G. Cohen & Lotan, 1995). At the same time, virtually any "cooperative" approach to instruction (cooperative learning, peer tutoring, reciprocal teaching) may help children begin to recognize that, despite the obvious diversity among them, they are ultimately more similar to one another than they are different (Schofield, 1995). Cooperative activities are usually most successful when children have a structure to follow (e.g., when each group member is given a specific role to perform) and are given some guidelines about appropriate group behavior (E. G. Cohen, 1994; Schofield, 1995; N. M. Webb & Palincsar, 1996).

■ *Label appropriate behaviors as they occur.* Practitioners can heighten children's awareness of effective social skills by identifying and praising behaviors that reflect those skills (Vorrath, 1985; Wittmer & Honig, 1994). For example, a teacher might say, "Thank you for *sharing* your art materials so helpfully," or, "I think that you two were able to write a more imaginative short story by *cooperating* on the project." Some researchers have found, too, that describing children as having desirable characteristics (generosity, empathy, etc.) has beneficial effects (R. S. L. Mills & Grusec, 1989). For example, 8-year-olds who are told, "You're the kind of person who likes to help others whenever you can," are more likely to share their belongings with others at a later date (Grusec & Redler, 1980).

■ *Ask young people to consider the effects their behaviors might have.* Children are more likely to behave prosocially when they are given reasons why certain behaviors are unacceptable (see the discussion of *induction* in Chapter 10). More generally, children are more likely to exhibit effective interpersonal behaviors and inhibit ineffective ones when they think about the consequences of their behaviors, whether they are actual past consequences or possible future ones (Guerra & Slaby, 1990; Myers, Shoffner, & Briggs, 2002; Rushton, 1980). For example, a teacher might say, "I'm sure you didn't mean to hurt Jamal's feelings, but he's pretty upset about what you said. Why don't you think about what you might do or say to make him feel better?"

■ *Develop a peer mediation program.* Elementary and secondary students can benefit from mediation training that teaches them how to intervene effectively in classmates' interpersonal disputes (M. Deutsch, 1993; D. W. Johnson, Johnson, Dudley, Ward, & Magnuson, 1995; Schumpf, Crawford, & Usadel, 1991). For example, in an experiment involving several second- through fifth-grade classes (D. W. Johnson et al., 1995), children were trained to help their peers resolve conflicts by asking the opposing sides to:

1. Define the conflict (the problem)
2. Explain their own perspectives and needs
3. Explain the other person's perspectives and needs
4. Identify at least three possible solutions to the conflict
5. Reach an agreement that addresses the needs of both parties

The students took turns serving as mediator for their classmates, so that each student had a chance to practice resolving the conflicts of others. At the end of the training program, the students more frequently resolved their own interpersonal conflicts in ways that addressed the needs of both parties, and they were less likely to ask for adult intervention, than students in an untrained control group. Similarly, in a case study involving adolescent gang members (Sanchez & Anderson, 1990), students were given mediation training and were asked to be responsible for mediating gang-related disputes. After a month of training, rival gang members were exchanging friendly greetings in the corridors, giving one another the "high five" sign, and interacting at lunch; meanwhile, gang-related fights virtually disappeared from the scene. Certainly it would be inappropriate to put peer mediators in potentially dangerous situations, and peer mediation is not always effective. Nonetheless, mediation training—preparing children to resolve their own conflicts and to help peers work through theirs—can be effectively applied in a wide range of settings.

■ *Enlist the support of children and families.* In setting up rules and consequences for misbehaviors, teachers and other practitioners can ask for input from parents. It is also desirable for practitioners to provide time for children to read discipline codes and to make recommendations for improving the rules they are being asked to follow. When policies are put into place, professionals can inform children and parents about these rules and consequences children will face if they violate them (Learning First Alliance, 2001).

◾ *Offer parenting classes and family therapy.* Many successful programs for preventing serious violence in youngsters target parents (Wasserman, Miller, & Cothern, 2000). As we learned in Chapter 12, many parents use disciplinary strategies that are reasonably effective, but some use techniques that are harsh, inconsistent, and physically injurious. These latter strategies are associated with aggression in children. Professionals can help children when they guide parents to communicate clear expectations to their children; express their affection to children and participate in mutually enjoyable activities with them; recognize, affirm, and reward their children's positive behaviors; and follow through with appropriate negative consequences when children misbehave.

◾ *Supervise young people when they are most likely to get in trouble.* The presence of adults can often deter aggression among children and adolescents. It is particularly important to supervise places such as hallways and playgrounds where rates of aggression are high. In addition, police officers and other community members can walk the streets and patrol the school vicinity before and after school and during school breaks, times when assaults are most likely to occur (Chaiken, 2000).

◾ *Offer emotional support and counseling to children who have been exposed to violence.* When children have been victimized by violence, seen family members affected, or been exposed to warfare, they need intensive support (Jersild, 1942). For example, counselors can provide therapy, and other practitioners can watch for signs of depression, offer appropriate reassurance, and help children to focus on things they can control. Writing and artistic expression can be helpful in allowing children to work through their anxieties and express hopes for a better world.

Another way to foster interpersonal skills is to help children make friends and in other ways get to know age-mates better. Friends and other peer relationships play an important—many theorists would say critical—role in social-emotional development. In the next section, we look at the nature of peer relationships in childhood and adolescence.

For most children and adolescents, peers are a primary source of companionship and recreation. Art by Madison, age 7.

Peer Relationships

Throughout the book we have seen many ways in which adults influence children and adolescents. *Peers,* people of approximately the same age and social status, make equally important contributions to development, especially in the social-emotional domain. In the next few pages, we look at the unique functions of peer relationships, consider the factors that affect popularity and social isolation, examine the nature of close friendships and larger social groups, and conclude with recommendations for supporting peer relationships.

Functions of Peer Relationships

Young people think of peers primarily as companions—as sources of amusement, excitement, and pleasure (Asher & Parker, 1989; Ginsberg, Gottman, & Parker, 1986). Most children and adolescents actively seek out peers, and play groups occur around the world (J. R. Harris, 1995). In fact, for many children and adolescents, interacting with friends at school is more important than completing classroom assignments (B. B. Brown, 1993; W. Doyle, 1986).

From a developmental standpoint, peer relationships serve multiple functions:

◾ *Peers serve as partners for practicing social skills.* When children and adolescents interact with their peers, they enter social exchanges on a more or less equal footing: No single individual has absolute power or authority. In their attempts to satisfy their own needs while also maintaining productive relationships with others, they acquire skills in perspective taking, persuasion, negotiation, compromise, and emotional control (Creasey, Jarvis, & Berk, 1998; Gottman, 1986b; Sutton-Smith, 1979). They make occasional social blunders while experimenting with emerging skills, but usually without the sanctions that parents and other adults might impose (Vandenberg, 1978).

■ *Peers socialize one another.* Children and adolescents socialize one another in several ways (Erwin, 1993; D. Ginsburg et al., 1986; J. R. Harris, 1998; A. M. Ryan, 2000). They define options for leisure time, perhaps jumping rope in a vacant lot, getting together in a study group, or smoking cigarettes on the corner. They offer new ideas and perspectives, perhaps demonstrating how to do an "Ollie" on a skateboard or presenting potent arguments for becoming a vegetarian. They serve as role models and provide standards for acceptable behavior, showing what is possible, what is admirable, and what is cool. Peers reinforce one another for acting in ways deemed appropriate for their age, gender, ethnic group, and cultural background. And they sanction one another for stepping beyond acceptable bounds, perhaps through ridicule (recall that Aqeelah was taunted in the opening case), gossip, or ostracism.

■ *Peers contribute to a sense of identity.* Association with a particular group of peers helps children and adolescents decide who they are and who they want to become (see Chapter 9). For instance, when Jeanne's son Alex was in middle school, he and his friends were avid skateboarders and spent long hours at a local skateboard ramp practicing and refining their technique. Alex proudly labeled himself as a "skater" and wore the extra-large T-shirts and wide-legged pants that conveyed this identity.

In addition to deriving identity from their solidarity with a particular group of peers, children and adolescents compare themselves to their peers and observe how their own characteristics (physical appearance, athletic prowess, school achievement, etc.) make them unique. The result of such comparisons is that, particularly in adolescence and young adulthood, young people increasingly look *inward* at their own characteristics, rather than *outward* toward their peers, to get a handle on who they are as individuals.

■ *Peers help one another make sense of their lives.* Recall the earlier conversation in which two girls (one of whom had just broken up with her boyfriend) shared their views about premarital intercourse. Growing up brings many confusing, ambiguous, and troubling events, and peers help one another sort through them. By sharing and critiquing others' ideas and values, children and adolescents construct increasingly complex and perceptive understandings of the world around them. This process is the *social construction of meaning* we discussed in Chapter 4.

■ *Peers provide emotional and social support.* Youngsters often seek comfort from peers when they are anxious or upset; for instance, preschoolers are more willing to explore a new environment if familiar playmates are nearby (Asher & Parker, 1989; Wentzel, 1999). Peers provide social support as well; for example, children who have one or more good friends are less likely to be victimized by bullies (D. Ginsburg et al., 1986; Pellegrini & Bartini, 2000; D. Schwartz et al., 1999). Although some youngsters adjust quite successfully on their own, as a general rule children and adolescents who have peers to turn to in times of trouble or stress have higher self-esteem, fewer emotional problems (e.g., depression), and higher school achievement (Buhrmester, 1992; Guay, Boivin, & Hodges, 1999; Levitt et al., 1999; R. M. Ryan et al., 1994).

Popularity and Social Isolation

Popularity among peers has definite advantages. By and large, when children and adolescents believe that their classmates accept and like them, they achieve at higher levels, have higher self-esteem, are happier at school, exhibit fewer problem behaviors, and have better attendance records (Guay et al., 1999; Harter, 1996; Reese & Thorkildsen, 1999; Wentzel, 1999).

Yet we have to be clear about the qualities represented by the term *popularity*. When researchers ask children to identify peers they would most like to do something with, they don't necessarily choose those whom they and their teachers perceive to be the most popular members of the student body (Lafontana & Cillessen, 1998; Parkhurst & Hopmeyer, 1998). This finding is consistent with the seemingly self-contradictory comment that Jeanne's daughter

Tina often made as a junior high school student: "No one likes the popular kids." Tina was talking about students who, in her eyes, had a dominant social status at school (perhaps they were star athletes or members of a prestigious social group) but were often aggressive or stuck-up. When we talk about **popular children** here, we are describing young people who are well liked, kind, and trustworthy—those who may or may not hold obvious high-status positions (Parkhurst & Hopmeyer, 1998). Children who are popular in this way typically have good social skills; for instance, they know how to initiate and sustain conversations, are sensitive to the subtle social cues that others give them, and adjust their behaviors to changing circumstances. They also tend to be quite prosocial; for instance, they are more likely to help, share, cooperate, and empathize with others (Caprara, Barbaranelli, Pastorelli, Bandura, & Zimbardo, 2000; Crick & Dodge, 1994; Wentzel & Asher, 1995).

In addition to asking children whom they would most like to do something with, researchers often ask them to identify peers whom they would least like to do something with. Those who are frequently selected are known as **rejected children**. Rejected children often have poor social skills (e.g., they may continually try to draw attention to themselves); they may also be impulsive and disruptive in the classroom (Asher & Renshaw, 1981; Pellegrini et al., 1999; Putallaz & Heflin, 1986). Many (but not all) aggressive children are also rejected, probably in part because they place higher priority on acquiring objects and gaining power over others than on establishing and maintaining congenial interpersonal relationships (Dodge, Bates, & Pettit, 1990; Ladd & Burgess, 1999; Patrick, 1997).

Researchers have identified a third group of children as well. **Neglected children** are those whom age-mates rarely select as someone they would either most like or least like to do something with (Asher & Renshaw, 1981). Neglected children tend to be quiet and keep to themselves. Some prefer to be alone, others may simply not know how to go about making friends, and still others may be quite content with the one or two close friends that they have (Guay et al., 1999; K. H. Rubin & Krasnor, 1986). Having "neglected" status is often only a temporary situation; children categorized as neglected at one time are not always the ones so categorized in follow-up assessments.

Not everyone falls neatly into one of these three categories. **Controversial children**, for example, are very well liked by some of their peers and intensely disliked by others. Yet others are, for lack of a better term, known simply as *average* children, in that some age-mates like them and others don't, but without the intensity of feelings shown for popular, rejected, or controversial children. In the Observation Guidelines table "Estimating Children's Social Acceptance Among Peers," we present common characteristics of popular, rejected, neglected, controversial, and average children and the implications for those who work with them.

The quality of young people's close friendships is probably even more important than popularity. We look now at the nature of friendships in childhood and adolescence.

Friendships

Healthy friendships come in many forms. Some are brief liaisons; others last a lifetime. Some are relatively casual; others are deep and intimate. Some children and adolescents have many friends; others invest steadfastly in a few close ones. Three qualities make friendships distinct from other kinds of peer relationships:

- *They are voluntary relationships.* Children and adolescents often spend time with peers strictly through happenstance: Perhaps they ride the same school bus, are members of the same class, or join the same sports team. In contrast, they *choose* their friends. Two or more youngsters remain friends as long as they continue to enjoy one another's company and can successfully resolve their differences.
- *They are powered by shared routines and customs.* Friends find activities that are mutually meaningful and enjoyable, and over time they acquire a common set of experiences that enable them to share certain perspectives on life (Gottman, 1986b; Suttles, 1970). As a result, they can easily communicate about many topics. For instance, children talk, smile, and laugh more often with friends than with nonfriends; they also engage in more complex fantasy play with friends (J. G. Parker, 1986).

popular children
Children whom many peers like and perceive to be kind and trustworthy.

rejected children
Children whom many peers identify as being unfavorable social partners.

neglected children
Children whom peers rarely select as someone they would either most like or least like to do something with.

controversial children
Children whom some peers really like and other peers strongly dislike.

OBSERVATION GUIDELINES

Estimating Children's Social Acceptance Among Peers

CHARACTERISTIC	LOOK FOR	EXAMPLE	IMPLICATION
"Popular" Children	• Good social and communication skills • Sensitivity and responsiveness to others' wishes and needs • Willingness to assimilate into ongoing activities • Signs of leadership potential	On the playground, 8-year-old Daequan moves easily from one group to another. Before joining a conversation, he listens to what others are saying and adds an appropriate comment. He doesn't draw much attention to himself but is well liked by most of his classmates.	Use popular children as leaders when trying to change other children's behavior. For example, when starting a recycling program, ask a well-regarded youngster to help get the program off the ground.
"Rejected" Children	• For some, high rates of aggression; for others, immature, anxious, or impulsive behavior • Disruptive behavior in class • Unwillingness of other children to play or work with them	Most children dislike 10-year-old Terra. She frequently calls other children insulting nicknames, threatens to beat them up, and noisily intrudes into their private conversations.	Help rejected children learn basic social skills, such as how to join a conversation. Place them in cooperative groups with children who are likely to be sensitive and accepting. If children are aggressive, give appropriate consequences, and teach self-regulatory strategies to help them keep their impulses in check. Publicly compliment all youngsters (including those who are rejected) about the things they do well.
"Neglected" Children	• Tendency to be relatively quiet; little or no disruptive behavior • Fewer than average interactions with age-mates, but possible friendships with one or two peers • For some, anxiety about interacting with others • Possible temporary nature of "neglected" status (this classification is not stable over time)	Fourteen-year-old Sedna is initially shy and withdrawn at her new school. Later in the year, however, she seems to be happier and more involved in school activities.	Identify group activities in which neglected children might feel comfortable and be successful. Arrange situations in which shy children with similar interests can get to know one another.
"Controversial" Children	• Acceptance by some peers, rejection by others • Possibly aggressive and disruptive in some situations yet helpful, cooperative, and socially sensitive in others	Thirteen-year-old Marcus can be disruptive, obnoxious, and manipulative, but his charm and sunny personality lead many classmates to forgive his transgressions.	Let controversial children know in no uncertain terms when their behaviors are inappropriate, but acknowledge their effective social skills as well.
"Average" Children	• Tendency to be liked by some peers but disliked by others • Average interpersonal skills (e.g., average levels of prosocial behavior and aggression) • Ability to find a comfortable social niche	Five-year-old Joachim doesn't draw much attention to himself. He's made a few friends in kindergarten and seems to get along fairly well with them, but he sometimes has conflicts with others.	Help average children refine their emerging social skills. Be sensitive to their occasional lapses in tact, kindness, and honesty.

Sources. Coie & Dodge, 1988; Coie & Kupersmidt, 1983; Dodge, 1983; Dodge, Coie, & Brakke, 1982; Dodge, Schlundt, Schocken, & Delugach, 1983; Newcomb & Bukowski, 1984; Newcomb, Bukowski, & Pattee, 1993; Putallaz & Gottman, 1981; Rubin, Bukowski, & Parker 1998.

■ *They are reciprocal relationships.* Friends spend time with one another and address one another's needs (J. L. Epstein, 1986; K. H. Rubin et al., 1998). But how they feel about one another, rather than what they do with or for one another, is arguably the primary basis of the friendship. Friends generally perceive their relationship to be deeper than the activities they share or the material goods and services they exchange.

We see such qualities in the three-way friendship depicted in our opening case study. In addition to going to school together, Aqeelah, Johanna, and Kelly shared many common

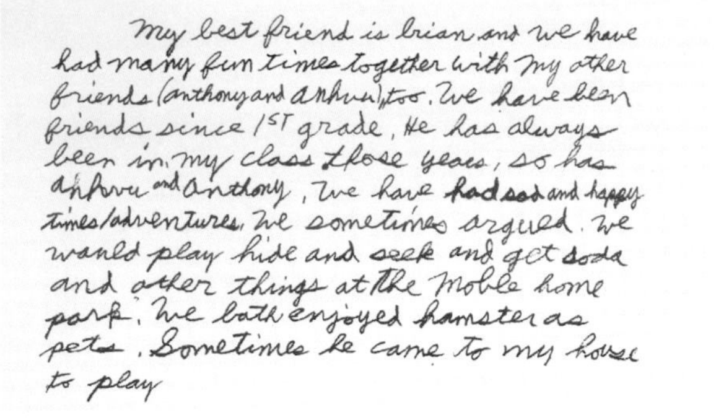

> My best friend is brian and we have had many fun times together with my other friends (anthony and anthony too. We have been friends since 1st grade. He has always been in my class those years, so has anthony and anthony. We have had sad and happy times/adventures. We sometimes argued. We would play hide and seek and get soda and other things at the moble home park. We both enjoyed hamster as pets. Sometimes he came to my house to play

FIGURE 13–6 Joseph, a 10-year-old boy, explains that he shared many experiences with his friend Brian.

Listen to 17-year-old Paul talk about resolving conflicts with friends in the Friendship/Late Adolescence clip of the Observation CD.

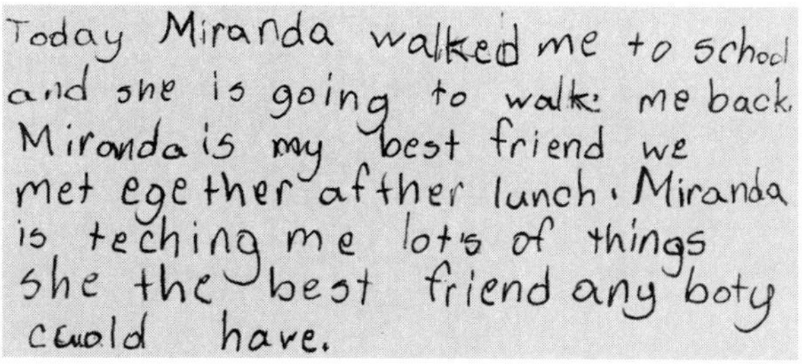

> Today Miranda walked me to school and she is going to walk me back. Miranda is my best friend we met egether afther lunch. Miranda is teching me lots of things she the best friend any boty could have.

FIGURE 13–7 Seven-year-old Jessica recognizes the value of a good friend.

routines (e.g., they regularly attended meetings of the Martin Luther King Association) and cared deeply for one another (T. Lewin, 2000). As they developed divergent interests, however, it became more difficult to sustain the friendship. Aqeelah was disappointed when she learned that Johanna and Kelly were not going out for the softball team with her: Without common activities, it seemed that they might grow apart. Similarly, 10-year-old Joseph explains that he experienced many good times as well as some difficult times with his friend Brian; having varied experiences together helped sustain their friendship (Figure 13–6).

Friends generally play a role in social-emotional development that surpasses that of casual peer relationships. Because friends have an emotional investment in their relationship, they work hard to look at situations from each other's point of view and to resolve disputes that threaten to be divisive. As a result, they develop enhanced perspective-taking and conflict resolution skills (Basinger et al., 1995; DeVries, 1997). In the Friendship/Late Adolescence clip of the Observation CD, 17-year-old Paul expresses an ability to adapt his conflict resolution skills to the different perspectives of male and female friends. Paul reports:

> Normally with my guy friends, we just get over it. I mean, there's no working it out, you just like fine, whatever, you know and we get over it. Girlfriends, you gotta like talk to them and work it out slowly, and apologize for whatever you did wrong. [He and the interviewer laugh.] There's a whole process.

Friends also help each other to cope with stressful events by providing emotional support (Berndt & Keefe, 1995; D. Ginsburg et al., 1986). In Figure 13–7, 7-year-old Jessica reveals her emerging understanding of the importance of a good friend in her life.

Close friends tend to be similar in age and are usually of the same sex and race (Hartup, 1992; Kovacs, Parker, & Hoffman, 1996; Roopnarine, Lasker, Sacks, & Stores, 1998). Cross-sex friendships are most common in the preschool years (e.g., recall 4-year-olds Eric and Naomi in their roles as "Bob" and "Claudia"), but some older children and adolescents have close friends of the opposite sex as well (Gottman, 1986b; Kovacs et al., 1996). Cross-race friendships (such as the friendship of Aqeelah, Johanna, and Kelly) are most often seen when the number of available peers is relatively small, as might occur in small classes or rural communities (Hallinan & Teixeria, 1987; Roopnarine et al., 1998).

Characteristics of Friendships at Different Ages Years ago, Jeanne asked her three children, "What are friends for?" Here are their responses:

Jeff (age 6): To play with.
Alex (age 9): Friends can help you in life. They can make you do better in school. They can make you feel better.
Tina (age 12): To be your friend and help you in good times and bad times. They're there so you can tell secrets. They're people that care. They're there because they like you. They're people you can trust.

Like Jeff, young children describe friends primarily as recreational companions and potential sources of shared playthings; thus, their understandings of friendship are relatively superficial and concrete. As they reach the upper elementary grades, they, like Alex, begin to understand that friends can help and depend on one another. Adolescents, like Tina, describe increasingly intimate friendships as they start to share their innermost secrets, fears, and dreams (Berndt, 1992; Damon, 1977; Gottman & Mettetal, 1986; G. P. Jones & Dembo, 1989; Youniss, 1980).

Such developmental trends in children's descriptions of friendships notwithstanding, even friendships in early childhood reflect some degree of mutual dependence and trust, as reflected in children's enjoyment of one another's company and their ability to coordinate their actions and make occasional compromises. As we look more closely at the nature of friendship across the five developmental periods, we will see how friendships grow in complexity and stability and how they increasingly reflect such characteristics as loyalty, trust, and intimacy.

Infancy (birth–2).   Primitive friendships emerge in the first year or two of life. As we mentioned earlier when describing developmental trends in interpersonal behaviors, infants sometimes smile at other infants and babble at and gesture to them. Toddlers respond differently to familiar and unfamiliar children: They are more likely to make social overtures, carry on complex interactions, and display positive emotions with children that they know (Howes, 1988). For example, when Teresa's son Connor was less than a year old, he became friends with Patrick, another boy at his child care center. The two boys established familiar play routines, often laughing and chasing one another as they crawled around the room. Although they weren't yet speaking, and they certainly didn't swap secrets, they were clearly attuned to each other's behaviors. After they moved on to separate elementary schools, they occasionally called one another to arrange play sessions and sleepovers. Even as adolescents, they stay in touch, albeit less often.

Early childhood (ages 2–6).   In the preschool years, children build on the rudimentary relationships of infancy. They also enrich their social interactions through their language, fantasy, and play, especially with people they know well. When 3- and 4-year-olds interact with familiar peers (rather than with strangers), they are more likely to offer social greetings and carry on a conversation, engage in more complex play, and exhibit better social skills (Charlesworth & LaFreniere, 1983; A. Doyle, 1982; Hinde, Titmus, Easton, & Tamplin, 1985). Figure 13–8 shows a picture drawn by 4-year-old Dana of herself and her friend, Dina. The two girls met in child care and became close companions; afterwards, they moved to separate towns but happily renewed their friendship when given the chance at summer camp.

Of course, early friendships also provide opportunities for disagreements, arguments, and even physical aggression (Hartup & Laursen, 1991). Such disputes can be quite heated, but young children are motivated to solve them. You can see this desire to resolve conflict in a young child by listening to 6-year-old Ying-Yu describe how she responds to an argument with a friend in the Friendship/Early Childhood clip of the Observation CD: "I let them choose. My friends choose first and then me 'cause I think that's the helpful thing to do."

When they have disagreements with nonfriends, preschoolers often stand firm; when they have conflicts with friends, they are more inclined to negotiate, compromise, or withdraw (Hartup, Laursen, Stewart, & Eastenson, 1988). Thus, young children seem to have different motives in their conflicts with nonfriends and friends. From an unfamiliar child, they want their toys back and their dignity reaffirmed; they also want that ill-tempered upstart out of sight! Although children may be angry with friends, they want to restore communication and good feelings. In the process of working through conflicts with friends, then, they begin to acquire an important skill: asserting themselves while maintaining productive relationships.

Middle childhood (ages 6–10).   During the elementary school years, children continue to act differently with friends than with peers who are not friends. For example, with friends, they are more likely to express their feelings (important capabilities described in Chapter 9) and to understand the other person's emotional states (Newcomb & Bagwell, 1995; Newcomb & Brady, 1982). In times of conflict, they strive to identify an equitable resolution and preserve the relationship (Hartup, 1996; Newcomb & Bagwell, 1995). At this age, friends develop a sense of loyalty to one another, and many of them, girls especially, use self-disclosure as a strategy for maintaining a friendship (Buhrmester, 1996; Diaz & Berndt, 1982).

Friendships are often more stable in middle childhood than in earlier years (Berndt & Hoyle, 1985). Children don't choose friends anymore simply because they just happen to live in the same apartment building, attend the same preschool, or have parents who are friends. They become deliberate in selecting their playmates and are usually attracted to peers who have similar interests and styles of behavior (K. H. Rubin, Lynch, Coplan, Rose-Krasnor, & Booth, 1994). For example, a child who is energetic and high-spirited

FIGURE 13–8   Four-year-old Dana drew a picture of herself and her friend, Dina. The two girls met in child care and became good friends.

Listen to 6-year-old Ying-Yu talk about resolving conflicts with friends in the Friendship/Early Childhood clip of the Observation CD.

Close friendships in the elementary and middle school years are typically between children of the same sex. Art by Andres, age 10.

and another who is quiet and sedate are each likely to seek a companion with a similar disposition. Youngsters in this age range typically choose friends of their own sex, perhaps in part because same-sex peers are more likely to be behaviorally compatible (Gottman, 1986b; Kovacs et al., 1996; E. E. Maccoby, 1990).

Early adolescence (ages 10–14). Differences in relationships between friends and nonfriends intensify during early adolescence (Basinger et al., 1995; J. G. Parker & Gottman, 1989). Many young adolescents let down their guard and reveal their weaknesses and vulnerabilities to close friends, even as they may try to maintain a demeanor of competence and self-confidence in front of most other age-mates. They begin to confront feelings of possessiveness and jealousy about friends, and after age 11 the number of close friends slowly declines (K. H. Rubin et al., 1998). Gradually, young adolescents learn that friendships don't have to be exclusive—that they are not necessarily jeopardized when one friend spends time with other people—and that friends are more likely to grow by having relationships with many individuals (K. H. Rubin et al., 1998). Thus, many friendship pairs gradually converge into larger groups, such as cliques (you will learn more about these shortly).

Late adolescence (ages 14–18). Older adolescents tend to be quite selective in their choice of friends (J. L. Epstein, 1986). Gone are the days when they ran out of fingers as they counted off their "close" friends. Instead, they tend to nurture relationships with a few friends that they keep for some time, perhaps throughout their lives, and having such friendships enhances their self-esteem (Berndt, 1992; Berndt & Hoyle, 1985).

Many friendships in late adolescence are enriched with self-disclosure, intimacy, and loyalty (Buhrmester, 1996; Newcomb & Bagwell, 1995). Older teenagers frequently turn to friends for emotional support in times of trouble or confusion, and they are likely to engage in lengthy discussions about personal problems and possible solutions (Asher & Parker, 1989; Buhrmester, 1992; J. G. Parker & Gottman, 1989; Seltzer, 1982). In the process, they often discover that they aren't as unique as they once thought, thereby poking holes in the *personal fable* we spoke of in Chapter 9 (Elkind, 1981a). For such reasons, friendships become especially important during the teenage years (Csikszentmihalyi, 1995; Wigfield, Eccles, & Pintrich, 1996).

Most children and adolescents interact regularly with, and clearly enjoy the company of, many peers besides their close friends. We look now at the nature of their larger social groups.

Larger Social Groups

In middle childhood, children enter elementary school and are increasingly able to travel independently in their neighborhoods. As a result of such changes, they come into contact with a greater number of peers, and many begin to form larger social groups that regularly fraternize (Eisenberg et al., 1996; Gottman & Mettetal, 1986). Initially, such groups are usually comprised of a single sex, but in adolescence they often include both boys and girls (Gottman & Mettetal, 1986; J. R. Harris, 1995).

Children's and adolescents' social groups vary considerably in size, function, and character. However, many have the following attributes:

■ *Group members share a common culture.* The group develops a general set of rules (often unspoken), expectations, and interpretations—a **peer culture**—that influences how group members behave (P. Davidson & Youniss, 1995; J. R. Harris, 1998; Knapp & Woolverton, 1995). This shared culture gives group members a sense of community, belonging, and identity. It also entices them to adopt the group's shared norms and values, that is, to *self-socialize* (Gottman & Mettetal, 1986; Kindermann, 1993). Other group members encourage such conformity as well, both by reinforcing behaviors that are appropriate in the eyes of the group and by discouraging behaviors that are not (Clasen & Brown, 1985; Dishion, Spracklen, Andrews, & Patterson, 1996). The composition of groups can be quite

peer culture
General set of rules, expectations, and interpretations that influence how members of a particular peer group behave.

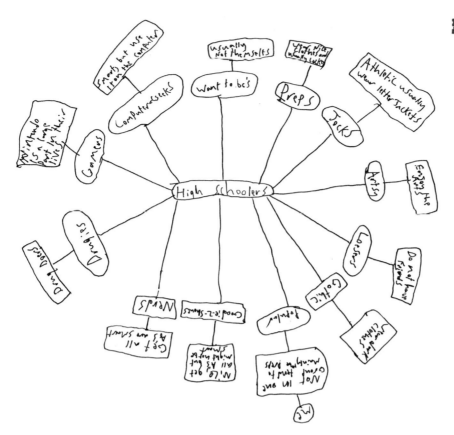

FIGURE 13-9 Fourteen-year-old Connor drew a map of the groups of students he observed during his freshman year in high school. In his inner circle he listed commonly used labels for different groups (e.g., *preps, jocks, gamers, gothic*), and in the outer circle he described each one (e.g., "wear nice clothes and usually cocky," "athletic, usually wear letter jackets," "Nintendo is a large part in their lives," "wear dark clothes").

complex, as 14-year-old Connor shows in his representation of the groups of students he noticed during his freshman year in high school (Figure 13–9).

Fortunately, many children's and adolescents' peer groups embrace productive and prosocial behaviors such as honesty, fairness, cooperation, academic achievement, and a sense of humor (Damon, 1988; Kindermann, 1993; McCallum & Bracken, 1993). Many others, however, encourage less worthy pursuits, such as aggression and violence, and discourage scholastic endeavors, perhaps by making fun of "brainy" students or endorsing such behaviors as cheating, cutting class, and skipping school (Berndt, 1992; B. B. Brown, 1993; Knapp & Woolverton, 1995; Lowry, Sleet, Duncan, Powell, & Kolbe, 1995).

Peer groups are particularly influential in matters of style—for example, in dress, music, and social activities. On the other hand, parents, teachers, and other significant adults continue to be influential in most young people's views about education, morality, religion, and careers (J. R. Harris, 1998; Hartup, 1983; Sewald, 1986). It's important to note, too, that many young people actively think about and evaluate what their peers ask them to do; they rarely accept anyone's suggestions without question (B. B. Brown, 1990).

■ *Group members have a sense of unity as a group.* Once children or adolescents gel as a group, they prefer other group members over nonmembers, and they develop feelings of loyalty to individuals within the group. In some cases, they also develop feelings of hostility and rivalry toward members of other groups (J. R. Harris, 1995, 1998; Sherif, Harvey, White, Hood, & Sherif, 1961). Such feelings toward *out-groups* are particularly intense when two or more groups must actively compete for status or resources, as rival athletic teams and adolescent gangs often do.

■ *Dominance hierarchies emerge within the group.* When children's groups continue for any length of time, a pecking order, or **dominance hierarchy**, gradually evolves (Strayer, 1991). Some group members rise to the top, leading the way and making decisions for the entire group. Other group members are followers rather than leaders: They look to those around them for guidance about how to behave and assume lesser roles in the group's activities. Sometimes these less dominant individuals find unique niches within the group, perhaps becoming the clown, daredevil, or brain of the group.

dominance hierarchy Relative standing of group members in terms of such qualities as leadership and popularity.

Social groups become a particularly prominent feature of children's social worlds once they reach puberty. Researchers have described three group phenomena that are significant during the adolescent years: cliques, subcultures, and gangs.

Cliques   Cliques are moderately stable friendship groups of perhaps 3 to 10 individuals; they provide the basis for most voluntary social interactions (Crockett, Losoff, & Peterson, 1984; J. L. Epstein, 1986; Kindermann, McCollom, & Gibson, 1996). Clique boundaries tend to be fairly rigid and exclusive (some people are "in," others are "out"), and membership in various cliques affects social status and dominance with peers (Wigfield et al., 1996). In early adolescence, cliques are usually comprised of a single sex; in later adolescence, cross-sex cliques become increasingly common (J. L. Epstein, 1986).

Although most middle school and high school students have friends, a smaller number of them belong to cliques (J. L. Epstein, 1986). Thus, the emergence of cliques in early adolescence heightens young people's concerns about acceptance and popularity (Gavin & Furman, 1989). Young adolescents wonder about their social standing: "Who likes me?" "Will I be popular at my new school?" "Why didn't Sal invite me to his party?" When they occasionally leave one clique to join another (perhaps more prestigious) one, they engender feelings of betrayal, hurt, and jealousy in the friends they leave behind (Kanner, Feldman, Weinberger, & Ford, 1987; K. H. Rubin et al., 1998).

Subcultures   Some adolescents affiliate with a well-defined **subculture**, a group that resists a powerful dominant culture by adopting a significantly different way of life (J. S. Epstein, 1998). Such a group may be considerably larger than a clique, and it does not always have the tight-knit cohesiveness and carefully drawn boundaries of a clique. Instead, it is defined by common values, beliefs, and behavior patterns. Some subcultures are relatively benign; for instance, a middle school skateboarders' subculture may simply espouse a particular mode of dress. Other subcultures, such as those who endorse racist and antisemitic behaviors (e.g., skinheads) or who practice Satanic worship and rituals, are worrisome to many adults (C. C. Clark, 1992).

Some adolescent subcultures, like this one, are distinguished by relatively superficial characteristics, such as hairstyle or mode of dress. Other subcultures that endorse dangerous or antisocial behaviors are more worrisome.

Adolescents are more likely to affiliate with subcultures when they feel alienated from the dominant culture (perhaps that of their school or that of society more generally) and want to distinguish themselves from it in some way (C. C. Clark, 1992; J. R. Harris, 1998). They also tend to develop subcultures when they are pessimistic or apathetic about their future (J. S. Epstein, 1998). For example, some subcultures within racial minority groups discourage "acting white," that is, displaying behaviors endorsed by the dominant European American culture (B. B. Brown, 1993; Ogbu, 1992). Individuals in these subcultures, especially boys, find little value in doing well at traditional academic tasks, which represent the culture from which they want to distance themselves (Graham, Taylor, & Hudley, 1998; Ogbu, 1992). Consider what happened to professional basketball player Kareem Abdul-Jabbar when, as a 9-year-old, he enrolled in a new, predominantly African American school:

> I got there and immediately found I could read better than anyone in the school. . . . When the nuns found this out they paid me a lot of attention, once even asking me, a fourth grader, to read to the seventh grade. When the kids found this out I became a target. . . . I got all A's and was hated for it; I spoke correctly and was called a punk. I had to learn a new language simply to be able to deal with the threats. I had good manners and was a good little boy and paid for it with my hide. (Abdul-Jabbar & Knobles, 1983, p. 16)

In his classmates' eyes, Abdul-Jabbar was, by reading so well, endorsing the value system of mainstream European American society and betraying the members of an African American subculture.

Gangs   A gang is a cohesive social group characterized by initiation rites, distinctive colors and symbols, ownership of a specific territory, and feuds with one or more rival groups (A. Campbell, 1984). Gangs have well-defined dominance hierarchies, with specific roles defined for each member (A. Campbell, 1984). Typically, they are governed by strict rules for behavior, with stiff penalties for breaking them.

Historically, gangs in the United States originated out of conflicts among immigrant ethnic groups (e.g., recall the case of Lun Cheung in Chapter 10). However, the appeal of gangs now extends well beyond immigrant ethnic groups; gangs have grown in number in recent decades, especially in lower-income inner-city areas (Parks, 1995). They have also become increasingly violent, in part as a result of greater drug use and access to more destructive weapons (Parks, 1995).

Adolescents (and sometimes children as well) affiliate with gangs for a variety of reasons (A. Campbell, 1984; C. C. Clark, 1992; Parks, 1995; Simons, Whitbeck, Conger, & Conger, 1991). Some do so to demonstrate their loyalty to family, friends, and neighborhood. Some seek the status and prestige that gang membership brings. Some have poor academic records and see the gang as an alternative arena in which they might gain recognition for accomplishments. Gangs may also promise financial rewards through criminal activities. Many members of gangs have had troubled relationships with their families or have been consistently rejected by peers, and so they turn to street gangs or other deviant subcultures to get missing emotional support.

Gangs traditionally have been dominated by young men, but young women have become increasingly active (Parks, 1995). In an in-depth case study of three gangs in New York, A. Campbell (1984) found that female gang members fit no single stereotype. Some joined a gang for a relatively short time, hoping to liberate a beloved boyfriend from the organization. Some joined a gang in a passing adolescent phase but quickly realized that long-term membership would be a dead-end street, perhaps leading to life "in a grubby apartment, taking the children upstate on a bus every weekend to visit their father in prison" (A. Campbell 1984, p. 7). Many others enjoyed the excitement and intrigue of the gang: "They like sharp clothes, loud music, alcohol, and soft drugs. They admire toughness and verbal 'smarts'" (A. Campbell, 1984, pp. 7–8).

In some instances, gang members endorse prosocial behaviors, but generally speaking, gangs do more harm than good: They have high levels of violent and criminal activity, making them a matter of great concern to law enforcement officers, community leaders, and educators.

Social institutions—schools, child care agencies, clubs, recreation centers, community organizations, and sports teams—provide important contexts in which children and adolescents establish peer relationships. They can be assisted in this process by the professionals who work with them in such settings. We look now at some practical strategies for helping young people to develop rewarding relationships with one another.

Supporting Peer Relationships

One obvious way to support positive peer interactions is to teach social skills to young people who seem to lack them (see the Development and Practice table "Fostering Effective Interpersonal Skills" on p. 568). But even when youngsters are able to relate effectively to one another, many of them interact almost exclusively within small, close-knit groups, leaving a few others socially isolated. For example, youngsters often divide along ethnic lines when they eat lunch and interact on the playground (Schofield, 1995). Immigrant youngsters rarely interact with long-term residents (Olneck, 1995). And children with special needs are often poorly accepted or even rejected by their peers (B. Cook & Semmel, 1999; Gresham & MacMillan, 1997; Morrison, Furlong, & Smith, 1994; Yude, Goodman, & McConachie, 1998).

Teachers and other practitioners can take proactive steps to broaden the base of social interactions among children and adolescents. Intervention is particularly important for youngsters who are rejected by their peers: Their tendency to alienate others leaves them few opportunities to develop the social skills they so desperately need, and they consequently often feel lonely and unhappy (Bullock, 1993; Coie & Cillessen, 1993). Hence we offer the following suggestions:

■ *Help young children ease into social groups.* Young children who are shy or new to a community can benefit from gentle actions of caregivers to insert them into a group. In the following anecdote, Mrs. Kusumoto, a Japanese preschool teacher, skillfully models desired behaviors and helps Fumiko enter into a group of peers:

Fumiko is sitting by herself, watching a group of girls play house while she dreamily shakes a maraca (plastic bottle filled with small beans) that was part of an earlier class project. Mrs. Kusumoto notices a few beans leaking from the bottle, and helps Fumiko seal it with tape. She sings a song to Fumiko, demonstrating how to shake the maraca in time to the music. At that point her attention is diverted by requests from other children. Fumiko follows her around, shaking the maraca but not engaging with any other children. Mrs. Kusumoto helps Fumiko put a cha-cha-cha tape in the portable cassette player, and calls a second girl to come over and join them on a small stage made of blocks. The two girls and Mrs. Kusumoto stand on the stage, singing and shaking their maracas. Then Mrs. Kusumoto steps down and faces them, singing along and encouraging them to continue. After a few minutes she attempts to melt away. The girls continue singing briefly, but when the song ends the second girl runs off, leaving Fumiko alone and unoccupied. She looks for Mrs. Kusumoto and begins following her around again. Mrs. Kusumoto approaches a small group of girls who are playing house, asking them: "Would you like to invite this girl over for dinner? After giving the concert, she is very hungry." One of the girls nods silently. Fumiko smiles and enters the "house." She stands there uncertainly, saying nothing. Mrs. Kusumoto inquires, "Fumiko-chan. Have you had your dinner? Why don't you join us? Don't you want something to eat? It looks good." Fumiko nods and the girls bring her a couple [of] dishes of clay "food." Mrs. Kusumoto looks on briefly, then moves quietly out of the scene. (Holloway, 2000, pp. 100–101)

■ *Set up situations in which youngsters can form new friendships.* Teachers and other practitioners can do many simple things to encourage children and adolescents to get to know one another, and in particular to get to know age-mates committed to education and productive activities. They can arrange situations that encourage children to work or play cooperatively with others. For example, they can develop structured cooperative learning activities that require all group members to share equal responsibility, or provide play equipment that requires the participation of several children (Banks, 1994; S. S. Martin, Brady, & Williams, 1991; Schofield, 1995; Slavin, 1990).[3] They can assign partners to youngsters with special needs, who can provide assistance when needed, perhaps reading to a peer with a visual impairment, signing to a child with hearing loss, tutoring a classmate with a learning disability, or taking notes for a child with a physical impairment. Even the simple practice of giving children assigned seats in class and then occasionally changing those assignments increases the number of friends that they make (Schofield, 1995).

■ *Minimize or eliminate barriers to social interaction.* Children and adolescents are less likely to interact with peers when impeded by physical, linguistic, or social barriers. For example, Jeanne recalls a junior high girl who could not negotiate the cafeteria steps with her wheelchair and always ended up eating lunch alone. Professionals who work with youngsters must be on the lookout for such physical impediments to interaction and campaign for their removal. They can also teach groups of youngsters who speak different languages (including American Sign Language, used by many children with hearing loss) some basic vocabulary and simple phrases in one another's native tongues. And, at a deeper level, they must actively address the prejudices and tensions that sometimes separate diverse ethnic groups (see Chapter 10).

■ *Encourage and facilitate participation in extracurricular activities.* Extracurricular activities provide additional opportunities for children to interact and work cooperatively with a wide range of peers (Genova & Walberg, 1984; Phelan, Yu, & Davidson, 1994; Schofield, 1995). (Sports and other extracurricular activities also can sometimes help to keep them out of trouble, as noted in Chapters 3 and 14.) Coaches and advisors must be careful, however, that no single group dominates in membership or leadership in any particular activity (Sleeter & Grant, 1999). For some children, schools may need to make special arrangements for after-school transportation (Schofield, 1995).

■ *Develop nondisabled children's understanding of their peers with special needs.* Nondisabled children sometimes feel resentment or anger about inappropriate behaviors they believe a peer with special needs should be able to control (Juvonen, 1991; Juvonen

---

[3] Adults need to supervise cooperative groups closely when a child with poor social skills is present. They can help the child to behave appropriately; they can also model effective ways for other group members to respond to antisocial behaviors.

& Weiner, 1993). Consequently, they are less likely to be tolerant of children with cognitive difficulties or emotional and behavioral disorders than they are of children with obvious physical disabilities (Madden & Slavin, 1983; Ysseldyke & Algozzine, 1984). Teachers and other practitioners must help nondisabled children understand the difficulties that peers may have as a result of a disability. At the same time, they can, perhaps through the paired or small-group activities they arrange, show nondisabled youngsters that their peers with disabilities have many of the same thoughts, feelings, and desires as they do (D. Staub, 1998).

■ *Help change the reputations of formerly antisocial children and adolescents.* Unfortunately, bad reputations often live on long after people's behavior has changed for the better. Even after young people show dramatic improvements in social behavior, their peers may continue to dislike and reject them (Bierman, Miller, & Staub, 1987; Juvonen & Hiner, 1991; Juvonen & Weiner, 1993). For example, in the case of formerly aggressive children, the perception of many peers is "once a bully, always a bully." So when teachers and other professionals work to improve the behaviors of antisocial youngsters, they must work to improve their reputations as well—for example, by placing them in structured cooperative learning groups where they can use their newly developed social skills or by encouraging their active involvement in extracurricular activities. In one way or another, adults must help youngsters show peers that they have changed and are worth getting to know better.

Support children who have developed a reputation for being aggressive by placing them in groups, monitoring their social interactions, and publicly recognizing their good behaviors.

■ *Encourage a general feeling of respect for others.* Adults who effectively promote friendships among diverse groups of children are often those who convey a consistent message over and over again: All members of their community deserve respect as human beings (Turnbull, Pereira, & Blue-Banning, 2000). Fernando Arias, a high school vocational education teacher, has put it this way:

In our school, our philosophy is that we treat everybody the way we'd like to be treated. . . . Our school is a unique situation where we have pregnant young ladies who go to our school. We have special education children. We have the regular kids, and we have the drop-out recovery program . . . we're all equal. We all have an equal chance. And we have members of every gang at our school, and we hardly have any fights, and there are close to about 300 gangs in our city. We all get along. It's one big family unit it seems like. (Turnbull et al., 2000, p. 67)

■ *Be a backup system when relationships with peers aren't going well.* Disruptions in peer relationships—perhaps because of interpersonal conflicts or a best friend's relocation to a distant city—are often a source of emotional distress (Wentzel, 1999). Warm, supportive adults can lessen the pain in such circumstances, and their ongoing gestures of affection and support can bolster the spirits of children who, for whatever reasons, have no close friends (Guay et al., 1999; Wentzel, 1999). Such overtures of caring and goodwill may be especially important for children who have little support at home and might otherwise turn to deviant subcultures or gangs to gain attention and affection (Parks, 1995).

So far we have limited our discussion to platonic peer relationships—relationships that are social, emotional, and perhaps cognitive, but rarely physical, in nature. In the final section of the chapter, we consider the nature of romantic relationships and the development of sexuality.

Romantic Relationships and Sexuality

Even preschoolers show considerable awareness of, as well as interest in, romantic relationships. Many, especially those living in traditional two-parent families, believe that getting married and having children is a normal, perhaps inevitable, part of growing up. They sometimes act out their fantasies and emerging understandings about romance in their sociodramatic play, as this episode involving Eric and Naomi (previously observed planning a shopping trip and killing robbers in the closet) illustrates:

E: Hey, Naomi, I know what we can play today.
N: What?
E: How about, um, the marry game. You like that.
N: Marry?
E: How about baker or something? How about this. Marry you? OK, Naomi, you want to pretend that?
N: Yes.
E: OK, Naomi, do you want to marry me?
N: Yeah.
E: Good, just a minute, Naomi, we don't have any marry place.
N: We could pretend this is the marry place.
E: Oh, well, pretend this, ah, there'll have to be a cake.
N: The wedding is here first.
E: OK, but listen to this, we have to have a baby, oh, and a pet.
N: This is our baby. (Gottman, 1986b, p. 157; reprinted with permission of Cambridge University Press)

Consistent with what we have learned about cognitive abilities at this age, young children's understandings of courtship and marriage are superficial and concrete. For example, in the preceding scenario, the children focus on having a "marry place" and wedding cake; jumping the gun a bit, they also make sure they have a baby and family pet.

As children grow older, they become increasingly aware of the romantic nature of many adult relationships. For instance, prior to puberty, some children practice courtship behaviors (Elkind, 1981b). Girls may vie for the attention of boys, use cosmetics, and choose clothing and hairstyles that make them look older. Boys, meanwhile, may flaunt whatever manly airs they can muster. Both sexes pay close heed to the romantic activities of those around them and absorb the many romantic images they see in the media (Connolly & Goldberg, 1999; Larson, Clore, & Wood, 1999).

As they reach adolescence, romance is increasingly on young people's minds and a frequent topic of conversation (B. B. Brown, Feiring, & Furman, 1999). The biological changes associated with puberty usher in romantic and sexual desires (Larson et al., 1999). Furthermore, in most Western cultures, social pressures mount to tempt, perhaps even push, young adolescents into dating and some degree of sexual activity (Larson et al., 1999; B. C. Miller & Benson, 1999).

Romantic relationships in adolescents have numerous benefits. From adolescents' own perspective, being one half of a couple addresses needs for companionship, affection, and security and may significantly enhance social status with peers (Collins & Sroufe, 1999; Furman & Simon, 1999; B. C. Miller & Benson, 1999). Such relationships also promote social-emotional development by providing opportunities for young people to experiment with new interpersonal behaviors and examine previously unexplored aspects of their own identity (Furman & Simon, 1999). Young adolescents' early ventures into cross-sex relationships are often awkward and unskilled. They might not know what to do or so, for example, when they receive phone calls or e-mail messages from admirers. With time and experience, however, many become adept at capturing and maintaining the interest and affections of potential or actual romantic partners.

At the same time, romantic relationships can wreak havoc with adolescents' emotions (Larson et al., 1999). As noted in Chapter 9, adolescents have more extreme mood swings than younger children or adults, and such instability is sometimes due to the excitement and frustrations of being romantically involved (or perhaps *not* involved) with another. The emotional highs and lows that come with romance—the roller coaster ride between exhilaration and disappointment—can cloud judgment and interfere with accurate information processing and reality testing (Larson et al., 1999). Romantic breakups can lead to severe depression and deficits in motivation.

Fortunately, most adolescents enter the world of romance slowly and cautiously (B. B. Brown, 1999; Connolly & Goldberg, 1999). Initially, their romances often exist more

Most preschoolers are very aware of and curious about courtship and marriage. Here Teresa's son Alex (age 5) depicts his image of his parents getting married. He created the drawing at school during a period when he and his classmates were especially fascinated with engagements and weddings.

in their minds than in reality, as the following conversation between two young teenagers illustrates:

A: How's Lance [*giggle*]? Has he taken you to a movie yet?
B: No. Saw him today but I don't care.
A: Didn't he say anything to you?
B: Oh . . .
A: Lovers!
B: Shut up!
A: Lovers at first sight! [*Giggle.*]
B: [*Giggle.*] Quit it! (Gottman & Mettetal, 1986, p. 210; reprinted with the permission of Cambridge University Press)

Young adolescents' romantic thoughts may also involve "crushes" on people who are out of reach—perhaps favorite teachers, movie idols, or rock stars (B. B. Brown, 1999; B. C. Miller & Benson, 1999). Slowly, young people become comfortable in spending time with peers of the opposite sex (B. B. Brown et al., 1999; B. C. Miller & Benson, 1999). These opposite-sex peers often become targets of desire. Eventually, many adolescents broaden their interpersonal worlds in two ways—by dating and experiencing sexual intimacy. Some of them also wrestle with new feelings about members of their own sex. Let's look more closely at developmental phenomena related to dating, sexual intimacy, and sexual orientation.

Dating

Dating is a developmental milestone for young people. It represents something new, a marker of adult status. Dating behaviors do have antecedents, however. Research suggests that teenagers bring their prior social experiences with family and friends into romantic relationships (Bigelow, Tesson, & Lewko, 1999; Collins & Sroufe, 1999; Leaper & Anderson, 1997). For instance, adolescents who have formed secure attachments to family members are more likely to have successful dating experiences, perhaps because they have greater self-confidence, better social skills, and more experience with trusting relationships. Adolescents who have grown up in an authoritative family (recall the discussion of authoritative parenting in Chapter 12) are accustomed to a balanced give-and-take in decision making and may use this same style with romantic partners, negotiating what movie to see, which party to attend, and so on. Conversely, teens who have repeatedly seen family violence may bring physical aggression into disagreements with dating partners, hitting, pushing or in other ways violating them (Wolfe & Wekerle, 1997); they may also tolerate and rationalize aggressive behavior from partners ("He didn't mean it"; "She was drunk"; "He'll outgrow it").

In the middle school years, young adolescents' forays into dating may initially consist of little more than being identified as a couple in the eyes of peers. For instance, in their seventh-grade year, Jeanne's daughter Tina and her friends talked about their various "boyfriends." Although the girls often described themselves as "going out" with this boy or that, in fact they never actually dated any of them. Eventually, however, most adolescents venture out on actual dates with one or more peers.

In general, beginning to date has more to do with social expectations than with the onset of puberty (Collins & Sroufe, 1999; Dornbusch et al., 1981; B. C. Miller & Benson, 1999). If adolescents have friends who are dating, odds are that they will also begin to date. Early dating partners are often chosen because of their physical attractiveness or social status, and dating relationships tend to be short-lived and involve only superficial interaction (B. B. Brown, 1999; Collins & Sroufe, 1999; G. Downey et al., 1999).

As teenagers move into the high school years, some begin to form more long-term, intimate relationships (B. B. Brown, 1999; Connolly & Goldberg, 1999). At this point, their choices of dating partners depend more on personality characteristics and compatibility, and peers' judgments are less influential. Relationships become more intense, sometimes stealing time away from other, more platonic friendships. Often, such relationships lead to varying degrees of sexual intimacy.

Sexual Intimacy

For many adolescents, sexual intimacy goes hand in hand with, and is a natural outgrowth of, long-term romantic relationships (Graber, Britto, & Brooks-Gunn, 1999; B. C. Miller & Benson, 1999). For many others, however, it is something that should be saved for the "right moment," or perhaps for after marriage. And for some, sexual intimacy is an activity completely separate from romantic involvement; rather, it may be a means of enhancing one's image and social status with peers, exploring one's sexual orientation, or gaining another's attention and affection (Collins & Sroufe, 1999; L. M. Diamond, Savin-Williams, & Dubé, 1999).

Both sexes have the capacity for sexual arousal before puberty (Conn & Kanner, 1940; Langfeldt, 1981). Children and preadolescents occasionally look at or touch one another in private places and play games (e.g., strip poker) that have sexual overtones (Dornbusch et al., 1981; Katchadourian, 1990). Except in cases of sexual abuse, however, sexuality before adolescence lacks the erotic features present in later development.

Sexual maturation is, like dating, a sign of adulthood and a harbinger of intimacies and pleasures to come. Even so, no one knows how best to handle adolescent sexuality—not parents, not teachers, and certainly not adolescents themselves (Katchadourian, 1990). Many adults ignore the topic, assuming (or perhaps hoping) it's not yet relevant for adolescents. Even teenagers who have good relationships with their parents have few chances to talk about sex (Brooks-Gunn & Furstenberg, 1990; Leite, Buoncompagno, Leite, & Mergulhao, 1995). When parents and teachers do broach the topic of sexuality, they often raise it in conjunction with problems, such as irresponsible behavior, substance abuse, disease, and unwanted pregnancy.

Adolescents, meanwhile, must come to terms with their emerging sexuality, either on their own or in collaboration with trusted peers. They must learn to accept their changing bodies, cope with unanticipated new feelings of sexual arousal and desire, and try to reconcile the conflicting messages they get from various sources—home, school, religious groups, peers, the media—about whether and under what circumstances varying degrees of sexual intimacy are appropriate (Brooks-Gunn & Paikoff, 1993).

Their early sexual experiences often add to the confusion; consider these varying recollections about a first kiss (Alapack, 1991):

> "It felt so smooth. I walked home on cloud nine immensely pleased with myself. Finally I had something to boast about. Mission accomplished!" (p. 58)

> "The experience was so gentle that I was in awe. I walked back to my cabin on weak knees. My girlfriends told me I was blushing furiously. I felt lightheaded, but oh so satisfied." (p. 58)

> "I found myself mentally stepping back, thinking: 'no rockets, fireworks, music or stars.' I had to fake enjoyment, humor him. But I felt nothing! Later I sat on my bed and contemplated becoming a nun!" (p. 60)

> "He kissed me violently and pawed me over. When I started to cry, he let me go . . . I didn't want it to count. I wanted to wipe it off as I rubbed off the saliva. I couldn't. It couldn't be reversed; I couldn't be unkissed again. And the moisture, I could feel it, smell it, even though it was wiped. It made me nauseous. I felt like I was going to throw up." (p. 62)

These varied accounts have little in common, except perhaps a common sense of discovery. Other first sexual experiences also reflect such variability. Some teens are moved by tenderness and shared pleasure, but others are disappointed or even repulsed.

Most adolescents add gradually to their repertoire of sexual behaviors. Typically, they initiate actual sexual intercourse (in teenage lingo, they "go all the way") only after several years of experience with less intimate contacts (DeLamater & MacCorquodale, 1979; Udry, 1988). The experience is usually a positive one for boys, but many girls have mixed feelings, sometimes even regret (Carns, 1973; Sorensen, 1983). Seventeen-year-old April expresses her regret:

> The first time I had sex I was fourteen. That was a real hurting experience. I was young and I wasn't ready for it. I had a lot of feelings for the guy. I wanted to be his only girlfriend, but he had many other girlfriends. I thought since it was special to me, it was special to him. But it wasn't. It wasn't his first time. It wasn't what I wished it was.[4]

---

[4] From *Girls in America: Their Stories, Their Words* (p. 40), by Carol Cassidy, 1999, New York: TV Books. Copyright 1999 by TV Books. Reprinted with permission of Carol Cassidy.

In the United States, boys are more likely than girls to have tried sexual intercourse early in their high school years, but girls catch up by late adolescence. During their freshman year of high school, 29% of girls and 41% of boys have had intercourse; by their senior year, 60% of girls and 61% of boys have tried it (Grunbaum, Kann, Kinchen, Williams, Ross, Lowry, & Kolbe, 2002). Average ages for first intercourse also vary as a function of socioeconomic status and ethnicity. These variations reflect differences in peer groups and cultural norms about when behaviors are acceptable (Goodson, Evans, & Edmundson, 1997; B. C. Miller & Benson, 1999; U.S. Department of Health and Human Services, 1998). In some societies, men are lauded for their sexual conquests, perhaps even as women are encouraged to remain chaste until marriage. In other cultures, it is rare for high school students to be sexually active, in part because dating couples are regularly accompanied by an adult chaperone (B. B. Brown et al., 1999). Early and frequent sexual activity is also associated with alcohol and drug use (M. L. Cooper & Orcutt, 1997).

Sexual Orientation

By **sexual orientation**, we mean the particular sex(es) to which an individual is romantically and sexually attracted. A small but sizable percentage of adolescents find themselves sexually attracted to their own sex either instead of or in addition to the opposite sex. Although it has been difficult to establish precise figures, researchers have estimated that 5% to 10% of the adult population may be gay, lesbian, or bisexual (Durby, 1994; C. J. Patterson, 1995).

Sexual orientation does not appear to be a voluntary decision: Some adolescents actively try to ignore or stifle what they perceive to be deviant urges, and intensive treatments to convert homosexual adults into heterosexual ones have been largely unsuccessful (Gabard, 1999; Halderman, 1991). The exact causes of sexual orientation remain elusive, however. Some evidence for a genetic component comes from twin studies: Monozygotic (identical) twins are more similar in their sexual orientation than dizygotic (fraternal) twins (Bailey & Pillard, 1997; Gabard, 1999). Nevertheless, even monozygotic twins are not always the same. For male twins, if one is homosexual, the other has a 50-50 chance of being so; for female twins, the probability is a bit lower. Some researchers have observed subtle differences between homosexual and heterosexual individuals in certain brain structures, and still others have found that varying levels of androgens (male hormones) during prenatal development affect sexual orientation in animals (Bailey & Pillard, 1997; Money, 1987). Yet such biological variables may be the result of environmental rather than genetic influences (Dickemann, 1995; Money, 1987, 1988). At this point, many theorists suspect that both genetic and environmental factors are involved in determining sexual orientation (Byne, 1997; De Cecco & Parker, 1995; Money, 1988; Savin-Williams & Diamond, 1997).

In some cultures, homosexuality is considered to be well within the bounds of acceptable behavior. For instance, on certain islands in the South Pacific, 9- to 19-year-old boys live together in a single large house at the center of their village. They participate in numerous homosexual activities, and *not* participating is considered deviant (Herdt, 1981; Money, 1987). In most Western societies, however, people who are gay, lesbian, or bisexual encounter considerable misunderstanding, prejudice, and discrimination (C. J. Patterson, 1995).

Many homosexual and bisexual young people recall feeling "different" from peers in their childhood days (D. A. Anderson, 1994; Savin-Williams, 1995). Adolescence is a particularly confusing time for them, as they struggle to form an identity while feeling different and isolated from peers (Morrow, 1997; C. J. Patterson, 1995). When their attractions to same-sex peers become stronger, they may initially work hard to ignore or discount such feelings. At an older age, they may begin to accept some aspects of their homosexuality, and later still, they may "come out" and identify fully and openly with other gay and lesbian individuals. To see an example, refer back to Figure 9–10 on page 403.

Yet they often find the road to self-acceptance to be a rocky one, and anger, depression, and suicidal thoughts are common along the way (Elia, 1994; C. J. Patterson, 1995). Adolescents with a homosexual or bisexual orientation are frequently harassed by peers and are occasionally the victims of hate crimes (R. A. Friend, 1993; Savin-Williams, 1995). When the topic of homosexuality comes up in the school curriculum, it is usually within

sexual orientation
Particular sex(es) to which an individual is romantically and sexually attracted.

the context of acquired immune deficiency syndrome (AIDS) and other risks; more often, it is not discussed at all. One 17-year-old student recalls:

> I don't remember any formal discussion of homosexuality in school. In fact, it's really surprising to me that we didn't discuss it. My required eleventh grade health class, come to think of it, covered everything but it. We did condoms, sex, teen pregnancy, suicide, eating disorders, every kind of cancer—you name it, we did it. But nothing on homosexuality. (Malinsky, 1997, p. 40)

Under such circumstances, gay, lesbian, and bisexual youths often feel "silent, invisible, and fearful" (M. B. Harris, 1997, p. xxi), and a higher than average proportion drop out of school (Elia, 1994). Furthermore, some school personnel offer little in the way of comfort. A young woman named Elise describes what happened when she shared her homosexuality with her high school counselor:

> I came out to my counselor in my freshman year in high school. I've told this story over and over because it cracks me up but it's also very scary. It's just that she told me first of all not to confuse being gay with masturbation. Uh, which confused me. I wasn't confused before [laughs] but I was after that. She said, "Don't let your gay friends pressure you into it." At this point in time I knew I was gay; I recognized that fact but I didn't have any gay friends. Nobody's pressuring me into it; I don't know any gay people—that's why I'm upset. "Don't make a decision like this until you're at least 18." . . . I was in there saying I'm gay, not I think I'm gay . . . I believe if I had not been secure in already recognizing who I was and very strong-minded . . . that would have probably pushed me back in the closet. If this wasn't misinformation. . . . " (Herr, 1997, p. 59)

While drawing attention to the negative experiences of many gay and lesbian adolescents, we must also point out that most are psychologically and socially healthy (Savin-Williams, 1989). Moreover, many gain considerable social and emotional support from their parents, teachers, counselors, and peers. For example, Elise's mother was more understanding than her counselor had been and eventually put Elise in touch with a local support group. Elise found long-sought contact with other gay and lesbian adolescents to be very reassuring:

> I was so happy to realize that—oh wow, it's very difficult to describe the feeling—realizing, feeling completely completely alone and then realizing that other people know exactly where you're at or what you're going through. I mean it was amazing. (Herr, 1997, p. 60)

Regardless of adolescents' sexual orientation, their sexuality is an important and sometimes all-consuming concern. We now look at some ways in which teachers and other school personnel can help teenagers come to terms with their changing bodies and feelings.

Addressing Sexuality Issues in Group Environments

When young people reach puberty, romance saturates their social environments. Adolescents become preoccupied with who harbors secret yearnings for whom, whether the targets of desire reciprocate the affection, and which friends have progressed to various points along the continuum of sexual exploration. Adults often find this undercurrent of romantic desire distracting, yet they cannot prevent teenagers from growing up or squash the instincts that energize their bodies. So what can teachers and other professionals do? We offer the following suggestions:

■ *Remember how you felt as an adolescent.* If romance was not a part of your own adolescence, we suspect that you longed for it or found yourself fantasizing about a particular "someone." If you dated occasionally or frequently, the depth of sentiments from your first experiences undoubtedly left a trace (we wager you can remember your first date, first kiss, first rejection). Distracting as they might be, romantic desires are a natural, healthy part of coming-of-age.

■ *Expect diversity in adolescents' romantic relationships.* Teenagers' romantic activities will, to some degree, reflect the cultural norms of the surrounding community. Yet within any given culture, individual differences are sizable. Some young people attract a series of steady admirers, whereas others may be inexperienced in, possibly even indifferent to, the world of romance. And a small percentage of adolescents will have yearnings for members of their own sex.

■ *Make information about human sexuality easily available.* A conventional belief has been that education about "the birds and the bees" is the prerogative of parents and has no place in schools or other institutions. Typically, if sex education is a part of the school curriculum at all, it focuses on the biological aspects of sexual intercourse and offers little information to help teens make sense of their conflicting thoughts and feelings about sex and romance. Furthermore, adolescents' participation in a sex education curriculum usually requires parents' approval, and many parents are loathe to give it. Less controversial alternatives are to let adolescents know that school counselors, nurses, social workers, and health educators are always willing to talk with them about matters of sexuality (and to listen to their concerns with an open mind) and to make literature about a variety of related issues accessible at school and community libraries. (For related suggestions, see the sections on "Sexual Activity" and "Health-Compromising Behaviors" in Chapter 3.)

■ *Work to create a supportive environment for all young people.* To adults, the romantic bonds and breakups of adolescents often seem trivial, but they may cause considerable stress and emotional volatility in teenagers. For instance, adolescents may feel deep humiliation after rejection from an elusive suitor or a profound sense of loss as a long-term relationship ends (Kaczmarek & Backlund, 1991). In such situations, teachers and other practitioners can help adolescents sort through their feelings and look forward with optimism to brighter days and new relationships ahead (Larson et al., 1999).

In addition, professionals must make sure that adolescents with diverse sexual orientations feel welcome, respected, and safe at school and elsewhere (Morrow, 1997). They may also need to confront misconceptions in some of their colleagues: Creating a climate that is tolerant of sexual diversity is *not* likely to increase the number of students who are gay and lesbian. What it may do, however, is keep these students productive and in school.

■ *Describe sexual harassment and indicate why it is prohibited.* **Sexual harassment** is any action that a target can reasonably construe as being hostile, humiliating, or sexually offensive (Sjostrom & Stein, 1996). It is a form of discrimination and therefore is prohibited by federal and state laws. Sexual harassment can be a problem at the late elementary, middle school, and high school levels, and children and adolescents must know that it will not be tolerated. They should be informed that under no circumstances can they degrade one another—by words, gestures, or actions—with regard to physical traits or sexual orientation. An example of a description of sexual harassment, appropriate for students at varying grade levels, appears in Figure 13–10.

■ *Explain that healthy relationships do not include harassment and violence.* Children and adolescents may have grown up hearing adults use derogatory words and watching them push one another around. When talking with these youngsters, make it clear that they themselves do not have to tolerate harassment or physical violence. In the discussion below, Doris, a staff member from Latina Womanfocus, is endeavoring to make these essential points to a group of eighth graders. Latina Womanfocus is a nonprofit agency that delivers a voluntary program to adolescent girls aimed at encouraging sexual abstinence, self-esteem, and self-sufficiency (Weis, 2000).

Doris: Is it good to be friends before having a boyfriend/girlfriend relationship?
Delores: I think you should be friends first, then if you don't work out, you can still be friends.
Ayisha: That don't work.
Patrice: I hate it when you make friends with a boy and then he doesn't want to take you out because he think you like a little sister.
Tonika: I hate it, most of the guys are taken, conceited, or gay [all laugh].
Doris: How old are you? [she already knows how old they are]
Response: Thirteen, thirteen, etc.
Doris: Don't you have a long way to go?
Tonika: No.
Ayisha: This one guy likes me. Everywhere I go he right there. When I go to my friend Phalla's, he right there.
Doris: Why is that a problem?
Ayisha: Cuz I don't like him. I don't want him to be around me.

sexual harassment
Form of discrimination in which a target individual perceives another's actions or statements to be hostile, humiliating, or offensive, especially pertaining to physical appearance or sexual matters.

SEXUAL HARASSMENT: IT'S NO JOKE!

- **Sexual harassment is unwanted and unwelcomed sexual behavior** which interferes with your right to get an education or to participate in school activities. In school, sexual harassment may result from someone's words, gestures or actions (of a sexual nature) that make you feel uncomfortable, embarassed, offended, demeaned, frightened, helpless or threatened. If you are the target of sexual harassment, it may be very scary to go to school or hard to concentrate on your school work.

- **Sexual harassment can happen once, several times, or on a daily basis.**

- **Sexual harassment can happen any time and anywhere** in school—in hallways or in the lunchroom, on the playground or the bus, at dances or on field trips.

- **Sexual harassment can happen to anyone!** Girls and boys both get sexually harassed by other students in school.

- **Agreement isn't needed.** The target of sexual harassment and the harasser do not have to agree about what is happening; sexual harassment is defined by the girl or boy who is targeted. The harasser may tell you that he or she is only joking, but if their words, gestures or actions (of a sexual nature) are making you uncomfortable or afraid, then you're being sexually harassed.

You do not have to get others, either your friends, teachers or school officials, to agree with you.

- **No one has the right to sexually harass another person!** School officials are legally responsible to guarantee that all students, you included, can learn in a safe environment which is free from sexual harassment and sex discrimination. If you are being sexually harassed, your student rights are being violated. Find an adult you trust and tell them what's happening, so that something can be done to stop the harassment.

- **Examples of sexual harassment in school:**
  - touching, pinching, and grabbing body parts
  - being cornered
  - sending sexual notes or pictures
  - writing sexual graffiti on desks, bathroom walls or buildings
  - making suggestive or sexual gestures, looks, jokes, or verbal comments (including "mooing," "barking" and other noises)
  - spreading sexual rumors or making sexual propositions
  - pulling off someone's clothes
  - pulling off your own clothes
  - being forced to kiss someone or do something sexual
  - attempted rape and rape

REMEMBER: SEXUAL HARASSMENT IS SERIOUS AND AGAINST THE LAW!

FIGURE 13-10 Example of how professionals might describe sexual harassment in language that children and adolescents understand

Originally appeared as "Stop Sexual Harassment in Schools," by N. Stein, May 18, 1993, *USA Today*. Copyright 1993 by Nan Stein. Reprinted with permission of the author.

Doris:	Is this a form of sexual harassment? We walk down the street and someone calls after us. Don't we want real romance? You meet and fall in love?
Tish:	But then you find out he's married.
Patrice:	He's married and he's got a girlfriend.
Delores:	He's married, got a girlfriend, and got kids by both of them.
Doris:	What do we do when someone is in an unhealthy relationship?
Tish:	Try to help them out.
Patrice:	Get a restraining order.
Tonika:	Talk about violence! When my mom was pregnant, her boyfriend hit her.
Patrice:	My mom got beat up, then she left.
Doris:	Well, we all know that relationships are bad if there is physical abuse. (Weis, 2000, pp. 640–641)

In this and other conversations, Doris helped the girls learn to resist physical abuse in their relationships. Notice also that she guided them to understand that they did not have to put up with sexual harassment.

- *Make appropriate referrals when necessary.* Teachers and other professionals who work with adolescents occasionally learn unexpectedly about aspects of youngsters' personal lives. For instance, students may tell teachers they are pregnant, have a pregnant girlfriend, or suspect they've contracted a sexually transmitted infection. Professionals need to be prepared to make immediate referrals to counselors who can offer guidance and encourage adolescents to talk with parents and other family members. Practitioners may also hear that adolescents have been raped (the percentage of adolescent girls and women who have been raped is difficult to estimate, but rates have ranged from 13% to 25%; Kahn & Mathie, 2000). In the case of rape, practitioners should suggest that adolescents talk with their families, counselors, and law enforcement officials; practitioners will also want to talk immediately with their own supervisors to determine how best to follow up.

In this chapter, we've seen the many changes in young people's social skills and peer relationships over the course of childhood and adolescence. In the Developmental Trends

DEVELOPMENTAL TRENDS

Peer Relationships at Different Age Levels

AGE	WHAT YOU MIGHT OBSERVE	DIVERSITY	IMPLICATIONS
Infancy (Birth–2) 	• Occasional exploration of other children by looking and touching • Some actions suggesting obliviousness to presence of other children, such as crawling over them to reach a toy • Rudimentary imitation of facial expressions and actions of other children • In second year, side-by-side play with awareness of one another's actions • In second year, conflicts over desirable toys • Different responses to familiar versus unfamiliar peers	• Some infants have not had social experiences with other children in their families or in child care; they may need time to adjust to the presence of other children. • Attachment security to parents and other caregivers may affect children's interaction style with peers. • Infants who are temperamentally inclined to be shy, fearful, or inhibited may be wary of unfamiliar peers.	• Place small babies side by side when they are calm and alert. • Talk about what children are doing (e.g., "Look at Willonda shaking that toy; let's go watch how she makes the beads spin"). • Always supervise small children to prevent them from hurting one another. When they accidentally bump into others, redirect them to a different path (e.g., "Come this way Tameika. Chloe doesn't like it when you bump into her.").
Early Childhood (2–6) 	• Increasing frequency and complexity of peer interactions as children gain experience with age-mates • Variability in styles of play (sometimes solitary, sometimes parallel, sometimes cooperative) • Ability to approach and watch a peer and then initiate conversation • Increase in complexity of sociodramatic play, which provides practice in communication and negotiation • Agreement on roles and willingness to take turns in play activities (ages 4–6)	• Children who know their classmates or have had earlier positive experiences with peers may be more socially oriented than children who are new to the group or have previously had negative experiences with peers. • Temperament affects children's interactive style. Some children may be drawn to peers yet have trouble controlling their emotions (e.g., they may be aggressive and disruptive). • Children who have insecure attachments to parents and other family members may be less knowledgeable about how to interact sensitively and may not expect kindness from others (Bretherton & Waters, 1985). • Children with language delays may have more difficulty interacting with peers effectively.	• Help shy children gain entry into groups, especially if they have previously had limited social experiences. • Let children bring one or two items from home (e.g., favorite snuggly toys for nap time) and maintain ownership of their possessions, but remind them to take turns and share school toys and equipment. • When necessary, help children resolve interpersonal conflicts, but encourage them to identify solutions that benefit everyone and let them do as much of the negotiation as possible. • Help children deal with anger and conflict constructively so that they learn strategies for maintaining productive interpersonal relationships.
Middle Childhood (6–10)	• Increase in time spent with peers; greater concern about being accepted by peers • Tendency to assemble in larger groups than in early childhood • Less need for adult supervision than in early childhood • Decline of pretend play and rough-and-tumble play across middle childhood (pretend play may continue in private, where there are unlikely to be social sanctions against it) • Less physical aggression, but more verbal aggression (e.g., threats, insults) than in earlier years • Increase in gossip, as children show concern over friends and enemies • Some social exclusiveness, with friends being reluctant to have others join in their activities • Predominance of same-sex friendships (especially after age 7)	• Boys tend to play in larger groups than girls. • Some children are temperamentally cautious and timid; they may stand at the periphery of groups and show little social initiative. • Some children are actively rejected by their peers, perhaps because they are perceived as odd or have poor social skills. • Bullying and other forms of victimization emerge during middle childhood. Some bullies are aggressive, show little self-control, and tend to seek victims who are insecure, anxious, and isolated. Some bullies use their social skills to maximize their ability to hurt victims.	• Supervise children's peer relationships from a distance; intervene when needed to defuse an escalating situation. Identify ways to resolve conflicts that ensure everyone's welfare and rights. • Help isolated and rejected children join games, work groups, and lunch groups, and teach them skills for interacting effectively with peers. • Teach aggressive children more productive ways to solve conflicts with peers.

(continued)

DEVELOPMENTAL TRENDS

Peer Relationships at Different Age Levels *(continued)*

AGE	WHAT YOU MIGHT OBSERVE	DIVERSITY	IMPLICATIONS
Early Adolescence (10–14) 	• Variety of contexts (e.g., competitive sports, extracurricular activities, parties) in which to interact with peers • Increased concern about acceptance and popularity among peers • Fads and conformity in dress and communication styles in peer groups • Same-sex cliques, often restricted to members of a single ethnic group • Increasing intimacy, self-disclosure, and loyalty among friends • New interest in members of the opposite sex; for gay and lesbian youths, interest in the same sex takes on new dimensions • For some, initiation of dating, often within the context of group activities	• Some young adolescents are very socially minded; others are more quiet and reserved. • Some young adolescents hold tenaciously to childhood interests, such as dolls or Lego blocks. • Some young adolescents become involved in gangs and other delinquent social activities. • A few young adolescents are sexually active. • A small percentage begin to construct an identity as a gay or lesbian individual. • Gossiping and social exclusion may continue in some groups.	• Make classrooms, schools, and other settings friendly, affirming places for all adolescents. Do not tolerate name calling, ethnic slurs, or sexual harassment. • Provide appropriate places for adolescents to "hang out" before and after school. • Identify mechanisms (e.g., cooperative learning groups, public service projects) through which teenagers can fraternize productively as they work toward academic or prosocial goals. Give teens sufficient structure to work together effectively. • On some occasions, decide which youngsters will work together in groups; on other occasions, let them choose their work partners. • Sponsor structured after-school activities (e.g., in sports, music, or academic interest areas).
Late Adolescence (14–18) 	• Emerging understanding that relationships with numerous peers do not necessarily threaten close friendships • Increasing dependence on friends for advice and emotional support; however, adults remain important in such matters as educational choices and career goals • Less cliquishness toward the end of high school; greater tendency to affiliate with larger, less exclusive crowds • Increasing amount of time spent in mixed-sex groups • Many social activities unsupervised by adults • Emergence of committed romantic couples, especially in the last two years of high school	• Some teenagers have parents who continue to monitor their whereabouts; others have little adult supervision. • Adolescents' choices of friends and social groups reflect their interests and values; these friends, in turn, affect their leisure activities, risk-taking behaviors, and attitudes about schoolwork. Some adolescents, known as thrill-seekers, actively seek out risky activities. • Teens who find themselves attracted to same-sex peers face additional challenges in constructing their adult identities, especially if others are not understanding and accepting.	• In literature and history, assign readings with themes of psychological interest to adolescents (e.g., loyalty among friends, self-disclosure of feelings, and vulnerability). • Be alert to the specific peer groups with which teenagers are associating. If they associate with troubled agemates who discourage academic achievement or prosocial behavior, encourage them to join extracurricular activities and in other ways make them feel an integral part of the school and community. • Sponsor dances and other supervised social events that give adolescents opportunities to socialize in safe and wholesome ways.

Sources: Baumeister & Senders, 1989; Bigelow, 1977; Bredekamp & Copple, 1997; Bretherton & Waters, 1985; Buhrmester, 1996; Coie & Dodge, 1998; Eder, 1985; J. L. Epstein, 1986; Furman & Buhrmester, 1992; Garvey, 1974, 1990; Göncü, 1993; Kindermann, McCollom, & Gibson, 1996; Leaper, 1994; O'Brien & Bierman, 1987; Olweus, 1993; C. J. Patterson, 1995; K. H. Rubin, Bukowski, & Parker, 1998; K. H. Rubin, Coplan, Fox, & Calkins, 1995; Selman & Schultz, 1990; Shrum & Cheek, 1987; Teasley & Parker, 1995; Youniss & Smollar, 1985; Zarbatany et al., 1990.

table "Peer Relationships at Different Age Levels," we summarize key characteristics of interpersonal relationships in the five age groups, from infancy through adolescence, and offer additional suggestions for practitioners. In the following, final chapter of the book, we go beyond family and peers to look at the larger contexts in which young people grow up.

CASE STUDY: AARON AND COLE

Aaron and Cole became friends when they were both students in Mr. Howard's fifth-grade class. Whereas Aaron was in most respects a typical fifth grader, Cole had significant developmental delays. Special educator Debbie Staub (1998) summed up both his special educational needs and his strengths as follows:

Cole has limited expressive vocabulary and uses one- or two-word sentences. He does not participate in traditional academic tasks, although he is included with his typically developing schoolmates for the entire school day. Cole has a history of behavioral problems that have ranged from mild noncompliance to adult requests to serious aggressive and destructive behavior such as throwing furniture at others. In spite of his occasional outbursts, however, it is hard not to like him. Cole is like an eager toddler who finds wonder in the world around him. The boys he has befriended in Mr. Howard's class bring him great joy. He appreciates their jokes and harmless teasing. Cole would like nothing better than to hang out with his friends all day, but if he had to choose just one friend, it would be Aaron. (p. 76)

Aaron and Cole remained close until Cole moved to a group home 30 miles away at the beginning of seventh grade. Throughout their fifth- and sixth-grade years, Aaron was both a good friend and a caring mentor to Cole.

Without prompting from adults, Aaron helped Cole with his work, included him at games at recess, and generally watched out for him. Aaron also assumed responsibility for Cole's behavior by explaining to Cole how his actions affected others. The following excerpt from a classroom observation illustrates Aaron's gentle way with Cole: "Cole was taking Nelle's [a classmate's] things out of her bag and throwing them on the floor. As soon as Aaron saw, he walked right over to Cole and started talking to him. He said, 'We're making a new rule—no being mean.' Then he walked with Cole to the front of the room and told him to tell another boy what the new rule was. Cole tapped the boy's shoulder to tell him but the boy walked away. Cole looked confused. Aaron smiled and put his hand on Cole's shoulder and told him, 'It's okay. Just remember the rule.' Then he walked Cole back to Nelle's stuff and quietly asked Cole to put everything back." (D. Staub, 1998, pp. 77–78)

But Aaron, too, benefited from the friendship, as his mother explained: "Our family has recently gone through a tough divorce and there are a lot of hurt feelings out there for everyone. But at least when Aaron is at school he feels good about being there and I think a big reason is because he has Cole and he knows that he is an important person in Cole's life" (D. Staub, 1998, pp. 90–91)

Dr. Staub observed that, despite their developmental differences, the boys' relationship was in many respects a normal one:

I asked Mr. Howard once, "Do you think Cole's and Aaron's friendship looks different from others' in your class?" Mr. Howard thought for a moment before responding: "No, I don't think it looks that different. Well, I was going to say one of the differences is that Aaron sometimes tells Cole to be quiet, or 'Hey Cole, I gotta do my work!' But I don't know if that is any different than what he might say to Ben leaning over and interrupting him. I think I would say that Aaron honestly likes Cole and it's not because he's a special-needs kid." (D. Staub, 1998, p. 78)

Excerpts from *Delicate Threads: Friendships Between Children With and Without Special Needs in Inclusive Settings*, by D. Staub, 1998, Bethesda, MD: Woodbine House. Reprinted with permission.

- In what ways did the friendship of Aaron and Cole promote each boy's social-emotional development?
- Was the boys' friendship a reciprocal one? Why or why not?

Now go to our Companion Website to assess your understanding of chapter content with a Practice Quiz, apply what you've learned in Essay Questions, and broaden your knowledge with links to related Developmental Psychology Web sites. Go to www.prenhall.com/mcdevitt.

SUMMARY

Development of Interpersonal Behaviors

Interpersonal behaviors begin in infancy, when children show an interest in one another and make simple social gestures. Young people continue to acquire and refine social skills (e.g., cooperation, negotiation, conflict resolution) throughout childhood and adolescence. Schools, child care settings, and other group environments provide important contexts in which such skills develop. Most children become increasingly prosocial over the years, propelled in part by their growing capacity for perspective taking and empathy. Some degree of aggression (especially verbal aggression) is common; however, a few youngsters display troublesome levels of physical or psychological aggression and may require interventions that teach effective social skills. Both prosocial behavior and aggression appear to have genetic roots, but environmental factors (e.g., parenting styles, exposure to prosocial and aggressive models) play crucial roles.

Peer Relationships

Peers serve important functions in social-emotional development. Not only do they offer companionship and pleasure, but peers create contexts for practicing social skills, helping one another make sense of social experiences, and influencing one another's habits and ideas. Peer relationships change systematically over childhood and adolescence; for instance, activities tend to shift from simple gestures and imitation (infancy), to pretend play (early childhood), to structured group games (middle childhood), to social activities within cliques (early adolescence), and finally to larger, mixed-sex groups (late adolescence). Friendships are especially important peer relationships in that they provide social and emotional support, motivation to resolve conflicts in mutually satisfying ways, and eventually, emotional intimacy.

Romantic Relationships and Sexuality

Although preschoolers and elementary school children are well aware that romantic relationships are common among teenagers and adults, young people do not appreciate the full significance of romance and sexuality until they reach adolescence. As they go through puberty, they must come to terms with their changing bodies, sexual drives, and increasing sexual attraction to peers. Romances, either actual or imagined, can wreak havoc with teenagers' emotions, which in turn may affect their behaviors at school and in the community. Some adolescents experiment with sexual intimacy with only limited information about the potential risks of doing so, and others wrestle with sexual feelings about members of their own sex. Such changes require sensitivity, understanding and in many cases, support on the part of teachers and other practitioners.

KEY CONCEPTS

social skills (p. 548)
aggressive behavior (p. 549)
sociodramatic play (p. 560)
social pretense (p. 561)

peer pressure (p. 563)
popular children (p. 572)
rejected children (p. 572)
neglected children (p. 572)

controversial children (p. 572)
peer culture (p. 576)
dominance hierarchy (p. 577)
clique (p. 578)

subculture (p. 578)
gang (p. 578)
sexual orientation (p. 585)
sexual harassment (p. 587)

Bradley, age 5

Sarae, age 7

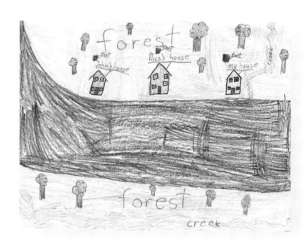

David, age 8

John, age 12

Growing Up in Context

CASE STUDY: THE NEW SCHOOL

In *The Dreamkeepers*, Gloria Ladson-Billings (1994) describes her childhood experiences as an African American student in American public schools. In the following excerpt, she tells what it was like to change schools—and simultaneously to change cultures—when she began seventh grade:

> I was sent to an integrated junior high school that was not in my neighborhood. I describe it as "integrated" rather than "desegregated" because no court mandates placed black children there. I was there because my mother was concerned about the quality of our neighborhood school.
>
> There were a handful of African American students in my seventh-grade class, but I knew none of them. They lived in a more affluent neighborhood than I did. Their parents had stable blue collar or white collar jobs. They had gone to better-equipped elementary schools than I had. The white students were even more privileged. Their fathers had impressive jobs as doctors, lawyers—one was a photojournalist. Most of their mothers were homemakers. In contrast, my mother and father both worked full-time. My father often even worked two jobs, yet we still lived more modestly than most of my classmates did.
>
> In seventh grade I learned what it means to be competitive. In elementary school my teachers did not seem to make a big deal out of my academic achievements. They encouraged me but did not hold me up as an example that might intimidate slower students. Although I suspect I was a recipient of a kind of sponsored mobility—perhaps because my mother always sent me to school neat and clean and with my hair combed—I don't think this preferential treatment was obvious to the other students. But in my new surroundings the competition was very obvious. Many of my white classmates made a point of showing off their academic skills. Further, their parents actively lent a hand in important class assignments and projects. For example, one boy had horrible penmanship. You could barely read what he scrawled in class, but he always brought in neatly typed homework. I asked him once if he did the typing and he told me his mother typed everything for him. She also did the typing of his cousin, who was also in our class and had beautiful penmanship. The teachers often commented on the high quality of these typed papers.
>
> I had come from a school where children learned and produced together. This competitiveness, further encouraged by the parents, was new to me. I could attempt to keep up with this unfair competition and "act white" or I could continue to work my hardest and hope I could still achieve. (Ladson-Billings, 1994, pp. 11–12)

or other young people at Gloria's new school, the focus on individual talents and accomplishments was a way of life that everyone took for granted. But this focus was out of sync with the emphasis at Gloria's previous schools, where children worked cooperatively toward common goals. Gloria's encounter with new and unsettling values illustrates just one of the innumerable ways in which culture affects children.

In preceding chapters, we often considered the role of culture in child development; in this chapter we look systematically at culture as a broad social environment, or *context*, in which youngsters grow. We look at other contexts as well, including historical events, religion, socioeconomic status, neighborhoods and communities, and the media. As we examine these contexts, we consider their effects on children and their implications for professionals who teach, guide, and nurture young people.

No single theoretical explanation accounts fully for the effects of context on children. However, as you read, you will see three recurring themes that are consistent with developmental viewpoints introduced in Chapter 1 and reviewed periodically throughout the book:

- Youngsters actively look for, and then interpret, messages in their world, a theme articulated by *cognitive-developmental* and *information processing perspectives*.
- The settings in which children live affect development, a result compatible with *ecological systems theory* and more broadly with *developmental systems perspectives*.
- Young people become increasingly responsible citizens by participating in countless informal lessons with neighbors, community leaders, and other adults, an idea embraced by *sociocultural perspectives*.

We begin our consideration of context by looking at *culture*, a concept that underlies the other contexts we will examine subsequently.

Culture and Ethnicity

By **culture**, we mean the *behaviors* and *beliefs* that characterize a social group. Cross-cultural differences in behavior—customs, traditions, and everyday practices—are often fairly concrete and easily observed. For instance, various cultural groups exhibit differences in meal practices (what, how, and with whom they eat), division of responsibility in families (who makes decisions about financial purchases, who disciplines the children, who prepares dinner and cares for the house, etc.), and social practices (how and with whom parents converse and children play). Cultural practices are also frequently seen in how people mark children's increasing age and responsibility. In some cultures, specific rituals and ceremonies mark an abrupt passage from childhood to adulthood. In others—in many Western societies, for example—numerous small events mark a more gradual transition from childhood to adolescence to adulthood. These may include acquisition of a driver's license, graduation from high school, a first intimate sexual experience, and eligibility to vote in national elections.

Belief systems, though not as obvious as behaviors, are an equally important part of a group's cultural heritage. Consider the following ideas:

- Babies are innocent at birth.
- As children grow, they should become increasingly self-reliant and independent.
- If people want something, they should say so.
- Some competition among individuals is healthy and productive.

Beliefs like these reflect some of the core ideas of mainstream Western culture (Hollins, 1996; Shweder et al., 1998), but they are far from universal. For example, some cultural groups believe that infants are not innocent but, rather, that they display inappropriate impulses that must be eradicated (Shweder et al., 1998). And as we saw in the opening case study, some groups value competition over cooperation while others value the reverse (Dien, 1998; Hollins, 1996; N. M. Webb & Palincsar, 1996).

The two bookends of culture—behaviors and beliefs—are closely related. Common practices stem from shared beliefs about what is true, healthy, appropriate, and rational (Shweder et al., 1998). Adults within a culture, therefore, can justify their typical ways of

culture
Behaviors and belief systems that characterize a social group and provide a framework for how group members decide what is normal and appropriate.

raising children, the number of children they give birth to, how they ask children to relate to them as authority figures, and which sports and leisure activities they encourage. As one specific illustration, consider the fact that most European American parents have their children sleep in rooms separate from their own, holding the belief that this practice provides nighttime privacy for adults and fosters independence in children (Shweder et al., 1998). Yet in other cultures, children sleep with parents who vigorously defend co-sleeping arrangements. For instance, Japanese parents may say, "I value and want to promote interdependency and feelings of closeness and solidarity among members of the family," and, "I know that co-sleeping will help children overcome feelings of distance and separation from members of the family who are older or of a different sex" (Shweder et al., 1998, p. 873).

Cultures differ in their practices and beliefs related to children's sleeping habits.

Ultimately, culture is fundamental to making a community meaningful for children. To a large extent, culture determines the ideas children acquire, the tools and actions they master, and the adult roles to which they aspire. It identifies problems worth solving and strategies for solving them. And it guides development of language and communication skills, expression and regulation of emotions, and formation of a sense of self.

Ethnicity and Race

Ethnicity refers to a group of individuals with common ancestors who have given their descendents values, beliefs, and behaviors that influence their lives. By maintaining these ethnic ties, members of the group share a sense of interdependence, a feeling that their lives are intertwined (Au, 1993; C. B. Fisher, Jackson, & Villarruel, 1998; NCSS Task Force on Ethnic Studies Curriculum Guidelines, 1992). An ethnic group may be comprised of people of the same race, national origin, or religious background.[1]

Sometimes members of a particular race are considered to be an ethnic group; for instance, in earlier chapters we have spoken of African Americans, Caucasians (using the term *European Americans*), or Asian Americans. The term *race* generally refers to a group of people who share certain physical similarities, such as skin color or eye shape, that have a genetic basis (C. B. Fisher et al., 1998). However, as noted in Chapter 6, race is not defined simply by biology: We cannot pinpoint a person's race by analyzing DNA.

Membership in a particular racial group is not always a good indication of children's ethnic culture.

We prefer the term *ethnicity* rather than *race* because *ethnicity* emphasizes important cultural dimensions without suggesting that differences are caused by biological factors. Yet *ethnicity*, too, is a broad descriptor with limited utility. Consider the terms *Hispanic* and *Latino/Latina*. The term *Hispanic* refers to any Spanish-speaking individual and includes people from Spain, Mexico, Central and South American countries, and Spanish-speaking Caribbean nations; it may also include Portuguese-speaking people of Portugal and Brazil. The terms *Latino* and *Latina* (for males and females, respectively) are more frequently limited to people whose origins are in Central and South America (C. B. Fisher et al., 1998). When such broad ethnic categories are used, they obscure the tremendous variation that exists within an ethnic culture. Even within homogeneous local ethnic groups, there are individual differences in how people manifest a cultural value, such as strong obligation to one's parents. For example, in a single family, one grown child may send home money, another may do repairs around the house, and another may visit the parents whenever possible.

Finally, many people have a rich ethnic heritage that cannot be compartmentalized into a single ethnic category. Today, many children are **multi-ethnic**: they claim ancestry from more than a single ethnic group.[2] For instance, a child whose mother has African

---

[1] The concepts *culture* and *ethnicity* overlap, with *culture* emphasizing characteristic beliefs and customs in a group and *ethnicity* emphasizing membership in a defined group of people.

[2] Some people prefer the term *biracial children* to describe children whose parents come from different racial backgrounds. Other relevant terms are *biethnicity* (the parents are from two different ethnic cultures) and *multiracial children* (one or both parents can claim more than one racial heritage; see King, 1999). We use the term *multi-ethnic children* to include all of these children; there may be occasions, however, when professionals, youngsters, and families prefer to use one of the other terms.

ethnicity
Membership in a group of people with a common set of values, beliefs, and behaviors. The group's roots either precede the creation of, or are external to, the country in which the group resides.

multi-ethnic child
A child who can claim ancestry from more than one ethnic group.

BASIC DEVELOPMENTAL ISSUES

Characterizing Culture and Ethnicity

ISSUE	CULTURE AND ETHNICITY
Nature and Nurture	The general capacity for culture has evolved over millions of years and is inscribed in the human genetic code. For example, children's desires to form attachments and to master language have a genetic basis. The particular cultural heritage of a given group, as reflected in language patterns, social hierarchies, interpersonal behaviors, chosen professions, priorities, and so on, is environmental in origin. Individual children's inherited temperaments and talents may influence the particular ways in which they manifest the teachings of their culture. Furthermore, racial heritage, which has some genetic origins, sometimes influences the particular groups with which children identify.
Universality and Diversity	All cultural and ethnic groups prescribe certain behaviors and belief systems for their members. These differ widely from one group to another. In multicultural countries, such as the United States, ethnic groups differ further in the opportunities each has within the dominant society; for example, some groups experience discrimination in housing, jobs, and educational opportunities. Additional diversity in behaviors and beliefs may exist within a particular group. Diversity between groups and within groups has implications for professionals, who must be sensitive to cultural differences yet not form rigid stereotypes of particular groups.
Qualitative and Quantitative Change	Some cultures and ethnic groups view development in terms of abrupt qualitative changes; for instance, rituals that signify passage from childhood to adulthood may be accompanied by an immediate and drastic change in young people's roles in the community and in others' expectations for their performance. Other cultures and ethnic groups view development as a series of smaller, more gradual steps—for instance, by allowing increasing responsibility and independence to unfold gradually.

American and Native American heritage and whose father is from England may be exposed to several distinct family traditions (E. W. King, 1999). Historically, actual numbers of multi-ethnic children have been difficult to estimate because government officials used simple ethnic categories (Hodgkinson, 1995). Beginning with the 2000 U.S. Census, however, respondents were given the option of selecting one or more categories to indicate their racial identities; 2.4% of American respondents identified themselves as being of two or more races (Grieco & Cassidy, 2001).

The Basic Developmental Issues table "Characterizing Culture and Ethnicity" looks at culture and ethnicity in terms of nature and nurture, universality and diversity, and qualitative and quantitative change. We now examine more closely the kinds of diversity we are likely to see among children of different ethnic groups.

Children's Ethnic Worlds

Cultural and ethnic differences are reflected in adults' ways of instructing, motivating, and nurturing children. For instance, in the opening case study, we saw that schools in different ethnic neighborhoods of a single American city had differing emphases on cooperation and competition. Ethnic cultures also vary in their models of instruction. In most Western schools, teachers use interactive verbal lessons to teach information and skills. In contrast, many Native American communities ask children to watch carefully as adults perform crafts and to listen quietly as adults tell lengthy stories (Tharp, 1994). Ethnic cultures also determine who is an acceptable caregiver. In Western countries, young children may have many experiences interacting with age-mates, but they typically do so with supervision from adults. In contrast, Nso children in rural Cameroon spend considerably more time with other children than with adults. For instance, numerous Nso children ranging in age from 1½ to 6 or 7 might play together under supervision of two older girls, who are perhaps 8 to 10 years old (Nsamenang & Lamb, 1994).

You might wonder why ethnic environments are so different from one another. Natural resources and forms of livelihood shape cultural practices (Kim & Choi, 1994). Having older children supervise younger ones is typical of rural agricultural groups comprised of large, close-knit families (Nsamenang & Lamb, 1994). Such a close-knit feeling would not be feasible for migratory tribes living in jungles, mountains, and deserts because people must pull up roots frequently to search for food and water. Under these circumstances, cultural groups socialize children to be assertive, venturesome, and self-reliant (Barry, Child, & Bacon, 1959). To some extent, ethnic culture is an outgrowth of a people's history of minimizing hardships, increasing physical comfort, and maintaining social harmony.

Children are profoundly influenced by such environmental adaptations. For example, a team of researchers examined cognitive abilities of 6- to 8-year-old children in three areas of Peru (Stevenson, Chen, Lee, & Fuligini, 1991). In these three areas, schools received little funding, class sizes were large (ranging from 38 to 47), and buildings lacked such basic features as roofs, furniture, and custodial care. In two areas, however, children received support for emerging academic skills, in one case by seeing written messages and mathematical calculations used by vendors and family members, and in the other case by participating in complex traditions celebrating history, crafts, and religious beliefs. Children in these two areas did reasonably well on tests of reading and cognitive tasks. In the third area, parents traveled outside the village to work. Apparently, their impoverished circumstances left parents with little energy to sing, dance, or worship when they were home on the weekend. Probably as a result of limited exposure to literate systems and cultural traditions, their children performed poorly on academic and cognitive tasks.

These comparisons illustrate the powerful effects of culture on children's learning, but they also raise questions about how children fare when families move from one region to another. We examine these issues now.

Ethnicity, Immigration, and Social Change

Cultural and ethnic differences become salient when people move from one cultural environment to another—for instance, when they immigrate to a new country. When families move, they often find that they are not embraced as full, privileged participants in their new setting. In the United States, for instance, public anxiety arises from misperceptions that immigrants come into the country illegally (not true for the majority) and that they take jobs away from native citizens (not supported by the data) (Board on Children and Families, Commission on Behavioral and Social Sciences and Education, National Research Council, & Institute of Medicine, 1995; Fix & Passel, 1994). Such anti-immigrant sentiments have led to legislation that limits immigrants' access to public services.

Acculturation, Assimilation, and Bicultural Orientation   When different cultural groups exist in the same region, the two groups interact and learn about one another (C. B. Fisher et al., 1998). As people participate in the customs and take on the values of a new culture, **acculturation** occurs. For different individuals, acculturation takes different forms:

- **Assimilation.** Some people totally embrace values and customs of the new culture, giving up their original cultural identity in the process (LaFromboise, Hardin, Coleman, & Gerton, 1993). For instance, the Irish and German groups who migrated to the United States in the early decades of the 20th century have been largely assimilated into mainstream American culture; the only obvious signs of their cultural backgrounds are Irish and German surnames and occasional celebrations of holidays from the homeland. Assimilation is typically a gradual process that occurs over several generations (Delgado-Gaitan, 1994).
- **Selective adoption.** Immigrants may acquire some customs of the new culture while retaining other customs from their homeland. They choose the traditions they like and disregard those with less appeal. For instance, Naomi Padilla, a Mexican American woman who lived next door to Jeanne for several years, enjoyed many American customs, such as celebrating the Fourth of July, yet every day made tortillas for her family, just as her mother had in Mexico.

acculturation
Taking on the customs and values of a new culture.

assimilation
Totally embracing a new culture, abandoning one's previous culture in the process.

selective adoption
Assuming some customs of a new culture while also retaining some customs of one's previous culture.

- **Rejection.** Sometimes people move to a new culture without taking on any of their new community's cultural practices (Kim & Choi, 1994). Complete rejection of a new culture is probably possible only when an individual has little need to interact with people in that culture. For example, a Mexican American colleague of ours had her elderly mother living with her for many years. The mother learned little English and rarely ventured outside the home except in the company of her daughter, and so her Mexican customs and beliefs remained intact throughout the many years that she lived in the United States.
- **Bicultural orientation.** Some people retain their original culture yet also acquire beliefs and master practices of their new culture, and they readily adjust behaviors to fit the particular contexts in which they find themselves (Hong, Morris, Chiu, & Benet-Martínez, 2000). For example, we think of two daughters of an American father and Japanese mother who once worked with us. The girls were born and raised in the United States, but they often lived with their maternal grandparents in Japan during the summer. They were fluent not only in two languages (English and Japanese) but also in both American and Japanese cultural practices, and they expertly adapted their speech and behaviors to the countries in which they were living at any particular time.

Sometimes two or more forms of acculturation can be seen in a single immigrant family. For example, imagine that a Vietnamese family, the Huongs, moves to a culturally diverse neighborhood in Los Angeles. Mr. and Mrs. Huong selectively take on some American cultural practices (e.g., learning American business practices so that they can operate a restaurant) while retaining many of their Vietnamese traditions both in their restaurant and at home. The Huong children, whose classmates hail from a variety of ethnic backgrounds, develop a bicultural orientation, so that they are equally comfortable at school and at home and know appropriate ways of behaving in each setting. When Mrs. Huong's elderly mother comes for a summer visit, she rejects all aspects of American culture—for instance, complaining about the high rates of crime in downtown Los Angeles, the unhealthy food offered at fast-food restaurants, and the video games that preoccupy her grandchildren.

At one time, total assimilation was considered to be the optimal situation for immigrants and other ethnic minority citizens, at least in the United States. The route to success was presumed to entail blending into the "melting pot" in which people of diverse backgrounds became increasingly similar. More recently, however, researchers have discovered that when young immigrants give up their family's cultural traditions, they are at greater risk for dangerous behaviors, such as using alcohol and drugs, having unprotected sex, and engaging in criminal activities (Caetanno, 1987; Gilbert & Cervantes, 1986; Neff, Hoppe, & Perea, 1987; Vega, Gil, Warheit, Zimmerman, & Apospori, 1993; Ventura & Tappel, 1985). Children and adolescents who reject traditional cultural values often find themselves in conflict with their parents and may lack the strong positive values they need to resist temptation (C. B. Fisher et al., 1998). Increasingly, therefore, the idea that the United States is a melting pot is giving way to the idea that the country can be more productively thought of as a "mosaic" of cultural and ethnic pieces that all legitimately contribute to the greater good of society (C. B. Fisher et al., 1998). Immigrant children appear to adjust most successfully when they learn certain aspects of their new culture while also retaining aspects of their original culture—that is, when they show a pattern of either selective adoption or bicultural orientation. For instance, adolescent immigrants who maintain allegiance to traditional values enjoy close, unstressed relationships with parents and support from extended family. As a general rule, they do well in school, have few behavioral or mental health problems, and express high life satisfaction (C. B. Fisher et al., 1998; Fuligni, 1998; Kim & Choi, 1994).

Children of diverse ethnic backgrounds often adjust well when they remain knowledgeable about their ethnic heritage and also master customs of mainstream society.

rejection
Refusing to learn or accept any customs and values found within a new cultural environment.

bicultural orientation
Ability to behave in accordance with two different cultural frameworks in appropriate contexts.

Developmental Issues for Children from Diverse Cultural Backgrounds

When children come from cultural backgrounds different from mainstream culture, they not only must tackle basic developmental tasks (e.g., mastering language, learning about the physical world, refining social skills) but they also face such challenges as learning a second language, contending with discrimination, and discerning the subtleties of new cultural practices. Many youngsters develop coping mechanisms that help them deal with such challenges. Nevertheless, their school performance is not always on a par with that of classmates from the majority group. In this section, we look at each of these interrelated issues: developmental challenges, coping mechanisms, and school performance.

Challenges for Ethnic Minority Children   As already noted in this and previous chapters, children from diverse cultural backgrounds have different kinds of experiences that may not be understood by people in the dominant groups. For example, in many ethnic minority groups in the United States, parents rarely engage children in the question-answer sessions ("What does a doggie say?" "Wuff!" "That's right! A dog says, 'Ruff, ruff!'") seen in many European American homes and in most American classrooms (Losey, 1995; L. S. Miller, 1995). Unaccustomed to this communication pattern, children may be puzzled when questioned in this way at school or in community settings.

Children also acquire culturally based beliefs about what constitutes acceptable behavior that may be poorly understood at school and in the community. The following incident reported by a preschool teacher illustrates a difference in viewpoints:

> Sarah signaled me that she felt faint. I rose and started toward Pedro. Suddenly I saw what Sarah had seen: around his neck, punched for stringing like mittens, were the two bloody ears of a deer. I had seconds to recover and speak. Grasping the psychiatrist's technique of reaching for the obvious, I asked, "Someone in your family, Pedro, has been deer hunting?"
>
> "Yup," he said, "my dad."
>
> Trying not to look too closely, I removed the strung ears, saying I would hang them where they would be safe, high above an out-of-the-way blackboard. With Sarah pale and off to the side and Pedro center stage, I sat on the floor with the children and invited Pedro to give us some details. With relish he did so, although briefly. The other children and I listened in rapt silence.
>
> I had recently learned one small fact about Alaskan Indian caribou hunting, so I felt I could ask Pedro if his mother did the butchering, the cutting up for roasts and steaks. "Yup," he answered, and we were launched on a discussion of the meat and its distribution. It would go to friends and family, primarily to the latter. Cousin Timmy showed us with his hands how big a roast would come to his family. (This was in response to a mistake I had made in assuming cousin Timmy's family might get a half. "No," corrected Pedro, "only a roast.") (Hawkins, 1997, pp. 329–330)

In Pedro's eyes, the deer ears were tokens of his father's skill as a hunter; his teacher acknowledged his feelings with sensitivity. However, a practitioner less sensitive to cultural differences might have rebuffed or punished Pedro for bringing in these "disgusting" trophies.

Another challenge that many children and families from minority groups face is *discrimination,* inequitable treatment as a result of their group membership. For example, data on home mortgage inquiries suggest that African Americans and Hispanic Americans are given less information about loan processes and options than are European Americans with comparable incomes and credit histories (Turner, Freiberg, Godfrey, Herbig, Levy, & Smith, 2002). Also, African Americans and Hispanic Americans have, on average, lower-paying jobs than European Americans and are underrepresented in managerial positions and professional occupations (Federal Glass Ceiling Commission, 1995). And of adolescents who use or sell drugs, African Americans are more likely than European Americans to get caught and contend with the juvenile justice system (C. B. Fisher et al., 1998).

When ethnic minority families have little discretionary income and limited housing options, their children often end up in schools that are poorly funded, inadequately equipped and staffed, and overcrowded (C. B. Fisher et al., 1998; Portes, 1996). For example, Cedric Jennings, the African American high school student introduced at the beginning of Chapter 12, had considerable difficulty during his first year at Brown University; his inner-city high school had simply not prepared him for the rigors of a challenging college curriculum (Suskind, 1998). (The story has a happy ending: With effort and perseverance, Cedric graduated with his class in 1999.)

Coping Mechanisms   How do children from ethnic minority groups deal with the special developmental challenges they face? Development of a strong sense of *ethnic identity* is one important way of coping. As you may recall from Chapter 9, ethnic identity refers to a child's awareness of being a member of a particular group and his or her willingness to adopt certain behaviors characteristic of that group. Youngsters develop a sense of ethnic identity out of the array of messages they receive from families, peers, community, and the media. For instance, they may hear tales of ancestors' struggles and victories in a discriminatory setting, and they may see media portrayals of their ethnic group in particular roles—perhaps as leaders and trailblazers for humane causes or, alternatively, as violent and deviant troublemakers (C. B. Fisher et al., 1998). The many messages children hear and see are not always consistent, and they struggle to form a coherent set of beliefs about their cultural group. Eventually, many reject messages from mainstream society that demean their own ethnic culture (Phinney, 1990).

A second coping mechanism entails development of a *cultural frame of reference*, a particular way of interpreting cultural differences between one's own group and the dominant society. John Ogbu (1994) has used this concept to explain why some minority cultural and ethnic groups gain fuller access to resources in mainstream society than others. He suggests that people (and their descendents) who have moved to a new country with hopes of economic prosperity and political freedom often consider themselves better off than in their former environment. Despite discrimination in the dominant society, they generally have confidence that they can succeed in their new country once they master English and learn skills needed for better-paying jobs. They are likely to emphasize education and teach their children the importance of studying hard and obeying school rules. In contrast, people (and their descendents) who became members of the new country against their will (through slavery, conquest, or colonization) compare their circumstances to those of majority group members and realize that they enjoy fewer economic, social, and political benefits. They are likely to interpret menial jobs and high unemployment rates in terms of long-term discrimination by the white majority. They tend not to trust the public schools to educate their children with the same quality and commitment afforded children from the dominant groups.

Because they perceive their difficulties to be the result of widespread discrimination, people in the latter group often establish clear psychological boundaries between themselves and the host society. They develop a particular cultural frame of reference, intentionally rejecting values and practices of the dominant group. For example, many African Americans use words and grammatical structures that are rarely if ever heard outside of their own communities (recall our discussion of African American English in Chapter 7). Ogbu suggests that such language provides a concrete way for people to maintain distance from mainstream culture. In fact, African American children often experience considerable social pressure to remain "different" from the mainstream. For instance, those who speak in a Standard English dialect (used in the media and most school systems; see Chapter 7) are often accused by other African Americans of "acting white" (Luster, 1992). Behaving in accordance with common practices of the mainstream culture (e.g., getting good grades, competing against classmates) is also a sign that one is acting white. Recall Gloria Ladson-Billings's concern about being competitive in the opening case study—she considered this style to be unfair but also to be acting white.

School Performance   Despite the challenges they face, many children and adolescents from diverse cultural and ethnic backgrounds manage to hold their own in the classroom. On average, children of immigrant families perform as well academically as native-born children of similar income backgrounds, and they stay in school longer. Children of Asian families and those of highly educated parents are especially successful (Davenport et al., 1998; Flynn, 1991; Fuligni, 1998; McDonnell & Hill, 1993). Not all ethnic groups enjoy academic success, however. African Americans, Native Americans, and Mexican Americans have historically performed at lower levels in the classroom than their classmates of European descent (L. S. Miller, 1995). Furthermore, students in these three groups are more likely to be identified as having special educational needs and to drop out prior to graduation (Portes, 1996; Rumberger, 1995; U.S. Department of Education, Office of Civil Rights, 1993).

The lower school achievement of members of some ethnic minority groups appears to be the result of several factors, including environmental stresses associated with economic hardship, limited access to good schools and educational opportunities, failures of schools to recognize their cultural strengths, and (in the case of recent immigrants from non-English-speaking countries) language barriers (McLoyd, 1998b; Stevenson, Chen, & Uttal, 1990). Furthermore, students who continually encounter teachers who hold low expectations for them become discouraged about what they can accomplish academically (Graham, 1989; Holliday, 1985).

Nonetheless, in any ethnic minority group, some children and adolescents do extremely well in school despite challenges. Furthermore, teachers and other professionals can use many strategies to help youngsters from diverse ethnic backgrounds achieve academic and social success. We consider these strategies now.

Integrating Culture and Ethnicity into Professional Practice

In the United States, children increasingly come from ethnic minority backgrounds. Between 1980 and 2000, percentages of children from European American families declined, children from African American and Native American families remained fairly steady, and children from Hispanic American and Asian American families increased (see Table 14–1; Federal Interagency Forum on Child and Family Statistics, 2002). A related diversity issue is the increase of children born to immigrant families. During 2001, 19% of American children lived with at least one parent who was foreign-born (Federal Interagency Forum on Child and Family Statistics, 2002).

Many professionals work quite effectively with children and adolescents from cultural backgrounds different from their own. Typically, they use strategies such as those described in the Development and Practice feature, "Accommodating Cultural and Ethnic Differences." In addition, they often follow these recommendations:

■ *Learn about the practices and values of children's cultures.* Some professionals, in an effort to treat everyone equitably, try to be "color blind" in their treatment of children. But in fact, professionals are most effective with youngsters when they tailor their practices to children's cultural backgrounds (Diller, 1999; Kottler, 1997; Pérez, 1998; L. Weiner, 1999). Consider Ed, a man of European American descent who is just beginning his first year teaching in a classroom of Native American children. Two researchers enter Ed's classroom:

> It is our first visit to Ed's room, and we have just finished introducing ourselves to the children. Ed turns to the class and tells them to introduce themselves to us. No one speaks. Ed calls on one of the children to begin. The boy is almost inaudible; we lean forward to hear better. The

TABLE 14–1 **Percentages of U.S. Children Who Belong to Ethnic Groups**

	ESTIMATES FOR YEAR			PROJECTED FOR YEAR
Ethnic Origin	*1980*	*1990*	*2000*	*2010*
White, Non-Hispanic	74	69	64	59
Black, Non-Hispanic	15	15	15	14
Hispanic	9	12	16	21
Asian/Pacific Islander, Non-Hispanic	2	3	4	5
Native American, Non-Hispanic	1	1	1	1

Note. Figures are for U.S. children 18 years and under. Persons of Hispanic origin may be of any race. In these data, children with Hispanic origins are considered having Hispanic ethnicity, regardless of their other ethnic or racial origins. Accumulated percentages may not equal 100 due to rounding error.
Source. Federal Interagency Forum on Child and Family Statistics, 2002.

DEVELOPMENT AND PRACTICE

Accommodating Cultural and Ethnic Differences

■ Think about how cultural beliefs and practices serve adaptive functions for children.

A girls' club leader notices that few of the girls are willing to answer her questions about gardening, even though it is clear from her conversations with them as individuals that they know the answers. She discovers that bringing attention to oneself is not appropriate in their culture and so modifies her style to allow for group responses.

■ Build on children's background experiences.

A teacher asks her class of inner-city African American children to translate a poem written in a local dialect by an African American scholar. She puts the words to the poem on an overhead transparency and asks children to translate each line for her into Standard English. In doing so, she cultivates a sense of pride about being "bilingual" (Ladson-Billings, 1994).

■ Use materials that represent all ethnic groups in a positive and competent light.

A history teacher peruses a history textbook to make sure that it portrays all ethnic groups in a nonstereotypical manner. He supple-

ments the text with readings that highlight important roles played by members of various ethnic groups throughout history.

■ Provide opportunities for children of different backgrounds to get to know one another better.

For a public service project, a community leader forms groups of children, each with a particular task to carry out, such as investigating a social problem, identifying existing services, or considering public figures that might be contacted. The leader is careful to form groups comprised of children from various neighborhoods and ethnic groups.

■ Expose youngsters to successful models from various ethnic backgrounds.

A high school teacher invites several successful professionals from minority groups to speak with her class about their careers. When some youngsters seem interested in particular careers, she arranges for them to spend time with these professionals in their workplaces.

next child is the same. None of the children makes eye contact with us, although they are glancing at one another. Finally, the last child has finished. Ed, sensing the same discomfort that we have, addresses the children, "Gee, maybe next time I should have you introduce each other. Maybe that would work better." (Suina & Smolkin, 1994, p. 125)

As a newcomer to the Pueblo community in which the children live, Ed has not yet learned the nuances of Pueblo culture, but he is aware that he has in some way violated the children's cultural norms. He will soon discover that Pueblo children believe it is inappropriate to single themselves out, and he will accommodate that belief in his instructional strategies.

Professionals become increasingly aware of youngsters' cultural backgrounds if they participate in local community activities and converse regularly with community members (McCarty & Watahomigie, 1998; H. L. Smith, 1998). In the process, they discover that virtually every group has certain traditions and values that have proven effective in sustaining it. For example, the Latin American value of *familism* establishes strong feelings of respect and responsibility among a child's family members. The strong multigenerational kinship networks among many African American families give children close family support from multiple, loving caregivers.

■ *Seek guidance from cultural authorities.* Professionals specializing in a given culture offer helpful viewpoints on designing schools and community groups. For instance, Madhubuti and Madhubuti (1994) describe African-centered schools in which group learning activities play a key role, African and African American history and traditions are incorporated into curricula, and African American role models are regularly invited into the classroom. Other specialists in African American education recommend acknowledging students' feelings of inequity and disenfranchisement regarding their schooling, describing struggles and contributions of students' ancestors, and conducting class discussions about how, together, they can all work toward a better society (Asante, 1991; Beauboeuf-LaFontant, 1999; Ladson-Billings, 1994; Mitchell, 1998). Extensive evaluation data are not yet available on achievement of students in African-centered schools, but preliminary data indicate that some African American students achieve at higher levels in these schools than in more traditional schools (Bakari, 2000).

■ *Adapt professional strategies to fit with children's cultural practices.* Professionals of all kinds can find ways to adapt their services to the cultural backgrounds of young people.

For example, counselors can learn about clients' cultural beliefs, discuss a full range of options for treatment, and help clients find protection from destructive environments, such as violent neighborhoods (LaFromboise, Foster, & James, 1996). Nurses and other health-care providers can ask children and families about their traditional remedies and health practices, such as special diets, herbs, amulets, and rituals (Berger & Williams, 1999). When cultural practices appear harmful, health providers can talk with families to determine acceptable solutions. For example, a school dietician might talk with parents to determine whether a diabetic adolescent can ask a religious leader for a temporary exemption from fasting (Leininger, 1995). Finally, social workers and other youth service providers may inform clients of cultural resources in their community, such as community action groups and churches (Berger & Williams, 1999).

In the Observation Guidelines table on page 304 of Chapter 7, we presented examples of cultural differences in sociolinguistic conventions. Additional examples of diverse cultural practices and strategies practitioners can use to accommodate them are presented in the Observation Guidelines "Identifying Cultural Practices and Beliefs." At the same time, it is important not to overgeneralize: Youngsters in any cultural group represent a collection of individuals; their specific behaviors, attitudes, and needs will vary considerably depending on their particular circumstances.

■ *Protect young people from discrimination.* When professionals find that ethnic minority children are treated unfairly, they can strive to establish fairer procedures. For example, the court systems sometimes treat young people of color more punitively than they treat European American juveniles (A. Liberman, Winterfield, & McElroy, 1996). To address this inequity, juvenile justice professionals can establish clear, systematic criteria to guide decisions about punishment so that personal, unconscious biases are less influential (Champion, 2001).

■ *Accept the validity of cultural viewpoints that differ from your own.* All professionals make assumptions that come from the cultural environments—mainstream or not—in which they grew up. Like all human beings, teachers, counselors, and other practitioners favor their own attitudes and see their ideas as the way things "should" be, particularly if they belong to the dominant culture (P. J. Miller & Goodnow, 1995). They then tend to interpret other people's actions accordingly (Hong et al., 2000). For instance, middle-income European American teachers sometimes judge low-income African American students as having lower maturity and social competence than middle-income European American students, even when the two groups of students are similar (Alexander, Entwisle, & Thompson, 1987). They are also more likely to attribute low achievement in ethnic minority students to problems in families rather than to problems in schools—racist behaviors of peers, ethnic stereotypes in curricula, or discrimination in special education placements (Kailin, 1999).

Furthermore, although very few professionals intentionally discriminate against young people based on the color of their skin (Sleeter & Grant, 1999), their actions sometimes perpetuate group differences. For instance, some teachers call on and praise students who are European American, male, and middle class more than other students (G. Jackson & Cosca, 1974; Sadker & Sadker, 1988). Other teachers rarely modify or individualize instruction for students with diverse needs; instead, they present instruction in a take-it-or-leave-it manner (Sleeter & Grant, 1999).

Many practitioners have become increasingly motivated to help children from diverse backgrounds achieve academic success. Yet considerable naïveté remains. In a study of teacher education students' attitudes toward working with African American students (Bakari, 2000), many prospective teachers expressed willingness to teach such students, for instance agreeing with such statements as "I would enjoy the opportunity to motivate African American students" and "I feel personally invested in helping African American children achieve." However, they less often agreed with statements that reflected sensitivity to African American perspectives, such as "I respect African American culture" and "African American literature is important when teaching African American children to read." Clearly, teaching and guiding children in a culturally sensitive manner requires more than giving lip service to cultural diversity; it requires a genuine commitment to modifying interactions with children so they can truly achieve their full academic potential.

Practitioners naturally make assumptions based on the cultural environment in which they grew up. They should be aware of this tendency and accept that others' cultural viewpoints are also valid.

OBSERVATION GUIDELINES

Identifying Cultural Practices and Beliefs

CHARACTERISTIC	LOOK FOR	EXAMPLE	IMPLICATION
Individualism (characteristic of many European American groups)	• Independence, assertiveness, and self-reliance • Eagerness to pursue individual assignments and tasks • Willingness to compete against others • Pride in one's own accomplishments	When given the choice of doing a project either by herself or with a partner in her girls' club, Melissa decides to work alone. She is thrilled when she earns a third-place ribbon in a statewide competition.	Provide time for independent work, and accommodate children's individual achievement levels. Give feedback about personal accomplishments in private rather than in front of peers.
Collectivism (characteristic of many African American, Asian, Hispanic, and Native American groups)	• Willingness to depend on others • Emphasis on group accomplishments over individual achievements • Preference for cooperative rather than competitive tasks • Concern about bringing honor to one's family • Strong sense of loyalty to other family members	Tsusha is a talented and hard-working seventh grader. She is conscientious about bringing home her graded work assignments to show her parents, but she appears uncomfortable when praised in front of classmates.	Stress group progress and achievement more than individual successes. Make frequent use of cooperative learning activities.
Behavior Toward Authority Figures	• Looking down in the presence of an authority figure (common in many Native American, African American, Mexican American, and Puerto Rican children) *vs.* looking an authority figure in the eye (common in many children of European American descent) • Observing an adult quietly (an expectation in some Native American and some Hispanic groups) *vs.* asking questions when one doesn't understand (common in many European American groups)	A Native American child named Jimmy never says a word to his teacher. He looks frightened when his teacher looks him in the eye and greets him each morning. One day, the teacher looks in another direction and says, "Hello, Jimmy" as he enters the classroom. "Why hello Miss Jacobs," he responds enthusiastically (Gilliland, 1988, p. 26).	Recognize that different cultures show respect for authority figures in different ways; don't misinterpret lack of eye contact or nonresponse as an indication of disinterest or disrespect.
Cognitive Tools	• Focus on the abstract properties of objects and ideas (common in many European American communities) • Preference for personal anecdotes about objects and events (common in some Native American and some African American groups)	A scout leader asks his boys to categorize rocks and minerals and guess how they were formed. Francisco talks about volcanoes and sandstone, whereas Seymour groups specimens based on ones similar to those in his grandmother's rock garden.	When presenting natural substances and materials, refer both to abstract concepts and ideas and to objects and experiences in children's everyday lives.
Valued Activities	• Hopes for high achievement in traditional academic areas (common in many cultural groups in Western countries) • Devaluing of school achievement as representative of white culture (evident in some students from minority groups) • Expectations for excellence in culture-specific activities, such as art or dance (often seen in traditional Native American and Polynesian communities)	Clarence is obviously a very bright young man, but he shows considerable ambivalence about doing well in his high school classes. He often earns high marks on quizzes and tests, but he rarely participates in class discussions or turns in homework assignments.	Show how academic subject matter relates to children's lives. Acknowledge youngsters' achievement in nonacademic as well as academic pursuits. Allow young people to keep their accomplishments confidential from age-mates so that they can maintain credibility with peers who don't value school achievement.
Conceptions of Time	• Concern for punctuality and acknowledgment of deadlines for assignments (common for many students of European descent) • Lack of concern for specific times and schedules (observed in some Hispanic and Native American communities)	Lucy is often late for her counseling appointments. Her parents are diligent about bringing her to appointments but do not always arrive at the time they have scheduled with the counselor.	Encourage punctuality as a way of enhancing children's long-term success in mainstream Western society. At the same time, recognize that not all children are especially concerned about clock time. Be flexible when parents seem to disregard strict schedules.

Sources: Banks & Banks, 1995; K. H. Basso, 1984; E. E. Garcia, 1994; Garrison, 1989; Gilliland, 1988; Grant & Gomez, 2001; Heath, 1983; Irujo, 1988; Kirschenbaum, 1989; Losey, 1995; McAlpine & Taylor, 1993; L. S. Miller, 1995; Ogbu, 1994; Reid, 1989; Shweder, Goodnow, Hatano, LeVine, Markus, & Miller, 1998; Tharp, 1994; Torres-Guzmán, 1998; Trawick-Smith, 2000; Triandis, 1995.

■ *Include numerous cultural perspectives in curricula and programs for young people.* Textbooks and other instructional materials almost invariably reflect the cultural biases of their authors. For example, when Sleeter and Grant (1991) analyzed American textbooks for students in grades 1 through 8, they found that certain themes, such as the following, were rarely stated overtly but were assumed:

> The United States is the land of wealth and opportunity . . . open to all who try.
>
> American history flowed from Europe to the east coast of North America; from there it flowed westward.
>
> American culture is of European origin; Europe is the main source of worthwhile cultural achievements.
>
> National ideals are (and should be) individual advancement, private accumulation, rule by the majority as well as by market demand, loyalty to the U.S. government, and freedom of speech.
>
> Americans share consensus about most things; differences are individual and can be talked out. . . .
>
> Other places in the world may have poverty and problems, but the United States does not; [America] tend[s] to solve other nations' problems. (Sleeter & Grant, 1999, p. 117)

As you read the list of themes, you undoubtedly found some (e.g., the "ideal" of individual advancement) that conflict with the values of certain cultural groups and others (e.g., the belief that Americans share consensus about most things) that fly in the face of what you know to be true.

To the extent that societies are the multicultural mosaic we spoke of earlier, it is essential that curricula, instructional methods, counseling techniques, and community programs reflect this diversity. True multicultural education is not limited to cooking ethnic foods, celebrating Cinco de Mayo, or studying famous African Americans during Black History Month—strategies that Ladson-Billings (1994) calls a "foods and festivals" approach. Rather, **multicultural education** includes experiences of numerous cultural groups—and also those of both men and women, people of varying sexual orientations, and people with disabilities—on a regular basis (Banks, 1995; E. E. García, 1995; Hollins, 1996; NCSS Task Force on Ethnic Studies Curriculum Guidelines, 1992). Following are examples of what teachers might do:

- In history, look at wars and other major events from diverse perspectives (e.g., the Spanish perspective of the Spanish-American War and Native American groups' views of pioneers' westward migration in North America).
- In social studies, examine discrimination and oppression.
- In literature, present the work of minority authors and poets.
- In art, consider creations and techniques by artists from around the world.
- In music, teach songs from many cultures and nations.
- In physical education, teach games or folk dances from other countries and cultures.

(Asai, 1993; Boutte & McCormick, 1992; Casanova, 1987; Cottrol, 1990; K. Freedman, 2001; Koza, 2001; NCSS Task Force on Ethnic Studies Curriculum Guidelines, 1992; Pang, 1995; Sleeter & Grant, 1999; Ulichny, 1994)

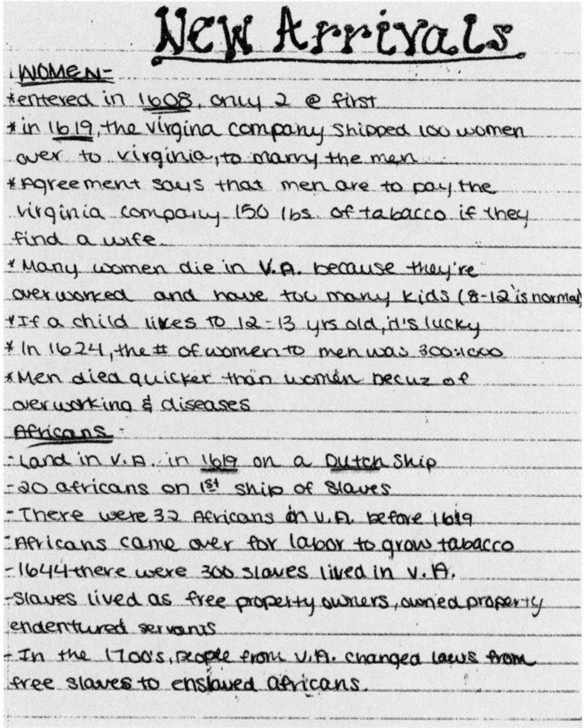
New Arrivals
WOMEN-
*entered in 1608, only 2 @ first
*in 1619, the virgina company shipped 100 women over to virginia, to marry the men
*Agreement says that men are to pay the virginia company 150 lbs. of tabacco if they find a wife.
*Many women die in V.A. because they're overworked and have too many kids (8-12 is normal)
*If a child likes to 12-13 yrs old, it's lucky
*In 1624, the # of women to men was 300:1000
*Men died quicker than women becuz of overworking & diseases
Africans-
-Land in V.A. in 1619 on a Dutch ship
-20 africans on 1st ship of slaves
-There were 32 Africans in V.A. before 1619
-Africans came over for labor to grow tabacco
-1644 there were 300 slaves lived in V.A.
-Slaves lived as free property owners, owned property endentured servants
-In the 1700's, people from V.A. changed laws from free slaves to enslaved africans.

FIGURE 14–1 Thirteen-year-old Carol took these notes in her American history class. Throughout the unit, her teacher made a point of discussing the perspectives of different groups. Carol's notes show that she learned about the hardships faced by men and women in the new world in the 1600s; she also learned about European settlers, African settlers, and enslaved Africans.

multicultural education
Education that includes the perspectives and experiences of numerous cultural groups on a regular basis.

One teacher's efforts to include perspectives of distinct groups are featured in Figure 14–1. The figure shows 13-year-old Carol's notes on her teacher's remarks during an eighth-grade American history class. In previous lessons, Carol learned about lasting contributions Native Americans made to American government, art, language, food, and sports. She also learned about the courageous voyage of Christopher Columbus and his abysmal treatment of Native Americans. Here, Carol has taken notes on the "New Arrivals" who came to the New World in the 1600s. Notice that her teacher spoke about experiences of men and women; she also referred to European settlers as well as African settlers and enslaved Africans.

As teachers and other practitioners explore cultures with youngsters, they should look for commonalities as well as differences. For example, they might study how various cultural groups celebrate the beginning of a new year, discovering that "out with the old and in with the new" is a common theme (Ramsey, 1987). At the secondary level, classes might explore issues faced by adolescents of all cultures: gaining the respect of elders, forming trusting relationships with peers, and finding a meaningful place in society (Ulichny, 1994). One important goal of multicultural education should be to communicate that people ultimately are more alike than different.

■ *Foster respect for diverse cultures and ethnic groups.* In addition to taking children's cultural backgrounds into account when interacting with them, teachers and other practitioners should convey that all cultural perspectives have merit. They should select materials that represent cultural groups in a positive and competent light—for instance, by choosing textbooks, works of fiction, and videotapes that portray people of varying ethnic backgrounds as legitimate participants in their society rather than as exotic "curiosities" who live in a separate world. Teachers and other professionals should also avoid or modify materials that portray members of minority groups in an overly simplistic, romanticized, exaggerated, or otherwise stereotypical fashion (Banks, 1994; Boutte & McCormick, 1992; Pang, 1995).

■ *Create opportunities for children with diverse backgrounds to interact.* When young people have positive interactions with people from backgrounds other than their own, they gain further respect for different cultures. In culturally heterogeneous schools, teachers and school counselors might promote friendships among students from different groups by using cooperative learning activities, teaching basic phrases in other students' native languages, and encouraging schoolwide participation in extracurricular activities. In culturally homogeneous schools, professionals might take youngsters, either physically or vicariously, beyond school boundaries—perhaps engaging them in community service projects that bring them outside their own neighborhoods.

■ *Accept that children may follow practices from two or more cultures.* Earlier we introduced the idea that immigrant children often adjust well when they hold onto their family's cultural beliefs rather than fully replacing them with ideas favored by the dominant society. You may find that children are selective in the customs they absorb from their new communities—remember that this is a healthy approach, not an indication that children are confused about their identity. The same principle holds for multi-ethnic children. Children raised with parents from different ethnic cultures are likely to value traditions from both sides of the family.

■ *When cultural conflicts occur, find constructive ways to address them.* Occasionally, children and families follow cultural practices that are contradictory—at least on the surface—to those followed by professionals. When this happens, it is a good idea to learn more about these practices. Investing this effort, professionals will be better prepared to appreciate why children act as they do ("OK, avoiding certain foods shows their religious devotion; they do not mean to be disrespectful, and I can certainly offer other snack choices").

Cultural conflicts may require discussions with colleagues and supervisors. For example, Antonia Lopez asked her child care staff to discuss a practice followed by parents in their Mexican American community (Bredekamp & Copple, 1997). Following a cultural custom, parents showed appreciation to teachers by giving them individual gifts. Teachers became concerned that parents felt pressure to give gifts and to compete against one another. Teachers wished to build a team spirit in families and worried that competition among families might undermine that goal. Yet teachers did not wish to reject parents' kind gestures:

> They worked out a strategy to accept gifts on behalf of the entire center. . . . Once they made a commitment to resolve the contradiction without choosing between the values of the families and the school, the question became, "How can we receive the gifts in the spirit in which they are offered?"[3]

---

[3] From *Developmentally Appropriate Practice in Early Childhood Programs, Revised Edition* (p. 47), by S. Bredekamp and C. Copple, 1997, Washington, D.C.: NAEYC. Reprinted with permission from the National Association for the Education of Young Children.

Showing respect for diverse cultural perspectives does not necessarily mean that "anything goes" or that there are no moral judgments to be made. No one, for example, needs to embrace a culture in which people's basic human rights are blatantly violated. It does mean, however, that adults and children must try to understand another cultural group's behaviors within the context of that culture's beliefs and assumptions (M. N. Cohen, 1998). Ultimately, any culturally sensitive group must espouse such democratic ideals as respect for human dignity, equality, and justice as well as tolerance for diverse points of view (Cottrol, 1990; NCSS Task Force on Ethnic Studies Curriculum Guidelines, 1992; Sleeter & Grant, 1999).

Cultural ideas and practices differ between groups but they also change over time. We now turn to historical events as additional contexts in which children develop.

Historical Era

In the field of child development, *history* means large-scale events that bring about social change, including war, famine, acts of terror, prosperity, and technological advances. Historical events dramatically affect socialization of children and adolescents, but their effects are tempered by gender, age, birth order, religious background, and family income (Levi & Schmitt, 1997). Consider the following contexts for young people during various periods in history:

- In ancient Rome, young men often entered into military service, where they were socialized to curb their impulses and comply with commands of leaders. As a mass of foot soldiers acting in unity, they were strong; as individuals acting on their own, they had little power (Fraschetti, 1997).
- In medieval Spain, age 10 marked the transition from childhood to adulthood for girls, and marriages of 10- to 12-year-old girls were common (Horowitz, 1997).
- In the 18th and 19th centuries, many African American children became indentured servants. These children were removed from their own family and placed in a new family, for whom they had to work hard doing chores, and by whom they were given housing, meals, and a basic education (Shannon, 2002).

These specific destinies for young people required distinct socialization patterns. Think about how the "right stuff" would vary for young people serving in the military, marrying at a young age, or being separated from their family while working for unfamiliar people. Some historical circumstances undoubtedly put a strain on children's coping skills; in many eras, extended family members and other concerned community members have stepped forward to help struggling children (Shannon, 2002).

What opportunities and liabilities do modern times offer young people? In some ways, our own children have had more opportunities and resources—school trips to France and Spain, handheld calculators that quickly graph complex algebraic formulas, access to a wealth of information on the World Wide Web—than we had as children. In a complex and increasingly international society, economic, political, and social conditions can change quickly, however. For example, with a stock market collapse or unexpected layoffs at a parent's workplace, a family's financial security can deteriorate overnight. During times of political upheaval, terrorism, and civil war, children may suddenly find themselves orphaned and homeless.

Historical events do not influence all children in the same way. For instance, war, economic collapses, and other traumatic circumstances often affect older children and adolescents more intensely than toddlers and preschoolers (Baltes, Reese, & Lipsitt, 1980). Teresa's two sons provide an illustration. On the first anniversary of the disaster at Columbine High School, in which two Colorado high school students shot and killed 12 of their classmates and one of their teachers, 12-year-old Connor was reluctant to attend school, as were many of his classmates. In comparison, 5-year-old Alex knew little of the event and showed no fear.

Older adolescents are perhaps the most thoughtful about historical events. For example, in 1985, Schuman and Scott (1989) asked a large sample of American adults about which national and world events in the past 50 years were most important. Most respondents chose events that had occurred when they were in their late teens or early 20s: Adults who were 70 and older tended to choose the Great Depression as the most important event;

adults in their 30s and 40s in 1985 chose the assassination of John F. Kennedy; adults between 18 and 23 identified terrorism.

Type of exposure to historical events is also an important factor in how young people respond. When children and adolescents personally experience traumatic historical events, such as war or violence, they initially respond in a disorganized fashion (perhaps appearing stunned or detached) and have trouble comprehending and believing what has happened. Later, they cycle through intense emotions such as anger, sadness, and depression (Casarez-Levison, 2000). Adults cannot assume that youngsters who recently experienced trauma or upheaval will rebound quickly. In fact, professionals can be helpful by offering reassurance over an extended period of time (see Chapter 9 for helping children deal with troubling emotions).

Even when young people are not themselves affected by current events, they often learn about them through school curricula and community programs. For instance, a natural disaster affecting a nearby region (e.g., an earthquake or hurricane) provides a chance for youngsters to organize fundraisers and in other ways help those who have suffered losses. When young people actively participate in such service, they often conclude that they can make positive contributions to society.

Religious Affiliation

Dear Mr. Lincoln,

you were a great presadent. I'm glad you freed the slaves is it fun up there in hevin

Yours truly,

Jared

As 7-year-old Jared's letter to Abraham Lincoln illustrates, religious beliefs affect many children's interpretations of the world.

For many children and adolescents, religious beliefs imbue everyday events with meaning. Fighting with your brother? God wants us to get along. Suffering from asthma? Seek a spiritual healer. Dad lost his job? We pray for God's guidance. Grandpa died last week? He's joined the great oneness of spirits. Victim of oppression? Come to church for comfort. Confused? Read the Bible, the Koran, the writings of Malcolm X, the scriptures of Buddha, the philosophy of Confucius, or one of many other sources of spiritual and humanitarian inspiration.

In an average week, 43% of adults in the United States visit a church or synagogue, and a larger percentage have religious beliefs that affect their actions in some way (Bezilla, 1993; Gallup, 1996). Of those who have a religious preference, the great majority of U.S. citizens align with a denomination of Christianity (e.g., they are Protestant, Roman Catholic, Eastern Orthodox, Latter Day Saint), Judaism (e.g., they are Orthodox, Reform, Conservative), or Islam (Gollnick & Chinn, 2002).

Religion affects roles that people adopt as marital partners, the ways in which they raise their children, and the expectations they have for school curricula. Religion is also correlated with the moral judgments they make (Narvaez, Getz, Rest, & Thoma, 1999). For growing children and adolescents, religion is a factor in dress and appearance, social activities, choice of friends, and decisions about smoking and alcohol consumption (Gollnick & Chinn, 2002). Children's religious affiliations (or lack thereof) may also affect relationships with peers: For instance, members of mainstream religious groups occasionally harass members of small religious sects (e.g., Jehovah's Witnesses, Children of God, the Unification Church) and children of atheistic parents (Gollnick & Chinn, 2002). And regrettably, in some families and organizations religion provides a pretext for articulating anti-Semitic, anti-Muslim, and anti-Catholic sentiments.

Because people often worship, reflect, and contemplate together, religious affiliation can lend social support to children and families. For example, many churches that serve predominantly African American populations offer members a safe haven from racism, a chance to be connected with a community committed to protecting one another's welfare, a forum for cultural self-expression, and the possibility of spiritual transcendence (Poole, 1990). Religious and nonreligious orientations also provide ways to think about social responsibility. In Figure 14–2, you can see how children holding distinct religious and philosophical beliefs share a disposition for caring for other people.

As with all aspects of development, children's spiritual and philosophical convictions evolve over time. We now examine one model that describes changes in children's thinking about religion, spirituality, and the meaning of life.

Thirteen-year-old Sajid, a Muslim boy from London, reflects on Allah's teachings as explained to him by his father:

> Either you give to the poor, to your neighbor, or you risk lots of trouble when you die …[My father] said I should still try to be very good in school, in all that I do; but I should help my friends, too. You should be generous; you should give help to others. (Coles, 1990, pp. 240–41)

Seven-year-old Fred describes the Christian values he has learned and his 6-year-old brother, Ray, draws a nativity scene.

Eleven-year-old Sylvia comes from an agnostic family and articulates her beliefs:

> I didn't say there's nothing out there; I know there is a lot to live for. I love my family, and I love my friends. I love it when we go to a new place on a trip, and I can see new people, and you can stand there—like up in Vermont or New Hampshire—and look at all

the land, for miles (if you're up a mountain), and the trees, and you're nearer the clouds. (Coles, 1990, p. 299)

Five-year-old Lindsey has drawn a picture of Buddha. Her drawing and commentary are posted to an online Buddhist website:

> If you look in the triangle, it will make you gooder …because there are people doing nice things in there. And thinking about it will make you nice. First when you look it is just scribble—but if you look closer (that is why the Buddha is closing one eye) you can seem [sic] them being nice. (The Online Buddhist Family Center, 2003; http://www.idsl.net/heather/onlinebuddhistcenter/welcome.html). Reprinted with permission of Heather K. Woollard.

On Yom Kippur, 12-year-old Maggie prepares for her Bat Mitzvah and learns moral lessons from her Rabbi:

> The rabbi explained that the point of our coming together for Yom Kippur was to think about what we had done wrong in the past year and to think about our relationships with each other, with friends and family. She said that sometimes the services get boring and that's when we're meant to think about who we are as people and how to help in our communities.

FIGURE 14–2 Children use their religious and nonreligious beliefs to help interpret life's meaning and obligations.

Fowler's Stages of Faith

James Fowler (1981) proposed that religious and philosophical beliefs develop in a predictable sequence. Initially, the trust that children establish with parents predisposes them to accept parents' beliefs. As children grow older, they make sense of preaching in accordance with their current reasoning abilities. Drawing from the theories of Jean Piaget, Erik Erikson, and Lawrence Kohlberg (see Chapters 4, 9, and 10, respectively) and from interviews with children and adolescents, Fowler proposed the following *stages of faith*:

Stage 1: Intuitive-projective faith. In early childhood, children apply an active imagination to construct their own interpretations of religious ideas and symbols. In the following interview, 6-year-old Freddy illustrates intuitive-projective faith in his description of a powerful God:

Interviewer:	When you do something bad, does God know?
Freddy:	Yes, He spreads all around the world in one day.
Interviewer:	He does? How does he do that?
Freddy:	He does 'cause he's smart.

Interviewer:	He's smart? How does he get all around the world in one day?
Freddy:	Uh—he can split or he can be like a God.
Interviewer:	He can split into a lot of things?
Freddy:	Yeah. (Fowler, 1981, p. 128)[4]

Stage 2: Mythic-literal faith.   In middle childhood, children continue to make sense of religion, now striving for logical coherence. Such reasoning is evident in an interview with 10-year-old Millie:

Interviewer:	. . . [T]ell me now why you think there are people here in the world. Are they here for any purpose?
Millie:	There—well, if there wasn't any people in the world, who would keep God company?
Interviewer:	Is that why people are here?
Millie:	I don't know, but that question just popped into my mind. How—how would God keep busy?
Interviewer:	And what does God do with people?
Millie:	He—he makes the people. He tries to give them good families. And he, he, um, made the world. He made trees and everything. If you didn't have trees you wouldn't have books. And if you didn't—like he made the whole world, which has a lot of beauty and that makes up things. Like rocks make metals and some kinds of rocks make metal. (Fowler, 1981, p. 138)[5]

Religious ideas in mythic-literal faith reflect a dependence on concrete reality that characterizes thinking during middle childhood. Consider what Millie says when the interviewer asks her to describe what God looks like:

Millie:	I imagine that he's an old man with a white beard and white hair wearing a long robe and that the clouds are his floor and he has a throne. And he has all these people and there's angels around him. And there's all the good people, angels and—and um, cupids and that he has like—I guess I—he has a nice face, nice blue eyes. (Fowler, 1981, p. 138)[6]

By and large, children in middle childhood unquestioningly accept religious doctrines and practices that their parents and others pass down to them, and the concrete aspects of religion are far more salient than the abstract—and ultimately more central—qualities. Nine-year-old Noah describes himself as both Jewish and Christian primarily because his mother and father are, respectively, Jewish and Christian; in Figure 14–3, he focuses on the concrete advantages of his affiliations.

Stage 3: Synthetic-conventional faith.   In adolescence, abstract understandings about religion become possible. Initially, however, adolescents have difficulty distinguishing between concrete religious symbols and abstract meanings they represent, and they do not seriously question beliefs that others have passed along to them. In the following interview, 15-year-old Linda reveals an abstract notion of God as well as an acceptance of what her parents have told her:

Interviewer:	Linda, when you say you *know* what you believe in . . . can you try to trace *how* you came to know what you believe in?
Linda:	I guess religion. I've always gone to church and everything. And my parents, they always guided me. . . . They've always taught me that God's always there and, you know, he's the only way that you can really make it. . . . You depend upon him and I really believe in him and, you know how they say God talks in many mysterious ways? Well, in a sense he's told me lots of times . . . I really think that he's led me to where I am today. 'Cause lots of times I've just thought the world is just, you know, I just don't feel anything. But then that morning I'll just have a feeling that . . . I guess there is Somebody, you know?
Interviewer:	What do you think God is?

FIGURE 14–3 In middle childhood, children's notions of religion are fairly concrete. Here 9-year-old Noah conceptualizes Christmas and Hanukkah as a time for getting presents.

[4, 5, 6] Excerpts from *Stages of Faith: The Psychology of Human Development and the Quest for Meaning* by James W. Fowler. Copyright © 1981 by James W. Fowler. Reprinted by permission of HarperCollins Publishers, Inc.

Linda: God is different to a lot of people. . . . I don't exactly go by the Bible. I think you should try to make the world . . . you should try to make people happy and at the same time enjoy yourself, you know? In a good kind way . . . (Fowler, 1981, pp. 155–156)[7]

According to Fowler, many young people stop at Stage 3: Although they may make minor adjustments to what others have told them (e.g., Linda acknowledges that she doesn't completely "go by the Bible"), by and large they accept their religious legacy. But some adolescents eventually become uncomfortable with what they've been told, as the next stage illustrates.

Stage 4: Individuative-reflective faith. In their late teens or early 20s, some young people critically examine their religious beliefs and assumptions. They place their religion within its historical context and begin to understand how it has been shaped by many social, political, and economic factors over the years. Thus, individuative-reflective faith is characterized by a more analytic attitude and more conscious decision making about one's own beliefs. Sixteen-year-old Brian, whom Fowler classified as still being in Stage 3, is beginning to show a critical attitude characteristic of individuative-reflective faith:

Interviewer: It bothers you, this sense of the unknown about what happens at death?
Brian: Right, because it's unexplainable. We only make up what we feel is the answer. Just take that. Maybe the answer is something that no one can grasp because no one is really smart enough or it's something completely beyond our conceptions of being able to grasp what life is about and something like that. It makes me think quite a bit; I don't know about anyone else, but not being able to grasp an idea—it's physically impossible to grasp that idea—really bothers me and makes me think about it. (Fowler, 1981, pp. 160–161)[8]

Some evidence is consistent with Fowler's belief that adolescents take a critical stance toward religion: The vast majority of teenagers (90%) report that they pray, but only 25% report that they are highly confident in organized religion (Gallup & Poling, 1980). Other teens who are inquisitive yet insecure may be attracted to small "cult" religions in which extensive training programs try to convert new members (Swope, 1980). Overall, religious development during adolescence appears to be related to other changes, such as an increasing capacity for abstract reasoning and emotional vulnerabilities (Elkind, 1978; Pipher, 1994).[9]

As you think about Fowler's stages, keep in mind that he based them on three theories that do not necessarily provide airtight explanations of child and adolescent development (see the critiques of Piaget, Erikson, and Kohlberg in Chapters 4, 9, and 10). Furthermore, his interviews with children were limited (Fowler does not say how many he interviewed) and apparently restricted to those raised in Christian, Jewish, and Unitarian homes; thus, his stages of faith do not necessarily characterize accurately the religious development of children around the world.

Religion in Schools and Other Settings

Religion is a positive guiding force in many children's lives. It is ironic, then, that religious affiliations can be a source of problems in the classroom and community (Gollnick & Chinn, 2002). Some children make inappropriate remarks based on their own religious beliefs or those of their peers ("Mei-Chang's a Buddhist. How weird!" "Those kids in the Bible Club are Jesus Freaks!"). And families' diverse beliefs can create controversies about appropriate curriculum and reading materials (Should evolution or biblical creationism be taught? Should sex education take place at school or home?).

[7,8] Excerpts from *Stages of Faith: The Psychology of Human Development and the Quest for Meaning* by James W. Fowler. Copyright © 1981 by James W. Fowler. Reprinted by permission of HarperCollins Publishers, Inc.
[9] Fowler believed that additional changes were possible in adulthood, such as formulating a deep commitment to one's beliefs.

In the United States, the First Amendment to the Constitution requires that matters of church and state be kept separate. Public school teachers can certainly discuss religions within the context of curricula about history, culture, or other appropriate academic topics. But teachers and other public figures cannot incorporate religious ideas or practices into classroom activities or community events in any way that shows preference for one religion over another, or even a preference for religion over atheism. Nevertheless, we acknowledge religion as an important source of diversity among children and families, and ask that you consider the following suggestions:

◾ *Become aware of religious diversity in the community where you work.* At the practical level, professionals should think about religious holidays and observances whenever they schedule meetings and conferences with families, school events, community celebrations, counseling sessions, and so on. Moreover, they must certainly avoid giving preferential treatment to youngsters from religious (or nonreligious) backgrounds similar to their own.

◾ *Foster a climate of religious tolerance.* Just as professionals foster respect for diverse cultural backgrounds, so, too, they should foster respect for diverse religious beliefs. If young people are to work effectively in adult society, they must learn that many different religious persuasions have value and that their nation guarantees citizens' right to religious freedom. Many school districts and other institutions have policies that prohibit any name-calling that denigrates others' religious beliefs, practices, and affiliations.

◾ *Work with your colleagues to cultivate productive communication with families about controversial issues.* Parents and other community members often participate in decisions about school curricula, and some have strong religious convictions about whether certain content (e.g., creationism, birth control) should be included. Crafting a reasonable compromise when people hold firmly to differing religious doctrines often takes hard work from professionals, but in many cases it can be done. Sometimes, of course, when children's safety or legal rights are at stake, compromise is out of the question. Even in these circumstances, however, professionals must never discredit parents' religious beliefs.

Socioeconomic Status

When Gloria Ladson-Billings enrolled in an integrated junior high school far from her own neighborhood, she noticed a clear difference between the jobs and income levels of her classmates' parents and those of her own mother and father. This difference reflected their unequal **socioeconomic status** (SES), their standing in the community based on such variables as occupation, income, and education level. A family's socioeconomic status—whether high-SES, middle-SES, or low-SES—gives us a sense of how much flexibility they have with regard to where they live and what they buy, how much influence they have in political decision making, what educational opportunities they can offer children, and so on. When we have spoken of "middle-income" and "low-income" families and children in previous chapters, we have been referring to socioeconomic status.

On average, children and adolescents from low-SES backgrounds achieve at lower levels than young people from middle-SES backgrounds, and the gap between the two groups widens as youngsters move through the grade levels (Jimerson, Egeland, & Teo, 1999; McLoyd, 1998b; L. S. Miller, 1995). Low-SES youngsters also exhibit more frequent and severe behavior problems at school and are more likely to drop out prior to high school graduation (McLoyd, 1998b; J. D. Nichols, Ludwin, & Iadicola, 1999; Rumberger, 1995). It's important to stress, however, that other factors—for instance, children's activities and the guidance they get from their parents—are far more predictive of academic accomplishments than is socioeconomic status per se (Hoover-Dempsey & Sandler, 1997; Jimerson et al., 1999; McLoyd, 1998b; Seaton et al., 1999; Walberg & Paik, 1997). For instance, like many others, Gloria Ladson-Billings achieved considerable success (she holds a Ph.D. from Stanford University and is a college professor) despite growing up poor. Her parents' decision to send her to a high-quality junior high school and her own motivations and abilities proved to be more important than her parents' socioeconomic status.

socioeconomic status (SES)
One's general social and economic standing in society, encompassing such variables as family income, occupation, and education level.

Low-income families are a diverse lot. They range from families who carefully watch their budgets but can afford basic necessities to families who live in abject poverty. In the following sections we look at effects of poverty on children's development, discover how some children successfully overcome the challenges of an economically impoverished environment, and identify strategies for working with children and adolescents from low-income families.

Poverty

Ideally, it's what you do, not what you have, that matters. But this generalization may not hold for the truly needy. Families living in poverty have so little that they have few options as to what they can do for their children. And there are many more children living in poverty than most people realize: During 2000, approximately 16% of American children lived in poverty (e.g., income rates were $17,602 or less for families with four people). An additional 21% of children live in low-income families who miss the poverty cutoff but nevertheless must struggle to make ends meet (e.g., incomes rates were between $17,603 and $35,205 for families of four). Thus, more than one in every three children lives in a low-income family (Federal Interagency Forum on Child and Family Statistics, 2002).

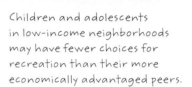

Children and adolescents in low-income neighborhoods may have fewer choices for recreation than their more economically advantaged peers.

In addition to being alarmingly high, poverty rates are disproportionate across ethnic groups: African American, Native American, and Hispanic children are far more likely to be poor than are children from European American backgrounds (McLoyd, 1998a; Sidel, 1996). Nonetheless, we must be careful not to overgeneralize, as poor people come from all walks of life:

> Poor . . . are young, they are middle-aged, and they are old. They are from rural Maine and Mississippi, from New York, Detroit, and Los Angeles, from small towns in the Midwest, from the mining towns of Appalachia, and from the suburban communities that ring the major cities. They are married, divorced, separated, widowed, and never married. They are from all backgrounds—white, African-American, Latina, Asian-American, Native American, and many others on whom the Census Bureau does not keep detailed data. They are full-time workers, part-time workers, the unemployed and the underemployed. They are high school dropouts and high school graduates; some have attended college, some have even completed college. (Sidel, 1996, p. 65)

Poverty is a brief experience for some and an ongoing way of life for others. Sadly, 5% of children—1 in 20—spend 10 years or more in poverty (Center for the Future of Children, 1997). Spending one's early childhood years in poverty seems to be particularly difficult. Low income during the preschool years is more predictive of low rates of high school completion than is low income during later childhood and adolescence (Baydar, Brooks-Gunn, & Furstenberg, 1993; Brooks-Gunn & Duncan, 1997; Center for the Future of Children, 1997; G. J. Duncan, Yeung, Brooks-Gunn, & Smith, 1998).

Risk Factors Associated with Poverty   Children and adolescents living in poverty face challenges beyond those normally associated with physical, cognitive, and social-emotional development:

- *Poor nutrition and health care.*   Some children are poorly fed and have little access to adequate health care; as a result, they may suffer from malnutrition and other chronic health problems (Center for the Future of Children, 1997; L. S. Miller, 1995). Children who receive inadequate nutrition during their prenatal development or first few years of life may experience one or more serious developmental problems, such as having a small brain, experiencing brain damage, being delayed in their cognitive and motor skills, and being too weak to explore the environment (Tanner & Finn-Stevenson, 2002).
- *Inadequate housing.*   Many children live in tight quarters, perhaps sharing one or two rooms with several other family members. For instance, teacher Frances

Hawkins describes what often happened when her inner-city Boston preschoolers played with a dollhouse:

When we furnished the dollhouse, the children would move all the furniture into one room. It was an "apartment" house to them. They knew no other. (Hawkins, 1997, p. 180)

Some children have no place to live at all, except, perhaps, the family car or a homeless shelter. Children of homeless families often have health problems, low self-esteem, a short attention span, poor language skills, and inappropriate behaviors (Coe, Salamon, & Molnar, 1991; McLoyd, 1998b; Pawlas, 1994). Some may be reluctant to go to school because they lack bathing facilities and presentable clothing (Gollnick & Chinn, 2002).

- *Gaps in background knowledge.* Teachers typically assume that children have had certain kinds of experiences before they begin school—for instance, that they have been read to, have seen many kinds of animals at farms or zoos, and have had ample opportunities to explore their physical environment. However, some children who live in extreme poverty miss out on such foundational experiences (Case, Okamoto, et al., 1996; McLoyd, 1998b). For example, Frances Hawkins reports how her inner-city preschoolers behaved when she gave them a chance to play with toy boats in a tub of water:

    Children *shoved* the boats along. Impatient with the slow floating motion—not familiar with the way things move in water, or just natural impatience with slowness? . . .

    As our understanding of how and where these children lived fell into place, we realized that the chance even to use water, to play with water, was rare. One kitchen, one bath—not always in working order—was normal in a house for three, four, or five families to share. (Hawkins, 1997, p. 187)

    Furthermore, when children move frequently from one school to another—as many homeless children do—they miss some of the early school experiences so essential to their success in later grades (Pawlas, 1994).

- *Increased probability of disabling conditions.* Children who live in poverty are more likely to have physical, mental, or social-emotional disabilities (McLoyd, 1998b; U.S. Department of Education, 1997). In some cases, disabilities are the result of poor nutrition (prenatally or later), exposure to lead paint, and other environmental hazards; in other cases, they may be the result of harsh and inconsistent parenting (Brooks-Gunn & Duncan, 1997; McLoyd, 1998b).

- *Emotional stress.* Children function less effectively when under stress, and many poor families live in chronically stressful conditions (Maccoby & Martin, 1983; Trueba, 1988). The lack of financial resources is one obvious source of anxiety; children may wonder where their next meal is coming from or how long the landlord will wait before evicting them for not paying the rent. The preponderance of single-parent homes among low-SES families is another stress-inducing factor; a single parent may be overwhelmed with worries about supporting the family (Scott-Jones, 1984). In addition, poor children are more likely to be subjected to maltreatment by parents and other adults and to encounter violent crimes in their neighborhoods (Center for the Future of Children, 1997; McLoyd, 1998b; R. A. Thompson & Wyatt, 1999).

- *Lower quality schools.* In the opening case, Gloria Ladson-Billings attended a high school in another part of town because her mother had concerns about the quality of the neighborhood school. Schools in low-income neighborhoods and communities are often poorly funded and equipped, and they have high teacher turnover rates. Furthermore, some teachers at these schools have lower expectations for students—and offer a less demanding curriculum, assign less homework, and set lower standards for performance—than teachers of middle-SES students (McLoyd, 1998b; Murdock, 1999; Portes, 1996).

- *Public misconceptions.* People from economically advantaged backgrounds often have mixed feelings about low-SES families: They may feel pity yet simultaneously believe that poor people are responsible for their misfortunes, perhaps because of laziness, promiscuity, or overdependence on social welfare programs (Chafel, 1997; McLoyd, 1998a; Sidel, 1996). Agents in social service and federal programs sometimes share these conflicted feelings and may come across to the people they serve as uncaring and punitive (McLoyd, 1998a). Teachers of lower-income children—especially teachers who come from upper- and middle-income backgrounds—often have such biases as well, particularly when they have limited knowledge of children's families and cultures (K. Alexander, Entwisle, & Thompson, 1987; McLoyd, 1998b).

The challenges facing children and adolescents living in poverty make it difficult for them to feel optimistic about the future. In Jonathan Kozol's *Amazing Grace*, a teenager named Maria describes her feeling of being ignored by a more affluent society:

> It's not like, "well, these babies just aren't dying fast enough," Maria says. "Let's figure out a way to kill some more." It's not like that at all. It's like—I don't know how to say this. . . . If you weave enough bad things into the fibers of a person's life—sickness and filth, old mattresses and other junk thrown in the streets and other ugly ruined things, and ruined people, a prison here, sewage there, drug dealers here, the homeless people over there, then give us the very worst schools anyone could think of, hospitals that keep you waiting for ten hours, police that don't show up when someone's dying, take the train that's underneath the street in the good neighborhoods and put it up above where it shuts out the sun, you can guess that life will not be very nice and children will not have much sense of being glad of who they are. (Kozol, 1995, pp. 39–40)

Many children and adolescents find the challenges of poverty so overwhelming that they engage in behaviors—dropping out of school, abusing drugs and alcohol, participating in criminal activities—that create further problems. However, the great majority of children and adolescents from poor families do well despite the adversities they face: They appear to be relatively *resilient* in confronting life's hardships.

Resilience

Although children who live in poverty have less reason to be optimistic about their future than their economically advantaged peers, a great number of them set their sights on a better life. For example, during 1996 almost half of 16- to 24-year-olds who completed high school and were from low-income families (those in the bottom 20% of income levels) enrolled in college the following autumn (National Center for Education Statistics, 2003).

The term **resilience** refers to the ability of many young people to beat the odds and succeed in life despite exceptional hardships such as poverty and parental maltreatment. Resilient youngsters develop particular characteristics and coping skills: They have likable personalities, positive self-concepts, strong motivation to succeed, and high yet realistic goals. They believe that success comes with hard work, and their bad experiences serve as constant reminders of the importance of getting a good education (English, 1998; Masten & Coatsworth, 1998; McMillan & Reed, 1994; E. E. Werner, 1995).

Resilient youngsters usually have one or more individuals in their lives whom they trust and know they can turn to in difficult times (English, 1998; Masten & Coatsworth, 1998; R. A. Thompson & Wyatt, 1999; E. E. Werner, 1995). These individuals may be family members, neighbors, or school personnel; for example, many resilient students have been encouraged by teachers who took a personal interest in them (McMillan & Reed, 1994; Paris & Cunningham, 1996). Consider how one teacher, Mr. Taylor, took an interest in Cedric Jennings, the inner-city high school student introduced in Chapter 12 (Suskind, 1998):

> Mr. Taylor . . . has personally invested in Cedric's future since the student appeared in his tenth grade chemistry class—back then, Cedric was a sullen ninth grader who had just been thrown out of biology for talking back to the teacher and needed somewhere to go. Taylor let him sit in, gave him a few assignments that the older kids were doing, and was soon marveling at flawless A papers. Taylor took Cedric for an after-school dinner at Western Sizzlin', and they were suddenly a team.
>
> In the last two years, Taylor has offered his charge a steady stream of extra-credit projects and trips, like a visit last month with scientists at the National Aeronautics and Space Administration. He challenges Cedric with elaborate intellectual puzzles, withholding praise and

resilience
Ability of some children and adolescents to thrive and achieve despite adverse environmental conditions.

daring the pupil to vanquish his theatrical doubting with a real display of intellectual muscle. It's call and response, combative but productive. (p. 6)[10]

Mr. Taylor also offered frequent words of encouragement, especially when Cedric encountered classmates' taunts that he was a "nerd" or acting white:

> "You see, Cedric, you're in a race, a long race. . . . You can't worry about what people say from the sidelines. They're already out of it. You, however, are still on the track. You have to just keep on running. . . . (pp. 6–7)[11]

Working with Children and Adolescents from Low-Income Families

Teaching, guiding, and counseling young people from low-income families can be challenging, but also highly rewarding. Adults who want to "make a difference" in children's lives are most likely to do so in schools, agencies, and other institutions serving low-SES populations. But to be effective, professionals must be committed to their jobs, hold high expectations for children's achievement and success, think creatively about how they can make the most of limited equipment and resources, and show a contagious enthusiasm for learning (L. W. Anderson & Pellicer, 1998; Ogden & Germinario, 1988). Experts offer these recommendations:

■ *Identify and build on the strengths of children and adolescents.* When professionals concentrate on weaknesses, young people easily become discouraged and may soon resign themselves to the idea that their efforts are in vain. In contrast, focusing on what's right with children can generate optimism, enthusiasm, and a definite commitment to learning on the part of adults and children alike.

Although many children from lower-SES backgrounds lag behind peers in such basic academic skills as reading, writing, and computation, they nevertheless bring strengths to the classroom and community. They may have strong social and leadership skills. They are often clever at improvising with everyday objects (Torrance, 1995). For instance, they might think of many functions for a worn-out pair of shoes, such as growing herbs in them or using them as a doorstop on a hot evening. If they work part-time to help their families make ends meet, they may have a good understanding of the working world. If they are children of single, working parents, they may know far more than peers about cooking, cleaning, and taking care of younger siblings (Whiting & Edwards, 1988). Some children know firsthand what it is like to be hungry for days at a time or to live in an unheated apartment in the winter; they may have a special appreciation for basic human needs and true empathy for victims of war and famine. Furthermore, those who are willing to talk about the challenges they've faced can sensitize peers to inequities in society.

When adults provide opportunities for children to build on their strengths, they increase the likelihood that children will be successful (Masten & Coatsworth, 1998). One elementary school established a singing group, called the "Jazz Cats," for low-income fourth and fifth graders (Jenlink, 1994). The group rehearsed regularly, performed at a variety of community events, and enjoyed visibility for its talent. The success of the program extended far beyond music: Many group members exhibited increased self-esteem, improvement in other school subjects, and greater teamwork and leadership skills (Jenlink, 1994). One child's mother reported on the difference she saw in her daughter after being in Jazz Cats:

> Abbey has completely turned around. . . . She's not shy to ask questions anymore. . . . I think the Jazz Cats have helped her with the idea that everything will work its way out. So she doesn't seem to be this angry, quiet little girl any more. She wants to be very loving, very outspoken. (Jenlink, 1994, p. 20)

■ *Create a sense of community.* In Chapter 11, we emphasized the importance of creating a *sense of community* in schools and classrooms. A sense of community is undoubtedly important in nonacademic contexts (community centers, clubs, scout troops, etc.) as well, and may be especially important for youngsters from low-income backgrounds

---

[10, 11] Reprinted with the permission of The Free Press, a Division of Simon & Schuster Adult Publishing Group, from *A Hope in the Unseen* by Ron Suskind. Copyright © 1998 by Ron Suskind.

(L. W. Anderson & Pellicer, 1998; J. Downey, 2000). It can be created by professionals in a variety of ways: They can assign chores on a rotating basis, ask youngsters to give input into the rules to be followed, use cooperative learning activities, involve children and adolescents in cross-grade tutoring, and encourage everyone's participation in extracurricular activities (J. Downey, 2000). Above all, adults must convey that they deeply care about all aspects of youngsters' development and encourage them to succeed both inside and outside of the classroom (Masten & Coatsworth, 1998; McMillan & Reed, 1994; E. E. Werner, 1995).

■ *Establish clear and consistent expectations for children's behavior.* For all children, and especially those who have had more than their share of life's challenges, knowing what's expected is important. It's not enough simply to ask for "responsibility" or "respect for others." Instead, adults should describe their expectations in clear, concrete terms (J. Downey, 2000). For instance, when finishing lunch in the cafeteria, children might be asked explicitly to "empty the napkins and leftovers into the trash bin, put the trays and dishes on the counter, and go quietly outside." When working in cooperative groups, young people might be reminded, "Everyone needs to participate in the discussions and contribute to the group project," and, "It's OK to find fault with ideas, but it's *not* OK to find fault with people." Ideally, professionals should convey such expectations in an informational, rather than controlling, manner (see Chapter 11).

■ *Place a high priority on developing reading skills.* Many children from low-SES backgrounds have poor reading skills, in part because their families may not have the skills or resources to teach them literacy basics at home (see Chapter 8). Yet reading proficiency seems to be a fundamental cornerstone on which many resilient students build their later successes (J. Downey, 2000; V. E. Lee, Winfield, & Wilson, 1991; E. E. Werner, 1993). It is therefore important to identify and address any deficiencies in emergent literacy or reading skills early, ideally in the preschool years or early elementary grades (Chall, 1996).

■ *Show relevance of academic skills to children's lives and needs.* Finding personal relevance in classroom activities and subject matter is important for any child, but it may be especially critical for children from low-SES backgrounds (L. W. Anderson & Pellicer, 1998; Lee-Pearce, Plowman, & Touchstone, 1998). Helping children see how they can use skills in their everyday lives outside the classroom makes learning more meaningful as well as more motivating.

■ *Communicate high expectations for children's success.* Children from low-SES backgrounds often do not expect much of their own academic performance. Typically they also have lower aspirations for higher education and possible careers (Knapp & Woolverton, 1995; S. Taylor, 1994). Yet practitioners can communicate a can-do attitude and back up the message by offering the extra support children may need to achieve ambitious goals. Offering help sessions for challenging classroom material, finding low-cost academic enrichment programs during the summer, and helping adolescents fill out applications for college scholarships are just a few of the forms that such support might take.

■ *Make sure children's basic needs are met.* Social workers and other community service providers can help economically disadvantaged families to find needed resources. For instance, social workers can inform families about food stamp benefits, public health insurance, housing subsidies, and utility assistance (Beverly, 2001). Unfortunately, many families not eligible for such assistance also have unmet basic needs. Many low-income working parents cannot afford adequate medical care or basic clothing for children after they have paid rent and utilities. Professionals can inform these families of community resources to contact.

Child care centers and schools in low-income neighborhoods often make sure children are well fed (e.g., through free or reduced-cost breakfast and lunch programs) and adequately clothed (e.g., through local "jackets for kids" programs). However, some economically disadvantaged children attend schools in more affluent neighborhoods, and teachers and other professionals must be alert for indications that these children need assistance.

■ *Ask children to tell you about their lives.* Asking children to talk about their experiences is a good way for virtually any professional to learn more about children. In one study, "street children" in Cameroon described their lives to researchers (Tchombe, Nuwanyakpa, & Etmonia, 2001). (Street children roam the streets instead of going to school; they sell goods, carry bags for adults, and sometimes steal.) These children talked about many problems, some of which—being hungry, for example—would have been known to community workers. Other problems, such as perceptions of police hostility, came to light only because children were given an opportunity to talk freely about their experiences.

■ *Give homeless children supplies and help them to ease into new communities.* Professionals who work with children of homeless families can help them to adjust to their new settings. For example, teachers, principals, and school counselors might pair homeless children with classmates who can explain school procedures and introduce them to peers; provide a notebook, clipboard, or other portable "desk" on which children can do their homework at the shelter; find adult or teenage volunteers to tutor them at the shelter; ask civic organizations to donate school supplies; meet with parents at the shelter rather than at school; and share copies of homework assignments, school calendars, and newsletters with shelter officials (Pawlas, 1994).

■ *Show compassion for parents' circumstances.* Most parents, including those living in extreme poverty, want their children to do well in school (Stevenson, Chen, & Uttal, 1990). However, many do not have the financial resources, emotional energy, or educational background to help their children achieve academic success (e.g., in the opening case study, Gloria Ladson-Billings could not bring in the neatly typed papers that some of her classmates did). It's all too easy for practitioners to find fault with parents—to think that parents are shirking their obligations to their children—when in fact parents may be doing all they possibly can. In many cases, a visit to children's homes or neighborhoods can give professionals a better understanding of the life challenges they and their families face, as well as insight into their native strengths (Belle, 1984; Hawkins, 1997). Ultimately, professionals work more effectively with parents when they strive to work in partnership with them, rather than placing blame for what parents may or may not do (see Chapter 12).

■ *Seek out good role models for children and adolescents.* Youngsters from some low-income neighborhoods encounter few good role models (Torrance, 1995). Young people are more likely to be optimistic about their future when they meet—and ideally establish close, trusting relationships with—people from their community who have succeeded despite limited financial resources.

Neighborhoods and communities not only can offer potential role models but also support children's development in other ways. We turn now to the numerous ways in which these settings serve as yet another context for development.

Neighborhood and Community

Children's experiences can be very, very different from one community to the next, and even within distinct neighborhoods in a single community. Neighborhoods and communities influence children's development in several ways:

As children gain increasing mobility with age, their neighborhoods expand, as shown in art by Marsalis, age 7½ (top) and by James, age 13 (bottom). Marsalis stays very close to home, but James can easily travel a mile or more on his bicycle.

■ *They affect the peer groups with whom children come into contact.* Children spend a great deal of time close to home, often within hollering distance when they are young, and within easy reach by bicycle, car, bus, or subway as they grow older. Occasionally children maintain long-distance friendships by telephone or the Internet, but such friendships usually supplement, rather than replace, face-to-face contact with age-mates in the local community.

As you should recall from Chapter 13, peer groups play key roles in children's development. They foster the development of social skills, provide companionship and social support, and help children and adolescents make sense of their lives. However, when social problems such as unemployment, violence, and drug use are prevalent in peer groups, then peers can foster social deviance and despair (Crane, 1991; J. R. Harris, 1998). In fact, when children and adolescents move from high-crime neighborhoods to law-abiding ones, their behavior sometimes improves dramatically. Consider Larry Ayuso, a 16-year-old New York City resident with low grades and heavy involvement in crime and drugs:

> Three of his friends had died in drug-related homicides. He was headed for high school dropout and a life (or death) of crime when he was rescued by a program that takes kids out of urban ghettos and puts them somewhere else—somewhere far away. Larry ended up in a small town in New Mexico, living with a middle-class . . . family. Two years later he was making A's and B's, averaging 28 points a game on his high school basketball team, and headed for college. (J. R. Harris, 1998, p. 212)[12]

■ *They affect choices for recreation.*   Children and adolescents make decisions about how to spend their spare time based largely on what opportunities are convenient and affordable. You can see how important recreational opportunities are to youngsters by listening to 14-year-old Brendan in the Neighborhood/Early Adolescence clip of the Observation CD. Here's how Brendan describes his neighborhood:

> There's a lot of people. Nice people. And there's fun stuff to do around here. . . . We play football or sports in the backyards, and we have playgrounds and a basketball court. . . .

Listen to 14-year-old Brendan talk about a sense of community and recreational opportunities in the Neighborhood/Early Adolescence clip of the Observation CD.

Recreational settings in the local neighborhood are especially important for children from low-income families, who rarely travel far from home (D. S. Elliott et al., 1996).

■ *They tell children what society expects them to be as adults.*   The activities in which local adults engage—whether productive employment and community volunteerism, on the one hand, or drug trafficking and gang affiliation, on the other—tell youngsters what behaviors are normal and desirable. When a high percentage of adults in a neighborhood have stable and high-status jobs, children are more likely to stay in school and aspire to similar types of employment (Jencks & Mayer, 1990). Adults who reach out to other people, perhaps doing errands for sick neighbors or hosting a block party, show young people how good citizens act. In the Neighborhood/Late Adolescence clip of the Observation CD, 15-year-old Robin is impressed by friendly gestures from her neighbors:

> Next door there is these two, this old couple. They're really, really nice . . . we went over to their house for a Christmas party one time. The entire neighborhood came.

Listen to 15-year-old Robin talk about friendly neighbors in the Neighborhood/Late Adolescence clip of the Observation CD.

■ *They offer formal support to families through their institutions.*   As we discovered in our discussion of ecological systems theory in Chapter 12, communities comprise the larger social systems within which families operate. Many agencies and institutions within the local community—schools, health clinics, social service agencies, homeless shelters, and so on—support families' ongoing efforts to help children grow into productive adults.

■ *They provide social support systems.*   The informal connections families make within their community indirectly affect, and often enhance, the lives of children. For example, community members may occasionally supervise children's activities, model and offer advice on effective parenting strategies, inform parents about employment opportunities, and provide emotional support that family members need in times of trouble and stress (Cochran, 1993; McLoyd, 1990; Simons, Lorenz, Wu, & Conger, 1993).

Neighborhoods and communities are most likely to foster children's development when people know and respect one another and work cooperatively to solve local problems (Sampson & Groves, 1989). When there is little sense of community—for example, when people move into and out of a neighborhood frequently, or when people in different ethnic

---

[12] Reprinted with the permission of The Free Press, a Division of Simon & Schuster Adult Publishing Group, from *The Nurture Assumption: Why Children Turn Out the Way They Do* by Judith Rich Harris. Copyright © 1998 by Judith Rich Harris.

DEVELOPMENT AND PRACTICE

Considering Contexts in Which Children Grow Up

■ Discuss current events in class.

A high school history teacher compares a recent riot in a nearby city to class conflicts in industrial England. Adolescents discuss their fears and concerns about the riot and think about the perspectives of all parties involved.

■ Be neutral, inclusive, and respectful regarding children's religious and nonreligious practices.

A community leader encourages children in her club to bring in artifacts that show how they celebrate holidays during the winter months. Children bring in decorations and religious symbols related to Christmas, Ramadan, Kwanzaa, Hanukkah, and the winter solstice.

■ Work closely with families of low-income children to ensure children's academic success.

A teacher working in a low-socioeconomic neighborhood regularly invites parents and guardians to participate in school events. He learns about the goals that family members have for their children, arranges for child care during meetings, and becomes familiar with community services that families might find helpful.

■ Establish connections with local communities.

A high school teacher encourages adolescents to engage in community service projects. Adolescents choose from a wide range of possibilities, including neighborhood cleanups, story time with preschoolers at the library, and volunteer work at a food bank or soup kitchen.

groups mistrust one another—youngsters are more likely to engage in delinquent behavior (Sampson & Groves, 1989).

The Development and Practice feature "Considering Contexts in Which Children Grow Up" offers suggestions to professionals for using information about communities, religious backgrounds, and historical events to help youngsters.

Types of Communities

Neighborhoods do not exist in isolation from the broader social landscape. Instead, each is nested within a particular geographical location. Furthermore, each community has a particular density of inhabitants. People in urban communities live in close proximity to one another; those in rural environments often live quite a distance from one another. Here we look briefly at the potential advantages and disadvantages of living in urban, rural, and suburban communities. Keep in mind that these descriptions are generalizations. Individual urban, rural, and suburban communities vary and are influenced by the region in which they are located and proximity to other types of communities. Also, in densely populated areas, demarcations between urban, rural, and suburban regions are often blurred.

Urban Communities A large city provides many sources of enrichment for young people. For instance, most major cities have ongoing events and resources related to music, art, drama, science, sports, and diverse cultures. Experiencing cultural events first-hand can be exciting and motivating for children. In Figure 14–4, 6-year-old Lee displays his enthusiasm for an art museum he visited in a large city. However, not every child in the big city can take advantage of its many splendors. Clearly, children's daily lives in urban communities are affected by their family's financial status. Some families can afford to make choices about where they live, which schools their children attend, and which resources they take advantage of, but many others must choose among less desirable alternatives.

Tragically, many inner-city neighborhoods are fraught with serious problems, including poverty, drugs, violence, crime, and racial segregation (Massey & Denton, 1993). Not surprisingly, these problems seep into schools. For instance, secondary school principals in inner-city public schools are more likely than their counterparts in rural and suburban schools to see poverty, inadequate academic skills, student apathy, and lack of parent involvement as serious problems affecting their schools (National Center for Education Statistics, 1999b). Partly because of such problems, many people in the public at large hold negative stereotypes of inner-city youths—especially those from ethnic and racial minority groups—and often think of these youngsters as being violent, drug-addicted, uneducated, and dependent on welfare (J. T. Gibbs, 1985; Way, 1998). In reality, many young people living in the inner city steer clear of delinquent activities, grad-

FIGURE 14–4 Six-year-old Lee displays his enthusiasm for an art museum he visited in a large city. In this artwork, he represents some of the themes he perceived, including warfare, religion, and community.

uate from high school, find jobs or pursue higher education, and live productive lives (Price & Clarke-McLean, 1997; Way, 1998).

Rural Communities Families living in rural settings, particularly farming communities, often foster a cooperative spirit and strong work ethic (E. E. García, 1994; Reynolds, 1999). For instance, farm families tend to structure chores so that all family members contribute to the family's economic livelihood. Furthermore, farm families often drop their own work to help other families with such activities as chopping wood and harvesting crops. Some rural neighbors exchange produce and hand-made goods and in the process deepen their community social ties.

Although a rural environment offers many advantages for children and adolescents, its recreational activities can be limited, leading young people to seek excitement through unproductive activities. For instance, school principals in rural areas and small towns are more likely than principals in central cities and suburban areas to identify student alcohol abuse as a serious problem (National Center for Education Statistics, 1999b).

Historically, members of rural communities have been actively involved in local schools, volunteering to organize social gatherings and help with school maintenance. Rural communities frequently have a limited budget for children's schooling, and so several communities may join forces to create large, consolidated school districts. In a consolidated school, students have access to more educational resources than they might otherwise, but some may need to travel many miles to attend school each day and so have limited opportunity to participate in extracurricular activities or in other ways socialize with classmates after school hours. Furthermore, parents may feel little connection to, or investment in, a distant school operated by teachers they do not know (National Center for Education Statistics, 1999b).

Suburban Communities On average, families in suburban communities have higher incomes than those who live in inner cities or rural areas, and schools are often better funded. In some people's minds, a suburban community is the "ideal" environment for growing children: There is easy access to the educational and cultural resources of the big city, yet everyone has a bit of backyard and some privacy.

However, economic resources are not equally distributed in suburban communities, and not all young people have an optimistic outlook about their chances for future success (Gaines, 1991). Furthermore, some children and adolescents in wealthier communities may reject their less financially advantaged peers, especially if those peers don't adhere to unspoken rules for acceptable behavior. Developmental psychologist Judith Harris (1998) describes such rejection in her own childhood:

> We moved around a lot, those early years, and several times I was taken out of a classroom in the middle of the school year and put into another one, but I had no trouble making new friends. My high spirits and outgoing nature made me popular with my peers, both boys and girls.
>
> Then we moved once more—as usual, after the school year had begun—and everything changed. I found myself the youngest and smallest child, and one of the few who wore glasses, in a fourth-grade classroom in a snooty suburb in the Northeast. The other girls were sophisticated little ladies, interested in hairstyles, proud of their pretty clothes. I wasn't like them, and they didn't like me.
>
> My family remained in that place for four years, and they were the worst four years of my life. I went to school each day with children from my neighborhood, but not one of them would play with me or talk to me. If I dared to say anything to them, it was ignored. Pretty soon I gave up trying. Within a year or two I went from being active and outgoing to being inhibited and shy. My parents knew nothing of this—they saw no major changes in my behavior at home. The only thing that changed, as far as they were concerned, was that I was spending a lot of time reading. Too much time, in their opinion. (J. R. Harris, 1998, pp. 146–147)[13]

Harris's experience is not unusual; regardless of the setting in which children live—whether urban, rural, or suburban—frequent moves from one community to another can

---

[13] Reprinted with the permission of The Free Press, a Division of Simon & Schuster Adult Publishing Group, from *The Nurture Assumption: Why Children Turn Out the Way They Do* by Judith Rich Harris. Copyright © 1998 by Judith Rich Harris.

disrupt peer relationships and support networks. Yet frequent mobility is becoming more typical in Western society. For example, in 1994, approximately one in six children had moved to a new home within the last year (Hernandez, 1997). Children who move frequently are at risk both academically and socially, in part because the frequent transition from one school to another often leaves gaps in their basic knowledge and skills and in part because they have little continuity in their peer support groups (J. R. Harris, 1998; Knutson & Mantzicopoulos, 1999). Nonetheless, children who move frequently often develop good coping skills, such as learning to make new friends.

Promoting Community Ties

"It takes a village to raise a child." This old African proverb is right on the mark: Children's development is fostered not only by family members but also by the community. We urge our readers to capitalize on the resources in their towns and cities, and also to encourage young people to give back to their communities. Following are some specific suggestions:

■ *Build a sense of community.* Most parents and guardians need ongoing social support from others who have children. Parent-teacher meetings, evening concerts and plays, school and community suppers, and award nights for club members give parents a chance to connect with one another and compare notes about their children's progress and struggles. Such gatherings may also give family members an opportunity to interact with public figures such as local government officials, school board members, law enforcement officers, and drug and crime prevention specialists.

■ *Take active measures to integrate new children and families into the community.* As our earlier example of the girl who moved to the "snooty" suburb illustrates, children's transitions to new schools and communities are not always easy. School personnel and community officials are often among the first people new residents meet. A few simple gestures—perhaps finding a group of boys or girls with whom a new student can eat lunch, inviting a new parent to help with a fund-raiser, or scheduling a potluck dinner to welcome the new family—can make a world of difference in helping newcomers establish social ties.

■ *Honor the accomplishments of local citizens.* Successful adults from the local community are valuable role models for all children and may be especially important for youngsters whose daily lives bring them into regular contact with deviant activities and lifestyles. In a few cases, conversations between children and successful citizens may even lead to productive apprenticeships (see Chapter 4) outside of school.

■ *Bring your own outside activities into your work with young people.* Professionals often have particular hobbies and service roles in the community that they can share with children. For example, Julia Devereaux, a teacher of children from low-income families, reports that she brings her outside volunteer role as a Girl Scout leader into the classroom, with positive results: "I just bring all of the membership information here and tell the girls how wonderful scouting can be. Frankly, by the time I describe the sleepovers—over-night camping—and the skating part, everyone says they want to be in the troop."[14]

■ *Get children and adolescents involved in community service projects.* Youngsters often feel more connected to their community when, in some small way, they give something back. Members of a school might conduct a neighborhood cleanup, volunteer in a nursing home or in a hospital pediatric ward, serve as readers at the local library, or raise funds to benefit community causes (Ladson-Billings, 1994). The city of Boston sponsors an after-school program called the Mural Crew, in which groups of teenagers replace graffiti on buildings with large-scale murals. Since 1991, adolescents in the program have created more than 60 public works of art. One of the murals appears in Figure 14–5.

---

[14] From *The Dreamkeepers: Successful Teachers of African American Children* (pp. 64–65), by G. Ladson-Billings, 1994, San Francisco: Jossey-Bass. Copyright © 1994 by Jossey-Bass, Inc., Publishers. This material is used by permission of John Wiley & Sons, Inc.

FIGURE 14–5 *Saturday in Jamaica Plain.* The Mural Crew program of the Boston Youth Clean-Up Corps (BYCC) enlists groups of teenagers to beautify the city with public works of art.

Artists: Antonio, Gabe, Awurama, Agapito, Nikia, Alyssa, Jon. Supervising artists: Heidi Schork and Teig Grennan.

Providing Community Support for Children and Adolescents

Neighborhood and community support is especially evident during times children are not attending school: throughout the day during the infant and preschool years, and before and after school hours and over the summer in children's later years. Here we look at three forms that such support might take—child care, early childhood intervention programs, and before- and after-school programs for older children and adolescents. We consider, as well, the potential role of neighbors when children take care of themselves. We also examine risks and benefits of part-time employment for adolescents, and the individualized services provided by community organizations.

Child Care Many young children are in **child care**—in the care of people other than their parents—for a significant portion of the work week. Mothers' increasing employment outside the home and the rise of single-parent families have contributed to use of child care in many Western countries. For example, in the United States, the majority of infants are regularly cared for by someone other than their mothers and fathers, and more than two-thirds of children under age 4 are routinely cared for by someone besides parents (M. E. Lamb, 1998). Most infants are cared for in home settings, their own or that of a caregiver. As children get older, attendance at child care centers becomes more common (Kisker, Hofferth, Phillips, & Farguhar, 1991; M. E. Lamb, 1998).

By and large, child care appears to be a mostly positive experience for children—if it is of good quality. Children who receive low quality care and those who spend long hours in child care face risks, however. Following are some key research findings:

■ *Child care does not undermine children's attachment to parents.* Many social commentators lament the trend for infants to be apart from their mothers during the day and suggest that nonparental care compromises the infant-mother bond. (Curiously, the same critics appear to think it quite natural for fathers to be off at work.) Research on quality child care has largely invalidated their concerns. Only when attachment relationships are already vulnerable—for instance, when mothers are insensitive and nonresponsive to their infants' needs—do young children in child care display insecure attachment to parents (M. E. Lamb, 1998).

Infants frequently become attached to employed caregivers in child care centers and home settings, especially when these individuals are stable, warm, sensitive, and actively involved in infants' care (Barnas & Cummings, 1994; Raikes, 1993). In some cases, a secure attachment to a teacher may actually enhance the infant's bond with parents. In a study of infants with depressed mothers, Cohn, Campbell, and Ross (1991) found a positive correlation between the number of hours infants spent in child care and security of their attachment to mothers.

child care
Care of children by nonparental adults for a significant portion of the workweek.

■ *High-quality child care can enhance cognitive and linguistic development of some children.* High-quality infant care seems to be especially beneficial for children's development when their alternative is a home environment that is not stimulating or challenging (M. E. Lamb, 1998; Ramey, 1992; Scarr, 1997). Its benefits have been observed primarily for children from low-income families; child care seems to have minimal effects, either positive or negative, on the cognitive development of children from middle- and upper-income homes (Scarr, 1998).

■ *Experience in child care may help children develop social skills and independence.* Children who have high-quality child care experiences are more likely to be socially competent (T. Field, 1991; T. Field, Masi, Goldstein, Perry, & Parl, 1988; Howes, 1988; Scarr, 1998; Scott-Little & Holloway, 1992). Child care may also foster self-confidence and self-reliance; for instance, in a study with 8-year-old Swedish children, those who had had out-of-home care as infants appeared to their teachers to be more persistent and independent, as well as less anxious, than those who did not have this experience (Andersson, 1989).

■ *Exposure to child care at a young age may increase aggression and noncompliance slightly.* In an ethnically diverse sample of over 1300 families, spending a long time in child care during the first few years of life predicted behavioral problems noticed by caregivers when the children were 4½ years old (NICHD Early Child Care Research Network, 2002a). Caregivers noticed both internalizing problems (e.g., being fearful and anxious) and externalizing problems (e.g., arguing a lot; see Chapter 9 for descriptions of emotional difficulties). This association held up when numerous variables were controlled for statistically, including children's temperament, mothers' psychological adjustment and anxiety in separating from children, and mothers' beliefs about employment.

These effects are not always seen, and when they are, they are smaller for high-quality than for low-quality care (Bagley, 1989; Clarke-Stewart, 1989; DiLalla, 1998; Hegland & Rix, 1990). The long-term impact of such effects is not known, although there is some evidence that overly aggressive behaviors decrease over time (Clarke-Stewart, 1989). It may be that children in child care settings learn more quickly to stand up for their own rights and needs—in other words, they become more *assertive*—and that researchers and teachers interpret their assertiveness as aggression or noncompliance (Hegland & Rix, 1990).

However, the fact that several researchers find associations between extended time in child care, particularly time in lower-quality child care, and elevated social problems concerns us. Professionals may not be able to curtail hours children spend in child care, but they can definitely advocate for quality. Moreover, when school-age children have experienced long hours in low-quality child care, professionals may need to teach them to cope with emotional stresses and to relate positively to peers and adults (see Chapters 9 and 13).

■ *Mothers' employment in the first year of life is associated with minor social and intellectual problems in children.* In Chapter 12, we learned that parents' employment can have positive effects on children: Parents teach youngsters about particular careers and expose them to valuable work habits, such as being punctual. But we also cited a less positive effect of parents' employment: When parents work long hours and are not permitted to stay home with sick children, parents feel stressed and children's health may be jeopardized.

Working long hours may also reduce parents' ability to give infants relaxed, stimulating, and loving care. A study with more than 1200 4- to 6-year-old children from European American and African American backgrounds found that mothers who worked full-time from the beginning of their children's first or second year had children who became less compliant than age-mates whose mothers did not work full-time (Belsky & Eggebeen, 1991). That is, rather than doing things their mothers asked, such as eating particular foods, going to bed, or turning off the television, children protested. In an investigation with 900 European American 3-year-old children, maternal employment by infants' 9th month was associated with somewhat low performance on school readiness tests (e.g., knowledge of color, letter identification, and counting) (Brooks-Gunn, Han, & Waldfogel, 2002).

These results can be interpreted as validating family leave policies that permit mothers—and fathers—to use flexible work time to care for infants. They do not, however, address the question of what exactly constitutes good quality in child care, which we take up next.

■ *Quality of care matters to children.* Advocates for high standards in child care have focused on two primary ways of defining quality. *Structural measures* include such objective indices as caregivers' training and experience, child-caregiver ratios, staff turnover, and number and complexity of toys and equipment (M. E. Lamb, 1998; Sims, Hutchins, & Taylor, 1997). For example, early childhood specialists recommend that the child-caregiver ratio be no more than three infants for each adult and no more than six toddlers for each adult (Bredekamp & Copple, 1997). *Process measures* of quality, which examine children's social and cognitive experiences in child care settings, include measures of child-caregiver relationships, child-peer interactions, and developmentally appropriate activities (Harms & Clifford, 1980; Sims et al., 1997). For example, the schedules of activities in a toddler room might be fairly predictable from day to day but are also flexible and guided by children's needs (Bredekamp & Copple, 1997). Thus, toddlers may be offered two snacks over the span of the morning even though only a few choose to eat twice.

Structural and process variables are related. For example, in one study, over 800 children who were in child care 10 or more hours per week at the age of four and a half years were examined in their child care settings (NICHD Early Child Care Research Network, 2002b). Both the training of caregivers and the child-staff ratio were related to caregivers' relationships with children. Caregivers with good training tended to show sensitivity and competence, having established a positive emotional climate that also stimulated children's cognitive growth. Caregivers' good relationships with children, in turn, were associated with positive teacher ratings of children's social competence and classroom behavior. It is possible that well-prepared teachers working in a setting with good child-staff ratios were able to facilitate children's friendships and conflict resolution skills. It is also possible that teachers with good training were somewhat biased, focusing on the positive sides of children. Although we cannot rule out the latter explanation, we note that numerous research studies show that lower child-staff ratios, smaller group sizes, and more caregiver education and training predict better child-caregiver interactions (e.g., Howes, Smith, & Galinsky, 1995; Phillips, Mekos, Scarr, McCartney, & Abbott-Shim, 2001).

Other process variables are close ties with local communities and respect for the cultural practices of families served. Local communities may have definite views about quality, as does the Meadow Lake Tribal Council of northern Saskatchewan, Canada:

Young children often benefit by experiences in high-quality child care, that is, settings in which caregivers are sensitive and have appropriate training, child-staff ratios are low, and caregivers focus on children's individual needs.

> The First Nations of the Meadow Lake Tribal Council believe that a child care program developed, administered and operated by their own people is a vital component to their vision of sustainable growth and development. It impacts every sector of their long-term plans as they prepare to enter the twenty-first century. It will be children who inherit the struggle to retain and enhance the people's culture, language and history; who continue the quest for economic progress for a better quality of life; and who move forward with a strengthened resolve to plan their own destiny. (Dahlberg, Moss, & Pence, 1999, p. 168)

The First Nations people did not accept the "best practices" model of child care that Canadian governmental authorities offered them. Instead, the tribal council decided to work with the School of Child and Youth Care at the University of Victoria, which agreed that the tribal council should plan its own child care. Eventually, the council designed a program that reflected research on child development, advice from elders in the community, and traditional practices, such as use of cradle boards to tightly hold swaddled infants. The result was a high-quality program that integrated local cultural practices and also revitalized the community by reaffirming traditional values (Dahlberg et al., 1999).

Unfortunately, some child care arrangements fit nobody's definition of quality. In these cases, caregivers have no education in child development, they do not care deeply about children, and facilities are dangerous. How do children fare in such settings? In fact, little research has been conducted on the outcomes of child care that is emotionally cold, punitive, or overpopulated. We suspect that low-quality child care—"care" in which children are inadequately nurtured, stimulated, and supervised—may seriously tax children's resilience, especially when children also lack nurturing family environments. Child care can be of benefit only when it addresses children's immediate physical needs and when it includes affection, regular social interaction, toys, healthy meals, and activities designed to foster children's development.

Early Childhood Intervention Programs   High-quality educational environments for young children routinely have positive effects on children's intellectual growth and may be particularly beneficial for children from low-SES backgrounds (Brooks-Gunn, 2003; M. E. Lamb, 1998; McLoyd, 1998a; Ramey & Ramey, 1998; Scarr, 1998). Accordingly, legislators and educators have joined forces to create centers that give young children from low-income families important foundational knowledge and skills. Such **early childhood intervention programs** typically combine an educational focus with other supports for children and their families, such as basic medical care, social services, and parenting guidance.

In the United States, the best-known model of early childhood intervention is Project Head Start. Established under federal legislation, Head Start was designed for 3- to 5-year-old low-income children and their families. Since 1965, it has served more than 13 million children, many of them from single-parent homes. A typical Head Start program includes early childhood education (preschool), health screening and referrals, mental health services, nutrition education, family support services, and parent involvement in decision making (McLoyd, 1998a; Washington & Bailey, 1995).

Numerous research studies have been conducted on the effectiveness of Head Start and similar early childhood intervention programs. The short-term effects of such programs are clear—children score higher on measures of cognitive ability and achieve at higher levels in school—but such advantages often disappear by the upper elementary grades (Lee, Brooks-Gunn, Schnur, & Liaw, 1990; McKey et al., 1985; McLoyd, 1998b; Ramey & Ramey, 1998). Other long-term benefits have been observed, however: Low-income children who attend Head Start or similar preschool programs are less likely to require special educational services and more likely to graduate from high school than similar children who have no preschool experience (Lazar, Darlington, Murray, Royce, & Snipper, 1982; McLoyd, 1998a; Schweinhart & Weikart, 1983; Washington & Bailey, 1995). Longer and more intensive programs (e.g., 2 or more years of full-time preschool rather than a single year of part-time schooling), as well as programs in which teachers are well trained and parents are actively involved, yield the greatest benefits (Ramey & Ramey, 1998; Ripple, Gilliam, Chanana, & Zigler, 1999).

Anecdotal evidence also attests to the potential benefits of early childhood intervention, as illustrated in these two testimonials from Head Start graduates (K. Mills, 1998):

- Pancho Mansera is a machinist in Santa Maria, California. As an adult, he went to night school to earn his high school diploma, and he now regularly helps his four children do their homework. Through the services of Head Start, he was diagnosed with a treatable thyroid condition. He says that Head Start "gave me a second chance in life. I started living like a normal kid" (K. Mills, 1998, p. 163).
- Rachel Jones is a journalist specializing in children's issues. One of 10 children, Rachel remembers going to bed hungry, "longing for the luxury of the hot dogs or Sloppy Joes they served at Head Start and kindergarten" (p. 172). Concerned about the fate of social programs for families, Jones reflects: "[W]hen I think of the smiles, the loving support, the hopeful, helpful moments doled out in a warm, bustling school basement 30 years ago, I know I'd gladly pay an extra dollar of taxes to provide Head Start to someone else's child" (pp. 172–173).

early childhood intervention program
Program for infants, toddlers, and preschool children designed to foster basic intellectual, social-emotional, and physical development in children whose home environments may not nurture such skills.

Given the generally positive effects of early childhood intervention, it is unfortunate that not all needy children are served. In fact, only 30% of eligible 3- to 5-year-old children participate in Head Start (McLoyd, 1998a).

Some educators suggest that quality care and education should be more universally available and start earlier than age 3. Accordingly, one model program, the Carolina Abecedarian Project, offers services to children of poor families beginning in infancy (F. A. Campbell & Ramey, 1994, 1995; Horacek, Ramey, Campbell, Hoffman, & Fletcher, 1987). In one longitudinal experimental study of the program's effectiveness, children were randomly assigned to one of four groups:

1. Those who attended a full-time intervention program from 4 months to 5 years of age
2. Those who received supplementary academic support in the early elementary grades, from age 5 through age 8
3. Those who both attended the intervention program and had supplementary academic support in the early elementary grades
4. Those who participated in neither program (the control group)

Children in all four groups received nutrition and health services, but children in the three treatment groups received educational enrichment as well. The intervention program (for Groups 1 and 3) was designed to stimulate children's motor, cognitive, language, and social skills; beginning at age 3, it also included activities to foster prereading and mathematical skills. The supplementary support during the early elementary years (for Groups 2 and 3) involved the services of a resource teacher, who regularly visited children's homes and provided educational activities tailored to individual needs.

Early intervention had a significant effect on cognitive development: Children who attended the early intervention program earned higher IQ scores from age 1½ until age 15, and they were less likely to require special educational services, than those who had no early intervention. The effects of the later, school-age intervention were positive but weaker than the effects of the early childhood intervention.

Other programs supporting children in the early elementary years have been instituted as well (e.g., A. Reynolds, 1994; E. Zigler & Muenchow, 1992). Although such programs appear to have positive effects, evaluations of them often lack the tight experimental controls (e.g., random assignment to groups) that make conclusions about cause-effect relationships possible. Increasingly, however, researchers are discovering that children make the most progress when interventions begin early (ideally in infancy) and continue throughout the school years. We agree with other theorists that it is virtually impossible to inoculate children against impoverished living conditions with a short intervention (Brooks-Gunn, 2003; Ramey & Ramey, 1998; Washington & Bailey, 1995).

In considering the potential benefits of early intervention, practitioners from middle- and upper-income backgrounds must be careful not to think of children from lower-SES neighborhoods as being "disadvantaged" or "deprived " (Bruer, 1999). In fact, children from low-income families often have a great deal of stimulation and many enriching experiences at home. What they lack may simply be certain kinds of knowledge and skills—for instance, in language, literacy, mathematics and, later on, perhaps in study skills and reading comprehension—that they need for academic success.

Before- and After-School Programs   Another way in which communities contribute to young people's development is through the programs they offer before and after school and during the summer—clubs, sports leagues, dance and martial arts lessons, scout troops, and so on. Many of these programs are located at public recreation facilities, youth centers, private businesses, and community members' homes. National organizations (e.g., the YMCA, Boys and Girls Clubs of America, National 4-H Council, and National Association of Police Athletic Leagues) also sponsor activities designed to meet youngsters' needs at a variety of developmental levels; these groups build skills, foster teamwork, and bring young people into regular contact with positive role models (Chaiken, 1998). Twelve-year-old Colin gives a sense of his rich learning experiences, made possible by his community, in an interview in the After School/Early Adolescence clip of the Observation CD:

Interviewer:	So you play basketball?
Colin:	Yeah. Yeah.
Interviewer:	What other. . . . Is that your favorite sport?
Colin:	I like basketball and track about the same.
Interviewer:	Do you play any other sports?

Effective after-school programs typically offer a variety of activities through which young people can pursue their individual interests and develop their unique talents. Art by Brandon, age 11.

Listen to 12-year-old Colin describe what he does outside of school in the After School/Early Adolescence clip of the Observation CD.

Colin:	Yeah. I play, basically, I play football, baseball, hockey. . . .
Interviewer:	Wow. What do you like about sports?
Colin:	Well, they're fun and just something to do. . . .
Interviewer:	So what kinds of clubs do you belong to?
Colin:	I belong to . . . well, I used to belong to 4-H. And I'm in the chess club, Boy Scouts, and sign language club.

More than 25% of before- and after-school programs are located in school buildings (Dryfoos, 1999). At the middle school and secondary level, most of these take the form of *extracurricular activities,* such as clubs and athletic teams. At the elementary level, extended-day programs often provide supervision, academic support, and recreational activities for children of working parents. With financial aid from federal, state, and local agencies, schools are opening their doors earlier in the morning and closing them later at night, and they are increasingly making their facilities available to students and families on weekends and during the summer (Dryfoos, 1999).

Some programs offered on school sites are operated by the schools themselves; others are offered with the assistance of community-based organizations (Dryfoos, 1999; National Center for Education Statistics, 1997). In one model (the CoZi Schools), school-based centers offer home visits to parents of children from birth to age 3, all-day child care for preschoolers ages 3 to 5, before- and after-school care and vacation care for school-age children, education for family members (e.g., home visits, referrals to community services), assistance with nutritional and health needs, and mental health services (Finn-Stevenson & Stern, 1996; B. M. Stern & Finn-Stevenson, 1999).

A growing body of research indicates that participation in after-school programs fosters children's cognitive and social-emotional development. For instance, extended-day programs for elementary students can cultivate positive feelings about school, better school attendance, higher grades and achievement test scores, better classroom behavior, greater conflict resolution skills, and decreased tension with family members (Charles A. Dana Center, 1999; Dryfoos, 1999; Vandell & Pierce, 1999). Regular communication between teachers and after-school caregivers helps to increase the likelihood of these good outcomes (Caplan, McElvain, & Walter, 2001). For instance, teachers and after-school caregivers can communicate about educational objectives using face-to-face meetings and two-way written forms such as the one shown in Figure 14–6. Summer school programs that focus on remedial or accelerated learning also appear to enhance students' academic knowledge and skills (H. Cooper, Charlton, Valentine, & Muhlenbruck, 2000).

Nonacademic programs, too, have benefits. For instance, high school students who participate in their school's extracurricular activities are more likely to achieve at high levels and graduate from high school, and they are less likely to smoke, use alcohol or drugs, join gangs, engage in criminal activities, or become teenage parents (Biddle, 1993; H. Cooper, Valentine, Nye, & Lindsay, 1999; Donato et al., 1997; Eppright, Sanfacon, Beck, & Bradley, 1998; Zill, Nord, & Loomis, 1995). Joining a club or team at school may also give students a productive peer group with which to associate and thereby indirectly promote greater attachment to school (H. Cooper et al., 1999; Zill et al., 1995).

The combination of caring adults and friendly peers can be a big draw to adolescents. For example, the majority (75%) of 10- to 18-year-olds who attended one of four inner-city sites of Boys and Girls Clubs of America described the setting as being like a home to them (Deutsch & Hirsch, 2001). Sammy, a 16-year-old African American young man, described his feeling about the club:

Directions: This form is to be used by the classroom teacher and after-school tutor to share information about an individual student's homework assignments and study habits. For each homework assignment, the teacher fills out the information in column one and gives the form to the tutor. After assisting the student, the tutor fills out the information in column two and returns the form to the teacher.

Today's Date:	
Student's Name:	
Teacher's Name:	
Tutor's Name:	
Completed by teacher.	**Completed by tutor.**
The homework for today is:	This student: ❏ Completed the homework easily and independently. ❏ Had difficulty *understanding* what was asked in the homework. ❏ Had difficulty *completing* the homework. ❏ Had difficulty *focusing* on the assignment.
Please pay special attention to:	This student required: ❏ No help with the assignment. ❏ A little help. ❏ Occasional help. ❏ A great deal of help. ❏ See comments on back.
This homework should take _____ minutes to complete.	The homework took _____ minutes to complete.

FIGURE 14–6 Homework sharing tool. Daytime teachers and after-school teachers who tutor children can use this form to communicate about homework.

From *Beyond the Bell: A Toolkit for Creating Effective After-School Programs,* 2e (p. 105), by Judith G. Caplan, Carol K. McElvain, and Katie E. Walter, 2001, Naperville, IL: NCREL. Copyright 2001 by the North Central Regional Educational Laboratory. All rights reserved. Reprinted by permission.

Some people do not have any home. I have been granted the gift of having two homes: my home and the Boys and Girls Club. [The club] allows me to express myself mentally, verbally, physically, and artistically. (p. 1)

Other young people are drawn to athletics. High school sports programs can foster a team spirit and a willingness to work hard, perform under pressure, and handle wins and losses constructively (Danish, Nellen, & Owens, 1996). But children of all ages can enjoy physical activity, as you may recall from Chapter 3. In the After-School module of the Observation CD, all four youngsters describe their participation in one or more sports after school; here is how 6-year-old Brent describes the sports he plays:

Listen to 6-year-old Brent talk about what he likes to do outside of school in the After School/Early Childhood clip of the Observation CD.

Football, and sometimes we kick, um, we throw the football and sometimes we kick it. Sometimes we do both . . . [and] we had a [soccer] game yesterday.

Giving back to the community is another worthwhile after-school activity for young people. Community service projects provide an opportunity for **service learning**, by which children and adolescents gain new knowledge and skills and increased self-confidence while assisting other people or in other ways contributing to the betterment of their community (Sheckley & Keeton, 1997; Stukas, Clary, & Snyder, 1999). Fifteen-year-old Connor volunteered to become the football coach for his seven-year-old brother's team when none of the team parents could do so. Here's his description of what the experience meant to him:

[I learned] just how to be a leader and a lot about football. You have to be nice to the little kids and when they make a good play, you gotta tell them about it and when they make a bad play, you gotta *not* tell them about it. I had fun doing it.

Effective after-school programs and community clubs typically offer the following elements (C. R. Cooper, Denner, & Lopez, 1999; Kerewsky & Lefstein, 1982; Lefstein & Lipsitz, 1995):

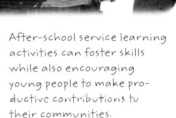

After-school service learning activities can foster skills while also encouraging young people to make productive contributions to their communities.

- A variety of activities, including recreation, academic and cultural enrichment, and opportunities for pursuit of individual interests
- Chances for meaningful participation, perhaps through service learning activities in which youngsters practice new skills while giving back to their neighborhoods or communities
- Opportunities for success, perhaps in domains where youngsters have previously unrecognized talents
- Positive interactions with others, helping youngsters to form friendships with peers and find appropriate role models or mentors in adults
- Structure and clear limits, with youngsters' active participation in planning and rule setting
- High regard from adults for the beliefs and practices young people have learned in their cultural communities

Many studies of extracurricular and other after-school activities are correlational in their research design, and so it is not possible to certify that participation in them actually *causes* the possible effects that we've listed. An alternative explanation might be that children and adolescents who participate in after-school programs are different from those who don't. For example, adolescents who join extracurricular clubs and athletic teams at school might feel more positively about their school and would be unlikely to smoke, use alcohol, or engage in criminal activity even if they didn't participate. Nonetheless, because of the potential—and, we suggest, likely—benefits, after-school programs certainly merit investment of time, energy, and financial resources until social scientists can evaluate them with more certainty.

Self-Care Learning to take care of oneself is a natural part of development. Choosing clothes, getting dressed, preparing snacks and simple meals, deciding what to do with free time, and avoiding dangerous situations are essential developmental tasks. Accordingly, as children grow older, parents, teachers, and other caregivers give them increasing autonomy in tending to their own needs. Children do not always act responsibly when the reins are

service learning
Activity that promotes learning and skill development through volunteerism or community service.

loosened, but eventually most learn to make decisions that assure their safety and physical well-being.

Questions arise, however, about the age at which children can safely engage in *self-care*, looking after themselves before or after school while their parents are away from home. Most parents and child development experts think that preschoolers are too young for self-care, yet one in a hundred is left alone regularly (Kerrebrock & Lewitt, 1999). Small as this proportion may seem, it indicates that tens of thousands of American preschoolers are frequently left home by themselves.

Self-care is more prevalent once children reach school age. Two national surveys indicate that approximately 12% of children between the ages of 5 and 12 care for themselves at least once a week; this figure may underestimate the actual percentage, however, as parents are often reluctant to admit that they leave their children unattended (Kerrebrock & Lewitt, 1999). By adolescence, some self-care is common (Medrich & Marzke, 1991).

Why do parents leave their children unattended? Many work, cannot afford after-school care, have children who resist having babysitters or attending child care centers, or are unaware of other options (Belle, 1999). While at work, many parents worry: What are their children doing in their absence? Are they safe? Is it legal to leave them alone? As one single mother with an 8-year-old at home put it, "All I do after 3:00 is worry" (Belle, 1999, p. 52).

Parents have reason to be concerned about leaving children home alone. In caring for themselves, young children are not always safety-minded. They may put themselves at risk by leaving a hot stove unattended, opening the door to a stranger, getting into fights with siblings, and in other ways making poor decisions. (At age 12, Teresa's son Connor once took a nap while babysitting his 5-year-old brother.) Older adolescents, who have greater mobility in the community, face additional temptations in the form of unhealthy or illegal activities with unsupervised age-mates. About half of all juvenile crime takes place after school hours, between 2:00 P.M. and 8:00 P.M. (J. A. Fox & Newman, 1997; Sickmund, Snyder, & Poe-Yamagata, 1997).

Correlational studies indicate that self-care may have some negative effects (remember, however, that correlational studies do not conclusively show cause-effect relationships). On average, children who spend considerable time in self-care in the early elementary grades show poorer academic performance and social skills, as well as more behavior problems, than children who are more closely supervised in the early years (Pettit, Laird, Bates, & Dodge, 1997; Vandell & Posner, 1999). But studies addressing the impact of self-care have not always found negative effects (Vandell & Shumow, 1999). Some children may, in fact, benefit from caring for themselves, in that they develop self-regulatory skills such as establishing a self-care routine, buckling down to do homework without parental prodding, and cooperating with siblings to complete household chores.

Children are more likely to succeed in self-care when parents maintain regular contact with them about their activities and whereabouts (Galambos & Maggs, 1991b; Goyette-Ewing, 2000; Pettit, Bates, Dodge, & Meece, 1999; Steinberg, 1986). They also are more likely to negotiate challenges of self-care when they are socially outgoing and emotionally well-adjusted and when they can take minor frustrations in stride (Goyette-Ewing & Knoebber, 1999).

Although youngsters in self-care are ostensibly on their own, in fact community contexts influence the success of such arrangements. For instance, some residential areas have caring adults who are at home during the day and keep an eye on younger neighbors, whereas other areas offer the company of drug dealers and adolescent gangs. Although any neighborhood harbors dangers for unsupervised youngsters, low-income urban neighborhoods are particularly threatening. Thus, children from low-income families who engage in self-care for part of the day often feel afraid and socially isolated (T. J. Long & Long, 1982; Marshall, White, Keefe, & Marx, 1999; Zill, 1983). Furthermore, they are more likely than unattended children from high-income families to show aggression and delinquent behavior in later years (Meece, Colwell, & Pettit, 1999).

Community agencies provide valuable backup services for children who arrive home before their parents do. For instance, homework hotlines, often staffed by parents or other volunteers, offer assistance when children encounter difficulty with classroom assignments. Phone calls to police stations, poison control centers, and "911" can bring rapid assistance or advice when emergencies arise.

DEVELOPMENT AND PRACTICE

Enhancing Students' Before- and After-School Experiences

■ Help children navigate transitions between school and child care.

After school, a kindergarten teacher walks out with children to make sure that each one successfully connects with family members or car pool drivers, gets on the appropriate bus, or begins walking home.

■ Inform parents and other family members about out-of-school programs in your area.

At a parent-teacher-student conference, a middle school teacher describes clubs and sports programs at school, as well as recreational opportunities in the local community.

■ Sponsor after-school clubs in your school and community.

A community leader organizes a Hispanic Cultures Club in her center. She encourages young people to speak only in Spanish but allows them to choose their own group activities—possibly cooking, discussing Spanish literature, or translating a newsletter into Spanish.

■ Be explicit about students' homework assignments, and provide sufficient guidance to allow youngsters to complete them on their own or with a tutor.

When an elementary teacher gives homework assignments, she cross-references each assignment to the textbook pages that provide explanations for the concepts.

■ Establish a team of school personnel and after-school providers to ensure that after-school programs use resources appropriately and meet children's physical, social-emotional, and academic needs.

Two school teachers, the principal, and the director of an after-school program meet regularly to discuss space, resources, and ways that the after-school program can give children needed rest, relaxation, snacks, and tutoring.

■ Encourage parents to set limits on their children's television viewing and to talk about TV programs with their children.

In a newsletter to students and their families, a third-grade teacher includes "TV Tips" that outline educational uses, restrictions, and benefits of television.

In summary, adults in the community can do a lot to support young people in the hours they spend outside of school. For young children, they can advocate for high-quality child care and preschool; for older children and adolescents, they can provide meaningful service activities, effective before- and after-school programs, and appealing clubs and back-up systems. In the Development and Practice feature, "Enhancing Students' Before- and After-School Experiences," you can see some specific things that professionals can do to help support children in their out-of-school hours.

Part-time Employment   Particularly in the high school years, many adolescents take on part-time jobs in their local communities. Such jobs have both advantages and disadvantages, as the following interview with 17-year-old Jeremy illustrates:

Adult: You've been working at the local grocery store for almost 2 years now. In what ways has it been worthwhile?

Jeremy: Oh, lots of ways. Real-world experience. The money, of course. Interaction with people, both customers and coworkers, in a setting other than school. It broadens my network of connections with other people. Development of social skills, teamwork, leadership skills.

Adult: Is there a downside to working while you're still in school?

Jeremy: Sometimes it's hard to get everything done, in schoolwork and in personal stuff I have to do. Also, sometimes it conflicts with other activities I'd rather do.

Adult: Has it been a good experience overall?

Jeremy: Definitely. I have more friends and acquaintances because of it. I have more real-world experience. I feel I'm better prepared for going off to college or another job.

At the time of this interview, Jeremy had a 3.1 grade-point average in a challenging high school curriculum, maintained a good relationship with his parents, was active in French Club and service activities at school, and went skiing with a friend every Saturday—all while working about 15 hours a week as a cashier at the grocery store.

Not all teens juggle the multiple demands of work, school, home, and a social life as successfully as Jeremy. Research on the potential effects of student employment has been somewhat inconclusive, perhaps in part because group averages mask the effects of individual teenagers' ability levels, temperaments, and inclinations. Many employed adolescents learn to be responsible: They get to work on time, adhere to required procedures and standards of the job, and use their wages judiciously. However, employment can adversely affect adolescents' grade-point-averages, decrease their attachment to school, and increase high-risk behaviors such as substance abuse (Charner & Fraser, 1988; Steinberg, Brown, Cider, Kaczmarek, & Lazzaro, 1988). Limiting work commitments to a maximum of 15 to 20 hours per week seems to minimize the possibility for such negative effects (Mortimer, Finch, Seongryeol, Shanahan, & McCall, 1993; Steinberg et al., 1988).

Individualized Services by Community Organizations A wide variety of community organizations provide individualized services to young people facing significant hardships. For example, some community youth groups offer **mentorships** to individual children and adolescents. An adult volunteer shows a personal interest in a young person, spends time with him or her, and serves as a role model.

Close relationships with adults through community organizations can help children become competent in life skills (Masten & Coatsworth, 1998). For example, Big Brothers/Big Sisters of America pairs up a child with a screened adult volunteer who develops a relationship with him or her (Thompson & Kelly-Vance, 2001). In one study, researchers compared boys participating in a Big Brothers program with boys who had attended an orientation to the program but had not yet received a mentor (Thompson & Kelly-Vance, 2001). The 7- to 15-year-old boys with mentors and control boys came from single-parent families; both sets of boys showed one or more risk factors such as living in poverty, using drugs, or falling behind at school. Boys with mentors saw them weekly and did such things as going to movies, working on homework, and playing miniature golf. These boys performed higher in reading and mathematics even when intelligence scores were controlled statistically. This research cannot rule out other factors causing the differences in boys' achievement (e.g., perhaps boys who sought mentors earlier were more invested in doing well at school), yet results do indicate that mentoring programs deserve continued investment and research.

Sometimes, individualized attention from adults comes through the **juvenile justice system**. The juvenile justice system is a network of personnel and agencies that work with young people accused of breaking a law or at risk for doing so. It includes law enforcement agents, prosecutors, judges, officials in treatment programs, and officers working in corrections, probation, and parole (Champion, 2001). Juvenile justice professionals try to persuade young offenders to relinquish inappropriate behaviors, although conditions have not always been optimal in their work. Historically, juvenile justice professionals have had to deal with overcrowded facilities and large case loads (Donziger, 1996).

The majority of juvenile arrests in the United States are for property crimes and other nonviolent offenses, but 6 out of every 100 juvenile arrests is for a violent crime such as rape or murder (Donziger, 1996). One recent trend has been to place violent youths into small and secure facilities that offer treatment for drug use, assistance with educational planning, and therapy. Nonviolent juvenile offenders may be placed in group homes with supervised programs, educational and vocational training, and individualized treatment programs (Donziger, 1996). Because of separation of these two groups, nonviolent offenders are less likely to be victimized by violent offenders or to witness their aggressive acts. At the same time, society is protected when violent offenders are securely confined and given rehabilitative services.

Another recent trend has been to transfer adolescents from juvenile courts to criminal courts, where they are prosecuted as adults. However, whereas juvenile courts are inclined to offer second chances to youth, criminal courts are adversarial and give lengthy prison sentences. Compared to adults, adolescents are at a disadvantage in criminal courts to the degree that they do not have the requisite abilities assumed by the legal system. For example, adolescents may be unable to weigh costs and benefits of different pleas, and they may misunderstand the motives of defense attorneys, prosecuting attorneys, and judges (Steinberg & Cauffman, 2001).

The majority of youngsters do not experience the juvenile justice system through these individualized services. More commonly, children learn about police officers and other practitioners in the field of juvenile justice through indirect and informal means. For ex-

mentorship
Relationship between an adult and youngster in which the adult takes a personal interest in the young person, serves as a role model, and cultivates the young person's career and educational aspirations.

juvenile justice system
Network of professionals and agencies that work with young people accused of, or at risk for, breaking a law.

ample, young people may observe police officers patrol the streets and watch actors on television in roles as detectives. Some children are suspicious of police officers or see them as ineffective, particularly if officers have failed to apprehend a perpetrator of a violent crime in their neighborhood (Marans & Berkman, 1997). Other children admire agents of law enforcement and some have had personal experience being helped by police officers.

Many law enforcement officials cultivate positive attitudes in young people by emphasizing their helping roles and by coordinating their services with those of other agencies. For example, the Child Development-Community Policing (CD-CP) program in New Haven, Connecticut, brought together police officers and mental health professionals for training and consultation (Marans & Berkman, 1997). Police officers received education in child development, clinicians spent time with police in squad cars and on the streets, joint seminars were offered to both groups, and consultation services were arranged so that police officers could refer families for immediate counseling services. Consider the following case that resulted from professionals' working together; a crime was solved, and the victim received valuable support:

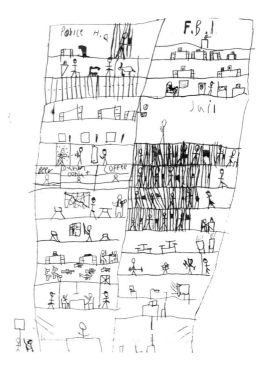

Nine-year-old Connor's image of law and order includes police headquarters, an office for the FBI, a jail, an interrogation room, an indoor rifle range, a storage area for weapons, and, curiously, a place where officers can eat donuts and drink beer and coffee.

> A 15-year-old boy was robbed at gunpoint by two men. In the immediate aftermath of the robbery, he was too shaken to say anything to police about what had happened. Officers referred him for an urgent clinical evaluation, which took place at the local hospital. During the course of the clinical interview, the boy reported wanting to get a gun and take revenge. By the end of the interview, however, he had recovered sufficient memory of the events to become an effective aid to investigating detectives, who were then able to arrest the robbers. Local community-based officers established regular contact with the boy, supporting him in the maintenance of his good school record and deterring an early-stage involvement with neighborhood drug dealers. (Marans & Berkman, 1997, p. 5)

As you have seen in the last few pages, people and institutions in the community influence children's development in numerous ways, both positive and negative. In fact, people across the nation and even across the world can influence growing children. The Developmental Trends table "Growing Up in Context at Different Age Levels" illustrates some of the ways that children in different age groups may respond to the varied contexts of their lives.

The Media

Television, films, radio, music, books, magazines, computers, the Internet—all give children and adolescents many options for entertainment, education, and communication. The media permeate young people's lives both inside and outside of formal school settings.

To some extent, children's minds are shaped by the messages that the media present. For instance, persuasive advertisements may influence their activities and eating habits; we recall our own children (and ourselves many years earlier) being absolutely certain that they (or we) would just *die* if they (we) didn't acquire a particular toy, game, breakfast cereal, or soft drink. Children also encounter certain social messages quite routinely in television shows, books, magazines, and song lyrics. Some of these messages (e.g., "Treat your neighbor as you yourself would like to be treated," "Every citizen should vote") are certainly beneficial, in that they promote prosocial behavior, citizenship, and other responsible actions, but others (e.g., "Violence resolves interpersonal conflicts," "Sexual promiscuity is safe and commonplace") give tacit approval to behaviors that are not in the best interests of children and adolescents. The media may also perpetuate stereotypes about particular groups of people. Frequently, television casts members of racial minority groups in bad-guy roles and portrays female characters as weak and passive, and academic textbooks more often portray men than women engaging in math and science (Eisenberg, Martin, & Fabes, 1996; Huston et al., 1992).

However, youngsters' own actions and thoughts mediate the effects that media and technology are likely to have. For example, most young people have considerable choice about the television programs they watch and actively interpret the content they view (Huston &

DEVELOPMENTAL TRENDS

Growing Up in Context at Different Age Levels

AGE	WHAT YOU MIGHT OBSERVE	DIVERSITY	IMPLICATIONS
Infancy (Birth–2) 	• Beginning awareness of cultural patterns, such as using tools in certain ways (e.g., putting a hairbrush to one's head) • Listening for sounds in languages used by families and caregivers • Growing familiarity with tastes and appearances of food served at home, in child care, and in the community.	• Infants differ in the number of languages they are exposed to at home and in child care. • Some infants may be comfortable with separations from parents, but others become quite distressed when dropped off at the child care setting. • Some infants are placed in front of the television as families go about their household routines.	• Use low child-staff ratios and employ staff trained in infant development and care. • Prioritize sensitive and responsive care so infants develop healthy and secure attachments to caregivers. • Staff child care with people who can speak languages spoken by families whenever possible. • Introduce new foods, experiences, and people gradually so infants feel safe and secure.
Early Childhood (2–6) 	• Strong motivation to learn the physical tools of one's culture (e.g., writing implements, computers) • Emerging but rudimentary understandings of gender and ethnic differences and of variations in religious practice • For many children, attendance at group child care or home care settings	• Children differ in their prior knowledge and skill-building experiences (e.g., storybook reading, visits to zoos and museums, travel to distant places). • Children celebrate holidays and birthdays differently depending on their families' cultural backgrounds. • Some children need extra reassurance from caregivers when saying good-bye to parents in the morning.	• Show respect for diverse backgrounds and perspectives (e.g., talk about the "holiday season" rather than Christmas). • Identify and build on the strengths that children from various cultural, religious, and socioeconomic backgrounds are likely to have. • Provide age-appropriate access to various media (books, computer programs, etc.).
Middle Childhood (6–10) 	• Increasing interest about people's differing cultural and religious beliefs and practices. • Increasing responsibility in decision making and self-care.	• Some children are more understanding and respectful than others of peers' backgrounds and income levels. • Some children can care for themselves responsibly, whereas others do not know or follow basic safety guidelines.	• Model and encourage respect for diverse practices and beliefs. • Incorporate multiple perspectives into the curriculum (e.g., in literature, history, music, art). • Provide a variety of activities in after-school programs so that all children can find enjoyment in at least one activity.
Early Adolescence (10–14) 	• Increasing identification with a particular ethnic group • Increasing ability to care for oneself; increasing independence from adult supervision • More time spent watching television and playing video games than in early or middle childhood	• Members of minority groups are more likely than members of the mainstream culture to form a strong ethnic identity (Phinney, 1989). • Some members of minority groups may see academic achievement in a negative light (i.e., as acting white). • With their increasing independence, some young adolescents come into contact with deviant adults and peers in their neighborhoods. • Some adolescents have few constructive after-school activities and resources in their neighborhoods.	• Stress the relevance of academic subjects for people from all backgrounds. • Let young adolescents make choices about some of their activities in after-school groups (Eccles, 1999). • Let young adolescents help establish goals and rules for their after-school clubs and programs. • Make regular use of newspaper and newsmagazine articles when exploring classroom topics.
Late Adolescence (14–18) 	• Increasing opportunities to explore the community and nearby cities independently of parents and other family members • Gradual decline in television viewing • Greater skill in accessing and exploring the Internet	• Some teenagers participate regularly in community activities (e.g., employment, public service activities); others rarely venture far from home in the after-school hours. • Adolescents differ considerably in their knowledge about and access to computers.	• Collaborate with community agencies to offer opportunities for career exploration and public service. • Encourage adolescents to use online sources to supplement rather than replace libraries and other traditional sources of information.

Wright, 1998). As a high school student, Jeanne's son Jeff was an avid viewer of *The Simpsons*, an animated cartoon series that depicts what some critics describe as a dysfunctional American family. Jeff certainly did not imitate Homer Simpson's alcoholic tendencies, Bart Simpson's delinquent activities, or Krusty the Clown's inappropriate interactions with children; he merely laughed at the characters' antics and found pleasure in the show's biting social commentary.

In the next section we review research related to two forms of media: television and computers. We then consider how professionals can take advantage of the benefits that the media have to offer.

Television

On average, television viewing time increases rapidly during early childhood, continues to increase in middle childhood and early adolescence (reaching a peak of almost 4 hours a day), and then declines gradually after about age 14 (Comstock, 1991; Medrich, Roizen, Rubin, & Buckley, 1982; Timmer, Eccles, & O'Brien, 1985). Children vary greatly in their television viewing habits, however: Some are glued to their TV sets for several hours a day while others rarely if ever watch television.

Television's increasing prominence in daily life has led many parents, teachers, and social activists to wonder about its possible negative effects on children and adolescents. They voice concerns not only about the graphic depictions of violence and sexual activity but also about the sheer number of hours children spend watching TV. In the following sections we look at television's possible negative effects and at its potential benefits for children's development.

What Harm Does Television Do and *Not* Do? Researchers have found that, overall, television viewing is not necessarily a bad thing, but that certain kinds of programs can have detrimental effects. Let's consider several common questions about the effects of television and the answers that emerge from the research.

■ *Does television take time away from more productive activities?* If so, the effects are small. In fact, the activities that seem most displaced by television are going to the movies and listening to the radio (Huston & Wright, 1998). Contrary to many people's assumptions, television does not substantially reduce time that would otherwise be spent reading. For example, when television satellite coverage was first introduced between 1995 and 1997 to St. Helena, a small island in the mid-South Atlantic, children began to watch television enthusiastically, but they also slightly increased the time they spent reading books, participating in sports, and enjoying indoor hobbies (Hannan & Carlton, 1999). On the other hand, they devoted somewhat less time to a few particular activities, such as sleeping, eating, walking, and watching videos. In other research, there is some evidence for an association between watching a lot of television during early childhood and spending little time in educational activities such as looking at books, being read to, and doing puzzles (e.g., Huston, Wright, Marquis, & Green, 1999). However, the correlational nature of these findings makes the results difficult to interpret. Watching television may leave children with less time to learn in other areas, but it is also possible that families who allow their children to watch a lot of television are not inclined to provide them with educational opportunities.

■ *Does television interfere with academic achievement?* Television does not interfere with the academic achievement of most children. Synthesizing the results of numerous studies, Huston and Wright (1998) concluded that watching television does not significantly interfere with school achievement except at very high levels of exposure—for instance, when students watch TV more than 4 hours a day or more than 30 hours a week. Extensive television viewing may inhibit the development of reading skills, although other factors—such as family background, exposure to print, and time spent doing homework—are far more influential factors in reading development (Huston & Wright, 1998; Ritchie, Price, & Roberts, 1987).

■ *Does television stifle imagination and breed mental passivity?* Not for most children. Contrary to public perceptions, children do not become "lumps on a log" when viewing television. They actively interpret programs, identify underlying themes, and show good recall for what they've seen (Huston & Wright, 1998). Nor does television automatically dampen children's imagination and creativity, although the content of programs does seem to have an impact. In particular, children who watch a lot of violence on television engage in less fantasy play than children who view little or no violence (Van der Voort & Valkenburg, 1994).

■ *Does television make children distractible?* Not really. Many educators believe that television's quick pace and frequent change of topics impair children's ability to focus thoughtfully and patiently on classroom lessons. However, there is no systematic evidence to support this assertion (Huston & Wright, 1998). For example, children who watch *Sesame Street,* which consists of many short segments, have been generally perceived by teachers to adjust well to the classroom setting (Wright & Huston, 1995).

■ *Do children learn the wrong social messages?* Possibly yes. Perhaps television's most negative impact resides in the content of its messages. Television often portrays people in ways that are arguably inappropriate. Television characters have been described as aggressive, stereotyped in gender and ethnic roles, and sexually active with partners they know only casually and with whom they do not use protective measures (Huston & Wright, 1998; Signorielli & Lears, 1992).

Children and adolescents show some understanding that television's social world is artificial. For instance, adolescents in grades 8 through 12 understand that sexual behavior on television does not mirror sexual behavior in everyday life (Silverman-Watkins & Sprafkin, 1983). They realize that the probability of having sex with someone one has just met is higher on television than in real life and that the negative consequences of unprotected sexual activity (e.g., an unwanted pregnancy or contraction of a sexually transmitted disease) are rarely shown on TV. However, despite such understandings, children and adolescents can still be influenced by television's social content, especially when they are heavy viewers (Huston & Wright, 1998).

■ *Does television lead to more aggression?* Although research results have not been 100% consistent, the general picture they paint makes us pause. Repeated exposure to violent acts on television seems to make children more aggressive, and it may be particularly harmful to those already predisposed to be aggressive (Andison, 1977; Eron, 1980; Hearold, 1986; Paik & Comstock, 1994; Van der Voort & Valkenburg, 1994; Wood, Wong, & Chachere, 1991). In other words, young children inclined to solve conflicts in physically aggressive ways may choose to watch programs that are particularly violent in content, and they become even more aggressive after viewing televised violence. Realistic violence seems to be more influential than the violence depicted in cartoons, though the latter appears to have an effect as well (Huston & Wright, 1998).

How Can Television Benefit Children? With its engaging combination of visual and auditory stimuli, television has tremendous potential to affect children's learning and development in a positive way (Comstock, 1991; Huston & Wright, 1998). It can teach basic skills; knowledge of current and historical events; understanding and problem solving in science and mathematics; and appreciation for literature, music, drama, and art. It can also promote greater awareness of the practices, language, and music of diverse cultures. For example, *Sesame Street* helps children learn their letters and numbers (Comstock, 1991; Huston & Wright, 1998). *Barney & Friends* promotes understanding of emotions, manners, nature, health, and cultural differences (D. G. Singer & Singer, 1994; J. L. Singer & Singer, 1994). *Reading Rainbow* piques interest in children's literature (RMC Research Corporation, 1989). Other programs have been found to enhance knowledge and attitudes about science and mathematics (Bennett, Debold, & Solan, 1991; M. Chen, 1984; Hall, Esty, & Fisch, 1990).

Unfortunately, most commercial television programming is not educational; those segments that do have educational value most often focus on natural and social science (Neapolitan & Huston, 1994). Furthermore, most families do little to steer children toward educational programming. In fact, parents rarely monitor or guide their children's viewing, nor do they generally sit down and watch television with their children (Comstock, 1991; Huston & Wright, 1998). Parents with new televisions can use "V-chip" technology to screen unwanted content, but few take advantage of this service. (Teresa confesses that her son Connor, then 12, showed her how to use the V-chip system.)

Although television is rarely used in schools and child care centers (Huston & Wright, 1998), it can be used productively in educational settings. For example, the benefits of watching *Barney & Friends* are greatest when preschool teachers plan classroom activities that build on what children learn from the program (D. G. Singer & Singer, 1994; J. L. Singer & Singer, 1994). Some distributors of educational programs offer suggestions for lesson plans and supplementary curriculum materials that complement what children see on television.[15]

Teachers and after-school caregivers must choose their selections carefully, however. One controversial program is *Channel One*, a program broadcast directly to middle and high schools that consists of 10 minutes of news and 2 minutes of advertisements (Huston & Wright, 1998; Wartella, 1995). Youngsters seem to gain knowledge of current events, but the advertisements influence their preferences for commercial products and may encourage them to become more avid consumers (Brand & Greenberg, 1994).

In industrialized societies, another medium, the computer, is gaining increasing prominence in many children's lives and, we suspect, is partly replacing television as a source of both entertainment and information.

Computers, the Internet, and New Technologies

Personal computers and their progeny seem to be just about everywhere these days. Computer technologies are changing the ways that adults communicate, make decisions, spend money, and entertain themselves. Children and adolescents follow suit and in many cases actually lead the pack.

One form of computer technology—video games—is a popular source of entertainment among American youth, especially boys between the ages of 5 and 12 (Huston & Wright, 1998). Video game systems can be found in many homes, and youngsters spend many hours clutching a controller as they engage in virtual karate matches, motorcycle races, and explorations of mythical environments. For example, 6-year-old Brent shows his enthusiasm for video games in the After School/Early Childhood clip from the Observation CD. He says:

Listen to Brent talk about video games in the After School/ Early Childhood clip of the Observation CD.

> I usually play video games. There's this army game and snowboard game and . . . and a game called "Smash Brothers." . . . They're cool.

Although video games may foster sensorimotor and spatial-visual skills (Greenfield, 1994b), those with violent content may desensitize children to violence and increase aggressive behavior (Cocking & Greenfield, 1996; Gailey, 1993; R. A. Irwin & Gross, 1995). Although some social critics worry that video games are replacing social play, it has been our observation as parents that children remain very social in their use of video games: They often share games with friends, watch one another in (virtual) action, compete with or against one another using two or more controllers, and eventually move on to other forms of recreation.

Other uses of computer technology are more beneficial than video games, however (Huston & Wright, 1998). Many computer programs make challenging cognitive demands and require considerable planning and strategy (Greenfield, 1994b). They can also be highly motivating. For instance, when her son Alex was 4, Teresa would routinely find him on the computer when she picked him up at his child care center, and Alex would insist on finishing what he was doing before they went home. Computers have an additional advantage in that, unlike television, communication goes two ways (from computer to child and from child to computer), and so children can see the immediate effects of their actions.

---

[15] For example, check out Websites for the Public Broadcasting Service, Discovery Channel, and Nickelodeon.

Gene drew this picture of his video game equipment from memory, showing his familiarity with the apparatus and a game's combat theme.

However, such interactivity does not always enhance learning, as images and sounds may captivate children more than the academic skills that program writers intend for them to master (Huston & Wright, 1998).

As youngsters make the transition from childhood to adolescence, many supplement or even replace interests in electronic games with social communication by e-mail and in chat rooms and MUDS (Multiuser Dungeons or Multiuser Dimensions) (Hellenga, 2002). Research on social relationships enabled by the Internet is in its infancy, but a preliminary case can be made for some positive effects. For example, a shy teenager may form relationships with a few individuals through regular e-mail and chat room exchanges; in these relationships the teenager learns to disclose personal information and to express feelings of anger, fear, and frustration. Other adolescents find like-minded individuals who support their interests and orientations (e.g., homosexuality). Adolescents may try on different personas at a time when they are wrestling with identity issues (e.g., some young people intentionally suggest that they are older than they really are, or accentuate their physical attractiveness) (Hellenga, 2002).

Some negative consequences are also possible. A teenager might withdraw from family and peers in favor of friends known only electronically; this desire to stay connected electronically may lead to excessively long hours on the computer (Hellenga, 2002). Other youngsters develop bad habits, such as "flaming" (verbally ridiculing someone in a public electronic site), "trolling" in newsgroups (making an inflammatory remark to provoke an argument), hacking into secured sites and trying to disrupt services or spread computer viruses, and plagiarizing the work of other people (Hellenga, 2002). Furthermore, adolescents who are regular users of the Internet often are sexually harassed or the recipients of sexual solicitation (Finkelhor, Mitchell, & Wolak, 2000). Also, some adolescents purposefully visit exploitative pornographic sites (R. E. Anderson, 2002).

Implications of Television and Technology for Children

Television, computers, the Internet, and other media have tremendous potential for educating children. You may hope, as we do, that corporate sponsors of television programming will increasingly support educational programs and that governments and international agencies will find ways to protect youths from vices of the World Wide Web (e.g., hacking, plagiarism, sexual predators). In addition, we offer the following suggestions:

■ *Encourage parents to regulate and monitor children's television viewing.* At meetings and events and in newsletters, professionals can encourage parents to set specific TV-viewing goals for their children. For instance, if parents find their children watching television 4 or more hours a day, they might want to set a 2-hour limit. Parents also may find it informative to watch television with their children. In the process, they can discover how their children interpret what they watch and provide a reality check when characters and story lines consistently violate norms for appropriate behavior ("Do you really think people should insult one another like that?").

■ *Teach critical viewing skills.* Practitioners can teach youngsters how to watch television with a critical eye. For example, preschool teachers can help young children understand that television commercials are designed to persuade them to buy toys and hamburgers. Teachers and community leaders working with older children and adolescents may point out more subtle advertising ploys, such as the use of color, images (e.g., sexual symbols), and endorsements by famous actors and athletes. And for any medium—television, computers, books, magazines, and so on—adults can help young people become more aware of stereotypes and negative portrayals of men and women, ethnic groups, and various professions.

■ *Use televised movies and computer programs that build on instructional units.* Some television programs and videos can make content in print more concrete and understandable. For instance, when Teresa and friend led a group of adolescents in a "Great Books" discussion of George Bernard Shaw's play *Pygmalion*, they all struggled to decipher the characters' dialects. Afterward, the group watched segments of *My Fair Lady*—a movie based on the play—and found dialects easier to understand. Furthermore, the different endings in the movie and the play provoked considerable discussion.

■ *Increase youngsters' familiarity and comfort with computers.* Although many middle- and upper-income families now have personal computers, many lower-income families cannot afford them. But as we look to the future, we anticipate that computer expertise, including Internet use, will be increasingly critical for everyone's success. Adults in many settings can find ways to incorporate computers and the Internet into lessons and activities. For instance, a preschool teacher might teach children how to play computer games that give practice in prereading and mathematical skills. An elementary school teacher might show students how to track the path of a hurricane using government weather maps. A coach might provide Internet Web sites where youngsters can find regulations for basketball. An after-school program provider might show young people how they can use the Internet to look up facts needed for homework.

■ *Teach young people to be critical users of the Internet.* Young people need to learn how to navigate through countless electronic sites. Because information is expanding exponentially on many significant topics, youngsters must learn (side-by-side with adults) to find, retrieve, organize, and evaluate information they find on the Internet. As young people begin to use the Internet for activities in classrooms and clubs, teachers and other professionals should give guidance for evaluating the quality of information on the World Wide Web (e.g., data provided by government agencies and well-known nonprofit organizations are fairly reliable, but opinion pieces on someone's personal home page may not be). Professionals can also ask youngsters to talk about the kinds of surfing they do on the Internet and the kinds of social contacts they make. Such conversations give adults a chance to point out that unscrupulous individuals may exploit young people commercially and sexually if given a chance.

■ *Encourage use of a wide range of media.* Television is the primary medium, and in some cases the only medium, through which many children and adolescents gain news and information about their region and country. Ideally, youngsters should learn to use the many other media available to them—not only the Internet but also books, newspapers, and newsmagazines—to gain the knowledge and skills they will need in the adult world.

A Place for Professionals in Children's Lives

In this chapter, we found many strong environmental influences on children's development. For example, we learned that adults' sensitivity in child care centers affects children's social and cognitive skills; a personal relationship with a stable, affectionate practitioner can help children overcome risks; cultural beliefs and practices prepare children to take up responsible positions in their society; and neighborhoods dictate children's choices for recreation, exposure to hazards, and access to role models. Furthermore, we learned that children themselves are a major factor in the contextual equation. Rather than passively submitting to environments, young people assert preferences for clubs and hobbies, wrestle with implications of religious and nonreligious doctrines, and select television programs to watch and Internet sites to visit (occasionally with family guidance).

Amidst these and other contextual influences, trained professionals offer needed services to children. This means that you, as someone potentially preparing to work with children, are about to become a vital part of children's landscape. As a caring adult, you can form personal relationships with children, cultivate their emerging strengths, and persuade them to find a good path. And when children stumble, you can nudge, persuade, insist, advocate—do whatever it takes—to help them get back on track.

To make a difference in the lives of children, you must surmount significant challenges. For example, you may confront serious social problems (e.g., poverty and racism), be obliged to allocate time to numerous duties (e.g., preparing reports, managing budgets, and caring for children), and have to come to terms with conflicting objectives (e.g., rehabilitating versus punishing delinquent youths). These formidable challenges can challenge the most dedicated child professional. The prize, of course, is worth it: watching children progress toward positive developmental outcomes.

Keep your eye on the prize. To make a difference to children, give your utmost attention to their developmental needs. We have offered recommendations throughout this book for supporting specific aspects of children's development. For maximum impact, you will need to adapt these strategies to the particular populations with whom you work. Moreover, your position will partly determine the specific effects you have on children. For example, as a teacher, you can have a strong impact on children's academic skills, sense of self, and peer relationships. As a family educator or youth service provider, you can document serious family problems, connect families with social service agencies, and give young people new hope. As a mental health professional, you can teach children how to cope with sadness, disappointment, and anger. As a community leader, you can give young people outlets for recreation and work experience. And as a health educator, you can persuade children and adolescents to care for their own physical needs and avoid risky behaviors.

Regardless of your exact job title or the specific community in which you work, however, you can apply your knowledge of child development and in particular your understanding of basic developmental issues. Think about these three issues one final time. First, the tendency for *nature and nurture* to be intertwined throughout development enables you to stay optimistic for children. A child's fate is never sealed—it always depends on care from adults and the child's own efforts. In addition, consider how you can acknowledge children's genetically based talents, dispositions, and limitations. When children's natural inclinations become stumbling blocks to positive growth, give them a supporting hand.

Second, both *universality and diversity* are important landmarks for professionals. Many variations in developmental pathways—the timing, appearance, and nature of changes—are normal and predictable. By becoming familiar with vast differences among children, you can learn to treat individual youngsters patiently and appropriately. However, when children are exceptionally late in reaching a basic milestone or adjust poorly to a developmental transition, intervention may be helpful or even necessary. For example, you may offer extra support to a 1-year-old child failing to explore the environment, a 5-year-old child showing no empathy for familiar people in distress, a 9-year-old child struggling to read, a 12-year-old adolescent feeling anxious after a full year in middle school, and a 16-year-old adolescent withdrawing suddenly from family and friends.

Finally, remember that children change both *qualitatively and quantitatively* as they learn about the world. As you teach children academic concepts, the benefits of physical activity, ways to get along with peers, and so on, you may find that they gradually accumulate new knowledge and skills. On other occasions, qualitative change is in order when children must reorganize their thinking and behavior, often to the beats of their own internal drum.

There are many obstacles, distractions, and stresses in any job. By focusing on children's developmental needs, you have one solid reason to confront these challenges: You know you can make a difference.

CASE STUDY: FRANK

In *Angela's Ashes*, Frank McCourt (1996) describes what it was like to be a small child in Ireland dealing with hunger, cold, inadequate housing, health problems, an alcoholic father, and an overwhelming sense of personal responsibility for his family.[16]

> I wish I could swing up into the sky, up into the clouds. I might be able to fly around the whole world and not hear my brothers, Oliver and Eugene, cry in the middle of the night anymore. My mother says they're always hungry. She cries in the middle of the night, too. She says she's worn out nursing and feeding and changing and four boys is too much for her. She wishes she had one little girl all for herself. She'd give anything for one little girl. . . . (p. 22)

> My mother tells me all the time, Never, never leave that playground except to come home. But what am I to do with the twins bawling with the hunger in the pram? I tell

---

[16] Extracts reprinted with permission of Scribner, a Division of Simon & Schuster, Inc., from *Angela's Ashes* by Frank McCourt. Copyright © 1996 by Frank McCourt.

Malachy I'll be back in a minute. I make sure no one is looking, grab a bunch of bananas outside the Italian grocery shop and run down Myrtle Avenue, away from the playground, around the block and back to the other end where there's a hole in the fence. We push the pram to a dark corner and peel the bananas for the twins. There are five bananas in the bunch and we feast on them in the dark corner. The twins slobber and chew and spread banana over their faces, their hair, their clothes. I realize then that questions will be asked. Mam will want to know why the twins are smothered in bananas, where did you get them? I can't tell her about the Italian shop on the corner. I will have to say, A man . . . (p. 32)

Dad and Mam lay at the head of the bed, Malachy and I at the bottom, the twins wherever they could find comfort. Malachy made us laugh again. Ye, ye, ye, he said, and oy oy oy, and then fell asleep. Mam made the little hink hink snore sound that told us she was sleeping. In the moonlight I could look up the length of the bed and see Dad still awake and when Oliver cried in his sleep Dad reached for him and held him. Whisht, he said. Whisht.

Then Eugene sat up, screaming, tearing at himself. Ah, ah, Mommy, Mommy. Dad sat up. What's up son? Eugene went on crying and when Dad leaped up from the bed and turned on the gaslight we saw the fleas, leaping, jumping, fastened to our flesh. We slapped at them and slapped but they hopped from body to body, hopping, biting. We tore at the bites till they bled. We jumped from the bed, the twins crying, Mam moaning. . . . (p. 59)

I'm seven, eight, nine going on ten and still Dad has no work. He drinks his tea in the morning, signs for the dole at the Labour Exchange, reads the papers at the Carnegie Library, goes for his long walks far into the country. If he gets a job at the Limerick Cement Company or Rank's Flour Mills he loses it in the third week. He loses it because he goes to the pubs on the third Friday of the job, drinks all his wages and misses the half day of work on Saturday morning. . . . (p. 145)

Having read these descriptions of Frank's childhood, you may wonder what transformed a poor child into the witty and successful author that Frank has become. What kind of education did Frank have? Did he have warm and sympathetic teachers? Did they help him build his confidence? We peek back into his school experiences looking for answers:

Mr. O'Neill is the master in the fourth class at school. We call him Dotty because he's small like a dot. He teaches in the one classroom with a platform so that he can stand above us and threaten us with his ash plant and peel his apple for all to see. The first day of school in September he writes on the blackboard three words which are to stay there for the rest of the year, Euclid, geometry, idiot. Now, repeat after me, Anyone who doesn't understand the theorems of Euclid is an idiot. Of course we all know what an idiot is because that's what the masters keep telling us we are.

Brendan Quigley raises his hand. Sir, what's a theorem and what's a Euclid?

We expect Dotty to lash at Brendan the way all masters do when you ask them a question but he looks at Brendan with a little smile. Ah, now, here's a boy with not one but two questions. What is your name, boy?

Brendan Quigley, sir.

This is a boy who will go far. Where will he go, boys?

Far, sir.

Indeed and he will. The boy who wants to know something about the grace, elegance and beauty of Euclid can go nowhere but up. In what direction and no other can this boy go, boys?

Up, sir.

Without Euclid, boys, mathematics would be a poor doddering thing. Without Euclid we wouldn't be able to go from here to there. Without Euclid the bicycle would have no wheel. Without Euclid St. Joseph could not have been a carpenter for carpentry is geometry and geometry is carpentry. Without Euclid this very school could never have been built. (McCourt, 1996, pp. 151–152)

- In what ways were daily hardship, poverty, and injustice part of Frank's education? How do Frank's experiences resemble those of children who live in poverty that you've read about in this chapter?
- How might Frank have used his peers as a source of social support?
- Frank eventually became a successful author. From what you learned about resilience in this chapter, how might you explain his success?

 Now go to our Companion Website to assess your understanding of chapter content with a Practice Quiz, apply what you've learned in Essay Questions, and broaden your knowledge with links to related Developmental Psychology Web sites. Go to www.prenhall.com/mcdevitt.

SUMMARY

Culture and Ethnicity

Children's cultural heritage helps them to derive meaning from their interactions with their physical and social worlds. Membership in a particular cultural or ethnic group gives them values, beliefs, and traditions that influence their daily behaviors both in and outside of school; it often becomes an important part of children's identity. Depending on circumstances, children from minority groups may embrace mainstream culture, find a workable balance between their own roots and mainstream practices, or reject mainstream ideals.

History

The significant social and political events that occur during childhood affect children's knowledge, skills, motives, attitudes, priorities, and goals. War, peace, famine, prosperity, the destructive forces of nature, technological advances—these and many other aspects of history influence children's development.

Religious Affiliation

Religious beliefs and philosophical ideas, like culture, help children impose meaning on their lives. Initially, children's religious beliefs are quite concrete in nature but in other ways tend to be similar to those of their parents. Adolescents form more abstract notions and begin to question the religious ideas and practices that their elders have handed down to them.

Socioeconomic Status

Economic well-being affects availability of resources and influences where families live and what schools children will attend. Children whose families live in poverty face numerous challenges, possibly including poor nutrition and health care, inadequate housing, gaps in background knowledge, increased risk for physical and mental disabilities, emotional stress, low-quality schools, and public misconceptions and disdain. Nevertheless, many children and adolescents are resilient to such environmental insults (particularly if they have one or more supportive people in their lives) and grow to be successful, productive adults.

Neighborhood and Community

Neighborhoods and communities affect children directly through the role models and peer groups they provide, as well as indirectly through the social and emotional support they offer families. Neighborhoods and communities contribute in significant ways to children's development—by providing child care centers, early intervention programs, after-school programs, employment opportunities, and access to services.

Media and Technology

Many children and adolescents spend after-school hours watching television and playing or working on the computer. Television, computers, and other media have considerable potential for fostering children's cognitive development, but their benefits have not yet been fully realized.

Professionals in Children's Lives

Professionals extend and enrich the contexts in which children live; sometimes professionals compensate for problems in youngsters' primary environments. Professionals are advised to focus on the important developmental tasks that children face and to surmount the many challenges and distractions they inevitably face in their work.

KEY CONCEPTS

culture (p. 596)
ethnicity (p. 597)
multi-ethnic child (p. 597)
acculturation (p. 599)
assimilation (p. 599)
selective adoption (p. 599)
rejection (of a new culture) (p. 600)
bicultural orientation (p. 600)
multicultural education (p. 607)
socioeconomic status (SES) (p. 614)
resilience (p. 617)
child care (pp. 625)
early childhood intervention program (p. 628)
service learning (p. 631)
mentorship (pp. 634)
juvenile justice system (pp. 634)

Glossary

accommodation   Dealing with a new event by either modifying an existing scheme or forming a new one.

acculturation   Taking on the customs and values of a new culture.

achievement motivation   Need for excellence for its own sake, without regard for any external rewards that one's accomplishments might bring.

action research   Systematic study of an issue or problem in one's own situation, with the goal of bringing about improved practice and more productive outcomes.

actual developmental level   Upper limit of tasks that a child can successfully perform independently.

adaptation   Developmental process of responding to the environment in an increasingly effective manner.

adaptive behavior   Behavior related to daily living skills and appropriate conduct in social situations.

addiction   Physical and psychological dependence on a substance, such that increasing quantities must be taken to produce the desired effect and withdrawal produces adverse physiological and psychological effects.

African American English   Dialect of some African American communities that includes some pronunciations, grammatical constructions, and idioms different from those of Standard English.

aggressive behavior   Action intentionally taken to hurt another, either physically or psychologically.

alleles   Genes located at the same point on corresponding (paired) chromosomes and related to the same physical characteristic.

androgyny   Tendency to have some characteristics that are stereotypically "female" (e.g., nurturance) and others that are stereotypically "male" (e.g., assertiveness).

anorexia nervosa   Eating disorder in which a person eats little or nothing for weeks or months and seriously jeopardizes health.

anxiety   Emotional state characterized by worry and apprehension.

anxiety disorder   Chronic emotional condition characterized by excessive, debilitating worry.

apprenticeship   Situation in which a novice works intensively with an expert to learn how to accomplish complex tasks.

assessment   Task that children complete and researchers use to make judgments of children's understandings and skills.

assimilation   In Piaget's theory, dealing with a new event in a way that is consistent with an existing scheme (Ch. 4). In cultural identity, totally embracing a new culture, abandoning one's previous culture in the process (Ch. 14).

attachment   An enduring emotional tie uniting one person to another.

attention-deficit hyperactivity disorder (ADHD)   Disability (probably biological in origin) characterized by inattention and/or hyperactivity and impulsive behavior.

attribution   Belief about the cause of one's success or failure.

authentic activity   Instructional activity similar to one that a child might eventually encounter in the outside world.

authoritarian style   Parenting style characterized by strict expectations for behavior and rigid rules that children are expected to obey without question.

authoritative parenting   Parenting style characterized by emotional warmth, high expectations and standards for behavior, consistent enforcement of rules, explanations regarding the reasons behind these rules, and the inclusion of children in decision making.

authoritative style   Parenting style characterized by emotional warmth, high expectations and standards for behavior, consistent enforcement of rules, explanations regarding the reasons behind these rules, and the inclusion of children in decision making.

autism   Disability (probably biological in origin) characterized by infrequent social interaction, little awareness of one's own and others' thoughts, communication impairments, repetitive behaviors, narrowly focused interests, and a strong need for a predictable environment.

automatization   Process of becoming able to respond quickly and efficiently while mentally processing or physically performing certain tasks.

axon   Armlike part of a neuron that sends information to other neurons.

babbling   Universal tendency for human beings to produce speechlike sounds in infancy.

behavioral learning perspective   Theoretical perspective that focuses on environmental stimuli and learning processes that lead to developmental change.

behaviorism   Theoretical perspective in which behavior is described and explained in terms of specific stimulus-response relationships.

bicultural orientation   Ability to behave in accordance with two different cultural frameworks in appropriate contexts.

bilingual education   Approach to second-language instruction in which students are instructed in academic subject areas in their native language while simultaneously being taught to speak and write in the second language.

bilingualism   Knowing and speaking two languages fluently.

biliteracy   Ability to read and write well in two languages.

blended family   Family created when one parent-child(ren) family structure combines with another parent figure and any children in his or her custody.

bulimia   Eating disorder in which a person, in an attempt to be thin, eats a large amount of food and then purposefully purges it from the body by vomiting or taking laxatives.

canalization   Tight genetic control of a particular aspect of development.

care orientation   Focus on nurturance and concern for others in moral decision making.

causal-comparative study   Research study in which relationships are identified between existing conditions in children's lives and one or more aspects of the children's behavior.

central conceptual structure   Integrated network of concepts and cognitive processes that forms the basis for much of one's thinking, reasoning, and learning in specific content domains.

central executive   Component of the human information processing system that oversees the flow of information throughout the system.

cephalocaudal trend   Vertical ordering of motor skills and physical development; order is head first to feet last.

child care   Care of children by nonparental adults for a significant portion of the workweek.

chromosome   Rodlike structure that resides in the nucleus of every cell of the body and contains genes that guide growth and development; each chromosome is made up of DNA.

class inclusion   Recognition that something simultaneously belongs to a particular category and to one of its subcategories.

classroom climate   General psychological atmosphere of the classroom.

clinical method   Procedure whereby a researcher probes a child's reasoning about a task or problem, tailoring questions to follow up on what the child has previously said or done.

clique   Moderately stable friendship group of perhaps 3 to 10 members.

codominance   Situation in which the two genes of an allele pair, though not identical, both have some influence on the characteristic they affect.

cognition   The various mental activities in which a person engages.

cognitive apprenticeship   Mentorship in which an expert and a novice work together on a challenging task and the expert suggests ways to think about the task.

cognitive development   Systematic changes in reasoning, concepts, memory, and language.

cognitive-developmental perspective   Theoretical perspective that focuses on qualitative changes in thinking processes over time.

cognitive strategy Specific mental process that people use to acquire or manipulate information.

colic Persistent crying by infants; it is most prevalent in the first three months of life.

comprehension monitoring Process of checking oneself to make sure one understands what one is learning.

conceptions of society Beliefs about the nature, structure, and operations of social institutions.

conceptual change Revising one's knowledge and understanding of a topic in response to new information about the topic.

conduct disorder Chronic emotional condition characterized by lack of concern for the rights of others.

conservation Realization that if nothing is added or taken away, amount stays the same regardless of any alterations in shape or arrangement.

constructivism Theoretical perspective proposing that learners construct a body of knowledge from their experiences, rather than absorbing information at face value.

context The broad social environments, including culture, ethnicity, neighborhood, family, community, socioeconomic status, religious affiliation, and historical events, that influence children's development.

control group A group of participants in a research study who do not receive the treatment under investigation; often used in an experimental study.

controversial children Children whom some peers really like and other peers strongly dislike.

conventional morality Acceptance of society's conventions regarding right and wrong; behaving to please others or to live up to society's expectations for appropriate behavior.

conventional transgression Action that violates society's general guidelines (often unspoken) for socially acceptable behavior.

cooing Making and repeating vowel sounds (e.g., "oooooo"); common in early infancy.

co-regulated learning Process through which an adult and child share responsibility for directing various aspects of the child's learning.

correlation Extent to which two variables are related to each other, such that when one variable increases, the other either increases or decreases in a somewhat predictable fashion.

correlational feature Characteristic present in many instances of a concept but not essential for concept membership.

correlational study Research study that explores relationships among variables.

correlation coefficient A statistic that indicates the nature of the relationship between two variables.

cortex Part of the forebrain that houses conscious thinking processes (executive functions).

cross-sectional study Research study in which the performance of individuals at different ages is compared.

crystallized intelligence Knowledge and skills accumulated from prior experience and schooling.

cultural bias Extent to which an assessment instrument offends or unfairly penalizes some individuals because of their ethnicity, gender, or socioeconomic status.

culture Behaviors and belief systems that characterize a social group and provide a framework for how group members decide what is normal and appropriate.

culture shock Sense of confusion that occurs when one encounters an environment with expectations for behavior very different from those in one's home environment.

deferred imitation Ability to recall and reproduce another person's behaviors after a delay of several hours or longer.

defining feature Characteristic that must be present in all instances of a concept.

delay of gratification Foregoing small immediate rewards for larger, more delayed ones.

dendrite Branchlike part of a neuron that receives information from other neurons.

depression Emotional condition characterized by significant sadness, discouragement, and hopelessness.

development Systematic, age-related changes in physical and psychological functioning.

developmentally appropriate practice Adapting instructional practices and materials to the age, characteristics, and developmental progress of children.

developmental systems perspective Theoretical perspective that focuses on the multiple factors, including systems inside and outside children, that combine to influence children's development.

dialect Form of a language characteristic of a particular geographic region or ethnic group.

differentiation An increase from general to more specific functioning over the course of development.

disequilibrium State of being unable to explain new events in terms of existing schemes.

disorganized and disoriented attachment Attachment classification in which children lack a single coherent way of responding to attachment figures.

distributed intelligence Thinking facilitated by physical objects and technology, social support, and concepts and symbols of one's culture.

distributive justice Beliefs about what constitutes people's fair share of a valued commodity.

diversity Characteristics and developmental progressions that differ from one individual to another.

dizygotic twins Twins that began as two separate zygotes and so are as genetically similar as two siblings conceived and born at different times.

DNA Short for deoxyribonucleic acid, a double-helix shaped "ladder" of four chemicals that specifies how to build specific proteins, which in turn direct growth and developmental change.

dominance hierarchy Relative standing of group members in terms of such qualities as leadership and popularity.

dominant gene Gene that overrides any competing instructions in an allele pair.

dynamic assessment Systematic examination of how a child's knowledge or reasoning

may change as a result of learning or performing a specific task.

dysgraphia Exceptional difficulty acquiring handwriting skills.

dyslexia Inability to master basic reading skills in a developmentally typical time frame.

early childhood intervention program Program for infants, toddlers, and preschool children designed to foster basic intellectual, social-emotional, and physical development in children whose home environments may not nurture such skills.

egocentric speech Speaking without taking the perspective and knowledge of the listener into account.

egocentrism Inability of a child in Piaget's preoperational stage to view situations from another person's perspective.

elaboration Using prior knowledge to expand on new information and thereby learn it more effectively.

emergent literacy Knowledge and skills that lay a foundation for reading and writing; typically develops in the preschool years from early experiences with written language.

emotion Affective response to an event that is personally relevant to one's needs and goals.

emotional contagion Tendency for infants to cry spontaneously when they hear other infants crying.

emotional regulation Strategies to manage responses to stressful events (also called coping).

empathy Capacity to experience the same feelings as another person, especially in pain or distress.

entity view of ability Belief that ability is a "thing" that is relatively permanent and unchangeable.

epistemological beliefs Beliefs regarding the nature of knowledge and knowledge acquisition.

equilibration Movement from equilibrium to disequilibrium and back to equilibrium; a process that promotes the development of increasingly complex forms of thought and knowledge.

equilibrium State of being able to explain new events in terms of existing schemes.

ethnic identity Awareness of one's membership in a particular ethnic or cultural group, and willingness to adopt certain behaviors characteristic of that group.

ethnicity Membership in a group of people with a common set of values, beliefs, and behaviors. The group's roots either precede the creation of, or are external to, the country in which the group resides.

ethological attachment theory Theoretical perspective that emphasizes the functional importance of caregiver-child bonds in protecting children and giving them a secure base from which to explore their surroundings.

evolutionary perspective Theoretical perspective that focuses on inherited behavior patterns that enhance the survival and reproduction of the species.

executive functions Conscious thinking processes within the brain (e.g., reasoning, communicating, decision making).

expansion Repeating a child's short utterances in a more complete and grammatically correct form.

experimental study Research study in which a researcher manipulates one aspect of the environment (a treatment), controls other aspects of the environment, and assesses the treatment's effects on participants' behavior.

expressive language Ability to communicate effectively through speaking and writing.

extrinsic motivation Motivation promoted by factors external to the individual and unrelated to the task being performed.

family One or more adults caring for offspring for a significant portion of their childhood.

fast mapping Inferring a word's general meaning after a single exposure.

fetal alcohol syndrome (FAS) Condition in which a child is born with distinctive facial features, delayed motor and language development, and mental retardation; results from excessive alcohol consumption throughout pregnancy.

figurative speech Speech that communicates meaning beyond a literal interpretation of its words.

fine motor skills Small, precise movements of particular parts of the body, especially the hands

fluid intelligence Ability to acquire knowledge quickly and thereby adapt readily to new situations.

Flynn effect Gradual increase in intelligence test performance observed worldwide over the past several decades.

forebrain Part of the brain responsible for complex thinking, emotions, and motivation.

fourth-grade slump Tendency for some children (especially those from low-income backgrounds) to experience greater difficulty with reading tasks as they encounter more challenging material in the upper elementary grades.

functionalism Theoretical perspective of language development that emphasizes the purposes language serves for human beings.

g General factor in intelligence that influences performance in a wide variety of tasks and content domains.

gamete Reproductive cell that, in humans, contains 23 chromosomes rather than the 46 present in other cells in the body; a male gamete (sperm) and a female gamete (ovum) join at conception.

gang Cohesive social group characterized by initiation rites, distinctive colors and symbols, territorial orientation, and feuds with rival groups.

gene Basic unit of genetic instruction in a living cell; segments of genes are contained on chromosomes.

giftedness Unusually high ability in one or more areas, to the point where children require special educational services to help them meet their full potential.

glial cell Cell in the brain or other part of the nervous system that provides structural or functional support for one or more neurons.

goal-directed behavior Intentional behavior aimed at bringing about an anticipated outcome.

grammatical word Word that affects the meanings of other words or the interrelationships among words in a sentence.

gross motor skills Large movements of the body that permit locomotion around the environment.

growth spurt Rapid increase in height and weight during puberty.

guided participation Active engagement in adult activities, typically with considerable direction and structure from an adult or other more advanced individual; children are given increasing responsibility and independence as they gain experience and proficiency.

guilt Feeling of discomfort when one inflicts damage or causes someone else pain or distress.

habituation Changes in children's physiological responses to repeated displays of the same stimulus; it reflects loss of interest.

hindbrain Part of the brain controlling the basic physiological processes that sustain survival.

holophrase A single word used to express a complete thought; commonly observed in children's earliest speech.

identity People's self-constructed definition of who they are, what they find important, what they believe, and what goals they want to accomplish in life.

identity crisis Period during which an individual actively struggles to choose a course in life.

imaginary audience Belief that one is the center of attention in any social situation.

immersion Approach to second-language instruction in which students hear and speak that language almost exclusively in the classroom.

inclusion Practice of educating all students, including those with severe and multiple disabilities, in neighborhood schools and general education classrooms.

incremental view of ability Belief that ability can and does improve with effort and practice.

individual constructivism Theoretical perspective that focuses on how people construct meaning from events without the assistance of others.

induction Explaining why a certain behavior is unacceptable, often with a focus on the pain or distress that someone has caused another.

infant-directed speech Short, simple, high-pitched speech often used when talking to young children.

infantile amnesia General inability to recall events that occurred in the early years of life.

information processing perspective Theoretical perspective that focuses on the precise nature of human cognitive processes.

information processing theory Theoretical perspective that focuses on the specific ways in which people mentally think about ("process") the information they receive.

inner speech "Talking" to oneself mentally rather than aloud.

insecure-avoidant attachment Attachment classification in which children appear

somewhat indifferent to attachment figures.

insecure-resistant attachment Attachment classification in which children are preoccupied with their attachment figures but gain little comfort from them when distressed.

integration An increasing coordination of body parts over the course of development.

intelligence Ability to modify and adjust one's behaviors in order to accomplish new tasks successfully.

intelligence test General measure of current cognitive functioning, used primarily to predict academic achievement over the short run.

intentionality Engaging in an action congruent with one's purpose or goal.

internalization In Vygotsky's theory, the gradual evolution of external, social activities into internal, mental activities (Ch. 4). In moral development, adopting society's rules and values about acceptable behavior as one's own (Ch. 10).

internalized motivation Adoption of behaviors that others value, even if those behaviors are not reinforced by environmental consequences.

intersubjectivity Shared understandings that provide the foundation for social interaction and communication.

interview Data collection technique that obtains self-report data through face-to-face conversation.

intrinsic motivation Internal desire to perform a particular task.

invented spelling Children's early, self-constructed word spellings, which may reflect only some of a word's phonemes.

IQ score Score on an intelligence test determined by comparing one's performance with the performance of same-age peers.

IRE cycle Adult-child interaction pattern marked by adult initiation, child response, and adult evaluation; in Western cultures, such a pattern is often seen in instructional settings.

joint attention Phenomenon in which two people (e.g., a child and caregiver) simultaneously focus on the same object or event, monitor each other's attention, and coordinate their responses.

justice orientation Focus on individual rights in moral decision making.

juvenile justice system Network of professionals and agencies that work with young people accused of, or at risk for, breaking a law.

knowledge base One's knowledge about specific topics and the world in general.

knowledge telling Writing down ideas in whatever order they come to mind, with little regard for communicating the ideas effectively.

knowledge transforming Writing ideas in such a way as to intentionally help the reader understand them.

language acquisition device Biologically built-in mechanism hypothesized to facilitate language learning.

learned helplessness General belief that one is incapable of accomplishing tasks and has little or no control of the environment.

learning disability   Significant deficit in one or more cognitive processes, to the point where special educational services are required.

learning strategy   Specific mental process used in acquiring new information.

left hemisphere   Left side of the cortex; largely responsible for sequential reasoning and analysis, especially in right-handed people.

level of potential development   Upper limit of tasks that a child can successfully perform with the assistance of a more competent individual.

lexical word   Word that in some way represents an aspect of one's physical, social, or psychological world.

lexicon   The words one knows in a particular language.

life-span perspective   Theoretical perspective that looks at developmental patterns from conception until death.

longitudinal study   Research study in which the performance of a single group of people is tracked over a period of time.

long-term memory   Component of memory that holds knowledge and skills for a relatively long period of time.

mastery goal   Desire to acquire additional knowledge or master new skills.

mastery orientation   General belief that one is capable of accomplishing challenging tasks, accompanied by the intent to master such tasks.

maturation   Genetically controlled changes that occur over the course of development.

maturational perspective   Theoretical perspective that emphasizes genetically guided unfolding of developmental structures, neurological organizations, and motor abilities.

mediated learning experience   Discussion between an adult and a child in which the adult helps the child make sense of an event they have mutually experienced.

meiosis   The process of cell reproduction and division by which gametes are formed.

menarche   First menstrual period in an adolescent female.

mental retardation   Condition marked by significantly below-average general intelligence and deficits in adaptive behavior.

mentorship   Relationship between an adult and a youngster in which the adult takes a personal interest in the young person, serves as a role model, and cultivates the young person's career and educational aspirations.

metacognition   Knowledge and beliefs about one's own cognitive processes, as well as efforts to regulate those cognitive processes to maximize learning and memory.

metacognitive awareness   Extent to which one is able to reflect on the nature of one's own thinking processes.

metalinguistic awareness   Extent to which one is able to think about the nature of language.

midbrain   Part of the brain that coordinates communication between the hindbrain and forebrain.

monozygotic twins   Twins that began as a single zygote and so share the same genetic makeup.

moral dilemma   Situation in which there is no clear-cut answer regarding the morally correct thing to do.

morality   General set of standards about right and wrong.

moral realism   Viewing rules for behavior as firm and inflexible, as having a life of their own separate from the purposes they serve.

moral transgression   Action that causes damage or harm or in some other way infringes on the needs and rights of others.

motivation   State that energizes, directs, and sustains behavior.

multicultural education   Education that includes the perspectives and experiences of numerous cultural groups on a regular basis.

multi-ethnic child   A child who can claim ancestry from more than one ethnic group.

myelination   The growth of a fatty sheath around neurons that allows them to transmit messages more quickly.

narrative   A temporal sequence of events that are logically interconnected; a story.

native language   The first language a child learns.

nativism   Theoretical perspective that some knowledge is biologically built in and present at birth.

naturalistic study   Research study in which individuals are observed in their natural environment.

nature   Effects of heredity and genetically controlled maturational processes on development.

need for affiliation   Consistent tendency in some individuals to seek out friendly relationships with others.

need for approval   Consistent desire in some individuals to gain the acceptance and positive judgments of others.

need for relatedness   Fundamental human need to feel socially connected and secure the love and respect of others.

negative reinforcement   Consequence that brings about the increase of a behavior through the removal (rather than presentation) of a stimulus.

neglected children   Children whom peers rarely select as someone they would either most like or least like to do something with.

neo-Piagetian theory   Theoretical perspective that combines elements of both Piaget's theory and information processing theory and portrays cognitive development as involving a series of distinct stages.

neuron   Cell that transmits information to other cells; also called nerve cell.

neurotransmitter   Chemical substance through which one neuron sends a message to another neuron.

niche-picking   Tendency to actively seek out environments that match one's inherited abilities.

nurture   Effects of environmental conditions on development.

obesity   Condition in which a person weighs at least 20% more than what is optimal for good health.

object permanence   Realization that objects continue to exist even after they are removed from view.

observation   Data collection technique whereby a researcher carefully observes and documents the behaviors of participants in a research study.

operant conditioning   Explanation of behavior change in which a response increases in frequency as a result of being followed by reinforcement.

operation   In Piaget's theory, an organized and integrated system of thought processes.

organization   Finding interrelationships among pieces of information as a way of learning them more effectively.

overgeneralization   Too broad a meaning for a word, such that it is used in situations to which it doesn't apply.

overregularization   Applying a syntactical rule in situations where exceptions to the rule apply.

parenting style   General pattern of behaviors that a parent uses to nurture and guide his or her children.

peer culture   General set of rules, expectations, and interpretations that influence how members of a particular peer group behave.

peer pressure   Tactics used to encourage some behaviors and discourage others in age-mates.

perception   Cognitive interpretation of stimuli that the body has sensed.

performance goal   Desire to look good and receive favorable judgments from others.

permissive style   Parenting style characterized by emotional warmth but few expectations or standards for children's behavior.

personal fable   Tendency for adolescents to think of themselves as unique beings invulnerable to normal risks and dangers.

personality   Characteristic way an individual person behaves, thinks, and feels.

personal space   Personally and culturally preferred distance between two people during social interaction.

person perception   Recognition and interpretation of people's basic characteristics, including their physical features, behaviors, and internal psychological states.

phonemes   Smallest units of a spoken language that signify differences in meaning.

phonological awareness   Ability to hear the distinct sounds within words.

phonology   The sound system of a language; how words sound and are produced.

physical development   Physical and neurological growth and age-related changes in motor skills.

physiological measure   Direct assessment of physical development or physiological functioning.

playing the dozens   Friendly, playful exchange of insults, common in some African American communities. Also called joaning or sounding.

polygenic inheritance   Situation in which many genes combine in their influence on a particular characteristic.

popular children   Children whom many peers like and perceive to be kind and trustworthy.

positive reinforcement   Consequence that brings about the increase of a behavior through the presentation (rather than removal) of a stimulus.

postconventional morality   Behaving in accordance with self-developed, fairly abstract principles regarding right and wrong.

pragmatics   Strategies and rules for effective and socially acceptable verbal interaction.

preconventional morality A lack of internalized standards about right and wrong; making decisions based on what is best for oneself, without regard for others' needs and feelings.

prejudice Exhibiting negative attitudes, feelings, and behaviors toward particular individuals because of their membership in a specific group.

primary reinforcer Stimulus that satisfies a built-in biological need.

prosocial behavior Action intended to benefit another, without regard for one's own needs.

proximodistal trend Inside-outside ordering of motor skills and physical development; order is inside first and outside last.

psychodynamic perspective Theoretical perspective that focuses on how early experiences affect social and personality development.

psychometric approach Approach to cognitive development that focuses on children's performance on intelligence tests.

psychosocial stages In Erikson's theory, eight periods of life that involve age-related tasks or dilemmas.

puberty Physiological changes that occur during adolescence and lead to reproductive maturation.

qualitative change Relatively dramatic developmental change that reflects considerable reorganization or modification of functioning.

qualitative research Research study in which the data collected are largely non-numerical in nature.

quantitative change Developmental change that involves a series of minor, trendlike modifications.

quantitative research Research study in which the data collected are predominantly numerical in nature.

quasi-experimental study Research study in which one or more experimental treatments are administered but in which random assignment to groups is not possible.

questionnaire Data collection technique that obtains self-report data through a paper-pencil inventory.

receptive language Ability to understand the language that one hears or reads.

recessive gene Gene that influences growth and development only if the other gene in the allele pair is identical to it.

reciprocal teaching Approach to teaching reading whereby students take turns asking teacherlike questions of their classmates.

recursive thinking Thinking about what other people may be thinking about oneself, possibly through multiple iterations.

reflex An automatic response to a particular kind of stimulation.

rehearsal Attempt to learn and remember information by repeating it over and over.

reinforcer Consequence of a response that leads to an increased frequency of that response.

rejected children Children whom many peers identify as being unfavorable social partners.

rejection Refusing to learn or accept any customs and values found within a new cultural environment.

reliability Extent to which a data collection technique yields consistent, dependable results—results that are only minimally affected by temporary and irrelevant influences.

resilience Tendency of some children and adolescents to thrive and develop despite adverse environmental conditions.

right hemisphere Right side of the cortex; largely responsible for simultaneous processing and synthesis, especially in right-handed people.

rough-and-tumble play Playful physical "fighting" typical in early and middle childhood.

sample The specific participants in a research study; their performance is often assumed to indicate how a larger population of individuals would perform.

scaffolding Support mechanism, provided by a more competent individual, that helps a child successfully perform a task within his or her zone of proximal development.

schema Tightly integrated set of ideas about a specific object or situation.

scheme In Piaget's theory, an organized group of similar actions or thoughts.

schizophrenia A psychiatric condition characterized by irrational ideas and disorganized thinking.

script Schema that involves a predictable sequence of events related to a common activity.

secondary reinforcer Stimulus that becomes reinforcing over time through its association with another reinforcer.

secure attachment Attachment classification in which children use attachment figures as a secure base from which to explore and as a source of comfort in times of distress.

selective adoption Assuming some customs of a new culture while also retaining some customs of one's previous culture.

self-concept Beliefs that people have about themselves, their characteristics, and their abilities.

self-conscious emotion Affective state that reflects awareness of a community's social standards (e.g., pride, guilt, shame).

self-efficacy Belief that one is capable of executing certain behaviors or reaching certain goals in a particular task or domain.

self-esteem Feelings that people have about their own capabilities and self-worth.

self-evaluation Judging one's own performance or behavior in accordance with predetermined criteria.

self-fulfilling prophecy Phenomenon in which an adult's expectations for a child's performance directly or indirectly bring about that level of performance.

self-instructions Instructions that people give themselves as they perform a complex behavior.

self-monitoring Process of observing and recording one's own behavior.

self-regulated learning Directing and regulating one's own cognitive processes in order to learn successfully.

self-regulation Directing and controlling one's own actions.

self-reinforcement Self-imposed pleasurable consequence for a desired behavior.

self-report Data collection technique whereby participants are asked to describe their own characteristics and performance.

self-talk Talking to oneself as a way of guiding oneself through a task.

semantic bootstrapping Using knowledge of word meanings to derive knowledge about syntactic categories and structures.

semantics The meanings of words and word combinations.

sensation Physiological detection of stimuli in the environment.

sense of competence Belief that one can deal effectively with a particular aspect of one's environment.

sense of self-determination Belief that one has some choice and control regarding the future course of one's life.

sensitive period A period in development when certain environmental experiences have a more pronounced influence than is true at other times.

sensory register Component of memory that holds incoming information in an unanalyzed form for a very brief time (2–3 seconds or less).

service learning Activity that promotes learning and skill development through volunteerism or community service.

sexual harassment Form of discrimination in which a target individual perceives another's actions or statements to be hostile, humiliating, or offensive, especially pertaining to physical appearance or sexual matters.

sexual orientation Particular sex(es) to which an individual is romantically and sexually attracted.

shame Feeling of embarrassment or humiliation after failing to meet the standards for moral behavior that others have set.

sight vocabulary Words that a child can recognize immediately while reading.

social cognition Thinking about people, self, and society.

social-cognitive bias Mental shortcut in thinking about social phenomena.

social cognitive theory Theoretical perspective that focuses on the roles of observation and modeling in learning and motivation.

social constructivism Theoretical perspective that focuses on people's collective efforts to impose meaning on the world.

social-emotional development Systematic changes in emotional, social, and moral functioning.

social information processing Series of cognitive steps applied to understanding of, and responding to, social events.

socialization Systematic efforts by other people and by institutions to prepare youngsters to act in ways deemed by society to be appropriate and responsible.

socialization agent Person who plays a key role in preparing youngsters to act in ways deemed by society to be appropriate and responsible.

social perspective taking Imagining what someone else is thinking or feeling.

social pretense Ability to share internal fantasies with a social partner.

social referencing Looking at someone else (e.g., a caregiver) for clues about how to respond to a particular object or event.

social skills Strategies that people use to interact effectively with others.

sociocognitive conflict Encountering and having to wrestle with ideas and viewpoints different from one's own.

sociocultural perspective Theoretical perspective that focuses on children's learning of tools and communication systems through practice in meaningful tasks with other people. More generally, theoretical perspective that emphasizes the importance of society and culture for promoting cognitive development.

sociodramatic play Play in which children take on assumed roles and act out a scenario of events.

socioeconomic status (SES) One's general social and economic standing in society, encompassing such variables as family income, occupation, and education level.

sociolinguistic behaviors Social and culturally specific conventions that govern appropriate verbal interaction.

specific ability test Test designed to assess a specific cognitive skill or the potential to learn and perform in a specific content domain.

speech and communication disorders Category of special needs characterized by abnormalities in spoken language that significantly interfere with children's performance and achievement.

spermarche First ejaculation in an adolescent male.

stage A period of development characterized by a particular way of behaving or thinking.

stage theory Theory that describes development as involving a series of qualitatively distinct changes, with these changes occurring in the same sequence for everyone.

Standard English Form of English generally considered acceptable in school (as reflected in textbooks, grammar instruction, etc.) and in the media.

stereotype Rigid, simplistic, and erroneous characterization of a particular group.

stereotype threat Reduction in performance (often unintentional) as a result of a belief that one's group typically performs poorly.

story schema Knowledge of the typical elements and sequence of a narrative.

stranger anxiety Fear of unfamiliar adults in the latter half of the first year and into the second year of life.

structure In neo-Piagetian theory, a specific system of concepts and thinking skills that influence thinking and reasoning in a particular content domain.

student at risk Student who has a high probability of failing to acquire the minimal

academic skills necessary for success in the adult world.

subculture Group that resists the ways of the dominant culture and adopts its own norms for behavior.

Sudden Infant Death Syndrome Death of infant in the first year of life, typically during sleep, that cannot be explained by a thorough medical examination; it peaks between 2 and 4 months.

symbol Mental entity that represents an external object or event, often without reflecting its perceptual and behavioral qualities.

symbolic thought Ability to represent and think about external objects and events in one's mind.

sympathy Feeling of sorrow or concern about another's problems or distress.

synapse Junction between two neurons.

synaptic pruning A universal process in brain development whereby many previously formed synapses wither away, especially if they have not been used frequently.

synaptogenesis A universal process in brain development whereby many new synapses appear, typically in the first 31/2 years of life.

syntax Rules used to put words together into sentences.

telegraphic speech Short, grammatically incomplete sentences that include lexical (rather than grammatical) words almost exclusively; common in toddlers.

temperament Constitutional ways of responding to emotional events and novel stimulation, and of regulating impulses.

test Instrument designed to assess knowledge, understandings, abilities, or skills in a consistent fashion across individuals.

theory Organized system of principles and explanations regarding a particular phenomenon.

theory of mind Awareness that people have an inner, psychological life (thoughts, beliefs, feelings, etc.).

theory theory Theoretical perspective proposing that children construct increasingly integrated and complex understandings of physical and mental phenomena.

trait theory Theoretical perspective focusing on stable individual differences in human behavior.

undergeneralization Overly restricted meaning for a word, excluding some situations to which the word applies.

uninvolved style Parenting style characterized by a lack of emotional support and a lack of standards regarding appropriate behavior.

Universal Grammar Hypothesized set of parameters within the language acquisition device that allow some grammatical structures but exclude others.

universality Characteristics and developmental progressions shared by virtually all human beings.

validity Extent to which a data collection technique actually assesses what it is intended to assess.

vicarious punishment Phenomenon in which a person decreases a certain response after seeing another person punished for that response.

vicarious reinforcement Phenomenon in which a person increases a certain response after seeing another person reinforced for that response.

wait time The length of time a teacher pauses, after either asking a question or hearing a student's comment, before saying something else.

whole-language perspective Theoretical perspective that proposes that children develop literacy skills most effectively within the context of authentic reading and writing tasks.

word decoding Identifying an unknown word by using letter-sound relationships, analogies, common letter patterns, and/or semantic and syntactic context.

working memory Component of memory that enables people to actively think about and process a small amount of information.

zone of proximal development (ZPD) Range of tasks that one cannot yet perform independently but can perform with the help and guidance of others.

zygote Cell formed when a male sperm joins with a female ovum; with healthy genes and nurturing conditions in the uterus, it may develop into a fetus and be born as a live infant.

References

Abdul-Jabbar, K., & Knobles, P. (1983). *Giant steps: The autobiography of Kareem Abdul-Jabbar.* New York: Bantam.

Abi-Nader, J. (1993). Meeting the needs of multi-cultural classrooms: Family values and the motivation of minority students. In M. J. O'Hair & S. J. Odell (Eds.), *Diversity and teaching: Teacher education yearbook I.* Fort Worth, TX: Harcourt Brace Jovanovich.

Aboud, F. E. (1988). *Children and prejudice.* Oxford, England: Blackwell.

Aboud, F. E. (1993). The developmental psychology of racial prejudice. *Transcultural Psychiatric Research Review, 30,* 229–242.

Adalbjarnardottir, S., & Selman, R. L. (1997). "I feel I have received a new vision": An analysis of teachers' professional development as they work with students on interpersonal issues. *Teaching and Teacher Education, 13,* 409–428.

Adams, G. R., Gullotta, T. P., & Markstrom-Adams, C. (1994). *Adolescent life experiences* (3rd ed.). Pacific Grove, CA: Brooks/Cole.

Adams, M. J. (1990). *Beginning to read: Thinking and learning about print.* Cambridge, MA: MIT Press.

Adams, R. J. (1987). An evaluation of color preference in early infancy. *Infant Behavior and Development, 10,* 143–150.

Adamson, L. B., & Bakeman, R. (1991). The development of shared attention during infancy. In R. Vasta (Ed.), *Annals of child development* (Vol. 8, pp. 1–41). London: Kingsley.

Adamson, L. B., & McArthur, D. (1995). Joint attention, affect, and culture. In C. Moore & P. J. Dunham (Eds.), *Joint attention: Its origins and role in development* (pp. 205–221). Hillsdale, NJ: Erlbaum.

Agency for Toxic Substances and Disease Registry (1999, June). ToxFAQs™ for Lead. Retrieved January 19, 2003, from http://www.atsdr.cdc.gov/tfacts13.html

Ainsworth, M. D. S. (1963). The development of infant-mother interaction among the Ganda. In B. M. Foss (Ed.), *Determinants of infant behavior* (Vol. 2, pp. 67–104). New York: Wiley.

Ainsworth, M. D. S. (1973). The development of infant-mother attachment. In B. Caldwell & H. Ricciuti (Eds.), *Review of child development research* (Vol. 3, pp. 1–94). Chicago: University of Chicago Press.

Ainsworth, M. D. S., Blehar, M. C., Waters, E., & Wall, S. (1978). *Patterns of attachment.* Hillsdale, NJ: Erlbaum.

Aitchison, J. (1996). *The seeds of speech: Language origin and evolution.* Cambridge, England: Cambridge University Press.

Akhtar, N., Carpenter, M., & Tomasello, M. (1996). The role of discourse novelty in early word learning. *Child Development, 67,* 635–645.

Akhtar, N., Jipson, J., & Callanan, M. A. (2001). Learning words through overhearing. *Child Development, 72,* 416–430.

Akiskal, H. S., & McKinney, W. T. (1973). Depressive disorders: Toward a unified hypothesis. *Science, 162,* 20–29.

Alapack, R. (1991). The adolescent first kiss. *Humanistic Psychologist, 19,* 48–67.

Alderman, M. K. (1990). Motivation for at-risk students. *Educational Leadership, 48*(1), 27–30.

Aldridge, M. A., Stillman, R. D., & Bower, T. G. R. (2001). Newborn categorization of vowel-like sounds. *Developmental Science, 4*(2), 220–232.

Alegria, J. (1998). The origin and functions of phonological representations in deaf people. In C. Hulme & R. M. Joshi (Eds.), *Reading and spelling: Development and disorders.* Mahwah, NJ: Erlbaum.

Alessi, N. E., Krahn, D., Brehm, D., & Wittekindt, J. (1989). Prepubertal anorexia nervosa and major depressive disorder. *Journal of the American Academy of Child and Adolescent Psychiatry, 28,* 380–384.

Alexander, K., Entwisle, D., & Thompson, M. (1987). School performance, status relations, and the structure of sentiment: Bringing the teacher back in. *American Sociological Review, 52,* 665–682.

Alexander, P. A. (1997). Mapping the multidimensional nature of domain learning: The interplay of cognitive, motivational, and strategic forces. In P. R. Pintrich & M. L. Maehr (Eds.), *Advances in motivation and achievement* (Vol. 10). Greenwich, CT: JAI Press.

Alexander, P. A., Graham, S., & Harris, K. R. (1998). A perspective on strategy research: Progress and prospects. *Educational Psychology Review, 10,* 129–154.

Alexander, P. A., & Jetton, T. L. (1996). The role of importance and interest in the processing of text. *Educational Psychology Review, 8,* 89–121.

Alfassi, M. (1998). Reading for meaning: The efficacy of reciprocal teaching in fostering reading comprehension in high school students in remedial reading classes. *American Educational Research Journal, 35,* 309–332.

Al-Krenawi, A., & Graham, J. R. (2000). Culturally sensitive social work practice with Arab clients in mental health settings. *Health & Social Work, 25*(1), 9–22.

Allen, L., Cipielewski, J., & Stanovich, K. E. (1992). Multiple indicators of children's reading habits and attitudes: Construct validity and cognitive correlates. *Journal of Educational Psychology, 84,* 489–503.

Alley, G., & Deshler, D. (1979). *Teaching the learning disabled adolescent: Strategies and methods.* Denver, CO: Love.

Allison, K. W. (1998). Stress and oppressed social category membership. In J. K. Swim & C. Stangor (Eds.), *Prejudice: The target's perspective* (pp. 149–170). San Diego, CA: Academic Press.

Almeida, D. M., Wethington, E., & Chandler, A. L. (1999). Daily transmission of tensions between marital dyads and parent-child dyads. *Journal of Marriage and the Family, 61,* 49–61.

Alvermann, D. E., & Moore, D. W. (1991). Secondary school reading. In R. Barr, M. L. Kamil, P. B. Mosenthal, & P. D. Pearson (Eds.), *Handbook of reading research* (Vol. II). New York: Longman.

Alvermann, D. E., Young, J. P., Green, C., & Wisenbaker, J. M. (1999). Adolescents' perceptions and negotiations of literacy practices in after-school read and talk clubs. *American Educational Research Journal, 36,* 221–264.

Ambrose, D., Allen, J., & Huntley, S. B. (1994). Mentorship of the highly creative. *Roeper Review, 17,* 131–133.

American Academy of Pediatrics Committee on Nutrition (1998). Soy protein-based formulas: Recommendations for use in infant feeding (RE9806). *Pediatrics, 101*(1), 148–153.

American Academy of Pediatrics Committee on Nutrition (1999). Iron fortification of infant formulas. *Pediatrics, 104*(1), 119–123.

American Academy of Pediatrics Committee on Pediatric AIDS and Committee on Adolescence (2001). Adolescents and Human Immunodeficiency Virus infection: The role of the pediatrician in prevention and intervention. *Pediatrics, 107*(1), 188–190.

American Academy of Pediatrics Committee on Pediatric AIDS and Committee on Infectious Diseases (1999). Issues related to Human Immunodeficiency Virus transmission in schools, child care, medical settings, home, and community. *Pediatrics, 104*(2), 318–324.

American Academy of Pediatrics Committee on Sports Medicine and Fitness (2000). Intensive training and sports specialization in young athletes. *Pediatrics, 106*(1), 154–157.

American Academy of Pediatrics Committee on Sports Medicine and Fitness and Committee on Injury and Poison Prevention (2000). Swimming programs for infants and toddlers (RE9940). *Pediatrics, 105*(4), 868–870.

American Academy of Pediatrics Task Force on Infant Sleep Position and Sudden Infant Death Syndrome (2000). Changing concepts of sudden infant death syndrome: Implications for infant sleeping environment and sleep position (RE9946). *Pediatrics, 105*(3), 650–656.

American Association on Mental Retardation. (1992). *Mental retardation: Definition, classification, and systems of supports* (9th ed.). Washington, DC: Author.

American Psychiatric Association (1994). *Diagnostic and statistical manual of mental disorders* (4th ed.). Washington, DC: Author.

American Speech-Language-Hearing Association (1993). Definitions of communication disorders and variations. *ASHA, 35*(Suppl. 10), 40–41.

Ames, C. (1984). Competitive, cooperative, and individualistic goal structures: A cognitive-motivational analysis. In R. Ames & C. Ames (Eds.), *Research on motivation in education: Vol. 1. Student motivation.* San Diego, CA: Academic Press.

Ames, C. (1992). Classrooms: Goals, structures, and student motivation. *Journal of Educational Psychology, 84,* 261–271.

Amirkhanian, Y. A., Tiunov, D. V., & Kelly, J. A. (2001). Risk factors for HIV and other sexually transmitted diseases among adolescents in St. Petersburg, Russia. *Family Planning Perspectives, 33*(3), 106–112.

Anastasi, A., & Urbina, S. (1997). *Psychological testing* (7th ed.). Upper Saddle River, NJ: Prentice Hall.

Anderman, E. M., & Maehr, M. L. (1994). Motivation and schooling in the middle grades. *Review of Educational Research, 64,* 287–309.

Anderman, L. H., & Anderman, E. M. (1999). Social predictors of changes in students' achievement goal orientation. *Contemporary Educational Psychology, 25,* 21–37.

Anderson, D. A. (1994). Lesbian and gay adolescents: Social and developmental considerations. *The High School Journal, 77* (1,2), 13–19.

Anderson, E. (1990). *Streetwise: Race, class, and change in an urban community.* Chicago: University of Chicago Press.

Anderson, J. R., Reder, L. M., & Simon, H. A. (1997). Situative versus cognitive perspectives: Form versus substance. *Educational Researcher, 26*(1), 18–21.

Anderson, J. C. (1983). *The architecture of cognition.* Cambridge, MA: Harvard University Press.

Anderson, J. R., Reder, L. M., & Simon, H. A. (1997). Situative versus cognitive perspectives: Form versus substance. *Educational Researcher, 26*(1), 18–21.

Anderson, L. W., & Pellicer, L. O. (1998). Toward an understanding of unusually successful programs for economically disadvantaged students. *Journal of Education for Students Placed at Risk, 3,* 237–263.

Anderson, R. C., Nguyen-Jahiel, K., McNurlen, B., Archodidou, A., Kim, S.-Y., Reznitskaya, A., et al. (2001). The snowball phenomenon: Spread of ways of talking and ways of thinking across groups of children. *Cognition and Instruction, 19,* 1–46.

Anderson, R. C., Shirey, L., Wilson, P., & Fielding, L. (1987). Interestingness of children's reading materials. In R. Snow & M. Farr (Eds.), *Aptitude, learning, and instruction: III. Conative and affective process analyses.* Hillsdale, NJ: Erlbaum.

Anderson, R. C., Wilson, P. T., & Fielding, L. G. (1988). Growth in reading and how children spend their time outside of school. *Reading Research Quarterly, 23,* 285–303.

Anderson, R. E. (2002). Youth and information technology. In J. T. Mortimer & R. W. Larson (Eds.), *The changing adolescent experience: Societal trends and the transition to adulthood* (pp. 175–207). Cambridge, England: Cambridge University Press.

Anderson, R. G., & Freebody, P. (1981). Vocabulary knowledge. In J. T. Guthrie (Ed.), *Comprehension and teaching: Research reviews.* Newark, DE: International Reading Association.

Andersson, B. E. (1989). Effects of public day care: A longitudinal study. *Child Development, 60,* 857–866.

Andison, F. S. (1977). TV violence and viewer aggression: Accumulation of study results 1956–1976. *Public Opinion Quarterly, 41,* 314–331.

Andrews, J. F., & Mason, J. M. (1986). Childhood deafness and the acquisition of print concepts. In D. B. Yaden, Jr., & S. Templeton (Eds.), *Metalinguistic awareness and beginning literacy: Conceptualizing what it means to read and write.* Portsmouth, NH: Heinemann.

Anglin, J. M. (1977). *Word, object, and conceptual development.* New York: Norton.

Anisfeld, E., Casper, V., Nosyce, M., & Cunningham, N. (1990). Does infant carrying promote attachment? An experimental study of the effects of increased physical contact on the development of attachment. *Child Development, 61,* 1617–1627.

Antelman, S., & Caggiula, A. (1977). Norepinephrine-dopamine interactions and behavior. *Science, 195,* 646–651.

Anthony, J. L., Lonigan, C. J., & Dyer, S.M. (1996, April). *The development of reading comprehension: Listening comprehension or basic language processes?* Paper presented at the annual meeting of the American Educational Research Association, New York.

Anyon, J. (1988). Social class and the hidden curriculum of work. In G. Handel (Ed.), *Childhood socialization.* New York: Aldine de Gruyter.

Archer, J. (1991). The influence of testosterone on human aggression. *British Journal of Psychology, 82,* 1–28.

Archer, S. L. (1982). The lower age boundaries of identity development. *Child Development, 53,* 1551–1556.

Arcus, D. M. (1991). *Experiential modification of temperamental bias in inhibited and uninhibited children.* Unpublished doctoral dissertation, Harvard University, Cambridge, MA.

Armstrong, T. (1994). *Multiple intelligences in the classroom.* Alexandria, VA: Association for Supervision and Curriculum Development.

Arnett, J. (1995). The young and the reckless: Adolescent reckless behavior. *Current Directions in Psychological Science, 4,* 67–71.

Arnett, J. J. (1999). Adolescent storm and stress, reconsidered. *American Psychologist, 54,* 317–326.

Arnold, A. P., & Gorski, R. A. (1984). Gonadal steroid induction of structural sex differences in the central nervous system. *Annual Review of Neuroscience, 7,* 413–442.

Arnold, M. L. (2000). Stage, sequence, and sequels: Changing conceptions of morality, post-Kohlberg. *Educational Psychology Review, 12,* 365–383.

Aronfreed, J. (1976). Moral development from the standpoint of a general psychological theory. In T. Lickona (Ed.), *Moral development and behavior: Theory, research, and social issues* (pp. 54–69). New York: Holt, Rinehart & Winston.

Artman, L., & Cahan, S. (1993). Schooling and the development of transitive inference. *Developmental Psychology, 29,* 753–759.

Asai, S. (1993). In search of Asia through music: Guidelines and ideas for teaching Asian music. In T. Perry & J. W. Fraser (Eds.), *Freedom's plow: Teaching in the multicultural classroom.* New York: Routledge.

Asante, M. K. (1991). Afrocentric curriculum. *Educational Leadership, 24*(4), 28–31.

Asher, S. R., & Coie, J. D. (Eds.). (1990). *Peer rejection in childhood.* Cambridge, England: Cambridge University Press.

Asher, S. R., & Parker, J. G. (1989). Significance of peer relationship problems in childhood. In B. H. Schneider, G. Attili, J. Nadel, & R. P. Weissberg (Eds.), *Social competence in developmental perspective.* Dordrecht, Netherlands: Kluwer.

Asher, S. R., & Renshaw, P. D. (1981). Children without friends: Social knowledge and social skill training. In S. R. Asher & J. M. Gottman (Eds.), *The development of children's friendships* (pp. 273–296). Cambridge, England: Cambridge University Press.

Ashmead, D. H., Davis, D. L., Whalen, T., & Odom, R. D. (1991). Sound localization and sensitivity to interaural time differences in human infants. *Child Development, 62,* 1211–1226.

Ashmore, R., & DelBoca, F. (1976). Psychological approaches. In P. A. Katz (Ed.), *Elimination of racism.* New York: Pergamon.

Ashton, P. (1985). Motivation and the teacher's sense of efficacy. In C. Ames & R. Ames (Eds.), *Research on motivation in education: Vol. 2. The classroom milieu.* San Diego, CA: Academic Press.

Aslin, R. N. (1993). Perception of visual direction in human infants. In C. E. Granrud (Ed.), *Visual perception and cognition in infancy.* Hillsdale, NJ: Erlbaum.

Aslin, R. N., Saffran, J. R., & Newport, E. L. (1998). Computation of conditional probability statistics by 8-month-old infants. *Psychological Science, 9,* 321–324.

Asmussen, L., & Larson, R. (1991). The quality of family time among adolescents in single-parent and married-parent families. *Journal of Marriage and the Family, 53,* 1021–1030.

Assor, A., & Connell, J. P. (1992). The validity of students' self-reports as measures of performance affecting self-appraisals. In D. H. Schunk & J. L. Meece (Eds.), *Student perceptions in the classroom.* Hillsdale, NJ: Erlbaum.

Astington, J. W. (1991). Intention in the child's theory of mind. In C. Moore & D. Frye (Eds.), *Children's theories of mind* (pp. 157–172). Hillsdale, NJ: Erlbaum.

Astington, J. W. (1993). *The child's discovery of the mind.* Cambridge, MA: Harvard University Press.

Astington, J. W., & Pelletier, J. (1996). The language of mind: Its role in teaching and learning. In D. R. Olson & N. Torrance (Eds.), *The handbook of education and human development: New models of learning, teaching and schooling* (pp. 593–619). Cambridge, MA: Blackwell.

Astor, R. A. (1994). Children's moral reasoning about family and peer violence: The role of provocation and retribution. *Child Development, 65,* 1054–1067.

Astor, R. A., Meyer, H. A., & Behre, W. J. (1999). Unowned places and times: Maps and interviews about violence in high schools. *American Educational Research Journal, 36,* 3–42.

Atkinson, J. W., & Feather, N. T. (Eds.). (1966). *A theory of achievement motivation.* New York: Wiley.

Atkinson, M. (1992). *Children's syntax: An introduction to principles and parameters theory.* Oxford, England: Blackwell.

Attie, I., & Brooks-Gunn, J. (1989). Development of eating problems in adolescent girls: A longitudinal study. *Developmental Psychology, 25,* 70–79.

Attie, I., Brooks-Gunn, J., & Petersen, A. (1990). A developmental perspective on eating disorders and eating problems. In M. Lewis & S. M. Miller (Eds.), *Handbook of developmental psychopathology* (pp. 409–420). New York: Plenum Press.

Attride-Stirling, J., Davis, H., Markless, G., Sclare, I., & Day, C. (2001). "Someone to talk to who'll listen": Addressing the psychosocial needs of children and families. *Journal of Community & Applied Social Psychology, 11,* 179–191.

Atwater, E. (1996). *Adolescence.* Upper Saddle River, NJ: Prentice Hall.

Au, K. H. (1980). Participation structures in a reading lesson with Hawaiian children: Analysis of a culturally appropriate instructional event. *Anthropology and Education Quarterly, 11,* 91–115.

Au, K. H. (1993). *Literacy instruction in multicultural settings.* Fort Worth, TX: Harcourt Brace Jovanovich.

Au, K. H. (1997). A sociocultural model of reading instruction: The Kamehameha Elementary Education Program. In S. A. Stahl & D. A. Hayes (Eds.), *Instructional models in reading* (pp. 181–202). Mahwah, NJ: Erlbaum.

Au, K. H., & Mason, J. (1981). Social organizational factors in learning to read: The balance of rights hypothesis. *Reading Research Quarterly, 17,* 115–152.

Au, T. K., & Glusman, M. (1990). The principle of mutual exclusivity in word learning: To honor or not to honor? *Child Development, 61,* 1474–1490.

Ausubel, D. P., Novak, J. D., & Hanesian, H. (1978). *Educational psychology: A cognitive view* (2nd ed.). New York: Holt, Rinehart & Winston.

Avis, J., & Harris, P. L. (1991). Belief-desire reasoning among Baka children: Evidence for a universal conception of mind. *Child Development, 62,* 460–467.

Babad, E. (1993). Teachers' differential behavior. *Educational Psychology Review, 5,* 347–376.

Bagley, C. (1989). Aggression and anxiety in day-care graduates. *Psychological Reports, 64,* 250.

Bahrick, L. E. (2002). Generalization of learning in three-and-a-half-month-old infants on the basis of amodal relations. *Child Development, 73,* 667–681.

Bailey, C. T., & Boykin, A. W. (2001). The role of task variability and home contextual factors in the academic performance and task motivation of African American elementary school children. *Journal of Negro Education, 70*(1–2), 84–95.

Bailey, D. B., Jr. (1996). Assessing family resources, priorities, and concerns. In M. McLean, D. B.

Bailey, Jr., & M. Wolery (Eds.), *Assessing infants and preschoolers with special needs* (2nd ed., pp. 202–234). Englewood Cliffs, NJ: Merrill/Prentice-Hall.

Bailey, J. M., Bobrow, D., Wolfe, M., & Mikach, S. (1995). Sexual orientation of adult sons of gay fathers. *Developmental Psychology, 31,* 124–129.

Bailey, J. M., & Pillard, R. C. (1997). The innateness of homosexuality. In M. R. Walsh (Ed.), *Women, men, and gender: Ongoing debates* (pp. 184–187). New Haven, CT: Yale University Press.

Baillargeon, R. (1994). How do infants learn about the physical world? *Current Directions in Psychological Science, 3,* 133–140.

Bakari, R. (2000). *The development and validation of an instrument to measure preservice teachers' attitudes toward teaching African American students.* Unpublished doctoral dissertation, University of Northern Colorado, Greeley.

Bakeman, R., & Brownlee, J. R. (1980). The strategic use of parallel play: A sequential analysis. *Child Development, 51,* 873–878.

Baker, C. (1993). *Foundations of bilingual education and bilingualism.* Clevedon, England: Multilingual Matters.

Baker, L., Scher, D., & Mackler, K. (1997). Home and family influences on motivations for reading. *Educational Psychologist, 32,* 69–82.

Baker, S. (2000). *School counseling for the twenty-first century* (3rd ed.). Upper Saddle River, NJ: Merrill/Prentice Hall.

Baker-Ward, L., Ornstein, P. A., & Holden, D. J. (1984). The expression of memorization in early childhood. *Journal of Experimental Child Psychology, 37,* 555–575.

Baldwin, D. A. (1993). Early referential understanding: Infants' ability to recognize referential acts for what they are. *Developmental Psychology, 29,* 832–843.

Baldwin, D. A. (2000). Interpersonal understanding fuels knowledge acquisition. *Current Directions in Psychological Science, 9,* 40–45.

Baldwin, M. W., Keelan, J. P. R., Fehr, B., Enns, V., & Koh-Rangarajoo, E. (1996). Social-cognitive conceptualization of attachment working models: Availability and accessibility effects. *Journal of Personality and Social Psychology, 71,* 94–109.

Baltes, P. B., Lindenberger, U., & Staudinger, U. M. (1998). Life-span theory in developmental psychology. In W. Damon (Editor-in-Chief), & R. M. Lerner (Vol. Ed.), *Handbook of child psychology. Vol. 1. Theoretical models of human development* (5th ed., pp. 1029–1143). New York: Wiley.

Baltes, P. B., Reese, H. W., & Lipsitt, L. P. (1980). Life-span developmental psychology. *Annual Review of Psychology, 31,* 65–110.

Bandura, A. (1973). *Aggression: A social learning analysis.* Englewood Cliffs, NJ: Prentice Hall.

Bandura, A. (1977). *Social learning theory.* Upper Saddle River, NJ: Prentice Hall.

Bandura, A. (1981). Self-referent thought: A developmental analysis of self-efficacy. In J. Flavell & L. Ross (Eds.), *Social cognitive development: Frontiers and possible futures.* Cambridge, England: Cambridge University Press.

Bandura, A. (1982). Self-efficacy mechanism in human agency. *American Psychologist, 37,* 122–147.

Bandura, A. (1986). *Social foundations of thought and action: A social cognitive theory.* Englewood Cliffs, NJ: Prentice Hall.

Bandura, A. (1991). Social cognitive theory of moral thought and action. In W. M. Kurtines & J. L. Gewirtz (Eds.), *Handbook of moral behavior and development: Vol. 1. Theory.* Hillsdale, NJ: Erlbaum.

Bandura, A. (1997). *Self-efficacy: The exercise of control.* New York: Freeman.

Bandura, A., Barbaranelli, C., Caprara, G. V., & Pastorelli, C. (2001). Self-efficacy beliefs as shapers of children's aspirations and career trajectories. *Child Development, 72,* 187–206.

Bandura, A., & Mischel, W. (1965). Modification of self-imposed delay of reward through exposure to live and symbolic models. *Journal of Personality and Social Psychology, 2,* 698–705.

Bandura, A., Ross, D., & Ross, S. A. (1963). Imitation of film-mediated aggressive models. *Journal of Abnormal and Social Psychology, 66,* 3–11.

Bandura, A., & Schunk, D. H. (1981). Cultivating competence, self-efficacy, and intrinsic interest through proximal self-motivation. *Journal of Personality and Social Psychology, 41,* 586–598.

Bank, S. (1992). Remembering and reinterpreting sibling bonds. In F. Boer & J. Dunn (Eds.), *Children's sibling relationships: Developmental and clinical issues.* Hillsdale, NJ: Erlbaum.

Banks, J. A. (1994). *An introduction to multicultural education.* Needham Heights, MA: Allyn & Bacon.

Banks, J. A. (1995). Multicultural education: Historical development, dimensions, and practice. In J. A. Banks & C. A. M. Banks (Eds.), *Handbook of research on multicultural education.* New York: Macmillan.

Banks, J. A., & Banks, C. A. M. (Eds.). (1995). *Handbook of research on multicultural education.* New York: Macmillan.

Bar-Tal, D., Raviv, A., & Leiser, T. (1980). The development of altruistic behavior: Empirical evidence. *Developmental Psychology, 16,* 516–524.

Barenboim, C. (1981). The development of person perception in childhood and adolescence: From behavioral comparisons to psychological constructs to psychological comparisons. *Child Development, 52,* 129–144.

Barga, N. K. (1996). Students with learning disabilities in education: Managing a disability. *Journal of Learning Disabilities, 29,* 413–421.

Barker, G. P., & Graham, S. (1987). Developmental study of praise and blame as attributional cues. *Journal of Educational Psychology, 79,* 62–66.

Barker, R. G., & Wright, H. F. (1951). *One boy's day: A specimen record of behavior.* New York: Harper & Brothers.

Barkley, R. A. (1997). *ADHD and the nature of self-control.* New York: Guilford Press.

Barkley, R. A. (1998). *Attention-deficit hyperactivity disorder: A handbook for diagnosis and treatment* (2nd ed.). New York: Guilford Press.

Barnas, M. V., & Cummings, E. M. (1994). Caregiver stability and toddlers' attachment-related behaviors towards caregivers in day care. *Infant Behavior and Development, 17*(2), 141–147.

Barnett, J. E. (2001, April). *Study strategies and preparing for exams: A survey of middle and high school students.* Paper presented at the annual meeting of the American Educational Research Association, Seattle, WA.

Baron, J. B. (1987). Evaluating thinking skills in the classroom. In J. B. Baron & R. J. Sternberg (Eds.), *Teaching thinking skills: Theory and practice.* New York: Freeman.

Baron-Cohen, S. (1991). The development of a theory of mind in autism: Deviance and delay? *Psychiatric Clinics of North America, 14,* 33–51.

Baron-Cohen, S., Tager-Flusberg, H., & Cohen, D. J. (1993). *Understanding other minds: Perspectives from autism.* Oxford, England: Oxford University Press.

Barr, H. M., Streissguth, A. P., Darby, B. L., & Sampson, P. D. (1990). Prenatal exposure to alcohol, caffeine, tobacco, and aspirin: Effects on fine and gross motor performance in 4-year-old children. *Developmental Psychology, 26,* 339–348.

Barr, R. (1999, April). *The role of siblings in the development of imitation.* Paper presented at the biennial meeting of the Society for Research in Child Development, Albuquerque, NM.

Barringer, C., & Gholson, B. (1979). Effects of type and combination of feedback upon conceptual learning by children: Implications for research in academic learning. *Review of Educational Research, 49,* 459–478.

Barron, R. W. (1998). Proto-literate knowledge: Antecedents and influences on phonological awareness and literacy. In C. Hulme & R. M. Joshi (Eds.), *Reading and spelling: Development and disorders.* Mahwah, NJ: Erlbaum.

Barry, H., III, Child, I. L., & Bacon, M. K. (1959). Relations of child training to subsistence economy. *American Anthropologist, 61,* 51–63.

Bartlett, E. J. (1982). Learning to revise: Some component processes. In M. Nystrand (Ed.), *What writers know: The language, process, and structure of written discourse.* New York: Academic Press.

Bartollas, C., & Miller, S. J. (2001). *Juvenile justice in America* (3rd ed.). Upper Saddle River, NJ: Prentice Hall.

Barton, K. C., & Levstik, L. S. (1996). "Back when God was around and everything": Elementary children's understanding of historical time. *American Educational Research Journal, 33,* 419–454.

Bartsch, K., & Wellman, H. M. (1995). *Children talk about the mind.* New York: Oxford University Press.

Basinger, K. S., Gibbs, J. C., & Fuller, D. (1995). Context and the measurement of moral judgment. *International Journal of Behavioral Development, 18,* 537–556.

Bassett, D. S., Jackson, L., Ferrell, K. A., Luckner, J., Hagerty, P. J., Bunsen, T. D., & MacIsaac, D. (1996). Multiple perspectives on inclusive education: Reflections of a university faculty. *Teacher Education and Special Education, 19,* 355–386.

Basso, K. (1972). To give up on words: Silence in western Apache culture. In P. Giglioli (Ed.), *Language and social context.* New York: Penguin Books.

Basso, K. H. (1984). Stalking with stories: Names, places, and moral narratives among the Western Apache. In E. M. Bruner & S. Plattner (Eds.), *Text, play and story: The construction and reconstruction of self and society* (pp. 19–55). Washington, DC: American Ethnological Society.

Bates, E., & MacWhinney, B. (1987). Competition, variation, and language learning. In B. MacWhinney (Ed.), *Mechanisms of language acquisition.* Hillsdale, NJ: Erlbaum.

Bates, J. E., Maslin, C. A., & Frankel, K. A. (1985). Attachment security, mother-child interaction, and temperament as predictors of behavior problem ratings at age three years. In L. Bretherton & E. Waters (Eds.), *Growing points of attachment theory and research. Monographs of the Society for Research in Child Development, 50*(1/2, Serial No. 209).

Bates, J. E., Viken, R. J., Alexander, D. B., Beyers, J., & Stockton, L. (2002). Sleep and adjustment in preschool children: Sleep diary reports by mothers relate to behavior reports by teachers. *Child Development, 73,* 62–74.

Batshaw, M. L., & Shapiro, B. K. (1997). Mental retardation. In M. L. Batshaw (Ed.), *Children with disabilities* (4th ed.). Baltimore: Brookes.

Batson, C. D. (1991). *The altruism question: Toward a social-psychological answer.* Hillsdale, NJ: Erlbaum.

Battistich, V., Solomon, D., Kim, D., Watson, M., & Schaps, E. (1995). Schools as communities, poverty levels of student populations, and students' attitudes, motives, and performance: A multilevel analysis. *American Educational Research Journal, 32,* 627–658.

Battistich, V., Solomon, D., Watson, M., & Schaps, E. (1997). Caring school communities. *Educational Psychologist, 32,* 137–151.

Bauer, P. J. (1995). Recalling past events: From infancy to early childhood. In R. Vasta (Ed.), *Annals of child development: A research annual* (Vol. 11, pp. 25–71). London: Jessica Kingsley.

Bauer, P. J., & Dow, G. A. (1994). Episodic memory in 16- and 20-month-old children: Specifics not generalized, but not forgotten. *Developmental Psychology, 30,* 403–417.

Bauer, P. J., & Mandler, J. M. (1990). Remembering what happened next: Very young children's recall of event sequences. In R. Fivush & J. A. Hudson (Eds.), *Knowing and remembering in young children* (pp. 9–29). Cambridge, England: Cambridge University Press.

Baumeister, R. F., & Senders, P. S. (1989). Identity development and the role of structure of children's games. *Journal of Genetic Psychology, 150,* 19–37.

Baumrind, D. (1967). Child care practices anteceding three patterns of preschool behavior. *Genetic Psychology Monographs, 75,* 43–88.

Baumrind, D. (1971). Current patterns of parental authority. *Developmental Psychology Monographs, 4*(1, Pt. 2).

Baumrind, D. (1980). New directions in socialization research. *American Psychologist, 35,* 639–652.

Baumrind, D. (1982). An explanatory study of socialization effects on black children: Some black-white comparisons. *Child Development, 43,* 261–267.

Baumrind, D. (1989). Rearing competent children. In W. Damon (Ed.), *Child development today and tomorrow.* San Francisco: Jossey-Bass.

Baumrind, D. (1991). Parenting styles and adolescent development. In R. Lerner, A. C. Petersen, & J. Brooks-Gunn (Eds.), *The encyclopedia of adolescence.* New York: Garland Press.

Baumrind, D., Larzelere, R. E., & Cowan, P. A. (2002). Ordinary physical punishment: Is it harmful? Comment on Gershoff (2002). *Psychological Bulletin, 128*(4), 580–589.

Bay-Hinitz, A. K., Peterson, R. F., & Quilitch, H. R. (1994). Cooperative games: A way to modify aggressive and cooperative behaviors in young children. *Journal of Applied Behavior Analysis, 27,* 435–446.

Baydar, N., Brooks-Gunn, J., & Furstenberg, F. F., Jr. (1993). Early warning signs of functional illiteracy: Predictors in childhood and adolescence. *Child Development, 64*(3), 815–829.

Bayley, N. (1993). *Bayley Scales of Infant Development* (2nd ed.). San Antonio, TX: The Psychological Corporation.

Beal, C. R. (1996). The role of comprehension monitoring in children's revision. *Educational Psychology Review, 8,* 219–238.

Bear, G. G., & Richards, H. C. (1981). Moral reasoning and conduct problems in the classroom. *Journal of Educational Psychology, 73,* 644–670.

Bearison, D., & Levey, L. (1977). Children's comprehension of referential communication: Decoding ambiguous messages. *Child Development, 48,* 716–720.

Bearison, D. J. (1998). Pediatric psychology and children's medical problems. In W. Damon (Editor-in-Chief), I. E. Sigel, & K. A. Renninger (Vol. Eds.), *Handbook of child psychology: Vol. 4. Child psychology in practice* (5th ed., pp. 635–711). New York: Wiley.

Beatty, B. (1996). Rethinking the historical role of psychology in educational reform. In D. R. Olson & N. Torrance (Eds.), *The handbook of education and human development: New models of learning, teaching and schooling* (pp. 100–116). Cambridge, MA: Blackwell.

Beaty, J. J. (1998). *Observing development of the young child* (4th ed.). Upper Saddle River, NJ: Merrill/Prentice Hall.

Beaty, L. A. (1999). Identity development of homosexual youth and parental and familial influences on the coming out process. *Adolescence, 34,* 597–601.

Beauboeuf-LaFontant, T. (1999). A movement against and beyond boundaries: "Politically relevant teaching" among African American teachers. *Teachers College Record, 100*(4), 702–723.

Beaudry, M., Dufour, R., & Marcoux, S. (1995). Relation between infant feeding and infections during the first six months of life. *Journal of Pediatrics, 126,* 191–197.

Bebko, J. M., Burke, L., Craven, J., & Sarlo, N. (1992). The importance of motor activity in sensorimotor development: A perspective from children with physical handicaps. *Human Development, 35*(4), 226–240.

Beck, I. L., McKeown, M. G., Sinatra, G. M., & Loxterman, J. A. (1991). Revising social studies text from a text-processing perspective: Evidence of improved comprehensibility. *Reading Research Quarterly, 26,* 251–276.

Beck, I. L., McKeown, M. G., Worthy, J., Sandora, C. A., & Kucan, L. (1996). Questioning the author: A yearlong classroom implementation to engage students with text. *The Elementary School Journal, 96,* 385–414.

Beck, M. (1999). *Expecting Adam: A true story of birth, rebirth, and everyday magic.* New York: Random House.

Becker, B. J. (1986). Influence again: An examination of reviews and studies of gender differences in social influence. In J. S. Hyde & M. C. Linn (Eds.), *The psychology of gender differences: Advances through meta-analysis.* Baltimore: Johns Hopkins University Press.

Beeman, M. J., & Chiarello, C. (1998). Complementary right- and left-hemisphere language comprehension. *Current Directions in Psychological Science, 7,* 2–8.

Beers, J. W. (1980). Developmental strategies of spelling competence in primary school children. In E. H. Henderson & J. W. Beers (Eds.), *Developmental and cognitive aspects of learning to spell: A reflection of word knowledge.* Newark, DE: International Reading Association.

Begg, I., Anas, A., & Farinacci, S. (1992). Dissociation of processes in belief: Source recollection, statement familiarity, and the illusion of truth. *Journal of Experimental Psychology: General, 121,* 446–458.

Behl-Chadha, G. (1996). Basic-level and superordinate-like categorical representations in early infancy. *Cognition, 60,* 105–141.

Beirne-Smith, M., Ittenbach, R., & Patton, J. R. (1998). *Mental retardation* (5th ed.). Upper Saddle River, NJ: Merrill/Prentice Hall.

Belenky, M. F., Bond, L. A., & Weinstock, J. S. (1997). *A tradition that has no name: Nurturing the development of people, families, and communities.* New York: Basic Books.

Belenky, M. F., Clinchy, B. M., Goldberger, N. R., & Tarule, J. M. (1986). *Women's ways of knowing: The development of self, voice, and mind.* New York: Basic Books.

Belfiore, P. J., & Hornyak, R. S. (1998). Operant theory and application to self-monitoring in adolescents. In D. H. Schunk and B. J. Zimmerman (Eds.), *Self-regulated learning: From teaching to self-reflective practice.* New York: Guilford Press.

Bell, C. C., & Jenkins, E. J. (1993). Community violence and children on Chicago's southside. *Psychiatry, 56,* 46–55.

Bell, L. A. (1989). Something's wrong here and it's not me: Challenging the dilemmas that block girls' success. *Journal for the Education of the Gifted, 12,* 118–130.

Bell, N., Grossen, M., & Perret-Clermont, A. (1985). Sociocognitive conflict and intellectual growth. In M. W. Berkowitz (Ed.), *Peer conflict and psychological growth.* San Francisco: Jossey-Bass.

Bell, R. Q. (1988). Contributions of human infants to caregiving and social interaction. In G. Handel (Ed.), *Childhood socialization* (pp. 103–122). New York: Aldine de Gruyter.

Bell-Scott, P., & Taylor, R. L. (1989). Introduction: The multiple ecologies of black adolescent development. *Journal of Adolescent Research, 4*(2), 119–124.

Belle, D. (1984). Inequality and mental health: Low income and minority women. In L. Walker (Ed.), *Women and mental health policy* (pp. 135–150). Beverly Hills, CA: Sage.

Belle, D. (1999). *The after-school lives of children: Alone and with others while parents work.* Mahwah, NJ: Erlbaum.

Belsky, J., & Eggebeen, D. (1991). Early and extensive maternal employment and young children's socioemotional development: Children of the National Longitudinal Survey of Youth. *Journal of Marriage and the Family, 53*(4), 1083–1098.

Belsky, J., Gilstrap, B., & Rovine, M. (1984). The Pennsylvania Infant and Family Development Project, I: Stability and change in mother-infant and father-infant interaction in a family setting at one, three, and nine months. *Child Development, 55,* 692-705.

Belzer, M., Rogers, A. S., Camarca, M., Fuschs, D., Peralta, L., Tucker, D., et al. (2001). Contraceptive choices in HIV infected and HIV at-risk adolescent females. *Journal of Adolescent Health, 29*(3 Suppl), 93–100.

Bem, S. L. (1977). On the utility of alternative procedures for assessing psychological androgyny. *Journal of Consulting and Clinical Psychology, 45,* 196–205.

Bem, S. L. (1981). Gender schema theory: A cognitive account of sex typing. *Psychological Review, 88,* 354–364.

Bem, S. L. (1989). Genital knowledge and gender constancy in preschool children. *Child Development, 60,* 649–662.

Benbow, C. P., Lubinski, D., Shea, D. L., & Eftekhari-Sanjani, H. (2000). Sex differences in mathematical reasoning ability at age 13: Their status 20 years later. *Psychological Science, 11,* 474–480.

Bender, T. A. (1997). Assessment of subjective well-being during childhood and adolescence. In G. D. Phye (Ed.), *Handbook of classroom assessment: Learning, achievement, and adjustment.* San Diego, CA: Academic Press.

Benes, F. (2001, May–June). Modern myelination: The brain at midlife. *Harvard Magazine, 103*(5), 9.

Bennett, D. T., Debold, E., & Solan, S. V. (1991, April). *Children and mathematics: Enjoyment, motivation, and Square One TV.* Paper presented at the biennial meeting of the Society for Research in Child Development, Seattle, WA.

Bennett, R. E., Gottesman, R. L., Rock, D. A., & Cerullo, F. (1993). Influence of behavior perceptions and gender on teachers' judgments of students' academic skill. *Journal of Educational Psychology, 85,* 347–356.

Benoit, D., & Parker, K. C. (1994). Stability and transmission of attachment across three generations. *Child Development, 65,* 1444–1456.

Benton, S. L. (1997). Psychological foundations of elementary writing instruction. In G. D. Phye (Ed.), *Handbook of academic learning: Construction of knowledge.* San Diego, CA: Academic Press.

Benware, C., & Deci, E. L. (1984). Quality of learning with an active versus passive motivational set. *American Educational Research Journal, 21,* 755–765.

Bereiter, C., & Scardamalia, M. (1987). *The psychology of written composition.* Hillsdale, NJ: Erlbaum.

Berenstain, S., & Berenstain, J. (1990). *The Berenstain Bears' Trouble with Pets.* New York: Random House.

Berg, I. K., & Kelly, S. (2000). *Building solutions in child protective services.* New York: W. W. Norton & Company.

Berger, K. J., & Williams, M. B. (1999). *Fundamentals of nursing: Collaborating for optimal health: Volume 1. Nursing, health, and the patient* (2nd ed.). Stamford, CT: Appleton & Lange.

Bergin, D. A. (1996, April). *Adolescents' out-of-school learning strategies.* Paper presented at the annual meeting of the American Educational Research Association, New York.

Berk, L. E. (1994). Why children talk to themselves. *Scientific American, 271,* 78–83.

Berk, L. E., & Spuhl, S. T. (1995). Maternal interaction, private speech, and task performance in preschool children. *Early Childhood Research Quarterly, 10,* 145–169.

Berkowitz, L. (1968). Responsibility, reciprocity, and social distance in help giving: An experimental investigation of English social class differences. *Journal of Experimental Social Psychology, 4,* 46–63.

Berkowitz, L. (1989). Frustration-aggression hypothesis: Examination and reformulation. *Psychological Bulletin, 106,* 59–73.

Berkowitz, L. (1993). Towards a general theory of anger and emotional expression: Implications of the cognitive-neoassociationist perspective for the analysis of anger and other emotions. In R. W. Wyer, Jr., & T. K. Srull (Eds.), *Advances in social cognition: Vol. 6. Perspectives on anger and emotion* (pp. 1–45). Hillsdale, NJ: Erlbaum.

Berkowitz, M. W., & Gibbs, J. C. (1985). The process of moral conflict resolution and moral development. In M. W. Berkowitz (Ed.), *Peer conflict and psychological growth.* San Francisco: Jossey-Bass.

Berkowitz, M. W., Guerra, N., & Nucci, L. (1991). Sociomoral development and drug and alcohol abuse. In W. M. Kurtines & J. L. Gewirtz (Eds.), *Moral behavior and development: Vol. 3. Application.* Hillsdale, NJ: Erlbaum.

Berndt, T. J. (1992). Friendship and friends' influence in adolescence. *Current Directions in Psychological Science, 1,* 156–159.

Berndt, T. J., & Hoyle, S. G. (1985). Stability and change in childhood and adolescent friendships. *Developmental Psychology, 21,* 1007–1015.

Berndt, T. J., & Keefe, K. (1995). Friends' influence on adolescents' adjustment to school. *Child Development, 66,* 1312–1329.

Berndt, T. J., & Keefe, K. (1996). Friends' influence on school adjustment: A motivational analysis. In J. Juvonen & K. R. Wentzel (Eds.), *Social motivation: Understanding children's school adjustment* (pp. 248–278). Cambridge, England: Cambridge University Press.

Berndt, T. J., Laychak, A. E., & Park, K. (1990). Friends' influence on adolescents' academic achievement motivation: An experimental study. *Journal of Educational Psychology, 82,* 664–670.

Berninger, V. W., Fuller, F., & Whitaker, D. (1996). A process model of writing development across the life span. *Educational Psychology Review, 8,* 193–218.

Bernstein, B. (1971). *Class codes and control: Vol. 1. Theoretical studies toward a sociology of language.* London: Routledge & Kegan Paul.

Bertenthal, B. I. (1993). Perception of biomechanical motions by infants: Intrinsic image and knowledge-based constraints. In C. E. Granrud (Ed.), *Visual perception and cognition in infancy* (pp. 175–214). Hillsdale, NJ: Erlbaum.

Bertenthal, B. I., & Campos, J. J. (1987). New directions in the study of early experience. *Child Development, 58,* 560–567.

Bertenthal, B. I., Campos, J. J., & Kermoian, R. (1994). An epigenetic perspective on the development of self-produced locomotion and its consequences. *Current Directions in Psychological Science, 3,* 140–145.

Bertenthal, B. I., & Pinto, J. (1993). Complementary processes in the perception and production of human movements. In E. Thelen & L. Smith (Eds.), *Dynamic approaches to development: Vol. 2. Applications.* Cambridge, MA: Bradford Books.

Berti, A. E., & Bombi, A. S. (1988). *The child's construction of economics.* Cambridge, England: Cambridge University Press.

Berzonsky, M. D. (1988). Self-theorists, identity status, and social cognition. In D. K. Lapsley &

F. C. Power (Eds.), *Self, ego, and identity: Integrative approaches* (pp. 243–261). New York: Springer-Verlag.

Best, D. L., & Ornstein, P. A. (1986). Children's generation and communication of mnemonic organizational strategies. *Developmental Psychology, 22,* 845–853.

Beverly, S. G. (2001). Material hardship in the United States: Evidence from the Survey of Income and Program Participation. *Social Work Research, 25*(3), 143–151.

Bezilla, R. (Ed.). (1993). *Religion in America.* Princeton, NJ: Princeton Religion Research Center.

Bialystok, E. (1994a). Representation and ways of knowing: Three issues in second language acquisition. In N. C. Ellis (Ed.), *Implicit and explicit learning of languages.* London: Academic Press.

Bialystok, E. (1994b). Towards an explanation of second language acquisition. In G. Brown, K. Malmkjær, A. Pollitt, & J. Williams (Eds.), *Language and understanding.* Oxford, England: Oxford University Press.

Bialystok, E. (2001). *Bilingualism in development: Language, literacy, and cognition.* Cambridge, England: Cambridge University Press.

Bibace, R., & Walsh, M. E. (1981). Children's conceptions of illness. In R. Bibace & M. E. Walsh (Eds.), *New directions for child development: Children's conceptions of health, illness, and bodily functions* (pp. 31–48). San Francisco: Jossey-Bass.

Biddle, S. J. (1993). Children, exercise and mental health. *International Journal of Sport Psychology, 24,* 200–216.

Bidell, T. R., & Fischer, K. W. (1997). Between nature and nurture: The role of human agency in the epigenesis of intelligence. In R. J. Sternberg & E. L. Grigorenko (Eds.), *Intelligence, heredity, and environment* (pp. 193–242). Cambridge, England: Cambridge University Press.

Biemiller, A. (1994). Some observations on beginning reading instruction. *Educational Psychologist, 29,* 203–209.

Biemiller, A., Shany, M., Inglis, A., & Meichenbaum, D. (1998). Factors influencing children's acquisition and demonstration of self-regulation on academic tasks. In D. H. Schunk & B. J. Zimmerman (Eds.), *Self-regulated learning: From teaching to self-reflective practice* (pp. 203–224). New York: Guilford.

Bierman, K. L., Miller, C. L., & Stabb, S. D. (1987). Improving the social behavior and peer acceptance of rejected boys: Effect of social skill training with instructions and prohibitions. *Journal of Consulting and Clinical Psychology, 55,* 194–200.

Biesheuvel, S. (1999). An examination of Jensen's theory concerning educability, heritability and population differences. In A. Montagu (Ed.), *Race and IQ* (expanded ed.; pp. 108–121). New York: Oxford University Press.

Bigelow, B. J. (1977). Children's friendship expectations: A cognitive developmental study. *Child Development, 48,* 246–253.

Bigelow, B. J., Tesson, G., & Lewko, J. H. (1999). The contextual influences of sibling and dating relations on adolescents' personal relations and their close friends, dating partners, and parents: The Sullivan-Piaget-Hartup hypothesis considered. In J. A. McLellan & M. J. V. Pugh (Eds.), The role of peer groups in adolescent social identity: Exploring the importance of stability and change. *New directions for child and adolescent development* (No. 84, pp. 71–86). San Francisco: Jossey-Bass.

Bijeljac-Babic, R., Bertoncini, J., & Mehler, J. (1993). How do 4-day-old infants categorize multisyllabic utterances? *Developmental Psychology, 29,* 711–721.

Binder, L. M., Dixon, M. R., & Ghezzi, P. M. (2000). A procedure to teach self-control to children with attention deficit hyperactivity disorder. *Journal of Applied Behavior Analysis, 33,* 233–237.

Binns, K., Steinberg, A., Amorosi, S., & Cuevas, A. M. (1997). *The Metropolitan Life survey of the American teacher 1997: Examining gender issues in public schools.* New York: Louis Harris and Associates.

Birch, S. A. J., & Bloom, P. (2002). Preschoolers are sensitive to the speaker's knowledge when learning proper names. *Child Development, 73,* 434–444.

Birnbaum, D. W., & Croll, W. L. (1984). The etiology of children's stereotypes about sex differences in emotionality. *Sex Roles, 10,* 677–691.

Bishop, S. J., Murphy, J. M., Hicks, R., Quinn, S. D., Lewis, P. D., Grace, M. P., & Jellinek, M. S. (2001). The youngest victims of maltreatment: What happens to infants in a court sample? *Child Maltreatment, 6*(3), 243–249.

Bivens, J. A., & Berk, L. E. (1990). A longitudinal study of the development of elementary school children's private speech. *Merrill-Palmer Quarterly, 36,* 443–463.

Bjorklund, D. F. (1987). How age changes in knowledge base contribute to the development of children's memory: An interpretive review. *Developmental Review, 7,* 93–130.

Bjorklund, D. F. (1997). In search for a metatheory for cognitive development (or, Piaget is dead and I don't feel so good myself). *Child Development, 68,* 144–148.

Bjorklund, D. F., & Brown, R. D. (1998). Physical play and cognitive development: Integrating activity, cognition, and education. *Child Development, 69,* 604–606.

Bjorklund, D. F., & Coyle, T. R. (1995). Utilization deficiencies in the development of memory strategies. In F. E. Weinert & W. Schneider (Eds.), *Research on memory development: State of the art and future directions.* Hillsdale, NJ: Erlbaum.

Bjorklund, D. F., & Green, B. L. (1992). The adaptive nature of cognitive immaturity. *American Psychologist, 47,* 46–54.

Bjorklund, D. F., & Jacobs, J. W. (1985). Associative and categorical processes in children's memory: The role of automaticity in the development of organization in free recall. *Journal of Experimental Child Psychology, 39,* 599–617.

Bjorklund, D. F., Schneider, W., Cassel, W. S., & Ashley, E. (1994). Training and extension of a memory strategy: Evidence for utilization deficiencies in high- and low-IQ children. *Child Development, 65,* 951–965.

Bjorkqvist, K., Osterman, K., & Kaukiainen, A. (1992). The development of direct and indirect aggressive strategies in males and females. In K. Bjorkqvist & P. Niemala (Eds.), *Of mice and women: Aspects of female aggression.* San Diego, CA: Academic Press.

Blachford, S. L. (2002). *The Gale encyclopedia of genetic disorders.* Detroit, MI: Gale Group.

Black, M. M., Hutcheson, J. J., Dubowitz, H., & Berenson-Howard, J. (1994). Parenting style and developmental status among children with nonorganic failure to thrive. *Journal of Pediatric Psychology, 19,* 689–707

Black-Gutman, D., & Hickson, F. (1996). The relationship between racial attitudes and social-cognitive development in children: An Australian study. *Developmental Psychology, 32,* 448–456.

Blackson, T. C., Butler, T., Belsky, J., Ammerman, R. T., Shaw, D. S., & Tarter, R. E. (1999). Individual traits and family contexts predict sons' externalizing behavior and preliminary relative risk ratios for conduct disorder and substance use disorder outcomes. *Drug & Alcohol Dependence, 56*(2), 115–131.

Blair, C. (2002). School readiness: Integrating cognition and emotion in a neurobiological conceptualization of children's functioning at school entry. *American Psychologist, 57,* 111–127.

Blakemore, C. (1976). The conditions required for the maintenance of binocularity in the kitten's visual cortex. *Journal of Physiology, 261*, 423–444.

Blasi, A. (1980). Bridging moral cognition and moral action: A critical review of the literature. *Psychological Bulletin, 88*, 593–637.

Blasi, A. (1995). Moral understanding and the moral personality: The process of moral integration. In W. M. Kurtines & J. L. Gewirtz (Eds.), *Moral development: An introduction*. Boston: Allyn & Bacon.

Block, J. H. (1979). Another look at sex differentiation in the socialization behaviors of mothers and fathers. In J. Sherman & F. L. Denmark (Eds.), *Psychology of women: Future of research*. New York: Psychological Dimensions.

Block, J. H. (1983). Differential premises arising from differential socialization of the sexes: Some conjectures. *Child Development, 54*, 1335–1354.

Block, N. (1999). How heritability misleads about race. In A. Montagu (Ed.), *Race and IQ* (expanded ed.; pp. 444–486). New York: Oxford University Press.

Bloom, B. S. (1964). *Stability and change in human characteristics*. New York: Wiley.

Bloom, K., Russell, A., & Wassnberg, K. (1987). Turn taking affects the quality of infant vocalizations. *Journal of Child Language, 14*, 211–227.

Bloom, L., & Lahey, M. (1978). *Language development and language disorders*. New York: Wiley.

Bloom, L., & Tinker, E. (2001). The intentionality model and language acquisition. *Monographs of the Society for Research in Child Development, 66*(4, Serial No. 267).

Blumberg, M. S., & Lucas, D. E. (1996). A developmental and component analysis of active sleep. *Developmental Psychobiology, 29*, 1–22.

Blyth, D. A., Simmons, R. G., & Zakin, D. F. (1985). Satisfaction with body image for early adolescent females: The impact of pubertal timing within different school environments. *Journal of Youth and Adolescence, 14*, 207–225.

Board on Children and Families, Commission on Behavioral and Social Sciences and Education, National Research Council, & Institute of Medicine. (1995). Immigrant children and their families: Issues for research and policy. *The Future of Children, 5*, 72–89.

Boccia, M., & Campos, J. J. (1989). Maternal emotional signals, social referencing, and infants' reactions to strangers. In N. Eisenberg (Ed.), *New directions for child development* (Vol. 44, pp. 25–49). San Francisco: Jossey-Bass.

Bodine, R. J., & Crawford, D. K. (1999). *Developing emotional intelligence: A guide to behavior management and conflict resolution in schools*. Champaign, IL: Research Press.

Boekaert, M. (1993). Being concerned with well-being and with learning. *Educational Psychologist, 28*, 149–167.

Bogin, B. (1988). *Patterns of human growth*. Cambridge, England: Cambridge University Press.

Bohan, J. S. (1995). *Re-placing women in psychology: Readings toward a more inclusive history* (2nd ed.). Dubuque, IA: Kendall/Hunt.

Bohannon, J. N., MacWhinney, B., & Snow, C. (1990). No negative evidence revisited: Beyond learnability, or who has to prove what to whom. *Developmental Psychology, 26*, 221–226.

Boldizar, J. P., Perry, D. G., & Perry, L. C. (1989). Outcome values and aggression. *Child Development, 60*, 571–579.

Bong, M. (2001). Between- and within-domain relations of academic motivation among middle and high school students: Self-efficacy, task-value, and achievement goals. *Journal of Educational Psychology, 93*, 23–34.

Boom, J., Brugman, D., & van der Heijden, P. G. M. (2001). Hierarchical structure of moral stages assessed by a sorting task. *Child Development, 72*, 535–548.

Booth, P. B., & Koller, T. J. (1998). Training parents of failure-to-attach children. In J. M. Briesmeister & C. E. Schaefer (Eds.), *Handbook of parent training: Parents as co-therapists for children's behavior problems* (2nd ed., pp. 308–342). New York: Wiley.

Borkowski, J. G., Bisconti, T., Willard, C. C., Keogh, D. A., Whitman, T. L., & Weed, K. (2002). The adolescent as parent: Influences on children's intellectual, academic, and socioemotional development. In J. G. Borkowski, S. L. Ramey, & M. Bristol-Power (Eds.), *Parenting and the child's world: Influences on academic, intellectual, and social-emotional development* (pp. 161–184). Mahwah, NJ: Erlbaum.

Bornstein, M. (1989). Information processing (habituation) and stability in cognitive development. *Human Development, 32*, 129–136.

Bornstein, M. H. (1978). Chromatic vision in infancy. In H. W. Reese & L. P. Lipsitt (Eds.), *Advances in child development and behavior* (Vol. 12). New York: Academic Press.

Bornstein, M. H., Haynes, O. M., Pascual, L., Painter, K. M., & Galperin, C. (1999). Play in two societies: Pervasiveness of process, specificity of structure. *Child Development, 70*, 317–331.

Bosacki, S. L. (2000). Theory of mind and self-concept in preadolescents: Links with gender and language. *Journal of Educational Psychology, 92*, 709–717.

Botvin, G. J., & Scheier, L. M. (1997). Preventing drug abuse and violence. In D. K. Wilson, J. R. Rodrigue, & W. C. Taylor (Eds.), *Health-promoting and health-compromising behaviors among minority adolescents* (pp. 55–86). Washington, DC: American Psychological Association.

Bouchard, T. J., & McGue, M. (1981). Familial studies of intelligence: A review. *Science, 212*, 1056.

Bouchard, T. J., Jr. (1997). IQ similarity in twins reared apart: Findings and responses to critics. In R. J. Sternberg & E. L. Grigorenko (Eds.), *Intelligence, heredity, and environment* (pp. 126–160). Cambridge, England: Cambridge University Press.

Boutte, G. S., & McCormick, C. B. (1992). Authentic multicultural activities: Avoiding pseudomulticulturalism. *Childhood Education, 68*(3), 140–144.

Bowen, M. (1978). *Family therapy in clinical practice*. New York: Jason Aaronson.

Bowey, J. (1986). Syntactic awareness and verbal performance from preschool to fifth grade. *Journal of Psycholinguistic Research, 15*, 285–308.

Bowlby, J. (1951). *Maternal care and mental health*. Geneva, Switzerland: World Health Organization.

Bowlby, J. (1958). The nature of the child's tie to his mother. *International Journal of Psycho-Analysis, 39*, 350–373.

Bowlby, J. (1969/1982). *Attachment and loss: Vol. 1. Attachment* (2nd ed.). New York: Basic Books.

Bowlby, J. (1973). *Attachment and loss: Vol. 2. Separation: Anxiety and anger*. New York: Basic Books.

Bowlby, J. (1988). *A secure base: Parent-child attachment and healthy human development*. New York: Basic Books.

Bowman, B. T. (1989). Educating language-minority children: Challenges and opportunities. *Phi Delta Kappan, 71*, 118–120.

Boyatzis, R. E. (1973). Affiliation motivation. In D. C. McClelland & R. S. Steele (Eds.), *Human motivation: A book of readings*. Morristown, NJ: General Learning Press.

Boykin, A. W. (1982). Task variability and the performance of Black and White schoolchildren: Vervistic explorations. *Journal of Black Studies, 12*, 469–485.

Boykin, A. W. (1994). Harvesting talent and culture: African-American children and educational reform. In R. J. Rossi (Ed.), *Schools and students at risk: Context and framework for positive change*. New York: Teachers College Press.

Bracken, B. A., & McCallum, R. S. (1998). *Universal Nonverbal Intelligence Test*. Itasca, IL: Riverside.

Bracken, B. A., McCallum, R. S., & Shaughnessy, M. F. (1999). An interview with Bruce A. Bracken and R. Steve McCallum, authors of the Universal Nonverbal Intelligence Test (UNIT). *North American Journal of Psychology, 1*, 277–288.

Bracken, B. A., & Walker, K. C. (1997). The utility of intelligence tests for preschool children. In D. P. Flanagan, J. L. Genshaft, & P. L. Harrison (Eds.), *Contemporary intellectual assessment: Theories, tests, and issues* (pp. 484–502). New York: Guilford Press.

Bradley, L., & Bryant, P. (1991). Phonological skills before and after learning to read. In S. A. Brady & D. P. Shankweiler (Eds.), *Phonological processes in literacy*. Hillsdale, NJ: Erlbaum.

Bradley, R. H., & Caldwell, B. M. (1984). The relation of infants' home environments to achievement test performance in first grade: A follow-up study. *Child Development, 55*, 803–809.

Brain Injury Association. (1999). *Kids' corner*. Retrieved from the World Wide Web: http://www.biausa.org/national.htm.

Brainerd, C. J. (1996). Piaget: A centennial celebration. *Psychological Science, 7*(4), 191–195.

Brand, J. E., & Greenberg, B. S. (1994). Commercials in the classroom: The impact of Channel One advertising. *Journal of Advertising Research, 34*, 18–27.

Brazelton, T. B., Koslowski, B., & Main, M. (1974). The origins of reciprocity: The early mother-infant interaction. In M. Lewis & L. A. Rosenblum (Eds.), *The origins of behavior: The effect of the infant on its caregiver* (pp. 49–76). New York: Wiley.

Brazelton Institute (2000). *The Neonatal Behavioral Assessment Scale (Revised)*. Boston, MA: Children's Hospital.

Bredekamp, S. (Ed.). (1987). Developmentally appropriate practice in early childhood programs serving children from birth through age 8. Washington, DC: National Association for the Education of Young Children.

Bredekamp, S., & Copple, C. (Eds.). (1997). *Developmentally appropriate practice in early childhood programs* (3rd ed.). Washington, DC: National Association for the Education of Young Children.

Brener, N. D., Simon, T. R., Krug, E. G., & Lowry, R. (1999). Recent trends in violence-related behaviors among high school students in the United States. *Journal of the American Medical Association, 282*, 440–446.

Brenner, E. M., & Salovey, P. (1997). Emotion regulation during childhood: Developmental, interpersonal, and individual considerations. In P. Salovey & D. J. Sluyter (Eds.), *Emotional development and emotional intelligence: Educational implications* (pp. 168–195). New York: Basic Books.

Brenner, L. A., Koehler, D. J., Liberman, V., & Tversky, A. (1996). Overconfidence in probability and frequency judgments: A critical examination. *Organizational Behavior and Human Decision Processes, 65*(3), 212–219.

Bretherton, I. (1991). Pouring new wine into old bottles: The social self as internal working model. In M. R. Gunnar & L. A. Sroufe (Eds.), *Self processes and development: The Minnesota Symposia on Child Development* (Vol. 23, pp. 1–42). Hillsdale, NJ: Erlbaum.

Bretherton, I., & Beeghly, M. (1982). Talking about internal states: The acquisition of an explicit theory of mind. *Developmental Psychology, 18*, 906–921.

Bretherton, I., Fritz, J., Zahn-Waxler, C., & Ridgeway, D. (1986). Learning to talk about emotions: A functionalist perspective. *Child Development, 57*, 529–548.

Bretherton, I., & Waters, E. (Eds.). (1985). Growing points in attachment theory and research.

Monographs of the Society for Research in Child Development, 50(Serial No. 209).

Bridges, L. J., Connell, J. P., & Belsky, J. (1988). Similarities and differences in infant-mother and infant-father interaction in the Strange Situation: A component process analysis. *Developmental Psychology, 24,* 92–100.

Brinton, B., & Fujiki, M. (1984). Development of topic manipulation skills in discourse. *Journal of Speech and Hearing Research, 27,* 350–358.

Bristol, M. M., Cohen, D. J., Costello, E. J., Denckia, M., Eckberg, T. J., Kallen, R., Kraemer, H. C., Lord, C., Maurer, R., McIlvane, W. J., Minsher, N., Sigman, M., & Spence, M. A. (1996). State of the science in autism: Report to the National Institutes of Health. *Journal of Autism and Developmental Disorders, 26,* 121–154.

Britt, M. A., Rouet, J-F., Georgi, M. C., & Perfetti, C. A. (1994). Learning from history texts: From causal analysis to argument models. In G. Leinhardt, I. L. Beck, & C. Stainton (Eds.), *Teaching and learning in history.* Hillsdale, NJ: Erlbaum.

Brody, G. H., & Shaffer, D. R. (1982). Contributions of parents and peers to children's moral socialization. *Developmental Review, 2,* 31–75.

Brody, G. H., Stoneman, Z., & McCoy, J. K. (1994). Forecasting sibling relationships in early adolescence from child temperament and family processes in middle childhood. *Child Development, 65,* 771–784.

Brody, N. (1985). The validity of tests of intelligence. In B. B. Wolman (Ed.), *Handbook of intelligence.* New York: Wiley.

Brody, N. (1992). *Intelligence.* New York: Academic Press.

Brody, N. (1997). Intelligence, schooling, and society. *American Psychologist, 52,* 1046–1050.

Brodzinsky, D. M. (1993). Long-term outcomes in adoption. *The Future of Children, 3*(1), 153–166.

Brodzinsky, D. M., Messer, S. M., & Tew, J. D. (1979). Sex differences in children's expression and control of fantasy and overt aggression. *Child Development, 50,* 372–379.

Bronfenbrenner, U. (1979). *The ecology of human development: Experiments by nature and design.* Cambridge, MA: Harvard University Press.

Bronfenbrenner, U. (1989). Ecological systems theory. In R. Vasta (Ed.), *Annals of child development* (Vol. 6, pp. 187–251). Greenwich, CT: JAI Press.

Bronfenbrenner, U. (1993). The ecology of cognitive development: Research models and fugitive findings. In R. H. Wozniak & K. W. Fischer (Eds.), *Development in context* (pp. 3–44). Hillsdale, NJ: Erlbaum.

Bronfenbrenner, U. (1999a). Is early intervention effective? Some studies of early education in familial and extra-familial settings. In A. Montagu (Ed.), *Race and IQ* (expanded ed.; pp. 343–378). New York: Oxford University Press.

Bronfenbrenner, U. (1999b). Nature with nurture: A reinterpretation of the evidence. In A. Montagu (Ed.), *Race and IQ* (expanded ed.; pp. 153–183). New York: Oxford University Press.

Bronfenbrenner, U., Alvarez, W. F., & Henderson, C. R., Jr. (1984). Working and watching: Maternal employment status and parents' perceptions of their three-year-old children. *Child Development, 55,* 1362–1379.

Bronfenbrenner, U., Kessel, F., Kessen, W., & White, S. (1986). Toward a critical social history of developmental psychology: A propaedeutic discussion. *American Psychologist, 41,* 1218–1230.

Bronson, M. B. (2000). *Self-regulation in early childhood: Nature and nurture.* New York: Guilford Press.

Bronson, W. C. (1981). Toddlers' behaviors with agemates: Issues of interaction, cognition, and affect. *Monographs of Infancy, 1,* 127.

Brook, J. S., Brook, D. W., Gordon, A. S., Whiteman, M., & Cohen, P. (1990). The psychological etiology of adolescent drug use: A family interactional approach. *Genetic Psychology Monographs, 116,* (No. 2).

Brookhart, S. M., & Freeman, D. J. (1992). Characteristics of entering teacher candidates. *Review of Educational Research, 62,* 36–60.

Brooks, G. (1995). *Nine parts of desire: The hidden world of Islamic women.* New York: Doubleday.

Brooks-Gunn, J. (1989). Pubertal processes and the early adolescent transition. In W. Damon (Ed.), *Child development today and tomorrow* (pp. 155–176). San Francisco: Jossey-Bass.

Brooks-Gunn, J. (2003). Do you believe in magic? What we can expect from early childhood intervention programs. *Social Policy Report, 17*(1). Ann Arbor, MI: Society for Research in Child Development.

Brooks-Gunn, J., & Duncan, G. J. (1997). The effects of poverty on children. *The Future of Children: Children and Poverty, 7*(2), 55–71.

Brooks-Gunn, J., & Furstenberg, F. F. (1990). Coming of age in the era of AIDS: Puberty, sexuality, and contraception. *Milbank Quarterly, 68* (Suppl 1), 59–84.

Brooks-Gunn, J., Han, W-J., & Waldfogel, J. (2002). Maternal employment and the child cognitive outcomes in the first three years of life: The NICHD study of early child care. *Child Development, 73*(4), 1052–1072.

Brooks-Gunn, J., Klebanov, P. K., & Duncan, G. J. (1996). Ethnic differences in children's intelligence test scores: Role of economic deprivation, home environment, and maternal characteristics. *Child Development, 67,* 396–408.

Brooks-Gunn, J., & Paikoff, R. L. (1992). Changes in self-feelings during the transition toward adolescence. In H. R. McGurk (Ed.), *Childhood social development: Contemporary perspectives* (pp. 63–97). Hillsdale, NJ: Erlbaum.

Brooks-Gunn, J., & Paikoff, R. L. (1993). "Sex is a gamble, kissing is a game": Adolescent sexuality and health promotion. In S. G. Millstein, A. C. Petersen, & E. O. Nightingale (Eds.), *Promoting the health of adolescents: New directions for the twenty-first century* (pp. 180–208). New York: Oxford University Press.

Brophy, J. E. (1987). Synthesis of research on strategies for motivating students to learn. *Educational Leadership, 45*(2), 40–48.

Brown, A. L. (1989). Analogical learning and transfer: What develops? In S. Vosniadou & A. Ortony (Eds.), *Similarity and analogical reasoning.* Cambridge, England: Cambridge University Press.

Brown, A. L., & Campione, J. C. (1994). Guided discovery in a community of learners. In K. McGilly (Ed.), *Classroom lessons: Integrating cognitive theory and classroom practice.* Cambridge, MA: MIT Press.

Brown, A. L., & Palincsar, A. S. (1987). Reciprocal teaching of comprehension strategies: A natural history of one program for enhancing learning. In J. Borkowski & J. D. Day (Eds.), *Cognition in special education: Comparative approaches to retardation, learning disabilities, and giftedness.* Norwood, NJ: Ablex.

Brown, A. L., & Palincsar, A. S. (1989). Guided, cooperative learning and individual knowledge acquisition. In L. B. Resnick (Ed.), *Knowing, learning, and instruction: Essays in honor of Robert Glaser.* Hillsdale, NJ: Erlbaum.

Brown, A. L., & Scott, M. S. (1971). Recognition memory for pictures in preschool children. *Journal of Experimental Child Psychology, 11,* 401–412.

Brown, A. L., Susser, E. S., Butler, P. D., Andrews, R. R., Kauffman, C. A., & Gorman, J. M. (1996). Neurobiological plausibility of prenatal nutritional deprivation as a risk factor for schizo-

phrenia. *Journal of Nervous and Mental Disease, 184*(2), 71–85.

Brown, B. (1999). Optimizing expression of the common human genome for child development. *Current Directions in Psychological Science, 8,* 37–41.

Brown, B. B. (1990). Peer groups and peer culture. In S. S. Feldman & G. R. Elliott (Eds.), *At the threshold: The developing adolescent* (pp. 171–196). Cambridge, MA: Harvard University Press.

Brown, B. B. (1993). School culture, social politics, and the academic motivation of U.S. citizens. In T. M. Tomlinson (Ed.), *Motivating students to learn: Overcoming barriers to high achievement.* Berkeley, CA: McCrutchan.

Brown, B. B. (1999). "You're going out with *who?*" Peer group influences on adolescent romantic relationships. In W. Furman, B. B. Brown, & C. Feiring (Eds.), *The development of romantic relationships in adolescence* (pp. 291–329). Cambridge, England: Cambridge University Press.

Brown, B. B., Eicher, S. A., & Petrie, S. (1986). The importance of peer group ("crowd") affiliation in adolescence. *Journal of Adolescence, 9,* 73–96.

Brown, B. B., Feiring, C., & Furman, W. (1999). Missing the love boat: Why researchers have shied away from adolescent romance. In W. Furman, B. B. Brown, & C. Feiring (Eds.), *The development of romantic relationships in adolescence* (pp. 1–16). Cambridge, England: Cambridge University Press.

Brown, J. D., & Siegel, J. D. (1988). Exercise as a buffer of life stress: A prospective study of adolescent health. *Health Psychology, 7,* 341–353.

Brown, J. R., & Dunn, J. (1996). Continuities in emotion understanding from three to six years. *Child Development, 67,* 789–802.

Brown, J. S., Collins, A., & Duguid, P. (1989). Situated cognition and the culture of learning. *Educational Researcher, 18*(1), 32–42.

Brown, L. M., Tappan, M. B., & Gilligan, C. (1995). Listening to different voices. In W. M. Kurtines & J. L. Gewirtz (Eds.), *Moral development: An introduction.* Boston: Allyn & Bacon.

Brown, R. (1973). *A first language: The early stages.* Cambridge, MA: Harvard University Press.

Brown, R., & Hanlon, C. (1970). Derivational complexity and order of acquisition in child speech. In J. R. Hayes (Ed.), *Cognition and the development of language.* New York: Wiley.

Brown, R. D., & Bjorklund, D. F. (1998). The biologizing of cognition, development, and education: Approach with cautious enthusiasm. *Educational Psychology Review, 10,* 355–373.

Brown, R. T., Reynolds, C. R., & Whitaker, J. S. (1999). Bias in mental testing since *Bias in Mental Testing. School Psychology Quarterly, 14,* 208–238.

Brown, T. A., Frederico, M., Hewitt, L., & Sheehan, R. (2001). The child abuse and divorce myth. *Child Abuse Review, 10*(2), 113–124.

Brown, V. A. (2002). *Child welfare case studies.* Boston, MA: Allyn & Bacon.

Brown-Mizuno, C. (1990). Success strategies for learners who are learning disabled as well as gifted. *Teaching Exceptional Children, 23*(1), 10–12.

Brownell, M. T., Mellard, D. F., & Deshler, D. D. (1993). Differences in the learning and transfer performance between students with learning disabilities and other low-achieving students on problem-solving tasks. *Learning Disabilities Quarterly, 16,* 138–156.

Bruck, M., & Ceci, S. J. (1997). The suggestibility of young children. *Current Directions in Psychological Science, 6,* 75–79.

Bruer, J. T. (1997). Education and the brain: A bridge too far. *Educational Researcher, 26*(8), 4–16.

Bruer, J. T. (1999). *The myth of the first three years: A new understanding of early brain development and lifelong learning.* New York: Free Press.

Bruner, J. S. (1983). The acquisition of pragmatic commitments. In R. M. Golinkoff (Ed.), *The transition from prelinguistic to linguistic communication* (pp. 27–42). Hillsdale, NJ: Erlbaum.

Bruner, J. S. (1972). The nature and uses of immaturity. *American Psychologist, 27*, 687–708.

Bruner, J. S., & Sherwood, V. (1976). Early rule structure: The case of "peekaboo." In R. Harre (Ed.), *Life sentences* (pp. 55–62). London: Wiley.

Bruni, M. (1998). *Fine-motor skills in children with Down syndrome: A guide for parents and professionals.* Bethesda, MD: Woodbine House.

Bryan, J. H., Redfield, J., & Mader, S. (1971). Words and deeds concerning altruism and subsequent reinforcement power of the model. *Child Development, 42*, 1501–1508.

Bryan, T., Burstein, K., & Bryan, J. (2001). Students with learning disabilities: Homework problems and promising practices. *Educational Psychologist, 36*, 167–180.

Bryant, A. L., & Zimmerman, M. A. (1999, April). *Adolescent substance use and school apathy: A developmental perspective examining motivational, peer, and family factors.* Paper presented at the Biennial Meeting of the Society for Research in Child Development, Albuquerque, NM.

Bryant, B. K. (1985). *The neighborhood walk: Sources of support in middle childhood.* Chicago: University of Chicago Press.

Bryant, P., Nunes, T., & Aidinis, A. (1999). Different morphemes, same spelling problems: Cross-linguistic developmental studies. In M. Harris & G. Hatano (Eds.), *Learning to read and write: A cross-linguistic perspective.* Cambridge, England: Cambridge University Press.

Bryson, S. E. (1997). Epidemiology of autism: Overview and issues outstanding. In D. J. Cohen & F. R. Volkmar (Eds.), *Handbook of autism and pervasive developmental disorders* (2nd ed.). New York: Wiley.

Buchanan, C. M. (1991). Pubertal status in early adolescent girls: Relations to moods, energy, and restlessness. *Journal of Early Adolescence, 11*(2), 185–200.

Buchanan, C. M., Eccles, J. S., & Becker, J. B. (1992). Are adolescents the victims of raging hormones: Evidence for activational effects of hormones on moods and behaviors at adolescence. *Psychological Bulletin, 111*(1), 62–107.

Buchoff, T. (1990). Attention deficit disorder: Help for the classroom teacher. *Childhood Education, 67*(2), 86–90.

Budwig, N. (1995). *A developmental-functionalist approach to child language.* Mahwah, NJ: Erlbaum.

Bugental, D. B., & Goodnow, J. J. (1998). Socialization processes. In W. Damon (Editor-in-Chief) and N. Eisenberg (Vol. Ed.), *Handbook of child psychology: Vol. 3. Social, emotional, and personality development* (5th ed., pp. 389–462). New York: Wiley.

Buhrmester, D. (1992). The developmental courses of sibling and peer relationships. In F. Boer and J. Dunn (Eds.), *Children's sibling relationships: Developmental and clinical issues.* Hillsdale, NJ: Erlbaum.

Buhrmester, D. (1996). Need fulfillment, interpersonal competence, and the developmental contexts of friendship. In W. M. Bukowski, A. F. Newcomb, & W. W. Hartup (Eds.), *The company they keep: Friendship during childhood and adolescence* (pp. 158–185). New York: Cambridge University Press.

Bullock, J. R. (1993). Children's loneliness and their relationships with family and peers. *Family Relations, 42*, 46–49.

Burhans, K. K., & Dweck, C. S. (1995). Helplessness in early childhood: The role of contingent worth. *Child Development, 66*, 1719–1738.

Burleson, B. R., & Kunkel, A. W. (1995, March). *Socialization of emotional support skills in childhood: The influence of parents and peers.* Paper presented at the biennial meeting of the Society for Research in Child Development, Indianapolis, Indiana.

Burnett, R. E., & Kastman, L. M. (1997). Teaching composition: Current theories and practices. In G. D. Phye (Ed.), *Handbook of academic learning: Construction of knowledge.* San Diego, CA: Academic Press.

Burns, C. E., Brady, M. A., Dunn, A. M., & Starr, N. B. (2000). *Pediatric primary care: A handbook for nurse practitioners* (2nd ed.). Philadelphia, PA: W. B. Saunders.

Burton, L. M. (1992). Black grandparents rearing children of drug addicted parents: Stressors, outcomes, and social service needs. *The Gerontologist, 32*(6), 744–751.

Burton, L. M., & Price-Spratlen, T. (1999). Through the eyes of children: An ethnographic perspective on neighborhoods and child development. In A. S. Masten (Ed.), Cultural processes in child development. *The Minnesota Symposia on Child Psychology, 29*, 77–96. Mahwah, NJ: Erlbaum.

Burton, R. V., & Kunce, L. (1995). Behavioral models of moral development: A brief history and integration. In W. M. Kurtines & J. L. Gewirtz (Eds.), *Moral development: An introduction.* Boston: Allyn & Bacon.

Bus, A. G., & van IJzendoorn, M. H. (1999). Phonological awareness and early reading: A meta-analysis of experimental training studies. *Journal of Educational Psychology, 91*, 403–414.

Bush, P. J., Zuckerman, A. E., Taggert, V. S., Theiss, P. K., Peleg, E. O., & Smith, S. A. (1989). Cardiovascular risk factor prevention in Black school children: The 'Know Your Body' evaluation project. *Health Education Quarterly, 16*, 215–227.

Butler, D. L., & Winne, P. H. (1995). Feedback and self-regulated learning: A theoretical synthesis. *Review of Educational Research, 65*, 245–281.

Butler, R. (1989). Mastery versus ability appraisal: A developmental study of children's observations of peers' work. *Child Development, 60*, 1350–1361.

Butler, R. (1994). Teacher communication and student interpretations: Effects of teacher responses to failing students on attributional inferences in two age groups. *British Journal of Educational Psychology, 64*, 277–294.

Butler, R. (1998). Age trends in the use of social and temporal comparison for self-evaluation: Examination of a novel developmental hypothesis. *Child Development, 69*, 1054–1073.

Butterfield, E. C., & Ferretti, R. P. (1987). Toward a theoretical integration of cognitive hypotheses about intellectual differences among children. In J. G. Borkowski & J. D. Day (Eds.), *Cognition in special children: Approaches to retardation, learning disabilities, and giftedness.* Norwood, NJ: Ablex.

Byne, W. (1997). Why we cannot conclude that sexual orientation is primarily a biological phenomenon. *Journal of Homosexuality, 34*, 73–80.

Byrne, B., Fielding-Barnsley, R., & Ashley, L. (2000). Effects of preschool phoneme identity training after six years: Outcome level distinguished from rate of response. *Journal of Educational Psychology, 92*, 659–667.

Byrnes, J. P. (1996). *Cognitive development and learning in instructional contexts.* Boston: Allyn & Bacon.

Caetanno, R. (1987). Acculturation and drinking patterns among U.S. Hispanics. *British Journal of Addiction, 82*, 789–799.

Cain, K., & Oakhill, J. (1998). Comprehension skill and inference-making ability: Issues of causality. In C. Hulme & R. M. Joshi (Eds.), *Reading and spelling: Development and disorders.* Mahwah, NJ: Erlbaum.

Cairns, H. S. (1996). *The acquisition of language* (2nd ed.). Austin, TX: Pro-Ed.

Cairns, R. B. (1979). *Social development: The origins and plasticity of interchanges.* San Francisco: Freeman.

Cairns, R. B. (1983). The emergence of developmental psychology. In W. Kessen (Ed.) & P. H. Mussen (Series Ed.), *Handbook of child psychology: Vol. 1. History, theory, and methods* (pp. 41–102). New York: Wiley.

Cairns, R. B., Cairns, B. D., Neckerman, H. J., Ferguson, L. L., & Gariépy, J.-L. (1989). Growth and aggression: 1. Childhood to early adolescence. *Developmental Psychology, 25*, 320–330.

Calfee, R. C., & Masuda, W. V. (1997). Classroom assessment as inquiry. In G. D. Phye (Ed.), *Handbook of classroom assessment: Learning, achievement, and adjustment.* San Diego, CA: Academic Press.

Callanan, M. A., & Oakes, L. M. (1992). Preschoolers' questions and parents' explanations: Causal thinking in everyday activity. *Cognitive Development, 7*, 213–233.

Cameron, C. A., Hunt, A. K., & Linton, M. J. (1996). Written expression as recontextualization: Children write in social time. *Educational Psychology Review, 8*, 125–150.

Campbell, A. (1984). *The girls in the gang: A report from New York City.* New York: Basil Blackwell.

Campbell, D. T., & Stanley, J. C. (1963). Experimental and quasi-experimental designs for research on teaching. In N. L. Gage (Ed.), *Handbook of research on teaching* (pp. 171–246). Chicago: Rand McNally.

Campbell, D. W., Eaton, W. O., McKeen, N. A., & Mitsutake, G. (1999, April). *The rise and fall of motor activity: Evidence of age-related change from 7 to 14 years.* Paper presented at the biennial meeting of the Society for Research in Child Development, Albuquerque, NM.

Campbell, F. A., & Ramey, C. T. (1994). Effects of early intervention on intellectual and academic achievement: A follow-up study of children from low-income families. *Child Development, 65*, 684–698.

Campbell, F. A., & Ramey, C. T. (1995). Cognitive and school outcomes for high-risk African-American students at middle adolescence: Positive effects of early intervention. *American Educational Research Journal, 32*, 742–772.

Campbell, L., Campbell, B., & Dickinson, D. (1998). *Teaching and learning through multiple intelligences* (2nd ed.). Boston: Allyn & Bacon.

Campione, J. C., Shapiro, A. M., & Brown, A. L. (1995). Forms of transfer in a community of learners: Flexible learning and understanding. In A. McKeough, J. Lupart, & A. Marini (Eds.), *Teaching for transfer: Fostering generalization in learning.* Mahwah, NJ: Erlbaum.

Campos, J. J., Bertenthal, B. I., & Kermoian, R. (1992). Early experiences and emotional development: The emergence of wariness of heights. *Psychological Science, 3*, 61–64.

Campos, R., Antunes, C. M., Raffaelli, M., Halsey, N., Ude, W., Greco, M., Greco, D., Ruff, A., Rolf, J., & Street Youth Study Group. (1994). Social networks and daily activities of street youth in Belo Horizonte, Brazil. *Child Development, 65*, 319–330.

Camras, L. A., Malatesta, C., & Izard, C. (1991). The development of facial expressions in infancy. In R. S. Feldman & B. Rime (Eds.), *Fundamentals of nonverbal behavior: Studies in emotion and social interaction* (pp. 73–105). New York: Cambridge University Press.

Camras, L. A., Oster, H., Campos, J., Campos, R., Ujiie, T., Miyake, K., et al. (1998). Production of emotional and facial expressions in European American, Japanese, and Chinese infants. *Developmental Psychology, 34*, 616–628.

Candler-Lotven, A., Tallent-Runnels, M. K., Olivárez, A., & Hildreth, B. (1994, April). *A comparison of learning and study strategies of gifted, average-ability, and learning-disabled ninth grade students.*

Paper presented at the annual meeting of the American Educational Research Association, New Orleans, LA.

Capelli, C. A., Nakagawa, N., & Madden, C. M. (1990). How children understand sarcasm: The role of context and intonation. *Child Development, 61,* 1824–1841.

Caplan, J. G., McElvain, C. K., & Walter, K. E. (2001). *Beyond the bell: A tool kit for creating after-school programs* (2nd ed.). Naperville, IL: North Central Regional Educational Laboratory.

Caplan, M., Vespo, J. E., Pedersen, J., & Hay, D. F. (1991). Conflict over resources in small groups of 1- and 2-year-olds. *Child Development, 62,* 1513–1524.

Caplow, T., Bahr, H. M., Chadwick, B. A., Hill, R., & Williamson, M. H. (1982). *Middletown families.* Minneapolis: University of Minnesota Press.

Caprara, G. V., Barbaranelli, C., Pastorelli, C., Bandura, A., & Zimbardo, P. G. (2000). Prosocial foundations of children's academic achievement. *Psychological Science, 11,* 302–306.

Capron, C., & Duyme, M. (1989). Assessment of effects of socio-economic status on IQ in a full cross-fostering study. *Nature, 340,* 552–554.

Carey, S. (1978). The child as word learner. In M. Halle, J. Bresnan, & G. Miller (Eds.), *Linguistic theory and psychological reality.* Cambridge, MA: MIT Press.

Carey, S. (1985a). Are children fundamentally different kinds of thinkers and learners than adults? In S. F. Chipman, J. W. Segal, & R. Glaser (Eds.), *Learning and thinking skills: Vol. 2. Research and open questions.* Hillsdale, NJ: Erlbaum.

Carey, S. (1985b). *Conceptual change in childhood.* Cambridge, MA: MIT Press.

Carey, S., & Bartlett, E. (1978). Acquiring a single new word. *Papers and Reports on Child Language Development, 15,* 17–29.

Carlson, C. L., Pelham, W. E., Milich, R., & Dixon, J. (1992). Single and combined effects of methylphenidate and behavior therapy on the classroom performance of children with attention deficit hyperactivity disorder. *Journal of Abnormal Child Psychology, 20,* 213–232.

Carlson, N. R. (1999). *Foundations of physiological psychology.* Boston: Allyn & Bacon.

Carlson, S. M., & Moses, L. J. (2001). Individual differences in inhibitory control and children's theory of mind. *Child Development, 72,* 1032–1053.

Carns, D. (1973). Talking about sex: Notes on first coitus and the double sexual standard. *Journal of Marriage and the Family, 35,* 677–688.

Caron, A. J., Caron, R. F., & MacLean, D. J. (1988). Infant discrimination of naturalistic emotional expressions: The role of face and voice. *Child Development, 59,* 604–616.

Carpenter, M., Nagell, K., & Tomasello, M. (1998). Social cognition, joint attention, and communicative competence from 9 to 15 months of age. *Monographs of the Society for Research in Child Development, 63*(Serial No. 255). Chicago: University of Chicago Press.

Carr, A. A. (1997, March). *The participation "race": Kentucky's site based decision teams.* Paper presented at the annual meeting of the American Educational Research Association, Chicago.

Carr, E. G., Levin, L., McConnachie, G., Carlson, J. I., Kemp, D. C., & Smith, C. E. (1994). *Communication-based intervention for problem behavior: A user's guide for producing positive change.* Baltimore: Brookes.

Carr, M., & Schneider, W. (1991). Long-term maintenance of organizational strategies in kindergarten children. *Contemporary Educational Psychology, 16,* 61–72.

Carraher, T. N., Carraher, D. W., & Schliemann, A. D. (1985). Mathematics in the streets and in the schools. *British Journal of Developmental Psychology, 3,* 21–29.

Carroll, J. B. (1992). Cognitive abilities: The state of the art. *Psychological Science, 3,* 266–270.

Carroll, L. (1872). *Through the looking glass and what Alice found there.* London: Macmillan.

Carroll, L. (1881). *Alice's adventures in Wonderland.* London: Macmillan.

Carter, D. B., & Levy, G. D. (1988). Cognitive aspects of early sex-role development: The influence of gender schemas on preschoolers' memories and preferences for sex-typed toys and activities. *Child Development, 59,* 782–792.

Carter, D. E., Detine-Carter, S. L., & Benson, F. W. (1995). Interracial acceptance in the classroom. In H. C. Foot, A. J. Chapman, & J. R. Smith (Eds.), *Friendship and social relations in children* (pp. 117–143). New Brunswick: Transaction Publishers.

Carter, K. R. (1991). Evaluation of gifted programs. In N. Buchanan & J. Feldhusen (Eds.), *Conducting research and evaluation in gifted education: A handbook of methods and applications.* New York: Teachers College Press.

Carter, K. R., & Ormrod, J. E. (1982). Acquisition of formal operations by intellectually gifted children. *Gifted Child Quarterly, 26,* 110–115.

Cartledge, G., & Milburn, J. F. (1995). *Teaching social skills to children and youth: Innovative approaches* (3rd ed.). Needham Heights, MA: Allyn & Bacon.

Casanova, U. (1987). Ethnic and cultural differences. In V. Richardson-Koehler (Ed.), *Educator's handbook: A research perspective.* White Plains, NY: Longman.

Casarez-Levison, R. (2000, April). *In the aftermath of the Columbine tragedy: An exploration of the psychological dimensions of victimization in school settings.* Paper presented at the annual meeting of the American Educational Research Association, New Orleans.

Case, R. (1985). *Intellectual development: Birth to adulthood.* Orlando, FL: Academic Press.

Case, R., & Edelstein, W. (1993). *The new structuralism in cognitive development: Theory and research on individual pathways.* Basel, Switzerland: Karger.

Case, R., & Mueller, M. P. (2001). Differentiation, integration, and covariance mapping as fundamental processes in cognitive and neurological growth. In J. L. McClelland & R. S. Siegler (Eds.), *Mechanisms of cognitive development: Behavioral and neural perspectives* (pp. 185–219). Mahwah, NJ: Erlbaum.

Case, R., & Okamoto, Y., in collaboration with Griffin, S., McKeough, A., Bleiker, C., Henderson, B., & Stephenson, K. M. (1996). The role of central conceptual structures in the development of children's thought. *Monographs of the Society for Research in Child Development, 61*(1–2, Serial No. 246).

Case, R., Okamoto, Y., Henderson, B., & McKeough, A. (1993). Individual variability and consistency in cognitive development: New evidence for the existence of central conceptual structures. In R. Case & W. Edelstein (Eds.), *The new structuralism in cognitive development: Theory and research on individual pathways.* Basel, Switzerland: Karger.

Case-Smith, J. (1996). Fine motor outcomes in preschool children who receive occupational therapy services. *American Journal of Occupational Therapy, 50*(1), 52–61.

Casey, B. J. (2001). Disruption of inhibitory control in developmental disorders: A mechanistic model of implicated frontostriatal circuitry. In J. L. McClelland & R. S. Siegler (Eds.), *Mechanisms of cognitive development: Behavioral and neural perspectives* (pp. 327–349). Mahwah, NJ: Erlbaum.

Casey, B. J., Giedd, J. N., & Thomas, K. M. (2000). Structural and functional brain development and its relation to cognitive development. *Biological Psychology, 54,* 241–257.

Casey, B. M., McIntire, D. D., & Leveno, K. J. (2001). The continuing value of the Apgar score for the assessment of newborn infants. *New England Journal of Medicine, 344,* 467–471.

Casey, W. M., & Burton, R. V. (1982). Training children to be consistently honest through verbal self-instructions. *Child Development, 53,* 911–919.

Caspi, A. (1998). Personality development across the life course. In W. Damon (Editor-in-Chief) & N. Eisenberg (Vol. Ed.), *Handbook of child psychology: Vol. 3. Social, emotional, and personality development* (5th ed., pp. 311–388). New York: Wiley.

Caspi, A., Taylor, A., Moffitt, T. E., & Plomin, R. (2000). Neighborhood deprivation affects children's mental health: Environmental risks identified in a genetic design. *Psychological Science, 11,* 338–342.

Cassidy, C. (1999). *Girls in America: Their stories, their words.* New York: TV Books.

Cassidy, M., & Berlin, L. J. (1994). The insecure/ambivalent pattern of attachment: Theory and research. *Child Development, 65,* 971–991.

Catania, J. A., Coates, T. J., Stall, R., Turner, H., Peterson, J., Hearst, N., Dolcini, M. M., Hudes, E., Gagnon, J., Wiley, J., & Groves, R. (1992). Prevalence of AIDS-related risk factors and condom use in the United States. *Science, 258,* 1101–1106.

Catron, T. F., & Masters, J. C. (1993). Mothers' and children's conceptualizations of corporal punishment. *Child Development, 64,* 1815–1828.

Cattell, R. B. (1963). Theory of fluid and crystallized intelligence: A critical experiment. *Journal of Educational Psychology, 54,* 1–22.

Cattell, R. B. (1980). The heritability of fluid, g_f, and crystallised, g_c, intelligence, estimated by a least squares use of the MAVA method. *British Journal of Educational Psychology, 50,* 253–265.

Cattell, R. B. (1987). *Intelligence: Its structure, growth, and action.* Amsterdam: North-Holland.

Cauce, A. M., Mason, C., Gonzales, N., Hiraga, Y., & Liu, G. (1994). Social support during adolescence: Methodological and theoretical considerations. In F. Nestemann & K. Hurrelmann (Eds.), *Social networks and social support in childhood and adolescence.* Berlin, Germany: Aldine de Gruyter.

Cazden, C. B. (1968). The acquisition of noun and verb inflections. *Child Development, 39,* 433–448.

Cazden, C. B. (1976). Play with language and metalinguistic awareness: One dimension of language experience. In J. Bruner, A. Jolly, & K. Sylva (Eds.), *Play: Its role in development and evolution.* New York: Basic Books.

Ceci, S. J., & Roazzi, A. (1994). The effects of context on cognition: Postcards from Brazil. In R. J. Sternberg & R. K. Wagner (Eds.), *Mind in context: Interactionist perspectives on human intelligence.* Cambridge, England: Cambridge University Press.

Ceci, S. J., Rosenblum, T., de Bruyn, E., & Lee, D. Y. (1997). A bio-ecological model of intellectual development: Moving beyond h^2. In R. J. Sternberg & E. L. Grigorenko (Eds.), *Intelligence, heredity, and environment* (pp. 303–322). Cambridge, England: Cambridge University Press.

Ceci, S. J., Rosenblum, T. B., & Kumpf, M. (1998). The shrinking gap between high- and low-scoring groups: Current trends and possible causes. In U. Neisser (Ed.), *The rising curve: Long-term gains in IQ and related measures* (pp. 287–302). Washington, DC: American Psychological Association.

Ceci, S. J., & Williams, W. M. (1997). Schooling, intelligence, and income. *American Psychologist, 52,* 1051–1058.

Center for the Future of Children. (1997). Executive Summary: Children and Poverty, *The Future of Children, 7*(2), 1–7.

Centers for Disease Control and Prevention (1997). *Pediatric nutrition surveillance: 1997 Executive summary*. Atlanta, GA: Centers for Disease Control and Prevention.

Centers for Disease Control and Prevention (2002, Fall). Body and Mind Teacher's Corner Resource: Planning for physical activity. Retrieved January 19, 2003, from *http://www.bam.gov/teachers*

Cerella, J., & Hale, S. (1994). The rise and fall in information-processing rates over the life span. *Acta Psychologia, 86*, 109–197.

Chafel, J. A. (1991). The play of children: Developmental processes and policy implications. *Child & Youth Care Forum, 20*, 115–132.

Chafel, J. A. (1997). Schooling, the hidden curriculum, and children's conceptions of poverty. *Social Policy Report: Society for Research in Child Development, 11*(1), 1–18.

Chaffee, S. H., & Yang, S. M. (1990). Communication and political socialization. In O. Ichilov (Ed.), *Political socialization, citizenship, education, and democracy* (pp. 137–157). New York: Teachers College Press.

Chaiken, M. R. (1998). Tailoring established after-school programs to meet urban realities. In D. S. Elliot & B. A. Hamburg (Eds.), *Violence in American schools: A new perspective* (pp. 348–375). New York: Cambridge University Press.

Chaiken, M. R. (2000, May). Violent neighborhoods, violent kids. *Juvenile Justice Bulletin*, NCJ 178248. Washington, DC: U.S. Department of Justice, Office of Juvenile Justice and Delinquency Prevention.

Chalfant, J. C. (1989). Learning disabilities: Policy issues and promising approaches. *American Psychologist, 44*, 392–398.

Chall, J. S. (1996). *Stages of reading development* (2nd ed.) Fort Worth, TX: Harcourt, Brace.

Chalmers, J., & Townsend, M. (1990). The effects of training in social perspective taking on socially maladjusted girls. *Child Development, 61*, 178–190.

Chamberlain, P., & Reid, J. (1998). Comparison of two community alternatives to incarceration for chronic juvenile offenders. *Journal of Consulting and Clinical Psychology, 6*(4), 624–633.

Chambliss, M. J. (1994). Why do readers fail to change their beliefs after reading persuasive text? In R. Garner & P. A. Alexander (Eds.), *Beliefs about text and instruction with text*. Hillsdale, NJ: Erlbaum.

Chambliss, M. J. (1998, April). *Children as thinkers composing scientific explanations*. Paper presented at the annual meeting of the American Educational Research Association, San Diego, CA.

Champagne, A. B., & Bunce, D. M. (1991). Learning-theory-based science teaching. In S. M. Glynn, R. H. Yeany, & B. K. Britton (Eds.), *The psychology of learning science*. Hillsdale, NJ: Erlbaum.

Champion, D. J. (2001). *The juvenile justice system: Delinquency, processing, and the law* (3rd ed.). Upper Saddle River, NJ: Prentice Hall.

Chan, C., Burtis, J., & Bereiter, C. (1997). Knowledge building as a mediator of conflict in conceptual change. *Cognition and Instruction, 15*, 1–40.

Chandler, M. (1982). Social cognition and social structure. In F. C. Serafica (Ed.), *Social cognitive development in context*. New York: Guilford Press.

Chandler, M., & Boyes, M. (1982). Social-cognitive development. In B. Wolman (Ed.), *Handbook of developmental psychology*. Upper Saddle River, NJ: Prentice Hall.

Chandler, M., & Moran, T. (1990). Psychopathy and moral development: A comparative study of delinquent and nondelinquent youth. *Development and Psychopathology, 2*, 227–246.

Chandler, M. J. (1973). Egocentrism and antisocial behavior: The assessment and training of social perspective-taking skills. *Developmental Psychology, 9*, 326–332.

Chandler, M. J. (1987). The Othello effect: Essay on the emergence and eclipse of skeptical doubt. *Human Development, 30*, 137–159.

Chandler, T. J. L., & Goldberg, A. D. (1990). The academic All-American as vaunted adolescent role-identity. *Sociology of Sport Journal, 7*, 287–293.

Chang, H., & Trehub, S. (1977). Infants' perception of temporal grouping in auditory patterns. *Child Development, 48*, 1666–1670.

Chang, J.-M. (1998). Language and literacy in Chinese American communities. In B. Pérez (Ed.), *Sociocultural contexts of language and literacy*. Mahwah, NJ: Erlbaum.

Chao, R. K. (1994). Beyond parental control and authoritarian parenting style: Understanding Chinese parenting through the cultural notion of training. *Child Development, 65*, 1111–1119.

Chao, R. K. (2000). Cultural explanations for the role of parenting in the school success of Asian-American children. In R. D. Taylor & M. C. Wang (Eds.), *Resilience across contexts: Family, work, culture, and community* (pp. 333–363). Mahwah, NJ: Erlbaum.

Chapman, C., Nolin, M., & Kline, K. (1997). *Student interest in national news and its relation to school courses* (NCES 97–970). Washington, DC: U.S. Department of Education, National Center for Education Statistics.

Charles A. Dana Center. (1999). *Hope for urban education: A study of nine high-performing, high-poverty, urban elementary schools*. Washington, DC: U.S. Department of Education, Planning and Evaluation Service.

Charlesworth, W. R. (1992). Charles Darwin and developmental psychology: Past and present. *Developmental Psychology, 28*, 5–16.

Charlesworth, W. R., & LaFreniere, P. (1983). Dominance, friendship, and resource utilization in preschool children's groups. *Ethology and Sociobiology, 4*, 175–186.

Charman, T., Swettenham, J., Baron-Cohen, S., Cox, A., Baird, G., & Drew, A. (1997). Infants with autism: An investigation of empathy, pretend play, joint attention, and imitation. *Developmental Psychology, 33*, 781–789.

Charner, I., & Fraser, B. S. (1988). *Youth and work: What we know, what we don't know, what we need to know*. Washington, DC: Commission on Work, Family, and Citizenship. (ERIC Document Service No. ED 292 980)

Chase-Lansdale, P. L., & Brooks-Gunn, J. (1994). Correlates of adolescent pregnancy and parenthood. In C. B. Fisher & R. M. Lerner (Eds.), *Applied developmental psychology* (pp. 207–236). New York: McGraw-Hill.

Chase-Lansdale, P. L., Brooks-Gunn, J., & Zamsky, E. S. (1994). Young African-American multigenerational families in poverty: Quality of mothering and grandmothering. *Child Development, 65*, 373–393.

Chasnoff, I. J., Burns, K. A., Burns, W. J., & Schnoll, S. H. (1986). Prenatal drug exposure: Effects on neonatal and infant growth and development. *Neurobehavioral Toxicology & Teratology, 8*(4), 357–362.

Chassin, L., Curran, P. J., Hussong, A. M., & Colder, C. R. (1996). The relation of parent alcoholism to adolescent substance use: A longitudinal follow-up study. *Journal of Abnormal Psychology, 105*, 70–80.

Clavez, A., Martinez, C., Soberanes, B. (1995). Effects of early malnutrition on late mental and behavioral performance. *Developmental Brain Dysfunction, 8*(2–3), 90–102.

Chavkin, N. F. (Ed.). (1993). *Families and schools in a pluralistic society*. Albany: State University of New York Press.

Chazan-Cohen, R., Jerald, J., & Stark, D. R. (2001). A commitment to supporting the mental health of our youngest children. *Zero to Three, 22*(1), 4–12.

Cheatham, S. K., Smith, J. D., Rucker, H. N., Polloway, E. A., & Lewis, G. W. (1995, September). Savant syndrome: Case studies, hypotheses, and implications for special education. *Education and Training in Mental Retardation*, 243–253.

Chen, J.-Q., Krechevsky, M., & Viens, J. (1998). *Building on children's strengths: The experience of Project Spectrum*. New York: Teachers College Press.

Chen, M. (1984). *A review of research on the educational potential of 3-2-1 Contact: A children's TV series on science and technology*. New York: Children's Television Workshop.

Chen, X., Rubin, K. H., & Li, Z. (1995). Social functioning and adjustment in Chinese children. *Developmental Psychology, 31*, 531–539.

Chen, X., Rubin, K. H., & Sun, Y. (1992). Social reputation and peer relationships in Chinese and Canadian children: A cross-cultural study. *Child Development, 63*, 1336–1343.

Chen, Z., Sanchez, R. P., & Campbell, T. (1997). From beyond to within their grasp: The rudiments of analogical problem solving in 10- and 13-month-olds. *Developmental Psychology, 33*, pp. 790–801.

Cherlin, A. J., & Furstenberg, F. F., Jr. (1988, September). The changing European family: Lessons for the American reader. *Journal of Family Issues, 9*, 291–297.

Chi, M. T. H. (1978). Knowledge structures and memory development. In R. S. Siegler (Ed.), *Children's thinking: What develops?* Hillsdale, NJ: Erlbaum.

Chiappe, P., & Siegel, L. S. (1999). Phonological awareness and reading acquisition in English- and Punjabi-speaking Canadian children. *Journal of Educational Psychology, 91*, 20–28.

Chilamkurti, C., & Milner, J. S. (1993). Perceptions and evaluations of child transgressions and disciplinary techniques in high- and low-risk mothers and their children. *Child Development, 64*, 1801–1814.

Chinn, C. A., & Brewer, W. F. (1993). The role of anomalous data in knowledge acquisition: A theoretical framework and implications for science instruction. *Review of Educational Research, 63*, 1–49.

Chisholm, J. S. (1996). The evolutionary ecology of attachment organization. *Human Nature, 1*, 1–37.

Chisholm, K., Carter, M. C., Ames, E. W., & Morison, S. J. (1995). Attachment security and indiscriminately friendly behavior in children adopted from Romanian orphanages. *Development and Psychopathology, 7*, 283–297.

Chomsky, C. S. (1969). *The acquisition of syntax in children from 5 to 10*. Cambridge, MA: MIT Press.

Chomsky, N. (1959). [Review of B. F. Skinner's *Verbal behavior*]. *Language, 35*, 26–58.

Chomsky, N. (1964). *Current issues in linguistic theory*. The Hague, Netherlands: Mouton.

Chomsky, N. (1965). *Aspects of the theory of syntax*. Cambridge, MA: MIT Press.

Chomsky, N. (1972). *Language and mind* (enlarged ed.). San Diego, CA: Harcourt Brace Jovanovich.

Chomsky, N. (1976). *Reflections on language*. London: Temple Smith.

Christie, J. F., & Johnsen, E. P. (1983). The role of play in social-intellectual development. *Review of Educational Research, 53*, 93–115.

Chu, Y.-W. (2000). *The relationships between domain-specific self-concepts and global self-esteem among adolescents in Taiwan*. Unpublished doctoral dissertation, University of Northern Colorado, Greeley.

Chugani, H. T. (1998). Biological bases of emotions: Brain systems and brain development. *Pediatrics, 102*(5 Suppl. E), 1225–1229.

Chukovsky, K. (1968). *From two to five* (M. Morton, Trans.). Berkeley: University of California Press.

Churchill, S. L. (1999, April). *Parent and teacher agreement on child and parenting behaviors as a predictor of child outcomes.* Paper presented at the biennial meeting of the Society for Research in Child Development, Albuquerque, NM.

Cialdini, R. B. (2001). *Influence: Science and practice.* Boston: Allyn & Bacon.

Cicchetti, D., & Garmezy, N. (1993). Prospects and promises in the study of resilience. *Development and Psychopathology, 5,* 497–502.

Cicchetti, D., Rogosch, F. A., & Toth, S. L. (1997). Ontogenesis, depressotypic organization, and the depressive spectrum. In S. S. Luthar, J. A. Burack, D. Cicchetti, & J. R. Weisz (Eds.), *Developmental psychopathology: Perspectives on adjustment, risk, and disorder* (pp. 273–313). Cambridge, England: Cambridge University Press.

Cicchetti, D., & Toth, S. L. (1998). Perspectives on research and practice in developmental psychopathology. In W. Damon (Editor-in-Chief), I. E. Sigel, & K. A. Renninger (Vol. Eds.), *Handbook of child psychology: Vol. 4. Child psychology in practice* (5th ed., pp. 479–583). New York: Wiley.

CJ Foundation for SIDS. (2002). SIDS Information. Retrieved January 19, 2003, from *http://www.cjsids.com/sids.htm*

Clark, B. (1997). *Growing up gifted* (5th ed.). Upper Saddle River, NJ: Merrill/Prentice Hall.

Clark, C. C. (1992). Deviant adolescent subcultures: Assessment strategies and clinical interventions. *Adolescence, 27*(106), 283–293.

Clark, E. V. (1971). On the acquisition of the meaning of "before" and "after." *Journal of Verbal Learning and Verbal Behavior, 10,* 266–275.

Clark, R. M. (1983). *Family life and school achievement: Why poor Black children succeed or fail.* Chicago: University of Chicago Press.

Clarke, L. K. (1988). Invented versus traditional spelling in first graders' writings: Effects on learning to spell and read. *Research in the Teaching of English, 22,* 281–309.

Clarke-Stewart, K. A. (1989). Infant day care: Maligned or malignant? *American Psychologist, 44,* 266–273.

Clasen, D. R., & Brown, B. B. (1985). The multidimensionality of peer pressure in adolescence. *Journal of Youth and Adolescence, 14,* 451–468.

Claude, D., & Firestone, P. (1995). The development of ADHD boys: A 12-year follow-up. *Canadian Journal of Behavioural Science, 27,* 226–249.

Clifford, M. M. (1990). Students need challenge, not easy success. *Educational Leadership, 48*(1), 22–26.

Clinchy, E. (1994). Higher education: The albatross around the neck of our public schools. *Phi Delta Kappan, 75,* 744–751.

Cochran, M. (1993). Personal networks in the ecology of human development. In M. Cochran, M. Larner, D. Riley, L. Gunnarsson, & C. R. Henderson, Jr. (Eds.), *Extending families: The social networks of parents and their children* (pp. 1–33). New York: Cambridge University Press.

Cochran-Smith, M. (1991). *The making of a reader.* Norwood, NJ: Ablex.

Cochran-Smith, M., & Lytle, S. (1993). *Inside out: Teacher research and knowledge.* New York: Teachers College Press.

Cocking, R. R., & Greenfield, P. M. (1996). Introduction. In P. M. Greenfield & R. Cocking (Eds.), *Interacting with video* (pp. 3–7). Norwood, NJ: Ablex.

Cody, H., & Kamphaus, R. W. (1999). Down syndrome. In S. Goldstein & C. R. Reynolds (Eds.), *Handbook of neurodevelopmental and genetic disorders* (pp. 385–405). New York: Guilford Press.

Coe, J., Salamon, L., & Molnar, J. (1991). *Homeless children and youth.* New Brunswick, NJ: Transaction.

Cohen, D., & Nisbett, R. E. (1994). Self-protection and the culture of honor: Explaining Southern violence. *Personality and Social Psychology Bulletin, 20,* 551–567.

Cohen, E. G. (1994). Restructuring the classroom: Conditions for productive small groups. *Review of Educational Research, 64,* 1–35.

Cohen, E. G., & Lotan, R. A. (1995). Producing equal-status interaction in the heterogeneous classroom. *American Educational Research Journal, 32,* 99–120.

Cohen, G. (1981). Culture and educational achievement. *Harvard Educational Review, 51,* 270–285.

Cohen, M. N. (1998). Culture, not race, explains human diversity. *The Chronicle of Higher Education,* April 17.

Cohen, M. R. (1997). Individual and sex differences in speed of handwriting among high school students. *Perceptual and Motor Skills, 84*(3, Pt. 2), 1428–1430.

Cohen, R. J., & Swerdlik, M. E. (1999). *Psychological testing and assessment.* Mountain View, CA: Mayfield.

Cohn, J. F., Campbell, S. B., & Ross, S. (1991). Infant response in the still-face paradigm at 6 months predicts avoidant and secure attachment at 12 months. *Development and Psychopathology, 3,* 367–376.

Coie, J. D., & Cillessen, A. H. N. (1993). Peer rejection: Origins and effects on children's development. *Current Directions in Psychological Science, 2,* 89–92.

Coie, J. D., & Dodge, K. A. (1988). Multiple sources of data on social behavior and social status. *Child Development, 59,* 815–829.

Coie, J. D., & Dodge, K. A. (1998). Aggression and antisocial behavior. In W. Damon (Editor in Chief) & N. Eisenberg (Vol. Ed.), *Handbook of child psychology: Vol. 3. Social, emotional, and personality development* (pp. 779–862). New York: Wiley.

Coie, J. D., Dodge, K. A., Terry, R., & Wright, V. (1991). The role of aggression in peer relations: An analysis of aggression episodes in boys' play groups. *Child Development, 62,* 812–826.

Coie, J. D., & Kupersmidt, J. (1983). A behavioral analysis of emerging social status in boys' groups. *Child Development, 54,* 1400–1416.

Colby, A., & Kohlberg, L. (1984). Invariant sequence and internal consistency in moral judgment stages. In W. M. Kurtines & J. L. Gewirtz (Eds.), *Morality, moral behavior, and moral development.* New York: Wiley.

Colby, A., Kohlberg, L., Gibbs, J., & Lieberman, M. (1983). A longitudinal study of moral judgment. *Monographs of the Society for Research in Child Development, 48*(1–2, Serial No. 200).

Cole, M., & Schribner, S. (1977). Cross-cultural studies of memory and cognition. In R. V. Kail & J. W. Hagen (Eds.), *Perspectives on the development of memory and cognition.* Hillsdale, NJ: Erlbaum.

Cole, N. S. (1990). Conceptions of educational achievement. *Educational Researcher, 19*(3), 2–7.

Cole, N. S. (1990). Conceptions of educational achievement. *Educational Researcher, 19*(3), 2–7.

Cole, P. (1986). Children's spontaneous control of facial expression. *Child Development, 57,* 1309–1321.

Coles, R. (1967). *Children of crisis: Vol. 1. A study of courage and fear.* Boston: Little, Brown.

Coles, R. (1971a). *Children of crisis: Vol. 2. Migrants, sharecroppers, mountaineers.* Boston: Little, Brown.

Coles, R. (1971b). *Children of crisis: Vol. 3. The South goes north.* Boston: Little, Brown.

Coles, R. (1977). *Children of crisis: Vol. 4. Eskimos, Chicanos, Indians.* Boston: Little, Brown.

Coles, R. (1997). *The youngest parents.* New York: W. W. Norton.

Coles, R. (1990). *The spiritual life of children.* Boston, MA: Houghton Mifflin Company.

Coley, R. L., & Chase-Lansdale, P. L. (1998). Adolescent pregnancy and parenthood. *American Psychologist, 53,* 152–166.

Coll, C. G., Crnic, K., Lamberty, G., Wasik, B. J., Jenkins, R., Garcia, H. V., & McAdoo, H. P. (1996). An integrative model for the study of developmental competencies in minority children. *Child Development, 67,* 1891–1914.

Collaer, M. L., & Hines, M. (1995). Human behavioral sex differences: A role for gonadal hormones during early development? *Psychological Bulletin, 118,* 55–107.

Collie, R., & Hayne, H. (1999). Deferred imitation by 6- and 9-month-old infants: More evidence for declarative memory. *Developmental Psychobiology, 35,* 83–90.

Collier, V. (1989). How long? A synthesis of research on academic achievement in a second language. *TESOL Quarterly, 23,* 509–523.

Collier, V. P. (1992). The Canadian bilingual immersion debate: A synthesis of research findings. *Studies in Second Language Acquisition, 14,* 87–97.

Collingwood, T. R. (1997). *Helping at-risk youth through physical fitness programming.* Champaign, IL: Human Kinetics.

Collins, A., Brown, J. S., & Newman, S. E. (1989). Cognitive apprenticeship: Teaching the crafts of reading, writing, and mathematics. In L. B. Resnick (Ed.), *Knowing, learning, and instruction: Essays in honor of Robert Glaser.* Hillsdale, NJ: Erlbaum.

Collins, R. (1999). The adoption and foster care analysis and reporting system: Implications for foster care policy. In P. A. Curtis, G. D. Dale, & J. C. Kendall (Eds.), *The foster care crisis: Translating research into policy and practice* (pp. 45–59). Lincoln: University of Nebraska Press.

Collins, W. A. (1990). Parent-child relationships in the transition to adolescence: Continuity and change in interaction, affects, and cognition. In R. Montemayor, G. Adams, & T. Gullota (Eds.), *Advances in adolescent development* (Vol. 2). Beverly Hills, CA: Sage.

Collins, W. A., Maccoby, E. E., Steinberg, L., Hetherington, E. M., & Bornstein, M. H. (2000). Contemporary research on parenting: the case for nature and nurture. *American Psychologist, 55,* pp. 218–232.

Collins, W. A., & Sroufe, L. A. (1999). Capacity for intimate relationships: A developmental construction. In W. Furman, B. B. Brown, & C. Feiring (Eds.), *The development of romantic relationships in adolescence* (pp. 125–147). Cambridge, England: Cambridge University Press.

Colombo, J. (1993). *Infant cognition: Predicting later intellectual functioning.* Newbury Park, CA: Sage.

Comeau, L., Cormier, P., Grandmaison, É., & Lacroix, D. (1999). A longitudinal study of phonological processing skills in children learning to read in a second language. *Journal of Educational Psychology, 91,* 29–43.

Commons, M. L., Richards, F. A., & Armon, C. (Eds.). (1984). *Beyond formal operations.* New York: Praeger.

Comstock, G., with H. Paik. (1991). *Television and the American child.* San Diego, CA: Academic Press.

Condon, J. C., & Yousef, F. S. (1975). *An introduction to intercultural communication.* Indianapolis, IN: Bobbs-Merrill.

Condry, J. C., & Ross, D. F. (1985). Sex and aggression: The influence of gender label on the perception of aggression in children. *Child Development, 56,* 225–233.

Conel, J. L. (1939–1967). *Postnatal development of the human cerebral cortex* (Vols. 1–8). Cambridge, MA: Harvard University Press.

Conn, J., & Kanner, L. (1940). Spontaneous erections in childhood. *Journal of Pediatrics, 16,* 237–240.

Connell, J. P. (1990). Context, self, and action: A motivational analysis of self-system processes across the life span. In D. Cicchetti & M. Beeghly (Eds.), *The self in transition: Infancy to childhood.* Chicago: University of Chicago Press.

Connell, J. P., & Wellborn, J. G. (1991). Competence, autonomy, and relatedness: A motivational analysis of self-system processes. In M. R. Gunnar & L. A. Sroufe (Eds.), *Self processes and development: The Minnesota Symposia on Child Psychology* (Vol. 23). Hillsdale, NJ: Erlbaum.

Connolly, J., & Goldberg, A. (1999). Romantic relationships in adolescence: The role of friends and peers in their emergence and development. In W. Furman, B. B. Brown, & C. Feiring (Eds.), *The development of romantic relationships in adolescence* (pp. 266–290). Cambridge, England: Cambridge University Press.

Conroy, M., Hess, R. D., Azuma, H., & Kashiwagi, K. (1980). Maternal strategies for regulating children's behavior: Japanese and American families. *Journal of Cross-Cultural Psychology, 11,* 153–172.

Consortium for Longitudinal Studies. (1983). *As the twig is bent: Lasting effects of preschool programs.* Hillsdale, NJ: Erlbaum.

Constantina, N. (1998). Adolescents' perceived attachment to parents and its relationship to depression. *Dissertation Abstracts International: Section B. The Sciences and Engineering, 58*(12–B), June, 6870.

Conte, R. (1991). Attention disorders. In B. Y. L. Wong (Ed.), *Learning about learning disabilities.* San Diego, CA: Academic Press.

Cook, B., & Semmel, M. (1999). Peer acceptance of included students with disabilities as a function of severity of disability and classroom composition. *Journal of Special Education, 33*(10), 50–62.

Cook, V., & Newson, M. (1996). *Chomsky's universal grammar: An introduction* (2nd ed.). Oxford, England: Blackwell.

Cook-Sather, A. (2002). Authorizing students' perspectives: Toward trust, dialogue, and change in education. *Educational Researcher, 31*(4), 3–14.

Cooper, C. R., Denner, J., & Lopez, E. M. (1999, Fall). Cultural brokers: Helping Latino children on pathways toward success. *The Future of Children: When School Is Out, 9,* 51–57.

Cooper, H. (1989). Synthesis of research on homework. *Educational Leadership, 47*(3), 85–91.

Cooper, H., Charlton, K., Valentine, J. C., & Muhlenbruck, L. (2000). Making the most of summer school: A meta-analytic and narrative review. *Monographs of the Society for Research in Child Development, 65*(1, Serial No. 260).

Cooper, H., & Dorr, N. (1995). Race comparisons on need for achievement: A meta-analytic alternative to Graham's narrative review. *Review of Educational Research, 65,* 483–508.

Cooper, H., & Valentine, J. C. (2001). Using research to answer practical questions about homework. *Educational Psychologist, 36,* 143–153.

Cooper, H., Valentine, J. C., Nye, B., & Lindsay, J. J. (1999). Relationships between five after-school activities and academic achievement. *Journal of Educational Psychology, 91,* 369–378.

Cooper, M. L., & Orcutt, H. K. (1997). Drinking and sexual experience on first dates among adolescents. *Journal of Abnormal Psychology, 106,* 191–202.

Cooper, R. P., & Aslin, R. N. (1990). Preference for infant-directed speech in the first month after birth. *Child Development, 61,* 1584–1595.

Coopersmith, S. (1967). *The antecedents of self-esteem.* San Francisco: Freeman.

Copeland, R. W. (1979). *How children learn mathematics: Teaching implications of Piaget's research* (3rd ed.). New York: Macmillan.

Cornell, D. G., Pelton, G. M., Bassin, L. E., Landrum, M., Ramsay, S. G., Cooley, M. R., Lynch, K. A., & Hamrick, E. (1990). Self-concept and peer status among gifted program youth. *Journal of Educational Psychology, 82,* 456–463.

Corsaro, W. A. (1985). *Friendship and peer culture in the early years.* Norwood, NJ: Ablex.

Cosden, M., Morrison, G., Albanese, A. L., & Macias, S. (2001). When homework is not home work: After-school programs for homework assistance. *Educational Psychologist, 36,* 211–221.

Cosmides, L., & Tooby, J. (1989). Evolutionary psychology and the generation of culture: II. Case study: A computational theory of social exchange. *Ethology and Sociobiology, 10,* 51–97.

Cossu, G. (1999). The acquisition of Italian orthography. In M. Harris & G. Hatano (Eds.), *Learning to read and write: A cross-linguistic perspective.* Cambridge, England: Cambridge University Press.

Costanzo, P. R., & Fraenkel, P. (1987). Social influence, socialization, and the development of social cognition: The heart of the matter. In N. Eisenberg (Ed.), *Contemporary topics in developmental psychology* (pp. 190–215). New York: Wiley.

Costin, S. E., & Jones, D. C. (1992). Friendship as a facilitator of emotional responsiveness and prosocial interventions among young children. *Developmental Psychology, 28,* 941–947.

Cota-Robles, S., & Neiss, M. (1999, April). *The role of puberty in non-violent delinquency among Anglo-American, Hispanic, and African American boys.* Paper presented at the Biennial Meeting of the Society for Research in Child Development, Albuquerque, NM.

Cottrol, R. J. (1990). America the multicultural. *American Educator, 14*(4), 18–21.

Council for Exceptional Children. (1995). *Toward a common agenda: Linking gifted education and school reform.* Reston, VA: Author.

Courage, M. L., & Adams, R. J. (1990). Visual acuity assessment from birth to three years using the acuity card procedures: Cross-sectional and longitudinal samples. *Optometry and Vision Science, 67,* 713–718.

Covill, A. E. (1997, March). *Students' revision practices and attitudes in response to surface-related feedback as compared to content-related feedback on their writing.* Paper presented at the annual meeting of the American Educational Research Association, Chicago.

Covington, M. V. (1987). Achievement motivation, self-attributions, and the exceptional learner. In J. D. Day & J. G. Borkowski (Eds.), *Intelligence and exceptionality.* Norwood, NJ: Ablex.

Covington, M. V. (1992). *Making the grade: A self-worth perspective on motivation and school reform.* Cambridge, England: Cambridge University Press.

Cowan, W. M. (1979). The development of the brain. *Scientific American, 241,* 106–117.

Cox, C. B. (2000). *Empowering grandparents raising grandchildren.* New York: Springer.

Craft, D. H. (1995). Visual impairments and hearing losses. In J. P. Winnick (Ed.), *Adapted physical education and sport* (2nd ed., pp. 143–166). Champaign, IL: Human Kinetics.

Craft, M. (1984). Education for diversity. In M. Craft (Ed.), *Educational and cultural pluralism.* London: Falmer Press.

Crago, M. B., Allen, S. E. M., & Hough-Eyamie, W. P. (1997). Exploring innateness through cultural and linguistic variation. In M. Gopnik (Ed.), *The inheritance and innateness of grammars.* New York: Oxford University Press.

Crago, M. B., Annahatak, B., & Ningiuruvik, L. (1993). Changing patterns of language socialization in Inuit homes. *Anthropology and Education Quarterly, 24,* 205–223.

Crane, J. (1991). The epidemic theory of ghettos and neighborhood effects on dropping out and teenage childbearing. *American Journal of Sociology, 64,* 32–41.

Crawley, A. M., Anderson, D. R., Wilder, A., Williams, M., & Santomero, A. (1999). Effects of repeated exposures to a single episode of the television program *Blue's Clues* on the viewing behaviors and comprehension of preschool children. *Journal of Educational Psychology 91,* 630–637.

Creasey, G. L., Jarvis, P. A., & Berk, L. E. (1998). Play and social competence. In O. N. Saracho & B. Spodek (Eds.), *Multiple perspectives on play in early childhood education.* Albany: State University of New York Press.

Crick, N. R., Casas, J. F., & Nelson, D. A. (2002). Toward a more comprehensive understanding of peer maltreatment: Studies of relational victimization. *Current Directions in Psychological Science, 11*(3), 98–101.

Crick, N. R., & Dodge, K. A. (1994). A review and reformulation of social information-processing mechanisms in children's social adjustment. *Psychological Bulletin, 115,* 74–101.

Crick, N. R., & Dodge, K. A. (1996). Social information-processing mechanisms in reactive and proactive aggression. *Child Development, 67,* 993–1002.

Crick, N. R., & Grotpeter, J. K. (1995). Relational aggression, gender, and social-psychological adjustment. *Child Development, 66,* 710–722.

Crockett, L., Losoff, M., & Peterson, A. C. (1984). Perceptions of the peer group and friendship in early adolescence. *Journal of Early Adolescence, 4,* 155–181.

Cromer, R. F. (1993). Language growth with experience without feedback. In P. Bloom (Ed.), *Language acquisition: Core readings.* Cambridge, MA: MIT Press.

Crouter, A. (1994). Processes linking families and work: Implications for behavior and development in both settings. In R. D. Parke & S. G. Killam (Eds.), *Exploring family relationships with other social contexts.* Hillsdale, NJ: Erlbaum.

Crouter, A. C., & Bumpus, M. F. (2001). Linking parents' work stress to children's and adolescents' psychological adjustment. *Current Directions in Psychological Science, 10*(5), 156–159.

Crowne, D. P., & Marlowe, D. (1964). *The approval motive: Studies in evaluative dependence.* New York: Wiley.

Csikszentmihalyi, M. (1995). Education for the twenty-first century. *Daedalus, 124*(4), 107–114.

Csikszentmihalyi, M., & Larson, R. (1984). *Being adolescent: Conflict and growth in the teenage years.* New York: Basic Books.

Cunningham, A. E., & Stanovich, K. E. (1997). Early reading acquisition and its relation to reading experience and ability. *Developmental Psychology, 33,* 934–945.

Cunningham, C. E., & Cunningham, L. J. (1998). Student-mediated conflict resolution programs. In R. A. Barkley (Ed.), *Attention-deficit hyperactivity disorder: A handbook for diagnosis and treatment* (2nd ed.; pp. 491–509). New York: Guilford Press.

Cunningham, T. H., & Graham, C. R. (2000). Increasing native English vocabulary recognition through Spanish immersion: Cognate transfer from foreign to first language. *Journal of Educational Psychology, 92,* 37–49.

Curtiss, S. (1977). *Genie: A psycholinguistic study of a modern-day "wild child."* New York: Academic Press.

Dacey, J., & Kenny, M. (1994). *Adolescent development.* Madison, WI: William C. Brown.

Dahlberg, G., Moss, P., & Pence, A. (1999). *Beyond quality in early childhood education and care: Postmodern perspectives.* London: Falmer Press.

Dale, P. S. (1976). *Language development: Structure and function* (2nd ed.). New York: Holt, Rinehart & Winston.

Dalrymple, N. J. (1995). Environmental supports to develop flexibility and independence. In K. A. Quill (Ed.), *Teaching children with autism: Strategies to enhance communication and socialization.* New York: Delmar.

Damon, W. (1977). *The social world of the child.* San Francisco: Jossey-Bass.

Damon, W. (1980). Patterns of change in children's social reasoning: A two-year longitudinal study. *Child Development, 51,* 1010–1017.

Damon, W. (1981). Exploring children's social cognitions on two fronts. In J. M. Flavell & L. Ross (Eds.), *Social cognitive development: Frontiers and possible futures* (pp. 154–175). Cambridge, England: Cambridge University Press.

Damon, W. (1984). Peer education: The untapped potential. *Journal of Applied Developmental Psychology, 5,* 331–343.

Damon, W. (1988). *The moral child: Nurturing children's natural moral growth.* New York: Free Press.

Damon, W. (1995). *Greater expectations: Overcoming the culture of indulgence in America's homes and schools.* New York: Free Press.

Damon, W., & Hart, D. (1988). *Self-understanding in childhood and adolescence.* New York: Cambridge University Press.

DanceSafe (2000a). *What is LSD?* Oakland, CA: Author. Retrieved from http://www.dancesafe.org/lsd.html

DanceSafe (2000b). *What is speed?* Oakland, CA: Author. Retrieved from http://www.dancesafe.org/speed.html

Danish, S. J., Nellen, V. C., & Owens, S. S. (1996). Teaching life skills through sport: Community based programs for adolescents. In J. V. Raalte & B. W. Brewer (Eds.), *Exploring sport and exercise psychology* (pp. 205–225). Washington, DC: American Psychological Association.

Dannemiller, J. L., & Stephens, B. R. (1988). A critical test of infant pattern preference models. *Child Development, 59,* 210–216.

Danner, F. W., & Day, M. C. (1977). Eliciting formal operations. *Child Development, 48,* 1600–1606.

Darling-Hammond, L. (1995). Inequality and access to knowledge. In J. A. Banks & C. A. M. Banks (Eds.), *Handbook of research on multicultural education.* New York: Macmillan.

Darwin, C. (1859). *On the origin of species by means of natural selection, or, the preservation of favored races in the struggle for life.* London: John Murray.

Dauber, S. L., & Epstein, J. L. (1993). Parents' attitudes and practices of involvement in inner-city elementary and middle schools. In N. F. Chavkin (Ed.), *Families and schools in a pluralistic society* (pp. 53–71). Albany: State University of New York Press.

Davenport, E. C., Jr., Davison, M. L., Kuang, H., Ding, S., Kim, S., & Kwak, N. (1998). High school mathematics course-taking by gender and ethnicity. *American Educational Research Journal, 35,* 497–514.

Davidson, F. H. (1976). Ability to respect persons compared to ethnic prejudice in childhood. *Journal of Personality and Social Psychology, 34,* 1256–1267.

Davidson, F. H., & Davidson, M. M. (1994). *Changing childhood prejudice: The caring work of the schools.* Westport, CT: Bergin & Garvey.

Davidson, P., Turiel, E., & Black, A. (1983). The effect of stimulus familiarity on the use of criteria and justification in children's social reasoning. *British Journal of Developmental Psychology, 1,* 49–65.

Davidson, P., & Youniss, J. (1995). Moral development and social construction. In W. M. Kurtines & J. L. Gewirtz (Eds.), *Moral development: An introduction.* Boston: Allyn & Bacon.

Davis, B. (2001). The restorative power of emotions in Child Protective Services. *Child and Adolescent Social Work Journal, 18*(6), 437–454.

Davis, G. A., & Rimm, S. B. (1998). *Education of the gifted and talented* (4th ed.). Boston: Allyn & Bacon.

Davis, G. A., & Thomas, M. A. (1989). *Effective schools and effective teachers.* Needham Heights, MA: Allyn & Bacon.

Dawson, D. A. (1991). Family structure and children's health and well-being: Data from the 1988 National Health Interview Survey on Child Health. *Journal of Marriage and the Family, 53,* 573–584.

Dawson, G., Carver, L., Meltzoff, A. N., Panagiotides, H., McPartland, J., & Webb, S. J. (2002). Neural correlates of face and object recognition in young children with autism spectrum disorder, developmental delay, and typical development. *Child Development, 73,* 700–717.

Dawson, G., Munson, J., Estes, A., Osterling, J., McPartland, J., Toth, K., Carver, L., & Abbott, R. (2002). Neurocognitive function and joint attention ability in young children with autism spectrum disorder versus developmental delay. *Child Development, 73,* 345–358.

Deal, L. W., Gomby, D. S., Zippiroli, L., & Behrman, R. E. (2000). Unintentional injuries in childhood: Analysis and recommendations. *Future of Children, 10*(1), 4–22.

Deater-Deakard, K., Dodge, K., Bates, J., & Pettit, G. (1996). Physical discipline among African American and European American mothers: Links to children's externalizing behaviors. *Developmental Psychology, 32*(6), 1065–1072.

Deaux, K. (1984). From individual differences to social categories: Analysis of a decade's research on gender. *American Psychologist, 39,* 105–116.

De Carvalho, M. E. P. (2001). *Rethinking family-school relations: A critique of family involvement in schooling.* Mahwah, NJ: Erlbaum.

DeCasper, A. J., & Fifer, W. P. (1980). Of human bonding: Newborns prefer their mothers' voices. *Science, 208,* 1174–1176.

DeCasper, A. J., & Spence, M. J. (1986). Prenatal maternal speech influences newborns' perception of speech sounds. *Infant Behavior and Development, 9,* 133–150.

De Cecco, J. P., & Parker, D. A. (1995). The biology of homosexuality: Sexual orientation or sexual preference? *Journal of Homosexuality, 28,* 1–27.

deCharms, R. (1984). Motivation enhancement in educational settings. In R. Ames & C. Ames (Eds.), *Research on motivation in education: Vol. 1. Student motivation.* Orlando, FL: Academic Press.

Deci, E. L. (1992). The relation of interest to the motivation of behavior: A self-determination theory perspective. In K. A. Renninger, S. Hidi, & A. Krapp (Eds.), *The role of interest in learning and development.* Hillsdale, NJ: Erlbaum.

Deci, E. L., & Ryan, R. M. (1985). *Intrinsic motivation and self-determination in human behavior.* New York: Plenum Press.

Deci, E. L., & Ryan, R. M. (1987). The support of autonomy and the control of behavior. *Journal of Personality and Social Psychology, 53,* 1024–1037.

Deci, E. L., & Ryan, R. M. (1992). The initiation and regulation of intrinsically motivated learning and achievement. In A. K. Boggiano & T. S. Pittman (Eds.), *Achievement and motivation: A social-developmental perspective.* Cambridge, England: Cambridge University Press.

Deci, E. L., & Ryan, R. M. (1995). Human autonomy: The basis for true self-esteem. In M. H. Kernis (Ed.), *Efficacy, agency, and self-esteem.* New York: Plenum Press.

DeKlynen, M., Speltz, M. L., & Greenberg, M. T. (1998). Fathering and early onset of conduct problems: Positive and negative parenting, father-son attachment, and the marital context. *Clinical Child & Family Psychology Review, 1*(1), 3–28.

Dekovic, M., & Janssens, J. M. (1992). Parents' child-rearing style and child's sociometric status. *Developmental Psychology, 28,* 925–932.

DeLain, M. T., Pearson, P. D., & Anderson, R. C. (1985). Reading comprehension and creativity in black language use: You stand to gain by playing the sounding game! *American Educational Research Journal, 22,* 155–173.

DeLamater, J., & MacCorquodale, P. (1979). *Premarital sexuality: Attitudes, relationships, behavior.* Madison: The University of Wisconsin Press.

De La Paz, S., Swanson, P. N., & Graham, S. (1998). The contribution of executive control to the revising by students with writing and learning difficulties. *Journal of Educational Psychology, 90,* 448–460.

DelCarmen-Wiggins, R., Huffman, L. C., Pedersen, F. A., & Bryan, Y. E. (2000). Mothers' and fathers' perceptions of three year olds' attachment behavior. *Journal of Developmental and Behavioral Pediatrics, 21*(2), 97–106.

Delgado-Gaitan, C. (1992). School matters in the Mexican-American home: Socializing children to education. *American Educational Research Journal, 29,* 495–513.

Delgado-Gaitan, C. (1994). Socializing young children in Mexican-American families: An intergenerational perspective. In P. M. Greenfield & R. R. Cocking (Eds.), *Cross-cultural roots of minority child development* (pp. 55–86). Hillsdale, NJ: Erlbaum.

DeLisi, R., & Gallagher, A. M. (1991). Understanding of gender stability and constancy in Argentinian children. *Merrill-Palmer Quarterly, 37,* 483–502.

DeLisi, R., & Golbeck, S. L. (1999). Implications of Piagetian theory for peer learning. In A. M. O'Donnell & A. King (Eds.), *Cognitive perspectives on peer learning* (pp. 3–37). Mahwah, NJ: Erlbaum.

DeLisle, J. R. (1984). *Gifted children speak out.* New York: Walker.

DeLoache, J. S., Cassidy, D. J., & Brown, A. L. (1985). Precursors of mnemonic strategies in very young children's memory. *Child Development, 56,* 125–137.

DeLoache, J. S., Miller, K. F., & Rosengren, K. S. (1997). The credible shrinking room: Very young children's performance with symbolic and nonsymbolic relations. *Psychological Science, 8,* 308–313.

DeLoache, J. S., & Todd, C. M. (1988). Young children's use of spatial categorization as a mnemonic strategy. *Journal of Experimental Child Psychology, 46,* 1–20.

DeMarie-Dreblow, D., & Miller, P. H. (1988). The development of children's strategies for selective attention: Evidence for a transitional period. *Child Development, 59,* 1504–1513.

deMarrais, K. B., Nelson, P. A., & Baker, J. H. (1994). Meaning in mud: Yup'ik Eskimo girls at play. In J. L. Roopnarine, J. E. Johnson, & F. H. Hooper (Eds.), *Children's play in diverse cultures.* Albany, NY: SUNY Press.

Dempster, F. N., & Corkill, A. J. (1999). Interference and inhibition in cognition and behavior: Unifying themes for educational psychology. *Educational Psychology Review, 11,* 1–88.

Denkla, M. B. (1986). New diagnostic criteria for autism and related behavioral disorders: Guidelines for research protocols. *Journal of the American Academy of Child Psychiatry, 25,* 221–224.

Dennis, W. (1960). Causes of retardation among institutionalized children: Iran. *Journal of Genetic Psychology, 96,* 47–59.

DeRidder, L. M. (1993). Teenage pregnancy: Etiology and educational interventions. *Educational Psychology Review, 5,* 87–107.

Derry, S. J. (1996). Cognitive schema theory in the constructivist debate. *Educational Psychologist, 31,* 163–174.

Deschenes, S., Tyack, D., & Cuban, L. (2001). Mismatch: Historical perspectives on schools and students who don't fit them. *Teachers College Record, 103,* 525–547.

Deshler, D. D., & Schumaker, J. B. (1988). An instructional model for teaching students how to learn. In J. L. Graden, J. E. Zins, & M. J. Curtis (Eds.), *Alternative educational delivery systems: Enhancing instructional options for all students.* Washington, DC: National Association of School Psychologists.

Deutsch, F. M., Ruble, N., Fleming, A., & Brooks-Gunn, J. (1988). Information-seeking and maternal self-definition during the transition to motherhood. *Journal of Personality and Social Psychology, 55*(3), 420–431.

Deutsch, M. (1993). Educating for a peaceful world. *American Psychologist, 48,* 510–517.

Deutsch, M. P. (1963). The disadvantaged child and the learning process. In A. H. Passow (Ed.), *Education in depressed areas.* New York: Teachers College Press.

Deutsch, N. L., & Hirsch, B. J. (2001, April). *A place to call home: Youth organizations in the lives of inner city adolescents.* Paper presented at the biennial meeting of the Society for Research in Child Development, Minneapolis.

DeVault, G., Krug, C., & Fake, S. (1996, September). Why does Samantha act that way: Positive behavioral support leads to successful inclusion. *Exceptional Parent,* 43–47.

de Villiers, J. (1995). Empty categories and complex sentences: The case of wh- questions. In P. Fletcher & B. MacWhinney (Eds.), *The handbook of child language* (pp. 508–540). Oxford, England: Blackwell.

Devine, P. G. (1995). Prejudice and out-group perception. In A. Tesser (Ed.), *Advanced social psychology.* New York: McGraw-Hill.

Devlin, B., Fienberg, S. E., Resnick, D. P., & Roeder, K. (1995). Galton redux: Intelligence, race, and society: A review of "The Bell Curve: Intelligence and Class Structure in American Life." *American Statistician, 90,* 1483–1488.

DeVoe, J. F., Peter, K., Kaufman, P., Ruddy, S. A., Miller, A. K., Planty, M., Snyder, T. D., Duhart, D. T., & Rand, M. R. (2002). *Indicators of school crime and safety: 2002.* NCES 2003-009/NCJ 196753. Washington, DC: U.S. Departments of Education and Justice.

DeVries, M. W., & Sameroff, A. J. (1984). Culture and temperament: Influences on infant temperament in three East-African societies. *American Journal of Orthopsychiatry, 54,* 83–96.

DeVries, R. (1997). Piaget's social theory. *Educational Researcher, 26*(2), 4–17.

DeVries, R., & Zan, B. (1996). A constructivist perspective on the role of the sociomoral atmosphere in promoting children's development. In C. T. Fosnot (Ed.), *Constructivism: Theory, perspectives, and practice.* New York: Teachers College Press.

Dewey, K. G., Heinig, M. J., & Nommsen-Rivers, L. A. (1995). Differences in morbidity between breast-fed and formula-fed infants. *Journal of Pediatrics, 126,* 696–702.

Diagram Group, The. (1983). *The human body on file.* New York: Facts on File.

Diamond, L. M., Savin-Williams, R. C., & Dubé, E. M. (1999). Sex, dating, passionate friendships, and romance: Intimate peer relations among lesbian, gay, and bisexual adolescents. In W. Furman, B. B. Brown, & C. Feiring (Eds.), *The development of romantic relationships in adolescence* (pp. 175–210). Cambridge, England: Cambridge University Press.

Diamond, M., & Hopson, J. (1998). *Magic trees of the mind.* New York: Dutton.

Diamond, S. C. (1991). What to do when you can't do anything: Working with disturbed adolescents. *Clearing House, 64,* 232–234.

Diaz, R. M. (1983). Thought and two languages: The impact of bilingualism on cognitive development. In E. W. Gordon (Ed.), *Review of research in education* (Vol. 10). Washington, DC: American Educational Research Association.

Diaz, R. M., & Berndt, T. J. (1982). Children's knowledge of best friend: Fact or fancy? *Developmental Psychology, 18,* 787–794.

Diaz, R. M., & Klingler, C. (1991). Toward an explanatory model of the interaction between bilingualism and cognitive development. In E. Bialystok (Ed.), *Language processing in bilingual children.* Cambridge, England: Cambridge University Press.

Dickemann, M. (1995). Wilson's panchreston: The inclusive fitness hypothesis of sociobiology re-examined. *Journal of Homosexuality, 28,* 147–183.

Dickinson, D., Wolf, M., & Stotsky, S. (1993). Words move: The interwoven development of oral and written language. In J. B. Gleason (Ed.), *The development of language.* Boston: Allyn & Bacon.

Dien, T. (1998). Language and literacy in Vietnamese American communities. In B. Pérez (Ed.), *Sociocultural contexts of language and literacy.* Mahwah, NJ: Erlbaum.

Digman, J. M. (1989). Five robust trait dimensions: Development, stability, and utility. *Journal of Personality, 57,* 195–214.

Diller, D. (1999). Opening the dialogue: Using culture as a tool in teaching young African American children. *The Reading Teacher, 52,* 820–828.

diSessa, A. A. (1996). What do "just plain folk" know about physics? In D. R. Olson & N. Torrance (Eds.), *The handbook of education and human development: New models of learning, teaching, and schooling.* Cambridge, MA: Blackwell.

Dishion, T. J., Andrews, D. W., & Crosby, L. (1995). Antisocial boys and their friends in early adolescence: Relationship characteristics, quality, and interactional process. *Child Development, 66,* 139–151.

Dishion, T. J., Spracklen, K. M., Andrews, D. W., & Patterson, G. R. (1996). Deviancy training in male adolescents' friendships. *Behavior Therapy, 27,* 373–390.

Dixon, R. A., & Lerner, R. M. (1992). A history of systems in developmental psychology. In M. H. Bornstein & M. E. Lamb (Eds.), *Developmental psychology: An advanced textbook* (3rd ed., pp. 3–58). Hillsdale, NJ: Erlbaum.

Dodge, K. A. (1980). Social cognition and children's aggressive behavior. *Child Development, 51,* 162–170.

Dodge, K. A. (1983). Behavioral antecedents of peer social status. *Child Development, 54,* 1386–1399.

Dodge, K. A. (1986). A social information processing model of social competence in children. In M. Perlmutter (Ed.), *Minnesota symposia on child psychology: Vol. 18. Cognitive perspectives in children's social and behavioral development.* Hillsdale, NJ: Erlbaum.

Dodge, K. A. (1991). Emotion and social information processing. In J. Garber & K. A. Dodge (Eds.), *The development of emotion regulation and dysregulation.* Cambridge, England: Cambridge University Press.

Dodge, K. A., Bates, J. E., & Pettit, G. S. (1990). Mechanisms in the cycle of violence. *Science, 250,* 1678–1683.

Dodge, K. A., Coie, J. D., & Brakke, N. P. (1982). Behavior patterns of socially rejected and neglected preadolescents: The role of social approach and aggression. *Journal of Abnormal Child Psychology, 10,* 389–410.

Dodge, K. A., Lochman, J. E., Harnish, J. D., Bates, J. E., & Pettit, G. S. (1997). Reactive and proactive aggression in school children and psychiatrically impaired chronically assaultive youth. *Journal of Abnormal Psychology, 106,* 37–51.

Dodge, K. A., Pettit, G. S., Bates, J. E., & Valente, E. (1995). Social information processing patterns partially mediate the effect of early physical abuse on later conduct problems. *Journal of Abnormal Psychology, 104,* 632–643.

Dodge, K. A., Schlundt, D. G., Schocken, I., & Delugach, J. D. (1983). Social competence and children's social status: The role of peer group entry strategies. *Merrill-Palmer Quarterly, 29,* 309–336.

Doescher, S. M., & Sugawara, A. I. (1989). Encouraging prosocial behavior in young children. *Childhood Education, 65,* 213–216.

Dole, J. A., Duffy, G. G., Roehler, L. R., & Pearson, P. D. (1991). Moving from the old to the new: Research on reading comprehension instruction. *Review of Educational Research, 61,* 239–264.

Donaldson, M. (1978). *Children's minds.* New York: Norton.

Donaldson, S. K., & Westerman, M. A. (1986). Development of children's understanding of ambivalence and causal theories of emotion. *Developmental Psychology, 22,* 655–662.

Donato, F., Assanelli, D., Chiesa, R., Poeta, M. L., Tomansoni, V., & Turla, C. (1997). Cigarette smoking and sports participation in adolescents: A cross-sectional survey among high school students in Italy. *Substance Use and Misuse, 32,* 1555–1572.

Donovan, C. A. (1999, April). *"Stories have a beginning, a middle, and an end. Information only has a beginning": Elementary school children's genre and writing development.* Paper presented at the annual meeting of the American Educational Research Association, San Diego, CA.

Donziger, S. R. (Ed.). (1996). *The real war on crime: The report of the National Criminal Justice Commission.* New York: HarperPerennial.

Dornbusch, S. M., Carlsmith, J. M., Gross, R. T., Martin, J. A., Jennings, D., Rosenberg, A., & Duke, P. (1981). Sexual development, age, and dating: A comparison of biological and social influences upon one set of behaviors. *Child Development, 52,* 179–185.

Dornbusch, S. M., Ritter, P. L., Leiderman, P. H., Roberts, D. F., & Fraleigh, M. J. (1987). The relation of parenting style to adolescent school performance. *Child Development, 58,* 1244–1257.

Dorris, M. (1989). *The broken cord.* New York: Harper & Row.

Dougherty, T. M., & Haith, M. M. (1997). Infant expectations and reaction time as predictors of childhood speed of processing and IQ. *Developmental Psychology, 33,* 146–155.

Dovidio, J. F., & Gaertner, S. L. (1999). Reducing prejudice: Combating intergroup biases. *Current Directions in Psychological Science, 8,* 101–105.

Downey, G., Bonica, C., & Rincón, C. (1999). Rejection sensitivity and adolescent romantic relationships. In W. Furman, B. B. Brown, & C. Feiring (Eds.), *The development of romantic relationships in adolescence* (pp. 148–174). Cambridge, England: Cambridge University Press.

Downey, G., Lebolt, A., Rincón, C., & Freitas, A. L. (1998). Rejection sensitivity and children's interpersonal difficulties. *Child Development, 69,* 1074–1091.

Downey, J. (2000, March). *The role of schools in adolescent resilience: Recommendations from the literature.* Paper presented at the International Association of Adolescent Health, Washington, DC.

Downing, J. (1986). Cognitive clarity: A unifying and cross-cultural theory for language awareness phenomena in reading. In D. B. Yaden, Jr., & S. Templeton (Eds.), *Metalinguistic awareness and beginning literacy: Conceptualizing what it means to read and write.* Portsmouth, NH: Heinemann.

Dowson, M., & McInerney, D. M. (2001). Psychological parameters of students' social and work avoidance goals: A qualitative investigation. *Journal of Educational Psychology, 93,* 35–42.

Doyle, A. (1982). Friends, acquaintances, and strangers: The influence of familiarity and ethnolinguistic background on social interaction. In K. H. Rubin & H. S. Ross (Eds.), *Peer relationships and social skills in childhood* (pp. 229–252). New York: Springer-Verlag.

Doyle, W. (1983). Academic work. *Review of Educational Research, 53,* 159–199.

Doyle, W. (1986). Classroom organization and management. In M. C. Wittrock (Ed.), *Handbook of research on teaching* (3rd ed.). New York: Macmillan.

Dozier, M., Stovall, K. C., Albus, K. E., & Bates, B. (2001). Attachment for infants in foster care: The role of caregiver state of mind. *Child Development, 72,* 1467–1477.

Dreman, S. B. (1976). Sharing behavior in Israeli school children: Cognitive and social learning factors. *Child Development, 47,* 186–194.

Dryden, M. A., & Jefferson, P. (1994, April). *Use of background knowledge and reading achievement among elementary school students.* Paper presented at the annual meeting of the American Educational Research Association, New Orleans, LA.

Dryfoos, J. G. (1999, Fall). The role of the school in children's out-of-school time. *The Future of Children: When School Is Out, 9,* 117–134.

Dube, E. F. (1982). Literacy, cultural familiarity, and "intelligence" as determinants of story recall. In U. Neisser (Ed.), *Memory observed: Remembering in natural contexts.* San Francisco: Freeman.

Dube, M., Julien, D., Lebeau, E., & Gagnon, I. (2000). Marital satisfaction of mothers and the quality of daily interaction with their adolescents. *Canadian Journal of Behavioural Science, 32*(1), 18–28.

Dufresne, A., & Kobasigawa, A. (1989). Children's spontaneous allocation of study time: Differential and sufficient aspects. *Journal of Experimental Child Psychology, 47,* 274–296.

Duit, R. (1991). Students' conceptual frameworks: Consequences for learning science. In S. M. Glynn, R. H. Yeany, & B. K. Britton (Eds.), *The psychology of learning science.* Hillsdale, NJ: Erlbaum.

Dunbar, N. D., Azmitia, M., & Brown, J. R. (1999, April). *Mexican-descent parents' beliefs and guidance strategies for their adolescent children's paths in life.* Paper presented at the biennial meeting of the Society for Research in Child Development, Albuquerque, NM.

Duncan, G. J., Yeung, W. J., Brooks-Gunn, J., & Smith, J. R. (1998). How much does childhood poverty affect the life chances of children? *American Sociological Review, 63*(3), 406–423.

Duncan, P. D., Ritter, P. L., Dornbusch, S. M., Gross, R. T., & Carlsmith, J. M. (1985). The effects of pubertal timing on body image, school behavior, and deviance. *Journal of Youth and Adolescence, 14,* 227–235.

Dunham, P. J., Dunham, F., & Curwin, A. (1993). Joint-attentional states and lexical acquisition at 18 months. *Developmental Psychology, 29,* 827–831.

Dunn, J. (1984). *Sisters and brothers.* Cambridge, MA: Harvard University Press.

Dunn, J. (1988). *The beginnings of social understanding.* Cambridge, MA: Harvard University Press.

Dunn, J. (1993). Social interaction, relationships, and the development of causal discourse and conflict management. *European Journal of Psychology of Education, 8,* 391–401.

Dunn, J. (1996). Sibling relationships and perceived self-competence: Patterns of stability between childhood and early adolescence. In A. J. Sameroff & M. M. Haith (Eds.), *The five to seven year shift* (pp. 253–270). Chicago: University of Chicago Press.

Dunn, J., Bretherton, I., & Munn, P. (1987). Conversations about feeling states between mothers and their young children. *Developmental Psychology, 23,* 132–139.

Dunn, J., Brown, J., & Beardsall, L. (1991). Family talk about feeling states and children's later understanding of others' emotions. *Developmental Psychology, 27,* 448–455.

Dunn, J., & Munn, P. (1987). Development of justification in disputes with mother and sibling. *Developmental Psychology, 23,* 791–798.

Dunton, K. J., McDevitt, T. M., & Hess, R. D. (1988). Origins of mothers' attributions about their daughters' and sons' performance in mathematics in sixth grade. *Merrill-Palmer Quarterly, 34,* 47–70.

DuPaul, G. J., & Eckert, T. L. (1994). The effects of social skills curricula: Now you see them, now you don't. *School Psychology Quarterly, 9,* 113–132.

DuPaul, G. J., Ervin, R. A., Hook, C. L., & McGoey, K. E. (1998). Peer tutoring for children with attention deficit hyperactivity disorder: Effects on classroom behavior and academic performance. *Journal of Applied Behavior Analysis, 31,* 579–592.

Duran, B. J., & Weffer, R. E. (1992). Immigrants' aspirations, high school process, and academic outcomes. *American Educational Research Journal, 29,* 163–181.

Durand, V. M. (1998). *Sleep better: A guide to improving sleep for children with special needs.* Baltimore: Brookes.

Durby, D. D. (1994). Gay, lesbian, and bisexual youth. In T. DeCrescenzo (Ed.), *Helping gay and lesbian youth: New policies, new programs, new practice* (pp. 1–37). New York: The Haworth Press.

Durkin, K. (1987). Social cognition and social context in the construction of sex differences. In M. A. Baker (Ed.), *Sex differences in human performance.* Chichester, England: Wiley.

Durkin, K. (1995). *Developmental social psychology: From infancy to old age.* Cambridge, MA: Blackwell.

Dweck, C. S. (1975). The role of expectations and attributions in the alleviation of learned helplessness. *Journal of Personality and Social Psychology, 31,* 674–685.

Dweck, C. S. (1978). Achievement. In M. E. Lamb (Ed.), *Social and personality development.* New York: Holt, Rinehart & Winston.

Dweck, C. S. (1986). Motivational processes affecting learning. *American Psychologist, 41,* 1040–1048.

Dweck, C. S. (1999). *Self-theories: Their role in motivation, personality, and development.* Philadelphia: Taylor & Francis.

Dweck, C. S., & Elliott, E. S. (1983). Achievement motivation. In E. M. Hetherington (Ed.), *Handbook of child psychology: Vol. 4. Socialization, personality, and social development* (4th ed.). New York: Wiley.

Dweck, C. S., & Leggett, E. L. (1988). A social-cognitive approach to motivation and personality. *Psychological Review, 95,* 256–273.

Dykens, E. M., & Cassidy, S. B. (1999). Prader-Willi syndrome. In S. Goldstein & C. R. Reynolds (Eds.), *Handbook of neurodevelopmental and genetic disorders* (pp. 525–554). New York: Guilford Press.

Dyson, A. H. (1986). Children's early interpretations of writing: Expanding research perspectives. In D. B. Yaden, Jr., & S. Templeton (Eds.), *Metalinguistic awareness and beginning literacy: Conceptualizing what it means to read and write.* Portsmouth, NH: Heinemann.

D'Amato, R. C., Chitooran, M. M., & Whitten, J. D. (1992). Neuropsychological consequences of malnutrition. In D. I. Templer, L. C. Hartlage, & W. G. Cannon (Eds.), *Preventable brain damage: Brain vulnerability and brain health.* New York: Springer.

Eacott, M. J. (1999). Memory for the events of early childhood. *Current Directions in Psychological Science, 8,* 46–49.

Eagly, A. H. (1987). *Sex differences in social behavior: A social-role interpretation.* Hillsdale, NJ: Erlbaum.

Eagly, A. H., & Crowley, M. (1986). Gender and helping behavior: A meta-analytic review of the social psychological literature. *Psychological Bulletin, 100,* 283–308.

Eaton, W. O., & Enns, L. R. (1986). Sex differences in human motor activity level. *Psychological Bulletin, 100,* 19–28.

Eccles, J. (1999, Fall). The development of children ages 6 to 14. *The Future of Children: When School Is Out, 9,* 30–44.

Eccles, J. S. (1989). Bringing young women to math and science. In M. Crawford & M. Gentry (Eds.), *Gender and thought: Psychological perspectives.* New York: Springer-Verlag.

Eccles, J. S., & Harold, R. D. (1993). Parent-school involvement during the early adolescent years. *Teachers College Record, 94,* 568–587.

Eccles, J. S., & Jacobs, J. E. (1986). Social forces shape math attitudes and performance. *Signs: Journal of Women in Culture and Society, 11,* 367–380.

Eccles, J. S., Jacobs, J., Harold-Goldsmith, R., Jayaratne, T., & Yee, D. (1989, April). *The relations between parents' category-based and target-based beliefs: Gender roles and biological influences.* Paper presented at the Society for Research in Child Development, Kansas City, MO.

Eccles, J. S., & Midgley, C. (1989). Stage-environment fit: Developmentally appropriate classrooms for young adolescents. In C. Ames & R. Ames (Eds.), *Research on motivation in education: Vol. 3. Goals and cognition.* San Diego, CA: Academic Press.

Eccles, J. S., & Wigfield, A. (1985). Teacher expectations and student motivation. In J. B. Dusek (Ed.), *Teacher expectancies.* Hillsdale, NJ: Erlbaum.

Eccles, J. S., Wigfield, A., & Schiefele, U. (1998). Motivation to succeed. In W. Damon (Editor-in-Chief) and N. Eisenberg (Vol. Ed.), *Handbook of child psychology: Vol 3: Social, emotional, and personality development* (5th ed., pp. 1017–1095). New York: Wiley.

Eccles (Parsons), J. S. (1983). Expectancies, values, and academic behaviors. In J. T. Spence (Ed.), *Achievement and achievement motivation.* San Francisco: Freeman.

Eccles (Parsons), J. S. (1984). Sex differences in mathematics participation. In M. Steinkamp & M. Maehr (Eds.), *Women in science.* Greenwich, CT: JAI Press.

Echols, L. D., West, R. F., Stanovich, K. E., & Kehr, K. S. (1996). Using children's literacy activities to predict growth in verbal cognitive skills: A longitudinal investigation. *Journal of Educational Psychology, 88,* 296–304.

Eckerman, C. O. (1979). The human infant in social interaction. In R. Cairns (Ed.), *The analysis of social interactions: Methods, issues, and illustrations* (pp. 163–178). Hillsdale, NJ: Erlbaum.

Eckerman, C. O., & Didow, S. M. (1996). Non-verbal imitation and toddlers' mastery of verbal means of achieving coordinated action. *Developmental Psychology, 32,* 141–152.

Eckerman, C. O. (1993). Imitation and toddlers' achievement of co-ordinated action with others. In J. Nadel & L. Camaioni (Eds.), *New perspectives in early communicative development* (pp. 116–156). New York: Routledge.

Eckman, P. (1972). Universals and cultural differences in facial expressions of emotion. In J. K. Cole (Ed.), *Nebraska symposium on motivation.* Lincoln: University of Nebraska Press.

Edelman, M. W. (1993, March). Investing in our children: A struggle for America's conscience and future. *USA Today, 121*(2574), 24–26.

Edelsky, C., Altwerger, B., & Flores, B. (1991). *Whole language: What's the difference?* Portsmouth, NH: Heinemann.

Eder, D. (1985). The cycle of popularity: Interpersonal relations among female adolescents. *Sociology of Education, 58,* 154–165.

Edmundson, P. J. (1990). A normative look at the curriculum in teacher education. *Phi Delta Kappan, 71,* 717–722.

Edwards , C. P., Gandini, L., & Giovaninni, D. (1996). The contrasting developmental timetables of parents and preschool teachers in two cultural communities. In Harkness, B., & Super, C. (Eds.). *Parents' cultural belief systems* (pp. 270–288). New York: Guilford Press.

Edwards, P. A., & Garcia, G. E. (1994). The implications of Vygotskian theory for the development of home-school programs: A focus on storybook reading. In V. John-Steiner, C. P. Panofsky, & L. W. Smith (Eds.), *Sociocultural approaches to language and literacy: An interactionist perspective.* Cambridge, England: Cambridge University Press.

Eeds, M., & Wells, D. (1989). Grand conversations: An explanation of meaning construction in literature study groups. *Research in the Teaching of English, 23,* 4–29.

Egami, Y., Ford, D., & Crum, R. (1996). Psychiatric profile and sociodemographic characteristics of adults who report physically abusing or neglecting children. *The American Journal of Psychiatry, 153,* 921–930.

Ehri, L. (1991). Development of the ability to read words. In P. D. Pearson (Ed.), *Handbook of reading research* (vol. II). New York: Longman.

Ehri, L. (1994). Development of the ability to read words: Update. In R. B. Ruddell, M. R. Ruddell, & H. Singer (Eds.), *Theoretical models and processes of reading* (4th ed.). Newark, DE: International Reading Association.

Ehri, L. C. (1998). Word reading by sight and by analogy in beginning readers. In C. Hulme & R. M. Joshi (Eds.), *Reading and spelling: Development and disorders.* Mahwah, NJ: Erlbaum.

Ehri, L. C., & Robbins, C. (1992). Beginners need some decoding skill to read words by analogy. *Reading Research Quarterly, 27,* 12–27.

Ehri, L. C., & Wilce, L. S. (1986). The influence of spellings on speech: Are alveolar flaps /d/ or /t/?. In D. B. Yaden, Jr., & S. Templeton (Eds.), *Metalinguistic awareness and beginning literacy: Conceptualizing what it means to read and write.* Portsmouth, NH: Heinemann.

Eilers, R. E., & Oller, D. K. (1994). Infant vocalizations and early diagnosis of severe hearing impairment. *Journal of Pediatrics, 124,* 199–203.

Eimas, P. D., & Quinn, P. C. (1994). Studies on the formation of perceptually based basic-level categories in young infants. *Child Development, 65,* 903–917.

Eisenberg, N. (1982). The development of reasoning regarding prosocial behavior. In N. Eisenberg (Ed.), *The development of prosocial behavior.* New York: Academic Press.

Eisenberg, N. (1987). The relation of altruism and other moral behaviors to moral cognition: Methodological and conceptual issues. In N. Eisenberg (Ed.), *Contemporary topics in developmental psychology* (pp. 165–189). New York: Wiley.

Eisenberg, N. (1992). *The caring child.* Cambridge, MA: Harvard University Press.

Eisenberg, N. (1995). Prosocial development: A multifaceted model. In W. M. Kurtines & J. L. Gewirtz (Eds.), *Moral development: An introduction.* Boston: Allyn & Bacon.

Eisenberg, N. (1998). Introduction. In W. Damon (Editor-in-Chief) & N. Eisenberg (Vol. Ed.), *Handbook of child psychology: Vol. 3. Social, emotional, and personality development* (5th ed., pp. 1–24). New York: Wiley.

Eisenberg, N., Carlo, G., Murphy, B., & Van Court, N. (1995). Prosocial development in late adolescence: A longitudinal study. *Child Development, 66,* 1179–1197.

Eisenberg, N., Cumberland, A., & Spinard, T. L. (1988). Parental socialization of emotion. *Psychological Inquiry, 9,* 241–273.

Eisenberg, N., & Fabes, R. A. (1991). Prosocial behavior: A multimethod developmental perspective. In M. S. Clark (Ed.), *Review of personality and social psychology* (Vol. 2, pp. 34–61). Newbury Park, CA: Sage.

Eisenberg, N., & Fabes, R. A. (1994). Mothers' reactions to children's negative emotions: Relations to children's temperament and anger behavior. *Merrill-Palmer Quarterly, 40,* 138–156.

Eisenberg, N., & Fabes, R. A. (1998). Prosocial development. In W. Damon (Editor-in-Chief), & N. Eisenberg (Vol. Ed.), *Handbook of child psychology: Vol. 3. Social, emotional, and personality development* (pp. 701–778). New York: Wiley.

Eisenberg, N., Fabes, R. A., Carlo, G., & Karbon, M. (1992). Emotional responsivity to others: Behavioral correlates and socialization antecedents. In N. Eisenberg & R. A. Fabes (Eds.), *New directions in child development* (No. 55, pp. 57–73). San Francisco: Jossey-Bass.

Eisenberg, N., Fabes, R. A., Schaller, M., Carlo, G., & Miller, P. A. (1991). The relations of parental characteristics and practices to children's vicarious emotional responding. *Child Development, 62,* 1393–1408.

Eisenberg, N., Lennon, R., & Pasternack, J. F. (1986). Altruistic values and moral judgment. In N. Eisenberg (Ed.), *Altruistic emotion, cognition, and behavior.* Hillsdale, NJ: Erlbaum.

Eisenberg, N., Losoya, S., & Guthrie, I. K. (1997). Social cognition and prosocial development. In S. Hala (Ed.), *The development of social cognition. Studies in developmental psychology* (pp. 329–363). Hove, England: Psychology Press/Erlbaum.

Eisenberg, N., Martin, C. L., & Fabes, R. A. (1996). Gender development and gender effects. In D. C. Berliner & R. C. Calfee (Eds.), *Handbook of educational psychology.* New York: Macmillan.

Eisenberg, N., Miller, P. A., Shell, R., McNalley, S., & Shea, C. (1991). Prosocial development in adolescence: A longitudinal study. *Developmental Psychology, 27,* 849–857.

Eisenberg, N., & Shell, R. (1986). Prosocial moral judgment and behavior in children: The mediating role of cost. *Personality and Social Psychology Bulletin, 12,* 426–433.

Eisenberg, N., Zhou, Q., & Koller, S. (2001). Brazilian adolescents' prosocial moral judgment and behavior: Relations to sympathy, perspective taking, gender-role orientation, and demographic characteristics. *Child Development, 72,* 518–534.

Eisenberger, R. (1992). Learned industriousness. *Psychological Review, 99,* 248–267.

Elia, J. P. (1994). Homophobia in the high school: A problem in need of a resolution. *Journal of Homosexuality, 77*(1), 177–185.

Elias, G., & Broerse, J. (1996). Developmental changes in the incidence and likelihood of simultaneous talk during the first two years: A question of function. *Journal of Child Language, 23,* 201–217.

Elicker, J., Englund, M., & Sroufe, L. A. (1992). Predicting peer competence and peer relationships in childhood from early parent-child relationships. In R. D. Parke & G. W. Ladd (Eds.), *Family-peer relationships: Modes of linkage* (pp. 77–106). Hillsdale, NJ: Erlbaum.

Elkind, D. (1978). Understanding the young adolescent. *Adolescence, 13,* 127–134.

Elkind, D. (1981a). *Children and adolescents: Interpretive essays on Jean Piaget* (3rd ed.). New York: Oxford University Press.

Elkind, D. (1981b). *The hurried child: Growing up too fast too soon.* Reading, MA: Addison-Wesley.

Elkind, D. (1984). *All grown up and no place to go.* Reading, MA: Addison-Wesley.

Ellenwood, S., & Ryan, K. (1991). Literature and morality: An experimental curriculum. In W. M. Kurtines & J. L. Gewirtz (Eds.), *Moral behavior and development: Vol. 3. Application.* Hillsdale, NJ: Erlbaum.

Elliot, A. J., & McGregor, H. A. (2000, April). Approach and avoidance goals and autonomous-controlled regulation: Empirical and conceptual relations. In A. Assor (Chair), *Self-determination theory and achievement goal theory: Convergences, divergences, and educational implications.* Symposium conducted at the annual meeting of the American Educational Research Association, New Orleans, LA.

Elliott, D. J. (1995). *Music matters: A new philosophy of music education.* New York: Oxford University Press.

Elliott, D. S. (1994). Serious violent offenders: Onset, developmental course, and termination—The American Society of Criminology 1993 Presidential Address. *Criminology, 32,* 1–21.

Elliott, D. S., Wilson, W. J., Huizinga, D., Sampson, R. J., Elliott, A., & Rankin, B. (1996). The effects of neighborhood disadvantage on adolescent development. *Journal of Research in Crime and Delinquency, 33,* 389–426.

Elliott, R., & Vasta, R. (1970). The modeling of sharing: Effects associated with vicarious reinforcement, symbolization, age, and generalization. *Journal of Experimental Child Psychology, 10,* 8–15.

Elliott, S. N., & Busse, R. T. (1991). Social skills assessment and intervention with children and adolescents. *School Psychology International, 12,* 63–83.

Ellis, E. S., & Friend, P. (1991). Adolescents with learning disabilities. In B. Y. L. Wong (Ed.), *Learning about learning disabilities.* San Diego, CA: Academic Press.

Ember, C. R., & Ember, M. (1994). War, socialization, and interpersonal violence. *Journal of Conflict Resolution, 38,* 620–646.

Emde, R., Gaensbauer, T., & Harmon, R. (1976). *Emotional expression in infancy: A biobehavioral study* (Psychological Issues, Vol. 10, No. 37). New York: International Universities Press.

Emde, R. N., & & Buchsbaum, H. (1990). "Didn't you hear my mommy?" Autonomy with connectedness in moral self-emergence. In D. Cicchetti & M. Beeghly (Eds.), *The self in transition: Infancy to adulthood* (pp. 35–60). Chicago: University of Chicago Press.

Emery, R. E., & Laumann-Billings, L. (1998). An overview of the nature, causes, and consequences of abusive family relationships. *American Psychologist, 53,* 121–135.

Emmer, E. T., Evertson, C. M., Clements, B. S., & Worsham, M. E. (1994). *Classroom management for secondary teachers* (3rd ed.). Needham Heights, MA: Allyn & Bacon.

Emmerich, W., Goldman, K. S., Kirsch, B., & Sharabany, R. (1977). Evidence of a transitional phase in the development of gender constancy. *Child Development, 48,* 930–936.

Empson, S. B. (1999). Equal sharing and shared meaning: The development of fraction concepts in a first-grade classroom. *Cognition and Instruction, 17,* 283–342.

Endicott, K. (1992). Fathering in an egalitarian society. In B. S. Hewlett (Ed.), *Father-child relations: Cultural and biosocial contexts* (pp. 281–295). New York: Aldine deGruyter.

Engle, P. L., & Breaux, C. (1998). Fathers' involvement with children: Perspectives from developing countries. *Social Policy Report: Society for Research in Child Development, 12*(1), 1–21.

Englert, C. S., Raphael, T. E., Anderson, L. M., Anthony, H. M., & Stevens, D. D. (1991). Making strategies and self-talk visible: Writing instruction in regular and special education classrooms. *American Educational Research Journal, 28,* 337–372.

English, D. J. (1998). The extent and consequences of child maltreatment. *The Future of Children: Protecting Children from Abuse and Neglect, 8*(1), 39–53.

Eppright, T. D., Sanfacon, J. A., Beck, N. C., & Bradley, S. J. (1998). Sport psychiatry in childhood and adolescence: An overview. *Child Psychiatry and Human Development, 28,* 71–88.

Epstein, J. A., Botvin, G. J., Diaz, T., Toth, V., & Schinke, S. P. (1995). Social and personal factors in marijuana use and intentions to use drugs among inner city minority youth. *Journal of Developmental and Behavioral Pediatrics, 16,* 14–20.

Epstein, J. L. (1983). Longitudinal effects of family-school-person interactions on student outcomes. *Research in Sociology of Education and Socialization, 4,* 101–127.

Epstein, J. L. (1986). Friendship selection: Developmental and environmental influences. In E. Mueller & C. Cooper (Eds.), *Process and outcome in peer relationships* (pp. 129–160). New York: Academic Press.

Epstein, J. L. (1996). Perspectives and previews on research and policy for school, family, and community partnerships. In A. Booth & J. F. Dunn (Eds.), *Family-school links: How do they affect educational outcomes?* Mahwah, NJ: Erlbaum.

Epstein, J. S. (1998). Introduction: Generation X, youth culture, and identity. In J. S. Epstein (Ed.), *Youth culture: Identity in a postmodern world.* Malden, MA: Blackwell.

Epstein, L. H. (1990). Behavioral treatment of obesity. In E. M. Stricker (Ed.), *Handbook of behavioral neurobiology: Vol. 10. Neurobiology of food and fluid intake* (pp. 61–73). New York: Plenum Press.

Epstein, L. H., Wing, R. R., & Valoski, A. (1985). Childhood obesity. *Pediatric Clinics of North America, 32,* 363–379.

Epstein, S., & Morling, B. (1995). Is the self motivated to do more than enhance and/or verify itself? In M. H. Kernis (Ed.), *Efficacy, agency, and self-esteem.* New York: Plenum Press.

Epstein, T. (2000). Adolescents' perspectives on racial diversity in U.S. history: Case studies from an urban classroom. *American Educational Research Journal, 37,* 185–214.

Erdley, C. A., & Asher, S. R. (1996). Children's social goals and self-efficacy perceptions as influences on their responses to ambiguous provocation. *Child Development, 67,* 1329–1344.

Erdley, C. A., Qualey, L. L., & Pietrucha, C. A. (1996, April). *Boys' and girls' attributions of intent and legitimacy of aggression beliefs as predictors of their social behavior.* Paper presented at the annual meeting of the American Educational Research Association, New York.

Ericsson, K. A., & Chalmers, N. (1994). Expert performance: Its structure and acquisition. *American Psychologist, 49,* 725–747.

Erikson, E. H. (1963). *Childhood and society* (2nd ed.). New York: Norton.

Erikson, E. H. (1972). Eight ages of man. In C. S. Lavatelli & F. Stendler (Eds.), *Readings in child behavior and child development.* San Diego, CA: Harcourt Brace Jovanovich.

Eron, L. D. (1980). Prescription for reduction of aggression. *American Psychologist, 35,* 244–252.

Eron, L. D. (1987). The development of aggressive behavior from the perspective of a developing behaviorism. *American Psychologist, 42,* 435–442.

Erwin, P. (1993). *Friendship and peer relations in children.* Chichester, England: Wiley.

Etaugh, C., Grinnell, K., & Etaugh, A. (1989). Development of gender labeling: Effect of age of pictured children. *Sex Roles, 21,* 769–773.

Eysenck, H. J., & Schoenthaler, S. J. (1997). Raising IQ level by vitamin and mineral supplementation. In R. J. Sternberg & E. L. Grigorenko (Eds.), *Intelligence, heredity, and environment* (pp. 363–392). Cambridge, England: Cambridge University Press.

Eysenck, M. W. (1992). *Anxiety: The cognitive perspective.* Hove, England: Erlbaum.

Fabes, R. A., Eisenberg, N., Jones, S., Smith, M., Guthrie, I., Poulin, R., Shepard, S., & Friedman, J. (1999). Regulation, emotionality, and preschoolers' socially competent peer interactions. *Child Development, 70,* 432–442.

Fabes, R. A., Fultz, J., Eisenberg, N., May-Plumlee, T., & Christopher, F. S. (1989). The effect of reward on children's prosocial motivation: A socialization study. *Developmental Psychology, 25,* 509–515.

Fabricius, W. V., & Hagen, J. W. (1984). Use of causal attributions about recall performance to assess metamemory and predict strategic memory behavior in young children. *Developmental Psychology, 20,* 975–987.

Fagan, J. F., & Singer, L. T. (1983). Infant recognition memory as a measure of intelligence. In L. P. Lipsitt (Ed.), *Advances in infancy research* (Vol. 2). Norwood, NJ: Ablex.

Fagot, B. I., & Leinbach, M. D. (1989). Gender-role development in young children: From discrimination to labeling. *Developmental Review, 13,* 205–224.

Fahrmeier, E. D. (1978). The development of concrete operations among the Hausa. *Journal of Cross-Cultural Psychology, 9,* 23–44.

Fairchild, H. H., & Edwards-Evans, S. (1990). African American dialects and schooling: A review. In A. M. Padilla, H. H. Fairchild & C. M. Valadez (Eds.), *Bilingual education: Issues and strategies.* Newbury Park, CA: Sage.

Faks, D. K., Filcher, I., Masterpasqua, E., & Joseph, G. (1995). Lesbians choosing motherhood: A comparative study of lesbian and heterosexual parents and their children. *Developmental Psychology, 31,* 105–114.

Falbo, T. (1992). Social norms and the one-child family: Clinical and policy implications. In F. Boer & J. Dunn (Eds.), *Children's sibling relationships* (pp. 71–82). Hillsdale, NJ: Erlbaum.

Falbo, T., & Polit, D. (1986). A quantitative review of the only child literature: Research evidence and theory development. *Psychological Bulletin, 100,* 176–189.

Famularo, R., Kinscherff, R., & Fenton, T. (1992). Psychiatric diagnoses of maltreated children: Preliminary findings. *Journal of the American Academy of Child and Adolescent Psychiatry, 31,* 863–867.

Fantini, A. E. (1985). *Language acquisition of a bilingual child: A sociolinguistic perspective.* Clevedon, England: Multilingual Matters. (Available from the SIT Bookstore, School for International Training, Kipling Road, Brattleboro, VT 05302)

Fantino, A. M., & Colak, A. (2001). Refugee children in Canada: Searching for identity. *Child Welfare, 80*(5), 587–596.

Faraone, S. V., Biederman, J., Chen, W. J., Milberger, S., Warburton, R., & Tsuang, M. T. (1995). Genetic heterogeneity in attention-deficit hyperactivity disorder (ADHD): Gender, psychiatric comorbidity, and maternal ADHD. *Journal of Abnormal Psychology, 104,* 334–345.

Farber, B., Mindel, C. H., & Lazerwitz, B. (1988). The Jewish American family. In C. H. Mindel, R. W. Habenstein, & R. Wright (Eds.), *Ethnic families in America: Patterns and variations.* New York: Elsevier.

Farrar, M. J., & Goodman, G. S. (1992). Developmental changes in event memory. *Child Development, 63,* 173–187.

Farrell, M. M., & Phelps, L. (2000). A comparison of the Leiter-R and the Universal Nonverbal Intelligence Test (UNIT) with children classified as language impaired. *Journal of Psychoeducational Assessment, 18,* 268–274.

Farver, J. A. M., & Branstetter, W. H. (1994). Preschoolers' prosocial responses to their peers' distress. *Developmental Psychology, 30,* 334–341.

Fausel, D. F. (1986). Loss after divorce: Helping children grieve. *Journal of Independent Social Work, 1*(1), 39–47.

Feather, N. T. (1982). *Expectations and actions: Expectancy-value models in psychology.* Hillsdale, NJ: Erlbaum.

Federal Glass Ceiling Commission. (1995). *Good for business: Making full use of the nation's human capital. The environmental scan.* Washington, DC: U.S. Government Printing Office.

Federal Interagency Forum on Child and Family Statistics (2002). *America's children: Key national indicators of well-being, 2002.* Washington, DC: U.S. Government Printing Office.

Feigenson, L., Carey, S., & Hauser, M. (2002). The representations underlying infants' choice of more: Object files versus analog magnitudes. *Psychological Science, 13,* 150–156.

Fein, G. G. (1979). Play and the acquisition of symbols. In L. Katz (Ed.), *Current topics in early childhood education.* Norwood, NJ: Ablex.

Feingold, A. (1993). Cognitive gender differences: A developmental perspective. *Sex Roles, 29,* 91–112.

Feinman, S. (1992). *Social referencing and the social construction of reality in infancy.* New York: Plenum Press.

Feld, S., Ruhland, D., & Gold, M. (1979). Developmental changes in achievement motivation. *Merrill-Palmer Quarterly, 25,* 43–60.

Feldhusen, J. F. (1989). Synthesis of research on gifted youth. *Educational Leadership, 26*(1), 6–11.

Feldhusen, J. F., Van Winkle, L., & Ehle, D. A. (1996). Is it acceleration or simply appropriate instruction for precocious youth? *Teaching Exceptional Children, 28*(3), 48–51.

Feldman, S. S., Gowen, L. K., & Fisher, L. (1998). Family relationships and gender as predictors of romantic intimacy in young adults: A longitudinal study. *Journal of Research on Adolescence, 8*(2), 263–286.

Feldman, S. S., & Wentzel, K. R. (1990). The relationship between parental styles, sons' self-restraint, and peer relations in early adolescence. *Journal of Early Adolescence, 10,* 439–454.

Feldman, S. S., & Wood, D. N. (1994). Parents' expectations for preadolescent sons' behavioral autonomy: A longitudinal study of correlates and outcomes. *Journal of Research on Adolescence, 4,*(1), 45–70.

Felton, R. H. (1998). The development of reading skills in poor readers: Educational implications. In C. Hulme & R. M. Joshi (Eds.), *Reading and spelling: Development and disorders.* Mahwah, NJ: Erlbaum.

Fennema, E. (1987). Sex-related differences in education: Myths, realities, and interventions. In V. Richardson-Koehler (Ed.), *Educators' handbook: A research perspective.* White Plains, NY: Longman.

Fenson, L., Dale, P., Reznick, J., Bates, E., Thal, D., & Pethick, S. (1994). Variability in early communicative development. *Monographs of the Society for Research in Child Development, 59*(5, Serial No. 242), 1–173.

Fenson, L., Vella, D., & Kennedy, M. (1989). Children's knowledge of thematic and taxonomic relations at two years of age. *Child Development, 60,* 911–919.

Ferguson, C. J. (1999). Building literacy with child-constructed sociodramatic play centers. *Dimensions of Early Childhood, 27,* 23–29.

Fernald, A. (1992). Human maternal vocalizations to infants as biologically relevant signals: An evolutionary perspective. In J. Barkow, L. Cosmides, & J. Tooby (Eds.), *Evolutionary psychology and the generation of culture.* New York: Oxford University Press.

Fernald, A., Swingley, D., & Pinto, J. P. (2001). When half a word is enough: Infants can recognize spoken words using partial phonetic information. *Child Development, 72,* 1003–1015.

Ferreiro, E. (1990). Literacy development: Psychogenesis. In Y. M. Goodman (Ed.), *How children construct literacy.* Newark, DE: International Reading Association.

Ferretti, R. P., MacArthur, C. A., & Dowdy, N. S. (2000). The effects of an elaborated goal on the persuasive writing of students with learning disabilities and their normally achieving peers. *Journal of Educational Psychology, 92,* 694–702.

Feshbach, N. (1997). Empathy: The formative years—Implications for clinical practice. In A. C. Bohart & L. S. Greenberg (Eds.), *Empathy reconsidered: New directions for psychotherapy* (pp. 33–59). Washington, DC: American Psychological Association.

Feuerstein, R. (1979). *The dynamic assessment of retarded performers: The Learning Potential Assessment Device, theory, instruments, and techniques.* Baltimore: University Park Press.

Feuerstein, R. (1980). *Instrumental enrichment: An intervention program for cognitive modifiability.* Baltimore: University Park Press.

Feuerstein, R. (1990). The theory of structural cognitive modifiability. In B. Z. Presseisen (Ed.), *Learning and thinking styles: Classroom interaction.* Washington, DC: National Education Association.

Feuerstein, R., Feuerstein, R., & Gross, S. (1997). The Learning Potential Assessment Device. In D. P. Flanagan, J. L. Genshaft, & P. L. Harrison (Eds.), *Contemporary intellectual assessment: Theories, tests, and issues* (pp. 297–313). New York: Guilford Press.

Feuerstein, R., Klein, P. R., & Tannenbaum, A. (Eds.). (1991). *Mediated learning experience: Theoretical, psychosocial, and learning implications.* London: Freund.

Fewell, R. R. & Sandall, S. R. (1983). Curricula adaptations for young children: Visually impaired, hearing impaired, and physically impaired. *Curricula in Early Childhood Special Education, 2*(4), 51–66.

Fey, M. E., Catts, H., & Larrivee, L. (1995). Preparing preschoolers for the academic and social challenges of school. In M. E. Fey, J. Windsor, & S. F. Warren (Eds.), *Language intervention: Preschool through elementary years.* Baltimore: Brookes.

Fiedler, E. D., Lange, R. E., & Winebrenner, S. (1993). In search of reality: Unraveling the myths about tracking, ability grouping and the gifted. *Roeper Review, 16*(1), 4–7.

Field, D. (1987). A review of preschool conservation training: An analysis of analyses. *Developmental Review, 7,* 210–251.

Field, S. L., Labbo, L. D., & Ash, G. E. (1999, April). *Investigating young children's construction of social studies concepts and the intersection of literacy learning.* Paper presented at the annual meeting of the American Educational Research Association, Montreal, Canada.

Field, T. (1991). Quality infant daycare and grade school behavior and performance. *Child Development, 62,* 863–870.

Field, T., Masi, W., Goldstein, D., Perry, S., & Parl, S. (1988). Infant daycare facilitates preschool behavior. *Early Childhood Research Quarterly, 3,* 341–359.

Field, T., Vega-Lahr, N., Scafidi, F., & Goldstein, S. (1986). Effects of maternal unavailability on mother-infant interactions. *Infant Behavior and Development, 9,* 473–478.

Field, T., Woodson, R., Greenberg, R., & Cohen, D. (1982). Discrimination and imitation of facial expressions by neonates. *Science, 218,* 179–81.

Fields, J. (2001, April). *Living arrangements of children: Fall 1996.* Current Population Reports, P70–74. Washington, CD: U.S. Census Bureau.

Fifer, W. P., & Moon, C. M. (1995). The effects of fetal experience with sound. In J.P. Lecanuet, W. P. Fifer, N. A. Krasnegor, & W. P. Smotherman (Eds.), *Fetal development: A psychobiological perspective.* Hillsdale, NJ: Erlbaum.

Finders, M., & Lewis, C. (1994). Why some parents don't come to school. *Educational Leadership, 51*(8), 50–54.

Fingerhut, L. A., Ingram, D. D., & Feldman, J. J. (1992). Firearm and nonfirearm homicide among persons 15 through 19 years of age: Differences by level of urbanization, United States, 1979 through 1989. *Journal of the American Medical Association, 267,* 3048–3053.

Finkelhor, D., & Dziuba-Leatherman, J. (1994). Victimization of children. *American Psychologist, 49*(3), 173–183.

Finkelhor, D., Mitchell, K. J., & Wolak, J. (2000). *Online victimization: A report on the nation's youth.* Durham, NH: Crimes Against Children Research Center. Retrieved March 7, 2003, from http://www.unh.edu/ccrc/Victimization_Online_Survey.pdf

Finkelhor, D., & Ormrod, R. (2000, December). *Juvenile victims of property crimes.* Washington, DC: U.S. Department of Justice, Office of Justice Programs, Office of Juvenile Justice and Delinquency Prevention.

Finn, J. D. (1989). Withdrawing from school. *Review of Educational Research, 59,* 117–142.

Finn-Stevenson, M., & Stern, B. (1996). CoZi: Linking early childhood and family support services. *Principal, 75*(5), 6–10.

Fischer, K. W., & Bidell, T. (1991). Constraining nativist inferences about cognitive capacities. In S. Carey & R. Gelman (Eds.), *The epigenesis of mind: Essays on biology and cognition.* Hillsdale, NJ: Erlbaum.

Fischer, K. W., Knight, C. C., & Van Parys, M. (1993). Analyzing diversity in developmental pathways: Methods and concepts. In R. Case & W. Edelstein (Eds.), *The new structuralism in cognitive development: Theory and research on individual pathways.* Basel, Switzerland: Karger.

Fisher, C. B., & Brone, R. J. (1991). Eating disorders in adolescence. In R. M. Lerner, A. C. Petersen, & J. Brooks-Gunn (Eds.), *Encyclopedia of adolescence* (Vol. 1). New York: Garland.

Fisher, C. B., Jackson, J. F., & Villarruel, F. A. (1998). The study of African American and Latin American children and youth. In W. Damon (Editor-in-Chief) & R. M. Lerner (Vol. Ed.), *Handbook of child psychology: Vol. 1. Theoretical models of human development* (5th ed., pp. 1145–1207). New York: Wiley.

Fisher, J. D., & Fisher, W. A. (1992). Changing AIDS-risk behavior. *Psychological Bulletin, 111,* 455–474.

Fiske, S. T., & Taylor, S. E. (1991). *Social cognition* (2nd ed.). New York: McGraw-Hill.

Fitzgerald, J. (1987). Research on revision in writing. *Review of Educational Research, 57,* 481–506.

Fitzgerald, J., & Markman, L. R. (1987). Teaching children about revision in writing. *Cognition and Instruction, 41,* 3–24.

Fivush, R., Haden, C., & Adam, S. (1995). Structure and coherence of preschoolers' personal narratives over time: Implications for childhood amnesia. *Journal of Experimental Child Psychology, 60,* 32–56.

Fivush, R., Haden, C., & Reese, E. (1996). Remembering, recounting, and reminiscing: The development of autobiographical memory in social context. In D. C. Rubin (Ed.), *Remembering our past: Studies in autobiographical memory* (pp. 341–359). Cambridge, England: Cambridge University Press.

Fix, M., & Passel, J. S. (1994, May). *Immigration and immigrants: Setting the record straight.* Washington, DC: Urban Institute.

Flanagan, C. (1995, March). *Adolescents' explanations for poverty, unemployment, homelessness, and wealth.* Paper presented at the biennial meeting of the Society for Research in Child Development, Indianapolis, Indiana.

Flanagan, C. A., & Faison, N. (2001). Youth civic development: Implications of research for social policy and programs. *Social Policy Report of the Society for Research in Child Development, 15*(1), 1–14.

Flanagan, C. A., & Tucker, C. J. (1999). Adolescents' explanations for political issues: Concordance with their views of self and society. *Developmental Psychology, 35,* 1198–1209.

Flannery, D. J., Vazsonyi, A. T., Torquati, J., & Fridrich, A. (1994). Ethnic and gender differences in risk for early adolescent substance use. *Journal of Youth and Adolescence, 23,* 195–213.

Flavell, J. H. (1992). Perspectives on perspective taking. In H. Beilin & P. Pufall (Eds.), *Piaget's theory: Prospects and possibilities* (pp. 107–139). Hillsdale, NJ: Erlbaum.

Flavell, J. H. (1994). Cognitive development: Past, present, and future. In R. D. Parke, P. A. Ornstein, J. J. Rieser, & C. Zahn-Waxler (Eds.), *A century of developmental psychology* (pp. 569–587). Washington, DC: American Psychological Association.

Flavell, J. H. (1996). Piaget's legacy. *Psychological Science, 7*(4), 200–203.

Flavell, J. H. (2000). Development of children's knowledge about the mental world. *International Journal of Behavioral Development, 24*(1), 15–23.

Flavell, J. H., Flavell, E. R., & Green, F. L. (2001). Development of children's understanding of connections between thinking and feeling. *Psychological Science, 12,* 430–432.

Flavell, J. H., Friedrichs, A. G., & Hoyt, J. D. (1970). Developmental changes in memorization processes. *Cognitive Psychology, 1,* 324–340.

Flavell, J. H., Green, F. L., & Flavell, E. R. (1995). Young children's knowledge about thinking. *Monographs of the Society for Research in Child Development, 60*(1, Serial No. 243).

Flavell, J. H., Green, F. L., & Flavell, E. R. (2000). Development of children's awareness of their own thoughts. *Journal of Cognitive Development, 1,* 97–112.

Flavell, J. H., & Miller, P. H. (1998). Social cognition. In W. Damon (Series Ed.) & D. Kuhn & R. S. Siegler (Vol. Eds.), *Handbook of child psychology: Vol. 2. Cognition, perception, and language* (5th ed.). New York: Wiley.

Flavell, J. H., Miller, P. H., & Miller, S. A. (1993). *Cognitive development* (3rd ed.). Upper Saddle River, NJ: Prentice Hall.

Fleege, P. O., Charlesworth, R., & Burts, D. C. (1992). Stress begins in kindergarten: A look at behavior during standardized testing. *Journal of Research in Childhood Education, 7*(1), 20–26.

Flege, J. E., Munro, M. J., & MacKay, I. R. A. (1995). Effects of age of second-language learning on the production of English consonants. *Speech Communication, 16*(1), 1–26.

Fletcher, K. L., & Bray, N. W. (1995). External and verbal strategies in children with and without mild mental retardation. *American Journal on Mental Retardation, 99,* 363–475.

Fletcher, K. L., & Bray, N. W. (1996). External memory strategy use in preschool children. *Merrill-Palmer Quarterly, 42,* 379–396.

Flieller, A. (1999). Comparison of the development of formal thought in adolescent cohorts aged 10 to 15 years (1967–1996 and 1972–1993). *Developmental Psychology, 35,* 1048–1058.

Flink, C., Boggiano, A. K., Main, D. S., Barrett, M., & Katz, P. A. (1992). Children's achievement-related behaviors: The role of extrinsic and intrinsic motivational orientations. In A. K. Boggiano & T. S. Pittman (Eds.), *Achievement and motivation: A social-developmental perspective.* Cambridge, England: Cambridge University Press.

Flower, L. S., & Hayes, J. R. (1981). A cognitive process theory of writing. *College Composition and Communication, 32,* 365–387.

Flynn, J. R. (1987). Massive IQ gains in 14 nations: What IQ tests really measure. *Psychological Bulletin, 101,* 171–191.

Flynn, J. R. (1991). *Asian Americans: Achievement beyond IQ.* Hillsdale, NJ: Erlbaum.

Flynn, J. R. (1999). Searching for justice: The discovery of IQ gains over time. *American Psychologist, 54,* 5–20.

Folds, T. H., Footo, M., Guttentag, R. E., & Ornstein, P. A. (1990). When children mean to remember: Issues of context specificity, strategy effectiveness, and intentionality in the development of memory. In D. F. Bjorklund (Ed.), *Children's strategies: Contemporary views of cognitive development.* Hillsdale, NJ: Erlbaum.

Forbes, M. L., Ormrod, J. E., Bernardi, J. D., Taylor, S. L., & Jackson, D. L. (1999, April). *Children's conceptions of space, as reflected in maps of their hometown.* Paper presented at the annual meeting of the American Educational Research Association, Montreal.

Ford, D. H., & Lerner, R. M. (1992). *Developmental systems theory: An integrative approach.* Newbury Park, CA: Sage.

Ford, D. Y. (1996). *Reversing underachievement among gifted black students.* New York: Teachers College Press.

Ford, M. E. (1996). Motivational opportunities and obstacles associated with social responsibility and caring behavior in school contexts. In J. Juvonen & K. R. Wentzel (Eds.), *Social motivation: Understanding children's school adjustment* (pp. 126–153). Cambridge, England: Cambridge University Press.

Ford, M. E. (1997). Developmental psychology. In H. J. Walberg & G. D. Haertel (Eds.), *Psychology and educational practice.* Berkeley, CA: McCrutchan.

Forehand, R., Biggar, H., & Kotchick, B. A. (1998). Cumulative risk across family stressors: Short- and long-term effects for adolescents. *Journal of Abnormal Child Psychology, 26*(2), 119–128.

Forehand, R., Wierson, M., Thomas, A. M., Fauber, R., Armistead, L., Kempton, T., & Long, N. (1991). A short-term longitudinal examination of young adolescent functioning following divorce: The role of family factors. *Journal of Abnormal Child Psychology, 19,* 97–111.

Forgey, M. A., Schinke, S., & Cole, K. (1997). School-based interventions to prevent substance use among inner-city minority adolescents. In D. K. Wilson, J. R. Rodrigue, & W. C. Taylor (Eds.), *Health-promoting and health-compromising behaviors among adolescents* (pp. 251–267). Washington, DC: American Psychological Association.

Fowler, J. W. (1981). *Stages of faith: The psychology of human development and the quest for meaning.* San Francisco: Harper & Row.

Fowler, S. A., & Baer, D. M. (1981). "Do I have to be good all day?" The timing of delayed reinforcement as a factor in generalization. *Journal of Applied Behavior Analysis, 14,* 13–24.

Fox, J. A., & Newman, S. A. (1997, September). *After-school programs or after-school crime.* Washington, DC: Fight crime: Invest in kids.

Fox, L. H. (1979). Programs for the gifted and talented: An overview. In A. H. Passow (Ed.), *The gifted and the talented: Their education and development. The seventy-eighth yearbook of the National Society for the Study of Education.* Chicago: University of Chicago Press.

Fox, N. A., Kimmerly, N. L., & Schafer, W. D. (1991). Attachment to mother/attachment to father: A meta-analysis. *Child Development, 52,* 210–225.

Francis, M., & McCutchen, D. (1994, April). *Strategy differences in revising between skilled and less skilled writers.* Paper presented at the annual meeting of the American Educational Research Association, New Orleans, LA.

Frank, A. (1967). *The diary of a young girl* (B. M. Mooyaart-Doubleday, Trans.). New York: Doubleday.

Frank, C. (1999). *Ethnographic eyes: A teacher's guide to classroom observation.* Portsmouth, NH: Heinemann.

Fraschetti, A. (1997). Roman youth. In G. Levi & J. C. Schmitt (Eds.), *A history of young people in the west: Vol. 1. Ancient and medieval rites of passage* (C. Naish, Trans.; pp. 51–82). Cambridge, MA: Belknap Press of Harvard University Press.

Freedman, K. (2001). The social reconstruction of art education: Teaching visual culture. In C. A. Grant & M. L. Gomez, *Campus and classroom: Making schooling multicultural* (2nd ed.). Upper Saddle River, NJ: Merrill/Prentice Hall.

Freedman, S. G. (1990). *Small victories: The real world of a teacher, her students, and their high school.* New York: Harper & Row.

French, E. G. (1956). Motivation as a variable in work partner selection. *Journal of Abnormal and Social Psychology, 53,* 96–99.

French, L., & Brown, A. (1977). Comprehension of "before" and "after" in logical and arbitrary sequences. *Journal of Child Language, 4,* 247–256.

Freud, S. (1959). *Collected papers.* New York: Basic Books.

Freund, L. (1990). Maternal regulation of children's problem solving behavior and its impact on children's performance. *Child Development, 61,* 113–126.

Friedel, M. (1993). *Characteristics of gifted/creative children.* Warwick, RI: National Foundation for Gifted and Creative Children.

Friend, M., & Davis, T. L. (1993). Appearance-reality distinction: Children's understanding of the physical and affective domains. *Developmental Psychology, 29,* 907–914.

Friend, R. A. (1993). Choices, not closets: Heterosexism and homophobia in schools. In L. Weis & M. Fine (Eds.), *Beyond silenced voices: Class, race, and gender in United States schools* (pp. 209–235). Albany, NY: SUNY Press.

Frijters, J. C., Barron, R. W., & Brunello, M. (2000). Direct and mediated influences of home literacy and literacy interest on prereaders' oral vocabulary and early written language skill. *Journal of Educational Psychology, 92,* 466–477.

Frith, U. (1985). Beneath the surface of surface dyslexia. In K. E. Patterson, J. C. Marshall, & M. Coltheart (Eds.), *Surface dyslexia: Neuropsychological and cognitive studies of phonological reading.* London: Routledge & Kegan Paul.

Frost, J. L., Shin, D., & Jacobs, P. J. (1998). Physical environments and children's play. In O. N. Saracho & B. Spodek (Eds.), *Multiple perspectives on play in early childhood education.* Albany: State University of New York Press.

Fry, A. F., & Hale, S. (1996). Processing speed, working memory, and fluid intelligence. *Psychological Science, 7,* 237–241.

Fuchs, D., Fuchs, L. S., Mathes, P. G., & Simmons, D. C. (1997). Peer-assisted learning strategies: Making classrooms more responsive to diversity. *American Educational Research Journal, 34,* 174–206.

Fuchs, D., Fuchs, L. S., Thompson, A., Al Otaiba, S., Yen, L., Yang, N. J., et al. (2001). Is reading important in reading-readiness programs? A randomized field trial with teachers as program implementers. *Journal of Educational Psychology, 93,* 251–267.

Fukkink, R. G., & de Glopper, K. (1998). Effects of instruction in deriving word meanings from context: A meta-analysis. *Review of Educational Research, 68,* 450–469.

Fuligni, A. J. (1998). The adjustment of children from immigrant families. *Current Directions in Psychological Science, 7,* 99–103.

Fuller, M. L. (2001). Multicultural concerns and classroom management. In C. A. Grant & M. L. Gomez, *Campus and classroom: Making school multicultural* (pp. 109–134). Upper Saddle River, NJ: Merrill/Prentice Hall.

Furman, W., & Buhrmester, D. (1992). Age and sex differences in perceptions of networks and personal relationships. *Child Development, 63,* 103–115.

Furman, W., & Simon, V. A. (1999). Cognitive representations of adolescent romantic relationships. In W. Furman, B. B. Brown, & C. Feiring (Eds.), *The development of romantic relationships in adolescence* (pp. 75–98). Cambridge, England: Cambridge University Press.

Furstenberg, F. F., Jr., & Cherlin, A. J. (1991). *Divided families: What happens to children when parents part.* Cambridge, MA: Harvard University Press.

Furstenberg, F. F., Jr., Nord, C., Peterson, J. L., & Zill, N. (1983). The life course of children and divorce: Marital disruption and parental conflict. *American Sociological Review, 48,* 656–668.

Furth, H. G. (1980). *The world of grown-ups: Children's conceptions of society.* New York: Elsevier.

Futterman, D., Chabon, B., & Hoffman, N. D. (2000). HIV and AIDS in adolescents. *Pediatric Clinics of North America, 47,* 171–188.

Gabard, D. L. (1999). Homosexuality and the Human Genome Project: Private and public choices. *Journal of Homosexuality, 37,* 25–51.

Gailey, C. W. (1993). Mediated messages: Gender, class, and cosmos in home video games. *Journal of Popular Culture, 27*(1), 81–97.

Galaburda, A. M., & Rosen, G. D. (2001). Neural plasticity in dyslexia: A window to mechanisms of learning disabilities. In J. L. McClelland & R. S. Siegler (Eds.), *Mechanisms of cognitive development: Behavioral and neural perspectives* (pp. 307–323). Mahwah, NJ: Erlbaum.

Galambos, N. L., Almeida, D. M., & Petersen, A. C. (1990). Masculinity, femininity, and sex role attitudes in early adolescence: Exploring gender intensification. *Child Development, 61,* 1905–1914.

Galambos, N. L., & Maggs, J. L. (1991a). Children in self-care: Figures, facts and fiction. In J. V. Verner & N. L. Galambos (Eds.), *Employed mothers and their children* (pp. 131–157). New York: Garland Press.

Galambos, N. L., & Maggs, J. L. (1991b). Out-of-school care of young adolescents and self-reported behavior. *Developmental Psychology, 27,* 644–655.

Gallagher, J. J. (1991). Personal patterns of underachievement. *Journal for the Education of the Gifted, 14,* 221–233.

Gallahue, D. L., & Ozmun, J. C. (1998). *Understanding motor development: Infants, children, adolescents, adults.* Boston: McGraw-Hill.

Gallimore, R., & Goldenberg, C. (2001). Analyzing cultural models and settings to connect minority achievement and school improvement research. *Educational Psychologist, 36,* 45–56.

Gallimore, R., & Tharp, R. (1990). Teaching mind in society: Teaching, schooling, and literate discourse. In L. C. Moll (Ed.), *Vygotsky and education: Instructional implications and applications of sociohistorical psychology.* Cambridge, England: Cambridge University Press.

Gallup, G. H., Jr. (1996). *Religion in America.* Princeton, NJ: Princeton Religious Research Center.

Gallup, G. H., Jr., & Poling, D. (1980). *The search for America's faith.* New York: Abington.

Galotti, K. M., Komatsu, L. K., & Voelz, S. (1997). Children's differential performance on deductive and inductive syllogisms. *Developmental Psychology, 33,* 70–78.

Gambrell, L. B., & Bales, R. J. (1986). Mental imagery and the comprehension-monitoring performance of fourth- and fifth-grade poor readers. *Reading Research Quarterly, 21,* 454–464.

Garbarino, J. (1981). *Successful schools and competent students.* Lexington, MA: Lexington Books.

Garbarino, J. (1995). The American war zone: What children can tell us about living with violence. *Developmental and Behavioral Pediatrics, 16,* 431–435.

Garbarino, J., & Abramowitz, R. H. (1992a). The family as a social system. In J. Garbarino (Ed.), *Children and families in the social environment* (pp. 72–98). New York: Aldine de Gruyter.

Garbarino, J., & Abramowitz, R. H. (1992b). Sociocultural risk and opportunity. In J. Garbarino (Ed.), *Children and families in the social environment* (pp. 35–70). New York: Aldine de Gruyter.

Garbarino, J., & Abramowitz, R. H. (1992c). The ecology of human development. In J. Garbarino (Ed.), *Children and families in the social environment* (pp. 11–33). New York: Aldine de Gruyter.

Garbarino, J., & Bronfenbrenner, U. (1976). The socialization of moral judgment and behavior in cross-cultural perspective. In T. Lickona (Ed.), *Moral development and behavior.* New York: Holt, Rinehart & Winston.

Garbarino, J., Kostelny, K., & Dubrow, N. (1991a). What children can tell us about living in danger. *American Psychologist, 46*(4), 376–383.

Garbarino, J., Kostelny, K., & Dubrow, N. (1991b). *No place to be a child: Growing up in a war zone.* Lexington, MA: Lexington Books.

García, E. E. (1992). "Hispanic" children: Theoretical, empirical, and related policy issues. *Educational Psychology Review, 4,* 69–93.

García, E. E. (1994). *Understanding and meeting the challenge of student cultural diversity.* Boston: Houghton Mifflin.

García, E. E. (1995). Educating Mexican American students: Past treatment and recent developments in theory, research, policy, and practice. In J. A. Banks & C. A. M. Banks (Eds.), *Handbook of research on multicultural education.* New York: Macmillan.

García, G. E., Jiménez, R. T., & Pearson, P. D. (1998). Metacognition, childhood bilingualism, and reading. In D. J. Hacker, J. Dunlosky, & A. C. Graesser (Eds.), *Metacognition in educational theory and practice.* Mahwah, NJ: Erlbaum.

Gardner, H. (1983). *Frames of mind: The theory of multiple intelligences.* New York: Basic Books.

Gardner, H. (1993). *Multiple intelligences: The theory in practice.* New York: Basic Books.

Gardner, H. (1995). Reflections on multiple intelligences: Myths and messages. *Phi Delta Kappan, 77,* 200–209.

Gardner, H. (1999). *Intelligence reframed: Multiple intelligences for the 21st century.* New York: Basic Books.

Gardner, H. (2000). *The disciplined mind: Beyond facts and standardized tests, the K–12 education that every child deserves.* New York: Penguin Books.

Gardner, H., & Hatch, T. (1990). Multiple intelligences go to school: Educational implications of the theory of multiple intelligences. *Educational Researcher, 18*(8), 4–10.

Gardner, H., Torff, B., & Hatch, T. (1996). The age of innocence reconsidered: Preserving the best of the progressive traditions in psychology and education. In D. R. Olson & N. Torrance (Eds.), *The handbook of education and human development: New models of learning, teaching and schooling* (pp. 28–55). Cambridge, MA: Blackwell.

Garibaldi, A. M. (1992). Educating and motivating African American males to succeed. *The Journal of Negro Education, 61*(1), 4–11.

Garner, R. (1987). Strategies for reading and studying expository texts. *Educational Psychologist, 22,* 299–312.

Garner, R. (1998). Epilogue: Choosing to learn or not-learn in school. *Educational Psychology Review, 10,* 227–237.

Garnier, H. E., Stein, J. A., & Jacobs, J. K. (1997). The process of dropping out of high school: A 19-year perspective. *American Educational Research Journal, 34,* 395–419.

Garrison, L. (1989). Programming for the gifted American Indian student. In C. J. Maker & S. W. Schiever (Eds.), *Critical issues in gifted education: Vol. 2. Defensible programs for cultural and ethnic minorities.* Austin, TX: Pro-Ed.

Garvey, C. (1974). Some properties of social play. *Merrill-Palmer Quarterly, 20,* 163–180.

Garvey, C. (1990). *Play.* Cambridge, MA: Harvard University Press.

Garvey, C., & Berninger, G. (1981). Timing and turn taking in children's conversations. *Discourse Processes, 4,* 27–59.

Garvey, C., & Horgan, R. (1973). Social speech and social interaction: Egocentrism revisited. *Child Development, 44,* 562–568.

Gathercole, S. E., & Hitch, G. J. (1993). Developmental changes in short-term memory: A revised working memory perspective. In A. F. Collins, S. E. Gathercole, M. A. Conway, & P. E. Morris (Eds.), *Theories of memory.* Hove, England: Erlbaum.

Gauvain, M. (1992). Social influences on the development of planning in advance and during action. *International Journal of Behavioral Development, 15,* 377–398.

Gauvain, M. (1999). Everyday opportunities for the development of planning skills: Sociocultural and family influences. In A. Göncü (Ed.), *Children's engagement in the world: Sociocultural perspectives* (pp. 173–201). Cambridge, England: Cambridge University Press.

Gauvain, M. (2001). *The social context of cognitive development.* New York: Guilford Press.

Gavin, L. A., & Fuhrman, W. (1989). Age differences in adolescents' perceptions of their peer groups. *Developmental Psychology, 25,* 827–834.

Gay, G. (1993). Building cultural bridges: A bold proposal for teacher education. *Education and Urban Society, 25*(3), 285–299.

Gelman, R. (1972). Logical capacity of very young children: Number invariance rules. *Child Development, 43,* 75–90.

Gelman, R., & Baillargeon, R. (1983). A review of some Piagetian concepts. In J. H. Flavell & E. M. Markman (Eds.), *Handbook of child psychology: Vol. 3. Cognitive development.* New York: Wiley.

Gelman, S. A., & Taylor, M. (1984). How two-year-old children interpret proper and common names for unfamiliar objects. *Child Development, 55,* 1535–1540.

Genesee, F. (1985). Second language learning through immersion: A review of U.S. programs. *Review of Educational Research, 55,* 541–561.

Genova, W. J., & Walberg, H. J. (1984). Enhancing integration in urban high schools. In D. E. Bartz & M. L. Maehr (Eds.), *Advances in motivation and achievement: Vol. 1. The effects of school desegregation on motivation and achievement.* Greenwich, CT: JAI Press.

Gentry, R. (1982). An analysis of the developmental spellings in *Gnys at Wrk. The Reading Teacher, 36,* 192–200.

Gephart, M. (1997). Neighborhoods and communities as contexts for development. In J. Brooks-Gunn, G. J. Duncan, & J. L. Aber (Eds.), *Neighborhood poverty: Context and consequences for children* (Vol. 1, pp. 1–43). New York: Russell Sage Foundation Press.

Gerber, M. (1998). *Dear parent: Caring for infants with respect.* Los Angeles: Resources for Infant Educators.

Gerken, L. (1994). Child phonology: Past research, present questions, future directions. In M. A. Gernsbacher (Ed.), *Handbook of psycholinguistics* (pp. 781–820). San Diego, CA: Academic Press.

Gershoff, E. T. (2002). Corporal punishment by parents and associated child behaviors and experiences: A meta-analytic and theoretical review. *Psychological Bulletin, 128*(4), 539–579.

Gesell, A. (1923). *The preschool child.* New York: Houghton Mifflin.

Gesell, A. (1928). *Infancy and human growth.* New York: Macmillan.

Gesell, A. (1929). The guidance nursery of the Yale Psycho-Clinic. In *Twenty-eighth yearbook of the National Society for the Study of Education.* Chicago: University of Chicago Press.

Ghodsian-Carpey, J., & Baker, L. A. (1987). Genetic and environmental influences on aggression in 4- to 7-year-old twins. *Aggressive Behavior, 13,* 173–186.

Gibbs, J. C. (1995). The cognitive developmental perspective. In W. M. Kurtines & J. L. Gewirtz (Eds.), *Moral development: An introduction.* Boston: Allyn & Bacon.

Gibbs, J. T. (1985). City girls: Psychosocial adjustment of urban black adolescent females. *Sage, 2*(2), 28–36.

Gibson, E. J., & Walk, R. D. (1960). The "visual cliff." *Scientific American, 202*(4), 64–71.

Gibson, J. J., (1979). *The ecological approach to visual perception.* Boston: Houghton-Mifflin.

Giedd, J. N., Blumenthal, J., Jeffries, N. O., Castellanos, F. X., Liu, H., Zijdenbos, A., Paus, T., Evans, A. C., & Rapoport, J. L. (1999). Brain development during childhood and adolescence: A longitudinal MRI study. *Nature Neuroscience, 2,* 861–863.

Giedd, J. N., Blumenthal, J., Jeffries, N. O., Rajapakse, J. C., Vaituzis, A. C., Liu, H., Berry, Y. C., Tobin, M., Nelson, J., & Castellanos, F. X. (1999). Development of the human corpus callosum during childhood and adolescence: A longitudinal MRI study. *Progress in Neuro-Psychopharmacology and Biological Psychiatry, 23,* 571–588.

Giedd, J. N., Jeffries, N. O., Blumenthal, J., Castellanos, F. X., Vaituzis, A. C., Fernandez, T., Hamburger, S. D., Liu, H., Nelson, J., Bedwell, J., Tran, L., Lenane, M., Nicolson, R., & Rapoport, J. L. (1999). Childhood-onset schizophrenia: Progressive brain changes during adolescence. *Biological Psychiatry, 46,* 892–898.

Gilbert, M. J., & Cervantes, R. (1986). Patterns and practices of alcohol use among Mexican Americans: A comprehensive review. *Hispanic Journal of Behavioral Sciences, 8,* 1–60.

Gillam, R. B., & Johnston, J. R. (1992). Spoken and written language relationships in language/learning-impaired and normal achieving school-age children. *Journal of Speech and Hearing Research, 35,* 1303–1315.

Gillberg, I. C., & Coleman, M. (1996). Autism and medical disorders: A review of the literature.

Developmental Medicine and Child Neurology, 38, 191–202.

Gillham, J. E., Reivich, K. J., Jaycox, L. H., & Seligman, M. E. P. (1995). Prevention of depressive symptoms in schoolchildren: Two-year follow-up. *Psychological Science, 6,* 343–351.

Gilligan, C. (1977). In a different voice: Women's conceptions of self and of morality. *Harvard Educational Review, 47,* 481–517.

Gilligan, C. (1982). *In a different voice: Psychological theory and women's development.* Cambridge, MA: Harvard University Press.

Gilligan, C. F. (1985, March). Keynote address. Conference on Women and Moral Theory, Stony Brook, NY.

Gilligan, C. F. (1987). Moral orientation and moral development. In E. F. Kittay & D. T. Meyers (Eds.), *Women and moral theory.* Totowa, NJ: Rowman & Littlefield.

Gilligan, C. F., & Attanucci, J. (1988). Two moral orientations. In C. F. Gilligan, J. V. Ward, & J. M. Taylor (Eds.), *Mapping the moral domain: A contribution of women's thinking to psychological theory and education.* Cambridge, MA: Center for the Study of Gender, Education, and Human Development (distributed by Harvard University Press).

Gilliland, H. (1988). Discovering and emphasizing the positive aspects of the culture. In H. Gilliland & J. Reyhner (Eds.), *Teaching the native American.* Dubuque, IA: Kendall/Hunt.

Gillis, J. J., Gilger, J. W., Pennington, B. F., & DeFries, J. C. (1992). Attention deficit disorder in reading-disabled twins: Evidence for a genetic etiology. *Journal of Abnormal Child Psychology, 20,* 303–315.

Ginsburg, D., Gottman, J. M., & Parker, J. G. (1986). The importance of friendship. In J. M. Gottman & J. G. Parker (Eds.), *Conversations of friends: Speculations on affective development* (pp. 3–48). Cambridge, England: Cambridge University Press.

Ginsburg, G. P., & Kilbourne, B. K. (1988). Emergence of vocal alternation in mother-infant interchanges. *Journal of Child Language, 15,* 221–235.

Ginsburg, M. B., & Newman, M. K. (1985). Social inequalities, schooling, and teacher education. *Journal of Teacher Education, 36*(2), 49–54.

Giordano, P. C., Cernkovich, S. A., & DeMaris, A. (1993). The family and peer relations of black adolescents. *Journal of Marriage and the Family, 55,* 277–287.

Gladwell, M. (1997, Feb. 24 and Mar. 3). Crime and science: Damaged. *The New Yorker.*

Glick, J. (1975). Cognitive development in cross-cultural perspective. In F. Horowitz (Ed.), *Review of child development research* (Vol. 4). Chicago: University of Chicago Press.

Glucksberg, S., & Krauss, R. M. (1967). What do people say after they have learned to talk? Studies of the development of referential communication. *Merrill-Palmer Quarterly, 13,* 309–316.

Glynn, S. M., Yeany, R. H., & Britton, B. K. (1991). A constructive view of learning science. In S. M. Glynn, R. H. Yeany, & B. K. Britton (Eds.), *The psychology of learning science.* Hillsdale, NJ: Erlbaum.

Gnepp, J. (1989). Children's use of personal information to understand other people's feelings. In C. Saarni & P. L. Harris (Eds.), *Children's understanding of emotion.* Cambridge, England: Cambridge University Press.

Gohm, C. L., Oishi, S., Darlington, J., & Diener, E. (1998). Culture, parental conflict, parental marital status, and the subjective well-being of young adults. *Journal of Marriage & the Family, 60*(2), 319–334.

Goldberg, E., & Costa, L. D. (1981). Hemisphere differences in the acquisition and use of descriptive systems. *Brain and Language, 14,* 144–173.

Goldenberg, C. (1992). The limits of expectations: A case for case knowledge about teacher expectancy effects. *American Educational Research Journal, 29,* 517–544.

Goldin-Meadow, S. (1997). When gestures and words speak differently. *Current Directions in Psychological Science, 6,* 138–143.

Goldin-Meadow, S. (2001). Giving the mind a hand: The role of gesture in cognitive change. In J. L. McClelland & R. S. Siegler (Eds.), *Mechanisms of cognitive development: Behavioral and neural perspectives* (pp. 5–31). Mahwah, NJ: Erlbaum.

Goldin-Meadow, S., & Mylander, C. (1993). Beyond the input given: The child's role in the acquisition of language. In P. Bloom (Ed.), *Language acquisition: Core readings.* Cambridge, MA: MIT Press.

Goldin-Meadow, S., Nusbaum, H., Kelly, S. D., & Wagner, S. (2001). Explaining math: Gesturing lightens the load. *Psychological Science, 12,* 516–522.

Goldsmith, H. H., & Gottesman, I. I. (1996). Heritable variability and variable heritability in developmental psychopathology. In M. F. Lenzenweger & J. J. Haugaard (Eds.), *Frontiers of developmental psychopathology* (pp. 5–43). New York: Oxford University Press.

Goldsmith-Phillips, J. (1989). Word and context in reading development: A test of the interactive-compensatory hypothesis. *Journal of Educational Psychology, 81,* 299–305.

Goleman, D. (1995). *Emotional intelligence.* New York: Bantam Books.

Golinkoff, R. M., Hirsh-Pasek, K., Bailey, L., & Wenger, N. (1992). Young children and adults use lexical principles to learn new nouns. *Developmental Psychology, 28,* 99–108.

Golinkoff, R. M., Hirsh-Pasek, K., Mervis, C. B., Frawley, W. B., & Parillo, M. (1995). Lexical principles can be extended to the acquisition of verbs. In M. Tomasello & W. E. Merriman (Eds.), *Beyond names for things: Young children's acquisition of verbs.* Hillsdale, NJ: Erlbaum.

Gollnick, D. M., & Chinn, P. C. (2002). *Multicultural education in a pluralistic society* (6th ed.). Upper Saddle River, NJ: Merrill/Prentice Hall.

Golombok, S., & Tasker, F. (1996). Do parents influence the sexual orientation of their children? Findings from a longitudinal study of lesbian families. *Developmental Psychology, 32,* 3–11.

Gomby, D. S., Culross, P. L., & Behrman, R. E. (1999). Home visiting: Recent program evaluations—Analysis and recommendations. *The Future of Children. Home Visiting: Recent Program Evaluations, 9*(1), 4–26.

Göncü, A. (1993). Development of intersubjectivity in the dyadic play of preschoolers. *Early Childhood Research Quarterly, 8,* 99–116.

Gonzalez-Mena, J. (2002). *The child in the family and the community* (3rd ed.). Upper Saddle River, NJ: Merrill/Prentice Hall.

Gonzales-Mena, J., & Widmeyer Eyer, D. (2001). *Infants, toddlers, and caregivers* (5th ed.). Mountain View, CA: Mayfield Publishing Company.

Good, T. L., & Brophy, J. E. (1994). *Looking in classrooms* (6th ed.). New York: Harper Collins.

Good, T. L., McCaslin, M. M., & Reys, B. J. (1992). Investigating work groups to promote problem solving in mathematics. In J. Brophy (Ed.), *Advances in research on teaching: Vol. 3. Planning and managing learning tasks and activities.* Greenwich, CT: JAI Press.

Good, T. L., & Nichols, S. L. (2001). Expectancy effects in the classroom: A special focus on improving the reading performance of minority students in first-grade classrooms. *Educational Psychologist, 36,* 113–126.

Goodenow, C. (1993). Classroom belonging among early adolescent students: Relationships to motivation and achievement. *Journal of Early Adolescence, 13*(1), 21–43.

Goodman, K. S. (1989). Whole-language research: Foundations and development. *Elementary School Journal, 90,* 207–221.

Goodman, K. S., & Goodman, Y. M. (1979). Learning to read is natural. In L. B. Resnick & P. A Weaver (Eds.), *Theory and practice of early reading* (Vol. 1). Hillsdale, NJ: Erlbaum.

Goodman, Y. M., & Goodman, K. S. (1990). Vygotsky in a whole-language perspective. In L. C. Moll (Ed.), *Vygotsky and education: Instructional implications and applications of sociohistorical psychology.* Cambridge, England: Cambridge University Press.

Goodnow, J. J., & Collins, W. A. (1990). *Development according to parents: The nature, sources, and consequences of parents' ideas.* East Sussex, England: Erlbaum.

Goodson, P., Evans, A., & Edmundson, E. (1997). Female adolescents and onset of sexual intercourse: A theory-based review of research from 1984 to 1994. *Journal of Adolescent Health, 21,* 147–156.

Gopnik, A., & Astington, J. W. (1988). Children's understanding of representational change and its relation to the understanding of false belief and the appearance-reality distinction. *Child Development, 59,* 26–37.

Gopnik, A., & Meltzoff, A. N. (1997). *Words, thoughts, and theories.* Cambridge, MA: MIT Press.

Gopnik, M. (Ed.). (1997). *The inheritance and innateness of grammars.* New York: Oxford University Press.

Gortmaker, S. L., Dietz, W. H., Sobol, A. M., & Wehler, C. A. (1987). Increasing pediatric obesity in the United States. *American Journal of Diseases of Children, 141,* 535–540.

Goswami, U. (1998). Rime-based coding in early reading development in English: Orthographic analogies and rime neighborhoods. In C. Hulme & R. M. Joshi (Eds.), *Reading and spelling: Development and disorders.* Mahwah, NJ: Erlbaum.

Goswami, U. (1999). The relationship between phonological awareness and orthographic representation in different orthographies. In M. Harris & G. Hatano (Eds.), *Learning to read and write: A cross-linguistic perspective.* Cambridge, England: Cambridge University Press.

Gottfredson, L. S. (1981). Circumscription and compromise: A developmental theory of occupational aspirations. *Journal of Counseling Psychology Monograph, 28,* 545–579.

Gottfried, A. E. (1990). Academic intrinsic motivation in young elementary school children. *Journal of Educational Psychology, 82,* 525–538.

Gottfried, A. E., Fleming, J. S., & Gottfried, A. W. (1994). Role of parental motivational practices in children's academic intrinsic motivation and achievement. *Journal of Educational Psychology, 86,* 104–113.

Gottfried, A. W., Gottfried, A. E., Bathurst, K., & Guerin, D. W. (1994). *Gifted IQ: Early developmental aspects.* New York: Plenum Press.

Gottlieb, D. (1964). Teaching and students: The views of Negros and white teachers. *Sociology of Education, 37,* 345–353.

Gottlieb, G. (1991). Experiential canalization of behavioral development: Theory. *Developmental Psychology, 27,* 4–13.

Gottlieb, G. (1992). *Individual development and evolution: The genesis of novel behavior.* New York: Oxford University Press.

Gottman, J. M. (1983). How children become friends. *Monographs of the Society for Research in Child Development, 48*(3, Serial No. 201).

Gottman, J. M. (1986a). The observation of social process. In J. M. Gottman & J. G. Parker (Eds.), *Conversations of friends: Speculations on affective development* (pp. 51–100). Cambridge, England: Cambridge University Press.

Gottman, J. M. (1986b). The world of coordinated play: Same- and cross-sex friendship in young children. In J. M. Gottman & J. G. Parker (Eds.), *Conversations of friends: Speculations on affective development* (pp. 139–191). Cambridge, England: Cambridge University Press.

Gottman, J. M., & Mettetal, G. (1986). Speculations about social and affective development: Friendship and acquaintanceship through adolescence. In J. M. Gottman & J. G. Parker (Eds.), *Conversations of friends: Speculations on affective development* (pp. 192–237). Cambridge, England: Cambridge University Press.

Gough, P. B., & Wren, S. (1998). The decomposition of decoding. In C. Hulme & R. M. Joshi (Eds.), *Reading and spelling: Development and disorders.* Mahwah, NJ: Erlbaum.

Gould, S. J. (1977). *Ontogeny and phylogeny.* Cambridge, MA: Harvard University Press.

Goyen, T. A., Lui, K., & Woods, R. (1998). Visual-motor, visual-perceptual, and fine-motor outcomes in very-low-birthweight children at 5 years. *Developmental Medicine and Child Neurology, 40*(2), 76–81.

Goyette-Ewing, M. (2000). Children's after school arrangements: A study of self-care and developmental outcomes. *Journal of Prevention and Intervention in the Community, 20*(1–2), 55–67.

Graber, J. A., Britto, P. R., & Brooks-Gunn, J. (1999). What's love got to do with it? Adolescents' and young adults' beliefs about sexual and romantic relationships. In W. Furman, B. B. Brown, & C. Feiring (Eds.), *The development of romantic relationships in adolescence* (pp. 364–395). Cambridge, England: Cambridge University Press.

Graesser, A., Golding, J. M., & Long, D. L. (1991). Narrative representation and comprehension. In R. Barr, M. L. Kamil, P. Mosenthal, & P. D. Pearson (Eds.), *Handbook of reading research* (Vol. II). New York: Longman.

Graham, S. (1989). Motivation in Afro-Americans. In G. L. Berry & J. K. Asamen (Eds.), *Black students: Psychosocial issues and academic achievement.* Newbury Park, CA: Sage.

Graham, S. (1990). Communicating low ability in the classroom: Bad things good teachers sometimes do. In S. Graham & V. S. Folkes (Eds.), *Attribution theory: Applications to achievement, mental health, and interpersonal conflict.* Hillsdale, NJ: Erlbaum.

Graham, S. (1991). A review of attribution theory in achievement contexts. *Educational Psychology Review, 3,* 5–39.

Graham, S. (1997). Using attribution theory to understand social and academic motivation in African American youth. *Educational Psychologist, 32,* 21–34.

Graham, S., & Harris, K. R. (1992). Self-regulated strategy development: Programmatic research in writing. In B. Y. L. Wong (Ed.), *Contemporary intervention research in learning disabilities: An international perspective.* New York: Springer-Verlag.

Graham, S., Harris, K. R., & Fink, B. (2000). Is handwriting causally related to learning to write? Treatment of handwriting problems in beginning writers. *Journal of Educational Psychology, 92,* 620–633.

Graham, S., & Hudley, C. (1994). Attributions of aggressive and nonaggressive African-American male early adolescents: A study of construct accessibility. *Developmental Psychology, 30,* 365–373.

Graham, S., Hudley, C., & Williams, E. (1992). Attributional and emotional determinants of aggression among African-American and Latino young adolescents. *Developmental Psychology, 28,* 731–740.

Graham, S., MacArthur, C., & Schwartz, S. (1995). Effects of goal setting and procedural facilitation on the revising behavior and writing performance of students with writing and learning problems. *Journal of Educational Psychology, 87,* 230–240.

Graham, S., Schwartz, S. S., & MacArthur, C. A. (1993). Knowledge of writing and the composing process, attitude toward writing, and self-efficacy for students with and without learning disabilities. *Journal of Learning Disabilities, 26,* 237–249.

Graham, S., Taylor, A. Z., & Hudley, C. (1998). Exploring achievement values among ethnic minority early adolescents. *Journal of Educational Psychology, 90,* 606–620.

Graham, S., & Weiner, B. (1996). Theories and principles of motivation. In D. C. Berliner & R. C. Calfee (Eds.), *Handbook of educational psychology.* New York: Macmillan.

Graham, S., & Weintraub, N. (1996). A review of handwriting research: Progress and prospects from 1980 to 1994. *Educational Psychology Review, 8,* 7–87.

Grandin, T. (1995). *Thinking in pictures and other reports of my life with autism.* New York: Random House.

Granger, R. C. (2002). A problem worth our sustained attention: Creating the conditions linked to successful youth development. In William T. Grant Foundation (Ed.), *The world through the eyes of young people: Report and resource guide.* New York: William T. Grant Foundation.

Grant, C. A., & Gomez, M. L. (2001). *Campus and classroom: Making schooling multicultural* (2nd ed.). Upper Saddle River, NJ: Merrill/Prentice Hall.

Graue, M. E., & Walsh, D. J. (1998). *Studying children in context.* Thousand Oaks, CA: Sage Publications.

Graves, D. (1983). *Writing: Teachers and children at work.* Portsmouth, NH: Heinemann.

Gray, C., & Garaud, J. D. (1993). Social stories: Improving responses of students with autism with accurate social information. *Focus on Autistic Behavior, 8,* 1–10.

Green, J., & Dixon, C. (1996). Language of literacy dialogues: Facing the future or reproducing the past. *Journal of Literacy Research, 28,* 290–301.

Green, L., Fry, A. F., & Myerson, J. (1994). Discounting of delayed rewards: A life-span comparison. *Psychological Science, 5,* 33–36.

Greenberg, D. J., & O'Donnell, W. J. (1972). Infancy and the optimal level of stimulation. *Child Development, 43,* 639–645.

Greenberg, M. T. (1999). Attachment and psychopathology in childhood. In J. Cassidy & P. R. Shaver (Eds.), *Handbook of attachment: Theory, research, and clinical applications* (pp. 469–496). New York: Guilford Press.

Greenberg, M. T., Domitrovich, C., & Bumbarger, B. (2000). *Preventing mental disorders in school-age children: A review of the effectiveness of prevention programs.* University Park, PA: Prevention Research Center for the Promotion of Human Development at Pennsylvania State University.

Greenberg, M. T., Kusche, C. A., Cook, E. T., & Quamma, J. P. (1995). Promoting emotional competence in school-aged children: The effects of the PATHS curriculum. *Development and Psychopathology, 7,* 117–136.

Greenberg, W. H., Levin-Epstein, J., Hutson, R. W., Ooms, T. J., Schumacher, R., Turetsky, V., & Engstrom, D. M. (2002). The 1996 Welfare Law: Key elements and reauthorization issues affecting children. *The Future of Children, 12,* 27–57.

Greene, B. A., & Royer, J. M. (1994). A developmental review of response time data that support a cognitive components model of reading. *Educational Psychology Review, 6,* 141–172.

Greene, S., & Ackerman, J. M. (1995). Expanding the constructivist metaphor: A rhetorical perspective on literacy research and practice. *Review of Educational Research, 65,* 383–420.

Greenfield, P. M. (1994a). Independence and interdependence as developmental scripts: Implications for theory, research, and practice. In P. M. Greenfield & R. R. Cocking (Eds.), *Cross-cultural roots of minority child development.* Hillsdale, NJ: Erlbaum.

Greenfield, P. M. (1994b). Video games as cultural artifacts. *Journal of Applied Developmental Psychology, 15,* 3–11.

Greenfield, P. M. (1998). The cultural evolution of IQ. In U. Neisser (Ed.), *The rising curve: Long-term gains in IQ and related measures* (pp. 81–123). Washington, DC: American Psychological Association.

Greenhoot, A. F., Ornstein, P. A., Gordon, B. N., & Baker-Ward, L. (1999). Acting out the details of a pediatric check-up: The impact of interview condition and behavioral style on children's memory reports. *Child Development, 70,* 363–380.

Greenman, J., & Stonehouse, A. (1996). *Prime times: A handbook for excellence in infant and toddler care.* St. Paul, MN: Redleaf Press.

Greeno, J. G. (1997). On claims that answer the wrong questions. *Educational Researcher, 26*(1), 5–17.

Greenough, W. T., & Black, J. E. (1992). Induction of brain structure by experience: Substrates for cognitive development. In M. R. Gunnar & C. A. Nelson (Eds.), *Developmental behavioral neuroscience. The Minnesota Symposium on Child Psychology* (Vol. 24, pp. 155–200). Mahwah, NJ: Erlbaum.

Greenough, W. T., Black, J. E., & Wallace, C. S. (1987). Experience and brain development. *Child Development, 58,* 539–559.

Greenspan, S., & Granfield, J. M. (1992). Reconsidering the construct of mental retardation: Implications of a model of social competence. *American Journal of Mental Retardation, 96,* 442–453.

Greenspan S. I., & Meisels, S. (1996). Toward a new vision for the developmental assessment of infants and young children. In S. J. Meisels and E. Fenichel (Eds.), *New visions for the developmental assessment of infants and young children.* Washington, DC: Zero to Three.

Greenwood, C. R., Carta, J. J., & Hall, R. V. (1988). The use of peer tutoring strategies in classroom management and educational instruction. *School Psychology Review, 17,* 258–275.

Gregg, M., & Leinhardt, G. (1994, April). *Constructing geography.* Paper presented at the annual meeting of the American Educational Research Association, New Orleans, LA.

Gresham, F. M., & MacMillan, D. L. (1997). Social competence and affective characteristics of students with mild disabilities. *Review of Educational Research, 67,* 377–415.

Gribov, I. (1992). Creativity and brain hemispheres: Educational implications. *European Journal for High Ability, 3*(1), 6–14.

Grieco, E. M., & Cassidy, R. C. (2001, March). *Overview of race and Hispanic origin.* Census 2000 Brief, C2KBR/01–1. Washington, DC: U.S. Census Bureau.

Griffin, S., Case, R., & Capodilupo, A. (1995). Teaching for understanding: The importance of the central conceptual structures in the elementary mathematics curriculum. In A. McKeough, J. Lupart, & A. Marini (Eds.), *Teaching for transfer: Fostering generalization in learning.* Mahwah, NJ: Erlbaum.

Griffin, S. A., Case, R., & Siegler, R. S. (1994). Rightstart: Providing the central conceptual prerequisites for first formal learning of arithmetic to students at risk for school failure. In K. McGilly (Ed.), *Classroom lessons: Integrating cognitive theory and classroom practice.* Cambridge, MA: MIT Press.

Griffith, P. L. (1991). Phonemic awareness helps first graders invent spellings and third graders remember correct spellings. *Journal of Reading Behavior, 23,* 215–233.

Griswold, K. S., & Pessar, L. F. (2000). Management of bipolar disorder. *American Family Physician, 62,* 1343–1356.

Grodzinsky, G. M., & Diamond, R. (1992). Frontal lobe functioning in boys with attention-deficit hyperactivity disorder. *Developmental Neuropsychology, 8,* 427–445.

Gropper, N., & Froschl, M. (1999, April). *The role of gender in young children's teasing and bullying behavior.* Paper presented at the annual meeting of the American Educational Research Association, Montreal.

Gross, R. T., & Duke, P. M. (1980). The effect of early versus late physical maturation in adolescent behavior. *Pediatric Clinics of North America, 27,* 71–77.

Grossman, H. L. (1994). *Classroom behavior management in a diverse society.* Mountain View, CA: Mayfield.

Grunbaum, J. A., Kann, L., Kinchen, S. A., Williams, B., Ross, J. G., Lowry, R., & Kolbe, L. (2002). Youth risk behavior surveillance: United States, 2001. *Surveillance Summaries, 51 (SS04),* 1–64, Centers for Disease Control and Prevention. Retrieved February 20, 2003, from http://www.cdc.gov/mmwr/preview/mmwrhtml/ ss5104a1.htm

Grusec, J. E., & Goodnow, J. J. (1994). Impact of parental discipline methods on the child's internalization of values: A reconceptualization of current points of view. *Developmental Psychology, 30,* 4–19.

Grusec, J. E., & Redler, E. (1980). Attribution, reinforcement, and altruism. *Developmental Psychology, 16,* 525–534.

Grych, J. H., & Finchman, F. D. (1997). Children's adaptation to divorce: From description to explanation. In S. A. Wolchik & I. N. Sandler (Eds.), *Handbook of children's coping: Linking theory to intervention* (pp. 159–193). New York: Plenum Press.

Guay, F., Boivin, M., & Hodges, E. V. E. (1999). Social comparison processes and academic achievement: The dependence of the development of self-evaluations on friends' performance. *Journal of Educational Psychology, 91,* 564–568.

Guberman, S. R., Rahm, J., & Menk, D. W. (1998). Transforming cultural practices: Illustrations from children's game play. *Anthropology and Education Quarterly, 29,* 419–445.

Guerra, N. G., & Slaby, R. G. (1989). Evaluative factors in social problem solving by aggressive boys. *Journal of Abnormal Child Psychology, 17,* 277–289.

Guerra, N. G., & Slaby, R. G. (1990). Cognitive mediators of aggression in adolescent offenders: 2. Intervention. *Developmental Psychology, 26,* 269–277.

Guerra, N. G., Huesmann, L. R., Tolan, P. H., Van Acker, R., & Eron, L. D. (1995). Stressful events and individual beliefs as correlates of economic disadvantage and aggression among urban children. *Journal of Consulting and Clinical Psychology, 63,* 518–528.

Gulya, M., Rovee-Collier, C., Galluccio, L., & Wilk, A. (1998). Memory processing of a serial list by young infants. *Psychological Science, 9,* 303–307.

Gundy, J. H. (1981). The pediatric physical examination. In R. A. Hoekelman, S. Blatman, S. B. Friedman, N. M. Nelson, & H. M. Seidel (Eds.), *Primary pediatric care.* Washington, DC: C. V. Mosby.

Gustafsson, J., & Undheim, J. O. (1996). Individual differences in cognitive functions. In D. C. Berliner & R. C. Calfee (Eds.), *Handbook of educational psychology.* New York: Macmillan.

Guthrie, B. J., Caldwell, C. H., & Hunter, A. G. (1997). Minority adolescent female health: Strategies for the next millennium. In D. K. Wilson, J. R. Rodrigue & W. C. Taylor (Eds.), *Health-promoting and health-compromising behaviors among minority adolescents* (pp. 153–171). Washington, DC: American Psychological Association.

Guthrie, J. T., Cox, K. E., Anderson, E., Harris, K., Mazzoni, S., & Rach, L. (1998). Principles of integrated instruction for engagement in reading. *Educational Psychology Review, 10,* 177–199.

Guttmacher, S., Lieberman, L., Ward, D., Freudenberg, N., Radosh, A., & DesJarlais, D. (1997). Condom availability in New York City public high schools: Relationships to condom use and sexual behavior. *American Journal of Public Health, 87,* 1427–1433.

Gyurke, J. S. (1991). The assessment of preschool children with the Wechsler Preschool and Primary Scale of Intelligence–Revised. In B. A. Bracken (Ed.), *The psychoeducational assessment of preschool children* (2nd ed., pp. 86–106). Boston: Allyn and Bacon.

Hacker, D. J. (1995, April). *Comprehension monitoring of written discourse across early-to-middle adolescence.* Paper presented at the annual meeting of the American Educational Research Association, San Francisco.

Hacker, D. J., Bol, L., Horgan, D. D., & Rakow, E. A. (2000). Test prediction and performance in a classroom context. *Journal of Educational Psychology, 92,* 160–170.

Haden, C. A., Ornstein, P. A., Eckerman, C. O., & Didow, S. M. (2001). Mother-child conversational interactions as events unfold: Linkages to subsequent remembering. *Child Development, 72,* 1016–1031.

Haenan, J. (1996). Piotr Gal'perin's criticism and extension of Lev Vygotsky's work. *Journal of Russian and East European Psychology, 34*(2), 54–60.

Hagen, J. W., & Stanovich, K. G. (1977). Memory: Strategies of acquisition. In R. V. Kail, Jr. & J. W. Hagen (Eds.), *Perspectives on the development of memory and cognition.* Hillsdale, NJ: Erlbaum.

Hagerman, R. J., & Lampe, M. E. (1999). Fragile X syndrome. In S. Goldstein & C. R. Reynolds (Eds.), *Handbook of neurodevelopmental and genetic disorders* (pp. 298–316). New York: Guilford Press.

Haight, W. L., & Miller, P. J. (1993). *Pretending at home: Early development in a sociocultural context.* Albany, NY: SUNY Press.

Haith, M. M. (1980). *Rules that babies look by: The organization of newborn visual activity.* Hillsdale, NJ: Erlbaum.

Haith, M. M. (1990). Perceptual and sensory processes in early infancy. *Merrill-Palmer Quarterly, 36,* 1–26.

Haith, M. M., Hazan, C., & Goodman, G. S. (1988). Expectation and anticipation of dynamic visual events by 3.5-month-old babies. *Child Development, 59,* 467–479.

Hakes, D. T. (1980). *The development of metalinguistic abilities in children.* Berlin, Germany: Springer-Verlag.

Hakuta, K., & McLaughlin, B. (1996). Bilingualism and second language learning: Seven tensions that define the research. In D. C. Berliner & R. C. Calfee (Eds.), *Handbook of educational psychology.* New York: Macmillan.

Halderman, D. C. (1991). Sexual orientation conversion therapy for gay men and lesbians: A scientific examination. In J. C. Gonsiorek & J. D. Weinrich (Eds.), *Homosexuality: Research implications for public policy* (pp. 149–160). Newbury Park, CA: Sage.

Hale-Benson, J. E. (1986). *Black children: Their roots, culture, and learning styles.* Baltimore: Johns Hopkins University Press.

Halford, G. S. (1989). Cognitive processing capacity and learning ability: An integration of two areas. *Learning and Individual Differences, 1,* 125–153.

Hall, E. R., Esty, E. T., & Fisch, S. M. (1990). Television and children's problem-solving behavior: A synopsis of an evaluation of the effects of Square One TV. *Journal of Mathematical Behavior, 9,* 161–174.

Hall, G. S. (1904). *Adolescence.* New York: Appleton-Century-Crofts.

Hall, R. V., Axelrod, S., Foundopoulos, M., Shellman, J., Campbell, R. A., & Cranston, S. S. (1971). The effective use of punishment to modify behavior in the classroom. *Educational Technology, 11*(4), 24–26.

Hall, W. S. (1989). Reading comprehension. *American Psychologist, 44,* 157–161.

Hallenbeck, M. J. (1996). The cognitive strategy in writing: Welcome relief for adolescents with learning disabilities. *Learning Disabilities Research and Practice, 11,* 107–119.

Hallinan, M. T., & Teixeria, R. A. (1987). Opportunities and constraints: Black-white differences in the formation of interracial friendships. *Child Development, 58,* 1358–1371.

Hallowell, E. (1996). *When you worry about the child you love.* New York: Simon and Schuster.

Halpern, D. F. (1992). *Sex differences in cognitive abilities* (2nd ed.). Hillsdale, NJ: Erlbaum.

Halpern, D. F. (1997). Sex differences in intelligence: Implications for education. *American Psychologist, 52,* 1091–1102.

Halpern, D. F., & LaMay, M. L. (2000). The smarter sex: A critical review of sex differences in intelligence. *Educational Psychology Review, 12,* 229–246.

Hamburg, D. A. (1992). *Children of urban poverty: Approaches to a critical American problem* (Report of the President, 1992). New York: Carnegie Corporation.

Hamers, J. H. M., & Ruijssenaars, A. J. J. M. (1997). Assessing classroom learning potential. In G. D. Phye (Ed.), *Handbook of academic learning: Construction of knowledge.* San Diego, CA: Academic Press.

Hamill, P. V., Drizd, T. A., Johnson, C. L., Reed, R. B., Roche, A. F., & Moore, W. M. (1979). Physical growth: National Center for Health Statistics percentiles. *American Journal of Clinical Nutrition, 32,* 607–629.

Hammer, D. (1994). Epistemological beliefs in introductory physics. *Cognition and Instruction, 12,* 151–183.

Hanley, J. R., Tzeng, O., & Huang, H.-S. (1999). Learning to read Chinese. In M. Harris & G. Hatano (Eds.), *Learning to read and write: A cross-linguistic perspective.* Cambridge, England: Cambridge University Press.

Hannan, A., & Charlton, T. (1999). Leisure activities of middle-school pupils of St Helena before and after the introduction of television. *Research Papers in Education, 14*(3), 257–274.

Hare, J. (1994). Concerns and issues faced by families headed by a lesbian couple. *Families in Society, 43,* 27–35.

Harlow, H. F. (1959). Love in infant monkeys. *Scientific American, 200,* 68–74.

Harlow, H. F., & Harlow, M. K. (1962). Social deprivation in monkeys. *Scientific American, 207,* 137–146.

Harms, T., & Clifford, R. M. (1980). *The early childhood environment rating scale.* New York: Teachers College Press.

Harris, C. R. (1991). Identifying and serving the gifted new immigrants. *Teaching Exceptional Children, 23*(4), 26–30.

Harris, J. R. (1995). Where is the child's environment? A group socialization theory of development. *Psychological Review, 102,* 458–489.

Harris, J. R. (1998). *The nurture assumption: Why children turn out the way they do.* New York: Free Press.

Harris, K. R. (1986). Self-monitoring of attentional behavior versus self-monitoring of productivity: Effects of on-task behavior and academic response rate among learning disabled children. *Journal of Applied Behavior Analysis, 19,* 417–423.

Harris, K. R., & Graham, S. (1992). Self-regulated strategy development: A part of the writing process. In M. Pressley, K. R. Harris, & J. T. Guthrie (Eds.), *Promoting academic competence and literacy in school.* San Diego, CA: Academic Press.

Harris, M. (1992). *Language experience and early language development: From input to uptake.* Hove, England: Erlbaum.

Harris, M., & Giannouli, V. (1999). Learning to read and spell in Greek: The importance of letter knowledge and morphological awareness. In M. Harris & G. Hatano (Eds.). *Learning to read and write: A cross-linguistic perspective.* Cambridge, England: Cambridge University Press.

Harris, M., & Hatano, G. (Eds.). (1999). *Learning to read and write: A cross-linguistic perspective.* Cambridge, England: Cambridge University Press.

Harris, M. B. (1997). Preface: Images of the invisible minority. In M. B. Harris (Ed.), *School experiences of gay and lesbian youth: The invisible minority* (pp. xiv–xxii). Binghamton, NY: Harrington Park Press.

Harris, M. J., & Rosenthal, R. (1985). Mediation of interpersonal expectancy effects: 31 meta-analyses. *Psychological Bulletin, 97,* 363–386.

Harris, N. G. S., Bellugi, U., Bates, E., Jones, W., & Rossen, M. (1997). Contrasting profiles of language development in children with Williams and Down syndromes. *Developmental Neuro-psychology, 13,* 345–370.

Harris, P. L. (1989). *Children and emotion: The development of psychological understanding.* Oxford, England: Basil Blackwell.

Harrison, A. O., Wilson, M. N., Pine, C. J., Chan, S. Q., & Buriel, R. (1990). Family ecologies of ethnic minority children. *Child Development, 61,* 347–362.

Hart, B., & Risley, T. R. (1995). *Meaningful differences in the everyday experiences of young American children.* Baltimore: Brookes.

Hart, C. H., Ladd, G. W., & Burleson, B. (1990). Children's expectations of the outcomes of social strategies: Relations with sociometric status and maternal disciplinary styles. *Child Development, 61,* 127–137.

Hart, D. (1988). The adolescent self-concept in social context. In D. K. Lapsley & F. C. Power (Eds.), *Self, ego, and identity: Integrative approaches* (pp. 71–90). New York: Springer-Verlag.

Hart, D., & Damon, W. (1986). Developmental trends in self-understanding. *Social Cognition, 4*(4), 388–407.

Hart, D., & Fegley, S. (1995). Prosocial behavior and caring in adolescence: Relations to self-understanding and social judgment. *Child Development, 66,* 1346–1359.

Hart, E. L., Lahey, B. B., Loeber, R., Applegate, B., & Frick, P. J. (1995). Developmental changes in attention-deficit hyperactivity disorder in boys: A four-year longitudinal study. *Journal of Abnormal Child Psychology, 23,* 729–750.

Harter, S. (1975). Mastery motivation and the need for approval in older children and their relationship to social desirability response tendencies. *Developmental Psychology, 11,* 186–196.

Harter, S. (1983a). Children's understanding of multiple emotions: A cognitive-developmental approach. In W. F. Overton (Ed.), *The relationship between social and cognitive development.* Hillsdale, NJ: Erlbaum.

Harter, S. (1983b). Developmental perspectives on the self-system. In P. M. Mussen (Series Ed.) & E. M. Hetherington (Vol. Ed.), *Handbook of child psychology: Vol. 4: Socialization, personality, and social development* (4th ed., pp. 275–385). New York: Wiley.

Harter, S. (1988). The construction and conservation of the self: James and Cooley revisited. In D. K. Lapsley & F. C. Power (Eds.), *Self, ego, and identity: Integrative approaches* (pp. 43–69). New York: Springer-Verlag.

Harter, S. (1990a). Causes, correlates, and the functional role of global self-worth: A life-span perspective. In R. J. Sternberg & J. Kolligian, Jr. (Eds.), *Competence considered.* New Haven, CT: Yale University Press.

Harter, S. (1990b). Processes underlying adolescent self-concept formation. In R. Montemayor, G. R. Adams, & T. P. Gullotta (Eds.), *From childhood to adolescence: A transitional period?* Newbury Park, CA: Sage.

Harter, S. (1992). The relationship between perceived competence, affect, and motivational orientation within the classroom: Processes and patterns of change. In A. K. Boggiano & T. S. Pittman (Eds.), *Achievement and motivation: A social-developmental perspective.* Cambridge, England: Cambridge University Press.

Harter, S. (1996). Teacher and classmate influences on scholastic motivation, self-esteem, and level of voice in adolescents. In J. Juvonen & K. Wentzel (Eds.), *Social motivation: Understanding children's school adjustment.* New York: Cambridge University Press.

Harter, S. (1998). The development of self-representations. In W. Damon (Editor-in-Chief) & N. Eisenberg (Vol. Ed.), *Handbook of child psychology: Vol. 3. Social, emotional, and personality development* (5th ed., pp. 553–617). New York: Wiley.

Harter, S. (1999). *The construction of the self.* New York: Guilford Press.

Harter, S., Bresnick, S., Bouchey, H., & Whitesell, N. R. (1997). The development of multiple role-related selves during adolescence. *Development and Psychopathology, 9,* 835–853.

Harter, S., & Monsour, A. (1992). Developmental analysis of conflict caused by opposing attributes in the adolescent self-portrait. *Developmental Psychology, 28*(2), 251–260.

Harter, S., Stocker, C., & Robinson, N. S. (1996). The perceived directionality of the link between approval and self-worth: The liabilities of a looking glad self-orientation among young adolescents. *Journal of Research on Adolescence, 6,* 285–308.

Harter, S., Waters, P. L., & Whitesell, N. R. (1997). Lack of voice as a manifestation of false self-behavior among adolescents: The school setting as a stage upon which the drama of authenticity is enacted. *Educational Psychologist, 32,* 153–173.

Harter, S., Waters, P. L., Whitesell, N. R., & Kastelic, D. (1998). Level of voice among female and male high school students: Relational context, support, and gender orientation. *Developmental Psychology, 34,* 892–901.

Harter, S., & Whitesell, N. R. (1989). Developmental changes in children's understanding of single, multiple, and blended emotion concepts. In C. Saarni & P. Harris (Eds.), *Children's understanding of emotion* (pp. 81–116). Cambridge, England: Cambridge University Press.

Harter, S., Whitesell, N. R., & Junkin, L. J. (1998). Similarities and differences in domain-specific and global self-evaluations of learning-disabled, behaviorally disordered, and normally achieving adolescents. *American Educational Research Journal, 35,* 653–680.

Hartmann, D. P., & George, T. P. (1999). Design, measurement, and analysis in developmental research. In M. H. Bornstein & M. E. Lamb (Eds.), *Developmental psychology: An advanced textbook* (4th ed., pp. 125–195). Mahwah, NJ: Erlbaum.

Hartup, W. W. (1974). Aggression in childhood: Developmental perspectives. *American Psychologist, 29,* 336–341.

Hartup, W. W. (1983). Peer relations. In P. H. Mussen (Ed.), *Handbook of child psychology: Vol. IV. Socialization* (4th ed.). New York: Wiley.

Hartup, W. W. (1984). The peer context in middle childhood. In A. Collins (Ed.), *Development during middle childhood: The years from six to twelve.* Washington, DC: National Academy Press.

Hartup, W. W. (1989). Social relationships and their developmental significance. *American Psychologist, 44,* 120–126.

Hartup, W. W. (1992). Friendships and their developmental significance. In H. McGurk (Ed.), *Contemporary issues in childhood social development.* London: Routledge.

Hartup, W. W. (1996). The company they keep: Friendships and their developmental significance. *Child Development, 67,* 1–13.

Hartup, W. W., & Laursen, B. (1991). Relationships as developmental contexts. In R. Cohen & W. A. Siegel (Eds.), *Context and development* (pp. 253–279). Hillsdale, NJ: Erlbaum.

Hartup, W. W., Laursen, B., Stewart, M. I., & Eastenson, A. (1988). Conflict and the friendship relations of young children. *Child Development, 59,* 1590–1600.

Harwood, R. L., Miller, J. G., & Irizarry, N. L. (1995). *Culture and attachment: Perceptions of the child in context.* New York: Guilford Press.

Hatano, G., & Inagaki, K. (1991). Sharing cognition through collective comprehension activity. In L. B. Resnick, J. M. Levine, & S. D. Teasley (Eds.), *Perspectives on socially shared cognition.* Washington, DC: American Psychological Association.

Hatano, G., & Inagaki, K. (1993). Desituating cognition through the construction of conceptual knowledge. In P. Light and G. Butterworth (Eds.), *Context and cognition: Ways of learning and knowing.* Hillsdale, NJ: Erlbaum.

Hatano, G., & Inagaki, K. (1996). Cognitive and cultural factors in the acquisition of intuitive biology. In D. R. Olson & N. Torrance (Eds.), *The handbook of education and human development: New models of learning, teaching, and schooling.* Cambridge, MA: Blackwell.

Hatfield, E., Cacioppo, J. T., & Rapson, R. L. (1994). *Emotional contagion.* Cambridge, England: Cambridge University Press.

Hattie, J., Biggs, J., & Purdie, N. (1996). Effects of learning skills interventions on student learning: A meta-analysis. *Review of Educational Research, 66,* 99–136.

Haviland, J. M., & Lelwica, M. (1987). The induced affect response: 10-week-old infants' responses to three emotional expressions. *Developmental Psychology, 23,* 97–104.

Hawkins, F. P. L. (1997). *Journal with children: The autobiography of a teacher.* Niwot: University Press of Colorado.

Hawkins, R. P. (1989). The nature and potential of therapeutic foster care programs. In R. P. Hawkins and J. Breiling (Eds.), *Therapeutic foster care: Critical issues.* Washington, DC: Child Welfare League of America.

Hay, D. A. (1999). Adolescent twins and secondary schooling. In A. C. Sandbank (Ed.), *Twin and triplet psychology: A professional guide to working with multiples* (pp. 119–142). London: Routledge.

Hay, D. F. (1979). Cooperative interactions and sharing between very young children and their parents. *Developmental Psychology, 15,* 647–653.

Hay, D. F., & Ross, H. S. (1982). The social nature of early conflict. *Child Development, 53,* 105–113.

Hayes, C. D., & Hofferth, S. L. (1987). *Risking the future: Adolescent sexuality, pregnancy, and child-*

bearing (Vol. 2). Washington, DC: National Academy Press.

Hayes, D. P., & Grether, J. (1983). The school year and vacations: When do students learn? *Cornell Journal of Social Relations, 17*(1), 56–71.

Hayne, H., Rovee-Collier, C., & Borza, M. (1991). Infant memory for place information. *Memory and Cognition, 19,* 378–386.

Hayslip, B., Jr. (1994). Stability of intelligence. In R. J. Sternberg (Ed.), *Encyclopedia of human intelligence* (Vol. 2). New York: Macmillan.

Hearold, S. (1986). A synthesis of 1,043 effects of television on social behavior. In G. Comstock (Ed.), *Public communication and behavior* (Vol. 1). New York: Academic Press.

Heath, S. B. (1980). Questioning at home and at school: A comparative study. In G. Spindler (Ed.), *The ethnography of schooling: Educational anthropology in action.* New York: Holt, Rinehart & Winston.

Heath, S. B. (1983). *Ways with words: Language, life, and work in communities and classrooms.* Cambridge, England: Cambridge University Press.

Heath, S. B. (1986). Taking a cross-cultural look at narratives. *Topics in Language Disorders, 7*(1), 84–94.

Heath, S. B. (1989). Oral and literate traditions among black Americans living in poverty. *American Psychologist, 44,* 367–373.

Heath, S. B. (1999). Dimensions of language development: Lessons from older children. In A. S. Masten (Ed.), *Cultural processes in child development: The Minnesota Symposium on Child Psychology* (Vol. 29, pp. 59–75). Mahwah, NJ: Erlbaum.

Heckenhausen, H. (1984). Emergent achievement behavior: Some early developments. In J. Nicholls (Ed.), *Advances in achievement motivation.* Greenwich, CT: JAI Press.

Heckenhausen, H. (1987). Emotional components of action: Their ontogeny as reflected in achievement behavior. In D. Girlitz & J. F. Wohlwill (Eds.), *Curiosity, imagination, and play.* Hillsdale, NJ: Erlbaum.

Hedges, L. V., & Nowell, A. (1995). Sex differences in mental test scores, variability, and numbers of high-scoring individuals. *Science, 269,* 41–45.

Hegarty, M., & Kozhevnikov, M. (1999). Types of visual-spatial representations and mathematical problem solving. *Journal of Educational Psychology, 91,* 684–689.

Hegland, S. M., & Rix, M. K. (1990). Aggression and assertiveness in kindergarten children differing in day care experiences. *Early Childhood Research Quarterly, 5,* 105–116.

Heibeck, T. H., & Markman, E. M. (1987). Word learning in children: An examination of fast mapping. *Child Development, 58,* 1021–1034.

Held, R. (1993). What can rates of development tell us about underlying mechanisms? In C. E. Granrud (Ed.), *Visual perception and cognition in infancy.* Hillsdale, NJ: Erlbaum.

Hellenga, K. (2002). Social space, the final frontier: Adolescents on the Internet. In J. T. Mortimer & R. W. Larson (Eds.), *The changing adolescent experience: Societal trends and the transition to adulthood* (pp. 208–249). Cambridge, England: Cambridge University Press.

Helwig, C. C. (1995). Adolescents' and young adults' conceptions of civil liberties: Freedom of speech and religion. *Child Development, 66,* 152–166.

Helwig, C. C., & Jasiobedzka, U. (2001). The relation between law and morality: Children's reasoning about socially beneficial and unjust laws. *Child Development, 72,* 1382–1393.

Helwig, C. C., Zelazo, P. D., & Wilson, M. (2001). Children's judgments of psychological harm in normal and noncanonical situations. *Child Development, 72,* 66–81.

Hembree, R. (1988). Correlates, causes, effects, and treatment of test anxiety. *Review of Educational Research, 58,* 47–77.

Hemphill, L., & Snow, C. (1996). Language and literacy development: Discontinuities and differences. In D. R. Olson & N. Torrance (Eds.), *The handbook of education and human development: New models of learning, teaching, and schooling.* Cambridge, MA: Blackwell Publishers.

Henderson, N. D. (1982). Human behavior genetics. *Annual Review of Psychology, 33,* 403–440.

Hennessey, B. A. (1995). Social, environmental, and developmental issues and creativity. *Educational Psychology Review, 7,* 163–183.

Henrich, C. C., Brown, J. L., & Aber, J. L. (1999). Evaluating the effectiveness of school-based violence prevention: Developmental approaches. *Social Policy Report, Society for Research in Child Development, 8*(3), 1–17.

Henshaw, S. K. (1997). Teenager abortion and pregnancy statistics by state, 1992. *Family Planning Perspectives, 29,* 115–122.

Herdt, G. H. (1981). *Guardians of the flutes: Idioms of masculinity.* New York: McGraw-Hill.

Hernandez, D. J. (1997). Child development and the social demography of childhood. *Child Development, 68,* 149–169.

Herr, K. (1997). Learning lessons from school: Homophobia, heterosexism, and the construction of failure. In M. B. Harris (Ed.), *School experiences of gay and lesbian youth: The invisible minority* (pp. 51–64). Binghamton, NY: Harrington Park Press.

Herrnstein, R. J., & Murray, C. (1994). *The bell curve: Intelligence and class structure in American life.* New York: Free Press.

Hertel, P. T. (1994). Depression and memory: Are impairments remediable through attentional control? *Current Directions in Psychological Science, 3,* 190–193.

Hess, E. H. (1958). "Imprinting" in animals. *Scientific American, 198*(3), 81–90.

Hess, R. D., Chang, C. M., & McDevitt, T. M. (1987). Cultural variations in family beliefs about children's performance in mathematics. Comparisons among People's Republic of China, Chinese-American, and Caucasian-American families. *Journal of Educational Psychology, 79,* 179–188.

Hess, R. D., & Holloway, S. D. (1984). Family and school as educational institutions. In R. D. Parke, R. N. Emde, H. P. McAdoo, & G. P. Sackett (Eds.), *Review of child development research* (Vol. 7). *The family* (pp. 179–222). Chicago: University of Chicago Press.

Hess, R. D., & McDevitt, T. M. (1989). Family. In E. Barnouw (Ed.), *International encyclopedia of communications.* New York: Oxford University Press.

Hetherington, E. M. (1988). Family relations six years after divorce. In E. M. Hetherington & R. D. Parke (Eds.), *Contemporary readings in child psychology.* New York: McGraw-Hill.

Hetherington, E. M. (1989). Coping with family transitions: Winners, losers, and survivors. *Child Development, 60,* 1–14.

Hetherington, E. M. (1999a). Should we stay together for the sake of the children? In E. M. Hetherington et al. (Eds.), *Coping with divorce, single parenting, and remarriage: A risk and resiliency perspective* (pp. 93–116). Mahwah, NJ: Erlbaum.

Hetherington, E. M. (1999b). Social capital and the development of youth from nondivorced, divorced and remarried families. In C. W. Andrew & L. Brett (Eds.), *The Minnesota Symposia on Child Psychology: Vol. 30. Relationships as developmental contexts* (pp. 177–209). Mahwah, NJ: Erlbaum.

Hetherington, E. M., Bridges, M., & Insabella, G. M. (1998). What matters? What does not? Five perspectives on the association between marital transitions and children's adjustment. *American Psychologist, 53,* 167–184.

Hetherington, E. M., & Clingempeel, W. G. (1992). Coping with marital transitions: A family systems perspective. *Monographs of the Society for Research in Child Development, 57*(2–3, Serial No. 227).

Hetherington, E. M., Cox, M., & Cox, R. (1978). The aftermath of divorce. In J. H. Stevens, Jr., & M. Matthews (Eds.), *Mother-child father-child relationships.* Washington, DC: National Association for the Education of Young Children.

Hetherington, E. M., Henderson, S. H., Reiss, D., Anderson, E. R., Bridges, M., Chan, R. W., Insabella, G. M., Jodl, K. M., Kim, J. E., Mitchell, A. S., O'Connor, T. G., Skaggs, M. J., & Taylor, L. C. (1999). Adolescent siblings in stepfamilies: Family functioning and adolescent adjustment. *Monographs of the Society for Research in Child Development, 64*(4, Serial No. 259).

Hetherington, E. M., & Stanley-Hagan, M. M. (1997). The effects of divorce on fathers and their children. In M. E. Lamb (Ed.), *The role of the father in child development* (pp. 191–211). New York: Wiley.

Hetherington, E. M., & Stanley-Hagan, M. M. (1999). Stepfamilies. In M. E. Lamb (Ed.), *Parenting and child development in "nontraditional" families* (pp. 137–159). Mahwah, NJ: Erlbaum.

Hettinger, H. R., & Knapp, N. F. (2001). Potential, performance, and paradox: A case study of J.P., a verbally gifted, struggling reader. *Journal for the Education of the Gifted, 24,* 248–289.

Heuwinkel, M. K. (1998). *An investigation of preservice teachers' interactive assessment of student understanding in a traditional program and a professional development school.* Unpublished doctoral dissertation, University of Northern Colorado, Greeley.

Heward, W. L. (1996). *Exceptional children: An introduction to special education* (5th ed.). Upper Saddle River, NJ: Merrill/Prentice Hall.

Hiatt, S., Campos, J., & Emde, R. (1979). Facial patterning and infant emotional expression: Happiness, surprise, and fear. *Child Development, 50,* 1020–1035.

Hickey, D. T. (1997). Motivation and contemporary socio-constructivist instructional perspectives. *Educational Psychologist, 32,* 175–193.

Hickey, T. L., & Peduzzi, J. D. (1987). Structure and development of the visual system. In P. Salapatek & L. Cohen (Eds.), *Handbook of infant perception: Vol. 1. From sensation to perception.* New York: Academic Press.

Hicks, L. (1997). Academic motivation and peer relationships—how do they mix in an adolescent world? *Middle School Journal, 28,* 18–22.

Hidalgo, N. M., Siu, S., Bright, J. A., Swap, S. M., & Epstein, J. L. (1995). Research on families, schools, and communities: A multicultural perspective. In J. A. Banks & C. A. M. Banks (Eds.), *Handbook of research on multicultural education.* New York: Macmillan.

Hide, D. W., & Guyer, B. M. (1982). Prevalence of infant colic. *Archives of Disease in Childhood, 57,* 559–560.

Hidi, S., & Anderson, V. (1992). Situational interest and its impact on reading and expository writing. In K. A. Renninger, S. Hidi, & A. Krapp (Eds.), *The role of interest in learning and development.* Hillsdale, NJ: Erlbaum.

Hidi, S., & Harackiewicz, J. M. (2000). Motivating the academically unmotivated: A critical issue for the 21st century. *Review of Educational Research, 70,* 151–179.

Hiebert, E. H., & Fisher, C. W. (1992). The tasks of school literacy: Trends and issues. In J. Brophy (Ed.), *Advances in research on teaching: Vol. 3: Planning and managing learning tasks and activities.* Greenwich, CT: JAI Press.

Hiebert, E. H., & Raphael, T. E. (1996). Psychological perspectives on literacy and extensions to educational practice. In D. C. Berliner & R. C. Calfee (Eds.), *Handbook of educational psychology.* New York: Macmillan.

Hiebert, J., Carpenter, T. P., Fennema, E., Fuson, K. C., Wearne, D., Murray, H., Olivier, A., & Human, P. (1997). *Making sense: Teaching and learning mathematics with understanding.* Portsmouth, NH: Heinemann.

Higgins, A. (1995). Educating for justice and community: Lawrence Kohlberg's vision of moral education. In W. M. Kurtines & J. L. Gewirtz (Eds.), *Moral development: An introduction.* Boston: Allyn & Bacon.

Higgins, A. T., & Turnure, J. E. (1984). Distractibility and concentration of attention in children's development. *Child Development, 55,* 1799–1810.

High, P. C., & Gorski, P. A. (1985). Womb for improvement—A study of preterm development in an intensive care nursery. In A. W. Gottfried & J. L. Gaiter (Eds.), *Infant stress under intensive care* (pp. 131–155). Baltimore, MD: University Park Press.

Hill, J. P., Holmbeck, G. N., Marlow, L., Green, T. M., & Lynch, M. E. (1985). Menarchal status and parent-child relations in families of seventh-grade girls. *Journal of Youth and Adolescence, 14,* 301–316.

Hilliard, A., & Vaughn-Scott, M. (1982). The quest for the minority child. In S. G. Moore & C. R. Cooper (Eds.), *The young child: Reviews of research* (Vol. 3). Washington, DC: National Association for the Education of Young Children.

Hillier, L., Hewitt, K. L., & Morrongiello, B. A. (1992). Infants' perception of illusions in sound localization: Reaching to sounds in the dark. *Journal of Experimental Child Psychology, 53,* 159–179.

Hillocks, G. (1989). Synthesis of research on teaching writing. *Educational Leadership, 44,* 71–82.

Hinde, R. A., Titmus, G., Easton, D., & Tamplin, A. (1985). Incidence of "friendship" and behavior with strong associates versus non-associates in preschoolers. *Child Development, 56,* 234–245.

Hine, P., & Fraser, B. J. (2002, April). *Combining qualitative and quantitative methods in a study of Australian students' transition from elementary to high school.* Paper presented at the annual meeting of the American Educational Research Association, New Orleans, LA.

Hinkley, J. W., McInerney, D. M., & Marsh, H. W. (2001, April). *The multi-faceted structure of school achievement motivation: A case for social goals.* Paper presented at the annual meeting of the American Educational Research Association, Seattle, WA.

Hinshaw, S. P., Zupan, B. A., Simmel, C., Nigg, J. T., & Melnick, S. (1997). Peer status in boys with and without Attention-Deficit Hyperactivity Disorder: Predictions from overt and covert antisocial behavior, social isolation, and authoritative parenting beliefs. *Child Development, 68,* 880–896.

Hirsh-Pasek, K., & Golinkoff, R. M. (1996). *The origins of grammar: Evidence from early language comprehension.* Cambridge, MA: MIT Press.

Hirsh-Pasek, K., Hyson, M., & Rescorla, L. (1990). Academic environments in preschool: Do they pressure or challenge young children? *Early Education and Development, 1*(6), 401–423.

Ho, D. Y. F. (1986). Chinese pattern of socialization: A critical review. In M. H. Bond (Ed.), *The psychology of Chinese people.* Oxford, England: Oxford University Press.

Ho, D. Y. F. (1994). Cognitive socialization in Confucian heritage cultures. In P. M. Greenfield & R. R. Cocking (Eds.), *Cross-cultural roots of minority child development.* Hillsdale, NJ: Erlbaum.

Ho, H.-Z., Hinckley, H. S., Fox, K. R., Brown, J. H., & Dixon, C. N. (2001, April). *Family literacy: Promoting parent support strategies for student success.* Paper presented at the annual meeting of the American Educational Research Association, Seattle, WA.

Hobson, R. P. (1993). *Autism and the development of mind.* London: Erlbaum.

Hodges, E., Malone, J., & Perry, D. (1997). Individual risk and social risk as interacting determinants of victimization in the peer group. *Developmental Psychology, 32,* 1033–1039.

Hodgkinson, H. (1995). What should we call people? Race, class and the census for 2000. *Phi Delta Kappan,* October, 173–179.

Hofer, B. K., & Pintrich, P. R. (1997). The development of epistemological theories: Beliefs about knowledge and knowing and their relation to learning. *Review of Educational Research, 67,* 88–140.

Hoff, E., & Naigles, L. (2002). How children use input to acquire a lexicon. *Child Development, 73,* 418–433.

Hofferth, S. L., & Hayes, C. D. (Eds.). (1987). *Risking the future: Adolescent sexuality, pregnancy, and childbearing,* (Vol. II). Washington, DC: National Academy of Sciences Press.

Hoffman, J. A. (1984). Psychological separation of late adolescents from their parents. *Journal of Counseling Psychology, 31,* 170–178.

Hoffman, L. W. (1988). Cross-cultural differences in childrearing goals. In R. A. LeVine, P. M. Miller, & M. M. West (Eds.), *Parental behavior in diverse societies* (pp. 99–122). San Francisco: Jossey-Bass.

Hoffman, M. L. (1970). Moral development. In P. H. Mussen (Ed.), *Carmichael's manual of child psychology* (Vol. 2). New York: Wiley.

Hoffman, M. L. (1975). Altruistic behavior and the parent-child relationship. *Journal of Personality and Social Psychology, 31,* 937–943.

Hoffman, M. L. (1981). Is altruism part of human nature? *Journal of Personality and Social Psychology, 40,* 121–137.

Hoffman, M. L. (1988). Moral development. In M. H. Bornstein & M. E. Lamb (Eds.), *Developmental psychology: An advanced textbook* (2nd ed.). Hillsdale, NJ: Erlbaum.

Hoffman, M. L. (1991). Empathy, social cognition, and moral action. In W. M. Kurtines & J. L. Gewirtz (Eds.), *Moral behavior and development: Vol. 1. Theory.* Hillsdale, NJ: Erlbaum.

Hoffman, M. L. (1998). Varieties of empathy-based guilt. In J. Bybee (Ed.), *Guilt and children* (pp. 91–112). San Diego, CA: Academic Press.

Hogan, K. (1997, March). *Relating students' personal frameworks for science learning to their cognition in collaborative contexts.* Paper presented at the annual meeting of the American Educational Research Association, Chicago.

Hokoda, A., & Fincham, F. D. (1995). Origins of children's helplessness and mastery achievement patterns in the family. *Journal of Educational Psychology, 87,* 375–385.

Holden, G. W. (1988). Adults' thinking about a child-rearing problem: Effects of experience, parental status, and gender. *Child Development, 59,* 1623–1632.

Holliday, B. G. (1985). Towards a model of teacher-child transactional processes affecting black children's academic achievement. In M. B. Spencer, G. K. Brookins, & W. R. Allen (Eds.), *Beginnings: The social and affective development of black children.* Hillsdale, NJ: Erlbaum.

Hollins, E. R. (1996). *Culture in school learning: Revealing the deep meaning.* Mahwah, NJ: Erlbaum.

Holloway, S. D. (2000). *Contested childhood: Diversity and change in Japanese preschools.* New York: Routledge.

Holloway, S. D., Fuller, B., Rambaud, M. F., & Eggers-Péirola, C. (1997). *Through my own eyes: Single mothers and the cultures of poverty.* Cambridge, MA: Harvard University Press.

Holmes, R. M. (1998). *Fieldwork with children.* Thousand Oaks, CA: Sage Publications.

Holtz, L. T. (1997). *The alphabet book.* London: DK Publishing.

Hom, A., & Battistich, V. (1995, April). *Students' sense of school community as a factor in reducing drug use and delinquency.* Paper presented at the annual meeting of the American Educational Research Association, San Francisco.

Hong, Y., Chiu, C., & Dweck, C. S. (1995). Implicit theories of intelligence: Reconsidering the role of confidence in achievement motivation. In M. H. Kernis (Ed.), *Efficacy, agency, and self-esteem.* New York: Plenum Press.

Hong, Y., Morris, M. W., Chiu, C., & Benet-Mart'nez, V. (2000). Multicultural minds: A dynamic constructivist approach to culture and cognition. *American Psychologist, 55,* 709–720.

Honig, A. S. (2002). *Secure relationships: Nurturing infant/toddler attachment in early care settings.* Washington D.C.: National Association for the Education of Young Children.

Hoover-Dempsey, K. V., & Sandler, H. M. (1997). Why do parents become involved in their children's education? *Review of Educational Research, 67,* 3–42.

Hopkins, B., & Westra, T. (1998). Maternal handling and motor development: An intracultural study. *Genetic, Social and General Psychology Monographs, 14,* 377–420.

Horacek, H., Ramey, C., Campbell, F., Hoffman, K., & Fletcher, R. (1987). Predicting school failure and assessing early intervention with high-risk children. *American Academy of Child and Adolescent Psychiatry, 26,* 758–763.

Horn, J. L., & Noll, J. (1997). Human cognitive capabilities: Gf-Gc theory. In D. P. Flanagan, J. L. Genshaft, & P. L. Harrison (Eds.), *Contemporary intellectual assessment: Theories, tests, and issues* (pp. 53–91). New York: Guilford.

Horowitz, E. (1997). The worlds of Jewish youth in Europe, 1300–1800. In G. Levi & J. C. Schmitt (Eds.), *A history of young people in the west: Vol. 1. Ancient and medieval rites of passage* (C. Naish, Trans.; pp. 83–119). Cambridge, MA: Belknap Press of Harvard University Press.

Hosley, C. A., & Montemayor, R. (1997). Fathers and adolescents. In M. E. Lamb (Ed.), *The role of the father in child development* (3rd ed., pp. 162–178). New York: Wiley.

Hossain, Z., & Roopnarine, J. L. (1994). African American fathers' involvement with infants: Relationship to their functioning style, support, education, and income. *Infant Behavior and Development, 17,* 175–184.

Hossler, D., & Stage, F. K. (1992). Family and high school experience influences on the postsecondary educational plans of ninth-grade students. *American Educational Research Journal, 29,* 425–451.

Howe, D. (1995). Adoption and attachment. *Adoption and Fostering, 19,* 7–15.

Howe, M. L., & Courage, M. L. (1993). On resolving the enigma of infantile amnesia. *Psychological Bulletin, 113,* 305–326.

Howes, C. (1987). Social competence with peers in young children: Developmental sequences. *Developmental Review, 7,* 252–272.

Howes, C. (1988). The peer interactions of young children. *Monographs of the Society for Research in Child Development, 53*(1, Serial No. 217).

Howes, C. (1992). *The collaborative construction of pretend.* Albany: State University of New York Press.

Howes, C. (1999). Attachment relationships in the context of multiple caregivers. In J. Cassidy & P. R. Shaver (Eds.), *Handbook of attachment: Theory, research, and clinical applications* (pp. 671–687). New York: Guilford Press.

Howes, C., & Matheson, C. C. (1992). Sequences in the development of competent play with peers: Social and social-pretend play. *Developmental Psychology, 28,* 961–974.

Howes, C., & Ritchie, S. (1998). Changes in child-teacher relationships in a therapeutic preschool program. *Early Education and Development, 9,* 411–422.

Howes, C., & Segal, J. (1993). Children's relationships with alternative caregivers: The special case of maltreated children removed from their homes. *Journal of Applied Developmental Psychology, 17,* 71–81.

Howes, C., Smith, E., & Galinsky, E. (1995). *The Florida child care quality improvement study.* New York: Families and Work Institute.

Huang, M.-H., & Hauser, R. M. (1998). Trends in Black-White test-score differentials: II. The WORDSUM vocabulary test. In U. Neisser (Ed.), *The rising curve: Long-term gains in IQ and related measures* (pp. 303–332). Washington, DC: American Psychological Association.

Hubel, D., & Wiesel, T. (1965). Binocular interaction in striate cortex of kittens reared with artificial squint. *Journal of Neurophysiology, 28,* 1041–1059.

Hughes, F. P. (1998). Play in special populations. In O. N. Saracho & B. Spodek (Eds.), *Multiple perspectives on play in early childhood education* (pp. 171–193). Albany: State University of New York Press.

Hulme, C., & Joshi, R. M. (Eds.). (1998). *Reading and spelling: Development and disorders.* Mahwah, NJ: Erlbaum.

Humphreys, A. P., & Smith, P. K. (1987). Rough-and-tumble play, friendship, and dominance in school children: Evidence for continuity and change with age. *Child Development, 58,* 201–212.

Humphreys, L. G. (1992). What both critics and users of ability tests need to know. *Psychological Science, 3,* 271–274.

Hunt, D. E. (1981). Teachers' adaptation: "Reading" and "flexing" to students. In B. R. Joyce, C. C. Brown, & L. Peck (Eds.), *Flexibility in teaching: An excursion into the nature of teaching and training* (pp. 59–71). New York: Longman.

Hunt, E. (1997). Nature vs. nurture: The feeling of *vujà dé.* In R. J. Sternberg & E. L. Grigorenko (Eds.), *Intelligence, heredity, and environment* (pp. 531–551). Cambridge, England: Cambridge University Press.

Hunt, E., Streissguth, A. P., Kerr, B., & Olson, H. C. (1995). Mothers' alcohol consumption during pregnancy: Effects on spatial-visual reasoning in 14-year-old children. *Psychological Science, 6,* 339–342.

Hunt, J. M. V. (1969). *The challenge of incompetence and poverty.* Urbana: University of Illinois Press.

Husman, J., & Freeman, B. (1999, April). *The effect of perceptions of instrumentality on intrinsic motivation.* Paper presented at the annual meeting of the American Educational Research Association, Montreal, Canada.

Hussong, A., Chassin, L., & Hicks, R. (1999, April). *The elusive relation between negative affect and adolescent substance use: Does it exist?* Paper presented at the Biennial Meeting of the Society for Research in Child Development, Albuquerque, NM.

Huston, A. C. (1983). Sex typing. In E. M. Hetherington (Ed.), *Handbook of child psychology: Vol.

4. Socialization, personality, and social development* (4th ed., pp. 387–467). New York: Wiley.

Huston, A. C., Donnerstein, E., Fairchild, H., Feshbach, N. D., Katz, P. A., Murray, J. P., Rubenstein, E. A., Wilcox, B. L., & Zuckerman, D. (1992). *Big world, small screen: The role of television in American society.* Lincoln: University of Nebraska Press.

Huston, A. C., & Wright, J. C. (1998). Mass media and children's development. In W. Damon (Editor-in-Chief), I. E. Sigel, & K. A. Renninger (Vol. Eds.), *Handbook of child psychology: Vol. 4. Child psychology in practice* (5th ed., pp. 999–1058). New York: Wiley.

Huston, A. C., Wright, J. C., Marquis, J., & Green, S. B. (1999). How young children spend their time: Television and other activities. *Developmental Psychology, 35*(4), 912–925.

Huttenlocher, J., Newcombe, N., & Vasilyeva, M. (1999). Spatial scaling in young children. *Psychological Science, 10,* 393–398.

Huttenlocher, P. R. (1979). Synaptic density in human frontal cortex: Developmental changes and effects of aging. *Brain Research, 163,* 195–205.

Huttenlocher, P. R. (1990). Morphometric study of human cerebral cortex development. *Neuropsychologia, 28,* 517–527.

Huttenlocher, P. R. (1993). Morphometric study of human cerebral cortex development. In M. H. Johnson (Ed.), *Brain development and cognition: A reader.* Cambridge, MA: Blackwell.

Huttenlocher, P. R. & De Courten, C. (1987). The development of synapses in striate cortex of man. *Human Neurobiology, 6,* 1–9.

Hyson, M. C., Hirsh-Pasek, K., Rescorla, L., Cone, J., & Martell-Boinske, L. (1991). Ingredients of parental "pressure" in early childhood. *Journal of Applied Developmental Psychology, 12*(3), 347–365.

Iannotti, R. J. (1978). Effects of role-taking experiences on role-taking, empathy, altruism, and aggression. *Developmental Psychology, 14,* 119–124.

Igoa, C. (1995). *The inner world of the immigrant child.* Mahwah, NJ: Erlbaum.

Igoe, A. R., & Sullivan, H. (1991, April). *Gender and grade-level differences in student attributes related to school learning and motivation.* Paper presented at the annual meeting of the American Educational Research Association, Chicago.

Inglehart, M., Brown, D. R., & Vida, M. (1994). Competition, achievement, and gender: A stress theoretical analysis. In P. R. Pintrich, D. R. Brown, & C. E. Weinstein (Eds.), *Student motivation, cognition, and learning: Essays in honor of Wilbert J. McKeachie.* Hillsdale, NJ: Erlbaum.

Inglis, A., & Biemiller, A. (1997, March). *Fostering self-direction in mathematics: A cross-age tutoring program that enhances math problem solving.* Paper presented at the annual meeting of the American Educational Research Association, Chicago.

Inhelder, B., & Piaget, J. (1958). *The growth of logical thinking from childhood to adolescence* (A. Parsons & S. Milgram, Trans.). New York: Basic Books.

Interagency Forum on Child and Family Statistics (1999). *America's children: Key national indicators of well-being, 1999.* Washington, DC: U.S. Government Printing Office. Retrieved from the World Wide Web: http://www.ChildStats.gov/ac1999/highlight.asp

Irujo, S. (1988). An introduction to intercultural differences and similarities in nonverbal communication. In J. S. Wurzel (Ed.), *Toward multiculturalism: A reader in multicultural education.* Yarmouth, ME: Intercultural Press.

Irvine, J. (1990). *Black students and school failure: Policies, practices, and prescriptions.* New York: Greenwood Press.

Irwin, C. E., Jr., & Millstein, S. G. (1992). Biopsychosocial correlates of risk-taking behaviors during adolescence: Can the physician intervene? *Journal of Adolescent Health Care, 7*(Suppl. 6), 82S–96S.

Irwin, R. A., & Gross, A. M. (1995). Cognitive tempo, violent video games, and aggressive behavior in young boys. *Journal of Family Violence, 10,* 337–350.

Isabella, R. A., & Belsky, J. (1991). Interactional synchrony and the origins of infant-mother attachment: A replication study. *Child Development, 62,* 373–384.

Isen, A., Daubman, K. A., & Gorgoglione, J. M. (1987). The influence of positive affect on cognitive organization: Implications for education. In R. E. Snow & M. J. Farr (Eds.), *Aptitude, learning and instruction: Vol. 3. Cognitive and affective process analysis.* Hillsdale, NJ: Erlbaum.

Isolauri, E., Sutas, Y., Salo, M. K., Isosonppi, R., & Kaila, M. (1998). Elimination diet in cow's milk allergy: Risk for impaired growth in young children. *Journal of Pediatrics, 132,* 1004–1009.

Jacklin, C. N. (1989). Female and male: Issues of gender. *American Psychologist, 44,* 127–133.

Jackson, D. L., & Ormrod, J. E. (1998). *Case studies: Applying educational psychology.* Upper Saddle River, NJ: Merrill/Prentice Hall.

Jackson, G., & Cosca, C. (1974). The inequality of educational opportunity in the Southwest: An observational study of ethnically mixed classrooms. *American Educational Research Journal, 11,* 219–229.

Jackson, J. F. (1986). Characteristics of Black infant attachment. *American Journal of Social Psychiatry, 6*(1), 32–35.

Jackson, J. F. (1993). Multiple caregiving among African Americans and infant attachment: The need for an emic approach. *Human Development, 35,* 87–102.

Jackson, P. W. (1988). The daily grind. In G. Handel (Ed.), *Childhood socialization.* New York: Aldine de Gruyter.

Jacobs, J. E., Lanza, S., Osgood, D. W., Eccles, J. S., & Wigfield, A. (2002). Changes in children's self-competence and values: Gender and domain differences across grades one through twelve. *Child Development, 73,* 509–527.

Jacobsen, B., Lowery, B., & DuCette, J. (1986). Attributions of learning disabled children. *Journal of Educational Psychology, 78,* 59–64.

Jacobsen, L. K., Giedd, J. N., Berquin, P. C., Krain, A. L., Hamburger, S. D., Kumra, S., & Rapoport, J. L. (1997). Quantitative morphology of the cerebellum and fourth ventricle in childhood-onset schizophrenia. *American Journal of Psychiatry, 154,* 1663–1669.

Jacobsen, L. K., Giedd, J. N., Castellanos, F. X., Vaituzis, A. C., Hamburger, S. D., Kumra, S., Lenane, M. C., & Rapoport, J. L. (1997). Progressive reduction of temporal lobe structures in childhood-onset schizophrenia. *American Journal of Psychiatry, 155,* 678–685.

Jacoby, R., & Glauberman, N. (Eds.). (1995). *The bell curve debate: History, documents, opinions.* New York: Random House.

Jahoda, G. (1979). The construction of economic reality by some Glaswegian children. *European Journal of Social Psychology, 9,* 115–127.

Jahoda, G. (1982). The development of ideas about an economic institution: A cross-national replication. *British Journal of Social Psychology, 21,* 337–338.

Jahoda, G. (1983). European "lag" in the development of an economic concept: A study in Zimbabwe. *British Journal of Developmental Psychology, 1*(2), 113–120.

Jalongo, M. R., Isenberg, J. P., & Gerbracht, G. (1995). *Teachers' stories: From personal narrative to professional insight.* San Francisco: Jossey-Bass.

James, W. T. (1890). *The principles of psychology.* Vol. II. New York: Henry Holt and Company.

Janowsky, J. S., & Carper, R. (1996). Is there a neural basis for cognitive transitions in school-age children? In A. J. Sameroff & M. M. Haith (Eds.), *The five to seven year shift: The age of reason and responsibility* (pp. 33–60). Chicago: The University of Chicago Press.

Jaswal, V. K., & Markman, E. M. (2001). Learning proper and common names in inferential versus ostensive contexts. *Child Development, 72,* 768–786.

Jencks, C. M., & Mayer, S. (1990). The social consequences of growing up in a poor neighborhood: A review. In M. McGreary & L. Lynn (Eds.), *Concentrated urban poverty in America.* Washington, DC: National Academy.

Jenkins, J. M., & Astington, J. W. (1996). Cognitive factors and family structure associated with theory of mind development in young children. *Developmental Psychology, 32,* 70–78.

Jenkins, S., Bax, M., & Hart, H. (1980). Behavior problems in preschool children. *Journal of Child Psychology and Psychiatry, 21,* 5–18.

Jenlink, C. L. (1994, April). *Music: A lifeline for the self-esteem of at-risk students.* Paper presented at the annual meeting of the American Educational Research Association, New Orleans, LA.

Jersild, A. T. (1942). Children and the war. *Teachers College Record, 44*(1), 7–20.

Jersild, A. T., & Markey, F. U. (1935). Conflicts between preschool children. *Child Development Monographs.*

Jessor, R., Donovan, J. E., & Costa, F. M. (1991). *Beyond adolescence: Problem behavior and young adult development.* New York: Academic Press.

Jessor, R., & Jessor, S. L. (1977). *Problem behavior and psychosocial development: A longitudinal study of youth.* San Diego, CA: Academic Press.

Jimerson, S., Egeland, B., & Teo, A. (1999). A longitudinal study of achievement trajectories: Factors associated with change. *Journal of Educational Psychology, 91,* 116–126.

Jiménez, R. T. (2000). Literacy and the identity development of Latina/o students. *American Educational Research Journal, 37,* 971–1000.

John, O. P. (1990). The "Big Five" factor taxonomy: Dimensions of personality in the natural language and in questionnaires. In L. Pervin (Ed.), *Handbook of personality: Theory and research* (pp. 66–100). New York: Guilford Press.

John, O. P., Caspi, A., Robins, R. W., Moffitt, T. E., & Stouthamer-Loeber, M. (1994). The "Little Five": Exploring the five-factor model of personality in adolescent boys. *Child Development, 65,* 160–178.

John-Steiner, V., & Mahn, H. (1996). Sociocultural approaches to learning and development: A Vygotskian framework. *Educational Psychologist, 31,* 191–206.

John-Steiner, V., Panofsky, C. P., & Smith, L. W. (Eds.). (1994). *Sociocultural approaches to language and literacy: An interactionist perspective.* Cambridge, England: Cambridge University Press.

Johnson, D. W., & Johnson, R. T. (2000). The three Cs of reducing prejudice and discrimination. In S. Oskamp (Ed.), *Reducing prejudice and discrimination* (pp. 239–268). Mahwah, NJ: Erlbaum.

Johnson, D. W., Johnson, R., Dudley, B., Ward, M., & Magnuson, D. (1995). The impact of peer mediation training on the management of school and home conflicts. *American Educational Research Journal, 32,* 829–844.

Johnson, H. C., & Friesen, B. J. (1993). Etiologies of mental and emotional disorders in children. In H. Johnson (Ed.), *Child mental health in the 1990s: Curricula for graduate and undergraduate.* Washington, DC: U.S. Department of Health and Human Services.

Johnson, J. S., & Newport, E. L. (1989). Critical period effects in second language learning: The influence of maturational state on acquisition of English as a second lanuage. *Cognitive Psychology, 21,* 60–99.

Johnson, M. H. (1998). The neural basis of cognitive development. In W. Damon (Series Ed.) & D. Kuhn & R. S. Siegler (Vol. Eds.), *Handbook of child psychology: Vol. 2. Cognition, perception, and language* (5th ed.). New York: Wiley.

Johnson, M. H. (1999). Developmental neuroscience. In M. H. Bornstein & M. E. Lamb (Eds.), *Developmental psychology: An advanced textbook* (4th ed., pp 199–230). Mahwah, NJ: Erlbaum.

Johnson, M. H., & de Haan, M. (2001). Developing cortical specialization for visual-cognitive function: The case of face recognition. In J. L. McClelland & R. S. Siegler (Eds.), *Mechanisms of cognitive development: Behavioral and neural perspectives* (pp. 253–270). Mahwah, NJ: Erlbaum.

Johnson, M. H., & Morton, J. (1991). *Biology and cognitive development: The case of face recognition.* Oxford, England: Blackwell.

Johnston, D. K. (1988). Adolescents' solutions to dilemmas in fables: Two moral orientations— two problem solving strategies. In C. Gilligan, J. V. Ward, J. M. Taylor, & B. Bardige (Eds.), *Mapping the moral domain: A contribution of women's thinking to psychological theory and education* (pp. 49–71). Cambridge, MA: Harvard University Press.

Johnston, J. R. (1994). High-conflict divorce. *The Future of Children: Children and Divorce, 4*(1), 164–182.

Johnston, J. R. (1997). Specific language impairment, cognition and the biological basis of language. In M. Gopnik (Ed.), *The inheritance and innateness of grammars.* New York: Oxford University Press.

Johnston, L. D., O'Malley, P. M., & Bachman, J. G. (2000). *The Monitoring the Future national results on adolescent drug use: Overview of the findings, 1999.* Bethesda, MD: National Institute on Drug Use. Retrieved from http://www.monitoringthefuture.org/pubs/keyfindings.pdf.

Johnston, L. D., O'Malley, P. M., Bachman, J. G., & Schulenberg, J. E. (1999). *Cigarette brand preferences among adolescents* (Monitoring the Future Occasional Paper 45). Ann Arbor: University of Michigan Institute for Social Research. Retrieved from the World Wide Web: http://www.isr.umich.edu/src/mtf/occpaper45/paper.html

Johnston, P., & Afflerbach, P. (1985). The process of constructing main ideas from text. *Cognition and Instruction, 2,* 207–232.

Jones, D., & Christensen, C. A. (1999). Relationship between automaticity in handwriting and students' ability to generate written text. *Journal of Educational Psychology, 91,* 44–49.

Jones, G. P., & Dembo, M. H. (1989). Age and sex role differences in intimate friendships during childhood and adolescence. *Merrill-Palmer Quarterly, 35,* 445–462.

Jones, H. F. (1949). Adolescence in our society. In *Anniversary Papers of the Community Service Society of New York: The family in a democratic society* (pp. 70–82). New York: Columbia University Press.

Jones, I., & Pellegrini, A. D. (1996). The effects of social relationships, writing media, and microgenetic development on first-grade students' written narratives. *American Educational Research Journal, 33,* 691–718.

Jones, M. S., Levin, M. E., Levin, J. R., & Beitzel, B. D. (2000). Can vocabulary-learning strategies and pair-learning formats be profitably combined? *Journal of Educational Psychology, 92,* 256–262.

Jordan, C. (1981). The selection of culturally compatible teaching practices. *Educational Perspectives, 20,* 16–19.

Joshi, M. S. & MacLean, M. (1994). Indian and English children's understanding of the distinction between real and apparent emotion. *Child Development, 65,* 1372–1384.

Josselson, R. (1988). The embedded self: I and Thou revisited. In D. K. Lapsley & F. C. Power (Eds.), *Self, ego, and identity: Integrative approaches* (pp. 91–106). New York: Springer-Verlag.

Jovanovic, J., & King, S. S. (1998). Boys and girls in the performance-based science classroom: Who's doing the performing? *American Educational Research Journal, 35,* 477–496.

Juel, C. (1991). Beginning reading. In R. Barr, M. Kamii, P. Mosenthal, & P. D. Pearson (Eds.), *Handbook of reading research* (Vol. II). New York: Longman.

Juel, C. (1998). What kind of one-on-one tutoring helps a poor reader? In C. Hulme & R. M. Joshi (Eds.), *Reading and spelling: Development and disorders.* Mahwah, NJ: Erlbaum.

Jusczyk, P. W. (1995). Language acquisition: Speech sounds and phonological development. In J. L. Miller & P. D. Eimas (Eds.), *Handbook of perception and cognition: Vol. 11. Speech, language, and communication.* Orlando, FL: Academic Press.

Jusczyk, P. W. (1997). Finding and remembering words: Some beginnings by English-learning infants. *Current Directions in Psychological Science, 6,* 170–174.

Jusczyk, P. W. (2002). How infants adapt speech-processing capacities to native-language structure. *Current Directions in Psychological Science, 11,* 15–18.

Jusczyk, P. W., & Aslin, R. N. (1995). Infants' detection of the sound patterns of words in fluent speech. *Cognitive Psychology, 29,* 1–23.

Jussim, L., Eccles, J., & Madon, S. (1996). Social perception, social stereotypes, and teacher expectations: Accuracy and the quest for the powerful self-fulfilling prophecy. In L. Berkowitz (Ed.), *Advances in experimental social psychology.* New York: Academic Press.

Juster, N. (1961). *The phantom tollbooth.* New York: Random House.

Juvonen, J. (1991). Deviance, perceived responsibility, and negative peer reactions. *Developmental Psychology, 27,* 672–681.

Juvonen, J. (2000). The social functions of attributional face-saving tactics among early adolescents. *Educational Psychology Review, 12,* 15–32.

Juvonen, J., & Hiner, M. (1991, April). *Perceived responsibility and annoyance as mediators of negative peer reactions.* Paper presented at the annual meeting of the American Educational Research Association, Chicago.

Juvonen, J., Nishina, A., & Graham, S. (2000). Peer harassment, psychological adjustment, and school functioning in early adolescence. *Journal of Educational Psychology, 92,* 349–359.

Juvonen, J., & Weiner, B. (1993). An attributional analysis of students' interactions: The social consequences of perceived responsibility. *Educational Psychology Review, 5,* 325–345.

Kaczmarek, M. G., & Backlund, B. A. (1991). Disenfranchised grief: The loss of an adolescent romantic relationship. *Adolescence, 26,* 253–259.

Kagan, D. (1992). Implications of research on teacher belief. *Educational Psychologist, 27,* 65–90.

Kagan, J. (1981). *The second year: The emergence of self-awareness.* Cambridge, MA: Harvard University Press.

Kagan, J. (1984). *The nature of the child.* New York: Basic Books.

Kagan, J. (1998a). Biology and the child. In W. Damon (Editor-in-Chief), and N. Eisenberg (Vol. Ed.), *Handbook of child psychology: Vol. 3. Social, emotional, and personality development* (pp. 177–235). New York: Wiley.

Kagan, J. (1998b). *Three seductive ideas.* Cambridge, MA: Harvard University Press.

Kahl, B., & Woloshyn, V. E. (1994). Using elaborative interrogation to facilitate acquisition of factual information in cooperative learning settings: One good strategy deserves another. *Applied Cognitive Psychology, 8,* 465–478.

Kahn, A. S., & Mathie, V. A. (2000). Understanding the unacknowledged rape victim. In C. T. Travis & J. W. White (Eds.), *Sexuality, society, and feminism* (pp. 377–403). Washington, DC: American Psychological Association.

Kahneman, D. (2000). Preface. In D. Kahneman, & A. Tversky (Eds.). *Choices, values, and frames* (pp. ix–xvii). New York: Russell Sage Foundation.

Kail, R. (1990). *The development of memory in children* (3rd ed.). New York: Freeman.

Kail, R. (1991). Developmental changes in speed of processing during childhood and adolescence. *Psychological Bulletin, 109,* 490–501.

Kail, R. (1993). The role of a global mechanism in developmental change in speed of processing. In M. L. Howe & R. Pasnak (Eds.), *Emerging themes in cognitive development: Vol. 1. Foundations.* New York: Springer-Verlag.

Kail, R., & Park, Y. (1994). Processing time, articulation time, and memory span. *Journal of Experimental Child Psychology, 57,* 281–291.

Kail, R. V. (1998). *Children and their development.* Upper Saddle River, NJ: Prentice Hall.

Kailin, J. (1999). How white teachers perceive the problem of racism in their schools: A case study in "liberal" Lakeview. *Teachers College Record, 100*(4), 724–750.

Kaler, S. R., & Kopp, C. B. (1990). Compliance and comprehension in very young toddlers. *Child Development, 61,* 1997–2003.

Kamerman, S. B. (2000). Parental leave policies: An essential ingredient in early childhood education and care policies. *Social Policy Report, 14*(2). Ann Arbor, MI: Society for Research in Child Development.

Kang-Ning, C. (1981). Education for Chinese and Indochinese. *Theory into Practice, 20*(1), 35–44.

Kanner, A. D., Feldman, S. S., Weinberger, D. A., & Ford, M. E. (1987). Uplifts, hassles, and adaptational outcomes in early adolescents. *Journal of Early Adolescence, 7,* 371–394.

Kaplan, A. (1998, April). *Task goal orientation and adaptive social interaction among students of diverse cultural backgrounds* Paper presented at the annual meeting of the American Educational Research Association, San Diego, CA.

Kaplan, A., & Maehr, M. L. (1999). Enhancing the motivation of African American students: An achievement goal theory perspective. *Journal of Negro Education, 68*(1), 23–41.

Kaplan, P. S., Goldstein, M. H., Huckeby, E. R., & Cooper, R. P. (1995). Habituation, sensitization, and infants' responses to motherese speech. *Developmental Psychobiology, 28,* 45–57.

Kapp-Simon, K., & Simon, D. J. (1991). Meeting the challenge: Social skills training for teens with special needs. *Connections: The Newsletter of the National Center for Youth and Disabilities, 2*(2), 1–5.

Karabenick, S. A., & Sharma, R. (1994). Seeking academic assistance as a strategic learning resource. In P. R. Pintrich, D. R. Brown, & C. E. Weinstein (Eds.), *Student motivation, cognition, and learning: Essays in honor of Wilbert J. McKeachie.* Hillsdale, NJ: Erlbaum.

Kardash, C. A. M., & Howell, K. L. (1996, April). *Effects of epistemological beliefs on strategies employed to comprehend dual-positional text.* Paper presented at the annual meeting of the American Educational Research Association, New York.

Karmiloff-Smith, A. (1979). Language development after five. In P. Fletcher & M. Garman (Eds.), *Language acquisition: Studies in first language development.* Cambridge, England: Cambridge University Press.

Karmiloff-Smith, A. (1993). Innate constraints and developmental change. In P. Bloom (Ed.),

Language acquisition: Core readings. Cambridge, MA: MIT Press.

Karp, J. M. (1996). Assessing environments. In M. McLean, D. B. Bailey, Jr., & M. Wolery (Eds.), *Assessing infants and preschoolers with special needs* (2nd ed., pp. 235–267). Englewood Cliffs, NJ: Merrill/Prentice-Hall.

Karpov, Y. V., & Haywood, H. C. (1998). Two ways to elaborate Vygotsky's concept of mediation: Implications for instruction. *American Psychologist, 53,* 27–36.

Katchadourian, H. (1990). Sexuality. In S. S. Feldman & G. R. Elliott (Eds.), *At the threshold: The developing adolescent* (pp. 330–351). Cambridge, MA: Harvard University Press.

Katkovsky, W., Crandall, V. C., & Good, S. (1967). Parental antecedents of children's beliefs in internal-external control of reinforcements in intellectual achievement situations. *Child Development, 38,* 765–776.

Katsurada, E., & Sugawara, A. I. (1998). The relationship between hostile attributional bias and aggressive behavior in preschoolers. *Early Childhood Research Quarterly, 13,* 623–636.

Katz, E. W., & Brent, S. B. (1968). Understanding connectives. *Journal of Verbal Learning and Verbal Behavior, 7,* 501–509.

Katz, L. F., & Gottman, J. M. (1991). Marital discord and child outcomes: A social psychophysiological approach. In J. Garber & K. A. Dodge (Eds.), *The development of emotion regulation and dysregulation.* Cambridge, England: Cambridge University Press.

Katz, L. G. (1999a). *Another look at what young children should be learning.* Champaign, IL. ERIC Clearing-house on Elementary and Early Childhood Education (ERIC Document Reproduction Service No. ED 430 735).

Katz, L. G. (1999b, November). *Current perspectives on education in the early years: Challenges for the new millennium.* Paper presented at the Annual Rudolph Goodridge Memorial Lecture, Barbados, West Indies. (ERIC Document Reproduction Service No. ED 437 212).

Kaufman, P., Chen, X., Choy, S. P., Chandler, K. A., Chapman, C. D., Rand, M. R., & Ringel, C. (1999). Indicators of school crime and safety, 1998. *Education Statistics Quarterly, 1*(1), 42–45.

Kazdin, A. E. (1997). Conduct disorder across the life-span. In S. S. Luthar, J. A. Burack, D. Cicchetti, & J. R. Weisz (Eds.), *Developmental psychopathology: Perspectives on adjustment, risk, and disorder* (pp. 248–272). Cambridge, England: Cambridge University Press.

Kazura, K. (2000). Fathers' qualitative and quantitative involvement: An investigation of attachment. *The Journal of Men's Studies, 9*(1), 41–57.

Kearins, J. M. (1981). Visual spatial memory in Australian aboriginal children of desert regions. *Cognitive Psychology, 13,* 434–460.

Keating, D. P. (1996a). A grand theory of development. In R. Case & Y. Okamoto, in collaboration with S. Griffin, A. McKeough, C. Bleiker, B. Henderson, & K. M. Stephenson. The role of central conceptual structures in the development of children's thought. *Monographs of the Society for Research in Child Development, 61*(1, Serial No. 246).

Keating, D. P. (1996b). Habits of mind for a learning society: Educating for human development. In D. R. Olson & N. Torrance (Eds.), *The handbook of education and human development: New models of learning, teaching and schooling* (pp. 461–481). Cambridge, MA: Blackwell.

Kedesdy, J. H., & Budd, K. S. (1998). *Childhood feeding disorders: Biobehavioral assessment and intervention.* Baltimore: Brookes.

Keeney, T. J., Canizzo, S. R., & Flavell, J. H. (1967). Spontaneous and induced verbal rehearsal in a recall task. *Child Development, 38,* 953–966.

Keil, F. C. (1987). Conceptual development and category structure. In U. Neisser (Ed.), *Concepts*

and conceptual development: Ecological and intellectual factors in categorization. Cambridge, England: Cambridge University Press.

Keil, F. C. (1989). *Concepts, kinds, and cognitive development.* Cambridge, MA: MIT Press.

Keil, F. C. (1991). Theories, concepts, and the acquisition of word meaning. In S. A. Gelman & J. P. Byrnes (Eds.), *Perspectives on language and thought: Interrelations in development.* Cambridge, England: Cambridge University Press.

Keil, F. C. (1994). The birth and nurturance of concepts by domains: The origins of concepts of living things. In L. A. Hirschfeld & S. A. Gelman (Eds.), *Mapping the mind: Domain specificity in cognition and culture.* New York: Cambridge University Press.

Kelemen, D. (1999). Why are rocks pointy? Children's preference for teleological explanations of the natural world. *Developmental Psychology, 35,* 1440–1452.

Kellam, S. G. (1990). Developmental epidemiological framework for family research on depression and aggression. In G. R. Patterson (Ed.), *Depression and aggression in family interaction* (pp. 11–48). Hillsdale, NJ: Erlbaum.

Kelley, M. L., Power, T. G., & Wimbush, D. D. (1992). Determinants of disciplinary practices in low-income Black mothers. *Child Development, 63,* 573–582.

Kellogg, R. (1967). *The psychology of children's art.* New York: CRM–Random House.

Kellogg, R. T. (1994). *The psychology of writing.* New York: Oxford University Press.

Kelly, A., & Smail, B. (1986). Sex stereotypes and attitudes to science among eleven-year-old children. *British Journal of Educational Psychology, 56,* 158–168.

Kelly, J. B., & Lamb, M. E. (2000). Using child development research to make appropriate custody and access decisions for young children. *Family and Conciliation Courts Review, 38*(3), 297–311.

Kelly, J. A. (1995). *Changing HIV risk behavior: Practical strategies.* New York: Guilford Press.

Kelly, J. A., Murphy, D. A., Sikkema, K. J., & Kalichman, S. C. (1993). Psychological interventions to prevent HIV infection are urgently needed. *American Psychologist, 48,* 1023–1034.

Kemper, S. (1984). The development of narrative skills: Explanations and entertainments. In S. Kuczaj (Ed.), *Discourse development: Progress in cognitive development research.* New York: Springer-Verlag.

Kemper, S., & Edwards, L. (1986). Children's expression of causality and their construction of narratives. *Topics in Language Disorders, 7*(1), 11–20.

Kenneth, K., Smith, P. K., & Palermiti, A. L. (1997). Conflict in childhood and reproductive development. *Evolution and Human Behavior, 18,* 109–142.

Keogh, B. K., & MacMillan, D. L. (1996). Exceptionality. In D. C. Berliner & R. C. Calfee (Eds.), *Handbook of educational psychology.* New York: Macmillan.

Kerewsky, W., & Lefstein, L. M. (1982). Young adolescents and their community: A shared responsibility. In L. M. Lefstein et al. (Eds.), *3:00 to 6:00 P.M.: Young adolescents at home and in the community.* Carrboro, NC: Center for Early Adolescence.

Kern, L., Dunlap, G., Childs, K. E., & Clark, S. (1994). Use of a classwide self-management program to improve the behavior of students with emotional and behavioral disorders. *Education and Treatment of Children, 17,* 445–458.

Kerns, L. L., & Lieberman, A. B. (1993). *Helping your depressed child.* Rocklin, CA: Prima.

Kerr, M. M., & Nelson, C. M. (1989). *Strategies for managing behavior problems in the classroom* (2nd ed.). Upper Saddle River, NJ: Merrill/Prentice Hall.

Kerrebrock, N., & Lewitt, E. M. (1999). Children in self-care. *The Future of Children: When School Is Out, 9,* 151–160.

Kestenbaum, R., Farber, E. A., & Sroufe, L. A. (1989). Individual differences in empathy among preschoolers: Relation to attachment history. In N. Eisenberg (Ed.), *Empathy and related emotional responses* (New Directions for Child Development, No. 44; pp. 51–64). San Francisco: Jossey-Bass.

Kidder, T. (1989). *Among schoolchildren.* New York: Avon Books.

Kienberger-Jaudes, R., Ekwo, E., & Van Voorhis, J. (1995). Association of drug abuse and child abuse. *Child Abuse and Neglect, 19*(5), 531–543.

Killen, M., & Nucci, L. P. (1995). Morality, autonomy, and social conflict. In M. Killen & D. Hart (Eds.), *Morality in everyday life: Developmental perspectives* (pp. 52–86). Cambridge, England: Cambridge University Press.

Killgore, W. D., Oki, M., & Yurgelun-Todd, D. A. (2001). Sex-specific developmental changes in amygdala responses to affective faces. *Neuroreport, 12*(2), 427–433.

Kim, D., Solomon, D., & Roberts, W. (1995, April). *Classroom practices that enhance students' sense of community.* Paper presented at the annual meeting of the American Educational Research Association, San Francisco.

Kim, J. M., & Turiel, E. (1996). Korean and American children's concepts of adult and peer authority. *Social Development, 5,* 310–329.

Kim, U., & Choi, S. H. (1994). Individualism, collectivism, and child development: A Korean perspective. In P. M. Greenfield & R. R. Cocking (Eds.), *Cross-cultural roots of minority child development* (pp. 227–257). Hillsdale, NJ: Erlbaum.

Kimball, M. M. (1986). Television and sex-role attitudes. In T. M. Williams (Ed.), *The impact of television.* New York: Academic Press.

Kimberg, D. Y., D'Esposito, M., & Farah, M. J. (1997). Cognitive functions in the prefrontal cortex—working memory and executive control. *Current Directions in Psychological Science, 6,* 185–192.

Kindermann, T. A. (1993). Natural peer groups as contexts for individual development: The case of children's motivation in school. *Developmental Psychology, 29,* 970–977.

Kindermann, T. A., McCollam, T. L., & Gibson, E., Jr. (1996). Peer networks and students' classroom engagement during childhood and adolescence. In J. Juvonen & K. R. Wentzel (Eds.), *Social motivation: Understanding children's school adjustment.* Cambridge, England: Cambridge University Press.

King, A. (1999). Discourse patterns for mediating peer learning. In A. M. O'Donnell & A. King (Eds.), *Cognitive perspectives on peer learning* (pp. 87–115). Mahwah, NJ: Erlbaum.

King, A. J. C. (1989). Changing sex roles, lifestyles and attitudes in an urban society. In K. Hurrelmann & U. Engel (Eds.), *The social world of adolescents: International perspectives.* New York: Aldine de Gruyter.

King, E. W. (1999). *Looking into the lives of children: A worldwide view.* Albert Park, Australia: James Nicholas Publishers.

Kinsey, A. C., Pomeroy, W. B., & Martin, C. E. (1948). *Sexual behavior in the human male.* Philadelphia: Saunders.

Kirschenbaum, R. J. (1989). Identification of the gifted and talented American Indian student. In C. J. Maker & S. W. Schiever (Eds.), *Critical issues in gifted education: Vol. 2. Defensible programs for cultural and ethnic minorities.* Austin, TX: Pro-Ed.

Kish, C. K., Zimmer, J. W., & Henning, M. J. (1994, April). *Using direct instruction to teach revision to novice writers: The role of metacognition.* Paper presented at the annual meeting of the American Educational Research Association, New Orleans, LA.

Kisker, E., Hofferth, S., Phillips, D., & Farguhar, E. (1991). *A profile of child care settings: Early education and care in 1990.* Princeton, NJ: Mathematica Policy Research.

Klaczynski, P. A. (2001). Analytic and heuristic processing influences on adolescent reasoning and decision-making. *Child Development, 72,* 844–861.

Klahr, D. (1982). Non-monotone assessment of monotone development: An information processing analysis. In S. Strauss & R. Stavy (Eds.), *U-shaped behavioral growth* (pp. 63–86). New York: Academic Press.

Klahr, D., & Robinson, M. (1981). Formal assessment of problem solving and planning processes in children. *Cognitive Psychology, 13,* 113–148.

Klassen, T. P., MacKay, J. M., Moher, D., Walker, A., & Jones, A. L. (2000). Community-based injury prevention interventions. *The Future of Children, 10*(1), 83–110.

Klein, P. D. (1999). Reopening inquiry into cognitive processes in writing-to-learn. *Educational Psychology Review, 11,* 203–270.

Klinnert, M. D. (1984). The regulation of infant behavior by maternal facial expression. *Infant Behavior and Development, 7,* 447–465.

Klinnert, M. D., Emde, R. N., Butterfield, P., & Campos, J. J. (1986). Social referencing: The infant's use of emotional signals from a friendly adult with mother present. *Developmental Psychology, 22,* 427–434.

Kluger, A. N., & DeNisi, A. (1998). Feedback interventions: Toward the understanding of a double-edged sword. *Current Directions in Psychological Science, 7,* 67–72.

Knapp, M. S., & Woolverton, S. (1995). Social class and schooling. In J. A. Banks & C. A. M. Banks (Eds.), *Handbook of research on multicultural education.* New York: Macmillan.

Knapp, N. F. (1995, April). *Tom and Joshua: Two at-risk readers at home and at school.* Paper presented at the annual meeting of the American Educational Research Association, San Francisco, CA.

Knowlton, D. (1995). Managing children with oppositional behavior. *Beyond Behavior, 6*(3), 5–10.

Knudson, R. E. (1992). The development of written argumentation: An analysis and comparison of argumentative writing at four grade levels. *Child Study Journal, 22,* 167–181.

Knutson, D. J., & Mantzicopoulos, P. Y. (1999, April). *Contextual factors of geographic mobility and their relation to the achievement and adjustment of children.* Paper presented at the annual meeting of the American Educational Research Association, Montreal.

Kochanska, G., Casey, R. J., & Fukumoto, A. (1995). Toddlers' sensitivity to standard violations. *Child Development, 66,* 643–656.

Kochanska, G., Coy, K. C., & Murray, K. T. (2001). The development of self-regulation in the first four years of life. *Child Development, 72,* 1091–1111.

Kochanska, G., Gross, J. N., Lin, M.-H., & Nichols, K. E. (2002). Guilt in young children: Development, determinants, and relations with a broader system of standards. *Child Development, 73,* 461–482.

Kochanski, G. (1993). Toward a synthesis of parental socialization and child temperament in early development of conscience. *Child Development, 64,* 325–347.

Koeppel, J., & Mulrooney, M. (1992). The Sister Schools Program: A way for children to learn about cultural diversity—when there isn't any in their school. *Young Children, 48*(1), 44–47.

Koestner, R., Ryan, R. M., Bernieri, F., & Holt, K. (1984). Setting limits on children's behavior: The differential effects of controlling versus informational styles on intrinsic motivation and creativity. *Journal of Personality, 52,* 233–248.

Kohlberg, L. (1963). Moral development and identification. In H. W. Stevenson (Ed.), *Child psychology: 62nd yearbook of the National Society for the Study of Education* (pp. 277–332). Chicago: University of Chicago Press.

Kohlberg, L. (1969). Stage and sequence: The cognitive-developmental approach to socialization. In D. A. Goslin (Ed.), *Handbook of socialization theory and research* (pp. 347–480). Chicago: Rand McNally.

Kohlberg, L. (1975). The cognitive-developmental approach to moral education. *Phi Delta Kappan, 57,* 670–677.

Kohlberg, L. (1976). Moral stages and moralization: The cognitive-developmental approach. In T. Lickona (Ed.), *Moral development and behavior: Theory, research, and social issues.* New York: Holt, Rinehart & Winston.

Kohlberg, L. (1981). *The philosophy of moral development: Moral stages and the idea of justice.* San Francisco: Harper & Row.

Kohlberg, L. (1984). *The psychology of moral development: The nature and validity of moral stages.* San Francisco: Harper & Row.

Kohlberg, L. (1986). A current statement on some theoretical issues. In S. Modgil & C. Modgil (Eds.), *Lawrence Kohlberg: Consensus and controversy.* Philadelphia: Falmer Press.

Kohlberg, L., & Candee, D. (1984). The relationship of moral judgment to moral action. In W. M. Kurtines & J. L. Gewirtz (Eds.), *Morality, moral behavior, and moral development.* New York: Wiley.

Kohlberg, L., & Fein, G. G. (1987). Play and constructive work as contributors to development. In L. Kohlberg (Ed.), *Child psychology and childhood education: A cognitive-developmental view* (pp. 392–440). New York: Longman.

Kohlberg, L., & Kramer, R. (1969). Continuities and discontinuities in childhood and adult moral development. *Human Development, 12,* 93–120.

Kohlberg, L., & Mayer, R. (1972). Development as the aim of education. *Harvard Educational Review, 42,* 449–496.

Kohn, M. L. (1977). *Class and conformity* (2nd ed.). Chicago: University of Chicago Press.

Kohut, S., Jr. (1988). *The middle school: A bridge between elementary and high schools* (2nd ed.). Washington, DC: National Education Association.

Kolb, B., & Fantie, B. (1989). Development of the child's brain and behavior. In C. R. Reynolds & E. F. Janzen (Eds.), *Handbook of clinical child neuropsychology* (pp. 17–40). New York: Plenum Press.

Kolb, B., & Whishaw, I. (1996). *Fundamentals of human neuropsychology* (3rd ed.). San Francisco: Freeman.

Konner, M. (1972). Aspects of the developmental ethology of a foraging people. In N. Blurton Jones (Ed.), *Ethological studies of child behavior* (pp. 285–304). Cambridge, England: Cambridge University Press.

Konopak, B. C., Martin, S. H., & Martin, M. A. (1990). Using a writing strategy to enhance sixth-grade students' comprehension of content material. *Journal of Reading Behavior, 22,* 19–37.

Kontos, S., Raikes, H., & Woods, A. (1983). Early childhood staff attitudes toward their parent clienteles. *Child Care Quarterly, 12,* 45–58.

Kontos, S., & Wells, W. (1986). Attitudes of caregivers and the day care experience of families. *Early Childhood Research Quarterly, 1,* 47–67.

Kopp, C. B. (1982). Antecedents of self-regulation: A developmental perspective. *Developmental Psychology, 18,* 199–214.

Kopp, C. B. (1992). Emotional distress and control in young children. In N. Eisenberg & R. A. Fabes (Eds.), *Emotion and its regulation in early development.* San Francisco: Jossey-Bass.

Koren-Karie, N., Oppenheim, D., Dolev, S., Sher, E., & Etzion-Carasso, A. (2002). Mothers' insightfulness regarding their infants' internal experience: Relations with maternal sensitivity and infant attachment. *Developmental Psychology, 38*(4), 534–542.

Korkman, M., Autti-Raemoe, I., Koivulehto, H., & Granstroem, M. L. (1998). Neuropsychological effects at early school age of fetal alcohol exposure of varying duration. *Child Neuropsychology, 4*(3), 199–212.

Kornhaber, A. (1996). *Contemporary grandparenting.* Thousand Oaks, CA: Sage.

Koskinen, P. S., Blum, I. H., Bisson, S. A., Phillips, S. M., Creamer, T. S., & Baker, T. K. (2000). Book access, shared reading, and audio models: The effects of supporting the literacy learning of linguistically diverse students in school and at home. *Journal of Educational Psychology, 92,* 23–36.

Kottler, J. A. (1997). *What's really said in the teachers' lounge: Provocative ideas about cultures and classrooms.* Thousand Oaks, CA: Corwin Press.

Kovacs, D. M., Parker, J. G., & Hoffman, L. W. (1996). Behavioral, affective, and social correlates of involvement in cross-sex friendship in elementary school. *Child Development, 67,* 2269–2286.

Koyanagi, C., & Gaines, S. (1993). *All systems failure: An examination of the results of neglecting the needs of children with serious emotional disturbance.* Alexandria, VA: National Mental Health Association.

Koza, J. E. (2001). Multicultural approaches to music education. In C. A. Grant & M. L. Gomez, *Campus and classroom: Making schooling multicultural* (2nd ed.). Upper Saddle River, NJ: Merrill/Prentice Hall.

Kozol, J. (1995). *Amazing grace: The lives of children and the conscience of a nation.* New York: Crown Publishers.

Kozulin, A., & Falik, L. (1995). Dynamic cognitive assessment of the child. *Current Directions in Psychological Science, 4,* 192–196.

Kraemingk, K., & Paquette, A. (1999). Effects of prenatal alcohol exposure on neuropsychological functioning. *Developmental Neuropsychology, 15*(1), 111–140.

Krampen, G. (1987). Differential effects of teacher comments. *Journal of Educational Psychology, 79,* 137–146.

Krapp, A., Hidi, S., & Renninger, K. A. (1992). Interest, learning, and development. In K. A. Renninger, S. Hidi, & A. Krapp (Eds.), *The role of interest in learning and development.* Hillsdale, NJ: Erlbaum.

Krashen, S. D. (1996). *Under attack: The case against bilingual education.* Culver City, CA: Language Education Associates.

Krebs, D. L., & Van Hesteren, F. (1994). The development of altruism: Toward an integrative model. *Developmental Review, 14,* 103–158.

Krebs, P. L. (1995). Mental retardation. In J. P. Winnick (Ed.), *Adapted physical education and sport* (2nd ed., pp. 93–109). Champaign, IL: Human Kinetics.

Kreutzer, M. A., Leonard, C., & Flavell, J. H. (1975). An interview study of children's knowledge about memory. *Monographs of the Society for Research in Child Development, 40*(1, Serial No. 159).

Krispin, O., Sternberg, K. J., & Lamb, M. E. (1992). The dimensions of peer evaluation in Israel: A cross-cultural perspective. *International Journal of Behavioral Development, 15,* 299–314.

Kroll, B. M. (1984). Audience adaptation in children's persuasive letters. *Written Communication, 1,* 407–427.

Kruger, A. C., & Tomasello, M. (1996). Cultural learning and learning culture. In D. R. Olson & N. Torrance (Eds.), *The handbook of education and human development: New models of learning, teaching and schooling* (pp. 369–387). Cambridge, MA: Blackwell.

Kuhl, J. (1985). Volitional mediators of cognition-behavior consistency: Self-regulatory processes and actions versus state orientation. In J. Kuhl & J. Beckmann (Eds.), *Action control: From cognition to behavior.* Berlin, Germany: Springer-Verlag.

Kuhl, P. K., & Meltzoff, A. N. (1997). Evolution, nativism and learning in the development of language and speech. In M. Gopnik (Ed.), *The inheritance and innateness of grammars.* New York: Oxford University Press.

Kuhl, P. K., Williams, K. A., Lacerda, F., Stevens, K. N., & Lindblom, B. (1992). Linguistic experience alters phonetic perception in infants by 6 months of age. *Science, 255,* 606–608.

Kuhn, D. (1997). Constraints or guideposts? Developmental psychology and science education. *Review of Educational Research, 67,* 141–150.

Kuhn, D. (2001a). How do people know? *Psychological Science, 12,* 1–8.

Kuhn, D. (2001b). Why development does (and does not) occur: Evidence from the domain of inductive reasoning. In J. L. McClelland & R. S. Siegler (Eds.), *Mechanisms of cognitive development: Behavioral and neural perspectives* (pp. 221–249). Mahwah, NJ: Erlbaum.

Kuhn, D., Amsel, E., & O'Loughlin, M. (1988). *The development of scientific thinking skills.* San Diego, CA: Academic Press.

Kuhn, D., Garcia-Mila, M., Zohar, A., & Andersen, C. (1995). Strategies of knowledge acquisition. *Monographs of the Society for Research in Child Development, 60* (4, Whole No. 245).

Kuhn, D., & Phelps, E. (1982). The development of problem-solving strategies. In H. Reese (Ed.), *Advances in child development and behavior* (Vol. 17). New York: Academic Press.

Kuhn, D., Shaw, V., & Felton, M. (1997). Effects of dyadic interaction on argumentative reasoning. *Cognition and Instruction, 15,* 287–315.

Kuklinski, M. R., & Weinstein, R. S. (2001). Classroom and developmental differences in a path model of teacher expectancy effects. *Child Development, 72,* 1554–1578.

Kulberg, A. (1986). Substance abuse: Clinical identification and management. *Pediatrics Toxicology, 33*(2), 325–361.

Kulik, J. A., & Kulik, C. C. (1988). Timing of feedback and verbal learning. *Review of Educational Research, 58,* 79–97.

Kunzinger, E. L., III (1985). A short-term longitudinal study of memorial development during early grade school. *Developmental Psychology, 21,* 642–646.

Kupersmidt, J. B., Buchele, K. S., Voegler, M. E., & Sedikides, C. (1996). Social self-discrepancy: A theory relating peer relations problems and school maladjustment. In J. Juvonen & K. R. Wentzel (Eds.), *Social motivation: Understanding children's school adjustment* (pp. 66–97). Cambridge, England: Cambridge University Press.

Kupersmidt, J. B., & Coie, J. D. (1990). Preadolescent peer status, aggression, and school adjustment as predictors of externalizing problems in adolescence. *Child Development, 61,* 1350–1362.

Kurtines, W. M., Berman, S. L., Ittel, A., & Williamson, S. (1995). Moral development: A co-constructivist perspective. In W. M. Kurtines & J. L. Gewirtz (Eds.), *Moral development: An introduction.* Boston: Allyn & Bacon.

Kurtines, W. M., & Gewirtz, J. L. (Eds.). (1991). *Moral behavior and development: Vol. 2. Research.* Hillsdale, NJ: Erlbaum.

Kurtz, B. E., Schneider, W., Carr, M., Borkowski, J. G., & Rellinger, E. (1990). Strategy instruction and attributional beliefs in West Germany and the United States: Do teachers foster metacognitive development? *Contemporary Educational Psychology, 15,* 268–283.

LaBlance, G. R., Steckol, K. F., & Smith, V. L. (1994). Stuttering: The role of the classroom teacher. *Teaching Exceptional Children, 26*(2), 10–12.

Laboratory of Human Cognition. (1982). Culture and intelligence. In R. J. Sternberg (Ed.), *Handbook of human intelligence.* Cambridge, England: Cambridge University Press.

Ladavas, E. (1988). Asymmetries in processing horizontal and vertical dimensions. *Memory and Cognition, 16*(4), 377–382.

Ladd, G. W. (1990). Having friends, keeping friends, making friends, and being liked by peers in the classroom: Predictors of children's early school adjustment? *Child Development, 61,* 1081–1100.

Ladd, G. W., & Burgess, K. B. (1999). Charting the relationship trajectories of aggressive, withdrawn, and aggressive/withdrawn children during early grade school. *Child Development, 70,* 910–929.

Ladson-Billings, G. (1994). *The dreamkeepers: Successful teachers of African American children.* San Francisco: Jossey-Bass.

Lafontana, K. M., & Cillessen, A. H. N. (1998). The nature of children's stereotypes of popularity. *Social Development, 7,* 301–320.

LaFromboise, T. D., Foster, S., & James, A. (1996). Ethics in multicultural counseling. In P. B. Pedersen, T. G. Draguns, W. J. Lonner, & J. E. Trimble (Eds.), *Counseling across cultures* (4th ed., pp. 47–72). Thousand Oaks, CA: Sage.

LaFromboise, T., Hardin, L., Coleman, K., & Gerton, J. (1993). Psychological impact of biculturalism: Evidence and theory. *Psychological Bulletin, 114,* 395–412.

La Guardia, J. G., Ryan, R. M., Couchman, C. E., & Deci, E. L. (2000). Within-person variation in security of attachment: A self-determination theory perspective on attachment, need fulfillment, and well-being. *Journal of Personality and Social Psychology, 79,* 367–384.

Lahey, B., Loeber, R., Quay, H. C., Frick, P. J., & Grimm, J. (1992). Oppositional defiant and conduct disorders: Issues to be resolved for DSM-IV. *Journal of the American Academy of Child and Adolescent Psychiatry, 31,* 539–546.

Lamb, M. E. (1976). Interactions between eight-month-old children and their fathers and mothers. In M. E. Lamb (Ed.), *The role of the father in child development* (pp. 307–327). New York: Wiley.

Lamb, M. E. (1997). The development of father-infant relationships. In M. E. Lamb (Ed.), *The role of the father in child development* (3rd ed., pp. 104–120). New York: Wiley.

Lamb, M. E. (1998). Nonparental child care: Context, quality, correlates, and consequences. In W. Damon (Editor-in-Chief), I. E. Sigel, & K. A. Renninger (Vol. Eds.), *Handbook of child psychology* (Vol. 4, pp. 73–133). New York: Wiley.

Lamb, M. E., Frodi, A. M., Hwang, C. P., Frodi, M., & Steinberg, J. (1982). Mother- and father-infant interactions involving play and holding in traditional and non-traditional Swedish families. *Developmental Psychology, 18,* 215–221.

Lamb, S. (1991). First moral sense: Aspects of and contributions to a beginning morality in the second year of life. In W. M. Kurtines & J. L. Gewirtz (Eds.), *Handbook of moral behavior and development: Vol. 2. Research.* Hillsdale, NJ: Erlbaum.

Lamb, S., & Feeny, N. C. (1995). Early moral sense and socialization. In W. M. Kurtines & J. L. Gewirtz (Eds.), *Moral development: An introduction.* Boston: Allyn & Bacon.

Lamborn, S. D., & Felbab, A. J. (2001, April). *Applying ethnic equivalence and cultural value models to African American teens' perceptions of parents.* Paper presented at the biennial meetings of the Society for Research in Child Development, Minneapolis.

Lamborn, S. D., Mounts, N. S., Steinberg, L., & Dornbusch, S. M. (1991). Patterns of competence and adjustment among adolescents from authoritative, authoritarian, indulgent, and neglectful families. *Child Development, 62,* 1049–1065.

Lampert, M. (1990). When the problem is not the question and the solution is not the answer: Mathematical knowing and teaching. *American Educational Research Journal, 27,* 29–64.

Landau, S., & McAninch, C. (1993). Young children with attention deficits. *Young Children, 48*(4), 49–58.

Landesman, S., & Ramey, C. (1989). Developmental psychology and mental retardation: Integrating scientific principles with treatment practices. *American Psychologist, 44,* 409–415.

Lane, D. M., & Pearson, D. A. (1982). The development of selective attention. *Merrill-Palmer Quarterly, 28,* 317–337.

Langacker, R. (1986). An introduction to cognitive grammar. *Cognitive Science, 10,* 1–40.

Lange, G., & Pierce, S. H. (1992). Memory-strategy learning and maintenance in preschool children. *Developmental Psychology, 28,* 453–462.

Langfeldt, T. (1981). Sexual development in children. In M. Cook & K. Howells (Eds.), *Adult sexual interest in children.* London: Academic Press.

Langlois, J. H. (1981). Beauty and the beast: The role of physical attractiveness in the development of peer relations and social behavior. In S. S. Brehm, S. M. Kassin, & F. X. Gibbons (Eds.), *Developmental social psychology: Theory and research* (pp. 47–63). New York: Oxford University Press.

Langlois, J. H., & Downs, A. C. (1980). Mothers, fathers, and peers as socialization agents of sex-typed play behaviors in young children. *Child Development, 51,* 1237–1247.

Lanza, E. (1992). Can bilingual two-year-olds code-switch? *Journal of Child Language, 19,* 633–658.

Lapsley, D. K. (1993). Toward an integrated theory of adolescent ego development: The "new look" at adolescent egocentrism. *American Journal of Orthopsychiatry, 63,* 562–571.

Lapsley, D. K., Jackson, S., Rice, K., & Shadid, G. (1988). Self-monitoring and the "new look" at the imaginary audience and personal fable: An ego-developmental analysis. *Journal of Adolescent Research, 3,* 17–31.

Lapsley, D. K., Milstead, M., Quintana, S., Flannery, D., & Buss, R. (1986). Adolescent egocentrism and formal operations: Tests of a theoretical assumption. *Developmental Psychology, 22,* 800–807.

Lareau, A. (1987). Social class differences in family-school relationships: The importance of cultural capital. *Sociology of Education, 60,* 73–85.

Lareau, A. (1989). *Home advantage: Social class and parental intervention in elementary education.* New York: Falmer Press.

Lareau, A. (2000). Social class and the daily lives of children: A study from the United States. *Childhood, 7*(2), 155–171.

Lareau, A., & Horvat, E. M. (1999). Moments of social inclusion and exclusion: Race, class, and cultural capital in family-school relationships. *Sociology of Education, 72,* 37–53.

Larkin, R. W. (1979). *Suburban youth in cultural crisis.* New York: Oxford University Press.

Larner, M. B., Stevenson, C. S., & Behrman, R. E. (1998). Protecting children from abuse and neglect: Analysis and recommendations. *The Future of Children: Protecting Children From Abuse and Neglect, 8*(1), 4–22.

Larson, R. W. (2000). Toward a psychology of positive youth development. *American Psychologist, 55,* pp. 170–183.

Larson, R. W. (2002). Globalization, societal change, and new technologies: What they mean for the future of adolescence. In R. W. Larson, B. B. Brown, & J. T. Mortimer (Eds.), *Adolescents' preparation for the future: Perils and promise (A*

report of the Study Group on Adolescence in the Twenty-First Century; pp. 1–30). Ann Arbor, MI: The Society for Research on Adolescence.

Larson, R. W., Clore, G. L., & Wood, G. A. (1999). The emotions of romantic relationships: Do they wreak havoc on adolescents? In W. Furman, B. B. Brown, & C. Feiring (Eds.), *The development of romantic relationships in adolescence* (pp. 19–49). Cambridge, England: Cambridge University Press.

Last, C. G., Hersen, M., Kazdin, A. E., Francis, G., & Grubb, H. J. (1987). Psychiatric illness in the mothers of anxious children. *American Journal of Psychiatry, 144,* 1580–1583.

Laupa, M. (1994). "Who's in charge?" Preschool children's concepts of authority. *Early Childhood Research Quarterly, 9,* 1–17.

Laupa, M., & Turiel, E. (1995). Social domain theory. In W. M. Kurtines & J. L. Gewirtz (Eds.), *Moral development: An introduction.* Boston: Allyn & Bacon.

Lauritsen, J. L., Laub, J. H., & Sampson, R. J. (1992). Conventional and delinquent activities: Implications for the prevention of violent victimization among adolescents. *Violence and Victims, 7*(2), 91–108.

Lautrey, J. (1993). Structure and variability: A plea for a pluralistic approach to cognitive development. In R. Case & W. Edelstein (Eds.), *The new structuralism in cognitive development: Theory and research on individual pathways.* Basel, Switzerland: Karger.

Lave, J. (1993). Word problems: A microcosm of theories of learning. In P. Light and G. Butterworth (Eds.), *Context and cognition: Ways of learning and knowing.* Hillsdale, NJ: Erlbaum.

Lave, J., & Wenger, E. (1991). *Situated learning: Legitimate peripheral participation.* Cambridge, England: Cambridge University Press.

Lazar, I., Darlington, R., Murray, H., Royce, J., & Snipper, A. (1982). Lasting effects of early education: A report from the Consortium for Longitudinal Studies. *Monographs of the Society for Research in Child Development, 47*(2–3, Serial No. 195).

Lazarus, R. S. (1991). *Emotion and adaptation.* New York: Oxford University Press.

Leakey, R. (1994). *The origin of humankind.* New York: Basic Books.

Leaper, C. (1994). Exploring the consequences of gender segregation on social relationships. In C. Leaper (Ed.), *Childhood gender segregation: Causes and consequences* (pp. 67–86). San Francisco: Jossey-Bass.

Leaper, C., & Anderson, K. J. (1997). Gender development and heterosexual romantic relationships during adolescence. In S. Shulman & W. A. Collins (Eds.), Romantic relationships in adolescence: Developmental perspectives. *New directions for child development* (No. 78, pp. 85–103). San Francisco: Jossey-Bass.

Learning First Alliance (2001). *Every child learning: Safe and supportive schools.* Washington, DC: Learning First Alliance and Association for Supervision and Curriculum Development.

Lee, C. D., & Slaughter-Defoe, D. T. (1995). Historical and sociocultural influences on African and American education. In J. A. Banks & C. A. M. Banks (Eds.), *Handbook of research on multicultural education.* New York: Macmillan.

Lee, O. (1999). Science knowledge, world views, and information sources in social and cultural contexts: Making sense after a natural disaster. *American Educational Research Journal, 36,* 187–219.

Lee, S. (1985). Children's acquisition of conditional logic structure: Teachable? *Contemporary Educational Psychology, 10,* 14–27.

Lee, V., Brooks-Gunn, J., Schnur, E., & Liaw, F. (1990). Are Head Start effects sustained? A

longitudinal follow-up comparison of disadvantaged children attending Head Start, no preschool, and other preschool programs. *Child Development, 61,* 495–507.

Lee, V. E., Winfield, L. F., & Wilson, T. C. (1991). Academic behaviors among high-achieving African American students. *Education and Urban Society, 24*(1), 65–86.

Lee-Pearce, M. L., Plowman, T. S., & Touchstone, D. (1998). Starbase-Atlantis, a school without walls: A comparative study of an innovative science program for at-risk urban elementary students. *Journal of Education for Students Placed at Risk, 3,* 223–235.

Leffert, J. S., Siperstein, G. N., & Millikan, E. (1999). *Social perception and strategy generation: Two key social cognitive processes in children with mental retardation.* Paper presented at the biennial meeting of the Society for Research in Child Development, Albuquerque, NM.

Lefstein, L. M., & Lipsitz, J. (1995). *3:00 to 6:00 P.M.: Programs for young adolescents.* Minneapolis, MN: Search Institute.

Lehman, D. R., & Nisbett, R. E. (1990). A longitudinal study of the effects of undergraduate training on reasoning. *Developmental Psychology, 26,* 952–960.

Leichtman, M. D., & Ceci, S. J. (1995). The effects of stereotypes and suggestions on preschoolers' reports. *Developmental Psychology, 31,* 568–578.

Leinhardt, G. (1994). History: A time to be mindful. In G. Leinhardt, I. L. Beck, & C. Stainton (Eds.), *Teaching and learning in history.* Hillsdale, NJ: Erlbaum.

Leininger, M. (1995). *Transcultural nursing: Concepts, theories, research, and practices.* New York: McGraw-Hill.

Leite, R. W., & McKenry, P. C. (2002). Aspects of father status and postdivorce father involvement with children. *Journal of Family Issues, 23*(5), 601–623.

Leite, R. M. C., Buoncompagno, E. M., Leite, A. C. C., & Mergulhao, E. A. (1995). Psychosexual characteristics of male university students in Brazil. *Adolescence, 30,* 363–380.

Leiter, J., & Johnsen, M. C. (1997). Child maltreatment and school performance declines: An event-history analysis. *American Educational Research Journal, 34,* 563–589.

Lenneberg, E. H. (1967). *Biological foundations of language.* New York: Wiley.

Lennon, R., & Eisenberg, N. (1987). Gender and age differences in empathy and sympathy. In N. Eisenberg & J. Strayer (Eds.), *Empathy and its development* (pp. 195–217). New York: Cambridge University Press.

Lennon, R., Eisenberg, N., & Carroll, J. L. (1983). The assessment of empathy in early childhood. *Journal of Applied Developmental Psychology, 4,* 295–302.

Lennox, C., & Siegel, L. S. (1998). Phonological and orthographic processes in good and poor spellers. In C. Hulme & R. M. Joshi (Eds.), *Reading and spelling: Development and disorders.* Mahwah, NJ: Erlbaum.

Leong, C. K. (1998). Strategies used by 9- to 12-year-old children in written spelling. In C. Hulme & R. M. Joshi (Eds.), *Reading and spelling: Development and disorders.* Mahwah, NJ: Erlbaum.

Leont'ev, A. N. (1981). *Problems of the development of mind.* Moscow: Progress.

Lerner, B. (1985). Self-esteem and excellence: The choice and the paradox. *American Educator, 9*(4), 10–16.

Lerner, J. W. (1985). *Learning disabilities: Theories, diagnosis, and teaching strategies* (4th ed.). Boston: Houghton Mifflin.

Lerner, R. M. (1989). Developmental contextualism and the life-span view of person-context interaction. In M. Bornstein & J. S. Bruner (Eds.), *Interaction in human development* (pp. 217–239). Hillsdale, NJ: Erlbaum.

Lerner, R. M. (1998). Theories of human development: Contemporary perspectives. In W. Damon (Editor-in-Chief), & R. M. Lerner (Vol. Ed.), *Handbook of child psychology. Vol. 1. Theoretical models of human development* (5th ed., pp. 1–24). New York: Wiley.

Leslie, A. M. (1991). The theory of mind impairment in autism: Evidence for a modular mechanism of development? In A. Whiten (Ed.), *Natural theories of mind: Evolution, development and simulation of everyday mindreading.* Oxford, England: Blackwell.

Levi, G., & Schmitt, J. C. (1997). Introduction: Paternal authority and freedom of choice in seventeenth-century Italy. In G. Levi & J. C. Schmitt (Eds.), *A history of young people in the west: Vol. 1. Ancient and medieval rites of passage* (C. Naish, Trans.; pp. 1–11). Cambridge, MA: Belknap Press of Harvard University Press.

Levine, D. U., & Lezotte, L. W. (1995). Effective schools research. In J. A. Banks & C. A. M. Banks (Eds.), *Handbook of research on multicultural education.* New York: Macmillan.

Levine, L. (1983). Mine: Self-definition in 2-year-old boys. *Developmental Psychology, 19,* 544–549.

LeVine, R. A. (1974). Parental goals: A cross-cultural view. *Teachers College Record, 76*(2), 226–239.

LeVine, R. A. (1988). Human parental care: Universal goals, cultural strategies, individual behavior. In R. A. LeVine, P. M. Miller, & M. M. West (Eds.), *Parental behavior in diverse societies* (pp. 5–12). San Francisco: Jossey-Bass.

Levitt, M. J., Guacci-Franco, N., & Levitt, J. L. (1993). Convoys of social support in childhood and early adolescence: Structure and function. *Developmental Psychology, 29,* 811–818.

Levitt, M. J., Levitt, J. L., Bustos, G. L., Crooks, N. A., Santos, J. D., Telan, P., & Silver, M. E. (1999, April). *The social ecology of achievement in pre-adolescents: Social support and school attitudes.* Paper presented at the annual meeting of the American Educational Research Association, Montreal.

Levitt, M. J., Weber, R. A., Clark, M. C., & McDonnell, P. (1985). Reciprocity of exchange in toddler sharing behavior. *Developmental Psychology, 21,* 122–123.

Levy, G. D., Taylor, M. G., & Gelman, S. A. (1995). Traditional and evaluative aspects of flexibility in gender roles, social conventions, moral rules, and physical laws. *Child Development, 66,* 515–531.

Levy, T. M., & Orlans, M. (2000). Attachment disorder and the adoptive family. In T. M. Levy et al. (Eds.), *Handbook of attachment interventions* (pp. 243–259). San Diego, CA: Academic Press.

Lewin, B., Siliciano, P., & Klotz, M. (1997). *Genes VI.* Oxford, England: Oxford University.

Lewin, T. (2000, June 25). Growing up, growing apart: Fast friends try to resist the pressure to divide by race. *The New York Times,* pp. 1, 18–20.

Lewis, C. (1981). The effects of firm control: A reinterpretation of findings. *Psychological Bulletin, 90,* 547–563.

Lewis, M. (1991). Self-knowledge and social influence. In M. Lewis & S. Feinman (Eds.), *Social influences and socialization in infancy: Vol. 6. Genesis of behavior* (pp. 111–134). New York: Plenum Press.

Lewis, M. (1993). Self-conscious emotions: Embarrassment, pride, shame, and guilt. In M. Lewis & J. Haviland (Eds.), *The handbook of emotions* (pp. 563–573). New York: Guilford Press.

Lewis, M. (1995). Embarrassment: The emotion of self-exposure and evaluation. In J. Tangney & K. Fischer (Eds.), *Self-conscious emotions: The psychology of shame, guilt, embarrassment and pride* (pp. 198–218). New York: Guilford Press.

Lewis, M. (2000). The emergence of human emotions. In M. Lewis & J. M. Haviland-Jones (Eds.), *Handbook of emotions* (2nd ed., pp. 265–280). New York: Guilford Press.

Lewis, M., & Brooks-Gunn, J. (1979). *Social cognition and the acquisition of self.* New York: Plenum.

Lewis, M., Feiring, C., & Rosenthal, S. (2000). Attachment over time. *Child Development, 71,* 707–720.

Lewkowicz, D. J., & Turkewitz, G. (1981). Intersensory interaction in newborns: Modification of visual preferences following exposure to sound. *Child Development, 52,* 827–832.

Liben, L. S., & Bigler, R. S. (2002). The developmental course of gender differentiation: Conceptualizing, measuring, and evaluating constructs and pathways. *Monographs of the Society for Research in Child Development, Serial No. 269, Vol. 67*(2).

Liben, L. S., Bigler, R. S., & Krogh, H. R. (2002). Language at work: Children's gendered interpretations of occupational titles. *Child Development, 73,* 810–828.

Liben, L. S., & Downs, R. M. (1989). Understanding maps as symbols: The development of map concepts in children. In H. W. Reese (Ed.), *Advances in child development and behavior* (Vol. 22). San Diego, CA: Harcourt Brace Jovanovich.

Liben, L. S., & Signorella, M. L. (1993). Gender-schematic processing in children: The role of initial interpretations of stimuli. *Developmental Psychology, 29,* 141–149.

Liberman, A., Winterfield, L., & McElroy, J. (1996). *Minority overrepresentation among juveniles in New York City's adult and juvenile court systems.* New York: New York City Criminal Justice Agency.

Liberman, A. M. (1998). Why is speech so much easier than reading and writing? In C. Hulme & R. M. Joshi (Eds.), *Reading and spelling: Development and disorders.* Mahwah, NJ: Erlbaum.

Lickona, T. (1991). Moral development in the elementary school classroom. In W. M. Kurtines & J. L. Gewirtz (Eds.), *Moral behavior and development: Vol. 3. Application.* Hillsdale, NJ: Erlbaum.

Lidz, C. S. (1991). Issues in the assessment of preschool children. In B. A. Bracken (Ed.), *The psychoeducational assessment of preschool children* (2nd ed., pp. 18–31). Boston: Allyn & Bacon.

Lidz, C. S. (1997). Dynamic assessment approaches. In D. P. Flanagan, J. L. Genshaft, & P. L. Harrison (Eds.), *Contemporary intellectual assessment: Theories, tests, and issues* (pp. 281–296). New York: Guilford Press.

Lieberman, A. (1993). *The emotional life of the toddler.* New York: Free Press.

Lieberman, A. F., Weston, D. R., & Pawl, J. H. (1991). Preventive intervention and outcome with anxiously attached dyads. *Child Development, 62,* 199–209.

Light, J. G., & Defries, J. C. (1995). Comorbidity of reading and mathematics disabilities: Genetic and environmental etiologies. *Journal of Learning Disabilities, 28,* 96–106.

Light, P., & Butterworth, G. (Eds.). (1993). *Context and cognition: Ways of learning and knowing.* Hillsdale, NJ: Erlbaum.

Lightfoot, C. (1992). Constructing self and peer culture: A narrative perspective on adolescent risk taking. In L. T. Winegar & J. Valsiner (Eds.), *Children's development within social context: Vol. 2. Research and methodology* (pp. 229–245). Hillsdale, NJ: Erlbaum.

Lightfoot, D. (1999). *The development of language: Acquisition, change, and evolution.* Malden, MA: Blackwell.

Lillard, A. S. (1993). Pretend play skills and the child's theory of mind. *Child Development, 64,* 348–371.

Lillard, A. S. (1997). Other folks' theories of mind and behavior. *Psychological Science, 8,* 268–274.

Lillard, A. S. (1998). Playing with a theory of mind. In O. N. Saracho & B. Spodek (Eds.), *Multiple perspectives on play in early childhood education.* Albany: State University of New York Press.

Lillard, A. S. (1999). Developing a cultural theory of mind: The CIAO approach. *Current Directions in Psychological Science, 8,* 57–61.

Lin, C. C., & Fu, V. R. (1990). A comparison of child-rearing practices among Chinese, immigrant Chinese, and Caucasian-American parents. *Child Development, 61,* 429–433.

Lindberg, M. (1991). A taxonomy of suggestibility and eyewitness memory: Age, memory process, and focus of analysis. In J. L. Doris (Ed.), *The suggestibility of children's recollections.* Washington, DC: American Psychological Association.

Linder, T. W. (1993). *Transdisciplinary play-based assessment: A functional approach to working with young children.* Baltimore, MD: Paul H. Brookes.

Linn, M. C., Clement, C., Pulos, S., & Sullivan, P. (1989). Scientific reasoning during adolescence: The influence of instruction in science knowledge and reasoning strategies. *Journal of Research in Science Teaching, 26,* 171–187.

Linn, M. C., & Hyde, J. S. (1989). Gender, mathematics, and science. *Educational Researcher, 18*(8), 17–19, 22–27.

Linn, M. C., Songer, N. B., & Eylon, B. (1996). Shifts and convergences in science learning and instruction. In D. C. Berliner & R. C. Calfee (Eds.), *Handbook of educational psychology.* New York: Macmillan.

Linn, R. L., & Gronlund, N. E. (2000). *Measurement and assessment in teaching* (8th ed.). Upper Saddle River, NJ: Merrill/Prentice Hall.

Linscheid, T. R., & Fleming, C. H. (1995). Anorexia nervosa, bulimia nervosa, and obesity. In M. C. Roberts (Ed.), *Handbook of pediatric psychology* (pp. 676–700). New York: Guilford Press.

Lipson, M. Y. (1983). The influence of religious affiliation on children's memory for text information. *Reading Research Quarterly, 18,* 448–457.

Liss, M. B. (Ed.). (1983). *Social and cognitive skills: Sex roles and children's play.* San Diego, CA: Academic Press.

Little, L. (2000a). *Differences in stress and coping for parents of children with Asperger-spectrum disorders.* Manuscript submitted for publication.

Little, L. (2000b, June). *Maternal discipline of children with Asperger-spectrum disorders.* Paper presented at the Youth and Victimization International Research Conference, Durham, NH.

Little, L. (2000c, June). *Peer victimization of children with Asperger-spectrum disorders.* Paper presented at the Youth and Victimization International Research Conference, Durham, NH.

Little, T. D., Oettingen, G., Stetsenko, A., & Baltes, P. B. (1995). Children's action-control beliefs about school performance: How do American children compare with German and Russian children? *Journal of Personality and Social Psychology, 69,* 686–700.

Littlewood, W. T. (1984). *Foreign and second language learning: Language-acquisition research and its implications for the classroom.* Cambridge, England: Cambridge University Press.

Livesley, W. J., & Bromley, D. B. (1973). *Person perception in childhood and adolescence.* New York: Wiley.

Livson, N., & Peshkin, H. (1980). Perspectives on adolescence from longitudinal research. In

J. Adelson (Ed.), *Handbook of adolescent psychology* (pp. 47–98). New York: Wiley.

Lobel, A. (1979). *Frog and Toad are friends.* New York: HarperCollins.

Lochman, J. E., & Dodge, K. A. (1994). Social–cognitive processes of severely violent, moderately aggressive, and nonaggressive boys. *Journal of Consulting and Clinical Psychology, 62,* 366–374.

Lochman, J. E., & Dodge, K. A. (1998). Distorted perceptions in dyadic interactions of aggressive and nonaggressive boys: Effects of prior expectations, context, and boys' age. *Development and Psychopathology, 10*(3), 495–512.

Lochman, J. E., Wayland, K. K., & White, K. J. (1993). Social goals: Relationship to adolescent adjustment and to social problem solving. *Journal of Abnormal Child Psychology, 21,* 1993.

Locke, E. A., & Latham, G. P. (1990). *A theory of goal setting and task performance.* Upper Saddle River, NJ: Prentice Hall.

Locke, E. A., & Latham, G. P. (1994). Goal setting theory. In H. F. O'Neil, Jr., & M. Drillings (Eds.), *Motivation: Theory and research.* Hillsdale, NJ: Erlbaum.

Locke, J. L. (1993). *The child's path to spoken language.* Cambridge, MA: Harvard University Press.

Loeb, R. C., Horst, L., & Horton, P. J. (1980). Family interaction patterns associated with self-esteem in preadolescent girls and boys. *Merrill-Palmer Quarterly, 26,* 205–217.

Loeber, R. (1982). The stability of antisocial child behavior. *Annals of Child Development, 2,* 77–116.

Loeber, R., & Hay, D. F. (1993). Developmental approaches to aggression and conduct problems. In M. Rutter & D. F. Hay (Eds.), *Development through life: A handbook for clinicians* (pp. 488–516). Oxford, England: Blackwell.

Loeber, R., Lahey, B. B., & Thomas, C. (1991). Diagnostic conundrum of oppositional defiant disorder. *Journal of Abnormal Psychology, 100,* 379–390.

Loeber, R., & Schmaling, K. B. (1985). Empirical evidence for overt and covert patterns of antisocial conduct problems: A meta-analysis. *Journal of Abnormal Child Psychology, 13,* 227–252.

Loeber, R., & Stouthamer-Loeber, M. (1998). Development of juvenile aggression and violence. *American Psychologist, 53,* 242–259.

Loehlin, J. C. (1992). *Genes and environment in personality development.* Newbury Park, CA: Sage.

Logan, K. R., Alberto, P. A., Kana, T. G., & Waylor-Bowen, T. (1994). Curriculum development and instructional design for students with profound disabilities. In L. Sternberg (Ed.), *Individuals with profound disabilities: Instructional and assistive strategies* (3rd ed.). Austin, TX: Pro-Ed.

Logsdon, B. J., Alleman, L. M., Straits, S. A., Belka, D. E., Clark, D. (1997). *Physical education unit plans for grades 5–6* (2nd ed.). Champaign, IL: Human Kinetics.

Lomawaima, K. T. (1995). Educating Native Americans. In J. A. Banks & C. A. M. Banks (Eds.), *Handbook of research on multicultural education.* New York: Macmillan.

Lombroso, P. J., & Sapolsky, R. (1998). Development of the cerebral cortex: XII. Stress and brain development: I. *Journal of the American Academy of Child and Adolescent Psychiatry, 37,* 1337–1339.

London, P. (1970). The rescuers: Motivational hypotheses about Christians who saved Jews from the Nazis. In J. Macaulay & L. Berkowitz (Eds.), *Altruism and helping behavior* (pp. 241–250). New York: Academic Press.

Long, M. (1995). The role of the linguistic environment in second language acquisition. In W. C. Ritchie & T. K. Bhatia (Eds.), *Handbook of language acquisition: Vol. 2. Second language acquisition.* San Diego, CA: Academic Press.

Long, T. J., & Long, L. (1982). Latchkey children: The child's view of self care. Washington, DC: Catholic University. (ERIC Document Reproduction Service No. ED 211 229).

Lonigan, C. J., Burgess, S. R., Anthony, J. L., & Barker, T. A. (1998). Development of phonological sensitivity in 2- to 5-year-old children. *Journal of Educational Psychology, 90,* 294–311.

Lopez, E. C. (1997). The cognitive assessment of limited English proficient and bilingual children. In D. P. Flanagan, J. L. Genshaft, & P. L. Harrison (Eds.), *Contemporary intellectual assessment: Theories, tests, and issues* (pp. 503–516). New York: Guilford Press.

López, G. R., Scribner, J. D., & Mahitivanichcha, K. (2001). Redefining parental involvement: Lessons from high-performing migrant-impacted schools. *American Educational Research Journal, 38*(2), 253–288.

López del Bosque, R. (2000). Sticks and stones: What words are to self-esteem. *Intercultural Development Research Association Newsletter, 27*(5), 4–7, 16.

Lorch, E. P., Diener, M. B., Sanchez, R. P., Milich, R., Welsh, R., & van den Broek, P. (1999). The effects of story structure on the recall of stories in children with attention deficit hyperactivity disorder. *Journal of Educational Psychology, 91,* 251–260.

Lorenz, K. (1966). *On aggression.* New York: Harcourt.

Lorenz, K. Z. (1981). *The foundations of ethology* (K. Z. Lorenz & R. W. Kickert, Trans.). New York: Springer-Verlag.

Lortie, D. (1975). *Schoolteacher: A sociological study.* Chicago: University of Chicago Press.

Losey, K. M. (1995). Mexican American students and classroom interaction: An overview and critique. *Review of Educational Research, 65,* 283–318.

Lou, Y., Abrami, P. C., Spence, J. C., Poulsen, C., Chambers, B., & d'Apollonia, S. (1996). Within-class grouping: A meta-analysis. *Review of Educational Research, 66,* 423–458.

Lounsbury, J. H. (Ed.) (1984). *Perspectives: Middle school education 1964–1984.* Columbus, OH: National Middle School Association.

Lovell, K. (1979). Intellectual growth and the school curriculum. In F. B. Murray (Ed.), *The impact of Piagetian theory: On education, philosophy, psychiatry, and psychology.* Baltimore: University Park Press.

Lovett, M. W., Lacerenza, L., Borden, S. L., Frijters, J. C., Steinbach, K. A., & De Palma, M. (2000). Components of effective remediation for developmental reading disabilities: Combining phonological and strategy-based instruction to improve outcomes. *Journal of Educational Psychology, 92,* 263–283.

Lovett, S. B., & Flavell, J. H. (1990). Understanding and remembering: Children's knowledge about the differential effects of strategy and task variables on comprehension and memorization. *Child Development, 61,* 1842–1858.

Lowry, R., Sleet, D., Duncan, C., Powell, K., & Kolbe, L. (1995). Adolescents at risk for violence. *Educational Psychology Review, 7,* 7–39.

Lozoff, B. (1989). Nutrition and behavior. *American Psychologist, 44,* 231–236.

Lucariello, J., Kyratzis, A., & Nelson, K. (1992). Taxonomic knowledge: What kind and when? *Child Development, 63,* 978–998.

Luckasson, R., Coulter, D. L., Polloway, E. A., Reiss, S., Schalock, R. L., Snell, M. E., Spitalnik, D. M., & Stark, J. A. (1992). *Mental retardation: Definition, classification, and systems of supports.* Washington, DC: American Association on Mental Retardation.

Lueptow, L. B. (1984). *Adolescent sex roles and social change.* New York: Columbia University Press.

Lupart, J. L. (1995). Exceptional learners and teaching for transfer. In A. McKeough, J. Lupart, & A. Marini (Eds.), *Teaching for transfer: Fostering generalization in learning.* Mahwah, NJ: Erlbaum.

Luster, L. (1992). *Schooling, survival, and struggle: Black women and the GED.* Unpublished doctoral dissertation, Stanford University, School of Education, Stanford, CA.

Lutke, J. (1997). Spider web walking: Hope for children with FAS through understanding. In A. Streissguth & J. Kanter (Eds.), *The challenge of fetal alcohol syndrome: Overcoming secondary disabilities* (pp. 181–188). Seattle: University of Washington Press.

Lykken, D. T. (1997). The American crime factory. *Psychological Inquiry, 8,* 261–270.

Lynd, R. S., & Lynd, H. M. (1929). *Middletown.* New York: Harcourt, Brace.

Lyon, T. D., & Flavell, J. H. (1994). Young children's understanding of "remember" and "forget." *Child Development, 65,* 1357–1371.

Lytton, H., & Romney, D. M. (1991). Parents' differential socialization of boys and girls: A meta-analysis. *Psychological Bulletin, 109,* 267–296.

Lyytinen, P. (1991). Developmental trends in children's pretend play. *Child: Care, Health, and Development, 17,* 9–25.

Ma, X., & Kishor, N. (1997). Attitude toward self, social factors, and achievement in mathematics: A meta-analytic review. *Educational Psychology Review, 9,* 89–120.

MacArthur, C., & Ferretti, R. P. (1997, March). *The effects of elaborated goals on the argumentative writing of students with learning disabilities and their normally achieving peers.* Paper presented at the annual meeting of the American Educational Research Association, Chicago.

MacArthur, C., & Graham, S. (1987). Learning disabled students' composing with three methods: Handwriting, dictation, and word processing. *Journal of Special Education, 21,* 22–42.

Maccoby, E., & Martin, J. (1983). Socialization in the context of the family: Parent-child interaction. In P. H. Mussen (Series Ed.) & E. M. Hetherington (Vol. Ed.), *Handbook of child psychology: Vol. 4. Socialization, personality and social development* (4th ed., pp. 1–102). New York: Wiley.

Maccoby, E. E. (1980). *Social development: Psychological growth and the parent-child relationship.* New York: Harcourt Brace Jovanovich.

Maccoby, E. E. (1984). Middle childhood in the context of the family. In W. A. Collins (Ed.), *Development during middle childhood* (pp. 184–239). Washington, DC: National Academy Press.

Maccoby, E. E. (1990). Gender and relationships: A developmental account. *American Psychologist, 45,* 513–520.

Maccoby, E. E., & Hagen, J. W. (1965). Effects of distraction upon central versus incidental recall: Developmental trends. *Journal of Experimental Child Psychology, 2,* 280–289.

Maccoby, E. E., & Jacklin, C. N. (1974). *The psychology of sex differences.* Stanford, CA: Stanford University Press.

MacDermid, S. M., Lee, M. D., & Smith, S. (2001). Forward into yesterday: Families and work in the 21st century. In K. J. Daly (Ed.), *Minding the time in family experience: Emerging perspectives and issues* (pp. 59–81). Amsterdam: Elsevier Science.

Mace, F. C., & Kratochwill, T. R. (1988). Self-monitoring. In J. C. Witt, S. N. Elliott, & F. M. Gresham (Eds.), *Handbook of behavior therapy in education.* New York: Plenum Press.

Macfarlane, J. W. (1971). From infancy to adulthood. In M. C. Jones, N. Bayley, J. W. Macfarlane, & M. P. Honzik (Eds.), *The course of human development* (pp. 406–410). Waltham, MA: Xerox College Publishing.

Mackey, W. C. (2001). Support for the existence of an independent man-to-child affiliative bond: Fatherhood as a biocultural invention. *Psychology of Men and Masculinity, 2(1),* 51–66.

Mackey, W. J., Fredericks, J., & Fredericks, M. A. (1993). *Urbanism as delinquency: Compromising the agenda for social change.* Lanham, MD: University Press of America.

Mackintosh, N. J. (1998). *IQ and human intelligence.* London: Oxford University Press.

MacWhinney, B., & Chang, F. (1995). Connectionism and language learning. In C. Nelson (Ed.), *Basic and applied perspectives on learning, cognition, and development: The Minnesota symposium on child psychology* (Vol. 28). Mahwah, NJ: Erlbaum.

Madden, N. A., & Slavin, R. E. (1983). Mainstreaming students with mild handicaps: Academic and social outcomes. *Review of Educational Research, 53,* 519–569.

Madhubuti, H., & Madhubuti, S. (1994). *African-centered education.* Chicago: Third World Press.

Magnusson, S. J., Boyle, R. A., & Templin, M. (1994, April). *Conceptual development: Re-examining knowledge construction in science.* Paper presented at the annual meeting of the American Educational Research Association, New Orleans, LA.

Mahoney, G., O'Sullivan, P., & Robinson, C. (1992). The family environments of children with disabilities: Diverse but not so different. *Topics in Early Childhood Special Education, 12,* 386–402.

Main, M. (1995). Recent studies in attachment: Overview, with selected implications for clinical work. In S. Goldberg, R. Muir, & J. Kerr (Eds.), *Attachment theory: Social, developmental, and clinical perspectives* (pp. 407–474). Hillsdale, NJ: Analytic Press.

Main, M., & Cassidy, J. (1988). Categories of response to reunion with the parent at age 6: Predictable from infant attachment classification and stable over a 1-month period. *Developmental Psychology, 24,* 415–426.

Main, M., Kaplan, N., & Cassidy, J. (1985). Security in infancy, childhood, and adulthood: A move to the level of representation. *Monographs of the Society for Research in Child Development, 50,* 66–104.

Main, M., & Solomon, J. (1986). Discovery of an insecure-disorganized/disoriented attachment pattern. In T. B. Brazelton & M. W. Yogman (Eds.), *Affective development in infancy* (pp. 95–124). Norwood, NJ: Ablex.

Main, M., & Solomon, J. (1990). Procedures for identifying infants as disorganized/disoriented during the Ainsworth Strange Situation. In M. T. Greenberg, D. Cicchetti, & E. M. Cummings (Eds.), *Attachment in the preschool years* (pp. 121–160). Chicago: University of Chicago Press.

Main, M., & Weston, D. (1981). The quality of the toddler's relationship to mother and father: Related to conflict behavior and readiness to establish new social relationships. *Child Development, 52,* 932–940.

Major, B., & Schmader, T. (1998). Coping with stigma through psychological disengagement. In J. K. Swim & C. Stangor (Eds.), *Prejudice: The target's perspective* (pp. 220–241). San Diego, CA: Academic Press.

Maker, C. J. (1993). Creativity, intelligence, and problem solving: A definition and design for cross-cultural research and measurement related to giftedness. *Gifted Education International, 9(2),* 68–77.

Maker, C. J., & Schiever, S. W. (Eds.). (1989). *Critical issues in gifted education: Vol. 2. Defensible programs for cultural and ethnic minorities.* Austin, TX: Pro-Ed.

Malatesta, C. Z., & Haviland, J. M. (1982). Learning display rules: The socialization of emotion expression in infancy. *Child Development, 53,* 991–1003.

Malinsky, K. P. (1997). Learning to be invisible: Female sexual minority students in America's public high schools. In M. B. Harris (Ed.), *School experiences of gay and lesbian youth: The invisible minority* (pp. 35–50). Binghamton, NY: The Harrington Park Press.

Maller, S. J. (2000). Item invariance of four subtests of the Universal Nonverbal Intelligence Test across groups of deaf and hearing children. *Journal of Psychoeducational Assessment, 18,* 240–254.

Malone, D. M., Stoneham, Z., & Langone, J. (1995). Contextual variation of correspondences among measures of play and developmental level of preschool children. *Journal of Early Intervention, 18,* 199–215.

Maloney, M. J., McGuire, J. B., & Daniels, S. R. (1988). Reliability testing of a children's version of the Eating Attitude Test. *Journal of the American Academy of Child and Adolescent Psychiatry, 27,* 541–543.

Mandel, D. R., Jusczyk, P. W., & Pisoni, D. B. (1995). Infants' recognition of the sound patterns of their own names. *Psychological Science, 6,* 314–317.

Manderson, L., Tye, L. C., & Rajanayagam, K. (1997). Condom use in heterosexual sex: A review of research, 1985–1994. In J. Catalan, L. Sherr, et al. (Eds.), *The impact of AIDS: Psychological and social aspects of HIV infection* (pp. 1–26). Singapore: Harwood Academic Publishers.

Mandler, J. M., Fivush, R., & Reznick, J. S. (1987). The development of contextual categories. *Cognitive Development, 2,* 339–354.

Mangelsdorf, S. C., Shapiro, J. R., & Marzolf, D. (1995). Developmental and temperamental differences in emotion regulation in infancy. *Child Development, 66,* 1817–1828.

Manis, F. R. (1996). Current trends in dyslexia research. In B. J. Cratty & R. L. Goldman (Eds.), *Learning disabilities: Contemporary viewpoints.* Amsterdam: Harwood Academic.

Marachi, R., Friedel, J., & Midgley, C. (2001, April). *"I sometimes annoy my teacher during math": Relations between student perceptions of the teacher and disruptive behavior in the classroom.* Paper presented at the annual meeting of the American Educational Research Association, Seattle, WA.

Marans, S., & Berkman, M. (1997, March). Child Development–Community Policing: Partnership in a climate of violence. *Juvenile Justice Bulletin,* 1–8.

Maratsos, M. (1998). Some problems in grammatical acquisition. In W. Damon (Series Ed.) & D. Kuhn & R. S. Siegler (Vol. Eds.), *Handbook of child psychology: Vol. 2. Cognition, perception, and language* (5th ed.). New York: Wiley.

Marcia, J. E. (1980). Identity in adolescence. In J. Adelson (Ed.), *Handbook of adolescent psychology.* New York: Wiley.

Marcia, J. E. (1988). Common processes underlying ego identity, cognitive/moral development, and individuation. In D. K. Lapsley & F. C. Power (Eds.), *Self, ego, and identity: Integrative approaches* (pp. 211–225). New York: Springer-Verlag.

Marcovitch, S., Goldberg, S., Gold, A., Washington, J., Wasson, C., Krekewich, K., et al. (1997). Determinants of behavioral problems in Romanian children adopted in Ontario. *International Journal of Behavioral Development, 20,* 17–31.

Marcus, G. F. (1996). Why do children say "breaked"? *Current Directions in Psychological Science, 5,* 81–85.

Marcus, G. F., Vijayan, S., Bandi Rao, S., & Vishton, P. M. (1999). Rule learning by seven-month-old infants. *Science, 283,* 77–80.

Marcus, R. F. (1980). Empathy and popularity of preschool children. *Child Study Journal, 10,* 133–145.

Markman, E. M. (1977). Realizing that you don't understand: A preliminary investigation. *Child Development, 48,* 986–992.

Markman, E. M. (1979). Realizing that you don't understand: Elementary school children's awareness of inconsistencies. *Child Development, 50,* 643–655.

Markman, E. M. (1989). *Categorization and naming in children: Problems of induction.* Cambridge, MA: MIT Press.

Markman, E. M. (1992). Constraints on word learning: Speculations about their nature, origins, and domain specificity. In M. R. Gunner & M. P. Maratsos (Eds.), *Modularity and constraints in language and cognition: The Minnesota Symposium on Child Psychology,* Hillsdale, NJ: Erlbaum.

Marks, J. (1995). *Human biodiversity: Genes, race, and history.* New York: Aldine de Gruyter.

Markus, H. R., & Kitayama, S. (1991). Culture and the self: Implications for cognition, emotion, and motivation. *Psychological Review, 98,* 224–253.

Marsh, H. W. (1990a). Causal ordering of academic self-concept and academic achievement: A multiwave, longitudinal panel analysis. *Journal of Educational Psychology, 82,* 646–656.

Marsh, H. W. (1990b). A multidimensional, hierarchical model of self-concept: Theoretical and empirical justification. *Educational Psychology Review, 2,* 77–172.

Marsh, H. W., & Craven, R. (1997). Academic self-concept: Beyond the dustbowl. In G. D. Phye (Ed.), *Handbook of classroom assessment: Learning, achievement, and adjustment.* San Diego, CA: Academic Press.

Marsh, H. W., & Yeung, A. S. (1998). Longitudinal structural equation models of academic self-concept and achievement: Gender differences in the development of math and English constructs. *American Educational Research Journal, 35,* 705–738.

Marshall, N. L., White, A. M., Keefe, N. E., & Marx, F. (1999, April). *When are children in self- or sibling care? Predicting entry into unsupervised care.* Paper presented at the biennial meeting of the Society for Research in Child Development, Albuquerque, New Mexico.

Martin, C., & Halverson, C. F. (1987). The roles of cognition in sex role acquisition. In D. B. Carter (Ed.), *Current conceptions of sex roles and sex typing: Theory and research.* New York: Praeger.

Martin, C. L. (1989). Children's use of gender-related information in making social judgments. *Developmental Psychology, 25,* 80–88.

Martin, C. L. (1991). The role of cognition in understanding gender effects. *Advances in Child Development and Behavior, 23,* 113–149.

Martin, C. L., & Halverson, C. F. (1981). A schematic processing model of sex typing and stereotyping in children. *Child Development, 52,* 1119–1134.

Martin, S. S., Brady, M. P., & Williams, R. E. (1991). Effects of toys on the social behavior of preschool children in integrated and noninte-grated groups: Investigation of a setting event. *Journal of Early Intervention, 15,* 153–161.

Martínez, M. A., Sauleda, N., & Huber, G. L. (2001). Metaphors as blueprints of thinking about teaching and learning. *Teaching and Teacher Education, 17,* 965–977.

Masataka, N. (1992). Pitch characteristics of Japanese maternal speech to infants. *Journal of Child Language, 19,* 213–224.

Mason, C. Y., & Jaskulski, T. (1994). HIV/AIDS prevention and education. In M. Agran, N. E. Marchand-Martella, & R. C. Martella (Eds.), *Promoting health and safety: Skills for independent living* (pp. 161–191). Baltimore: Brookes.

Massey, D. S., & Denton, N. A. (1993). *American apartheid: Segregation and the making of the underclass.* Cambridge, MA: Cambridge University Press.

Massimini, K. (2000). *Genetic disorders sourcebook* (2nd ed.). Detroit, MI: Omnigraphics.

Masten, A. S., & Coatsworth, J. D. (1998). The development of competence in favorable and unfavorable environments. *American Psychologist, 53,* 205–220.

Masten, A. S., Neemann, J., & Andenas, S. (1994). Life events and adjustment in adolescents: The significance of event independence, desirability, and chronicity. *Journal of Research on Adolescence, 4,* 71–97.

Mastropieri, M. A., & Scruggs, T. E. (1992). Science for students with disabilities. *Review of Educational Research, 62,* 377–411.

Masur, E. F., McIntyre, C. W., & Flavell, J. H. (1973). Developmental changes in apportionment of study time among items in a multitrial free recall task. *Journal of Experimental Child Psychology, 15,* 237–246.

Matheny, A. P. (1989). Children's behavioral inhibition over age and across situations: Genetic similarity for a trait during change. *Journal of Personality, 57,* 215–226.

Matthews, K. A., Batson, C. D., Horn, J., & Rosenman, R. H. (1981). Principles in his nature which interest him in the fortune of others: The heritability of empathic concern for others. *Journal of Personality, 49,* 237–247.

Mattison, R. E. (1992). Anxiety disorders. In S. R. Hooper, G. W. Hynd, & R. E. Mattison (Eds.), *Child psychopathology: Diagnostic criteria and clinical assessment* (pp. 179–202). Hillsdale, NJ: Erlbaum.

Maurer, D., & Maurer, C. (1988). *The world of the newborn.* New York: Basic Books.

Mayall, B., Bendelow, G., Barker, S., Storey, P., & Veltman, M. (1996). *Children's health in primary schools.* London: Falmer Press.

Mayer, J. D. (2001). Emotion, intelligence, and emotional intelligence. In J. P. Forgas (Ed.), *Handbook of affect and social cognition* (pp. 410–431). Mahwah, NJ: Erlbaum

Mayer, R. E. (1992). *Thinking, problem solving, cognition* (2nd ed.). New York: Freeman.

Mayer, R. E. (1996). Learning strategies for making sense out of expository text: The SOI model for guiding three cognitive processes in knowledge construction. *Educational Psychology Review, 8,* 357–371.

Mayer, R. E. (1998). Does the brain have a place in educational psychology? *Educational Psychology Review, 10,* 389–396.

Mayes, L. C., & Bornstein, M. H. (1997). The development of children exposed to cocaine. In S. S. Luthar, J. A. Burack, D. Cicchetti, & J. R. Weisz (Eds.), *Developmental psychopathology: Perspectives on adjustment, risk, and disorder* (pp. 166–188). Cambridge, England: Cambridge University Press.

Maynard, A. E. (2002). Cultural teaching: The development of teaching skills in Maya sibling interactions. *Child Development, 73,* 969–982.

Mazza, J. J., & Overstreet, S. (2000). Children and adolescents exposed to community violence: A mental health perspective for school psychologists. *School Psychology Review, 29,* 86–101.

McAdoo, H. P. (1985). Racial attitude and self-concept of young Black children over time. In H. P. McAdoo & J. L. McAdoo (Eds.), *Black children: Social, educational, and parental environments.* Newbury Park, CA: Sage.

McAlpine, L. (1992). Language, literacy and education: Case studies of Cree, Inuit and Mohawk communities. *Canadian Children, 17*(1), 17–30.

McAlpine, L., & Taylor, D. M. (1993). Instructional preferences of Cree, Inuit, and Mohawk teachers. *Journal of American Indian Education, 33*(1), 1–20.

McBride-Chang, C., & Ho, C. S. (2000). Developmental issues in Chinese children's character acquisition. *Journal of Educational Psychology, 92,* 50–55.

McCall, R. B. (1993). Developmental functions for general mental performance. In D. K. Detterman (Ed.), *Current topics in human intelligence* (Vol. 3). Norwood, NJ: Ablex.

McCall, R. B. (1994). Academic underachievers. *Current Directions in Psychological Science, 3,* 15–19.

McCall, R. B., & Kagan, J. (1967). Stimulus-schema discrepancy and attention in the infant. *Journal of Experimental Child Psychology, 5,* 381–390.

McCall, R. B., Kennedy, C. B., & Applebaum, M. I. (1977). Magnitude of discrepancy and the distribution of attention in infants. *Child Development, 48,* 772–786.

McCall, R. B., & Mash, C. W. (1995). Infant cognition and its relation to mature intelligence. *Annals of Child Development, 4,* 27–56.

McCallum, R. S. (1991). The assessment of preschool children with the Stanford-Binet Intelligence Scale: Fourth Edition. In B. A. Bracken (Ed.), *The psychoeducational assessment of preschool children* (2nd ed., pp. 107–132). Boston: Allyn and Bacon.

McCallum, R. S. (1999). A "baker's dozen" criteria for evaluating fairness in nonverbal testing. *The School Psychologist, 53*(2), 41–60.

McCallum, R. S., & Bracken, B. A. (1993). Interpersonal relations between school children and their peers, parents, and teachers. *Educational Psychology Review, 5,* 155–176.

McCallum, R. S., & Bracken, B. A. (1997). The Universal Nonverbal Intelligence Test. In D. P. Flanagan, J. L. Genshaft, & P. L. Harrison (Eds.), *Contemporary intellectual assessment: Theories, tests, and issues* (pp. 268–280). New York: Guilford Press.

McCann, T. M. (1989). Student argumentative writing knowledge and ability at three grade levels. *Research in the Teaching of English, 23,* 62–72.

McCarty, T. L., & Watahomigie, L. J. (1998). Language and literacy in American Indian and Alaska Native communities. In B. Pérez (Ed.), *Sociocultural contexts of language and literacy.* Mahwah, NJ: Erlbaum.

McCaslin, M., & Good, T. L. (1996). The informal curriculum. In D. C. Berliner & R. C. Calfee (Eds.), *Handbook of educational psychology.* New York: Macmillan.

McCauley, R. N. (1987). The role of theories in a theory of concepts. In U. Neisser (Ed.), *Concepts and conceptual development: Ecological and intellectual factors in categorization.* Cambridge, England: Cambridge University Press.

McClelland, D. C., Atkinson, J. W., Clark, R. A., & Lowell, E. L. (1953). *The achievement motive.* New York: Appleton-Century-Crofts.

McCloskey, M. (1983). Naïve theories of motion. In D. Genter & A. L. Stevens (Eds.), *Mental models* (pp. 299–324). Hillsdale, NJ: Erlbaum.

McCormick, C. B., Busching, B. A., & Potter, E. F. (1992). Children's knowledge about writing: The development and use of evaluative criteria. In

M. Pressley, K. R. Harris, & J. T. Guthrie (Eds.), *Promoting academic competence and literacy in school.* San Diego, CA: Academic Press.

McCourt, F. (1996). *Angela's ashes: A memoir.* New York: Scribner.

McCoy, K. (1994). *Understanding your teenager's depression.* New York: Perigee.

McCrae, R. R., Costa, P. T. Jr., & Busch, C. M. (1986). Evaluating comprehensiveness in personality systems: The California Q-Set and the five-factor model. *Journal of Personality, 54,* 430–446.

McCreary, M. L., Slavin, L. A., & Berry, E. J. (1996). Predicting problem behavior and self-esteem among African-American adolescents. *Journal of Adolescent Research, 11,* 216–234.

McCutchen, D. (1987). Children's discourse skill: Form and modality requirements of schooled writing. *Discourse Processes, 10,* 267–286.

McCutchen, D. (1996). A capacity theory of writing: Working memory in composition. *Educational Psychology Review, 8,* 299–325.

McDevitt, M., & Chaffee, S. H. (1998). Second chance political socialization: "Trickle-up" effects of children on parents. In T. J. Johnson, C. E. Hays, & S. P. Hays (Eds.), *Engaging the public: How government and the media can reinvigorate American democracy.* Lanhan, MD: Rowman & Littlefield.

McDevitt, T. M. (1990). Encouraging young children's listening skills. *Academic Therapy, 25,* 569–577.

McDevitt, T. M., & Ford, M. E. (1987). Processes in young children's communicative functioning and development. In M. E. Ford & D. H. Ford (Eds.), *Humans as self-constructing systems: Putting the framework to work.* (pp. 145–175). Hillsdale, NJ: Erlbaum.

McDevitt, T. M., Spivey, N., Sheehan, E. P., Lennon, R., & Story, R. (1990). Children's beliefs about listening: Is it enough to be still and quiet? *Child Development, 61,* 713–721.

McDonnell, L. M., & Hill, P. T. (1993). *Newcomers in American schools: Meeting the educational needs of immigrant youth.* Santa Monica, CA: RAND.

McGee, K. D., Knight, S. L., & Boudah, D. J. (2001, April). *Using reciprocal teaching in secondary inclusive English classroom instruction.* Paper presented at the annual meeting of the American Educational Research Association, Seattle, WA.

McGill, D. E. (1997). *Big Brothers Big Sisters of America.* Boulder, CO: Center for the Study and Prevention of Violence, University of Colorado at Boulder, Institute of Behavioral Science.

McGinn, P. V., Viernstein, M. C., & Hogan, R. (1980). Fostering the intellectual development of verbally gifted adolescents. *Journal of Educational Psychology, 72,* 494–498.

McGowan, R. J., & Johnson, D. L. (1984). The mother-child relationship and other antecedents of childhood intelligence: A causal analysis. *Child Development, 55,* 810–820.

McGrew, K. S., Flanagan, D. P., Zeith, T. Z., & Vanderwood, M. (1997). Beyond g: The impact of Gf-Gc specific cognitive abilities research on the future use and interpretation of intelligence tests in the schools. *School Psychology Review, 26,* 189–210.

McGue, M., Bouchard, T. J., Jr., Iacono, W. G., & Lykken, D. T. (1993). Behavioral genetics of cognitive ability: A life-span perspective. In R. Plomin & G. E. McClearn (Eds.), *Nature, nurture, and psychology.* Washington, DC: American Psychological Association.

McHale, J. P., & Rasmussen, J. L. (1998). Coparental and family group-level dynamics during infancy: Early family precursors of child and family functioning during preschool. *Development and Psychopathology, 10,* 39–59.

McHale, S. M., Bartko, W. T., Crouter, A. C., & Perry-Jenkins, M. (1990). Children's housework and psychosocial functioning: The mediating effects of parents' sex-role behaviors and attitudes. *Child Development, 61,* 1413–1426.

McKay, A. (1993). Research supports broadly-based sex education. *The Canadian Journal of Human Sexuality,* 2(2), 89–98.

McKenzie, J. K. (1993). Adoption of children with special needs. *The Future of Children,* 3(1), 26–42.

McKeough, A. (1995). Teaching narrative knowledge for transfer in the early school years. In A. McKeough, J. Lupart, & A. Marini (Eds.), *Teaching for transfer: Fostering generalization in learning.* Mahwah, NJ: Erlbaum.

McKeown, M. G., & Beck, I. L. (1994). Making sense of accounts of history: Why young students don't and how they might. In G. Leinhardt, I. L. Beck, & C. Stainton (Eds.), *Teaching and learning in history.* Hillsdale, NJ: Erlbaum.

McKey, R., Condelli, L., Ganson, H., Barrett, B., McConkey, C., & Plantz, M. (1985). *The impact of Head Start on children, families, and communities* (DHHS Publication No. OHDS 90-31193). Washington, DC: U.S. Government Printing Office.

McLane, J. B., & McNamee, G. D. (1990). *Early literacy.* Cambridge, MA: Harvard University Press.

McLoyd, V. C. (1990). The impact of economic hardship on black families and children: Psychological distress, parenting, and socioemotional development. *Child Development, 61,* 311–346.

McLoyd, V. C. (1998a). Children in poverty: Development, public policy, and practice. In W. Damon (Editor-in-Chief), I. E. Sigel, & K. A. Renninger (Vol. Eds.), *Handbook of child psychology: Vol. 4. Child psychology in practice* (5th ed., pp. 135–208). New York: Wiley.

McLoyd, V. C. (1998b). Socioeconomic disadvantage and child development. *American Psychologist, 53,* 185–204.

McMahon, S. (1992). Book club: A case study of a group of fifth graders as they participate in a literature-based reading program. *Reading Research Quarterly,* 27(4), 292–294.

McMillan, J. H., & Reed, D. F. (1994). At-risk students and resiliency: Factors contributing to academic success. *Clearing House,* 67(3), 137–140.

McMillan, J. H., Singh, J., & Simonetta, L. G. (1994). The tyranny of self-oriented self-esteem. *Educational Horizons, 72,* 141–145.

McNeill, D. (1966). Developmental psycholinguistics. In F. Smith & G. A. Miller (Eds.), *The genesis of language.* Cambridge, MA: MIT Press.

McNeill, D. (1970). *The acquisition of language: The study of developmental psycholinguistics.* New York: Harper & Row.

Mead, M. (1930). *Growing up in New Guinea.* New York: Mentor.

Mead, M. (1935). *Sex and temperament in three primitive societies.* New York: American Library.

Medrich, E., & Marzke, C. (1991). *Young adolescents and discretionary time use: The nature of life outside school.* Washington, DC: Carnegie Council on Adolescent Development.

Medrich, E. A., Roizen, J. A., Rubin, V., & Buckley, S. (1982). *The serious business of growing up: A study of children's lives outside school.* Berkeley, CA: University of California Press.

Meece, D., Colwell, M. J., & Pettit, G. (1999, April). *Infant-care, self-care, and early adolescent peer contact: A longitudinal study of developmental risk and continuity in nonparental care.* Paper presented at the biennial meeting of the Society for Research in Child Development, Albuquerque, NM.

Meece, J. L. (1994). The role of motivation in self-regulated learning. In D. H. Schunk & B. J. Zimmerman (Eds.), *Self-regulation of learning and performance: Issues and educational applications.* Hillsdale, NJ: Erlbaum.

Mehan, H. (1979). *Social organization in the classroom.* Cambridge, MA: Harvard University Press.

Meichenbaum, D. (1977). *Cognitive-behavior modification: An integrative approach.* New York: Plenum Press.

Meichenbaum, D. (1985). Teaching thinking: A cognitive-behavioral perspective. In S. F. Chipman, J. W. Segal, & R. Glaser (Eds.), *Thinking and learning skills: Vol. 2. Research and open questions.* Hillsdale, NJ: Erlbaum.

Meichenbaum, D., & Goodman, J. (1971). Training impulsive children to talk to themselves: A means of developing self-control. *Journal of Abnormal Psychology, 77,* 115–126.

Meindl, R. S. (1992). Human populations before agriculture. In S. Jones, R. Martin, D. Pilbeam, & S. Bunney (Eds.), *Cambridge encyclopedia of human evolution* (pp. 406–410). Cambridge, England: Cambridge University Press.

Meltzoff, A. N. (1988). Infant imitation after a 1-week delay: Long-term memory for novel acts and multiple stimuli. *Developmental Psychology, 24,* 470–476.

Meltzoff, A. N. (1990). Foundations for developing a concept of self: The role of imitation in relating self to other and the value of social mirroring, social modeling, and self practice in infancy. In D. Cicchetti & M. Beeghly (Eds.), *The self in transition: Infancy to childhood* (pp. 139–164). Chicago: University of Chicago Press.

Meltzoff, A. N., & Borton, R. W. (1979). Intermodal matching by human neonates. *Nature, 282,* 403–404.

Meltzoff, A. N. & Moore, M. K. (1977). Imitation of facial and manual gestures by human neonates, *Science, 198,* pp. 75–78.

Meltzoff, A. N., & Moore, M. K. (1994). Imitation, memory, and the representation of persons. *Infant Behavior and Development, 17,* 83–99.

Mence, V. H., & Schonwetter, D. J. (1994, April). *Action control, motivation, and academic achievement.* Paper presented at the annual meeting of the American Educational Research Association, New Orleans, LA.

Menyuk, P., & Menyuk, D. (1988). Communicative competence: A historical and cultural perspective. In J. S. Wurzel (Ed.), *Toward multiculturalism: A reader in multicultural education.* Yarmouth, ME: Intercultural Press.

Mercer, C. D. (1997). *Students with learning disabilities* (5th ed.). Upper Saddle River, NJ: Merrill/Prentice Hall.

Mercer, C. D., Jordan, L., Allsopp, D. H., & Mercer, A. R. (1996). Learning disabilities definitions and criteria used by state education departments. *Learning Disabilities Quarterly, 19,* 217–231.

Merrill, M. D., & Tennyson, R. D. (1977). *Concept teaching: An instructional design guide.* Englewood Cliffs, NJ: Educational Technology.

Mervis, C. B. (1987). Child-basic object categories and early lexical development. In U. Neisser (Ed.), *Concepts and conceptual development: Ecological and intellectual factors in categorization.* Cambridge, England: Cambridge University Press.

Merzenich, M. M. (2001). Cortical plasticity contributing to child development. In J. L. McClelland & R. S. Siegler (Eds.), *Mechanisms of cognitive development: Behavioral and neural perspectives* (pp. 67–95). Mahwah, NJ: Erlbaum.

Metz, K. E. (1995). Reassessment of developmental constraints on children's science instruction. *Review of Educational Research, 65,* 93–127.

Metz, K. E. (1997). On the complex relation between cognitive developmental research and children's science curricula. *Review of Educational Research, 67,* 151–163.

Meyer, D. K., Turner, J. C., & Spencer, C. A. (1994, April). *Academic risk taking and motivation in an elementary mathematics classroom.* Paper presented at the annual meeting of the American Educational Research Association, New Orleans, LA.

Meyer, D. K., Turner, J. C., & Spencer, C. A. (1997). Challenge in a mathematics classroom: Students' motivation and strategies in project-based learning. *Elementary School Journal, 97,* 501–521.

Meyer, M. S. (2000). The ability-achievement discrepancy: Does it contribute to an understanding of learning disabilities? *Educational Psychology Review, 12,* 315–337.

Meyers, D. T. (1987). The socialized individual and individual autonomy: An intersection between philosophy and psychology. In E. F. Kittay and D. T. Meyers (Eds.), *Women and moral theory.* Totowa, NJ: Rowman & Littlefield.

Michel, C. (1989). Radiation embryology. *Experientia, 45,* 69–77.

Micheli, L. J., & Melhonian, N. (1987). The child is sport. In *Proceedings of the Pan American Sports Medicine Congress XII.* Bloomington: Indiana University.

Middleton, M. J. (1999, April). *Classroom effects on the gender gap in middle school students' math self-efficacy.* Paper presented at the annual meeting of the American Educational Research Association, Montreal, Canada.

Midgley, C., Feldlaufer, H., & Eccles, J. S. (1989). Change in teacher efficacy and student self- and task-related beliefs in mathematics during the transition to junior high school. *Journal of Educational Psychology, 81,* 247–258.

Milch-Reich, S., Campbell, S. B., Pelham, W. E., Jr., Connelly, L. M., & Geva, D. (1999). Developmental and individual differences in children's on-line representations of dynamic social events. *Child Development, 70,* 413–431.

Miller, B. C., & Benson, B. (1999). Romantic and sexual relationship development during adolescence. In W. Furman, B. B. Brown, & C. Feiring (Eds.), *The development of romantic relationships in adolescence* (pp. 99–121). Cambridge, England: Cambridge University Press.

Miller, C. T., & Myers, A. M. (1998). Compensating for prejudice: How heavyweight people (and others) control outcomes despite prejudice. In J. K. Swim & C. Stangor (Eds.), *Prejudice: The target's perspective* (pp. 191–218). San Diego, CA: Academic Press.

Miller, D. (1994). Suicidal behavior of adolescents with behavior disorders and their peers without disabilities. *Behavioral Disorders,* 20(1), 61–68.

Miller, G. A., & Gildea, P. M. (1987). How children learn words. *Scientific American, 257,* 94–99.

Miller, J. G. (1997). A cultural-psychology perspective on intelligence. In R. J. Sternberg & E. L. Grigorenko (Eds.), *Intelligence, heredity, and environment* (pp. 269–302). Cambridge, England: Cambridge University Press.

Miller, J. G., & Bersoff, D. M. (1992). Culture and moral judgment: How are conflicts between justice and interpersonal responsibilities resolved? *Journal of Personality and Social Psychology, 62,* 541–554.

Miller, J. G., & Bersoff, D. M. (1995). Development in the context of everyday family relationships: Culture, interpersonal morality, and adaptation. In M. Killen & D. Hart (Eds.), *Morality in everyday life: Developmental perspectives* (pp. 259–282). Cambridge, England: Cambridge University Press.

Miller, L. S. (1995). *An American imperative: Accelerating minority educational advancement.* New Haven, CT: Yale University Press.

Miller, N., & Maruyama, G. (1976). Ordinal position and peer popularity. *Journal of Personality and Social Psychology, 33,* 123–131.

Miller, P., & Seier, W. (1994). Strategy utilization deficiencies in children: when, where, and why. In H. Reese (Ed.), *Advances in child development and behavior* (Vol. 25). New York: Academic Press.

Miller, P., & Sperry, L. L. (1987). The socialization of anger and aggression. *Merrill-Palmer Quarterly, 33,* 1–31.

Miller, P. A., Eisenberg, N., Fabes, R. A., & Shell, R. (1996). Relations of moral reasoning and vicarious emotion to young children's prosocial behavior toward peers and adults. *Developmental Psychology, 32,* 210–219.

Miller, P. J. (1982). *Amy, Wendy, and Beth: Learning language in South Baltimore.* Austin: University of Texas Press.

Miller, P. J., & Goodnow, J. J. (1995). Cultural practices: Toward an integration of culture and development. In J. J. Goodnow & P. J. Miller (Eds.), *Cultural practices as contexts for development* (New Directions for Child Development, No. 67; pp. 5–16). San Francisco, CA: Jossey-Bass.

Miller, P. M., Danaher, D. L., & Forbes, D. (1986). Sex-related strategies of coping with interpersonal conflict in children aged five to seven. *Developmental Psychology, 22,* 543–548.

Miller-Jones, D. (1989). Culture and testing. *American Psychologist, 44,* 360–366.

Mills, G. E. (2003). *Action research: A Guide for the teacher researcher* (2nd ed.). Upper Saddle River, NJ: Merrill/Prentice Hall.

Mills, K. (1998). *Something better for my children: The history and people of Head Start.* New York: Penguin/Dutton Books.

Mills, R. S. L., & Grusec, J. E. (1989). Cognitive, affective, and behavioral consequences of praising altruism. *Merrill-Palmer Quarterly, 35,* 299–326.

Milroy, L. (1994). Sociolinguistics and second language learning: Understanding speakers from different speech communities. In G. Brown, K. Malmkjær, A. Pollitt, & J. Williams (Eds.), *Language and understanding.* Oxford, England: Oxford University Press.

Minami, M., & Ovando, C. J. (1995). Language issues in multicultural contexts. In J. A. Banks & C. A. M. Banks (Eds.), *Handbook of research on multicultural education.* New York: Macmillan.

Mintzes, J. J., Trowbridge, J. E., Arnaudin, M. W., & Wandersee, J. H. (1991). Children's biology: Studies on conceptual development in the life sciences. In S. M. Glynn, R. H. Yeany, & B. K. Britton (Eds.), *The psychology of learning science.* Hillsdale, NJ: Erlbaum.

Mischel, W. (1974). Processes in delay of gratification. In L. Berkowitz (Ed.), *Advances in experimental social psychology* (Vol. 7, pp. 249–292). New York: Academic Press.

Mischel, W., & Ebbesen, E. (1970). Attention in delay of gratification. *Journal of Personality and Social Psychology, 16,* 329–337.

Mischel, W., Shoda, Y., & Rodriguez, M. L. (1989). Delay of gratification in children. *Science, 244,* 933–938.

Mitchell, A. (1998). African American teachers: Unique roles and universal lessons. *Education and Urban Society, 31*(1), 104–122.

Miyake, K., Campos, J., Kagan, J., & Bradshaw, D. (1986). Issues in socioemotional development in Japan. In H. Azuma, K. Hakuta, & H. Stevenson (Eds.), *Kodomo: Child development and education in Japan* (pp. 238–261). San Francisco: Freeman.

Miyake, K., Chen, S.-J., & Campos, J. J. (1985). Infant temperament, mother's mode of interaction, and attachment in Japan: An interim report. In I. Bretherton & E. Waters (Eds.), Growing points of attachment theory and research. *Monographs of the Society for Research in Child Development, 50*(1–2, Serial No. 209), 276–297.

Mize, J., Pettit, G. S., & Brown, E. G. (1995). Mothers' supervision of their children's peer play: Relations with beliefs, perceptions, and knowledge. *Developmental Psychology, 31,* 311–321.

Moen, P., & Erickson, M. A. (1995). Linked lives: A transgenerational approach to resilience. In P. Moen, G. H. Elder, Jr., & K. Luscher (Eds.), *Examining lives in context: Perspectives on the ecology of human development* (pp. 169–207). Washington, DC: American Psychological Association.

Mohatt, G., & Erickson, F. (1981). Cultural differences in teaching styles in an Odawa school: A sociolinguistic approach. In H. T. Trueba, G. P. Guthrie, & K. H. Au (Eds.), *Culture and the bilingual classroom: Studies in classroom ethnography.* Rowley, MA: Newbury House.

Money, J. (1987). Sin, sickness, or status? Homosexual gender identification and psychoneuroendocrinology. *American Psychologist, 42,* 384–399.

Money, J. (1988). *Gay, straight, and in-between: The sexology of erotic orientation.* New York: Oxford University Press.

Montagu, A. (1999a). Introduction. In A. Montagu (Ed.), *Race and IQ* (expanded ed.; pp. 1–18). New York: Oxford University Press.

Montagu, A. (Ed.). (1999b). *Race and IQ* (expanded ed.). New York: Oxford University Press.

Montague, D. P. F., & Walker-Andrews, A. S. (2001). Peekaboo: A new look at infants' perceptions of emotion expressions. *Developmental Psychology, 37,* 826–838.

Montemayor, R. (1982). The relationship between parent-adolescent conflict and the amount of time adolescents spend with parents, peers, and alone. *Child Development, 53,* 1512–1519.

Montemayor, R. (1983). Parents and adolescents in conflict. *Journal of Early Adolescence, 3,* 83–103.

Montgomery, D. (1989). Identification of giftedness among American Indian people. In C. J. Maker & S. W. Schiever (Eds.), *Critical issues in gifted education: Vol. 2. Defensible programs for cultural and ethnic minorities.* Austin, TX: Pro-Ed.

Moon, S. M., Feldhusen, J. F., & Dillon, D. R. (1994). Long term effects of an enrichment program based on the Purdue three-stage model. *Gifted Child Quarterly, 38,* 38–47.

Moore, G. A., Cohn, J. F., & Campbell, S. B. (2001). Infant affective responses to mother's still face at 6 months differentially predict externalizing and internalizing behaviors at 18 months. *Developmental Psychology, 37,* 706–714.

Moore, K. L., & Persaud, T. V. N. (1998). *Before we are born: Essentials of embryology and birth defects* (5th ed.). Philadelphia, PA: W. B. Saunders Company.

Moore, S. M., & Rosenthal, D. A. (1991). Condoms and coitus: Adolescents' attitudes to AIDS and safe sex behavior. *Journal of Adolescence, 14,* 211–227.

Moorehouse, M. J. (1991). Linking maternal employment patterns to mother-child activities and children's school competence. *Developmental Psychology, 27,* 295–303.

Moran, C. E., & Hakuta, K. (1995). Bilingual education: Broadening research perspectives. In J. A. Banks & C. A. M. Banks (Eds.), *Handbook of research on multicultural education.* New York: Macmillan.

Morgan, J. L., & Demuth, K. (Eds.). (1996). *Signal to syntax: Bootstrapping from speech to grammar in early acquisition.* Mahwah, NJ: Erlbaum.

Morgan, M. (1985). Self-monitoring of attained subgoals in private study. *Journal of Educational Psychology, 77,* 623–630.

Morris, D. (1977). *Manwatching: A field guide to human behaviour.* New York: Harry N. Abrams.

Morris, D., Tyner, B., & Perney, J. (2000). Early steps: Replicating the effects of a first-grade reading intervention program. *Journal of Educational Psychology, 92,* 681–693.

Morris, R. D., Stuebing, K. K., Fletcher, J. M., Shaywitz, S. E., Lyon, G. R., Shankweiler, D. P., Katz, L., Francis, D. J., & Shaywitz, B. A. (1998). Subtypes of reading disability: Variability around a phonological core. *Journal of Educational Psychology, 90,* 347–373.

Morrison, G., Furlong, M., & Smith, G. (1994). Factors associated with the experience of school violence among general education, leadership class, opportunity class, and special day class pupils. *Education and Treatment of Children, 17,* 356–369.

Morrongiello, B. A., Fenwick, K. D., Hillier, L., & Chance, G. (1994). Sound localization in newborn human infants. *Developmental Psychobiology, 27,* 519–538.

Morrow, S. L. (1997). Career development of lesbian and gay youth: Effects of sexual orientation, coming out, and homophobia. In M. B. Harris (Ed.), *School experiences of gay and lesbian youth: The invisible minority* (pp. 1–15). Binghamton, NY: Harrington Park Press.

Mortimer, J. T., Finch, M., Seongryeol, R., Shanahan, M. J., & McCall, K. T. (1993). *The effects of work intensity on adolescent mental health, achievement and behavioral adjustment: New evidence from a prospective study.* Paper presented at the biennial meeting of the Society for Research in Child Development, New Orleans, LA.

Mortimer, J. T., Shanahan, M., & Ryu, S. (1994). The effects of adolescent employment on school-related orientation and behavior. In R. K. Silbereisen & E. Todt (Eds.), *Adolescence in context: The interplay of family, school, peers and work in adjustment.* New York: Springer-Verlag.

Moses, L., Baldwin, D. A., Rosicky, J. G., & Tidball, G. (2001). Evidence for referential understanding in the emotions domain at twelve and eighteen months. *Child Development, 72,* 718–735.

Mueller, E. (1972). The maintenance of verbal exchanges between young children. *Child Development, 43,* 930–938.

Mueller, E., & Brenner, J. (1977). The origins of social skills and interaction among playgroup toddlers. *Child Development, 48,* 854–861.

Mueller, E., & Silverman, N. (1989). Peer relations in maltreated children. In D. Cicchetti & V. Carlson (Eds.), *Child maltreatment: Theory and research on the causes and consequences of child abuse and neglect* (pp. 529–579). New York: Cambridge University Press.

Mühlnickel, W., Elbert, T., Taub, E., & Flor, H. (1998). Reorganization of auditory cortex in tinnitus. *Proceedings of the National Academy of Sciences, USA, 95,* 10340–10343.

Mullen, M. K., & Yi, S. (1995). The cultural context of talk about the past: Implications for the development of autobiographical memory. *Cognitive Development, 10,* 407–419.

Munro, E. (2001). Empowering looked-after children. *Child and Family Social Work, 6*(2), 129–137.

Munroe, R. L., & Munroe, P. J. (1992). Fathers in children's environments: A four culture study. In B. S. Hewlett (Ed.), *Father-child relations:*

Cultural and biosocial contexts (pp. 213–230). New York: Aldine de Gruyter.

Murdock, T. B. (1999). The social context of risk: Status and motivational predictors of alienation in middle school. *Journal of Educational Psychology, 91,* 62–75.

Murphy, D. A., Durako, S. J., Moscicki, A. B., Vermund, S. H., Ma, Y., Schwarz, D. F., et al. (2001). No change in health risk behaviors over time among HIV infected adolescents in care: Role of psychological distress. *Journal of Adolescent Health, 29(3 Suppl),* 57–63.

Murray, F. B. (1978). Teaching strategies and conservation training. In A. M. Lesgold, J. W. Pellegrino, S. D. Fokkema, & R. Glaser (Eds.), *Cognitive psychology and instruction.* New York: Plenum Press.

Muter, V. (1998). Phonological awareness: Its nature and its influence over early literacy development. In C. Hulme & R. M. Joshi (Eds.), *Reading and spelling: Development and disorders.* Mahwah, NJ: Erlbaum.

Myers, J. E., Shoffner, M. E., & Briggs, M. K. (2002). Developmental counseling and therapy: An effective approach to understanding and counseling children. *Professional School Counseling, 5(3),* 194–202.

Nagy, L. (1912). *Psychologie des kindlichen Interesses.* Leipzig, Germany: Nemnich.

Nagy, W. E., Herman, P. A., & Anderson, R. C. (1985). Learning words from context. *Reading Research Quarterly, 20,* 233–253.

Narvaez, D. (1998). The influence of moral schemas on the reconstruction of moral narratives in eighth graders and college students. *Journal of Educational Psychology, 90,* 13–24.

Narvaez, D., Getz, I., Rest, J. R., & Thoma, S. J. (1999). Individual moral judgment and cultural ideologies. *Developmental Psychology, 35,* 477–488.

Narvaez, D., & Rest, J. (1995). The four components of acting morally. In W. M. Kurtines & J. L. Gewirtz (Eds.), *Moral development: An introduction.* Boston: Allyn & Bacon.

Nation, K., & Hulme, C. (1998). The role of analogy in early spelling development. In C. Hulme & R. M. Joshi (Eds.), *Reading and spelling: Development and disorders.* Mahwah, NJ: Erlbaum.

National Assessment of Educational Progress. (1985). *The reading report card: Progress toward excellence in our schools; trends in reading over four national assessments, 1971–1984.* Princeton, NJ: Author.

National Association of Secondary School Principals (NASSP). (1996). *Breaking ranks: Changing an American institution.* Reston, VA: Author.

National Center for Education Statistics. (1997). *Issue brief: Schools serving family needs: Extended-day programs in public and private schools.* Washington, DC: U.S. Department of Education.

National Center for Education Statistics. (1999a). *Digest of Education Statistics 1998* (NCES Publication No. 1999-036). Washington, DC: U.S. Department of Education.

National Center for Education Statistics. (1999b, August). *Snapshots of public schools in the United States: Results from the Schools and Staffing Survey.* Washington, DC: Author.

National Center for Education Statistics. (2003). *Percentage of high school completers ages 16–24 who were enrolled in college the October after completing high school, by type of institution, family income, and race/ethnicity: October 1972–96.* Washington, DC: Author. Retrieved February 24, 2003, from http://nces.ed.gov/quicktables/Detail.asp?Key=147

National Council for Accreditation of Teacher Education. (2000). *Program Standards for Elementary Teacher Preparation.* Retrieved from the World Wide Web: http://www.ncate.org/elemstds.pdf.

National Joint Committee on Learning Disabilities (1994). Learning disabilities: Issues on definition, a position paper of the National Joint Committee on Learning Disabilities. In *Collective perspectives on issues affecting learning disabilities: Position papers and statements.* Austin, TX: Pro-Ed.

National Middle School Association (NMSA). (1995). *This we believe: Developmentally responsive middle-level schools.* Columbus, OH: Author.

National Research Council. (1993a). *Losing generations: Adolescents in high risk settings.* Washington, DC: National Academy of Sciences.

National Research Council. (1993b). *Understanding child abuse and neglect.* Washington, DC: National Academy Press.

National Research Council (1999). *How people learn: Brain, mind, experience, and school.* Washington, DC: Author.

Navarro, R. A. (1985). The problems of language, education, and society: Who decides. In E. E. Garcia & R. V. Padilla (Eds.), *Advances in bilingual education research.* Tucson: University of Arizona Press.

NCSS Task Force on Ethnic Studies Curriculum Guidelines. (1992). Curriculum guidelines for multicultural education. *Social Education, 56,* 274–294.

Neapolitan, D. M., & Huston, A. C. (1994). *Educational content of children's programs on public and commercial television.* Lawrence, KS: Center for Research on the Influences of Television on Children, University of Kansas.

Neff, J. A., Hoppe, S. K., & Perea, P. (1987). Acculturation and alcohol use: Drinking patterns and problems among Anglo- and Mexican-American male drinkers. *Hispanic Journal of Behavioral Sciences, 9,* 151–181.

Neisser, U. (1998a). Introduction: Rising test scores and what they mean. In U. Neisser (Ed.), *The rising curve: Long-term gains in IQ and related measures* (pp. 3–22). Washington, DC: American Psychological Association.

Neisser, U. (Ed.) (1998b). *The rising curve: Long-term gains in IQ and related measures.* Washington, DC: American Psychological Association.

Neisser, U., Boodoo, G., Bouchard, T. J., Boykin, A. W., Brody, N., Ceci, S. J., Halpern, D. F., Loehlen, J. C., Perloff, R., Sternberg, R. J., & Urbina, S. (1996). Intelligence: Knowns and unknowns. *American Psychologist, 51,* 77–101.

Nel, J. (1993). Preservice teachers' perceptions of the goals of multicultural education: Implications for the empowerment of minority students, *Educational Horizons, 71,* 120–125.

Nelson, C. A. (1995). The ontogeny of human memory: A cognitive neuroscience perspective. *Developmental Psychology, 31,* 723–738.

Nelson, C. A. (1999). Neural plasticity and human development. *Current Directions in Psychological Science, 8,* 42–45.

Nelson, K. (1973). Structure and strategy in learning to talk. *Monographs of the Society for Research in Child Development, 38*(1–2, Serial No. 149).

Nelson, K. (1993). Events, narratives, memory: What develops? In C. A. Nelson (Ed.), *Memory and affect: Minnesota Symposia on Child Psychology* (Vol. 26, pp. 1–24). Hillsdale, NJ: Erlbaum.

Nelson, K. (1996). Memory development from 4 to 7 years. In A. J. Sameroff & M. M. Haith (Eds.), *The 5 to 7 shift* (pp. 141–160). Chicago: University of Chicago Press.

Nelson, K. E. (Ed.). (1986). *Event knowledge: Structure and function in development.* Hillsdale, NJ: Erlbaum.

Neubauer, G., Mansel, J., Avrahami, A., & Nathan, M. (1994). Family and peer support of Israeli and German adolescents. In F. Nestemann & K. Hurrelmann (Eds.), *Social networks and social support in childhood and adolescence.* Berlin, Germany: Aldine de Gruyter.

Neville, H. J., & Bavelier, D. (2001). Variability of developmental plasticity. In J. L. McClelland & R. S. Siegler (Eds.), *Mechanisms of cognitive development: Behavioral and neural perspectives* (pp. 271–287). Mahwah, NJ: Erlbaum.

Newcomb, A. F., & Bagwell, C. L. (1995). Children's friendship relations: A meta-analysis review. *Psychological Bulletin, 117,* 306–347.

Newcomb, A. F., & Brady, J. E. (1982). Mutuality in boys' friendship relations. *Child Development, 53,* 392–395.

Newcomb, A. F., & Bukowski, W. M. (1984). A longitudinal study of the utility of social preference and social impact sociometric classification schemes. *Child Development, 55,* 1434–1447.

Newcomb, A. F., Bukowski, W. M., & Pattee, L. (1993). Children's peer relations: A meta-analytic review of popular, rejected, controversial, and average sociometric status. *Psychological Bulletin, 113,* 99–128.

Newcombe, N., & Huttenlocher, J. (1992). Children's early ability to solve perspective-taking problems. *Developmental Psychology, 28,* 635–643.

Newcombe, N. S., Drummey, A. B., Fox, N. A., Lie, E., & Ottinger-Albergs, W. (2000). Remembering early childhood: How much, how, and why (or why not). *Current Directions in Psychological Science, 9,* 55–58.

Newman, L. S. (1990). Intentional and unintentional memory in young children: Remembering vs. playing. *Journal of Experimental Child Psychology, 50,* 243–258.

Newman, L. S. (1991). Why are traits inferred spontaneously? A developmental approach. *Social Cognition, 9,* 221–253.

Newman, R. S., & Schwager, M. T. (1992). Student perceptions and academic help seeking. In D. Schunk & J. Meece (Eds.), *Student perceptions in the classroom.* Hillsdale, NJ: Erlbaum.

Newport, E. L. (1990). Maturational constraints on language learning. *Cognitive Science, 14,* 11–28.

Newport, E. L. (1993). Maturational constraints on language learning. In P. Bloom (Ed.), *Language acquisition: Core readings.* Cambridge, MA: MIT Press.

Newson, J., & Newson, E. (1975). Intersubjectivity and the transmission of culture: On the origins of symbolic functioning. *Bulletin of the British Psychological Society, 28,* 437–446.

NICHD Early Child Care Research Network (1997). The effects of infant child care on infant-mother attachment security: Results of the NICHD study of early child care. *Child Development, 68,* 860–879.

NICHD Early Child Care Research Network. (2002a). Early child care and children's development prior to school entry: Results from the NICHD study of early child care. *American Educational Research Journal, 39*(1), 133–164.

NICHD Early Child Care Research Network. (2002b). Child care structure→ process→ outcome: Direct and indirect effects of child care quality on young children's development. *Psychological Science, 13*(3), 199–206.

Nicholls, J. G. (1979). Development of perception of own attainment and causal attributions for success and failure in reading. *Journal of Educational Psychology, 71,* 94–99.

Nicholls, J. G. (1984). Conceptions of ability and achievement motivation. In R. Ames & C. Ames (Eds.), *Research on motivation in education: Vol. 1. Student motivation.* San Diego, CA: Academic Press.

Nicholls, J. G. (1990). What is ability and why are we mindful of it? A developmental perspective. In R. J. Sternberg & J. Kolligian (Eds.), *Competence considered.* New Haven, CT: Yale University Press.

Nicholls, J. G., Cobb, P., Yackel, E., Wood, T., & Wheatley, G. (1990). Students' theories of mathematics and their mathematical knowledge: Multiple dimensions of assessment. In G. Kulm (Ed.), *Assessing higher order thinking in mathematics.* Washington, DC: American Association for the Advancement of Science.

Nichols, J. D., Ludwin, W. G., & Iadicola, P. (1999). A darker shade of gray: A year-end analysis of discipline and suspension data. *Equity and Excellence in Education, 32*(1), 43–55.

Nichols, M. L., & Ganschow, L. (1992). Has there been a paradigm shift in gifted education? In N. Coangelo, S. G. Assouline, & D. L. Ambroson (Eds.), *Talent development: Proceedings from the 1991 Henry B. and Jocelyn Wallace National Research Symposium on Talent Development.* New York: Trillium.

Nichols, P. D., & Mittelholtz, D. J. (1997). Constructing the concept of aptitude: Implications for the assessment of analogical reasoning. In G. D. Phye (Ed.), *Handbook of academic learning: Construction of knowledge.* San Diego, CA: Academic Press.

Nicklas, T. A., Webber, L. S., Johnson, C. C., Srinivasan, S. R., & Berenson, G. S. (1995). Foundations for health promotion with youth: A review of observations from the Bogalusa Heart Study. *Journal of Health Education, 26*(Suppl. 2), 18–26.

Nicolson, S., & Shipstead, S. G. (2002). *Through the looking glass: Observations in the early childhood classroom* (3rd ed.). Upper Saddle River, NJ: Merrill/Prentice Hall.

Niemi, R. G., & Junn, J. (1998). *Civic education: What makes students learn.* New Haven: Yale University Press.

Nieto, S. (1995a). *Affirming diversity* (2nd ed.). White Plains, NY: Longman.

Nieto, S. (1995b). A history of the education of Puerto Rican students in U.S. mainland schools: "Losers," "outsiders," or "leaders"? In J. A. Banks & C. A. M. Banks (Eds.), *Handbook of research on multicultural education.* New York: Macmillan.

Nilsson, D. E., & Bradford, L. W. (1999). Neurofibromatosis. In S. Goldstein & C. R. Reynolds (Eds.), *Handbook of neurodevelopmental and genetic disorders* (pp. 350–367). New York: Guilford Press.

Nippold, M. A. (1988). The literate lexicon. In M. A. Nippold (Ed.), *Later language development: Ages nine through nineteen.* Boston: Little, Brown.

Nix, R. L., Pinderhughes, E. E., Dodge, K. A., Bates, J. E., Pettit, G. S., & McFadyen-Ketchum, S. A. (1999). The relation between mothers' hostile attribution tendencies and children's externalizing behavior problems: The mediating role of mothers' harsh discipline practices. *Child Development, 70,* 896–909.

Noffke, S. (1997). Professional, personal, and political dimensions of action research. *Review of Research in Education, 22,* 305–343.

Nolen, S. B. (1996). Why study? How reasons for learning influence strategy selection. *Educational Psychology Review, 8,* 335–355.

Nolen-Hoeksema, S. (1987). Sex differences in unipolar depression: Evidence and theory. *Journal of Personality and Social Psychology, 101,* 259–282.

Norton, A. J., & Moorman, J. E. (1987). Current trends in marriage and divorce among American women. *Journal of Marriage and the Family, 49,* 3–14.

Nottelmann, E. D. (1987). Competence and self-esteem during transition from childhood to adolescence. *Developmental Psychology, 23,* 441–450.

Nsamenang, A. B., & Lamb, M. E. (1994). Socialization of the Nso children in the Bamenda Grassfields of northwest Cameroon. In P. M. Greenfield & R. R. Cocking (Eds.), *Cross-cultural roots of minority child development* (pp. 133–146). Hillsdale, NJ: Erlbaum.

Nucci, L. P., & Nucci, M. S. (1982a). Children's responses to moral and social conventional transgressions in free-play settings. *Child Development, 53,* 1337–1342.

Nucci, L. P., & Nucci, M. S. (1982b). Children's social interactions in the context of moral and conventional transgressions. *Child Development, 53,* 403–412.

Nucci, L. P., & Turiel, E. (1978). Social interactions and the development of social concepts in preschool children. *Child Development, 49,* 400–407.

Nucci, L. P., & Weber, E. K. (1991). The domain approach to values education: From theory to practice. In W. M. Kurtines & J. L. Gewirtz (Eds.), *Handbook of moral behavior and development: Vol. 3. Application* (pp. 251–266). Hillsdale, NJ: Erlbaum.

Nucci, L. P., & Weber, E. K. (1995). Social interactions in the home and the development of young children's conceptions of the personal. *Child Development, 66,* 1438–1452.

Nunner-Winkler, G. (1984). Two moralities? A critical discussion of an ethic of care and responsibility versus an ethic of rights and justice. In W. M. Kurtines & J. L. Gewirtz (Eds.), *Morality, moral behavior, and moral development.* New York: Wiley.

Nuthall, G. (1996). Commentary: Of learning and language and understanding the complexity of the classroom. *Educational Psychologist, 31,* 207–214.

Nybell, L. (2001). Meltdowns and containments: Constructions of children at risk as complex systems. *Childhood, 8*(2), 213–230.

Oakes, J., & Guiton, G. (1995). Matchmaking: The dynamics of high school tracking decisions. *American Educational Research Journal, 32,* 3–33.

Oakhill, J., Cain, K., & Yuill, N. (1998). Individual differences in children's comprehension skill: Toward an integrated model. In C. Hulme & R. M. Joshi (Eds.), *Reading and spelling: Development and disorders.* Mahwah, NJ: Erlbaum.

Oatley, K., & Nundy, S. (1996). Rethinking the role of emotions in education. In D. R. Olson & N. Torrance (Eds.), *The handbook of education and human development: New models of learning, teaching, and schooling.* Cambridge, MA: Blackwell.

O'Boyle, M. W., & Gill, H. S. (1998). On the relevance of research findings in cognitive neuroscience to educational practice. *Educational Psychology Review, 10,* 397–409.

O'Brien, S. F., & Bierman, K. L. (1987). Conceptions and perceived influence of peer groups: Interviews with preadolescents and adolescents. *Child Development, 59,* 1360–1365.

Ochs, E. (1982). Talking to children in western Samoa. *Language and Society, 11,* 77–104.

Ochs, E. (1988). *Culture and language development: Language acquisition and language socialization in a Samoan village.* New York: Cambridge University Press.

Ochs, E., & Schieffelin, B. (1995). The impact of language socialization on grammatical development. In P. Fletcher & B. MacWhinney (Eds.), *The handbook of child language.* Cambridge, MA: Blackwell.

O'Connor, M. J., Sigman, N., & Kasari, C. (1993). Attachment behavior of infants exposed prenatally to alcohol: Mediating effects of infant affect and mother-infant interaction. *Development and Psychopathology, 4,* 243–256.

Ogbu, J. U. (1992). Understanding cultural diversity and learning. *Educational Researcher, 21*(8), 5–14, 24.

Ogbu, J. U. (1994). From cultural differences to differences in cultural frames of reference. In P. M. Greenfield & R. R. Cocking (Eds.), *Cross-cultural roots of minority child development* (pp. 365–391). Hillsdale, NJ: Erlbaum.

Ogbu, J. U. (1999). Beyond language: Ebonics, proper English, and identity in a Black-American speech community. *American Educational Research Journal, 36,* 147–184.

Ogden, E. H., & Germinario, V. (1988). *The at-risk student: Answers for educators.* Lancaster, PA: Technomic.

O'Grady, W. (1997). *Syntactic development.* Chicago: University of Chicago Press.

Okagaki, L., & Diamond, K. E. (2000, May). Responding to cultural and linguistic differences in the beliefs and practices of families with young children. *Young Children,* 74–80.

Okagaki, L., & Frensch, P. A. (1998). Parenting and children's achievement: A multiethnic perspective. *American Educational Research Journal, 35,* 123–144.

Okagaki, L., & Sternberg, R. J. (1993). Parental beliefs and children's school performance. *Child Development, 64,* 36–56.

Oldfather, P., & West, J. (1999). *Learning through children's eyes: Social constructivism and the desire to learn.* Washington, DC: American Psychological Association.

O'Leary, K. D., & O'Leary, S. G. (Eds.). (1972). *Classroom management: The successful use of behavior modification.* New York: Pergamon Press.

Oliner, S. P., & Oliner, P. M. (1988). *The altruistic personality: Rescuers of Jews in Nazi Europe.* New York: Free Press.

Oliver, J. M., Cole, N. H., & Hollingsworth, H. (1991). Learning disabilities as functions of familial learning problems and developmental problems. *Exceptional Children, 57,* 427–440.

Olneck, M. R. (1995). Immigrants and education. In J. A. Banks & C. A. M. Banks (Eds.), *Handbook of research on multicultural education.* New York: Macmillan.

Olson, D. R. (1994). *The world on paper: The conceptual and cognitive implications of writing and reading.* New York: Cambridge University Press.

Olson, D. R., & Bruner, J. S. (1996). Folk psychology and folk pedagogy. In D. R. Olson & N. Torrance (Eds.), *The handbook of education and human development: New models of learning, teaching and schooling* (pp. 9–27). Cambridge, MA: Blackwell.

Olweus, D. (1993). *Bullying at school: What we know and what we can do.* Oxford, England: Blackwell.

Olweus, D., Mattson, A., Schalling, D., & Low, H. (1988). Circulating testosterone levels and aggression in adult males: A causal analysis. *Psychosomatic Medicine, 42,* 253–269.

O'Malley, P. M., & Bachman, J. G. (1983). Self-esteem: Change and stability between ages 13 and 23. *Developmental Psychology, 19,* 257–268.

Oppenheimer, L. (1986). Development of recursive thinking: Procedural variations. *International Journal of Behavioral Development, 9,* 401–411.

Oppenheimer, L., & de Groot, W. (1981). Development of concepts about people in interpersonal situations. *European Journal of Social Psychology, 11,* 209–225.

O'Reilly, A. W. (1995). Using representations: Comprehension and production of actions with imagined objects. *Child Development, 66,* 999–1010.

Ornstein, P. A., & Haden, C. A. (2001). *Memory development or the development of memory?*

Current Directions in Psychological Science, 10, 202–205.

Ornstein, R. (1997). *The right mind: Making sense of the hemispheres.* San Diego, CA: Harcourt Brace.

Ortony, A., Turner, T. J., & Larson-Shapiro, N. (1985). Cultural and instructional influences on figurative comprehension by inner city children. *Research in the Teaching of English, 19*(1), 25–36.

Osborne, J. W., & Simmons, C. M. (2002, April). *Girls, math, stereotype threat, and anxiety: Physiological evidence.* Paper presented at the annual meeting of the American Educational Research Association, New Orleans, LA.

Oskamp, S. (Ed.) (2000). *Reducing prejudice and discrimination.* Mahwah, NJ: Erlbaum.

Osofsky, J. D. (1995). The effects of exposure to violence on young children. *American Psychologist, 50,* 782–788.

Osterman, K. F. (2000). Students' need for belonging in the school community. *Review of Educational Research, 70,* 323–367.

Owens, C. R., & Ascione, F. R. (1991). Effects of the model's age, perceived similarity, and familiarity on children's donating. *Journal of Genetic Psychology, 152,* 341–357.

Owens, R. E., Jr. (1995). *Language disorders: A functional approach to assessment and intervention* (2nd ed.). Boston: Allyn & Bacon.

Owens, R. E., Jr. (1996). *Language development* (4th ed.). Boston: Allyn & Bacon.

Owens, S. A., Steen, F., Hargrave, J., Flores, N., & Hall, P. (2000). *Chase play: The neglected structure of a type of physical activity play.* Manuscript submitted for publication.

Packard, V. (1983). *Our endangered children: Growing up in a changing world.* Boston: Little, Brown.

Paget, K. F., Kritt, D., & Bergemann, L. (1984). Understanding strategic interactions in television commercials: A developmental study. *Journal of Applied Developmental Psychology, 5,* 145–161.

Page-Voth, V., & Graham, S. (1999). Effects of goal setting and strategy use on the writing performance and self-efficacy of students with writing and learning problems. *Journal of Educational Psychology, 91,* 230–240.

Paik, H., & Comstock, G. (1994). The effects of television violence on antisocial behavior: A meta-analysis. *Communication Research, 21,* 516–546.

Paikoff, R. L., & Brooks-Gunn, J. (1991). Do parent-child relationships change during puberty? *Psychological Bulletin, 110,* 47–66.

Pajares, F. (1996). Self-efficacy beliefs in academic settings. *Review of Educational Research, 66,* 543–578.

Pajares, F., & Valiante, G. (1999). *Writing self-efficacy of middle school students: Relation to motivation constructs, achievement, gender, and gender orientation.* Paper presented at the annual meeting of the American Educational Research Association, Montreal, Canada.

Pajares, M. F. (1992). Teachers' beliefs and educational research: Cleaning up a messy construct. *Review of Educational Research, 62,* 307–332.

Palermo, D. S. (1974). Still more about the comprehension of "less." *Developmental Psychology, 10,* 827–829.

Paley, V. G. (1984). *Boys and girls: Superheroes in the doll corner.* Chicago: University of Chicago Press.

Palincsar, A. S., & Brown, A. L. (1984). Reciprocal teaching of comprehension-fostering and comprehension-monitoring activities. *Cognition and Instruction, 1,* 117–175.

Palincsar, A. S., & Brown, A. L. (1989). Classroom dialogues to promote self-regulated comprehension. In J. Brophy (Ed.), *Advances in research on teaching* (Vol. 1). Greenwich, CT: JAI Press.

Palincsar, A. S., & Herrenkohl, L. R. (1999). Designing collaborative contexts: Lessons from

three research programs. In A. M. O'Donnell & A. King (Eds.), *Cognitive perspectives on peer learning* (pp. 151–177). Mahwah, NJ: Erlbaum.

Pang, V. O. (1995). Asian Pacific American students: A diverse and complex population. In J. A. Banks & C. A. M. Banks (Eds.), *Handbook of research on multicultural education.* New York: Macmillan.

Panksepp, J. (1998). Attention deficit hyperactivity disorders, psychostimulants, and intolerance of childhood playfulness: A tragedy in the making? *Current Directions in Psychological Science, 7,* 91–98.

Panofsky, C. P. (1994). Developing the representational functions of language: The role of parent-child book-reading activity. In V. John-Steiner, C. P. Panofsky, & L. W. Smith (Eds.), *Sociocultural approaches to language and literacy: An interactionist perspective.* Cambridge, England: Cambridge University Press.

Papernow, P. (1988). Stepparent role development: From outsider to intimate. In W. R. Beer (Ed.), *Relative strangers* (pp. 54–82). Totowa, NJ: Rowman & Littlefield.

Papousek, M., & Papousek, H. (1996). Infantile persistent crying, state regulation, and interaction with parents: A systems view. In M. H. Bornstein & J. L. Genevro (Eds.), *Child development and behavioral pediatrics* (pp. 11–33). Mahwah, NJ: Erlbaum.

Paris, S. G., & Ayres, L. R. (1994). *Becoming reflective students and teachers with portfolios and authentic assessment.* Washington, DC: American Psychological Association.

Paris, S. G., & Cunningham, A. E. (1996). Children becoming students. In D. C. Berliner & R. C. Calfee (Eds.), *Handbook of educational psychology.* New York: Macmillan.

Paris, S. G., & Jacobs, J. E. (1984). The benefits of informed instruction for children's reading awareness and comprehension skills. *Child Development, 55,* 2083–2093.

Paris, S. G., & Turner, J. C. (1994). Situated motivation. In P. R. Pintrich, D. R. Brown, & C. E. Weinstein (Eds.), *Student motivation, cognition, and learning: Essays in honor of Wilbert J. McKeachie.* Hillsdale, NJ: Erlbaum.

Paris, S. G., & Upton, L. R. (1976). Children's memory for inferential relationships in prose. *Child Development, 47,* 660–668.

Parish, P. (1985). *Amelia Bedelia goes camping.* New York: William Morrow.

Parke, R. D., & Bhavnagri, N. P. (1989). Parents as managers of children's peer relationships. In D. Belle (Ed.), *Children's social networks and social supports.* New York: Wiley.

Parke, R. D., & Buriel, R. (1998). Socialization in the family: Ethnic and ecological perspectives. In W. Damon (Editor-in-Chief) & N. Eisenberg (Vol. Ed.), *Handbook of child psychology: Vol. 3. Social, emotional, and personality development* (5th ed., pp. 463–552). New York: Wiley.

Parke, R. D., Ornstein, P. A., Rieser, J. J., & Zahn-Waxler, C. (1994). The past as prologue: An overview of a century of developmental psychology. In R. D. Parke, P. A. Ornstein, J. J. Rieser, & C. Zahn-Waxler (Eds.), *A century of developmental psychology* (pp. 1–70). Washington, DC: American Psychological Association.

Parke, R. D., & Tinsley, B. R. (1981). The father's role in infancy: Determinants of involvement in caregiving and play. In M. E. Lamb (Ed.), *The role of the father in child development* (pp. 429–458). New York: Wiley.

Parke, R. D., & Tinsley, B. R. (1987). Family interaction in infancy. In J. D. Osofsky (Ed.), *Handbook of infant development* (pp. 429–458). New York: Wiley.

Parke, R. D., & Walters, R. M. (1967). Some factors influencing the efficacy of punishment training for inducing response inhibition. *Monographs of the Society for Research in Child Development, 32*(1).

Parker, J. G. (1986). Becoming friends: Conversational skills for friendship formation in young children. In J. M. Gottman & J. G. Parker (Eds.), *Conversations of friends: Speculations on affective development* (pp. 103–138). Cambridge, England: Cambridge University Press.

Parker, J. G., & Gottman, J. M. (1989). Social and emotional development in a relational context: Friendship interaction from early childhood to adolescence. In T. J. Berndt & G. W. Ladd (Eds.), *Peer relations in child development* (pp. 95–131). New York: Wiley.

Parker, W. D. (1997). An empirical typology of perfectionism in academically talented children. *American Educational Research Journal, 34,* 545–562.

Parkhurst, J., & Gottman, J. M. (1986). How young children get what they want. In J. M. Gottman & J. G. Parker (Eds.), *Conversations of friends: Speculations on affective development* (pp. 315–345). Cambridge, England: Cambridge University Press.

Parkhurst, J. T., & Hopmeyer, A. (1998). Sociometric popularity and peer-perceived popularity: Two distinct dimensions of peer status. *Journal of Early Adolescence, 18,* 125–144.

Parks, C. P. (1995). Gang behavior in the schools: Reality or myth? *Educational Psychology Review, 7,* 41–68.

Parsons, J. E., Adler, T. F., & Kaczala, C. M. (1982). Socialization of achievement attitudes and beliefs: Parental influences. *Child Development, 53,* 310–321.

Parsons, J. E., Kaczala, C. M., & Meece, J. L. (1982). Socialization of achievement attitudes and beliefs: Classroom influences. *Child Development, 53,* 322–339.

Parten, M. B. (1932). Social participation among preschool children. *Journal of Abnormal and Social Psychology, 27,* 243–269.

Pascarella, E. T., & Terenzini, P. T. (1991). *How college affects students: Findings and insights from twenty years of research.* San Francisco: Jossey-Bass.

Passler, M., Isaac, W., & Hynd, G. W. (1985). Neuropsychological development of behavior attributed to frontal lobe functioning in children. *Developmental Neuropsychology, 1,* 349–370.

Pate, R. R., Long, B. J., & Heath, G. (1994). Descriptive epidemiology of physical activity in adolescents. *Pediatric Exercise Science, 6,* 434–447.

Patrick, H. (1997). Social self-regulation: Exploring the relations between children's social relationships, academic self-regulation, and school performance. *Educational Psychologist, 32,* 209–220.

Patterson, C. J. (1992). Children of lesbian and gay parents. *Child Development, 63,* 1025–1042.

Patterson, C. J. (1995). Sexual orientation and human development: An overview. *Developmental Psychology, 31,* 3–11.

Patterson, C. J., & Chan, R. W. (1997). Gay fathers. In M. E. Lamb (Ed.), *The role of the father in child development* (3rd ed., pp. 245–360). New York: Wiley.

Patterson, G. R. (1986). Performance models for antisocial boys. *American Psychologist, 41,* 432–444.

Patterson, G. R. (1995). Coercion as a basis for early age of onset for arrest. In J. McCord (Ed.), *Coercion and punishment in long-term perspectives* (pp. 81–105). New York: Cambridge University Press.

Patterson, G. R., DeBaryshe, B. D., & Ramsey, E. (1989). A developmental perspective on antisocial behavior. *American Psychologist, 44,* 329–335.

Patterson, G. R., Littman, R., & Bricker, W. (1967). Assertive behavior in children: A step toward a theory of aggression. *Monographs of the Society for Research in Child Development, 32*(Serial No. 113).

Patterson, G. R., & Reid, J. B. (1970). Reciprocity and coercion: Two facets of social systems. In C. Neuringer & J. Michael (Eds.), *Behavior modification in clinical psychology.* New York: Appleton-Century-Crofts.

Patton, J. R., Blackbourn, J. M., & Fad, K. (1996). *Exceptional individuals in focus* (6th ed.). Upper Saddle River, NJ: Merrill/Prentice Hall.

Paul, R. (1990). Comprehension strategies: Interactions between world knowledge and the development of sentence comprehension. *Topics in Language Disorders, 10*(3), 63–75.

Paus, T., Zijdenbos, A., Worsley, K., Collins, D. I., Blumenthal, J., Giedd, J. N., et al. (1999). Structural maturation of neural pathways in children and adolescents: in vivo study. *Science, 283,* 1908–1911.

Pawlas, G. E. (1994). Homeless students at the school door. *Educational Leadership, 51*(8), 79–82.

Pea, R. D. (1993). Practices of distributed intelligence and designs for education. In G. Salomon (Ed.), *Distributed cognitions: Psychological and educational considerations.* Cambridge, England: Cambridge University Press.

Peak, L. (1993). Academic effort in international perspective. In T. M. Tomlinson (Ed.), *Motivating students to learn: Overcoming barriers to high achievement.* Berkeley, CA: McCutchan.

Pearson, P. D., Hansen, J., & Gordon, C. (1979). The effect of background knowledge on young children's comprehension of explicit and implicit information. *Journal of Reading Behavior, 11,* 201–209.

Pederson, D. R., Rook-Green, A., & Elder, J. L. (1981). The role of action in the development of pretend play in young children. *Developmental Psychology, 17,* 756–759.

Peiper, A. (1963). *Cerebral function in infancy and childhood.* New York: Consultants Bureau.

Peláez-Nogueras, M., & Gewirtz, J. L. (1995). The learning of moral behavior: A behavior-analytic approach. In W. M. Kurtines & J. L. Gewirtz (Eds.), *Moral development: An introduction.* Boston: Allyn & Bacon.

Pellegrini, A. D. (1996). *Observing children in their natural worlds: A methodological primer.* Mahwah, NJ: Erlbaum.

Pellegrini, A. D. (1998). Play and the assessment of young children. In O. N. Saracho & B. Spodek (Eds.), *Multiple perspectives on play in early childhood education.* Albany: State University of New York Press.

Pellegrini, A. D., & Bartini, M. (2000). A longitudinal study of bullying, victimization, and peer affiliation during the transition from primary school to middle school. *American Educational Research Journal, 37,* 699–725.

Pellegrini, A. D., Bartini, M., & Brooks, F. (1999). School bullies, victims, and aggressive victims: Factors relating to group affiliation and victimization in early adolescence. *Journal of Educational Psychology, 91,* 216–224.

Pellegrini, A. D., & Bjorklund, D. F. (1997). The role of recess in children's cognitive performance. *Educational Psychologist, 32,* 35–40.

Pellegrini, A. D., & Horvat, M. (1995). A developmental contextualist critique of attention deficit hyperactivity disorder. *Educational Researcher, 24*(1), 13–19.

Pellegrini, A. D., & Smith, P. K. (1998). Physical activity play: Consensus and debate. *Child Development, 69,* 609–610.

Peña, E. (1993). Learning strategies checklist. In V. F. Gutiérrez-Clellan & E. Peña (2001), Dynamic assessment of diverse children: A tutorial. *Language, Speech and Hearing Services in Schools, 32,* 212–224.

Pennington, B. F., & Bennetto, L. (1993). Main effects of transactions in the neuropsychology of conduct disorder. Commentary on "The neuropsychology of conduct disorder." *Development and Psychopathology, 5,* 153–164.

Pérez, B. (Ed.). (1998). *Sociocultural contexts of language and literacy.* Mahwah, NJ: Erlbaum.

Perez-Granados, D. R., & Callanan, M. A. (1997). Parents and siblings as early resources for young children's learning in Mexican-descent families. *Hispanic Journal of Behavioral Sciences, 19,* 3–33.

Perfetti, C. A. (1985). Reading ability. In R. J. Sternberg (Ed.), *Human abilities: An information-processing approach.* New York: Freeman.

Perfetti, C. A. (1992). The representation problem in reading acquisition. In P. B. Gough, L. C. Ehri, & R. Treiman (Eds.), *Reading acquisition.* Hillsdale, NJ: Erlbaum.

Perfetti, C. A., & McCutchen, D. (1987). Schooled language competence: Linguistic abilities in reading and writing. In S. Rosenberg (Ed.), *Advances in applied psycholinguistics.* Cambridge, England: Cambridge University Press.

Perkins, D. N., (1992). *Smart schools: From training memories to educating minds.* New York: Free Press/Macmillan.

Perkins, D. N. (1995). *Outsmarting IQ: The emerging science of learnable intelligence.* New York: Free Press.

Perkins, D. N., & Grotzer, T. A. (1997). Teaching intelligence. *American Psychologist, 52,* 1125–1133.

Perkins, D. N., Tishman, S., Ritchhart, R., Donis, K., & Andrade, A. (2000). Intelligence in the wild: A dispositional view of intellectual traits. *Educational Psychology Review, 12,* 269–293.

Perlmutter, M., & Lange, G. A. (1978). A developmental analysis of recall-recognition distinctions. In P. A. Ornstein (Ed.), *Memory development in children.* Hillsdale, NJ: Erlbaum.

Perner, J. (1991). *Understanding the representational mind.* Cambridge, MA: MIT Press.

Perner, J., Lang, B., & Kloo, D. (2002). Theory of mind and self-control: More than a common problem of inhibition. *Child Development, 73,* 752–767.

Perner, J., Ruffman, T., & Leekam, S. R. (1994). Theory of mind is contagious: You catch it from your sibs. *Child Development, 65,* 1228–1238.

Perner, J., & Wimmer, H. (1985). "John *thinks* that Mary *thinks* that. . ." Attribution of second-order beliefs by 5- to 10-year-old children. *Journal of Experimental Child Psychology, 39,* 437–471.

Perry, C. L., Luepker, R. V., Murray, D. M., Hearn, M. D., Halper, A., Dudvitz, B., Mailie, M. C., & Smyth, M. (1989). Parent involvement with children's health promotion: A one-year follow-up of the Minnesota Home Team. *Health Education Quarterly, 16,* 71–180.

Perry, N. E. (1998). Young children's self-regulated learning and contexts that support it. *Journal of Educational Psychology, 90,* 715–729.

Perry, W. G., Jr. (1968). *Forms of intellectual and ethical development in the college years.* Cambridge, MA: President and Fellows of Harvard College.

Peters, A. M. (1983). *The units of language acquisition.* New York: Cambridge University Press.

Peterson, A. C., & Taylor, B. (1980). The biological approach to adolescence: Biological change and psychological adaptation. In J. Adelson (Ed.), *Handbook of adolescent psychology* (pp. 117–155). New York: Wiley.

Peterson, C. (1990). Explanatory style in the classroom and on the playing field. In S. Graham & V. S. Folkes (Eds.), *Attribution theory: Applications to achievement, mental health, and interpersonal conflict.* Hillsdale, NJ: Erlbaum.

Peterson, C., Maier, S. F., & Seligman, M. E. P. (1993). *Learned helplessness: A theory for the age of personal control.* New York: Oxford University Press.

Peterson, L. (1980). Developmental changes in verbal and behavioral sensitivity to cues of social norms of altruism. *Child Development, 51,* 830–838.

Peterson, M. E., & Haines, L. P. (1992). Orthographic analogy training with kindergarten children: Effects of analogy use, phonemic segmentation, and letter-sound knowledge. *Journal of Reading Behavior, 24,* 109–127.

Peterson, P. L. (1992). Revising their thinking: Keisha Coleman and her third-grade mathematics class. In H. H. Marshall (Ed.), *Redefining student learning: Roots of educational change.* Norwood, NJ: Ablex.

Petrill, S. A., & Wilkerson, B. (2000). Intelligence and achievement: A behavioral genetic perspective. *Educational Psychology Review, 12,* 185–199.

Pettit, G. S., Bates, J. E., Dodge, K. A., & Meece, D. W. (1999). The impact of after-school peer contact on early adolescent externalizing problems is moderated by parental monitoring, perceived neighborhood safety, and prior adjustment. *Child Development, 70,* 768–778.

Pettit, G. S., Brown, E. G., Mize, J., & Lindsey, E. (1998). Mothers and fathers socializing behaviors in three contexts: Links with children's peer competence. *Merrill-Palmer Quarterly, 44*(2), 173–193.

Pettit, G. S., Laird, R. D., Bates, J. E., & Dodge, K. A. (1997). Patterns of after-school care in middle childhood: Risk factors and developmental outcomes. *Merrill-Palmer Quarterly, 43*(3), 515–538.

Pettito, A. L. (1985). Division of labor: Procedural learning in teacher-led small groups. *Cognition and Instruction, 2,* 233–270.

Pettito, L. A. (1997). In the beginning: On the genetic and environmental factors that make early language acquisition possible. In M. Gopnik (Ed.), *The inheritance and innateness of grammars.* New York: Oxford University Press.

Phelan, P., Yu, H. C., & Davidson, A. L. (1994). Navigating the psychosocial pressures of adolescence: The voices and experiences of high school youth. *American Educational Research Journal, 31,* 415–447.

Phillips, D., Mekos, D., Scarr, S., McCartney, K., & Abbott-Shim, M. (2001). Within and beyond the classroom door: Assessing quality in child care centers. *Early Childhood Research Quarterly, 15,* 475–496.

Phillips, M. (1997). What makes schools effective? A comparison of the relationships of communitarian climate and academic climate to mathematics achievement and attendance during middle school. *American Educational Research Journal, 34,* 633–662.

Phinney, J. S. (1989). Stages of ethnic identity development in minority group adolescents. *Journal of Early Adolescence, 9,* 34–49.

Phinney, J. S. (1990). Ethnic identity in adolescents and adults: Review of research. *Psychological Bulletin, 108,* 499–514.

Phinney, J. S., & Tarver, S. (1988). Ethnic identity search and commitment in Black and White eighth graders. *Journal of Early Adolescence, 8,* 265–277.

Piaget, J. (1928). *Judgment and reasoning in the child* (M. Warden, Trans.). New York: Harcourt, Brace.

Piaget, J. (1929). *The child's conception of the world.* New York: Harcourt, Brace.

Piaget, J. (1952a). *The child's conception of number* (C. Gattegno & F. M. Hodgson, Trans.). London: Routledge & Kegan Paul.

Piaget, J. (1952b). *The origins of intelligence in children.* New York: International Universities Press.

Piaget, J. (1959). *The language and thought of the child* (3rd ed.; M. Gabain, Trans.). London: Routledge & Kegan Paul.

Piaget, J. (1960a). *The child's conception of physical causality* (M. Gabain, Trans.). Paterson, NJ: Littlefield, Adams.

Piaget, J. (1960b). *The moral judgment of the child* (M. Gabain, Trans.). Glencoe, IL: Free Press. (First published in 1932)

Piaget, J., & Inhelder, B. (1969). *The psychology of the child* (H. Weaver, Trans.). New York: Basic Books.

Piaget, J. (1970). Piaget's theory. In P. H. Mussen (Ed.), *Carmichael's manual of psychology.* New York: Wiley.

Piaget, J. (1985). *The equilibration of cognitive structures: The central problem of intellectual development.* Chicago: University of Chicago Press.

Pianko, S. (1979). A description of the composing processes of college freshmen writers. *Research in the Teaching of English, 13,* 5–22.

Piche, C., & Plante, C. (1991). Perceived masculinity, femininity, and androgyny among primary school boys: Relationships with the adaptation level of these students and the attitudes of the teachers towards them. *European Journal of Psychology of Education, 6,* 423–435.

Piirto, J. (1999). *Talented children and adults: Their development and education* (2nd ed.). Upper Saddle River, NJ: Merrill/Prentice Hall.

Pillow, B. H. (2002). Children's and adults' evaluation of the certainty of deductive inferences, inductive inferences, and guesses. *Child Development, 73,* 779–792.

Pillow, B. H., & Henrichon, A. J. (1996). There's more to the picture than meets the eye: Young children's difficulty understanding biased interpretation. *Child Development, 67,* 803–819.

Pinker, S. (1982). A theory of the acquisition of lexical interpretive grammars. In J. Bresnan (Ed.), *The mental representation of grammatical notions.* Cambridge, MA: MIT Press.

Pinker, S. (1984). *Language learnability and language development.* Cambridge, MA: Harvard University Press.

Pinker, S. (1987). The bootstrapping problem in language acquisition. In B. MacWhinney (Ed.), *Mechanisms of language acquisition.* Hillsdale, NJ: Erlbaum.

Pinker, S. (1993). Rules of language. In P. Bloom (Ed.), *Language acquisition: Core readings.* Cambridge, MA: MIT Press.

Pinker, S. (1997). Evolutionary biology and the evolution of language. In M. Gopnik (Ed.), *The inheritance and innateness of grammars.* New York: Oxford University Press.

Pinnegar, S. E. (1988, April). *Learning the language of practice from practicing teachers: An exploration of the term "with me."* Paper presented at the annual meeting of the American Educational Research Association, New Orleans.

Pintrich, P. R. (2000). Multiple goals, multiple pathways: The role of goal orientation in learning and achievement. *Journal of Educational Psychology, 92,* 544–555.

Pintrich, P. R., & Garcia, T. (1994). Regulating motivation and cognition in the classroom: The role of self-schemas and self-regulatory strategies. In D. Schunk & B. Zimmerman (Eds.), *Self-regulation of learning and performance: Issues and educational applications.* Hillsdale, NJ: Erlbaum.

Pintrich, P. R., & Schrauben, B. (1992). Students' motivational beliefs and their cognitive engagement in academic tasks. In D. Schunk & J. Meece (Eds.), *Students' perceptions in the classroom: Causes and consequences.* Hillsdale, NJ: Erlbaum.

Pintrich, P. R., & Schunk, D. H. (1996). *Motivation in education: Theory, research, and applications.* Upper Saddle River, NJ: Merrill/Prentice Hall.

Pipher, M. (1994). *Reviving Ophelia: Saving the selves of adolescent girls.* New York: Putnam.

Plomin, R. (1989). Environment and genes: Determinants of behavior. *American Psychologist, 44,* 105–111.

Plomin, R. (1994). *Genetics and experience: The interplay between nature and nurture.* Thousand Oaks, CA: Sage.

Plomin, R., & DeFries, J. C. (1985). *Origins of individual differences in infancy.* New York: Academic Press.

Plomin, R., Emde, R. N., Braungart, J. M., Campos, J., Kagan, J., Reznick, J. S., Robinson, J., Zahn-Waxler, C., & DeFries, J. C. (1993). Genetic change and continuity from fourteen to twenty months: The MacArthur Longitudinal Twin Study. *Child Development, 64,* 1354–1376.

Plomin, R., Fulker, D. W., Corley, R., & DeFries, J. C. (1997). Nature, nurture, and cognitive development from 1 to 16 years: A parent-offspring adoption study. *Psychological Science, 8,* 442–447.

Plomin, R., Owen, M. J., & McGuffin, P. (1994). The genetic basis of complex human behaviors. *Science, 24,* 1733–1739.

Plomin, R., & Petrill, S. A. (1997). Genetics and intelligence: What's new? *Intelligence, 24,* 53–77.

Plumert, J. M. (1994). Flexibility in children's use of spatial and categorical organizational strategies in recall. *Developmental Psychology, 30,* 738–747.

Pogrow, S., & Londer, G. (1994). The effects of an intensive general thinking program on the motivation and cognitive development of at-risk students: Findings from the HOTS program. In H. F. O'Neil, Jr., & M. Drillings (Eds.), *Motivation: Theory and research.* Hillsdale, NJ: Erlbaum.

Pollack, W. (1998). *Real boys: Rescuing our sons from the myths of boyhood.* New York: Henry Holt.

Pollard, S. R., Kurtines, W. M., Carlo, G., Dancs, M., & Mayock, E. (1991). Moral education from the perspective of psychosocial theory. In W. M. Kurtines & J. L. Gewirtz (Eds.), *Moral behavior and development: Vol. 3. Application.* Hillsdale, NJ: Erlbaum.

Pollitt, E., & Oh, S. (1994). Early supplemental feeding, child development and health policy. *Food & Nutrition Bulletin, 15,* 208–214.

Poole, T. G. (1990). Black families and the Black church: A sociocultural perspective. In H. Cheatham & J. Stewart (Eds.), *Black families: Interdisciplinary perspectives* (pp. 33–48). New Brunswick, NJ: Transaction Publishers.

Poresky, R. H., Daniels, A. M., Mukerjee, J., & Gunnell, K. (1999, April). *Community and family influences on adolescents' use of alcohol and other drugs: An exploratory ecological analysis.* Paper presented at the Biennial Meeting of the Society for Research in Child Development, Albuquerque, NM.

Portes, P. R. (1996). Ethnicity and culture in educational psychology. In D. C. Berliner & R. C. Calfee (Eds.), *Handbook of educational psychology.* New York: Macmillan.

Posner, G. J., Strike, K. A., Hewson, P. W., & Gertzog, W. A. (1982). Accommodation of a scientific conception: Toward a theory of conceptual change. *Science Education, 66,* 211–227.

Poulin, F., & Boivin, M. (1999). Proactive and reactive aggression and boys' friendship quality in mainstream classrooms. *Journal of Emotional and Behavioral Disorders, 7,* 168–177.

Poulin-Dubois, D. (1999). Infants' distinction between animate and inanimate objects: The origins of naive psychology. In P. Rochat (Ed.), *Early social cognition* (pp. 257–280). Mahwah, NJ: Erlbaum.

Powell, G. J. (1983). *The psychosocial development of minority children.* New York: Brunner/Mazel.

Powell, M. P., & Schulte, T. (1999). Turner syndrome. In S. Goldstein & C. R. Reynolds (Eds.), *Handbook of neurodevelopmental and genetic disorders* (pp. 277–297). New York: Guilford Press.

Power, F. C., Higgins, A., & Kohlberg, L. (1989). *Lawrence Kohlberg's approach to moral education.* New York: Columbia University Press.

Powers, L. E., Sowers, J. A., & Stevens, T. (1995). An exploratory, randomized study of the impact of mentoring on the self-efficacy and community-based knowledge of adolescents with severe physical challenges. *Journal of Rehabilitation, 61*(1), 33–41.

Powers, S. M. (1974). The validity of the Vane Kindergarten Test in predicting achievement in kindergarten and first grade. *Educational and Psychological Measurement, 34,* 1003–1007.

Powers, S. I., Hauser, S. T., & Kilner, L. A. (1989). Adolescent mental health. *American Psychologist, 44,* 200–208.

Powlishta, K. K. (1995). Intergroup processes in childhood: Social categorization and sex role development. *Developmental Psychology, 31,* 781–788.

Powlishta, K. K., Serbin, L. A., Doyle, A.-B., & White, D. R. (1994). Gender, ethnic, and body type biases: The generality of prejudice in childhood. *Developmental Psychology, 30,* 526–536.

Pramling, I. (1996). Understanding and empowering the child as learner. In D. R. Olson & N. Torrance (Eds.), *The handbook of education and human development: New models of learning, teaching, and schooling.* Cambridge, MA: Blackwell.

Prawat, R. S. (1989). Promoting access to knowledge, strategy, and disposition in students: A research synthesis. *Review of Educational Research, 59,* 1–41.

Preedy, P. (1999). Meeting the educational needs of pre-school and primary aged twins and higher multiples. In A. C. Sandbank (Ed.), *Twin and triplet psychology: A professional guide to working with multiples* (pp. 70–99). London: Routledge.

Pressley, M. (1982). Elaboration and memory development. *Child Development, 53,* 296–309.

Pressley, M. (1994). State-of-the-science primary-grades reading instruction or whole language? *Educational Psychologist, 29,* 211–215.

Pressley, M., Almasi, J., Schuder, T., Bergman, J., Hite, S., El-Dinary, P. B., & Brown, R. (1994). Transactional instruction of comprehension strategies: The Montgomery County Maryland SAIL program. *Reading and Writing Quarterly, 10,* 5–19.

Pressley, M., Borkowski, J. G., & Schneider, W. (1987). Cognitive strategies: Good strategy users coordinate metacognition and knowledge. In R. Vasta (Ed.), *Annals of child development* (Vol. 4). Greenwich, CT: JAI Press.

Pressley, M., El-Dinary, P. B., Marks, M. B., Brown, R., & Stein, S. (1992). Good strategy instruction is motivating and interesting. In K. A. Renninger, S. Hidi, & A. Krapp (Eds.), *The role of interest in learning and development.* Hillsdale, NJ: Erlbaum.

Pressley, M., Goodchild, F., Fleet, J., Zajchowski, R., & Evans, E. D. (1989). The challenges of classroom strategy instruction. *Elementary School Journal, 89,* 301–342.

Pressley, M., Levin, J. R., & Ghatala, E. S. (1984). Memory strategy monitoring in adults and children. *Journal of Verbal Learning and Verbal Behavior, 23,* 270–288.

Pressley, M., & McCormick, C. B. (1995). *Advanced educational psychology for educators, researchers, and policymakers.* New York: HarperCollins.

Pressley, M., Ross, K. A., Levin, J. R., & Ghatala, E. S. (1984). The role of strategy utility knowledge in children's strategy decision making. *Journal of Experimental Child Psychology, 38,* 491–504.

Pribilsky, J. (2001). Nervios and 'modern childhood': Migration and shifting contexts of child life in the Ecuadorian Andes. *Childhood, 8(2),* 251–273.

Price, L. N., & Clarke-McLean, J. G. (1997, April). *Beyond stereotypes: Configurations and competence among African American inner city youth.* Poster presented at the biennial meeting of the Society for Research in Child Development, Washington, DC.

Price-Williams, D. R., Gordon, W., & Ramirez, M. (1969). Skill and conservation. *Developmental Psychology, 1,* 769.

Pritchard, R. (1990). The effects of cultural schemata on reading processing strategies. *Reading Research Quarterly, 25,* 273–295.

Proctor, R. W., & Dutta, A. (1995). *Skill acquisition and human performance.* Thousand Oaks, CA: Sage.

Pulkkinen, L. (1982). Self-control and continuity from childhood to adolescence. In P. B. Baltes & O. G. Brim (Eds.), *Life-span development and behavior* (Vol. 4). Orlando, FL: Academic Press.

Pulos, S., & Linn, M. C. (1981). Generality of the controlling variables scheme in early adolescence. *Journal of Early Adolescence, 1,* 26–37.

Purcell-Gates, V. (1995). *Other people's words: The cycle of low literacy.* Cambridge, MA: Harvard University Press.

Purcell-Gates, V., McIntyre, E., & Freppon, P. A. (1995). Learning written storybook language in school: A comparison of low-SES children in skills-based and whole language classrooms. *American Educational Research Journal, 32,* 659–685.

Purdie, N., & Hattie, J. (1996). Cultural differences in the use of strategies for self-regulated learning. *American Educational Research Journal, 33,* 845–871.

Purdie, N., Hattie, J., & Douglas, G. (1996). Student conceptions of learning and their use of self-regulated learning strategies: A cross-cultural comparison. *Journal of Educational Psychology, 88,* 87–100.

Putallaz, M., & Gottman, J. M. (1981). Social skills and group acceptance. In S. R. Asher & J. M. Gottman (Eds.), *The development of children's friendships* (pp. 116–149). New York: Cambridge University Press.

Putallaz, M., & Heflin, A. H. (1986). Toward a model of peer acceptance. In J. M. Gottman & J. G. Parker (Eds.), *Conversations of friends: Speculations on affective development* (pp. 292–314). Cambridge, England: Cambridge University Press.

Quinn, P. C. (2002). Category representation in young infants. *Current Directions in Psychological Science, 11,* 66–70.

Quinn, P. C. (2003). Concepts are not just for objects: Categorization of spatial relation information by young infants. In D. H. Rakison & L. M. Oakes (Eds.), *Early category and concept development: Making sense of the blooming,*

buzzing confusion. Oxford, England: Oxford University Press.

Rabinowitz, M., & Glaser, R. (1985). Cognitive structure and process in highly competent performance. In F. D. Horowitz & M. O'Brien (Eds.), *The gifted and the talented: Developmental perspectives.* Washington, DC: American Psychological Association.

Radziszewska, B., & Rogoff, B. (1988). Influence of adult and peer collaborators on children's planning skills. *Developmental Psychology, 24,* 840–848.

Radziszewska, B., & Rogoff, B. (1991). Children's guided participation in planning imaginary errands with skilled adult or peer partners. *Developmental Psychology, 27,* 381–389.

Rahm, J. (2002). Emergent learning opportunities in an inner-city youth gardening program. *Journal of Research in Science Teaching, 39(2),* 164–184.

Raikes, H. (1993). Relationship duration in infant care: Time with high-ability teacher and infant-teacher attachment. *Early Childhood Research Quarterly, 8(3),* 309–325.

Raine, A., & Scerbo, A. (1991). Biological theories of violence. In J. S. Milner (Ed.), *Neuropsychology of aggression* (pp. 1–25). Boston: Kluwer Academic Press.

Rakic, P. (1995). Corticogenesis in human and nonhuman primates. In M. S. Gazzaniga (Ed.), *The cognitive neurosciences* (pp. 127–145). Cambridge, MA: MIT Press.

Rallison, M. L. (1986). *Growth disorders in infants, children, and adolescents.* New York: Churchill Livingstone.

Ramachandran, V. S., Rogers-Ramachandran, D., & Stewart, M. (1992). Perceptual correlates of massive cortical reorganization. *Science, 258,* 1159–1160.

Ramey, C. T. (1992). High-risk children and IQ: Altering intergenerational patterns. *Intelligence, 16,* 239–256.

Ramey, C. T., & Ramey, S. L. (1998). Early intervention and early experience. *American Psychologist, 53,* 109–120.

Ramsey, P. G. (1987). *Teaching and learning in a diverse world: Multicultural education for young children.* New York: Teachers College Press.

Ramsey, P. G. (1995). Growing up with the contradictions of race and class. *Young Children, 50,* 18–22.

Ratcliff, N. (2001). Use the environment to prevent discipline problems and support learning. *Young Children,* 84–88.

Ratner, H. H. (1984). Memory demands and the development of young children's memory. *Child Development, 55,* 2173–2191.

Raudenbush, S. W. (1984). Magnitude of teacher expectancy effects on pupil IQ as a function of credibility induction: A synthesis of findings from 18 experiments. *Journal of Educational Psychology, 76,* 85–97.

Raver, C. C. (2002). Emotions matter: Making the case for the role of young children's emotional development for early school readiness. *Social Policy Report of the Society for Research in Child Development, 16(3),* 1, 3–6, 8–10, 12–18.

Rayner, K., Foorman, B. R., Perfetti, C. A., Pesetsky, D., & Seidenberg, M. S. (2001). How psychological science informs the teaching of reading. *Psychological Science in the Public Interest, 2,* 31–74.

Rayport, S. G. (1992). Cellular and molecular biology of the neuron. In S. C. Yudofsky & R. E. Hales (Eds.), *The American Psychiatric Press textbook of neuropsychiatry* (2nd ed., pp. 3–28). Washington, DC: American Psychiatric Press.

Reese, D. F., & Thorkildsen, T. A. (1999, April). *Perceptions of exclusion among eighth graders from low-income families.* Paper presented at the annual meeting of the American Educational Research Association, Montreal.

Reese, E., & Fivush, R. (1993). Parental styles of talking about the past. *Developmental Psychology, 29,* 596–606.

Reese, L., Garnier, H., Gallimore, R., & Goldenberg, C. (2000). Longitudinal analysis of the antecedents of emergent Spanish literacy and middle-school English reading achievement of Spanish-speaking students. *American Educational Research Journal, 37,* 633–662.

Reeve, J., Bolt, E., & Cai, Y. (1999). Autonomy-supportive teachers: How they teach and motivate students. *Journal of Educational Psychology, 91,* 537–548.

Reich, P. A. (1986). *Language development.* Englewood Cliffs, NJ: Prentice Hall.

Reid, N. (1989). Contemporary Polynesian conceptions of giftedness. *Gifted Education International, 6(1),* 30–38.

Reid, P. T. (1985). Sex-role socialization of black children: A review of theory, family, and media influences. *Academic Psychology Bulletin, 7,* 201–212.

Reifman, A., Barnes, G. M., & Hoffman, J. H. (1999, April). *Physical maturation and problem behaviors in male adolescents: A test of peer and parent relations as mediators.* Paper presented at the Biennial Meeting of the Society for Research in Child Development, Albuquerque, NM.

Reimer, J., Paolitto, D. P., & Hersh, R. H. (1983). *Promoting moral growth: From Piaget to Kohlberg* (2nd ed.). White Plains, NY: Longman.

Reis, S. M. (1989). Reflections on policy affecting the education of gifted and talented students: Past and future perspectives. *American Psychologist, 44,* 399–408.

Reiss, I. R. (1980). *Family systems in America* (3rd ed.). New York: Holt, Rinehart & Winston.

Reissland, N. (1988). Neonatal imitation in the first hour of life: Observations in rural Nepal. *Developmental Psychology, 24,* 464–469.

Renninger, K. A., Hidi, S., & Krapp, A. (Eds.). (1992). *The role of interest in learning and development.* Hillsdale, NJ: Erlbaum.

Renzulli, J. S. (1978). What makes giftedness? Reexamining a definition. *Phi Delta Kappan, 60,* 180–184.

Renzulli, J. S., & Reis, S. M. (1986). The enrichment triad/revolving door model: A school wide plan for the development of creative productivity. In J. Renzulli (Ed.), *Systems and models for developing programs for the gifted and talented.* Mansfield Center, CT: Creative Learning Press.

Repacholi, B. M., & Gopnik, A. (1997). Early reasoning about desires: Evidence from 14- and 18-month-olds. *Developmental Psychology, 33,* 12–21.

Reschly, D. J. (1997). Diagnostic and treatment utility of intelligence tests. In D. P. Flanagan, J. L. Genshaft, & P. L. Harrison (Eds.), *Contemporary intellectual assessment: Theories, tests, and issues* (pp. 437–456). New York: Guilford Press.

Resnick, L. B. (1989). Developing mathematical knowledge. *American Psychologist, 44,* 162–169.

Resnick, L. B. (1995). From aptitude to effort: A new foundation for our schools. *Daedalus, 124(4),* 55–62.

Resnicow, K., Cross, D., & Wynder, E. (1991). The role of comprehensive school-based interventions. *Annals of the New York Academy of Sciences, 623,* 285–298.

Rest, J. R., Narvaez, D., Bebeau, M., & Thoma, S. (1999). A neo-Kohlbergian approach: The DIT and schema theory. *Educational Psychology Review, 11,* 291–324.

Reutzel, D. R., & Cooter, R. B., Jr. (1999). *Balanced reading strategies and practices.* Upper Saddle River, NJ: Merrill/Prentice Hall.

Reyna, C. (2000). Lazy, dumb, or industrious: When stereotypes convey attribution information in the classroom. *Educational Psychology Review, 12,* 85–110.

Reyna, V. F. (1996, May 2). Fuzzy-trace theory, reasoning, and decision-making. Presentation at the University of Northern Colorado, Greeley.

Reynolds, A. (1994). Effects of a preschool plus follow-on intervention for children at risk. *Developmental Psychology, 30*, 787–804.

Reynolds, A. J., Mavrogenes, N. A., Bezruczko, N., & Hagemann, M. (1996). Cognitive and family-support mediators of preschool effectiveness: A confirmatory analysis. *Child Development, 67*, 1119–1140.

Reynolds, R. E., Taylor, M. A., Steffensen, M. S., Shirey, L. L., & Anderson, R. C. (1982). Cultural schemata and reading comprehension. *Reading Research Quarterly, 17*, 353–366.

Reznick, J. S., & Goldfield, B. A. (1992). Rapid change in lexical development in comprehension and production. *Developmental Psychology, 28*, 408–414.

Ricciuti, H. N. (1993). Nutrition and mental development. *Current Directions in Psychological Science, 2*, 43–46.

Rice, M., Hadley, P. A., & Alexander, A. L. (1993). Social biases toward children with speech and language impairments: A correlative causal model of language limitations. *Applied Psycholinguistics, 14*, 445–471.

Rice, M. L., Huston, A. C., Truglio, R., & Wright, J. (1990). Words from "Sesame Street": Learning vocabulary while viewing. *Developmental Psychology, 26*, 421–428.

Richards, J. E., & Turner, E. D. (2001). Extended visual fixation and distractibility in children from six to twenty-four months of age. *Child Development, 72*, 963–972.

Richman, A. L., Miller, P. M., & Solomon, M. J. (1988). The socialization of infants in suburban Boston. In R. A. LeVine, P. M. Miller, & M. M. West (Eds.), *Parental behavior in diverse societies* (pp. 65–74). San Francisco, CA: Jossey-Bass.

Richman, N., Stevenson, J., & Graham, P. J. (1982). *Preschool to school: A behavioural study*. London: Academic Press.

Ridderinkhof, K. R., & van der Molen, M. (1995). A psychophysiological analysis of developmental differences in the ability to resist interference. *Child Development, 60*, 1040–1056.

Rimm, D. C., & Masters, J. C. (1974). *Behavior therapy: Techniques and empirical findings*. San Diego, CA: Academic Press.

Rinehart, S. D., Stahl, S. A., & Erickson, L. G. (1986). Some effects of summarization training on reading and studying. *Reading Research Quarterly, 21*, 422–438.

Ripple, C. H., Gilliam, W. S., Chanana, N., & Zigler, E. (1999). Will fifty cooks spoil the broth? The debate over entrusting Head Start to the states. *American Psychologist, 54*, 327–343.

Ritchie, D., Price, V., & Roberts, D. F. (1987). Television, reading, and reading achievement: A reappraisal. *Communication Research, 14*, 292–315.

Rittle-Johnson, B., & Siegler, R. S. (1999). Learning to spell: Variability, choice, and change in children's strategy use. *Child Development, 70*, 332–348.

Ritts, V., Patterson, M. L., & Tubbs, M. E. (1992). Expectations, impressions, and judgments of physically attractive students: A review. *Review of Educational Research, 62*, 413–426.

RMC Research Corporation. (1989). *The impact of Reading Rainbow on libraries*. Hampton, NH: RMC Corporation.

Robbins, W. J., Brody, S., Hogan, A. G., Jackson, C. M., & Green, C. W. (Eds.) (1928). *Growth*. New Haven, CT: Yale University Press.

Roberge, J. J. (1970). A study of children's abilities to reason with basic principles of deductive reasoning. *American Educational Research Journal, 7*, 583–596.

Roberts, D. F., Christenson, P., Gibson, W. A., Mooser, L., & Goldberg, M. E. (1980). Developing discriminating consumers. *Journal of Communication, 30*, 94–105.

Robertson, J. S. (2000). Is attribution training a worthwhile classroom intervention for K–12 students with learning difficulties? *Educational Psychology Review, 12*, 111–134.

Robin, D. J., Berthier, N. E., & Clifton, R. K. (1996). Infants' predictive reaching for moving objects in the dark. *Developmental Psychology, 32*, 824–835.

Robinson, T. N., & Killen, J. D. (1995). Ethnic and gender differences in the relationship between television viewing and obesity, physical activity, and dietary fat intake. *Journal of Health Education, 26*(Suppl. 2), S91–S98.

Robinson, T. R., Smith, S. W., Miller, M. D., & Brownell, M. T. (1999). Cognitive behavior modification of hyperactivity-impulsivity and aggression: A meta-analysis of school-based studies. *Journal of Educational Psychology, 91*, 195–203.

Rochat, P., & Bullinger, A. (1994). Posture and functional action in infancy. In A. Vyt, H. Bloch, & M. H. Bornstein (Eds.), *Early child development in the French tradition: Contributions from current research*. Hillsdale, NJ: Erlbaum.

Rochat, P., & Goubet, N. (1995). Development of sitting and reaching in 5- to 6-month-old infants. *Infant behavior and development, 18*, 53–68.

Roderick, M., & Camburn, E. (1999). Risk and recovery from course failure in the early years of high school. *American Educational Research Journal, 36*, 303–343.

Roffwarg, H. P., Muzio, J. N., & Dement, W. C. (1966). Ontogenetic development of the human sleep-dream cycle. *Science, 152*, 604–619.

Rogoff, B. (1990). *Apprenticeship in thinking: Cognitive development in social context*. New York: Oxford University Press.

Rogoff, B. (1991). Social interaction as apprenticeship in thinking: Guidance and participation in spatial planning. In L. B. Resnick, J. M. Levine, & S. D. Teasley (Eds.), *Perspectives on socially shared cognition*. Washington, DC: American Psychological Association.

Rogoff, B. (1995). Observing sociocultural activity on three planes: Participatory appropriation, guided participation, and apprenticeship. In J. V. Wertsch, P. del Rio, & A. Alvarez (Eds.), *Sociocultural studies of mind*. Cambridge, England: Cambridge University Press.

Rogoff, B. (1996). Developmental transitions in children's participation in sociocultural activities. In A. J. Sameroff & M. M. Haith (Eds.), *The five to seven year shift: The age of reason and responsibility* (pp. 273–294). Chicago: University of Chicago Press.

Rogoff, B., Mistry, J., Göncü, A., & Mosier, C. (1993). Guided participation in cultural activity by toddlers and caregivers. *Monographs of the Society for Research in Child Development, 58* (8, Serial No. 236).

Rogoff, B., & Morelli, G. (1989). Perspectives on children's development from cultural psychology. *American Psychologist, 44*, 343–348.

Rohner, R. P. (1998). Father love and child development: History and current evidence. *Current Directions in Psychological Science, 7*, 157–161.

Rohner, R. P., & Rohner, E. C. (1981). Parental acceptance-rejection and parental control: Cross-cultural codes. *Ethnology, 20*, 245–260.

Roid, G. (2003). *Stanford-Binet Intelligence Scales* (5th ed.). Itasca, IL: Riverside.

Rommetveit, R. (1985). Language acquisition as increasing linguistic structuring of experience and symbolic behavior control. In J. V. Wertsch (Ed.), *Culture, communication, and cognition: Vygotskian perspectives* (pp. 183–204). Cambridge, England: Cambridge University Press.

Rondal, J. A. (1985). *Adult-child interaction and the process of language acquisition*. New York: Praeger.

Roopnarine, J. L., Lasker, J., Sacks, M., & Stores, M. (1998). The cultural contexts of children's play. In O. N. Saracho & B. Spodek (Eds.), *Multiple perspectives on play in early childhood education*. Albany: State University of New York Press.

Rose, A. J., & Asher, S. R. (1999). Children's goals and strategies in response to conflicts within a friendship. *Developmental Psychology, 35*, 69–79.

Rose, S. A. (1994). Relation between physical growth and information processing in infants born in India. *Child Development, 65*, 889–903.

Rose, S. A., & Feldman, J. F. (1995). Prediction of IQ and specific cognitive abilities at 11 years from infancy measures. *Developmental Psychology, 31*, 685–696.

Rose, S. C., & Thornburg, K. R. (1984). Mastery motivation and need for approval in young children: Effects of age, sex, and reinforcement condition. *Educational Research Quarterly, 9*(1), 34–42.

Rosenberg, M. (1986). Self-concept from middle childhood through adolescence. In S. Suls & A. Greenwald (Eds.), *Psychological perspectives on the self* (Vol. 3, pp. 107–135). Hillsdale, NJ: Erlbaum.

Rosenberg, M. L., O'Carroll, P., & Powell, K. (1992). Let's be clear: Violence is a public health problem. *Journal of the American Medical Association, 267*, 3071–3072.

Rosenhan, D. L. (1970). The natural socialization of altruistic autonomy. In J. Macaulay & L. Berkowitz (Eds.), *Altruism and helping behavior* (pp. 251–268). New York: Academic Press.

Rosenshine, B., & Meister, C. (1992). The use of scaffolds for teaching higher-level cognitive strategies. *Educational Leadership, 49*(7), 26–33.

Rosenshine, B., & Meister, C. (1994). Reciprocal teaching: A review of the research. *Review of Educational Research, 64*, 479–530.

Rosenshine, B., Meister, C., & Chapman, S. (1996). Teaching students to generate questions: A review of the intervention studies. *Review of Educational Research, 66*, 181–221.

Rosenstein, D., & Oster, H. (1988). Differential facial responses to four basic tastes in newborns. *Child Development, 59*, 1555–1568.

Rosenthal, R. (1994). Interpersonal expectancy effects: A 30-year perspective. *Current Directions in Psychological Science, 3*, 176–179.

Rosenthal, T. L., & Bandura, A. (1978). Psychological modeling: Theory and practice. In S. L. Garfield & A. E. Begia (Eds.), *Handbook of psychotherapy and behavior change: An empirical analysis* (2nd ed.). New York: Wiley.

Ross, H. N., Conant, C. L., Cheyne, J. A., & Alevizos, E. (1992). Relationships and alliances in the social interactions of kibbutz toddlers. *Social Development, 1*, 1–17.

Ross, J. A. (1988). Controlling variables: A meta-analysis of training studies. *Review of Educational Research, 58*, 405–437.

Ross, S. M., Smith, L. J., Casey, J., & Slavin, R. E. (1995). Increasing the academic success of disadvantaged children: An examination of alternative early intervention programs. *American Educational Research Journal, 32*, 773–800.

Rosser, R. (1994). *Cognitive development: Psychological and biological perspectives*. Boston: Allyn & Bacon.

Rossi, A. S., & Rossi, P. H. (1990). *Of human bonding: Parent-child relations across the life course*. New York: Aldine de Gruyter.

Rossman, B. R. (1992). School-age children's perceptions of coping with distress: Strategies for emotion regulation and the moderation of adjustment. *Journal of Child Psychology and Psychiatry, 33*, 1373–1397.

Rotenberg, K. J., & Mayer, E. V. (1990). Delay of gratification in Native and White children:

A cross-cultural comparison. *International Journal of Behavioral Development, 13,* 23–30.

Roth, K. J. (1990). Developing meaningful conceptual understanding in science. In B. F. Jones & L. Idol (Eds.), *Dimensions of thinking and cognitive instruction.* Hillsdale, NJ: Erlbaum.

Roth, K. J., & Anderson, C. (1988). Promoting conceptual change learning from science textbooks. In P. Ramsden (Ed.), *Improving learning: New perspectives.* London: Kogan Page.

Roth, W., & Bowen, G. M. (1995). Knowing and interacting: A study of culture, practices, and resources in a grade 8 open-inquiry science classroom guided by a cognitive apprenticeship metaphor. *Cognition and Instruction, 13,* 73–128.

Rothbart, M. K., & Ahadi, S. A. (1994). Temperament and the development of personality. *Journal of Abnormal Psychology, 103,* 55–66.

Rothbart, M. K., & Bates, J. E. (1998). Temperament. In W. Damon (Editor-in-Chief) & N. Eisenberg (Vol. Ed.), *Handbook of child psychology: Vol. 3. Social, emotional, and personality development* (5th ed., pp. 105–176). New York: Wiley.

Rothbart, M. K., Hanley, D., & Albert, M. (1986). Gender differences in moral reasoning. *Sex Roles, 15,* 645–653.

Rothbaum, F., Weisz, J., Pott, M., Miyake, K., & Morelli, G. (2000). Attachment and culture: Security in the United States and Japan. *American Psychologist, 55,* 1093–1104.

Rovee-Collier, C. (1999). The development of infant memory. *Current Directions in Psychological Science, 8,* 80–85.

Rowe, D., Vazsonyi, A., & Flannery, D. (1994). No more than skin deep: Ethnic and racial similarity in developmental processes. *Psychological Review, 101,* 396–413.

Rowe, D. C., Almeida, D. M., & Jacobson, K. C. (1999). School context and genetic influences on aggression in adolescence. *Psychological Science, 10,* 277–280.

Rowe, D. C., Jacobson, K. C., & Van den Oord, E. J. C. G. (1999). Genetic and environmental influences on Vocabulary IQ: Parental education level as moderator. *Child Development, 70,* 1151–1162.

Rowe, D. W., & Harste, J. C. (1986). Metalinguistic awareness in writing and reading: The young child as curricular informant. In D. B. Yaden, Jr., & S. Templeton (Eds.), *Metalinguistic awareness and beginning literacy: Conceptualizing what it means to read and write.* Portsmouth, NH: Heinemann.

Rowe, E. (1999, April). *Gender differences in math self-concept development: The role of classroom interaction.* Paper presented at the annual meeting of the American Educational Research Association, Montreal, Canada.

Rowe, M. B. (1974). Wait-time and rewards as instructional variables, their influence on language, logic, and fate control: Part one—wait time. *Journal of Research in Science Teaching, 11,* 81–94.

Rowe, M. B. (1987). Wait-time: Slowing down may be a way of speeding up. *American Educator, 11,* 38–43, 47.

Rowland, T. W. (1990). *Exercise and children's health.* Champaign, IL: Human Kinetics.

Royce, J. M., Darlington, R. B., & Murray, H. W. (1983). Pooled analyses: Findings across studies. In Consortium for Longitudinal Studies (Ed.), *As the twig is bent: Lasting effects of preschool programs.* Hillsdale, NJ: Erlbaum.

Rubin, K., Fein, G., & Vandenberg, B. (1983). Play. In E. M. Hetherington (Ed.), *Handbook of child psychology: Vol. 4. Socialization, personality, and social development* (pp. 693–774). New York: Wiley.

Rubin, K. H., Bukowski, W., & Parker, J. G. (1998). Peer interactions, relationships, and groups. In W. Damon (Editor in Chief) & N. Eisenberg (Vol. Ed.), *Handbook of child psychology: Vol. 3.*

Social, emotional, and personality development (pp. 619–700). New York: Wiley.

Rubin, K. H., Coplan, R. J., Fox, N. A., & Calkins, S. (1995). Emotionality, emotion regulation, and preschoolers' social adaptation. *Development and Psychopathology, 7,* 49–62.

Rubin, K. H., & Krasnor, L. R. (1986). Social-cognitive and social behavioral perspectives on problem solving. In M. Perlmutter (Ed.), *Minnesota symposia on child psychology: Vol. 19. Cognitive perspectives on children's social and behavioral development.* Hillsdale, NJ: Erlbaum.

Rubin, K. H., Lynch, D., Coplan, R., Rose-Krasnor, L., & Booth, C. L. (1994). "Birds of a feather": Behavioral concordances and preferential personal attraction in children. *Child Development, 65,* 1778–1785.

Rubin, K. H., & Pepler, D. J. (1995). The relationship of child's play to social-cognitive growth and development. In H. C. Foot, A. J. Chapman, & J. R. Smith (Eds.), *Friendship and social relations in children* (pp. 209–233). New Brunswick, NJ: Transaction.

Ruble, D. N., & Martin, C. L. (1998). Gender development. In W. Damon (Editor-in-Chief) & N. Eisenberg (Vol. Ed.), *Handbook of child psychology: Vol. 3. Social, emotional, and personality development* (5th ed., pp. 933–1016). New York: Wiley.

Rudlin, C. R. (1993). Growth and sexual development: What is normal, and what is not? *Journal of the American Academy of Physician Assistants, 6,* 25–35.

Rudolph, K. D., Lambert, S. F., Clark, A. G., & Kurlakowsky, K. D. (2001). Negotiating the transition to middle school: The role of self-regulatory processes. *Child Development, 72,* 929–946.

Rueda, R., & Moll, L. C. (1994). A sociocultural perspective on motivation. In H. F. O'Neil, Jr., & M. Drillings (Eds.), *Motivation: Theory and research.* Hillsdale, NJ: Erlbaum.

Ruff, H. A., & Lawson, K. R. (1990). Development of sustained, focused attention in young children during free play. *Developmental Psychology, 26,* 85–93.

Ruff, H. A., & Rothbart, M. K. (1996). *Attention in early development: Themes and variations.* New York: Oxford University Press.

Ruffman, T., Perner, J., Naito, M., Parkin, L., & Clements, W. A. (1998). Older (but not younger) siblings facilitate false belief understanding. *Developmental Psychology, 34*(1), 161–174.

Ruffman, T., Perner, J., Olson, D. R., & Doherty, M. (1993). Reflecting on scientific thinking: Children's understanding of the hypothesis-evidence relation. *Child Development, 64,* 1617–1636.

Ruffman, T., Slade, L., & Crowe, E. (2002). The relation between children's and mothers' mental state language and theory-of-mind understanding. *Child Development, 73,* 734–751.

Ruhm, C. J. (1998, May). *Parental leave and child health* (NBER Working Paper No. W6554). Cambridge, MA: National Bureau of Economic Research.

Rumberger, R. W. (1995). Dropping out of middle school: A multilevel analysis of students and schools. *American Educational Research Journal, 32,* 583–625.

Rushton, J. P. (1980). *Altruism, socialization, and society.* Upper Saddle River, NJ: Prentice Hall.

Rushton, J. P., Fulkner, D. W., Neal, M. C., Nias, D. K. B., & Eysenck, H. J. (1986). Altruism and aggression: The heritability of individual differences. *Journal of Personality and Social Psychology, 50,* 1192–1198.

Rushton, J. P., & Teachman, G. (1978). The effects of positive reinforcement, attributions, and punishment on model induced altruism in children. *Personality and Social Psychology Bulletin, 4,* 322–325.

Russell, A., & Russell, G. (1994). Coparenting early school-age children: An examination of mother-father independence within families. *Developmental Psychology, 30,* 757–770.

Rutter, M. (1989). Pathways from childhood to adult life. *Journal of Child Psychology and Psychiatry, 31,* 5–37.

Rutter, M., Champion, L., Quinton, D., Maughan, B., & Pickles, A. (1995). Understanding individual differences in environmental-risk exposure. In P. Moen, G. H. Elder, Jr., & K. Lüscher (Eds.), *Examining lives in context: Perspectives on the ecology of human development* (pp. 61–93). Washington, DC: American Psychological Association.

Rutter, M., & Garmezy, N. (1983). Developmental psychopathology. In P. H. Mussen (Series Ed.) & E. M. Hetherington (Vol. Ed.), *Handbook of child psychology: Vol. 4. Socialization, personality, and social development* (4th ed., pp. 775–911). New York: Wiley.

Rutter, M., & O'Connor, T. G. (1999). Implications of attachment theory for child care policies. In J. Cassidy & P. R. Shaver (Eds.), *Handbook of attachment: Theory, research, and clinical applications* (pp. 823–844). New York: Guilford Press.

Rutter, M. L. (1997). Nature-nurture integration: The example of antisocial behavior. *American Psychologist, 52,* 390–398.

Ryan, A. M. (2000). Peer groups as a context for the socialization of adolescents' motivation, engagement, and achievement in school. *Educational Psychologist, 35,* 101–111.

Ryan, A. M., & Patrick, H. (2001). The classroom social environment and changes in adolescents' motivation and engagement during middle school. *American Educational Research Journal, 38,* 437–460.

Ryan, E. B., Ledger, G. W., & Weed, K. A. (1987). Acquisition and transfer of an integrative imagery strategy by young children. *Child Development, 58,* 443–452.

Ryan, R. M., Connell, J. P., & Grolnick, W. S. (1992). When achievement is *not* intrinsically motivated: A theory of internalization and self-regulation in school. In A. K. Boggiano & T. S. Pittman (Eds.), *Achievement and motivation: A social-developmental perspective.* Cambridge, England: Cambridge University Press.

Ryan, R. M., & Kuczkowski, R. (1994). The imaginary audience, self-consciousness, and public individuation in adolescence. *Journal of Personality, 62,* 219–237.

Ryan, R. M., & Lynch, J. H. (1989). Emotional autonomy versus detachment: Revisiting the vicissitudes of adolescence and young adulthood. *Child Development, 60,* 340–356.

Ryan, R. M., Mims, V., & Koestner, R. (1983). Relation of reward contingency and interpersonal context to intrinsic motivation: A review and test using cognitive evaluation theory. *Journal of Personality and Social Psychology, 45,* 736–750.

Ryan, R. M., Stiller, J. D., & Lynch, J. H. (1994). Representations of relationships to teachers, parents, and friends as predictors of academic motivation and self-esteem. *Journal of Early Adolescence, 14,* 226–249.

Saarni, C. (2000). The social context of emotional development. In M. Lewis & J. M. Haviland-Jones (Eds.), *Handbook of emotions* (2nd ed., pp. 306–322). New York: Guilford Press.

Saarni, C., Mumme, D. L., & Campos, J. J. (1998). Emotional development: Action, communication, and understanding. In W. Damon (Editor-in-Chief) & N. Eisenberg (Vol. Ed.), *Handbook of child psychology: Vol. 3. Social, emotional, and personality development* (5th ed., pp. 237–309). New York: Wiley.

Sacks, C. H., & Mergendoller, J. R. (1997). The relationship between teachers' theoretical orientation toward reading and student outcomes in kindergarten children with different initial reading abilities. *American Educational Research Journal, 34,* 721–739.

Sadeh, A., Gruber, R., & Raviv, A. (2002). Sleep, neurobehavioral functioning, and behavior problems in school-age children. *Child Development, 73,* 405–417.

Sadker, M., & Sadker, A. (1988). *Sex equity handbook for schools* (2nd ed.). New York: Longman.

Sadker, M. P., & Sadker, D. (1994). *Failing at fairness: How our schools cheat girls.* New York: Touchstone.

Sadler, T. W. (2000). *Langman's medical embryology* (8th ed.). Philadelphia, PA: Lippincott Williams & Wilkins.

Saffran, J. R., Aslin, R. N., & Newport, E. L. (1996). Statistical learning by 8-month-old infants. *Science, 274,* 1926–1928.

Salend, S. J., & Taylor, L. (1993). Working with families: A cross-cultural perspective. *Remedial and Special Education, 14*(5), 25–32, 39.

Salisbury, C. L., Evans, I. M., & Palombaro, M. M. (1997). Collaborative problem solving to promote the inclusion of young children with significant disabilities in primary grades. *Exceptional Children, 63,* 195–210.

Sallis, J. F. (1993). Epidemiology of physical activity and fitness in children and adolescents. *Critical Reviews in Food Science and Nutrition, 33*(4–5), 403–408.

Saltz, E. (1971). *The cognitive bases of human learning.* Homewood, IL: Dorsey.

Sameroff, A., Seifer, R., Barocas, R., Zax, M., & Greenspan, S. (1987). Intelligent quotient scores of 4-year-old children: Social environmental risk factors. *Pediatrics, 79*(3), 343–360.

Sameroff, A. J., Seifer, R., Baldwin, A., & Baldwin, C. (1993). Stability of intelligence from preschool to adolescence: The influence of social and family risk factors. *Child Development, 64,* 80–97.

Sampson, R. J., & Groves, W. B. (1989). Community structure and crime: Testing social disorganization theory. *American Journal of Sociology, 94,* 774–802.

Sanborn, M. P. (1979). Counseling and guidance needs of the gifted and talented. In A. H. Passow (Ed.), *The gifted and the talented: Their education and development. The seventy-eighth yearbook of the National Society for the Study of Education.* Chicago: University of Chicago Press.

Sanchez, F., & Anderson, M. L. (1990). Gang mediation: A process that works. *Principal, 69*(4), 54–56.

Sanders, M. G. (1996). Action teams in action: Interviews and observations in three schools in the Baltimore School-Family-Community Partnership Program. *Journal of Education for Students Placed at Risk, 1,* 249–262.

Sands, D. J., & Wehmeyer, M. L. (Eds.). (1996). *Self-determination across the life span: Independence and choice for people with disabilities.* Baltimore: Brookes.

Sasso, G. M., Melloy, K. J., & Kavale, K. A. (1990). Generalization, maintenance, and behavior covariation associated with social skills training through structured learning. *Behavioral Disorders, 16*(1), 9–22.

Sattler, J. M. (2001). *Assessment of children: Cognitive applications* (4th ed.). San Diego, CA: Author.

Savin-Williams, R. C. (1995). Lesbian, gay male, and bisexual adolescents. In R. D'Augelli & C. J. Patterson (Eds.), *Lesbian, gay, and bisexual identities over the lifespan: Psychological perspectives* (pp. 165–189). New York: Oxford University Press.

Savin-Williams, R. C., & Demo, D. H. (1984). Developmental change and stability in adolescent self-concept. *Developmental Psychology, 20,* 1100–1110.

Savin-Williams, R. C., & Diamond, L. M. (1997). Sexual orientation as a developmental context for lesbians, gays, and bisexuals: Biological perspectives. In N. L. Segal, G. E. Weisfeld, & C. C. Weisfeld (Eds.), *Uniting psychology and biology: Integrative perspectives on human development* (pp. 217–238). Washington, DC: American Psychological Association.

Sawyer, R. J., Graham, S., & Harris, K. R. (1992). Direct teaching, strategy instruction, and strategy instruction with explicit self-regulation: Effects on the composition skills and self-efficacy of students with learning disabilities. *Journal of Educational Psychology, 84,* 340–352.

Scardamalia, M., & Bereiter, C. (1985). Fostering the development of self-regulation in children's knowledge processing. In S. F. Chipman, J. W. Segal, & R. Glaser (Eds.), *Thinking and learning skills: Vol. 2. Research and open questions.* Hillsdale, NJ: Erlbaum.

Scardamalia, M., & Bereiter, C. (1986). Research on written composition. In M. C. Wittrock (Ed.), *Handbook of research on teaching* (3rd ed.). New York: Macmillan.

Scardamalia, M., Bereiter, C., & Goelman, H. (1982). The role of production factors in writing ability. In M. Nystrand (Ed.), *What writers know: The language, process, and structure of written discourse.* New York: Academic Press.

Scarr, S. (1992). Developmental theories for the 1990s: Development and individual differences. *Child Development, 63,* 1–19.

Scarr, S. (1993). Biological and cultural diversity: The legacy of Darwin for development. *Child Development, 64,* 1333–1353.

Scarr, S. (1997). Behavior-genetic and socialization theories of intelligence: Truce and reconciliation. In R. J. Sternberg & E. L. Grigorenko (Eds.), *Intelligence, heredity, and environment* (pp. 3–41). Cambridge, England: Cambridge University Press.

Scarr, S. (1998). American child care today. *American Psychologist, 53,* 95–108.

Scarr, S., & McCartney, K. (1983). How people make their own environments: A theory of genotype environment effects. *Child Development, 54,* 424–435.

Scarr, S., & Weinberg, R. A. (1976). IQ test performance of black children adopted by white families. *American Psychologist, 31,* 726–739.

Schaffer, H. R. (1996). *Social development.* Cambridge, MA: Blackwell.

Schaie, K. W., & Willis, S. L. (2000). A stage theory model of adult cognitive development revisited. In R. L. Rubinstein, M. Moss, & M. H. Klebans (Eds.), *The many dimensions of aging* (pp. 175–193). New York: Springer.

Schauble, L. (1990). Belief revision in children: The role of prior knowledge and strategies for generating evidence. *Journal of Experimental Child Psychology, 49,* 31–57.

Schauble, L. (1996). The development of scientific reasoning in knowledge-rich contexts. *Developmental Psychology, 32,* 102–119.

Scherer, N., & Olswang, L. (1984). Role of mothers' expansions in stimulating children's language production. *Journal of Speech and Hearing Research, 27,* 387–396.

Schiefele, U. (1996). Topic interest, text representation, and quality of experience. *Contemporary Educational Psychology, 21,* 3–18.

Schimmoeller, M. A. (1998, April). *Influence of private speech on the writing behaviors of young children: Four case studies.* Paper presented at the annual meeting of the American Educational Research Association, San Diego, CA.

Schinke, S. P., Moncher, M. S., & Singer, B. R. (1994). Native American youths and cancer risk prevention. *Journal of Adolescent Health, 15,* 105–110.

Schlaefli, A., Rest, J. R., & Thoma, S. J. (1985). Does moral education improve moral judgment? A meta-analysis of intervention studies using the defining issues test. *Review of Educational Research, 55,* 319–352.

Schliemann, A. D., & Carraher, D. W. (1993). Proportional reasoning in and out of school. In P. Light and G. Butterworth (Eds.), *Context and cognition: Ways of learning and knowing.* Hillsdale, NJ: Erlbaum.

Schloss, P. J., & Smith, M. A. (1994). *Applied behavior analysis in the classroom.* Needham Heights, MA: Allyn & Bacon.

Schneider, J. J. (1998, April). *Developing multiple perspectives and audience awareness in elementary writers.* Paper presented at the annual meeting of the American Educational Research Association, San Diego, CA.

Schneider, W., Korkel, J., & Weinert, F. E. (1989). Domain-specific knowledge and memory performance: A comparison of high- and low-aptitude children. *Journal of Educational Psychology, 81,* 306–312.

Schneider, W., & Pressley, M. (1989). *Memory development between 2 and 20.* New York: Springer-Verlag.

Schneider, W., Roth, E., & Ennemoser, M. (2000). Training phonological skills and letter knowledge in children at risk for dyslexia: A comparison of three kindergarten intervention programs. *Journal of Educational Psychology, 92,* 284–295.

Schneider, W., & Shiffrin, R. M. (1977). Controlled and automatic human information processing: I. Detection, search, and attention. *Psychological Review, 84,* 1–66.

Schnur, E., Brooks-Gunn, J., & Shipman, V. C. (1992). Who attends programs serving poor children? The case of Head Start attendees and nonattendees. *Journal of Applied Developmental Psychology, 13,* 405–421.

Schofield, J. W. (1995). Improving intergroup relations among students. In J. A. Banks & C. A. M. Banks (Eds.), *Handbook of research on multicultural education.* New York: Macmillan.

Schommer, M. (1994a). An emerging conceptualization of epistemological beliefs and their role in learning. In R. Garner & P. A. Alexander (Eds.), *Beliefs about text and instruction with text.* Hillsdale, NJ: Erlbaum.

Schommer, M. (1994b). Synthesizing epistemological belief research: Tentative understandings and provocative confusions. *Educational Psychology Review, 6,* 293–319.

Schommer, M. (1997). The development of epistemological beliefs among secondary students: A longitudinal study. *Journal of Educational Psychology, 89,* 37–40.

Schonert-Reichl, K. A. (1993). Empathy and social relationships in adolescents with behavioral disorders. *Behavioral Disorders, 18,* 189–204.

Schore, A. N. (1994). *Affect regulation and the origin of the self: The neurobiology of emotional development.* Hillsdale, NJ: Erlbaum.

Schratz, M. (1978). A developmental investigation of sex differences in spatial (visual-analytic) and mathematical skills in three ethnic groups. *Developmental Psychology, 14,* 263–267.

Schraw, G., Potenza, M. T., & Nebelsick-Gullet, L. (1993). Constraints on the calibration of performance. *Contemporary Educational Psychology, 18,* 455–463.

Schreibman, L. (1988). *Autism.* Newbury Park, CA: Sage.

Schroth, M. L. (1992). The effects of delay of feedback on a delayed concept formation transfer task. *Contemporary Educational Psychology, 17,* 78–82.

Schulhofer, S. J. (1998). *Unwanted sex: The culture of intimidation and the failure of law.* Cambridge, MA: Harvard University Press.

Schultz, G. F., & Switzky, H. N. (1990). The development of intrinsic motivation in students with learning problems: Suggestions for more effective instructional practice. *Preventing School Failure, 34*(2), 14–20.

Schuman, H., & Scott, J. (1989). Generations and collective memories. *American Sociological Review, 54,* 359–381.

Schumpf, F., Crawford, D., & Usadel, H. C. (1991). *Peer mediation: Conflict resolution in schools.* Champaign, IL: Research Press.

Schunk, D. H. (1989). Self-efficacy and cognitive skill learning. In C. Ames & R. Ames (Eds.), *Research on motivation in education: Vol. 3. Goals and cognitions.* San Diego, CA: Academic Press.

Schunk, D. H. (1990, April). *Socialization and the development of self-regulated learning: The role of attributions.* Paper presented at the annual meeting of the American Educational Research Association, Boston.

Schunk, D. H. (1996). Goal and self-evaluative influences during children's cognitive skill learning. *American Educational Research Journal, 33,* 359–382.

Schunk, D. H., & Hanson, A. R. (1985). Peer models: Influence on children's self-efficacy and achievement. *Journal of Educational Psychology, 77,* 313–322.

Schunk, D. H., Hanson, A. R., & Cox, P. D. (1987). Peer-model attributes and children's achievement behaviors. *Journal of Educational Psychology, 79,* 54–61.

Schunk, D. H., & Rice, J. (1989). Learning goals and children's reading comprehension. *Journal of Reading Behavior, 21,* 279–293.

Schunk, D. H., & Swartz, C. W. (1993). Goals and progress feedback: Effects on self-efficacy and writing achievement. *Contemporary Educational Psychology, 18,* 337–354.

Schunk, D. H., & Zimmerman, B. J. (1997). Social origins of self-regulatory competence. *Educational Psychologist, 32,* 195–208.

Schutz, P. A. (1994). Goals as the transactive point between motivation and cognition. In P. R. Pintrich, D. R. Brown, & C. E. Weinstein (Eds.), *Student motivation, cognition, and learning: Essays in honor of Wilbert J. McKeachie.* Hillsdale, NJ: Erlbaum.

Schutz, P. A., & Davis, H. A. (2000). Emotions and self-regulation during test taking. *Educational Psychologist, 35,* 243–256.

Schwartz, D., Dodge, K. A., Coie, J. D., Hubbard, J. A., Cillessen, A. H., Lemerise, E. A., & Bateman, H. (1998). Social-cognitive and behavioral correlates of aggression and victimization in boys' play groups. *Journal of Abnormal Child Psychology, 26*(6), 431–440.

Schwartz, D., Dodge, K. A., Pettit, G. S., & Bates, J. E. (1997). The early socialization of aggressive victims of bullying. *Child Development, 68,* 665–675.

Schwartz, D., McFadyen-Ketchum, S., Dodge, K. A., Pettit, G. S., & Bates, J. E. (1999). Early behavior problems as a predictor of later peer victimization: Moderators and mediators in the pathways of social risk. *Journal of Abnormal Child Psychology, 27,* 191–201.

Schwartz, G. M., Izard, C. E., & Ansul, S. E. (1985). The 5-month-old's ability to discriminate facial expressions of emotion. *Infant Behavior and Development, 8,* 65–67.

Schweinhart, L. J., Barnes, H. V., & Weikart, D. P. (1993). *Significant benefits: The High/Scope Perry Preschool Study through age 27.* Ypsilanti, MI: High/Scope.

Schweinhart, L. J., & Weikart, D. (1983). The effects of the Perry Preschool Program on youths through age 15: A summary. In Consortium for Longitudinal Studies (Eds.), *As the twig is bent: Lasting effects of preschool programs* (pp. 71–101). Hillsdale, NJ: Erlbaum.

Scott-Jones, D. (1984). Family influences on cognitive development and school achievement.

In E. W. Gordon (Ed.), *Review of research in education* (Vol. 11). Washington, DC: American Educational Research Association.

Scott-Jones, D. (1991). Black families and literacy. In S. B. Silvern (Eds.), *Advances in reading/language research: Literacy through family, community, and school interaction* (pp. 173–200). Greenwich, CT: JAI Press.

Scott-Little, M., & Holloway, S. (1992). Child care providers' reasoning about misbehaviors: Relation to classroom control strategies and professional training. *Early Childhood Research Quarterly, 7,* 595–606.

Seaton, E., Rodriguez, A., Jacobson, L., Taylor, R., Caintic, R., & Dale, P. (1999, April). *Influence of economic resources on family organization and achievement in economically disadvantaged African-American families.* Paper presented at the annual meeting of the American Educational Research Association, Montreal.

Seefeldt, C., Denton, K., Galper, A., & Younoszai, T. (1999). The relation between Head Start parents' participation in a transition demonstration, education, efficacy, and their children's academic abilities. *Early Childhood Research Quarterly, 14*(1), 99–109.

Seeley, K. (1989). Facilitators for the gifted. In J. Feldhusen, J. VanTassel-Baska, & K. Seeley, *Excellence in educating the gifted.* Denver, CO: Love.

Segal, B. M., & Stewart, J. C. (1996). Substance use and abuse in adolescence: An overview. *Child Psychiatry and Human Development, 26,* 193–210.

Segal, N. L. (2000). Virtual twins: New findings on within-family environmental influences on intelligence. *Journal of Educational Psychology, 92,* 442–448.

Segal, N. L., & Russell, J. M. (1992). Twins in the classroom: School policy issues and recommendations. *Journal of Educational & Psychological Consultation, 3*(1), 69–84.

Seitz, V., Rosenbaum, L. K., & Apfel, N. H. (1985). Effects of family support intervention: A ten-year follow-up. *Child Development, 56,* 376–391.

Seligman, M. E. P. (1975). *Helplessness: On depression, development, and death.* San Francisco: Freeman.

Seligman, M. E. P. (1991). *Learned optimism.* New York: Knopf.

Selman, R. L. (1980). *The growth of interpersonal understanding.* San Diego, CA: Academic Press.

Selman, R. L., & Byrne, D. F. (1974). A structural-developmental analysis of levels of role taking in middle childhood. *Child Development, 45,* 803–806.

Selman, R. L., & Schultz, L. J. (1990). *Making a friend in youth: Developmental theory and pair therapy.* Chicago: University of Chicago Press.

Seltzer, V. C. (1982). *Adolescent social development: Dynamic functional interaction.* Lexington, MA: Heath.

Semb, G. B., Ellis, J. A., & Araujo, J. (1993). Long-term memory for knowledge learned in school. *Journal of Educational Psychology, 85,* 305–316.

Semrud-Clikeman, M., & Hynd, G. W. (1991). Specific nonverbal and social skills deficits in children with learning disabilities. In J. E. Obrzut & G. W. Hynd (Eds.), *Neuropsychological foundations of learning disabilities: A handbook of issues, methods, and practice* (pp. 603–630). San Diego, CA: Academic Press.

Sénéchal, M., & LeFevre, J.-A. (2002). Parental involvement in the development of children's reading skill: A five-year longitudinal study. *Child Development, 73,* 445–460.

Sénéchal, M., Thomas, E., & Monker, J. (1995). Individual differences in 4-year-old children's acquisition of vocabulary during storybook reading. *Journal of Educational Psychology, 87,* 218–229.

Seuss, Dr. (1960). *One fish two fish red fish blue fish.* New York: Beginner Books.

Sewald, H. (1986). Adolescents' shifting orientation toward parents and peers: A curvilinear trend over recent decades. *Journal of Marriage and the Family, 48,* 5–13.

Shaffer, D. R. (1988). *Social and personality development* (2nd ed.). Pacific Grove, CA: Brooks/Cole.

Shanahan, T., & Tierney, R. J. (1990). Reading-writing connections: The relations among three perspectives. In J. Zutell & S. McCormick (Eds.), *Literacy theory and research: Analyses from multiple paradigms. Thirty-ninth yearbook of the National Reading Conference.* Chicago: National Reading Conference.

Shannon, J. H. (2002). African-American childhood in early Philadelphia. In C. J. Trotman (Ed.), *Multiculturalism: Roots and realities* (pp. 187–202). Bloomington, IN: Indiana University Press.

Share, D. L. (1995). Phonological recoding and self-teaching: Sine qua non of reading acquisition. *Cognition, 55,* 151–218.

Share, D. L., & Gur, T. (1999). How reading begins: A study of preschoolers' print identification strategies. *Cognition and Instruction, 17,* 177–213.

Shatz, M., & Gelman, R. (1973). The development of communication skills: Modifications in the speech of young children as a function of the listener. *Monographs of the Society for Research in Child Development, 38*(5, Serial No. 152).

Shavers, C. A. (2000). *The interrelationships of exposure to community violence and trauma to the behavioral patterns and academic performance among urban elementary school-aged children.* Dissertation Abstracts International: Section B: the Sciences and Engineering. Vol 61(4-B), Oct 2000, 1876.

Shaw, C. C. (1993). Multicultural teacher education: A call for conceptual change. *Multicultural Education, 1*(2), 22–26.

Shaw, D. S., Vondra, J. I., Hommerding, K. D., Keenan, K., & Dunn, M. (1994). Chronic family adversity and early child behavior problems: A longitudinal study of low income families. *Journal of Child Psychology and Psychiatry, 35,* 1109–1122.

Shaywitz, S. E., Escobar, M. D., Shaywitz, B. A., Fletcher, J. M., & Makuch, R. (1992). Evidence that dyslexia may represent the lower tail of a normal distribution of reading ability. *The New England Journal of Medicine, 326,* 145–150.

Shealy, C. N. (1995). From *Boys Town* to *Oliver Twist:* Separating fact and fiction in welfare reform and out-of-home placement of children and youth. *American Psychologist, 50,* 565–580.

Shechtman, Z. (2001). Prevention groups for angry and aggressive children. *Journal for Specialists in Group Work, 26*(3), 228–236.

Sheckley, B. G., & Keeton, M. T. (1997). Service learning: A theoretical model. In J. Schine (Ed.), *Service learning.* Chicago: The National Society for the Study of Education.

Shedler, J., & Block, J. (1990). Adolescent drug use and psychological health. *American Psychologist, 45,* 612–630.

Sheehan, E. P., & Smith, H. V. (1986). Cerebral lateralization and handedness and their effects on verbal and spatial reasoning. *Neuropsychologia, 24,* 531–540.

Sheldon, A. (1974). The role of parallel function in the acquisition of relative clauses in English. *Journal of Verbal Learning and Verbal Behavior, 13,* 272–281.

Shephard, L., & Smith, M. L. (1987, October). Effects of kindergarten retention at the end of the first grade. *Psychology in the Schools, 24,* 346–357.

Shephard, L., & Smith, M. L. (Eds.). (1989). *Flunking grades: Research and policy on retention.* Philadelphia: Falmer Press.

Shephard, L. A., & Smith, M. L. (1988). Escalating academic demand in kindergarten: Counterproductive policies. *The Elementary School Journal, 89,* 135–144.

Sheridan, M. D. (1975). *Children's developmental progress from birth to five years: The Stycar Sequences.* Windsor, England: NFER.

Sherif, M., Harvey, O. J., White, B. J., Hood, W. R., & Sherif, C. (1961). *Inter-group conflict and cooperation: The Robbers Cave experiment.* Norman: University of Oklahoma Press.

Sherrill, D., Horowitz, B., Friedman, S. T., & Salisbury, J. L. (1970). Seating aggregation as an index of contagion. *Educational and Psychological Measurement, 30,* 663–668.

Sheveland, D. E. (1994, April). *Motivational factors in the development of independent readers.* Paper presented at the annual meeting of the American Educational Research Association, New Orleans, LA.

Shi, R., & Werker, J. F. (2001). Six-month-old infants' preference for lexical words. *Psychological Science, 12,* 70–75.

Shoda, Y., Mischel, W., & Peake, P. K. (1990). Predicting adolescent cognitive and self-regulatory competencies from preschool delay of gratification: Identifying diagnostic conditions. *Developmental Psychology, 26,* 978–986.

Shonkoff, J. P. & Phillips, D. A. (Eds.) (2000). *From neurons to neighborhoods: The science of early childhood development.* Washington, DC: National Academy of Sciences.

Short, E. J., & Ryan, E. B. (1984). Metacognitive differences between skilled and less skilled readers: Remediating deficits through story grammar and attribution training. *Journal of Educational Psychology, 76,* 225–235.

Short, E. J., Schatschneider, C. W., & Friebert, S. E. (1993). Relationship between memory and metamemory performance: A comparison of specific and general strategy knowledge. *Journal of Educational Psychology, 85,* 412–423.

Shrum, W., & Cheek, N. H. (1987). Social structure during the school years: Onset of the degrouping process. *American Sociological Review, 52,* 218–223.

Shuell, T. J. (1996). Teaching and learning in a classroom context. In D. C. Berliner & R. C. Calfee (Eds.), *Handbook of educational psychology.* New York: Macmillan.

Shultz, T. R. (1974). Development of the appreciation of riddles. *Child Development, 45,* 100–105.

Shultz, T. R., & Horibe, F. (1974). Development of the appreciation of verbal jokes. *Developmental Psychology, 10,* 13–20.

Shure, M. B., & Spivack, G. (1980). Interpersonal problem-solving as a mediator of behavioral adjustment in preschool and kindergarten children. *Journal of Applied Developmental Psychology, 1,* 29–44.

Shweder, R. A., Goodnow, J., Hatano, G., LeVine, R. A., Markus, H., & Miller, P. (1998). The cultural psychology of development: One mind, many mentalities. In W. Damon (Editor-in-Chief) & R. M. Lerner (Vol. Ed.), *Handbook of child psychology: Vol. 1. Theoretical models of human development* (5th ed., pp. 865–937). New York: Wiley.

Shweder, R. A., Mahapatra, M., & Miller, J. G. (1987). Culture and moral development. In J. Kagan & S. Lamb (Eds.), *The emergence of morality in young children* (pp. 1–83). Chicago: University of Chicago Press.

Shweder, R. A., & Miller, J. G. (1985). The social construction of the person: How is it possible? In K. J. Gergen & K. Davis (Eds.), *The social construction of the person* (pp. 41–69). New York: Springer-Verlag.

Shweder, R. A., Much, N. C., Mahapatra, M., & Park, L. (1997). The "big three" of morality (autonomy, community, and divinity) and the "big three" explanations of suffering. In A. Brandt & P. Rozin (Eds.), *Morality and health* (pp. 119–169). Stanford, CA: Stanford University Press.

Sickmund, M., Snyder, H. N., & Poe Yamagata, E. (1997). *Juvenile offenders and victims: 1997 Update on violence.* Washington, DC: Office of Juvenile Justice and Delinquency Prevention.

Sidel, R. (1996). *Keeping women and children last: America's war on the poor.* New York: Penguin Books.

Siegler, R. S. (1976). Three aspects of cognitive development. *Cognitive Psychology, 8,* 481–520.

Siegler, R. S. (1978). The origins of scientific reasoning. In R. S. Siegler (Ed.), *Children's thinking: What develops?* Hillsdale, NJ: Erlbaum.

Siegler, R. S. (1994). Cognitive variability: A key to understanding cognitive development. *Current Directions in Psychological Science, 3,* 1–5.

Siegler, R. S. (1996a). A grand theory of development. In R. Case & Y. Okamoto, in collaboration with S. Griffin, A. McKeough, C. Bleiker, B. Henderson, & K. M. Stephenson (1996). The role of central conceptual structures in the development of children's thought. *Monographs of the Society for Research in Child Development, 61*(1, Serial No. 246).

Siegler, R. S. (1996b). *Emerging minds: The process of change in children's thinking.* New York: Oxford University Press.

Siegler, R. S. (1998). *Children's thinking* (3rd ed.). Upper Saddle River, NJ: Prentice Hall.

Siegler, R. S., & Jenkins, E. (1989). *How children discover new strategies.* Hillsdale, NJ: Erlbaum.

Siegler, R. S., & Richards, D. D. (1982). The development of intelligence. In R. J. Sternberg (Ed.), *Handbook of human intelligence.* Cambridge, England: Cambridge University Press.

Siegler, R. S., & Stern, E. (1998). Conscious and unconscious strategy discoveries: A microgenetic analysis. *Journal of Experimental Psychology: General, 127*(4), 377–397.

Siever, L., & Davis, K. (1985). Overview: Toward a dysregulation hypothesis of depression. *American Journal of Psychiatry, 142,* 1017–1031.

Sigman, M. (1995). Nutrition and child development: Food for thought. *Current Directions in Psychological Science, 4,* 52–55.

Sigman, M. D., Kasari, C., Kwon, J. H., & Yirmiya, N. (1992). Responses to the negative emotions of others by autistic, mentally retarded, and normal children. *Child Development, 63,* 786–807.

Sigman, M., & Whaley, S. E. (1998). The role of nutrition in the development of intelligence. In U. Neisser (Ed.), *The rising curve: Long-term gains in IQ and related measures* (pp. 155–182). Washington, DC: American Psychological Association.

Signorielli, N., & Lears, M. (1992). Children, television, and conceptions about chores: Attitudes and behaviors. *Sex Roles, 27,* 157–170.

Silver, E. A., & Kenney, P. A. (1995). Sources of assessment information for instructional guidance in mathematics. In T. Romberg (Ed.), *Reform in school mathematics and authentic assessment.* Albany: State University of New York Press.

Silverman, I. W., & Ragusa, D. M. (1990). Child and maternal correlates of impulse control in 24-month-old children. *Genetic, Social, and General Psychology Monographs, 116,* 435–473.

Silverman-Watkins, T., & Sprafkin, J. N. (1983). Adolescents' comprehension of televised sexual innuendoes. *Journal of Applied Developmental Psychology, 4,* 359–369.

Simcock, G., & Hayne, H. (2002). Breaking the barrier? Children fail to translate their preverbal memories into language. *Psychological Science, 13,* 225–231.

Simmons, R. G., & Blyth, D. A. (1987). *Moving into adolescence: The impact of pubertal change in school context.* New York: Aldine de Gruyter.

Simner, M. L. (1971). Newborn's response to the cry of another infant. *Developmental Psychology, 5,* 136–150.

Simons, R. L., Lorenz, F. O., Wu, C. I., & Conger, R. D. (1993). Social network and marital support as mediators and moderators of the impact of stress and depression on parental behavior. *Developmental Psychology, 29,* 368–381.

Simons, R. L., Robertson, J. F., & Downs, W. R. (1989). The nature of the association between parental rejection and delinquent behavior. *Journal of Youth and Adolescence, 18,* 297–310.

Simons, R. L., Whitbeck, L. B., Conger, R. D., & Conger, K. J. (1991). Parenting factors, social skills, and value commitments as precursors to school failure, involvement with deviant peers, and delinquent behavior. *Journal of Youth and Adolescence, 20,* 645–664.

Simons-Morton, B. G., Baranowski, T., Parcel, G. S., O'Hara, N. M., & Matteson, R. C. (1990). Children's frequency of consumption of foods high in fat and sodium. *American Journal of Preventive Medicine, 6,* 218–227.

Simons-Morton, B. G., Taylor, W. C., Snider, S. A., & Huang, I. W. (1993). The physical activity of fifth-grade students during physical education classes. *American Journal of Public Health, 83,* 262–264.

Simons-Morton, B. G., Taylor, W. C., Snider, S. A., Huang, I. W., & Fulton, J. E. (1994). Observed levels of elementary and middle school children's physical activity during physical education classes. *Preventive Medicine, 23,* 437–441.

Simonton, D. K. (2001). Talent development as a multidimensional, multiplicative, and dynamic process. *Current Directions in Psychological Science, 10,* 39–42.

Sims, M. (1993). How my question keeps evolving. In Cochran-Smith, M., & Lytle, S. L. (Eds.), *Inside/outside: Teacher research and knowledge* (pp. 283–289). New York: Teachers College Press.

Sims, M., Hutchins, T., & Taylor, M. (1997). Classroom "culture" and children's conflict behaviours. *Early Child Development and Care, 134,* 43–59.

Singer, D. G., & Singer, J. L. (1994). *Barney & Friends as education and entertainment: Phase 3. A national study: Can preschoolers learn through exposure to Barney & Friends?* New Haven, CT: Yale University Family Television Research and Consultation Center.

Singer, J. L., & Singer, D. G. (1994). *Barney & Friends as education and entertainment: Phase 2. Can children learn through preschool exposure to Barney & Friends?* New Haven, CT: Yale University Family Television Research and Consultation Center.

Singer, L. M., Burkowski, M., & Waters, E. (1985). Mother-infant attachment in adoptive families. *Child Development, 56,* 1543–1551.

Sinnott, J. D. (1998). *The development of logic in adulthood: Postformal thought and its applications.* New York: Plenum.

Sisk, D. A. (1989). Identifying and nurturing talent among American Indians. In C. J. Maker & S. W. Schiever (Eds.), *Critical issues in gifted education: Vol. 2. Defensible programs for cultural and ethnic minorities.* Austin, TX: Pro-Ed.

Sissel, P. A. (2000). *Staff, parents, and politics in Head Start: A case study in unequal power, knowledge, and material resources.* New York: Falmer Press.

Sitko, B. M. (1998). Knowing how to write: Metacognition and writing instruction. In D. J. Hacker, J. Dunlosky, & A. C. Graesser (Eds.), *Metacognition in educational theory and practice* (pp. 93–115). Mahwah, NJ: Erlbaum.

Sjostrom, L., & Stein, N. (1996). *Bully proof: A teacher's guide on teasing and bullying for use with fourth and fifth grade students.* Wellesley, MA: Wellesley College Center for Women.

Skinner, B. F. (1953). *Science and human behavior.* New York: Macmillan.

Skinner, B. F. (1957). *Verbal behavior.* New York: Appleton-Century-Crofts.

Skinner, B. F. (1968). *The technology of teaching.* New York: Appleton-Century-Crofts.

Skinner, B. F. (1971). *Beyond freedom and dignity.* New York: Knopf.

Slaby, R. G., & Frey, K. S. (1975). Development of gender constancy and selective attention to same-sex models. *Child Development, 52,* 849–856.

Slater, A. M., Mattock, A., & Brown, E. (1990). Size constancy at birth: Newborn infants' responses to retinal and real size. *Journal of Experimental Child Psychology, 49,* 314–322.

Slater, A. M., & Morison, V. (1985). Shape constancy and slant perception at birth. *Perception, 14,* 337–344.

Slavin, R. E. (1989). Students at risk of school failure: The problem and its dimensions. In R. E. Slavin, N. L. Karweit, & N. A. Madden (Eds.), *Effective programs for students at risk.* Needham Heights, MA: Allyn & Bacon.

Slavin, R. E. (1990). *Cooperative learning: Theory, research, and practice.* Upper Saddle River, NJ: Prentice Hall.

Sleeter, C. E., & Grant, C. A. (1991). Race, class, gender, and disability in current textbooks. In M. W. Apple & L. K. Christian-Smith (Eds.), *The politics of the textbook* (pp. 78–110). New York: Routledge.

Sleeter, C. E., & Grant, C. A. (1999). *Making choices for multicultural education: Five approaches to race, class, and gender* (3rd ed.). Upper Saddle River, NJ: Merrill/Prentice Hall.

Slonim, M. B. (1991). *Children, culture, ethnicity: Evaluating and understanding the impact.* New York: Garland.

Slonim, N. (2001). *Children's and adolescents' understandings of society and government.* Unpublished master's thesis, Ontario Institute for Studies in Education, University of Toronto.

Slonim, N., & Case, R. (2002, April). *Children's and adolescents' understandings of society and government.* Paper presented at the annual meeting of the American Educational Research Association, New Orleans, LA.

Slusher, M. P., & Anderson, C. A. (1996). Using causal persuasive arguments to change beliefs and teach new information: The mediating role of explanation availability and evaluation bias in the acceptance of knowledge. *Journal of Educational Psychology, 88,* 110–122.

Smart, C., Neale, B., & Wade, A. (2001). *The changing experience of childhood: Families and divorce.* Cambridge, England: Polity.

Smetana, J. G. (1981). Preschool children's conceptions of moral and social rules. *Child Development, 52,* 1333–1336.

Smetana, J. G. (1989). Toddlers' social interactions in the context of moral and conventional transgressions in the home. *Developmental Psychology, 25,* 499–508.

Smetana, J. G., & Asquith, P. (1994). Adolescents' and parents' conceptions of parental authority and adolescent autonomy. *Child Development, 65,* 1147–1162.

Smetana, J. G., & Braeges, J. L. (1990). The development of toddlers' moral and conventional judgments. *Merrill-Palmer Quarterly, 36,* 329–346.

Smetana, J. G., Killen, M., & Turiel, E. (1991). Children's reasoning about interpersonal and moral conflicts. *Child Development, 62,* 629–644.

Smith, C., Maclin, D., Grosslight, L., & Davis, H. (1997). Teaching for understanding: A study of students' preinstruction theories of matter and a comparison of the effectiveness of two approaches to teaching about matter and density. *Cognition and Instruction, 15,* 317–393.

Smith, C. L., Maclin, D., Houghton, C., & Hennessey, M. G. (2000). Sixth-grade students' epistemologies of science: The impact of school science experiences on epistemological development. *Cognition and Instruction, 18,* 349–422.

Smith, H. L. (1998). Literacy and instruction in African American communities: Shall we overcome? In B. Pérez (Ed.), *Sociocultural contexts of language and literacy.* Mahwah, NJ: Erlbaum.

Smith, J., & Russell, G. (1984). Why do males and females differ? Children's beliefs about sex differences. *Sex Roles, 11,* 1111–1120.

Smith, J. T. (1999). Sickle cell disease. In S. Goldstein & C. R. Reynolds (Eds.), *Handbook of neurodevelopmental and genetic disorders* (pp. 368–384). New York: Guilford Press.

Smith, L. (1994, February 16). Bad habits: Testament to the downward spiral of drugs and teen angst. *Los Angeles Times,* p. 1.

Smith, M. A., & Schloss, P. (1998). *Applied behavior analysis in the classroom* (2nd ed.). Needham Heights, MA: Allyn & Bacon.

Smith, N. R., Cicchetti, L., Clark, M. C., Fucigna, C., Gordon-O'Connor, B., Halley, B. A., & Kennedy, M. (1998). *Observation drawing with children: A framework for teachers.* New York: Teachers College Press.

Smith, P. B., & Bond, M. H. (1994). *Social psychology across cultures: Analysis and perspectives.* Needham Heights, MA: Allyn & Bacon.

Smith, R. E., & Smoll, F. L. (1997). Coaching the coaches: Youth sports as a scientific and applied behavioral setting. *Current Directions in Psychological Science, 6*(1), 16–21.

Smitherman, G. (1994). "The blacker the berry the sweeter the juice": African American student writers. In A. H. Dyson & C. Genishi (Eds.), *The need for story: Cultural diversity in classroom and community.* Urbana, IL: National Council of Teachers of English.

Snarey, J. (1995). In a communitarian voice: The sociological expansion of Kohlbergian theory, research, and practice. In W. M. Kurtines & J. L. Gewirtz (Eds.), *Moral development: An introduction.* Boston: Allyn & Bacon.

Snell, M. E., & Janney, R. (2000). *Social relationships and peer support.* Baltimore: Brookes.

Snow, C., & Ninio, A. (1986). The contracts of literacy: What children learn from learning to read books. In W. Teale & E. Sulzby (Eds.), *Emergent literacy: Writing and reading.* Norwood, NJ: Ablex.

Snow, C. E. (1990). Rationales for native language instruction: Evidence from research. In A. M. Padilla, H. H. Fairchild, & C. M. Valadez (Eds.), *Bilingual education: Issues and strategies.* Newbury Park, CA: Sage.

Snow, C. E., & Hoefnagel-Höhle, M. (1978). The critical period for language acquisition: Evidence from second language learning. *Child Development, 49,* 1114–1128.

Snyder, H., Finnegan, T., Nimick, E., Sickmund, D., & Tierney, N. (1987). *Juvenile Court Statistics, 1984.* Pittsburgh: National Center for Juvenile Justice.

Solomon, D., Watson, M., Battistich, E., Schaps, E., & Delucchi, K. (1992). Creating a caring community: Educational practices that promote children's prosocial development. In F. K. Oser, A. Dick, & J. L. Patry (Eds.), *Effective and responsible teaching: The new synthesis.* San Francisco: Jossey-Bass.

Solomons, H. C., & Elardo, R. (1989). Bite injuries at a day care center. *Early Childhood Research Quarterly, 4*(1), 89–96.

Sonnenschein, S. (1988). The development of referential communication: Speaking to different listeners. *Child Development, 59,* 694–702.

Sorce, J. F., Emde, R. N., Campos, J., & Klinnert, M. D. (1985). Maternal emotional signaling: Its effects on the visual cliff behavior of 1-year-olds. *Developmental Psychology, 21,* 195–200.

Sorensen, R. (1983). *Adolescent sexuality in contemporary society.* New York: World Books.

Sosniak, L. A., & Stodolsky, S. S. (1994). Making connections: Social studies education in an urban fourth-grade classroom. In J. Brophy (Ed.), *Advances in research on teaching: Vol. 4. Case studies of teaching and learning in social studies.* Greenwich, CT: JAI Press.

South, D. (2000). What motivates unmotivated students? In G. Mills, *Action research: A guide for the teacher researcher* (2nd ed, pp. 1–2). Upper Saddle River, NJ: Merrill/Prentice Hall.

Sowell, E. R., Delis, D., Stiles, J., & Jernigan, T. L. (2001). Improved memory functioning and frontal lobe maturation between childhood and adolescence: A structural MRI study. *Journal of the International Neuropsychological Society, 7,* 312–322.

Sowell, E. R., & Jernigan, T. L. (1998). Further MRI evidence of late brain maturation: Limbic volume increases and changing asymmetries during childhood and adolescence. *Developmental Neuropsychology, 14,* 599–617.

Sowell, E. R., Thompson, P. M., Holmes, C. J., Jernigan, T. L., & Toga, A. W. (1999). In vivo evidence for post-adolescent brain maturation in frontal and striatal regions. *Nature Neuroscience, 2,* 859–861.

Sowell, E. R., Thompson, P. M., Rex, D., Kornsand, D., Tessner, K. D., Jernigan, T. L., & Toga, A. W. (2002). Mapping sulcal pattern asymmetry and local cortical surface gray matter distribution in vivo: Maturation in the perisylvian cortices. *Cerebral Cortex, 12,* 17–26.

Sowell, E. R., Thompson, P. M., Tessner, K. D., & Toga, A. W. (2001). Mapping continued brain growth and gray matter density reduction in dorsal frontal cortex: Inverse relationships during postadolescent brain maturation. *Journal of Neuroscience, 21,* 8819–8829.

Spaulding, C. L. (1992). *Motivation in the classroom.* New York: McGraw-Hill.

Spearman, C. (1904). General intelligence, objectively determined and measured. *American Journal of Psychology, 15,* 201–293.

Spearman, C. (1927). *The abilities of man: Their nature and measurement.* New York: Macmillan.

Spelke, E. (1976). Infants' intermodal perception of events. *Cognitive Psychology, 8,* 553–560.

Spelke, E. S. (1994). Initial knowledge: Six suggestions. *Cognition, 50,* 431–445.

Spelke, E. S. (2000). Core knowledge. *American Psychologist, 55,* pp. 1233–1243.

Spelke, E. S., Breinlinger, K., Macomber, J., & Jacobson, K. (1992). Origins of knowledge. *Psychological Review, 99,* 605–632.

Spencer, M. B., & Markstrom-Adams, C. (1990). Identity processes among racial and ethnic minority children in America. *Child Development, 61,* 290–310.

Spencer, M. B., Noll, E., Stoltzfus, J., & Harpalani, V. (2001). Identity and school adjustment: Revisiting the "acting White" phenomenon. *Educational Psychologist, 36,* 21–30.

Sperling, M. (1996). Revisiting the writing-speaking connection: Challenges for research on writing and writing instruction. *Review of Educational Research, 66,* 53–86.

Spicker, H. H. (1992). Identifying and enriching: Rural gifted children. *Educational Horizons, 70*(2), 60–65.

Spivey, N. N. (1997). *The constructivist metaphor: Reading, writing, and the making of meaning.* San Diego, CA: Academic Press.

Sprafkin, C., Serbin, L. A., Denier, C., & Connor, J. M. (1983). Sex-differentiated play: Cognitive consequences and early interventions. In M. B. Liss (Ed.), *Social and cognitive skills: Sex roles and children's play.* San Diego, CA: Academic Press.

Squires, D. A., Howley, J. P., & Gahr, R. K. (1999). The developmental pathways study group. In J. P. Comer, M. Ben-Avie, N. M. Haynes, & E. T. Joyner (Eds.), *Child by child: The Comer process in education* (pp. 193–207). New York: Teachers College Press.

Sroufe, L. A. (1983). Infant-caregiver attachment and patterns of adaptation in preschool: The roots of maladaptation and competence. In M. Perlmutter (Ed.), *Development and policy concerning children with special needs. Minnesota Symposium on Child Psychology, 16,* 41–83. Hillsdale, NJ: Erlbaum.

Sroufe, L. A., Carlson, E., & Shulman, S. (1993). Individuals in relationships: Development from infancy through adolescence. In D. C. Funder, R. D. Parke, C. Tomlinson-Keasey, & K. Widaman (Eds.), *Studying lives through time: Personality and development* (pp. 315–342). Washington, DC: American Psychological Association.

Sroufe, L. A., & Fleeson, J. (1986). Attachment and the construction of relationships. In W. W. Hartup & Z. Rubin (Eds.), *Relationships and development* (pp. 51–71). New York: Cambridge University Press.

St. James-Roberts, I., & Halil, T. (1991). Infant crying patterns in the first year of life: Normal community and clinical findings. *Journal of Child Psychology and Psychiatry, 32,* 951–968.

St. James-Roberts, I., & Plewis, I. (1996). Individual differences, daily fluctuations, and developmental changes in amounts of infant waking, fussiness, crying, feeding, and sleeping. *Child Development, 67,* 2527–2540.

Stack, C. B., & Burton, L. M. (1993). Kinscripts. *Journal of Comparative Family Studies, 24,* 157–170.

Stahl, S. A., & Miller, P. D. (1989). Whole language and language experience approaches for beginning reading: A quantitative research synthesis. *Review of Educational Research, 59,* 87–116.

Stanley, J. C. (1980). On educating the gifted. *Educational Researcher, 9*(3), 8–12.

Stanovich, K. E. (1986). Matthew effects in reading: Some consequences of individual differences in the acquisition of literacy. *Reading Research Quarterly, 21,* 360–407.

Stanovich, K. E. (2000). *Progress in understanding reading: Scientific foundations and new frontiers.* New York: Guilford Press.

Stanovich, K. E., West, R. F., & Harrison, M. R. (1995). Knowledge growth and maintenance across the life span: The role of print exposure. *Developmental Psychology, 31,* 811–826.

Starr, E. J., & Lovett, S. B. (2000). The ability to distinguish between comprehension and memory: Failing to succeed. *Journal of Educational Psychology, 92,* 761–771.

Stattin, H., & Magnusson, D. (1989). The role of early aggressive behavior in the frequency, seriousness, and types of later crime. *Journal of Consulting and Clinical Psychology, 57,* 710–718.

Staub, D. (1998). *Delicate threads: Friendships between children with and without special needs in inclusive settings.* Bethesda, MD: Woodbine House.

Staub, E. (1995). The roots of prosocial and antisocial behavior in persons and groups: Environmental influence, personality, culture, and socialization. In W. M. Kurtines & J. L. Gewirtz (Eds.), *Moral development: An introduction.* Boston: Allyn & Bacon.

Staudt, M. M. (2001). Use of services prior to and following intensive family preservation services. *Journal of Child and Family Studies, 10*(1), 101–114.

Steele, C. M. (1997). A threat in the air: How stereotypes shape intellectual identify and performance. *American Psychologist, 52,* 613–629.

Steen, F., & Owens, S. A. (2000, March). *Implicit pedagogy: From chase play to collaborative worldmaking.* Paper presented at the Evolution and Social Mind Speaker Series, University of California at Santa Barbara.

Stein, D. M., & Reichert, P. (1990). Extreme dieting behaviors in early adolescence. *Journal of Early Adolescence, 10,* 108–121.

Stein, N. (1993). Stop sexual harassment in schools. *USA Today,* May 18.

Stein, N. L. (1982). What's in a story: Interpreting the interpretations of story grammars. *Discourse Processes, 5,* 319–335.

Stein, N. L., & Glenn, C. G. (1979). An analysis of story comprehension in elementary school children. In R. O. Freedle (Eds.), *New directions in discourse processing* (Vol. 2). Norwood, NJ: Ablex.

Stein, R. (1996). Physical self-concept. In B. A. Bracken (Ed.), *Handbook of self-concept: Developmental, social, and clinical considerations* (pp. 374–394). New York: Wiley.

Steinberg, L. Latchkey children and susceptibility to peer pressure: An ecological analysis. *Developmental Psychology, 22,* 433–439.

Steinberg, L. (1993). *Adolescence* (3rd ed.). New York: McGraw-Hill.

Steinberg, L. (1996). *Beyond the classroom: Why school reform has failed and what parents need to do.* New York: Touchstone.

Steinberg, L., Blinde, P. L., & Chan, K. S. (1984). Dropping out among language minority youth. *Review of Educational Research, 54,* 113–132.

Steinberg, L., Brown, B. B., Cider, M., Kaczmarek, N., & Lazzaro, C. (1988). *Noninstructional influences on high school student achievement: The contributions of parents, peers, extracurricular activities, and part-time work.* Madison, WI: National Center on Effective Secondary Schools. (ERIC Document Reproduction Service No. ED 307 509)

Steinberg, L., & Cauffman, E. (2001). Adolescents as adults in court: A developmental perspective on the transfer of juveniles to criminal court. *Social Policy Report, 15*(4), 1, 3–13

Steinberg, L., Elmen, J., & Mounts, N. (1989). Authoritative parenting, psychosocial maturity, and academic success among adolescents. *Child Development, 60,* 1424–1436.

Steinberg, L., Lamborn, S., Darling, N., Mounts, S., & Dornbusch, S. (1994). Over time change in adjustment and competence among adolescents from authoritative, authoritarian, indulgent, and neglectful families. *Child Development, 65,* 754–770.

Steiner, J. E. (1979). Human facial expression in response to taste and smell stimulation. In H. W. Reese & L. P. Lipsitt (Eds.), *Advances in child development and behavior* (Vol. 13). New York: Academic Press.

Stenberg, C. R., & Campos, J. J. (1990). The development of anger expressions in infancy. In N. L. Stein, B. Leventhal, & T. Trabasso (Eds.), *Psychological and biological approaches to emotion* (pp. 247–282). Hillsdale, NJ: Erlbaum.

Stern, B. M., & Finn-Stevenson, M. (1999). Preregistered for success: The Comer/Zigler initiative. In J. P. Comer, M. Ben-Avie, N. M. Haynes, & E. T. Joyner (Eds.), *Child by child: The Comer process for change in education* (pp. 63–77). New York: Teachers College Press.

Stern, D. N. (1977). *The first relationship: Mother and infant.* Cambridge, MA: Harvard University Press.

Stern, W. (1912). *Die psychologischen Methoden der Intelligenzprufung.* Leipzig, Germany: Barth.

Sternberg, R. J. (1984). Toward a triarchic theory of human intelligence. *Behavioral and Brain Sciences, 7,* 269–287.

Sternberg, R. J. (1985). *Beyond IQ: A triarchic theory of human intelligence.* Cambridge, England: Cambridge University Press.

Sternberg, R. J. (1996). Myths, countermyths, and truths about intelligence. *Educational Researcher, 25*(2), 11–16.

Sternberg, R. J. (1997). The concept of intelligence and its role in lifelong learning and success. *American Psychologist, 52,* 1030–1037.

Sternberg, R. J. (1998). Abilities are forms of developing expertise. *Educational Researcher, 27*(3), 11–20.

Sternberg, R. J., & Detterman, D. K. (Eds.). (1986). *What is intelligence? Contemporary views on its nature and definition.* Norwood, NJ: Ablex.

Sternberg, R. J., Forsythe, G. B., Hedlund, J., Horvath, J. A., Wagner, R. K., Williams, W. M., et al. (2000). *Practical intelligence in everyday life.* Cambridge, England: Cambridge University Press.

Sternberg, R. J., & Grigorenko, E. L. (2000). Theme-park psychology: A case study regarding human intelligence and its implications for education. *Educational Psychology Review, 12,* 247–268.

Sternberg, R. J., & Wagner, R. K. (Eds.). (1994). *Mind in context: Interactionist perspectives on human intelligence.* Cambridge, England: Cambridge University Press.

Sternberg, R. J., & Zhang, L. (1995). What do we mean by giftedness? A pentagonal implicit theory. *Gifted Child Quarterly, 39,* 88–94.

Stevens, R. J., & Slavin, R. E. (1995). The cooperative elementary school: Effects of students' achievement, attitudes, and social relations. *American Educational Research Journal, 32,* 321–351.

Stevenson, H. C. (1995). Relationships of adolescent perceptions of racial socialization to racial identity. *Journal of Black Psychology, 21,* 49–70.

Stevenson, H. W., Chen, C., Lee, S-Y., & Fuligini, A. J. (1991). Schooling, culture, and cognitive development. In L. Okagaki & R. J. Sternberg (Eds.), *Directors of development: Influences on the development of children's thinking* (pp. 243–268). Hillsdale, NJ: Erlbaum.

Stevenson, H. W., Chen, C., & Uttal, D. H. (1990). Beliefs and achievement: A study of black, white, and Hispanic children. *Child Development, 61,* 508–523.

Stewart, R. B. (1983). Sibling interaction: The role of the older child as teacher for the younger. *Merrill-Palmer Quarterly, 29,* 47–68.

Stiles, J., & Thal, D. (1993). Linguistic and spatial cognitive development following early focal brain injury: Patterns of deficit and recovery. In M. Johnson (Ed.), *Brain development and cognition.* Oxford, England: Blackwell.

Stipek, D. (2002). At what age should children enter kindergarten? A question for policy makers and parents. *Social Policy Report, 16,* 1, 3–16. Ann Arbor, MI: Society for Research in Child Development.

Stipek, D. J. (1981). Children's perceptions of their own and their classmates' ability. *Journal of Educational Psychology, 73,* 404–410.

Stipek, D. J. (1984). Sex differences in children's attributions for success and failure on math and spelling tests. *Sex Roles, 11,* 969–981.

Stipek, D. J. (1993). *Motivation to learn: From theory to practice* (2nd ed.). Needham Heights, MA: Allyn & Bacon.

Stipek, D. J. (1996). Motivation and instruction. In D. C. Berliner & R. C. Calfee (Eds.), *Handbook of educational psychology.* New York: Macmillan.

Stipek, D. J., & Kowalski, P. S. (1989). Learned helplessness in task-orienting versus performance-orienting testing conditions. *Journal of Educational Psychology, 81,* 384–391.

Stipek, D. J., Recchia, S., & McClintic, S. M. (1992). Self-evaluation in young children. *Monographs of* the Society for Research in Child Development, 57(2, Serial No. 226).

Stodolsky, S. S. (1974). How children find something to do in preschools. *Genetic Psychology Monographs, 90,* 245–303.

Stolley, K. S. (1993). Statistics on adoption in the United States. *The Future of Children, 3*(1), 26–42.

Storfer, M. D. (1995). Problems in left-right discrimination in a high-IQ population. *Perceptual & Motor Skills, 81*(2), 491–497.

Strage, A., & Brandt, T. S. (1999). Authoritative parenting and college students' academic adjustment and success. *Journal of Educational Psychology, 91,* 146–156.

Statistical Abstract of the United States (111th ed.). (1991). Washington, DC: Department of Commerce, Bureau of the Census.

Status of the American school teacher 1990–1991 (1992). Washington, DC: National Education Association, Research Division.

Straus, M. A. (2000). The benefits of never spanking: New and more definitive evidence. In M. A. Straus, *Beating the devil out of them: Corporal punishment by American families and its effects on children.* New Brunswick, NJ: Transaction Publications.

Strauss, S., & Shilony, T. (1994). Teachers' models of children's mind and learning. In L. A. Hirschfeld & S. A. Gelman (Eds.), *Mapping the mind: Domain specificity in cognition and culture* (pp. 455–473). New York: Cambridge University Press.

Strayer, F. F. (1991). The development of agonistic and affiliative structures in preschool play groups. In J. Silverberg & P. Gray (Eds.), *To fight or not to fight: Violence and peacefulness in humans and other primates.* Oxford: Oxford University Press.

Strayer, F. F., & Trudel, M. (1984). Developmental changes in the nature and function of social dominance among young children. *Ethology and Sociobiology, 5,* 279–295.

Streigel-Moore, R., Silberstein, L. R., & Rodin, J. (1986). Toward an understanding of bulimia. *American Psychologist, 41,* 246–263.

Streissguth, A. P., Barr, H. M., Sampson, P. D., & Bookstein, F. L. (1994). Prenatal alcohol and offspring development: The first fourteen years. *Drug & Alcohol Dependence, 36,* 89–99.

Streri, A., & Spelke, E. S. (1988). Haptic perception of objects in infancy. *Cognitive Psychology, 20,* 1–23.

Strike, K. A., & Posner, G. J. (1992). A revisionist theory of conceptual change. In R. A. Duschl & R. J. Hamilton (Eds.), *Philosophy of science, cognitive psychology, and educational theory and practice.* Albany: State University of New York Press.

Strozer, J. R. (1994). *Language acquisition after puberty.* Washington, DC: Georgetown University Press.

Stukas, A. A., Jr., Clary, E. G., & Snyder, M. (1999). Service learning: Who benefits and why. *Social Policy Report, Society for Research in Child Development, 13*(4), 1–19.

Subar, A. F., Heimendinger, J., Krebs-Smith, S. M., Patterson, B. H., Kessler, R., & Pivonka, E. (1992). *Five a day for better health: A baseline study of American's fruit and vegetable consumptions.* Rockville, MD: National Cancer Institute.

Sue, D. W. (1990). Culture-specific strategies in counseling: A conceptual framework. *Professional Psychology: Research and Practice, 21,* 424–433.

Sue, S., & Chin, R. (1983). The mental health of Chinese-American children: Stressors and resources. In G. J. Powell (Ed.), *The psychosocial development of minority children.* New York: Brunner/Mazel.

Sugar, W. A., & Bonk, C. J. (1998). Student role play in the World Forum: Analyses of an Arctic learning apprenticeship. In C. J. Bonk & K. S. King (Eds.), *Electronic collaborators: Learner-centered technologies for literacy, apprenticeship, and discourse.* Mahwah, NJ: Erlbaum.

Sugarman, S. (1983). *Children's early thought: Developments in classification.* New York: Cambridge University Press.

Suhr, D. D. (1999). *An investigation of mathematics and reading achievement of 5- through 14-year olds using latent growth curve methodology.* Unpublished doctoral dissertation, University of Northern Colorado, Greeley.

Suina, J. H., & Smolkin, L. B. (1994). From natal culture to school culture to dominant society culture: Supporting transitions for Pueblo Indian students. In P. M. Greenfield & R. R. Cocking (Eds.), *Cross-cultural roots of minority child development* (pp. 115–130). Hillsdale, NJ: Erlbaum.

Sullivan, F. M., & Barlow, S. M. (2001). Review of risk factors for sudden infant death syndrome. *Paediatric & Perinatal Epidemiology, 15*(2), 144–200.

Sullivan, L. W. (1987). The risks of the sickle-cell trait: Caution and common sense. *New England Journal of Medicine, 317,* 830–831.

Sullivan, P., & Knutson, J. F. (1998). The association between child maltreatment and disabilities in a hospital based epidemiological study. *Child Abuse and Neglect, 22,* 271–288.

Sullivan, R. C. (1994). Autism: Definitions past and present. *Journal of Vocational Rehabilitation, 4,* 4–9.

Sullivan-DeCarlo, C., DeFalco, K., & Roberts, V. (1998). Helping students avoid risky behavior. *Educational Leadership, 56*(1), 80–82.

Sulzby, E. (1985). Children's emergent reading of favorite storybooks: A developmental study. *Reading Research Quarterly, 20,* 458–481.

Sulzby, E. (1986). Children's elicitation and use of metalinguistic knowledge about *word* during literacy interactions. In D. B. Yaden, Jr., & S. Templeton (Eds.), *Metalinguistic awareness and beginning literacy: Conceptualizing what it means to read and write.* Portsmouth, NH: Heinemann.

Sulzby, E., & Teale, W. (1991). Emergent literacy. In R. Barr, M. L. Kamil, P. B. Mosenthal, & P. D. Pearson (Eds.), *Handbook of reading research* (Vol. II). New York: Longman.

Sund, R. B. (1976). *Piaget for educators.* Columbus, OH: Charles E. Merrill.

Super, C. M. (1981). Behavioral development in infancy. In R. H. Munroe, R. L. Munroe, & B. B. Whiting (Eds.), *Handbook of cross-cultural human development* (pp. 181–270). New York: Garland STPM Press.

Suskind, R. (1998). *A hope in the unseen: An American odyssey from the inner city to the Ivy League.* New York: Broadway Books.

Susman, E. J., Inoff-Germain, G., Nottelmann, E. D., Loriaux, D. L., Cutler, J., Gordon, B., & Chrousos, G. P. (1987). Hormones, emotional dispositions, and aggressive attributes in young adolescents. *Child Development, 58,* 1114–1134.

Susman, E. J., Nottelmann, E. D., Inhoff-Germain, G., Dorn, L. D., & Chrousos, G. P. (1987). Hormonal influences on aspects of psychological development during adolescence. *Journal of Adolescent Health Care, 8,* 492–504.

Susman, E. J., Nottelmann, E. D., Inhoff-Germain, G. E., Dorn, L. D., Cutler, G. B. Jr., Loriaux, D. L., & Chrousos, G. P. (1985). The relation of development and social-emotional behavior in young adolescents. *Journal of Youth and Adolescence, 14,* 245–264.

Suttles, G. D. (1970). Friendship as a social institution. In G. J. McCall, M. McCall, N. K. Denzin, G. D. Scuttles, & S. Kurth (Eds.), *Social relationships* (pp. 95–135). Chicago: Aldine de Gruyter.

Sutton, J., Smith, P. K., & Swettenham, J. (1999). Bullying and 'theory of mind': A critique of the 'social skills deficit' view of anti-social behaviour. *Social Development, 8*(1), 117–127.

Sutton-Smith, B. (Ed.). (1979). *Play and learning.* New York: Gardner Press.

Sutton-Smith, B. (1986). The development of fictional narrative performances. *Topics in Language Disorders, 7*(1), 1–10.

Svirsky, M. A., Robbins, A. M., Kirk, K. I., Pisoni, D. B., & Miyamoto, R. T. (2000). Language development in profoundly deaf children with cochlear implants. *Psychological Science, 11,* 153–158.

Swanborn, M. S., L., & de Glopper, K. (1999). Incidental word learning while reading: A meta analysis. *Review of Educational Research, 69,* 261–285.

Swann, W. B., Jr. (1997). The trouble with change: Self-verification and allegiance to the self. *Psychological Science, 8,* 177–180.

Swanson, H. L. (1993). An information processing analysis of learning disabled children's problem solving. *American Educational Research Journal, 30,* 861–893.

Swanson, H. L., Mink, J., & Bocian, K. M. (1999). Cognitive processing deficits in poor readers with symptoms of reading disabilities and ADHD: More alike than different? *Journal of Educational Psychology, 91,* 321–333.

Swim, J. K., Cohen, L. L., & Hyers, L. L. (1998). Experiencing everyday prejudice and discrimination. In J. K. Swim & C. Stangor (Eds.), *Prejudice: The target's perspective* (pp. 38–60). San Diego, CA: Academic Press.

Swope, G. W. (1980). Kids and cults: Who joins and why? *Media and Methods, 16,* 18–21.

Sylvester, R. (1995). *A celebration of neurosis: An educator's guide to the human brain.* Alexandria, VA: Association for Supervision and Curriculum Development.

Szynal-Brown, C., & Morgan, R. R. (1983). The effects of reward on tutor's behaviors in a cross-age tutoring context. *Journal of Experimental Child Psychology, 36,* 196–208.

Tager-Flusberg, H. (1993). Putting words together: Morphology and syntax in the preschool years. In J. Berko-Gleason (Ed.), *The development of language* (3rd ed.). Upper Saddle River, NJ: Merrill/Prentice Hall.

Takahashi, K. (1990). Are the key assumptions of the "Strange Situation" procedure universal? A view from Japanese research. *Human Development, 33,* 23–30.

Tallman, I., Gray, L. N., Kullberg, V., & Henderson, D. (1999). The intergenerational transmission of marital conflict: Testing a process model. *Social Psychology Quarterly, 62*(3), 219–239.

Tamburrini, J. (1982). Some educational implications of Piaget's theory. In S. Modgil and C. Modgil (Eds.), *Jean Piaget: Consensus and controversy.* New York: Praeger.

Tamis-LeMonda, C. S., & Cabrera, N. (1999). Perspectives on father involvement: Research and policy. *Social Policy Report, 13*(2), 1–25.

Tannen, D. (1990). *You just don't understand: Talk between the sexes.* New York: Ballantine.

Tanner, E. M., & Finn-Stevenson, M. (2002). Nutrition and brain development: Social policy implications. *American Journal of Orthopsychiatry, 72*(2), 182–193.

Tanner, J. M. (1990). *Foetus into man: Physical growth from conception to maturity* (Rev. ed.). Cambridge, MA: Harvard University Press.

Tate, W. F. (1995). Returning to the root: A culturally relevant approach to mathematics pedagogy. *Theory into Practice, 34,* 166–173.

Taylor, J. M. (1994). *MDMA frequently asked questions list.* Retrieved from the World Wide Web: http://ibbserver.ibb.uu.nl/jboschma/ecstasy/xtc01.

Taylor, M., Esbensen, B. M., & Bennett, R. T. (1994). Children's understanding of knowledge acquisition: The tendency for children to report that they have always known what they have just learned. *Child Development, 65,* 1581–1604.

Taylor, R. D., Casten, R., Flickinger, S. M., Roberts, D., & Fulmore, C. D. (1994). Explaining the school performance of African American adolescents. *Journal of Research on Adolescence, 4,* 21–44.

Taylor, R. D., & Roberts, D. (1995). Kinship support and maternal and adolescent well-being in economically disadvantaged African-American families. *Child Development, 66,* 1585–1597.

Taylor, S. E., & Brown, J. D. (1988). Illusion and well-being: A social-psychological perspective on mental health. *Psychological Bulletin, 103,* 193–210.

Taylor, S. M. (1994, April). *Staying in school against the odds: Voices of minority adolescent girls.* Paper presented at the annual meeting of the American Educational Research Association, New Orleans.

Taylor, W. C., Beech, B. M., & Cummings, S. S. (1998). Increasing physical activity levels among youth: A public health challenge. In D. K. Wilson, J. R. Rodrigue, & W. C. Taylor (Eds.), *Health-promoting and health-compromising behaviors among minority adolescents* (pp. 107–128). Washington, DC: American Psychological Association.

Tchombe, T. M., Nuwanyakpa, M., & Etmonia, T. (2001). Street children in Cameroon: Problems and perspectives. *Journal of Psychology in Africa, 11*(2), 101–125.

Teale, W. H. (1978). Positive environments for learning to read: What studies of early readers tell us. *Language Arts, 55,* 922–932.

Teale, W. H. (1986). Home background and young children's literacy development. In W. H. Teale & E. Sulzby (Eds.), *Emergent literacy: Writing and reading.* Norwood, NJ: Ablex.

Teasley, S. D., & Parker, J. G. (1995, March). *The effects of gender, friendship, and popularity on the targets and topics of preadolescents' gossip.* Paper presented at the biennial meeting of the Society for Research in Child Development, Indianapolis, IN.

Teeter, P. A., & Semrud-Clikeman, M. (1997). *Child neuropsychology: Assessment and interventions for neurodevelopmental disorders.* Boston: Allyn & Bacon.

Tellegren, A., Lykken, D. T., Bouchard, T. J., & Wilcox, K. J. (1988). Personality similarity in twins reared apart and together. *Journal of Personality and Social Psychology, 54,* 1031–1039.

Tennenbaum, H. R., & Leaper, C. (2002). Are parents' gender schemas related to their children's gender-related cognitions? A meta-analysis. *Developmental Psychology, 38,* 615–630.

Tennyson, R. D., & Cocchiarella, M. J. (1986). An empirically based instructional design theory for teaching concepts. *Review of Educational Research, 56,* 40–71.

Terman, L. M. (1916). *The measurement of intelligence.* Boston: Houghton Mifflin.

Terman, L. M., & Merrill, M. A. (1972). *Stanford-Binet Intelligence Scale* (3rd ed.). Boston: Houghton Mifflin.

Terrell, S. L., & Terrell, F. (1993). African-American cultures. In D. E. Battles (Ed.), *Communication disorders in multicultural populations.* Stoneham, MA: Butterworth-Heinemann.

Tessler, M., & Nelson, K. (1994). Making memories: The influence of joint encoding on later recall by young children. *Consciousness and Cognition, 3,* 307–326.

Teti, D. M., Gelfand, D., Messinger, D. S., & Isabella, R. (1995). Maternal depression and the quality of early attachment: An examination of infants, preschoolers and their mothers. *Developmental Psychology, 31,* 364–376.

Thaler, R. H. (2000). Mental accounting matters. In D. Kahneman & A. Tversky (Eds.), *Choices,*

values, and frames (pp. 241–287). New York: Russell Sage Foundation.

Tharp, R. G. (1989). Psychocultural variables and constants: Effects on teaching and learning in schools. *American Psychologist, 44,* 349–359.

Tharp, R. G. (1994). Intergroup differences among Native Americans in socialization and child cognition: An ethnogenetic analysis. In P. M. Greenfield & R. R. Cocking (Eds.), *Cross-cultural roots of minority child development* (pp. 87–105). Hillsdale, NJ: Erlbaum.

Tharp, R. G., & Gallimore, R. (1988). *Rousing minds to life: Teaching, learning, and schooling in social context.* Cambridge, England: Cambridge University Press.

Thatcher, R. W. (1994). Cyclic cortical reorganization: Origins of human cognitive development. In G. Dawson & K. W. Fischer (Eds.), *Human behavior and the developing brain* (pp. 232–266). New York: Guilford.

Thelen, E., Corbetta, D., Kamm, K., Spencer, J. P., Schneider, K., & Zernicke, R. F. (1993). The transition to reaching: Mapping intention and intrinsic dynamics. *Child Development, 64,* 1058–1098.

Thelen, E., Corbetta, D., & Spencer, J. (1996). The development of reaching during the first year: The role of movement speed. *Journal of Experimental Psychology: Human Perception and Performance, 22,* 1059–1076.

Thelen, E., & Smith, L. B. (1998). Dynamic systems theories. In W. Damon (Editor-in-Chief), & R. M. Lerner (Vol. Ed.), *Handbook of child psychology. Vol. 1. Theoretical models of human development* (5th ed., pp. 563–634). New York: Wiley.

Thiede, H., Romero, M., Bordelon, K., Hagan, H., & Murrill, C. S. (2001). Using a jail-based survey to monitor HIV and risk behaviors among Seattle area injection users. *Journal of Urban Health, 78*(2), 264–287.

Thomas, A., & Chess, S. (1977). *Temperament and development.* New York: Brunner/Mazel.

Thomas, A., Chess, S., & Birch, H. (1968). *Temperament and behavior disorders in children.* New York. New York University Press.

Thomas, J. R., & French, K. E. (1985). Gender differences across age in motor performance: A meta-analysis. *Psychological Bulletin, 98,* 260–282.

Thomas, J. W. (1993). Promoting independent learning in the middle grades: The role of instructional support practices. *Elementary School Journal, 93,* 575–591.

Thomas, S., & Oldfather, P. (1997). Intrinsic motivations, literacy, and assessment practices: "That's my grade. That's me." *Educational Psychologist, 32,* 107–123.

Thomas, S. P., Groër, M., & Droppleman, P. (1993). Physical health of today's school children. *Educational Psychology Review, 5,* 5–33.

Thomas, W. P., Collier, V. P., & Abbott, M. (1993). Academic achievement through Japanese, Spanish, or French: The first two years of partial immersion. *Modern Language Journal, 77,* 170–179.

Thompson, H., & Carr, M. (1995, April). *Brief metacognitive intervention and interest as predictors of memory for text.* Paper presented at the annual meeting of the American Educational Research Association, San Francisco.

Thompson, L. A., Fagan, J. F., & Fulker, D. W. (1991). Longitudinal prediction of specific cognitive abilities from infant novelty preference. *Child Development, 62,* 530–538.

Thompson, L. A., & Kelly-Vance, L. (2001). The impact of mentoring on academic achievement of at-risk youth. *Children and Youth Services Review, 23*(3), 227–242.

Thompson, P. M., Giedd, J. N., Woods. R. P., MacDonald, D., Evans, A. C., Toga, A. W. (2000). Growth patterns in the developing brain detected

by using continuum mechanical tensor maps. *Nature, 404,* 190–193.

Thompson, R. A. (1994). The role of the father after divorce. *The Future of Children: Children and Divorce, 4*(1), 210–235.

Thompson, R. A. (1998). Early sociopersonality development. In W. Damon (Editor-in-Chief) & N. Eisenberg (Vol. Ed.), *Handbook of child psychology: Vol. 3. Social, emotional, and personality development* (5th ed., pp. 25–104). New York: Wiley.

Thompson, R. A., & Wyatt, J. M. (1999). Current research on child maltreatment: Implications for educators. *Educational Psychology Review, 11,* 173–201.

Thompson, R. F. (1975). *Introduction to physiological psychology.* New York: Harper & Row.

Thorkildsen, T. A. (1995). Conceptions of social justice. In W. M. Kurtines & J. L. Gewirtz (Eds.), *Moral development: An introduction.* Boston: Allyn & Bacon.

Thorndike, R. M. (1997). *Measurement and evaluation in psychology and education* (6th ed.). Upper Saddle River, NJ: Merrill/Prentice Hall.

Thorndike, R., Hagen, E., & Sattler, J. (1986). *Stanford-Binet Intelligence Scale* (4th ed.). Chicago: Riverside.

Thornton, M. C., Chatters, L. M., Taylor, R. J., & Allen, W. (1990). Sociodemographic and environmental correlates of racial socialization by Black parents. *Child Development, 61,* 401–409.

Timmer, S. G., Eccles, J., & O'Brien, K. (1985). How children use time. In F. T. Juster & F. P. Stafford (Eds.), *Time, goods, and well-being* (pp. 353–383). Ann Arbor, MI: Survey Research Center, Institute for Social Research.

Tincoff, R., & Jusczyk, P. W. (1999). Some beginnings of word comprehension in 6-month-olds. *Psychological Science, 10,* 172–175.

Tisak, M. (1993). Preschool children's judgments of moral and personal events involving physical harm and property damage. *Merrill-Palmer Quarterly, 39,* 375–390.

Tobias, S. (1977). A model for research on the effect of anxiety on instruction. In J. E. Sieber, H. F. O'Neil, Jr., & S. Tobias (Eds.), *Anxiety, learning, and instruction.* Hillsdale, NJ: Erlbaum.

Tobias, S. (1994). Interest, prior knowledge, and learning. *Review of Educational Research, 64,* 37–54.

Tomblin, J. B. (1997). Epidemiology of specific language impairment. In M. Gopnik (Ed.), *The inheritance and innateness of grammars.* New York: Oxford University Press.

Tompkins, G. E., & McGee, L. M. (1986). Visually impaired and sighted children's emerging concepts about written language. In D. B. Yaden, Jr., & S. Templeton (Eds.), *Metalinguistic awareness and beginning literacy: Conceptualizing what it means to read and write.* Portsmouth, NH: Heinemann.

Torgesen, J. K., Wagner, R. K., Rashotte, C. A., Rose, E., Lindamood, P., Conway, T., et al. (1999). Preventing reading failure in young children with phonological processing disabilities: Group and individual responses to instruction. *Journal of Educational Psychology 91,* 579–593.

Torney-Purta, J. (1990). Youth in relation to social institutions. In S. S. Feldman & G. R. Elliott (Eds.), *At the threshold: The developing adolescent* (pp. 457–477). Cambridge, MA: Harvard University Press.

Torquati, J. C. (2002). Personal and social resources as predictors of parenting in homeless families. *Journal of Family Issues, 23*(4), 463–485.

Torrance, E. P. (1989). A reaction to "Gifted black students: Curriculum and teaching strategies." In C. J. Maker & S. W. Schiever (Eds.), *Critical issues in gifted education: Vol. 2. Defensible programs for cultural and ethnic minorities.* Austin, TX: Pro-Ed.

Torrance, E. P. (1995). Insights about creativity: Questioned, rejected, ridiculed, ignored. *Educational Psychology Review, 7,* 313–322.

Torres-Guzmán, M. E. (1998). Language, culture, and literacy in Puerto Rican communities. In B. Pérez (Ed.), *Sociocultural contexts of language and literacy.* Mahwah, NJ: Erlbaum.

Tourniaire, F., & Pulos, S. (1985). Proportional reasoning: A review of the literature. *Educational Studies in Mathematics, 16,* 181–204.

Touwen, B. C. L. (1974). The neurological development of the infant. In J. A. Davis & J. Dobbing (Eds.), *Scientific foundations of pediatrics.* Philadelphia: W. B. Saunders.

Trainor, L. J., Austin, C. M., & Desjardins, R. N. (2000). Is infant-directed speech prosody a result of the vocal expression of emotion? *Psychological Science, 11,* 188–195.

Trawick-Smith, J. (2003). *Early childhood development: A multicultural perspective* (3rd ed.). Upper Saddle River, NJ: Merrill/Prentice Hall.

Treffert, D. A. (1989). *Extraordinary people: Understanding Savant syndrome.* New York: Harper & Row.

Treiman, R. (1993). *Beginning to spell: A study of first-grade children.* New York: Oxford University Press.

Treiman, R. (1998). Beginning to spell in English. In C. Hulme & R. M. Joshi (Eds.), *Reading and spelling: Development and disorders.* Mahwah, NJ: Erlbaum.

Trelease, J. (1982). *The read-aloud handbook.* New York: Penguin Books.

Tremblay, L. (1999, April). *Acceleration hypothesis: A meta-analysis of environmental stressors impact on puberty onset.* Paper presented at the Biennial Meeting of the Society for Research in Child Development, Albuquerque, NM.

Trevarthen, C. (1980). The foundations of intersubjectivity: Development of interpersonal and cooperative understandings in infants. In D. R. Olson (Ed.), *The social foundations of language and thought* (pp. 316–342). New York: Norton.

Trevarthen, C., & Hubley, P. (1978). Secondary intersubjectivity: Confidence, confiding and acts of meaning in the first year. In A. Lock (Ed.), *Action, gesture, and symbol: The emergence of language.* London: Academic Press.

Triandis, H. C. (1995). *Individualism and collectivism.* Boulder, CO: Westview Press.

Tronick, E. Z., Als, H., Adamson, L., Wise, S., & Brazelton, B. (1978). The infants' response to entrapment between contradictory messages in face-to-face interaction. *American Academy of Child Psychiatry, 1,* 1–13.

Tronick, E. Z., Cohn, J., & Shea, E. (1986). The transfer of affect between mother and infant. In T. B. Brazelton & M. W. Yogman (Eds.), *Affective development in infancy* (pp. 11–25). Norwood, NJ: Ablex.

Trueba, H. T. (1988). Peer socialization among minority students: A high school dropout prevention program. In H. T. Trueba & C. Delgado-Gaitan (Eds.), *School and society: Learning content through culture.* New York: Praeger.

Tunmer, W. E., & Bowey, J. A. (1984). Metalinguistic awareness and reading acquisition. In W. E. Tunmer, C. Pratt, & M. L. Herriman (Eds.), *Metalinguistic awareness in children: Theory, research, and implications.* Berlin, Germany: Springer-Verlag.

Tunmer, W. E., Pratt, C., & Herriman, M. L. (Eds.), (1984). *Metalinguistic awareness in children: Theory, research, and implications.* Berlin, Germany: Springer-Verlag.

Turiel, E. (1983). *The development of social knowledge: Morality and convention.* Cambridge, England: Cambridge University Press.

Turiel, E. (1998). The development of morality. In W. Damon (Editor-in-Chief) & N. Eisenberg (Vol. Ed.), *Handbook of child psychology: Vol. 3. Social,*

emotional, and personality development (pp. 863–932). New York: Wiley.

Turiel, E., Killen, M., & Helwig, C. C. (1987). Morality: Its structure, function, and vagaries. In J. Kagan & S. Lamb (Eds.), *The emergence of morality in young children* (pp. 155–243). Chicago: University of Chicago Press.

Turiel, E., Smetana, J. G., & Killen, M. (1991). Social contexts in social cognitive development. In W. M. Kurtines & J. L. Gewirtz (Eds.), *Moral behavior and development: Vol. 2. Research.* Hillsdale, NJ: Erlbaum.

Turkheimer, E. (2000). Three laws of behavior genetics and what they mean. *Current Directions in Psychological Science, 9,* 160–164.

Turnbull, A. P. (1974). Teaching retarded persons to rehearse through cumulative overt labeling. *American Journal of Mental Deficiency, 79,* 331–337.

Turnbull, A. P., Pereira, L., & Blue-Banning, M. (2000). Teachers as friendship facilitators: Respeto and personalismo. *Teaching Exceptional Children, 32*(5), 66–70.

Turnbull, R., Turnbull, A., Shank, M., Smith, S., & Leal, D. (2002). *Exceptional lives: Special education in today's schools* (3rd ed.). Upper Saddle River, NJ: Merrill/Prentice Hall.

Turner, J. C. (1995). The influence of classroom contexts on young children's motivation for literacy. *Reading Research Quarterly, 30,* 410–441.

Turner, M. A., Freiberg, F., Godfrey, E., Herbig, C., Levy, D. K., & Smith, R. R. (2002). *All other things being equal: A paired testing study of mortgage lending institutions.* Washington, DC: The Urban Institute.

Tversky, A., & Kahneman, D. (1990). Judgment under uncertainty: Heuristics and biases. In P. K. Moser (Ed.), *Rationality in action: Contemporary approaches* (pp. 171–188). New York: Cambridge University Press.

Tzuriel, D. (2000). Dynamic assessment of young children: Educational and intervention perspectives. *Educational Psychology Review, 12,* 385–435.

Uba, L., & Huang, K. (1999). *Psychology.* New York: Longman.

Udall, A. J. (1989). Curriculum for gifted Hispanic students. In C. J. Maker & S. W. Schiever (Eds.), *Critical issues in gifted education: Vol. 2. Defensible programs for cultural and ethnic minorities.* Austin, TX: Pro-Ed.

Udry, J. R. (1988). Biological predispositions and social control in adolescent sexual behavior. *American Sociological Review, 53*(5), 709–722.

Ulichny, P. (1994, April). *Cultures in conflict.* Paper presented at the annual meeting of the American Educational Research Association, New Orleans, LA.

Underwood, B., & Moore, B. (1982). Perspective-taking and altruism. *Psychological Bulletin, 91,* 143–173.

Upchurch, D. M., & McCarthy, J. (1990). The timing of first birth and high school completion. *American Sociological Review, 55,* 224–234.

Urban, J., Carlson, E., Egeland, B., & Sroufe, L. A. (1991). Patterns of individual adaptation across childhood. *Development and Psychopathology, 3,* 445–460.

Urdan, T. (1997). Achievement goal theory: Past results, future directions. In M. L. Maehr & P. R. Pintrich (Eds.), *Advances in motivation and achievement* (Vol. 10). Greenwich, CT: JAI Press.

Urdan, T. C., & Maehr, M. L. (1995). Beyond a two-goal theory of motivation and achievement: A case for social goals. *Review of Educational Research, 65,* 213–243.

U.S. Bureau of the Census. (1995). *Statistical Abstracts of the United States, 1995.* Washington, DC: U.S. Government Printing Office.

U.S. Bureau of the Census. (1996). *Statistical Abstracts of the United States, 1996.* Washington, DC: U.S. Government Printing Office.

U.S. Census Bureau (2000a). *Table FG1. Married Couple Family Groups, by Labor Force Status of Both Spouses, and Race and Hispanic Origin/1 of the Reference Person: March 2000.* Retrieved January 31, 2003, from *http://www.census. gov/population/socdemo/hh-fam/p20-537/2000/ tabFG1.txt*

U.S. Census Bureau (2000b). *Table FG5. One-Parent Family Groups with Own Children Under 18, by Labor Force Status, and Race and Hispanic Origin/1 of the Reference Person: March 2000.* Retrieved January 31, 2003, from *http://www.census.-gov/population/socdemo/hh-fam/p20-537/2000/tabFG5.txt*

U.S. Census Bureau (2003a). *Historical Table. Primary Child Care Arrangements Used by Employed Mothers of Preschoolers: 1985 to 1999.* Retrieved January 31, 2003, from *http://www. census.gov/population/socdemo/child/ pp1-168/tabH-1.pdf*

U.S. Census Bureau (2003b). *PPL Table 3B: Child Care Arrangements for Gradeschoolers by Family Characteristics and Employment Status of Mother: Spring 1999.* Retrieved January 31, 2003, from *http://www.census.gov/population/socdemo/ child/pp1-168/tab03B.pdf*

U.S. Department of Education. (1993). *National excellence: A case for developing America's talent.* Washington, DC: Office of Educational Research and Improvement.

U.S. Department of Education. (1996). *To assure the free appropriate public education of all children with disabilities: Eighteenth annual report to Congress on the implementation of the Individuals with Disabilities Education Act.* Washington, DC: Author.

U.S. Department of Education. (1997). *To assure the free appropriate public education of all children with disabilities: Nineteenth annual report to Congress on the implementation of the Individuals with Disabilities Education Act.* Washington, DC: Author.

U.S. Department of Education, Office of Civil Rights. (1993). *Annual report to Congress.* Washington, DC: Author.

U.S. Department of Health and Human Services. (1994, April/May). *Reducing teenage pregnancy increases life options for youth* (U.S. Public Health Service Prevention Report, pp. 1–4). Washington, DC: Author.

U.S. Department of Health and Human Services. (1996). *Physical activity and health: A report of the Surgeon General. Executive Summary.* Washington, DC: Author.

U.S. Department of Health and Human Services. (1997). *Youth risk behavior surveillance—United States* (CDC MMWR Surveillance Summaries Vol. 45, No. SS-4). Washington, DC: Author.

U.S. Department of Health and Human Services. (1998). Youth risk behavior surveillance—United States, 1997. *Morbidity and Mortality Weekly Report, 47*(No. SS-3).

U.S. Department of Health and Human Services (2001). *Prevention works! A practitioner's guide to achieving outcomes.* Rockville, MD: Author.

U.S. Department of Health and Human Services (2002, August). *The AFCARS report 7.* Retrieved January 25, 2003, from *http://www.acf.hhs.gov/ programs/cb/dis/afcars/cwstats.htm*

U.S. Drug Enforcement Administration (2002). *Team up: A drug prevention manual for high school athletic coaches.* Washington, DC: U.S. Department of Justice Drug Enforcement Administration.

Uttal, D. H., Marzolf, D. P., Pierroutsakos, S. L., Smith, C. M., Troseth, G. L., Scudder, K. V., & DeLoache, J. S. (1998). Seeing through symbols: The development of children's understanding of symbolic relations. In O. N. Saracho & B.

Spodek (Eds.), *Multiple perspectives on play in early childhood education*. Albany: State University of New York Press.

van Andel, J. (1990). Places children like, dislike, and fear. *Children's Environment Quarterly, 7*(4), 24–31.

Vandell, D. L., & Mueller, D. C. (1995). Peer play and friendships during the first two years. In H. C. Foot, A. J. Chapman, & J. R. Smithe (Eds.), *Friendship and social relations in children* (pp. 181–208). New Brunswich, NJ: Transaction.

Vandell, D. L., & Pierce, K. M. (1999, April). *Can after-school programs benefit children who live in high-crime neighborhoods?* Paper presented at the biennial meeting of the Society for Research in Child Development, Albuquerque, NM.

Vandell, D. L., & Posner, J. (1999). Conceptualization and measurement of children's after-school environments. In S. L. Friedman & T. D. Wachs (Eds.), *Assessment of the environment across the lifespan* (pp. 167–197). Washington, DC: American Psychological Association Press.

Vandell, D. L., & Shumow, L. (1999, Fall). After-school child care programs. *The Future of Children: When School Is Out, 9,* 64–80.

Vandell, D. L., Wilson, K. S., & Buchanan, N. R. (1980). Peer interaction in the first year of life: An examination of its structure, content, and sensitivity to toys. *Child Development, 51,* 481–488.

Vandenberg, B. (1978). Play and development from an ethological perspective. *American Psychologist, 33,* 724–738.

VandenBerg, K. A. (1982). Humanizing the intensive care nursery. In A. Waldstein, D. Gilderman, D. Taylor-Hersel, S. Prestridge, & J. Anderson (Eds.), *Issues in neonatal care* (pp. 83–105). Chapel Hill, NC: TADS, University of North Carolina.

van den Broek, P., Bauer, P. J., & Bourg, T. (Eds.) (1997). *Developmental spans in event comprehension and representation: Bridging fictional and actual events.* Mahwah, NJ: Erlbaum.

Van der Voort, T. H. A., & Valkenburg, P. M. (1994). Television's impact on fantasy play: A review of research. *Developmental Review, 14*(1), 227–251.

van Heteren, C. F., Boekkooi, P. F., Jongsma, H. W., & Nijhuis, J. G. (2001). Fetal habituation to vibroacoustic stimulation in relation to fetal states and fetal heart rate parameters. *Early Human Development, 61,* 135–145.

Van Hoorn, J., Nourot, P. M., Scales B., & Alward, K. R. (1999). *Play at the center of the curriculum* (2nd ed.). Upper Saddle River, NJ: Merrill/Prentice Hall.

van IJzendoorn, M. H., Goldberg, S., Kroonenberg, P. M., & Frenkel, O. J. (1992). The relative effects of maternal and child problems on the quality of attachment: A meta-analysis of attachment in clinical samples. *Child Development, 63,* 840–858.

van IJzendoorn, M. H., Sagi, A., Lambermon, M. (1992). The multiple caregiver paradox: Data from Holland and Israel. In R. C. Pianta (Ed.), *New directions for child development: No. 57. Beyond the parent: The role of other adults in children's lives* (pp. 5–27). San Francisco, CA: Jossey-Bass.

van Kraayenoord, C. E., & Paris, S. G. (1997). Children's self-appraisal of their worksamples and academic progress. *Elementary School Journal, 97,* 523–537.

van Laar, C. (2000). The paradox of low academic achievement but high self-esteem in African American students: An attributional account. *Educational Psychology Review, 12,* 33–61.

Vasquez, J. A. (1990). Teaching to the distinctive traits of minority students. *Clearing House, 63,* 299–304.

Vaughn, B. E., Egeland, B., Sroufe, L. A., & Waters, E. (1979). Individual differences in infant-mother attachment at twelve and eighteen months: Stability and change in families under stress. *Child Development, 50,* 971–975.

Vaughn, B. E., Kopp, C. B., & Krakow, J. B. (1984). The emergence and consolidation of self-control from eighteen to thirty months of age: Normative trends and individual differences. *Child Development, 55,* 990–1004.

Vaughn, S. (1991). Social skills enhancement in students with learning disabilities. In B. Y. L. Wong (Ed.), *Learning about learning disabilities.* San Diego, CA: Academic Press.

Vega, W. A., Gil, A. G., Warheit, G. J., Zimmerman, R. S., & Apospori, E. (1993). Acculturation and delinquent behavior among Cuban American adolescents: Toward an empirical model. *American Journal of Community Psychology, 21,* 113–125.

Ventura, S. J., & Tappel, S. M. (1985). Child bearing characteristics of U.S. and foreign born Hispanic mothers. *Public Health Reports, 100,* 647–652.

Vermeer, H. J., Boekaerts, M., & Seegers, G. (2000). Motivational and gender differences: Sixth-grade students' mathematical problem-solving behavior. *Journal of Educational Psychology, 92,* 308–315.

Vernon, P. A. (1993). Intelligence and neural efficiency. In D. K. Detterman (Ed.), *Current topics in human intelligence* (Vol. 3). Norwood, NJ: Ablex.

Veroff, J., McClelland, L., & Ruhland, D. (1975). Varieties of achievement motivation. In M. T. S. Mednick, S. S. Tangri & L. W. Hoffman (Eds.), *Women and achievement: Social and motivational analyses.* New York: Halsted.

Vignau, J., Bailly, D., Duhamel, A., Vervaecke, P., Beuscart, R., & Collinet, C. (1997). Epidemiologic study of sleep quality and troubles in French secondary school adolescents. *Journal of Adolescent Health, 21*(5), 343–350.

Viorst, Judith. (1972). *Alexander and the terrible, horrible, no good, very bad day.* New York: Atheneum.

Vitaro, F., Gendreau, P. L., Tremblay, R. E., & Oligny, P. (1998). Reactive and proactive aggression differentially predict later conduct problems. *Journal of Child Psychology and Psychiatry and Allied Disciplines, 39,* 377–385.

Voelkl, K. E., & Frone, M. R. (2000). Predictors of substance use at school among high school students. *Journal of Educational Psychology, 92,* 583–592.

Vogel, G. (1997). Cocaine wreaks subtle damage on developing brains. *Science, 278,* 38–39.

Volling, B. L. (2001). Early attachment relationships as predictors of preschool children's emotion regulation with a distressed sibling. *Early Education and Development, 12*(2), 185–207.

Vorhees, C. V., & Mollnow, E. (1987). Behavioral teratogenesis: Long-term influences on behavior from early exposure to environmental agents. In J. D. Osofsky (Ed.), *Handbook of infant development* (2nd ed., pp. 913–971). New York: Wiley.

Vorrath, H. (1985). *Positive peer culture.* New York: Aldine de Gruyter.

Vosniadou, S. (1991). Conceptual development in astronomy. In S. M. Glynn, R. H. Yeany, & B. K. Britton (Eds.), *The psychology of learning science.* Hillsdale, NJ: Erlbaum.

Vosniadou, S. (1994). Universal and culture-specific properties of children's mental models of the earth. In L. A. Hirschfeld & S. A. Gelman (Eds.), *Mapping the mind: Domain specificity in cognition and culture.* Cambridge, England: Cambridge University Press.

Vosniadou, S., & Brewer, W. F. (1987). Theories of knowledge restructuring in development. *Review of Educational Research, 57,* 51–67.

Voss, J. F., & Schauble, L. (1992). Is interest educationally interesting? An interest-related model of learning. In K. A. Renninger, S. Hidi, & A. Krapp (Eds.), *The role of interest in learning and development.* Hillsdale, NJ: Erlbaum.

Vygotsky, L. S. (1962). *Thought and language* (E. Haufmann & G. Vakar, Eds. and Trans.). Cambridge, MA: MIT Press.

Vygotsky, L. S. (1978). *Mind in society: The development of higher psychological processes.* Cambridge, MA: Harvard University Press.

Vygotsky, L. S. (1987a). *The collected works of L. S. Vygotsky* (R. W. Rieber & A. S. Carton, Eds.). New York: Plenum Press.

Vygotsky, L. S. (1987b). Thinking and speech. In R. W. Rieber & A. S. Carton (Eds.), *The collected works of L. S. Vygotsky.* New York: Plenum Press.

Vygotsky, L. S. (1997). *Educational psychology.* Boca Raton, FL: St. Lucie Press.

Waddington, C. H. (1957). *The strategy of the genes.* London: Allyn & Bacon.

Wagner, L. S., Carlin, P. L., Cauce, A. M., & Tenner, A. (2001). A snapshot of homeless youth in Seattle: Their characteristics, behaviors and beliefs about HIV protective strategies. *Journal of Community Health, 26*(3), 219–232.

Wagner, M. M. (1995a). *The contributions of poverty and ethnic background to the participation of secondary school students in special education.* Washington, DC: U.S. Department of Education.

Wagner, M. M. (1995b). Outcomes for youths with serious emotional disturbance in secondary school and early childhood. *Critical Issues for Children and Youths, 5*(2), 90–112.

Wagner, R. K., Torgesen, J. K., & Rashotte, C. A. (1994). Development of reading-related phonological processing abilities: New evidence of bidirectional causality from a latent variable longitudinal study. *Developmental Psychology, 30,* 73–87.

Wahlsten, D., & Gottlieb, G. (1997). The invalid separation of effects of nature and nurture: Lessons from animal experimentation. In R. J. Sternberg & E. L. Grigorenko (Eds.), *Intelligence, heredity, and environment* (pp. 163–192). Cambridge, England: Cambridge University Press.

Waisbren, S. E. (1999). Phenylketonuria. In S. Goldstein & C. R. Reynolds (Eds.), *Handbook of neurodevelopmental and genetic disorders* (pp. 433–458). New York: Guilford Press.

Walberg, H. J., & Paik, S. J. (1997). Home environments for learning. In H. J. Walberg & G. D. Haertel (Eds.), *Psychology and educational practice* (pp. 356–368). Berkeley, CA: McCrutchan.

Waldman, I. D., Weinberg, R. A., & Scarr, S. (1994). Racial-group differences in IQ in the Minnesota Transracial Adoption Study: A reply to Levin and Lynn. *Intelligence, 19,* 29–44.

Walker, J. E., & Shea, T. M. (1999). *Behavior management: A practical approach for educators* (7th ed.). Upper Saddle River, NJ: Merrill/Prentice Hall.

Walker, J. M. T. (2001, April). *A cross-sectional study of student motivation, strategy knowledge and strategy use during homework: Implications for research on self-regulated learning.* Paper presented at the annual meeting of the American Educational Research Association, Seattle, WA.

Walker, L. J. (1991). Sex differences in moral reasoning. In W. M. Kurtines & J. L. Gewirtz (Eds.), *Handbook of moral behavior and development: Vol. 2. Research* (pp. 333–364). Hillsdale, NJ: Erlbaum.

Walker, L. J. (1995). Sexism in Kohlberg's moral psychology? In W. M. Kurtines & J. L. Gewirtz

(Eds.), *Moral development: An introduction.* Boston: Allyn & Bacon.

Walker, L. J., & Taylor, J. H. (1991). Family interactions and the development of moral reasoning. *Child Development, 62,* 264–283.

Wallerstein, J. S. (1984). Children of divorce: The psychological tasks of the child. *Annual Progress in Child Psychiatry & Child Development,* 263–280.

Wallerstein, J. S., & Kelly, J. B. (1980). *Surviving the break-up: How children and parents cope with divorce.* New York: Basic Books.

Walters, G. C., & Grusec, J. E. (1977). *Punishment.* San Francisco: Freeman.

Walton, G. E., Bower, N. J. A., & Bower, T. G. R. (1992). Recognition of familiar faces by newborns. *Infant Behavior and Development, 15,* 265–269.

Wang, P. P., & Baron, M. A. (1997). Language and communication: Development and disorders. In M. L. Batshaw (Ed.), *Children with disabilities* (4th ed.). Baltimore: Brookes.

Want, S. C., & Harris, P. L. (2001). Learning from other people's mistakes: Causal understanding in learning to use a tool. *Child Development, 72,* 431–443.

Ward, R. A., & Spitze, G. (1998). Sandwiched marriages: The implications of child and parent relations for marital quality in midlife. *Social Forces, 77*(2), 647–666.

Warren, A. R., & McCloskey, L. A. (1993). Pragmatics: Language in social contexts. In J. Berko-Gleason (Ed.), *The development of language* (3rd ed.). New York: Macmillan.

Warren-Leubecker, A., & Bohannon, J. N. (1989). Pragmatics: Language in social contexts. In J. Berko-Gleason (Ed.), *The development of language* (2nd ed.). Upper Saddle River, NJ: Merrill/Prentice Hall.

Wartella, E. (1995). The commercialization of youth: Channel One in context. *Phi Delta Kappan, 76,* 448–451.

Warton, P. M., & Goodnow, J. J. (1991). The nature of responsibility: Children's understanding of "Your Job." *Child Development, 62,* 156–165.

Washington, V., & Bailey, U. J. O. (1995). *Project Head Start: Models and strategies for the twenty-first century.* New York: Garland.

Wasik, B. A., & Bond, M. A. (2001). Beyond the pages of a book: Interactive book reading and language development in preschool classrooms. *Journal of Educational Psychology, 93,* 243–250.

Wasik, B., Karweit, N., Burns, L., & Brodsky, E. (1998, April). *Once upon a time: The role of rereading and retelling in storybook reading.* Paper presented at the annual meeting of the American Educational Research Association, San Diego, CA.

Wasserman, G. A., Miller, L. S., & Cothern, L. (2000, May). Prevention of serious and violent juvenile offending. *Juvenile Justice Bulletin,* NCJ 178898. Washington, DC: U.S. Department of Justice, Office of Juvenile Justice and Delinquency Prevention.

Waters, E., Merrick, S., Treboux, D., Crowell, J., Albersheim, L. (2000). Attachment security in infancy and early adulthood: A twenty-year longitudinal study. *Child Development, 71,* 684–689.

Waters, H. S. (1982). Memory development in adolescence: Relationships between metamemory, strategy use, and performance. *Journal of Experimental Child Psychology, 33,* 183–195.

Watson, J. (1928). *The psychological care of the infant and child.* New York: Norton.

Watson, R. (1996). Rethinking readiness for learning. In D. R. Olson & N. Torrance (Eds.), *The handbook of education and human development: New models of learning, teaching and*

schooling (pp. 148–172). Cambridge, MA: Blackwell.

Waxman, S. R. (1990). Linguistic biases and the establishment of conceptual hierarchies: Evidence from preschool children. *Cognitive Development, 5,* 123–150.

Way, N. (1998). *Everyday courage: The lives and stories of urban teenagers.* New York: New York University Press.

Weaver, C. (1990). *Understanding whole language: From principles to practice.* Portsmouth, NH: Heinemann.

Weaver, C. A., III, & Kintsch, W. (1991). Expository text. In R. Barr, M. L. Kamil, P. B. Mosenthal, & P. D. Pearson (Eds.), *Handbook of reading research* (Vol. II). New York: Longman.

Webb, J. T., Meckstroth, E. A., & Tolan, S. S. (1982). *Guiding the gifted child: A practical source for parents and teachers.* Dayton: Ohio Psychology Press.

Webb, N. M., & Farivar, S. (1994). Promoting helping behavior in cooperative small groups in middle school mathematics. *American Educational Research Journal, 31,* 369–395.

Webb, N. M., & Palincsar, A. S. (1996). Group processes in the classroom. In D. C. Berliner & R. C. Calfee (Eds.), *Handbook of educational psychology.* New York: Macmillan.

Webber, J., Scheuermann, B., McCall, C., & Coleman, M. (1993). Research on self-monitoring as a behavior management technique in special education classrooms: A descriptive review. *Remedial and Special Education, 14*(2), 38–56.

Webster-Stratton, C., & Hammond, M. (1999). Marital conflict management skills, parenting style, and early-onset conduct problems: Processes and pathways. *Journal of Child Psychology & Psychiatry & Allied Disciplines, 40,* 917–927.

Wechsler, D. (1989). *Wechsler Preschool and Primary Scale of Intelligence—Revised.* San Antonio, TX: The Psychological Corporation.

Wechsler, D. (1991). *Wechsler Intelligence Scale for Children* (3rd ed.). San Antonio, TX: Psychological Corporation.

Weinberg, R. A. (1989). Intelligence and IQ: Landmark issues and great debates. *American Psychologist, 44,* 98–104.

Weiner, B. (1984). Principles for a theory of student motivation and their application within an attributional framework. In R. Ames & C. Ames (Eds.), *Research on motivation in education: Vol. 1. Student motivation.* San Diego, CA: Academic Press.

Weiner, B. (1986). *An attributional theory of motivation and emotion.* New York: Springer-Verlag.

Weiner, B. (2000). Intrapersonal and interpersonal theories of motivation from an attributional perspective. *Educational Psychology Review, 12,* 1–14.

Weiner, L. (1999). *Urban teaching: The essentials.* New York: Teachers College Press.

Weinfeld, N. S., Sroufe, L. A., & Egeland, B. (2000). Attachment from infancy to early adulthood in a high-risk sample: Continuity, discontinuity, and their correlates. *Child Development, 71,* 695–702.

Weinstein, C. S. (1988). Preservice teachers' expectations about their first year of teaching. *Teaching and Teacher Education, 40*(2), 53–60.

Weinstein, R. S. (1993). Children's knowledge of differential treatment in school: Implications for motivation. In T. M. Tomlinson (Ed.), *Motivating students to learn: Overcoming barriers to high achievement.* Berkeley, CA: McCutchan.

Weinstein, R. S., Madison, S. M., & Kuklinski, M. R. (1995). Raising expectations in schooling: Obstacles and opportunities for change.

American Educational Research Journal, 32, 121–159.

Weis, L. (2000). Learning to speak out in an abstinence based sex education group: Gender and race work in an urban magnet school. *Teachers College Record, 102*(3), 620–650.

Weisner, T. S. (1997). Why ethnography and its findings matter. *Ethos, 25,* 177–190.

Weisner, T. S., & Gallimore, R. (1977). My brother's keeper: Child and sibling caregiving. *Current Anthropology, 18,* 169–190.

Weisner, T. S., Gallimore, R., & Jordan, C. (1988). Unpackaging cultural effects on classroom learning: Hawaiian peer assistance and child-generated activity. *Anthropology and Education Quarterly, 19,* 327–352.

Weiss, M. J., & Hagen, R. (1988). A key to literacy: Kindergartners' awareness of the functions of print. *The Reading Teacher, 41,* 574–578.

Weissglass, J. (1998). *Ripples of hope: Building relationships for educational change.* Santa Barbara, CA: Center for Educational Change in Mathematics and Science, University of California.

Wellman, H. M. (1985). The child's theory of mind: The development of conceptions of cognition. In S. R. Yussen (Ed.), *The growth of reflection in children.* San Diego, CA: Academic Press.

Wellman, H. M. (1990). *The child's theory of mind.* Cambridge, MA: MIT Press.

Wellman, H. M., Cross, D., & Watson, J. (2001). Meta-analysis of theory-of-mind development: The truth about false belief. *Child Development, 72,* 655–684.

Wellman, H. M., & Estes, D. (1986). Early understanding of mental entities: A reexamination of childhood realism. *Child Development, 57,* 910–923.

Wellman, H. M., & Gelman, S. A. (1992). Cognitive development: Foundational theories of core domains. In M. R. Rosenzweig & L. W. Porter (Eds.), *Annual review of psychology* (Vol. 43). Palo Alto, CA: Annual Reviews, Inc.

Wellman, H. M., & Gelman, S. A. (1998). Knowledge acquisition in functional domains. In W. Damon (Series Ed.), D. Kuhn & R. S. Siegler (Vol. Eds.), *Handbook of child psychology: Vol. 2. Cognition, perception, and language* (5th ed., pp. 523–573). New York: Wiley.

Wellman, H. M., Harris, P. L., Banerjee, M., & Sinclair, A. (1995). Early understanding of emotion: Evidence from natural language. *Cognition and Emotion, 9,* 117–149.

Wellman, H. M., & Hickling, A. K. (1994). The mind's "I": Children's conception of the mind as an active agent. *Child Development, 65,* 1564–1580.

Wellman, H. M., Phillips, A. T., & Rodriguez, T. (2000). Young children's understanding of perception, desire, and emotion. *Child Development, 71,* 895–912.

Wells, Y. D., & Johnson, T. M. (2001). Impact of parental divorce on willingness of young adults to provide care for parents in the future. *Journal of Family Studies, 7*(2), 160–170.

Welsh, M. C. (1991). Rule-guided behavior and self-monitoring on the tower of Hanoi disk-transfer task. *Cognitive Development, 4,* 59–76.

Wenar, C. (1972). Executive competence and spontaneous social behavior in 1–year-olds. *Child Development, 43,* 256–260.

Wentzel, K. R. (1999). Social-motivational processes and interpersonal relationships: Implications for understanding motivation at school. *Journal of Educational Psychology, 91,* 76–97.

Wentzel, K. R., & Asher, S. R. (1995). The academic lives of neglected, rejected, popular, and controversial children. *Child Development, 66,* 754–763.

Wentzel, K. R., & Wigfield, A. (1998). Academic and social motivational influences on students' academic performance. *Educational Psychology Review, 10,* 155–175.

Werker, J. F., & Lalonde, C. E. (1988). Cross-language speech perception: Initial capabilities and developmental change. *Developmental Psychology, 24,* 672–683.

Werner, E. (1989). High-risk children in adulthood: A longitudinal study from birth to 32 years. *American Journal of Orthopsychiatry, 59*(1), 72–81.

Werner, E. (1993). Risk, resilience, and recovery: Perspectives from the Kauai longitudinal study. *Development and Psychopathology, 5,* 505–515.

Werner, E., & Smith, R. (1992). *Overcoming the odds: High risk children from birth to adulthood.* Ithaca, NY: Cornell University Press.

Werner, E. E. (1995). Resilience in development. *Current Directions in Psychological Science, 4,* 81–85.

Werner, E. E., & Smith, R. S. (1982). *Vulnerable but invincible: A longitudinal study of resilient children.* New York: McGraw-Hill. Reprinted 1989, 1998. New York: Adams, Bannister, Cox.

Wertsch, J. V. (1984). The zone of proximal development: Some conceptual issues. *Children's learning in the zone of proximal development: New directions for child development* (No. 23). San Francisco: Jossey-Bass.

Wertsch, J. V., & Tulviste, P. (1994). Lev Semyonovich Vygotsky and contemporary developmental psychology. In R. D. Parke, P. A. Ornstein, J. J. Rieser, & C. Zahn-Waxler (Eds.), *A century of developmental psychology* (pp. 333–355). Washington, DC: American Psychological Association.

West, M. J., & Rheingold, H. L. (1978). Infant stimulation of maternal instruction. *Infant Behavior and Development, 1,* 205–215.

Whalen, C. K., Jamner, L. D., Henker, B., Delfino, R. J., & Lozano, J. M. (2002). The ADHD spectrum and everyday life: Experience sampling of adolescent moods, activities, smoking, and drinking. *Child Development, 73,* 209–227.

White, R. (1959). Motivation reconsidered: The concept of competence. *Psychological Review, 66,* 297–333.

White, R., & Cunningham, A. M. (1991). *Ryan White: My own story.* New York: Signet.

White, S. H. (1992). G. Stanley Hall: From philosophy to developmental psychology. *Developmental Psychology, 28,* 25–34.

Whitehurst, G. J., Arnold, D. S., Epstein, J. N., Angell, A. L., Smith, M., & Fischel, J. E. (1994). A picture book reading intervention in day care and home for children from low-income families. *Developmental Psychology, 30,* 679–689.

Whiting, B. B., & Edwards, C. P. (1988). *Children of different worlds.* Cambridge, MA: Harvard University Press.

Whiting, B. B., & Whiting, J. W. M. (1975). *Children of six cultures: A psycho-cultural analysis.* Cambridge, MA: Harvard University Press.

Whiting, J. (1981). Environmental constraint on infant care practices. In R. H. Munroe, R. L. Munroe, & B. Whiting (Eds.), *Handbook of cross-cultural development.* New York: Garland STPM Press.

Wiesel, T. N., & Hubel, D. H. (1965). Extent of recovery from the effects of visual deprivation in kittens. *Journal of Neurophysiology, 28,* 1060–1072.

Wigfield, A. (1994). Expectancy-value theory of achievement motivation: A developmental perspective. *Educational Psychology Review, 6,* 49–78.

Wigfield, A. (1997). Reading motivation: A domain-specific approach to motivation. *Educational Psychologist, 32,* 59–68.

Wigfield, A., & Eccles, J. (2000). Expectancy-value theory of achievement motivation. *Contemporary Educational Psychology, 25,* 68–81.

Wigfield, A., Eccles, J., Mac Iver, D., Reuman, D., & Midgley, C. (1991). Transitions at early adolescence: Changes in children's domain-specific self-perceptions and general self-esteem across the transition to junior high school. *Developmental Psychology, 27,* 552–565.

Wigfield, A., & Eccles, J. S. (1994). Children's competence beliefs, achievement values, and general self-esteem: Change across elementary and middle school. *Journal of Early Adolescence, 14,* 107–138.

Wigfield, A., & Karpathian, M. (1991). Who am I and what can I do? Children's self-concepts and motivation in achievement situations. *Educational Psychologist, 26,* 233–262.

Wigfield, A., Eccles, J. S., & Pintrich, P. R. (1996). Development between the ages of 11 and 25. In D. C. Berliner & R. C. Calfee (Eds.), *Handbook of educational psychology.* New York: Macmillan.

Wiig, E. H., Gilbert, M. F., & Christian, S. H. (1978). Developmental sequences in perception and interpretation of ambiguous sentences. *Perceptual and Motor Skills, 46,* 959–969.

Wilcox, S. (1994). Struggling for a voice: An interactionist view of language and literacy in Deaf education. In V. John-Steiner, C. P. Panofsky, & L. W. Smith (Eds.), *Sociocultural approaches to language and literacy: An interactionist perspective.* Cambridge, England: Cambridge University Press.

Wilder, D. A., & Shapiro, P. N. (1989). Role of competition-induced anxiety in limiting the beneficial impact of positive behavior by an out-group member. *Journal of Personality and Social Psychology, 56,* 60–69.

Willatts, P. (1990). Development of problem solving strategies in infancy. In D. F. Bjorklund (Ed.), *Children's strategies* (pp. 23–66). Hillsdale, NJ: Erlbaum.

Williams, D. (1996). *Autism: An inside-outside approach.* London: Kingsley.

Williams, D. E., & D'Alessandro, J. D. (1994). A comparison of three measures of androgyny and their relationship to psychological adjustment. *Journal of Social Behavior and Personality, 9,* 469–480.

Williams, E., & Radin, N. (1993). Parental involvement, maternal employment, and adolescents' academic achievement: An 11-year follow-up. *American Journal of Orthopsychiatry, 63,* 306–312.

Williams, G., Donley, C. R., & Keller, J. W. (2000). Teaching children with autism to ask questions about hidden objects. *Journal of Applied Behavior Analysis, 33,* 627–630.

Williams, J., & Williamson, K. (1992). "I wouldn't want to shoot nobody": The out-of-school curriculum as described by urban students. *Action in Teacher Education, 14*(2), 9–15.

Willig, A. C. (1985). A meta-analysis of selected studies on the effectiveness of bilingual education. *Review of Educational Research, 55,* 269–317.

Willis, W. (1992). Families with African American roots. In E. W. Lynch & M. J. Hanson (Eds.), *Developing cross-cultural competence: A guide for working with young children and their families* (pp. 121–150). Baltimore: Brookes.

Wills, T. A., McNamara, G., Vaccaro, D., & Hirky, A. E. (1996). Escalated substance use: A longitudinal grouping analysis from early to middle adolescence. *Journal of Abnormal Psychology, 105,* 166–180.

Wilson, B. L., & Corbett, H. D. (2001). *Listening to urban kids: School reform and the teachers they want.* Albany, NY: State University of New York Press.

Wilson, C. C., Piazza, C. C., & Nagle, R. (1990). Investigation of the effect of consistent and inconsistent behavioral example upon children's donation behavior. *Journal of Genetic Psychology, 151,* 361–376.

Wilson, D. K., Nicholson, S. C., & Krishnamoorthy, J. S. (1998). The role of diet in minority adolescent health promotion. In D. K. Wilson, J. R. Rodrigue, & W. C. Taylor (Eds.), *Health-promoting and health-compromising behaviors among minority adolescents* (pp. 129–151). Washington, DC: American Psychological Association.

Wilson, J. D., & Foster, D. W. (1985). *Williams textbook of endocrinology* (7th ed.). Philadelphia: Saunders.

Wilson, M. (1989). Child development in the context of the black extended family. *American Psychologist, 44,* 380–383.

Wilson, S. M., Shulman, L. S., & Richert, A. E. (1987). "150 different ways" of knowing: Representations of knowledge in teaching. In J. Calderhead (Ed.), *Exploring teachers' thinking* (pp. 104–124). London: Cassell Educational Limited.

Wimmer, H., Landerl, K., & Frith, U. (1999). Learning to read German: Normal and impaired acquisition. In M. Harris & G. Hatano (Eds.), *Learning to read and write: A cross-linguistic perspective.* Cambridge, England: Cambridge University Press.

Wimmer, H., Mayringer, H., & Landerl, K. (2000). The double-deficit hypothesis and difficulties in learning to read a regular orthography. *Journal of Educational Psychology, 92,* 668–680.

Wimmer, H., & Perner, J. (1983). Beliefs about beliefs: Representation and constraining function of wrong beliefs in young children's understanding of deception. *Cognition, 13,* 103–128.

Winer, G. A., Craig, R. K., & Weinbaum, E. (1992). Adults' failure on misleading weight-conservation tests: A developmental analysis. *Developmental Psychology, 28,* 109–120.

Winne, P. H. (1995a). Inherent details in self-regulated learning. *Educational Psychologist, 30,* 173–187.

Winne, P. H. (1995b). Self-regulation is ubiquitous but its forms vary with knowledge. *Educational Psychologist, 30,* 223–228.

Winne, P. H., & Marx, R. W. (1989). A cognitive-processing analysis of motivation with classroom tasks. In C. Ames & R. Ames (Eds.), *Research on motivation in education* (Vol. 3). San Diego, CA: Academic Press.

Winner, E. (1988). *The point of words.* Cambridge, MA: Harvard University Press.

Winner, E. (1997). Exceptionally high intelligence and schooling. *American Psychologist, 52,* 1070–1081.

Winner, E. (2000a). Giftedness: Current theory and research. *Current Directions in Psychological Science, 9,* 153–156.

Winner, E. (2000b). The origins and ends of giftedness. *American Psychologist, 55,* pp. 159–169.

Winsler, A., Díaz, R. M., Espinosa, L., & Rodriguez, J. L. (1999). When learning a second language does not mean losing the first: Bilingual language development in low-income, Spanish-speaking children attending bilingual preschool. *Child Development, 70,* 349–362.

Winslow, G. R. (1984). From loyalty to advocacy: A new metaphor for nursing. *Hastings Center Report, 14*(3), 32–40.

Winston, P. (1973). Learning to identify toy block structures. In R. L. Solso (Ed.), *Contemporary issues in cognitive psychology: The Loyola Symposium.* Washington, DC: V. H. Winston.

Wise, F., & Miller, N. B. (1983). The mental health of the American Indian child. In G. J. Powell

(Ed.), *The psychosocial development of minority children*. New York: Brunner/Mazel.

Witelson, S. F. (1985). The brain connection: The corpus callosum is larger in left-handers. *Science, 229*(4714), 665–668.

Wittmer, D. S., & Honig, A. S. (1994). Encouraging positive social development in young children. *Young Children, 49*(5), 4–12.

Wlodkowski, R. J., & Ginsberg, M. B. (1995). *Diversity and motivation: Culturally responsive teaching.* San Francisco: Jossey-Bass.

Wodtke, K. H., Harper, F., & Schommer, M. (1989). How standardized is school testing? An exploratory observational study of standardized group testing in kindergarten. *Educational Evaluation and Policy Analysis, 11*, 223–235.

Wolf, M., & Bowers, P. G. (1999). The double-deficit hypothesis for the developmental dyslexias. *Journal of Educational Psychology, 91*, 415–438.

Wolfe, D. A., & Wekerle, C. (1997). Pathways to violence in teen dating relationships. In D. Cicchetti & S. L. Toth (Eds.), *Developmental perspectives on trauma: Theory, research, and intervention. Rochester symposium on developmental psychology, 8*, 315–341. Rochester, NH: University of Rochester Press.

Wolff, P. G. (1966). The causes, controls, and organization of behavior in the neonate. *Psychological Issues, 5* (1, Serial No. 17).

Wolock, I., Sherman, P., Feldman, L. H., & Metzger, B. (2001). Child abuse and neglect referral patterns: A longitudinal study. *Children and Youth Services Review, 23*(1), 21–47.

Wong, B. Y. L. (Ed.). (1991). *Learning about learning disabilities.* San Diego, CA: Academic Press.

Wong Fillmore, L. (1993). Educating citizens for a multicultural 21st century. *Multicultural Education, 1*, 10–12, 37.

Wood, D., Bruner, J. S., & Ross, G. (1976). The role of tutoring in problem-solving. *Journal of Child Psychology and Psychiatry, 17*, 89–100.

Wood, E., Motz, M., & Willoughby, T. (1997, April). *Examining students' retrospective memories of strategy development.* Paper presented at the annual meeting of the American Educational Research Association, Chicago.

Wood, E., Willoughby, T., McDermott, C., Motz, M., Kaspar, V., & Ducharme, M. J. (1999). Developmental differences in study behavior. *Journal of Educational Psychology, 91*, 527–536.

Wood, E., Willoughby, T., Reilley, S., Elliott, S., & DuCharme, M. (1994, April). *Evaluating students' acquisition of factual material when studying independently or with a partner.* Paper presented at the annual meeting of the American Educational Research Association, New Orleans, LA.

Wood, J. W. (1998). *Adapting instruction to accommodate students in inclusive settings* (3rd ed.). Upper Saddle River, NJ: Merrill/Prentice Hall.

Wood, R. M., & Gustafson, G. E. (2001). Infant crying and adults' anticipated caregiving responses: Acoustic and contextual influences. *Child Development, 72*, 1287–1300.

Wood, W., Wong, F. Y., & Chachere, J. G. (1991). Effects of media violence on viewers' aggression in unconstrained social interaction. *Psychological Bulletin, 109*, 371–383.

Woodward, A. L. (1998). Infants selectively encode the goal object of an actor's reach. *Cognition, 69*, 1–34.

Woodward, A. L., Markman, E. M., & Fitzsimmons, C. M. (1994). Rapid word learning in 13- and 18-month-olds. *Developmental Psychology, 30*, 553–566.

Woodward, A. L., & Sommerville, J. A. (2000). Twelve-month-old infants interpret action in context. *Psychological Science, 11*, 73–77.

Woody-Ramsey, J., & Miller, P. H. (1988). The facilitation of selective attention in preschoolers. *Child Development, 59*, 1497–1503.

Woolfe, T., Want, S. C., & Siegal, M. (2002). Signposts to development: Theory of mind in deaf children. *Child Development, 73*, 768–778.

Woolley, J. D. (1995). The fictional mind: Young children's understanding of pretense, imagination, and dreams. *Developmental Review, 15*, 172–211.

Wright, J. C., & Huston, A. C. (1995, June). *Effects of educational TV viewing of lower income preschoolers on academic skills, school readiness, and school adjustment one to three years later* (report to Children's Television Workshop). Lawrence, KS: Center for Research on the Influences of Television on Children, University of Kansas.

Wright, R. (1994). *The moral animal: The new science of evolutionary psychology.* New York: Pantheon Books.

Wright, S., & Taylor, D. (1995). Identity and the language of the classroom: Investigating the impact of heritage versus second-language instruction on personal and collective self-esteem. *Journal of Educational Psychology, 87*, 241–252.

Wright, S. C., Taylor, D. M., & Macarthur, J. (2000). Subtractive bilingualism and the survival of the Inuit language: Heritage- versus second-language education. *Journal of Educational Psychology, 92*, 63–84.

Wu, Z. (1995). The stability of cohabitation relationships: The role of children. *Journal of Marriage and the Family, 57*(1), 231–236.

Wynbrandt, J., & Ludman, M. D. (2000). *The encyclopedia of genetic disorders and birth defects* (2nd ed.). New York: Facts on File, Inc.

Xu, F., & Spelke, E. S. (2000). Large number discrimination in 6-month-old infants. *Cognition, 74*, B1–B11.

Yaden, D. B., Jr., & Templeton, S. (Eds.). (1986). *Metalinguistic awareness and beginning literacy: Conceptualizing what it means to read and write.* Portsmouth, NH: Heinemann.

Yakovlev, P. I., & Lecours, A. R. (1967). The myelogenetic cycles of regional maturation of the brain. In A. Minkowski (Ed.), *Regional development of the brain in early life* (pp. 3–70). Oxford, UK: Blackwell Scientific.

Yarrow, M. R., Scott, P. M., & Waxler, C. Z. (1973). Learning concern for others. *Developmental Psychology, 8*, 240–260.

Yates, M., & Youniss, J. (1996). A developmental perspective on community service in adolescence. *Social Development, 5*, 85–111.

Yeager, E. A., Foster, S. J., Maley, S. D., Anderson, T., Morris, J. W., III, & Davis, O. L., Jr. (1997, March). *The role of empathy in the development of historical understanding.* Paper presented at the annual meeting of the American Educational Research Association, Chicago.

Yee, A. H. (1992). Asians as stereotypes and students: Misperceptions that persist. *Educational Psychology Review, 4*, 95–132.

Yell, M. L., Robinson, T. R., & Drasgow, E. (2001). Cognitive behavior modification. In T. J. Zirpoli & K. J. Melloy, *Behavior management: Applications for teachers* (3rd ed.). Upper Saddle River, NJ: Merrill/Prentice Hall.

Young, E. L., & Assing, R. (2000). Review of *The Universal Nonverbal Intelligence Test. Journal of Psychoeducational Assessment, 18*, 280–288.

Youniss, J. (1980). *Parents and peers in social development.* Chicago: University of Chicago Press.

Youniss, J. (1983). Social construction of adolescence by adolescents and their parents. In H. D. Grotevant & C. R. Cooper (Eds.), *Adolescent development in the family: New directions for child development* (No. 22). San Francisco: Jossey-Bass.

Youniss, J., & Smollar, J. (1985). *Adolescent relations with mothers, fathers, and friends.* Chicago: University of Chicago Press.

Youniss, J., & Yates, M. (1999). Youth service and moral-civic identity: A case of everyday morality. *Educational Psychology Review, 11*(4), 361–376.

Ysseldyke, J. E., & Algozzine, B. (1984). *Introduction to special education.* Boston: Houghton Mifflin.

Yu, S. L., Elder, A. D., & Urdan, T. C. (1995, April). *Motivation and cognitive strategies in students with a "good student" or "poor student" self-schema.* Paper presented at the annual meeting of the American Educational Research Association, San Francisco.

Yude, C., Goodman, R., & McConachie, H. (1998). Peer problems of children with hemiplegia in mainstream primary schools. *Journal of Child Psychology and Psychiatry, 39*, 533–541.

Zahn-Waxler, C., Mayfield, A., Radke-Yarrow, M., McKnew, D. H., Cytryn, L., & Davenport, Y. B. (1988). A follow-up investigation of offspring of parents with bipolar disorder. *American Journal of Psychiatry, 145*, 506–509.

Zahn-Waxler, C., & Radke-Yarrow, M. (1982). The development of altruism: Alternative research strategies. In N. Eisenberg-Berg (Ed.), *The development of prosocial behavior.* Lincoln: University of Nebraska Press.

Zahn-Waxler, C., Radke-Yarrow, M., Wagner, E., & Chapman, M. (1992). Development of concern for others. *Developmental Psychology, 28*, 126–136.

Zahn-Waxler, C., Robinson, J., & Emde, R. N. (1992). The development of empathy in twins. *Developmental Psychology, 28*, 1038–1047.

Zahn-Waxler, C., & Smith, K. D. (1992). The development of prosocial behavior. In V. B. Van Hasselt & M. Hersen (Eds.), *Handbook of social development: A lifespan perspective* (Perspectives in Developmental Psychology, pp. 229–256). New York: Plenum Press.

Zajonc, R. B., & Mullally, P. R. (1997). Birth order: Reconciling conflicting effects. *American Psychologist, 52*, 685–699.

Zarbatany, L., Hartmann, D. P., & Rankin, D. B. (1990). The psychological function of preadolescent peer activities. *Child Development, 61*, 1067–1080.

Zeanah, C. H. (2000). Disturbances of attachment in young children adopted from institutions. *Journal of Developmental and Behavioral Pediatrics, 21*, 230–236.

Zelli, A., Dodge, K. A., Lochman, J. E., & Laird, R. D. (1999). The distinction between beliefs legitimizing aggression and deviant processing of social cues: Testing measurement validity and the hypothesis that biased processing mediates the effects of beliefs on aggression. *Journal of Personality and Social Psychology, 77*, 150–166.

Zero to Three: National Center for Infants, Toddlers, and Families (2002). *Temperament.* Retrieved January 16, 2003, from http://www.zerotothree.org/Archive/TEMPERAM.HTM

Zervigon-Hakes, A. (1984). Materials mastery and symbolic development in construction play: Stages of development. *Early Child Development and Care, 17*, 37–47.

Zhou, Q., Eisenberg, N., Losoya, S. H., Fabes, R. A., Reiser, M., Guthrie, et al. (2002). The relations of parental warmth and positive expressiveness to children's empathy-related responding and social functioning: A longitudinal study. *Child Development, 73*, 893–915.

Ziegert, D. I., Kistner, J. A., Castro, R., & Robertson, B. (2001). Longitudinal study of young children's responses to challenging achievement situations. *Child Development, 72*, 609–624.

Ziegler, J. C., Tan, L. H., Perry, C., & Montant, M. (2000). Phonology matters: The phonological frequency effect in written Chinese. *Psychological Science, 11,* 234–238.

Ziegler, S. G. (1987). Effects of stimulus cueing on the acquisition of groundstrokes by beginning tennis players. *Journal of Applied Behavior Analysis, 20,* 405–411.

Zigler, E., & Muenchow, S. (1992). *Head Start: The inside story of America's most successful educational experiment.* New York: Basic Books.

Zigler, E. F., & Finn-Stevenson, M. (1987). *Children: Development and social issues.* Lexington, MA: Heath.

Zigler, E. F., & Finn-Stevenson, M. (1992). Applied developmental psychology. In M. H. Bornstein & M. E. Lamb (Eds.), *Developmental psychology: An advanced textbook.* Hillsdale, NJ: Erlbaum.

Zill, N. (1983). *American children: Happy, healthy and insecure.* New York: Doubleday/Anchor Press.

Zill, N. (1985, April). *Behavior and learning problems among adopted children: Findings from a national survey of child health.* Paper presented at the meeting of the Society for Research in Child Development, Toronto.

Zill, N., Nord, C., & Loomis, L. (1995, September). *Adolescent time use, risky behavior, and outcomes: An analysis of national data.* Rockville, MD: Westat.

Zimmerman, B. J. (1998). Developing self-fulfilling cycles of academic regulation: An analysis of exemplary instructional models. In D. H. Schunk & B. J. Zimmerman (Eds.), *Self-regulated learning: From teaching to self-reflective practice* (pp. 1–19). New York: Guilford.

Zimmerman, B. J., & Bandura, A. (1994). Impact of self-regulatory influences on writing course attainment. *American Educational Research Journal, 31,* 845–862.

Zimmerman, B. J., & Kitsantas, A. (1999). Acquiring writing revision skill: Shifting from process to outcome self-regulatory goals. *Journal of Educational Psychology, 91,* 241–250.

Zimmerman, B. J., & Risemberg, R. (1997). Self-regulatory dimensions of academic learning and motivation. In G. D. Phye (Ed.), *Handbook of academic learning: Construction of knowledge.* San Diego, CA: Academic Press.

Zirpoli, T. J., & Melloy, K. J. (1993). *Behavior management: Applications for teachers and parents.* Upper Saddle River, NJ: Merrill/Prentice Hall.

Zuckerman, G. A. (1994). A pilot study of a ten-day course in cooperative learning for beginning Russian first graders. *Elementary School Journal, 94,* 405–420.

Zwaan, R. A., Langston, M. C., & Graesser, A. C. (1995). The construction of situation models in narrative comprehension: An event-indexing model. *Psychological Science, 6,* 292–297.

Photo Credits

Mark Adams/Getty Images, Inc.–Taxi, p. 164; Davis Barber/PhotoEdit, pp. 49, 392; Albert Bandura, p. 57; Billy E. Barnes/PhotoEdit, p. 116; Susan Burger, p. 169; Berkeley Police Department, p. 127; David Blume/The Image Works, p. 143; Boston Youth Clean-up Corps, p. 625; Michelle D. Bridwell /PhotoEdit, p. 507; Robert Burke/Getty Images Inc., Stone Allstock, p. 305; Mark Burnett/Stock Boston, p. 536; Myrleen Ferguson Cate/PhotoEdit, pp. 153, 205; Courtesy of *Child Development*, p. 63 (top); CNRI/Science Photo Library/Photo Researchers, p. 81 (left); Courtesy Dr. Carolyn Rovee Collier, p. 194; Paul Conklin/PhotoEdit, pp. 170 (bottom), 514; Corbis Digital Stock, p. 524; Scott Cunningham/Merrill, pp. 10, 254, 340, 370, 468 (left), 494, 597 (bottom); Bob Daemmrich/The Image Works, p. 31; Deborah Davis/PhotoEdit, p. 600; Tim Davis/Photo Researchers, Inc., p. 263; Mary Kate Denny/PhotoEdit, pp. 8, 39, 83, 104, 299, 563; Laima Druskis/PH College, pp. 19, 88, 329, 334; Laura Dwight, p. 485; Laura Dwight/Laura Dwight Photography, pp. 87, 284; Laura Dwight/Omni–Photo Communications, Inc., pp. 119, 554; Laura Dwight/PhotoEdit, pp. 18 (top), 51 (top), 505; Laura Elliot/Comstock Images, p. 105 (top); John Paul Endress/Silver Burdett Ginn, p. 270; Rachel Epstein/The Image Works, p. 252; Courtesy of Dan Erdman, p. 176; Amy Etra/PhotoEdit, p. 282;

EyeWire Collection/Getty Images/EyeWire, Inc., pp. 395, 519; FBI, p. 81 (right); Myrleen Ferguson/PhotoEdit, pp. 288, 291; Fotopic/Omni–Photo Communications, Inc., p. 333; Hunter Freeman/Getty Images Inc.–Stone Allstock, p. 66; Tony Freeman/PhotoEdit, pp. 114, 167 (bottom), 279, 365, 564, 597 (top); S. Gazin/The Image Works, p. 517; Getty Images, Inc.–Photodisc, pp. 222 (center), 458; Mike Good/Dorling Kindersley Media Library, pp. 90, 463; Spencer Grant/PhotoEdit, p. 295; Jeff Greenberg/PhotoEdit, pp. 214, 415; Will Hart/PhotoEdit, p. 257; Richard Hutchings/PhotoEdit, p. 301; Richard Hutchings/Photo Researchers, p. 222 (left); Bonnie Kamin /PhotoEdit, p. 511; Catherine Karnow/Corbis, p. 15; Catherine Karnow/Woodfin Camp & Associates, p. 578; KS Studios/Merrill, p. 350; Richard Lord/The Image Works, p. 420; Anthony Magnacca/Merrill, pp. 20, 209, 222 (right), 233, 325, 424, 440, 479, 550; B. Mahoney/The Image Works, p. 65; Michael Malyszko/Getty Images, Inc.–Taxi, p. 399; Karen Mancinelli/Pearson Learning, p. 461; Renzo Mancini/Getty Images, Inc.–Image Bank, p. 448; Teresa McDevitt, p. 92; Ericka McConnell/Getty Images, Inc.–Taxi, p. 459; Kent Meireis/The Image Works, p. 227; Laurence Monneret/Getty Images Inc.–Stone Allstock, p. 559; Andrew Moore, p. 344; Joseph Nettis/Stock Boston, p. 264; Michael Newman/PhotoEdit,

pp. 21, 89, 121, 158, 170 (top), 373, 404, 581, 615; Jonathan Nourok/PhotoEdit, p. 384; Novastock/PhotoEdit, p. 239; Page Poore/PH College, p. 508; Tom Prettyman/PhotoEdit, pp. 167 (top), 470; Mike Provost/Silver Burdett Ginn, p. 197 (top); Seth Resnick/Stock Boston, p. 627; Mark Richards/PhotoEdit, p. 631; Mark Richards/PhotoEdit/Courtesy of Joe Campos & Rosanne Kermoian, p. 135; Nancy Richmond/The Image Works, p. 391; Oliver Rigardiere/Getty Images, Inc., p. 18 (bottom); Andy Sacks/Getty Images Inc.–Stone Allstock, p. 387; David J. Sams/Getty Images Inc.–Stone Allstock, p. 18 (center); Valerie Schultz/Merrill, p. 192; Silver Burdett Ginn, pp. 243, 262; Frank Siteman/Omni–Photo Communications, Inc., p. 501; Jim Smith/Photo Researchers, Inc., p. 436; Courtesy of Elizabeth Sowell, pp. 51, 102; Ken Straitor/Corbis/Stock Market, p. 380; SuperStock, Inc., p. 231; SW Productions/Getty Images, Inc., p. 379; Tom Watson/Merrill, p. 430; David Young/PhotoEdit, p. 133; Courtesy of *Young Child Magazine*, p. 63 (bottom); David Young-Wolff/Getty Images Inc.–Stone Allstock, pp. 73, 353; David Young-Wolf/PhotoEdit, pp. 105 (bottom), 197 (bottom), 312, 313, 366, 409, 427, 446, 468 (right), 476, 489, 552, 605; Courtesy of *ZeroToThree*, p. 33; and Elizabeth Zuckerman/PhotoEdit, p. 537.

Subject Index